Lecture Notes in Computer Science   16505

Founding Editors

Gerhard Goos
Juris Hartmanis

Editorial Board Members

Elisa Bertino, USA
Wen Gao, China

Bernhard Steffen, Germany
Moti Yung, USA

Advanced Research in Computing and Software Science

Subline of Lecture Notes in Computer Science

Subline Series Editors

Giorgio Ausiello, *University of Rome 'La Sapienza', Italy*
Vladimiro Sassone, *University of Southampton, UK*

Subline Advisory Board

Susanne Albers, *TU Munich, Germany*
Benjamin C. Pierce, *University of Pennsylvania, USA*
Bernhard Steffen, *University of Dortmund, Germany*
Deng Xiaotie, *Peking University, Beijing, China*
Jeannette M. Wing, *Microsoft Research, Redmond, WA, USA*

More information about this series at https://link.springer.com/bookseries/558

Sebastian Junges · Guy Katz
Editors

Tools and Algorithms for the Construction and Analysis of Systems

32nd International Conference, TACAS 2026
Held as Part of the International Joint Conferences
on Theory and Practice of Software, ETAPS 2026
Turin, Italy, April 11–16, 2026
Proceedings, Part I

 Springer

Editors
Sebastian Junges 
Radboud University
Nijmegen, The Netherlands

Guy Katz
The Hebrew University of Jerusalem
Jerusalem, Israel

ISSN 0302-9743   ISSN 1611-3349 (electronic)
Lecture Notes in Computer Science
ISBN 978-3-032-22751-5   ISBN 978-3-032-22752-2 (eBook)
https://doi.org/10.1007/978-3-032-22752-2

ETAPS Foreword

Welcome to the 29th edition of ETAPS, which took place as an on-site event in Turin, Italy during April 11–16, 2026!

ETAPS 2026 was the 29th instance of the International Joint Conferences on Theory and Practice of Software (ETAPS). ETAPS is an annual federated conference established in 1998, and consists of four main conferences: ESOP, FASE, FoSSaCS, and TACAS. Each conference has its own Program Committee (PC) and its own Steering Committee (SC). The ETAPS main conferences cover various aspects of software systems, ranging from theoretical computer science to foundations of programming languages, tools and algorithms for system analysis, and formal approaches to software engineering. Organizing these conferences in a coherent, highly synchronized conference programme enables researchers to participate in an exciting event, having the possibility to meet many colleagues working in different directions in the field, and to easily attend talks of different conferences. In addition to its four main conferences, ETAPS 2026 also hosted fifteen satellite workshops and two colocated events, which together further attracted many researchers from all over the globe.

ETAPS 2026 received 456 submissions in total, 138 of which were accepted, yielding an overall acceptance rate of 30%. Out of the 138 accepted papers, 16 papers were selected as ETAPS distinguished papers. I thank all the authors of submitted papers for their interest in ETAPS, all the reviewers for their reviewing efforts, the PC members for their contributions, and in particular the PC (co-)chairs for their hard work in running this entire intensive process in a constructive, objective and timely manner. I congratulate all authors of the ETAPS 2026 accepted papers!

ETAPS 2026 featured the unifying invited keynotes by

- Monika Henzinger (Institute of Science and Technology Austria, Austria), delivering a talk about "Guarding Privacy Over Time: Challenges and Solutions in Continuous Data Observation",
- Einar Broch Johnsen (University of Oslo, Norway), discussing "Formal Methods Meet Digital Twins: Challenges and Opportunities".

ETAPS 2026 hosted the invited keynote speakers

- Christel Baier (Technische Universität Dresden, Germany) for FoSSaCS, presenting "Verification of Infinite-horizon Properties of Dynamic Bayesian Networks",
- Guy Van den Broeck (University of California, Los Angeles, USA) for TACAS, introducing "Symbolic Reasoning in the Age of Large Language Models".

The ETAPS 2026 invited tutorials were provided by

- Mieke Massink (CNR-ISTI Pisa, Italy) on "Model Checking in Space with Applications to Medical Image Analysis",
- Leonardo de Moura (Amazon Web Services, USA) surveying "The Lean Programming Language and Theorem Prover".

The ETAPS 2026 programme also featured a lively Ask-Me-Anything session, interactive tool demos, a Diversity, Equity, and Inclusion session, SV-Comp and Test-Comp community building events, and the ETAPS industry day. The goal of the ETAPS industry day is to bring industrial practitioners into the heart of the research community and to catalyze the interaction between industry and academia. The ETAPS 2026 industry day was organized by Giorgio Audrito (University of Turin, Italy), Sean Kauffman (Queen's University, Kingston, Canada), and Nikolai Kosmatov (Thales Research and Technology, Palaiseau, France).

ETAPS 2026 was organized by the Department of Computer Science of the University of Turin, which is the center for coordinating research, teaching, dissemination and technological transfer in computer science in Turin, Italy. The department covers both methodological and application oriented aspects of computer science, and performs research in several interdisciplinary areas. This is reflected in the collaborations with other research centers and companies in many scientific areas and in its participation in national, European and international projects.

ETAPS 2026 was further supported by the following associations and societies: ETAPS e. V. (the ETAPS Association), EATCS (European Association for Theoretical Computer Science), EAPLS (European Association for Programming Languages and Systems), and EASST (European Association of Software Science and Technology).

The ETAPS Steering Committee consists of an Executive Board, and representatives of the individual ETAPS conferences, as well as representatives of EATCS, EAPLS, and EASST. The Executive Board consists of Laura Kovács (TU Wien, chair), Andrzej Wąsowski (IT University of Copenhagen, vice-chair), Thomas Noll (RWTH Aachen, treasurer), Arnd Hartmanns (University of Twente, artifact evaluation coordinator), Barbara König (University of Duisburg-Essen, proceedings coordination), Caterina Urban (Inria, PhD activities), Elizabeth Polgreen (University of Edinburgh, social media), Jan Kofroň (Charles University Prague, organisational support, website), Jan Křetínský (Masaryk University Brno and TU Munich, diversity & inclusion), and Marieke Huisman (University of Twente, blog, awards). Further members of the ETAPS Steering Committee committee are: Robbert Krebbers (Radboud University Nijmegen), Azalea Raad (Imperial College London), Luís Caires (Tecnico ULisboa), Elvira Albert (Universidad Complutense de Madrid), Corina Păsăreanu (Carnegie Mellon University), Erika Ábrahám (RWTH Aachen), Marsha Chechik (University of Toronto), Marie-Christine Jakobs (LMU Munich), Nathalie Bertrand (Inria Rennes), Stefan Milius (Friedrich-Alexander Universität Erlangen-Nürnberg), Alexandra Silva (Cornell University), Joël Ouaknine (MPI-SWS Saarbrücken), Andrzej Murawski (University of Oxford), Sebastian Junges (Radboud University Nijmegen), Guy Katz (The Hebrew University of Jerusalem), Christian Schilling (Aalborg University), Naijun Zhan (Peking University), Joost-Pieter Katoen (RWTH Aachen and University of Twente), Dirk Beyer (LMU Munich), Fabrice Kordon (Sorbonne University Paris), Laure Petrucci (Université Paris 13), Peter Y.A. Ryan (University of Luxembourg), Claudio Menghi (University of Bergamo and McMaster University Hamilton), Mark Lawford (McMaster University Hamilton), Maurice ter Beek (CNR-ISTI Pisa), Ferruccio Damiani (University of Turin), Kim Guldstrand Larsen (Aalborg University), Bernhard Beckert (KIT Karlsruhe), Mattias Ulbrich (KIT Karlsruhe), Reiko Heckel (University of Leicester), Vladimiro Sassone

(University of Southampton), Anton Wijs (Eindhoven University of Technology), and Nikolai Kosmatov (Thales Research and Technology, Palaiseau).

The ETAPS 2026 local organization team consisted of Maurice ter Beek (CNR-ISTI Pisa, general co-chair), Ferruccio Damiani (University of Turin, general co-chair), Barbara Boni (Synesthesia Turin, local organization chair), Vincenzo Ciancia (CNR-ISTI Pisa, satellite events co-chair), Luca Paolini (University of Turin, satellite events co-chair), Maria Tacconi (Synesthesia Turin, satellite events co-chair and publicity co-chair), Francesco Brocero (Synesthesia Turin, web co-chair and volunteers co-chair), José Proença (University of Porto, web co-chair), Gianluca Torta (University of Turin, publicity co-chair and local proceedings co-chair), Lucy James (Synesthesia Turin, sponsor chair), Giovanna Broccia (CNR-ISTI Pisa, local proceedings co-chair), Giorgio Audrito (University of Turin, volunteers co-chair), Riccardo Sieve (UiO Oslo, volunteers co-chair), and Reiner Hähnle (TU Darmstadt, wine chair).

I would like to take this opportunity to thank all authors, keynote speakers, invited tutorial speakers, and attendees. Special thanks goes to the organizers of the ETAPS 2026 satellite workshops and colocated events. ETAPS 2026 is grateful for the generous support of Amazon Web Services, AccessiWay, Camera di Commercio Industria Artigianato e Agricoltura di Torino, the Department of Computer Science of the University of Turin, Springer Nature, and Turismo Torino e provincia Convention Bureau. I thank our general co-chairs Maurice ter Beek (CNR-ISTI Pisa) and Ferruccio Damiani (University of Turin), who made it all happen in Turin, and their local organization team for their enormous efforts to make ETAPS 2026 a fantastic event. I am especially grateful to Barbara Boni, Maria Tacconi, and Lucy James (Synesthesia Turin) for handling the organizational process in a smooth and reliable way. Last but not least, a big thanks to Jan Kofroň for all his help as an ETAPS Fellow and providing online presence support for the ETAPS conferences and the ETAPS Association.

I hope you all enjoyed ETAPS 2026!

April 2026
Laura Kovács
ETAPS SC Chair, President of the ETAPS
Association

Preface

This two-volume proceedings contains the papers presented at the 32nd International Conference on Tools and Algorithms for the Construction and Analysis of Systems (TACAS 2026). TACAS 2026 was part of the 29th International Joint Conferences on Theory and Practice of Software (ETAPS 2026), which was held between April 11–16, 2026, in Turin, Italy.

TACAS is a forum for researchers, developers and users interested in rigorous tools and algorithms for the construction and analysis of systems. The conference aims to bridge the gaps between different communities with this common interest and to support them in their quest to improve the utility, reliability, flexibility, and efficiency of tools and algorithms for building systems. TACAS 2026 interleaves and integrates various disciplines, including formal verification of software and hardware systems, static analysis, probabilistic programming, program synthesis, concurrency, testing, simulations, verification of machine learning/autonomous systems, cyber-physical systems, SAT/SMT solving, automated and interactive theorem proving, and proof checking.

There were four submission categories for TACAS 2026:

1. Regular research papers, identifying and justifying a principled advance to the theoretical foundations for the construction and analysis of systems.
2. Case study papers, describing the application of techniques developed by the community to a single problem or a set of problems of practical importance, preferably in a real-world setting.
3. Regular tool papers, presenting a novel tool or a new version of an existing tool, built using novel algorithmic and engineering techniques.
4. Tool demonstration papers, demonstrating a new tool or application of an existing tool on a significant case-study.

Regular research, case study, and regular tool paper submissions were restricted to 16 pages, whereas tool demonstration papers were restricted to 6 pages, excluding the bibliography and the data availability statement. An extra page was allowed for the final version of each accepted paper.

TACAS 2026 received 190 submissions, consisting of 117 regular research papers, 11 case study papers, 33 regular tool papers, and 16 tool demonstration papers. 13 papers were desk-rejected for being out-of-scope or for violating anonymity requirements as outlined in the CfP. Each submission was assigned for review to at least three Program Committee (PC) members, who made use of subreviewers. In total, we obtained 566 reviews, of which 260 were contributed by subreviewers and/or external experts. Regular research papers were reviewed in double-blind mode, whereas case study, regular tool, and tool-demonstration papers were reviewed using a single-blind reviewing process.

Similarly to previous years, it was possible to submit an artifact alongside a paper. Artifact submission was mandatory for regular tool and tool demo papers, and was voluntary, but encouraged, for regular research and case study papers. An artifact might consist of a tool, models, proofs, or other data required for validation of the results of the paper. The Artifact Evaluation Committee (AEC) was tasked with reviewing the artifacts, based on their documentation, ease of use, and, most importantly, whether the results presented in the corresponding paper could be accurately reproduced. When relevant, AEC reviewers also assessed whether the tool could easily be extended to novel examples and future research. The evaluation was carried out using either a standardized virtual machine or a Docker image to ensure the consistency of the results. The virtual machine used this year included, for the first time, support for ARM architectures, in addition to x86 architectures supported previously. Exceptions were made for those artifacts that had special hardware or software requirements.

Artifact evaluation at TACAS 2026 consisted of two rounds. The first round implemented the mandatory artifact evaluation of regular tool and tool demonstration papers; this round was carried out in parallel with the work of the PC. The judgment of the AEC was communicated to the PC and weighed in their discussion. In particular, regular tool papers and tool demo papers whose artifacts did not earn the "Available" and "Functional" badges were rejected. The second round of artifact evaluation carried out the voluntary artifact evaluation of regular research and case study papers, and took place after paper acceptance notifications were sent out; authors of accepted regular research and case study papers were invited to submit artifacts for this purpose. In both rounds, the AEC provided 2–4 reviews (typically 3) and a summary meta-review for each artifact, and communicated anonymously with the authors to resolve any apparent technical issues. In total, the AEC performed 227 reviews and evaluated a total of 77 artifacts regarding their availability, functionality, and/or reusability. 48 artifacts were submitted to the first round and 29 to the second round. Papers with an artifact that were successfully evaluated include one or more badges on the first page, certifying the respective properties. 71 artifacts were awarded the "Available" badge, 66 the "Functional" badge and 34 were awarded the "Reusable" badge.

All authors were given a chance to provide a rebuttal response to questions raised in the PC discussions. Using the review reports and rebuttals, the PC had a thorough discussion on each paper. For regular tool and tool demonstration papers, the PC also discussed the corresponding artifact, using the AEC recommendations. The papers were discussed during a short but lively online discussion phase with over 1,400 posts, followed by a virtual meeting with the area chairs and PC chairs. As a result, the PC decided to accept 56 papers, which consisted of 34 regular research papers, 15 regular tool papers, 3 case study papers, and 4 tool demonstration papers. This corresponds to an overall acceptance rate slightly lower than 30%. Each accepted paper at TACAS 2026 had either all positive reviews and/or a "championing" PC member who argued in favor of accepting the paper. All papers received a meta-review with a summary of the discussion phase.

TACAS 2026 also hosted SV-COMP 2026, the 15th International Competition on Software Verification. This event evaluated 72 tools for automatic verification of C and Java programs and 19 tools for witness validation, where 43 verification and 13 validation tools were registered and actively supported by development teams. Besides the languages C and Java, the competition now includes a category for the language SV-LIB, a new exchange format for verification of imperative programs. This demonstration category attracted 3 verifiers and 1 validator. In total, SV-COMP included 12 verifiers and

3 validators that participated for the first time. The TACAS 2026 proceedings contain a competition report by the SV-COMP chairs and 15 short papers selected by the competition jury. The 15 short papers were reviewed by a separate Program Committee (jury); each was assessed by at least three jury members. Two sessions in the TACAS 2026 program were reserved for SV-COMP: (1) a presentation session on Monday afternoon with a report by the competition chairs and summaries by the development teams of participating tools, and (2) an open community meeting on Thursday afternoon.

We would like to thank everyone who helped to make TACAS 2026 a success. We thank the authors for submitting their papers to TACAS 2026. The PC members and additional reviewers did an excellent job in reviewing papers: they provided detailed reports and engaged in the PC discussions. We thank our six area chairs: Roderick Bloem, Dana Drachsler Cohen, Anastasia Mavridou, Dave Parker, Natasha Sharygina and Yoni Zohar, who proved invaluable in moderating the various PC discussions and pushing them forward. Likewise, we thank the AEC members for their thorough evaluation of all artifacts. We thank the TACAS Steering Committee, and especially its chair, Joost-Pieter Katoen, for his valuable advice. We are grateful to the ETAPS Steering Committee, and in particular its chairs, Marieke Huisman and Laura Kovács, for supporting our changes and suggestions on the TACAS 2026 review process and final program; to Jan Kofroň, for help in updating and maintaining the web presence; to Arnd Hartmanns as AE coordinator, and to Barbara König as publication coordinator. We also acknowledge the support provided by the EasyChair and HotCRP developers, and by Loes Kruger in checking the camera-ready versions. Lastly, we would like to thank the overall organization team of ETAPS 2026, in particular the proceedings co-chairs Giovanna Broccia and Gianluca Torta, for their help in creating these proceedings. Some of the Alt Texts used in the figures in this volume were generated using the publisher's automation, they were not author-generated.

April 2026

Sebastian Junges
Guy Katz
PC Chairs

Guy Amir
Matthias Volk
AEC Chairs

Dirk Beyer
Jan Strejček
SV-COMP Chairs

Organization

Program Committee Chairs

Sebastian Junges	Radboud University, Netherlands
Guy Katz	The Hebrew University of Jerusalem, Israel

Area Chairs

Roderick Bloem	Graz University of Technology, Austria
Dana Drachsler Cohen	Technion, Israel
Anastasia Mavridou	KBR/NASA Ames Research Center, USA
Dave Parker	University of Oxford, UK
Natasha Sharygina	Università della Svizzera italiana, Italy
Yoni Zohar	Bar-Ilan University, Israel

Program Committee

Erika Ábrahám	RWTH Aachen University, Germany
S. Akshay	IIT Bombay, India
Elvio Gilberto Amparore	Università di Torino, Italy
Étienne André	Nantes Université, France
Christel Baier	TU Dresden, Germany
Haniel Barbosa	Universidade Federal de Minas Gerais, Brazil
Clark Barrett	Stanford University, USA
Dirk Beyer	LMU Munich, Germany
Armin Biere	University of Freiburg, Germany
Luca Bortolussi	University of Trieste, Italy
Milan Češka	Brno University of Technology, Czechia
Supratik Chakraborty	IIT Bombay, India
Mingshuai Chen	Zhejiang University, China
Yu-Fang Chen	Academia Sinica, Taiwan
Wei-Ngan Chin	National University of Singapore, Singapore
Alessandro Cimatti	Fondazione Bruno Kessler, Italy
Rayna Dimitrova	CISPA Helmholtz Center for Information Security, Germany
Dana Fisman	Ben-Gurion University, Israel
Hadar Frenkel	Bar-Ilan University, Israel

Florian Frohn	RWTH Aachen University, Germany
Mirco Giacobbe	University of Birmingham, UK
Arie Gurfinkel	University of Waterloo, Canada
Arnd Hartmanns	University of Twente, Netherlands
Marijn Heule	Carnegie Mellon University, USA
Falk Howar	TU Dortmund University, Germany
Omri Isac	The Hebrew University of Jerusalem, Israel
Nils Jansen	Ruhr University Bochum, Germany
Daniela Kaufmann	TU Wien, Austria
Orna Kupferman	The Hebrew University of Jerusalem, Israel
Alfons Laarman	Leiden University, Netherlands
Aina Niemetz	Stanford University, USA
Petr Novotný	Masaryk University, Czechia
Guillermo Perez	University of Antwerp, Belgium
Andrea Pferscher	University of Oslo, Norway
Kristin Yvonne Rozier	Iowa State University, USA
Ocan Sankur	Mitsubishi Electric R&D Centre Europe, France
Christian Schilling	Aalborg University, Denmark
Anne-Kathrin Schmuck	Max-Planck-Institute for Software Systems, Germany
Mihaela Sighireanu	ENS Paris-Saclay, LMF, France
Sadegh Soudjani	Newcastle University, UK
Jiri Srba	Aalborg University, Denmark
Armando Tacchella	Università di Genova, Italy
Hazem Torfah	Chalmers University of Technology, Sweden
Yakir Vizel	Technion, Israel
Bow-Yaw Wang	Academia Sinica, Taiwan
Naijun Zhan	Institute of Software, Chinese Academy of Sciences, China
Lijun Zhang	Institute of Software, Chinese Academy of Sciences, China
Djordje Zikelic	Singapore Management University, Singapore

Artifact Evaluation Committee Chairs

Guy Amir	Cornell University, USA
Matthias Volk	Eindhoven University of Technology, Netherlands

Artifact Evaluation Committee

Abha Chaudhary	Binghamton University, USA
Abhishek Singh	IIIT Hyderabad, India
Aditya Senthilnathan	Cornell University, USA
Alberto Bombardelli	Fondazione Bruno Kessler, Italy
Alejandro Hernández-Cerezo	Complutense University of Madrid, Spain
Alexander Stekelenburg	University of Twente, Netherlands
Andy Oertel	Lund University, Sweden
Aron Ricardo Perez-Lopez	Stanford University, USA
Aosen Xiong	University of Waterloo, Canada
Arshia Rafieioskouei	Michigan State University, USA
Åsmund Aqissiaq Arild Kløvstad	University of Oslo, Norway
Ayaka Yorihiro	Cornell University, USA
Benedikt Peterseim	Universiteit Twente, Netherlands
Benjamin Przybocki	Carnegie Mellon University, USA
Bob Rubbens	University of Twente, Netherlands
Bruno Andreotti	Universidade Federal de Minas Gerais, Brazil
Charles de Haro	École Normale Supérieure, Université PSL, France
Chris Johannsen	Iowa State University, USA
Christoph Wernhard	University of Potsdam, Germany
Clara Rodríguez Núñez	Universidad Complutense de Madrid, Spain
Dapeng Zhi	East China Normal University, Jiangsu University of Technology, China
Divyesh Unadkat	Synopsys Inc, India
Edward Wang	MIT, USA
Elizaveta Pertseva	Stanford University, USA
Étienne André	Nantes Université, France
Evgenii Vinarskii	Télécom SudParis/Institut Polytechnique de Paris, France
Filip Cano	Institute of Science and Technology, Austria
Filip Macák	Brno University of Technology, Czechia
Geoff Sutcliffe	University of Miami, USA
Hanna Lachnitt	Stanford University, USA
Hassan Mousavi	University of Tehran and Tehran Institute for Advanced Studies, Iran
Hichem Rami Ait-El-Hara	OCamlPro, France
Ian Dardik	Carnegie Mellon University, USA
Idan Refaeli	The Hebrew University of Jerusalem, Israel

Jiong Yang	Georgia Institute of Technology, USA
Jonathan Spiegelman	The Hebrew University of Jerusalem, Israel
Juliane Päßler	University of Oslo, Norway
Kartik Sabharwal	University of Iowa, USA
Karthik Nukala	SRI International, USA
Kevin Van de Glind	Eindhoven University of Technology, Netherlands
Leyi Cui	Carnegie Mellon University, USA
Luca Marzari	University of Verona, Italy
Mara Miulescu	Eindhoven University of Technology, Netherlands
Marco Campion	Sorbonne Université, France
Marco Lewis	INRIA, France
Mariem Hammami	UPEC, France
Mark Peyrer	Johannes Kepler University, Austria
Martin Kristjansen	Aalborg University, Denmark
Matthias Hetzenberger	TU Wien, Austria
Max Fan	Cornell University, USA
Mahboubeh Samadi	Tehran Institute for Advanced Studies, Iran
Maria Belen Rodriguez	University of Twente, Netherlands
Maurice Laveaux	Eindhoven University of Technology, Netherlands
Miguel Isabel	Universidad Complutense de Madrid, Spain
Mingkai Miao	The Hong Kong University of Science and Technology (Guangzhou), China
Mohammad Afzal	TCS Research Pune and IIT Bombay, India
Neea Rusch	Uppsala University, Sweden
Nicolas Amat	ONERA — The French Aerospace Lab, France
Nils Lommen	RWTH Aachen, Germany
Oyendrila Dobe	Amazon Web Services, USA
Pablo Gordillo	Complutense University of Madrid, Spain
Philipp Schlehuber-Caissier	Telecom SudParis/Samovar, France
Raya Elsaleh	The Hebrew University of Jerusalem, Israel
Reza Soltani	University of Twente, Netherlands
Robert Modderman	University of Twente, Netherlands
Rui Ge	University of British Columbia, Canada
Samuel Akinwande	Stanford University, USA
Sarat Chandra Varanasi	GE Aerospace Research, USA
Sergei Novozhilov	The Hong Kong University of Science and Technology, China
Simon Robillard	LIRMM, Université de Montpellier & CNRS, France
Syyeda Zainab Fatmi	University of Oxford, UK
Tobias Seufert	University of Freiburg, Germany
Tom Yaacov	Ben-Gurion University, Israel

Tudor Braicu	Cornell University, USA
Vaibhav Mehta	Cornell University, USA
Vlad-Constantin Craciun	Bitdefender, Romania
Weiyi Chen	Purdue University, USA
Wietze Koops	Lund University and University of Copenhagen, Denmark
Xuyang Li	Purdue University, USA
Yonghui Liu	Australian National University, Australia
Yusen Su	University of Waterloo, Canada
Yun Chen Tsai	National Institute of Informatics, Japan
Zvika Berger	Bar-Ilan University, Israel

SV-COMP Organization Committee

Chairs

Dirk Beyer	LMU Munich, Germany
Jan Strejček	Masaryk University, Brno, Czechia

Benchmark Quality Assurance

Zsófia Ádám	BME Budapest, Hungary
Raphaël Monat	Inria and University of Lille, France
Simmo Saan	University of Tartu, Estonia
Frank Schüssele	University of Freiburg, Germany

Benchmark Categories

Thomas Lemberger	LMU Munich, Germany

Infrastructure

Philipp Wendler	LMU Munich, Germany (BenchExec)
Po-Chun Chien	LMU Munich, Germany (BenchCloud)
Marek Jankola	LMU Munich, Germany (BenchCloud)
Henrik Wachowitz	LMU Munich, Germany (FM-Weck)
Matthias Kettl	LMU Munich, Germany (Competition Scripts)
Marian Lingsch-Rosenfeld	LMU Munich, Germany (WitnessLint)

Reproducibility

Levente Bajczi   BME Budapest, Hungary

Qualification

Paulína Ayaziová   Masaryk University, Brno, Czechia
Matthias Heizmann   University of Freiburg, Germany
Marian Lingsch-Rosenfeld   LMU Munich, Germany
Felix Mächtle   University of Luebeck, Germany
Raphaël Monat   Inria and University of Lille, France
Malte Mues   Bergische Universität Wuppertal, Germany
Jan-Niclas Serr   University of Luebeck, Germany

SV-COMP Program Committee and Jury

Dirk Beyer (Co-chair)   LMU Munich, Germany
Jan Strejček (Co-chair)   Masaryk University, Brno, Czechia
Zsófia Ádám   BME Budapest, Hungary
Paulína Ayaziová   Masaryk University, Brno, Czechia
Levente Bajczi   BME Budapest, Hungary
Max Barth   LMU Munich, Germany
Manuel Bentele   University of Freiburg, Germany
Martin Blicha   Charles University, Czechia
Lei Bu   Nanjing University, China
Zhenbang Chen   National University of Defense Technology,
                                          China
Po-Chun Chien   LMU Munich, Germany
Tomáš Dacík   Brno University of Technology, Czechia
Paolo Di Biase   Unimol, Italy
Daniel Dietsch   University of Freiburg, Germany
Marcel Ebbinghaus   University of Freiburg, Germany
Gidon Ernst   LMU Munich, Germany
Fei He   Tsinghua University, China
Matthias Heizmann   University of Freiburg, Germany
Karoliine Holter   University of Tartu, Estonia
Omar Inverso   Gran Sasso Science Institute, Italy
Marek Jankola   LMU Munich, Germany
Martin Jonáš   Masaryk University, Brno, Czechia
Dominik Klumpp   University of Freiburg, Germany
Xianzhiyu Li   University of Manchester, UK

Marian Lingsch-Rosenfeld	LMU Munich, Germany
Nils Lommen	RWTH Aachen, Germany
Nils Loose	University of Luebeck, Germany
Felix Mächtle	University of Luebeck, Germany
Ravindra Metta	Tata Consultancy Services, India
Raphaël Monat	Inria and University of Lille, France
Hassan Mousavi	University of Tehran and Tehran Institute for Advanced Studies, Iran
Naïm Moussaoui Remil	Inria Paris and École Normale Supérieure, France
Malte Mues	Bergische Universität Wuppertal, Germany
Hernán Ponce de León	Huawei Dresden Research Center, Germany
Ali Rasim Koçal	Technische Universität München, Germany
Matthew Richards	University of New South Wales, Australia
Simmo Saan	University of Tartu, Estonia
Peter Schrammel	Diffblue, UK
Frank Schüssele	University of Freiburg, Germany
Adéla Štěpková	Masaryk University, Brno, Czechia
Csanád Telbisz	BME Budapest, Hungary
Hiroshi Unno	Tohoku University, Japan
Vesal Vojdani	University of Tartu, Estonia
Henrik Wachowitz	LMU Munich, Germany
Tong Wu	University of Manchester, UK
Zuchao Yang	Xidian University, China
Giacomo Zanatta	Ca' Foscari University of Venice, Italy

Steering Committee

Dirk Beyer	LMU Munich, Germany
Dana Fisman	Ben-Gurion University, Israel
Holger Hermanns	Universität des Saarlandes, Germany
Joost-Pieter Katoen (Chair)	RWTH Aachen, Germany
Kim G. Larsen	Aalborg Universitet, Denmark
Corina Păsăreanu	NASA Ames, USA

Additional Reviewers

Miriam Ackermann	Jie An
Rajab Aghamov	Ashwani Anand
Amir Ahmadian	Elli Anastasiadi
Daneshvar Amrollahi	Bruno Andreotti

Roman Andriushchenko
Himanshu Arora
Nicola Assolini
Thom Badings
Daniel Baier
Nikhil Balaji
Ludovico Battista
Chanan Ben Tal
Zvika Berger
Martin Blicha
Eline Bovy
Marco Bozzano
Konstantin Britikov
Asger Horn Brorholt
Francesca Cairoli
Calvin Chau
Po-Chun Chien
Rachel Cleaveland
Robin Coutelier
Loris D'Antoni
Gabriel Dengler
Laurens Devos
Alastair Donaldson
Romina Doz
Kevin Dubrulle
Yizhak Elboher
Constantin Enea
Zainab Fatmi
Shenghua Feng
Mathias Fleury
Darius Foo
Markus Frohme
Maris Galesloot
Laura P. Gamboa Guzman
Xinyu Ge
Christina Gehnen
Enrico Ghiorzi
Juergen Giesl
Andrea Gimelli
Ehsan Goharshady
R Govind
Alberto Griggio
Thomas Hader
Edwin Hamel-de Le Court
Jonas Hansen
Ichiro Hasuo
Steef Hegeman
Philippe Heim
Denghang Hu
Marieke Huisman
Antti Hyvärinen
Emilio Incerto
Shachar Itzhaky
Michael Jacks Jr
Marek Jankola
David N. Jansen
Nicolaj Østerby Jensen
Somesh Jha
Taylor T. Johnson
Aniruddha Joshi
Benjamin Lucien Kaminski
Jan-Christoph Kassing
Chantal Keller
Matthias Kettl
Åsmund Aqissiaq Arild Kløvstad
Sascha Klüppelholz
Paul Kobialka
Bram Kohlen
Tomas Kolarik
Igor Konnov
Merlijn Krale
Srdan Krstic
Konstantin Kueffner
Martin Kurečka
Robert Künnemann
Zbyněk Křivka
Hanna Lachnitt
Jean-Marie Lagniez
Min Lai
Engel Lefaucheux
Thomas Lemberger
Matthieu Lemerre
Moritz Leven Rosarius
Bohan Li
Renjue Li
Xie Li
Yong Li
Zhiyang Li
Shaokai Lin
Yi-Fan Lin

Marian Lingsch-Rosenfeld
Fang-Yi Lo
Nils Lommen
Alejandro Luque Cerpa
Filip Macák
Benedikt Maderbacher
Assia Mahboubi
Muhammad Mahmoud
Claude Marché
Jan Martens
Agustín E. Martínez-Suñé
Tomaz Mascarenhas
Kuldeep S. Meel
Jingyi Mei
Roland Meyer
Éléanore Meyer
Robert Modderman
Federico Mora
Harshit Jitendra Motwani
Vojtech Mrazek
Marco Muniz
Vít Musil
Alexander Nadel
Jasper Nalbach
Massimo Narizzano
Mahdi Nazeri
Grigory Neustroev
Sergei Novozhilov
Dirk Nowotka
Tommaso Padoan
Alasdair Paren
Julie Parreaux
Karim Pedemonte
David Perera
Elizaveta Pertseva
Annabell Petri
Ramchandra Phawade
Nir Piterman
Francesco Pontiggia
Danny Bøgsted Poulsen
Satya Prakash Nayak
Valentin Promies
Ritam Raha
Francesca Randone
Gianluca Redondi
Idan Refaeli
Andrew Reynolds
Alec Rosentrater
Nikolaj Rossander Kristensen
Diptarko Roy
Pedro Saccomani
Irmak Saglam
Mahmoud Salamati
Michael Sammler
Sriram Sankaranarayanan
Dominik Schmid
Jule Schmidt
Yannik Schnitzer
Morten Konggaard Schou
Peter Schrammel
Johann Schumann
Arijit Shaw
Riccardo Sieve
Simone Silvetti
Nikhil Singh
Antonina Skurka
Mallku Soldevila
Sylvain Soliman
Gaëtan Staquet
Richard Stewing
Han Su
Yusen Su
Elina Sudit
Marnix Suilen
Amrita Suresh
Juraj Síč
Fouzi Tabouri
Rasmus Tollund
Stefano Tonetta
Wei-Lun Tsai
Max Tschaikowski
Nestan Tsiskaridze
Andrea Turrini
Viktor Vafeiadis
Niels van der Weide
Tom van Dijk
Mark van Wijk
Marcell Vazquez-Chanlatte
Freek Verbeek
Henrik Wachowitz

Zili Wang
Ziran Wang
Lennart Weingarten
Maximilian Weininger
Joshua Wendland
Philipp Wendler
Tim Willemse
Amalee Wilson
Thorsten Wißmann
Boris Wu
Hao Wu

Haoze Wu
Yu-Hsuan Wu
Akihisa Yamada
Mingqi Yang
Qiusong Yang
Wenzhang Yang
Robin Ziemek
Markel Zubia
Michal Šedý
Jakub Šárník

Contents

Proofs and Quantifier Elimination

Automata

SAT/SMT

Robustness Verification of Graph Neural Networks Via Lightweight Satisfiability Testing

Chia-Hsuan Lu[1], Tony Tan[2], and
Michael Benedikt[1]

[1] University of Oxford, UK
[2] University of Liverpool, UK

Abstract. Graph neural networks (GNNs) are the predominant architecture for learning over graphs. As with any machine learning model, an important issue is the detection of attacks, where an adversary can change the output with a small perturbation of the input. Techniques for solving the *adversarial robustness problem* – determining whether an attack exists – were originally developed for image classification. In the case of graph learning, the attack model usually considers changes to the graph structure in addition to or instead of the numerical features of the input, and the state of the art techniques proceed via reduction to constraint solving, working on top of powerful solvers, e.g. for mixed integer programming. We show that it is possible to improve on the state of the art in structural robustness by replacing the use of powerful solvers by calls to efficient *partial solvers*, which run in polynomial time but may be incomplete. We evaluate our tool RobLight on a diverse set of GNN variants and datasets.

1 Introduction

Graph neural networks (GNNs) have become the dominant model for graph learning, used in many critical applications, such as physical and life sciences [26, 5, 15]. An important issue in safety of machine learning is *robustness verification*: verifying that small changes to an input do not change the systems' classification. Robustness verification of machine learning systems emerged in image recognition [4, 20, 18], and has since been explored for a variety of neural architectures. In particular, robustness has been extended to GNNs, where new issues arise as one should consider attacks consisting of small perturbations to the graph structure. Indeed, it has been shown that small structural perturbations can represent effective attacks on common graph learning architectures [7]. The past literature has considered a variety of models for graph structure perturbation, including the addition and deletion of edges [3, 28, 12, 16], or even node injection [17]. Robustness verification makes sense in the context of every graph learning problem, including node classification and graph classification.

State of the art robustness verification techniques for GNNs are based on two ideas. First one iteratively computes upper and lower bounds to arrive at constraints capturing the existing of a suitable attack. For example the constraint

S. Junges and G. Katz (Eds.): TACAS 2026, LNCS 16505, pp. 3–22, 2026.
https://doi.org/10.1007/978-3-032-22752-2_1

might have variables indexed by edges, representing whether the edge is present or not. Secondly, one solves these constraints, using a general-purpose constraint solver. A canonical example is [11], which reduces robustness verification to mixed integer linear programming (MIP). The MIP problems are formed by approximating the behaviour of the GNN, and their satisfiability is tested using the MIP solver Gurobi.

The robustness problem is easily seen to be NP-complete, and thus reducing to a generic solver for another NP-hard problem is natural. But it is not clear that these reductions allow the solvers to exploit the structure of the robustness problem. And indeed, despite advances, robustness verification is currently limited to very small GNNs: e.g. 3 layers. Here we take an alternative approach, and make use of *lightweight solvers*. As in prior approaches we iteratively refine approximations to the evaluation of a GNN on a set of graphs obtained from small perturbations, expressing our approximation as a set of constraints. Unlike prior approaches, we test satisfiability of the constraints only approximately, developing our own *partial oracles* that can efficiently determine whether constraints are satisfiable or not, but may return unknown. Although the lightweight solver approach may seem simpler than one based on existing general-purpose solvers, we show that its performance is significantly better than state-of-the-art.

This paper is organised as follows. In Section 2 we introduce the necessary notations and review GNNs and the robustness problem. In Section 3 we present our notion of partial oracles and how they can be used for robustness analysis. We present our experimental results in Section 4. Finally, we conclude in Section 5. Missing proofs, additional variations of the problems that our tool can handle, and experimental results can be found in the full version [21].

2   Preliminaries

Throughout the paper we deal with directed graphs in which each node is associated with a vector of reals.

Definition 1 (Featured graphs). *A* featured graph $\mathcal{G}$, *or simply graph for short, is a tuple* $\langle V, E, X \rangle$, *where V is the set of vertices, $E \subseteq V \times V$ is the set of edges, and $X : V \to \mathbb{R}^m$ is the input feature mapping.*

For a vertex $v \in V$, we denote the set of incoming neighbors of v, or simply neighbors for short, in a graph $\mathcal{G}$ by $\mathcal{N}_{\mathcal{G}}(v)$, i.e., $\mathcal{N}_{\mathcal{G}}(v) := \{u \in V \mid (u, v) \in E\}$.

We need to analyze the behavior of a network on a collection of graphs obtained through edge insertions and deletions. We will abstract the inputs using the following notion of incomplete graphs, a variant of the general notion of incomplete dataset in database theory [1]:

Definition 2 (Incomplete graphs). *An* incomplete graph $\mathcal{H}$ *is a tuple* $\langle V, E, E^{\mathsf{Unk}}, E^{\mathsf{Non}}, X \rangle$, *where V is the set of vertices, E is the set of* normal *edges, E^{Unk} is the set of* unknown *edges, E^{Non} is the set of* non-edges, *and $X : V \to \mathbb{R}^m$ is the input feature mapping, with E, E^{Unk}, and E^{Non} forming a partition of $V \times V$.*

For a vertex $v \in V$, we denote the set of incoming normal and incoming unknown neighbors of v in $\mathcal{H}$ by $\mathcal{N}_{\mathcal{H}}^{\mathsf{Norm}}(v)$ and $\mathcal{N}_{\mathcal{H}}^{\mathsf{Unk}}(v)$. We will sometimes abuse notation by treating a graph as a special kind of incomplete graph where $E^{\mathsf{Unk}} = \emptyset$.

We denote the set of all incomplete graphs with vertex set V and input feature mapping X by $\mathfrak{H}_{V,X}$. We denote by $\mathfrak{G}_{V,X}$ the subset of "normal graphs" – those with no unknown edges. We will use $\mathcal{H}$ to denote an incomplete graph, and often assume a vertex set V and feature map X.

Incomplete graphs on the same vertex set have a natural "information order", a partial order relation on the set $\mathfrak{H}_{V,X}$.

Definition 3 (Refinement). *For incomplete graphs $\mathcal{H}_1, \mathcal{H}_2 \in \mathfrak{H}_{V,X}$, we say that $\mathcal{H}_2$ refines $\mathcal{H}_1$, denoted by $\mathcal{H}_2 \sqsubseteq \mathcal{H}_1$, if:*

$$E_2 \subseteq E_1 \cup E_1^{\mathsf{Unk}}, \quad E_2^{\mathsf{Unk}} \subseteq E_1^{\mathsf{Unk}}, \quad and \quad E_2^{\mathsf{Non}} \subseteq E_1^{\mathsf{Non}} \cup E_1^{\mathsf{Unk}}.$$

Intuitively, $\mathcal{H}_2 \sqsubseteq \mathcal{H}_1$ means $\mathcal{H}_2$ can be obtained from $\mathcal{H}_1$ through a sequence converting an unknown edge into a normal edge and converting an unknown edge into a non-edge. Featured graphs are the minimal elements of this order.

Definition 4 (Completion). *For an incomplete graph $\mathcal{H} \in \mathfrak{H}_{V,X}$, the completions of $\mathcal{H}$, denoted by $\mathsf{COMP}(\mathcal{H})$, is the set of graphs that refine $\mathcal{H}$.*

It is easy to see that $\mathcal{H}_2 \sqsubseteq \mathcal{H}_1$ if and only if $\mathsf{COMP}(\mathcal{H}_2) \subseteq \mathsf{COMP}(\mathcal{H}_1)$.

Definition 5 (Grounding). *For an incomplete graph $\mathcal{H} \in \mathfrak{H}_{V,X}$, and a graph $\mathcal{G} \in \mathfrak{G}_{V,X}$, the grounding $\mathcal{G}'$ of $\mathcal{H}$ to $\mathcal{G}$ is the completion of $\mathcal{H}$ obtained by the procedure: for every edge $e \in E^{\mathsf{Unk}}$, if e is an edge in $\mathcal{G}$, then e is converted to a normal edge in $\mathcal{G}'$; otherwise, if e is not an edge in $\mathcal{G}$, then e is converted to a non-edge in $\mathcal{G}'$.*

Intuitively, grounding of $\mathcal{H}$ to $\mathcal{G}$ is the completion of $\mathcal{H}$ that is closest to $\mathcal{G}$. We will formalize this once we define a notion of distance.

We will also need a way of introducing incompleteness:

Definition 6 (Relaxation). *For a graph $\mathcal{G} \in \mathfrak{G}_{V,X}$ and a set $E_p \subseteq V \times V$ the relaxation of $\mathcal{G}$ by E_p, denoted by $\mathcal{H}_{\mathcal{G},E_p}$, is the incomplete graph obtained from $\mathcal{G}$ by making all the edges in E_p unknown, and subtracting off any edges in E_p from both the edge set E and the set of non-edges.*

Next, we define the notion of distance on the set of incomplete graphs.

Definition 7 (Distance). *For incomplete graphs $\mathcal{H}_1, \mathcal{H}_2 \in \mathfrak{H}_{V,X}$, for vertices $v, u \in V$, we say that (v, u) is inconsistent between $\mathcal{H}_1$ and $\mathcal{H}_2$ if either: $(v, u) \in E_1$ and $(v, u) \in E_2^{\mathsf{Non}}$; or $(v, u) \in E_1^{\mathsf{Non}}$ and $(v, u) \in E_2$. The distance between $\mathcal{H}_1$ and $\mathcal{H}_2$, denoted by $\mathsf{dist}(\mathcal{H}_1, \mathcal{H}_2)$ is defined as*

$$\mathsf{dist}(\mathcal{H}_1, \mathcal{H}_2) := |\{(v, u) \in V \times V \mid (v, u) \text{ is inconsistent between } \mathcal{H}_1 \text{ and } \mathcal{H}_2\}|.$$

Note that the distance between $\mathcal{H}_1$ and $\mathcal{H}_2$ can equivalently be defined as the minimum of the distances between completions of $\mathcal{H}_1$ and of $\mathcal{H}_2$. One can check that for all incomplete graphs $\mathcal{H}, \mathcal{H}_1, \mathcal{H}_2 \in \mathfrak{H}_{n,X}$: (a) $\mathsf{dist}\,(\mathcal{H}, \mathcal{H}) = 0$. (b) $\mathsf{dist}\,(\mathcal{H}_1, \mathcal{H}_2) = \mathsf{dist}\,(\mathcal{H}_2, \mathcal{H}_1)$. (c) $\mathcal{H}_2 \subseteq \mathcal{H}_1$ implies $\mathsf{dist}\,(\mathcal{H}_2, \mathcal{H}) \geq \mathsf{dist}\,(\mathcal{H}_1, \mathcal{H})$.

A way to achieve the minimal distance from a graph to an incomplete graph is to use the grounding:

Lemma 1. *For every incomplete graph $\mathcal{H} \in \mathfrak{H}_{V,X}$ and graph $\mathcal{G} \in \mathfrak{G}_{V,X}$, letting $\mathcal{G}'$ be the grounding of $\mathcal{H}$ to $\mathcal{G}$, $\mathsf{dist}\,(\mathcal{G}', \mathcal{G}) = \mathsf{dist}\,(\mathcal{H}, \mathcal{G})$.*

The incomplete graph generated by relaxing a graph $\mathcal{G}$ has distance zero to the graph, since $\mathcal{G}$ is one of its completions:

Lemma 2. *For every graph $\mathcal{G} \in \mathfrak{G}_{V,X}$ and every set E_p of pairs of nodes, $\mathcal{G}$ is a completion of its relaxation with respect to E_p, and hence $\mathsf{dist}\,\left(\mathcal{H}_{\mathcal{G},E_p}, \mathcal{G}\right) = 0$.*

Graph Neural Networks Graph neural networks are neural network architectures that can be used for a variety of machine learning tasks, including node-level classification: in this context, they take a featured graph as input and output predictions for each node. We focus on *message-passing neural networks* [8, 10], which are architectures with a fixed number of layers. Following the literature on robustness of GNNs [11], we use a variation that involves directed graphs, with aggregation over incoming nodes. We discuss modifications for undirected graphs and for graph-level classification in the appendix of [21].

Intuitively, at each layer, a GNN produces a new feature vector for each node, aggregating the previous-layer features from its incoming neighbors and applying a feedforward neural networks to the node's own previous-layer features.

Definition 8 (Graph neural network). *An L-layer graph neural network $\mathcal{A}$ consists of a sequence of dimensions $d^{(0)}, d^{(1)}, \ldots, d^{(L)} \in \mathbb{N}^+$, an aggregation function $\mathbf{aggr} \in \{\mathbf{sum}, \mathbf{max}, \mathbf{mean}\}$, and, for each $1 \leq \ell \leq L$, learnable coefficient matrices $\mathbf{C}^{(\ell)}, \mathbf{A}^{(\ell)} \in \mathbb{R}^{d^{(\ell)} \times d^{(\ell-1)}}$ together with bias vectors $\mathbf{b}^{(\ell)} \in \mathbb{R}^{d^{(\ell)}}$.*

Definition 9 (Computation of a GNN). *For an L-layer GNN $\mathcal{A}$ and a featured graph $\mathcal{G} \in \mathfrak{G}_{V,X}$, the computation of $\mathcal{A}$ on $\mathcal{G}$ is a sequence of features $\xi_{\mathcal{G}}^{(\ell)}(v)$ for $0 \leq \ell \leq L$ and $v \in V$. For $\ell = 0$, we set $\xi_{\mathcal{G}}^{(0)}(v) := X(v)$. For $1 \leq \ell \leq L$,*

$$\xi_{\mathcal{G}}^{(\ell)}(v) := \mathsf{ReLU}\left(\mathbf{C}^{(\ell)} \cdot \xi_{\mathcal{G}}^{(\ell-1)}(v) + \mathbf{A}^{(\ell)} \cdot \mathbf{aggr}\left(\left\{\!\!\left\{ \xi_{\mathcal{G}}^{(\ell-1)}(u) \,\middle|\, u \in \mathcal{N}_{\mathcal{G}}(v) \right\}\!\!\right\}\right) + \mathbf{b}^{(\ell)}\right),$$

where $\left\{\!\!\left\{ \cdot \right\}\!\!\right\}$ denotes a multiset.

Once the features are computed, we can apply a threshold to produce a classification of nodes. The GNN assigns each node to one of the classes $\left\{1, \ldots, d^{(L)}\right\}$ based on its final-layer features.

Definition 10 (Classifier induced by a GNN). *Let $\mathcal{A}$ be an L-layer GNN and $\mathcal{G} \in \mathfrak{G}_{V,X}$. For a vertex $v \in V$, the predicted class of $\mathcal{A}$ on v, denoted by $\hat{c}(\mathcal{G}, v)$, is*

$$\hat{c}(\mathcal{G}, v) := \arg\max_{1 \leq i \leq d^{(L)}} \left(\xi_{\mathcal{G}}^{(L)}(v) \right)[i].$$

Adversarial Robustness of GNNs Unlike standard feedforward neural networks, whose features and predictions depend only on the input features; GNN computation depends on both the input features and the structure of the input graph. Consequently, GNN features and predictions may change under two types of perturbations [3, 11, 19]: (i) *feature perturbations*, where an adversary modifies node features, and (ii) *structural perturbations*, where an adversary inserts or deletes edges. In this work we study adversarial robustness under *structural perturbations only*: given a GNN $\mathcal{A}$, a featured graph $\mathcal{G}$, and an admissible perturbation budget, we ask whether the prediction of $\mathcal{A}$ remains unchanged for *every* graph within the admissible perturbation margin around $\mathcal{G}$.

We formalize admissible perturbations via an *admissible perturbation space of graphs*, following prior work [3, 11, 19]. We restrict to structural perturbations — edge insertions and deletions — while keeping node features fixed.

Definition 11 (Admissible perturbation space of a graph). *Given a featured graph* $\mathcal{G} = \langle V, E, X \rangle$, *a set of fragile edges* $F \subseteq V \times V$, *a global perturbation budget* Δ, *and a local perturbation budget* δ, *the* admissible perturbation space $\mathfrak{Q}(\mathcal{G}, F, \Delta, \delta)$ *of* $\mathcal{G}$ *with respect to* F, Δ, *and* δ *is the set of graphs* $\langle V, E', X \rangle$ *that satisfy:*

1. $E \backslash F \subseteq E' \subseteq E \cup F.$
2. $|E \backslash E'| + |E' \backslash E| \leq \Delta.$
3. *For every* $v \in V$, $|\mathcal{N}_{\mathcal{G}}(v) \backslash \mathcal{N}_{\mathcal{G}'}(v)| + |\mathcal{N}_{\mathcal{G}'}(v) \backslash \mathcal{N}_{\mathcal{G}}(v)| \leq \delta.$

The conditions above are equivalent to requiring that $\mathcal{G}'$ can be obtained from $\mathcal{G}$ by converting at most Δ edges from F. Moreover, for each $v \in V$, at most δ of its incident edges are converted. We also consider the admissible perturbation space without local budget limitations. In this case, we simply write $\mathfrak{Q}(\mathcal{G}, F, \Delta)$.

The choice of the fragile-edge set F captures different scenarios. For example, in the *deletion-only* case, setting $F = E$ allows the adversary to delete existing edges but not insert new ones; if we set $F = (V \times V) \setminus \{(v, v) : v \in V\}$, the adversary may insert or delete any non-self-loop edge.

We now formalize the notion of adversarial robustness for GNNs.

Definition 12 (Adversarial robustness of GNNs). *Let* $\mathcal{A}$ *be an* L-*layer GNN,* $\mathcal{G}$ *a featured graph,* $F \subseteq V \times V$ *a set of fragile edges,* $\Delta \in \mathbb{N}$ *a global budget, and* $\delta \in \mathbb{N}$ *a local budget. For a class* $1 \leq c \leq d^{(L)}$, *we define the adversarial robustness of* $\mathcal{A}$ *with respect to* c *as follows:*

For a vertex $v \in V$, *we say that* $\mathcal{A}$ *is* adversarially robust *for* v *with class* c, *(w.r.t.* F, Δ, *and* δ*) if, for every perturbed graph* $\mathcal{G}' \in \mathfrak{Q}(\mathcal{G}, F, \Delta, \delta)$, $\hat{c}(\mathcal{G}', v) = c$. *When the limitation on local budget* δ *is dropped, the perturbed graph* $\mathcal{G}'$ *is taken from* $\mathfrak{Q}(\mathcal{G}, F, \Delta)$.

Note that the condition in the above definition is equivalent to requiring that, for every $1 \leq c' \neq c \leq d^{(L)}$, $\xi_{\mathcal{G}'}^{(L)}(v)[c] \geq \xi_{\mathcal{G}'}^{(L)}(v)[c']$. This formulation requires robustness against *every* alternative class $c' \neq c$. These problems are easily seen to be NP-complete even for a fixed GNN and a very simple update model: see the full version for a precise statement and a proof, which follows along the lines of similar results for feedforward networks [13, 24].

Definition 13 (Adversarial robustness radius of GNNs). *Let $\mathcal{A}$ be an L-layer GNN, $\mathcal{G}$ a featured graph, and $F \subseteq V \times V$ a set of fragile edges. For a class $1 \leq c \leq d^{(L)}$, for a vertex $v \in V$, the* adversarial robustness radius *of $\mathcal{A}$ for v with class c is the maximum global budget Δ such that $\mathcal{A}$ is adversarial robust for v with class c (w.r.t. F and Δ).*

We focus on the node classification case. The variation for graph classification is similar: see the appendix of [21].

3   Lightweight robustness analysis graph neural networks

We overview our approach to robustness analysis. Consider the following generalization of the robustness verification problem:

Definition 14 (d-radius satisfaction). *Given property $\mathcal{Q}$, a normal graph $\mathcal{G} \in \mathfrak{G}_{V,X}$, an incomplete graph $\mathcal{H} \in \mathfrak{H}_{V,X}$, and a vertex $v \in V$, we say that property $\mathcal{Q}$ is* satisfied within radius d of $\mathcal{G}$ at v with respect to $\mathcal{H}$ *if there is a completion $\mathcal{G}'$ of $\mathcal{H}$ with $\mathsf{dist}\,(\mathcal{G}', \mathcal{G}) \leq \mathsf{dist}\,(\mathcal{H}, \mathcal{G}) + d$ and $\langle \mathcal{G}', v \rangle$ satisfies $\mathcal{Q}$.*

We will also consider the following search problem variant.

Definition 15 (Radius of satisfaction). *Given property $\mathcal{Q}$, a normal graph $\mathcal{G} \in \mathfrak{G}_{V,X}$, an incomplete graph $\mathcal{H} \in \mathfrak{H}_{V,X}$, a vertex $v \in V$, and a maximum budget $d_m \in \mathbb{N}$, the* radius of satisfaction *of $\mathcal{Q}$ of $\mathcal{G}$ at v with respect to $\mathcal{H}$ is the largest $d \leq d_m$, such that for every completion $\mathcal{G}'$ of $\mathcal{H}$ with $\mathsf{dist}\,(\mathcal{G}', \mathcal{G}) \leq d$, $\langle \mathcal{G}', v \rangle$ does not satisfy $\mathcal{Q}$.*

Assuming membership in the property $\mathcal{Q}$ is decidable, we can decide the problems defined above, since a naive algorithm can enumerate completions of $\mathcal{H}$, and check whether they satisfy $\mathcal{Q}$ and the distance constraint. Rather than using a naïve algorithm, we aim to solve these problems by employing a *partial oracle*.

Definition 16 (Partial oracle). *For a node property $\mathcal{Q}$, a normal graph $\mathcal{G} \in \mathfrak{G}_{V,X}$, and a vertex $v \in V$, a* partial oracle *for $\mathcal{Q}$, $\mathcal{G}$, and v, denoted by $\mathcal{O}_{\mathcal{Q},\mathcal{G},v}$, is a function that receives an incomplete graph $\mathcal{H} \in \mathfrak{H}_{V,X}$ and a budget $d \in \mathbb{N}$ as input, and which outputs either* SAT, UNSAT, *or* UNKNOWN, *and satisfy the following conditions:*

1. *(Correctness for* SAT*) If $\mathcal{O}_{\mathcal{Q},\mathcal{G},v}(\mathcal{H}, d)$ returns* SAT, *then there is a completion $\mathcal{G}'$ of $\mathcal{H}$ with $\mathsf{dist}\,(\mathcal{G}', \mathcal{G}) \leq \mathsf{dist}\,(\mathcal{H}, \mathcal{G}) + d$ and $\langle \mathcal{G}', v \rangle$ satisfies $\mathcal{Q}$.*
2. *(Correctness for* UNSAT*) If $\mathcal{O}_{\mathcal{Q},\mathcal{G},v}(\mathcal{H}, d)$ returns* UNSAT, *then for each completion $\mathcal{G}'$ of $\mathcal{H}$ with $\mathsf{dist}\,(\mathcal{G}', \mathcal{G}) \leq \mathsf{dist}\,(\mathcal{H}, \mathcal{G}) + d$, $\langle \mathcal{G}', v \rangle$ does not satisfy $\mathcal{Q}$.*
3. *(Soundness on normal graphs or zero budget) If $\mathcal{H}$ is normal or $d = 0$, then $\mathcal{O}_{\mathcal{Q},\mathcal{G},v}(\mathcal{H}, d)$ never returns* UNKNOWN.

We can solve the d-radius satisfaction problem by the following depth-first search (DFS) Algorithm 1, which searches through completions of $\mathcal{H}$ for boosting a partial oracle into an exact solution. The search procedure is guided by the partial oracle $\mathcal{O}_{\mathcal{Q},\mathcal{G},v}$, that is, if the oracle returns either SAT or UNSAT, then the search procedure returns from the current branch with SAT or UNSAT immediately. If the oracle returns UNKNOWN, the algorithm converts an unknown edge to either a non-edge or a normal edge and proceeds recursively. The correctness can be established by induction on the number of unknown edges.

The runtime of Algorithm 1 is exponential in the number of unknown edges in $\mathcal{H}$ in the worst case. Since the partial oracle is complete for normal graphs, when the incomplete graph $\mathcal{H}$ is normal, it will return SAT at line 4 or UNSAT at line 6. The partial oracle will only return UNKNOWN when the incomplete graph $\mathcal{H}$ is not normal. The graphs $\mathcal{H}_1$ and $\mathcal{H}_2$ are obtained by converting an unknown edge in $\mathcal{H}$ into a normal edge or a non-edge, respectively, which implies that the number of unknown edges in $\mathcal{H}_1$ or $\mathcal{H}_2$ is one less than in $\mathcal{H}$. Thus the number of recursive calls is bounded by $2^{|E_{\mathsf{Unk}}|}$.

Designing a higher-quality oracle can significantly reduce the number of oracle calls compared to the naïve approach. However, there is always a trade-off between the quality of the oracle and its cost: an exact oracle can be obtained by exhaustively checking all exponentially many normal graphs, whereas a trivial sloppy oracle may simply return UNKNOWN for every non-normal graph.

Algorithm 1 Algorithm for solving the d radius satisfaction problem.

1: **procedure** CHECK($\mathcal{Q}$, $\mathcal{G}$, v, $\mathcal{H}$, d)
2:    OracleResult $\leftarrow \mathcal{O}_{\mathcal{Q},\mathcal{G},v}(\mathcal{H}, d)$
3:    **if** OracleResult is SAT **then**
4:       **return** SAT
5:    **else if** OracleResult is UNSAT **then**
6:       **return** UNSAT
7:    **else**
8:       Pick $e \in E_{\mathsf{Unk}}$
9:       **if** e is an edge in $\mathcal{G}$ **then**
10:         $\mathcal{H}_1 \leftarrow \mathcal{H}$ by converting e into a normal edge.
11:         $\mathcal{H}_2 \leftarrow \mathcal{H}$ by converting e into a non-edge.
12:       **else**
13:         $\mathcal{H}_1 \leftarrow \mathcal{H}$ by converting e into a non-edge.
14:         $\mathcal{H}_2 \leftarrow \mathcal{H}$ by converting e into a normal edge.
15:       **end if**
16:       **if** (CHECK($\mathcal{Q}$, $\mathcal{G}$, v, $\mathcal{H}_1$, d) **return** SAT) or (CHECK($\mathcal{Q}$, $\mathcal{G}$, v, $\mathcal{H}_2$, $d-1$) **return** SAT) **then**
17:         **return** SAT
18:       **else**
19:         **return** UNSAT
20:       **end if**
21:    **end if**
22: **end procedure**

We will solve the adversarial robustness problem for GNNs via Algorithm 1, using a polynomial time partial oracle. We focus on node classification under an unbounded local budget: no per-vertex constraint on the number of perturbed edges. Once we have obtained a partial oracle for the d-radius satisfaction problem, we could apply it naïvely to compute the distance for satisfaction, which corresponds to the adversarial robustness radius problem.

We fix an L-layer GNN $\mathcal{A}$, a graph $\mathcal{G}$ with set of vertices V and feature mapping X, a vertex $v_0 \in V$, a set of fragile edges $F \subseteq V \times V$, a global budget Δ, and a class $1 \leq c \leq d^{(L)}$.

Consider the relaxation of $\mathcal{G}$ with respect to F, which is denoted by $\mathcal{H}_{\mathcal{G},F}$. Recall that $\mathcal{H}_{\mathcal{G},F}$ is the incomplete graph obtained by converting all the edges and non-edges in F into unknown edges. By Lemma 2, we have $\mathsf{dist}\,(\mathcal{H}_{\mathcal{G},F}, \mathcal{G}) = 0$. We first observe that the admissible perturbation space $\mathfrak{Q}(\mathcal{G}, F, \Delta)$ coincides with the set of completions $\mathcal{G}'$ of $\mathcal{H}_{\mathcal{G},F}$ satisfying $\mathsf{dist}\,(\mathcal{G}', \mathcal{G}) \leq \Delta$.

Let $\mathcal{Q}_{\mathcal{A},c}$ be the node property that holds on node v_0 in $\mathcal{G}'$ when there exist $1 \leq c' \neq c \leq d^{(L)}$ such that $\xi_{\mathcal{G}'}^{(L)}(v_0)[c] < \xi_{\mathcal{G}'}^{(L)}(v_0)[c']$. If there exists a perturbed graph $\mathcal{G}' \in \mathfrak{Q}(\mathcal{G}, F, \Delta)$, such that $\langle \mathcal{G}', v_0 \rangle$ satisfies $\mathcal{Q}$, then $\mathcal{A}$ is not adversarially robust for v_0 with class c. Thus, verifying the *non-adversarial robustness* of $\mathcal{A}$ for v_0 with class c can be reduced to solving the d-radius satisfaction problem as follows:

> Does there exist a normal graph $\mathcal{G}' \subseteq \mathcal{H}_{\mathcal{G},F}$ with $\mathsf{dist}\,(\mathcal{G}', \mathcal{G}) \leq \Delta$ such that $\langle \mathcal{G}', v \rangle$ satisfies $\mathcal{Q}_{\mathcal{A},c}$?

We next present a polynomial time partial oracle for the node property $\mathcal{Q}_{\mathcal{A},c}$. We will describe it for general incomplete graphs $\mathcal{H}$, not just for $\mathcal{H}_{\mathcal{G},F}$. The partial oracle consists of two sequential components: a non-robustness tester, and a bound propagator. It returns SAT (resp. UNSAT) if any of the components returns SAT (resp. UNSAT). Otherwise, it returns UNKNOWN.

Non-robustness tester The non-robustness tester evaluates the grounding $\mathcal{G}'$ of $\mathcal{H}$ with respect to $\mathcal{G}$ and returns SAT if the grounding $\mathcal{G}'$ satisfies $\mathcal{Q}_{\mathcal{A},c}$; otherwise, it returns UNKNOWN. Recall that the grounding is the completion of $\mathcal{H}$ that is closest to $\mathcal{G}$. By Lemma 1, we have $\mathsf{dist}\,(\mathcal{G}', \mathcal{G}) = \mathsf{dist}\,(\mathcal{H}, \mathcal{G}) \leq \mathsf{dist}\,(\mathcal{H}, \mathcal{G}) + d$ for any $d \in \mathbb{N}$. Therefore, if $\mathcal{G}'$ satisfies $\mathcal{Q}_{\mathcal{A},c}$, then $\mathcal{G}'$ is a non-robust normal graph within the admissible perturbation space.

Bound propagator For the bound propagator, we abstract the computation of a GNN on an incomplete graph by computing upper and lower bounds for features at each vertex v and each layer ℓ: we denote these by $\bar{\xi}_{\mathcal{H}}^{(\ell)}(v)$ and $\underline{\xi}_{\mathcal{H}}^{(\ell)}(v)$. The bounds are computed in a bottom-up manner, with the correctness condition being that for every completion $\mathcal{G}'$ of $\mathcal{H}$,

$$\underline{\xi}_{\mathcal{H}}^{(\ell)}(v) \leq \xi_{\mathcal{G}'}^{(\ell)}(v) \leq \bar{\xi}_{\mathcal{H}}^{(\ell)}(v).$$

Note that vector comparisons are performed entrywise. After computing the over-approximated bounds, we check that, for every $1 \leq c' \neq c \leq d^{(L)}$,

$$\overline{\xi}_{\mathcal{H}}^{(L)}(v_0)[c] \;<\; \underline{\xi}_{\mathcal{H}}^{(L)}(v_0)[c'].$$

If this condition holds, then for every completion $\mathcal{G}'$ of $\mathcal{H}$, we have

$$\xi_{\mathcal{G}'}^{(L)}(v_0)[c] \;\leq\; \overline{\xi}_{\mathcal{H}}^{(L)}(v_0)[c] \;<\; \underline{\xi}_{\mathcal{H}}^{(L)}(v_0)[c'] \;\leq\; \xi_{\mathcal{G}'}^{(L)}(v_0)[c'],$$

which implies that $\langle \mathcal{G}', v_0 \rangle$ do not satisfy $\mathcal{Q}_{\mathcal{A},c}$.

We need functions for capturing bound propagation for matrix multiplication and aggregation functions. First, for $\mathbf{A} \in \mathbb{R}^{m \times n}$ and $\overline{\mathbf{v}}, \underline{\mathbf{v}} \in \mathbb{R}^n$, we define

$$\overline{\mathrm{relax}}(\mathbf{A}, \overline{\mathbf{v}}, \underline{\mathbf{v}}) \;:=\; \mathbf{A}^+ \cdot \overline{\mathbf{v}} + \mathbf{A}^- \cdot \underline{\mathbf{v}} \quad \text{and} \quad \underline{\mathrm{relax}}(\mathbf{A}, \overline{\mathbf{v}}, \underline{\mathbf{v}}) \;:=\; \mathbf{A}^+ \cdot \underline{\mathbf{v}} + \mathbf{A}^- \cdot \overline{\mathbf{v}},$$

where $\mathbf{A}^+, \mathbf{A}^- \in \mathbb{R}^{m \times n}$ are defined entrywise by $\mathbf{A}^+ := \max(\mathbf{A}, 0)$ and $\mathbf{A}^- := \min(\mathbf{A}, 0)$. These are lower and upper approximations for matrix multiplication, as captured in the following lemma:

Lemma 3. *For every* $\mathbf{A} \in \mathbb{R}^{m \times n}$ *and* $\overline{\mathbf{v}}, \mathbf{v}, \underline{\mathbf{v}} \in \mathbb{R}^n$ *with* $\underline{\mathbf{v}} \leq \mathbf{v} \leq \overline{\mathbf{v}}$,

$$\underline{\mathrm{relax}}(\mathbf{A}, \overline{\mathbf{v}}, \underline{\mathbf{v}}) \;\leq\; \mathbf{A} \cdot \mathbf{v} \;\leq\; \overline{\mathrm{relax}}(\mathbf{A}, \overline{\mathbf{v}}, \underline{\mathbf{v}}).$$

Next, we define approximations for the aggregation functions.

Definition 17. *Let* S_1 *and* S_2 *be multisets of reals.*
— *For* **sum** *aggregation, we define*

$$\overline{\mathrm{sum}}(S_1, S_2) \;:=\; \sum_{s \in S_1} s + \sum_{s \in S_2} \max(s, 0)$$

$$\underline{\mathrm{sum}}(S_1, S_2) \;:=\; \sum_{s \in S_1} s + \sum_{s \in S_2} \min(s, 0).$$

— *For* **max** *aggregation, we define* $\overline{\mathrm{max}}(S_1, S_2) := \max(S_1 \cup S_2)$. *If* $S_1 = \emptyset$, *then we set* $\underline{\mathrm{max}}(S_1, S_2) := \min(0, \min(S_2))$; *otherwise* $\underline{\mathrm{max}}(S_1, S_2) := \max(S_1)$. *For convention, we let* $\max(\emptyset) = 0$.
— *For* **mean** *aggregation, let* $s_1, \ldots, s_{|S_2|}$ *be the elements of* S_2 *arranged in descending order. We define*

$$\overline{\mathrm{mean}}(S_1, S_2) \;:=\; \max_{1 \leq i \leq |S_2|} \left(\left(\sum_{s \in S_1} s + \sum_{1 \leq j \leq i} s_j \right) / (|S_1| + i) \right)$$

$$\underline{\mathrm{mean}}(S_1, S_2) \;:=\; \max_{1 \leq i \leq |S_2|} \left(\left(\sum_{s \in S_1} s + \sum_{|S_2|-i \leq j \leq |S_2|} s_j \right) / (|S_1| + i) \right).$$

We now define the over-approximated upper and lower bounds for GNN computation. For $\ell = 0$, $\overline{\xi}_{\mathcal{H}}^{(0)}(v) = \underline{\xi}_{\mathcal{H}}^{(0)}(v) := X(v)$. For $1 \leq \ell \leq L$ and $v \in V$,

$$\overline{\xi}_{\mathcal{H}}^{(\ell)}(v) := \mathsf{ReLU}\left(\overline{\mathbf{relax}}\left(\mathbf{C}^{(\ell)}, \overline{\xi}_{\mathcal{H}}^{(\ell-1)}(v), \underline{\xi}_{\mathcal{H}}^{(\ell-1)}(v)\right) + \overline{\mathbf{relax}}\left(\mathbf{A}^{(\ell)}, \overline{\mathbf{s}}, \underline{\mathbf{s}}\right) + \mathbf{b}^{(\ell)}\right)$$

$$\underline{\xi}_{\mathcal{H}}^{(\ell)}(v) := \mathsf{ReLU}\left(\underline{\mathbf{relax}}\left(\mathbf{C}^{(\ell)}, \overline{\xi}_{\mathcal{H}}^{(\ell-1)}(v), \underline{\xi}_{\mathcal{H}}^{(\ell-1)}(v)\right) + \underline{\mathbf{relax}}\left(\mathbf{A}^{(\ell)}, \overline{\mathbf{s}}, \underline{\mathbf{s}}\right) + \mathbf{b}^{(\ell)}\right),$$

where

$$\overline{\mathbf{s}} := \overline{\mathbf{aggr}}\left(\overline{S}^{\mathsf{Norm}}, \overline{S}^{\mathsf{Unk}}\right) \quad \text{and} \quad \underline{\mathbf{s}} := \underline{\mathbf{aggr}}\left(\underline{S}^{\mathsf{Norm}}, \underline{S}^{\mathsf{Unk}}\right),$$

$$\overline{S}^{\mathsf{Norm}} := \left\{\!\!\left\{\overline{\xi}_{\mathcal{H}}^{(\ell-1)}(u) \,\middle|\, u \in \mathcal{N}_{\mathcal{H}}^{\mathsf{Norm}}(v)\right\}\!\!\right\} \text{ and } \underline{S}^{\mathsf{Norm}}, \overline{S}^{\mathsf{Unk}}, \underline{S}^{\mathsf{Unk}} \text{ defined analogously.}$$

The upper and lower bounds are computed in a bottom-up manner. For each layer ℓ and each vertex v:

- With **sum** and **max** aggregations, the bounds can be obtained in time linear in the number of neighbors of v.
- With **mean** aggregation, the bounds are computed by first sorting the neighbor bounds from the previous layer, with this sorting step dominating the overall cost.

Combining these results, the total time complexity is $O\left(L\,|V|^2\right)$ for **sum** and **max**, and $O\left(L\,|V|^2 \log|V|\right)$ for **mean**, where $|V|$ denotes the number of vertices in the graph and L denotes the number of GNN layers. The correctness of the over-approximated upper and lower bounds can be proven inductively.

Lemma 4. *For every completion $\mathcal{G}'$ of $\mathcal{H}$, $0 \leq \ell \leq L$, and vertex $v \in V$,*

$$\underline{\xi}_{\mathcal{H}}^{(\ell)}(v) \;\leq\; \xi_{\mathcal{G}'}^{(\ell)}(v) \;\leq\; \overline{\xi}_{\mathcal{H}}^{(\ell)}(v).$$

We also implement several optimizations to improve the efficiency of the naïve algorithm. For example, for GNNs with **sum** or **mean** aggregations, instead of computing first the aggregation over the neighbors and then the matrix multiplication, we can exchange the order of these two operations due to the linearity of matrix multiplication:

$$\mathbf{A}^{(\ell)} \cdot \mathbf{aggr}\left(\left\{\!\!\left\{\xi_{\mathcal{G}}^{(\ell-1)}(u) \,\middle|\, u \in \mathcal{N}_{\mathcal{G}}(v)\right\}\!\!\right\}\right) = \mathbf{aggr}\left(\left\{\!\!\left\{\mathbf{A}^{(\ell)} \cdot \xi_{\mathcal{G}}^{(\ell-1)}(u) \,\middle|\, u \in \mathcal{N}_{\mathcal{G}}(v)\right\}\!\!\right\}\right)$$

where **aggr** is either **sum** or **mean**. This reordering improves the efficiency of bound propagator by allowing us to shrink the over-approximated upper and lower bounds. Intuitively, over-approximated upper bounds for **aggr** are computed for each entry by selecting certain neighbors. If we perform the aggregation first, each entry is chosen independently, and the resulting bounds are later obtained through matrix multiplication. But we know that once a neighbor is chosen for the ith entry, the corresponding j^{th} entry is also determined. By performing the matrix multiplication first, we preserve this dependency between entries, which leads to tighter bounds.

We also exploit graph structure to accelerate termination. The high-level algorithm is order-sensitive: the amount of branch pruning depends heavily on which unknown edge is selected next (cf. line 8). One optimization strategy is to pick the edge whose resolution is expected to affect most amount of features. For example, for node classification, for target vertex v_0, we prioritize unknown edges that are *closest* to v_0. If an edge is at distance r from v_0, it can influence the feature of v_0 only starting from layer $L - r$, where L is the GNN depth. Choosing small-r edges typically maximizes the impact on the final-layer feature of v_0 and tends to minimize the connected region that contains v_0.

In the appendix of the full version, we discuss several optimizations of the naïve algorithm. In total we have five optimization strategies. Some, like the operations reordering described above, are based on the architecture of GNNs, while others, like the heuristics to pick unknown edges, leverage the structure of the input graph.

4   Experiments

Implementation of RobLight and Setup Our method is implemented as RobLight, which supports GNN robustness problems with a variety of aggregation functions (**sum**, **max**, and **mean**) for both node classification and graph classification; for both directed and undirected graphs; and for both deletion-only as well as deletion and insertion perturbations. RobLight is implemented in C, and all experiments were conducted using the version compiled with GCC 11.4. Experiments were performed on a cluster with Intel Xeon Platinum 8268 CPU @ 2.90GHz with AVX2 support enabled running CentOS 8. Each instance was solved using a single thread with 8GB of RAM. The time limit was set to 300s for node classification instances and 600s for graph classification instances.

Datasets and Models We evaluate the performance of RobLight on GNN models with various numbers of layers and aggregation functions, built and trained using PyG (PyTorch Geometric) 2.6 [6], on the benchmarks: Cora, CiteSeer [25, 27], Cornell, Texas, and Wisconsin [23] for node classification, and MUTAG and ENZYMES [22] for graph classification. Note that Cornell, Texas, and Wisconsin are different from the citation-based benchmarks in that they are *heterophilic*: the existence of an edge between two nodes is not tightly connected to the node labels. We summarize the information on benchmarks in Table 1.

All models are trained for 1000 epochs with a learning rate of 0.001 and a weight decay of 5×10^{-5}. For node datasets, we randomly select 30% of the nodes as the training set, 20% as the validation set, and the remaining 50% as the test set. For graph datasets, we use 80%, 10%, and 10% of the graphs for training, validation, and testing, respectively. The dimensions of hidden layers are set to 32 for node classification and 16 for graph classification. We conduct experiments on directed graphs with deletion-only perturbations for node classification; that is, the set of fragile edges F corresponds to the set of edges of the input graph. For graph classification, we perform both deletion and insertion perturbations on

Table 1: Information for benchmarks, where Degree denotes the average incoming degree of vertices. For graph datasets, #Vertices and #Edges represent the average number of vertices and edges per graph, respectively.

Dataset	#Vertices	#Edges	Degree	#Features	#Classes	Dataset	#Graphs	#Vertices	#Edges	Degree	#Features	#Classes
Cora	2,708	5,429	2.00	1,433	7	MUTAG	188	17.9	39.6	2.21	7	2
CiteSeer	3,312	4,715	1.42	3,703	6	ENZYMES	600	32.6	124.3	3.81	3	6
Cornell	183	298	1.63	1,703	5							
Texas	183	325	1.78	1,703	5							
Wisconsin	251	515	2.05	1,703	5							

undirected graphs; that is, the set of fragile edges F includes all edges excluding self-loops.

Recall that the condition of the robustness of a vertex v with respect to the class c is that, for *every* $1 \leq c' \neq c \leq d^{(L)}$, $\xi_{\mathcal{G}'}^{(L)}(v)[c] \geq \xi_{\mathcal{G}'}^{(L)}(v)[c']$. We also consider *weak robustness*, in which we only consider perturbations to one fixed target class c'. In our experiments, we set c to be the predicted class by the GNN and $c' = \left(c \mod d^{(L)}\right) + 1$.

Baselines We compare our RobLight with the most recent available exact tools for GNN robustness checking, SCIP-MPNN [11] and GNNev [19], both of which are based on translating the robustness problem into mixed-integer programming (MIP). SCIP-MPNN implements a solver for the weaker version of the GNN robustness problem, supporting node classification for directed graphs with deletion-only perturbations, and graph classification for undirected graphs with both deletion and insertion perturbations; both use **sum** aggregation only. It relies on the open-source MIP solver SCIP [2]. In our experiments, we run SCIP-MPNN using the SCIPsbt setting for node classification and the SCIPabt setting for graph classification. Note that SCIP-MPNN also provides options to solve the MIP instance with the commercial MIP solver Gurobi [9]. However, this implementation is buggy, as mentioned in Appendix B.2 of [11], and can incorrectly report a feasible instance as infeasible. For consistency, we do not run SCIP-MPNN with Gurobi. GNNev implements a solver for the GNN robustness problem for node classification on directed graphs with both deletion and insertion perturbation, supporting aggregation functions **sum**, **max**, and **mean**, relying on Gurobi [9]. We run GNNev with incremental solving enabled.

End to End Performance on Node Classification We first looked to answer the question of how our lightweight solve-based methods compares to the state of the art on standard node classification benchmarks, focusing on the Cora, CiteSeer, Cornell, Texas, and Wisconsin datasets. The number of GNN layers is set to 4, noting that no prior tool has shown consistent performance passed 3 layers. We apply the analysis on each vertex with budgets 1, 2, 5, and 10. We summarize the results on weak robustness for the **sum** aggregation as well as the results on general robustness for the **sum**, **max**, and **mean** aggregations in Table 2, where we sum the number of instances with different budgets. For the shifted geometric mean, we set the shiftb to 10. For the full results for each

Table 2: Comparison results of RobLight, GNNev, and SCIP-MPNN for weak and general robustness on the Cora, CiteSeer, Cornell, Texas, and Wisconsin datasets with various aggregation functions. Note that SCIP-MPNN only implements weak robustness for **sum** aggregation. t_a denotes the average runtime, and t_g denotes the shifted geometric mean of the runtime.

| | | | RobLight | | | | | | GNNev | | | | | | SCIP-MPNN | | | | | |
| | | | All instances | | | Robust instances | | | All instances | | | Robust instances | | | All instances | | | Robust instances | | |
		#Instances	#Solved	$t_a(s)$	$t_g(s)$	#Solved	$t_a(s)$	$t_g(s)$	#Solved	$t_a(s)$	$t_g(s)$	#Solved	$t_a(s)$	$t_g(s)$	#Solved	$t_a(s)$	$t_g(s)$	#Solved	$t_a(s)$	$t_g(s)$
sum (Weak)	Cora	10,832	10,812	0.36	0.12	9,132	0.32	0.13	7,509	27.13	11.55	6,101	27.36	10.57	8,912	53.63	19.91	7,641	49.09	17.35
	CiteSeer	13,248	13,222	0.13	0.04	11,930	0.14	0.05	12,193	14.70	7.58	10,936	13.77	6.73	12,935	13.06	4.17	11,720	11.32	3.52
	Cornell	732	732	0.01	0.01	413	0.01	0.01	627	15.68	8.37	331	16.46	7.36	691	25.94	7.66	411	22.38	6.45
	Texas	732	731	0.72	0.22	578	0.77	0.20	611	14.21	6.19	494	9.28	3.95	650	26.52	7.97	537	15.96	4.46
	Wisconsin	1,004	992	1.17	0.26	815	1.42	0.32	768	18.26	8.92	626	15.62	7.11	844	38.93	12.58	723	34.13	10.79
sum	Cora	10,832	10,826	0.22	0.07	6,824	0.27	0.08	8,122	23.27	11.11	4,741	17.98	7.17						
	CiteSeer	13,248	13,228	0.13	0.04	10,216	0.17	0.05	12,367	15.20	8.09	9,439	13.33	6.34						
	Cornell	732	732	0.01	0.01	327	0.01	0.01	675	14.39	8.54	292	15.18	6.76						
	Texas	732	732	0.01	0.01	305	0.02	0.02	655	10.42	6.09	273	5.96	3.17						
	Wisconsin	1,004	1,001	0.30	0.13	645	0.42	0.18	853	22.11	10.58	547	14.81	6.57						
max	Cora	10,832	10,813	0.36	0.14	7,096	0.51	0.19	7,092	93.64	29.53	4,394	55.68	13.75						
	CiteSeer	13,248	13,206	0.26	0.09	10,303	0.32	0.11	11,020	71.44	19.23	8,512	45.48	12.38						
	Cornell	732	732	0.16	0.05	390	0.30	0.09	559	41.00	18.09	267	27.93	9.98						
	Texas	732	730	0.76	0.25	548	0.72	0.21	551	48.44	11.32	438	27.05	5.36						
	Wisconsin	1,004	993	1.69	0.44	727	2.05	0.52	621	77.87	17.24	471	52.91	9.97						
mean	Cora	10,832	10,832	0.11	0.03	6,873	0.14	0.04	7,473	24.00	12.05	4,235	16.89	7.12						
	CiteSeer	13,248	13,234	0.09	0.04	10,215	0.11	0.04	11,708	13.90	7.62	8,887	11.97	5.87						
	Cornell	732	732	0.01	0.01	440	0.02	0.01	579	13.96	8.16	311	12.01	6.00						
	Texas	732	731	0.44	0.09	412	0.77	0.16	624	14.67	7.04	343	11.29	4.51						
	Wisconsin	1,004	1,000	0.38	0.14	633	0.31	0.17	741	20.96	9.86	439	13.86	5.71						

distinguished budget, see [21]. Figure 1 gives a different view, showing how many instances for each budget can be completed as time increases.

Takeaways The first conclusion is that RobLight outperforms the baselines by more than an order of magnitude for every set up. In particular, it shows that it can handle 4 layer GNNs, which were beyond the scope of the prior art. In the case of larger budgets, the competitors cannot complete a significant portion of the instances – note that we are showing the average time only for completed instances.

In our algorithm we are also doing constraint-solving. Our advantage is that we are using the structure of the GNN – in each call to our partial oracle and in the optimizations (e.g. caching) of the high-level algorithm. This structure is not transparent to a constraint solver like Gurobi.

For MIP-based solvers, robust instances are easier than non-robust ones, roughly corresponding to unsat vs. sat. For RobLight, non-robust instances are easier, since on non-robust instances our naïve counterexample finder turns out to be sufficient.

To fairly compare weak robustness and general robustness, we summarize the runtime of instances that are both weakly and generally robust (or non-robust) with budget 10 in Table 3. For instances that are both weakly and generally robust, the runtime increases for both RobLight and GNNev, as expected. However, for non-robust instances, compared with GNNev, whose runtime remains roughly the same, the runtime for general robustness decreases significantly for RobLight. This is again because our lightweight non-robust tester can quickly find counterexamples.

In terms of the impact of the aggregation function, we see that max is the hardest for RobLight, and this is because we cannot apply the re-ordering optimization.

Fig. 1: The number of instances solved by each tool plotted against runtime under different aggregations and budgets. The solid line denotes RobLight, the dashed line denotes GNNEv, and the dotted line denotes SCIP-MPNN. The blue, orange, green, and red lines correspond to budgets of 1, 2, 5, and 10, respectively. Note that the x axis is in logarithmic scale.

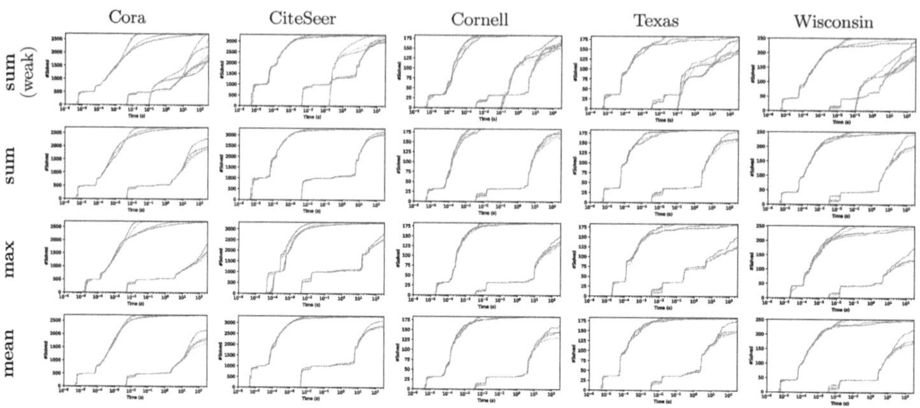

Evaluation of Optimization Strategies Our second experiment evaluates the optimization strategies described in Section 3. Recall that the runtime of Algorithm 1 depends on both the number of recursive calls and the runtime of each call. We introduce the notion of the *exploration ratio* to quantify how these optimization strategies affect the number of recursive calls. Let F denote the set of fragile edges. Since the number of recursive calls grows exponentially with $|F|$, we define the exploration ratio α to be such that $2^{\alpha \cdot (|F|+1)}$ is the number of recursive calls. That is, the exploration ratio is defined as the logarithm of the number of recursive calls divided by $(|F| + 1)$. In the worst case, Algorithm 1 explores all possible $2^{|F|}$ graphs, resulting in $2^{(|F|+1)} - 1$ recursive calls, which implies an exploration ratio close to 1.

We conducted experiments on several variants of RobLight that exclude the optimizations mentioned in Section 3. Table 4 summarizes the results for the variant without operator reordering, without heuristic edge picking, and without all optimization strategies, while the full results for all variants are provided in [21]. The experiments were performed on the Cora, CiteSeer, Cornell, Texas, and Wisconsin datasets using 4-layer GNNs with different aggregation functions, with both global and local budgets set to 10.

Takeaways The results show that the overall improvement exceeds an order of magnitude. Here we focus on the impact of the operator reordering optimization. A more detailed analysis of other optimizations is provided in [21].

With the operator reordering optimization, the average runtime per call decrease as expected. The average exploration ratio also decreases. For bound tightening with budgets, the overall runtime remains roughly the same or slightly

Table 3: Detailed comparison results of RobLight and GNNev for weak and general robustness on the Cora, CiteSeer, Cornell, Texas, and Wisconsin datasets with **sum** aggregation for global and local budget 10.

| | | RobLight | | | | GNNev | | | |
| | | Robust instances | | Non-robust instances | | Robust instances | | Non-robust instances | |
		$t_a(s)$	$t_g(s)$	$t_a(s)$	$t_g(s)$	$t_a(s)$	$t_g(s)$	$t_a(s)$	$t_g(s)$
sum	Cora	0.38	0.19	1.58	0.29	6.31	2.89	22.02	15.02
(Weak)	CiteSeer	0.19	0.07	0.02	0.01	7.63	4.19	22.84	17.64
	Cornell	0.01	0.01	0.01	0.01	13.34	5.42	12.73	9.13
	Texas	0.02	0.02	1.61	0.92	0.93	0.67	13.28	12.08
	Wisconsin	0.08	0.06	0.02	0.02	6.08	3.55	30.86	20.24
sum	Cora	1.02	0.34	0.06	0.03	10.44	3.49	25.01	15.95
	CiteSeer	0.38	0.10	0.01	0.01	12.90	5.35	26.55	18.45
	Cornell	0.01	0.01	0.01	0.01	8.62	4.06	11.17	9.04
	Texas	0.02	0.02	0.01	0.01	1.09	0.95	19.19	13.58
	Wisconsin	0.22	0.14	0.01	0.01	8.80	4.10	30.47	19.09

Table 4: The detailed comparison results of variants of RobLight on the Cora and CiteSeer datasets using 4-layer GNNs of varying aggregation function, with both global and local budgets set to 10. t_a denotes the average overall runtime, t_c denotes the average runtime per call, and ER denoted the average exploration ratio. N/A indicates that the strategy is not applicable in this case.

| | | RobLight | | | RobLight w/o operator reorder | | | RobLight w/o heuristic picking | | | RobLight w/o all optimizations | | |
		$t_a(s)$	$t_c(ms)$	ER	$t_a(s)$	$t_c(ms)$	ER	$t_a(s)$	$t_c(ms)$	ER	$t_a(s)$	$t_c(ms)$	ER
sum	Cora	0.002	0.005	0.29	0.021	0.031	0.30	0.048	0.002	0.34	5.143	0.209	0.34
	CiteSeer	0.001	0.005	0.42	0.037	0.159	0.43	0.002	0.003	0.44	1.111	1.052	0.44
	Cornell	0.001	0.022	0.32	0.001	0.042	0.32	0.001	0.010	0.32	0.006	0.155	0.32
	Texas	0.001	0.004	0.30	0.017	0.026	0.30	0.010	0.002	0.31	1.852	0.440	0.31
	Wisconsin	0.001	0.008	0.39	0.003	0.029	0.39	0.003	0.003	0.41	0.287	0.192	0.41
max	Cora	0.022	0.033	0.31	N/A	N/A	N/A	0.622	0.022	0.36	6.771	0.239	0.36
	CiteSeer	0.033	0.156	0.43	N/A	N/A	N/A	0.163	0.119	0.45	1.574	1.147	0.45
	Cornell	0.003	0.030	0.38	N/A	N/A	N/A	0.006	0.013	0.39	0.066	0.143	0.39
	Texas	0.040	0.035	0.49	N/A	N/A	N/A	0.139	0.033	0.50	1.282	0.285	0.50
	Wisconsin	0.005	0.033	0.45	N/A	N/A	N/A	0.128	0.012	0.48	2.645	0.254	0.48
mean	Cora	0.001	0.015	0.27	0.011	0.056	0.28	0.042	0.004	0.33	6.183	0.322	0.34
	CiteSeer	0.001	0.008	0.42	0.044	0.241	0.43	0.003	0.004	0.44	1.720	1.330	0.45
	Cornell	0.001	0.006	0.39	0.007	0.038	0.40	0.003	0.003	0.41	0.221	0.199	0.41
	Texas	0.001	0.006	0.37	0.012	0.043	0.37	0.007	0.005	0.38	0.616	0.225	0.38
	Wisconsin	0.001	0.016	0.38	0.002	0.058	0.39	0.002	0.004	0.40	0.204	0.332	0.41

increases; this may be because the benefit from shrinking is limited, as indicated by the exploration ratio remaining nearly unchanged.

Results on Robustness Radius The third experiment is about the robustness radius, which RobLight can compute using a variation of the top-level algorithm We conduct experiments on the Cora, CiteSeer, Cornell, Texas, and Wisconsin datasets with 4-layer GNNs with varying aggregation functions with timeout 600s. We summarize the results in Table 5.

Note that the true radius in each of these benchmarks is not large: at most 11. Despite this, to our knowledge, *no prior tool can compute the radius exactly.*

End to End Performance on Graph Classification Finally, we conduct experiments on the MUTAG and ENZYMES datasets, which are undirected and involve graph-level classification instances. In these cases, a final sum pooling operation is applied to obtain a single graph-level output. Details of graph-level robustness and set up for undirected graphs can be found in [21]. We consider

Table 5: Robustness radius of the Cora, CiteSeer, Cornell, Texas, and Wisconsin datasets using 4-layer GNNs of varying aggregation function. TO denotes time out, # is the number of instances, and t_a is the average overall runtime. Note that – indicates that there is no solved instance for this radius.

| | | TO | Robust | | $r=0$ | | $r=1$ | | $r=2$ | | $r=3$ | | $r=4$ | | $r=5$ | | $r=6$ | | $r=7$ | | $r=8$ | | $r=9$ | | $r=10$ | | $r=11$ | |
		#	#	$t_a(s)$	#	$t_a(s)$	#	$t_a(s)$	#	$t_a(s)$	#	$t_a(s)$	#	$t_a(s)$	#	$t_a(s)$	#	$t_a(s)$	#	$t_a(s)$	#	$t_a(s)$	#	$t_a(s)$	#	$t_a(s)$	#	$t_a(s)$
sum	Cora	17	1,447	1.67	580	0.01	349	0.02	172	0.47	94	0.47	39	0.14	7	0.25	2	0.79	1	0.97	–	–	–	–	–	–	–	–
	CiteSeer	26	2,388	0.38	521	0.01	206	0.01	87	0.01	40	0.01	12	0.10	9	0.21	11	14.77	5	54.93	2	3.90	2	265.39	3	150.66	–	–
	Cornell	0	69	0.01	73	0.01	31	0.01	7	0.01	2	0.01	1	0.04	–	–	–	–	–	–	–	–	–	–	–	–	–	–
	Texas	0	61	0.27	77	0.01	31	0.01	9	0.01	3	4.48	–	–	1	3.42	1	0.06	–	–	–	–	–	–	–	–	–	–
	Wisconsin	7	141	0.85	62	0.01	23	0.01	10	0.02	1	0.09	4	2.19	2	59.99	–	–	1	18.83	–	–	–	–	–	–	–	–
max	Cora	18	1,520	3.39	529	0.10	330	1.03	178	4.01	82	0.24	37	0.81	7	2.86	2	1.78	4	23.97	1	596.55	–	–	–	–	–	–
	CiteSeer	38	2,438	1.01	537	0.01	159	0.08	85	0.12	27	0.86	14	4.45	10	105.20	2	10.67	2	132.81	–	–	–	–	–	–	–	–
	Cornell	0	89	2.41	71	0.01	13	0.01	5	0.02	3	0.04	1	0.02	–	–	–	–	–	–	–	–	1	30.10	–	–	–	–
	Texas	7	127	4.74	32	5.62	12	41.31	5	0.12	–	–	–	–	–	–	–	–	–	–	–	–	–	–	–	–	–	–
	Wisconsin	14	160	1.49	48	0.42	13	0.57	8	0.78	3	4.75	2	40.46	1	1.17	2	69.81	–	–	–	–	–	–	–	–	–	–
mean	Cora	2	1,422	1.08	535	0.01	356	0.01	212	1.48	97	0.15	47	0.07	23	0.41	7	2.53	6	1.77	–	–	–	–	1	166.18	–	–
	CiteSeer	18	2,418	1.05	568	0.02	153	0.01	77	0.01	30	0.01	25	0.07	8	0.69	4	8.04	6	62.78	5	92.31	–	–	–	–	–	–
	Cornell	0	97	0.08	53	0.01	16	0.01	7	0.01	5	0.01	3	0.68	1	0.11	–	–	–	–	1	0.08	–	–	–	–	–	–
	Texas	2	87	6.42	56	0.01	23	0.01	8	0.01	1	0.01	2	0.84	–	–	2	0.04	1	2.55	–	–	1	0.13	–	–	–	–
	Wisconsin	7	133	1.14	65	0.01	19	0.03	14	0.08	3	0.05	4	0.86	4	6.54	–	–	1	19.35	–	–	–	–	–	–	1	111.57

Table 6: Comparison results of RobLight and SCIP-MPNN for weak and general robustness on the MUTAG and ENZYMES datasets with various aggregation functions. Note that SCIP-MPNN only implements weak robustness for **sum** aggregation, thus other entries in the table for SCIP-MPNN are left blank. t_a denotes the average runtime, and t_g denotes the shifted geometric mean of the runtime.

| | | | RobLight | | | | | | SCIP-MPNN | | | | | |
| | | | All instances | | | Robust instances | | | All instances | | | Robust instances | | |
		#Instances	#Solved	$t_a(s)$	$t_g(s)$	#Solved	$t_a(s)$	$t_g(s)$	#Solved	$t_a(s)$	$t_g(s)$	#Solved	$t_a(s)$	$t_g(s)$
sum	MUTAG	1,128	1,128	0.14	0.11	58	0.36	0.31	478	128.72	49.44	5	357.92	341.21
(Weak)	ENZYMES	3,600	3,385	15.94	4.10	559	38.20	9.47	672	113.98	50.65	48	188.68	104.27
sum	MUTAG	1,128	1,128	0.14	0.11	58	0.36	0.31						
	ENZYMES	3,600	3,556	3.66	1.04	160	16.95	5.08						
max	MUTAG	1,128	1,128	0.01	0.01	3	0.04	0.04						
	ENZYMES	3,600	3,586	0.52	0.20	115	2.18	1.19						
mean	MUTAG	1,128	1,094	5.03	1.56	224	2.32	1.98						
	ENZYMES	3,600	3,487	8.60	2.16	280	23.34	5.40						

both deletion and insertion perturbations, as well as a local budget constraint — that is, a local budget smaller than the global one— to demonstrate that RobLight can effectively handle robustness constraints under various settings. We conduct the experiments with pairs of global and local budget of $(1, 1)$, $(2, 1)$, $(2, 2)$, $(5, 1)$, $(5, 2)$, and $(5, 5)$, respectively. Table 6 summarizes the results, and Figure 2 gives a different view, showing how many instances for each budget can be completed as time increases. For the full results for each distinguished budget, see [21].

Graph classification is more challenging. Due to this final aggregation layer, we need to keep features and bounds up to date in each layer for every vertices in the graph. Again, we find that RobLight can handle up to four layers (excluding the final aggregation layer), surpassing the state of the art. Our method can in fact go beyond four layers, but we did not include a comparison since other solvers timed out on all examples.

Fig. 2: The number of instances solved by each tool plotted against runtime under different aggregations and budgets. The solid line denotes RoBLight and the dotted line denotes SCIP-MPNN. The blue, orange, green, red, purple, and brown lines correspond to pairs of global and local budget of $(1,1)$, $(2,1)$, $(2,2)$, $(5,1)$, $(5,2)$, and $(5,5)$, respectively. Note that the x axis is in logarithmic scale.

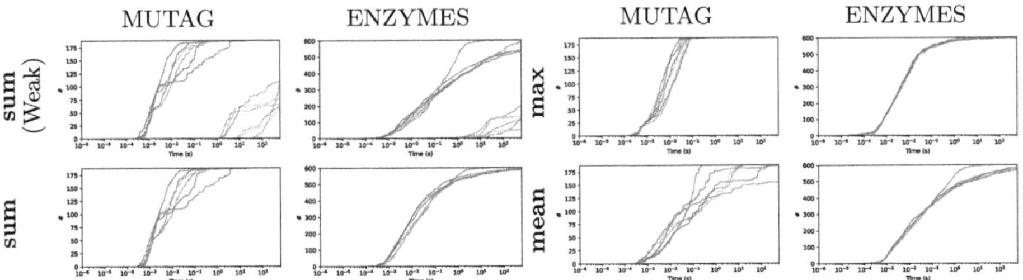

5   Conclusion

Adversarial robustness problems for discrete settings, such as graph learning, are examples of computationally hard problems, and it is thus natural that prior methods for attacking robustness work on top of solvers for classic hard problems, such as integer programming or SAT. Surprisingly, we show that direct approaches that apply heuristic search on top of lightweight solvers can outperform the state of the art. This indicates that solvers still lack the ability to recognize and exploit structure inherent arising from problems in neural verification, and may prompt investigation in how to adapt general purpose solving tools with these applications in mind.

We note that our work does not consider perturbation both to both the features and the edges. For feature perturbation, the graph neural network robustness problem is quite similar to the robustness problem for standard feedforward neural networks, and so it is natural to proceed via reduction to one of the tools available for analyzing feedforward networks, such as Marabou [14]. We also note that, while our work increases the range of robustness analysis for GNNs, the scalability of such systems is still extremely limited. We know of no tools that report exact analysis beyond GNNs with 4 layers and dimension of the hidden channel in each layer equal to 32.

Acknowledgements We thank the anonymous reviewers for their insightful comments and suggestions. We also thank Marta Kwiatkowska, Minghao Liu and Xiaowei Huang for insightful discussions.

Data-Availability Statements The data and code used in this paper are available at https://zenodo.org/records/17485304.

Bibliography

[1] Serbe Abiteboul, Richard Hull, and Victor Vianu. *Foundations of Databases*. Addison-Wesley, 1995.

[2] Ksenia Bestuzheva, Mathieu Besançon, Wei-Kun Chen, Antonia Chmiela, Tim Donkiewicz, Jasper van Doornmalen, Leon Eifler, Oliver Gaul, Gerald Gamrath, Ambros Gleixner, Leona Gottwald, Christoph Graczyk, Katrin Halbig, Alexander Hoen, Christopher Hojny, Rolf van der Hulst, Thorsten Koch, Marco Lübbecke, Stephen J. Maher, Frederic Matter, Erik Mühmer, Benjamin Müller, Marc E. Pfetsch, Daniel Rehfeldt, Steffan Schlein, Franziska Schlösser, Felipe Serrano, Yuji Shinano, Boro Sofranac, Mark Turner, Stefan Vigerske, Fabian Wegscheider, Philipp Wellner, Dieter Weninger, and Jakob Witzig. Enabling Research through the SCIP Optimization Suite 8.0. *ACM Trans. Math. Softw.*, 49(2), June 2023.

[3] Aleksandar Bojchevski and Stephan Günnemann. Certifiable robustness to graph perturbations. In *NeurIPS*, 2019.

[4] Houssem Ben Braiek and Foutse Khomh. Machine learning robustness: A primer, 2024.

[5] David Duvenaud, Dougal Maclaurin, Jorge Aguilera-Iparraguirre, Rafael Gómez-Bombarelli, Timothy Hirzel, Alán Aspuru-Guzik, and Ryan P. Adams. Convolutional networks on graphs for learning molecular fingerprints. In *NeurIPS*, 2015.

[6] Matthias Fey and Jan E. Lenssen. Fast graph representation learning with PyTorch Geometric. *arXiv:1903.02428*, 2019.

[7] Ben Finkelshtein, Chaim Baskin, Evgenii Zheltonozhskii, and Uri Alon. Single-node attacks for fooling graph neural networks. *Neurocomputing*, 513:1–12, 2022.

[8] Justin Gilmer, Samuel S. Schoenholz, Patrick F. Riley, Oriol Vinyals, and George E. Dahl. Neural message passing for quantum chemistry. In *ICML*, 2017.

[9] Gurobi Optimization, LLC. Gurobi Optimizer Reference Manual, 2024.

[10] William L. Hamilton, Zhitao Ying, and Jure Leskovec. Inductive representation learning on large graphs. In *NeurIPS*, 2017.

[11] Christopher Hojny, Shiqiang Zhang, Juan S. Campos, and Ruth Misener. Verifying message-passing neural networks via topology-based bounds tightening. In *ICML*, 2024.

[12] Hongwei Jin, Zhan Shi, Venkata Jaya Shankar Ashish Peruri, and Xinhua Zhang. Certified robustness of graph convolution networks for graph classification under topological attacks. In *NeurIPS*, 2020.

[13] Guy Katz, Clark W. Barrett, David L. Dill, Kyle Julian, and Mykel J. Kochenderfer. Reluplex: An efficient SMT solver for verifying deep neural networks. In *CAV*, 2017.

[14] Guy Katz, Derek A. Huang, Duligur Ibeling, Kyle Julian, Christopher Lazarus, Rachel Lim, Parth Shah, Shantanu Thakoor, Haoze Wu, Aleksan-

dar Zeljic, David L. Dill, Mykel J. Kochenderfer, and Clark Barrett. The Marabou Framework for Verification and Analysis of Deep Neural Networks. In *CAV*, 2019.

[15] Steven M. Kearnes, Kevin McCloskey, Marc Berndl, Vijay S. Pande, and Patrick Riley. Molecular graph convolutions: moving beyond fingerprints. *Journal of Computer Aided Molecular Design*, 30(8):595–608, 2016.

[16] Tobias Ladner, Michael Eichelbeck, and Matthias Althoff. Formal verification of graph convolutional networks with uncertain node features and uncertain graph structure. *Trans. Mach. Learn. Res.*, 2025, 2025.

[17] Yuni Lai, Yulin Zhu, Bailin Pan, and Kai Zhou. Node-aware bi-smoothing: Certified robustness against graph injection attacks. In *IEEE SP*, 2024.

[18] Chang Liu, Yinpeng Dong, Wenzhao Xiang, Xiao Yang, Hang Su, Jun Zhu, Yuefeng Chen, Yuan He, Hui Xue, and Shibao Zheng. A comprehensive study on robustness of image classification models: Benchmarking and rethinking. *Int. J. Comput. Vision*, 133(2):567–589, August 2024.

[19] Minghao Liu, Chia-Hsuan Lu, and Marta Kwiatkowska. Exact verification of graph neural networks with incremental constraint solving, 2025. https://www.arxiv.org/abs/2508.09320.

[20] Nikolaos Louloudakis, Perry Gibson, Jose Cano, and Ajitha Rajan. Assessing robustness of image recognition models to changes in the computational environment. In *NeurIPS ML Safety Workshop*, 2022.

[21] Chia-Hsuan Lu, Tony Tan, and Michael Benedikt. Robustness Verification of Graph Neural Networks Via Lightweight Satisfiability Testing, 2025. arxiv.

[22] Christopher Morris, Nils M. Kriege, Franka Bause, Kristian Kersting, Petra Mutzel, and Marion Neumann. TUDataset: A collection of benchmark datasets for learning with graphs. *ArXiv*, abs/2007.08663, 2020.

[23] Hongbin Pei, Bingzhen Wei, Kevin Chen-Chuan Chang, Yu Lei, and Bo Yang. Geom-gcn: Geometric graph convolutional networks. In *ICLR*, 2020.

[24] Marco Sälzer and Martin Lange. Reachability is np-complete even for the simplest neural networks. In *RP*, 2021.

[25] Prithviraj Sen, Galileo Namata, Mustafa Bilgic, Lise Getoor, Brian Gallagher, and Tina Eliassi-Rad. Collective classification in network data. *AI Mag.*, 29(3):93–106, September 2008.

[26] Jonathan Shlomi, Peter Battaglia, and Jean-Roch Vlimant. Graph neural networks in particle physics. *Machine Learning: Science and Technology*, 2(2):021001, 2021.

[27] Renchi Yang, Jieming Shi, Xiaokui Xiao, Yin Yang, Sourav S. Bhowmick, and Juncheng Liu. PANE: scalable and effective attributed network embedding. *The VLDB Journal*, 32(6):1237–1262, March 2023.

[28] Daniel Zügner and Stephan Günnemann. Certifiable robustness of graph convolutional networks under structure perturbations. In *KDD*, 2020.

SMT.ML: A Multi-Backend Frontend for SMT Solvers in OCaml

João Madeira Pereira[1,2,3], Filipe Marques[1,2], Pedro Adão[1,4],
Hichem Rami Ait-El-Hara[5], Léo Andrès[5], Arthur Carcano[5], Pierre Chambart[5],
Petar Maksimović[6], Nuno Santos[1,2], and José Fragoso Santos[1,2]

[1] INESC-ID, Lisbon, Portugal
[2] Instituto Superior Técnico, Universidade de Lisboa, Lisbon, Portugal
[3] Carnegie Mellon University, Pittsburgh, USA
[4] Instituto de Telecomunicações, Lisbon, Portugal
[5] OCamlPro, Paris, France
[6] Nethermind and Imperial College, London, UK

Abstract. SMT solvers are essential for applications in artificial intelligence, software verification, and optimisation. However, no single solver excels across all formula types, and different applications may require the use of different solvers. While the SMT-LIB language enables multi-solver support, it also incurs heavy I/O overhead. To address this, we introduce SMT.ML, an SMT-solver frontend for OCaml that simplifies integration with various solvers through a consistent interface. Its parametric encoding facilitates the easy addition of new solver backends, while optimisations like formula simplification, result caching, and detailed error feedback enhance performance and usability. Furthermore, SMT.ML is the only SMT frontend that includes a simplification-management engine for streamlining the integration of new formula simplifications and the verification of their correctness. Our evaluation demonstrates that SMT.ML's results are consistent with those of its backend solvers and that its optimisations are highly effective on formulas generated from the symbolic execution of an extensive program-analysis benchmark.

Keywords: SMT Solvers · Symbolic Execution · OCaml · SMT-LIB

1 Introduction

Since their emergence in the early 2000s, SMT solvers have become increasingly relevant and are now fundamental to numerous applications in modern life. They are applied in various scientific and industrial domains, ranging from planning problems in artificial intelligence [15] to software verification and test generation in software engineering [7,16,28,38], and even the optimisation of production chains in operations research [12].

While there are now multiple industry-strength SMT solvers for one to choose from, none of them is perfect for all applications. For example, recent SMT-COMP [14] results reveal considerable differences in solver ranking across various

© The Author(s) 2026
S. Junges and G. Katz (Eds.): TACAS 2026, LNCS 16505, pp. 23–44, 2026.
https://doi.org/10.1007/978-3-032-22752-2_2

theories. Hence, even within a single application, there may be benefits to using multiple solvers for tackling different types of formulas. However, switching between solvers often entails costly and error-prone integration work.

A common approach to interfacing with multiple solvers is to use SMT-LIB [9], a solver-agnostic textual format supported by almost all leading SMT solvers. In this approach, the given formula is serialised into an SMT-LIB formula and then the generated file is passed to the most appropriate solver for analysis. This textual interface, however, introduces I/O overhead, which can make it less suitable for performance-critical applications such as symbolic execution, program analysis, or synthesis engines. For efficiency, it is therefore often preferable for solvers to be integrated into the codebase as external libraries, linked directly via their native APIs. Unfortunately, these APIs differ widely in, for example, naming conventions, data representations, and type safety, making them challenging to understand and use in a uniform way.

While shared APIs for multiple solvers exist for some languages, such as Python and C++, they lack mechanisms to verify the correctness of any internal simplifications and do not address performance bottlenecks caused by repeated or redundant solver queries. Moreover, the OCaml ecosystem, which is home to a number of program-analysis and verification tools, has, until now, lacked a unified frontend for integrating multiple SMT solvers efficiently and safely.

To address these challenges, we introduce SMT.ML, a new SMT solver frontend for OCaml. SMT.ML simplifies the integration of OCaml programs with multiple SMT solvers by providing a consistent SMT-LIB-compatible language connected to five state-of-the-art solver backends: Alt-Ergo [21], Bitwuzla [48], Colibri2 [13], cvc5 [6], and Z3 [24]. With SMT.ML, OCaml developers do not need to understand any intricate detail of the API of these solvers to use them; they only have to create an SMT.ML formula and select the desired solver backend. Importantly, as part of the SMT.ML development effort, we created, for the first time, OCaml APIs for two SMT solvers: Colibri2 [13] and cvc5 [6].

The key novelties of SMT.ML when compared to other SMT frontends are:

1. a *parametric encoding* that relies on a common solver API to translate SMT.ML formulas into the native logic of each backend solver (§4);
2. a *simplification-management system* that allows developers to specify simplification rules using a new declarative domain-specific language (DSL), from which both their OCaml implementations and corresponding Lean [47] proof skeletons are automatically generated (§5.1);
3. a *caching system* for satisfiability results, which normalises SMT queries to maximise cache hits and avoid redundant computation (§5.2).

To the best of our knowledge, SMT.ML is the first SMT frontend to provide all these features simultaneously. The parametric encoding streamlines addition of new solvers to SMT.ML by requiring the developer to implement only a small, uniform set of functions, avoiding code duplication. The simplification management and caching systems are both solver-agnostic and together lead to a substantial increase in SMT performance on realistic program-analysis workloads. In addition, the former enables systematic verification of simplification correctness and provides a framework for extending the system with new verified simplifications.

We perform a comprehensive evaluation of SMT.ML on approximately 206K formulas from the official SMT-LIB benchmark [55] and 2.3M formulas obtained from symbolically executing the Test-Comp 2023 dataset [11] (§6). The results show that the behaviour of SMT.ML is fully consistent with the behaviour of the supported solvers, that the overhead of SMT.ML is negligible w.r.t. overall solving time (below 1% on average), and that the simplifications and caching of SMT.ML yield up to a 1.6x speed-up on formulas produced by symbolic execution.

We have made SMT.ML fully accessible to the OCaml and research communities. It is actively used in research projects across both academia [44,45] and industry [3], and has been integrated into OPAM [61], the OCaml package manager, simplifying its incorporation into future OCaml projects.

2   Why use SMT.ML?

In this section, we discuss in more detail the three main advantages that SMT.ML introduces for developers working with SMT solvers in OCaml.

Solver Independence. A key advantage of SMT.ML is its ability to interface with multiple SMT solvers through a single solver-independent frontend. In doing so, SMT.ML eliminates the need for developers to tailor their code to a specific solver API and lets them transparently switch between solvers, selecting whichever one is best for a given problem. This decision can even be made at runtime, allowing for the application of customised portfolio strategies [60].

Performance Optimisations. Interactions with SMT solvers are computationally expensive and can become a bottleneck in client applications. For instance, these interactions are known to be one of the main performance degradation factors in symbolic execution tools [45]. Our evaluation, described in detail in §6, shows that SMT.ML, with its solver-agnostic formula simplifications and caching of satisfiability results, can introduce substantial performance improvements when compared to using any single SMT solver directly.

Usability. OCaml bindings for SMT solvers often provide few type safety guarantees, with many using one generic OCaml type to represent SMT expressions denoting different types of values, such as integers or strings. For instance, OCaml bindings for Z3 [24] use a single type for all general expressions regardless of

---

Listing 1 Type violation of the addition operator using Z3 OCaml bindings.

```
1 (* String value -> "4" *)
2 let four = Seq.mk_string ctx "4"
3 (* Integer value -> 2 *)
4 let two = Arithmetic.Integer.mk_numeral_i ctx 2
5 (* "4" + 2 >= 2 *)
6 let formula = Arithmetic.mk_ge ctx (Arithmetic.mk_add ctx [ four; two ]) two
```

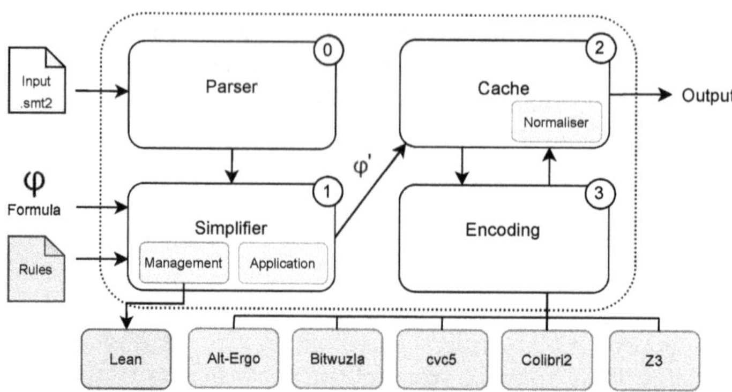

Fig. 1: Overview: Architecture of SMT.ML.

their underlying sort. This leads to ill-typed expressions not being detected at compile-time leading to hard-to-debug runtime errors. Listing 1 illustrates this issue by applying the addition operator, which expects two numeral arguments, to a string constant (line 6). This results in a runtime error indicating that the expected and actual argument types do not match. In contrast, SMT.ML features a typed API, ensuring that expressions are well-typed by construction, avoiding this class of bugs and promoting code correctness and reliability in the development process.

3   Architecture

Figure 1 presents an overview of the architecture of SMT.ML. While SMT.ML was primarily conceived to be used as a library within an OCaml application, it could, in principle, also be used as a standalone tool. Therefore, it accepts inputs either in the form of native SMT.ML formulas or SMT-LIB [9] textual formulas. In the case of the latter, the SMT-LIB formula is first parsed by the *Parser module (Step 0)* and converted into an SMT.ML native formula. Given a native formula, SMT.ML performs the following steps:

- *Simplifier module (Step 1):* This module applies a range of transformations to the given formula to reduce its complexity while preserving its original semantics. For instance, it applies the following algebraic identity to simplify bit-vector formulas:

$$\texttt{concat}(\texttt{extract}(x, h, m), \texttt{extract}(x, m, l)) \to \texttt{extract}(x, h, l)$$

  where the `concat` operator concatenates the two given bit-vectors and the `extract` operator returns the slice of the given bit-vector corresponding to the specified bounds, padding with additional zeros if necessary.
- *Cache module (Step 2):* This module normalises the given formula, checks if its satisfiability was already computed, and if so, returns the stored result. As part of the normalisation process, we rename symbolic variables in a standardised way to maximise cache hits.

TYPES
$t ::=$ Tunit | Tbool | Tint | Treal | Tbitv int | Tfp 32 | Tfp 64 | Tstr | Tregexp | Tapp | Tlist

VALUES
$v \in \mathcal{V}_{smt} ::=$ unit | true | false | int | real | bitv n | $f32$ | $f64$ | str | regexp | list v

EXPRESSIONS
$e \in \mathcal{E}_{smt} ::= v \mid x_t \mid$ unop(op, t, e) | binop(op, t, e, e) | triop(op, t, e, e, e)
$\qquad\qquad$ | naryop(op, t, list e) | relop(op, t, e, e) | cvtop(op, t, e) | list e

COMMANDS
$c \in \mathcal{C}_{smt} ::=$ declare(x_t) | assert e | check_sat (list e) | get_model
$\qquad\qquad$ | get_value e | pop int | push int | reset | exit

---

Fig. 2: The syntax of SMT.ML.

– *Encoding module (Step 3):* This module encodes SMT.ML expressions using the native OCaml bindings of the selected solver. It is parametric on a Core Solver API, simplifying the addition of new solver backends.

The simplifier module is also responsible for managing simplification rules, both converting them into the executable OCaml code that applies them and generating the Lean proof skeletons that, once completed, establish their correctness.

3.1 Syntax of SMT.ML

The syntax of SMT.ML is presented in Figure 2. There are two main syntactic categories: expressions, which denote values, and commands, which represent instructions given to the solver. SMT.ML currently supports the theories of quantifier-free linear integer and real arithmetic (**QF_LIA** and **QF_LRA**), bit-vectors (**QF_BV**), floating-point arithmetic (**QF_FP**), and strings (**QF_S**). These are the theories most commonly required for software verification and analysis tasks [5,17], which is the main application of SMT.ML. However, SMT.ML has a modular and extensible architecture, making it easy to add support for other theories.

Values. SMT.ML values, $v \in \mathcal{V}_{smt}$, include the unit value, booleans (**true** and **false**), integers, reals, machine integers (**bitv** n, where n denotes an arbitrary bit-width), IEEE 754 floating-point numbers (32 and 64-bit) [34], strings, regular expressions, and lists.

Expressions. Expressions, $e \in \mathcal{E}_{smt}$, consist of: values; typed symbolic variables x_t, where x denotes the variable identifier and t its type; and operators, which can be unary (**unop**, such as logical negation), binary (**binop**, such as addition), ternary (**triop**, such as bit-vector slicing), n-ary (**naryop**, such as list concatenation), relational (**relop**, such as comparisons), conversion-related (**cvtop**, such as casting from an integer to a string), or a special **list** operator that creates lists of expressions. Importantly, expression constructors enforce well-typedness by explicitly carrying the expression type.

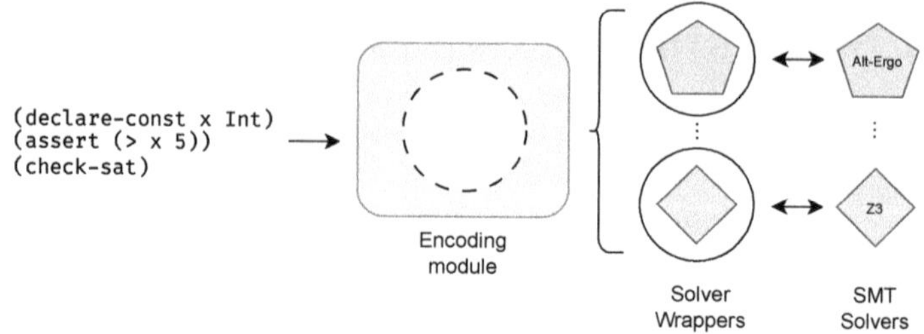

Fig. 3: The parametric Encoding module of SMT.ML.

Commands. SMT.ML provides the developer with a set of commands for interacting with SMT solvers. In particular, one can: declare a symbolic variable x of a given type t; assert that a given Boolean expression (i.e., formula) holds; check satisfiability of the current solver state additionally assuming a given list of formulas; get a model for the last satisfiability check; get a model for a given expression in the context of the last satisfiability check; introduce/remove a number of assertion levels; and reset/terminate the interaction with the solver.

4 Encoding

The Encoding Module is the core component of SMT.ML that is responsible for translating native SMT.ML expressions and commands into the expressions and commands of the solver backends. Instead of having a separate encoding process for each backend, we identify a set of fundamental functionalities required for solver interaction and bring them together to form a parametric *Core Solver API*, which we then use to define a solver-independent encoding. For a solver to be integrated into SMT.ML, all that it needs to do is: support integration with OCaml via native bindings; implement our Core Solver API as a wrapper around these bindings; and plug this implementation into SMT.ML. This parametric approach, which is illustrated in Figure 3, substantially streamlines the addition of new solver backends to SMT.ML and avoids code duplication.

Importantly, extending a given solver with the wrapper code that implements the Core Solver API is significantly easier than implementing a solver-specific encoding from scratch. In particular, as nearly all the functions required by the Core Solver API are typically present in native solver APIs, implementing the wrapper code only amounts to mapping their native names to those expected by the Core Solver API.

The Core Solver API, denoted by $\mathcal{S}$, encompasses all functions on solver values, expressions, and commands on which the encoding of SMT.ML expressions and commands depends. These functions can be divided into the following four main categories:

- *Values:* these functions are responsible for mapping SMT.ML primitive values, $v \in \mathcal{V}_{smt}$, into values from the corresponding target solver;

$$\text{VALUES} \qquad \cfrac{\mathcal{S}.val(v) = v'}{T_{\mathcal{S}}(v) = v'}$$

$$\text{SYMBOLS} \qquad \cfrac{\mathcal{S}.symbol(s) = s'}{T_{\mathcal{S}}(s) = s'}$$

$$\text{UNARY OPERATORS} \qquad \cfrac{T_{\mathcal{S}}(e) = te \qquad \mathcal{S}.unop(uop, te) = e'}{T_{\mathcal{S}}(uop\ e) = e'}$$

$$\text{N-ARY OPERATORS} \qquad \cfrac{T_{\mathcal{S}}(e_i) = e'_i \mid_{i=1}^{n} \qquad \mathcal{S}.naryop(nop, [e'_1, \ldots, e'_n]) = e'}{T_{\mathcal{S}}(nop\ [e_1, \ldots, e_n]) = e'}$$

Fig. 4: Parametric translation rules for SMT.ML (excerpt).

- *Operators:* these functions map SMT.ML operators to the corresponding solver operators: for example, solver wrappers are expected to implement the addition operator, which, when given two solver expressions, returns a target solver expression representing their sum;
- *Commands:* these functions map SMT.ML commands, $c \in \mathcal{C}_{smt}$, into commands that manipulate and interact with the target solver; and
- *Lifting:* these functions map solver values back to SMT.ML values, and are essential when performing model extraction, as they allow models to be constructed using native SMT.ML values.

Parametric Translation. Using the API described above, we implement a generic translation from SMT.ML constructs to the corresponding solver-specific constructs. Expression translation is formalised as a function $T_{\mathcal{S}} : \mathcal{E}_{smt} \to \mathcal{S}.Expr$ that receives an SMT.ML expression $e \in \mathcal{E}_{smt}$ and generates a target solver expression $te \in \mathcal{S}.Expr$. An excerpt of the translation rules is shown in Figure 4.

Values v and symbols s are translated into their counterparts in the target solver $\mathcal{S}$, using the functions $\mathcal{S}.val(v)$ and $\mathcal{S}.symbol(s)$, respectively. Unary operators, $uop\ e$, are translated by applying the solver's unary operator to the translated argument using the Core Solver API function $\mathcal{S}.unop(uop, te)$, which produces the solver expression denoting uop applied to te. The translation proceeds similarly for all other kinds of operators.

SMT.ML supports five backend solvers: Alt-Ergo, Bitwuzla, Colibri2, cvc5, and Z3. For each of these solvers we have implemented the Core Solver API. Furthermore, for Colibri2 we needed to implement a user-facing API to enable solver interaction, and for cvc5 we had to implement OCaml bindings from scratch [41], as none were originally available. In this way, we allow for cvc5 to be natively integrated not only into SMT.ML but also into any other OCaml-based tool.

5   Backend-independent Optimisations

The usefulness of SMT.ML extends beyond its capability to interact with multiple SMT solvers through a unified syntax. A significant aspect of its design is the inclusion of backend-independent optimisations that enhance performance when checking satisfiability. Here, we discuss the two most important such optimisations: expression simplifications (§5.1) and caching (§5.2).

5.1   Expression Simplifications

In applications that interact with SMT solvers, the size and complexity of the problem at hand can significantly affect solver efficiency, making performance the primary bottleneck [2,64]. To address this, SMT.ML tries to reduce expression complexity by applying a set of semantics-preserving simplifications before these expressions are passed to a solver. Currently, SMT.ML comes with 42 simplification rules, spanning the theories of bit-vectors (11 rules), strings (3 rules), booleans (2 rules), and 26 generic rules that are applicable to multiple theories.

Importantly, instead of hardcoding these simplifications directly into the OCaml codebase, we design a simple domain-specific language (DSL) that enables their declarative specification. This allows users of SMT.ML to easily examine, add, or remove simplifications by need. From these specifications, we automatically generate the corresponding OCaml implementations and, if applicable, Lean [47] proof skeletons, allowing users to formally prove simplification correctness by hand, thereby reducing the trusted computing base of SMT.ML. While there is prior work on declarative languages for specifying SMT simplifications [50] and on methods for their validation [37], SMT.ML is the first SMT frontend to adopt this approach.

Simplification management. SMT.ML simplification rules, $r \in \mathcal{R}$, are of the form $e_1 \Rightarrow e_2$ **when** e_f, meaning that if the boolean expression e_f holds, then the expression e_1 can be rewritten to e_2. For instance, consider the simplification rule:

$$\mathbf{Extract}(bv, h, l) \Rightarrow bv$$
$$\mathbf{when} \quad h < \mathtt{size}(bv) \ \&\& \ l \geq 0 \ \&\& \ \mathtt{size}(bv) = h - l + 1 \tag{1}$$

where **Extract** is an SMT.ML operator that returns the slice of a given bit-vector x from bit l to bit h inclusive, padding with zeros if the slice falls outside x. This rule says that $\mathbf{Extract}(x, h, l)$ can be rewritten to x when l is non-negative, h is within the bounds of x and $h - l + 1$ equals the size of x. From this rule, SMT.ML automatically generates the OCaml code that implements it (Fig. 5, left), as well as the corresponding Lean proof skeleton (Fig. 5, right).

```
1 let simplify_triop ty op hte1 hte2 hte3 =        1 lemma simplification_triop_000004
2   match op, hte1, hte2, hte3 with                2   {w : Nat}
3   | ... (* other simplification cases *)          3   {h l : Int}
4   | Extract, bv, Val (Int h), Val (Int l)         4   (n : BitVec w)
5     when l >= 0                                   5   (h0 : l >= 0)
6       and h < Ty.size (ty bv)                     6   (h1 : h < w)
7       and h - 1 + 1 = Ty.size (ty bv)             7   (h2 : (w : Int) = h - l + 1) :
8     -> bv                                         8 BitVec.extractLsb h l n = n := by ...
```

Fig. 5: Example: generated OCaml code (left) and Lean proof skeleton (right).

Simplification application. At runtime, SMT.ML takes the formulas that are to be checked for satisfiability and, for each such formula, keeps looping over the simplification rules, applying those whose constraints are satisfied until no further rules can be applied; this process is illustrated in Algorithm 1. Importantly, SMT.ML keeps track of simplified expressions and, when a new expression is simplified,

---

Algorithm 1 Expression simplification algorithm.

```
1:  procedure SIMPLIFY(e)
2:      e' ← e
3:      for all r ∈ Rules do
4:          e' ← apply r to e'
5:      if e' ≠ e then
6:          return SIMPLIFY(e')
7:      else
8:          return e'
```

---

it checks if it has occurred before ensuring that the collective application rules does not result in infinite loops, such as $e \xrightarrow{r_1} e' \xrightarrow{r_2} e$, where e is the original expression, e' the simplified expression, and r_1 and r_2 two simplification rules.

To apply a simplification rule $e_1 \implies e_2$ **when** e_f to a given expression e in execution context e'_f, SMT.ML proceeds as follows:

1. find a substitution θ such that $\theta(e_1) = e$;
2. if successful, check that $e'_f \models \theta(e_f)$;
3. if successful, replace e with $\theta(e_2)$.

For instance, in execution context $\pi \equiv |z| = 2$, applying the simplification from Equation 1 to the expression $\texttt{extract}(\texttt{concat}(y, z), |y|+2, 0)$ yields the expression $\texttt{concat}(y, z)$ with substitution $\theta = [x \mapsto \texttt{concat}(y, z), h \mapsto |y| + 2, l \mapsto 0]$.

Lean correctness proofs. We generate Lean proof skeletons for 33 out of the 42 simplifications and provide the corresponding proofs. As all of our simplifications describe basic properties of the underlying datatypes, their proofs are very simple and highly automated, relying on the comprehensive mathematical library of Lean. The remaining 9 simplifications are purely *definitional*, in that they describe the behaviour of SMT.ML operators on concrete inputs in terms of the corresponding OCaml operators. One such simplification, for example, is:

$$\texttt{Length}(l) \Rightarrow \texttt{List.length } l \textbf{ when } \texttt{concrete}(l) \tag{2}$$

which declares that the SMT.ML `Length` operator coincides with the OCaml `List.length` operator. Note that this simplification uses the $\texttt{concrete}(x)$ predicate in the **when** clause, which holds if and only if x is concrete.

5.2 Caching

Caching of intermediate satisfiability results is a standard technique used in SMT solvers and solver clients to improve performance [52,56]. However, it is not common for identical formulas to be queried multiple times, even in applications that make an intensive use of SMT solvers. To address this, formula caching systems [2,62] typically implement normalisation strategies [33] with the goal of maximising cache hits. SMT.ML comes with its own formula caching system equipped with a normalisation procedure that performs:

- *Standardisation of associative operators:* a standard order is imposed on expressions that include such operators. For instance, considering the disjunction operator, $\vee$, we have that $(x \vee y) \vee z = x \vee (y \vee z)$. In SMT.ML, expressions that include chained associative operators are always rewritten to ensure that the leftmost operations are performed first.
- *Variable renaming:* variables are renamed to ensure structurally identical formulas with different variable names are considered equal.

In addition to minimising the number of queries, one can also enhance the performance of solver clients by reducing the number of expressions created at runtime. In fact, solver clients often generate a large number of expressions, frequently with repeated elements. As the number of queries grows, memory consumption increases, impacting client performance; a prime example of this are symbolic execution engines [18]. The standard approach to reducing the memory impact of such systems is *hash-consing* [27], a technique that ensures that no two physical copies of the same expression are ever created by storing expressions in a hash table. SMT.ML includes a hash-consing module that prevents duplication of identical expressions. To this end, whenever an SMT.ML expression constructor is called, it checks whether the expression already exists, and, if it does, returns the previously stored expression.

Listing 2 illustrates this process for the `Or` constructor. We define the `mk_or` hash-consing constructor, which builds a boolean disjunction of two hash-consed expressions. In line 3, we construct the binary expression, and in line 4, we attempt to retrieve a previously constructed expression from the hash-consing table. If the expression is not found, we add it to the table and return the value constructed in line 3. One might notice that in line 3 we allocate memory to construct an expression, only to later use an existing one retrieved from the hash-consing table. However, as OCaml initially allocates values in the minor heap using a bump allocator [46], this allocation incurs no cost. Additionally, OCaml will collect the temporarily allocated values during minor garbage collection.

Listing 2 Hash-consing constructor for boolean disjunction.

```
1 let table = Hashtbl.create 251
2 let mk_or hte1 hte2 =
3   let x = Binary (Or, hte1, hte2) in
4   try Hashtbl.find table x with Not_found -> Hashtbl.add table x x; x
```

---

6 Evaluation

We evaluate SMT.ML with respect to the five following questions:

- *EQ1:* Does SMT.ML exhibit behaviour consistent with the supported solvers?
- *EQ2:* How much does SMT.ML's overhead impact overall performance?
- *EQ3:* How do SMT.ML's optimisations impact its overall performance?
- *EQ4:* Are SMT.ML's simplifications transparent and trustworthy?
- *EQ5:* How does SMT.ML compare to other SMT frontends?

All experiments were performed on a server with a 12-core Intel Xeon E5-2620 v4 CPU and 32GB of RAM, running Ubuntu 24.04.1 LTS. We compiled Smt.ml using the OCaml 5.3.0 compiler. For the SMT solvers, we used Alt-Ergo v2.6.2, Bitwuzla v0.8.0, Colibri2 development version (commit `1feba887`), cvc5 v1.3.0, and Z3 v4.13.0. Each benchmark was run with a timeout of 60s and 10GB memory limit. The benchmarking code, reproducibility scripts, and diagram generation scripts are all available at [29].

6.1   Datasets

To assess the correctness (§6.2) and performance overhead (§6.3) of Smt.ml, we used a subset of the official SMT-LIB benchmark [55]. In particular, we used approximately 206K SMT formulas that comprise the (quantifier-free) theories of: linear integer arithmetic (`QF_LIA`), floating-point arithmetic (`QF_FP`), bit-vector arithmetic (`QF_BV`), string theory (`QF_S`), and string theory with linear integer arithmetic (`QF_SLIA`). We chose these theories as they are the ones both most commonly used in practice [14] and well-supported by the Smt.ml backends.

To assess how the optimisations of Smt.ml impact performance (§6.4), we used a dataset of approximately 2.3M SMT formulas generated through symbolic execution of the following sub-categories from the `c/ReachSafety` category of the official Test-Comp 2023 benchmark suite [11]: Arrays, Bit-vectors, Heap, ProductLines, and Sequentialized. These categories provide a diverse set of formulas commonly encountered during symbolic execution of binary code. For formula generation, we used the Owi symbolic execution engine [3] as it does not implement its own formula caching system and includes only a small set of built-in optimisations, thereby allowing for a more trustworthy assessment of the true impact of Smt.ml.

Note that the formulas found in the SMT-LIB benchmarks by design share few commonalities and lack redundancies by design. This is the exact opposite of our intended use case for Smt.ml, which is integration with tools that interact multiple times with a solver during execution and generate similar formulas in doing so, such as symbolic execution tools. For this reason, we do not evaluate the optimisations of Smt.ml against the SMT-LIB benchmarks.

6.2   EQ1: Behaviour consistency

To assess the correctness of Smt.ml, we compared the results obtained when running Smt.ml and when running each supported solver directly on the targeted SMT-LIB benchmarks. This cross-validation is facilitated by the fact that most SMT-LIB benchmarks are annotated with their expected outcome.

Results. All results produced by Smt.ml matched those directly produced by the solvers and were aligned with the provided expected outcomes.

Takeaway 1: The behaviour of Smt.ml is fully consistent with the behaviour of its backend solvers.

Table 1: Average times on SMT-LIB benchmarks: SMT.ML vs. backend solvers.

Theory	SMT.ML		Backend solver check-sat	
	avg. (ms)	(%)	avg. (ms)	(%)
QF_BV	33.90	0.97	3460.69	99.03
QF_FP	0.36	0.01	9794.61	99.99
QF_LIA	20.97	3.13	648.97	96.87
QF_S	0.93	0.38	238.27	99.62
QF_SLIA	0.56	0.37	155.02	99.63
Total	11.09	0.50	2215.12	99.50

6.3 EQ2: Performance overhead

To quantify the overhead introduced by SMT.ML, we measured the time spent in SMT.ML versus the time spent in the backend solvers on the SMT-LIB benchmarks. SMT.ML's tasks include parsing SMT-LIB formulas, applying simplifications, and encoding formulas for each of the backend solver APIs. For each theory, we used the times obtained when using the solver that performed best on average for that theory. Table 1 reports the average time spent in SMT.ML and in the solvers for each theory, along with the corresponding percentages.

Results. The obtained results show that the overhead of SMT.ML is minimal when compared to solver runtime, staying below 1% for all theories except QF_LIA and rising to at most 3.13%, for QF_LIA. This larger percentage is due to the corresponding formulas being larger, and thus their parsing times.

Takeaway 2: SMT.ML introduces only negligible overhead on top of the time spent in its respective backend solvers.

6.4 EQ3: Performance impact on symbolic execution benchmarks

We evaluated the impact of the SMT.ML backend-independent optimisations through an ablation study using a dataset of SMT formulas generated by the Owi symbolic execution engine [3] while executing the Test-Comp 2023 benchmark suite [11]. We considered the following three configurations:

- *Raw*: no optimisations, formulas are sent directly to the backend solver;
- *Simplifications*: formulas are simplified before being sent to the solver;
- *Simplifications and caching*: simplified formulas are also cached to avoid redundant computation.

Figure 6 summarises the cumulative runtime for each configuration across the selected benchmark categories. We consider only cvc5 and Z3 as they support all of the theories required for the dataset at hand and are also the most performant.

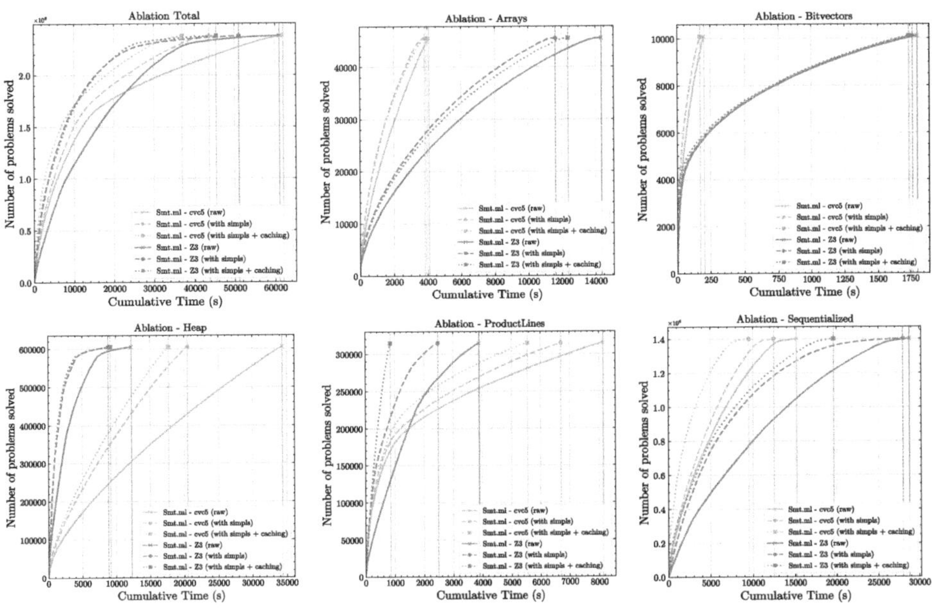

Fig. 6: Ablation study results by Test-Comp 2023 benchmark category.

Results. The results indicate that, on the whole, the backend-independent optimisations significantly improve performance. In particular, the total results for the considered dataset (Figure 6, top left), show that the two optimisations together yield a 1.59× speedup with Z3 and 1.54× with cvc5 relative to the Raw configuration baseline. When examining categories in isolation, we can see, for example, that for `c/ReachSafety-Arrays` and `c/ReachSafety-Heap` simplifications alone account for most of the performance improvement, whereas for `c/ReachSafety-ProductLines` and `c/ReachSafety-Sequentialized` it is the caching that dominantly speeds up the execution. In particular, for the latter category, caching exhibits 1.42× and 1.31× speedups over the Simplifications only configuration for Z3 and cvc5, respectively. These differences can be attributed to the nature of the formulas in each category: categories with many repeated sub-expressions benefit more from caching, whereas categories with complex but less repetitive formulas benefit primarily from simplifications.

Takeaway 3: The backend-independent optimisations significantly improve the performance of Smt.ml on symbolic execution benchmarks.

6.5   EQ4: Transparency and trustworthiness of simplifications

By developing a DSL for writing simplifications and a mechanism for automatic generation of corresponding OCaml code and Lean proof skeletons, we have provided users of Smt.ml with an easy-to-use simplification management system. When it comes to simplification correctness, on the one hand, the definitional

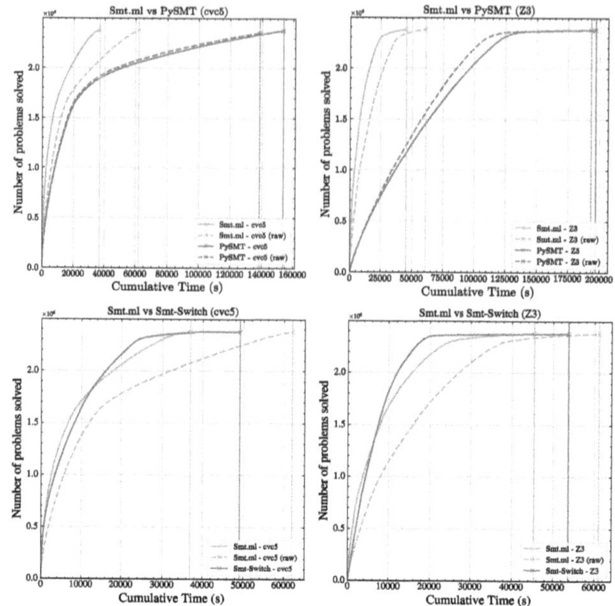

Fig. 7: Comparison: SMT.ML vs. PySMT (top); SMT.ML vs. Smt-Switch (bottom).

simplifications only connect SMT.ML operators to basic OCaml data-structure operators in a way that if one trusts the latter, one should also trust the former. On the other hand, the correctness of all 33 non-definitional simplifications has been fully proven in Lean. At a higher level, we opted to prove simplification correctness in a proof assistant rather than using SMT as some simplifications require inductive reasoning. For instance, to prove that reversing a list twice yields the original list, $\mathtt{Rev}(\mathtt{Rev}(l)) \Rightarrow l$, one must induct on the size of the list.

Takeaway 4: Users can easily examine and manage SMT.ML simplifications. All of these simplifications are trustworthy: most are formally verified in Lean, and the remaining ones rely on the correctness of fundamental OCaml operators.

6.6   EQ5: Comparison with other SMT frontends

We identified six relevant open-source SMT frontends: JavaSMT [4], PySMT [31], rsmt2 [19], SBV [26], Smt-Switch [43], and what4 [35]. We excluded JavaSMT, rsmt2, SBV, and what4 as they do not accept SMT-LIB input, making it impossible to measure their performance using standard benchmarks.

We compare SMT.ML against the remaining frontends: PySMT [31] and Smt-Switch [43]. For Smt-Switch we found an issue when trying to process multiple formulas with the same solver instance, as it would throw an error when given two independent formulas in which there is a shared variable name. To perform the comparison, we therefore create a new solver instance and SMT-LIB reader for each formula. We evaluated both frontends on the symbolic execution dataset described in §6.4, using cvc5 and Z3 as backend solvers, as they are the only common solvers supported by both SMT.ML, PySMT, and Smt-Switch. We evaluated both SMT.ML and PySMT under two settings: one with all optimisations enabled and one without any optimisations. Smt-Switch was evaluated only in its standard configuration, as it does not support optimisations.

Results. Figure 7 shows the comparisons between SMT.ML and PySMT (top diagrams), and between SMT.ML and Smt-Switch (bottom diagrams). The results show that, using the configuration with the most optimisations enabled, SMT.ML substantially outperforms PySMT, with speedups of 4.34× and 4.25× with Z3 and cvc5, respectively. On the other hand, disabling optimisations on both frontends narrows the gap between them, with speedups of 3.16× and 2.26× with Z3 and cvc5, respectively. This can be partly attributed to the implementation languages: SMT.ML is implemented in OCaml, a compiled language, whereas PySMT is written in Python, an interpreted language that incurs additional overhead. We note that the raw configuration for PySMT outperforms its optimised configuration possibly indicating that the simplifications implemented by PySMT are not effective on the Test-Comp formulas. The results also show that, with optimisations enabled, SMT.ML outperforms Smt-Switch, with speedups of 1.18× for Z3 and 1.33× for cvc5. However, under the raw configuration, SMT.ML is slower than Smt-Switch, with slowdowns of 0.88× and 0.79× for Z3 and cvc5, respectively. This can be attributed to the fact that Smt-Switch is implemented in C++, which is a more performant language than OCaml.

Takeaway 5: With optimisations enabled, SMT.ML outperforms both PySMT and Smt-Switch on symbolic execution benchmarks.

7   Related Work

SMT Solvers. SMT solvers have seen significant advancements since their emergence in the early 2000s [6,8,10,24,25], such as support for new theories, like strings [40] and quantified arithmetic [1], and new optimisation techniques, like new caching mechanisms [62] and portfolio strategies [54,59]. As a result, they are now used across the entire computer science community, with a wide variety of applications ranging from software verification and test generation [30,36,39] to combinatorial optimisation and classical operations research [12].

Currently, many SMT solvers are actively maintained, with 20 submitted to the 2024 edition of SMT-COMP [14]. Importantly, there is no one-size-fits-all solver: some excel in handling certain theories, others excel in handling others. Our solver selection for SMT.ML integration is guided by our specific needs. Initially, we supported Z3 [24] and Colibri2 [13], as they were already being used in our ongoing projects. Subsequently, we added support for cvc5 [6] and Bitwuzla [48], due to their excellent performance with bit-vectors and floating-point arithmetic, which are frequently required in symbolic execution. Most recently, we have also interfaced with Alt-Ergo [21], because it is the only SMT solver implemented entirely in OCaml. This makes it particularly attractive for our ecosystem, as it enables applications depending on Alt-Ergo to be compiled with `js_of_ocaml` [63], allowing native execution directly within the browser.

Frontends for SMT Solvers. Frontends [4,19,26,31,35,43] play an essential role in making SMT solvers more accessible to the broader computer science audience. These interfaces often come with user-friendly input languages that are both more expressive and closer to real-world problem domains than the logics of existing solvers, streamlining user interaction. Frontends also facilitate integration with high-level programming languages, allowing SMT-solving capabilities to be seamlessly embedded into applications and formal verification processes.

The two solver frontends closest to SMT.ML in spirit are PySMT [31] and Smt-Switch [43]. They are written in Python and C++, respectively, and equip users with a high-level API for interacting with various SMT solvers, abstracting low-level solver-specific details. PySMT supports five solvers, while Smt-Switch supports six. In particular, PySMT supports Z3, cvc5, Yices2 [25], Boolector [49], and MathSAT5 [20], whereas Smt-Switch supports Z3, cvc5, Yices2, MathSAT5, Bitwuzla, and Boolector. PySMT further implements a solver-agnostic optimisation layer that uses a set of simplification rules not unlike ours before passing the formulas to the solvers. However, SMT.ML is the only SMT frontend that includes a simplification-management engine for streamlining the integration of new simplifications and the verification of their correctness. Furthermore, unlike PySMT and Smt-Switch, SMT.ML also includes an integrated caching system, which is essential for containing memory consumption in our target applications and further improves performance. Finally, as the first SMT-solver frontend for OCaml, SMT.ML makes it easier for program analysis and verification tools implemented in OCaml (e.g., Frama-C [22], Binsec [23], Gillian [30]) to interface with multiple SMT solvers and take advantage of its optimisations.

Caching and Simplifications for SMT Solvers. While most SMT solvers apply some built-in simplifications as part of a preprocessing step before the core satisfiability check [6,24], the practical scope of these simplifications is often limited. For this reason, prior work has explored augmenting SMT workflows with additional simplification capabilities by either integrating them into the solver codebase [51] or applying them as a preprocessing stage before invoking the solver [30,32,42]. Empirical evidence shows that such simplifications are important for tool performance: for example, the verification of the real-world AWS code done in [42] would not have been tractable without simplifications. Prior work has also explored the use of domain-specific languages for specifying simplifications [50] and proving them using theorem provers [37]. Our contribution differs from these systems in that we propose a declarative DSL for specifying simplifications, from which we generate *both* their implementations and proof skeletons. This design streamlines the management and verification of simplifications, keeping them out of the trusted computing base.

The primary SMT application that benefits from formula caching is symbolic execution [5,17]. Symbolic execution of a program produces path formulas that record the branch conditions encountered during execution; these formulas often contain redundancies across different executions and even within the same one. For this reason, many high-profile symbolic execution tools implement formula caching [16,53,58], often reimplementing similar code. To address this, the Green system was proposed to factor formula caching out of individual symbolic execution tools so that different tools can share a common cache [62]. We follow the same philosophy in SMT.ML, shifting the responsibility for caching from SMT clients to SMT.ML. Unlike Green, however, we combine formula caching with hash-consing to reduce memory footprint.

8 Conclusions

We presented SMT.ML, a novel OCaml frontend for multiple SMT solvers. In contrast to existing frontends for SMT solvers in other languages, SMT.ML incorporates a solver-agnostic caching system and introduces a simplification-management engine that allows users to specify formula simplifications and prove their correctness. Our evaluation shows that SMT.ML's maintains consistent behaviour with its backend SMT solvers and introduces no significant overhead. We further demonstrate that, for formulas generated from the symbolic execution of programs, SMT.ML's optimisations are highly effective, leading to significant performance improvements.

In the future, we plan to explore a number of pathways for advancing the work on SMT.ML. Firstly, we will continue to add support for new solver backends and also offer developers the option to create solver portfolios parameterised on solver selection strategies. Moreover, we plan to improve our simplification module by adding further, more complex, simplifications, based on those currently present in state-of-the-art symbolic executors [30,57]. Finally, we will also investigate the option of integrating large language models with SMT.ML, with the aim of automating the proofs of simplification correctness.

Acknowledgements

The authors would like to thank the anonymous reviewers for their insightful comments and suggestions. This work was supported by Portuguese national funds through Fundação para a Ciência e a Tecnologia, I.P. (FCT) via grants 2024.18500.PRT and PRT/BD/154029/2022, as well as the projects UID/50021/2025 (DOI: https://doi.org/10.54499/UID/50021/2025), UID/PRR/50021/2025 (DOI: https://doi.org/10.54499/UID/PRR/50021/2025), and Web-CAP (ref. 2024.07393.IACDC, DOI: https://doi.org/10.54499/2024.07393.IACDC), and by IAPMEI under grant ref. C6632206063-00466847 (SmartRetail).

Data Availability Statement

The artifact associated with this paper, including the implementation of the tool and scripts for reproducing the experimental results, is available at https:

//doi.org/10.5281/zenodo.17489264. The benchmarks used in the evaluation are available at https://doi.org/10.5281/zenodo.16740866 (SMT-LIB benchmark suite) and https://doi.org/10.5281/zenodo.17474996 (dataset of formulas generated from the symbolic execution of subset of the Test-Comp 2023 benchmark suite). For reuse and further development, the current version of the SMT.ML's source code is maintained in a public GitHub repository at [29].

References

1. Ábrahám, E., Kremer, G.: SMT solving for arithmetic theories: Theory and tool support. In: 2017 19th International Symposium on Symbolic and Numeric Algorithms for Scientific Computing (SYNASC). pp. 1–8. IEEE (2017)
2. Amrollahi, D., Preiner, M., Niemetz, A., Reynolds, A., Charikar, M., Tinelli, C., Barrett, C.: Towards smt solver stability via input normalization (2025), https://arxiv.org/abs/2410.22419
3. Andrès, L., Marques, F., Carcano, A., Chambart, P., Fragoso Femenin dos Santos, J., Filliâtre, J.C.: Owi: Performant Parallel Symbolic Execution Made Easy, an Application to WebAssembly. The Art, Science, and Engineering of Programming **9**(2) (Oct 2024), https://hal.science/hal-04627413
4. Baier, D., Beyer, D., Friedberger, K.: Javasmt 3: Interacting with smt solvers in java. In: International Conference on Computer Aided Verification. pp. 195–208. Springer (2021)
5. Baldoni, R., Coppa, E., D'elia, D.C., Demetrescu, C., Finocchi, I.: A survey of symbolic execution techniques. ACM Computing Surveys (CSUR) **51**(3), 1–39 (2018)
6. Barbosa, H., Barrett, C., Brain, M., Kremer, G., Lachnitt, H., Mann, M., Mohamed, A., Mohamed, M., Niemetz, A., Nötzli, A., et al.: cvc5: A versatile and industrial-strength SMT solver. In: International Conference on Tools and Algorithms for the Construction and Analysis of Systems. pp. 415–442. Springer (2022)
7. Barnett, M., Chang, B.Y.E., DeLine, R., Jacobs, B., Leino, K.R.M.: Boogie: A modular reusable verifier for object-oriented programs. In: Formal Methods for Components and Objects: 4th International Symposium, FMCO 2005, Amsterdam, The Netherlands, November 1-4, 2005, Revised Lectures 4. pp. 364–387. Springer (2006)
8. Barrett, C., Conway, C.L., Deters, M., Hadarean, L., Jovanović, D., King, T., Reynolds, A., Tinelli, C.: Cvc4. In: Computer Aided Verification: 23rd International Conference, CAV 2011, Snowbird, UT, USA, July 14-20, 2011. Proceedings 23. pp. 171–177. Springer (2011)
9. Barrett, C., Stump, A., Tinelli, C., et al.: The SMT-LIB standard: Version 2.0. In: Proceedings of the 8th international workshop on satisfiability modulo theories (Edinburgh, UK). vol. 13, p. 14 (2010)
10. Barrett, C., Tinelli, C.: CVC3. In: Computer Aided Verification. Lecture Notes in Computer Science, vol. 4590, pp. 298–302. Springer (2007). https://doi.org/10.1007/978-3-540-73368-3_34, https://doi.org/10.1007/978-3-540-73368-3_34
11. Beyer, D.: Software testing: 5th comparative evaluation: Test-Comp 2023. Fundamental Approaches to Software Engineering LNCS 13991 p. 309 (2023)
12. Bjørner, N., Levatich, M., Lopes, N.P., Rybalchenko, A., Vuppalapati, C.: Supercharging Plant Configurations Using Z3. In: Proc. of the 18th International Conference on Integration of Constraint Programming, Artificial Intelligence, and Operations Research (CPAIOR) (Jul 2021). https://doi.org/10.1007/978-3-030-78230-6_1

13. Bobot, F., Marre, B., Bury, G., Graham-Lengrand, S., Ait El Hara, H.R.: Colibri2. webpage: https://colibri.frama-c.com, source code: https://git.frama-c.com/pub/colibrics
14. Bromberger, M., Bobot, F., , et al.: The International Satisfiability Modulo Theories Competition (SMT-COMP)(2024). https://smt-comp.github.io/
15. Bryce, D., Gao, S., Musliner, D., Goldman, R.: SMT-based nonlinear PDDL+ planning. In: Proceedings of the AAAI Conference on Artificial Intelligence. vol. 29 (2015)
16. Cadar, C., Dunbar, D., Engler, D.R., et al.: KLEE: unassisted and automatic generation of high-coverage tests for complex systems programs. In: OSDI. vol. 8, pp. 209–224 (2008)
17. Cadar, C., Sen, K.: Symbolic execution for software testing: three decades later. Communications of the ACM $\mathbf{56}$(2), 82–90 (2013)
18. Cha, S.K., Avgerinos, T., Rebert, A., Brumley, D.: Unleashing Mayhem on Binary Code. In: 2012 IEEE Symposium on Security and Privacy. pp. 380–394 (2012). https://doi.org/10.1109/SP.2012.31
19. Champion, A.: rsmt2. webpage: https://docs.rs/rsmt2/latest/rsmt2/index.html, source code: https://github.com/kino-mc/rsmt2
20. Cimatti, A., Griggio, A., Schaafsma, B.J., Sebastiani, R.: The mathsat5 SMT solver. In: Piterman, N., Smolka, S.A. (eds.) Tools and Algorithms for the Construction and Analysis of Systems - 19th International Conference, TACAS 2013, Held as Part of the European Joint Conferences on Theory and Practice of Software, ETAPS 2013, Rome, Italy, March 16-24, 2013. Proceedings. Lecture Notes in Computer Science, vol. 7795, pp. 93–107. Springer (2013). https://doi.org/10.1007/978-3-642-36742-7_7, https://doi.org/10.1007/978-3-642-36742-7_7
21. Conchon, S., Coquereau, A., Iguernlala, M., Mebsout, A.: Alt-Ergo 2.2. In: SMT Workshop: International Workshop on Satisfiability Modulo Theories (2018)
22. Cuoq, P., Kirchner, F., Kosmatov, N., Prevosto, V., Signoles, J., Yakobowski, B.: Frama-c: A software analysis perspective. In: International conference on software engineering and formal methods. pp. 233–247. Springer (2012)
23. Daniel, L.A., Bardin, S., Rezk, T.: Binsec/rel: Efficient relational symbolic execution for constant-time at binary-level. In: 2020 IEEE Symposium on Security and Privacy (SP). pp. 1021–1038. IEEE (2020)
24. De Moura, L., Bjørner, N.: Z3: An efficient SMT solver. In: International conference on Tools and Algorithms for the Construction and Analysis of Systems. pp. 337–340. Springer (2008)
25. Dutertre, B.: Yices 2.2. In: International Conference on Computer Aided Verification. pp. 737–744. Springer (2014)
26. Erkok, L.: SBV. webpage: https://hackage.haskell.org/package/sbv, source code: https://github.com/LeventErkok/sbv
27. Filliâtre, J.C., Conchon, S.: Type-safe modular hash-consing. In: Proceedings of the 2006 Workshop on ML. p. 12–19. ML '06, Association for Computing Machinery, New York, NY, USA (2006). https://doi.org/10.1145/1159876.1159880, https://doi.org/10.1145/1159876.1159880
28. Filliâtre, J.C., Paskevich, A.: Why3—where programs meet provers. In: Programming Languages and Systems: 22nd European Symposium on Programming, ESOP 2013, Held as Part of the European Joint Conferences on Theory and Practice of Software, ETAPS 2013, Rome, Italy, March 16-24, 2013. Proceedings 22. pp. 125–128. Springer (2013)
29. formalsec: smtml: An smt solver frontend for ocaml. https://github.com/formalsec/smtml

30. Fragoso Santos, J., Maksimović, P., Ayoun, S.É., Gardner, P.: Gillian, part i: a multi-language platform for symbolic execution. In: Proceedings of the 41st ACM SIGPLAN Conference on Programming Language Design and Implementation. pp. 927–942 (2020)
31. Gario, M., Micheli, A.: PySMT: a solver-agnostic library for fast prototyping of SMT-based algorithms. In: SMT workshop. vol. 2015 (2015)
32. Grannan, Z., Vazou, N., Darulova, E., Summers, A.J.: Rest: Integrating term rewriting with program verification (extended version). arXiv preprint arXiv:2202.05872 (2022)
33. Guilloud, S., Bucev, M., Milovančević, D., Kunčak, V.: Formula normalizations in verification. In: International Conference on Computer Aided Verification. pp. 398–422. Springer (2023)
34. IEEE: IEEE Standard for Floating-Point Arithmetic. IEEE Std 754-2019 (Revision of IEEE 754-2008) (2019)
35. Inc., G.: What4. source code: https://github.com/GaloisInc/what4
36. Jacobs, B., Smans, J., Philippaerts, P., Vogels, F., Penninckx, W., Piessens, F.: VeriFast: A powerful, sound, predictable, fast verifier for C and Java. In: NASA formal methods symposium. pp. 41–55. Springer (2011)
37. Lachnitt, H., Fleury, M., Aniva, L., Reynolds, A., Barbosa, H., Nötzli, A., Barrett, C., Tinelli, C.: IsaRare: Automatic verification of SMT rewrites in Isabelle/HOL. In: International Conference on Tools and Algorithms for the Construction and Analysis of Systems. Lecture Notes in Computer Science, vol. 14570, pp. 311–330. Springer (Apr 2024). https://doi.org/10.1007/978-3-031-57246-3_17, http://theory.stanford.edu/~barrett/pubs/LFA+24.pdf
38. Lee, J., Kim, D., Hur, C.K., Lopes, N.P.: An SMT encoding of LLVM's memory model for bounded translation validation. In: Proc. of the 33rd International Conference on Computer-Aided Verification (CAV) (Jul 2021). https://doi.org/10.1007/978-3-030-81688-9_35
39. Leino, K.R.M., Wüstholz, V.: The Dafny integrated development environment. arXiv preprint arXiv:1404.6602 (2014)
40. Liang, T., Reynolds, A., Tsiskaridze, N., Tinelli, C., Barrett, C., Deters, M.: An efficient SMT solver for string constraints. Formal Methods in System Design **48**, 206–234 (2016)
41. Madeira Pereira, J., Marques, F.: cvc5 OCaml bindings. source code: https://github.com/formalsec/ocaml-cvc5
42. Maksimovic, P., Ayoun, S., Santos, J.F., Gardner, P.: Gillian, part II: real-world verification for javascript and C. In: Computer Aided Verification - 33rd International Conference, CAV 2021, Virtual Event, July 20-23, 2021, Proceedings, Part II. Lecture Notes in Computer Science, vol. 12760, pp. 827–850. Springer (2021)
43. Mann, M., Wilson, A., Zohar, Y., Stuntz, L., Irfan, A., Brown, K., Donovick, C., Guman, A., Tinelli, C., Barrett, C.: SMT-switch: a solver-agnostic C++ API for SMT solving. In: International Conference on Theory and Applications of Satisfiability Testing. pp. 377–386. Springer (2021)
44. Marques, F., Ferreira, M., Nascimento, A., Coimbra, M.E., Santos, N., Jia, L., Fragoso Santos, J.: Automated exploit generation for node. js packages. Proceedings of the ACM on Programming Languages **9**(PLDI), 1341–1366 (2025)
45. Marques, F., Fragoso Santos, J., Santos, N., Ad ão, P.: Concolic Execution for WebAssembly. In: 36th European Conference on Object-Oriented Programming (ECOOP 2022). Schloss Dagstuhl-Leibniz-Zentrum für Informatik (2022)
46. Minsky, Y., Madhavapeddy, A., Hickey, J.: Real World OCaml: Functional programming for the masses. " O'Reilly Media, Inc." (2013)

47. de Moura, L., Kong, S., Avigad, J., van Doorn, F., von Raumer, J.: The lean theorem prover (system description). In: Felty, A.P., Middeldorp, A. (eds.) Automated Deduction - CADE-25. pp. 378–388. Springer International Publishing, Cham (2015)

48. Niemetz, A., Preiner, M.: Bitwuzla. In: International Conference on Computer Aided Verification. pp. 3–17. Springer (2023)

49. Niemetz, A., Preiner, M., Wolf, C., Biere, A.: Btor2, btormc and boolector 3.0. In: International Conference on Computer Aided Verification. pp. 587–595. Springer (2018)

50. Nötzli, A., Barbosa, H., Niemetz, A., Preiner, M., Reynolds, A., Barrett, C.W., Tinelli, C.: Reconstructing fine-grained proofs of rewrites using a domain-specific language. In: FMCAD. pp. 65–74 (2022)

51. Nötzli, A., Reynolds, A., Barbosa, H., Niemetz, A., Preiner, M., Barrett, C., Tinelli, C.: Syntax-guided rewrite rule enumeration for smt solvers. In: International Conference on Theory and Applications of Satisfiability Testing. pp. 279–297. Springer (2019)

52. Palikareva, H., Cadar, C.: Multi-solver support in symbolic execution. In: Computer Aided Verification: 25th International Conference, CAV 2013, Saint Petersburg, Russia, July 13-19, 2013. Proceedings 25. pp. 53–68. Springer (2013)

53. Păsăreanu, C.S., Rungta, N.: Symbolic pathfinder: symbolic execution of java bytecode. In: Proceedings of the 25th IEEE/ACM International Conference on Automated Software Engineering. pp. 179–180 (2010)

54. Pimpalkhare, N., Mora, F., Polgreen, E., Seshia, S.A.: MedleySolver: online SMT algorithm selection. In: Theory and Applications of Satisfiability Testing–SAT 2021: 24th International Conference, Barcelona, Spain, July 5-9, 2021, Proceedings 24. pp. 453–470. Springer (2021)

55. Preiner, M., Schurr, H.J., Barrett, C., Fontaine, P., Niemetz, A., Tinelli, C.: SMT-LIB release 2025 (non-incremental benchmarks) (Aug 2025). https://doi.org/10.5281/zenodo.16740866, https://doi.org/10.5281/zenodo.16740866

56. Rakadjiev, E., Shimosawa, T., Mine, H., Oshima, S.: Parallel SMT solving and concurrent symbolic execution. In: 2015 IEEE Trustcom/BigDataSE/ISPA. vol. 3, pp. 17–26. IEEE (2015)

57. Roșu, G., Șerbănuță, T.F.: An overview of the k semantic framework. The Journal of Logic and Algebraic Programming **79**(6), 397–434 (2010)

58. Ryan, K., Sturton, C.: Sylq-sv: Scaling symbolic execution of hardware designs with query caching. In: Proceedings of the 30th ACM International Conference on Architectural Support for Programming Languages and Operating Systems, Volume 3. pp. 195–211 (2025)

59. Scott, J., Niemetz, A., Preiner, M., Nejati, S., Ganesh, V.: Algorithm selection for SMT: MachSMT: machine learning driven algorithm selection for SMT solvers. International Journal on Software Tools for Technology Transfer **25**(2), 219–239 (2023)

60. Slivkins, A., et al.: Introduction to multi-armed bandits. Foundations and Trends® in Machine Learning **12**(1-2), 1–286 (2019)

61. Tuong, F., Le Fessant, F., Gazagnaire, T.: OPAM: an OCaml packa manager. In: ACM SIGPLAN OCaml Users and Developers Workshop (2012)

62. Visser, W., Geldenhuys, J., Dwyer, M.B.: Green: reducing, reusing and recycling constraints in program analysis. In: Proceedings of the ACM SIGSOFT 20th International Symposium on the Foundations of Software Engineering. pp. 1–11 (2012)

63. Vouillon, J., Balat, V.: From bytecode to javascript: the js_of_ocaml compiler. Software: Practice and Experience **44**(8), 951–972 (2014)
64. Wilson, A., Noetzli, A., Reynolds, A., Cook, B., Tinelli, C., Barrett, C.W.: Partitioning Strategies for Distributed SMT Solving. In: FMCAD. pp. 199–208 (2023)

Syntactically Convex Model-Based Projection for Linear Real Arithmetic

Anna Becchi[1] , Grigory Fedyukovich[2] ,
Arie Gurfinkel[3] , and Lev Nachmanson[4]

[1] Università della Svizzera italiana, Switzerland**, anna.becchi@usi.ch
[2] Florida State University, FL, USA, grigory@cs.fsu.edu
[3] University of Waterloo, Canada, arie.gurfinkel@uwaterloo.ca
[4] Microsoft Research, USA, levnach@microsoft.com

Abstract. Quantifier elimination (QE) is a key task in formal verification algorithms, and the ability to return partial results, such as under-approximations, is beneficial for many QE clients. In Linear Real Arithmetic (LRA), existing QE methods often fail to preserve syntactic convexity, that is, they return a disjunction even for a conjunctive input, or they return a large non-minimal representation. We define the novel concept of Bidirectional Model-Based Projection and a new QE algorithm for LRA (BMBP-QE) that (i) returns a conjunctive over-approximation and a disjunctive under-approximation when interrupted early, (ii) returns a minimal conjunction when the input is conjunctive, and (iii) applies to arbitrary LRA formulae. We show that BMBP-QE outperforms SMT-based QE algorithms, offering improvements in both runtime and result size.

Keywords: Quantifier Elimination · Model-Based Projection · Linear Real Arithmetic · Satisfiability Modulo Theories

1 Introduction

Quantifier elimination (QE) is the problem of deriving a quantifier-free formula equivalent to a quantified one within a given theory. QE is a crucial step in many automated verification tasks, including SMT-based model checking [3, 7], Constrained Horn Clauses (CHC) solving [5, 25], functional synthesis [13], reachability analysis of cyber-physical systems [16, 20], and static analysis [1, 10]. Various first-order theories admit a QE procedure. In this paper, we focus on the theory of Linear Real Arithmetic (LRA), which expresses linear relations between real-valued variables and Boolean combinations thereof. Since QE is computationally expensive, several automated verification algorithms have been adapted to work with partial results of QE, typically under-approximations. A notable example is the Spacer [25] model checker which uses *Model-Based Projection* (MBP).

** While writing this paper, Anna Becchi was affiliated with Fondazione Bruno Kessler, Italy.

S. Junges and G. Katz (Eds.): TACAS 2026, LNCS 16505, pp. 45–65, 2026.
https://doi.org/10.1007/978-3-032-22752-2_3

MBP constructs an *under-approximation* of QE based on a model extracted by an SMT solver. Spacer opportunistically exploits these under-approximations, which may be sufficient to solve a verification problem without requiring the full QE computation. The ability to return partial results while computing makes a MBP-based QE procedure (called, MBP-QE) an *anytime* algorithm.

Existing MBP-QE algorithms for LRA have a serious flaw: even when the input formula is conjunctive, the result of MBP-QE might be disjunctive. Losing conjunctiveness complicates the use of QE, as the resulting formula has unnecessarily large size and forces the caller to proceed disjunct-wise. While there are QE procedures for LRA that preserve a conjunctive form, they are either syntactic and yield many redundant constraints, or limited to convex formulae. For example, the Fourier-Motzkin method [21] combines syntactically the linear expressions appearing in the input formula and generates a quadratic number of inequalities for each quantified variable. Conversely, the Double Description method [1, 17, 29] applies specifically to convex polyhedra and does not handle arbitrary Boolean structures.

In this paper, we introduce a QE algorithm for LRA that (a) preserves the conjunctiveness of the input formula, (b) applies to formulae of arbitrary shape, and (c) can be interrupted at any time, yielding over- and under-approximations.

Our novel concept of *Bidirectional Model-Based Projection* (BMBP) extends the notion of MBP by simultaneously computing both over- and under-approximations of QE. The key intuition is that some of the literals in the under-approximation computed by MBP are entailed by the complete projection. Identifying such entailed literals while collecting under-approximations allows us to efficiently build an *over-approximation* of QE.

We use BMBP to construct a new QE algorithm (called, BMBP-QE) that monotonically refines both an *Over*- and an *Under*-approximation of QE. BMBP-QE capitalizes on the same SMT-based search performed by MBP-QE. While building a disjunctive *Under*, as the union of the collected under-approximations, it also maintains a conjunctive *Over*, as the intersection of the corresponding over-approximations. We define a *converging* property of BMBP: when a converging BMBP-QE terminates, the two approximations coincide and the result is available in both disjunctive and conjunctive forms. BMBP-QE is therefore an extension of MBP-QE that produces richer partial results with little overhead. Any QE client that is currently using MBP can benefit from the twofold approximations of the bidirectional version and implement new strategies.

BMBP is independent of any specific theory. In this paper, we present a *converging* BMBP procedure for LRA. Since our algorithm returns a minimal representation for conjunctive inputs, the QE client is spared from performing additional minimization steps or proceeding disjunct-wise.

We implemented BMBP-QE in a prototype tool called HENOSIS and evaluated it on benchmarks of LRA QE (both convex and arbitrary) including some arising in CHC solving. HENOSIS solves more instances than QE implementations of mature SMT solvers such as z3 and MATHSAT5. HENOSIS also outperforms approaches specialized for convex polyhedra, such as FMPLEX-QE and PPLITE, in cases where the QE result is much smaller (syntactically) than the input formula. For example, HENOSIS produces results that are up to three/four orders of magnitude smaller (syntactically) than those produced by z3/FMPLEX-QE.

Related work. Other QE methods on LRA include the Fourier-Motzkin elimination [21, 22], which produces many redundant constraints, and the Loos-Weispfenning method [27,30] and its model-based variant MBP-QE [4,25], which do not preserve the conjunctiveness of the input. MBP has many applications in formal verification and synthesis. In verification, MBP is used to generate phase guards for implication invariants [11,35,37] and in property directed reachability [5,7,23,25,26,32]. In functional synthesis [9,12], MBPs are used as guards in decision trees that represent implementations meeting a given specification [24]. Our approach is an improvement of MBP-QE that exploits the enumeration of model-based under-approximations to simultaneously enumerate adequate over-approximations that eventually yield a conjunctive result.

QE on conjunctive LRA formulae can be performed relying on the Double Description conversion procedure [6, 29]: while its implementations have been progressively optimized [1,2,17,19,38], it suffers from an exponential complexity and is suitable for convex polyhedra only. In contrast, our method leverages a lazy model enumeration procedure similar to the one proposed in [28] to address QE of arbitrary Boolean combinations and arbitrary quantifier alternation.

The idea of identifying entailed literals from under-approximations is similar to the intuition behind the recently proposed FMplex [33] QE method for LRA. However, FMplex-QE explores all under-approximations produced with *syntactic* substitutions from the original formula, potentially enumerating projections already covered by others or producing unnecessary literals in the result. In contrast, our method capitalizes on the SMT-based enumeration of model-based projections: we show how models can be used to avoid producing redundant combinations, and we construct only the under-approximations needed to semantically cover the QE result. A central contribution of this work is to prove that the under-approximations explored through model-driven search are sufficient to identify all literals required for a conjunctive description of the QE. Moreover, FMplex-QE is limited to syntactically convex formulae.

Outline of the paper. Sec. 2 provides background on existing QE methods for LRA. Sec. 3 introduces the concept of Bidirectional Model-Based Projection (BMBP) and describes a quantifier elimination algorithm based on it. Sec. 4 defines a BMBP for conjunctive LRA, and shows its extension to arbitrary LRA formulae. Sec. 5 reports our experimental evaluation. Sec. 6 concludes and outlines directions for future work.

2   Background

Let $\mathbb{R}, \mathbb{Q}$ and $\mathbb{N}$ be the sets of real, rational and natural numbers respectively. A function is *image-finite* if the set of possible distinct outputs is finite. For a set B and $n \in \mathbb{N}$ with $n > 0$, $\boldsymbol{b} \in B^n$ is a vector $(b_0, \ldots, b_{n-1})^{\mathrm{T}}$, where $b_i \in B$ for all $0 \le i < n$, and $|\boldsymbol{b}|$ is its cardinality n. Let $\boldsymbol{x} = (x_0, \ldots, x_{n-1})^{\mathrm{T}}$ be a vector of n real-valued variables. A linear expression, or term, on $\boldsymbol{x}$ variables is $\boldsymbol{a}^{\mathrm{T}} \boldsymbol{x} = \sum_i a_i x_i$, where $\boldsymbol{a} \in \mathbb{Q}^n$ is the vector of coefficients. In the following, we denote terms over $\boldsymbol{x}$ variables as $t(\boldsymbol{x})$, dropping $\boldsymbol{x}$ when clear from the context. A linear inequality over $\boldsymbol{x}$ variables is a predicate $t(\boldsymbol{x}) \bowtie 0$, where t is a linear term on $\boldsymbol{x}$ and $\bowtie\, \in \{<, \le\}$. We use standard Boolean connectives $\neg, \wedge, \vee$. A linear formula $\Psi(\boldsymbol{x})$ is a Boolean combination of linear inequalities over $\boldsymbol{x}$. Let $\mathrm{ineqs}(\Psi)$ return such set of inequalities. For a variable $x_i \in \boldsymbol{x}$, a linear term $\boldsymbol{a}^{\mathrm{T}} \boldsymbol{x}$ is x_i-free if $a_i = 0$. A linear formula $\Psi(\boldsymbol{x})$ is x_i-free, if every linear inequality occurring in Ψ is x_i-free. For a set of terms T and $t \in T$, $\mathrm{ismax}(t, T)$ and $\mathrm{ismin}(t, T)$ are $\bigwedge_{t' \in T} t' \le t$ and $\bigwedge_{t' \in T} t \le t'$, respectively. For sets of terms T_1, T_2, let $T_1 \le T_2$ be the conjunction of $t_1 \le t_2$ for all $t_1 \in T_1$ and $t_2 \in T_2$. Similarly, for $T_1 < T_2$.

In the setting of Satisfiability Modulo Theory (SMT), we use '$\models$' and '$\equiv$', for the entailment and equivalence, resepectively. We do not distinguish between a formula and the set of its satisfying assignments. In the context of LRA, we call *point* or *model* an interpretation $\boldsymbol{p} \in \mathbb{R}^n$ of the variables $\boldsymbol{x}$.

An LRA formula Ψ is *syntactically convex* (or conjunctive) if it is a conjunction of linear inequalities. Quantifier elimination over a conjunctive LRA formula reduces to the homogeneous, topologically closed case, thus we consider formulae of the form $A\boldsymbol{x} \le \boldsymbol{0}$, where matrix $A \in \mathbb{Q}^{m \times n}$ is the matrix of coefficients and $n = |\boldsymbol{x}|$ (standard procedures exists to take care of in-homogenous terms and strict inequalities [1,2]). For Farkas Lemma, every inequality entailed by $A\boldsymbol{x} \le 0$ can be expressed as $\boldsymbol{c}^{\mathrm{T}} A\boldsymbol{x} \le 0$ for some $\boldsymbol{c} \in \mathbb{R}_{\ge 0}^m$. Two inequalities $t_1 \le x$ and $x \le t_2$, where t_1, t_2 are x-free, *resolve* on variable x to a new inequality $t_1 \le t_2$. The inequality $t_1 \le t_2$ is x-free, it is implied by the conjunction $t_1 \le x \wedge x \le t_2$, and it is called a *resolvent*.

We now briefly describe existing methods for quantifier elimination on conjunctive LRA formulae by showing their application on a running example. Consider the formula $\mathcal{P}(x, y, z)$ defined as the conjunction of the 7 inequalities shown in Fig. 1 (top right) and graphed by the pyramid shown in Fig. 1 (top left). We want to existentially eliminate z by computing $\exists z.\mathcal{P}$, shown in Fig. 1 (bottom right) and graphed by the (gray) rectangle shown under the pyramid.

Double Description. The Double Description method for QE (DD-QE) [17,29] is based on the fact that a polyhedron $\mathcal{P}$ can be described with a constraint system (a set of linear inequalities) or a generator system (a set of points or rays such that $\mathcal{P}$ is the set of their positive linear combinations). Starting from one representation, the other can be obtained via an (exponential) conversion procedure [6]. In our example, $\mathcal{P}$ is provided with the 7 inequalities in Fig. 1 top right. DD-QE computes $\exists z.\mathcal{P}$ as follows. First, find the coordinates for the vertices $\boldsymbol{a}, \boldsymbol{b}, \boldsymbol{c}, \boldsymbol{d}$ and $\boldsymbol{e}$ [5] (this first conversion procedure enables identifying that constraints $z \le 10$ and $z \ge 0$ were redundant); second, remove the z coordinate from all vertices; third, find a constraint representation for them.

---

[5] $\boldsymbol{a} = (0, 1, 2)$, $\boldsymbol{b} = (2, 4, 2)$, $\boldsymbol{c} = (6, 3, 4)$, $\boldsymbol{d} = (4, 0, 4)$ and $\boldsymbol{e} = (3, 2, 6)$.

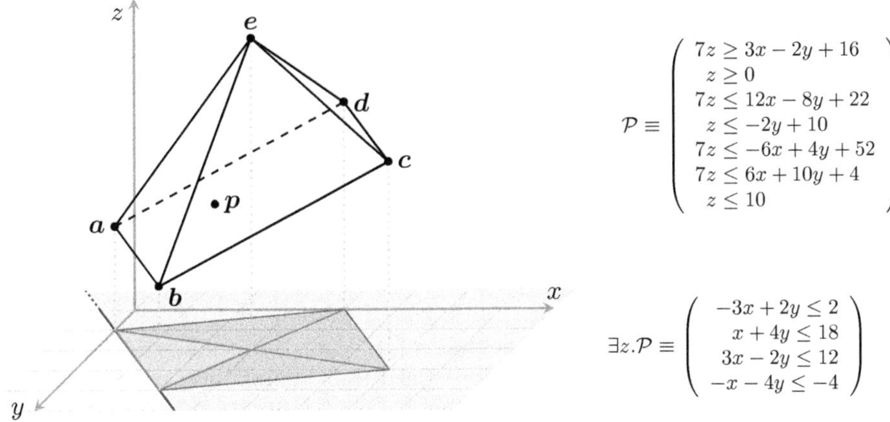

$$\mathcal{P} \equiv \begin{pmatrix} 7z \geq 3x - 2y + 16 \\ z \geq 0 \\ 7z \leq 12x - 8y + 22 \\ z \leq -2y + 10 \\ 7z \leq -6x + 4y + 52 \\ 7z \leq 6x + 10y + 4 \\ z \leq 10 \end{pmatrix}$$

$$\exists z.\mathcal{P} \equiv \begin{pmatrix} -3x + 2y \leq 2 \\ x + 4y \leq 18 \\ 3x - 2y \leq 12 \\ -x - 4y \leq -4 \end{pmatrix}$$

Fig. 1. Example of $\mathcal{P}$ in $\mathbb{R}^3$ and its projection in $\mathbb{R}^2$ by eliminating z.

Since DD-QE relies on two calls to the conversion procedure, it is forced to compute the (possibly large) generator system of $\mathcal{P}$ even when the projection is much simpler. A notable example of this limitation is hypercubes which are known to have exponentially many (irredundant) generators in the number of (irredundant) constraints.

Before discussing the other methods, let us display the sets L and U of z-free terms appearing in $\mathcal{P}$ constraints as lower and upper bounds for z:

$$L = \{1/7(3x - 2y + 16), 0\}$$
$$U = \{1/7(12x - 8y + 22), -2y + 10, 1/7(-6x + 4y + 52), 1/7(6x + 10y + 4), 10\}$$

Fourier-Motzkin. The Fourier-Motzkin procedure for QE (FM-QE) [21] applies to a conjunction of inequalities and is based on progressively resolving two inequalities into a new one. For each quantified variable, a quadratic number of inequalities is generated, among which many can be redundant. In our example, FM-QE computes $\exists z.\mathcal{P}$ as $L \leq U$. It does not recognize $z \geq 0$ and $z \leq 10$ as redundant for $\mathcal{P}$: out of the 10 combinations in $L \leq U$, only 4 are irredundant.

Loos-Weispfenning. The Loos-Weispfenning method [27] for QE (LW-QE) is based on (virtual) substitution. LW-QE computes $\exists z.\mathcal{P}$ as a *disjunction* of formulae of the form $\mathcal{P}[z \mapsto_v \mu]$, where μ is a z-free term, and $z \mapsto_v \mu$ indicates a virtual substitution of variable z with term μ. Such μ terms are derived from $\mathcal{P}$ (see [30] for a complete description of the approach). In our example, LW-QE returns the disjunction $\bigvee_{u \in U} \mathcal{P}[z \mapsto_v u]$. Unlike FM-QE and DD-QE, LW-QE returns a non-conjunctive formula even when the input is conjunctive.

Model-Based Projection (MBP). MBP is defined by Komuravelli et al. in [25].

Definition 1 (Model-Based Projection (MBP)). *Given an existentially quantified formula $\Psi_y(y) \equiv \exists x.\Psi(x, y)$ where Ψ is quantifier-free, an MBP is a function uProj from models of Ψ to x-free quantifier-free formulae such that*

- *uProj is image-finite;*
- *for every model $p \models \Psi : p \models uProj(p)$ and $uProj(p) \models \Psi_y$.*

That is, *uProj* is a function that takes a model of Ψ as input and returns an under-approximation of the quantifier elimination as output. It follows that $\Psi_y \equiv \bigvee_{p \models \Psi} uProj(p)$. Since the number of distinct under-approximations returned by *uProj* must be finite, there is a finite set of models $P \subseteq \Psi$ such that $\Psi_y \equiv \bigvee_{p \in P} uProj(p)$. MBP naturally defines a QE algorithm (called MBP-QE) that searches for new under-approximations until their disjunction covers the Ψ_y.

In [25], an MBP for LRA is defined as a function *LRAProj* such that: given a model p, function *LRAProj* selects one upper-bound $u \in U$ such that $p \models \mathrm{ismin}(u, U)$, and returns $LRAProj(p) \doteq \mathcal{P}[z \mapsto_v u]$. Consider point $p = (^5/_2, ^5/_2, 3)$ shown in Fig. 1. Upper-bound $u \doteq {}^1/_7(12x - 8y + 22)$ is such that $p \models \mathrm{ismin}(u, U)$, i.e., it corresponds to the closest face above p. Formula $LRAProj(p) = \mathcal{P}[z \mapsto_v u]$ is graphically rendered by the triangle below face **abe** (shown in red in Fig. 1): some of its constraints are resolvents (like the blue constraint in Fig. 1), and other constraints cut through the projection (like the red inequalities with hyper-spaces **aec** and **bed**). For a geometric intuition of the result, $\bigvee_{p \models \mathcal{P}} LRAProj(p)$ is a disjunction of four formulae corresponding to the four triangles below the faces **abe, bce, cde, dae**.

In LRA, MBP-QE can be seen as a variant of LW-QE that is "guided by models". Unlike LW-QE, MBP-QE avoids the substitution of upper-bound $10 \in U$ (since there are no models of $\mathcal{P}$ where $\mathrm{ismin}(10, U)$) and thus prevents the construction of unnecessary disjuncts. However, like LW-QE, MBP-QE does not preserve the conjunctiveness of the input formula.

In the next section, we show how to extend MBP-QE in a way that preserves the conjunctiveness of the input Ψ in the output $\exists x.\Psi$.

3 Bidirectional Model-Based Projection

In this section, we propose a new scheme for incrementally computing quantifier elimination based on a novel concept called *Bidirectional Model-Based Projection* (BMBP). BMBP extends the idea of MBP by simultaneously under- and over-approximating the quantifier elimination of a formula based on one of its models.

Definition 2 (Bidirectional Model-Based Projection (BMBP)). *Given an existentially quantified formula $\Psi_y(y) \equiv \exists x.\Psi(x, y)$ where Ψ is quantifier-free, a Bidirectional Model-Based Projection is a pair of functions $\langle oProj, uProj \rangle$ both from models of Ψ to quantifier-free and x-free formulae such that:*

- *oProj and uProj are image-finite;*
- *for all $p \models \Psi : p \models uProj(p)$, $uProj(p) \models \Psi_y$ and $\Psi_y \models oProj(p)$.*

Algorithm 1 Compute a quantifier-free formula $\Psi_y \equiv \exists \boldsymbol{x}.\Psi(\boldsymbol{x}, \boldsymbol{y})$ by progressively refining under- and over-approximations, given a BMBP π.

1: **function** BMBP-QE($\exists \boldsymbol{x}.\Psi(\boldsymbol{x}, \boldsymbol{y})$, π)
2:     **if** not exists $\boldsymbol{p}$ s.t. $\boldsymbol{p} \models \Psi$ **then return** $\langle \bot, \bot \rangle$
3:     let $\pi = \langle oProj, uProj \rangle$
4:     $\langle Over, Under \rangle := \langle \top, \bot \rangle$
5:     **while** exists $\boldsymbol{p}$ s.t. $\boldsymbol{p} \models \Psi \wedge \neg Under$ **do**
6:         $Over := Over \wedge oProj(\boldsymbol{p})$
7:         $Under := Under \vee uProj(\boldsymbol{p})$
8:     **return** $\langle Over, Under \rangle$ $\triangleright\ Under \equiv \Psi_y \models Over$

Given a model $\boldsymbol{p}$ of Ψ, the Bidirectional MBP from Def. 2 yields two formulae: one entailing, the other entailed by $\exists \boldsymbol{x}.\Psi$. The under-approximation is obtained with an MBP $uProj$ (from Def. 1), while the over-approximation is obtained with a new function called $oProj$.

It follows that, for any set of points P, the disjunction $\bigvee_{\boldsymbol{p} \in P} uProj(\boldsymbol{p})$ entails Ψ_y, while Ψ_y entails the conjunction $\bigwedge_{\boldsymbol{p} \in P} oProj(\boldsymbol{p})$.

Property 1 (Converging BMBP). A BMBP $\langle oProj, uProj \rangle$ for $\Psi_y \equiv \exists \boldsymbol{x}.\Psi$ is *converging* if and only if for any set of models $P \subseteq \Psi$

$$\left(\Psi_y \equiv \bigvee_{\boldsymbol{p} \in P} uProj(\boldsymbol{p}) \right) \implies \left(\Psi_y \equiv \bigwedge_{\boldsymbol{p} \in P} oProj(\boldsymbol{p}) \right)$$

With a converging BMBP, as soon as the disjunction of under-approximations covers Ψ_y, the conjunction of over-approximations is an equivalent formula to it.

Procedure BMBP-QE from Alg. 1 uses a BMBP $\pi = \langle oProj, uProj \rangle$ to iteratively compute $\Psi_y \equiv \exists \boldsymbol{x}.\Psi$. It iteratively looks for a new model of Ψ outside the current under-approximation (line 5) in order to avoid computing redundant $uProj$, and, therefore, finds a finite set of models that makes the under-approximation converge to Ψ_y. At any iteration of the while loop at line 5, the current $Under$ and $Over$ are valid under- and over-approximations of QE. When BMBP-QE terminates, (i.e., an unsat answer is obtained at line 5), $Under$ is a disjunctive description of Ψ_y, and, if it also holds that the input BMBP π is converging, then $Over$ is a conjunctive equivalent description for Ψ_y.

Theorem 1. *At any iteration of Alg. 1, at line 5, $Under \models \Psi_y \models Over$ holds. When Ψ is satisfiable, line 8 is reached after a finite number of iterations, and it holds that $Under \equiv \Psi_y \models Over$. Furthermore, if the input BMBP π is converging (Prop. 1), then at line 8, $\Psi_y \equiv Over$ holds.*

4   BMBP Quantifier Elimination for LRA

In this section, we first show a BMBP for a single quantified variable in a conjunctive formula (Sec. 4.1), then extend to multiple variables (Sec. 4.3), and finally show an algorithm handling arbitrary LRA formulae (Sec. 4.4).

4.1   A BMBP for Conjunctive LRA Formulae with One Quantifier

We consider $\Psi_{\boldsymbol{y}} \equiv \exists x.\Psi$, where Ψ is an LRA formula of the form

$$\Psi(x, \boldsymbol{y}) \doteq \psi(\boldsymbol{y}) \wedge \left(\bigwedge_{l \in L} l(\boldsymbol{y}) \leq x \right) \wedge \left(\bigwedge_{u \in U} x \leq u(\boldsymbol{y}) \right)$$

where ψ is conjunctive and x-free. In the following, we identify with L (resp. U) the set of x-free linear expressions that play the role of lower-bounds (resp. upper-bounds) for variable x in Ψ. Formula ψ will also be called the *background* for variable x in Ψ.

Intuition. Each irredundant constraint of a polyhedron Ψ identifies a face of Ψ. Faces $l \leq x$ and $x \leq u$ intersect in Ψ if there is a $\boldsymbol{p} \in \Psi$ with $l(\boldsymbol{p}) = u(\boldsymbol{p})$. We show that if $l \leq x$ and $x \leq u$ are not intersecting in Ψ, then the resolvent $l \leq u$ is certainly redundant in $\exists x.\Psi$. Hence, the search for irredundant resolvents can be guided by models: a model $\boldsymbol{p}$ identifies the faces that are the closest to $\boldsymbol{p}$ along the dimension to remove, e.g., from above and below as in $\exists z.\mathcal{P}$ from Fig. 1, and, thus, identifies a possibly irredundant resolvent.

In the following, we build on this intuition to define a BMBP that selects resolvents based on $\boldsymbol{p}$, and meanwhile builds an under-approximation around $\boldsymbol{p}$. This allows for looking for irredundant resolvents capitalizing on the standard collection of under-approximations.

Definition 3 (*ConvProj*). *Let ConvProj $= \langle \mathcal{O}, \mathcal{U} \rangle$ be a pair of functions from models of Ψ to quantifier-free and $\boldsymbol{x}$-free formulae such that for any model $\boldsymbol{p} \in \Psi$, if $L = \emptyset$ or $U = \emptyset$ then $\mathcal{O}(\boldsymbol{p}) \doteq \mathcal{U}(\boldsymbol{p}) \doteq \psi$, otherwise*

$$\mathcal{O}(\boldsymbol{p}) \doteq \psi \wedge L_M \leq U_m \qquad \mathcal{U}(\boldsymbol{p}) \doteq \psi \wedge L_M \leq U_m \wedge L' < L_M \wedge U_m < U'$$

where

$$L_M \doteq \{l \in L \mid \boldsymbol{p} \models \mathrm{ismax}(l, L)\} \qquad U_m \doteq \{u \in U \mid \boldsymbol{p} \models \mathrm{ismin}(u, U)\}$$
$$L' \doteq L \setminus L_M \qquad\qquad\qquad U' \doteq U \setminus U_m$$

The terms in the sets L and U are sorted according to their evaluation on $\boldsymbol{p}$: L_M is the set of greatest lower-bounds and U_m is the set of least upper-bounds for $\boldsymbol{p}$. Then, $\mathcal{O}(\boldsymbol{p})$ is the set of resolvents combining L_M and U_m, while $\mathcal{U}(\boldsymbol{p})$ is the set of points sharing with $\boldsymbol{p}$ the same sets of L_M and U_m.

Example 1. Recall $\mathcal{P}$ from Fig. 1. Let $\boldsymbol{p} = (5/2, 5/2, 3) \in \mathcal{P}$, so the sets of greatest lower bounds and least upper bounds on $\boldsymbol{p}$ are $L_M = \{1/7(3x - 2y + 16)\}$ and $U_m = \{1/7(12x - 8y + 22)\}$, resp. Def. 3 gives the following over-approximation $\mathcal{O}_{\exists z.\mathcal{P}}(\boldsymbol{p})$ and under-approximation $\mathcal{U}_{\exists z.\mathcal{P}}(\boldsymbol{p})$:

$$\mathcal{O}_{\exists z.\mathcal{P}}(\boldsymbol{p}) \equiv (-3x + 2y \leq 2) \qquad \mathcal{U}_{\exists z.\mathcal{P}}(\boldsymbol{p}) \equiv \begin{pmatrix} -3x + 2y \leq 2 \\ 2x + y < 8 \\ x - 3y < -3 \end{pmatrix}$$

Note that $\mathcal{O}_{\exists z.\mathcal{P}}(\boldsymbol{p})$ is the z-free resolvent corresponding to edge $\boldsymbol{ab}$, while $\mathcal{U}_{\exists z.\mathcal{P}}(\boldsymbol{p})$ is a triangle corresponding to the projection of face $\boldsymbol{abe}$. $\mathcal{U}_{\exists z.\mathcal{P}}(\boldsymbol{p})$ has strict inequalities corresponding to segments $\boldsymbol{ae}$ and $\boldsymbol{be}$, originating from a strict comparison between the upper-bounds in U' and U_m. $\qquad\square$

Theorem 2. *ConvProj is a* BMBP.

To prove that *ConvProj* is converging (Prop. 1), we need the following.

Lemma 1. *Formula $\Psi_{\boldsymbol{y}}$ is equivalent to $\mathcal{Q} \doteq \psi \wedge \bigwedge\{l \leq u \mid \langle l, u \rangle \in \mathrm{Core}\}$, where*

$$\mathrm{Core} \doteq \left\{ \langle l, u \rangle \in L \times U \;\middle|\; \boldsymbol{p} \models \Psi, l(\boldsymbol{p}) = u(\boldsymbol{p}) \right\}.$$

Lemma 1 shows that if two bounds $l \in L$ and $u \in U$ are not intersecting in Ψ, then the resolvent $l \leq u$ is redundant in $\Psi_{\boldsymbol{y}}$.

Lemma 2. *For any pair of points $\boldsymbol{p}, \boldsymbol{q} \models \Psi$, if $\boldsymbol{q} \models \mathcal{U}(\boldsymbol{p})$, then $\mathcal{O}(\boldsymbol{p}) \models \mathcal{O}(\boldsymbol{q})$.*

Lemma 2 states that in polyhedron $\mathcal{U}(\boldsymbol{p})$, no point would give a tighter over-approximation than $\mathcal{O}(\boldsymbol{p})$. In other words, $\mathcal{U}(\boldsymbol{p})$ generalizes $\boldsymbol{p}$ with a set of points $\boldsymbol{q}$ such that $\mathcal{O}(\boldsymbol{q})$ is weaker or equal than $\mathcal{O}(\boldsymbol{p})$.

Theorem 3. *ConvProj is converging (Prop. 1).*

Proof. Consider a set of points P such that $\Psi_{\boldsymbol{y}} \equiv \bigvee_{\boldsymbol{p} \in P} \mathcal{U}(\boldsymbol{p})$. We need to show that $\bigwedge_{\boldsymbol{p} \in P} \mathcal{O}(\boldsymbol{p}) \models \Psi_{\boldsymbol{y}}$. Let EP be the set of points in Ψ lying on an irredundant resolvent for Lemma 1:

$$EP \doteq \left\{ \boldsymbol{e} \in \Psi \;\middle|\; l \in L, u \in U, l(\boldsymbol{e}) = u(\boldsymbol{e}) \right\} \qquad (1)$$

Since $\Psi \models \bigvee_{\boldsymbol{p} \in P} \mathcal{U}(\boldsymbol{p})$, every $\boldsymbol{e} \in EP$ belongs to some $\mathcal{U}(\boldsymbol{p})$ for a $\boldsymbol{p} \in P$. Then,

$$
\begin{aligned}
\bigwedge\{\mathcal{O}(\boldsymbol{p}) \mid \boldsymbol{p} \in P\} &\models \bigwedge\{\mathcal{O}(\boldsymbol{e}) \mid \boldsymbol{e} \in EP\} && \text{[Lemma 2]} \\
&\models \psi \wedge \bigwedge\{l \leq u \mid \boldsymbol{e} \in EP, \boldsymbol{e} \models \mathrm{ismax}(l, L) \wedge \mathrm{ismin}(u, U)\} && \text{[Def 3]} \\
&\models \psi \wedge \bigwedge\{l \leq u \mid \boldsymbol{e} \in EP, l \in L, u \in U, l(\boldsymbol{e}) = u(\boldsymbol{e})\} && \text{[For (1)]} \\
&\equiv \Psi_{\boldsymbol{y}} && \text{[Lemma 1]}
\end{aligned}
$$

Corollary 1. *For a conjunctive LRA formula Ψ, BMBP-QE($\exists x.\Psi$, ConvProj) from Alg. 1, terminates with $\mathcal{U}nder \equiv \Psi_{\boldsymbol{y}} \equiv \mathcal{O}ver$, where $\mathcal{O}ver$ is conjunctive and $\mathcal{U}nder$ is in disjunctive normal form.*

Namely, when using *ConvProj* $= \langle \mathcal{O}, \mathcal{U} \rangle$ as the parameter π in BMBP-QE, $\mathcal{O}$ progressively adds new resolvents to $\mathcal{O}ver$, while $\mathcal{U}$ adds new under-approximations to $\mathcal{U}nder$. *ConvProj* guarantees that BMBP-QE terminates when $\mathcal{O}ver$ is a conjunctive formula equivalent to $\Psi_{\boldsymbol{y}}$.

4.2   Accelerating convergence in BMBP-QE

The BMBP *ConvProj* from Def. 3 is fully symmetric, meaning that upper-bounds and lower-bounds are treated in the same way. However, a valid variation is to opportunistically sort only one set of bounds, thus finding only L_M or U_m, depending on the cardinality of sets L and U. Another variation is given by breaking the ties found when sorting bounds in L_M or U_m. Namely, an element l_M can be picked from L_M based, for example, on lexicographical ordering.

The breaking symmetry and breaking ties variations can be combined in a new BMBP version: if $|L| \leq |U|$, then

$$\mathcal{O}(\boldsymbol{p}) \doteq \psi \wedge L_M \leq U \qquad \mathcal{U}(\boldsymbol{p}) \doteq \psi \wedge L_M \leq U \wedge L' < l_M \wedge L_M \leq l_M$$

where $l_M \in L_M$; otherwise, when $|L| > |U|$, then only U_m is considered, u_m is selected from U_m and the dual version is returned.

Intuitively, in this variant, polyhedron $\mathcal{U}(\boldsymbol{p})$ includes all the points that share with $\boldsymbol{p}$ the chosen greatest lower-bound l_M (or the least upper-bound u_m), without requiring to have exactly L_M as the set of greatest lower-bounds and U_m as the set of least upper-bounds. This effectively increases the size of the under-approximation, potentially accelerating convergence in Alg. 1.

4.3   Removing Multiple Existentially Quantified Variables

In this section, we consider the quantifier elimination of multiple variables, that is, $\exists \boldsymbol{x}.\Psi(\boldsymbol{x}, \boldsymbol{y})$, with $|\boldsymbol{x}| \geq 1$.

A standard way to remove multiple quantifiers is to apply QE $|\boldsymbol{x}|$ times. The classical MBP-QE algorithm follows a "depth-first search" strategy: based on a single model $\boldsymbol{p}$, all variables are removed based on $\boldsymbol{p}$ in a sequence of calls of *uProj*: starting from $u_{\boldsymbol{p}}^0 \equiv \Psi$, MBP-QE produces the sequence $u_{\boldsymbol{p}}^0, \ldots, u_{\boldsymbol{p}}^{|\boldsymbol{x}|}$, where each $u_{\boldsymbol{p}}^{i+1}$ under-approximates $\exists x_i.u_{\boldsymbol{p}}^i$. The last element $u_{\boldsymbol{p}}^{|\boldsymbol{x}|}$ is $\boldsymbol{x}$-free and is used to prune the search space for the next model. At the end, the projection is as usual the disjunction of the $u_{\boldsymbol{p}}^{|\boldsymbol{x}|}$.

We now adapt this strategy to produce over-approximations and preserve the convergence property. We use the BMBP $\langle \mathcal{O}_{\exists x.\phi}, \mathcal{U}_{\exists x.\phi} \rangle$ from Def. 3. The subscript makes explicit which formula BMBP is applied to and which variable is removed. Given a conjunctive formula ϕ, let filter.entailed(ϕ, Ψ) denote $\bigwedge \left\{ \ell \in \mathrm{ineqs}(\phi) \,\middle|\, \Psi \models \ell \right\}$.

Definition 4 (BMBP *ConvProj*$_{\exists \boldsymbol{x}.\Psi}$). *For a conjunctive LRA formula $\Psi(\boldsymbol{x}, \boldsymbol{y})$, ConvProj$_{\exists \boldsymbol{x}.\Psi}$ is a pair of functions $\langle \mathcal{O}_{\exists \boldsymbol{x}.\Psi}, \mathcal{U}_{\exists \boldsymbol{x}.\Psi} \rangle$ from models of Ψ to quantifier-free and $\boldsymbol{x}$-free formulae such that for any model $\boldsymbol{p} \models \Psi$:*

$$\mathcal{U}_{\exists \boldsymbol{x}.\Psi}(\boldsymbol{p}) \doteq u^{|\boldsymbol{x}|} \qquad\qquad \mathcal{O}_{\exists \boldsymbol{x}.\Psi}(\boldsymbol{p}) \doteq o^{|\boldsymbol{x}|}$$

where $u^0 \ldots u^{|\boldsymbol{x}|}$ and $o^0 \ldots o^{|\boldsymbol{x}|}$ are sequences of formulae with $u^0 = o^0 = \Psi$ and, for every $0 \leq i < |\boldsymbol{x}|$,

$$u^{i+1} \doteq \mathcal{U}_{\exists x_i.u^i}(\boldsymbol{p}) \qquad\qquad o^{i+1} \doteq \mathrm{filter.entailed}(\mathcal{O}_{\exists x_i.u^i}(\boldsymbol{p}), \Psi)$$

At every step i, a new variable is removed from the last under-approximation, so that $u^{i+1} \models (\exists x_i.u^i)$ and $(\exists x_i.u^i) \models o^{i+1}$. In order to guarantee that o^{i+1} is a sound over-approximation of $(\exists x_0, \ldots x_i.\Psi)$, it is filtered by preserving only the literals entailed by Ψ.

Theorem 4. *ConvProj$_{\exists \boldsymbol{x}.\Psi}$ is a BMBP.*

Example 2. Consider removing both variables z and y, based on point $\boldsymbol{p}$ from the pyramid $\mathcal{P}$ of Fig. 1. We start with $o^0 = u^0 = \mathcal{P}$.

We have that $|L| < |U|$, and that the greatest lower-bound is the base of the pyramid $\boldsymbol{abcd}$, thus, $L_M = \{1/7(3x - 2y + 16)\}$ with no ties. By breaking symmetry and considering all resolvents $L_M \leq U$, convergence is reached with only one point: $u_{\boldsymbol{p}}^1 \equiv o_{\boldsymbol{p}}^1 \equiv \exists z.\mathcal{P}$.

When removing the next variable y, we again break symmetry and only sort the lower bounds, picking as greatest lower-bound constraint $\boldsymbol{ad}$.

$$o_{\boldsymbol{p}}^2 = \text{filter.entailed}(\mathcal{O}_{\exists y.u_{\boldsymbol{p}}^1}(\boldsymbol{p}), \mathcal{P}) = (0 \leq x) \qquad u_{\boldsymbol{p}}^2 = \mathcal{U}_{\exists y.u_{\boldsymbol{p}}^1}(\boldsymbol{p}) = \begin{pmatrix} 0 \leq x \\ x < 4 \end{pmatrix}$$

This concludes the first iteration of BMBP-QE for $\exists z, y.\mathcal{P}$. Then, a new point is sought outside the interval $[0, 4)$. Assume that $\boldsymbol{d}$ is picked. We have that $u_{\boldsymbol{d}}^1 = u_{\boldsymbol{p}}^1$, from which we need to remove y. For symmetry breaking, only lower bounds are sorted, and for tie breaking, assume $\boldsymbol{cd}$ is picked as l_M:

$$o_{\boldsymbol{d}}^2 = \text{filter.entailed}(\mathcal{O}_{\exists y.u_{\boldsymbol{d}}^1}(\boldsymbol{d}), \mathcal{P}) = (x \leq 6) \qquad u_{\boldsymbol{d}}^2 = \mathcal{U}_{\exists y.u_{\boldsymbol{d}}^1}(\boldsymbol{d}) = \begin{pmatrix} 4 \leq x \\ x \leq 6 \end{pmatrix}$$

Since the union of the two found under-approximations $\mathcal{U}_{\exists z,y.\mathcal{P}}(\boldsymbol{p})$ and $\mathcal{U}_{\exists z,y.\mathcal{P}}(\boldsymbol{d})$ covers $\mathcal{P}$, BMBP-QE terminates. Two equivalent representation for $\exists z, y.\mathcal{P}$ are returned: $\mathcal{U}nder = (0 \leq x \wedge x < 4) \vee (4 \leq x \wedge x \leq 6)$ and $\mathcal{O}ver = (0 \leq x \wedge x \leq 6)$.
$\square$

Theorem 5. *ConvProj$_{\exists \boldsymbol{x}.\Psi}$ is converging (Prop. 1).*

4.4   The Algorithms

In this section, we show our algorithm for computing the BMBP *ConvProj* from Sec. 4.3 and discuss applications of Alg. 1 to arbitrary LRA formulae (Alg. 3).

BMBP for syntactically convex LRA formulae. Function *ConvProj* takes as input a conjunctive LRA formula Ψ, a set of variables $\boldsymbol{x}$ to be eliminated from Ψ, and a model $\boldsymbol{p}$ satisfying Ψ. As output, *ConvProj* returns two formulae corresponding to an over- and an under-approximation of $\exists \boldsymbol{x}.\Psi$.

Formulae are represented with matrices of coefficients $\mathsf{A}, \mathsf{U}, \mathsf{O}$, intended to be multiplied with a vector of variables $\boldsymbol{xy}\varepsilon$ [6]: ε is a fresh variable added[7] for

---

[6] Here, $\boldsymbol{xy}\varepsilon$ is the single column vector $(\boldsymbol{x}^{\mathrm{T}}, \boldsymbol{y}^{\mathrm{T}}, \varepsilon)^{\mathrm{T}}$.
[7] Initially, it is enough to add a zero column in A.

Algorithm 2 Compute $\mathcal{O}_{\exists x.\Psi}(p), \mathcal{U}_{\exists x.\Psi}(p)$ breaking ties and symmetry.

1: **function** $ConvProj(\Psi, x, p)$
2:      let $\Psi(x, y) = A \cdot xy\varepsilon \leq 0$
3:      $U := A; O := A$ $\triangleright$ Initially: $u = o = \Psi$
4:      **for** $x_i \in x$ **do**
5:          $\mathtt{Zer}, \mathtt{Pos}, \mathtt{Neg} := \mathtt{normalize\text{-}and\text{-}classify}\,(U, x_i)$
6:          **if** $|\mathtt{Pos}| = 0$ **or** $|\mathtt{Neg}| = 0$ **then** $O := U := \mathtt{Zer}$; **continue**
7:          **if** $|\mathtt{Neg}| < |\mathtt{Pos}|$ **then** swap $\mathtt{Neg}, \mathtt{Pos}$ $\triangleright$ Symmetry breaking
8:          $\mathtt{MaxPos}, \mathtt{OtherPos} := \mathtt{sort\text{-}rows}(\mathtt{Pos}, \lambda c.c \cdot p)$ $\triangleright$ MaxPos are ties
9:          $\mathtt{maxpos} := \mathtt{MaxPos}[0]$ $\triangleright$ Tie breaking
10:         $O := \mathtt{filter\text{-}rows}\left(\begin{bmatrix} \mathtt{Zer} \\ \mathtt{combine}^+(\mathtt{MaxPos}, \mathtt{Neg}) \end{bmatrix}, \mathtt{is\text{-}entailed\text{-}by}(A)\right)$

11:         $U := \begin{bmatrix} \mathtt{Zer} \\ \mathtt{combine}^+(\mathtt{MaxPos}, \mathtt{Neg}) \\ \mathtt{combine}^-_{\leq}(\mathtt{MaxPos}, \mathtt{maxpos}) \\ \mathtt{combine}^-_{<}(\mathtt{OtherPos}, \mathtt{maxpos}) \end{bmatrix}$

12:     **return** $O \cdot xy\varepsilon \leq 0, U \cdot xy\varepsilon \leq 0$

---

creating strict inequalities when needed. Initially U and O are both equal to A: this corresponds to initializing $u^0 = o^0 = \Psi$ in Def. 4. Then, the loop at line 4 scans the quantified variables x. Each iteration preserves as loop invariant that columns $0, \ldots, i$ in O and U are zeroes. Namely, at the i-th iteration, U is split into three sub-matrices, $\mathtt{Zer}, \mathtt{Pos}, \mathtt{Neg}$, whose rows are normalized to have $0, +1, -1$ in column i respectively. Matrix $\mathtt{Zer}$ defines the constraints where x_i does not occur (called ψ in Sec. 4), while $\mathtt{Pos}$ and $\mathtt{Neg}$ are the upper- and lower-bounds constraints for x_i, respectively. At line 8, the rows in $\mathtt{Pos}$ are sorted according to their interpretation on model p, and two matrices are generated: $\mathtt{MaxPos}$ and $\mathtt{OtherPos}$, representing L_M and L' from Def. 4, respectively. Symmetry is broken at line 7 based on the sizes of $\mathtt{Pos}$ and $\mathtt{Neg}$, while ties are broken at line 9 by picking one row $\mathtt{maxpos}$ from $\mathtt{MaxPos}$.

Then, O and U are created as in Def. 4 leveraging helper functions: $\mathtt{combine}^+$ for row-wise sum; $\mathtt{combine}^-_{\leq}$ for row-wise subtraction, forcing the created constraints to be non-strict (by setting ε coefficients to be 0); $\mathtt{combine}^-_{<}$ for row-wise subtraction forcing the created constraints to be strict (by forcing ε coefficients to be 1). Finally, O rows are filtered by preserving only the ones generating an inequality entailed by Ψ (line 10).

Alg. 2 assumes that Ψ is pre-processed by splitting equalities in two inequalities, adding a variable for the inhomogeneous term, and possibly adding a slack variable (not to be confused with the ε variable used inside the procedure) transforming a strict inequality to a non-strict one. A post-processing removes such additional variables and merges inequalities in an equality when possible.

Instead of manipulating matrices O and U, Alg. 2 could manipulate matrices of coefficients $\mathtt{C\_Over}$ and $\mathtt{C\_Under}$ such that $O = \mathtt{C\_Over} \cdot A$, and $U = \mathtt{C\_Under} \cdot A$. Inspired from [33], this improves the efficiency of the function $\mathtt{is\text{-}entailed\text{-}by}$ called to filter rows of O: in fact, if a row $\mathtt{c}$ in $\mathtt{C\_Over}$ is non-negative, then the

---

Algorithm 3 Using BMBP-QE to compute QE of an arbitrary LRA formula.

1: **function** LRA-BMBP-QE($\exists \boldsymbol{x}.\Psi(\boldsymbol{x}, \boldsymbol{y})$, π)
2:     $\mathcal{M} := \bot$
3:     **if** not exists $\boldsymbol{p}$ s.t. $\boldsymbol{p} \models \Psi$ **then return** $\mathcal{M}$
4:     **while** exists $\boldsymbol{p}$ s.t. $\boldsymbol{p} \models \Psi \wedge \neg \mathcal{M}$ **do**
5:         $\phi := $ GET-IMPLICANT-POLY$(\Psi, \boldsymbol{p})$
6:         $\mathcal{O}ver, \mathcal{U}nder := $ BMBP-QE$(\exists \boldsymbol{x}.\phi, \pi)$
7:         $\mathcal{M} := \mathcal{M} \vee \mathcal{O}ver$
8:     **return** $\mathcal{M}$
9: **function** GET-IMPLICANT-POLY$(\Psi, \boldsymbol{p})$
10:     $\phi := \bigwedge \{\ell \mid \ell \in \text{ineqs}(\Psi), \boldsymbol{p} \models \ell\} \wedge \bigwedge \{\neg\ell \mid \ell \in \text{ineqs}(\Psi), \boldsymbol{p} \not\models \ell\}$
11:     **return** unsat-core$(\phi, \neg\Psi)$

---

corresponding constraint $\ell \doteq (\mathbf{c} \cdot \mathbf{A} \cdot \boldsymbol{xy}\varepsilon \leq 0)$ is known to be entailed by Ψ for Farkas Lemma. Otherwise, an SMT check is required to determine $\Psi \models \ell$.

After some iterations of Alg. 2, the number of rows in C_Under may increase due to the propagation of redundant constraints. When the number of rows of C_Under is above a certain threshold[8], or when the last iteration has been completed, C_Under is minimized by removing redundant rows. Minimization is done by checking, for each row, if the represented inequality is entailed by the conjunction of the other rows, using SMT solving under-assumptions. This allows to keep the size of C_Under and C_Over manageable throughout the execution of Alg. 2. At the end of Alg. 1, when all over-approximations are conjoined in $\mathcal{O}ver = \bigwedge_{\boldsymbol{p} \in P} \mathcal{O}(\boldsymbol{p})$, then $\mathcal{O}ver$ is minimized again, thus returning a formula without redundancies.

Another design choice is to pick a quantified variable from $\boldsymbol{x}$ that has the minimal product $|\text{Pos}| \cdot |\text{Neg}|$ as the next one to be eliminated.

Main QE algorithm for LRA. Since BMBP-QE is SMT-based, it can be easily integrated in a QE algorithm for arbitrary LRA formulae, by using an SMT solver to lazily enumerate disjuncts in a DNF of the formula, e.g., as in Monniaux [28]. Alg. 3 shows such an extension in procedure LRA-BMBP-QE. When a model $\boldsymbol{p}$ is found, a convex polyhedron ϕ such that $\boldsymbol{p} \models \phi$ and that $\phi \models \Psi$ is obtained in function GET-IMPLICANT-POLY by conjoining the literals in Ψ that satisfy $\boldsymbol{p}$. In practice, ϕ can be further reduced by taking the unsat core of ϕ and $\neg\Psi$. Then, Alg. 1 with *ConvProj* is called to obtain a conjunctive representation $\mathcal{O}ver = \exists \boldsymbol{x}.\phi$, which is added to a formula $\mathcal{M}$ (that is initially $\bot$). The procedure terminates when there are no models of Ψ outside $\mathcal{M}$ to be explored.

One of the interesting advantages of Alg. 3 compared to [28] is that in each iteration the blocking is done by a single clause (the negation of $\mathcal{O}ver$), as opposed to by a possibly (syntactically) large formula $\mathcal{U}nder$.

---

[8] This threshold is progressively harmonized during Alg. 1 run.

5 Experimental Evaluation

We implemented Alg. 1, Alg. 2, and Alg. 3 in a new prototype tool called
HENOSIS in Python. HENOSIS uses SYMPY (v1.13.3) for symbolic matrices and
PYSMT [18,34] (v0.9.6) for making calls to the MATHSAT5 [8] (v5.6.10) SMT
solver and unsat core extractor. We evaluated HENOSIS against 5 competitors:

- Z3 (v4.13) implementation of MBP-QE called through PYSMT;
- MFM: a FM-QE with a post-processing removal of redundancies imple-
  mented in MATHSAT5 and called through PYSMT;
- MLW: a LW-QE with a post-processing simplification [36] implemented in
  MATHSAT5 and called through PYSMT;
- PPLITE [2,31] (v0.12), a C++ library for DD of polyhedra;
- FMPLEX-QE [15,33] implemented in SMT-RAT.

We considered 5 categories of benchmarks.

Rand: 2250 syntactically convex formulae taken from [33] from 6 to 30 variables (half are existentially quantified) and from 6 to 30 constraints.

DDhard: 364 syntactically convex formulae including hypercubes with up
to 30 variables (all but one are existentially quantified) and polyhedra with
hundreds of constraints. In these benchmarks, the projection is very simple (like
an interval in $\mathbb{R}^1$) while the input formula is described by many constraints
and/or generators.

NCRand: 1418 LRA formulae with up to 30 variables (half are existentially
quantified): these formulae are of the form $\exists x_0 \ldots x_{|x|/2}. \bigwedge_{i \leq k} \phi_i \wedge \bigwedge_{k < i \leq 10} \neg \phi_i$,
where the ϕ_is are randomly generated polyhedra on x variables and k is a ran-
domly generated integer.

chc-trans: 305 LRA formulae extracted by unrollings of Constrained Horn
Clauses [14] that represent safety verification problems.

SMTlib: 1903 benchmarks taken from the LRA category of SMT-comp,
which includes the tests for quantifier alternation from [28]. These benchmarks
were modified to extract a single QE problem, thus possibly producing more
tests from a single original SMT-comp benchmark.

We experimented on an AMD EPYC 7413 hardware, with a timeout of 300s
(as done in [28,33]) and memory limit of 16GB. All results produced by HENOSIS
were verified to be equivalent to those produced by the other competitors, with
an external SMT solver.

BMBP-QE preserves conjunctiveness and minimizes the output. Column "size
ratios" of Table 1 reports for each benchmark category the minimal and maximal
ratios between the DAG size[9] of each tool's output and the DAG size of the
result produced by HENOSIS. In the conjunctive benchmark categories, HENOSIS
returns the same minimized polyhedron that PPLITE produces, thus, the ratios
with respect to PPLITE are always equal to 1. The same holds for MFM, which

---

[9] The DAG size is the number of distinct nodes in the syntax tree of the formula.

Table 1. Number of solved benchmarks and size ratio against HENOSIS's result.

category	tot	HENOSIS nr solv	z3 nr solv	z3 size ratio	MLW nr solv	MLW size ratio	MFM nr solv	MFM size ratio	PPLITE nr solv	PPLITE size ratio	FMPLEX-QE nr solv	FMPLEX-QE size ratio
Rand	2250	1772	1077	$[1\text{-}10^2]$	1556	$[1\text{-}10^2]$	1305	1	2093	1	**2209**	$[1\text{-}98]$
DDhard	364	**364**	29	$[1\text{-}10^3]$	**364**	$[1\text{-}2]$	48	1	135	1	327	$[1\text{-}10^4]$
NCRand	1418	**1272**	943	$[0.1\text{-}10^2]$	1241	$[0.1\text{-}10^2]$	1133	$[0.1\text{-}16]$	-	-	-	-
chc-trans	305	299	**305**	$[0.1\text{-}9]$	251	$[0.3\text{-}9]$	304	$[0.3\text{-}7]$	-	-	-	-
SMTlib	1903	1486	**1659**	$[10^{-2}\text{-}10^2]$	1534	$[10^{-2}\text{-}94]$	684	$[0.1\text{-}10^2]$	-	-	-	-

constructs a conjunction using FM-QE and subsequently removes redundant constraints as a post-processing step.

By contrast, z3, MLW and FMPLEX-QE produce formulae with substantially larger DAGs. Specifically, z3 and MLW introduce unnecessary disjunctions (thereby failing in preserving convexity), while FMPLEX-QE includes a large number of redundant inequalities. Returning a result that is up to 10^3 times larger than necessary is clearly impractical for the QE caller.

Overhead of BMBP-QE with respect to MBP-QE. BMBP-QE extends MBP-QE by handling over-approximations while preserving the desirable property of being an anytime algorithm. We are now interested in evaluating the computational costs associated with maintaining the over-approximations.

As shown in Table 1, on conjunctive benchmarks, HENOSIS actually outperforms both z3 and MLW, which are based on MBP-QE. Specifically, HENOSIS solves 1030 more instances than z3, and 218 more instances than MLW.

The plots in Fig. 2 compare the numbers of solved instances on the convex benchmark categories by each tool. Given the different implementation languages (HENOSIS is written in Python, while z3 and MLW are implemented in C++), running times below 1 second are not meaningful for comparison.

The fact that MLW and HENOSIS both explore under-approximations and prune the projection tree in a comparable manner is highlighted by the similar behavior on the **DDhard** benchmarks. In particular, in the **DDhard** tests, the large size of the input formulae has little impact on the enumeration of under-approximations.

Comparison with methods for convex instances. For completeness, Fig. 2 compares HENOSIS with methods specialized for convex instances, namely PPLITE and FMPLEX-QE. It is important to note that PPLITE and FMPLEX-QE are *not* anytime algorithms and therefore cannot be used in SMT-based verification algorithms leveraging partial results. Moreover, as discussed previously, FMPLEX-QE relies on syntactic manipulations of the input formula and does not minimize the output. Therefore, it is generally expected that FMPLEX-QE and PPLITE are faster than HENOSIS.

However, it appears that PPLITE struggles on the **DDhard** benchmarks (see Table 1) with hypercubes and formulae with many generators even when the number of variables is small. Overall, HENOSIS solves 242 more instances than

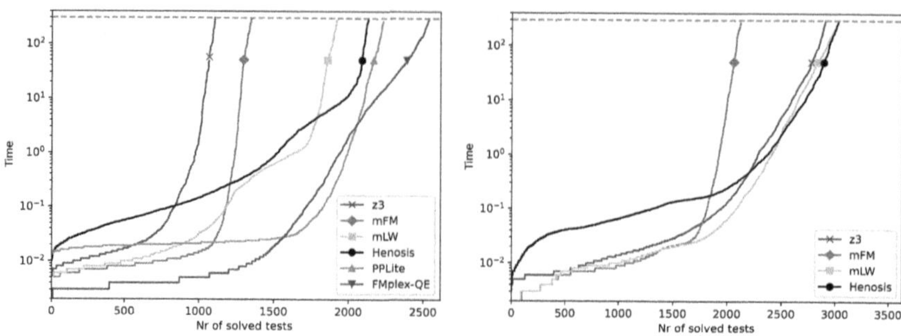

Fig. 2. Number of solved instances by each tool. Convex instances on the left, and arbitrary LRA instances on the right.

PPLite, including 33 cases in which PPLite ran out of memory. Similarly, FMplex-QE exhibits increased runtime on these benchmarks and produces results with on the order of 10^4 constraints, of which only 2 are irredundant. In total, HENOSIS solves 39 instances more than FMplex-QE including 36 cases in which FMplex-QE ran out of memory.

We also included a comparison with mFM. Like FMplex-QE, mFM generates a large number of resolvents when the input formula contains many constraints. Unlike FMplex-QE, however, mFM removes redundant constraints in a post-processing step. This post-processing frequently times out, for example on **DDhard** benchmarks, demonstrating how difficult it is to eliminate redundancies after they have been introduced. Overall, HENOSIS solves 796 more convex instances than mFM.

Breaking symmetry and ties accelerates convergence. We compared HENOSIS against its variant without symmetry and tie breaking (see Sec. 4.2), which we call HENOSIS*. Overall, HENOSIS solves 491 more instances than HENOSIS*. In terms of number of internal iterations of BMBP-QE, for the instances solved by both HENOSIS and HENOSIS*, HENOSIS requires an average of 2.6 iterations (with a maximum of 108 iterations), while HENOSIS* requires an average of 23 iterations (with a maximum of 3581 iterations). Notably, both HENOSIS and HENOSIS* return the same conjunctive and minimized formula.

Comparison on arbitrary LRA formulae. PPLite and FMplex-QE do not apply to this type of formulae. We compare with the remaining three tools. The ability to process benchmarks from category **chc-trans**, in particular, demonstrates the applicability of HENOSIS to real QE tasks in verification routines.

HENOSIS outperforms mFM and exhibits partial orthogonality with respect to the other MBP-QE based methods z3 and mLW. We attribute this behavior to the fact that the exploration strategy of HENOSIS differs substantially from that of common implementations of MBP-QE. HENOSIS enumerates implicant polyhedra (see Alg. 3) and computes QE for each of them using BMBP-QE.

This potentially leads to explore some overlapping regions twice, but it also avoids overloading the SMT solver with a large number of blocking lemmas.

Overall, HENOSIS solves 396 more instances than Z3, 160 more instances than MLW, and 944 more instances than MFM. On average, HENOSIS explored 45 convex polyhedra per test, with a maximum of 2842 explored polyhedra in a test from **SMTlib** category. For each polyhedron, HENOSIS collected an average of 1.7 models, with a maximum of 133 models.

6   Conclusion

We introduced a new QE method for LRA that preserves the syntactic convexity of the input while maintaining the benefits of an anytime QE algorithm using MBP. We defined Bidirectional Model Based Projection (BMBP), and an algorithm (BMBP-QE) where a conjunctive over- and a disjunctive under-approximations of QE are progressively refined. We formalized the conditions guaranteeing convergence. BMBP-QE naturally lifts to arbitrary LRA formulae with a lazy exploration of their DNF. In our experiments, BMBP-QE outperforms other SMT-based methods on convex and arbitrary LRA benchmarks, improving run time and the conciseness of the result. While it is in general less efficient than existing methods specialized for convex instances, BMBP-QE outperforms them when the input is larger than the QE result.

Future works include the integration of BMBP-QE inside a verification engine that could benefit from the twofold partial results ($Over$ and $Under$). For example, in SMT-based model checking one can try to block the over-approximation of the pre-image of a bad state, possibly learning more interesting lemmas if this succeeds. Other directions include leveraging the availability of a conjunctive description for the final output, and the extension to formulae with Boolean variables, integer and modular arithmetic.

Acknowledgments. The first author was partially supported by the "Formal Reasoning on Neural Networks" project funded by the Hasler Foundation, Switzerland, and Swiss National Science Foundation grant 200021-236601 – "Cross theory rigorous program verification using Constrained Horn clauses". The second author was partially supported by the National Science Foundation grant 2106949. We also acknowledge the support of the Natural Sciences and Engineering Research Council of Canada (NSERC), [funding reference number RGPIN-04029-2024.]

Data-Availability Statement. Henosis implementation and benchmarks are available at https://github.com/annabeks/convexQE.

References

1. Roberto Bagnara, Patricia M. Hill, and Enea Zaffanella. The Parma Polyhedra Library: Toward a complete set of numerical abstractions for the analysis and verification of hardware and software systems. *Sci. Comput. Program.*, 72(1-2):3–21, 2008.

2. Anna Becchi and Enea Zaffanella. PPLite: Zero-overhead encoding of NNC polyhedra. *Inf. Comput.*, 275:104620, 2020.

3. Nikolaj S. Bjørner and Arie Gurfinkel. Property directed polyhedral abstraction. In Deepak D'Souza, Akash Lal, and Kim Guldstrand Larsen, editors, *Verification, Model Checking, and Abstract Interpretation - 16th International Conference, VMCAI 2015, Mumbai, India, January 12-14, 2015. Proceedings*, volume 8931 of *Lecture Notes in Computer Science*, pages 263–281. Springer, 2015.

4. Nikolaj S. Bjørner and Mikolás Janota. Playing with quantified satisfaction. In Ansgar Fehnker, Annabelle McIver, Geoff Sutcliffe, and Andrei Voronkov, editors, *20th International Conferences on Logic for Programming, Artificial Intelligence and Reasoning - Short Presentations, LPAR 2015, Suva, Fiji, November 24-28, 2015*, volume 35 of *EPiC Series in Computing*, pages 15–27. EasyChair, 2015.

5. Martin Blicha, Grigory Fedyukovich, Antti E. J. Hyvärinen, and Natasha Sharygina. Transition power abstractions for deep counterexample detection. In Dana Fisman and Grigore Rosu, editors, *Tools and Algorithms for the Construction and Analysis of Systems - 28th International Conference, TACAS 2022, Held as Part of the European Joint Conferences on Theory and Practice of Software, ETAPS 2022, Munich, Germany, April 2-7, 2022, Proceedings, Part I*, volume 13243 of *Lecture Notes in Computer Science*, pages 524–542. Springer, 2022.

6. N. V. Chernikova. Algorithm for discovering the set of all solutions of a linear programming problem. *U.S.S.R. Computational Mathematics and Mathematical Physics*, 8(6):282–293, 1968.

7. Alessandro Cimatti and Alberto Griggio. Software model checking via IC3. In P. Madhusudan and Sanjit A. Seshia, editors, *Computer Aided Verification - 24th International Conference, CAV 2012, Berkeley, CA, USA, July 7-13, 2012 Proceedings*, volume 7358 of *Lecture Notes in Computer Science*, pages 277–293. Springer, 2012.

8. Alessandro Cimatti, Alberto Griggio, Bastiaan Joost Schaafsma, and Roberto Sebastiani. The mathsat5 SMT solver. In Nir Piterman and Scott A. Smolka, editors, *Tools and Algorithms for the Construction and Analysis of Systems - 19th International Conference, TACAS 2013, Held as Part of the European Joint Conferences on Theory and Practice of Software, ETAPS 2013, Rome, Italy, March 16-24, 2013. Proceedings*, volume 7795 of *Lecture Notes in Computer Science*, pages 93–107. Springer, 2013.

9. Byron Cook, Sumit Gulwani, Tal Lev-Ami, Andrey Rybalchenko, and Mooly Sagiv. Proving conditional termination. In Aarti Gupta and Sharad Malik, editors, *Computer Aided Verification, 20th International Conference, CAV 2008, Princeton, NJ, USA, July 7-14, 2008, Proceedings*, volume 5123 of *Lecture Notes in Computer Science*, pages 328–340. Springer, 2008.

10. Patrick Cousot and Nicolas Halbwachs. Automatic discovery of linear restraints among variables of a program. In Alfred V. Aho, Stephen N. Zilles, and Thomas G. Szymanski, editors, *Conference Record of the Fifth Annual ACM Symposium on Principles of Programming Languages, Tucson, Arizona, USA, January 1978*, pages 84–96. ACM Press, 1978.

11. Azadeh Farzan and Zachary Kincaid. Compositional recurrence analysis. In Roope Kaivola and Thomas Wahl, editors, *Formal Methods in Computer-Aided Design, FMCAD 2015, Austin, Texas, USA, September 27-30, 2015*, pages 57–64. IEEE, 2015.

12. Grigory Fedyukovich and Aarti Gupta. Functional synthesis with examples. In Thomas Schiex and Simon de Givry, editors, *Principles and Practice of Con-*

      straint Programming - 25th International Conference, CP 2019, Stamford, CT, USA, September 30 - October 4, 2019, Proceedings, volume 11802 of *Lecture Notes in Computer Science*, pages 547–564. Springer, 2019.

13. Grigory Fedyukovich, Arie Gurfinkel, and Aarti Gupta. Lazy but effective functional synthesis. In Constantin Enea and Ruzica Piskac, editors, *Verification, Model Checking, and Abstract Interpretation - 20th International Conference, VM-CAI 2019, Cascais, Portugal, January 13-15, 2019, Proceedings*, volume 11388 of *Lecture Notes in Computer Science*, pages 92–113. Springer, 2019.

14. Grigory Fedyukovich, Samuel J. Kaufman, and Rastislav Bodík. Sampling invariants from frequency distributions. In Daryl Stewart and Georg Weissenbacher, editors, *2017 Formal Methods in Computer Aided Design, FMCAD 2017, Vienna, Austria, October 2-6, 2017*, pages 100–107. IEEE, 2017.

15. FMplex. https://github.com/ths-rwth/smtrat/tree/pub/fmplex-qe-3.

16. Goran Frehse. Phaver: algorithmic verification of hybrid systems past hytech. *Int. J. Softw. Tools Technol. Transf.*, 10(3):263–279, 2008.

17. K. Fukuda and A. Prodon. Double description method revisited. In M. Deza, R. Euler, and Y. Manoussakis, editors, *Combinatorics and Computer Science, 8th Franco-Japanese and 4th Franco-Chinese Conference, Brest, France, July 3-5, 1995, Selected Papers*, volume 1120 of *Lecture Notes in Computer Science*, pages 91–111. Springer-Verlag, Berlin, 1996.

18. Marco Gario and Andrea Micheli. PySMT: a solver-agnostic library for fast prototyping of SMT-based algorithms. In *SMT Workshop 2015*, 2015.

19. Blagoy Genov. *The Convex Hull Problem in Practice: Improving the Running Time of the Double Description Method (Das Problem der konvexen Hülle in der Praxis)*. PhD thesis, Bremen University, Germany, 2015.

20. Nicolas Halbwachs, Yann-Eric Proy, and Pascal Raymond. Verification of linear hybrid systems by means of convex approximations. In Baudouin Le Charlier, editor, *Static Analysis, First International Static Analysis Symposium, SAS'94, Namur, Belgium, September 28-30, 1994, Proceedings*, volume 864 of *Lecture Notes in Computer Science*, pages 223–237. Springer, 1994.

21. Jean-Louis Imbert. Fourier's elimination: Which to choose? In *Principles and Practice of Constraint Programming, PPCP 1993, Newport, Rhode Island*, pages 117–129, 1993.

22. Rui-Juan Jing, Marc Moreno Maza, and Delaram Talaashrafi. Complexity estimates for fourier-motzkin elimination. In François Boulier, Matthew England, Timur M. Sadykov, and Evgenii V. Vorozhtsov, editors, *Computer Algebra in Scientific Computing - 22nd International Workshop, CASC 2020, Linz, Austria, September 14-18, 2020, Proceedings*, volume 12291 of *Lecture Notes in Computer Science*, pages 282–306. Springer, 2020.

23. Hari Govind V. K., Grigory Fedyukovich, and Arie Gurfinkel. Word level property directed reachability. In *IEEE/ACM International Conference On Computer Aided Design, ICCAD 2020, San Diego, CA, USA, November 2-5, 2020*, pages 107:1–107:9. IEEE, 2020.

24. Andreas Katis, Grigory Fedyukovich, Jeffrey Chen, David A. Greve, Sanjai Rayadurgam, and Michael W. Whalen. Synthesis of infinite-state systems with random behavior. In *35th IEEE/ACM International Conference on Automated Software Engineering, ASE 2020, Melbourne, Australia, September 21-25, 2020*, pages 250–261. IEEE, 2020.

25. Anvesh Komuravelli, Arie Gurfinkel, and Sagar Chaki. SMT-based model checking for recursive programs. In Armin Biere and Roderick Bloem, editors, *Computer*

Aided Verification - 26th International Conference, CAV 2014, Held as Part of the Vienna Summer of Logic, VSL 2014, Vienna, Austria, July 18-22, 2014. Proceedings, volume 8559 of *Lecture Notes in Computer Science*, pages 17–34. Springer, 2014.

26. Hari Govind Vediramana Krishnan, Yuting Chen, Sharon Shoham, and Arie Gurfinkel. Global guidance for local generalization in model checking. In Shuvendu K. Lahiri and Chao Wang, editors, *Computer Aided Verification - 32nd International Conference, CAV 2020, Los Angeles, CA, USA, July 21-24, 2020, Proceedings, Part II*, volume 12225 of *Lecture Notes in Computer Science*, pages 101–125. Springer, 2020.

27. Rüdiger Loos and Volker Weispfenning. Applying linear quantifier elimination. *Comput. J.*, 36(5):450–462, 1993.

28. David Monniaux. Quantifier elimination by lazy model enumeration. In Tayssir Touili, Byron Cook, and Paul B. Jackson, editors, *Computer Aided Verification, 22nd International Conference, CAV 2010, Edinburgh, UK, July 15-19, 2010. Proceedings*, volume 6174 of *Lecture Notes in Computer Science*, pages 585–599. Springer, 2010.

29. T. S. Motzkin, H. Raiffa, G. L. Thompson, and R. M. Thrall. The double description method. In H. W. Kuhn and A. W. Tucker, editors, *Contributions to the Theory of Games – Volume II*, number 28 in Annals of Mathematics Studies, pages 51–73. Princeton University Press, Princeton, New Jersey, 1953.

30. Tobias Nipkow. Linear quantifier elimination. *J. Autom. Reason.*, 45(2):189–212, 2010.

31. PPLite. https://github.com/ezaffanella/pplite.

32. Sumanth Prabhu, Deepak D'Souza, Supratik Chakraborty, R. Venkatesh, and Grigory Fedyukovich. Weakest precondition inference for non-deterministic linear array programs. In Bernd Finkbeiner and Laura Kovács, editors, *Tools and Algorithms for the Construction and Analysis of Systems - 30th International Conference, TACAS 2024, Held as Part of the European Joint Conferences on Theory and Practice of Software, ETAPS 2024, Luxembourg City, Luxembourg, April 6-11, 2024, Proceedings, Part II*, volume 14571 of *Lecture Notes in Computer Science*, pages 175–195. Springer, 2024.

33. Valentin Promies and Erika Ábrahám. A divide-and-conquer approach to variable elimination in linear real arithmetic. In André Platzer, Kristin Yvonne Rozier, Matteo Pradella, and Matteo Rossi, editors, *Formal Methods - 26th International Symposium, FM 2024, Milan, Italy, September 9-13, 2024, Proceedings, Part I*, volume 14933 of *Lecture Notes in Computer Science*, pages 131–148. Springer, 2024.

34. PySMT. https://github.com/pysmt/pysmt.

35. Daniel Riley and Grigory Fedyukovich. Multi-phase invariant synthesis. In Abhik Roychoudhury, Cristian Cadar, and Miryung Kim, editors, *Proceedings of the 30th ACM Joint European Software Engineering Conference and Symposium on the Foundations of Software Engineering, ESEC/FSE 2022, Singapore, Singapore, November 14-18, 2022*, pages 607–619. ACM, 2022.

36. Christoph Scholl, Stefan Disch, Florian Pigorsch, and Stefan Kupferschmid. Computing optimized representations for non-convex polyhedra by detection and removal of redundant linear constraints. In Stefan Kowalewski and Anna Philippou, editors, *Tools and Algorithms for the Construction and Analysis of Systems, 15th International Conference, TACAS 2009, Held as Part of the Joint European Conferences on Theory and Practice of Software, ETAPS 2009, York, UK, March 22-*

29, 2009. Proceedings, volume 5505 of *Lecture Notes in Computer Science*, pages 383–397. Springer, 2009.

37. Jake Silverman and Zachary Kincaid. Loop summarization with rational vector addition systems. In Isil Dillig and Serdar Tasiran, editors, *Computer Aided Verification - 31st International Conference, CAV 2019, New York City, NY, USA, July 15-18, 2019, Proceedings, Part II*, volume 11562 of *Lecture Notes in Computer Science*, pages 97–115. Springer, 2019.

38. N. Yu. Zolotykh. New modification of the double description method for constructing the skeleton of a polyhedral cone. *Computational Mathematics and Mathematical Physics*, 52(1):146–156, 2012.

Bit-Precise Interpolation in Bitwuzla[*]

Aina Niemetz and Mathias Preiner

Stanford University, Stanford, USA
{niemetz, preiner}@cs.stanford.edu

Abstract. Bitwuzla is a state-of-the-art SMT solver specialized in theories relevant to bit-precise reasoning. The main bit-vector solving procedure of Bitwuzla is based on bit-blasting, a reduction of bit-vector constraints to propositional logic (SAT). Until now, Bitwuzla did not support interpolant generation, which is a key requirement for many verification applications that rely on bit-precise reasoning. We present an extension of Bitwuzla with the capability to produce interpolants and interpolation sequences for quantifier-free bit-vector formulas. Our interpolation workflow extracts bit-level interpolants from proofs produced by the back-end SAT solver, which are lifted to the word-level and post-processed to recover and simplify word-level structure. We evaluate our new bit-vector interpolation engine in the context of various interpolation-based algorithms for symbolic model checking.

1 Introduction

Many applications in computer-aided verification rely on bit-precise reasoning at the back end. One prominent example is symbolic model checking [19], both in the context of software and hardware verification, where the representation of machine integers with bit-precise semantics is a key requirement. In recent years, advances in Satisfiability Modulo Theories (SMT) research and solving enabled the lifting of classic SAT-based model checking techniques to SMT [9]. This allows for modeling of systems that require more expressive reasoning.

Interpolation-based verification techniques that utilize Craig interpolants [20] to generalize abstractions are the basis for many state-of-the-art model checking algorithms (e.g., [16, 42, 50, 51]). Applications that implement such algorithms based on bit-precise reasoning as provided by the SMT theory of fixed-size bit-vectors therefore require the solver back end to produce bit-vector interpolants. Producing interpolants, however, is a feature that is not standardized in the SMT-LIB format [8] and not widely supported by SMT solvers.

Bitwuzla [44] is a state-of-the-art SMT solver specialized in theories relevant for bit-precise reasoning. It supports the theories of fixed-size bit-vectors, arrays, floating-point arithmetic and uninterpreted functions and their combinations. The main bit-vector solving procedure in Bitwuzla is an abstraction

---

[*] This work was supported in part by the Stanford Center for Automated Reasoning, the Stanford Center for Blockchain Research, and a gift from Amazon Web Services.

S. Junges and G. Katz (Eds.): TACAS 2026, LNCS 16505, pp. 66–88, 2026.
https://doi.org/10.1007/978-3-032-22752-2_4

refinement approach based on bit-blasting [46], which reduces bit-vector constraints to propositional logic (SAT).

In this paper, we extend Bitwuzla with the capability to produce interpolants and interpolation sequences for quantifier-free bit-vector formulas. Our interpolation workflow computes bit-level interpolants from the proofs produced by the back-end SAT solver of the bit-vector solver. These bit-level interpolants are then lifted to the word-level and post-processed to recover and simplify word-level structure. We evaluate our interpolation engine in the context of various interpolation-based engines implemented in the model checkers Pono [40] and Kind2 [14, 39], which both integrate Bitwuzla as one of their back-end solvers.

Related Work. Interpolation techniques for other theories, e.g., linear integer arithmetic, have been investigated in great detail [12]. Bit-vector interpolation, on the other hand, and especially techniques based on bit-blasting, have received relatively little attention over the years. The majority of interpolation techniques for quantifier-free bit-vector formulas rely on a reduction of bit-vector constraints to integer arithmetic [6, 28, 47]. Techniques based on such a reduction are not applicable in our context since Bitwuzla does not support integer arithmetic.

The main bit-vector interpolation technique for bit-blasting-based SMT procedures is a naive reconstruction of propositional bit-level interpolants on the word-level via bit extraction, Boolean conjunction and negation. This technique is complete but results in purely bit-level interpolants and a loss of word-level structure. Kroening et al. [37] attempted to mitigate this loss of word-level structure by lifting the propositional proof of unsatisfiability of a bit-vector interpolation problem to the word-level, prior to extracting the interpolant. This technique is, however, limited to the fragment of equality logic. The same authors later proposed an interpolation procedure based on a specialized, rewriting-based decision procedure [38], but limited to a fragment of the bit-vector theory. Our technique is also based on lifting bit-level interpolants to the word-level, augmented with additional post-processing and simplification strategies to recover more word-level structure, and not limited to a fragment of the bit-vector theory.

Few state-of-the-art SMT solvers provide support for bit-vector interpolation. MathSAT [17] implements a layered approach [28] where various incomplete interpolation techniques, including via a reduction to linear integer arithmetic, are combined with the standard bit-level technique as a fallback. Interpolants produced by the fallback technique are purely bit-level interpolants as no strategies to recover word-level structure are applied to the interpolant.

cvc5 [7] implements a generic interpolation approach where the interpolation query is translated into a Syntax-Guided Synthesis (SyGuS) query whose solutions are interpolants. SMTInterpol [15] and Princess [6] compute bit-vector interpolants via a reduction of the interpolation query to non-linear integer arithmetic. Yices2 [22] produces so-called model interpolants [27], which are derived within the MCSAT framework as explanations for why a partial model of formula B (over common symbols) cannot be extended to a full model of formula A.

Z3 [43] exposes interpolation as a reduction to solving non-recursive Constrained Horn Clauses (CHC) via its CHC solver Spacer [36]. Spacer implements a model-based projection procedure for the arithmetic fragment of the bit-vector theory (which falls back to value-based projection for operators outside of the fragment) to avoid bit-blasting-based interpolation techniques [34]. This approach iteratively approximates quantifier elimination. A layered, quantifier-elimination-based approach that also avoids bit-blasting but is limited to the linear arithmetic bit-vector fragment was proposed in [33].

2   Preliminaries

We assume the usual notions and terminology of many-sorted first-order logic with equality (see, e.g., [24, 41]). A *theory* is a pair $(\Sigma, \mathcal{I})$ where Σ is a signature consisting of sort symbols and sorted function symbols, and $\mathcal{I}$ is a class of Σ-interpretations. We assume that Σ includes equality and a designated sort Bool, values $\top$ (true) and $\bot$ (false) of sort Bool, and Boolean connectives defined as usual. We use the usual inductive definition of the satisfiability relation between Σ-interpretations and Σ-formulas. A Σ-formula is *T-satisfiable* (resp. *T-unsatisfiable*) if it is satisfied by some (resp. no) interpretation in $\mathcal{I}$; it is *T-valid* if it is satisfied by all interpretations in $\mathcal{I}$. We assume the usual definition of well-sorted terms, literals, and formulas.

We refer to 0-arity function symbols as *constants* and use $\mathcal{S}(t)$ and $\mathcal{S}(\varphi)$ for the set of uninterpreted symbols that appear in term t and formula φ, respectively. Similarly, for a formula $\varphi = \varphi_1 \wedge \ldots \wedge \varphi_n$, also denoted as $\{\varphi_1, \ldots, \varphi_n\}$, we use $\mathcal{S}(\varphi)$ for the set of uninterpreted symbols in $\mathcal{S}(\varphi_1) \cup \ldots \cup \mathcal{S}(\varphi_n)$. We write $\varphi[x_1, \ldots, x_n]$ to denote a formula φ defined over (a subset of) uninterpreted symbols $\{x_1, \ldots, x_n\}$. We further use $\varphi[x_1 \mapsto a_1, \ldots, x_n \mapsto a_n]$ for the formula obtained from φ by simultaneously replacing each occurrence of x_i with a_i.

We focus on the theory of fixed-size bit-vectors $T_{BV} = (\Sigma_{BV}, \mathcal{I}_{BV})$ as defined by the SMT-LIB 2 standard [8]. Signature Σ_{BV} includes a unique sort $\sigma_{[w]}$ for each bit-width w, function symbols overloaded for every $\sigma_{[w]}$, and all *bit-vector values* of sort $\sigma_{[w]}$ for each w. We denote a *bit-vector term* x of sort $\sigma_{[w]}$ as $x_{[w]}$, and omit w from the notation when it is clear from the context. We refer to the bit at index i of $x_{[w]}$ as $x[i]$ and represent a bit-vector value $v_{[w]}$ as a bit-string of 0s and 1s, with the most significant bit (MSB) as the left-most bit at index $w - 1$, and the least significant bit (LSB) as the right-most bit at index 0.

3   Interpolation

We briefly review background and definitions relevant to interpolation for quantifier-free bit-vector formulas as implemented in our SMT solver Bitwuzla [44]. The main procedure for solving quantifier-free bit-vector formulas in Bitwuzla is based on bit-blasting, which reduces bit-vector constraints to SAT. Our interpolation procedure is based on extracting an interpolant for the original bit-vector problem from the resolution refutation of its reduction to SAT. It integrates both Pudlák's [49] and McMillan's [42] interpolation systems for computing propositional interpolants from clausal resolution proofs of unsatisfiability.

Definition 1 (Craig Interpolant [20]). *Given T-formula $\varphi = \{\varphi_1, \ldots, \varphi_n\}$ such that φ is T-unsatisfiable, i.e., $\bigwedge_1^n \varphi_i \models \bot$. Let (A, B) be a partitioning of φ into formulas A and B with $A \cap B = \emptyset$, i.e., $A \wedge B$ is T-unsatisfiable and $A \Rightarrow \neg B$ is T-valid. An* interpolant *of A and B is a T-formula I such that*

(i) *$A \Rightarrow I$ is T-valid,*

(ii) *$I \wedge B$ is T-unsatisfiable, and*

(iii) *$\mathcal{S}(I) \subseteq \mathcal{S}(A) \cap \mathcal{S}(B)$.*

Given an (A, B) partitioning of φ, we use $\mathcal{S}_G = \mathcal{S}(A) \cap \mathcal{S}(B)$ for the set of *global symbols* in φ. We further denote the sets of A-*local* and B-*local* symbols as $\mathcal{S}_A = \mathcal{S}(A) \setminus \mathcal{S}_G$ and $\mathcal{S}_B = \mathcal{S}(B) \setminus \mathcal{S}_G$, respectively.

Based on such an (A, B) partitioning, a *term* t is global or local depending on its uninterpreted symbols: if $\mathcal{S}(t) \subseteq \mathcal{S}_G$, it is *global*; if its set of local symbols $\mathcal{S}_L(t) = \mathcal{S}(t) \setminus \mathcal{S}_G$ is non-empty and $\mathcal{S}_L(t) \subseteq \mathcal{S}_A$ or $\mathcal{S}_L(t) \subseteq \mathcal{S}_B$, it is A-*local* or B-*local*; and if $\mathcal{S}_L(t) \subseteq \mathcal{S}_A \cup \mathcal{S}_B$, it is AB-*mixed*. We use $t \in \mathcal{S}_A$, $t \in \mathcal{S}_B$ and $t \in \mathcal{S}_G$ as shorthand for *labeling* t as A-local, B-local and global, respectively.

Definition 2 (Interpolation Sequence [31]). *Given T-formula $\varphi = \{\varphi_1, \ldots, \varphi_n\}$ such that $\bigwedge_1^n \varphi_i \models \bot$. Let $\langle (A_1, B_1), \ldots, (A_n, B_n) \rangle$ be a sequence of n partitions of φ with $A_i = \{\varphi_1, \ldots, \varphi_i\}$ and $B_i = \{\varphi_{i+1}, \ldots, \varphi_n\}$ for $1 \leq i < n$. An* interpolation sequence *$\langle I_0, \ldots, I_n \rangle$ is a sequence of T-formulas such that*

(i) *$I_0 = \top$ and $I_n = \bot$,*

(ii) *I_i is an interpolant for (A_i, B_i), and*

(iii) *$I_i \wedge \varphi_{i+1} \Rightarrow I_{i+1}$.*

Note that by definition, terms in A and B are never AB-mixed. However, solving procedures for SMT may introduce AB-mixed terms (e.g., via lemmas) that appear in a proof of unsatisfiability for $A \wedge B$. In the context of our bit-vector interpolation procedure, we never encounter AB-mixed terms. We explain in more detail why this is the case in Section 4.

3.1 SAT-Based Interpolation

A *literal* l is either a propositional variable v or its negation $\neg v$. A *clause* $C = l_1 \vee \ldots \vee l_n$, also denoted as $\{l_1, \ldots, l_n\}$, is a disjunction of literals l_i. A formula $\phi = C_1 \wedge \ldots \wedge C_m$, also denoted as $\{C_1, \ldots, C_m\}$, in Conjunctive Normal Form (CNF) is a conjunction of clauses C_j. Given two clauses $C_1 = v \vee D_1$ and $C_2 = \neg v \vee D_2$, with D_1 and D_2 clauses that do not contain complementary literals. Then $D_1 \vee D_2$ is the *resolvent* of C_1 and C_2, also denoted as $res(C_1, C_2, v)$.

Given an unsatisfiable formula ϕ, partitioned into two clause sets A and B with $A \cap B = \emptyset$, an interpolant for A and B is defined as in Definition 1. Labeling of symbols and terms as A-local, B-local and global as above naturally extends to propositional variables and literals.

Definition 3 (Clausal Resolution Proof). *Given an unsatisfiable formula ϕ in CNF, a clausal resolution proof Π for ϕ is a directed acyclic graph (DAG) with clauses $V_\Pi = \{C_1, \ldots, C_k, D_{k+1}, \ldots, D_n\}$ as vertices such that*

(a) *root vertices $\{C_1, \ldots, C_k\} \subseteq \phi$,*
(b) *each $D \in \{D_{k+1}, \ldots, D_n\}$ has exactly two antecedents $A_1, A_2 \in V_\Pi$,*
(c) *$D = res(A_1, A_2, v)$, and*
(d) *the single leaf vertex of Π is $\{\}$ (the empty clause).*

Our interpolation procedure integrates the interpolation system proposed by McMillan [42] as the main procedure for computing propositional interpolants from a clausal resolution proof. Given $\phi = A \wedge B$ and a proof $\Pi(\phi)$, McMillan's algorithm recursively constructs an interpolant I from partial interpolants of every resolvent in Π based on the following, *asymmetric* construction rules.

Definition 4. *Let A and B be the disjoint partitions of a CNF formula ϕ, and let C be a clause in $\Pi(\phi)$. A **partial interpolant** I_p of C is defined via McMillan's asymmetric construction as follows.*

$$
I_p(C) = \begin{cases}
\{l \mid l \in C \wedge l \in \mathcal{S}_G\} & C \in A \\
\top & C \in B \\
I_p(C_1) \vee I_p(C_2) & C = res(C_1, C_2, v), v \in \mathcal{S}_A \\
I_p(C_1) \wedge I_p(C_2) & C = res(C_1, C_2, v), v \notin \mathcal{S}_A
\end{cases}
$$

Optionally, our interpolation procedure supports the interpolation system based on *symmetric* construction of partial interpolants proposed by Pudlák [49]. Pudlák's construction rules are similar to McMillan's rules but differ for A-clauses and in the case when pivot v of a resolved clause is not labeled as A-local.

Definition 5. *Let partitions A and B and clause C be defined as in Definition 4. If C is a resolvent $res(C_1, C_2, v)$, recall that $v \in C_1$ and $\neg v \in C_2$. A **partial interpolant** I_p of C is defined via Pudlák's symmetric construction as follows.*

$$
I_p(C) = \begin{cases}
\bot & C \in A \\
\top & C \in B \\
I_p(C_1) \vee I_p(C_2) & C = res(C_1, C_2, v), v \in \mathcal{S}_A \\
I_p(C_1) \wedge I_p(C_2) & C = res(C_1, C_2, v), v \in \mathcal{S}_B \\
(I_p(C_1) \vee v) \wedge (I_p(C_2) \vee \neg v) & C = res(C_1, C_2, v), v \in \mathcal{S}_G
\end{cases}
$$

4   Bit-Vector Interpolation Workflow

Our bit-vector interpolation procedure is implemented in Bitwuzla [44], an SMT solver for the (quantified and quantifier-free) theory of fixed-size bit-vectors and combinations with arrays, floating-point arithmetic and uninterpreted functions. The main solving procedure for quantifier-free bit-vector formulas in Bitwuzla is a CEGAR-style abstraction refinement procedure based on bit-blasting [46], combined with term rewriting and preprocessing techniques to simplify input constraints prior to the actual reduction step to SAT. This procedure introduces abstractions for arithmetic operations defined over large bit-widths that are expensive for the underlying SAT solver when translated to the bit-level.

The workflow of our interpolation procedure is given in Figure 2. The main components of the procedure are the *Solver*, which determines the satisfiability of the input formula, and the *Interpolator*, which extracts a bit-level interpolant from the SAT proof, and post-processes and lifts it back to the word-level. In the following, we discuss the relevant components of our workflow in more detail.

4.1 SMT-LIB and API Interface

The SMT-LIB 2.7 language [8] does not yet standardize interactions with the solver in case of interpolant generation. Previous extensions to support interpolation implemented by cvc5 [7], MathSAT [17], OpenSMT2 [32] and SMT-Interpol [15] only agree on enabling interpolant generation via (set-option :produce-interpolants true). We extended Bitwuzla's SMT-LIB interface in a similar way to SMTInterpol's extension by introducing a new command (get-interpolants $\langle terms \rangle^{+}$), with *terms* defined as a list of terms ($\langle term \rangle^{+}$) (corresponding to a conjunction of terms), and *term* defined as in SMT-LIB.

For an input formula $\varphi = A \wedge B$, we require that A and B are asserted, and that the T-unsatisfiability of φ has been determined via check-sat. Command get-interpolants must be issued after a check-sat command but prior to any subsequent pop commands. A *single* interpolant is queried with a single term list, which represents the A partition of the interpolation query. Assertions not in A make up partition B. An *interpolation sequence* is queried by specifying the list of A increments of the sequence. For example, (get-interpolants (a_1) (a_2) (a_3)) computes interpolants $\langle I_1, I_2, I_3 \rangle$ for A-partitions $\{a_1\}$, $\{a_1, a_2\}$ and $\{a_1, a_2, a_3\}$ such that $I_1 \wedge a_2 \Rightarrow I_2$ and $I_2 \wedge a_3 \Rightarrow I_3$. The resulting sequence of interpolants is returned as a term list. Figure 1 shows an example in SMT-LIB format, with the output of the query shown as comments below the corresponding command. We extended the API of Bitwuzla to support single and sequence interpolation queries in a similar way.

4.2 Bit-Vector Solving in Bitwuzla

Adding support for generating bit-vector interpolants in Bitwuzla requires the extension of its bit-blasting pipeline with capabilities to produce SAT proofs. The bit-vector solver and its extensions for interpolation are shown on the left in Figure 2. In this section, we briefly review the main workflow of its bit-vector solving procedure. We discuss its extension to produce SAT proofs in Section 4.3.

Given a bit-vector formula φ, as the first step, Bitwuzla applies various *preprocessing* techniques to simplify φ. These techniques can be divided into *local* and *global* simplifications. Local simplifications, e.g., term rewriting, are independent from the current set of assertions, while global simplifications are not.

```
(set-logic QF_BV)
(set-option :produce-interpolants true)
(declare-const x1 (_ BitVec 2))
(declare-const x2 (_ BitVec 2))
(declare-const x3 (_ BitVec 2))
(assert (! (bvslt (_ bv0 4) (bvsub (concat (_ bv0 2) x1) (_ bv1 4))) :named a1))
(assert (! (= x2 x1) :named a2))
(assert (! (= x3 ((_ extract 1 0) (bvneg (concat (_ bv0 2) x2)))) :named a3))
(assert (= x3 (_ bv0 2)))
(check-sat)
; unsat
(get-interpolants (a1 a2))
; (
; (not (= x2 #b00))
; )
(get-interpolants (a1) (a2) (a3))
; (
; (= #b0 ((_ extract 3 3) (bvadd (concat #b00 x1) #b1111)))
; (not (= x2 #b00))
; (not (= x3 #b00))
; )
```

Fig. 1: Interpolation example.

As a consequence, when applied *across* partitions, global simplifications may "pollute" the A-partition with B-local symbols and vice versa. Safely applying simplifications across partitions therefore requires tracking of such transformations during solving, and reconstructing the resulting SAT proof with respect to these simplifications when extracting the interpolant. Vizel et al. [52] address a similar problem in the context of interpolant generation for SAT-based bounded model checking. Limiting global simplifications to within a partition, on the other hand, requires that the partition is known at the time of preprocessing. Since the partitioning is defined by interpolation queries after the satisfiability check and queries for interpolation sequences require a dynamic AB-partitioning we cannot apply global preprocessing techniques within a partition. Thus, when interpolant generation is enabled, we currently only apply preprocessing passes that perform local simplifications. Extending our interpolation procedure to allow for application of global simplifications is non-trivial and left to future work.

As mentioned above, Bitwuzla implements a counterexample-guided abstraction refinement (CEGAR) [18] procedure for bit-vector arithmetic based on bit-blasting [46]. Thus, in the next step, the abstraction module replaces abstracted terms in the preprocessed formula φ' with fresh (uninterpreted) constants, yielding bit-vector formula φ'', which is an over-approximation of φ'. This over-approximation is iteratively refined with lemmas L until its reduction to SAT is *unsat*, or its satisfying assignment is consistent for all abstracted terms.

The bit-blasting pipeline of Bitwuzla consists of two stages. In the first stage, an And-Inverter Graph (AIG) representation of $\varphi'' \wedge L$ is constructed while applying AIG-level rewriting techniques [13]. In the second stage, this AIG circuit is converted to CNF via Tseitin transformation and sent to the SAT solver.

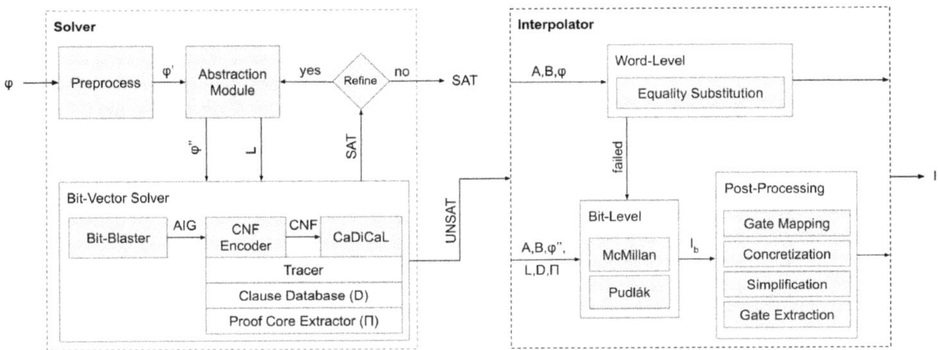

Fig. 2: The bit-vector interpolation workflow in Bitwuzla.

4.3   SAT Proofs via Tracer Interface of CaDiCaL

Bitwuzla supports multiple off-the-shelf SAT solvers as SAT back end and uses CaDiCaL [10] as its main SAT Solver. CaDiCaL provides an interface for *tracing* proof-related events such as clause addition and deletion via notifications and callbacks. This allows to define proof tracers for specific purposes and is utilized by CaDiCaL to provide user-facing printers and checkers for different proof formats, including the LRAT format [21]. For this format, CaDiCaL is required to provide justification derivation (resolution) chains for each derived clause, which was shown to only add a 5% overhead on average to solving time [48].

In its full expressive power, the LRAT format not only tracks resolution chains of clauses derived via reverse unit propagation (RUP) [25], but additional hints if the clause addition relied on the stronger resolution asymmetric tautology (RAT) property. CaDiCaL does not implement any reasoning techniques that require the latter, and thus effectively does not produce LRAT but *LRUP* proofs, i.e., RUP proofs augmented with clause ids and resolution chains [48].

As shown in Figure 2, we instrument the bit-blasting pipeline of Bitwuzla to facilitate recording proofs produced by CaDiCaL with three components: the proof tracer, the clause database, and the proof core extraction.

Tracer. The proof tracer is responsible for tracking and recording original and derived clauses and is implemented utilizing CaDiCaL's `Tracer` API. Each clause is assigned a unique identifier and stored in a clause database. Derived clauses are mapped to their antecedents, which are recorded in order of derivation. Additionally, each clause also maps to the AIG it corresponds to. Together with the bit-blaster's mapping from AIGs to T_{BV}-terms in $\varphi'' \wedge L$, this facilitates a dynamic back-mapping from clause to A/B-partition, which is required for generating sequence interpolants. We discuss partitioning of assertions and clauses, and labeling of symbols in more detail in Section 4.4.

Clause Database. Since the satisfiability query preceding an interpolation query may be non-trivial, for interpolation sequences it is desirable to not require indi-

ID	Label	Clause	Antecedents	ID	Label	Clause	Antecedents
3	A	{ 7, 2, 3 }		47	B	{ -27 }	
11	A	{ -7 }		49	B	{ -22 }	
18	A	{ 13, -2, 10 }		50		{ -21 }	{ 49, 45, 35 }
24	A	{ 16, -3, 11 }		51	B	{ -23 }	
26	A	{ -13 }		52		{ -11 }	{ 51, 47, 41 }
28	A	{ -16 }		53		{ -3 }	{ 52, 28, 24 }
31	B	{ 21, -10, 11 }		54		{ -10 }	{ 52, 50, 31 }
35	B	{ 24, -21, 22 }		55		{ 2 }	{ 53, 11, 3 }
41	B	{ 27, -11, 23 }		56		{ }	{ 55, 54, 26, 18 }
45	B	{ -24 }					

Fig. 3: Proof core of the first interpolation query in Figure 1.

vidual satisfiability queries for each interpolant. This, however, requires dynamic A/B-partitioning, decoupled from solving and proof generation. To achieve this, the bit-level interpolant is computed from the proof core, depending on the A/B-partitioning for each individual interpolation query. Since the proof core is extracted from the full proof, until CaDiCaL concludes *unsat*, we keep all recorded clauses in memory and ignore notifications about clause deletions.

Proof Core Extraction. The clause database represents the recorded proof as a DAG as in Definition 3, but with $n \geq 2$ instead of $n = 2$ antecedents for derived clauses. When CaDiCaL concludes unsat, a proof core is extracted by traversing the proof in reverse topological order, starting from the empty clause. The proof core of the first example interpolation query in Figure 1, augmented with the partition labeling for the given query, is given in Figure 3.

Discussion. The integration of CaDiCaL in Bitwuzla utilizes incremental SAT solving via solving under assumptions [23]. Recently, Khouri et al. [35] presented a CaDiCaL proof tracer implementation for producing interpolants from DRUP proofs that incorporates the proof core minimization technique presented in [29]. The authors argue that especially in the incremental case, this can lead to better interpolants for model checking applications. We leave the investigation of the impact of proof core minimization on our interpolation workflow to future work.

CaDiCaL provides a proof tracer implementation for extracting CNF interpolants [10], which supports both McMillan's and Pudlák's interpolation systems. This tracer, however, requires that the AB-partitioning is known at solve time, and is thus not suitable for our use case.

4.4 Interpolant Generation

After concluding that bit-vector formula φ is unsatisfiable and proof core Π is extracted, given a partitioning of φ into A and B, the Interpolator processes the proof core to compute interpolant I as shown in Figure 2 on the right. The Interpolator consists of three components: the *word-level* interpolator, the *bit-level* interpolator, and a *post-processor* for bit-level interpolants. Interpolant I is extracted either via word-level interpolation or our bit-level interpolation work-flow. Word-level interpolation is optional and implements a substitution-based technique that is not always applicable. If enabled and not applicable, we fall back to bit-level interpolation.

A/B-Partitioning. Word-level interpolation operates on the original input for-mula φ partitioned into A and B as given by the interpolation query and natively constructs a word-level interpolant. Bit-level interpolation, on the other hand, first computes a bit-level interpolant from the SAT proof core, which is then lifted to the word-level. That is, the recorded proof core is a proof for $\varphi'' \wedge L$. Thus, prior to computing the bit-level interpolant, the A/B-partitioning of φ must first be mapped to $\varphi'' \wedge L$ before mapping it to the bit-level.

Partitioning the set of clauses sent to the SAT solver into A and B partitions is straight forward: original assertions in φ are mapped to preprocessed assertions in φ'', which are then mapped to SAT clauses via the bit-blaster's mapping from T_{BV}-terms to AIGs and the clause database's mapping from AIGs to clauses.

Labeling SAT variables as A-local, B-local and global is more involved, as each stage of the bit-blasting pipeline introduces auxiliary constructs (AIGs when bit-blasting to AIG circuits, and Tseitin variables when translating these AIGs to CNF). We first partition $\mathcal{S}(\varphi)$ into $\mathcal{S}_A(\varphi)$, $\mathcal{S}_B(\varphi)$ and $\mathcal{S}_G(\varphi)$, and la-bel all terms in φ'' based on this partitioning as described in Section 3. Term abstractions, which are fresh uninterpreted bit-vector constants from the point of view of the bit-blaster, are labeled according to the label of the correspond-ing abstracted term. The labeling of uninterpreted constants is mapped to the bits of their AIG representation, and each AND-gate in these AIGs is labeled based on its inputs. The AIG-labeling is then mapped to the SAT variables of its corresponding CNF translation. Note that our labeling workflow ensures that auxiliary constructs are only labeled as global if they appear in both A and B.

As a final step, we assign each lemma to partition A or B, depending on the labeling of its symbols, and label their SAT variables as above. Note that in the context of our bit-vector solving procedure, lemmas always appear as either A-local, B-local, or global, and cannot be AB-mixed. This is due to the fact that we only introduce abstractions for arithmetic operations $x \diamond s$ with $\diamond \in \{\cdot, \div, \bmod\}$, while preserving the original label of the abstracted term for its abstraction t. Refinement lemmas for these abstractions are defined over only x, s, and t (for details, see [46]), and are therefore, by construction, never AB-mixed.

Word-Level Interpolation. Our bit-vector interpolation workflow optionally sup-ports a simple word-level interpolation technique, referred to as *equality substi-tution* in [28], which constructs a word-level interpolant via term substitution of local symbols. Given $A = \{a = t, A'\}$ with $a \in \mathcal{S}_A$, then $A'[a \mapsto t]$ is an interpolant for A and B if it does not contain any A-local symbols. Similarly, if $B = \{b = t, B'\}$ and $b \in \mathcal{S}_B$, then $\neg B'[b \mapsto t]$ is an interpolant for A and B if it does not contain any B-local symbols. This technique exploits a corner case of the more general fact that existential quantifier elimination of all A-local symbols in A (or all B-local symbols in $\neg B$) yields an interpolant. In Bitwuzla, equality substitution is implemented by utilizing its substitution preprocessing pass [44], which applies syntactic substitutions based on existing equalities and new equalities inferred based on a set of normalization techniques. In practice, we apply equality substitution to the A/B-partitions of φ' (rather than φ).

Bit-Level Interpolation. Given a SAT proof core Π and the A/B-partitioning of the set of clauses corresponding to formula φ as described above, our workflow extracts a bit-level interpolant I_b using either McMillan's (default) or Pudlák's interpolation algorithm as defined in Section 3.1. Recall that Π is represented as a DAG with $n \geq 2$ antecedents for derived clauses. These antecedents, recorded in the clause database in order of derivation, form a chain derivation [26]. Partial interpolant computation as defined in Section 3 is naturally lifted to such chains of length $n > 2$ without the need for fully expanding the recorded LRUP proof into a clausal resolution proof. Partial interpolants and the resulting bit-level interpolant I_b are constructed as AIGs. We utilize structural hashing when constructing AIGs, across the bit-blasted AIG representation of the bit-vector abstraction and the partial interpolants generated during interpolant extraction.

Post-Processing. Bit-level interpolant I_b is represented as an AIG, which must be lifted back to the word-level in the final stage of our interpolation workflow. Intuitively, the easiest way to lift back I_b is the naive approach where its AIG structure is reconstructed on the T_{BV}-level from the input bits, which correspond to bits of uninterpreted T_{BV}-constants. This would, however, result in a complete loss of word-level structure, which may not be desirable for techniques that exploit the structure of the interpolant. An example of such a technique is IC3+IA [16], which extracts and filters predicates from the interpolant to be used as an abstraction refinement. And even for techniques that use the interpolant as-is, subsequent reasoning in the back-end SMT solver may exploit structure.

In the post-processing stage of our workflow, we therefore do not naively lift I_b back to the word-level, but try to recover as much word-level structure as possible. We describe our post-processing pipeline in detail in Section 4.5.

4.5   From Bit-Level to Word-Level Interpolants

Given a bit-level interpolant I_b, in the post-processing stage of our interpolation workflow we lift I_b back to the word-level while recovering and simplifying word-level structure. Our post-processing pipeline consists of several stages, some optional, which are processed in order as follows.

Gate Mapping. In the first stage, we construct a T_{BV}-representation of I_b, starting from the input bits, while mapping AND-gates back to bits in corresponding T_{BV}-terms when possible. This back-mapping is the main difference to naively reconstructing the AIG structure on the node level by means of only Boolean conjunction and negation on top of the input bits, as outlined above.

Gate mapping already recovers some word-level structure, albeit potentially still sliced into individual bits. Note that mapping AND-gates back to terms is only possible for gates that represent "output" bits of the AIG circuit representation of a T_{BV}-term, with the additional constraint that the term only involves global symbols. AND-gates that map to bits of terms that involve local symbols may occur in I_b as a consequence of simplifications due to AIG-level rewriting when bit-blasting. Gates that cannot be mapped to bits of terms with only global symbols are reconstructed via Boolean conjunction and negation as expected.

As an example, consider bit-level interpolant I_b as given in Figure 4a. For this example, the original interpolation query is not relevant, it is only important to note that $\mathcal{S}(\varphi) = \{x, a, t\}$ with local symbol x (Boolean) and global bit-vector symbols $a_{[1]}$ and $t_{[2]}$. Interpolant I_b is an AIG with AND-gates $\{6, 7\}$ and constants $\{2, 4, 5\}$, labeled with the identifiers of the SAT variables in the CNF translation, which represent a, $t[1]$ and $t[0]$, respectively. Assume that AND-gate 6 maps to $t \approx 00$, and AND-gate 7 maps to the *msb* of term $ite(t \approx 00, ite(x, 00, 01), ite(a \approx 1, 10, 00))$. Figure 4b shows the word-level interpolant constructed from I_b via the naive construction, without gate mapping. When constructing the interpolant with gate mapping, gate 7 maps back to a term that involves local symbol x, thus we only map gate 6 to term $t \approx 00$. The resulting interpolant is given in Figure 4c.

Concretization. Recall that Bitwuzla's abstraction module may have replaced bit-vector arithmetic operations that occur in the original formula with fresh uninterpreted constants as abstractions. Each occurrence of such an abstraction in the interpolant must be concretized, i.e., replaced with the term it abstracts.

Simplification. In the simplification stage, we utilize Bitwuzla's preprocessor to simplify the concretized interpolant I_c. For this purpose, we create a fresh preprocessor instance and apply a pipeline of preprocessing passes to I_c in a predefined order until fixed-point. The passes configured in this pipeline are *term rewriting, and-flattening, term substitution, Boolean skeleton preprocessing, embedded constraints* and *arithmetic normalization* as described in [44]. The preprocessor may transform I_c into a set of simplified formulas $\{F_1, \ldots, F_n\}$,

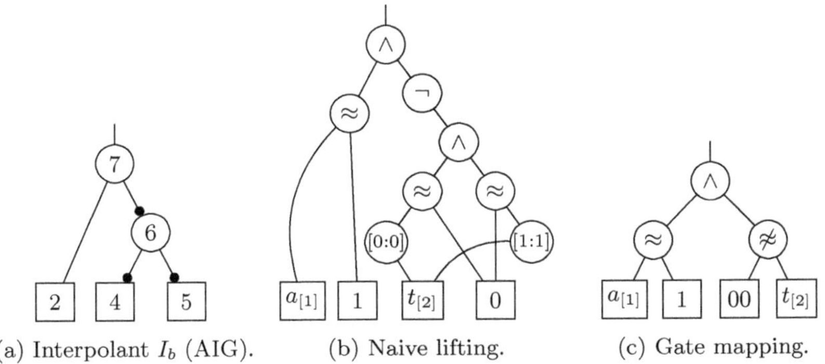

(a) Interpolant I_b (AIG).   (b) Naive lifting.   (c) Gate mapping.

Fig. 4: Gate mapping example.

	Condition	Extracted
(1)	$\sim(\sim x \,\&\, \sim y) \in \mathcal{C} \,\wedge\, \sim(x \,\&\, y) \in \mathcal{C}$	$x \oplus y$
(2)	$\sim(\sim x \,\&\, y) \in \mathcal{C} \,\wedge\, \sim(x \,\&\, \sim y) \in \mathcal{C}$	$\sim(x \oplus y)$
(3)	$\sim x \oplus y \in \mathcal{C}$	$\sim(x \oplus y)$
(4)	$x[i] \in \mathcal{C}$	$\mathtt{cmp}(x[i], 1)$
(5)	$\sim x[i] \in \mathcal{C}$	$\mathtt{cmp}(x[i], 0)$
(6)	$\sim(x[i] \oplus t) \in \mathcal{C}$	$\mathtt{cmp}(x[i], t)$
(7)	$\mathtt{cmp}(x[i\!:\!j], t_1) \in \mathcal{C} \,\wedge\, \mathtt{cmp}(x[k\!:\!l], t_2) \in \mathcal{C} \,\wedge\, j = k + 1$	$\mathtt{cmp}(x[i\!:\!l], t_1 \circ t_2)$

Table 1: Gate extraction rewrite rules applied on n-ary AND-gate with conjuncts $\mathcal{C}$. A rewrite rule applies if the conjuncts given in column Condition appear in $\mathcal{C}$. When applied, these conjuncts are replaced with the extracted expression.

which yields the resulting simplified interpolant $\bigwedge_1^n F_i$. If I_c is of the form $\neg F$, we first preprocess F, and construct $\neg(\bigwedge_1^n F_i)$ as the simplified interpolant.

Gate Extraction. Bit-level interpolants extracted from the SAT proof as described above usually contain multiple bit-level equalities over consecutive bits of a bit-vector term. If such equalities occur within an n-ary AND-gate, they can be lifted to word-level equalities over bit ranges. The goal of the gate extraction stage is to recover as many word-level equalities over bit ranges as possible.

In a first step, we flatten binary AND-gates to n-ary AND-gates if flattening does not destroy sharing of common subexpressions. For example, $(x \,\&\, (y \,\&\, z))$ is flattened to $(x \,\&\, y \,\&\, z)$ only if $(y \,\&\, z)$ does not occur in other subexpressions of the interpolant. Next, since XNOR-gates correspond to bit-level equalities, for every n-ary AND-gate G in the interpolant I, we extract XOR-gates and XNOR-gates from the bit-level structure. Note that when we reach this stage, the AIG representation of the bit-level interpolant has already been lifted to the T_{BV}-level and simplified. Thus, to allow for a uniform gate extraction process, in this stage, we treat Booleans as bit-vector of size 1.

As an example, consider $(\sim(x[0] \oplus y[0]) \,\&\, \sim(x[1] \oplus y[1]) \,\&\, \sim(x[2] \oplus y[2]))$ over single bits of bit-vector constants x and y. This can be lifted to the bitwise comparison $\mathtt{cmp}(x[2\!:\!0], y[2\!:\!0])$. Similarly, $(\sim x[0] \,\&\, \sim x[1] \,\&\, x[2] \,\&\, x[3])$ is lifted to $\mathtt{cmp}(x[3\!:\!0], 1100)$. Note that bitwise comparison (as defined in SMT-LIB) is similar to bitwise equality, but defined over bit-vector sorts $\sigma_{[w]} \times \sigma_{[w]} \to \sigma_{[1]}$.

We extract bitwise comparison operations by applying the rewrite rules shown in Table 1 until fixed point. Rules (1)-(3) are the main rules for extracting XOR and XNOR gates, while rules (4-6) are responsible for extracting bit-level comparisons. Rule (7) combines bit-level comparisons to comparisons over ranges of consecutive bits via the concatenation operator $\circ$, and is only applied if it preserves sharing of common subexpressions. When no more rules can be applied, we create a new n-ary AND-gate G' from the (sorted) rewritten conjuncts $\mathcal{C}'$ and substitute G with G' in I. Note that Table 1 omits symmetric rewrite rules.

As a last step, we lift operations over bit-vectors of size 1 back to Boolean and translate bitwise comparison operations to word-level equalities, if applicable.

5   Evaluation

We evaluate our bit-vector interpolator as implemented in Bitwuzla in the context of the interpolation-based engines implemented in the SMT-based model checkers Pono [40] and Kind2 [14, 39]. Pono primarily targets hardware verification problems and implements four interpolation-based algorithms as engines *interp* [42], *ismc* [50], *ic3ia* [16], and *dar* [51]. We evaluate these engines on the benchmarks used in the bit-vector track of the hardware model checking competitions 2019 [1], 2020 [2], and 2024 [11]. After removing duplicates, this combined set contains 839 benchmarks in BTOR2 [45] format. Kind2 is a model checker for finite-state and infinite-state synchronous reactive systems, which also features an *ic3ia* engine. We evaluate Kind2 on a set of 786 Lustre models [30] for verifying integer arithmetic properties represented as bit-vectors of size 32.

We ran our experiments on a cluster of 48 compute nodes with AMD Ryzen 9 7950X CPUs and 128GB of RAM. For each model checker and benchmark pair, we allocated one CPU core and 16GB of memory with a time limit of 600 seconds. We implemented our approach on top of Bitwuzla commit 28c4d80 [3], as integrated in Pono on top of version v2.0.0-beta.1 [5] and in Kind2 on top of commit cce530b [4]. We compare our interpolation engine against MathSAT [17] version 5.6.12, which is the default interpolation engine for both tools.

We use a combination of three options to configure our interpolation engine and use + and − to indicate that an option is enabled and disabled, respectively. Option *map* configures the gate mapping stage of our bit-level interpolation pipeline, option *post* the simplification and gate extraction stage, and option *subst* the word-level equality substitution interpolation.

Preliminary experiments have shown that gate mapping has in general a positive impact on the evaluated interpolation-based algorithms. We thus only disable gate mapping for configuration *-map-post-subst*, which corresponds to producing *purely bit-level* interpolants. Additional experiments with Pono across all four interpolation engines also showed that on average, the size of interpolants produced by Pudlák's interpolation system is 2.9x on the bit-level and 3.7x after post-processing over using McMillan's system. In general, configurations using McMillan's system significantly outperform configurations using Pudlak's system. We thus use McMillan's system in the following and by default.

In our first experiment, we evaluate the performance of our interpolation engine against MathSAT in the context of Pono as shown in Figure 5. Overall, Pono with Bitwuzla as the interpolator significantly outperforms Pono with MathSAT as the interpolator in all configurations for all engines except the *ic3ia* engine. For the *ic3ia* engine, *Bzla:Bzla+post+subst* outperforms *Bzla:MSat*, but *MSat:MSat* performs best and better than any other *ic3ia* configuration. This could be due to Pono using a custom configuration of MathSAT as the solver specifically for *ic3ia* which was tuned for combination with MathSAT as the interpolator, whereas Bitwuzla is used in default configuration.

In the context of Kind2's *ic3ia* engine, using MathSAT as the interpolator clearly outperforms Bitwuzla as the interpolation engine, as shown in Figure 6. The *ic3ia* algorithm heavily relies on extracting predicates from interpolants and

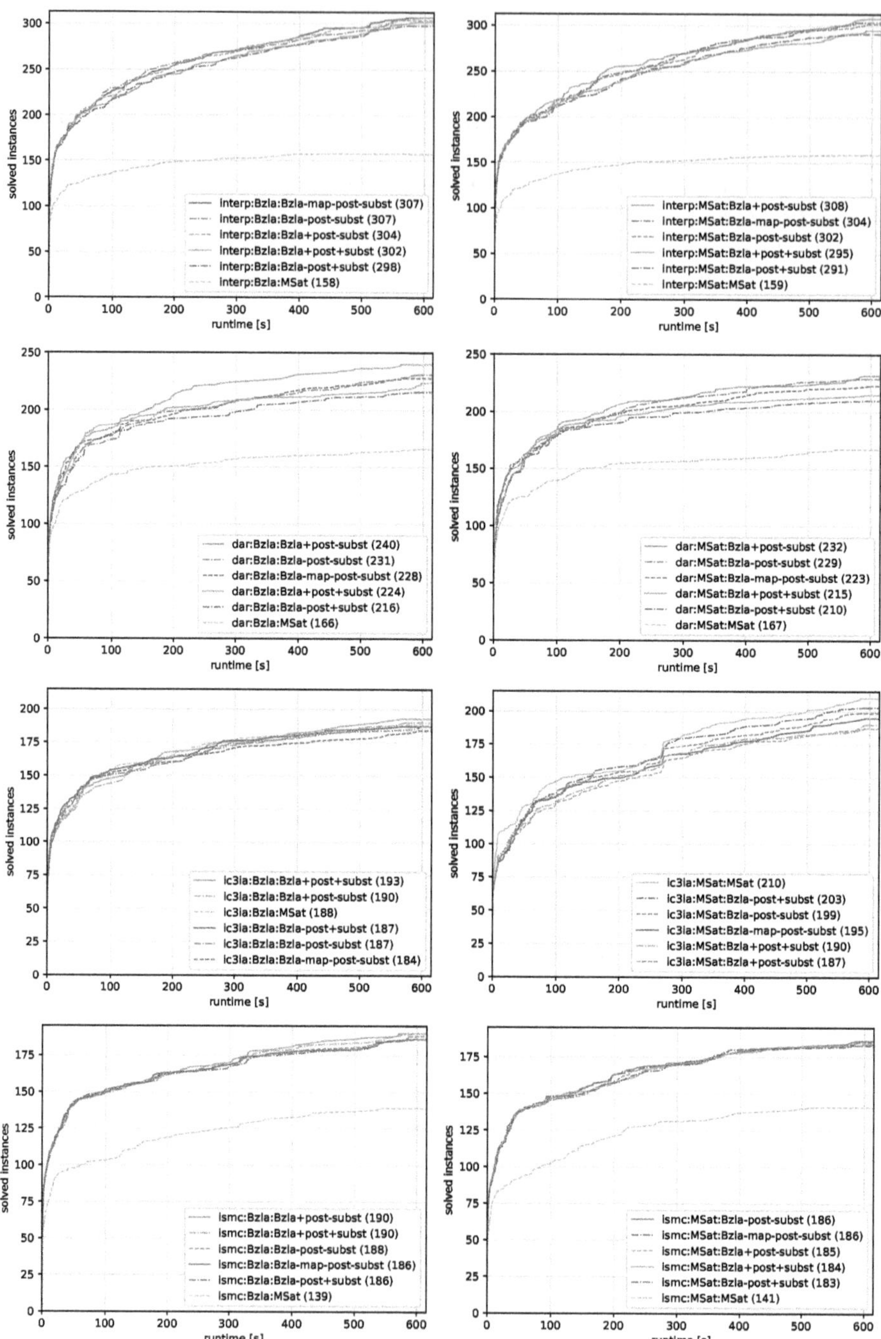

Fig. 5: Pono engines (E) with Bitwuzla (Bzla) and MathSAT (MSat) as solver (S) and interpolator (I) back ends. Configurations are given as E:S:I with Bitwuzla interpolator options gate mapping (map), post-processing (post), word-level substitution (subst) enabled (+) or disabled (-). Number of solved instances given in parentheses.

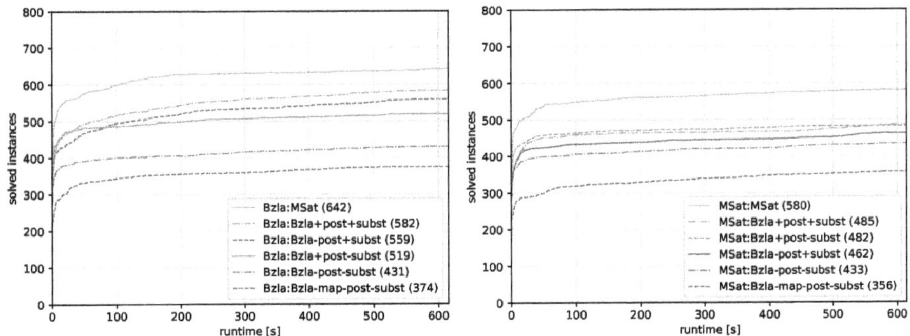

Fig. 6: Kind2 IC3IA engine with Bitwuzla (Bzla) and MathSAT (MSat) as solver (S) and interpolator (I) backends. Configurations given as S:I, with Bitwuzla interpolator options as in Figure 5. Number of solved instances given in parentheses.

can get overwhelmed if too many bit-level predicates are present. The Lustre benchmarks are bit-vector encodings of problems that were originally encoded in integer arithmetic and are thus arithmetic-heavy, with little bitwise reasoning. Hence, it is not too surprising that for *ic3ia*, the structure of these benchmarks seems to favor the arithmetic-based interpolation technique of MathSAT's layered interpolation approach, which produces predicates with potentially more word-level structure, especially in terms of bit-vector arithmetic. Further, Math-SAT's technique also constructs bit-vector inequalities, which our approach does not recover if they cannot be mapped back in the gate mapping stage.

In general, we observe that different configurations of our interpolator, corresponding to varying degrees of how much word-level structure is reconstructed, perform best across different interpolation-based word-level model checking techniques. Term substitution-based interpolation, if successful, preserves the word-level structure of the original problem and is especially beneficial for the *ic3ia* engines. Interpolator configurations that extract more word-level structure generally perform better for *ic3ia* engines than configurations that produce interpolants with less structure, while bit-level interpolant configurations perform worse. Our post-processing pipeline is especially beneficial for engine *dar*, while for engine *interp*, less word-level structure seems to lead to better performance.

In our second experiment, we measure the impact of our simplification and gate extraction stages in our post-processing pipeline on the size of the produced interpolants. We measure the size of an interpolant in terms of the number of AND-gates. For this purpose, we analyzed the 371,592 interpolation queries issued by the interpolation engines of Pono in configuration *Bzla:Bzla+post-subst* on all 839 HWMCC benchmarks within the given time and memory limits. For each interpolation query, we computed the size of the initial bit-level interpolant, the size after the simplification stage, and the size after the gate extraction stage. After each stage, we compute the number of AND-gates in the bit-blasted AIG representation of the interpolant. Figure 7 (left) compares the interpolant size of the initial interpolant with the size of the interpolant after the simplifica-

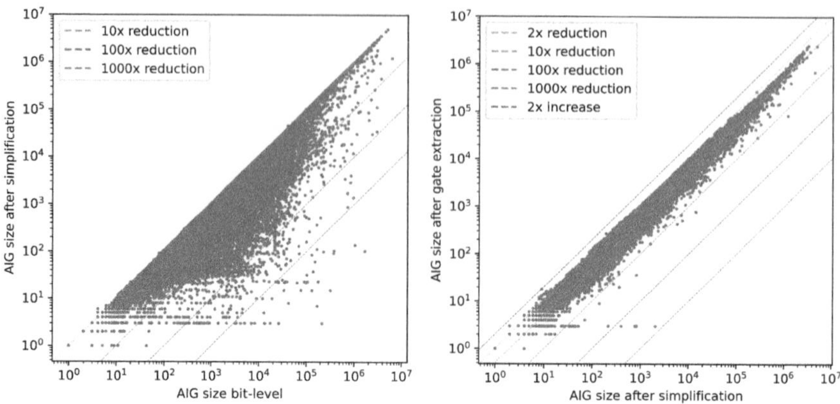

Fig. 7: Interpolant size comparison for our post-processing pipeline.

tion stage, and Figure 7 (right) compares the size of the interpolants after the simplification stage and after the gate extraction stage.

In the simplification stage, the preprocessor of Bitwuzla is able to consistently reduce the size of the interpolant, sometimes more than three orders of magnitude. The gate extraction stage further reduces the size of the simplified interpolant for 59.8% of the queries, up to two orders of magnitude.

We also measured the time spent in interpolant generation, not including the time for the satisfiability check that must precede the interpolation query. On average, 7.4% (6.3% total) of the total runtime of Pono is attributed to interpolant generation, including 2.0% (2.3% total) spent in our post-processing pipeline. For the 44,100 (out of 371,592) queries that were generated for solved benchmarks, interpolant generation is on average 7.8% (4.4% total), and our post-processing 0.9% (0.6% total) of the total runtime.

6   Conclusion

We have presented an extension of Bitwuzla with a new bit-vector interpolation engine, based on extracting interpolants from proofs produced by CaDiCaL as the back-end SAT engine of the bit-blasting bit-vector solver. Our interpolation engine supports the quantifier-free fragment of the theory of fixed-size bit-vectors. Interpolation for other theories supported by Bitwuzla, including arrays and uninterpreted functions, is currently limited to queries without occurrences of AB-mixed lemmas in the proof core. We leave extending our procedure to lift this limitation as future work.

Acknowledgement. We thank Po-Chun Chien and Áron Ricardo Perez-Lopez for their work on integrating Bitwuzla as an interpolator in Pono. We also thank Daniel Larraz for integrating Bitwuzla as interpolator in Kind2.

Data Availability Statement. The artifact accompanying this paper is archived and available in the Zenodo repository at https://zenodo.org/record/17427360.

References

1. Hardware Model Checking Competition 2019. https://fmv.jku.at/hwmcc19/ (2019)
2. Hardware Model Checking Competition 2020. https://hwmcc.github.io/2020/ (2020)
3. Bitwuzla on GitHub. https://github.com/bitwuzla/bitwuzla/ (2026)
4. Kind2 on GitHub. https://github.com/kind2-mc/kind2/ (2026)
5. Pono on GitHub. https://github.com/stanford-centaur/pono/ (2026)
6. Backeman, P., Rümmer, P., Zeljic, A.: Interpolating bit-vector formulas using uninterpreted predicates and presburger arithmetic. Formal Methods Syst. Des. **57**(2), 121–156 (2021). https://doi.org/10.1007/S10703-021-00372-6
7. Barbosa, H., Barrett, C.W., Brain, M., Kremer, G., Lachnitt, H., Mann, M., Mohamed, A., Mohamed, M., Niemetz, A., Nötzli, A., Ozdemir, A., Preiner, M., Reynolds, A., Sheng, Y., Tinelli, C., Zohar, Y.: cvc5: A versatile and industrial-strength SMT solver. In: Fisman, D., Rosu, G. (eds.) Tools and Algorithms for the Construction and Analysis of Systems - 28th International Conference, TACAS 2022, Held as Part of the European Joint Conferences on Theory and Practice of Software, ETAPS 2022, Munich, Germany, April 2-7, 2022, Proceedings, Part I. Lecture Notes in Computer Science, vol. 13243, pp. 415–442. Springer (2022). https://doi.org/10.1007/978-3-030-99524-9_24
8. Barrett, C., Fontaine, P., Tinelli, C.: The SMT-LIB Standard: Version 2.7. Tech. rep., Department of Computer Science, The University of Iowa (2025), available at http://smt-lib.org
9. Barrett, C.W., Tinelli, C.: Satisfiability modulo theories. In: Clarke, E.M., Henzinger, T.A., Veith, H., Bloem, R. (eds.) Handbook of Model Checking, pp. 305–343. Springer (2018). https://doi.org/10.1007/978-3-319-10575-8_11
10. Biere, A., Faller, T., Fazekas, K., Fleury, M., Froleyks, N., Pollitt, F.: Cadical 2.0. In: Gurfinkel, A., Ganesh, V. (eds.) Computer Aided Verification - 36th International Conference, CAV 2024, Montreal, QC, Canada, July 24-27, 2024, Proceedings, Part I. Lecture Notes in Computer Science, vol. 14681, pp. 133–152. Springer (2024). https://doi.org/10.1007/978-3-031-65627-9_7
11. Biere, A., Froleyks, N., Preiner, M.: Hardware model checking competition 2024. In: Narodytska, N., Rümmer, P. (eds.) Formal Methods in Computer-Aided Design, FMCAD 2024, Prague, Czech Republic, October 15-18, 2024. p. 1. IEEE (2024). https://doi.org/10.34727/2024/ISBN.978-3-85448-065-5_6
12. Bonacina, M.P., Johansson, M.: Interpolation systems for ground proofs in automated deduction: a survey. J. Autom. Reason. **54**(4), 353–390 (2015). https://doi.org/10.1007/S10817-015-9325-5
13. Brummayer, R., Biere, A.: Local Two-Level And-Inverter Graph Minimization without Blowup. In: 2nd Doctoral Workshop on Mathematical and Engineering Methods in Computer Science (MEMICS'06), Mikulov, Czechia, October 2006, Proceedings (2006)
14. Champion, A., Mebsout, A., Sticksel, C., Tinelli, C.: The Kind 2 model checker. In: Chaudhuri, S., Farzan, A. (eds.) Computer Aided Verification - 28th International Conference, CAV 2016, Toronto, ON, Canada, July 17-23, 2016, Proceedings, Part

II. Lecture Notes in Computer Science, vol. 9780, pp. 510–517. Springer (2016). https://doi.org/10.1007/978-3-319-41540-6_29

15. Christ, J., Hoenicke, J., Nutz, A.: SMTInterpol: An interpolating SMT solver. In: Donaldson, A.F., Parker, D. (eds.) Model Checking Software - 19th International Workshop, SPIN 2012, Oxford, UK, July 23-24, 2012. Proceedings. Lecture Notes in Computer Science, vol. 7385, pp. 248–254. Springer (2012). https://doi.org/10.1007/978-3-642-31759-0_19

16. Cimatti, A., Griggio, A., Mover, S., Tonetta, S.: IC3 modulo theories via implicit predicate abstraction. In: Ábrahám, E., Havelund, K. (eds.) Tools and Algorithms for the Construction and Analysis of Systems - 20th International Conference, TACAS 2014, Held as Part of the European Joint Conferences on Theory and Practice of Software, ETAPS 2014, Grenoble, France, April 5-13, 2014. Proceedings. Lecture Notes in Computer Science, vol. 8413, pp. 46–61. Springer (2014). https://doi.org/10.1007/978-3-642-54862-8_4

17. Cimatti, A., Griggio, A., Schaafsma, B.J., Sebastiani, R.: The mathsat5 SMT solver. In: Piterman, N., Smolka, S.A. (eds.) Tools and Algorithms for the Construction and Analysis of Systems - 19th International Conference, TACAS 2013, Held as Part of the European Joint Conferences on Theory and Practice of Software, ETAPS 2013, Rome, Italy, March 16-24, 2013. Proceedings. Lecture Notes in Computer Science, vol. 7795, pp. 93–107. Springer (2013). https://doi.org/10.1007/978-3-642-36742-7_7

18. Clarke, E.M., Grumberg, O., Jha, S., Lu, Y., Veith, H.: Counterexample-guided abstraction refinement. In: Emerson, E.A., Sistla, A.P. (eds.) Computer Aided Verification, 12th International Conference, CAV 2000, Chicago, IL, USA, July 15-19, 2000, Proceedings. Lecture Notes in Computer Science, vol. 1855, pp. 154–169. Springer (2000). https://doi.org/10.1007/10722167_15

19. Clarke, E.M., Henzinger, T.A., Veith, H., Bloem, R. (eds.): Handbook of Model Checking. Springer (2018). https://doi.org/10.1007/978-3-319-10575-8

20. Craig, W.: Three uses of the herbrand-gentzen theorem in relating model theory and proof theory. J. Symb. Log. **22**(3), 269–285 (1957). https://doi.org/10.2307/2963594

21. Cruz-Filipe, L., Heule, M.J.H., Jr., W.A.H., Kaufmann, M., Schneider-Kamp, P.: Efficient certified RAT verification. In: de Moura, L. (ed.) Automated Deduction - CADE 26 - 26th International Conference on Automated Deduction, Gothenburg, Sweden, August 6-11, 2017, Proceedings. Lecture Notes in Computer Science, vol. 10395, pp. 220–236. Springer (2017). https://doi.org/10.1007/978-3-319-63046-5_14

22. Dutertre, B.: Yices 2.2. In: Biere, A., Bloem, R. (eds.) Computer Aided Verification - 26th International Conference, CAV 2014, Held as Part of the Vienna Summer of Logic, VSL 2014, Vienna, Austria, July 18-22, 2014. Proceedings. Lecture Notes in Computer Science, vol. 8559, pp. 737–744. Springer (2014). https://doi.org/10.1007/978-3-319-08867-9_49

23. Eén, N., Sörensson, N.: An extensible sat-solver. In: Giunchiglia, E., Tacchella, A. (eds.) Theory and Applications of Satisfiability Testing, 6th International Conference, SAT 2003. Santa Margherita Ligure, Italy, May 5-8, 2003 Selected Revised Papers. Lecture Notes in Computer Science, vol. 2919, pp. 502–518. Springer (2003). https://doi.org/10.1007/978-3-540-24605-3_37

24. Enderton, H.B.: A mathematical introduction to logic. Academic Press (1972)

25. Gelder, A.V.: Verifying RUP proofs of propositional unsatisfiability. In: International Symposium on Artificial Intelligence and Math-

ematics, ISAIM 2008, Fort Lauderdale, Florida, USA, January 2-4, 2008 (2008), http://isaim2008.unl.edu/PAPERS/TechnicalProgram/ISAIM2008_0008_60a1f9b2fd607a61ec9e0feac3f438f8.pdf

26. Goldberg, E.I., Novikov, Y.: Verification of proofs of unsatisfiability for CNF formulas. In: 2003 Design, Automation and Test in Europe Conference and Exposition (DATE 2003), 3-7 March 2003, Munich, Germany. pp. 10886–10891. IEEE Computer Society (2003). https://doi.org/10.1109/DATE.2003.10008

27. Graham-Lengrand, S., Jovanovic, D., Dutertre, B.: Solving bitvectors with MC-SAT: explanations from bits and pieces. In: Peltier, N., Sofronie-Stokkermans, V. (eds.) Automated Reasoning - 10th International Joint Conference, IJCAR 2020, Paris, France, July 1-4, 2020, Proceedings, Part I. Lecture Notes in Computer Science, vol. 12166, pp. 103–121. Springer (2020). https://doi.org/10.1007/978-3-030-51074-9_7

28. Griggio, A.: Effective word-level interpolation for software verification. In: Bjesse, P., Slobodová, A. (eds.) International Conference on Formal Methods in Computer-Aided Design, FMCAD '11, Austin, TX, USA, October 30 - November 02, 2011. pp. 28–36. FMCAD Inc. (2011), http://dl.acm.org/citation.cfm?id=2157662

29. Gurfinkel, A., Vizel, Y.: Druping for interpolates. In: Formal Methods in Computer-Aided Design, FMCAD 2014, Lausanne, Switzerland, October 21-24, 2014. pp. 99–106. IEEE (2014). https://doi.org/10.1109/FMCAD.2014.6987601

30. Hagen, G., Tinelli, C.: Scaling up the formal verification of lustre programs with smt-based techniques. In: Cimatti, A., Jones, R.B. (eds.) Formal Methods in Computer-Aided Design, FMCAD 2008, Portland, Oregon, USA, 17-20 November 2008. pp. 1–9. IEEE (2008). https://doi.org/10.1109/FMCAD.2008.ECP.19

31. Henzinger, T.A., Jhala, R., Majumdar, R., McMillan, K.L.: Abstractions from proofs. In: Jones, N.D., Leroy, X. (eds.) Proceedings of the 31st ACM SIGPLAN-SIGACT Symposium on Principles of Programming Languages, POPL 2004, Venice, Italy, January 14-16, 2004. pp. 232–244. ACM (2004). https://doi.org/10.1145/964001.964021

32. Hyvärinen, A.E.J., Marescotti, M., Alt, L., Sharygina, N.: Opensmt2: An SMT solver for multi-core and cloud computing. In: Creignou, N., Berre, D.L. (eds.) Theory and Applications of Satisfiability Testing - SAT 2016 - 19th International Conference, Bordeaux, France, July 5-8, 2016, Proceedings. Lecture Notes in Computer Science, vol. 9710, pp. 547–553. Springer (2016). https://doi.org/10.1007/978-3-319-40970-2_35

33. John, A.K., Chakraborty, S.: A layered algorithm for quantifier elimination from linear modular constraints. Formal Methods Syst. Des. **49**(3), 272–323 (2016). https://doi.org/10.1007/S10703-016-0260-9

34. K., H.G.V., Fedyukovich, G., Gurfinkel, A.: Word level property directed reachability. In: IEEE/ACM International Conference On Computer Aided Design, ICCAD 2020, San Diego, CA, USA, November 2-5, 2020. pp. 107:1–107:9. IEEE (2020). https://doi.org/10.1145/3400302.3415708

35. Khouri, B., Vizel, Y.: Revisiting drup-based interpolants with cadical 2.0. In: Gurfinkel, A., Heule, M. (eds.) Tools and Algorithms for the Construction and Analysis of Systems - 31st International Conference, TACAS 2025, Held as Part of the International Joint Conferences on Theory and Practice of Software, ETAPS 2025, Hamilton, ON, Canada, May 3-8, 2025, Proceedings, Part II. Lecture Notes in Computer Science, vol. 15697, pp. 88–107. Springer (2025). https://doi.org/10.1007/978-3-031-90653-4_5

36. Komuravelli, A., Gurfinkel, A., Chaki, S.: Smt-based model checking for recursive programs. In: Biere, A., Bloem, R. (eds.) Computer Aided Verification - 26th International Conference, CAV 2014, Held as Part of the Vienna Summer of Logic, VSL 2014, Vienna, Austria, July 18-22, 2014. Proceedings. Lecture Notes in Computer Science, vol. 8559, pp. 17–34. Springer (2014). https://doi.org/10.1007/978-3-319-08867-9_2

37. Kroening, D., Weissenbacher, G.: Lifting propositional interpolants to the word-level. In: Formal Methods in Computer-Aided Design, 7th International Conference, FMCAD 2007, Austin, Texas, USA, November 11-14, 2007, Proceedings. pp. 85–89. IEEE Computer Society (2007). https://doi.org/10.1109/FAMCAD.2007.13

38. Kroening, D., Weissenbacher, G.: An interpolating decision procedure for transitive relations with uninterpreted functions. In: Namjoshi, K.S., Zeller, A., Ziv, A. (eds.) Hardware and Software: Verification and Testing - 5th International Haifa Verification Conference, HVC 2009, Haifa, Israel, October 19-22, 2009, Revised Selected Papers. Lecture Notes in Computer Science, vol. 6405, pp. 150–168. Springer (2009). https://doi.org/10.1007/978-3-642-19237-1_15

39. Larraz, D., Viswanathan, A., Tinelli, C., Laurent, M.: Beyond model checking of idealized lustre in Kind 2. Ada Lett. **42**(2), 40–44 (Apr 2023). https://doi.org/10.1145/3591335.3591338

40. Mann, M., Irfan, A., Lonsing, F., Yang, Y., Zhang, H., Brown, K., Gupta, A., Barrett, C.W.: Pono: A flexible and extensible smt-based model checker. In: Silva, A., Leino, K.R.M. (eds.) Computer Aided Verification - 33rd International Conference, CAV 2021, Virtual Event, July 20-23, 2021, Proceedings, Part II. Lecture Notes in Computer Science, vol. 12760, pp. 461–474. Springer (2021). https://doi.org/10.1007/978-3-030-81688-9_22

41. Manzano, M.: Introduction to many-sorted logic. In: Many-sorted logic and its applications, pp. 3–86. John Wiley & Sons, Inc., New York, NY, USA (1993)

42. McMillan, K.L.: Interpolation and sat-based model checking. In: Jr., W.A.H., Somenzi, F. (eds.) Computer Aided Verification, 15th International Conference, CAV 2003, Boulder, CO, USA, July 8-12, 2003, Proceedings. Lecture Notes in Computer Science, vol. 2725, pp. 1–13. Springer (2003). https://doi.org/10.1007/978-3-540-45069-6_1

43. de Moura, L.M., Bjørner, N.S.: Z3: an efficient SMT solver. In: Ramakrishnan, C.R., Rehof, J. (eds.) Tools and Algorithms for the Construction and Analysis of Systems, 14th International Conference, TACAS 2008, Held as Part of the Joint European Conferences on Theory and Practice of Software, ETAPS 2008, Budapest, Hungary, March 29-April 6, 2008. Proceedings. Lecture Notes in Computer Science, vol. 4963, pp. 337–340. Springer (2008). https://doi.org/10.1007/978-3-540-78800-3_24

44. Niemetz, A., Preiner, M.: Bitwuzla. In: Enea, C., Lal, A. (eds.) Computer Aided Verification - 35th International Conference, CAV 2023, Paris, France, July 17-22, 2023, Proceedings, Part II. Lecture Notes in Computer Science, vol. 13965, pp. 3–17. Springer (2023). https://doi.org/10.1007/978-3-031-37703-7_1

45. Niemetz, A., Preiner, M., Wolf, C., Biere, A.: Btor2 , BtorMC and Boolector 3.0. In: Chockler, H., Weissenbacher, G. (eds.) Computer Aided Verification - 30th International Conference, CAV 2018, Held as Part of the Federated Logic Conference, FloC 2018, Oxford, UK, July 14-17, 2018, Proceedings, Part I. Lecture Notes in Computer Science, vol. 10981, pp. 587–595. Springer (2018). https://doi.org/10.1007/978-3-319-96145-3_32

46. Niemetz, A., Preiner, M., Zohar, Y.: Scalable bit-blasting with abstractions. In: Gurfinkel, A., Ganesh, V. (eds.) Computer Aided Verification - 36th International Conference, CAV 2024, Montreal, QC, Canada, July 24-27, 2024, Proceedings, Part I. Lecture Notes in Computer Science, vol. 14681, pp. 178–200. Springer (2024). https://doi.org/10.1007/978-3-031-65627-9_9

47. Okudono, T., King, A.: Mind the gap: Bit-vector interpolation recast over linear integer arithmetic. In: Biere, A., Parker, D. (eds.) Tools and Algorithms for the Construction and Analysis of Systems - 26th International Conference, TACAS 2020, Held as Part of the European Joint Conferences on Theory and Practice of Software, ETAPS 2020, Dublin, Ireland, April 25-30, 2020, Proceedings, Part I. Lecture Notes in Computer Science, vol. 12078, pp. 79–96. Springer (2020). https://doi.org/10.1007/978-3-030-45190-5_5

48. Pollitt, F., Fleury, M., Biere, A.: Faster LRAT checking than solving with cadical. In: Mahajan, M., Slivovsky, F. (eds.) 26th International Conference on Theory and Applications of Satisfiability Testing, SAT 2023, July 4-8, 2023, Alghero, Italy. LIPIcs, vol. 271, pp. 21:1–21:12. Schloss Dagstuhl - Leibniz-Zentrum für Informatik (2023). https://doi.org/10.4230/LIPICS.SAT.2023.21

49. Pudlák, P.: Lower bounds for resolution and cutting plane proofs and monotone computations. J. Symb. Log. **62**(3), 981–998 (1997). https://doi.org/10.2307/2275583

50. Vizel, Y., Grumberg, O.: Interpolation-sequence based model checking. In: Proceedings of 9th International Conference on Formal Methods in Computer-Aided Design, FMCAD 2009, 15-18 November 2009, Austin, Texas, USA. pp. 1–8. IEEE (2009). https://doi.org/10.1109/FMCAD.2009.5351148

51. Vizel, Y., Grumberg, O., Shoham, S.: Intertwined forward-backward reachability analysis using interpolants. In: Piterman, N., Smolka, S.A. (eds.) Tools and Algorithms for the Construction and Analysis of Systems - 19th International Conference, TACAS 2013, Held as Part of the European Joint Conferences on Theory and Practice of Software, ETAPS 2013, Rome, Italy, March 16-24, 2013. Proceedings. Lecture Notes in Computer Science, vol. 7795, pp. 308–323. Springer (2013). https://doi.org/10.1007/978-3-642-36742-7_22

52. Vizel, Y., Gurfinkel, A., Malik, S.: Fast interpolating BMC. In: Kroening, D., Pasareanu, C.S. (eds.) Computer Aided Verification - 27th International Conference, CAV 2015, San Francisco, CA, USA, July 18-24, 2015, Proceedings, Part I. Lecture Notes in Computer Science, vol. 9206, pp. 641–657. Springer (2015). https://doi.org/10.1007/978-3-319-21690-4_43

Orbitopal Fixing in SAT

Markus Anders[1], Cayden Codel[2], and Marijn J. H. Heule[2]

[1] RPTU Kaiserslautern-Landau, Kaiserslautern, Germany
anders@cs.uni-kl.de
[2] Carnegie Mellon University, Pittsburgh, PA, United States
{ccodel,mheule}@cs.cmu.edu

Abstract. Despite their sophisticated heuristics, boolean satisfiability (SAT) solvers are still vulnerable to symmetry, causing them to visit search regions that are symmetric to ones already explored. While symmetry handling is routine in other solving paradigms, integrating it into state-of-the-art proof-producing SAT solvers is difficult: added reasoning must be fast, non-interfering with solver heuristics, and compatible with formal proof logging. To address these issues, we present a practical static symmetry breaking approach based on *orbitopal fixing*, a technique adapted from mixed-integer programming. Our approach adds only *unit clauses*, which minimizes downstream slowdowns, and it emits succinct proof certificates in the substitution redundancy proof system. Implemented in the SATSUMA tool, our methods deliver consistent speedups on symmetry-rich benchmarks with negligible regressions elsewhere.

1   Introduction

Boolean satisfiability (SAT) solvers power a wide range of industrial and academic applications [9]. Yet despite decades of innovation, state-of-the-art SAT solvers still lack robust, broadly deployed mechanisms for symmetry reasoning, even though such mechanisms are commonplace in other paradigms [19, 33]. Without explicit symmetry reasoning, solvers can waste significant amounts of time exploring search regions that are isomorphic to ones already ruled out, leading to substantial slowdowns on highly symmetric instances.

To address this problem, prior work in SAT has explored both preprocessing (static) and on-the-fly (dynamic) symmetry-breaking techniques [1, 3, 14–17, 24, 36]. The most used approach in SAT is *static symmetry breaking*, which adds constraints to the formula before solving to avoid isomorphic solutions. For example, in graph coloring, one can fix the color of a designated vertex, since any valid coloring can be permuted accordingly. Static methods are attractive in practice because their overhead is often modest [3].

Although these techniques can yield substantial speedups on highly symmetric formulas, they can also incur severe regressions elsewhere. A key culprit of this slowdown is overly aggressive symmetry breaking: Adding too many clauses to the formula often causes the solver's performance to degrade, especially when the formula is *satisfiable*. (For instance, see work by Aloul et al. [1].) Overall,

S. Junges and G. Katz (Eds.): TACAS 2026, LNCS 16505, pp. 89–109, 2026.
https://doi.org/10.1007/978-3-032-22752-2_5

symmetry handling techniques must strike a delicate balance between reasoning strength, computational cost, and minimal interference with solver heuristics.

Complicating this trade-off even further, SAT symmetry-breaking techniques must also be compatible with proof production. This is because modern SAT solvers (since 2016) are *certifying algorithms* [29], meaning that they emit formally checkable proofs that their answers are correct. Any additional symmetry reasoning must therefore integrate cleanly with proof generation and verification.

Today, practical SAT symmetry-breaking tools suffer from several drawbacks. All current tools produce structured lex-leader constraints [14], which can blow up the size of the formula and degrade learned clause quality when encoded into SAT. Proof logging is also problematic. Proof logging for practical symmetry-breaking tools was only introduced very recently by means of the dominance rule [10]. This approach has received notable success, with an implementation in BREAKID [17] earning a special prize at SAT Competition 2023. But while dominance-based rules are very general, the new proof systems needed to support them are complicated to implement, and their proofs are slow to check.

Interestingly, some symmetry-breaking techniques for mixed-integer programming (MIP) avoid the problems of using large lex-leader constraints by applying symmetry reasoning in a more surgical manner. For formulas that exhibit so-called row symmetry, *orbitopal fixing* [27] breaks symmetries by adding only *unit clauses*. This is accomplished by combining insights on symmetry with insights on cardinality. Adapting such a technique to SAT should have far fewer downsides than introducing long, structured constraints, such as lex-leader constraints.

Contribution. To tackle the challenges discussed above, we adapt orbitopal fixing from MIP to SAT to introduce three new methods of practical symmetry handling. All of our methods follow three guiding principles:

1. They exclusively add *unit clauses* to the formula.
2. They simultaneously exploit *symmetry* and *cardinality*.
3. They generate succinct proof certificates in the substitution redundancy (SR) proof system [12, 20], without the need for dominance-based rules.

We implement our new techniques in the state-of-the-art symmetry breaking tool SATSUMA [3].[1] Despite the apparent restrictions—foregoing lex-leader constraints and feature-rich proof systems—it turns out that, indeed, our approach produces strong practical results:

1. The performance of the state-of-the-art SAT solver CADICAL [8] is substantially improved on the SAT Competition 2025, the SAT anniversary track of 2022, and a set of highly symmetric crafted benchmarks.
2. The preprocessing overhead is negligible (less than 1% of average solve time).
3. The performance regression on *satisfiable instances* is significantly smaller than for lex-leader constraints (even though lex-leader constraints achieve overall better pruning than our techniques on *unsatisfiable* instances).
4. The SR proofs are succinct, easy to generate, and efficient to check.

---

[1] https://github.com/markusa4/satsuma.

Overall, our techniques offer a more lightweight, surgical, and stable approach to SAT symmetry breaking than lex-leader constraints, and our techniques can be easily combined with other symmetry handling methods.

2 Preliminaries

We assume that the reader is generally familiar with concepts from SAT solving. For a broad introduction to the topic, see the Handbook of Satisfiability [9].

The propositional formulas we consider in this paper are all in *conjunctive normal form* (CNF), meaning that they are conjunctions of disjunctive *clauses* containing *literals*. A literal ℓ is either a variable v or its negation $\overline{v}$. In this paper, we interpret clauses and formulas as sets. For example, we sometimes write the clause $(x \vee \overline{y} \vee z)$ as $\{x, \overline{y}, z\}$. Let $\mathrm{Var}(F)$ and $\mathrm{Lit}(F)$ be the set of variables and literals occurring in F, respectively.

Two formulas F and F' are *equisatisfiable* if F is satisfiable iff F' is satisfiable. This definition is bidirectional, but since we only consider formulas F' that are formed by adding clauses to F (i.e., $F \subseteq F'$), the reverse direction is trivial, and thus we omit it in our proofs.

2.1 Unique Literal Clauses

A clause $C \in F$ is a *unique literal clause* (ULC) with respect to F if none of its literals $\ell \in C$ appear elsewhere in $F \setminus C$. ULCs enjoy the following property, which is key to adapting orbitopal fixing to SAT (see Section 3.1).

Lemma 1 ([38], Lemma 4). *Let F be a formula, and let $C \in F$ be a ULC. If F is satisfiable, then it can be satisfied by a truth assignment that sets exactly one literal in C to true.*

Another nice property of ULCs is that the set of ULCs in a formula F can be computed in linear time: First store how many times each literal appears in F, and then check each clause to see if all of its literals appear exactly once in F.

2.2 Syntactic Symmetry of Formulas

A symmetry σ of a formula F is a permutation of $\mathrm{Lit}(F)$ that maps F to itself. Formally, let σ be a permutation of $\mathrm{Lit}(F)$, and define $\sigma(F)$ as the formula created by relabeling the literals of F under σ. Then σ is a *syntactic symmetry* of F if:

1. $\sigma(F) = F$, and
2. $\neg\sigma(l) = \sigma(\overline{\ell})$ for all $\ell \in \mathrm{Lit}(F)$ (i.e., σ commutes with negation).

When defining a symmetry σ, condition (2) says it is sufficient to specify $\sigma(\ell)$ for only positive literals ℓ. We will write symmetries as $\sigma := (\ell \mapsto \ell', \ldots)$, meaning that $\sigma(\ell) = \ell'$. All literals not explicitly listed are assumed to map back to themselves, i.e., $\sigma(x) = x$.

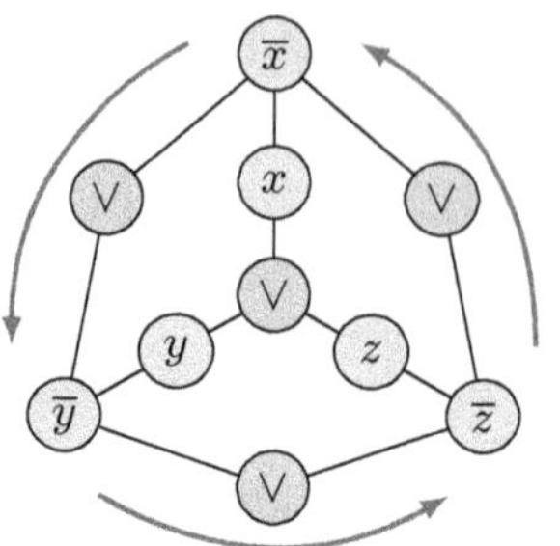
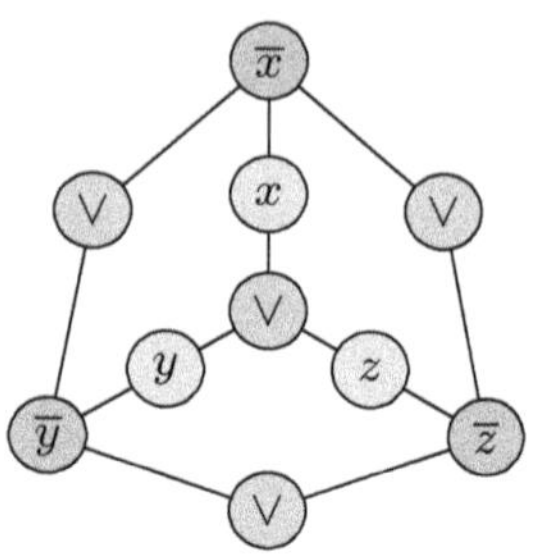

Fig. 1. A graph modeling the symmetries of the formula $(x \vee y \vee z) \wedge (\overline{x} \vee \overline{y}) \wedge (\overline{x} \vee \overline{z}) \wedge (\overline{y} \vee \overline{z})$. Every clause is connected to its component literals, and every literal is adjacent to its negation. On the left, the green arrows indicate the symmetry mapping x to y, y to z, and z to x. On the right, the colors indicate the orbits of the vertices.

Example 1. Let $F = (x \vee y \vee z) \wedge (\overline{x} \vee \overline{y}) \wedge (\overline{x} \vee \overline{z}) \wedge (\overline{y} \vee \overline{z})$. Then the permutation $\sigma := (x \mapsto y, y \mapsto z, z \mapsto x)$ is a symmetry of F, since

$$\sigma(F) = (y \vee z \vee x) \wedge (\overline{y} \vee \overline{z}) \wedge (\overline{y} \vee \overline{x}) \wedge (\overline{z} \vee \overline{x}) = F.$$

In practice, the symmetries of a CNF formula are computed by modeling the formula as a graph and then giving that graph to an off-the-shelf graph isomorphism solver, such as NAUTY [30, 31], BLISS [25, 26], TRACES [31, 34], or DEJAVU [4, 5]. Figure 1 (left) illustrates a graph modeling the symmetries of Example 1. More-compact graph representations are typically used in practice [2].

As it turns out, the symmetries of a formula $\mathrm{Aut}(F)^2$ form a *permutation group*, which means we can use concepts from group theory to reason about them. In this paper, we use two such concepts: stabilizers and orbits.

Stabilizers are sets of symmetries that map literals back to themselves in certain ways. The *pointwise stabilizer* $\mathrm{Aut}(F)_{(L)}$ contains all symmetries of F that stabilize each individual literal in a set of literals L, while the *setwise stabilizer* $\mathrm{Aut}(F)_{\{L\}}$ contains all symmetries of F that map L back to itself. Formally,

$$\mathrm{Aut}(F)_{(L)} := \{\sigma \in \mathrm{Aut}(F) \mid \sigma(\ell) = \ell \text{ for all } \ell \in L\}, \quad \text{(Pointwise)}$$
$$\mathrm{Aut}(F)_{\{L\}} := \{\sigma \in \mathrm{Aut}(F) \mid \sigma(L) = L\}. \quad \text{(Setwise)}$$

Since the condition for pointwise stabilizers is stronger than the one for setwise stabilizers, we have that $\mathrm{Aut}(F)_{(L)} \subseteq \mathrm{Aut}(F)_{\{L\}}$. Each set is always nonempty, since the identity permutation is a member of both stabilizers.

The *orbit* of a literal ℓ is the set of literals that can be reached from ℓ by a permutation group G of symmetries of F. Often, $G = \mathrm{Aut}(F)$, but G is allowed

---

² The notation Aut() is due to how the symmetries of F are also its **aut**omorphisms.

to be any subgroup of $\mathrm{Aut}(F)$. Two literals ℓ_1 and ℓ_2 are *in the same orbit* with respect to G if there exists a symmetry $\sigma \in G$ such that $\sigma(\ell_1) = \ell_2$. The orbits under G form a partition of the literals, where literals in the same orbit are in the same equivalence class. Figure 1 (right) illustrates the orbits of Example 1.

For a more general introduction to permutation groups, we refer the reader to work by Seress [37].

2.3   Substitution Redundancy Proofs

When performing static symmetry breaking for SAT, we add *symmetry-breaking clauses* to a CNF formula F to forbid symmetric solutions. For the additions to be valid, we must prove that each addition preserves the equisatisfiability of F. We can write such a proof of equisatisfiability in a *clausal proof system*, and we can check the proof with a formally-verified proof checker. In this paper, we use the *substitution redundancy* (SR) proof system [12, 20, 35], which is a generalization of the popular RAT [23] and PR [21] proof systems.

In a clausal proof system, each proof step either adds a clause or deletes a clause. Added clauses C must be *redundant*, meaning that F and $(F \wedge C)$ are equisatisfiable. Addition steps may also include a *witness* ω that helps prove that C is redundant. Crucially, these witnesses allow for efficient proof checking.

In SR, the witness is a substitution $\omega : \mathrm{Var}(F) \to \mathrm{Lit}(F) \cup \{\top, \bot\}$ that maps each variable to a literal or to a fixed truth value.[3] This substitution extends to literals in the natural way. As it turns out, substitutions can express the symmetry reasoning involved in orbitopal fixing, which makes it easy to generate SR proofs for the symmetry-breaking clauses we discuss in this paper.

To show that C is redundant, it is sufficient to show that C is *substitution redundant* (SR) for F. In the definition below, we use the following notation. We write $\neg C$ for the negation of the disjunctive clause C, i.e., $\neg C := \bigwedge_{\ell \in C} \bar{\ell}$. We write $F_{|\omega}$ for the reduction of the formula F under the substitution ω, where every literal ℓ in F is replaced with $\omega(\ell)$. We write $\vdash_1$ for entailment via unit propagation, where $F \vdash_1 \bot$ means that F causes a contradiction under unit propagation, $F \vdash_1 C$ means that $F \wedge \neg C \vdash_1 \bot$, and $F \vdash_1 G$ means that $F \wedge \neg D \vdash_1 \bot$ for all $D \in G$.

Definition 1 (Substitution redundant). *A clause C is* substitution redundant *for a formula F if there exists a substitution ω such that $F \wedge \neg C \vdash_1 (F \wedge C)_{|\omega}$.*

Intuitively, the witness ω provides a way to repair any assignment τ that satisfies F but not C into an assignment that satisfies both. If ω expresses a symmetry of F, then it suffices to show that the repaired assignment $\tau \circ \omega$ satisfies C, where "$\circ$" acts as a kind of function composition, with $(\tau \circ \omega)(\ell) = \omega(\ell)$ if $\omega(\ell) \in \{\top, \bot\}$ and $(\tau \circ \omega)(\ell) = \tau(\omega(\ell))$ otherwise.

The SR rule uses unit propagation $\vdash_1$ rather than general entailment $\vDash$ because the use of unit propagation enables the SR rule to be checked efficiently by proof

---

[3]   PR witnesses are partial assignments, and RAT witnesses are partial assignments on a single literal. Thus, SR is a natural generalization of these two systems.

checkers. Today, only the DSR/LSR [13] and VERIPB [20] proof formats support SR reasoning. Our tool can generate proofs in either format.

Example 2. Consider the pigeonhole problem (PHP) of placing m pigeons into n holes such that each pigeon gets its own hole. Whenever $m > n$, this task is impossible. A common SAT encoding of PHP is:

$$\text{PHP}(m,n) = \bigwedge_{j=1}^{m} \left(\bigvee_{i=1}^{n} p_{i,j} \right) \wedge \bigwedge_{i=1}^{n} \bigwedge_{1 \leq j < k \leq m} \left(\overline{p}_{i,j} \vee \overline{p}_{i,k} \right),$$

where the variables $p_{i,j}$ mean that pigeon j is placed in hole i. When visualized as a matrix, the m columns contain the at-least-one constraints, and the n rows contain the at-most-one constraints.

This encoding exhibits a lot of symmetry. In particular, we are free to relabel the holes or the pigeons however we wish. (In other words, the encoding exhibits *row symmetry*; see Section 3.1.) The presence of this symmetry allows us to use SR reasoning to add redundant clauses to the formula.

Suppose we want to use the SR rule to show that pigeon 1 does not go in hole 1, i.e., that the unit clause $C = \{\overline{p}_{1,1}\}$ is SR. Since the left-hand side of the $\vdash_1$ turnstile in the SR rule assumes $\neg C$, we are essentially assuming that pigeon 1 gets placed in hole 1. To "repair" this situation, we will use the witness ω that swaps holes 1 and 2, meaning that pigeon 1 now gets placed in hole 2. Formally, $\omega := (p_{1,1} \mapsto \bot,\ p_{2,1} \mapsto \top,\ p_{1,j} \mapsto p_{2,j},\ p_{2,j} \mapsto p_{1,j})$. Note that ω explicitly sets the truth values for $p_{1,1}$ and $p_{2,1}$, which forces pigeon 1 to be placed in hole 2. All other variables for holes 1 and 2 get swapped. Viewing the variables as a matrix, ω swaps rows 1 and 2.

We now show that C and ω satisfy the SR condition. The good news is that most clauses in $(F \wedge C)_{|\omega}$ have a trivial unit propagation refutation. In general, any clause $D \in F \wedge C$ where $D_{|\omega} = \top$ or $D_{|\omega} = D$ has a trivial refutation. Here, the at-least-one column constraint containing $p_{2,1}$ and any at-most-one row constraints containing $\overline{p}_{1,1}$ are satisfied by ω, and the remaining column constraints and the constraints for rows 3 through n are mapped back to themselves under ω. That leaves the at-most-one constraints for rows 1 and 2.

The row 1 constraints are easy. Either they contain $\overline{p}_{1,1}$ and are satisfied by ω, or they are mapped to a row 2 constraint, which causes a trivial refutation.

Finally, for the row 2 constraints, we do some unit propagation. By assuming $\neg C = \{p_{1,1}\}$ on the left-hand side of $\vdash_1$, we can derive $\{\overline{p}_{1,j}\}$ for all $j \neq 1$ via unit propagation on $\{\overline{p}_{1,1}, \overline{p}_{1,j}\}$. This lets us derive a refutation with the row 2 constraints on the right-hand side of $\vdash_1$, since any constraint $\{\overline{p}_{2,k}, \overline{p}_{2,k'}\}$, mapped under ω will contain $\overline{p}_{1,j}$ for some j, conflicting with the $\{\overline{p}_{1,j}\}$ unit we derived.

3   Fixing Rules

In this section, we introduce our new symmetry-breaking techniques. Notably, our techniques exclusively *assign* or *fix variables*, i.e., they exclusively add unit clauses to the formula. We also prove that each technique preserves equisatisfiability and is compatible with SR proof production.

3.1   Orbitopal Fixing

Our first symmetry-breaking technique is *orbitopal fixing*, which combines row symmetry in a matrix of literals M with the presence of unique literal clauses (ULCs) in the formula to fix literals of M. Our technique is inspired by a procedure of the same name used in MIP [27, 32].

Intuitively, a subset of a formula's literals exhibit row symmetry if they can be arranged into a rectangular matrix M such that there exist symmetries that swap any two rows of M. Formally, let F be a formula, and let $M := (\ell_{i,j})$ be an $n \times m$ matrix comprising a subset of $\mathrm{Lit}(F)$. Then M exhibits *row symmetry* [18] if there are symmetries $\{\sigma_{i_1,i_2}\}_{i_1,i_2 \in [1,n]} \subseteq \mathrm{Aut}(F)$ that swap rows i_1 and i_2 via:

$$\sigma_{i_1,i_2}(\ell) = \begin{cases} \ell_{i_2,j} & \text{if } \ell = \ell_{i_1,j} \text{ for some } j \in [1,m] \\ \ell_{i_1,j} & \text{if } \ell = \ell_{i_2,j} \text{ for some } j \in [1,m] \\ \ell_{i,j} & \text{if } \ell = \ell_{i,j} \in M \text{ and } i \notin \{i_1,i_2\} \end{cases} .$$

Note that for our purposes, row swaps are free to affect literals $\mathrm{Lit}(F) \setminus M$ that lie outside of the matrix. By composing row swaps, every possible reordering of the rows can be achieved. In group-theoretic terms, these swaps generate the symmetric group over the rows. Row symmetry and related structures are crucial for practical symmetry-handling algorithms, and they can be detected by generator-based [16, 22, 33] or more-recently developed graph-based approaches [3].

We now turn to orbitopal fixing. Suppose our formula F has a matrix of literals M that exhibits row symmetry. If each column of M is a unique literal clause of F, then we may fix the bottom literal in the first column $\ell_{n,1}$ to true and all literals in the upper-triangular portion above $\ell_{n,1}$ to false. Figure 2 shows an example of orbitopal fixing. More formally:

Definition 2 (Orbitopal fixing). *Let F be a formula, and let $M := (\ell_{i,j})$ be an $n \times m$ matrix that exhibits row symmetry in F. If every column of M is ULC with respect to F, i.e., if $C_j := \{\ell_{i,j}\}_{i \in [1,n]} \in F$ is ULC for every j, then orbitopal fixing derives unit clauses $(\ell_{n,1})$ and $(\overline{\ell}_{i,j})$ for every $j \in [1, \min(n,m)]$ and $i \leq n - j$.*

At first, it might be surprising that we may fix so many literals at once. But by using the property of ULCs from Lemma 1, we may assume that every column of M is satisfied by exactly one literal. This assumption allows us to strategically swap the rows with the satisfied literals into the lower-triangular portion of M, thus allowing us to fix the upper-triangular portion to false. This argument is formalized in the following lemma.

Theorem 1. *Let F be a formula with the conditions from Definition 2, and let $F \wedge L$ be the formula obtained by applying the orbitopal fixing rule to F. Then the following hold:*

1. F and $F \wedge L$ are equisatisfiable.

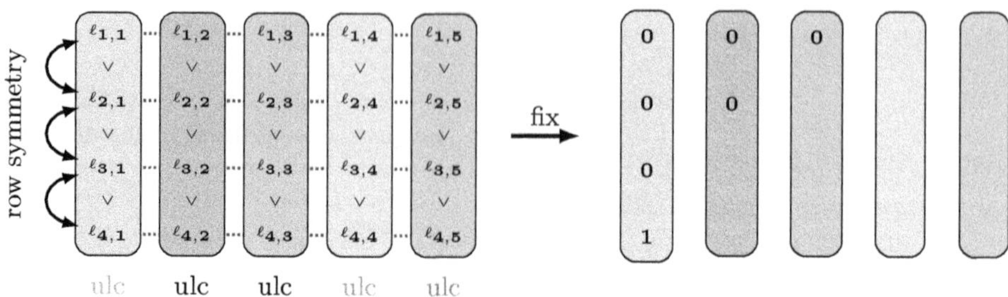

Fig. 2. An example of orbitopal fixing applied to a 4×5 matrix of literals from some formula F. The matrix exhibits row symmetry, and the columns are ULCs of F. Putting these two conditions together, we may fix the bottom-left literal $\ell_{4,1}$ to true and the upper-triangular portion of literals above $\ell_{4,1}$ to false.

 2. *There exists an* SR *proof that adds the unit clauses of L to F in a particular order, namely, column-wise, top to bottom, left to right.*

Proof. **(1).** By Lemma 1, let τ be a satisfying assignment for F that satisfies each column C_j of the matrix M with exactly one true literal. We will now transform τ into a new assignment that also satisfies the additional constraints in $F \wedge L$.

First, consider the leftmost column. Let i be the row containing the satisfied literal of C_1 under τ. If $i \neq n$, then we may use the row symmetry $\sigma_{i,n}$ to change τ into a new assignment $\tau \circ \sigma_{i,n}$ by swapping the truth values for rows i and n. Since $\sigma_{i,n}$ is a symmetry of F, the assignment $\tau \circ \sigma_{i,n}$ still satisfies F, and by our assumption that τ satisfies exactly one literal of C_1, it also satisfies the unit clauses in L setting $\ell_{n,1}$ to true and $\ell_{i,1}$ to false for all $i < n$.

Now consider the j-th column, and let i be the row containing the satisfied literal of C_j. If $i \leq n - j$, then we may do the same thing as before and swap rows i and $n - j + 1$ to form $\tau \circ \sigma_{i,n-j+1}$. Note that swapping these two rows exchanges only falsified literals in the columns to the left, since their true literals lie beneath the $(n - j + 1)$-th row. As a result, we still satisfy the constraints in these columns. And since the true literal of C_j is now beneath row $n - j$, the new assignment sets every literal at and above this row to false, which satisfies the unit clauses in L corresponding to column j.

By applying this procedure to the columns in order from left to right, we obtain a modified τ that satisfies both F and $F \wedge L$.

(2). The series of SR clause additions generated by orbitopal fixing follows the proof of **(1)** exactly, except we must add the clauses in order (top to bottom, left to right), and we must provide a row-permutation witness for each unit clause. More specifically, when we add the unit clause $\{\overline{\ell}_{i,j}\}$, we use the witness ω with

$$\omega(\ell) := \begin{cases} \bot & \text{if } \ell = \ell_{i,j} \\ \top & \text{if } \ell = \ell_{i+1,j} \\ \sigma_{i,i+1}(\ell) & \text{otherwise.} \end{cases}$$

Let $F \wedge L'$ be the formula constructed so far by adding unit clauses.

According to Definition 1, for us to show that $\{\overline{\ell}_{i,j}\}$ is SR, we must show that $F \wedge L' \wedge \{\ell_{i,j}\} \vdash_1 (F \wedge L' \wedge \{\overline{\ell}_{i,j}\})_{|\omega}$. For most clauses, this is trivial: any clauses $C \in F$ whose literals are not modified by ω, i.e., where $C \cap \{\ell \in \mathrm{Lit}(F) \mid \ell \neq \sigma(\ell)\} = \varnothing$, are immediately entailed. The new unit clause $\{\overline{\ell}_{i,j}\}$ is also trivially satisfied, since $\omega(\ell_{i,j}) = \bot$.

The remaining types of clauses modified by the witness are: (i) previously added unit literals L', (ii) clauses of F *not* containing the variables of $\ell_{i,j}$ and $\ell_{i+1,j}$, and (iii) clauses of F containing the variables of $\ell_{i,j}$ and $\ell_{i+1,j}$.

(Case i.) The order of the unit additions ensures that all previously added unit literals $\ell_{i,j'}$ for $1 \leq j' < j$ are mapped to other propagated literals $\ell_{i+1,j'}$. Hence, they also entail each other.

(Case ii.) For every clause $C \in F$ not containing the variables of $\ell_{i,j}$ or $\ell_{i+1,j}$, we observe that the symmetry $\sigma_{i,i+1}$ applies, and $\omega(C) \in F$ holds.

(Case iii.) The ULC containing $\ell_{i,j}$ and $\ell_{i+1,j}$ is entailed, since $\omega(\ell_{i+1,j}) = \top$. And because this clause is a ULC, all other clauses may only contain $\overline{\ell}_{i,j}$ and $\overline{\ell}_{i+1,j}$. All clauses containing $\overline{\ell}_{i,j}$ are immediately entailed.

It remains to show that clauses C containing $\overline{\ell}_{i+1,j}$ but not $\overline{\ell}_{i,j}$ are entailed. Consider the clause C' we obtain by mapping C under the row swap exchanging rows i and $i+1$, that is, $C' = \sigma_{i,i+1}(C)$. Since the row swap is a symmetry of F, $C' \in F$ holds. In other words, C' is a premise.

By assumption, $C \cap \{\overline{\ell}_{i,j}, \ell_{i,j}, \ell_{i+1,j}\} = \varnothing$ and $\overline{\ell}_{i+1,j} \in C$ hold, and thus we can conclude $C' = C_{|\omega} \cup \{\overline{\ell}_{i,j}\}$. Assuming $\neg C_{|\omega}$ together with the additional premise $\ell_{i,j}$ thus contradicts the premise C'. Hence, $C_{|\omega}$ is entailed. $\square$

Example 3. The pigeonhole problem with m pigeons and n holes exhibits row symmetry when encoded as in Example 2, with the rows corresponding to the holes and the columns corresponding to the pigeons. Thus, orbitopal fixing may be applied. Figure 2 illustrates the case of 5 pigeons and 4 holes. When applying orbitopal fixing to this formula, we end up with the following formula:

$$\mathrm{PHP}(5,4) \wedge \overline{p}_{1,1} \wedge \overline{p}_{2,1} \wedge \overline{p}_{3,1} \wedge p_{4,1} \wedge \overline{p}_{1,2} \wedge \overline{p}_{2,2} \wedge \overline{p}_{3,1}.$$

3.2 Clausal Fixing

Our second symmetry-breaking technique, called *clausal fixing*, is based on the observation that every clause must contain at least one satisfied literal. When all literals of a clause belong to the same orbit under the formula's symmetries, a representative literal can be fixed without loss of generality.

Definition 3 (Clausal fixing). *Let F be a formula with clause $\{\ell_1, \ldots, \ell_k\} \in F$ where all ℓ_i are in the same orbit of $\mathrm{Aut}(F)$. That is, there are symmetries σ with $\sigma(\ell_1) = \ell_i$ for each i. Then* clausal fixing *derives the unit clause $\{\ell_1\}$.*

Intuitively, if we have any satisfying assignment, we know that there must be at least one satisfied literal in that clause. Using the orbit, we can always swap the satisfied literal with ℓ_1. Thus, we can just assign ℓ_1 directly.

We now formally prove the correctness of the clausal fixing rule.

Theorem 2. *Let $F \wedge \{\ell_1\}$ be the formula obtained from F by an application of the clausal fixing rule to clause $C = \{\ell_1, \ldots, \ell_k\}$. Then the following hold:*

1. *F and $F \wedge \{\ell_1\}$ are equisatisfiable.*
2. *There is an SR proof deriving $F \wedge \{\ell_1\}$ from F in k steps.*

Proof. **(1).** Let τ be a satisfying assignment of F. We show how to transform τ into an assignment that satisfies $F \wedge \{\ell_1\}$.

Let ℓ_i be a satisfied literal of C. If $\ell_i = \ell_1$, then τ would already satisfy $F \wedge \{\ell_1\}$, so assume otherwise. By definition of the clausal fixing rule, for every literal $\ell_i \in C$, there exists a symmetry σ with $\sigma(\ell_1) = \ell_i$. Using this symmetry, we obtain $\tau' = \tau \circ \sigma$, which now sets ℓ_1 to true. Since σ is a symmetry, the resulting assignment τ' still satisfies F.

(2). We obtain an SR proof as follows. First, the proof derives binary symmetry-breaking clauses $\{\ell_1, \overline{\ell}_i\}$ for all $i \in [2, k]$. Each of these clauses is SR using the symmetry ω_i mapping $\omega_i(\ell_1) = \ell_i$. After that, we may derive the unit clause $\{\ell_1\}$ by resolution on the added binary clauses.

It suffices to show that each binary clause $\{\ell_1, \overline{\ell}_i\}$ is SR. Let L' be the set of binary clauses we have already added. We must show that

$$F \wedge L' \wedge \{\overline{\ell}_1\} \wedge \{\ell_i\} \vdash_1 (F \wedge L' \wedge \{\ell_1, \overline{\ell}_1\})_{|\omega_i}.$$

The result is immediate: Every clause in F is entailed, since ω_i is a symmetry of F, and every clause in $C \in L' \cup \{\ell_1, \overline{\ell}_1\}$ is entailed by the unit clause $\{\ell_i\}$, since $\ell_1 \in C$ and $\omega_i(\ell_1) = \ell_i$. $\qquad\square$

3.3 Negation Fixing

Lastly, we describe the *negation fixing* rule. When a literal can be mapped to its negation, we can fix it without loss of generality.

Definition 4 (Negation fixing). *Let F be a formula, let $\ell \in \mathrm{Lit}(F)$ be a literal, and let $\sigma \in \mathrm{Aut}(F)$ be a symmetry that maps $\sigma(\ell) = \overline{\ell}$. Then negation fixing derives the unit clause $\{\ell\}$.*

In a sense, the negation fixing rule also exploits cardinality: trivially, at least one of ℓ and $\overline{\ell}$ must be true. We prove the correctness of the rule.

Theorem 3. *Let $F \wedge \{\ell\}$ be a formula obtained from F by an application of the negation fixing rule. Then the following hold:*

1. *F and $F \wedge \{\ell\}$ are equisatisfiable.*
2. *The unit clause $\{\ell\}$ is SR.*

Proof. **(1.)** Let τ be a satisfying assignment of F. If τ sets ℓ to true, then we're done, so assume otherwise. Then the assignment $\tau \circ \sigma$ satisfies $F \wedge \{\ell\}$, where σ is the symmetry from the negation fixing rule swapping ℓ with $\overline{\ell}$.

(2.) The clause $\{\ell\}$ is SR using as witness the symmetry mapping $\sigma(\ell) = \overline{\ell}$. $\square$

3.4   Repeated Applications of Rules

All of our rules use the symmetries of a formula F to add a set of unit clauses L to the formula, yielding a new formula $F \wedge L$. In turn, subsequent rule applications would use the symmetries of $F \wedge L$. However, recomputing formula symmetries after *every* rule application is not practical.

Instead of recomputing symmetries, we can *update* the set of applicable symmetries using pointwise and setwise stabilizers (see Section 2.2). This approach may indeed yield fewer applicable symmetries than computing the full group $\mathrm{Aut}(F \wedge L)$, but it's cheaper to do so.

Let us now observe that by stabilizing the set of added unit literals L, we obtain symmetries of $F \wedge L$ from the symmetries of F.

Lemma 2. *Let F be a CNF formula and $L \subseteq \mathrm{Lit}(F)$ a subset of its literals. It holds that* $\mathrm{Aut}(F)_{\{L\}} \subseteq \mathrm{Aut}(F \wedge \{\{\ell\} \mid \ell \in L\})$.

Proof. Let $\sigma \in \mathrm{Aut}(F)_{\{L\}}$. This means that $\sigma(F) = F$ and $\sigma(L) = L$. Consider a clause C of the formula $F \wedge \{\{\ell\} \mid \ell \in L\}$. If $C \in F$, then $\sigma(C) \in F \wedge L$ follows. If $C = \{\ell\}$ is one of the unit clauses from L, then $\sigma(\ell) \in L$ follows, and $\{\sigma(\ell)\} \in \{\{\ell\} \mid \ell \in L\}$. Hence, σ is a symmetry of $F \wedge \{\{\ell\} \mid \ell \in L\}$. $\qquad\square$

Unfortunately, setwise stabilizers are also expensive to compute. (In fact, the problem of computing them is at least as hard as computing symmetries [28].) However, since $\mathrm{Aut}(F)_{(L)} \subseteq \mathrm{Aut}(F)_{\{L\}}$ holds, we can use pointwise stabilizers instead. Polynomial-time algorithms exist to find pointwise stabilizers [37], and they are often efficient in practice.

4   Implementation Details

We implemented our new fixing algorithms in the existing SATSUMA symmetry breaking tool [3]. The tool is implemented in C++.

To enable efficient symmetry handling, SATSUMA simplifies the formula in various ways: Duplicate literals are removed from clauses, duplicate clauses and tautological clauses are removed from the formula, and unit propagation is applied until fixpoint. But other than these simplifications, the tool only adds symmetry-breaking clauses. In particular, the ordering of literals and clauses in the formula remains unchanged.

Orbitopal Fixing. For the orbitopal fixing approach, we leverage the existing structure detection of SATSUMA for row symmetry, row-column symmetry, and the symmetries of so-called Johnson graphs [3].[4] Although orbitopal fixing is only defined over row symmetry, the more complex structures identified by SATSUMA

---

[4]   A Johnson graph $J(n, k)$ represents the k-element subsets of an n-element set, where two vertices share an edge if their set intersection has cardinality $(k - 1)$. Intuitively, Johnson graphs model the symmetries of the edges of complete graphs, or, more generally, relational structures.

often *contain* a row symmetry. In particular, row-column symmetry is inherently composed of two row symmetries. For Johnson symmetry, the relationship is more intricate, but certain instances of this structure can also contain an underlying row symmetry.

Once a structure is identified as potentially having row symmetry, we check its columns to see if they coincide with a unique literal clause in the formula. Orbitopal fixing is applied to columns that fulfill the condition.

Clausal Fixing. Our implementation of clausal fixing follows a four-step procedure:

1. *(Orbits.)* We first compute the orbits of the currently considered group.
2. *(Check clauses.)* Each clause is considered once. If all of its literals belong to the same orbit, then the clausal fixing rule is applied and one literal is propagated. Since orbit partitions refine strictly under pointwise stabilizers, a clause that does not qualify at this stage will not qualify at any later stage.
3. *(Witness.)* To generate SR proofs, we must identify symmetries that can act as witnesses. When we apply clausal fixing to a literal ℓ in a clause C, we explicitly compute symmetries σ such that $\sigma(\ell) = \ell'$ for each $\ell' \in C$.
4. *(Stabilize.)* Whenever propagation occurs, we update the group by taking the pointwise stabilizer of the propagated literals. Then we go back to Step 1 and recompute the orbits for the refined group.

The process stops once each clause has been checked once.

We employ two different algorithms to compute pointwise stabilizers and witness symmetries: a more involved Schreier-Sims-based implementation, and a faster heuristic for binary clauses.

1. The Schreier-Sims algorithm [37,39] computes pointwise stabilizers. Internally, it stores a so-called transversal which can immediately provide the necessary witness symmetries. While it tends to be quite fast for many groups, it often exhibits quadratic scaling in practice. As a result, we set computational limits on the use of Schreier-Sims in our implementation. We use the Schreier-Sims implementation of the DEJAVU [4] library.
2. For large groups, we implement a more rudimentary heuristic which only tests binary clauses. It greedily searches for an existing generator that can serve as the witness symmetry. The heuristic takes pointwise stabilizers by filtering generators to ones that stabilize the desired points.

Negation Fixing. Negation fixing follows a very similar strategy to clausal fixing, except instead of iterating over clauses, it iterates over variables. For each variable v, we check if v and $\bar{v}$ are in the same orbit. As with clausal fixing, we employ both a Schreier-Sims based implementation and a more efficient heuristic.

5   Experimental Evaluation

We evaluated the effectiveness of our fixing techniques as implemented in SATSUMA on three benchmark suites. The first suite is from the anniversary track of the

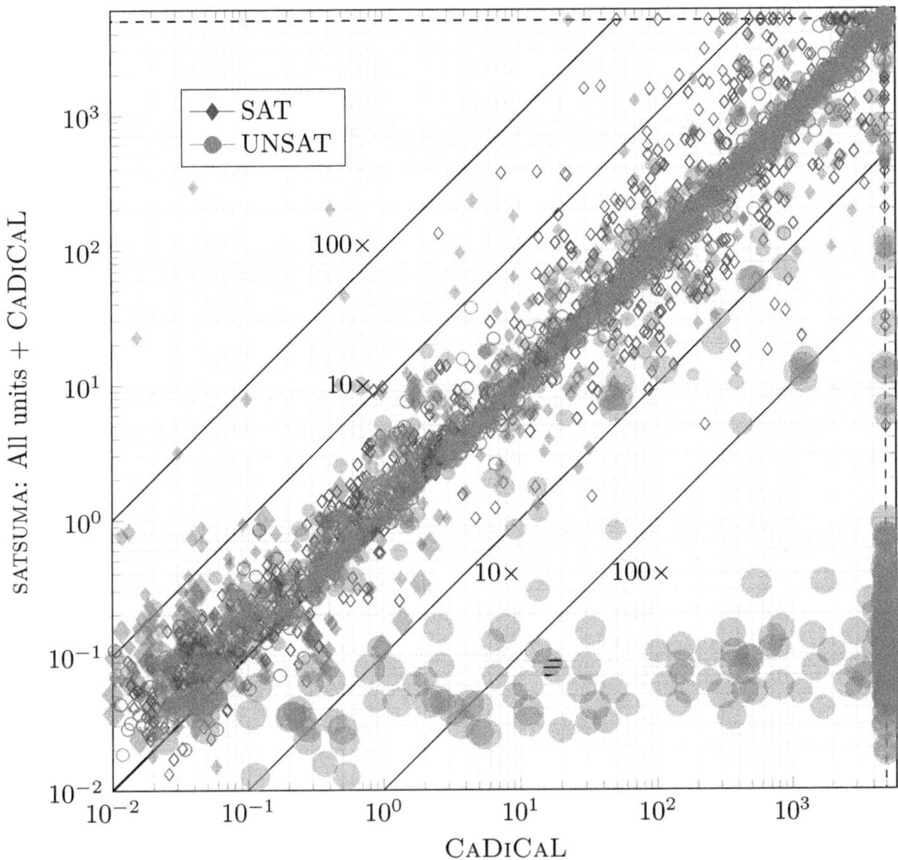

Fig. 3. A scatter plot of CaDiCaL with and without fixing on the anniversary suite. The times are in seconds and include preprocessing time. Empty marks denote that no units were added. The size of the marks correlates to the number of fixed units relative to the number of formula variables. Points below the diagonal benefited from fixing.

SAT Competition 2022 [6], comprising non-random benchmarks from the SAT Competitions 2002 to 2021, duplicates excluded. The second suite comprises the benchmarks from the main track of the SAT Competition 2025. The third suite comprises highly symmetric synthetic benchmarks that have appeared in various papers on symmetry breaking, including pigeonhole, Tseitin, clique coloring, and graph coloring formulas, as well as multiple instances from Ramsey theory.

For each suite, we filtered out all formulas larger than 1 GB in size, since for such large formulas symmetry handling often incurs prohibitive computational overhead, and are thus skipped by the symmetry breaking tools anyway. After this filter, the anniversary suite has 5344 formulas, the 2025 suite has 386 formulas, and the synthetic suite has 137 formulas.

We ran our experiments on the cluster at the Pittsburgh Supercomputing Center [11]. Each machine has 128 cores and 256 GB of RAM. We ran every tool in parallel across all cores. We used a timeout of 5000 seconds for CaDiCaL[5] (which matches the official timeout for the SAT competitions), as well as a 300 second timeout for SATSUMA and DSR-TRIM [13],[6] an (unverified) SR proof checker. Notably, all SATSUMA runs finished before timeout.

We ran SATSUMA with five different settings: each of our three fixing techniques individually, all of our techniques combined ("all-units"), and a control version of SATSUMA that produces lex-leader constraints. We checked all SATSUMA-generated SR proofs with DSR-TRIM. Then we ran CaDiCaL on all formulas.

Figure 3 shows the results of applying all fixing techniques to the anniversary benchmarks. Our fixing techniques allow CaDiCaL to solve many dozens of formulas very quickly, including 67 formulas that can be solved in a second of preprocessing time, while CaDiCaL without symmetry breaking times out after 5000 seconds. Many empty points below the diagonal are due to SATSUMA's formula simplification (especially on satisfiable instances). Note that few points are clearly above the diagonal, thereby showing that our techniques have minimal negative impact on the performance across the anniversary benchmarks.

Figure 4 shows similar results on the synthetic and 2025 suites. Notably, most of the synthetic benchmarks become easy after fixing, showing, somewhat surprisingly, that symmetry breaking is all that is needed to solve these instances.

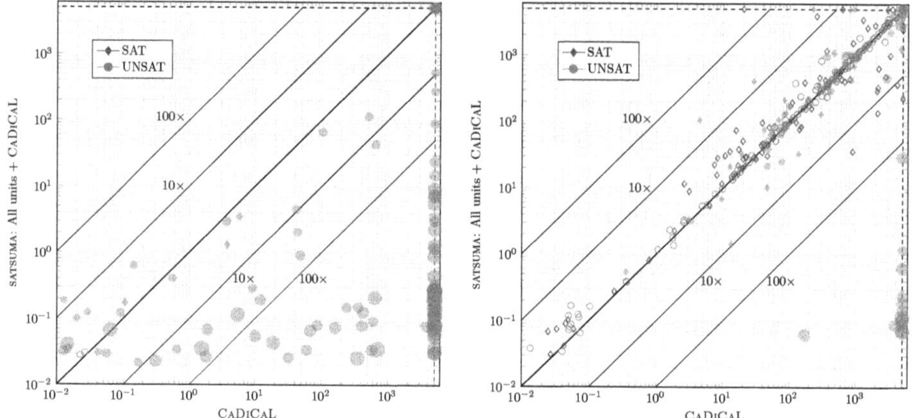

Fig. 4. Scatter plots of CaDiCaL with and without fixing on the synthetic suite (left) and the 2025 suite (right). The times are in seconds and include preprocessing time.

Figure 5 shows a cumulative solved formulas (CSF) plot comparing the runtimes of CaDiCaL with each SATSUMA setting against base CaDiCaL on the anniversary suite. The left CSF plot shows the regression due to symmetry

---

[5]   https://github.com/arminbiere/cadical. We used version 2.1.3.
[6]   https://github.com/ccodel/dsr-trim.

breaking on satisfiable instances, since symmetry breaking on satisfiable formulas typically has no benefit and can be harmful instead. The plot shows that the lex-leader setting performs the worst, while the new techniques limit the amount of regression. The regression is similar across SATSUMA settings, which suggests that SATSUMA's formula preprocessing and simplification dominate the costs.

The right CSF plot of Figure 5 shows the runtime performance on unsatisfiable instances. Lex-leader performs the best, but the all-units setting is close behind. Below them, each individual setting performs similarly, with clausal fixing performing the worst. All techniques outperform base CaDiCaL.

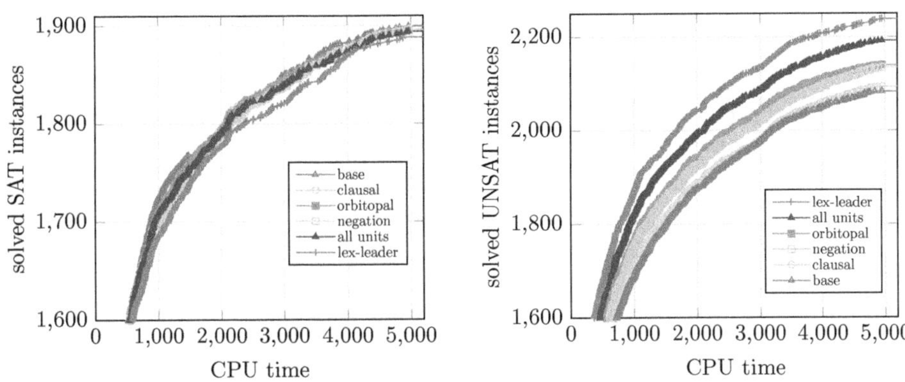

Fig. 5. CSF plots on SAT (left) and UNSAT (right) formulas of the anniversary suite

Figure 6 shows the CSF plots for the synthetic and 2025 suites. On the synthetic instances, the all-units configuration performs the best. The main reason for its success is that negation fixing can easily solve all Tseitin formulas, in contrast to lex-leader. (A similar approach could be implemented for lex-leader, but this is currently not present in SATSUMA.) On the 2025 suite, lex-leader shows the strongest performance, followed by the all-units configuration.

Table 1 summarizes the data shown in the figures.

As part of our experiments, we generated and checked SR and DRAT proofs. SATSUMA generated SR proofs when applying our fixing techniques, and CaDiCaL generated DRAT proofs for unsatisfiable formulas. All proofs were either accepted by the DSR-TRIM and LSR-CHECK proof checkers, or caused a memout/timeout. Proof checking time was generally low, with most proofs finishing in under 15 seconds. Table 2 summarizes the times taken for proof checking.

One particular advantage of SATSUMA's SR proof generation is that it composes with CaDiCaL's DRAT proof generation. For any unsatisfiable symmetry-broken formula, we appended the DRAT proof to the end of its SR proof, and then checked the proof with respect to the original formula. In this way, the two proofs form a complete proof of unsatisfiability of the original formula.

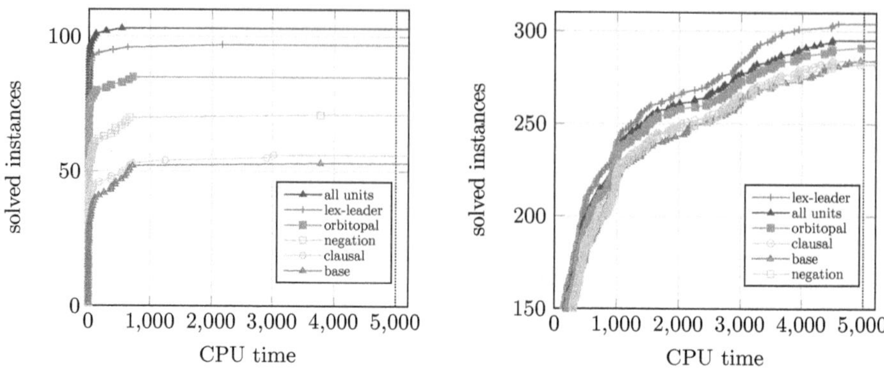

Fig. 6. CSF plots on the synthetic suite (left) and the 2025 suite (right)

Table 1. Results across the benchmark suites for the average preprocessing time in seconds (PPT), the average CaDiCaL runtime with preprocessing in seconds (CRT), and the average number of units added to the formula by the fixing technique (#U).

Suite	Anni22			Satcomp25			Synth		
Setting	PPT	CRT	#U	PPT	CRT	#U	PPT	CRT	#U
Orbitopal	2.51	1555.5	11.23	8.06	1746.7	8.37	0.44	1919.2	743.0
Negation	1.93	1572.0	32.59	5.77	1870.6	52.15	0.32	2469.4	16.5
Clausal	1.83	1605.7	23.64	5.45	1845.3	14.33	0.73	3041.0	15.2
All	1.81	1504.5	67.30	5.27	1694.3	71.48	0.76	1250.0	768.6
Lex-leader	1.73	1472.4	–	4.85	1593.7	–	0.32	1486.6	–
CaDiCaL	–	1607.8	–	–	1882.9	–	–	3138.6	–

Table 2. Results for SR proof checking times across the various benchmark suites and settings, showing the average DSR-TRIM checking time in seconds (DCT) and the average LSR-CHECK checking time in seconds (LCT).

Suite	Anni22		Satcomp25		Synth	
Setting	DCT	LCT	DCT	LCT	DCT	LCT
Orbitopal	5.35	0.76	15.15	1.36	8.42	4.19
Negation	5.76	1.43	16.80	1.64	0.04	0.01
Clausal	6.76	0.86	16.13	1.29	5.29	0.16
All	7.48	1.41	15.91	1.48	8.67	3.18

6 Conclusion

We presented new static symmetry-breaking techniques based solely on introducing unit clauses to a given formula, which we implemented in the state-of-the-art tool SATSUMA. The key insight behind these techniques was to combine symmetry and cardinality reasoning. This combination enabled us to, for the first time, implement meaningful, practical symmetry breaking that produces SR proofs instead of dominance-based proofs. Our experiments demonstrate significant performance improvements across a wide variety of benchmarks, with reduced regression compared to the lex-leader approach.

As for future work, we hope to expand the present techniques further to close the gap with the lex-leader approach on unsatisfiable instances. While this may be difficult by using only unit clauses, it would be interesting to achieve this without incurring any additional performance regression on satisfiable instances while still using lightweight SR proofs. Indeed, it would be intriguing to find concrete benchmark families that *can* be efficiently solved in practice using lex-leader constraints, but evade serious attempts at efficient, practical symmetry handling in SR. A concrete candidate might be small Ramsey numbers: while a very short SR proof for $R(4,4,18)$ is known [13], it is possible to easily solve the slightly harder $R(3,7,23)$ within few minutes using lex-leader constraints. We wonder if it is possible to generalize the symmetry breaking from the $R(4,4,18)$ proof to larger numbers. Separately, in MIP, orbitopal fixing can be used under more general conditions [7,27], which may be interesting to adapt to SAT.

7 Data Availability and Reproducibility

All of our source code, benchmark formulas, and experimental results can be found at our artifact on Zenodo.[7] The artifact contains detailed instructions for how to download the formulas and compile the source code in a Docker container. The artifact also contains scripts to run experiments and compare the results to the ones from our paper.

Acknowledgements

We thank Christopher Hojny for pointing out important literature in MIP. This work has benefited substantially from Dagstuhl Seminar 25231 "Certifying Algorithms for Automated Reasoning." This work was supported by the National Science Foundation (NSF) under grant CCF-2415773 and funding from AFRL and DARPA under Agreement FA8750-24-9-1000.

References

1. Aloul, F.A., Markov, I.L., Sakallah, K.A.: Shatter: efficient symmetry-breaking for boolean satisfiability. In: Proceedings of the 40th Design Automation Conference, DAC 2003, Anaheim, CA, USA, June 2-6, 2003. pp. 836–839. ACM (2003). https://doi.org/10.1145/775832.776042
2. Aloul, F.A., Ramani, A., Markov, I.L., Sakallah, K.A.: Solving difficult instances of boolean satisfiability in the presence of symmetry. IEEE Trans. Comput. Aided Des. Integr. Circuits Syst. **22**(9), 1117–1137 (2003). https://doi.org/10.1109/TCAD.2003.816218

---

[7] https://doi.org/10.5281/zenodo.17491222.

3. Anders, M., Brenner, S., Rattan, G.: Satsuma: Structure-based symmetry breaking in SAT. In: 27th International Conference on Theory and Applications of Satisfiability Testing, SAT 2024, August 21-24, 2024, Pune, India. LIPIcs, vol. 305, pp. 4:1–4:23. Schloss Dagstuhl - Leibniz-Zentrum für Informatik (2024). https://doi.org/10.4230/LIPICS.SAT.2024.4

4. Anders, M., Schweitzer, P.: Parallel computation of combinatorial symmetries. In: 29th Annual European Symposium on Algorithms, ESA 2021, September 6-8, 2021, Lisbon, Portugal (Virtual Conference). LIPIcs, vol. 204, pp. 6:1–6:18. Schloss Dagstuhl - Leibniz-Zentrum für Informatik (2021). https://doi.org/10.4230/LIPICS.ESA.2021.6

5. Anders, M., Schweitzer, P.: Search problems in trees with symmetries: Near optimal traversal strategies for individualization-refinement algorithms. In: 48th International Colloquium on Automata, Languages, and Programming, ICALP 2021, July 12-16, 2021, Glasgow, Scotland (Virtual Conference). LIPIcs, vol. 198, pp. 16:1–16:21. Schloss Dagstuhl - Leibniz-Zentrum für Informatik (2021). https://doi.org/10.4230/LIPICS.ICALP.2021.16

6. Balyo, T., Heule, M.J.H., Iser, M., Järvisalo, M., Suda, M. (eds.): Proceedings of SAT Competition 2022: Solver and Benchmark Descriptions. Department of Computer Science Series of Publications B, Helsinki Institute for Information Technology (2022)

7. Bendotti, P., Fouilhoux, P., Rottner, C.: Orbitopal fixing for the full (sub-)orbitope and application to the unit commitment problem. Mathematical Programming **186**(1), 337–372 (2021). https://doi.org/10.1007/s10107-019-01457-1

8. Biere, A., Faller, T., Fazekas, K., Fleury, M., Froleyks, N., Pollitt, F.: CaDiCaL 2.0. In: Gurfinkel, A., Ganesh, V. (eds.) Computer Aided Verification - 36th International Conference, CAV 2024, Montreal, QC, Canada, July 24-27, 2024, Proceedings, Part I. Lecture Notes in Computer Science, vol. 14681, pp. 133–152. Springer (2024). https://doi.org/10.1007/978-3-031-65627-9_7

9. Biere, A., Heule, M., van Maaren, H., Walsh, T. (eds.): Handbook of Satisfiability - Second Edition, Frontiers in Artificial Intelligence and Applications, vol. 336. IOS Press (2021). https://doi.org/10.3233/FAIA336

10. Bogaerts, B., Gocht, S., McCreesh, C., Nordström, J.: Certified dominance and symmetry breaking for combinatorial optimisation. J. Artif. Intell. Res. **77**, 1539–1589 (2023). https://doi.org/10.1613/JAIR.1.14296

11. Brown, S.T., Buitrago, P., Hanna, E., Sanielevici, S., Scibek, R., Nystrom, N.A.: Bridges-2: A platform for rapidly-evolving and data intensive research. In: Practice and Experience in Advanced Research Computing 2021: Evolution Across All Dimensions. PEARC '21, Association for Computing Machinery, New York, NY, USA (2021). https://doi.org/10.1145/3437359.3465593

12. Buss, S., Thapen, N.: DRAT and propagation redundancy proofs without new variables. Logical Methods in Computer Science **Volume 17, Issue 2** (Apr 2021). https://doi.org/10.23638/LMCS-17(2:12)2021

13. Codel, C.R., Avigad, J., Heule, M.J.H.: Verified substitution redundancy checking. In: Formal Methods in Computer-Aided Design, FMCAD 2024, Prague, Czech Republic, October 15-18, 2024. pp. 186–196. IEEE (2024). https://doi.org/10.34727/2024/ISBN.978-3-85448-065-5_24

14. Crawford, J.M., Ginsberg, M.L., Luks, E.M., Roy, A.: Symmetry-breaking predicates for search problems. In: Proceedings of the Fifth International Conference on Principles of Knowledge Representation and Reasoning (KR'96), Cambridge, Massachusetts, USA, November 5-8, 1996. pp. 148–159. Morgan Kaufmann (1996)

15. Devriendt, J., Bogaerts, B., Bruynooghe, M.: Symmetric explanation learning: Effective dynamic symmetry handling for SAT. In: Theory and Applications of Satisfiability Testing - SAT 2017 - 20th International Conference, Melbourne, VIC, Australia, August 28 - September 1, 2017, Proceedings. Lecture Notes in Computer Science, vol. 10491, pp. 83–100. Springer (2017). https://doi.org/10.1007/978-3-319-66263-3_6

16. Devriendt, J., Bogaerts, B., Bruynooghe, M., Denecker, M.: Improved static symmetry breaking for SAT. In: Theory and Applications of Satisfiability Testing - SAT 2016 - 19th International Conference, Bordeaux, France, July 5-8, 2016, Proceedings. Lecture Notes in Computer Science, vol. 9710, pp. 104–122. Springer (2016). https://doi.org/10.1007/978-3-319-40970-2_8

17. Devriendt, J., Bogaerts, B., Cat, B.D., Denecker, M., Mears, C.: Symmetry propagation: Improved dynamic symmetry breaking in SAT. In: IEEE 24th International Conference on Tools with Artificial Intelligence, ICTAI 2012, Athens, Greece, November 7-9, 2012. pp. 49–56. IEEE Computer Society (2012). https://doi.org/10.1109/ICTAI.2012.16

18. Flener, P., Frisch, A.M., Hnich, B., Kiziltan, Z., Miguel, I., Pearson, J., Walsh, T.: Breaking row and column symmetries in matrix models. In: Principles and Practice of Constraint Programming - CP 2002, 8th International Conference, CP 2002, Ithaca, NY, USA, September 9-13, 2002, Proceedings. Lecture Notes in Computer Science, vol. 2470, pp. 462–476. Springer (2002). https://doi.org/10.1007/3-540-46135-3_31

19. Gent, I.P., Petrie, K.E., Puget, J.: Symmetry in constraint programming. In: Rossi, F., van Beek, P., Walsh, T. (eds.) Handbook of Constraint Programming, Foundations of Artificial Intelligence, vol. 2, pp. 329–376. Elsevier (2006). https://doi.org/10.1016/S1574-6526(06)80014-3

20. Gocht, S., Nordström, J.: Certifying parity reasoning efficiently using pseudo-boolean proofs. In: Thirty-Fifth AAAI Conference on Artificial Intelligence, AAAI 2021, Thirty-Third Conference on Innovative Applications of Artificial Intelligence, IAAI 2021, The Eleventh Symposium on Educational Advances in Artificial Intelligence, EAAI 2021, Virtual Event, February 2-9, 2021. pp. 3768–3777. AAAI Press (2021). https://doi.org/10.1609/AAAI.V35I5.16494

21. Heule, M.J.H., Kiesl, B., Biere, A.: Strong extension-free proof systems. Journal of Automated Reasoning **64**(3), 533–554 (2020). https://doi.org/10.1007/s10817-019-09516-0

22. Hojny, C., Pfetsch, M.E.: Polytopes associated with symmetry handling. Math. Program. **175**(1-2), 197–240 (2019). https://doi.org/10.1007/S10107-018-1239-7

23. Järvisalo, M., Heule, M.J.H., Biere, A.: Inprocessing rules. In: Automated Reasoning. pp. 355–370 (2012)

24. Junttila, T.A., Karppa, M., Kaski, P., Kohonen, J.: An adaptive prefix-assignment technique for symmetry reduction. J. Symb. Comput. **99**, 21–49 (2020). https://doi.org/10.1016/J.JSC.2019.03.002

25. Junttila, T.A., Kaski, P.: Engineering an efficient canonical labeling tool for large and sparse graphs. In: Proceedings of the Nine Workshop on Algorithm Engineering and Experiments, ALENEX 2007, New Orleans, Louisiana, USA, January 6, 2007. SIAM (2007). https://doi.org/10.1137/1.9781611972870.13

26. Junttila, T.A., Kaski, P.: Conflict propagation and component recursion for canonical labeling. In: Theory and Practice of Algorithms in (Computer) Systems - First International ICST Conference, TAPAS 2011, Rome, Italy, April 18-20, 2011. Proceedings. Lecture Notes in Computer Science, vol. 6595, pp. 151–162. Springer (2011). https://doi.org/10.1007/978-3-642-19754-3_16

27. Kaibel, V., Peinhardt, M., Pfetsch, M.E.: Orbitopal fixing. Discrete Optimization **8**(4), 595–610 (2011). https://doi.org/https://doi.org/10.1016/j.disopt.2011.07.001

28. Luks, E.M.: Permutation groups and polynomial-time computation. In: Groups And Computation, Proceedings of a DIMACS Workshop, New Brunswick, New Jersey, USA, October 7-10, 1991. DIMACS Series in Discrete Mathematics and Theoretical Computer Science, vol. 11, pp. 139–175. DIMACS/AMS (1991). https://doi.org/10.1090/DIMACS/011/11

29. McConnell, R.M., Mehlhorn, K., Näher, S., Schweitzer, P.: Certifying algorithms. Comput. Sci. Rev. **5**(2), 119–161 (2011). https://doi.org/10.1016/J.COSREV.2010.09.009

30. McKay, B.D.: Practical graph isomorphism. In: 10th. Manitoba Conference on Numerical Mathematics and Computing (Winnipeg, 1980). pp. 45–87 (1981)

31. McKay, B.D., Piperno, A.: Practical graph isomorphism, II. J. Symb. Comput. **60**, 94–112 (2014). https://doi.org/10.1016/J.JSC.2013.09.003

32. Mexi, G., Kamp, D., Shinano, Y., Pu, S., Hoen, A., Bestuzheva, K., Hojny, C., Walter, M., Pfetsch, M.E., Pokutta, S., Koch, T.: State-of-the-art methods for pseudo-boolean solving with SCIP (2025), https://arxiv.org/abs/2501.03390

33. Pfetsch, M.E., Rehn, T.: A computational comparison of symmetry handling methods for mixed integer programs. Math. Program. Comput. **11**(1), 37–93 (2019). https://doi.org/10.1007/S12532-018-0140-Y

34. Piperno, A.: Search space contraction in canonical labeling of graphs (preliminary version). CoRR **abs/0804.4881** (2008), http://arxiv.org/abs/0804.4881

35. Rebola-Pardo, A.: Even shorter proofs without new variables. In: Mahajan, M., Slivovsky, F. (eds.) 26th International Conference on Theory and Applications of Satisfiability Testing (SAT 2023). Leibniz International Proceedings in Informatics (LIPIcs), vol. 271, pp. 22:1–22:20. Schloss Dagstuhl – Leibniz-Zentrum für Informatik, Dagstuhl, Germany (2023). https://doi.org/10.4230/LIPIcs.SAT.2023.22

36. Sabharwal, A.: SymChaff: exploiting symmetry in a structure-aware satisfiability solver. Constraints An Int. J. **14**(4), 478–505 (2009). https://doi.org/10.1007/S10601-008-9060-1

37. Seress, Á.: Permutation Group Algorithms. Cambridge Tracts in Mathematics, Cambridge University Press (2003). https://doi.org/10.1017/CBO9780511546549

38. Sheng, A., Reeves, J.E., Heule, M.J.H.: Reencoding unique literal clauses. In: 28th International Conference on Theory and Applications of Satisfiability Testing, SAT 2025, August 12-15, 2025, Glasgow, Scotland. LIPIcs, vol. 341, pp. 29:1–29:21. Schloss Dagstuhl - Leibniz-Zentrum für Informatik (2025). https://doi.org/10.4230/LIPICS.SAT.2025.29

39. Sims, C.C.: Computational methods in the study of permutation groups. In: Computational Problems in Abstract Algebra, pp. 169–183. Pergamon (1970). https://doi.org/https://doi.org/10.1016/B978-0-08-012975-4.50020-5

Automatically Tightening Access Control Policies with RESTRICTER [*]

Ka Lok Wu[1], Christa Jenkins[2][**], Scott D. Stoller[1],
and Omar Chowdhury[1][***]

[1] Stony Brook University, Stony Brook NY 11794, USA
{kalowu,stoller,omar}@cs.stonybrook.edu
[2] Galois, Inc. Portland, OR 97204, USA
christa.jenkins@galois.com

Abstract. Robust access control is a cornerstone of secure software, systems, and networks. An access control mechanism is as effective as the policy it enforces. However, authoring effective policies that satisfy desired properties such as the *principle of least privilege* is a challenging task even for experienced administrators. In this paper, we set out to address this pain point by proposing RESTRICTER, which *automatically* tightens each (permit) policy rule of a policy with respect to an access log, which captures some already exercised access requests and their corresponding access decisions (*i.e.*, allow or deny). RESTRICTER achieves policy tightening by reducing the number of access requests permitted by a policy rule without sacrificing the functionality of the underlying system it is regulating. We implement RESTRICTER for Amazon's Cedar policy language and demonstrate its effectiveness through two realistic case studies.

Keywords: Security Policy · Access Control · SyGuS.

1 Introduction

An access control mechanism is a critical defense for ensuring the resilient security posture of software, systems, and networks. In the 2024 CWE Top 25 Most Dangerous Software Weaknesses published by MITRE [25], three of them were related to access control and authorization management. In the similar vein, OWASP's Top 10 list of critical web application security risks published in 2021 ranks "*Broken Access Control*" at the top [27]. One reason for such access control-related vulnerabilities can be attributed to access control checks being intertwined with application logic in source code, making it challenging for maintaining and understanding the access control being enforced. It is well understood that decoupling the access control checks from the application business logic ensures better management and

---

[*] This material is based on work supported in part by an Amazon Research Award and NSF award CCF-1954837.

[**] Work done while the author was at Stony Brook University.

[***] Corresponding author.

S. Junges and G. Katz (Eds.): TACAS 2026, LNCS 16505, pp. 110–129, 2026.
https://doi.org/10.1007/978-3-032-22752-2_6

maintainability. To promote such decoupling, many access control systems have been developed (*e.g.*, Casbin [13], Open Policy Agent [15], Amazon's Cedar [7]).

At the heart of an access control system is an *access control policy*, which aims to precisely capture the conditions under which users may access critical resources. Designing such policies to prevent unauthorized access and allow legitimate users to carry out their business obligations is a challenging task. Misconfiguring a policy can lead to the following pitfalls: ❶ overly permissive policies violate the *principle of least privilege* (*i.e.*, granting users only necessary privileges) and allow unauthorized users to access critical resources, opening the door to misuse; ❷ overly restrictive policies prevent legitimate users from accessing resources necessary for performing their business tasks. Although policy misconfigurations of type ❷ often get rectified due to user complaining due to failure to carry out business operations, type ❶ misconfiguration can remain undetected, waiting to be exploited. Examples of type ❶ policy misconfigurations abound in practice [25]. For instance, exploitable misconfigurations of type ❶ were identified in mandatory access control policies written by experts for Android's SELinux [14]. *This paper designs, develops, and evaluates* RESTRICTER, *an automated technique, based on Satisfiability Modulo Theory (SMT) [10] and Syntax-guided Synthesis (SyGuS) [6], for reducing over-permissiveness in policies.*

Designing a policy that follows the principle of least privilege, which we call the *tightest policy*, is a challenging and error-prone task. Over-privileges (*i.e.*, requests permitted by the policy but not needed for any current business use case) can easily creep in as policies evolve. Over-privileges can also result from imprecision in identifying the permissions required for a use case and imprecision in formulating policy rules that grant those permissions. RESTRICTER addresses over-privileges by ① inferring such unintended over-privileges permitted by the current policy and then ② refining (*tightening*) the policy by removing them.

Besides scalability, the main technical challenge in realizing RESTRICTER's approach is identifying over-privileges (step ①). Unfortunately, a precise characterization of over-privileges in the current policy is often unavailable in practice. RESTRICTER's over-privilege inference is based on analysis of the current policy together with an *access log* in which all attempted access requests and their current policy decisions are logged. RESTRICTER's over-privilege inference is based on the insight that *the over-privileges are a subset of the permissions granted by the current policy and not exercised in the log.*

RESTRICTER focuses on Attribute-based Access Control (ABAC) [22]. It formulates ABAC policy tightening as a *program synthesis problem* and solves it using a Syntax-Guided Synthesis (SyGuS) solver. Unfortunately, tightening an entire policy at once with SyGuS does not scale even for moderate-sized policies. RESTRICTER addresses the scalability challenges by limiting the size and number of terms that are enumerated and by adopting a *rule-level analysis*, tightening permit rules individually. Rule-level analysis is also amenable to parallelization.

RESTRICTER is instantiated for a large subset of Cedar [18], an ABAC system developed by Amazon Web Services. It is then evaluated on two case studies. It is able to scalably infer the potential over-privileges and refine most (6 out of 8)

```
entity User { isPCChair: Bool, isPcMember: Bool};
entity Paper { authors: Set<User>, reviewers: Set<User>};
entity Review { ofPaper: Paper, author: User, isMetaReview: Bool };
action Read appliesTo {
principal: User, resource: [Review, Paper], context: {isReleased?: Bool}};
```

(a) Conference management system schema (snippet)

```
permit (principal, action == Action::"Read", resource is Paper)
when { principal.isPcMember };

permit (principal, action, resource is Review)
when { principal in resource.ofPaper.authors };
```

(b) Conference management system policies (snippet)

Fig. 1: Example Cedar schemas and policies

of the deliberately loose permit rules by adding appropriate general conditions instead of point-solutions, while also removing some over-privileges in the other cases. In summary, this paper makes the following contributions:

1. We formulate and formally define the access control policy tightening problem with respect to a given policy, access log, and policy state.
2. We present an approach that can incrementally tighten each policy rule using automated reasoning (*i.e.*, SyGuS, SMT).
3. We empirically demonstrate RESTRICTER's effectiveness and scalability on two realistic case studies.

2   Background on Cedar

This section presents a primer on Cedar. Due to space restrictions, we assume readers have some familiarity with ABAC, SyGuS, and SMT solvers. Further details on Cedar and these other topics are available from other sources [18,29,5,4,23,9,31]. Cedar [7] is an open-source authorization policy language developed (and used at scale, especially, to protect customer API end-points) by Amazon Web Services (AWS). We chose Cedar as the target of RESTRICTER to show that our approach is applicable to an authorization policy language that is practical, expressive, and actively used in industry, but RESTRICTER can also be extended to work on other ABAC policy languages.

2.1   Cedar Primer

We introduce some of Cedar's salient language features, using a conference management system inspired by HotCRP as a motivating example. This example comes from one of our case studies, which is described further in Section 7.1. **Schemas.** Cedar schemas define the data model for the entities and actions to which policies apply. Declarations of entity types specify the names and types of the entities' attributes. Valid attribute types include Booleans, entity types, and sets. Attributes can be *mandatory* or *optional*, indicated resp. by the absence or presence of the suffix ? in their name. As an example, in Figure 1a, the entity type `Paper` declares that each paper has two attributes: its sets of authors and reviewers.

Schemas also list the set of *actions* and the types of entities to which each action applies. Optionally, action declarations may specify the type of contexts associated with the action. For example, Figure 1a declares the action `Read`, which a `User` may take on a `Paper` or `Review`, and which comes with a context containing an optional Boolean attribute indicating whether the resource has been released.

Policies. A Cedar policy is composed of *rules*[3]. Each rule is a Boolean-valued function of four parameters — `principal`, `action`, `resource`, and `context` (implicit) — comprising:

- an **effect**, `permit` or `deny`, indicating whether to allow or prohibit requests to which the rule applies;
- a **scope** constraining the principals, actions, and resources to which the rule applies; and
- a **body** (optional), which places further constraints on the parameters, usually involving their attributes.

Example: In Figure 1b, the second rule has **effect** `permit`, a **scope** applying to any `principal` and `action` but only `resources` of type `Review`, and a **body** further constraining the rule to only those `principals` which are authors of the paper the review concerns.

Composing rule effects. When Cedar's authorization engine is given a request and policy, conceptually it applies each rule in the policy to the request. To assemble these results into a final decision, it resolves ambiguous cases as follows. ❶ *Default Deny:* If no `permit` rule applies, the request is denied. ❷ *Deny Overrides Permit:* If a `forbid` rule applies, the request is always denied.

Entity Hierarchies. Entity type declarations can also specify the types of *parent* entities. Each entity has zero or more parents. The reflexive transitive closure of the *parent of* relation comprises Cedar's *ancestor hierarchy*. This hierarchy provides support for role-based access control: the ancestor-descendant relationship can express membership of users in roles as well as role hierarchy.

3   Problem Definition

This section presents a motivating example and then formally defines the policy tightening problem that RESTRICTER aims to solve.

3.1   Motivating Example

Suppose the program committee (PC) chairs of a popular computer security conference are setting up the HotCRP conference review system instance for this year.

---

[3] In Cedar, these are called "policy set" and "policy," resp. For our presentation, we choose the terms more commonly used in access control literature.

The current PC chairs obtained the policy from the previous year's chairs; this policy is the one from which the listing in Figure 1 samples. However, the chairs anticipate receiving a substantial number of paper submissions this year, which induced the decision of partitioning the papers into mutually disjoint areas (*e.g.*, usable security, software security, network security, *etc.*). In addition, they decided to have a decentralized administration by assigning an area to each reviewer. It is analogous to having a set of small conferences under a bigger conference.

In preparation, they extended every `Paper` to have an `area` attribute of type `Area`, denoting the area assigned to a paper. The `User` type is updated to include a new Boolean attribute `isAreaChair` and to replace the `isPcMember` attribute with an optional attribute `pcMember` of type `Area`, which when set indicates the user is a PC member for that area. The first rule in the example is modified to reflect the change. These modifications are shown in Figure 2.

```
// modified schema (snippet)
entity User { isPCChair: Bool, isAreaChair: Bool, pcMember?: Area};
entity Area;
entity Paper { authors: Set<User>, reviewers: Set<User>, area: Area};
// modified policy (snippet)
permit (principal, action == Action::"Read", resource is Paper)
when { principal has pcMember };
```

Fig. 2: Modified Cedar policy

We may observe in the log that each reviewer accesses only papers in their area. After simplification, RESTRICTER is able to tighten the modified rule in Figure 2 to:

```
permit(principal, action == Action::"Read", resource is Paper)
when { principal has pcMember && principal.pcMember == resource.area};}
```

which exactly captures the semantics of our observation.

3.2   Notations and Problem Definition

Notations. Let Σ be the schema that specifies the entity types, the attributes associated with them, the allowed hierarchies, and the allowed principals and resources for each action. Let $\mathcal{E}$ be the environment, also known as the entity store, that consists of the principals, resources, and their attributes. Let $\text{req} = \langle prin, act, obj \rangle$ be an access request that consists of the principal, action, and resource, respectively. Let $\mathcal{R}$ be the universe of all requests consistent with the schema. Let $\text{PolicyEval}(\text{req}, \mathcal{P}, \mathcal{E})$ be the function that evaluates a request req with respect to a policy $\mathcal{P}$ and environment $\mathcal{E}$ according to Cedar's semantics, returning an access decision $d \in \{\text{allowed}, \text{denied}\}$. Let $[\![\mathcal{P}]\!]$ be the set of requests allowed by $\mathcal{P}$, i.e., $[\![\mathcal{P}]\!] \overset{\Delta}{=} \{\text{req} \mid \text{req} \in \mathcal{R} \wedge \text{PolicyEval}(\text{req}, \mathcal{P}, \mathcal{E}) = \text{allowed}\}$. If R^+

is one of the permit rules in $\mathcal{P}$, then we can similarly define the set of requests allowed by R^+ as $[\![R^+]\!] \overset{\Delta}{=} \{\mathsf{req} \mid \mathsf{req} \in \mathcal{R} \wedge \mathsf{PolicyEval}(\mathsf{req}, \{R^+\}, \mathcal{E}) = \mathsf{allowed}\}$.

An access log $\mathcal{L} \subset \mathcal{R} \times \{\mathsf{allowed},\mathsf{denied}\}$ is a set of requests labeled with the decision for that request from the initial policy $\mathcal{P}_{\mathsf{init}}$. Policy $\mathcal{P}$ is *consistent* with $\mathcal{L}$, denoted $\mathcal{P} \sim \mathcal{L}$, *iff* $\forall \langle \mathsf{req},d \rangle \in \mathcal{L}.\mathsf{PolicyEval}(\mathsf{req},\mathcal{P},\mathcal{E}) = d$. We assume $\mathcal{P}_{\mathsf{init}} \sim \mathcal{L}$.

The Policy Tightening Problem. Given a type-safe Cedar policy $\mathcal{P}_{\mathsf{init}}$, an access log $\mathcal{L}$, a universe of access requests $\mathcal{R}$, an entity schema Σ, and an environment $\mathcal{E}$, the *policy tightening problem* is to synthesize a type-safe Cedar policy $\mathcal{P}_\star$ such that: (I) $\mathcal{P}_\star \sim \mathcal{L}$, and (II) $[\![\mathcal{P}_\star]\!] \subseteq [\![\mathcal{P}_{\mathsf{init}}]\!]$. The rationale for (II) is to avoid violating the least privilege principle. In what follows, "*policy*" refers to a type-safe Cedar policy unless mentioned otherwise. When not explicitly identified, we consider a fixed schema Σ and an environment $\mathcal{E}$. We use $\mathcal{P}_\star$ to denote the tightened policy throughout the paper.

It is easy to see that the policy-tightening problem is under-constrained, since any subset of the unexercised permissions can be removed. A trivial solution is to return $\mathcal{P}_{\mathsf{init}}$; our algorithm is designed to remove unexercised permissions without changing the size of the policy too much and modifying the structure of the policy.

4   Design Dimensions

We discuss three design dimensions and their trade-offs that one may consider in developing an approach like RESTRICTER.

Global vs. Local Tightening. The first dimension is to consider whether to tighten the whole policy at once (*global*) or each policy rule individually (*local*).

- While costly, global tightening has the benefit of simplifying and minimizing the *entire* policy during tightening.
- Despite having a narrower view, local tightening can be more scalable: one can focus on the portions of $\mathcal{L}$ and entity store that are relevant to individual rules.

The local approach is further facilitated by Cedar's *default deny, deny overrides permit* semantics (Section 2.1): *as permit rules are the only ones allowing accesses, it is sufficient to tighten only permit rules locally.* We can refine the policy tightening problem as follows.

Let the set of allowed log requests be $\mathcal{L}^+ \overset{\Delta}{=} \{\mathsf{req} \mid \langle \mathsf{req},d \rangle \in \mathcal{L} \wedge d = \mathsf{allowed}\}$, and the log slice with respect to permit rule R^+ be $\mathcal{L}{\downarrow}_{R^+} \overset{\Delta}{=} \mathcal{L}^+ \cap [\![R^+]\!]$. For policy tightening, it suffices to find a permit rule $R^+_\star$ for each permit rule R^+ in the input policy such that:

(I'): $R^+_\star \sim \mathcal{L}{\downarrow}_{R^+} \times \{\mathsf{allowed}\}$, and

(II'): $\forall \mathsf{req} \in \mathcal{R}, \mathsf{PolicyEval}(\mathsf{req}, \{R^+\}, \mathcal{E}) = \mathsf{denied} \implies \mathsf{PolicyEval}(\mathsf{req}, \{R^+_\star\}, \mathcal{E}) = \mathsf{denied}$.

Here, we need to focus only on the permitted part of the log in (I') as the denied part is guaranteed to be consistent by (II').

Synthesizing vs. Incremental Strengthening. The next design dimension is whether to generate a new policy or rule, replacing the previous one, or strengthen the current policy or rule incrementally.

- Synthesizing new policies or rules is *prima facie* a more general approach, and has a larger search space.
- Incremental strengthening has a much more tractable search space.

Permit vs. Deny. Even when one chooses the latter approach, there are two alternatives: (i) adding or broadening deny rules to remove over-privileges, or (ii) strengthening permit rules to reduce over-privilege. From the perspective of scalability, the search space for (ii) can be further reduced as it suffices to identify additional conditions to be imposed on the permit rules. The additional conditions can be in the form of restricting the **scope** or **body** of the permit rule. The conditions one can place in the **scope** of a Cedar rule are restricted to certain forms — too restrictive for productively tightening. For the **body**, one can always add a conjunctive formula (any Boolean-valued Cedar expression) to a rule to tighten it. This has the benefit of being amenable to incremental tightening of a rule by adding one conjunct at a time.

Encoding Approaches. Irrespective of global/local, and synthesis/refinement approaches to tightening, a primary challenge is to ensure that any automated reasoning approaches for policy tightening not only scale with the size of the input but also generate a tightened Cedar policy that is both type-safe and satisfies the restrictions (I) and (II) (or their primed versions) discussed above.

- We can take a *syntactic approach* to policy encoding, modeling the abstract syntax tree (AST) of our supported subset of Cedar as an algebraic datatype (ADT); or
- We can take a *semantic approach*, translating the policy as a quantifier-free first-order logic (QF-FOL) formula.

The *syntactic approach* (a.k.a. *deep embedding*) is natural: the policy to be synthesized is a constant of the ADT type, and PolicyEval is a recursive function over values of the ADT expressing Cedar's operational semantics. One can then invoke the SMT solver's finite model finding capability for policy tightening. In our evaluation, such an approach suffered from severe scalability issues, as *user-defined ADTs are not amenable to optimizations enjoyed by native SMT theories.*

In the *semantic approach* (a.k.a a *shallow embedding*) a Cedar policy $\mathcal{P}$ with a set of permit rules $\{R_1^+, R_2^+, ..., R_m^+\}$ and a set of forbid rules $\{R_1^-, R_2^-, ..., R_n^-\}$, can be viewed as a QF-FOL formula: $\bigwedge_{i=1}^{n} \boxminus(R_i^-) \wedge \bigvee_{j=1}^{m} \boxplus(R_j^+)$. Here, $\boxplus(\cdot)$ and $\boxminus(\cdot)$ are functions that take a permit and deny policy rule, respectively, and return their QF-FOL representation. A rule has the form $\langle p,a,o,\phi \rangle$, where p,a,o represent conditions on principals, actions, and resources respectively, and ϕ represents the body. A permit rule $R^+ = \langle p,a,o,\phi \rangle$ is translated to $\Box p \wedge \Box a \wedge \Box o \wedge \Box \phi$, where $\Box c$ is the translation (as a conjunctive formula in the QF-FOL fragment) of a Cedar condition c. Similarly, a forbid policy rule $R^- = \langle p,a,o,\phi \rangle$ is translated to $\Box p \wedge \Box a \wedge \Box o \to \neg \Box \phi$ (notice the negation).

Therefore, we can represent a Cedar policy as an SMT term mimicking the above QF-FOL form and restricting ourselves mostly to native theories when possible. PolicyEval conceptually reduces to the evaluation of an SMT term. Finding a policy/rule becomes an instance of a SyGuS problem where the function to be synthesized is a QF-FOL formula that captures the evaluation of all the

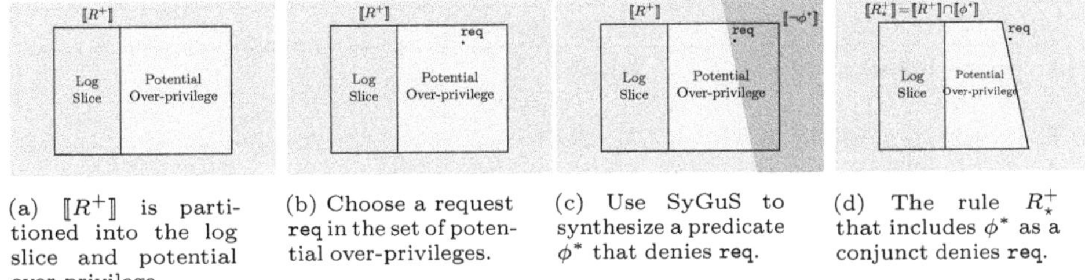

(a) $[\![R^+]\!]$ is partitioned into the log slice and potential over-privilege.

(b) Choose a request **req** in the set of potential over-privileges.

(c) Use SyGuS to synthesize a predicate ϕ^* that denies **req**.

(d) The rule $R^+_\star$ that includes ϕ^* as a conjunct denies **req**.

Fig. 3: An illustration of RESTRICTER's main idea for Step ❷. RESTRICTER chooses requests in the set of potential over-privileges to be denied by a conjunct ϕ (to be synthesized with SyGuS) while keeping the log slices permitted.

policies. We can also encode the original policy rules as SMT terms and use them as semantic constraints. A challenge still remains: *capturing Cedar type-safety as semantic constraints does not scale.*

5   RESTRICTER's Approach

RESTRICTER takes as input the current policy $\mathcal{P}_{\mathsf{init}}$, an environment $\mathcal{E}$, and an access log $\mathcal{L}$, and generates a tightened policy $\mathcal{P}_\star$. Out of the design choices mentioned in Section 4, RESTRICTER's approach embraces the following choices: (a) local, rule-based tightening; (b) incremental strengthening of each permit rule of the input policy through the introduction of conjunctive conditions; and (c) SyGuS-based approach for identifying the conjunctive conditions for rule strengthening. *By adding conjunctive formulas to permit rules, RESTRICTER syntactically guarantees that the tightened policy $\mathcal{P}_\star$ satisfies $[\![\mathcal{P}_\star]\!] \subseteq [\![\mathcal{P}_{\mathsf{init}}]\!]$.*

Sketch of RESTRICTER's Approach. RESTRICTER's algorithm is presented in Algorithm 1. At a high level, RESTRICTER's approach is as follows: ❶ collect each permit rule R^+_i from $\mathcal{P}_{\mathsf{init}}$; ❷ iteratively strengthen each permit rule R^+_i from $\mathcal{P}_{\mathsf{init}}$ *in parallel* to obtain a tighter permit rule $R^+_{i\star}$; and ❸ collect all the forbid rules of $\mathcal{P}_{\mathsf{init}}$ and combine them with the newly strengthened permit rules $R^+_{i\star}$ to obtain the tightened policy $\mathcal{P}_\star$. We mainly discuss Step ❷ of the overall approach.

High-level View of Tightening a Permit Rule (Step ❷). Before delving into the details, we first present a high-level view of RESTRICTER's approach to Step ❷; an illustration of the ideas is also presented in Figure 3. The rest of this section expands upon each of the following steps. RESTRICTER iteratively performs the following steps, while using the obtained strengthened policy of an iteration as input to the next, until some termination condition is met.

i. Calculate Relevant Log Slice: We first calculate $\mathcal{L}\!\downarrow_{R^+_i}$, the set of permitted requests in $\mathcal{L}$ that are also permitted by R^+_i.

ii. Calculate Approximate Over-Privileges in R^+_i: We then calculate an over-approximation of the set of over-privilege requests $\mathbb{R}$, such that all $\mathbf{req} \in \mathbb{R}$ satisfies $\mathbf{req} \notin \mathrm{dom}(\mathcal{L})$ (**req** is not in the log) and **req** is permitted by R^+_i.

Algorithm 1 Main algorithm of Restricter

1: **procedure** Restrict($\mathcal{P}_{\mathsf{init}}$, $\mathcal{L}$, $\mathcal{R}$, Σ, $\mathcal{E}$, t)
2:     $\mathcal{P}_* \leftarrow \emptyset$
3:     **for all** positive rule R^+ of $\mathcal{P}_{\mathsf{init}}$ **do**
4:         $R_\star^+ \leftarrow R^+$
5:         **repeat**
6:             **if** $[\![R_\star^+]\!] \setminus \mathcal{L}{\downarrow}_{R^+} = \emptyset$ **then break**
7:             $\mathsf{POP} \leftarrow [\![R_\star^+]\!] \setminus \mathcal{L}{\downarrow}_{R^+}$ ▷ *Steps i. and ii.*
8:             Pick requests $\{\mathtt{req}_i\}_i \subset \mathsf{POP}$
9:             $R_\star^+ \leftarrow$ Restrict_one($R_\star^+$, $\mathcal{L}{\downarrow}_{R^+}$, Σ, $\mathcal{E}$, $\{\mathtt{req}_i\}_i$)   ▷ *Steps iii. and iv.*
10:            **if** $R_\star^+ = \bot$ **then** restore the previous $R_\star^+$
11:        **until** $R_\star^+ = \bot$ for t times
12:        Insert the previous value of $R_\star^+$ into $\mathcal{P}_*$
13:    Insert all negative rules R^- into $\mathcal{P}_*$
14:    **return** $\mathcal{P}_*$

---

iii. Calculate Type-safe Cedar Predicate List: We precalculate the candidate predicates that SyGuS enumerates over. This approach avoids needing to encode Cedar's type checking rules into SyGuS, and instead delegate it to the meta-program generating the SyGuS problem instance.

iv. Invoke SyGuS: We finally invoke SyGuS to generate a type-safe Cedar predicate p such that $\boxplus(R_i^+) \wedge \square(p)$ (*i.e.*, the tighter rule $R_{i\star}^+$) allows every request in $\mathcal{L}{\downarrow}_{R_i^+}$, and denies at least one request in $\mathbb{R}$.

5.1   Synthesizing a tighter permit rule (Step ❷).

We now present descriptions of Steps (i) - (iii). Details of Step (iv) are in Section 6.

Finding a Separating Predicate for Tightening. Figure 3 shows the main idea of tightening a permit rule. We over-approximate the over-privileges as the accesses that do not appear in the log. Given the log and the permit rule, we compute the slice $\mathcal{L}{\downarrow}_{R^+}$. Then, the set of *potential unexercised over-privileges* $\mathsf{POP} \triangleq [\![R^+]\!] \setminus \mathcal{L}{\downarrow}_{R^+}$ consists of the requests permitted by the rule but not in $\mathcal{L}{\downarrow}_{R^+}$ (Figure 3a).

Given a permit rule $R^+ = \langle p,a,o,\phi \rangle$, we use SyGuS to find a *separating* predicate ϕ^* such that $R_\star^+ = \langle p,a,o,\phi \wedge \phi^* \rangle$ is consistent with the log slice, and denies some requests in POP (Figure 3c), Here, the restrictiveness requirement (II') can be dropped because $R_\star^+$ is syntactically guaranteed to be more restrictive. Denying some requests in POP makes $R_\star^+$ *strictly* more restrictive than R^+. We curate a list of candidate predicates that are type-safe, and the syntactic constraint becomes choosing one of the candidate predicates. If there is a predicate that satisfies the constraints, then $R_\star^+$ is the solution. Otherwise, $\bot$ is returned.

Avoiding Existential Quantification. To formulate that the separating predicate denies *some* (unspecified) request, we would need existential quantification. To avoid this, we explicitly choose some requests $\{\mathtt{req}_i\}_i$ in POP, and assert that at least one of them is denied in $R_\star^+$ (Figure 3b). The new rule $R_\star^+$ (if SyGuS

Algorithm 2 Restrict a rule by adding one conjunct

1: **procedure** RESTRICT_ONE(R^+, **Log_Slice**, Σ, $\mathcal{E}$, D)
2:    $\langle p,a,o,\phi \rangle \leftarrow$ symbolic encoding of R^+ under Σ
3:    $P \leftarrow$ Set of type-safe candidate predicates   ▷ *Step iii.*
4:    Ask SyGuS to construct a function $f : \mathcal{R} \rightarrow \{\text{allowed},\text{denied}\}$ that takes the form
      of a rule $\langle p,a,o,\phi \wedge \phi^* \rangle$ where $\phi^* \in P$, such that

       1. $\forall \text{req} \in \text{Log\_Slice}, f(\text{req}) = \text{allowed}$, and
       2. $\bigvee_{\text{req}^* \in D} (f(\text{req}^*) = \text{denied})$ holds   ▷ *Step iv.*

5:    **if** SyGuS fails **then return** $\bot$
6:    $R^+_\star \leftarrow$ encoding of $\langle p,a,o,\phi \wedge \phi^* \rangle$ in Cedar
7:    **return** $R^+_\star$

---

returns one) is strictly more restrictive than R^+ (Figure 3d). We can repeat this process until either POP is empty, or we fail to generate a predicate for a specified number of iterations (with different chosen requests req_i). The former means that we have obtained the tightest rule that only permits everything in the $\mathcal{L}\!\downarrow_{R^+}$. Section 9 discusses other termination conditions.

Generating Type-safe Predicates. To generate type-safe predicates, we analyze the Cedar schema and policy in the meta-program that generates candidate predicates. Then, we enumerate relevant type-safe predicates (Section 6.1) in our own symbolic encoding to be fed to SyGuS as syntactic constraints.

5.2   Choosing Concrete Requests to Deny

Explicit Enumeration. We can choose a random point in POP, or try to restrict every point in POP in parallel (see Figure 3b). Both would require explicit computation of the set POP, which entails enumerating over the set of requests $\mathcal{R}$ (with types restricted when possible) and checking whether $R^+_\star$ applies. As the size of $\mathcal{R}$ grows with the number of entities, this would introduce a large overhead.

Request Generation with SMT Solver. Alternatively, we can take the SMT encoding of the permit rule R^+, and ask the SMT solver to generate a concrete request req that satisfies R^+ and is not in $\mathcal{L}\!\downarrow_{R^+}$. If SyGuS fails to produce a tightened rule, then we add the picked request to the set of requests to be blocked and repeat. To reduce the likelihood of the SMT solver returning similar requests in different iterations, we randomize the entity encoding in our SMT representation, specifically, the mapping from entities to integers (discussed in Section 6.1).

6   Implementation

RESTRICTER is implemented in $\sim$2100 lines of Python and $\sim$400 lines of Rust. The main challenge is to implement the function RESTRICT_ONE (Algorithm 2). We first encode the input Cedar policy using our symbolic compiler as an SMT term. Along with the encoded policy, entity store and problem constraints, we invoke CVC5's [8] SyGuS engine [28], which takes semantic constraints and syntactic constraints in the form of SMT terms, to solve the tightening problem. The resulting rule, encoded as an SMT term, is translated back to a Cedar rule as output. The request generation routine also uses a fragment of the symbolic compiler to encode the policy rules.

6.1   Symbolic Encoding of Cedar

We now discuss our encoding of entity stores and policies as SMT terms to make them amenable to constraint solving (See Section 5.2) and synthesis (Finding separating predicate as discussed in Section 5.1). We also discuss how our approach differs from that of Cutler *et al.*'s symbolic compiler [18, Section 4].

There are three main ways that our encoding differs from the one in Cutler *et al. First*, Cutler *et al.*'s encoding does not consider specific entity stores, so operators like hierarchy relations are left as uninterpreted functions. We are given a concrete entity store, and can encode the hierarchy with concrete values.

Second, Cutler *et al.*'s *encoder* treat different entities as different types. The encoder meta-program instantiates the concrete types and pre-evaluate some expressions into the SMT solver. In contrast, the policy evaluation function in the *SMT solver* should take all possible entity types that are permitted by the schema as possible inputs. Therefore, we define one general entity type in the encoder and allow entities of any type to act as input to our function to synthesize, then make sure we only produce cedar-type-safe predicates in the encoder. As an example, consider the expression "`resource has ofPaper`" using the schema in 1a that is true when the type of `resource` is `Review`, and false otherwise. It is not possible to reason on the types of SMT terms using SMT terms. The approach in Cutler *et al.* tries each instantiation of types for `resource`. For type `Review`, for example, the expression is compiled directly to the SMT term `true`. In contrast, we have to evaluate this expression inside the SMT solver, since we cannot determine the concrete type of `resource` that goes into the policy evaluation beforehand. Therefore, our encoding of `has` would be a function that takes the entity type and consists of `ite`'s that test on the `type` (which is an element in the constructor of the one general entity type) and the name of the attribute.

Finally, we try to use simpler theories when possible in our encoding. As an example, we encode the name of the entities as integers instead of strings as the entity store only contains a small number of entities, and we can avoid invoking the string solver that may be expensive.

General entity type. In Cedar, an entity has a type and a name string. In our approach, all entities are encoded using a single datatype E that has a single constructor with `type` and `name` as integer arguments instead of the string type used in Cedar. We map each type in the schema and entity name in the entity store to an integer. In the semantic constraint, we state that the range of type and id of principals and resources is bounded by the image of these mappings. Equalities

Feature Support Examples

Equality	●	`principal.role == Role::"Teacher"`
Inequality	●	`User::"Alice" != User::"Bob"`
Attribute presence	●	`principal has pcMember`
Entity type test	●	`principal is Student`
Boolean negation	●	`!(principal in resource.authors)`
Integer comparison	◑	`principal.balance >= resource.cost`
Hierarchy membership	◑	`principal in resource.course`
Set membership	◑	`principal in resources.authors`
Conjunction, Disjunction	○	`true && true   true || true`
Integer operators	○	`4 * 10 + 5 - 3`

●: Full predicate generation support   ◑: Limited predicate generation support
○: No predicate generation support

Table 1: Summary of RESTRICTER's support for Cedar.

over entities are simply equalities over the type and id in the constructors. Representing these as integers rather than finite strings makes reasoning more efficient.

Entity attributes. The attributes of each entity type are defined in the schema with the name f and type t. For each attribute name-type pair $f:t$ in the entity store, we define a function $get_{f,t}: E \rightarrow \text{Option } t$ that takes an entity of any type that are in the entity store and returns either the value of the attribute of the entity or **None** when either (1) the attribute does not exist for the type, or (2) the attribute is marked optional for the entity in the store, and the given entity does not have the attribute. We also have for every attribute a predicate $has_f: E \rightarrow \text{Bool}$ that returns $true$ if $f:t$ is an attribute for e in the entity store for some type t.

Entity Hierarchy. We encode a given entity store's hierarchy relation as a concrete predicate by pre-computing the relation's reflexive, transitive closure.

6.2   Syntactic Constraints

We now describe the syntactic constraints that are posed to SyGuS to restrict candidate rules. If the original rule is $\langle p,a,o,\phi \rangle$, then the output rule has the form $\langle p,a,o,\phi \wedge \phi^* \rangle$, where ϕ^* is a type-safe Cedar predicate. We pre-compute the list of candidate type-safe Cedar predicates. Table 1 shows the subset of Cedar that RESTRICTER can parse, as well as the degree of RESTRICTER's ability to generate predicates utilizing the listed features. The features with only partial support for predicate generation, such as set membership tests, are intentionally limited to avoid enumerating arbitrary constants and instead only search applicable combinations of parameters, their attributes, and constants that appear in the entity store. Features not listed in Table 1, such as Cedar's various extension types, cannot be consumed by the current version of RESTRICTER.

Type-safety. For scalability, our encoding ensures type-safety outside SyGuS. As an example, the rule permit(principal,action,resource) when {principal.isAdmin} is not type-safe in Cedar unless all entity types that can be principals have the Boolean attribute `isAdmin`. In contrast, the following permit rule in Cedar `permit(principal,action,resource) when {`**`principal is User`**`&&principal.isAdmin};` is type-safe if `User` has the Boolean attribute `isAdmin`. To ensure our predicates are type-safe in Cedar, we syntactically restrict the types appearing in the expressions.

Equality. Since equality requires both sides to have the same type, we can enumerate possible equalities by enumerating all constants of each type, identifying entities with attributes of that type, and generating equalities between them. Enumerating the constants is straightforward, since the environment is known, and we can collect the values that appear in attributes of known entities. The main challenge is identifying when an entity has an attribute of a given type. To ensure an entity e has a given attribute f of type t, we can add a guard $has_f(e)$ at the front. Alternatively, for an entity e of type t_e, if t_e has a (required) attribute $f:t$, we can add the guard e `is` t_e. Now, for every entity $e_1:t_1$ and entity $e_2:t_2$ that have attributes $f_1:t$ and $f_2:t$, respectively, we can write the following type-safe predicate as a candidate predicate for RESTRICTER: e_1 `is` $t_1 \wedge e_2$ `is` $t_2 \longrightarrow e_1.f_1 == e_2.f_2$. We also consider equality where one side is a constant like e `is` $t \longrightarrow e.f == const$ where f and $const$ have the same type.

Similar constructions work for set membership and hierarchies. For example, for set membership, we can write the type-safe predicate for RESTRICTER: e_1 `is` $t_1 \wedge e_2$ `is` $t_2 \longrightarrow e_1.f_1 \in e_2.f_2$ if the type of f_1 is t and type of f_2 is `Set` t.

Attribute Chains. In Cedar, we can chain attributes together when the intermediate attributes have Entity or Record types. Using the schema in Figure 1a, if `resource` has type `Review`, we can write `resource.author.isPCChair`. It may be possible, depending on the schema, to have arbitrary nested or even cyclic attribute chains. For example, if `Paper` has a `metareview` attribute of type `Review`, then we can nest an arbitrary number of `.ofPaper.metareview` in `resource.ofPaper.metareview`.

While generating candidate expressions, instead of leaving the attribute accesses recursive on the grammar level, we enumerate all type-safe attribute chains up to a specified depth, which is a parameter of our algorithm, to limit our search space. We can ensure that the attribute chains are well-typed in Cedar, because we know the exact type of each attribute from the schema.

7   Evaluation

This section details our evaluation of RESTRICTER, beginning with our guiding research questions.

Q1: How frequently does RESTRICTER produce desired tightenings? When it fails to do so, how much over-privilege does it eliminate, and how much legitimate privilege does it preserve?

Q2: How well does the performance of RESTRICTER scale with respect to entity store size and log size (*i.e.*, the numbers of entities in the entity store and access requests in the access log)?

Some challenges arise in answering these questions which further influence our case study design and evaluations.

```
// P_tight
permit (principal, action in Action::"Read",resource is Paper)
when { principal has isPcMember && principal.pcMember == resource.area };
// P_init
permit (principal, action in Action::"Read",resource is Paper)
when { principal has isPcMember };
```

Fig. 4: Example corresponding rule pair (HotCRP)

Challenge 0: Unfortunately, none of the previous works on policy tightening [19,20,24] open source the tools or the test cases they used for evaluation. As such, we are not able to benchmark against the previous works.

Challenge 1: Due to their sensitive nature, it is difficult to obtain real-world examples of access control policies or logs. *Solution:* Our case studies are based on real-world management systems or examples found in the access control literature [1,2].

Challenge 2: Quantifying the answer to **Q1** requires a precise characterization of a policy's over-privilege. In practice, this is usually not available. *Solution:* Our case studies are designed with a loose initial policy and an intended tight policy. This intent is reflected indirectly in the access log and used to evaluate the policy rules produced by RESTRICTER, but is never given to it directly.

Challenge 3: The sizes of the entity store and log are not the only factors impacting the performance. The shape of the entity store (*i.e.,* the number and structure of relationships between entities) also affects performance. *Solution:* Our input generation approach is highly flexible, allowing control over the shape as well as the size of the entity store.

7.1   Design of Case Studies

We now overview the high-level design of our case studies, while the details can be found in the full version of the paper [32]. The two case studies used to evaluate RESTRICTER are a classroom management system inspired by Google Classroom [1] and a conference management system inspired by HotCRP [2]. Figure 4 shows an example for the HotCRP case study. For each case study, we crafted a schema and two policies: $\mathcal{P}_{tight}$, the desired tight policy; and $\mathcal{P}_{init}$, which we derived by deliberately introducing over-privilege in some rules of $\mathcal{P}_{tight}$ by dropping a conjunct. We generate the random entity stores and access logs for our case studies with a bespoke program ($\sim$3K LoC in Haskell). The program can generate sets—a.k.a. "families"—of related entity stores and logs of varying size, where entities and log entries in smaller members also appear in larger members. The members are indexed by a `size` parameter. The size of the entity store and logs are roughly linear to the `size` parameter.

7.2   Evaluation Results

We ran our experiments on a server with two Xeon Gold 5418Y CPUs totaling 96 threads and 256GB of RAM. We used cvc5 version 1.2.0 and the Cedar authorization engine version 3.2.1. For each test case, we invoke RESTRICTER to tighten every permit rule sequentially to obtain accurate measurements, even though RESTRICTER is parallelizable. We set the termination condition to 2 total failures, and generate three requests as a potential over-privilege to be denied in each iteration. For the datasets, we generated 100 dataset families using distinct seeds and varying log density from 30 to 100 percent with 10 percent increments. We repeat each experiment three times, taking the median running time (CPU time), among other statistics, as measurements. The full experimental results are in the full version of the paper [32].

Q1: Effectiveness. We run RESTRICTER on the input policy and compare its output to $\mathcal{P}_{\text{tight}}$. For cases where we do not get the intended tightening, we can still compute semantic similarities between the generated tightening and the intended tightening by enumerating all the over-privileges and intended privileges for each test case, and computing, for the generated tightening, the percentage of over-privileges remaining and intended (but unexercised) privileges removed. In the Google Classroom case study, all loosened rules are tightened with the expected conjunct (except with added type guards). For the HotCRP case study, two out of the five loosened rules were tightened to the ideal tight rules, while the other three still achieved good semantic similarity. Figure 5a shows the semantic similarity from one rule (with `size`=30) of the HotCRP case study. For this rule, both semantic similarity metrics improve (lower is better) as the log density increases, most likely because the real over-privileges got chosen instead of intended privileges in the request selection stage. Our results also confirm that our approach of adding one conjunct at a time discourages point solutions where we end up with an expression that denies one specific point.

In short, in our case studies, RESTRICTER successfully tightens most of the loose rules, and preserves most rules that were not loosened. On the few loosened rules where it was not tightened ideally, it still removes some over-privileges while keeping most intended privileges, even when the log density is low.

Q2: Scalability. To evaluate scalability, we measure RESTRICTER's running time. We vary the problem size in two dimensions: the `size` parameter and the log density. Figure 5b shows the time for each successful and failed tightening from SyGuS when varying the `size` parameter and the log density (ld). Figure 5b is representative, showing that in general, RESTRICTER runs in sub-exponential time when increasing the number of entities while being generally unaffected by the size of the log, which is proportional to the log density. This shows that RESTRICTER can handle problems of larger sizes efficiently.

8   Related Work

Manually developing access control policies is well-known to be challenging. There is a sizable body of literature on algorithms for mining (*a.k.a.* learning) access control policies. Work on learning ABAC or ReBAC policies starts with Xu et al. [34,33] and now spans many papers (*e.g.*, [26,21,30,11,17,12,16]). The

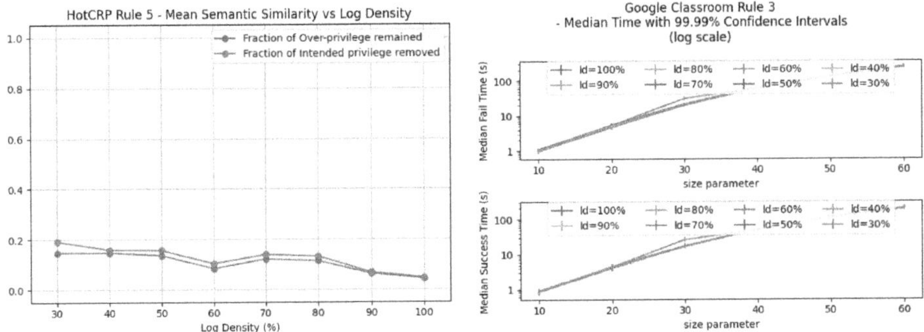

(a) Semantic Similarity of the synthesized rule as a function of the log density, in terms of the fraction of the over-privilege remained and the intended privilege removed (lower is better) in the HotCRP conference management case study.

(b) Running time (log scale) as a function of the size parameter and the log density (ld) with the 99.99% confidence intervals (stemming from the sign test for the median) of the median shown as error bars when SyGuS succeeds and fails to produce a tightening one of the rules in the Google classroom case study.

Fig. 5: Excerpt of the evaluation results in terms of semantic similarity of the generated rules versus the ideal ones and the running time.

general problem, like the policy tightening problem and for similar reasons, is under-constrained. None of these algorithms are based on SyGuS.

There are only a few efforts on algorithmically refining a given ABAC policy. IAM-PolicyRefiner [19] and Eiers *et al.* [20] both tighten AWS IAM policies whereas Mitani et al. [24] use machine learning to refine ABAC policies. IAM-PolicyRefiner and Eiers *et al.*, like RESTRICTER, tighten one rule at a time. However, both restrict the changes to a rule to *local* changes to predicates that appear in the original rule. RESTRICTER is able to introduce predicates absent in the original policy. This makes tightening possible in more cases. They mainly focus on generating regular expressions that restricts the names of the principal and resource, which is the main feature of IAM policies. We target Cedar, which is more expressive. Mitani *et al.* relies on "qualitative intention" as extra input, which RESTRICTER does not. This makes Mitani *et al.* less suitable for cloud access control providers, where user intent is not known a priori.

9 Discussion

Assumptions and Limitations. RESTRICTER assumes the input policy is type-safe, and that the schema and environment are fixed. A limitation of RESTRICTER is that it only considers tightening by adding a conjunction of atomic predicates to a rule. Extending RESTRICTER to consider more complex changes, such as adding arbitrary Boolean combinations of atomic predicates, is future work. We also assume that all permitted requests in the log should be permitted in the tightened policy. However, this may not be always true in practice. This is because there might be accidental or malicious accesses in the log that exercise permissions that are not intended. It is feasible to extend RESTRICTER to consider this case by loosening our semantic constraints to allow some of the entries in the log to not be permitted in the tightened rule.

Termination Criterion. By default, RESTRICTER stops tightening a permit rule when SyGuS fails a specified number of times. RESTRICTER supports other termination criteria, such as a preset timeout or termination when a certain percentage of tightening has been achieved (*i.e.*, a certain percentage of POP has been removed). Exploring such termination conditions is future work.

Rule overlap. If there is overlap between rules (*i.e.*, a request is permitted because of two or more permit rules), then RESTRICTER's rule-level tightening may not produce a policy that is as tight as expected. This is because, in order to remove this overlap, RESTRICTER would need to successfully tighten all such rules, and each such tightening must exclude the overlap. This difficulty gives rise to an interesting, orthogonal direction of future work: *can the techniques employed by RESTRICTER be effectively adapted to reducing overlap between rules, as an aid for policy maintainability?*

Manual Vetting. Our intention with RESTRICTER is for it to propose tightened rules that need to be vetted by administrators to ensure that tightening does not remove intended privileges. Manual vetting is practical, as RESTRICTER preserves the original rule's readability by limiting changes to each rule by adding conjuncts.

Using SyGuS. Using a SyGuS solver to choose from a set of pre-computed predicates, as RESTRICTER currently does, is one of many methods to consider for generating and evaluating potential tightenings. Although we do not currently use SyGuS for predicate generation, we wish to keep this open for further extension, since a bespoke term enumerator will likely be more difficult to extend.

Concerning the evaluation stage, one can encode the predicate directly into SMT constraints, but this would also require encoding *type safety* constraints. RESTRICTER avoids this difficulty by providing the SyGuS solver with *type-safe predicates*, effectively enforcing type safety through the grammar.

Missing features of Cedar. Currently, there are features in Cedar for which RESTRICTER does generate predicates during tightening. RESTRICTER can be modularly extended, under some assumptions, to support some of them. For example, predicates of the form $x \in S$ where S is a constant set can be generated by limiting the cardinality of S and considering only constants that appear in the log and entity store. Among the missing Cedar features, a notably challenging feature to support is linear integer arithmetic (LIA) predicates of the form $x + y < c$, where c is a symbolic constant to be synthesized. One can consider existing approaches to this problem to support this feature [3].

Data-Availability Statement

We have open-sourced RESTRICTER. RESTRICTER, the case studies, and the test case generation code can be found at https://github.com/REASONERSLab/Restricter.

References

1. Google Classroom. https://edu.google.com/intl/ALL_us/workspace-for-education/products/classroom/, accessed: 2025-05-08
2. HotCRP. https://hotcrp.com/, accessed: 2025-05-08
3. Abate, A., Barbosa, H., Barrett, C., David, C., Kesseli, P., Kroening, D., Polgreen, E., Reynolds, A., Tinelli, C.: Synthesising programs with non-trivial constants. Journal of automated reasoning $67(2)$, 19 (2023)
4. Abate, A., David, C., Kesseli, P., Kroening, D., Polgreen, E.: Counterexample guided inductive synthesis modulo theories. In: Chockler, H., Weissenbacher, G. (eds.) Computer Aided Verification. pp. 270–288. Springer International Publishing, Cham (2018)
5. Alur, R., Bodik, R., Juniwal, G., Martin, M.M., Raghothaman, M., Seshia, S.A., Singh, R., Solar-Lezama, A., Torlak, E., Udupa, A.: Syntax-guided synthesis. IEEE (2013)
6. Alur, R., Singh, R., Fisman, D., Solar-Lezama, A.: Search-based program synthesis. Communications of the ACM $61(12)$, 84–93 (Nov 2018). https://doi.org/10.1145/3208071, https://doi.org/10.1145/3208071
7. Amazon Web Services, Inc.: Cedar Language. https://www.cedarpolicy.com/en (2025), Accessed: Jan 2025
8. Barbosa, H., Barrett, C.W., Brain, M., Kremer, G., Lachnitt, H., Mann, M., Mohamed, A., Mohamed, M., Niemetz, A., Nötzli, A., Ozdemir, A., Preiner, M., Reynolds, A., Sheng, Y., Tinelli, C., Zohar, Y.: cvc5: A versatile and industrial-strength SMT solver. In: Fisman, D., Rosu, G. (eds.) Tools and Algorithms for the Construction and Analysis of Systems - 28th International Conference, TACAS 2022, Held as Part of the European Joint Conferences on Theory and Practice of Software, ETAPS 2022, Munich, Germany, April 2-7, 2022, Proceedings, Part I. Lecture Notes in Computer Science, vol. 13243, pp. 415–442. Springer (2022). https://doi.org/10.1007/978-3-030-99524-9_24, https://doi.org/10.1007/978-3-030-99524-9_24
9. Barrett, C.W., de Moura, L.M., Ranise, S., Stump, A., Tinelli, C.: The SMT-LIB initiative and the rise of SMT - (HVC 2010 award talk). In: Barner, S., Harris, I.G., Kroening, D., Raz, O. (eds.) Hardware and Software: Verification and Testing - 6th International Haifa Verification Conference, HVC 2010, Haifa, Israel, October 4-7, 2010. Revised Selected Papers. Lecture Notes in Computer Science, vol. 6504, p. 3. Springer (2010). https://doi.org/10.1007/978-3-642-19583-9_2, https://doi.org/10.1007/978-3-642-19583-9_2
10. Barrett, C.W., Sebastiani, R., Seshia, S.A., Tinelli, C.: Satisfiability modulo theories. In: Biere, A., Heule, M., van Maaren, H., Walsh, T. (eds.) Handbook of Satisfiability - Second Edition, Frontiers in Artificial Intelligence and Applications, vol. 336, pp. 1267–1329. IOS Press (2021). https://doi.org/10.3233/FAIA201017, https://doi.org/10.3233/FAIA201017
11. Bui, T., Stoller, S.D., Li, J.: Mining relationship-based access control policies. In: Proceedings of the 22nd ACM on Symposium on Access Control Models and Technologies. pp. 239–246 (2017)

12. Bui, T., Stoller, S.D., Li, J.: Greedy and evolutionary algorithms for mining relationship-based access control policies. Computers & Security **80**, 317–333 (jan 2019)
13. Casbin Organization: Casbin. https://casbin.org/ (2025), Accessed: Jul 2025
14. Chen, H., Li, N., Enck, W., Aafer, Y., Zhang, X.: Analysis of SEAndroid Policies: Combining MAC and DAC in Android. In: Proceedings of the 33rd Annual Computer Security Applications Conference. pp. 553–565 (2017)
15. Cloud Native Computing Foundation: Open Policy Agent. https://www.openpolicyagent.org/ (2025), Accessed: Jul 2025
16. Cotrini, C., Corinzia, L., Weghorn, T., Basin, D.: The next 700 policy miners: A universal method for building policy miners. In: Proceedings of the 2019 ACM SIGSAC Conference on Computer and Communications Security. pp. 95–112 (2019)
17. Cotrini, C., Weghorn, T., Basin, D.: Mining ABAC rules from sparse logs. In: 2018 IEEE European Symposium on Security and Privacy (EuroS&P). pp. 31–46. IEEE (2018)
18. Cutler, J.W., Disselkoen, C., Eline, A., He, S., Headley, K., Hicks, M., Hietala, K., Ioannidis, E., Kastner, J., Mamat, A., McAdams, D., McCutchen, M., Rungta, N., Torlak, E., Wells, A.M.: Cedar: A new language for expressive, fast, safe, and analyzable authorization. Proc. ACM Program. Lang. **8**(OOPSLA1) (apr 2024). https://doi.org/10.1145/3649835, https://doi.org/10.1145/3649835
19. D'Antoni, L., Ding, S., Goel, A., Ramesh, M., Rungta, N., Sung, C.: Automatically Reducing Privilege for Access Control Policies. Proceedings of the ACM on Programming Languages **8**(OOPSLA2), 763–790 (2024)
20. Eiers, W., Sankaran, G., Bultan, T.: Quantitative policy repair for access control on the cloud. In: Proceedings of the 32nd ACM SIGSOFT International Symposium on Software Testing and Analysis. pp. 564–575 (2023)
21. Gautam, M., Jha, S., Sural, S., Vaidya, J., Atluri, V.: Poster: Constrained policy mining in attribute based access control. In: Proceedings of the 22nd ACM on Symposium on Access Control Models and Technologies. p. 121–123. SACMAT '17 Abstracts, Association for Computing Machinery, New York, NY, USA (2017). https://doi.org/10.1145/3078861.3084163, https://doi.org/10.1145/3078861.3084163
22. Hu, V.C., Ferraiolo, D., Kuhn, R., Friedman, A.R., Lang, A.J., Cogdell, M.M., Schnitzer, A., Sandlin, K., Miller, R., Scarfone, K., et al.: Guide to Attribute Based Access Control (ABAC) Definition and Considerations (Aug 2019). https://doi.org/https://doi.org/10.6028/NIST.SP.800-162
23. Jha, S., Gulwani, S., Seshia, S.A., Tiwari, A.: Oracle-guided component-based program synthesis. In: Proceedings of the 32nd ACM/IEEE International Conference on Software Engineering-Volume 1. pp. 215–224 (2010)
24. Mitani, S., Kwon, J., Ghate, N., Singh, T., Ueda, H., Perrig, A.: Qualitative intention-aware attribute-based access control policy refinement. In: Proceedings of the 28th ACM Symposium on Access Control Models and Technologies. pp. 201–208 (2023)
25. MITRE: CWE Top 25 Most Dangerous Software Weaknesses. https://cwe.mitre.org/top25/archive/2024/2024_cwe_top25.html (2024)
26. Mocanu, D., Turkmen, F., Liotta, A.: Towards ABAC policy mining from logs with deep learning. In: The 18th International Multiconference, IS2015, Intelligent Systems, Ljubljana, Slovenia. (2015)
27. OWASP: Top 10 web application security risks. https://owasp.org/Top10/ (2021)
28. Reynolds, A., Barbosa, H., Nötzli, A., Barrett, C.W., Tinelli, C.: cvc4sy: Smart and fast term enumeration for syntax-guided synthesis. In: Dillig, I., Tasiran, S. (eds.) Computer Aided Verification - 31st International Conference, CAV 2019, New York City,

NY, USA, July 15-18, 2019, Proceedings, Part II. Lecture Notes in Computer Science, vol. 11562, pp. 74–83. Springer (2019). https://doi.org/10.1007/978-3-030-25543-5_5, https://doi.org/10.1007/978-3-030-25543-5_5

29. Standard, O.: eXtensible Access Control Markup Language (XACML) Version 3.0. A:(22 January 2013). URl: http://docs.oasis-open. org/xacml/3.0/xacml-3.0-core-spec-os-en. html (2013)

30. Talukdar, T., Batra, G., Vaidya, J., Atluri, V., Sural, S.: Efficient bottom-up mining of attribute based access control policies. In: 2017 IEEE 3rd International Conference on Collaboration and Internet Computing (CIC). pp. 339–348. IEEE (2017)

31. The SMT-Lib Initiative: SMT-Lib The Satisfiability Modulo Theories Library. https://smt-lib.org (2025), Accessed: Jan 2025

32. Wu, K.L., Jenkins, C., Stoller, S.D., Chowdhury, O.: Automatically tightening access control policies with restricter (2026), https://arxiv.org/abs/2601.14582

33. Xu, Z., Stoller, S.D.: Mining attribute-based access control policies. IEEE Transactions on Dependable and Secure Computing (2014). https://doi.org/http://dx.doi. org/10.1109/TDSC.2014.2369048, http://dx.doi.org/10.1109/TDSC.2014.2369048

34. Xu, Z., Stoller, S.D.: Mining attribute-based access control policies from logs. In: Proceedings of the 28th Annual IFIP WG 11.3 Working Conference on Data and Applications Security and Privacy (DBSec 2014). Lecture Notes in Computer Science, vol. 8566, pp. 276–291. Springer (2014)

Parallel SMT Solving
via Iterative Tree Partitioning

Tomáš Kolárik[1], Antti E.J. Hyvärinen[2], Seyedmasoud Asadzadeh[3], and
Natasha Sharygina[1]

[1] University of Lugano (USI), Lugano, Switzerland
[2] Certora Ltd
[3] Validas AG, Germany

Abstract. We present a novel algorithm for parallel solving of SMT
problems based on a partitioning process that divides the original problem into a tree structure in an iterative way. By enabling node revisiting,
the new method addresses the problem of partitioning divergence found
in prior approaches that frequently leads to longer runtimes compared to
sequential results. The resulting algorithm is highly flexible, offers a combination of partitioning, portfolio solving, and clause sharing, allows the
use of various partitioning functions, and scales gracefully with the available resources. We implemented the new approach in the tool SMTS on
top of the efficient sequential SMT solver OPENSMT. Our experimental results demonstrate a substantial improvement over OPENSMT in
logics QF_LRA and QF_LIA even when the partitioning approach utilizes
just a single solver. Notably, SMTS has consistently dominated several
divisions of the annual competition of parallel SMT solvers.

1 Introduction

Distributed SMT solving has remained a longstanding challenge [28,14,27,3].
A conventional approach is the *portfolio method* [26,10], where multiple SMT
solvers are run in parallel with differently seeded pseudorandom generators,
and possibly different configurations. Subsequent improvements add an efficient clause sharing mechanism [28,3] for communicating learned information.
However, these methods do not explicitly split the searched state space between the workers and therefore typically have a limited scalability [12]. Other
works [14,21,27,29] have studied partitioning the input problem, but they do
not revisit already attempted partitions (including the original problem), and
some also keep the structure fixed. As a consequence, in practice, such methods
often yield higher runtimes compared to a sequential approach [15], especially
within unsatisfiable benchmarks. A strong theoretical argument supports this
observation in Section 2.

Parallelizing the solving of a given, fixed SMT problem instance using a
divide-and-conquer approach is an elusive goal because of at least four reasons:
(1) It is hard to partition the search space so that each partition is, on average,
easier to solve than the original search space. (2) The runtime of SMT solvers

S. Junges and G. Katz (Eds.): TACAS 2026, LNCS 16505, pp. 130–149, 2026.
https://doi.org/10.1007/978-3-032-22752-2_7

is highly erratic [30]. Trivial changes in the input or random changes in the search algorithm typically result in a change of runtime up to orders of magnitude. For some problems, the erratic runtime is known to follow a Pareto–Lévy distribution [11,20], and it is very hard to estimate when this is the case for an arbitrary formula. (3) Combined with (1), the erratic runtime distributions of unsatisfiable instances behave particularly badly. It is helpful to interpret the combined runtime of instances tending toward the maximum runtime of an individual partition. (4) There are significant engineering challenges related to both SMT solving and parallel programming. In particular, to understand performance issues and ensure the correctness of the architecture, it is critical to implement low-level instrumentation in the solvers. This is all time-consuming and tedious.

Parallel SMT solver SMTS[4] is based on sequential solver OPENSMT [13,7], a consistent winner of several divisions in the annual competition [4,6]. Recently [2], the competition introduced tracks on parallel SMT solving, advancing the agenda of efficient distributed solutions. In the parallel tracks, SMTS consistently dominates similar divisions as OPENSMT. Moreover, in our experiments, SMTS also improves over the successful, yet sequential OPENSMT. These successes suggest that a promising approach for tackling the discussed issues of parallel SMT solving has been found. This paper presents, for the first time, the algorithms behind the competing tool SMTS. The novel approach is a specific combination of partitioning, portfolio solving, and clause sharing. The search is organised so that the system profits from the speedup available through the runtime distributions without making significant assumptions about the distribution shape, while still profiting from speedup available from search space partitioning. The approach is scalable both in the sense that it can maximally benefit from available resources, does not place limitations on the proportion between partitioning and portfolio solving, and is independent of the partitioning functions, SMT solvers, and the underlying theory. The central point of the algorithms is a *partition tree* [14] which logically divides the problem, allowing fine-grained allocation and cooperation of resources. The resulting parallel algorithm contributes with the following properties:

- Individual solvers are *never idle* and not restarted from scratch.
- Solvers *share* their *knowledge* efficiently according to the position in the tree.
- Partition tree *expands iteratively*, attempting gradually easier subproblems: Instances at a higher depth of the tree are often easier to solve, although there are important counterexamples (cf. Section 2).
- Partition tree *expansion* is *general*, allowing various partitioning functions.
- The tree is *not overexpanded*, and the expansion rate is configurable.
- Random seed and/or parameters of solvers are *not fixed* but change regularly. Particular instances may be *revisited* (i.e., reattempted) with a different setup and knowledge.
- The approach is *highly flexible* in the configuration of particular tasks.

---

[4] The competing tool inherits its name from the older system [22,21] but shares with it only the infrastructure for communicating with the underlying OPENSMT solvers.

The experiments, as well as the success in the past SMT competitions, confirm that the new parallel approach improves substantially over the long-standing sequential baseline OPENSMT, scales gracefully with an increasing number of solvers, and outperforms competitors. Moreover, the experiments demonstrate that the partitioning remains efficient despite limited resources, showing an improvement over OPENSMT with as few as a single solver.

Related Work. The most similar approach [27] (CVC5-CLOUD) to the one presented in this paper applies a portfolio of multiple partitioning strategies and builds the partition tree iteratively, but does not incorporate clause sharing. A further partitioning method [29] (Z3-PARTI-Z3++) targets the level of arithmetic variables: the partitioning is not done on existing atoms, but it splits to cases within the arithmetic domain of the variables, possibly creating brand new atoms. Yet, likewise, it omits clause sharing. In contrast, a recent work [3] (SMT-D) focuses on portfolio-based solving with extensive clause sharing and employs simple heuristics to assess clause usefulness, but does not partition. All three works have in common that they are not as general and do not combine all the issues this paper addresses at once. In particular, they do not apply partitioning together with clause sharing and do not revisit already attempted instances.

An earlier work [21] aimed at a combination of partitioning and clause sharing, but built the partition tree statically [14] using a size fixed to the available resources, which is fundamentally different than iterative partitioning that must manage and balance the tree on-the-run. It also used a binary format for clause sharing, which made the approach unportable for other underlying SMT solvers. Now obsolete for years, it was formerly implemented in SMTS and is now replaced by the new algorithms presented in this paper.

Other parallel SMT solvers focus on certain logics. For example, some solvers are focused on bitvectors or floating-point numbers (BITWUZLA [23], or [25]) or equalities with uninterpreted functions [8]. The theorem provers iPROVER [9] and VAMPIRE [19] support parallel solving in logics with quantifiers. Other approaches support simple portfolio solving (e.g., YICES2 [10], PAR4 [26], or [28]), or parallelize the underlying theory solvers (e.g., the simplex algorithm [1]).

Acknowledgement. This work was conducted as part of the "Formal Reasoning on Neural Networks" project funded by the Hasler Foundation, Switzerland and Swiss National Science Foundation grant 200021-236601 "Cross theory rigorous program verification using Constrained Horn clauses".

2   Background

Partitioning. A given input SMT formula φ can be partitioned into a *partition tree* [14] where the root node represents φ. Given a parent node associated with formula P, its i-th child represents a formula $P \wedge C_i$ produced by a *partitioning function* [17] such that for all i, the disjunction $\bigvee_i C_i$ holds, and for all $j \neq i$, $\neg(C_i \wedge C_j)$. Both *scattering* [17] and variable-level partitioning [29] are special cases of such a function. Hence, each node of the tree represents a logical subproblem of the original formula φ and is not directly coupled to computational resources. For each node, the associated formula is satisfiable iff any formula within the subtree is satisfiable. Unsatisfiable formula of a parent node implies unsatisfiability in *all* child nodes and vice versa. A *solver* is an SMT solver in the form of a computational resource along with its internal state, that is dynamically assigned to a node in the partition tree.

Runtime Distribution. Given a fixed formula, the runtime of a solver on the formula follows essentially a random distribution. While most SMT solvers aim to be deterministic, their runtime is unstable [30] w.r.t. small changes in the input formula (including the order of constraints) that change the runtime in such a way that it is practical to model it using a runtime distribution. In portfolio-based SMT solving, it is common to introduce this randomness deliberately in the solving process to gain speedup. This is typically done either through transformations on the formula or using deterministically seeded pseudorandom number generators for breaking ties in heuristics. Consider the case where for solving a fixed formula, the randomness is obtained in one of the above mentioned processes. We write that the probability of the runtime being less than or equal to t is $q(t)$. Assuming no delays in communication, the expected runtime is $\int_0^\infty tq'(t)\,dt$, where q' is the differential of q, i.e., the (differential) probability that the runtime is exactly t. Based on this, we can derive the expected runtime of a portfolio of n solvers as $\int_0^\infty ntq'(t)(1-q(t))^{n-1}\,dt = \int_0^\infty (1-q(t))^n\,dt$, where the integral over t is weighted by the probability that any of the n solvers finishes exactly at time t and that no other solver did before that time: $(1-q(t))^{n-1}$.

A similar formula can be derived for the runtime of a single partition. An instance is *perfectly partitioned* to n if for every run of a randomized solver that solves the original instance in time t, there is a corresponding run in all the partitioned instances that takes time $\bar{t} \leq t$. A reasonable relationship between $\bar{t}$ and t is given by $\bar{t} = t/n^\alpha$, where $0 \leq \alpha \leq 1$ is a constant. Here, the expected runtime of a single instance is $\int_0^\infty tq'(n^\alpha t)\,dt$. Assuming now an unsatisfiable problem on the input perfectly partitioned to n, the distribution of the runtime of solving all the resulting partitions in parallel with no delays is $q(n^\alpha t)^n$. That is, by time t, all n instances have been solved and the expected runtime is given by $\int_0^\infty tq'(n^\alpha t)^n\,dt = n^{1-\alpha}\int_0^\infty tq(t)^{n-1}q'(t)\,dt$. The efficiency of a parallel portfolio and the perfect partitioning described above depend on the shape of the distribution q, α and n. Notably, unless $\alpha = 1$, there is always a distribution where the partitioning approach is not only worse than the corresponding portfolio, but even worse than sequential solving [12,16]. While this is a theoretical argument, similar behavior is observable also in practical examples [15]. Intuitively, the issue is that the factor $n^{1-\alpha}$ increases the expected runtime at most linearly (with $\alpha = 0$) w.r.t. the number of solvers, and this increase needs to be counteracted by the exponential attenuation inside the integral in order to gain an efficient partitioning. A possible improvement is solving the instance at the root node in parallel with the leaves. The idea can be generalized recursively.

These observations motivate the treatment of partitioning discussed in this paper, with the key insights that the number of created partitions is not fixed, the partitions are organised into a tree, and that also internal nodes of the tree are revisited, that is, reattempted, which addresses the requirement to solve all partition leaves of the tree of unsatisfiable instances.

3   Partitioning SMT Problems

The partition tree can be fixed [14], that is, built only during the initial phase based on the available resources. This paper presents a different, *iterative* process of building the partition tree, offering more fine-grained partitioning not limited by the number of available solvers. In the following, this section describes in detail how such a tree is expanded and pruned on demand, as well as the schedule that determines the order of solving the instances in the tree. Overall, the partitioning process is divided into four main components:

- *Node selection algorithm* selects a list of nodes in the partition tree for the placement of solvers, preferring nodes with a higher depth since they are on average easier to solve. Furthermore, nodes can be revisited later, that is, they can be attempted repeatedly.
- *Solver placement* maps concrete solvers to the selected nodes. Notably, the placement supports solver preemption: a solver may be relocated once a computational time budget expires. Solvers do not start from scratch after moving but maintain their solving state. Placement aims at maximizing the reuse of the state when moving solvers to different nodes by choosing solvers from the close neighborhood of the selected nodes by exploiting the incrementality of SMT solvers. Even multiple solvers can be placed into a single node, achieving (partial) portfolio solving.
- *Partition tree expansion* expands the tree iteratively. The activation of the partitioning is heuristic. The tree is kept balanced, and it avoids rapid expansion (i.e., the size of the tree is bounded) to allow revisiting internal nodes, otherwise, only new nodes would be attempted.
- *Partition tree pruning* removes all nodes from the tree that are already (transitively) solved.

This results in a flexible approach that allows scaling gracefully even on difficult problems and using extensive computational resources. The presented algorithms are parametrized and thus configurable on demand. The list of all available parameters, along with their description and suggested default values, is available online [18]. We first present a sequential version of the top-level algorithm, and then a derived parallel version.

Sequential Partitioning. The sequential algorithm is described in Alg. 1. The algorithm takes as input a formula φ and an overall (wall) runtime limit T_W that can be infinite. The algorithm outputs **sat** or **unsat**, or **unknown** if the elapsed time since the start of the program reaches T_W.

Algorithm 1: Sequential Partitioning

Input: formula φ, overall timeout $T_W > 0$
Global: solver timeout $T_S > 0$
Output: sat, unsat or unknown

1   $tree \leftarrow \text{PARTITIONTREE}(\varphi)$ $\triangleright$ initial tree having only the root node of φ

2   **loop**
3     $(node) \leftarrow \text{SELECTNODES}(tree, 1)$ $\triangleright \approx$ DFS traverse of unsolved nodes (Alg. 2)
4   **const** $(s, t) \leftarrow \text{SOLVE}(node)$
5   **assert** $s = \texttt{TIMEOUT} \iff t \geq T_S$
6     $node.status \leftarrow s;\ node.time \leftarrow node.time + t$

7   **if** $\text{RUNTIME}() \geq T_W$ **then** $\triangleright$ overall time including expansions
8 | **return** unknown
9   **if** $s = \texttt{SAT}$ **then**
10 | **return** sat
11   **assert** $s \in \{\texttt{UNSAT}, \texttt{TIMEOUT}\}$

12    $\text{PRUNEUNSATBRANCHES}(tree)$ $\triangleright$ remove already solved branches (Alg. 3)
13   **assert** $\forall\, node \in tree : node.status \in \{\texttt{TIMEOUT}, \texttt{NEW}\}$
14   **if** $\text{EMPTY}(tree)$ **then**
15 | **return** unsat

16    $\text{TRYEXPANDTREE}(tree, 1)$ $\triangleright \approx$ BFS traverse of $\texttt{TIMEOUT}$ leaves (Alg. 4)

All presented algorithms may use the field *global* which stands for global configuration variables. These variables are not necessarily fixed and can be modified during the computation, by the user or by an automated algorithm, providing further flexibility. After initializing the partition tree *tree* from φ, the algorithm enters the main loop. First, the loop calls SELECTNODES (see Alg. 2), the node selection algorithm, which takes *tree* and a number n as input and returns a list of n nodes where the solvers will be placed. Note that multiple appearance of nodes in the list is allowed. In the sequential version, $n = 1$. The function prefers the nodes with the highest depth, intuition being that they correspond to the most reduced portions of the original formula.

Given the selected node, Alg. 1 runs the (only available) solver on the corresponding formula. Note that the solver parameters, such as the random seed, are not fixed for these executions and can vary over time. The solver returns the resulting status $s \in \{\texttt{SAT}, \texttt{UNSAT}, \texttt{TIMEOUT}\}$ and the computing time t spent in the node. The *solver timeout* T_S is the maximum allowed runtime spent in a particular node. Status s is $\texttt{TIMEOUT}$ if and only if t reaches the solver timeout (i.e., $t \geq T_S$). The status is stored in the node variable *node.status* and the computing time is accumulated into the runtime spent in the node in total, *node.time*. If the overall timeout T_W is reached, the procedure is aborted and the algorithm returns unknown. If the status is $\texttt{SAT}$, the algorithm returns sat since proving a satisfying model for any node in the tree satisfies the root. If the status is not $\texttt{SAT}$, the algorithm prunes all nodes that have already been shown unsatisfiable in $\text{PRUNEUNSATBRANCHES}$ (Alg. 3). After that, all remaining nodes are guaranteed to be either in the state TIMEOUT or NEW assigned to newly created nodes. The original formula is proved unsatisfiable if and only if PRUNEUNSATBRANCHES removes all nodes from the partition tree.

Finally, the partition tree may be expanded in function TRYEXPANDTREE (Alg. 4), parameterized by a number n, the minimum size of the tree that blocks rapid expansion. In the case of one solver, again $n = 1$. When expanding the tree, the algorithm selects a node with the status TIMEOUT and prefers the lowest depth in the tree (contrary to SELECTNODES), resembling a breadth-first search. Alg. 1 loops until it finds a solution or times out. Details on Algs. 2–4 follow.

Algorithm 2: Selection Algorithm (SELECTNODES)

Input: partition tree *tree*, $n \geq 1$ #nodes to return
Global: solver timeout $T_S > 0$
Output: selected nodes *nodes* for the placement of solvers ($|nodes| = n$)

```
1  function SELECTNODES(tree, n)
2      nodes ← ()                                    ▷ start with an empty list
3      const maxDepth ← MAXDEPTH(tree)

       ▷ loop forever over max. allowed #timeouts
4      for maxTouts ← 0; ⊤; maxTouts ← maxTouts + 1 do
5          for d ← maxDepth; d ≥ 0; d ← d − 1 do          ▷ prefer the deepest nodes
6              foreach node ∈ NODESATDEPTH(tree, d) do
7                  if node.time ≤ maxTouts · T_S then  ▷ total time spent in the node
8                      nodes.APPEND(node)
9                      if |nodes| = n then
10                         return nodes
```

Alg. 2 describes function SELECTNODES, the key novel technique in efficient distribution of the available solvers across the partitions. The function is parameterized by the number of nodes n it should return. At the top level, it loops over *maxTouts*, the maximum number of allowed timeouts in particular nodes: in line 7, it considers only those nodes with accumulated computing times below a multiple of the solver timeout T_S. Recall that only nodes that have not yet been solved are handled here (cf. Alg. 1, line 13). At the beginning, *maxTouts* is zero, meaning that nodes that have not been visited (i.e., nodes with the status NEW) are preferred. The second criterion is the depth of the nodes: given that two nodes have similar accumulated computing time, the one with a higher depth is strictly preferred. Within the same depth, the order of the nodes is arbitrary. Nodes that satisfy the criteria are appended to the list of nodes that is returned once the desired number of nodes n is reached. Although the function loops unconditionally at the top level, it always terminates because all *node.time* values are finite. Observe that (a) a node may be selected *multiple times* within a function call, in cases of an insufficient number of available alternative nodes, and (b) nodes may be *revisited* after failed attempts of solving the instance, which is useful due to the runtime distribution of SMT instances. Revisiting is meaningful if the instance is reattempted with a different random seed, different parameters of a solver, or a different set of learned clauses.

Algorithm 3: Partition Tree Pruning (PRUNEUNSATBRANCHES)

Input: partition tree *tree*

```
1  function PruneUnsatBranches(tree)
2  │   tree.root ← PruneUnsatBranchesRec(tree.root)

3  function PruneUnsatBranchesRec(node)
4  │   if node.status = UNSAT then
5  │   │   return None
6  │   assert node.status ∈ {TIMEOUT, NEW}
7  │   if |node.children| = 0 then
8  │   │   return node                              ▷ keep unsolved leaf
9  │   foreach child ∈ node.children do
10 │   │   child ← PruneUnsatBranchesRec(child)
11 │   if |node.children| = 0 then
12 │   │   return None                 ▷ all children eliminated: recursively UNSAT
13 │   return node                              ▷ keep unsolved parent node
```

Alg. 3 describes function PRUNEUNSATBRANCHES. At the beginning, all nodes of the partition tree are in one of the states {UNSAT, TIMEOUT, NEW}. The function ensures that no nodes associated with a transitively unsatisfiable formula remain in the tree. Nodes assigned to None are not counted as if they were removed. It is implementation-dependent whether the node is removed, overwritten, or else. Hence, the function recursively removes all UNSAT nodes and parent nodes that become childless. Nodes with pruned children are not reexpanded because the function ensures that parent nodes never become leaves again.

Finally, Alg. 4 describes the function TRYEXPANDTREE that is responsible for the expansion of the partition tree. Importantly, the function tries to avoid rapid expansion using multiple factors. First, the algorithm may abort the expansion based on the parameter n—the minimum size of the tree. If the tree is small enough, it is always expanded. The size of the tree changes dynamically: it is increased by TRYEXPANDTREE but also reduced by PRUNEUNSATBRANCHES. When expanding, it selects one of the leaf nodes closest to the root. One is guaranteed to exist[5] because the tree is finite. Such a selection also guarantees that the tree remains more or less *balanced*, because it does not increase the depth difference between the shallowest and deepest leaves. The expansion applies the partitioning function on the node and creates p children. If the tree is larger

---

[5] In an edge case when no more partitioning constraints can be generated, and therefore a node cannot be expanded further, such nodes should be skipped. The expansion should be skipped altogether if the tree is already maximal.

Algorithm 4: Partition Tree Expansion (TRYEXPANDTREE)

Input: partition tree *tree*, $n \geq 1$ minimum size of the tree
Global: $k \geq 1$ maximum factor of the size of the tree (default: 2),
$\quad\quad p \geq 2$ #created child nodes when partitioning (default: 2)

```
 1 function TryExpandTree(tree, n)
 2 │   if |tree| ≥ n then                              ▷ may abort expansion for large trees
 3 │   │   if |tree| ≥ k · n then                      ▷ abort for too large trees
 4 │   │   │   return
 5 │   │   if ∃ node ∈ tree : node.status = NEW then   ▷ abort on fresh nodes
 6 │   │   │   return
 7 │   │   const r ← Random()                          ▷ r ∈ ]0, 1[
 8 │   │   if r ≥ 1/p then                             ▷ sometimes abort based on p
 9 │   │   │   return
10 │   node ← SelectShallowestLeaf(tree)              ▷ guaranteed to exist
11 │   Expand(tree, node)                             ▷ split the node to p children
```

---

than n, the algorithm still needs to provide sufficient opportunities for the distribution of the solvers, while avoiding excessive growth of the tree with respect to the available solvers. If the relative size exceeds the configured maximum factor k, or if there are any unvisited nodes, the expansion aborts. Finally, the expansion may also be aborted based on a random choice and parameter p.

Optimizations. Alg. 4 may sometimes restrict tree expansion excessively. For example, having just one solver (i.e., $n = 1$), and with the default $k = 2$, the tree would be expanded at most once, resulting in a fixed tree. Using a fixed solver timeout T_S here could even result in nontermination. Notably, the choice of T_S is crucial in general, since low values are often suitable for easy problems but insufficient for difficult ones. To address all these issues, T_S dynamically and indefinitely increases over time, which also ensures termination of Alg. 1. As another optimization, Alg. 4 excludes nodes that have already timed out a certain number of times when computing the size of the tree $|tree|$ (e.g., when $node.time \geq 4 \cdot T_S$). Further optimizations can be found online [18].

Parallel Partitioning. The parallel version of Alg. 1 is presented in Alg. 5. There are several differences between them. Most importantly, multiple CPUs are allocated, for each of which it assigns a standalone solver, resulting in C parallel solvers. The number of selected nodes n for function SELECTNODES (Alg. 2) depends on C and also on a new global parameter *minPortfolio*. If *minPortfolio* $= 1$, exactly one solver is allocated to each selected node (i.e., $n = C$). Still, multiple solvers may be placed into one node if it is selected multiple times. When *minPortfolio* > 1, (partial) portfolio solving is used: multiple solvers solve a node simultaneously at the expense of solving fewer nodes.

Consequently, the placement algorithm, which is omitted in the sequential partitioning, becomes important in the parallel version. Function PLACE-

---

Algorithm 5: Parallel Partitioning

Input: formula φ, $C \geq 1$ #allocated CPUs, overall timeout $T_W > 0$
Global: minimum size of internal portfolios $minPortfolio \geq 1$ (default: 1)
Output: sat, unsat or unknown

---

1   $tree \leftarrow \text{PARTITIONTREE}(\varphi)$
2   $S \leftarrow \text{SOLVERS}(C)$ ▷ initialize C parallel solvers
3   **const** $n \leftarrow \lceil C/minPortfolio \rceil$ ▷ #nodes required for placement

4   **loop**
5 | $nodes \leftarrow \text{SELECTNODES}(tree, n)$ ▷ Alg. 2
6 | $\text{PLACESOLVERS}(S, nodes)$ ▷ map the nodes to the closest solvers
7 | **if** $|tree| \geq n$ **then**   ▷ if the tree is large enough …
8 | | $\text{WAITONEVENT}(tree, S, T_W)$ ▷ … wait for a change (up until T_W)
9 | **if** $\text{RUNTIME}() \geq T_W$ **then**
10 | | **return** unknown
11 | $\text{GETSTATUS}(tree, S)$ ▷ update the status of all solvers and nodes in the tree
12 | **if** $\exists\, node \in tree : node.status = \text{SAT}$ **then**
13 | | **return** sat
14 | $\text{PRUNEUNSATBRANCHES}(tree)$ ▷ Alg. 3
15 | **assert** $\forall\, node \in tree : node.status \in \{\text{TIMEOUT}, \text{NEW}\}$
16 | **if** $\text{EMPTY}(tree)$ **then**
17 | | **return** unsat
18 | $\text{TRYEXPANDTREE}(tree, n)$ ▷ Alg. 4

SOLVERS maps C solvers to n nodes. At that moment, all solvers and nodes have a fixed position in the partition tree. For every node, we select the solver located closest to the node. These paths may include upward edges as well, and it is undefined how the function should prioritize downward edges over upward, if at all. A path with only downward edges means that the solver is moved from a parent node to a descendant, ensuring full logical overlap of both instances. With upward edges, on the other hand, a part of the formula must be backtracked.

Another important difference with Alg. 1 is that function PLACESOLVERS runs the solvers in the background. Hence, rapid executions of the busy loop are avoided using a sleep. Furthermore, in a stable state when the partition tree is large enough and all solvers are distributed, it is worthless to execute anything until some of the solvers finish or time out, or new nodes from the expansion are delivered. Therefore, in such cases, it uses a function WAITONEVENT. However, if the tree is small, it does not wait because it may be useful to expand the tree. After that, the state of the tree must be synchronized with the solvers, using a function GETSTATUS. This call updates the status and the computing time of all nodes. If any of the nodes is in the SAT state, the algorithm returns sat. Otherwise, it removes all unsatisfiable branches in the tree and may conclude unsat, the same way as in the sequential algorithm.

Finally, the function calls TRYEXPANDTREE (Alg. 4), this time using parameter n, which is the same as in SELECTNODES because it also represents the sufficient number of nodes in the tree. The expansion in line 11, similarly to solving, does not block the execution and is resolved concurrently in the background, while ensuring that every node is expanded at most once. Note that line 7 in Alg. 5 is the same as line 2 in Alg. 4: Alg. 5 calls WAITONEVENT only if the tree is large enough, which is when it also tries to avoid rapid expansion.

Incremental Solving. In order to maintain efficient placement and execution of the solvers in the nodes of the partition tree, the SMT solvers are run *incrementally* and are never restarted from scratch. The root node defines the input formula φ and all descendant nodes only incrementally define additional constraints that stem from the expansion of the tree done by a partitioning function. Hence, any relocation of a solver in the tree corresponds to manipulating the assertion stack [5]: every descend to a child node corresponds to a push operation, while an ascend to a parent corresponds to a pop. The overhead of incremental solving is negligible: the traversal of the tree is logarithmic. Moreover, incremental solving is also useful for learning clauses from other solvers.

4   Lemma Sharing

In this paper, we assume that every shared lemma is a clause generated by the SAT solver. Hence, we do not distinguish between clause sharing and lemma sharing. The lemma-sharing system is based on SMT solvers sending some clauses to a central server, and on the other end on distributing some of these clauses back. A few critical parts need to be addressed carefully for this to work: (a) ability to serialize any possible clause, (b) efficient sharing of clauses learned at various parts of the partition tree in an incremental way, (c) efficient management of the central database of shared lemmas w.r.t. the partition tree, and (d) filtering which clauses to send from solvers to the server (and vice versa).

Serializing Clauses. We assume that the SMT solvers provide a representation in SMT-LIB2 [5] for any literal, and therefore any clause as well. This is available using a mapping from Boolean atoms in the underlying CDCL solver to terms at the theory level. Since SMT terms may have an arbitrarily shared structure, the serialization uses `let` terms, guaranteeing a representation linear in the number of nodes in a DAG representation of the term. As a result, the serialized clauses can even be shared among completely different SMT solvers that comply with the representation. A similar approach appears also in [3].

Learning Shared Clauses. To keep track of the assumptions in the partition tree, the SMT solvers introduce *frame literals*. They might appear in learned clauses and determine for which nodes in the partition tree the clause is valid, depending on the depth of the nodes. All such literals are filtered from the clause before being sent to the server. When another solver receives the clause, it inserts the clause in the disjunction with a frame literal that is unique to the node in the partition tree where the solver is located[6]. These clauses are enabled by assuming the negation of all the frame literals. This gives a direct way of identifying the deepest node in the partition tree where the clause is valid[7].

The lemmas sent to the server are pairs (*string, node*), where *string* is the serialized SMT-LIB representation of the lemma and *node* is a unique representation of the node within the tree. The node representation also determines the path to the subtree rooted at the node within which the lemma is valid. For example, *node* at depth n can be a sequence of integers $[i_k]_{k=0}^n$ that directly encodes the path to the node, or the integer $\frac{p^n-1}{p-1} + i$ where p is the arity of the tree and $i \in \{0, \ldots, p^n - 1\}$ is the ordinal number of the node within depth n.

Lemma Server. The lemma server collects and distributes back lemmas to the solvers. The solvers either *pull* lemmas (i.e., submit a request for lemmas), or *push* new lemmas. The lemmas are maintained in a structure reflecting the partition tree—a *lemma database*—so that each node contains the lemmas that are valid for all nodes of the subtree rooted at the node. Hence, the lemmas are not distributed to the ancestor nodes. The path to this subtree is extracted from the serialized lemmas.

Lemmas in the database are scored so that lemmas that have been learned several times have a higher score. When a pull request comes from a solver, the lemma server collects all eligible lemmas from the tree structure that have not yet been sent to this solver. If the number of lemmas exceeds the number requested by the solver, only the highest-scored lemmas are sent to the solver.

Filtering Clauses. SMT solvers must avoid the accumulation of too many clauses in the server. The first filtering of the clauses to share is done by the CDCL algorithm: Only clauses that are currently in the CDCL clause database (e.g., based on their activity score) are considered. These include all unit clauses found by the solver (that are valid for every node in the partition tree) and other clauses with a certain limited length. Given these clauses, solvers share only those where no literal has more than a certain number of nodes in the DAG representation of the term. Solvers also ensure that unit clauses generated in the preprocessing stage, or that are created after the first unit propagation, are not shared. Initial learned clauses are found by every solver, so there is no need to share them [3].

---

[6] The solver can remember the case when the clause originated from an ancestor node, and every time the solver is moved to a parent in the path to the ancestor, the clause can be readded with an additional frame literal that corresponds to the parent node.

[7] Because all theory lemmas are valid and frame literals cannot be removed by resolution as they only appear positive in the input, the depth of the deepest frame literal corresponds to the subtree rooted at the node for which the clause is valid.

Table 1: SMT-COMP results of the parallel tracks in 2024 and 2025 in two logics

Solver	2025 Parallel Track 128 cores				2024 Cloud Track 100 × 16 cores			
	QF_LRA		QF_LIA		QF_LRA		QF_LIA	
	Solved (/38)	AWT (s)	Solved (/44)	AWT (s)	Solved (/46)	AWT (s)	Solved (/123)	AWT (s)
SMTS	**21**	**275.7**	**19**	**191.6**	**33**	**149.2**	**30**	**49.3**
z3-Parti-z3++ [29]	7	725.1	12	237.4	16	509.5	27	452.8
Yices2 [10]	12	496.3	3	484.7	†	†	†	†
cvc5-cloud [27]	†	†	†	†	11	585.8	0	0

Legend: Solved $(/n)$: no. solved benchmarks out of n; AWT: Average Wall runtime of solved benchmarks in seconds; †: the solver did not participate.

5   Experimental Results

This section presents extensive experiments showing significant improvement over the baseline sequential SMT solver, OpenSMT [13,7], and compares it to a portfolio approach, demonstrates the effect of lemma sharing, and shows how the new algorithm scales gracefully w.r.t. increasing number of solvers. Moreover, the experiments show an encouraging result that the partitioning approach improves over the sequential solver even when using a single solver, demonstrating that the new approach is also meaningful when using limited resources. The experiments include results from the recent SMT-COMP [4,6] that compare state-of-the-art approaches within selected logics and using extensive computational resources.

Using the parallel solver SMTS [22], we replaced nowadays obsolete algorithms from [21] and implemented the novel algorithms presented in Section 3 and the lemma sharing presented in Section 4, in C++ and Python. SMTS uses instances of OpenSMT as the underlying SMT solvers and the default values of the configuration variables from Section 3. The solver timeout is initially $T_S = 32$ seconds, and is doubled every time the elapsed time since the start of the program reaches $4 \cdot T_S$. To partition a node, the system relocates an existing solver, forks its process, and scatters the formula within the new process. Only clauses of at most length 3 are shared with the lemma server.

SMT-COMP. SMT-COMP is an annual competition of state-of-the-art SMT solvers that is divided into the Cloud, Parallel, and sequential tracks, and further into SMT-LIB [5] logics, and divisions that gather specific groups of logics. Parallel and Cloud tracks consist of selected benchmarks that are either unsolved or very difficult for most sequential solvers. OpenSMT has consistently dominated logics QF_LRA and QF_LIA in the sequential tracks since 2022. Since 2021, when the new algorithms presented in this paper were implemented, SMTS has dominated most of the participated divisions in the parallel tracks[8], including

---

[8] In 2023, SMTS did not participate at all. In 2025, only Parallel Track was hosted.

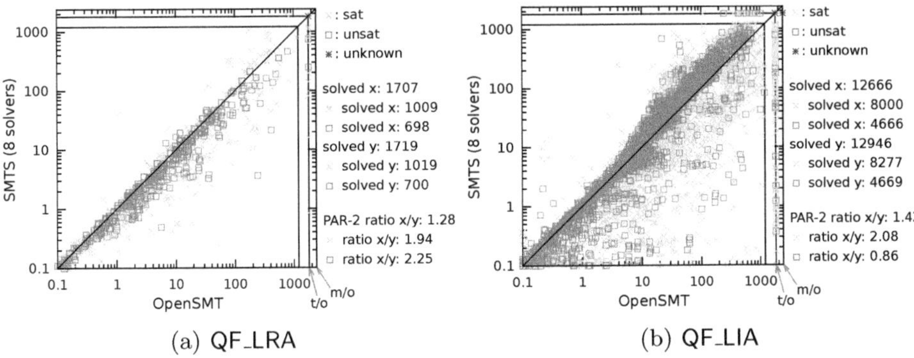

(a) QF_LRA   (b) QF_LIA

Fig. 1: Performance comparison between SMTS and OpenSMT in two logics

logics QF_LRA and QF_LIA. Table 1, compiled from the results of 2024 and 2025 in QF_LRA and QF_LIA, shows that SMTS solved substantially more benchmarks in total than the competitors using lower average runtimes of solved benchmarks. The Parallel Track in 2025 used 128 virtual cores and 2 TB of memory, and the Cloud Track in 2024 used 100 machines, each having 16 virtual cores and 64 GB of memory. The time limit per benchmark was 20 minutes. The results for the parallel tracks are available at `smt-comp.github.io`[9].

The portfolio-based state-of-the-art solver with lemma sharing SMT-D [3] has not participated in the competition. In [3], it compared to the new SMTS in portfolio-only mode (i.e., with no partitioning) in how the target lemma-sharing systems scale w.r.t. the number of solvers. Using selected benchmarks and 64 solvers, [3] showed that it does not beat the SMTS portfolio—since the base solver CVC5 is weaker within the logics than OpenSMT—but scales better: SMT-D improved the overall PAR-2 score by 52% over CVC5, while SMTS improved by 28% over OpenSMT. More details can be found in [3, Table I and Figure 4].

The rest of the section compares partitioning and lemma-sharing SMTS to OpenSMT or a differently configured SMTS. Since SMTS uses OpenSMT as the baseline solver, the results are indicative of the parallelization approach. The experiments were run on *all* SMT-LIB 2025 single-query benchmarks [24] within the logics QF_LRA (1753 benchmarks) and QF_LIA (13224), using computational nodes equipped with two sockets of Intel Xeon E5-2650 v3 (10 cores, 25M Cache, 2.3 GHz), 64GB memory, and CentOS 8.2.2004.x86_64. The wall time limit was 20 minutes per benchmark, and the experiments used 1, 2, 4, or 8 solvers.

Fig. 1 compares SMTS using 8 solvers with sequential OpenSMT in two *scatter plots* per logic, where ⨯ denotes a satisfiable benchmark solved by either of the tools, □ denotes an unsatisfiable one, and ✳ denotes a benchmark

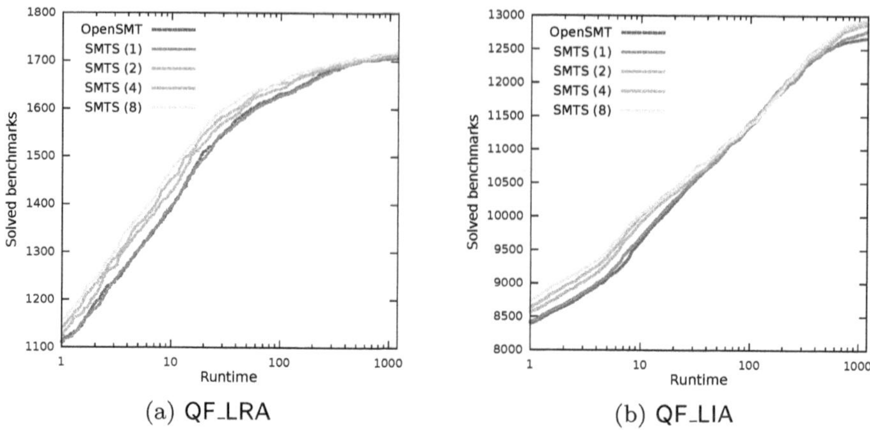

(a) QF_LRA   (b) QF_LIA

Fig. 2: Scaling of SMTS using 1 to 8 solvers against OPENSMT in two logics

where both tools timed out (t/o) or ran out of memory (m/o). The plots use a logarithmic scale for both axes that denote the runtime in seconds for each benchmark within the range $[0, 1200]$, meaning that the diagonal denotes equal runtimes of both tools. It also shows the number of solved benchmarks for each axis, distinguishing × and □ benchmarks as well. Finally, it displays the ratio between the PAR-2 scores of both tools, which is the sum of runtimes while using the double of the time limit for unsolved benchmarks; in the case of × and □ ratios, only the cases where either of the tools solved the benchmark are included. For both logics, and QF_LRA in particular, the figure clearly shows the improving trend of SMTS over OPENSMT, solving more benchmarks and having lower PAR-2 scores, especially within × benchmarks. Many points are located in the lower triangular part, sometimes providing a substantial speedup. In QF_LIA, though, SMTS has a higher PAR-2 score within □ benchmarks, due to numerous points located just above the diagonal and several instances where it timed out while OPENSMT did not. In QF_LIA, SMTS solved 277 more × benchmarks than OPENSMT, but only 3 more □ benchmarks.

Scalability. Fig. 2 compares OPENSMT with SMTS using also lower numbers of solvers in a cactus plot. It uses a logarithmic x-axis for runtime in seconds, starting from 1, and a y-axis representing the cumulative number of benchmarks each solved within the given runtime. It shows that SMTS scales gracefully with increasing number of solvers and that even using a single solver performs similarly or better than OPENSMT. Interestingly, QF_LIA benchmarks in the region around runtime 100 usually do not benefit from the parallelization.

Sequential Use. Fig. 3 provides further details on the comparison between OPENSMT and partitioning SMTS using one solver, again in the form of a scatter plot. Even now, the new approach improves over the baseline solver, solving more benchmarks—more than 100 benchmarks in the case of QF_LIA—and also having lower PAR-2 scores. The reason may be that the partitioning does not fix

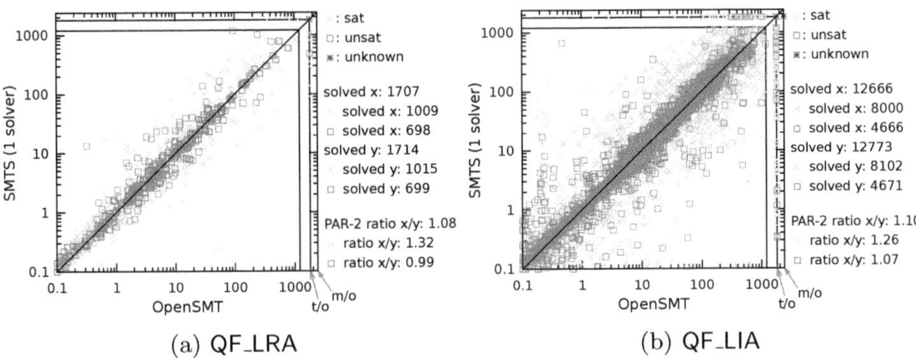

(a) QF_LRA   (b) QF_LIA

Fig. 3: Performance comparison of SMTS using 1 solver vs. OPENSMT

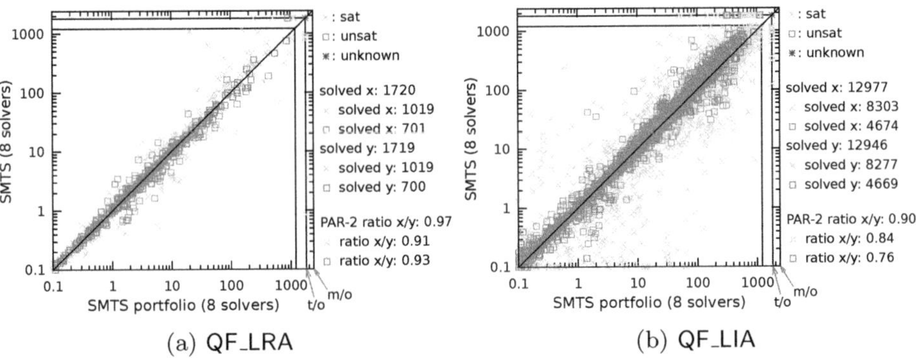

(a) QF_LRA   (b) QF_LIA

Fig. 4: Performance comparison of SMTS in portfolio vs. partitioning mode

the random seed of particular runs, and also balances between the breadth-first and depth-first search of the state space, as opposed to sequential approaches that rather resemble DFS and may get lost. Thus, it might be that using some of the new principles makes sense even within traditional SMT implementations. Notably, here SMTS solved 2 more □ benchmarks in QF_LIA than with 8 solvers in Fig. 1, suggesting that the parallel configuration can be improved.

Portfolio Solving. SMTS supports portfolio solving through changing the random seed of OPENSMT solvers. Fig. 4 compares partitioning to portfolio, each using lemma sharing and 8 solvers, in a scatter plot. Both approaches perform similarly in QF_LRA. In QF_LIA, partitioning significantly improves many × benchmarks, but overall solves fewer benchmarks and often remains slightly above the diagonal, resulting in worse average PAR-2 scores. The results suggest that the partitioning implementation may benefit from longer solving times for sequential solvers (as done in the portfolio), and that experimenting with different values of *minPortfolio* might be useful.

Lemma Sharing. The scatter plot in Fig. 5 demonstrates the effect of turning lemma sharing off in the partitioning approach. In QF_LRA, clause sharing is

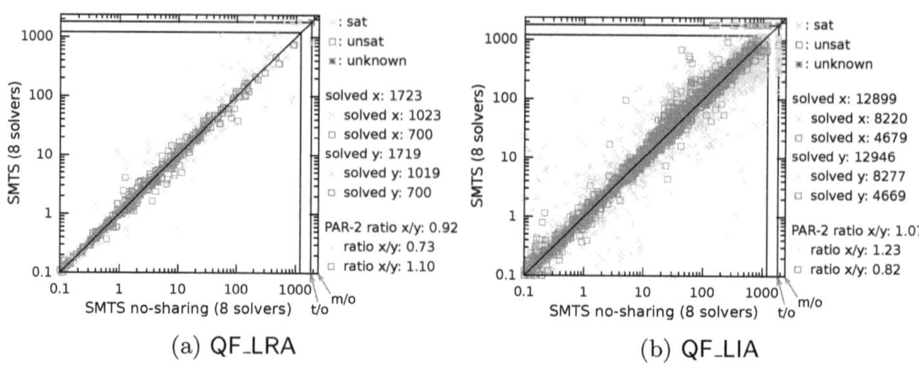

Fig. 5: Performance comparison of SMTS with or without lemma sharing

usually helpful for □ benchmarks, but often detrimental for ×—while in QF_LIA, the trend is the exact opposite and more conclusive. This suggests that a balance needs to be found between moving the solvers in the tree dynamically, which is efficient for partitioning and exploration of the tree, and carefully, such that shared clauses in different parts of the tree are not invalidated too frequently.

6   Conclusion and Future Work

This paper presented a novel algorithm for parallel SMT solving via iterative partitioning of the input formula into a tree structure using various partitioning functions, portfolio solving, and clause sharing, connecting all into one flexible system compatible with diverse SMT solvers and arbitrary theories. The approach also allows revisiting nodes in the tree, addressing the problem in prior works with poor performance on unsatisfiable benchmarks, both in theory and practice. The experiments demonstrate a substantial improvement of the new parallel system, which we implemented in SMTS, over our successful sequential solver, OPENSMT, solving 292 more out of 14977 benchmarks in QF_LRA and QF_LIA when using 8 solvers, and 114 more benchmarks even when using just a single solver. We also showed that the new approach scales gracefully with the available solvers. Moreover, SMTS, which implements the new algorithms presented in this paper, has consistently dominated the divisions in which it participated in the annual competition of parallel SMT solvers.

In the future, we will investigate closely the reasons behind some of the identified slowdowns, especially within unsatisfiable benchmarks, and aim at improving the clause sharing hand-in-hand with efficient partitioning. We will conduct a thorough experimentation in the rich configuration space of the parallel system, specifically examining the parameters solver timeout T_S and the portfolio size *minPortfolio*, as well as the use of additional parallel resources. Finally, we will address engineering issues of SMTS in a new, more efficient implementation.

Data Availability Statement. The experimental data and software are available at the permanent artifact located at https://zenodo.org/records/18330747.

References

1. Banković, M.: Parallelizing simplex within SMT solvers. Artificial Intelligence Review **48**, 83–112 (2017), https://doi.org/10.1007/s10462-016-9495-5
2. Barbosa, H., Hoenicke, J., Hyvärinen, A.E.J.: 16th international satisfiability modulo theories competition (SMT-COMP 2021): Rules and procedures (2021), https://smt-comp.github.io/2021/rules.pdf
3. Barrett, C., Chen, P.W., Cook, B., Dutertre, B., Jones, R., Le, N., Reynolds, A., Sheth, K., Stephens, C., Whalen, M.: SMT-D: New strategies for portfolio-based SMT solving. In: 2024 Formal Methods in Computer-Aided Design (FMCAD) (2024), https://www.amazon.science/publications/smt-d-new-strategies-for-portfolio-based-smt-solving
4. Barrett, C., Deters, M., de Moura, L., Oliveras, A., Stump, A.: 6 years of SMT-COMP. Journal of Automated Reasoning **50**(3), 243–277 (2013), https://doi.org/10.1007/s10817-012-9246-5
5. Barrett, C., Fontaine, P., Tinelli, C.: The SMT-LIB Standard: Version 2.6. Tech. rep., Department of Computer Science, The University of Iowa (2017), https://smt-lib.org
6. Bobot, F., Déharbe, D., Jonáš, M., Winterer, D.: 20th international satisfiability modulo theories competition (SMT-COMP 2025): Rules and procedures (2025), https://smt-comp.github.io/2025/rules.pdf
7. Bruttomesso, R., Pek, E., Sharygina, N., Tsitovich, A.: The OpenSMT Solver. In: Tools and Alg. for the Const. and Anal. of Systems (TACAS '10). LNCS, vol. 6015, pp. 150–153 (2010)
8. Cheng, X., Zhou, M., Song, X., Gu, M., Sun, J.: Parallelizing SMT solving: Lazy decomposition and conciliation. Artificial Intelligence **257**, 127–157 (2018), https://doi.org/10.1016/j.artint.2018.01.001
9. Duarte, A., Korovin, K.: Implementing superposition in iProver (system description). In: International Joint Conference on Automated Reasoning. pp. 388–397. Springer (2020)
10. Dutertre, B.: Yices 2.2. In: International Conference on Computer Aided Verification. pp. 737–744. Springer (2014)
11. Huberman, B.A., Lukose, R.M., Hogg, T.: An economics approach to hard computational problems. Science **275**(5296), 51 – 54 (1997)
12. Hyvärinen, A.E.J.: Grid Based Propositional Satisfiability Solving. Ph.D. thesis, Aalto University, Finland (2011)
13. Hyvärinen, A.E.J., Marescotti, M., Alt, L., Sharygina, N.: OpenSMT2: An SMT solver for multi-core and cloud computing. In: Creignou, N., Le Berre, D. (eds.) SAT 2016. LNCS, vol. 9710, pp. 547–553. Springer, Cham (2016)
14. Hyvärinen, A.E.J., Marescotti, M., Sharygina, N.: Search-space partitioning for parallelizing SMT solvers. In: Heule, M., Weaver, S.A. (eds.) Proc. SAT 2015. LNCS, vol. 9340, pp. 369–386. Springer (2015)
15. Hyvärinen, A.E.J., Marescotti, M., Sharygina, N.: Lookahead in partitioning SMT. In: Formal Methods in Computer Aided Design, FMCAD 2021, New Haven, CT, USA, October 19-22, 2021. pp. 271–279. IEEE (2021)

16. Hyvärinen, A.E.J., Wintersteiger, C.M.: Parallel satisfiability modulo theories. In: Hamadi, Y., Sais, L. (eds.) Handbook of Parallel Constraint Reasoning, pp. 141–178. Springer (2018)
17. Hyvärinen, A.E., Junttila, T., Niemelä, I.: Partitioning search spaces of a randomized search. Fundamenta Informaticae **107**(2-3), 289–311 (2011), https://doi.org/10.3233/FI-2011-404
18. Kolárik, T., Asadzadeh, S., Hyvärinen, A.E.J.: SMTS: Cloud and parallel smt solver (2025), https://verify.inf.usi.ch/smts
19. Kovács, L., Voronkov, A.: First-order theorem proving and Vampire. In: International Conference on Computer Aided Verification. pp. 1–35. Springer (2013)
20. Mandelbrot, B.: The pareto–lévy law and the distribution of income. International Economic Review **1**(2), 79–106 (1960)
21. Marescotti, M., Hyvärinen, A.E.J., Sharygina, N.: Clause sharing and partitioning for cloud-based SMT solving. In: Artho, C., Legay, A., Peled, D. (eds.) Automated Technology for Verification and Analysis. pp. 428–443. Springer International Publishing, Cham (2016)
22. Marescotti, M., Hyvärinen, A.E.J., Sharygina, N.: SMTS: distributed, visualized constraint solving. In: LPAR-22. 22nd International Conference on Logic for Programming, Artificial Intelligence and Reasoning, Awassa, Ethiopia, 16-21 November 2018 (2018)
23. Niemetz, A., Preiner, M.: Bitwuzla. In: Enea, C., Lal, A. (eds.) Computer Aided Verification - 35th International Conference, CAV 2023, Paris, France, July 17-22, 2023, Proceedings, Part II. Lecture Notes in Computer Science, vol. 13965, pp. 3–17. Springer (2023), https://doi.org/10.1007/978-3-031-37703-7_1
24. Preiner, M., Schurr, H.J., Barrett, C., Fontaine, P., Niemetz, A., Tinelli, C.: Smt-lib release 2025 (non-incremental benchmarks) (2025), https://doi.org/10.5281/zenodo.16740866
25. Reisenberger, C.: PBoolector: A Parallel SMT Solver for QF_BV by Combining Bit-Blasting with Look-Ahead. Master's thesis (2014)
26. Weber, T.: Par4. Tech. rep., Uppsala University (2019), http://smt2019.galois.com/papers/tool_paper_9.pdf
27. Wilson, A., Noetzli, A., Reynolds, A., Cook, B., Tinelli, C., Barrett, C.: Partitioning strategies for distributed SMT solving. In: 2023 Formal Methods in Computer-Aided Design (FMCAD). pp. 199–208 (2023), https://doi.org/10.34727/2023/isbn.978-3-85448-060-0_28
28. Wintersteiger, C.M., Hamadi, Y., de Moura, L.M.: A concurrent portfolio approach to SMT solving. In: Bouajjani, A., Maler, O. (eds.) Computer Aided Verification, 21st International Conference, CAV 2009, Grenoble, France, June 26 - July 2, 2009. Proceedings. Lecture Notes in Computer Science, vol. 5643, pp. 715–720. Springer (2009), https://doi.org/10.1007/978-3-642-02658-4_60
29. Zhao, M., Cai, S., Qian, Y.: Distributed SMT solving based on dynamic variable-level partitioning. In: Gurfinkel, A., Ganesh, V. (eds.) Computer Aided Verification. pp. 68–88. Springer Nature Switzerland, Cham (2024)
30. Zhou, Y., Bosamiya, J., Takashima, Y., Li, J., Heule, M., Parno, B.: Mariposa: Measuring SMT instability in automated program verification. In: 2023 Formal Methods in Computer-Aided Design (FMCAD). pp. 178–188 (2023), https://doi.org/10.34727/2023/isbn.978-3-85448-060-0_26

Exploring the SMT-LIB Benchmark Library*

Hans-Jörg Schurr[1] , François Bobot[2] , Mathias Preiner[3] , Aina Niemetz[3] ,
Clark Barrett[3] , Pascal Fontaine[4] , and Cesare Tinelli[1]

[1] The University of Iowa, Iowa, USA
[2] Université Paris-Saclay, CEA, List, FR
[3] Stanford University, Stanford, USA
[4] Université de Liège, Liege, BE

Abstract. The SMT-LIB benchmark collection is a large set of problems for SMT solvers. It has been continuously maintained and expanded since its creation in the early 2000s by the SMT-LIB initiative. It has been used since 2005 by the annual SMT solver competition to compare the performance of SMT solvers, and by researchers to study novel solving techniques. Effective use of the collection often requires access to benchmark metadata (e.g., date, source, satisfiability status, theory symbol count, and so on). Furthermore, this metadata and the past competition results contain a wealth of historical information about the development of SMT solving. In this paper, we report on our efforts to collect and curate all metadata from the SMT-LIB benchmarks together with the results of all past SMT-COMP competitions in a single SQLite database. We also present tools to explore this database and extract relevant insights. Since APIs for SQLite databases are available for all major programming languages, the database makes it easy to add features using SMT benchmark metadata to SMT development tools. To illustrate the structure of the collected data we perform multiple case studies. In particular, we present a comparison of SMT solvers that is independent of the changing hardware and benchmarks used by the competition. The database is released annually on Zenodo, and serves as an archive of the state of SMT-LIB and, by extension, of the state of the art in SMT.

Keywords: SMT · SMT-LIB benchmarks · data integration · SQLite · database · automated reasoning

1 Introduction

The SMT-LIB [5] initiative is an ongoing international effort started in 2003 whose goal is to facilitate research and development in Satisfiability Modulo Theories (SMT). Part of this initiative is the development of the SMT-LIB language [6] for specifying SMT problems in a textual format and the collection

* This work was supported in part by the Stanford Center for Automated Reasoning, the Stanford Center for Blockchain Research, Defense Advanced Research Projects Agency (DARPA) contract FA875024-2-1001, National Science Foundation (NSF) grant number 2303489, and a gift from Amazon Web Services.

S. Junges and G. Katz (Eds.): TACAS 2026, LNCS 16505, pp. 150–169, 2026.
https://doi.org/10.1007/978-3-032-22752-2_8

and maintenance of a large library of benchmark problems written in that format. The benchmark library, currently maintained by the authors of this paper, is curated and continually extended with contributions from the SMT community and published online in yearly releases. The 2025 release of the library, the latest one to date, contains a total of 495,180 benchmarks divided into two categories: *non-incremental* benchmarks (450,472), which consists of problems with a single satisfiability query, and *incremental* benchmarks (44,708), which contain multiple satisfiability queries.

The library is used to evaluate and improve SMT solving techniques on problems relevant to users or developers of SMT solvers. A large-scale evaluation is done annually by SMT solver competition SMT-COMP [21], which started in 2005. Overall, the benchmarks and the competition results provide a wealth of information on the structure of SMT problems (the majority of which come from real-world applications) and the development of SMT solving over time.

Data about SMT benchmarks is useful to SMT solver users and developers who often rely on advanced metadata for their work. For instance, when evaluating the performance of a procedure or solver configuration that targets a specific fragment of a theory, it may be desirable to only include benchmarks that contain only symbols of that fragment. Other examples are identifying benchmarks that are uniquely solved by a solver configuration, or not solved by any known configuration—both corner cases that may serve as important starting points for developing new solving techniques. Metadata can also be used for solving itself, e.g., to guide automatic selection of solving strategies [26].

However, until now this metadata was not easily accessible to SMT developers and users. Competition results were stored in different formats and different archives. The results of the competitions from 2007 to 2012 were lost due to a server migration. The benchmark metadata was commonly collected on demand, via ad-hoc scripts. This was not only error-prone but also inconvenient.

To address these issues, we have collected and integrated benchmark metadata, results from all past SMT competitions, and hand-curated data. The result is now publicly available as a single SQLite database together with the annual release of the benchmark library [25]. The database available under the terms of the CC-BY 4.0 license.

Since software libraries for interacting with SQLite databases exist for all major programming languages, the database can be integrated with existing benchmarking and testing systems easily. Furthermore, since every SQLite database is stored as a single file, the benchmark database is also easy to share.

As we discuss in Section 5, we have used the database to perform multiple case studies and to visualize the historical development of SMT solving. We first focus on simple investigations, such as the growth of the library over time. One difficulty when working with historical competition results is that the competition hardware changed over time. Hence, runtimes are not always directly comparable. Furthermore, the competitions used different subsets of the benchmarks. We illustrate how this can be addressed by comparing the relative performance of SMT solvers.

The database also serves an archival purpose: each annual release on Zenodo is a snapshot of past competition results and benchmark metadata. In the past, results from historical SMT competitions (2007-2012) became unavailable. Furthermore, the StarExec service [27], which partially served as an archive of the various releases of the library, has been recently discontinued. Our database helps to fill these gaps. To simplify the annual update of the database, we implemented the data integration pipeline through a collection of flexible Python scripts. For benchmark metadata extraction, we developed an optimized standalone tool called *Klammerhammer*. Klammerhammer and the Python pipeline are available under the terms of the 3-Clause BSD license.

Section 2 of this paper discusses related work. Then, Section 3 describes how benchmarks are represented in the database and gives a few example scenarios of its usage. In Section 4, we describe our data integration pipeline. There are two sources of data: the benchmark metadata (Section 4.1) and the outcome of SMT evaluations (Section 4.2). In Section 5, we discuss multiple studies we did on the collected data. Finally, we suggest future directions of research in Section 6.

2   Related Work

Benchmark libraries are common in the automated reasoning and theorem proving communities. Among those, the TPTP library [28] is close to SMT-LIB in spirit, but it precedes it and targets theorem provers instead of SMT solvers. TPTP problems store metadata in their header, including syntactic features such as symbol counts. The metadata header also contains a difficulty rating that inspired our rating (see Section 4.2). Instead of a standalone database, TPTP organizes benchmarks into folders and subfolders, and provides tools to search the library for benchmarks with specific characteristics. This is possible because the TPTP policy is to carefully curate the benchmark set and admit fewer benchmarks (the 9.2.1 release has 26,264 benchmarks).

The Global Benchmark Database [15] (GBD) catalogs benchmarks for propositional satisfiability (SAT). GBD is focused on a flexible data model where benchmarks are associated with different contexts, and contexts are associated with data fields. For example, the cnf context represents benchmarks in conjunctive normal form, and contains fields like the number of clauses and variables. To support this model, GBD's intended interface is a custom tool and query language. The GBD tool can be connected to different data sources using file formats such as SQLite and CSV. Hence, our database could be connected to GBD. However, our tables do not correspond to GBD contexts, and it would be necessary to present a denormalized schema. For example, each symbol count would be a dedicated field, instead of a relation between queries and the symbols list. GBD uses the concept of an *identification function* that maps benchmarks to identifiers. Such a function would help with the benchmark identification problems discussed in Section 4.2. However, we cannot use this approach, since we do not have archives of all benchmarks for every competition, and finding an iden-

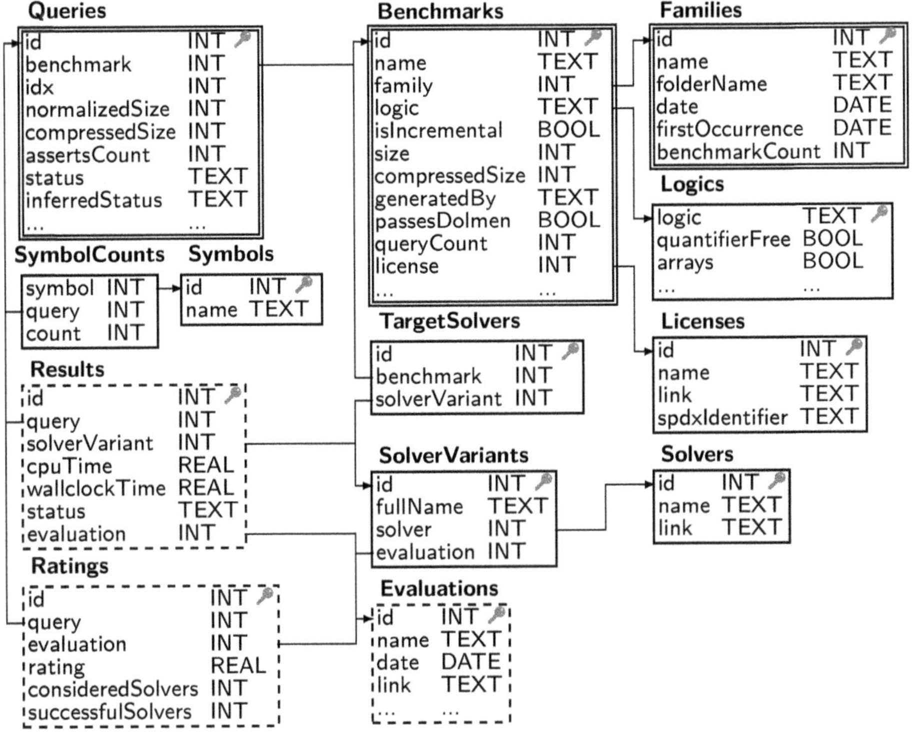

Fig. 1. Database schema of the catalog with some fields omitted.

tification function that is not affected by common benchmark editing operations is challenging due to the syntactic complexity of SMT problems.

SMTQuery [16] is a SMT benchmark analysis tool focused on the theory of strings. It uses a custom, SQL-like, language. The focus on strings and the custom implementation allows SMTQuery to support complex queries on the metadata. For example, it is possible to search for benchmarks with word equations that have a specific shape. Metadata like symbol frequency has been used for machine learning-based SMT solver selection [26].

A few retrospectives of the SMT competition have been published over the years. This includes the first six years of SMT-COMP [8] and the competitions between 2015 and 2018 [31]. Most notably, in 2013 a large scale evaluation was performed instead of an SMT competition [13]. This included an evaluation using all benchmarks on all solvers from prior years.

3   The Structure of the Database

Figure 1 shows the schema of the SQLite database that stores the collected data. The database tables of the schema fall into three categories, distinguished visually by their border. The three tables highlighted with ▣ form the core of the database and list the benchmarks and the queries they contain; the tables marked by ☐ store static metadata, such as symbol frequencies; and the tables shown as ⌐⌐ boxes store the results of large scale evaluations.

Every row of the **Benchmarks** table represents one SMT-LIB benchmark, and each benchmark belongs to exactly one *family*, stored in the **Families** table. This classification follows the folder structure of the benchmark library. There, each benchmark is uniquely identified by its file path, for example:

$$\underbrace{\texttt{non-incremental}}_{\text{isIncremental}} / \underbrace{\texttt{UFNIA}}_{\text{logic}} / \overbrace{\underbrace{\texttt{2019}}_{\text{date}} - \underbrace{\texttt{Preiner}}_{\text{name}}}^{\text{family}} / \underbrace{\texttt{partial/t3\_rw617.smt2}}_{\text{name}}$$

The topmost folder indicates whether the benchmark is incremental or not. The next subfolder is named after the SMT-LIB *logic* used in the benchmark. A logic indicates the SMT theories referred to by the benchmark and the language fragment its queries belongs to (e.g., quantifier-free, linear, . . .). A benchmark's logic is stored in the field logic of the **Benchmarks** table. The third component of the file path is the name of the benchmark's *family*. A family usually collects benchmarks with some property in common. For instance, they originate from the same application, or are generated by the same tool. Note that a family may contain benchmarks from several SMT-LIB logics. Hence, every benchmark refers to an entry in the **Families** table. The value of the field date (either a full date, or just a year) is chosen by the person who contributed the benchmarks, and is usually the date on which the benchmark family was generated.[5] The field firstOccurence records the date of the first competition that used a benchmark from the family. Overall, there are currently 287 families. Finally, the benchmark name is the path fragment following the family. It is stored in the name field of **Benchmarks**.

Incremental benchmarks contain more than one satisfiability query expressed with a check-sat command. Each check-sat command corresponds to a row in the **Queries** table. The command instructs the solver to determine the satisfiability of a set of formulas previously asserted with one or more assert commands. Asserted formulas are stored on a stack, which can be manipulated using the push and pop commands. The idx field of the **Queries** table is the index of the query in the benchmark. For example, if idx is 3, the query corresponds to the third check-sat call. Overall, there are 34,614,311 queries. Some benchmarks individually contain thousands of queries. The benchmark currently with the highest number of queries has 2,630,828 of them.

---

[5] Some benchmark families are not associated with a date for historical reasons.

```
(set-info :smt-lib-version 2.6)
(set-logic UFNIA)
(set-info :source |
  Generated by: Mathias Preiner
  Generated on: 2019-03-22
  Application: Verifying bit-vector rewrite rule candidates.
  Target solver: CVC4, Z3, Vampire |)
(set-info :license "https://creativecommons.org/licenses/by/4.0/")
(set-info :category "crafted")
(assert [...]) [...]
(set-info :status unknown)
(check-sat) (exit)
```

Listing 1.1. Abridged content of the SMT-LIB file from Section 3.

Exploring the Database The SMT-LIB benchmark library is released on the
open-access repository Zenodo [22,23]. Starting 2025, the metadata database is
released as an additional Zenodo artifact "SMT-LIB Catalog" [25] consisting of a
compressed archive containing the SQLite database proper as well as a number
of helper files. Since this archive is large (currently, around 1.5 GiB, 5.4 GiB
uncompressed), we expect users to download the database and perform queries
locally. To reduce the file size, the database has no query indexes. However, the
archive contains a script for generating default indexes.

The most basic way to explore the database is to use the SQLite command
line tool to perform queries. Alternatively, one can use language bindings, such
as Python's sqlite3 module, and graphical tools, such as the DB Browser for
SQLite. For example, the following query returns the number of non-incremental
benchmarks containing at least 100 bvxor calls (currently, 7, 130).

```sql
SELECT COUNT(Benchmarks.id) FROM Benchmarks
  JOIN Queries         ON Queries.benchmark = Benchmarks.id
  JOIN SymbolCounts    ON SymbolCounts.query = Queries.id
  JOIN Symbols         ON Symbols.id = SymbolCounts.symbol
 WHERE isIncremental = False AND Symbols.name = 'bvxor'
   AND SymbolCounts.count > 100;
```

The following query returns the number of benchmarks (currently 6,525) solved
by the solver SONOLAR but not by Abziz at SMT-COMP 2014 (with id 10).

```sql
WITH Eval AS (
  SELECT Queries.id, Solvers.name AS sn FROM Queries
  JOIN Results         ON Results.query = Queries.id
  JOIN SolverVariants ON SolverVariants.id = Results.solverVariant
  JOIN Solvers         ON Solvers.id = SolverVariants.solver
  WHERE Results.evaluation = 10 AND Results.status != 'unknown' )
SELECT COUNT(DISTINCT ev.id) FROM Eval AS ev
  WHERE (sn == 'SONOLAR') AND
  NOT EXISTS (SELECT * FROM Eval WHERE sn == "Abziz" AND ev.id == id);
```

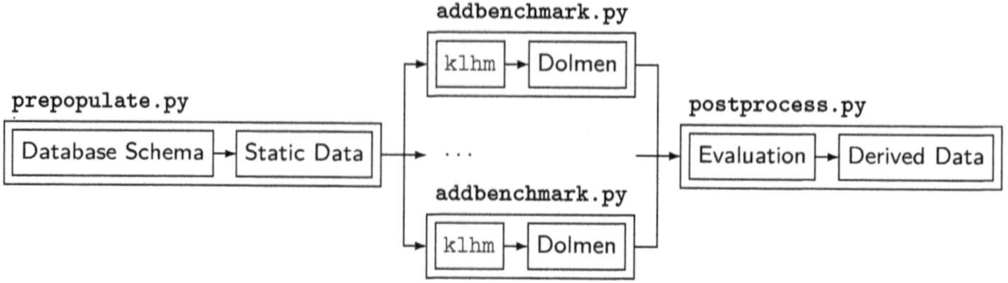

Fig. 2. The data integration pipeline.

Website. We also provide webpages generated from the database at explore.smt-lib.org, which allow one to quickly explore the SMT-LIB benchmarks. Users can browse benchmarks by logic and family. Once a benchmark is selected, a dedicated page shows the related metadata. Beyond the header data, and symbol counts, the page also lists all competitions where the benchmark was used, and the response by the participating solver variants. Every benchmark has a static URL based on its id. For example, the benchmark sketched in Listing 1.1 is available at explore.smt-lib.org/benchmark/111937.html. The website also shows data visualizations like those we present in Section 5 for all logics.

4   Data Integration

We collect metadata from two main sources: the individual benchmark files and the SMT competition data. The data collection from these sources and its integration into the database is implemented as a modular and easy-to-extend pipeline, written in Python.[6] Figure 2 depicts the workflow of the pipeline. It is divided into three stages, each implemented as a Python script. In the first stage, the script prepopulate.py creates the database scheme, and initializes the database with static data, such as the list of licenses and logics used in SMT-LIB benchmarks, the names of SMT solvers that participated in SMT-COMP, and so on. In the second stage, the script addbenchmark.py parses the individual benchmark files to extract the benchmark metadata. Since this stage is the most time consuming, to speed-up the data collection the user can run a provided auxiliary script to launch multiple copies of addbenchmark.py in parallel on different parts of the benchmark library. As a final step, the script postprocess.py integrates the SMT-COMP results data into the database and computes and stores additional data derived from these results.

4.1   Integrating Benchmark Metadata

The metadata tables (□) store data associated with benchmarks or queries. Each benchmark includes a header section that stores metadata (see Listing 1.1).

---

[6] Available at github.com/SMT-LIB/SMT-LIB-db.

The header uses the `set-info` command to declare metadata fields. This command can specify a `:source` field, which contains sub-fields that give information about the source of the benchmark. Most of these fields relate to the entire benchmark. Hence, most metadata fields are mapped directly to a corresponding field in the **Benchmarks** table. The entry for the example benchmark would store `Mathias Preiner` in the generatedBy field. The `:status` field relates to a specific *query*. It indicates whether the next query is known to be satisfiable or unsatisfiable. This is stored in the status field in the **Queries** table.

The license field associates one license to the benchmark, currently among a list of eleven, in the manually curated **Licenses** table. The license is usually identified by a short code, such as GPL, or by a link. However, some benchmarks (e.g., the *CPAchecker_kInduction-SoSy_Lab* family) contain the entire license text. We shorten this to a license code ("CMU SoSy Lab" in this case). The `Target solver` entry lists the solvers targeted by the benchmark creator. We store this list in the **TargetSolvers** table that maps solver variants to benchmarks. Solver variants are also used for SMT competition results (Section 4.2).

A key data point about an SMT query is which theory symbols and SMT-LIB features are used, and how often they occur in a benchmark. While these counts are not directly available in the benchmark header, they can be computed by scanning the benchmark. There are two different categories of SMT-LIB constructs that can be counted. On the one hand, there are commands such as `assert` which asserts formulas. On the other hand, there are predefined theory symbols that appear in formulas. The first category is small and fixed, while the second category is large and grows as new theories are added to SMT-LIB. Counts from the first category are therefore fields of the **Queries** table, e.g., assertsCount gives the number of `assert` commands used by a query. For the second category, we use the **Symbols** and **SymbolCounts** tables. The former lists all theory symbols we consider. We extracted this table from the SMT-LIB parser of the *cvc5* SMT solver [3]. The **SymbolCounts** has one entry for each symbol that appears at least once in a query. To simplify the scanner, we do not distinguish theory symbols from user declared symbols. Hence, the **SymbolCounts** table may contain entries for symbols that are not part of the benchmark logic.

The normalizedSize field of the **Queries** table is the logical *size* of a query in bytes. A query is identified with each `check-sat` command and encompasses all the commands that assert in the stack information relevant to that `check-sat` command. We handle the push and pop commands to ensure that we do not take the size of inactive assertions into account. The compressedSize field is the size of the query after compression with the *zstd* algorithm. This field is intended to measure the problem size independent of factors such as the length of symbol names. The size and compressedSize fields of the **Benchmarks** table are the logical sizes of the entire benchmark.

Finally, the passesDolmen field of the **Benchmark** table records whether Dolmen, the reference parser and type checker for SMT-LIB [11], reports no error for the benchmark.

Klammerhammer. To extract the metadata quickly we developed *Klammerhammer*, a standalone tool that performs a simple scan of the benchmark. It stores symbol counts on a stack. SMT-LIB push commands push a copy of the counts onto the stack, while pop commands remove the topmost entry. Whenever a `check-sat` command is encountered, the tool prints the current counts as JSON data. After scanning the entire benchmark, the tool prints the metadata fields for the entries in the **Benchmarks** table. To compute the query size we also store the byte offset of push and pop calls on the stack.

The tool is implemented in the low level programming language Zig, and uses the zstd library to compute the compressed sizes. It can be used independently of our data integration pipeline to extract benchmark metadata on demand, for instance, from non-public benchmarks or to implement strategy selection tools.

4.2   Integrating SMT-COMP Results

The database not only stores metadata on individual benchmarks in the SMT-LIB library, but also combines it with the historical data from all SMT competitions. This allows users to get answers for questions like "Did solver X solve benchmark Y in the past?" or "How difficult is this benchmark?". Normally, to answer these questions one must evaluate SMT solvers on the benchmarks. Instead of performing their own evaluations, users of our database can rely on historical results of the yearly SMT competition [21].

SMT-COMP participants can compete in multiple tracks. For instance the *single query* (resp. *incremental*) track tasks solvers with solving non-incremental (resp. *incremental*) benchmarks. Integrating multiple competition years also allows us to cover more benchmarks, since recent competitions use only a random subset of the benchmarks from the SMT-LIB library due it its increasingly large size. In recent years, the competition organizers publish sanitized results for the non-incremental track. Unfortunately, they only provided summary results for the incremental track, without the solvers answers for each individual query. The 2025 release of the database contains results for the incremental track of SMT-COMP 2024 generated from raw logs. We plan to include results for the years 2019 to 2023 in the 2026 release based on backups of raw competition logs.

Each competition year is a row in the **Evaluations** table. In the future, we can also use this table to store the results of other evaluations. This row stores some basic data about the competition, such as a link to its website. We also store the *hardware generation* used by the competition. This number is increased whenever the competition changed computation hardware (see Table 1). The solvers that participate in an evaluation are collected in the **Solvers** and **SolverVariants** tables. A solver variant is a concrete version of a solver that participated in an evaluation (or is mentioned as a target solver in a benchmark). Since solvers have different versioning schemes, we do not attempt to record solver *versions*. Instead, the different variant can represent solver versions, but also the different names used to refer to the same solver (e.g., `cvc5` and `CVC5`). Both the **Solvers** and the **SolverVariants** tables are manually curated. Overall, we record 82 solvers and 484 variants.

For each evaluation, the **Results** table connects queries to solvers. The status field is sat, unsat, or unknown, depending on the answer of the solver. Furthermore, we record both the wall-clock time and the CPU time when available from historical data.[7] Note that, due to the changing competition hardware, runtimes cannot be compared naively between arbitrary years.

A major challenge is that the structure of the SMT-LIB benchmark collection has also changed over the years. For example, the logic field of misclassified benchmarks was updated. Benchmarks were also removed if they were found not to comply with the SMT-LIB standard. To address this, when extracting information from the raw data of a particular edition of SMT-COMP we search for benchmarks from the SMT-LIB library heuristically in multiple steps. First we do a selection based only on the benchmark's name field since that seldom changes. If that returns a single benchmark, we used that benchmark. Otherwise, we narrow down the search by adding also the family, and finally the logic. If we were unable to uniquely determine the benchmark using this method, we discard the result. Our goal is not to record the entire evaluation, but to collect the results related to benchmarks in the current release. The missing benchmarks often correspond to a cleanup of the benchmark library. For example, from 2014 to 2016 the *AProVE* family contained duplicate benchmarks, and, in 2018, the missing benchmarks are in the QF_SLIA logic that was experimental that year.

Table 1 lists competition years and the missing results. The second column shows the benchmark file format. The first two competitions are published as HTML websites. From 2007 until 2012 the competition used SMTExec [4]. Since this platform is no longer online, these results are not publicly available. We used an archived backup of the SMTExec database to add those years and are currently working on restoring the public results. The SMT-EVAL in 2013 [13] and the competitions between 2014 and 2017 use very similar CSV formats, with different column names. Since 2018, all results are available as JSON files.

We compute derived fields from the evaluation results. The firstOccurence field of the **Families** table is the date of the first evaluation where any benchmark of the family was used. This is useful for benchmarks without metadata header or date in the file path. The inferredStatus field is a status (sat or unsat), if at a single evaluation two distinct solvers agreed on that status, and there was no disagreement by a third solver. Hence, this field allows users to know the likely status of a query if no status is explicitly provided in the benchmark itself.

Finally, we compute a difficulty *rating* for each query at each evaluation. This rating is the fraction of solvers that solved a benchmark over the solvers that attempted it: successfulSolvers/consideredSolvers. We *consider* a solver if any of its variants responded to any benchmark in the same logic. This excludes solvers that do not support the benchmark logic. A solver is *successful* if any of its variants gave a sat/unsat answer that did not contradict the status or inferredStatus value. This rating is inspired by the TPTP library. Our calculation, however, is slightly different. TPTP ignores solvers that solve only a strict subset of queries solved by another solver. We keep these solvers, because a superseded

---

[7] Not all competitions recorded both.

			Results			Benchmarks		
Year	Format	Generation	Missing	Total	Percent	Missing	Total	Percent
2005	HTML	1	10	3,299	0.30%	1	355	0.28%
2006	↓	2	158	7,067	2.24%	58	1,127	5.15%
2007	SQL	3	684	12,370	5.53%	149	2,297	6.49%
2008		↓	933	16,110	5.79%	253	2,993	8.45%
2009		4	471	14,948	3.15%	232	3,711	6.25%
2010			684	12,898	5.30%	208	3,731	5.57%
2011			380	18,588	2.04%	88	3,779	2.33%
2012	↓	↓	496	8,020	6.18%	90	1,557	5.78%
2013	CSV$_1$	5	1,370	1,663,472	0.08%	87	95,491	0.09%
2014	CSV$_2$		38,160	347,147	10.99%	9,097	67,426	13.49%
2015			68,675	980,235	7.01%	9,255	154,238	6.00%
2016			68,757	1,003,075	6.85%	9,274	154,424	6.01%
2017	↓		435	1,186,056	0.04%	117	238,758	0.05%
2018	JSON		29,789	1,388,191	2.15%	29,475	333,241	8.84%
2019			91	730,685	0.01%	13	64,154	0.02%
2020			878	563,052	0.16%	175	89,910	0.19%
2021			7	772,681	0.00%	1	99,254	0.00%
2022			0	658,873	0.00%	0	93,791	0.00%
2023		↓	9	740,591	0.00%	1	111,285	0.00%
2024		6	0	491,221	0.00%	0	123,486	0.00%
2025	↓	↓	0	823,169	0.00%	0	129,361	0.00%

Table 1. Evaluations: data format, hardware generation, and missed benchmarks.

solver is nonetheless typically the result of a serious research effort. Its inability to solve a query provides evidence of the difficulty of that query. One motivation for ignoring superseded solvers in TPTP is that the weaker solver is often a specialized variant of a stronger solver. We sidestep this consideration in our computation by grouping variants of the same solver into a single virtual solver.

5   Case Studies

In this section, we explain how we have used the collected data to better understand the development of the benchmark collection and SMT solvers over time. A key challenge in analyzing the date comes from the heterogeneity of SMT solving. Many solvers support only some theories, and research interests in different theories varies over time. Hence, we will focus on the big picture provided by the data. As mentioned in Section 3, the project webpage hosts graphs for all logics.

In Section 5.1 we visualize key data points from the database. Our goal is to understand how the library evolved over time. In Section 5.2 we study the development of solvers over time. Since the competition hardware and benchmark sets changed, we cannot compute a performance ranking. However, we can determine how *similar* their performance is.

5.1 Evolution of the Library

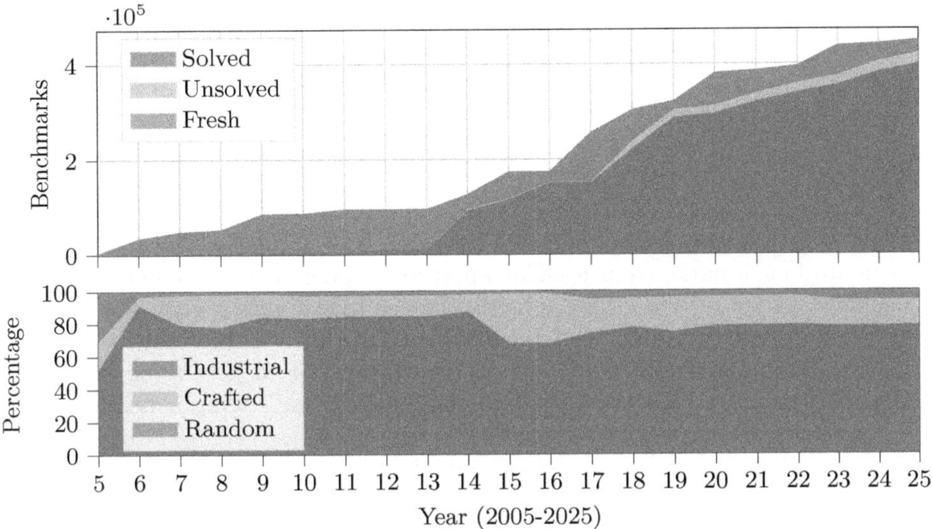

Fig. 3. Benchmarks and categories over time.

Figure 3 shows the growth of the benchmark collection over time. To compute this timeline we use the firstOccurence field of the benchmark families. Since this field uses competition results, and we only have limited competition data for incremental benchmarks, we restrict ourselves to non-incremental benchmarks.

The first graph shows how many benchmarks are added each year and how many benchmarks get solved. Benchmarks are *fresh* if they have never been used at a competition, benchmarks are *solved* if at least one solver gave a response not contradicting the benchmark status, and benchmarks are *unsolved* otherwise. Initially, the competitions used only a small subset of the available benchmarks every year. The 2013 SMT evaluation then used all existing benchmarks. Subsequent competitions always used all or large subsets of the benchmarks. It is remarkable that there are relatively few unsolved benchmarks. We suspect that benchmark contributors might be hesitant to submit difficult benchmarks, because they cannot identify whether the benchmark is simply too large, or whether it has any interesting properties.

The second graph shows the indicated benchmark categories over time. Most benchmarks are classified as *industrial*, which in SMT-LIB means that they were generated by client applications of SMT solvers, such as software verification

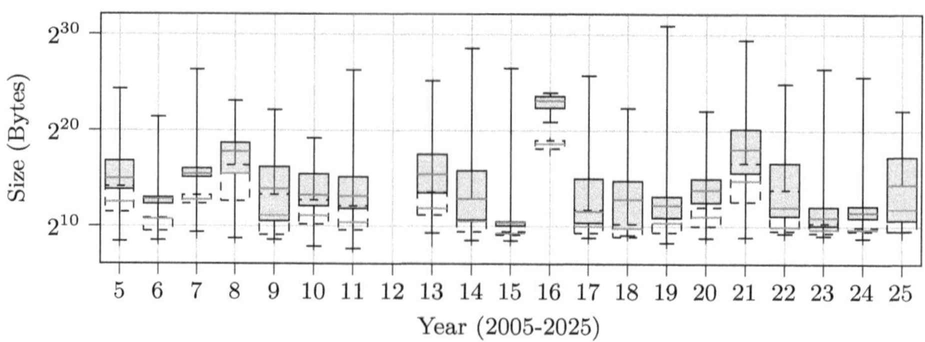

Fig. 4. Size of new benchmarks.

tools. It is not surprising that this category is dominating, since it is easy to generate benchmarks from a client application once it is implemented. *Crafted* benchmarks are benchmarks explicitly created to evaluate specific algorithms or to verify solver compliance to the SMT-LIB standard. One benefit of crafted benchmarks is that their difficulty is typically easier to determine in advance. Hence, they can be a source of interesting and/or challenging benchmarks.

An interesting question is whether benchmarks are getting larger. Figure 4 indicates that they are not. This figure is a box-plot of the size in bytes of benchmarks added to the benchmark collection. The plot is semi-logarithmic. The center line represents the mean, and the boxes extend from the first quartile to the third quartile. Differently from most box-plots, the caps here represent the smallest and largest benchmark. The dashed box shows the sizes after compression. Note that no new benchmarks were added in 2012, and only two were added in 2016. While the size of new benchmarks varies significantly from year to year, there is no clear trend towards larger benchmarks.

When benchmarks are sampled uniformly from all benchmarks of a logic, larger benchmark families are overrepresented. This can be problematic, since benchmarks from the same family share characteristics. In Figure 5 we explore the size of the benchmark families. This diagram shows histograms for all logics with at least five families (semi-logarithmic scale). While family sizes are generally well distributed, most logics also have some huge families.

Figure 6 shows the number of solvers that participated with at least one variant at the competition year by year. This also includes non-competing solvers, for instance from previous editions, that were included by the organizers for comparison purposes. In 2024, this practice changed and fewer solvers from older competitions were included.

5.2   Similarities Between Solvers

The database includes a wealth of information about how the solvers fare on the benchmarks. This information can be visualized effectively using cactus plots,

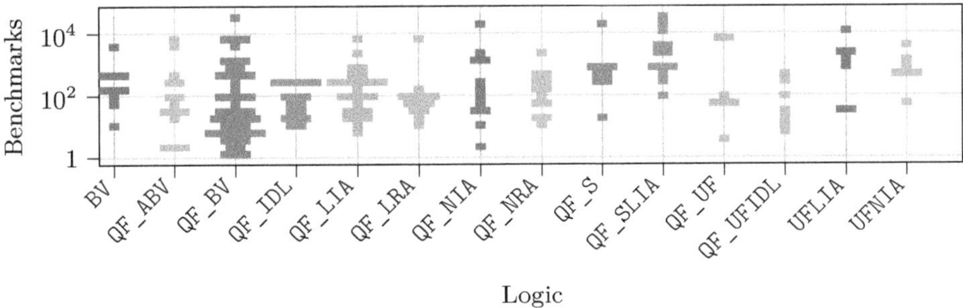

Fig. 5. Histogram of the number of benchmarks in the families.

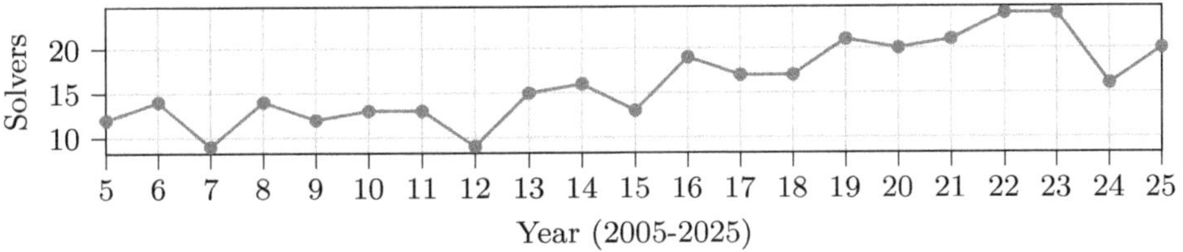

Fig. 6. Solvers over time.

even when many solvers are used [9]. However, we want further insights beyond observing the number of solved instances.

The database is also helpful to answer community-wide questions that are highly relevant for users and their choice of a solver for a particular application: Do solvers handle the same problems? Are solvers complementary? The usual representation using scatter plots would be impractical due to the large number of solvers involved. We rather use data analysis techniques that are naturally able to represents similarities and dissimilarities. Different algorithms exist that map a high dimension feature space with a distance metric into a lower dimension feature space using the Euclidean distance while preserving the initial distance as much as possible. Many choices for the selected features, the distance metric, and the algorithm are possible. We choose the established isomap algorithm as implemented in *scikit-learn* [1, 29]. Since the challenge is to aggregate results from two decades of competitions that considered different benchmark sets and used different computer hardware, the other choices need careful consideration.

As features, we choose just the *wall-clock* time taken by a solver on each benchmark because that information has been available since the first competition. The status *solved/unsolved* alone would be too limited to measure the difficulty of a benchmark. Still, in order to differentiate a solver that solved a goal in one second, say, from a solver that gave up in one second by answering unknown, we set the wall-clock time for unknown answers to 40 min as done for the PAR-2 score considered by the competition (last year's timeout was 20 min).

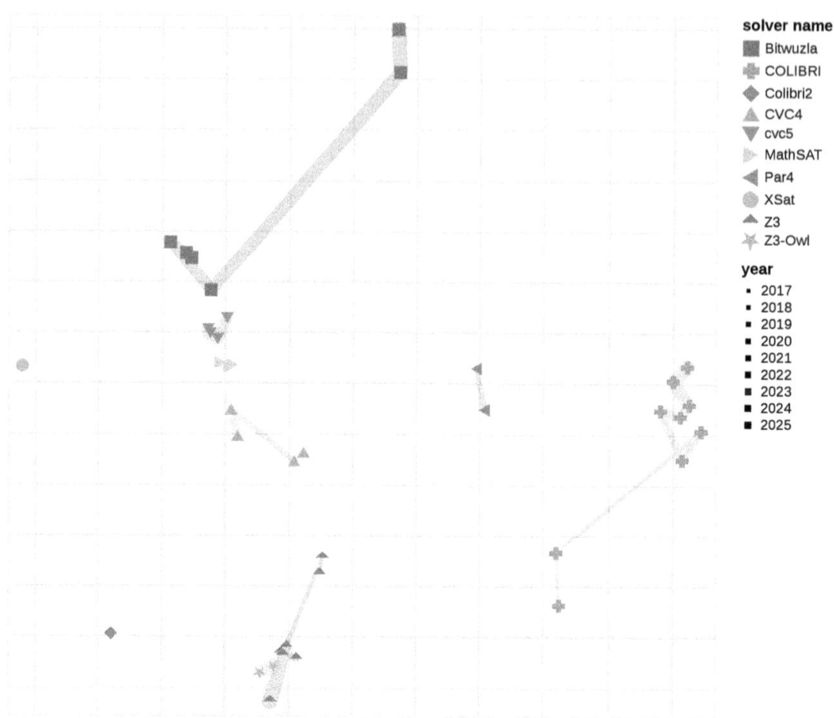

Fig. 7. Isomap for QF_FP: a version of a solver is a mark. The versions of the same solver are linked line growing with the competition years they appeared in.

To compute the similarity between two solvers we use the *cosine distance*, the cosine of the angle between two feature vectors (the distance between x and y is $1 - \frac{x\,y}{\llbracket x \rrbracket \llbracket y \rrbracket}$). The cosine distance allows us to reduce the impact of the changing competition hardware on the measure. For example, since the cosine distance between a vector and one that is twice as long is zero. This means that, if the hardware of a competition is twice as fast as the hardware of an earlier competition, all cosine distances remain the same across the two competitions. We point out that the Manhattan distance (L1) used by Biere et.al. [9] for a similar purpose in SAT solving does not have this property. Moreover, it does not differentiate well between many small differences and a few large ones.

Missing feature values, in our case for benchmarks that were not selected in a competition or were added later to SMT-LIB, are usually completed using an *imputer*. Imputer can consist of a first data analysis phase using a distance that handles missing values, such as the *NaN-Euclidean* distances of scikit-learn [2]. To keep the analysis straightforward, we directly compute the distance as the cosine distance on the common benchmarks and do not use an imputer.

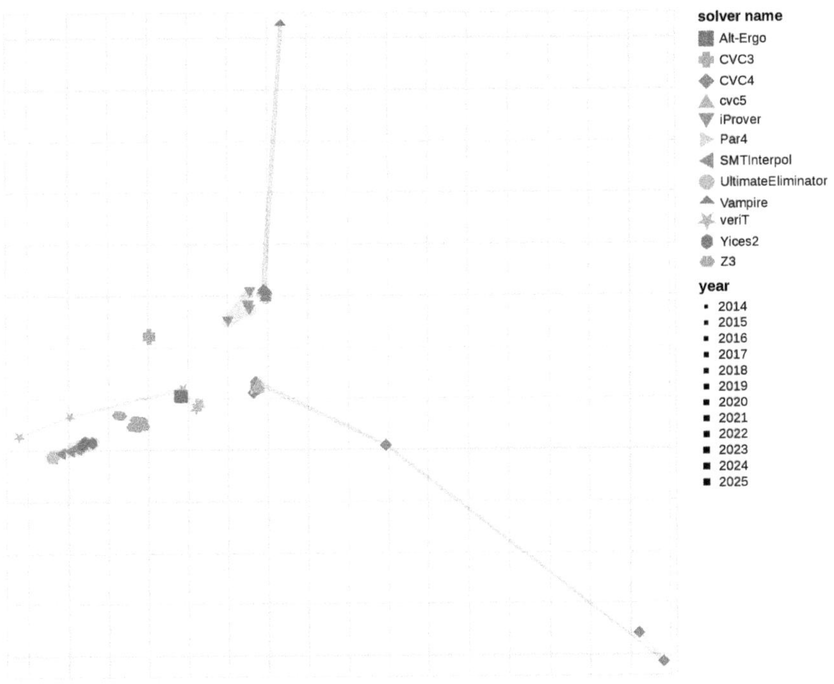

Fig. 8. Isomap for UF.

Figure 7 and Figure 8 show the isomap analysis for the logics QF_FP[8] and UF[9]. The trails show the evolution of each solver over the years.

The graphs have some easily identifiable characteristics. Solvers that implement similar techniques are, in general, close to each other. In QF_FP, solvers that are based on word-blasting, i.e., a reduction of floating-point arithmetic to bit-vectors, are gathered and aligned (Bitwuzla [19], CVC4 [7], cvc5 [3], MathSAT [12], Z3 [18]). Solvers that implement techniques different from word-blasting (COLIBRI [17], Colibri2 [10], and XSat [14]), on the other hand, are farther removed from each other and the word-blasting solvers. The portfolio-based solver Par4 [30], which includes configurations of COLIBRI, CVC4 and Z3, lies between COLIBRI and the word-blasting solvers. We observe that, in the graph, Bitwuzla and COLIBRI make a very distinct jump from one year to the other. For Bitwuzla, this can be attributed to a new solving procedure for bit-vectors based on abstraction-refinement [20], which has a beneficial impact on performance for floating-point arithmetic. For COLIBRI, according to its main developer Bruno Marre,[10] this can be explained by various major improvements

---

[8] Interactive chart: explore.smt-lib.org/isomap/QF_FP.html

[9] Interactive chart: explore.smt-lib.org/isomap/UF.html

[10] Private communication.

to the system, which is reflected in the graph. We want to emphasize, though, that while we can recognize these patterns in the isomaps for most logics, our assessment is only preliminary and should be extended in the future.

We can also see a stark contrast in the isomap of different logics. In QF_FP the solvers spread all over the map, suggesting that different solvers implement different techniques. The QF_FP ecosystem is quite active and solvers are typically complementary in terms of solved instances. In contrast, the solvers for UF are more clustered together. In addition, later versions of solvers do not move away much. This shows that the various solvers implement similar techniques, or that the benchmarks cannot distinguish among them (they are all solved).

We claim that studies performing data analysis like those above can help the community focus on logics in need of new benchmarks or new research.

6   Conclusion and Future Work

We have presented a new resource for the SMT community consisting of a database that seamlessly integrates data on SMT-LIB benchmarks from different sources, including historical data from 20 years of SMT competitions. We believe the new database and the tooling around it will be useful to both SMT solver users and developers. Our initial case studies also show that this data is useful to compare and understand SMT solvers, their performance and their evolution over time. We consider these studies just a first step towards a more systematic exploration of the collected data.

The first version of the database was released on Zenodo [25] earlier this year. We plan to release annual updates to the database in sync with the annual release of the SMT-LIB benchmark library. New releases will also provide an opportunity to add metadata requested by the community and integrate new data sources. An expected major change will be the transition to the upcoming Version 3 of the SMT-LIB language. Since Version 3 is substantially different from the current version, this will require updates to the data integration pipeline, and possible changes to the metadata fields, notably for the logic identifier.

We are also considering using the database to improve the consistency of the benchmark library and identify other errors in it. For example, using the inferredStatus field to update the status in the benchmark would make it easier for solver developers to detect classification errors.

Data-Availability Statement The experiments conducted for this paper used the 2025 release of the SMT-LIB benchmark library available on Zenodo [22,23]. The code to perform the experiments is available on Github [24].

Acknowledgments. We thank the many contributors of SMT-LIB benchmarks, and the organizers of the SMT competition. Geoff Sutcliffe provided valuable insights into benchmark difficulty ratings. We also thank the anonymous reviewers for their valuable feedback on the paper and the design of the database.

References

1. 2.2 manifold learning – scikit-learn 1.7.2 documentation. https://scikit-learn.org/stable/modules/manifold.html#isomap, accessed: 2025-10-16
2. nan_euclidean_distances – scikit-learn 1.7.2 documentation. https://scikit-learn.org/stable/modules/generated/sklearn.metrics.pairwise.nan_euclidean_distances.html, accessed: 2025-10-16
3. Barbosa, H., Barrett, C.W., Brain, M., Kremer, G., Lachnitt, H., Mann, M., Mohamed, A., Mohamed, M., Niemetz, A., Nötzli, A., Ozdemir, A., Preiner, M., Reynolds, A., Sheng, Y., Tinelli, C., Zohar, Y.: cvc5: A versatile and industrial-strength SMT solver. In: Fisman, D., Rosu, G. (eds.) Tools and Algorithms for the Construction and Analysis of Systems - 28th International Conference, TACAS 2022. Lecture Notes in Computer Science, vol. 13243, pp. 415–442. Springer (2022). https://doi.org/10.1007/978-3-030-99524-9_24
4. Barrett, C., Deters, M., de Moura, L., Oliveras, A., Stump, A.: 6 years of SMT-COMP. vol. 50, pp. 243–277 (Mar 2013). https://doi.org/10.1007/s10817-012-9246-5
5. Barrett, C., Fontaine, P., Tinelli, C.: The Satisfiability Modulo Theories Library (SMT-LIB). www.SMT-LIB.org (2016)
6. Barrett, C., Fontaine, P., Tinelli, C.: The SMT-LIB Standard: Version 2.7. Tech. rep., Department of Computer Science, The University of Iowa (2025), available at www.SMT-LIB.org
7. Barrett, C.W., Conway, C.L., Deters, M., Hadarean, L., Jovanovic, D., King, T., Reynolds, A., Tinelli, C.: CVC4. In: Gopalakrishnan, G., Qadeer, S. (eds.) Computer Aided Verification - 23rd International Conference, CAV 2011, Snowbird, UT, USA, July 14-20, 2011. Proceedings. Lecture Notes in Computer Science, vol. 6806, pp. 171–177. Springer (2011). https://doi.org/10.1007/978-3-642-22110-1_14
8. Barrett, C.W., Deters, M., de Moura, L.M., Oliveras, A., Stump, A.: 6 years of SMT-COMP. J. Autom. Reason. **50**(3), 243–277 (2013). https://doi.org/10.1007/S10817-012-9246-5
9. Biere, A., Fleury, M., Froleyks, N., Heule, J.M.: The SAT museum. In: Järvisalo, M., Le Berre, D. (eds.) Proceedings of the 14th International Workshop on Pragmatics of SAT Co-located with the 26th International Conference on Theory and Applications of Satisfiability Testing (SAT 2023), Alghero, Italy, July, 4, 2023. CEUR Workshop Proceedings, vol. 3545, pp. 72–87. CEUR-WS.org (2023), http://ceur-ws.org/Vol-3545/paper6.pdf
10. Bobot, F., Hara, H.R.A.E., Correnson, A., Junke, C.: colibri2 (Jun 2025). https://doi.org/10.5281/zenodo.15769941
11. Bury, G.: Dolmen: A validator for SMT-LIB and much more. In: Nadel, A., Niemetz, A. (eds.) Proceedings of the 19th International Workshop on Satisfiability Modulo Theories. CEUR Workshop Proceedings, vol. 2908, pp. 32–39. CEUR-WS.org (2021)
12. Cimatti, A., Griggio, A., Schaafsma, B.J., Sebastiani, R.: The MathSAT5 SMT solver. In: Piterman, N., Smolka, S.A. (eds.) Tools and Algorithms for the Construction and Analysis of Systems - 19th International Conference, TACAS 2013, Held as Part of the European Joint Conferences on Theory and Practice of Software, ETAPS 2013, Rome, Italy, March 16-24, 2013. Proceedings. Lecture Notes in Computer Science, vol. 7795, pp. 93–107. Springer (2013). https://doi.org/10.1007/978-3-642-36742-7_7

13. Cok, D.R., Stump, A., Weber, T.: The 2013 evaluation of SMT-COMP and SMT-LIB. J. Autom. Reason. **55**(1), 61–90 (2015). https://doi.org/10.1007/S10817-015-9328-2

14. Fu, Z., Su, Z.: Xsat: A fast floating-point satisfiability solver. In: Chaudhuri, S., Farzan, A. (eds.) Computer Aided Verification - 28th International Conference, CAV 2016, Toronto, ON, Canada, July 17-23, 2016, Proceedings, Part II. Lecture Notes in Computer Science, vol. 9780, pp. 187–209. Springer (2016). https://doi.org/10.1007/978-3-319-41540-6_11

15. Iser, M., Jabs, C.: Global Benchmark Database. In: Chakraborty, S., Jiang, J.H.R. (eds.) 27th International Conference on Theory and Applications of Satisfiability Testing (SAT 2024). Leibniz International Proceedings in Informatics (LIPIcs), vol. 305, pp. 18:1–18:10. Schloss Dagstuhl – Leibniz-Zentrum für Informatik, Dagstuhl, Germany (2024). https://doi.org/10.4230/LIPIcs.SAT.2024.18

16. Kulczynski, M., Lotz, K., Manea, F., Poulsen, D.B., Sarnighausen-Cahn, P.: SMT-Query: Analysing SMT-LIB string benchmarks. In: C. Nogueira, S., Teodorov, C. (eds.) Formal Methods: Foundations and Applications. pp. 22–34. Springer Nature Switzerland, Cham (2025). https://doi.org/10.1007/978-3-031-78116-2_2

17. Marre, B., Blanc, B., Mouy, P., Chihani, Z., Vedrine, F., Bobot, F.: Colibri (2019), https://smt-comp.github.io/2019/system-descriptions/colibri.pdf

18. de Moura, L.M., Bjørner, N.S.: Z3: an efficient SMT solver. In: Ramakrishnan, C.R., Rehof, J. (eds.) Tools and Algorithms for the Construction and Analysis of Systems, 14th International Conference, TACAS 2008, Held as Part of the Joint European Conferences on Theory and Practice of Software, ETAPS 2008, Budapest, Hungary, March 29-April 6, 2008. Proceedings. Lecture Notes in Computer Science, vol. 4963, pp. 337–340. Springer (2008). https://doi.org/10.1007/978-3-540-78800-3_24

19. Niemetz, A., Preiner, M.: Bitwuzla. In: Enea, C., Lal, A. (eds.) Computer Aided Verification - 35th International Conference, CAV 2023, Paris, France, July 17-22, 2023, Proceedings, Part II. Lecture Notes in Computer Science, vol. 13965, pp. 3–17. Springer (2023). https://doi.org/10.1007/978-3-031-37703-7_1

20. Niemetz, A., Preiner, M., Zohar, Y.: Scalable bit-blasting with abstractions. In: Gurfinkel, A., Ganesh, V. (eds.) Computer Aided Verification - 36th International Conference, CAV 2024, Montreal, QC, Canada, July 24-27, 2024, Proceedings, Part I. Lecture Notes in Computer Science, vol. 14681, pp. 178–200. Springer (2024). https://doi.org/10.1007/978-3-031-65627-9_9

21. Organizers, S.C.: The SMT competition. https://smt-comp.github.io (2025)

22. Preiner, M., Schurr, H.J., Barrett, C., Fontaine, P., Niemetz, A., Tinelli, C.: SMT-LIB release 2025 (incremental benchmarks) (May 2025). https://doi.org/10.5281/zenodo.15493096

23. Preiner, M., Schurr, H.J., Barrett, C., Fontaine, P., Niemetz, A., Tinelli, C.: SMT-LIB release 2025 (non-incremental benchmarks) (Aug 2025). https://doi.org/10.5281/zenodo.15493089

24. Schurr, H.J., Bobot, F.: Github reporsitory: SMT-LIB / SMT-LIB-db. https://github.com/SMT-LIB/SMT-LIB-db/releases/tag/tacas26 (2026)

25. Schurr, H.J., Preiner, M., Niemetz, A., Barrett, C., Fontaine, P., Tinelli, C.: SMT-LIB catalog 2025 (Jul 2025). https://doi.org/10.5281/zenodo.16290040

26. Scott, J., Niemetz, A., Preiner, M., Nejati, S., Ganesh, V.: Algorithm selection for SMT. Int. J. Softw. Tools Technol. Transf. **25**(2), 219–239 (2023). https://doi.org/10.1007/S10009-023-00696-0

27. Stump, A., Sutcliffe, G., Tinelli, C.: StarExec: A cross-community infrastructure for logic solving. In: Demri, S., Kapur, D., Weidenbach, C. (eds.) Automated Reasoning - 7th International Joint Conference, IJCAR 2014, Held as Part of the Vienna Summer of Logic, VSL 2014, Vienna, Austria, July 19-22, 2014. Proceedings. Lecture Notes in Computer Science, vol. 8562, pp. 367–373. Springer (2014). https://doi.org/10.1007/978-3-319-08587-6_28

28. Sutcliffe, G.: The TPTP Problem Library and Associated Infrastructure. From CNF to TH0, TPTP v6.4.0. J. Autom. Reason. **59**(4), 483–502 (2017). https://doi.org/10.1007/s10817-017-9407-7

29. Tenenbaum, J.B., de Silva, V., Langford, J.C.: A global geometric framework for nonlinear dimensionality reduction. Science **290**(5500), 2319–2323 (2000). https://doi.org/10.1126/science.290.5500.2319

30. Weber, T.: Par4 system description (2019), https://smt-comp.github.io/2019/system-descriptions/Par4.pdf

31. Weber, T., Conchon, S., Déharbe, D., Heizmann, M., Niemetz, A., Reger, G.: The SMT competition 2015–2018. J. Satisf. Boolean Model. Comput. **11**(1), 221–259 (2019). https://doi.org/10.3233/SAT190123

Massively Parallel Bit-Precise Verification with Bitwuzla and Mallob[*]

Dominik Schreiber[1] , Aina Niemetz[2] , and Mathias Preiner[2]

[1] Karlsruhe Institute of Technology, Karlsruhe, Germany
`dominik.schreiber@kit.edu`
[2] Stanford University, Stanford, CA, USA
`{niemetz, preiner}@cs.stanford.edu`

Abstract. We present a distributed platform for massively parallel SMT solving that supports various theories for bit-precise reasoning, with and without quantifiers and push-pop incrementality. Our system is based on an integration of the state-of-the-art SMT solver Bitwuzla into the distributed job scheduling and automated reasoning platform Mallob, which allows Bitwuzla to make heavy use of Mallob's distributed incremental SAT solving engine. Our experimental evaluation shows that this approach outperforms prior SMT parallelization approaches and achieves unprecedented speedups at up to 768 cores.

Keywords: SMT solving · Distributed computing · Verification · Propositional satisfiability

1   Introduction

Satisfiability Modulo Theories (SMT) solvers are integrated as the back-end reasoning engines in a wide range of applications of computer-aided verification, both in academia and industry. For many of these applications, bit-precise reasoning in the theory of fixed-size bit-vectors is a key requirement.

The dominant, state-of-the-art approach for solving bit-vector formulas in SMT is a technique called *bit-blasting* [23], an eager reduction of bit-vector constraints to propositional satisfiability (SAT). Bit-blasting is usually combined with aggressive simplifications of the input constraints prior to the actual reduction step. This technique is surprisingly efficient in practice, mainly due to the fact that state-of-the-art SAT solvers are able to efficiently deal with complex formulas over millions of variables. To render interrelated calls to the SAT solver more efficient, SMT solvers commonly exploit *incremental SAT solving*, where the SAT solver state is preserved across solving calls [3,13]. In the context of bit-blasting, such interrelated calls occur not only in incremental SMT solving, but also for abstraction-refinement-based techniques such as [32], and when combining the theory of fixed-size bit-vectors with other theories. Regardless, the back-end SAT solver of the procedure remains its main potential bottleneck.

[*] This work was supported in part by the Stanford Center for Automated Reasoning, the Stanford Center for Blockchain Research, and a gift from Amazon Web Services.

S. Junges and G. Katz (Eds.): TACAS 2026, LNCS 16505, pp. 170–191, 2026.
https://doi.org/10.1007/978-3-032-22752-2_9

In recent years, parallel and distributed SAT solvers have increasingly gained traction [11, 20, 43]. Some of the best available systems use careful *clause sharing* across SAT solver threads to solve challenging problems hundreds of times faster than their state-of-the-art sequential counterparts [42, 44]. In particular, the state-of-the-art distributed SAT solving platform Mallob [44] allows to solve many SAT tasks in parallel and on demand, balances the available computational resources among them in a flexible fashion [37], and efficiently handles *incremental* SAT solving queries at a distributed scale for individual tasks [40, 41]. Still, as of yet, we are unaware of any published works that exploit this power for SMT.

In this work, we specifically focus on accelerating the state-of-the-art SMT solver Bitwuzla [29], which supports reasoning over the (quantified and quantifier-free) theories of fixed-size bit-vectors and floating-point arithmetic, in combination with arrays and uninterpreted functions. The architecture of Bitwuzla is based on the counter-example guided abstraction refinement (CEGAR) paradigm [10]. Specifically, Bitwuzla implements the lazy SMT technique *lemmas on demand* [6, 28], but with a bit-blasting bit-vector solver (instead of a propositional abstraction) at its core. At the back end, the SAT solver is integrated in an offline fashion. This is in contrast to the classic $CDCL(\mathcal{T})$ framework [15, 33], which refines a propositional abstraction of the input via low-level, fine-grained interactions between the SAT solver and the theory solvers.

Contribution. We present an integration of the bit-blasting SMT solver Bitwuzla with distributed, on-demand incremental SAT solving in Mallob. Our work takes advantage of recent advances in parallel and distributed SAT solving in the context of SMT solving based on bit-blasting. This yields a scalable, parallel and distributed SMT solver for bit-precise reasoning.

Bitwuzla is integrated as a new application engine of the Mallob system and submits incremental SAT solving tasks to the distributed scheduler. This not only combines the advantages of bit-precise reasoning as implemented in Bitwuzla and parallel and distributed SAT solving as provided by Mallob, but offers remarkable synergies. First, we exploit the fact that almost all of Bitwuzla's non-trivial reasoning, and thus the vast majority of its solving time, is spent in plain incremental SAT solving, which is much easier to parallelize than the fine-grained interactions loop of $CDCL(\mathcal{T})$. Second, using a flexible on-demand scheduler allows to maintain several distinct SAT solving tasks (a common pattern when spawning sub-solvers in quantified reasoning) and to shift the distributed resources to the task that has use for them. Third, the use of *incremental* SAT solving enables highly efficient and low-latency SAT queries while keeping distributed communication at a minimum. Finally, in contrast to more theory-specific parallelization efforts targeting the bit-vector theory [36, 49], replacing the bit-blasting solver's back-end SAT solver with a parallel and distributed SAT solver is theory agnostic. Parallelization on the SAT level benefits every supported theory (and combination) while retaining the full expressive power and versatility of Bitwuzla.

We evaluate our system, which we refer to as BITWUZLLOB, on up to 768 cores (16 compute nodes) and show that it outperforms and outscales prior related parallel SMT approaches significantly. Our results suggest that BITWUZLLOB promises to serve as a solid base for future, theory-specific parallelization efforts in the context of bit-precise reasoning.

Related Work. State-of-the-art parallel and distributed SMT solving strategies can largely be divided into *portfolio* solving and *partitioning*. Portfolio solving configures multiple different solvers (or configurations of a solver) that attempt to solve the same SMT problem in parallel. Partitioning is a divide-and-conquer strategy where a problem is partitioned into independent subproblems that are solved in parallel. Some parallel SMT techniques are based on partitioning only [22,48], but the majority relies (at least partly) on a portfolio strategy, in combination with information sharing and partitioning [5,21,25,26,46]. Most of these approaches are in principle theory agnostic, but have not been evaluated in the context of incremental SMT solving and bit-precise reasoning. Furthermore, none of them exploit parallel and distributed SAT solving techniques.

Parallelization techniques for the theory of fixed-size bit-vectors have received little attention so far. Reisenberger [36] explored a cube-and-conquer-style partitioning technique, implemented as a prototype on top of an outdated version of Boolector [31], with limited success. STP-Parti-Bitwuzla [49], a recent participant in the parallel bit-vector track of SMT-COMP 2025 [1], implements a partitioning strategy similar to [48] on top of Bitwuzla. Recently, the shared-memory parallel SAT solver Gimsatul [16] was integrated as a SAT backend of Bitwuzla [30]. Gimsatul, however, does not support incremental solving, and is thus reinitialized for every SAT query.

2   Parallel and Distributed SAT Solving with Mallob

Consider a *propositional* formula $\phi = \bigwedge_{i=1}^{n} C_i$ in conjunctive normal form (CNF) where clauses $C_i = \bigvee_{j=1}^{k_i} l_{ij}$ are disjunctions of literals and each literal l_{ij} is a Boolean variable or its negation. The problem of *propositional satisfiability* (SAT) is to decide whether there exists a variable assignment that satisfies ϕ. Today's most efficient SAT solvers are based on Conflict-Driven Clause Learning (CDCL) [27], which involves a search over the space of partial variable assignments while bookkeeping *conflict clauses* derived from logical conflicts.

Many applications of SAT solvers exploit a mode of operation called *incremental SAT solving* [3,13] where, once a solver returns a satisfiability result for some formula ϕ, the user can specify additional clauses C and query the same solver instance on the resulting formula $\phi' := \phi \cup C$. Furthermore, each satisfiability query can be supplied with a number of *assumption literals*, which are enforced to hold for this query *only*. Incremental SAT solving offers efficient interaction schemes on interrelated and evolving problems since it allows the solver to preserve its knowledge base across incremental solving calls.

In parallel and distributed SAT solving, a common approach is to run a sequential SAT solver thread on each available core and let the solver threads *cooperate* by means of exchanging useful *conflict clauses* they find during their search [2,8,19,38,45,47]. Recent insights indicate that this *clause-sharing* strategy [44] can lead to good scalability up to hundreds, and even thousands of cores, even if all solver threads operate on the same, original formula and are configured and initialized in (almost) the exact same way [42].

Mallob is a distributed job scheduling and automated reasoning platform [44] that allows to schedule, balance, and solve many SAT (and other) tasks at once, in an on-demand fashion. The amount of computational resources allotted to a certain task can increase or decrease *during the task's execution* via so-called *malleable job scheduling*, subject to the overall system state (i.e., the number and demands of active jobs vs. the amount of available computational resources) [37]. The state-of-the-art parallel and distributed SAT solving engine MallobSat is tightly integrated in Mallob and offers full support for incremental SAT solving [40]. Recently, Mallob's combination of distributed incremental SAT solving with flexible multi-tasking was exploited for distributed MaxSAT solving [41].

3   Bit-Precise SMT Solving in Bitwuzla

Satisfiability Modulo Theories (SMT) is the problem of determining whether a *first-order* formula is satisfiable with respect to some background *theories* (for an introduction to SMT, see, e.g., [7]). Prominent examples of such background theories are the theories of fixed-size bit-vectors, arrays, integer arithmetic, real arithmetic and strings. In the following, we consider background theories as defined in SMT-LIB [4] and assume the usual notions and terminology of many-sorted first-order logic with equality (see, e.g., [14,24]).

Bitwuzla [29] is a state-of-the-art SMT solver specialized for bit-precise reasoning. It supports the theories of fixed-size bit-vectors and floating-point arithmetic, in combination with arrays and uninterpreted functions, with and without quantifiers. Bitwuzla implements an abstraction-refinement-based SMT paradigm called *lemmas on demand* [6,28], but with a bit-vector abstraction (and thus a bit-vector solver) instead of a propositional abstraction at its core. Atoms and terms that do not belong to the bit-vector theory are abstracted as uninterpreted Boolean and bit-vector constants, respectively. These abstracted terms are then handled by the corresponding theory solvers. The bit-vector abstraction is bit-blasted to propositional logic, and deciding its satisfiability is delegated to the back-end SAT solver. The general architecture of Bitwuzla is shown in Figure 1.

Given a formula ϕ, prior to solving, Bitwuzla aggressively applies simplification techniques as a preprocessing step. In the refinement loop of the lemmas on demand architecture, given the preprocessed formula ϕ' and the current set of refinement lemmas $\mathcal{L}$, the bit-vector solver is responsible for deciding the satisfiability of the bit-vector abstraction $\mathcal{A}(\phi' \cup \mathcal{L})$ (initially, $\mathcal{L} = \emptyset$). If the bit-vector solver determines that the abstraction is unsatisfiable, it concludes with *unsat* (since $\mathcal{A}$ is an over-approximation of the original problem ϕ). Otherwise, it produces a model for $\mathcal{A}$, which must be checked for consistency with respect to theory axioms by each theory solver. If a theory solvers determines that the model is inconsistent, it generates and adds a theory lemma to $\mathcal{L}$, thus refin-

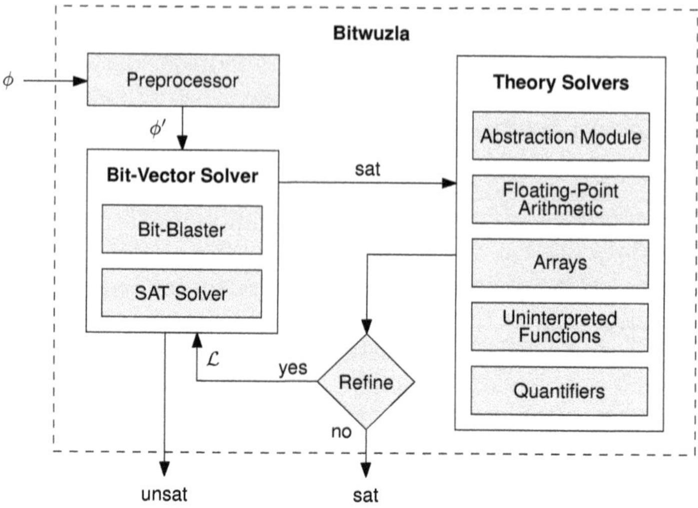

Fig. 1. Bitwuzla solver architecture.

ing $\mathcal{A}$ and ruling out the spurious model. This loop incrementally refines $\mathcal{A}$ until either $\mathcal{A}$ is determined to be unsatisfiable, or all theory solvers agree that the current model is consistent with their theory axioms, and thus, ϕ is *sat*.

Note that for floating-point arithmetic, Bitwuzla implements a technique called *word-blasting*, which translates floating-point terms to bit-vectors terms, thus heavily relying on the bit-vector solver. A more detailed introduction to Bitwuzla's architecture and theory solvers can be found in [29].

The main bit-vector solving procedure in Bitwuzla implements a CEGAR-based abstraction-refinement approach for bit-vector arithmetic based on bit-blasting [32]. This technique introduces and iteratively refines abstractions for arithmetic operations $\{\cdot, \div, \mathrm{mod}\}$, which are expensive for bit-blasting for large bit-widths due to the complexity of their bit-level circuit representation. It seamlessly integrates into Bitwuzla's lemmas on demand architecture.

Bitwuzla's bit-vector solver is used incrementally on different levels. On the user-facing side, Bitwuzla provides incremental solving capabilities via push-pop incrementality and solving under assumptions. But even for non-incremental SMT queries, Bitwuzla's bit-vector solver is used incrementally within the lemmas on demand loop. Consequently, Bitwuzla's bit-blasting solver heavily relies on the incremental solving capabilities of its default SAT backend CaDiCaL [9].

4   Integrating Bitwuzla with Mallob

We now describe our parallel and distributed SMT solver, which we refer to as BITWUZLLOB, as an integration of Bitwuzla into the Mallob platform.

Figure 2 provides a general overview of our system. At the top level, the system can be used as a plain SMT solver similar to unmodified Bitwuzla: it

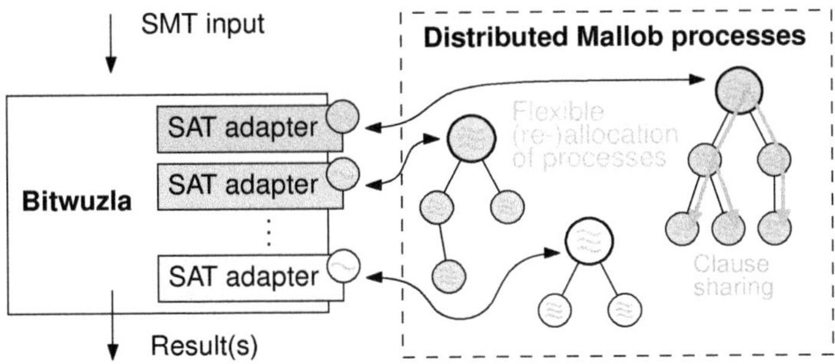

Fig. 2. Overview of our system's architecture (inspired by [41]). While only one SMT interaction is displayed, a single execution of the system can also handle several such interactions concurrently while balancing the available distributed resources among them. Each "$\sim$" illustrates an incremental SAT solver thread.

processes user input in the SMT-LIB format and provides the expected output, e.g., the model of a satisfiable query after a (get-model) command. At the back end, however, we reworked how Bitwuzla performs SAT solving.

Depending on the input problem, Bitwuzla's execution involves either one single or several co-existing SAT solver instances. Since Bitwuzla is purely sequential, *at most one* of these instances is *active* at any point in time. In BITWUZL-LOB, each of Bitwuzla's SAT solver instances now corresponds to a more complex *SAT adapter* object in the Mallob system instead of a plain CaDiCaL instance. We describe in Section 4.2 how we interfaced the two systems.

Each SAT adapter processes incoming SAT solving calls in two orthogonal ways in parallel. First, a *latency hiding head thread* runs a sequential CaDiCaL instance to intercept trivial SAT calls, as explained in more detail in Section 4.3. Second, a distributed incremental SAT solving task is deployed in Mallob to conquer non-trivial SAT calls. There is a 1:1 correspondence between SAT adapters and distributed incremental SAT solving tasks. However, a distributed task may be delayed in its deployment (if all SAT solving calls thus far are trivial, see Section 4.3) and a deployed, yet inactive distributed task may be terminated if too many inactive tasks are present in the system. Terminated tasks are potentially re-deployed at a later point (see Section 4.4 for further details).

4.1 User Interface

Launching BITWUZLLOB is done in the same way as launching Mallob. Since Mallob is based on the Message Passing Interface (MPI), an MPI wrapper such as mpirun or mpiexec is used to run $p \geq 1$ interconnected incarnations of the mallob executable, which can be distributed across $1 \leq m \leq p$ physical machines. The mapping of the p MPI processes to machines and cores can be configured via additional arguments to the MPI wrapper. For $m = p = 1$ (single-node, single-process), mallob can be executed directly without using an MPI wrapper.

```
$ mpirun -np 4 build/mallob -q -t=48 &   # Launch Mallob/Bitwuzllob
[1] 129857
$ mkfifo smt-output.pipe   # Create named pipe for output
$ cat job.json   # Show JSON submission file
{
    "user": "myname",
    "name": "job1",
    "application": "SMT",
    "files": ["smt-input.smt2"],
    "priority": 1.0,
    "configuration": {"smt-out-file": "smt-output.pipe"}
}
$ cp job.json .api/jobs.0/in/   # Submit SMT job
$ cat smt-output.pipe   # Fetch SMT solver output
sat
(
  (define-fun s () (_ BitVec 512) #b00000000 ... 00000110)
  (define-fun t () (_ BitVec 512) #b00000000 ... 00000000)
)
$ pkill -2 mpirun ; rm smt-output.pipe   # Clean up
```

Fig. 3. Example user interaction with BITWUZLLOB in its *on-demand* mode of operation. After launching BITWUZLLOB as a service (with four processes à 48 threads), an SMT solving task is submitted by copying a basic JSON file describing the task to a watched API directory. The output is then read from the specified output file (which, in this case, was set to a *named pipe* special file for direct inter-process communication). Note that the SMT input (specified as `smt-input.smt2` here) could also be set to a named pipe to feed SMT commands to BITWUZLLOB interactively.

Just like Mallob [39, 43], BITWUZLLOB supports two modes of operation: **mono** and **on-demand**. In the *mono* mode of operation, a path to a single SMT instance is given via the command-line (`-mono-app=SMT -mono=<file>`) when launching the system. BITWUZLLOB solves this instance and then terminates. In the *on-demand* mode, the system is launched without providing such a single instance to solve. Instead, a configurable subset of the system's processes, called **client processes**, *listen* for incoming SMT tasks, which users can submit to the system at any time over a filesystem-based JSON interface. Whenever a client receives an SMT task, it locally launches a procedure as shown in Figure 2 (left). Figure 3 illustrates an example for launching and using BITWUZLLOB in its *on-demand* mode to solve an SMT task. Internally, the *mono* mode is in fact only a special case of the *on-demand* mode, where exactly one client process is initialized and programmatically receives the singular input instance to process.

The distributed computational resources are balanced dynamically among all distributed SAT tasks spawned by the active SMT task(s) (cf. [37, 41]). If desired, the output of the internal Bitwuzla procedure of an SMT task can be directed to an output file by the client process that hosts the SMT task (specified via command-line option `-smt-out-file` in the *mono* setting, and JSON option "`smt-out-file`" in the *on-demand* setting). For incremental and interactive SMT solving use cases, the SMT input file and/or output file are initialized as *named pipes*, which allows interacting with BITWUZLLOB by successively reading from and/or writing to these pipes. SMT solving can be configured globally via the command-line option `-bitwuzla-args`, or locally (i.e., specific to a certain SMT task) via statements in the SMT-LIB input.

4.2   Interfacing Bitwuzla and Mallob

In the following, we describe the interface we established between the Bitwuzla and Mallob systems, as well as the underlying rationale.

Exploiting Mallob for an application of incremental SAT solving is possible via (at least) two avenues. The first option is to *connect* the application to a running client process via Mallob's provided *bridge interface* [40] or similar interfacing code. Internally, the application uses a file system to submit tasks to a Mallob process and receive corresponding feedback. The application (Bitwuzla) and the distributed program (Mallob) thus remain as separate systems.

The second option is to *integrate* the application into Mallob itself (cf. [41]). This requires adding application code to the Mallob project, to be executed whenever a job for the target application arrives. This option allows the application to deploy sub-tasks (such as incremental SAT solving tasks) to Mallob *programmatically* and thus much more efficiently than with the first option.

For the sake of efficiency and ease of use, we decided on the second option and implemented BITWUZLLOB as a stand-alone distributed SMT solver by integrating Bitwuzla into Mallob as a new application engine. For this purpose, we extended the public API of Bitwuzla to allow the injection of an external SAT solver factory for constructing SAT solver instances. We further added an application handler for SMT to Mallob, which executes Bitwuzla on the input problem in a dedicated thread within the hosting client process. Instead of using Bitwuzla's internal SAT solver factory to create SAT solver instances, Mallob now acts as the SAT solver factory, constructing instances of our SAT adapter.

4.3   Latency Reduction

Bitwuzla commonly produces incremental SAT queries that feature a large number (potentially thousands) of solving calls, many of which are trivial. In practice, low latencies for individual, trivial SAT solving calls are as crucial for performance as high parallel speedups for challenging ones. Mallob has been tuned to reduce latencies for trivial SAT calls before [40, 41], but we observed that latencies of around 5-10 ms per call were still common.

In order to reduce latencies even further, we therefore introduce a so-called *latency-hiding head thread* within the host process. In addition to the distributed SAT job dispatch, we locally run a single sequential SAT solver thread that attempts to solve the same problems as the distributed solver in the background. As such, we have two independent SAT solver actors, a local one and a distributed one, for each incremental stream of SAT calls. If one of these actors succeeds in solving incremental revisions 0 through k while the other actor is still occupied with revision $j < k$, the actor is interrupted. Subsequently, the interrupted actor receives revisions $j, j + 1, \ldots, k$ as a single *contracted increment* that features the clauses of revision j to k and the assumption literals of k.

As a result, if an SMT input yields thousands of trivial SAT calls followed by a single challenging call, the distributed solver receives only one single, challenging increment. We even take this a step further by deferring the initialization of the distributed incremental SAT task alltogether, until an increment that cannot be solved by the latency-hiding head thread within a few milliseconds is reached.

In order to account for the high number of incremental revisions arising from some Bitwuzla runs, we also refactored Mallob's inter-process communication. In prior versions of Mallob, each MPI process transfers each formula increment to its dedicated SAT solving sub-process by means of *shared memory*: the MPI process allocates an appropriately sized shared memory segment, populates it with the clauses of the next increment, and then notifies the SAT sub-process that the segment can now be read. This eventually results in a large number of concurrently open shared-memory segments and corresponding (virtual) files in `/dev/shm/` that require significant amounts of RAM, which may become detrimental to performance. Instead, Mallob now transfers formula information in a buffered manner over a single, fixed-size shared memory segment. Double buffering and dedicated I/O threads are utilized to transfer data as fast as possible.

4.4 Limiting Concurrent Distributed Tasks

On SMT input problems with quantifiers, in each iteration of the lemmas on demand loop, Bitwuzla creates an internal sub-solver instance for performing checks on quantified formulas arising from model-based quantifier instantiation (MBQI) [17]. The number of incremental sub-solver checks depends on the number of active quantified formulas, and while performing an MBQI check for a quantified formula, a sub-solver may create nested sub-solver instances if the checked quantified formula contains nested quantified formulas. As a consequence, the quantifiers module may create a large hierarchy of sub-solvers. Each sub-solver is a fully functional (internal) Bitwuzla instance with a fresh SAT solver, potentially resulting in a large number of SAT solver instances.

While at most one SAT solver instance is active at any point in time, each suspended distributed solving task in Mallob *exclusively* blocks one MPI process, until the task is terminated. As such, in a naïve implementation, an execution with p Mallob processes will run into issues once Bitwuzla has created and used, but not destroyed, SAT adapters $T_1, \ldots, T_p$, and then creates and uses another SAT adapter T_{p+1}. While the latency-hiding solver thread of T_{p+1} still progresses, the corresponding distributed task's deployment is stalled indefinitely since no process is available to deploy T_{p+1} to.

We mitigate this issue by limiting the number of deployed distributed tasks per SMT solving task to a user-defined parameter $s \leq p$. If some SAT adapter is about to deploy a distributed task that would exceed this limit, another adapter's inactive distributed task is *evicted*, i.e., terminated and cleaned up. In principle, any inactive task can be evicted since it can be re-deployed at a later point if and when the corresponding adapter receives another SAT call. In practice, choosing which task is best to evict can be non-trivial. Aspects to consider include the size of a task's formula (large problems take longer to re-deploy), the time of the task's creation (old solver instances might lose relevance), and the task's total solving time until now (significant knowledge may be lost when evicting a long running task). Considering Bitwuzla's approach to spawning sub-solvers, where the oldest SAT task may often correspond to Bitwuzla's main solver and is thus likely to be reused, we decided on an eviction strategy that picks the task with the *lowest total runtime* so far. We recommend to set $s \leq p/T$, where T is the maximum anticipated number of parallel SMT solving tasks, so that at least s processes per SMT solving task are in fact available. In our experiments, where only one SMT task is active at a time, we chose a conservative limit of $s = p/2$, thus ensuring that an active SAT task can exploit at least half of all processes.

5 Evaluation

We evaluate BITWUZLLOB in terms of SMT solving performance and scaling behavior on non-incremental and incremental benchmarks of all supported logics of the SMT-LIB benchmark library [34,35]. Runs in distributed environments are costly and resource intensive, which requires a responsible use of computational resources in our experimental design. As in previous work on distributed SAT and MaxSAT solving [40, 41, 44], we therefore limit the wallclock runtime per instance to 300 s. This time limit is justified not only by saving resources but also by the observation that investing large amounts of resources should be traded off with much lower wallclock runtimes (when considering the same inputs).

Further, the set of benchmarks in supported logics contains 156,307 non-incremental and 25,464 incremental instances. Since considering the whole set is not feasible for our experimental evaluation, we selected a modestly sized but diverse and representative benchmark set as follows. We first ran sequential Bitwuzla on all non-incremental and incremental benchmarks with a time limit of 1200 seconds and a memory limit of 8GB. For each logic, we then grouped all benchmarks into six sets S_1–S_5 and S_u based on the observed runtime. Sets S_1–S_5 contain all *solved* benchmarks that were solved in more than n and at most m seconds, whereas S_u contains all *unsolved* benchmarks. We used the following runtime distribution for these sets: $(n, m) \in \{(5, 10), (10, 100), (100, 300), (300, 600), (600, 1200)\}$. As a final step, we randomly sampled benchmarks from each group with a distribution of 10/10/25/25/35/50 for $S_1/S_2/S_3/S_4/S_5/S_u$. In total, we selected 1098 (96/134/180/117/116/455) non-incremental and 288 (60/64/63/28/16/57) incremental benchmarks. Selecting benchmarks that were solved quickly by the sequential version allows us to measure the overhead of our distributed setup on easy instances, while more difficult benchmarks enable us to measure and analyze its scaling behavior. Overall, we selected a larger number of harder benchmarks, since our approach is more likely to be applied to hard instances.

We compare our system against several existing approaches. As a most natural comparison, we run plain, sequential Bitwuzla, i.e., with its default CaDiCaL backend. In addition, we test the three most relevant competitors in the parallel track of the 2025 SMT competition: (1) Bitwuzla+Gimsatul (*Gims+Bzla*), a version of Bitwuzla with the shared-memory parallel SAT solver Gimsatul [16] instead of CaDiCaL as its SAT backend [30]; (2) STP-Parti-Bitwuzla (*STP-P-Bzla*), a recent partitioning-based parallel SMT solver [48] that uses Bitwuzla (with CaDiCaL) as its sequential SMT backend and participated in the non-incremental QF_BV logic [49]; and (3) Yices2 (*Yices*), a parallel portfolio of Yices2 configurations that participated in the QF_ABV, QF_AUFBV, QF_BV, and QF_UFBV logics (among other logics not supported by Bitwuzla) [12].

We ran all experiments on the cluster SuperMUC-NG, where each node features a two-socket Intel Skylake Xeon Platinum 8174 processor clocked at 2.7 GHz with a total of 48 physical cores (96 hardware threads) and 96 GB of main memory. Nodes are interconnected via Intel OmniPath and run Linux SLES.[3]

5.1 Solving Performance

In our first experiment, we compare BITWUZLLOB to existing approaches on commonly supported logics. Figure 4 (left) shows the results of all considered systems on the commonly supported non-incremental QF_BV logic on a single node with 48 cores. We ran this experiment on a single node since the competing approaches are not distributed. The explicit search space partitioning approach of STP-Parti-Bitwuzla results in a clear and consistent improvement over sequential Bitwuzla, but is outperformed by Bitwuzla with the parallel SAT solver Gimsatul as a backend. BITWUZLLOB performs similar to Gims+Bzla at lower runtimes ($< 20\,$s) and significantly outperforms all other approaches for higher runtimes. The comparatively low number of instances solved by Yices can be attributed to the fact that its parallel portfolio consists of one default configuration for each logic, complemented with additional, orthogonal MCSAT-based [18] configurations. These MCSAT-based configurations are highly efficient on some fragments of QF_BV and less efficient on others, and our benchmark selection for this logic seems to be less favorable for MCSAT-based approaches.

Figure 4 (right) complements our comparison on QF_BV with a comparison of sequential Bitwuzla with the systems that support the entire set of selected benchmarks. Interestingly, Bitwuzla's parallel Gimsatul backend seems ineffective if evaluated over a combination of theories as it is outperformed by Bitwuzla with the sequential CaDiCaL backend by a significant margin. This is likely due to the fact that Gimsatul does not support incremental solving, and thus, Bitwuzla creates a fresh Gimsatul instance for each incremental SAT call. As a consequence, the performance of Gims+Bzla suffers on incremental (SAT) workloads, which are higher on instances that involve arrays, uninterpreted functions, and quantifiers, even on the non-incremental benchmarks. BITWUZLLOB, in contrast, manages to drastically outperform sequential Bitwuzla.

---

[3] https://doku.lrz.de/supermuc-ng-10745965.html

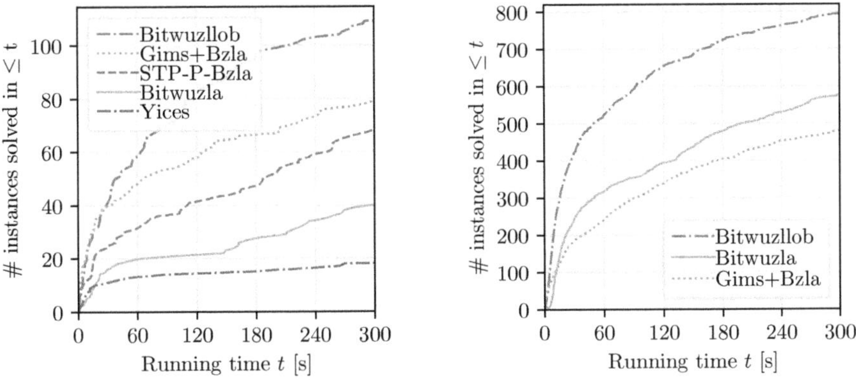

Fig. 4. Performance on non-incremental `QF_BV` instances (left) and the entire benchmark set (right) on a single node with 48 cores, with Bitwuzla as the sequential baseline.

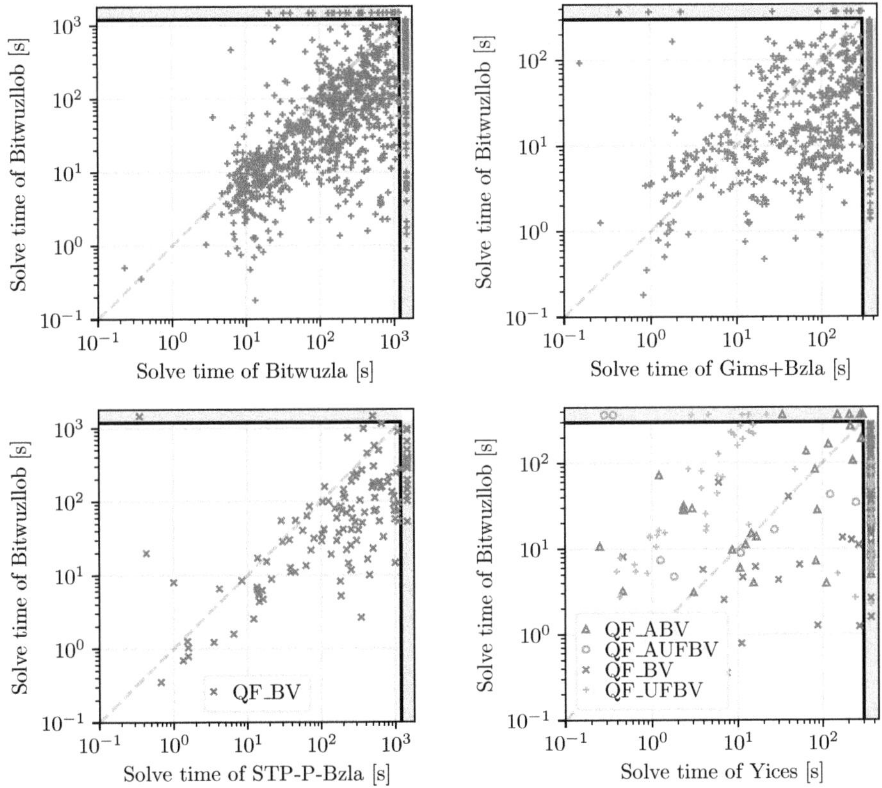

Fig. 5. Bitwuzllob versus Bitwuzla (top left), Gims+Bzla (top right), STP-Parti-Bzla (bottom left), and Yices (bottom right), on 48 cores, showing all instances from commonly supported logics. Left (right) plots use a time limit of 1200 s (300 s).

Figure 5 shows a per-instance comparison of our approach on a single node (48 cores) with the individual considered systems on the benchmarks of commonly supported logics. While we generally imposed a time limit of 300 s per instance, we also conducted additional runs with an increased time limit of 1200 s for a comparison of single-node BITWUZLLOB with sequential Bitwuzla and STP-Parti-Bitwuzla (the winner in logic QF_BV of the parallel track of SMT-COMP 2025) for a more complete picture, given in the left column of Figure 5. Overall, BITWUZLLOB clearly outperforms all other approaches. There are a few instances on which BITWUZLLOB seems to struggle that other parallel approaches solve quickly, indicated by points at the top-left corner of plots. On these instances, sequential Bitwuzla has a similarly bad performance behavior, which is also suggested by the comparison plot on the top left of Figure 5, as it does not show this behavior. We expect that improving the performance of the sequential solver on these instances will also improve the performance of BITWUZLLOB.

Tables 1 and 2 summarize the results of all considered systems with a time limit of 300 s on a single node with 48 cores in terms of solved instances, solved individual queries (for the case of incremental SMT instances), and Penalized Average Runtime (PAR-2), which penalizes each timeout with twice the time limit (i.e., 600 s). Logics not supported by a solver are indicated with a '–', and best results for each logic and metric are highlighted.

5.2 Scaling Performance

In our second experiment, we assess the scaling performance of our system. Figure 6 (left) provides a general overview for runs scaling from 4–768 cores on 1–16 nodes. Even at the lowest scale (1x4), our approach significantly outperforms sequential Bitwuzla.[4] We also observe consistent scaling-up to the highest scale (16x48), with clear diminishing returns beyond four nodes (192 cores).

Table 3 complements these findings with detailed *speedups* achieved over sequential Bitwuzla grouped by logic. Given a single SMT instance solved by the sequential baseline as well as the parallel run, the parallel speedup is the ratio between the sequential and the parallel (wallclock) runtime. We aggregate these speedup measures, using the geometric mean, while only considering instances of a certain minimum difficulty. For this, we first consider all *non-trivial* instances, i.e., instances that sequential Bitwuzla solved in ≥ 1 s, and then narrow this set down to the more *challenging* instances, i.e., instances solved by Bitwuzla in ≥ 60 s. Across the majority of logics, our system scales consistently when increasing the available computational resources, and also scales better for more challenging instances. The non-incremental logics that benefit the most from our parallelization are QF_BV, FP, and QF_BVFPLRA. Our system generally achieves lower speedups for incremental instances, albeit still very respectable in some cases (e.g., a speedup of 25.4 at 16 nodes for QF_BVFP).

---

[4] Note that comparing a run of our system with < 48 solver threads to a run on ≥ 1 entire nodes is not entirely fair because the run with fewer threads has access to relatively more resources (RAM, cache, hardware-threads for background tasks).

Table 1. Performance on *non-incremental* benchmarks in terms of number of solved instances (#) and Penalized Average Runtime (PAR-2) with a time limit of 300 s on a single node with 48 cores. The best result for each logic and metric is highlighted.

	Bitwuzla		Gim+B		B'b 1x48		B'b 4x48		B'b 16x48		Yices		STPPB	
# Logic	#	PAR-2	#	PAR-2	#	PAR-2	#	PAR-2	#	PAR-2	#	PAR-2	#	PAR-2
80 QF_ABV	38	361.2	23	467.7	42	317.4	46	287.8	**47**	**280.2**	30	404.2	–	–
26 QF_ABVFP	21	141.9	21	147.5	23	84.1	**24**	66.8	**24**	**61.4**	–	–	–	–
1 QF_ABVFPLRA	**1**	85.9	**1**	49.4	**1**	17.5	**1**	**13.9**	**1**	**13.9**	–	–	–	–
23 QF_AUFBV	13	298.1	8	420.1	13	276.4	**14**	267.7	**14**	**259.7**	8	409.2	–	–
155 QF_BV	40	474.8	79	332.2	109	233.5	118	191.9	**122**	**169.3**	18	538.1	63	398.8
23 QF_BVFP	22	73.1	22	36.6	22	36.0	**23**	18.0	**23**	**14.1**	–	–	–	–
12 QF_BVFPLRA	8	248.8	**12**	75.8	**12**	11.4	**12**	9.0	**12**	**6.8**	–	–	–	–
73 QF_FP	38	348.0	26	409.9	51	217.5	**55**	189.9	**55**	**179.1**	–	–	–	–
10 QF_FPLRA	9	127.1	4	434.7	**10**	20.7	**10**	11.9	**10**	**11.3**	–	–	–	–
105 QF_UFBV	52	356.2	27	465.2	70	233.9	**76**	208.8	75	**201.6**	39	383.4	–	–
51 ABV	0	600.0	**6**	**529.4**	0	600.0	0	600.0	0	600.0	–	–	–	–
4 ABVFP	**1**	**455.0**	0	600.0	1	465.5	1	465.5	1	465.5	–	–	–	–
151 AUFBV	**51**	429.6	28	506.3	48	435.1	47	435.6	**51**	**424.6**	–	–	–	–
31 AUFBVFP	10	421.1	0	600.0	11	401.1	11	409.3	**14**	**368.1**	–	–	–	–
109 BV	43	398.6	36	427.9	50	359.8	**56**	**319.7**	54	324.2	–	–	–	–
20 BVFP	3	513.0	0	600.0	11	362.6	**13**	**323.3**	10	387.8	–	–	–	–
10 BVFPLRA	2	487.2	1	540.0	**3**	**465.1**	**3**	465.4	**3**	**465.1**	–	–	–	–
153 FP	42	465.4	74	352.4	**102**	**241.2**	91	268.7	94	254.9	–	–	–	–
4 FPLRA	**0**	**600.0**	**0**	**600.0**	**0**	**600.0**	**0**	**600.0**	**0**	**600.0**	–	–	–	–
56 UFBV	10	497.7	8	526.4	11	484.7	11	484.2	**11**	**483.3**	–	–	–	–
1 UFBVFP	0	600.0	0	600.0	1	277.9	**1**	**156.1**	0	600.0	–	–	–	–

Table 2. Performance on *incremental* benchmarks in terms of number of solved *check-sat* queries (q) and Penalized Average Runtime (PAR-2) with a time limit of 300 s on a single node with 48 cores. The best result for each logic and metric is highlighted.

	Bitwuzla		Gim+B		B'b 1x48		B'b 4x48		B'b 16x48	
q # Logic	q	PAR-2	q	PAR-2	q	PAR-2	q	PAR-2	q	PAR-2
1017 79 QF_ABV	839	385.5	764	528.0	**944**	**260.4**	936	302.8	937	317.1
1040 45 QF_ABVFP	1014	321.1	856	493.1	**1016**	287.4	**1016**	**286.4**	925	297.5
1707 3 QF_ABVFPLRA	**1707**	29.6	583	600.0	**1707**	24.5	**1707**	25.1	**1707**	**24.4**
898 16 QF_AUFBV	887	248.9	834	481.3	889	234.5	893	182.0	**897**	**132.8**
14592 66 QF_BV	5819	291.4	2926	296.8	9700	226.2	9972	221.2	**9998**	**220.6**
53 31 QF_BVFP	36	224.2	39	210.5	**42**	97.3	**42**	89.8	**42**	**88.9**
26252 8 QF_BVFPLRA	**26252**	**17.9**	10487	487.2	**26252**	20.2	**26252**	20.2	**26252**	20.3
818 13 QF_UFBV	815	121.6	586	217.1	**818**	63.7	**818**	53.2	**818**	**46.3**
2108 2 ABVFPLRA	**2108**	**71.6**	450	600.0	**2108**	74.8	**2108**	73.3	**2108**	73.2
38856 18 BV	**35070**	**233.3**	23174	555.7	34931	273.4	34539	299.7	34678	275.2
458 1 BVFP	**458**	12.9	354	600.0	**458**	12.7	**458**	12.9	**458**	**12.5**
4855 6 BVFPLRA	3690	**213.9**	768	600.0	4047	216.1	3821	216.4	**4086**	216.5

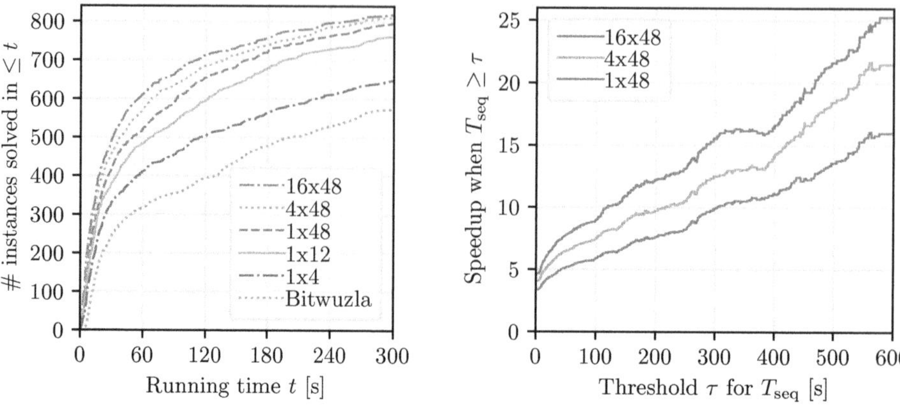

Fig. 6. Left: Scaling of our approach over all instances, with Bitwuzla as a sequential baseline. Right: *Weak scaling* of our approach. Each point (x, y) on a curve indicates that BITWUZLLOB achieved a mean speedup of y when only considering the (commonly solved) instances that took sequential Bitwuzla $\geq x$ seconds to solve.

Next, we analyze BITWUZLLOB's *Weak Scaling* behavior, i.e., how its speedups develop as the input difficulty is increased. While Table 3 shows speedups over instances with a runtime of sequential Bitwuzla of at least $\tau = 1$ s and $\tau = 60$ s, Figure 6 (right) shows BITWUZLLOB's mean speedups for *all* runtimes $0 \leq \tau \leq 600\,s$. For instance, when considering the instances solved by Bitwuzla in ≥ 300 s, BITWUZLLOB at 1, 4, and 16 nodes achieves a geometric mean speedup over sequential Bitwuzla of 9.9, 12.5, and 15.6, respectively. Overall, the speedups achieved by BITWUZLLOB consistently increase with increasing input difficulty, while investing more resources also consistently results in higher speedups. At a threshold of 300 and 600 seconds, the single-node run achieves a mean resource-efficiency (i.e., ratio between speedup and number of cores) of 21% and 33%, respectively. While the runs at higher scales cannot yet reach such remarkably high (cf. [44]) efficiencies, we still consider the observed scaling highly encouraging for developing our approach further in the future.

5.3   Latency Hiding

In our last experiment, we analyze the impact of our techniques to reduce the minimum latencies of SAT calls (Section 4.3). Figure 7 shows the relative improvement in terms of runtime achieved by latency-hiding threads (LHT), based on how many SAT calls per instance were issued (geometric mean) for each incremental and non-incremental logic. Clearly, logics with a very high number of SAT calls per instance (hundreds to thousands) profit significantly from the LHT, with mean accelerations ranging from 60% to 590%. In particular, the four points in the upper right correspond to the *incremental* logics ABVFPLRA, BV, BVFP and QF_BVFPLRA, all with more than 1,000 incremental SAT calls per instance on average. For logics with less than a few hundred SAT calls per instance, LHT are

Table 3. Mean speedups of Bitwuzllob on 1/4/16 nodes over sequential Bitwuzla. For each logic, we consider commonly solved instances with a minimum sequential runtime of $\{1, 60\}$ s and show the geometric mean speedup over the resulting instance set.

	Logic	#	Seq. time ≥ 1 s			#	Seq. time ≥ 60 s		
			1x48	4x48	16x48		1x48	4x48	16x48
Non-incremental	QF_ABV	40	2.50	3.20	3.54	22	3.69	5.19	6.35
	QF_ABVFP	23	3.27	4.62	5.29	5	7.14	11.65	14.23
	QF_ABVFPLRA	1	4.89	6.17	6.20	1	4.89	6.17	6.20
	QF_AUFBV	13	2.07	1.76	2.16	4	3.18	1.90	3.67
	QF_BV	97	7.84	11.76	14.12	79	9.07	13.77	17.04
	QF_BVFP	22	4.14	6.61	7.75	3	6.47	12.48	20.21
	QF_BVFPLRA	11	9.05	10.86	14.06	5	34.28	42.60	65.58
	QF_FP	45	3.86	5.46	7.87	29	4.91	6.81	10.66
	QF_FPLRA	10	4.19	6.05	6.52	4	8.12	11.15	12.42
	QF_UFBV	53	2.26	2.41	3.17	32	3.70	4.24	5.77
	ABVFP	1	0.32	0.32	0.32	0	–	–	–
	AUFBV	35	2.03	2.11	2.15	19	3.30	3.08	3.49
	AUFBVFP	9	2.11	1.98	1.90	3	2.72	2.77	4.26
	BV	43	2.48	3.68	3.67	26	3.20	4.59	4.90
	BVFP	2	0.82	1.11	1.20	0	–	–	–
	BVFPLRA	2	0.38	0.38	0.38	0	–	–	–
	FP	91	8.94	11.95	15.12	75	10.62	14.75	19.21
	UFBV	10	4.07	5.24	7.10	1	27.02	8.88	76.09
Incremental	QF_ABV	37	1.61	1.79	1.67	22	1.86	2.13	2.02
	QF_ABVFP	24	1.87	1.91	2.01	7	3.11	3.50	4.13
	QF_ABVFPLRA	3	1.36	1.32	1.34	0	–	–	–
	QF_AUFBV	11	1.26	1.52	1.71	7	1.27	1.66	1.90
	QF_BV	44	2.60	2.87	2.93	21	4.47	5.26	5.37
	QF_BVFP	26	3.75	5.91	6.57	10	10.67	21.13	25.36
	QF_BVFPLRA	8	0.89	0.88	0.88	0	–	–	–
	QF_UFBV	13	1.50	1.79	1.80	6	1.72	2.23	2.56
	ABVFPLRA	2	0.99	0.99	1.00	1	0.95	0.98	0.98
	BV	10	0.65	0.66	0.65	2	0.78	0.78	0.78
	BVFP	1	1.01	1.00	1.03	0	–	–	–
	BVFPLRA	4	0.96	0.99	0.98	0	–	–	–

not significantly beneficial, and sometimes even detrimental, to performance. In particular, for non-incremental logics **ABVFP**, **BVFP** and **BVFPLRA**, the LHT incur extreme performance degradation (a mean slowdown of 50 to over 100).

This may be due to the fact that the behavior of the abstraction-refinement loop and the MBQI procedure in Bitwuzla are sensitive to the models of the intermediate SAT calls. Examining some of the concerned instances, we found that MallobSat's distributed SAT solver portfolio used by Bitwuzllob reproducibly returns a different satisfying assignment to certain SAT queries than the LHT's default sequential CaDiCaL solver. Different satisfying assignments may guide Bitwuzla's search into different search spaces, leading to faster convergence of the search than others. Note that the affected logics for which the LHT models seem to have a higher-than-average negative impact contain only a small

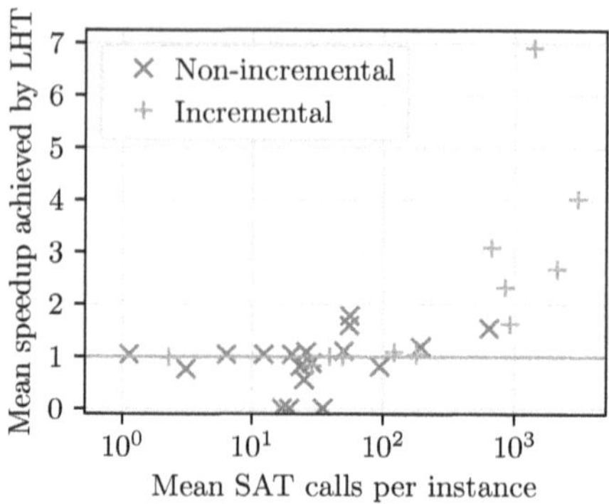

Fig. 7. Impact of latency-hiding threads (LHT), with one data point per logic. The x-coordinate denotes the geometric mean number of SAT calls across solved instances (without LHT), the y-coordinate denotes the geometric mean speedup achieved by enabling LHT over the commonly solved instances of the logic.

number of solved instances (15 in total). Overall, enabling the LHT significantly improves performance for instances with a high number of (fast) SAT calls. Exploiting the model sensitivity of our approach by retrieving *several* satisfying assignments from a single SAT query and then carefully branching the program flow over the resulting refinements in parallel may be an interesting direction for future work.

6   Conclusion

We have presented BITWUZLLOB, a system for massively parallel SMT solving specialized for bit-precise reasoning. Our tool features the bit-blasting SMT solver Bitwuzla as an integrated module and deploys its (incremental) SAT queries to the distributed SAT solving system Mallob. Experiments with up to 768 cores of a distributed environment show that our system outperforms existing parallel SMT solvers for bit-precise reasoning, with unprecedented scaling on a wide range of incremental and non-incremental logics.

For future work, BITWUZLLOB will serve as a solid foundation for exploring more advanced methods to further increase scalability. In particular, this may include modifying Bitwuzla's program flow to make *asynchronous* SAT calls (which would allow our system to actually solve several SAT tasks in parallel), as well as integrating theory-specific parallelization methods. Another promising direction could be to retrieve several different satisfying assignments from the distributed SAT solver and then branch over the respectively resulting refinements.

Acknowledgments. The authors gratefully acknowledge the Gauss Centre for Supercomputing e.V. (www.gauss-centre.eu) for funding parts of this project by providing computing time on the GCS Supercomputer SuperMUC-NG at Leibniz Supercomputing Centre (www.lrz.de).

Data Availability Statement. The artifact accompanying this paper is archived and available in the Zenodo repository at https://zenodo.org/records/17478480.

References

1. SMT Competition 2025. https://smt-comp.github.io/2025 (2025)
2. Audemard, G., Hoessen, B., Jabbour, S., Lagniez, J.M., Piette, C.: Revisiting clause exchange in parallel SAT solving. In: Theory and Applications of Satisfiability Testing (SAT). pp. 200–213. Springer (2012). https://doi.org/10.1007/978-3-642-31612-8_16
3. Balyo, T., Biere, A., Iser, M., Sinz, C.: SAT race 2015. Artificial Intelligence **241**, 45–65 (2016). https://doi.org/10.1016/j.artint.2016.08.007
4. Barrett, C., Fontaine, P., Tinelli, C.: The SMT-LIB Standard: Version 2.7. Tech. rep., Department of Computer Science, The University of Iowa (2025), available at http://smt-lib.org
5. Barrett, C.W., Chen, P., Cook, B., Dutertre, B., Jones, R.B., Le, N., Reynolds, A., Sheth, K., Stephens, C., Whalen, M.W.: SMT-D: new strategies for portfolio-based SMT solving. In: Narodytska, N., Rümmer, P. (eds.) Formal Methods in Computer-Aided Design, FMCAD 2024, Prague, Czech Republic, October 15-18, 2024. pp. 1–10. IEEE (2024). https://doi.org/10.34727/2024/ISBN.978-3-85448-065-5_10
6. Barrett, C.W., Dill, D.L., Stump, A.: Checking satisfiability of first-order formulas by incremental translation to SAT. In: Brinksma, E., Larsen, K.G. (eds.) Computer Aided Verification, 14th International Conference, CAV 2002,Copenhagen, Denmark, July 27-31, 2002, Proceedings. Lecture Notes in Computer Science, vol. 2404, pp. 236–249. Springer (2002). https://doi.org/10.1007/3-540-45657-0_18
7. Barrett, C.W., Tinelli, C.: Satisfiability modulo theories. In: Clarke, E.M., Henzinger, T.A., Veith, H., Bloem, R. (eds.) Handbook of Model Checking, pp. 305–343. Springer (2018). https://doi.org/10.1007/978-3-319-10575-8_11
8. Biere, A.: Lingeling, Plingeling and Treengeling entering the SAT competition 2013. In: SAT Competition 2013: Solver and Benchmark Descriptions. p. 1 (2013)
9. Biere, A., Faller, T., Fazekas, K., Fleury, M., Froleyks, N., Pollitt, F.: Cadical 2.0. In: Gurfinkel, A., Ganesh, V. (eds.) Computer Aided Verification - 36th International Conference, CAV 2024, Montreal, QC, Canada, July 24-27, 2024, Proceedings, Part I. Lecture Notes in Computer Science, vol. 14681, pp. 133–152. Springer (2024). https://doi.org/10.1007/978-3-031-65627-9_7
10. Clarke, E.M., Grumberg, O., Jha, S., Lu, Y., Veith, H.: Counterexample-guided abstraction refinement. In: Emerson, E.A., Sistla, A.P. (eds.) Computer Aided Verification, 12th International Conference, CAV 2000, Chicago, IL, USA, July 15-19, 2000, Proceedings. Lecture Notes in Computer Science, vol. 1855, pp. 154–169. Springer (2000). https://doi.org/10.1007/10722167_15
11. Cook, B.: Automated reasoning's scientific frontiers. https://www.amazon.science/blog/automated-reasonings-scientific-frontiers (2021), Amazon Science

12. Dutertre, B., Goel, A., Graham-Lengrand, S., Hader, T., Irfan, A., Jovanović, D., Lipparini, E., Mason, I.A., Nukala, K., Ruess, H.: Yices2 in SMT-COMP 2025. https://ahmed-irfan.github.io/smtcomp/yices2-smtcomp-2025.pdf (2025)

13. Eén, N., Sörensson, N.: Temporal induction by incremental SAT solving. Electronic Notes in Theoretical Computer Science **89**(4), 543–560 (2003). https://doi.org/10.1016/s1571-0661(05)82542-3

14. Enderton, H.B.: A mathematical introduction to logic. Academic Press (1972)

15. Fazekas, K., Niemetz, A., Preiner, M., Kirchweger, M., Szeider, S., Biere, A.: IPASIR-UP: user propagators for CDCL. In: Mahajan, M., Slivovsky, F. (eds.) 26th International Conference on Theory and Applications of Satisfiability Testing, SAT 2023, July 4-8, 2023, Alghero, Italy. LIPIcs, vol. 271, pp. 8:1–8:13. Schloss Dagstuhl - Leibniz-Zentrum für Informatik (2023). https://doi.org/10.4230/LIPICS.SAT.2023.8

16. Fleury, M., Biere, A.: Scalable proof producing multi-threaded SAT solving with Gimsatul through sharing instead of copying clauses. In: Pragmatics of SAT (2022)

17. Ge, Y., de Moura, L.M.: Complete instantiation for quantified formulas in satisfiabiliby modulo theories. In: Bouajjani, A., Maler, O. (eds.) Computer Aided Verification, 21st International Conference, CAV 2009, Grenoble, France, June 26 - July 2, 2009. Proceedings. Lecture Notes in Computer Science, vol. 5643, pp. 306–320. Springer (2009). https://doi.org/10.1007/978-3-642-02658-4_25

18. Graham-Lengrand, S., Jovanovic, D., Dutertre, B.: Solving bitvectors with MCSAT: explanations from bits and pieces. In: Peltier, N., Sofronie-Stokkermans, V. (eds.) Automated Reasoning - 10th International Joint Conference, IJCAR 2020, Paris, France, July 1-4, 2020, Proceedings, Part I. Lecture Notes in Computer Science, vol. 12166, pp. 103–121. Springer (2020). https://doi.org/10.1007/978-3-030-51074-9_7

19. Hamadi, Y., Jabbour, S., Sais, L.: ManySAT: a parallel SAT solver. JSAT **6**(4), 245–262 (2010). https://doi.org/10.3233/sat190070

20. Heisinger, M., Fleury, M., Biere, A.: Distributed Cube and Conquer with Paracooba. In: Pulina, L., Seidl, M. (eds.) Theory and Applications of Satisfiability Testing - SAT 2020 - 23rd International Conference, Alghero, Italy, July 3-10, 2020, Proceedings. Lecture Notes in Computer Science, vol. 12178, pp. 114–122. Springer (2020). https://doi.org/10.1007/978-3-030-51825-7_9

21. Hyvärinen, A.E.J., Marescotti, M., Sharygina, N.: Search-space partitioning for parallelizing SMT solvers. In: Heule, M., Weaver, S.A. (eds.) Theory and Applications of Satisfiability Testing - SAT 2015 - 18th International Conference, Austin, TX, USA, September 24-27, 2015, Proceedings. Lecture Notes in Computer Science, vol. 9340, pp. 369–386. Springer (2015). https://doi.org/10.1007/978-3-319-24318-4_27

22. Hyvärinen, A.E.J., Marescotti, M., Sharygina, N.: Lookahead in partitioning SMT. In: Formal Methods in Computer Aided Design, FMCAD 2021, New Haven, CT, USA, October 19-22, 2021. pp. 271–279. IEEE (2021). https://doi.org/10.34727/2021/ISBN.978-3-85448-046-4_37

23. Kroening, D., Strichman, O.: Decision Procedures - An Algorithmic Point of View, Second Edition. Texts in Theoretical Computer Science. An EATCS Series, Springer (2016). https://doi.org/10.1007/978-3-662-50497-0

24. Manzano, M.: Introduction to many-sorted logic. In: Many-sorted Logic and its Applications, pp. 3–86. John Wiley & Sons, Inc., New York, NY, USA (1993)

25. Marescotti, M., Hyvärinen, A.E.J., Sharygina, N.: Clause sharing and partitioning for cloud-based SMT solving. In: Artho, C., Legay, A., Peled, D. (eds.) Au-

tomated Technology for Verification and Analysis - 14th International Symposium, ATVA 2016, Chiba, Japan, October 17-20, 2016, Proceedings. Lecture Notes in Computer Science, vol. 9938, pp. 428–443 (2016). https://doi.org/10.1007/978-3-319-46520-3_27

26. Marescotti, M., Hyvärinen, A.E.J., Sharygina, N.: SMTS: distributed, visualized constraint solving. In: Barthe, G., Sutcliffe, G., Veanes, M. (eds.) LPAR-22. 22nd International Conference on Logic for Programming, Artificial Intelligence and Reasoning, Awassa, Ethiopia, 16-21 November 2018. EPiC Series in Computing, vol. 57, pp. 534–542. EasyChair (2018). https://doi.org/10.29007/FHGN

27. Marques-Silva, J., Lynce, I., Malik, S.: CDCL SAT solving. In: Handbook of Satisfiability. pp. 131–153. IOS Press (2021). https://doi.org/10.3233/faia200987

28. Moura, L.D., Rueß, H.: Lemmas on demand for satisfiability solvers. In: The 5th International Symposium on the Theory and Applications of Satisfiability Testing, SAT 2002, Cincinnati, USA, May 15, 2002 (2002)

29. Niemetz, A., Preiner, M.: Bitwuzla. In: Enea, C., Lal, A. (eds.) Computer Aided Verification - 35th International Conference, CAV 2023, Paris, France, July 17-22, 2023, Proceedings, Part II. Lecture Notes in Computer Science, vol. 13965, pp. 3–17. Springer (2023). https://doi.org/10.1007/978-3-031-37703-7_1

30. Niemetz, A., Preiner, M.: Bitwuzla at the SMT-COMP 2025. https://bitwuzla.github.io/data/smtcomp2025/paper.pdf (2025)

31. Niemetz, A., Preiner, M., Wolf, C., Biere, A.: Btor2 , BtorMC and Boolector 3.0. In: Chockler, H., Weissenbacher, G. (eds.) Computer Aided Verification - 30th International Conference, CAV 2018, Held as Part of the Federated Logic Conference, FloC 2018, Oxford, UK, July 14-17, 2018, Proceedings, Part I. Lecture Notes in Computer Science, vol. 10981, pp. 587–595. Springer (2018). https://doi.org/10.1007/978-3-319-96145-3_32

32. Niemetz, A., Preiner, M., Zohar, Y.: Scalable bit-blasting with abstractions. In: Gurfinkel, A., Ganesh, V. (eds.) Computer Aided Verification - 36th International Conference, CAV 2024, Montreal, QC, Canada, July 24-27, 2024, Proceedings, Part I. Lecture Notes in Computer Science, vol. 14681, pp. 178–200. Springer (2024). https://doi.org/10.1007/978-3-031-65627-9_9

33. Nieuwenhuis, R., Oliveras, A., Tinelli, C.: Solving SAT and SAT modulo theories: From an abstract Davis–Putnam–Logemann–Loveland procedure to DPLL(T). J. ACM **53**(6), 937–977 (2006). https://doi.org/10.1145/1217856.1217859

34. Preiner, M., Schurr, H., Barrett, C.W., Fontaine, P., Niemetz, A., Tinelli, C.: SMT-LIB release 2025 (incremental benchmarks) (May 2025). https://doi.org/10.5281/ZENODO.15493095

35. Preiner, M., Schurr, H., Barrett, C.W., Fontaine, P., Niemetz, A., Tinelli, C.: SMT-LIB release 2025 (non-incremental benchmarks) (Aug 2025). https://doi.org/10.5281/ZENODO.15493089

36. Reisenberger, C.: PBoolector: A Parallel SMT Solver for QF_BV by Combining Bit-Blasting with Look-Ahead. Master's thesis, Johannes Kepler University Linz (Nov 2014)

37. Sanders, P., Schreiber, D.: Decentralized online scheduling of malleable NP-hard jobs. In: Euro-Par 2022: Parallel Processing. pp. 119–135. Springer (2022). https://doi.org/10.1007/978-3-031-12597-3_8

38. Saoudi, M., Baarir, S., Sopena, J., Lejemble, T.: D-Painless: A framework for distributed portfolio SAT solving. In: Gurfinkel, A., Heule, M. (eds.) Tools and Algorithms for the Construction and Analysis of Systems - 31st International Conference, TACAS 2025, Held as Part of the International Joint Conferences on Theory

and Practice of Software, ETAPS 2025, Hamilton, ON, Canada, May 3-8, 2025, Proceedings, Part II. Lecture Notes in Computer Science, vol. 15697, pp. 45–64. Springer (2025). https://doi.org/10.1007/978-3-031-90653-4_3

39. Schreiber, D.: Engineering HordeSat towards malleability: mallob-mono in the SAT 2020 cloud track. In: Proc. SAT Competition. pp. 45–46 (2020)

40. Schreiber, D.: Distributed incremental SAT solving with Mallob: Report and case study with hierarchical planning. CoRR **abs/2505.18836** (2025), https://doi.org/10.48550/arXiv.2505.18836

41. Schreiber, D., Jabs, C., Berg, J.: From scalable SAT to MaxSAT: Massively parallel solution improving search. In: Symposium on Combinatorial Search (SoCS) (2025). https://doi.org/10.1609/socs.v18i1.35984

42. Schreiber, D., Rigi-Luperti, N., Biere, A.: Streamlining Distributed SAT Solver Design. In: Berg, J., Nordström, J. (eds.) 28th International Conference on Theory and Applications of Satisfiability Testing (SAT 2025). Leibniz International Proceedings in Informatics (LIPIcs), vol. 341, pp. 27:1–27:23. Schloss Dagstuhl – Leibniz-Zentrum für Informatik, Dagstuhl, Germany (2025). https://doi.org/10.4230/LIPIcs.SAT.2025.27

43. Schreiber, D., Sanders, P.: Scalable SAT solving in the cloud. In: Li, C.M., Manyà, F. (eds.) Theory and Applications of Satisfiability Testing – SAT 2021. pp. 518–534. Springer International Publishing, Cham (2021). https://doi.org/10.1007/978-3-030-80223-3_35

44. Schreiber, D., Sanders, P.: MallobSat: Scalable SAT solving by clause sharing. Journal of Artificial Intelligence Research **80**, 1437–1495 (2024). https://doi.org/10.1613/jair.1.15827

45. Sinz, C., Blochinger, W., Küchlin, W.: PaSAT – parallel SAT-checking with lemma exchange: Implementation and applications. Electronic Notes in Discrete Mathematics **9**, 205–216 (2001). https://doi.org/10.1016/s1571-0653(04)00323-3

46. Wilson, A., Nötzli, A., Reynolds, A., Cook, B., Tinelli, C., Barrett, C.W.: Partitioning strategies for distributed SMT solving. In: Nadel, A., Rozier, K.Y. (eds.) Formal Methods in Computer-Aided Design, FMCAD 2023, Ames, IA, USA, October 24-27, 2023. pp. 199–208. IEEE (2023). https://doi.org/10.34727/2023/ISBN.978-3-85448-060-0_28

47. Zhang, X., Chen, Z., Cai, S.: PRS: A new parallel/distributed framework for SAT. In: SAT Competition 2023: Benchmark, Solver and Proof Checker Descriptions. pp. 39–40 (2023)

48. Zhao, M., Cai, S., Qian, Y.: Distributed SMT solving based on dynamic variable-level partitioning. In: Gurfinkel, A., Ganesh, V. (eds.) Computer Aided Verification - 36th International Conference, CAV 2024, Montreal, QC, Canada, July 24-27, 2024, Proceedings, Part I. Lecture Notes in Computer Science, vol. 14681, pp. 68–88. Springer (2024). https://doi.org/10.1007/978-3-031-65627-9_4

49. Zhao, M., Xu, Z., Lin, J., Cai, S.: STP-Parti-Bitwuzla at SMT-COMP 2025. https://github.com/shaowei-cai-group/STP-Parti-Bitwuzla-at-SMT-COMP-2025/blob/master/STP_Parti_Bitwuzla_at_SMT_COMP_2025.pdf (2025)

SMT(LIA) Sampling with High Diversity[*]

Yong Lai[1], Junjie Li[2], and Chuan Luo[3] (✉)

[1] Key Laboratory of Symbolic Computation and Knowledge Engineering Ministry of Education, Jilin University, China
[2] College of Software, Jilin University, Changchun, China
[3] School of Software, Beihang University, Beijing, China
laiy@jlu.edu.cn, junjieli2026@gmail.com, chuanluo@buaa.edu.cn

Abstract. SMT sampling refers to the task of generating a set of satisfying assignments (samples) for a given SMT formula. An effective SMT sampler should be capable of producing samples with high diversity to maximize coverage of the solution space. However, most SMT samplers struggle to adequately cover the solution space and fail to generate sufficiently diverse solutions.

To address these limitations, we propose *HighDiv*, the first iterative sampling framework that integrates CDCL(T) and local search in a bidirectional guided manner. During the bidirectional guidance process, solutions generated by CDCL(T) guide the variable initialization of the local search. Conversely, solutions produced by the local search guide CDCL(T) to further explore the solution space. Additionally, we design a novel local search algorithm, *Context-Constrained Stochastic Search* (*CCSS*), which introduces the *Constraint-Partitioned Variable Initialization* and the *boundary-aware move* operator. These components effectively balance exploration and feasibility throughout the search process. We conduct an extensive evaluation on QF_LIA formulas from the SMT-LIB benchmark. The results demonstrate that *HighDiv* achieves substantial improvements in diversity over the state-of-the-art SMT sampling tools.

1 Introduction

Satisfiability Modulo Theories (SMT) is the problem of deciding the satisfiability of a first-order logic formula with respect to certain background theories. Modern software/hardware testing widely leverages SMT solvers to generate assignments that satisfy specified constraints, which are then used to construct test suites. In software testing, symbolic execution employs SMT solvers to solve collected path constraints, thereby producing new inputs that cover unexplored paths [4, 40, 42]; in hardware testing, constrained-random verification (CRV) encodes the functional model and verification scenarios of a hardware design as an SMT formula, whose solutions correspond to stimuli for the design under test (DUT) [38].

---

[*] The author list has been sorted alphabetically by last name.

© The Author(s) 2026
S. Junges and G. Katz (Eds.): TACAS 2026, LNCS 16505, pp. 192–212, 2026.
https://doi.org/10.1007/978-3-032-22752-2_10

Although SMT solving has been extensively studied and mainstream solvers typically return a single solution within acceptable time, software/hardware testing often requires multiple solutions. In software testing, prior work has shown that obtaining multiple solutions for the same constraint during symbolic execution can substantially improve testing effectiveness [19,20,28,48]. In hardware testing, within CRV, diversity among solutions directly translates into richer stimuli, thereby increasing the likelihood of exposing bugs [38].

The task of generating a set of highly diverse solutions for a given SMT formula is known as the sampling problem, which has attracted more attention in the community in recent years [7,10,11,39]. Although using a solver to enumerate solutions (by adding blocking constraints) for a formula is operationally straightforward, this approach is generally costly, and after multiple invocations, most solvers tend to return similar solutions. This prevalence of similar solutions is largely attributed to the fact that many solver techniques (e.g., the general simplex method for linear theories) tend to favor extreme values at the boundaries of the feasible region [1,8,36]. Therefore, there is a practical need to efficiently generate a highly diverse set of solutions for SMT formulas.

Existing SMT samplers typically treat SMT solvers as black boxes [10,11,39]. Their core strategy involves obtaining solutions from SMT solvers as initial seeds, which are then used to generate additional solutions. However, this approach inherently limits the diversity of generated samples as a large number of samples originate from a very limited set of seeds.

Recent studies on Boolean satisfiability (SAT) sampling have demonstrated that treating the solving procedure as a white-box and deliberately introducing diversification during search can substantially improve both effectiveness and efficiency [17,30,31]. In the context of finding a single solution of SMT problems, Conflict-Driven Clause Learning with Theory (CDCL(T)) and local search are two widely recognized and effective algorithmic frameworks. These two approaches are highly complementary, as demonstrated by their combined use in various recent studies [5,47]. Specifically, CDCL(T) leverages its powerful CDCL engine to perform efficient reasoning at the propositional logic level, while local search achieves rapid solving by flexibly modifying the current assignment. However, existing SMT solvers focus only on quickly finding a satisfying assignment without considering solution diversity during the assignment generation process. Consequently, striking an appropriate balance between sample diversity and search efficiency remains a challenge in SMT sampling tasks. This raises a fundamental question: *Can we combine CDCL(T) with local search in a white-box way to design high-diversity SMT sampling?*

In this paper, we introduce *HighDiv*, a novel sampling framework for the theory of *linear integer arithmetic* (SMT(LIA)) that is designed to tackle the aforementioned challenge in SMT sampling. We focus on SMT(LIA) because it is widely used in software and hardware testing and verification [9,15,29,32]. The framework utilizes bidirectional guidance between local search and CDCL(T) for iterative sampling, aiming to enhance sample diversity while maintaining solving efficiency. Specifically, the solution from CDCL(T) guides variable initialization during the local search phase, while the solution generated by local search is fed back into CDCL(T) to further explore the solution space.

In addition, for the local search component, we designed *Context-Constrained Stochastic Search* (*CCSS*), which introduces a novel variable initialization strategy called the *Constraint-Partitioned Variable Initialization*. This strategy partitions the constraints into different subsystems and initializes each subsystem based on its specific characteristics. Furthermore, to allow more flexible modifications of integer variables during the search, we introduced a new operator, *boundary-aware move*. The operator performs random moves within the interval determined by contextual boundary information. For the CDCL(T) component, we modified its *branching heuristic* and *phase selection heuristic*, enabling more flexible exploration of the solution space at the propositional level.

Under a 900-second time limit, *HighDiv* covers approximately 53% of the SMT-formula AST space, whereas state-of-the-art SMT(LIA) samplers average about 34%. Under a fixed sampling budget of 1000 samples, *HighDiv* reaches roughly 53% coverage, while competitors remain below 35%. These results clearly indicate that *HighDiv* is significantly more diverse than state-of-the-art SMT(LIA) samplers.

The primary contributions of this work are outlined below.

- We propose *HighDiv*, a SMT sampling framework that combines CDCL(T) and local search with bidirectional guided iteration, and treats the search process as a white-box, thereby advancing SMT(LIA) sampling.
- We investigate the trade-off between sample diversity and search efficiency in our local search algorithm, Context-Constrained Stochastic Search (*CCSS*), featuring a novel variable initialization strategy and the *boundary-aware move* operator.
- We implement *HighDiv* and compare it against state-of-the-art SMT(LIA) samplers. The results demonstrate that *HighDiv* generates more diverse samples under both fixed-time and fixed-sample-size conditions.

The structure of this paper is as follows: Section 2 introduces the relevant definitions and the frameworks of local search and CDCL(T); Section 3 presents the overall framework of *HighDiv*, as well as the interaction between stochastic CDCL(T) and *CCSS*; Section 4 introduces the stochastic CDCL(T) component; Section 5 provides a detailed explanation of *CCSS*; Section 6 presents the experiments; Section 7 discusses related work; Section 8 concludes.

2   Preliminary

2.1   SMT(LIA)

A formula under the Linear Integer Arithmetic (LIA) theory is constructed from *atomic formulas* using Boolean connectives, where an atomic formula is either a Boolean variable or an arithmetic formula. Arithmetic formulas can be consistently expressed in the standard form $\sum_{i=0}^{n-1} a_i x_i \leq k$ or $\sum_{i=0}^{n-1} a_i x_i = k$, where x

represents an integer variable, with a and k as constants. A *literal* can be either an atomic formula or its negated form. A *clause* is composed of the disjunction of a set of literals, and a formula in *Conjunctive Normal Form* (CNF) consists of the conjunction of a set of such clauses. Given sets of propositional variables $\mathcal{P}$ and integer variables $\mathcal{X}$, which are integral components of the SMT(LIA) formula F, an *assignment* α of F maps each $x \in \mathcal{X}$ to an integer in $\mathbb{Z}$ and each $p \in \mathcal{P}$ to *true* or *false*. Under this assignment, $\alpha(x)$ and $\alpha(p)$ represent the values of x and p, respectively.

Example 1. Given a set of integer variables $\mathcal{X} = \{x_1, x_2, x_3, x_4\}$ and a set of Boolean variables $\mathcal{P} = \{p_1, p_2\}$, the following F is a SMT(LIA) CNF formula,

$$
\begin{aligned}
F = \ & (p_1 \vee \neg p_2) \\
& \wedge \left(\neg(x_1 + x_2 \leq 2) \vee (-2x_1 + 3x_3 \leq 0)\right) \\
& \wedge \left(p_2 \vee (3x_2 - 7x_3 \leq 3)\right).
\end{aligned}
$$

2.2   SMT Sampling

Let φ be an SMT formula and $\mathrm{Sol}(\varphi)$ denote the set of all its satisfying assignments. The *SMT sampling problem* aims to construct, under limited resources (e.g., a sample-size bound or a time limit), a solution set $\mathcal{S} \subseteq \mathrm{Sol}(\varphi)$. Unlike conventional SMT solving, which returns an arbitrary satisfying assignment, sampling focuses on the diversity of solutions.

To measure diversity, we adopt the abstract syntax tree (AST) coverage metric proposed in prior work [10]. Specifically, we consider nodes in the AST of the SMT formula. Each Boolean node is treated as a single bit, while for integer nodes, only the least significant 64 bits of their values are considered. A bit is regarded as covered if it takes both values 0 and 1 across the sample set of satisfying models [39]. The overall coverage is defined as the ratio between the number of covered bits and the total number of bits. Note that under this metric, the maximum achievable coverage is not necessarily 100%, since some AST node values may be constrained by the input formula and thus take the same value for all assignments in $\mathrm{Sol}(\varphi)$.

2.3   CDCL(T) Framework

Most modern SMT solvers—e.g., Z3 [36] and CVC5 [1]—solve SMT(LIA) formulas using the CDCL(T) framework: a CDCL SAT engine reasons over the formula's Boolean skeleton while a LIA theory solver checks consistency, performs theory propagation, and returns theory lemmas to guide the SAT search [3, 14, 23].

The efficiency of CDCL critically depends on two heuristics: (i) *branching heuristics*, which choose the next decision variable (e.g., VSIDS [35]), and (ii) *phase selection heuristics*, which decide the sign of that variable (e.g., phase saving [41]). Once a complete assignment satisfying the formula is found, CDCL(T) returns the current assignment α, which serves as a *model* of the formula. More details about the CDCL(T) algorithm can be found in the references [3, 14, 23].

2.4 Local Search Framework for SMT(LIA)

The local search component of *HighDiv* uses the two-mode framework of LS-LIA, the first local search algorithm for SMT(LIA) [5]. We briefly introduce LS-LIA.

This algorithm divides its search process into two modes: *Boolean mode* and *Integer mode*. In different modes, operations on variables of the appropriate data type are selected to modify the current assignment. In each mode, when the number of *non-improving steps* reaches the threshold, it switches to another mode. This threshold is defined as $L \times P_b$ for the Boolean mode and $L \times P_i$ for the Integer mode, where P_b and P_i represent the proportion of Boolean and Integer literals, respectively, in the falsified clauses, and L is a parameter.

Within a local search algorithm, the pivotal element is the *operator*, which prescribes the manner in which the current solution may be altered. Once the operator is concretized by selecting a particular variable and designating a value to assign, it materializes as a specific *operation*. In Boolean mode, the *flip* operator turns a Boolean variable to its opposite value. The Integer mode introduces a unique operator called the *critical move* (cm), which is defined below.

Definition 1. *The critical move operator, represented as $cm(x, \ell)$, sets the integer variable x to a threshold value that satisfies the literal ℓ, where ℓ is a falsified literal that includes x.*

The threshold mentioned above refers to the minimal modification required to make the literal ℓ true for x. Example 2 is provided to assist readers in understanding the definition.

Example 2. Given the SMT(LIA) formula, which includes a literal, $\ell : (x_1 - 5x_2 \leq -5)$, the initial variable assignments are $\{x_1 = 0, x_2 = 0\}$. The operations $cm(x_1, \ell)$ and $cm(x_2, \ell)$ involve assigning -5 to x_1 and 1 to x_2, respectively, making the literal ℓ true.

Whenever a $cm(x, \ell)$ operation is performed, the corresponding literal ℓ is set to *true*. Therefore, during the algorithm search process, falsified literals are consistently selected and a *cm* operation is applied to make ℓ true.

For an assignment α, its *cost* is the number of clauses falsified under α; when clause weighting is enabled, the *cost* equals the total weight of all falsified clauses [6, 46].

During local search, the *score* of a candidate operation *op* is usually defined as

$$score(op) = cost(\alpha) - cost(\alpha'),$$

where α' is the assignment obtained by applying *op* to the current assignment α. If $score(op) > 0$, the operation *op* is called a *decreasing* move.

3 The Framework of *HighDiv*

We combine CDCL(T) and local search in a white-box way to design a high-diversity SMT(LIA) sampling method called *HighDiv*. Figure 1 provides an overview of the general structure and sequence of operations within *HighDiv*. The sampling framework is composed of two distinct components: stochastic CDCL(T) (Section 4) and Context-Constrained Stochastic Search (*CCSS*), a novel local search algorithm for sampling SMT(LIA) formulas and achieving high diversity (Section 5). The two components interact through bidirectional guidance: the solutions generated by *CCSS* dynamically guide the stochastic CDCL(T) to further explore the solution space, while the solutions obtained from the stochastic CDCL(T) are used to guide the variable initialization in *CCSS*.

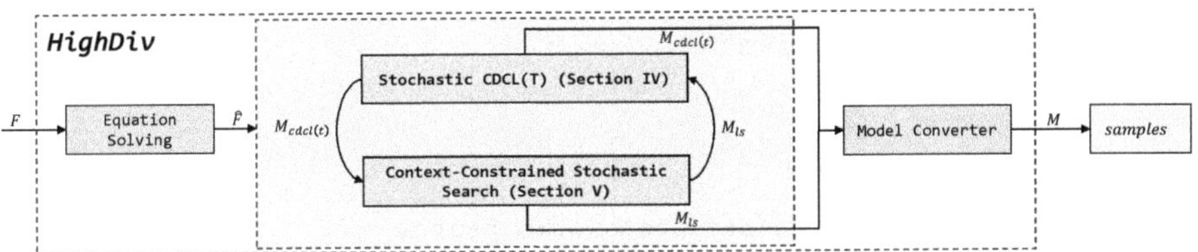

Fig. 1. Framework of *HighDiv*

Algorithm 1 presents the top-level framework of *HighDiv*. It takes two inputs: 1) the SMT(LIA) formula F, and 2) the desired number of solutions k.

HighDiv alternates between a CDCL(T) phase (lines 5-10) and a *CCSS* phase (lines 11-15). First, equalities are simplified using Z3's *solve-eqs* tactic [36], resulting in the pre-processed formula $\hat{F}$ (line 2). Next, a stochastic CDCL(T) solver attempts to solve the current under-approximation $\hat{F}_{under}$. If successful, the resulting model $M_{cdcl(t)}$ is mapped back to the original formula F and added to $\mathcal{S}$ (lines 7-8). Guided by $M_{cdcl(t)}$, the algorithm then executes *CCSS* on $\hat{F}$ (line 11). Upon success, *CCSS* returns a model M_{ls}, which is likewise converted and appended to $\mathcal{S}$ (lines 13-14). To build the next under-approximation formula, each variable in $\hat{F}$ is independently selected with a probability of P and fixed to its value in M_{ls}, yielding $\hat{F}_{under}$ (line 15). These two phases iterate, enlarging $\mathcal{S}$ until the desired sample count is reached ($|\mathcal{S}| = k$) or the time limit expires.

4   The Stochastic CDCL(T) Component

Previous studies have demonstrated that CDCL(T) and local search methods complement each other effectively [5]. A primary reason is the powerful reasoning capabilities of the CDCL engine at the propositional logic level. Inspired by SAT sampling algorithms based on stochastic CDCL [17], we implemented the stochastic CDCL(T) algorithm in Z3. Specifically, we modified the *branching heuristic* and *phase selection heuristic* in Z3, randomly selecting undecided variables at each decision point and assigning them a random phase.

Algorithm 1: The Framework of *HighDiv* (described in Section 3)

Input: F: An SMT(LIA) formula;
k: Allowed number of samples;
Output: S: The set of samples, i.e., solutions of F;

1 $S \leftarrow \emptyset$;

2 $\hat{F} \leftarrow equation\_solving(F)$;

3 $\hat{F}_{under} \leftarrow \hat{F}$;

4 **while** $|S| < k$ **and** *time limit not reached* **do**

    // Stochastic CDCL(T)

5      $M_{cdcl(t)} \leftarrow stochastic\_cdcl(t)\_solving(\hat{F}_{under})$;

6   **if** $M_{cdcl(t)} \neq \emptyset$ **then**

7          $M \leftarrow model\_convert(M_{cdcl(t)}, F)$;

8          $S \leftarrow S \cup \{M\}$;

9   **if** $|S| = k$ **then**

10   **return** S;

    // Context-Constrained Stochastic Search

11      $M_{ls} \leftarrow CCSS(\hat{F}, M_{cdcl(t)})$;

12   **if** $M_{ls} \neq \emptyset$ **then**

13          $M \leftarrow model\_convert(M_{ls}, F)$;

14          $S \leftarrow S \cup \{M\}$;

15          $\hat{F}_{under} \leftarrow fix\_partial\_assignment(\hat{F}, M_{ls})$;

16 **return** S;

Stochastic CDCL(T) plays a pivotal role in *HighDiv*. On one hand, the model generated by CDCL(T) can guide the variable initialization in *CCSS*; on the other hand, the integrated theory solvers within CDCL(T), such as the general simplex method, offer a perspective on the solution space that differs from *CCSS*, thereby enabling *HighDiv* to produce more diverse solutions.

5   Context-Constrained Stochastic Search

In this section, we first introduce Context-Constrained Stochastic Search (*CCSS*); we then detail its variable-initialization strategy and the *boundary-aware move* operator, and finally demonstrate how these components jointly mediate the trade-off between sample diversity and algorithmic scalability.

CCSS uses the basic two-mode framework of LS-LIA [5], i.e., Integer mode and Boolean mode for searching. While *CCSS* retains the LS-LIA search strategy in Boolean mode, we propose new techniques described in Sections 5.1–5.2 to improve sampling diversity in Integer mode. Algorithm 2 describes the Integer mode of *CCSS* algorithm. Line 1 generates the initial assignment α using the *Constraint-Partitioned Variable Initialization*. Lines 2-13 iteratively refine α until the number of consecutive non-improving steps exceeds the threshold *MaxSteps* or the current assignment satisfies the formula F. In lines 5-6,

---

Algorithm 2: Integer Mode of *CCSS* (described in Section 5)

Input: F: SMT(LIA) formula;
        M: A model of F;
Output: α: the solution of F;

1   $constraint\_partitioned\_variable\_initialization(\alpha, M)$;
2   **while** $Step_{total} \leq MaxSteps$ **do**
3   **if** α *satisfies* F **then return** α ;
4     $\mathcal{B} \leftarrow \emptyset$;
5   **foreach** *literal* ℓ *in falsified clauses* **do**
6       $\mathcal{B} \leftarrow \mathcal{B} \cup \{bam(\alpha, x, \ell) \mid x$ appears in $\ell\}$;
7   **if** $\exists$ *decreasing bam operation in* $\mathcal{B}$ **then**
8       $op \leftarrow$ select such an operation with the greatest *score*;
9   **else**
10   update clauses penalty weights;
11       $c \leftarrow$ a random falsified clause with integer variable;
12       $op \leftarrow$ the *bam* operation with the greatest score in c;
13     $\alpha \leftarrow \alpha$ with op performed;

---

boundary-aware moves are constructed for every literal in the falsified clause and inserted into the candidate set $\mathcal{B}$. Each iteration selects from $\mathcal{B}$ the highest-scoring *boundary-aware move* that decreases the number of falsified clauses (lines 7-8). If no such decreasing *boundary-aware move* exists, the search is deemed stuck in a local optimum; the algorithm then updates the penalty weights (line 10) and picks a random falsified clause with integer literals and chooses a *boundary-aware move* operation with the greatest score (lines 11-12).

5.1 Constraint-Partitioned Variable Initialization

In local search algorithms, the quality of variable initializations significantly impacts search efficiency [13, 27]. Traditional variable initialization methods typically rely solely on boundary information provided by the formula [5]. In the context of sampling problems, when initializing variables, it is essential to consider not only the impact of the initial values on search efficiency but also the potential detrimental effect of uniform initialization on the diversity of the solutions.

When solving constraint satisfaction problems (CSP), the constraint system can typically be decomposed into multiple independent subsystems for tailored solving. We propose a similar strategy called *Constraint-Partitioned Variable Initialization* to obtain an initialized assignment in line 1 in Algorithm 2. Specifically, we partition the integer variables into three independent constraint subsystems: the *equality system*, the *high-frequency system*, and the *general system*. Then, decomposing SMT(LIA) formulas into multiple sub-constraint systems and initializing variables based on the specific properties of the constraints achieves a better balance between sample diversity and search efficiency.

Initialization of Variables in Equality System Since *HighDiv* is integrated into Z3, we leverage Z3's equality-solving preprocessing tactic, *solve-eqs* [36]. This tactic simplifies the linear equalities in the conjunction, but may leave some equalities unresolved, which are then carried into the subsequent local search phase. Because equality constraints admit a much smaller solution space than inequality constraints, a bad initial assignment can substantially degrade the efficiency of the subsequent search.

We now define the *equality system* variable set. Let $\mathcal{C}_=$ denote equality constraints, and let $\mathcal{C}_{\neq}$ denote all remaining constraints. For a constraint c, let $\mathrm{vars}(c)$ denote the set of variables occurring in c. The equality system variable set $\mathcal{E}_{eq}$ is defined as the smallest set of variables satisfying:

1. $\bigcup_{c \in \mathcal{C}_=} \mathrm{vars}(c) \subseteq \mathcal{E}_{eq}$;
2. for every $c \in \mathcal{C}_{\neq}$, if $\mathrm{vars}(c) \cap \mathcal{E}_{eq} \neq \varnothing$, then $\mathrm{vars}(c) \subseteq \mathcal{E}_{eq}$.

To improve the efficiency of subsequent search, we initialize all variables in $\mathcal{E}_{eq}$ to zero during the variable initialization phase.

Initialization of Variables in High-frequency System In *CCSS*, each operation modifies the value of variable x to satisfy a literal ℓ that contains x. However, when x appears in multiple literals, changing its value can inadvertently disrupt the satisfaction of other literals.

For clarity, we define the frequency of a variable x, denoted by $freq(x)$, as the number of literals containing x. Let $\mathcal{C}$ be the set of constraints appearing in the formula, and let $\mathcal{E}_{eq}$ denote the set of variables in the equality system. Given a frequency threshold λ, the high-frequency variable set $\mathcal{E}_{hf}$ is defined as the smallest set of variables such that:

1. $\{v \mid freq(v) > \lambda\} \setminus \mathcal{E}_{eq} \subseteq \mathcal{E}_{hf}$;
2. for every constraint $c \in \mathcal{C} \setminus \mathcal{C}_=$, if $\mathrm{vars}(c) \cap \mathcal{E}_{hf} \neq \varnothing$, then $\mathrm{vars}(c) \setminus \mathcal{E}_{eq} \subseteq \mathcal{E}_{hf}$.

When initializing the variables in $\mathcal{E}_{hf}$, we first compute their value intervals based on the model obtained from the CDCL(T) phase, and then uniformly sample values within these intervals. Specifically, for each variable x to be initialized in $\mathcal{E}_{hf}$, we define the set of inequalities containing x that are true under the model M obtained in the CDCL(T) phase as $lit_{true}(x)$. For each $\ell_i \in lit_{true}(x)$, we substitute the values from M to calculate a feasible interval I_i for x under the interpretation of M with respect to ℓ_i. Therefore, each ℓ_i corresponds to a feasible interval I_i. Subsequently, the feasible intervals are merged based on the logical relationships between the literals: for conjunctions of literals ℓ_i and ℓ_j, the intervals are intersected, i.e., $I(x) = I_i \cap I_j$; for disjunctions of literals ℓ_i and ℓ_j, the intervals are united, i.e., $I(x) = I_i \cup I_j$. Finally, we obtain the initialization interval $I(x)$ for x. A specific example is given in Example 3.

Example 3. Given the SMT(LIA) formula $(\ell_1 \vee \ell_2) \wedge \ell_3 \wedge \ell_4 = (x_2 - x_1 \leq -1 \vee -x_1 \leq -10) \wedge (x_2 - x_3 \leq 0) \wedge (x_1 - x_3 \leq 3)$ and the model $M := \{x_1 = 10, x_2 = 7, x_3 = 7\}$. The literals $\{\ell_1, \ell_2, \ell_4\}$, which contain x_1 and are true under the model M, are used to compute the initialization interval of x_1 as follows:

- $\ell_1 := x_1 \geq x_2 + 1$, corresponding to $I_1 := [8, +\infty)$.
- $\ell_2 := x_1 \geq 10$, corresponding to $I_2 := [10, +\infty)$.
- $\ell_4 := x_1 \leq x_3 + 3$, corresponding to $I_4 := (-\infty, 10]$.

Therefore, the initialization interval for x_1 is $I(x_1) := (I_1 \cup I_2) \cap I_4 = [8, 10]$.

Initialization of Variables in General System Apart from the cases mentioned above, other constraints are generally easier to satisfy, and their initial states have a smaller impact on subsequent searches. Therefore, for the variables in these constraints, their values can be initialized to be far from the model obtained in the previous round of sampling.

Following Example 3, if x_1 is a general variable, the initialization interval for x_1 is set to the complement of the computed interval, i.e., $(-\infty, 7] \cup [11, +\infty)$.

5.2   Boundary-Aware Move

Previous research on local search for SMT(LIA) has introduced the *critical move* (cm) operator. Given a literal ℓ containing x and currently falsified, each operation $cm(x, \ell)$ modifies the assignment of x to make ℓ satisfied [5]. However, this operator always modifies the variable x to the boundary value that satisfies ℓ, which clearly imposes a strong restriction on the possible modified values of the variable. In fact, the value of the variable x that satisfies the literal ℓ is not unique. For example, consider the formula in Example 3 with the current assignment $\alpha := \{x_1 = 0, x_2 = 0, x_3 = 0\}$. As illustrated in Figure 2, performing the operation $cm(x_1, x_2 - x_1 \leq -1)$ assigns x_1 to 1. In fact, any value within the interval $[1, +\infty]$ for x_1 will satisfy $x_2 - x_1 \leq -1$.

However, note that when x_1 is assigned a value within the interval $[4, +\infty]$, another constraint $x_1 - x_3 \leq 3$ is no longer satisfied. In SMT(LIA) sampling, such an operation of modifying the assignment must balance search efficiency and solution diversity. To achieve a better trade-off, we propose a new operator, *boundary-aware move* (bam).

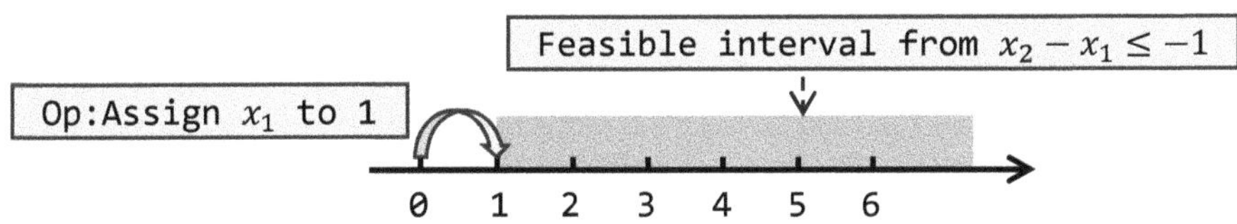

Fig. 2. When performing the operation $cm(x_1, x_2 - x_1 \leq -1)$, any assignment of the variable x_1 within $[1, +\infty]$ will make $x_2 - x_1 \leq -1$ true.

To facilitate describing bam, we first define the set of *contextual literals* for an integer variable x under assignment α as $\mathcal{L}^{\text{ctx}}(x, \alpha) = \{\ell \in \mathcal{L} \mid x \in \text{vars}(\ell) \text{ and } \alpha \models \ell\}$, where $\mathcal{L}$ is the set of all inequality literals occurring in the formula. Then, we introduce the *feasible interval* for the variable x with respect to the inequality literal ℓ: We substitute the current assignment α for every variable in ℓ except x, thereby obtaining x's *feasible interval* I_ℓ. Under linear integer arithmetic, I_ℓ can only be $[l, \infty)$ or $(-\infty, u]$; any integer chosen from that interval guaranties that ℓ becomes true after the operation. For instance, consider the literal $\ell : (x + y \geq 5)$ and the current assignment $\alpha = \{x = 0, y = 0\}$. Clearly, assigning any value from the interval $[5, \infty)$ to x satisfies the inequality. Therefore, the *feasible interval* for x with respect to ℓ is $[5, \infty)$.

We next describe how to construct the *sampling interval* I_s for the variable x with respect to the literal ℓ, where ℓ is the falsified literal that contains x.

- If $I_\ell = [l, \infty)$, we select contextual literals ℓ_i whose feasible intervals are of the form $(-\infty, u]$ and intersect I_ℓ with the minimal upper bound from these intervals.
- If $I_\ell = (-\infty, u]$, we select contextual literals ℓ_i whose feasible intervals are $[l, \infty)$ and intersect I_ℓ with the maximum lower bound from these intervals.

From this, we obtain the sampling interval I_s for x with respect to ℓ.

Definition 2. *To satisfy a currently falsified literal ℓ with variable x, the boundary-aware move operator, denoted as $bam(\alpha, x, \ell)$, obtains a new assignment by modifying the value of x in α as an integer uniformly sampled within the sampling interval I_s determined by ℓ and $\mathcal{L}^{\text{ctx}}(x, \alpha)$.*

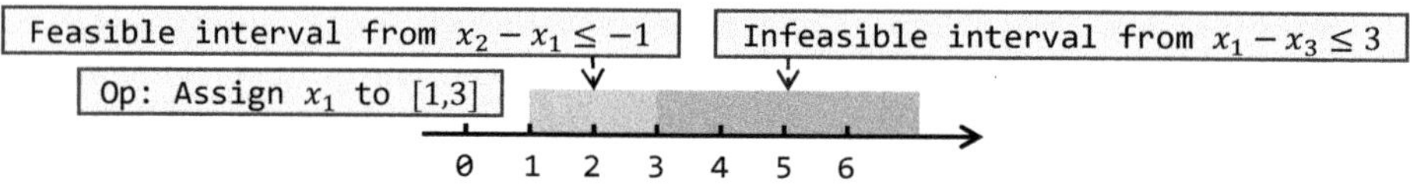

Fig. 3. During the operation $bam(\alpha, x, \ell_1)$, the infeasible interval specified by $\ell_4 := x_1 - x_3 \leq 3$ restricts the sampling interval of x_1.

Referring to the formula given in Example 3, the current assignment is $\alpha := \{x_1 = 0, x_2 = 0, x_3 = 0\}$. When performing the operation $bam(\alpha, x_1, \ell_1)$, the initial step involves determining the feasible interval to make ℓ_1 true, resulting in $[1, \infty)$. As illustrated in Figure 3, the contextual literal ℓ_4 supplies the opposite boundary, giving $(-\infty, 3]$. Therefore, $bam(\alpha, x_1, \ell_1)$ samples a random integer for x_1 from the interval $[1, 3]$.

6   Experiments

6.1   Setup

We describe the compared state-of-the-art SMT(LIA) sampling methods, the implementation of *HighDiv*, and the benchmark suites. All experiments were conducted on a workstation equipped with with a 13th-Generation Intel Core i7-13700F CPU and 32 GB RAM.

Competitors

- **MeGASampler** [39] is a recently proposed SMT(LIA) sampling tool and is among the most advanced tools for SMT(LIA) sampling. Additionally, it implements two distinct strategies, both of which we evaluate in our experiments.
- **SMTSampler(Int)**, the integer-logic variant of SMTSampler [10], has been reported to outperform MeGASampler in terms of coverage on certain benchmarks [39], and is therefore included in our evaluation.

Implementation We implemented *HighDiv* on top of Z3 version 4.14.2 [4]. To ensure a fair comparison, we used the same Z3 version (4.14.2) for MeGASampler and SMTSampler(Int).

Benchmarks To verify the effectiveness of the proposed method, we evaluated it on the same QF_LIA benchmark suite previously used to evaluate MeGASampler [39]. These benchmarks, sourced from the QF_LIA directory in SMT-LIB [2], were filtered to exclude unreasonable cases based on the following criteria: (1) marked as unsatisfiable or unknown; (2) unable to produce at least 100 samples with any technique; and (3) requiring more than one minute to solve using an SMT solver [39]. Following their methodology, they randomly selected 15 representative benchmarks from each of nine directories, yielding 345 instances, since benchmarks within the same directory tend to be similar.

6.2   Experimental Results

In this section, we first present the results of the experiment and then discuss threats to its validity.

Coverage Comparison within Fixed Time Limits To comprehensively compare state-of-the-art SMT(LIA) sampling methods, we followed the experimental setup of Peled et al. [39], setting the time limit to 900 seconds.

Table 1 presents the average coverage comparison among *HighDiv*, MeGASampler, and SMTSampler(Int) across 9 selected benchmark folders. To conserve

---

[4] *HighDiv* is open-sourced at `https://github.com/laigroup/HighDiv`.

Benchmarks	Coverage with fixed time				Coverage with fixed size			
	HighDiv	MeGA	MeGA[b]	SMTInt	*HighDiv*	MeGA	MeGA[b]	SMTInt
CAV2009-slacked	**93.15**	70.15	44.77	64.24	**93.16**	38.03	23.56	63.71
CAV2009	**76.79**	44.58	69.84	55.98	**76.79**	34.22	40.74	52.04
convert	**20.69**	9.23	8.48	15.02	**20.78**	4.04	5.95	19.84
dillig	**93.41**	33.58	89.75	44.83	**93.41**	32.87	42.19	41.01
prime-cone	**75.31**	46.14	30.37	46.28	**75.30**	28.49	21.94	40.60
slacks	**95.11**	71.39	47.04	64.27	**95.11**	39.73	25.41	62.64
pb2010	**4.45**	4.41	4.39	2.92	4.73	4.68	5.70	**5.09**
bofill-sched-random	11.06	**13.14**	9.56	9.86	10.84	**13.20**	11.16	12.35
bofill-sched-real	10.30	**11.46**	9.72	8.85	10.72	**11.52**	10.38	11.00
Average Coverage	**53.36**	33.79	34.88	34.69	**53.43**	22.98	20.78	34.25

Table 1. Comparative results (averaged) across the benchmarks with fixed Sampling Time (900s), fixed sample size (1000), and percentage coverage.

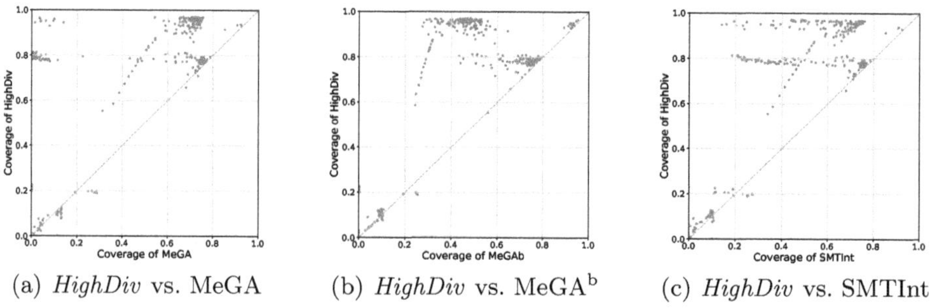

(a) *HighDiv* vs. MeGA   (b) *HighDiv* vs. MeGA[b]   (c) *HighDiv* vs. SMTInt

Fig. 4. Comparative Coverage Performance of *HighDiv* Against Competitors ($t = 900$ seconds).

space, only the average values for these 9 folders are shown. **MeGA** refers to the MeGASampler method based on random sampling, while **MeGA[b]** denotes the blocking-based variant. **SMTInt** indicates the integer logic version of SMT-Sampler. The best coverage results are highlighted in **bold**.

As shown in Table 1, *HighDiv* achieves higher coverage than its competitors across most benchmark categories. However, for two **bofill** categories, *HighDiv* achieves lower coverage than MeGA. We attribute this result to the high proportion of equality constraints in these instances, which limits *HighDiv*'s ability to introduce diversity during the search process.

To present detailed results for each individual benchmark file, we depict scatter plots in Figure 4 to provide a benchmark-wise comparison. It can be observed that, under the same time limit, *HighDiv* yields higher coverage in most benchmarks compared to MeGASampler and SMTSampler(Int).

Coverage Comparison within Fixed Sample Size We compare the performance of *HighDiv* with its competitors using a fixed-size sample set. In practice, solutions generated via sampling are typically embedded in the test suite, and executing even a single test campaign is computationally expensive. Therefore, a fixed-size set of test cases is commonly adopted for evaluation [31].

Following prior SAT sampling studies, we set the solution set size to $k = 1000$ [31] and limited the sampling time to one hour. From Table 1, it can be seen that with $k = 1000$, *HighDiv* significantly outperforms MeGASampler and SMTSampler(Int) in terms of coverage in most benchmarks. Figure 5 shows a scatter plot comparing the coverage of *HighDiv* with its competitors, where each point represents a benchmark file.

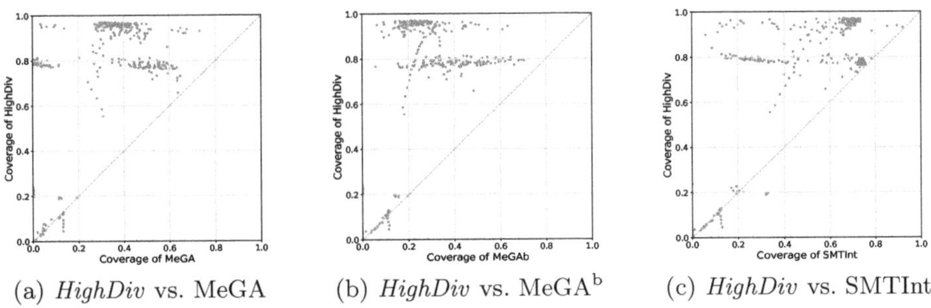

(a) *HighDiv* vs. MeGA   (b) *HighDiv* vs. MeGA^b (c) *HighDiv* vs. SMTInt

Fig. 5. Comparative Coverage Performance of *HighDiv* Against Competitors ($k = 1000$).

Effects of Algorithmic Components To analyze the effectiveness of each algorithmic component in *HighDiv*, we modify *HighDiv* to obtain seven alternative versions as follows.

- **init2zero**: In the local search phase, all integer variables are initially set to zero.
- **init2CD**: In the local search phase, all integer variables are initialized through guidance from CDCL(T).
- **init2rCD**: In the local search phase, all integer variables are initialized through reverse guidance from CDCL(T).
- **init2R**: In the local search phase, all integer variables are initialized randomly.
- **no_bam**: Removing the *boundary-aware move* operator and using the critical move operator.
- **no_cdcl**: Removing the stochastic CDCL(T) component and use only the local search component for iteration.
- **no_eqs**: Removing Z3's *solve-eqs* tactic in the pre-processing stage.

coverage	*HighDiv*	init2zero	init2CD	init2rCD	init2R	no_bam	no_cdcl	no_eqs
$t = 900s$	**53.36%**	47.75%	38.93%	51.09%	51.36%	33.82%	49.27%	49.71%
$k = 1000$	**53.43%**	47.42%	37.90%	51.15%	51.51%	33.44%	50.30%	49.86%

Table 2. Ablation study showing the effectiveness of each algorithmic component.

Table 2 presents the average coverage of each version across 9 benchmark categories. It can be observed that, under both the 900-second time limit and the 1000-sample constraint, *HighDiv* achieves higher coverage compared to the various variants. This demonstrates the effectiveness of each core algorithmic component in *HighDiv*.

Effect of Hyper-Parameter Setting Table 3 reports the average coverage of *HighDiv* across all benchmarks under fixed time and sample-size budgets, for different choices of λ and P. With our default setting ($\lambda = 50$), *HighDiv* attains the highest coverage in both experimental configurations. This matches our intuition: a smaller λ initializes the local search closer to the previous iteration's solution, which speeds up solving at the cost of reduced diversity; a larger λ yields an initialization farther from the previous model, improving diversity but reducing solving efficiency. Moreover, coverage varies little across different values of P, suggesting that *HighDiv* is insensitive to this parameter.

coverage	λ			P				
	20	50	80	0.1	0.3	0.5	0.7	0.9
$t = 900s$	48.31%	**53.36%**	53.27%	53.35%	**53.36%**	**53.36%**	**53.36%**	53.34%
$k = 1000$	48.38%	**53.43%**	53.08%	**53.43%**	**53.43%**	**53.43%**	**53.43%**	53.42%

Table 3. Average coverage of sampling results by *HighDiv* under different hyperparameter settings.

6.3   Threats to Validity

The validity of our evaluation may be subject to the following potential threats:

Correctness of Implementation. To ensure the correctness of our implementation, we validated all generated samples to confirm their satisfaction of the given formulas, thereby guaranteeing the robustness and accuracy of the results.

Validity of the Experimental Setup. Different experimental configurations may pose potential threats to the validity of our evaluation. Therefore, following previous studies [39], we conducted experiments with a time limit of 900 seconds;

and, in accordance with recent recommendations [31], we set the sample size k to 1000 to mitigate this risk. The results in Tables 1 and 2 demonstrate that under both configurations, *HighDiv* significantly outperforms MeGASampler and SMTSampler(Int) in terms of diversity on most benchmarks.

Diversity Metric Bias. The definition and emphasis of "diversity" vary across application scenarios; thus, evaluation conclusions may depend on the chosen metric. To assess the applicability of our method under different measures, we further consider two widely used diversity metrics—Hamming Distance [37] and 2-wise Coverage [31]—and evaluate them under two settings: fixed sampling time and fixed sample size. The results show that, under both metrics, HighDiv outperforms MeGASampler and SMTSampler(Int) on most benchmarks. Detailed results are reported in the appendix of an extended version of this paper [24].

7   Related Works

The constrained sampling problem is a significant research topic in software testing [16, 18, 43]. Over the past decades, satisfiability (SAT) sampling has been extensively studied. Current SAT sampling methods include Markov-Chain Monte-Carlo (MCMC) [21, 22], heuristic local search [30, 31], universal hashing [12, 33, 34], and knowledge compilation [25, 26, 44], all of which can effectively perform SAT sampling with various balances between solving efficiency and theoretical guarantees. While SMT formula sampling can be tackled using existing SAT methods by encoding SMT formulas into SAT [45], this transformation loses the formulas' high-level structure, which could otherwise improve sampling efficiency and diversity [10, 11, 39].

Dutra et al. introduced SMTSampler, the first sampler designed specifically for sampling SMT bit-vector theory formulas [10]. SMTSampler uses MaxSAT modulo theories (MAX-SMT) to generate initial random seeds and then obtains a set of solutions through syntactic mutation and combination. Subsequent research, GuidedSampler, allows for the setting of coverage metrics specific to certain problems and aims to optimize these metrics [11]. These methods primarily handle fixed-width bit-vector theory formulas, but this approach is unable to efficiently sample the linear integer constraints. Subsequently, Peled et al. proposed an effective sampling method for SMT(LIA) formula, named MeGASampler [39]. This method first uses an existing SMT solver to solve constraints, then generates an under-approximation formula of the original formula by adding extra constraints to the obtained solutions, and finally performs sampling based on this under-approximation formula. This is considered the state-of-the-art solution to SMT(LIA) sampling problems. However, these SMT samplers regard SMT solvers as black boxes and fail to introduce diversity into the solving process, thereby limiting the diversity of the generated solutions. Furthermore, these samplers frequently invoke MaxSMT to increase the randomness of the initial seeds, but using MaxSMT is very expensive, thus creating substantial overhead.

8   Conclusion

Previous SMT sampling algorithms often struggle to generate diverse samples as they treat the SMT solver as a black box and rely on extending a single model, limiting the coverage of the solution space. To overcome this, we propose *HighDiv*, the first iterative SMT sampling framework that integrates CDCL(T) and local search in a bidirectional guided manner. In the local search phase, *HighDiv* introduces an *Constraint-Partitioned Variable Initialization* strategy and the *boundary-aware move* operator, effectively balancing sample diversity and search efficiency. Experimental results show that *HighDiv* produces significantly more diverse samples than MeGASampler and SMTSampler(Int).

It is important to note that *HighDiv* is orthogonal to existing SMT sampling algorithms such as MeGASampler and SMTSampler. By generating initial models with *HighDiv* and then applying model-guided approximation or combinatorial mutation techniques, overall sampling efficiency can be greatly improved. In future work, we plan to extend *HighDiv* to support additional theories, such as Linear Real Arithmetic and Quantifier-Free Bit-Vectors, and explore integrating model-guided approximation and combinatorial mutation strategies to further enhance its scalability.

Acknowledgements

We thank the anonymous reviewers for their helpful feedback and Zizhao Han for artifact testing. This work was supported in part by National Key Research and Development Program of China [2023YFB3307500], Jilin Provincial Natural Science Foundation [20240101378JC], Jilin Provincial Education Department Research Project [JJKH20241286KJ], National Natural Science Foundation of China [62522201, 62202025, U22A2098, and 62172185], Young Elite Scientist Sponsorship Program by CAST [YESS20230566], Beijing Natural Science Foundation [L241050], CCF-Huawei Populus Grove Fund [CCF-HuaweiFM2024005], and Fundamental Research Fund Project of Beihang University.

References

1. Barbosa, H., Barrett, C.W., Brain, M., Kremer, G., Lachnitt, H., Mann, M., Mohamed, A., Mohamed, M., Niemetz, A., Nötzli, A., Ozdemir, A., Preiner, M., Reynolds, A., Sheng, Y., Tinelli, C., Zohar, Y.: cvc5: A versatile and industrial-strength SMT solver. In: Fisman, D., Rosu, G. (eds.) Tools and Algorithms for the Construction and Analysis of Systems - 28th International Conference, TACAS 2022. Lecture Notes in Computer Science, vol. 13243, pp. 415–442 (2022)
2. Barrett, C., Fontaine, P., Tinelli, C.: The Satisfiability Modulo Theories Library (SMT-LIB). www.SMT-LIB.org (2016)
3. Barrett, C.W., Sebastiani, R., Seshia, S.A., Tinelli, C.: Satisfiability modulo theories. In: Biere, A., Heule, M., van Maaren, H., Walsh, T. (eds.) Handbook of Satisfiability - Second Edition, Frontiers in Artificial Intelligence and Applications, vol. 336, pp. 1267–1329 (2021)

4. Cadar, C., Dunbar, D., Engler, D.R.: KLEE: unassisted and automatic generation of high-coverage tests for complex systems programs. In: Draves, R., van Renesse, R. (eds.) 8th USENIX Symposium on Operating Systems Design and Implementation, OSDI 2008. pp. 209–224 (2008)

5. Cai, S., Li, B., Zhang, X.: Local search for SMT on linear integer arithmetic. In: Shoham, S., Vizel, Y. (eds.) Computer Aided Verification - 34th International Conference, CAV 2022. Lecture Notes in Computer Science, vol. 13372, pp. 227–248 (2022)

6. Cai, S., Su, K.: Local search for boolean satisfiability with configuration checking and subscore. Artificial Intelligence

7. Carrasco, M., Cadar, C., Donaldson, A.: Scalable smt sampling for floating-point formulas via coverage-guided fuzzing. In: IEEE International Conference on Software Testing, Verification, and Validation (ICST 2025) (2025)

8. Cimatti, A., Griggio, A., Schaafsma, B.J., Sebastiani, R.: The mathsat5 SMT solver. In: Piterman, N., Smolka, S.A. (eds.) Tools and Algorithms for the Construction and Analysis of Systems - 19th International Conference, TACAS 2013. Lecture Notes in Computer Science, vol. 7795, pp. 93–107 (2013)

9. Codish, M., Fekete, Y., Fuhs, C., Giesl, J., Waldmann, J.: Exotic semi-ring constraints. In: Fontaine, P., Goel, A. (eds.) 10th International Workshop on Satisfiability Modulo Theories, SMT 2012. EPiC Series in Computing, vol. 20, pp. 88–97 (2012)

10. Dutra, R., Bachrach, J., Sen, K.: Smtsampler: efficient stimulus generation from complex SMT constraints. In: Bahar, I. (ed.) Proceedings of the International Conference on Computer-Aided Design, ICCAD 2018. p. 30 (2018)

11. Dutra, R., Bachrach, J., Sen, K.: GUIDEDSAMPLER: coverage-guided sampling of SMT solutions. In: Barrett, C.W., Yang, J. (eds.) 2019 Formal Methods in Computer Aided Design, FMCAD 2019. pp. 203–211 (2019)

12. Ermon, S., Gomes, C.P., Sabharwal, A., Selman, B.: Embed and project: Discrete sampling with universal hashing. In: Burges, C.J.C., Bottou, L., Ghahramani, Z., Weinberger, K.Q. (eds.) Advances in Neural Information Processing Systems 26: 27th Annual Conference on Neural Information Processing Systems 2013. pp. 2085–2093 (2013)

13. Fröhlich, A., Biere, A., Wintersteiger, C.M., Hamadi, Y.: Stochastic local search for satisfiability modulo theories. In: Bonet, B., Koenig, S. (eds.) Proceedings of the Twenty-Ninth AAAI Conference on Artificial Intelligence. pp. 1136–1143 (2015)

14. Ganzinger, H., Hagen, G., Nieuwenhuis, R., Oliveras, A., Tinelli, C.: DPLL(T): fast decision procedures. In: Alur, R., Peled, D.A. (eds.) Computer Aided Verification, 16th International Conference, CAV 2004. Lecture Notes in Computer Science, vol. 3114, pp. 175–188 (2004)

15. Gavrilenko, N., de León, H.P., Furbach, F., Heljanko, K., Meyer, R.: BMC for weak memory models: Relation analysis for compact SMT encodings. In: Dillig, I., Tasiran, S. (eds.) Computer Aided Verification - 31st International Conference, CAV 2019. Lecture Notes in Computer Science, vol. 11561, pp. 355–365 (2019)

16. Godefroid, P., Klarlund, N., Sen, K.: DART: directed automated random testing. In: Sarkar, V., Hall, M.W. (eds.) Proceedings of the ACM SIGPLAN 2005 Conference on Programming Language Design and Implementation. pp. 213–223 (2005)

17. Golia, P., Soos, M., Chakraborty, S., Meel, K.S.: Designing samplers is easy: The boon of testers. In: Formal Methods in Computer Aided Design, FMCAD 2021. pp. 222–230 (2021)

18. Holler, C., Herzig, K., Zeller, A.: Fuzzing with code fragments. In: Kohno, T. (ed.) Proceedings of the 21th USENIX Security Symposium. pp. 445–458 (2012)

19. Huang, H., Yao, P., Wu, R., Shi, Q., Zhang, C.: Pangolin: Incremental hybrid fuzzing with polyhedral path abstraction. In: 2020 IEEE Symposium on Security and Privacy, SP 2020. pp. 1613–1627 (2020)
20. Jiang, L., Yuan, H., Wu, M., Zhang, L., Zhang, Y.: Evaluating and improving hybrid fuzzing. In: 45th IEEE/ACM International Conference on Software Engineering, ICSE 2023. pp. 410–422 (2023)
21. Kitchen, N.: Markov Chain Monte Carlo Stimulus Generation for Constrained Random Simulation. Ph.D. thesis, University of California, Berkeley, USA (2010)
22. Kitchen, N., Kuehlmann, A.: Stimulus generation for constrained random simulation. In: Gielen, G.G.E. (ed.) 2007 International Conference on Computer-Aided Design, ICCAD 2007. pp. 258–265 (2007)
23. Kroening, D., Strichman, O.: Decision Procedures - An Algorithmic Point of View, Second Edition. Texts in Theoretical Computer Science. An EATCS Series, Springer (2016)
24. Lai, Y., Li, J., Luo, C.: SMT(LIA) sampling with high diversity. arXiv preprint arXiv:2503.04782 (2025)
25. Lai, Y., Liu, D., Yin, M.: New canonical representations by augmenting obdds with conjunctive decomposition. vol. 58, pp. 453–521 (2017)
26. Lai, Y., Meel, K.S., Yap, R.H.: Panini: an efficient and flexible knowledge compiler. In: International Conference on Computer Aided Verification. pp. 92–105. Springer (2025)
27. Liu, C., Liu, G., Luo, C., Cai, S., Lei, Z., Zhang, W., Chu, Y., Zhang, G.: Optimizing local search-based partial maxsat solving via initial assignment prediction. Sci. China Inf. Sci. **68**(2) (2025)
28. Liu, D., Ernst, G., Murray, T., Rubinstein, B.I.P.: LEGION: best-first concolic testing. In: 35th IEEE/ACM International Conference on Automated Software Engineering, ASE 2020. pp. 54–65 (2020)
29. Lopes, N.P., Monteiro, J.: Automatic equivalence checking of programs with uninterpreted functions and integer arithmetic. Int. J. Softw. Tools Technol. Transf. **18**(4), 359–374 (2016)
30. Luo, C., Song, J., Zhao, Q., Sun, B., Chen, J., Zhang, H., Lin, J., Hu, C.: Solving the t-wise coverage maximum problem via effective and efficient local search-based sampling. ACM Trans. Softw. Eng. Methodol. **34**(1), 13:1–13:64 (2025)
31. Luo, C., Sun, B., Qiao, B., Chen, J., Zhang, H., Lin, J., Lin, Q., Zhang, D.: Lssampling: an effective local search based sampling approach for achieving high t-wise coverage. In: Spinellis, D., Gousios, G., Chechik, M., Penta, M.D. (eds.) ESEC/FSE '21: 29th ACM Joint European Software Engineering Conference and Symposium on the Foundations of Software Engineering. pp. 1081–1092 (2021)
32. McCarthy, J.: Towards a mathematical science of computation. In: Information Processing, Proceedings of the 2nd IFIP Congress 1962, pp. 21–28 (1962)
33. Meel, K.S.: Sampling techniques for boolean satisfiability. CoRR **abs/1404.6682** (2014)
34. Meel, K.S., Vardi, M.Y., Chakraborty, S., Fremont, D.J., Seshia, S.A., Fried, D., Ivrii, A., Malik, S.: Constrained sampling and counting: Universal hashing meets SAT solving. In: Darwiche, A. (ed.) Beyond NP, Papers from the 2016 AAAI Workshop. AAAI Technical Report, vol. WS-16-05 (2016)
35. Moskewicz, M.W., Madigan, C.F., Zhao, Y., Zhang, L., Malik, S.: Chaff: Engineering an efficient sat solver. In: Proceedings of the 38th annual Design Automation Conference. pp. 530–535 (2001)

36. de Moura, L.M., Bjørner, N.S.: Z3: an efficient SMT solver. In: Ramakrishnan, C.R., Rehof, J. (eds.) Tools and Algorithms for the Construction and Analysis of Systems, 14th International Conference, TACAS 2008. Lecture Notes in Computer Science, vol. 4963, pp. 337–340 (2008)

37. Nadel, A.: Generating diverse solutions in sat. In: International Conference on Theory and Applications of Satisfiability Testing. pp. 287–301. Springer (2011)

38. Naveh, Y., Rimon, M., Jaeger, I., Katz, Y., Vinov, M., Marcus, E., Shurek, G.: Constraint-based random stimuli generation for hardware verification pp. 1720–1727 (2006)

39. Peled, M., Rothenberg, B., Itzhaky, S.: SMT sampling via model-guided approximation. In: Chechik, M., Katoen, J., Leucker, M. (eds.) Formal Methods - 25th International Symposium, FM 2023. Lecture Notes in Computer Science, vol. 14000, pp. 74–91 (2023)

40. Peleska, J., Vorobev, E., Lapschies, F.: Automated test case generation with smt-solving and abstract interpretation. In: Bobaru, M.G., Havelund, K., Holzmann, G.J., Joshi, R. (eds.) NASA Formal Methods - Third International Symposium, NFM 2011. Lecture Notes in Computer Science, vol. 6617, pp. 298–312 (2011)

41. Pipatsrisawat, K., Darwiche, A.: A lightweight component caching scheme for satisfiability solvers. In: International conference on theory and applications of satisfiability testing. pp. 294–299. Springer (2007)

42. Poeplau, S., Francillon, A.: Symbolic execution with symcc: Don't interpret, compile! In: Capkun, S., Roesner, F. (eds.) 29th USENIX Security Symposium, USENIX Security 2020. pp. 181–198 (2020)

43. Sen, K., Marinov, D., Agha, G.: CUTE: a concolic unit testing engine for C. In: Wermelinger, M., Gall, H.C. (eds.) Proceedings of the 10th European Software Engineering Conference held jointly with 13th ACM SIGSOFT International Symposium on Foundations of Software Engineering, 2005. pp. 263–272 (2005)

44. Sharma, S., Gupta, R., Roy, S., Meel, K.S.: Knowledge compilation meets uniform sampling. In: Barthe, G., Sutcliffe, G., Veanes, M. (eds.) LPAR-22. 22nd International Conference on Logic for Programming, Artificial Intelligence and Reasoning. EPiC Series in Computing, vol. 57, pp. 620–636 (2018)

45. Shaw, A., Meel, K.S.: CSB: A counting and sampling tool for bit-vectors. In: Reger, G., Zohar, Y. (eds.) Proceedings of the 22nd International Workshop on Satisfiability Modulo Theories co-located with the 36th International Conference on Computer Aided Verification (CAV 2024). CEUR Workshop Proceedings, vol. 3725, pp. 36–43 (2024)

46. Thornton, J., Pham, D.N., Bain, S., Ferreira Jr, V.: Additive versus multiplicative clause weighting for sat. In: AAAI. vol. 4, pp. 191–196 (2004)

47. Zhang, X., Li, B., Cai, S.: Deep combination of CDCL(T) and local search for satisfiability modulo non-linear integer arithmetic theory. In: Proceedings of the 46th IEEE/ACM International Conference on Software Engineering, ICSE 2024. pp. 125:1–125:13 (2024)

48. Zhang, Y., Chen, Z., Shuai, Z., Zhang, T., Li, K., Wang, J.: Multiplex symbolic execution: Exploring multiple paths by solving once. In: Proceedings of the 35th IEEE/ACM International Conference on Automated Software Engineering. pp. 846–857 (2020)

BDD-Based Formula Approximations
for Quantified Bit-Vector Satisfiability*

Jakub Horák and Martin Jonáš

Masaryk University, Brno, Czechia
`536519@mail.muni.cz, martin.jonas@mail.muni.cz`

Abstract. We propose a technique that combines a BDD-based solver for quantified bit-vector formulas with an arbitrary other solver. The main idea is to employ the BDD-based solver on subformulas of the problem and then add the obtained information back to the original formula. The technique relies on a preexisting algorithm for computing approximate BDDs for the given quantified bit-vector formula and on a novel algorithm that translates the resulting BDD back to a bit-vector formula while preserving some word-level information. The experimental evaluation shows that the proposed technique can improve performance of existing state-of-the-art SMT solvers and can decide satisfiability of some formulas that were beyond reach of all the compared solvers.

1 Introduction

Solving satisfiability of bit-vector formulas *without quantifiers* is crucial for many approaches to hardware and software verification, including techniques such as bounded model checking [4], k-induction [20], SMT-based IC3 [7], or symbolic execution [12]. For other use cases, quantifier-free formulas are not sufficient and deciding satisfiability of *quantified* bit-vector formulas is needed. This includes applications such as comparison of symbolic states [16], checking correctness of program or formula rewrites [19], or summarizing program loops [14,21].

For solving satisfiability of quantified bit-vector formulas, modern Satisfiability Modulo Theories (SMT) solvers rely mostly on two approaches. The first is *quantifier instantiation*, where the solver maintains a set of quantifier-free *quantifier instances*, obtained by substituting universally quantified variables in the input formula by suitable ground terms. These quantifier instances can then be handled by an SMT solver for quantifier-free bit-vector formulas. The set of quantifier instances can be refined if it is not sufficient to decide satisfiability of the original formula. We note that there are several variants of quantifier instantiation [22,18,19], but their specific details are not important for this paper. The approach based on quantifier instantiation is implemented in SMT solvers such as Bitwuzla [17], CVC5 [1], and Z3 [15]. The second approach to solving satisfiability of quantified bit-vector formulas relies on *binary decision diagrams*

---

* This work has been supported by the Czech Science Foundation grant GA26-22640S.

S. Junges and G. Katz (Eds.): TACAS 2026, LNCS 16505, pp. 213–232, 2026.
https://doi.org/10.1007/978-3-032-22752-2_11

(BDD). In this approach, the entire input formula is converted to a corresponding BDD, which is trivial to check for satisfiability. There are several ingredients that make the approach efficient, including good variable ordering, variable approximations, or operation abstractions [10,11]. The approach based on BDDs is implemented in the SMT solver Q3B [9].

The two approaches are incomparable in strength. Solvers based on quantifier instantiation can handle complex arithmetic and other complicated constraints, because they offload the hard reasoning about those to a solver for quantifier-free formulas and, in turn, to an efficient propositional satisfiability (SAT) solver. On the other hand, they tend to struggle when the quantifier structure is complicated. Conversely, the approach based on BDDs can handle a large number of quantifiers and their alternations, because with BDDs, it is possible to directly reason about quantifiers. On the other hand, the BDD-based algorithms struggle with presence of complicated (especially non-linear) arithmetic.

In this paper, we propose an approach that can combine the respective strengths of the two approaches within a single input formula. Essentially, the idea is to use BDDs for a formula preprocessing step. Instead of using a BDD-based solver only on the entire input formula, we apply it also to its individual quantified subformulas. Even when the solver does not solve satisfiability of the entire input formula, it can still obtain useful BDDs for some of its subformulas. To share the obtained information with a solver based on quantifier instantiation, we convert the BDDs for the subformulas back to bit-vector formulas. Note that these bit-vector formulas will be *quantifier-free*, because the quantifiers have been applied during BDD construction. These quantifier-free bit-vector formulas can then be added back to the original formula and subsequently leveraged by a solver based on quantifier instantiation or any other technique, when executed on the modified formula.

Importantly, even when a BDD-based SMT solver cannot compute the precise BDD for some subformula, it still can compute *approximations* of the precise BDD. In particular, it can compute an *underapproximating* BDD that describes a subset of the actual models of the subformula and an *overapproximating* BDD that describes a superset of its actual models. While these approximations do not describe the original subformula precisely, they can still contain useful information about its models, e.g., that some particular bits must be zero in all models or that some particular pairs of bits must always be equal, which can be leveraged by the quantifier-instantiation-based solver. Also the approximated BDDs can be converted to (quantifier-free) bit-vector formulas and added to the original formula.

Our experimental evaluation shows that while the approach is conceptually simple, it offers benefits over a straightforward combination of the two approaches, i.e., their parallel portfolio. In particular, it can be used to decide satisfiability of several quantified bit-vector formulas that cannot be solved by any of the combined solvers on their own.

Contributions. The paper makes the following contributions:

1. We propose an algorithm for translating BDDs to bit-vector formulas that reconstructs some word-level information from the input BDD.
2. We show how to combine this algorithm with existing approaches that convert bit-vector formulas to approximating BDDs. This allows using BDDs to compute approximating bit-vector formulas and to obtain new information that can be used to improve effectiveness of quantified bit-vector solvers that do not use BDDs.
3. We implement the proposed approach and experimentally evaluate it on a large number of formulas. We show that by using the algorithm, state-of-the-art SMT solvers for quantified bit-vectors can decide satisfiability of some formulas that were previously beyond their reach.

Paper structure. The paper is structured as follows. Section 2 briefly recalls logical preliminaries, BDDs, and existing algorithms for conversion of bit-vector formulas to BDDs. In Section 3, we propose a translation of BDDs back to bit-vector formulas. In Section 4, we develop an algorithm that uses the translations to enrich a given bit-vector formula with information obtained using BDDs. In Section 5, we describe our implementation of the algorithm and we evaluate its effectiveness in Section 6. Finally, the last section concludes the paper.

2   Preliminaries

Bit-Vector Logic We assume that the reader is familiar with the standard notions of many-sorted first-order logic, such as signatures, terms and formulas. The precise definitions of these terms can be found, for example, in Barrett and Tinelli [3]. We briefly recall the *theory of fixed sized bit-vectors* (*BV* or *bit-vector theory* for short). The bit-vector theory is a many-sorted first-order theory with infinitely many sorts that correspond to bit-vectors of various lengths, which are called *bit-widths*. Its signature contains only three predicates, namely *equality* $(=)$, *unsigned inequality* of bit-vectors interpreted as binary-encoded natural numbers $(\leq)$, and *signed inequality* of bit-vectors interpreted as integers in two's complement representation $(\leq_s)$. The theory contains various binary arithmetic functions including *addition* $(+)$ and *multiplication* $(\times)$, *bit-wise operations* $(\mathtt{bvand}, \mathtt{bvor}, \mathtt{bvxor})$, *shifts* $(\ll, \gg)$, and *concatenation* $(\mathtt{concat})$. Except for concatenation, all predicates and binary functions take two terms of the same bit-width. The theory also includes several unary functions including *extraction* of bits from position i to position j ($\mathtt{extract}_j^i$ with $i \leq j$) or *extension with n zeroes* ($\mathtt{zeroExtend}_n$). For convenience, we use the notation $x[i{:}j]$ for $\mathtt{extract}_j^i(x)$ and $x[i]$ for $\mathtt{extract}_i^i(x)$. It is standard to index the bits from the least significant, i.e., $x[0]$ extracts the least-significant bit of x.

Further, the signature of BV theory contains a constant $c^{[n]}$ for each bit-width $n > 0$ and a number $0 \leq c \leq 2^n - 1$, interpreted as the binary representation of c. Finally, we also allow the *if-then-else* construct $\mathtt{ite}(\varphi, t_1, t_2)$ that evaluates to t_1 if φ holds and as t_2 otherwise.

The precise description of bit-vector theory and its operations can be found for example in the paper describing complexity of quantified bit-vector theory by Kovásznai et al. [13] or in SMT-LIB [2].

If φ is a formula, ψ is its subformula and ρ is an arbitrary formula, we denote as $\varphi[\psi \leftarrow \rho]$ the result of replacing each occurrence of ψ in φ by ρ. We denote the set of all free variables in the formula φ as $Vars(\varphi)$. Since the theory does not contain uninterpreted functions, given an assignment μ to all variables $Vars(\varphi)$, it is possible to evaluate the formula φ to $[\![\varphi]\!]_\mu \in \{0, 1\}$.

Binary Decision Diagrams A *binary decision diagram* (BDD) is a data structure that can succinctly represent Boolean functions. Formally, a BDD is a rooted directed acyclic graph that has at most two leaves, which are labeled by 0 and 1. Each inner node n is labeled by a Boolean variable x, denoted as $var(n) = x$. It has two outgoing edges, which correspond to setting the Boolean variable x to 0 and 1, respectively. The successors of b under those edges are traditionally called *low child* and *high child* and are denoted $lo(b)$ and $hi(b)$, respectively. In the graphical representation, it is traditional to depict high children with solid edges and low children with dotted edges. The BDD maps each assignment μ of Boolean variables either to 0 or to 1. The value can be determined by following the unique path that starts in the root node and in each inner node labeled by x with $\mu(x) = 0$ goes to the low child and in each node labeled by x with $\mu(x) = 1$ goes to the high child. The final leaf node of this path, i.e., either 0 or 1, is then the result. The value to which a BDD b maps an assignment μ is denoted by $[\![b]\!]_\mu$.

We denote the leaf nodes as $\boxed{0}$ and $\boxed{1}$. These nodes also correspond to BDDs for constant Boolean functions *false* (0) and *true* (1), respectively.

In this paper, we suppose that all binary decision diagrams are *reduced* and *ordered*. A BDD is *ordered* if, for any two paths in the BDD, the order of the variables that occur on both paths is the same. A BDD is *reduced* if it does not contain isomorphic subgraphs and there is no inner node with the same low and high child. It has been shown that reduced and ordered BDDs are *canonical*, i.e., for each given function and a variable ordering, there is exactly one reduced and ordered BDD [5].

From Formulas to BDDs Binary decision diagrams can be used to represent sets of models of bit-vector formulas by a process called *bit-blasting*. Each bit-vector variable x of bit-width k can be represented by k Boolean variables, i.e., $x = x_{k-1}x_{k-2}\ldots x_1 x_0$, where x_0 is the least significant bit and x_{k-1} is the most significant bit. Using these variables, it is possible to construct the BDD for φ bottom-up. More precisely, it is possible to define bit-vector operations that operate on BDDs rather than on individual bit values and using those, one can construct BDDs that correspond to the individual bits of each subterm of the formula φ and, in turn, the BDDs for all subformulas of φ. The BDD that corresponds to the formula φ, i.e., describes all its models, is denoted $\texttt{f2BDD}(\varphi)$. We note that there are efficient implementations of this conversion [10], but their details are not important for this paper.

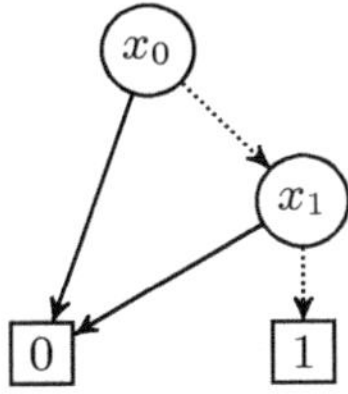

Fig. 1. An overapproximating BDD for $\forall z\,.(x \times z = 0^{[32]})$.

The function $\mathtt{f2BDD}(\varphi)$ has been used on its own as a core part of some SMT solvers. Clearly, if $\mathtt{f2BDD}(\varphi)$ has a path to the node $\boxed{1}$, the input formula φ is satisfiable and it is unsatisfiable otherwise.

There are both practical and theoretical limits for this approach. If the input formula φ contains complicated arithmetic, the BDD $\mathtt{f2BDD}(\varphi)$ tends to be impractically large. In fact, it is proven that given variables x, y, z of bit-width k, the BDD $\mathtt{f2BDD}(x \times y = z)$ is bound to have exponentially many nodes with respect to k, regardless the ordering of the BDD variables [6]. To partially mitigate this problem in practice, it has been proposed to use *variable approximations* [10] and *operation abstractions* [11] that trade off the size of the BDD for its precision. Given a precision parameter p, the techniques compute a pair of potentially smaller BDDs $\mathtt{f2ApproxBDD}(\varphi, p) = (b_u, b_o)$, where b_u underapproximates the set of models of φ and b_o overapproximates the set of models of φ. I.e., for each valuation μ, it holds that $[\![b_u]\!]_\mu \Rightarrow [\![\mathtt{f2BDD}(\varphi)]\!]_\mu$ and $[\![\mathtt{f2BDD}(\varphi)]\!]_\mu \Rightarrow [\![b_o]\!]_\mu$. The parameter p controls the precision: with larger p, the returned BDDs (b_u, b_o) can be larger, but more closely corresponds to the precise BDD $\mathtt{f2BDD}(\varphi)$.

As an example, consider the formula $\varphi \overset{\text{def}}{=} \forall z\,.(x \times z = 0^{[32]})$, where both variables are bit-vectors of bit-with 32. As noted earlier, it is infeasible to compute the precise BDD $\mathtt{f2BDD}(\varphi)$ because the BDD representation of $x \times z$ has exponential size. However, given a small precision p, it is possible to compute $\mathtt{f2ApproxBDD}(\varphi, p) = (b_u, b_o)$ by, for instance, applying operation abstractions and computing only two bits of the result of $x \times z$. In that case, the underapproximating BDD is the false BDD $b_u = \boxed{0}$, because when only two bits of $x \times z$ are known, no values of x are *guaranteed* to satisfy $x \times z = 0^{[32]}$. More interestingly, an overapproximating BDD b_o is presented in Figure 1. It shows that in any model of φ, the two least significant bits of x, i.e., x_0 and x_1 must be set to the value 0.

3   From BDDs to Formulas

In this section, we propose an algorithm to convert a BDD into an equivalent (quantifier-free) bit-vector formula. We first present a straightforward approach and then extend it with pattern detection in order to improve the word-level information of the resulting formula. For convenience, we use the Boolean BDD variable x_i and the 1-bit term $x[i]$ over the original bit-vector variables inter-

---

Algorithm 1 Straightforward conversion of a BDD-node to an equivalent formula.

1: **procedure** BDDNODE2FORMULA(*node*, *cache*)
2:    **if** *node* in *cache* **then return** *cache*[*node*]
3:    $\varphi_h \leftarrow$ BDDNODE2FORMULA(*hi*(*node*), *cache*)
4:    $\varphi_l \leftarrow$ BDDNODE2FORMULA(*lo*(*node*), *cache*)
5:    $t_x \leftarrow var(node)$
6:    $\psi \leftarrow \mathtt{ite}(t_x = 1^{[1]}, \varphi_h, \varphi_l)$
7:    *cache*[*node*] $\leftarrow \psi$
8:    **return** ψ
9: **end procedure**

Algorithm 2 Converting a BDD to an equivalent formula.

1: **procedure** BDD2FORMULA(*bdd*)
2:    *cache* $\leftarrow$ {}
3:    *cache*[1] $\leftarrow$ *true*
4:    *cache*[0] $\leftarrow$ *false*
5:    **return** BDDNODE2FORMULA(*root*(*bdd*), *cache*)
6: **end procedure**

---

changeably throughout this section. In particular, we assume that $var(node)$ returns the associated 1-bit bit-vector term.

3.1 Straightforward Implementation

A straightforward conversion of a BDD to a bit-vector formula can be implemented as in Algorithms 1 and 2. To convert a given node with variable x_i into a formula, we recursively convert its children and subsequently combine the obtained formulas using the **ite** function with the condition $x[i] = 1^{[1]}$, i.e., whether the i-th bit of the bit-vector variable x is set to 1. This exactly corresponds to the semantics of a BDD. The base case for the recursion are the leaf nodes 0 and 1, which are converted into the formulas *false* and *true*, respectively.

The result can be further improved by basic simplifications for cases where some argument to the **ite** function is a Boolean constant *false* or *true*. In these cases, the resulting formula can be expressed as a conjunction or disjunction of the two remaining arguments or their negations.

Since the BDD is not necessarily a tree, it is important to store computed formulas for all nodes in a cache. Without the use of the cache, the time complexity of the presented algorithm would be exponential in the number of nodes. When the cache is employed, the time complexity of the algorithm is linear.

3.2 Pattern Detection

The formulas produced by the previous algorithm perform operations directly on the bit level, i.e., using the individual bits of the bit-vector variables. To improve

---

Algorithm 3 Converting a BDD-node to a formula using pattern detection.

1: **procedure** BDDNODE2FORMULAPATTERNS($node$, $cache$)
2:     **if** $node$ in $cache$ **then return** $cache[node]$
3:     $n_h, n_l, \varphi_c \leftarrow$ DETECTPATTERN($node$)
4:     $\varphi_h \leftarrow$ BDDNODE2FORMULAPATTERNS(n_h, $cache$)
5:     $\varphi_l \leftarrow$ BDDNODE2FORMULAPATTERNS(n_l, $cache$)
6:     $\psi \leftarrow \texttt{ite}(\varphi_c, \varphi_h, \varphi_l)$
7:     $\psi' \leftarrow$ TRYMERGE(ψ)
8:     $cache[node] \leftarrow \psi'$
9:     **return** ψ'
10: **end procedure**

---

the word-level information of the formulas, we propose a more sophisticated version of the algorithm that can detect some frequently occurring patterns in the BDD and convert them to more descriptive formulas.

The pattern detection for an operation consists of two parts. First, we detect the base case, that is, the operation applied to a single bit. Then, we try to merge already detected operations by combining two operations applied to consecutive parts of a variable into one operation applied to the union of these parts.

To achieve this, we create a new procedure BDDNODE2FORMULAPATTERNS, presented in Algorithm 3 that proceeds as follows. First, it detects which base-case is $node$ a part of. This is based purely on the structure of the sub-BDD rooted in $node$. It then recursively calls itself on some nodes n_h and n_l in this sub-BDD, obtaining formulas φ_h and φ_l, respectively. The choice of n_h and n_l depends on the detected base case. After that, a new formula $\psi = \texttt{ite}(\varphi_c, \varphi_h, \varphi_l)$ is constructed, where the formula φ_c depends on the detected base-case, such that $\psi \equiv$ BDDNODE2FORMULA($node$), i.e., ψ is the correct conversion of $node$ to formula. Lastly, it attempts to merge adjacent operations in ψ, obtaining ψ', which is then returned from the procedure.

For each pattern we therefore have to specify how to detect the base case, how to obtain n_h, n_l, and φ_c given $node$, and how to merge adjacent operations of the given type. We now describe several useful patterns. For convenience, let $x_{node} = var(node)$ be the bit-vector term corresponding to the node's variable.

Equality Between a Variable and a Numeral (EqNum) The goal of *EqNum* pattern is to detect subformulas of form $x[i{:}j] = c^{[n]}$, where c is a numeral. This is the default pattern, as every node can be thought of as an equality check between the term $x_{node} = x[i{:}i]$ and the numeral $1^{[1]}$. The algorithm falls back to this case if no other pattern base case is detected. If the pattern is used, we set $\varphi_c \stackrel{\text{def}}{=} (x_{node} = 1^{[1]})$, $n_h \stackrel{\text{def}}{=} hi(node)$ and $n_l \stackrel{\text{def}}{=} lo(node)$. This exactly corresponds to what the straightforward algorithm does.

For operation merging, we can merge each ψ equivalent to $x[i{:}j] = c \wedge x[j+1{:}k] = d$ with $i \leq j < k$ to the equivalent formula $x[i{:}k] = \texttt{concat}(d, c)$.

Equality Between Two Variables (EqVar) The goal of *EqVar* pattern is to detect subformulas of form $x[i{:}j] = y[k{:}l]$. For *node* to be part of this pattern, the following conditions have to hold:

- $var(hi(node)) = var(lo(node))$, i.e., the low and high children of *node* test the same variable, further denoted as x_{child}.
- $hi(hi(node)) = lo(lo(node))$, i.e., the result node is the same when x_{node} and x_{child} have the same value, denote this node n_{same}.
- $hi(lo(node)) = lo(hi(node))$, i.e., the result node is the same when x_{node} and x_{child} have different values, denote this node $n_{different}$.

Intuitively, this exactly corresponds to comparing x_{node} and x_{child} for equality. Therefore, we set $\varphi_c \overset{\text{def}}{=} (x_{node} = x_{child})$, $n_h \overset{\text{def}}{=} n_{same}$ and $n_l \overset{\text{def}}{=} n_{different}$.

Similarly to the previous case, we can merge each ψ equivalent to $x[i{:}j] = y[i{:}j] \land x[j+1{:}k] = y[j+1{:}k]$ with $i \le j < k$ to the equivalent formula $x[i{:}k] = y[i{:}k]$.

Inequality Between Two Variables (IneqVar) The goal of *IneqVar* pattern is to detect subformulas of form $x[i{:}j] \le y[k{:}l]$. It contains two symmetrical base cases.

- If $hi(hi(node)) = lo(node)$, denote this node n_{leq}, the node $lo(hi(node))$ as n_{gt} and let $x_{child} = var(hi(node))$. According to the base case condition, the result node should be the same if x_{node} is false, or both x_{node} and x_{child} are true. This exactly corresponds to the condition $x_{node} \le x_{child}$. Therefore, we set $\varphi_c \overset{\text{def}}{=} (x_{node} \le x_{child})$, $n_h \overset{\text{def}}{=} n_{leq}$, and $n_l \overset{\text{def}}{=} n_{gt}$.
- If $lo(lo(node)) = hi(node)$, denote this node n_{leq}, the node $hi(lo(node))$ as n_{gt} and let $x_{child} = var(lo(node))$. According to the base case condition, the result node should be the same if x_{node} is true, or both x_{node} and x_{child} are false. This exactly corresponds to the condition $x_{child} \le x_{node}$. Therefore, we set $\varphi_c \overset{\text{def}}{=} (x_{child} \le x_{node})$, $n_h \overset{\text{def}}{=} n_{leq}$, and $n_l \overset{\text{def}}{=} n_{gt}$.

For merging of adjacent operations of this type, we use the following two rewrites (for all $k \ge j > i$) and their other symmetric variations:

$$\mathtt{ite}\Big(x[i{:}j-1] \le y[i{:}j-1],\ x[j{:}k] \le y[j{:}k],\ x[j{:}k] < y[j{:}k]\Big) \rightsquigarrow x[i{:}k] \le y[i{:}k],$$

$$\mathtt{ite}\Big(x[i{:}j-1] < y[i{:}j-1],\ x[j{:}k] \le y[j{:}k],\ x[j{:}k] < y[j{:}k]\Big) \rightsquigarrow x[i{:}k] < y[i{:}k].$$

We now show a few examples of the pattern detection and then a theorem that claims that the conversion is correct.

Example 1. As an example, consider again the BDD in Figure 1. The algorithm BDDNODE2FORMULA in this example returns the formula

$$\mathtt{ite}(x[0] = 1^{[1]}, \textit{false}, \mathtt{ite}(x[1] = 1^{[1]}, \textit{false}, \textit{true})).$$

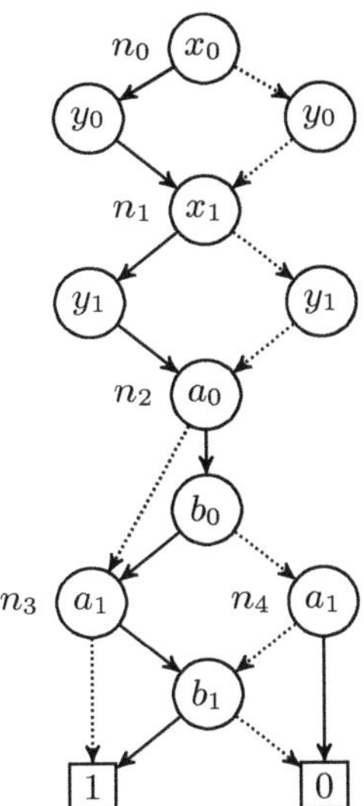

Fig. 2. An example BDD for pattern detection. Omitted edges lead to the leaf $\boxed{0}$.

With the constant-formula simplifications, this gets reduced to $x[0] = 0^{[1]} \wedge x[1] = 0^{[1]}$. When employing pattern detection, the *EqNum* pattern base case is detected in both nodes, as it is the default one. In the root node, the adjacent operations get merged and the final formula becomes $x[0:1] = 0^{[2]}$.

Example 2. Now consider the more complicated BDD shown in Figure 2. Note that some edges that lead to $\boxed{0}$ are not shown for clarity. On this example, we will demonstrate the pattern detection for *EqVar* and *IneqVar*.

Let us first examine the detected patterns and recursive calls in this example. When called on the root node n_0, the *EqVar* pattern base case is detected with $\varphi_c = (x[0] = y[0])$, $n_h = n_1$ and $n_l = \boxed{0}$. A recursive call on the node n_1 is therefore made, which again detects the *EqVar* pattern base case, this time with $\varphi_c = (x[1] = y[1])$, $n_h = n_2$ and $n_l = \boxed{0}$. Another recursive call is made on n_2, which detects the *IneqVar* pattern base case with $\varphi_c = (a[0] \leq b[0])$, $n_h = n_3$ and $n_l = n_4$. Two recursive calls on the nodes n_3 and n_4 are made this time. The call on n_3 detects the *IneqVar* pattern base case with $\varphi_c = (a[1] \leq b[1])$, $n_h = \boxed{1}$ and $n_l = \boxed{0}$, while the call on n_4 detects the same pattern base case but with $\varphi_c = (b[1] \leq a[1])$, $n_h = \boxed{0}$ and $n_l = \boxed{1}$. At this point, no more recursive calls on nodes are made.

Knowing this, we can now go from the bottom of the graph and construct the resulting formula. In the following, the important simplification steps are shown. For brevity reasons, the names of the nodes and their equivalent formulas are used interchangeably. From the nodes n_4, n_3, and n_2, we can detect inequality as follows:

$$n_4 \;\equiv\; \mathtt{ite}(b[1] \leq a[1], \mathit{false}, \mathit{true}) \;\equiv\; a[1] < b[1]$$
$$n_3 \;\equiv\; \mathtt{ite}(a[1] \leq b[1], \mathit{true}, \mathit{false}) \;\equiv\; a[1] \leq b[1]$$
$$n_2 \;\equiv\; \mathtt{ite}(a[0] \leq b[0], a[1] \leq b[1], a[1] < b[1]) \;\equiv\; a[0{:}1] \leq b[0{:}1]$$

Continuing the computation, we further detect a variable comparison in the remaining nodes and combine it with the inequality from n_2.

$$n_1 \;\equiv\; \mathtt{ite}(x[1] = y[1], a[0{:}1] \leq b[0{:}1], \mathit{false}) \;\equiv\; x[1] = y[1] \wedge a[0{:}1] \leq b[0{:}1]$$
$$n_0 \;\equiv\; \mathtt{ite}(x[0] = y[0], x[1] = y[1] \wedge a[0{:}1] \leq b[0{:}1], \mathit{false})$$
$$\equiv\; (x[0] = y[0]) \wedge (x[1] = y[1]) \wedge (a[0{:}1] \leq b[0{:}1])$$
$$\equiv\; (x[0{:}1] = y[0{:}1]) \wedge (a[0{:}1] \leq b[0{:}1]).$$

The final returned formula is therefore $x[0{:}1] = y[0{:}1] \wedge a[0{:}1] \leq b[0{:}1]$. Note that when constructing the formula for n_2 and n_0, the adjacent operations were merged by directly by applying the observation for the given pattern.

Theorem 1. *The proposed algorithm that uses patterns is correct, i.e., for any* BDD *b and any valuation μ we have that $[\![b]\!]_\mu = [\![BDD2\textsc{Formula}(b)]\!]_\mu$.*

Proof. Can be proven by simple induction on the structure of the BDD and by case distinction of the described patterns.

4   Main Algorithm

Using the function BDD2FORMULA with pattern detection, we can readily devise an algorithm that computes quantifier-free approximations for subformulas of the input formula φ using BDDs. These quantifier-free approximations can then be added back to the original formula to obtain a new formula φ'. It is then possible to employ any state-of-the-art SMT solver for quantified bit-vectors to check the satisfiability of φ'. As a result, this SMT solver can then directly leverage the added quantifier-free information that was computed using BDDs.

Consider an arbitrary formula φ and its subformula ψ. The formula ψ can be converted to approximating BDDs (b_u, b_o) using the function $\mathtt{f2ApproxBDD}(\psi, p)$ with a desired approximation precision p. Note that the quantifiers in ψ are applied during the BDD construction, and thus the BDDs b_u and b_o only contain variables corresponding to bits of bit-vector variables that are free in ψ. The approximating BDDs can be converted back to formulas $\psi_u \stackrel{\text{def}}{=} \text{BDD2FORMULA}(b_u)$ and $\psi_o \stackrel{\text{def}}{=} \text{BDD2FORMULA}(b_o)$ that are quantifier-free approximations of the original subformula ψ. In particular, both ψ_u and ψ_o contain only bit-vector variables from $\mathit{Vars}(\psi)$ and satisfy $\psi_u \models \psi \models \psi_o$. It is therefore possible to add the obtained quantifier-free information back to the original formula φ by replacing all occurrences of ψ by an equivalent formula $(\psi \wedge \psi_o) \vee \psi_u$. We note that in some cases, the approximations yield no additional information, i.e., $\psi_u = \mathit{false}$ or $\psi_o = \mathit{true}$, in which case they can be omitted.

Example 3. Consider the following quantified bit-vector formula with 32-bit variables x, y, z:

$$\varphi \stackrel{\text{def}}{=} x = (2^{[32]} \times y + 1^{[32]}) \,\wedge\, \underbrace{\forall z. (x \times z = 0^{[32]})}_{\psi}.$$

and its subformula ψ depicted above. Given a low precision p, for which only some bits of the product $x \times z$ are computed, suppose that $\texttt{f2ApproxBDD}(\psi, p)$ is (b_u, b_o) where $b_u = \boxed{0}$ is the false BDD and b_o is the BDD from Figure 1.

The result of $\text{BDD2FORMULA}(b_o)$ is $x[0{:}1] = 0^{[2]}$, which exactly says that two least significant bits of x are 0. The formula φ can thus be transformed to

$$\varphi' \stackrel{\text{def}}{=} x = (2^{[32]} \times y + 1^{[32]}) \,\wedge\, \forall z. (x \times z = 0^{[32]}) \,\wedge\, x[0{:}1] = 0^{[2]},$$

which can be decided as unsatisfiable without the need of any quantifier reasoning.   □

Additionally, it might happen that the BDD computation for ψ is actually *precise*, i.e., the approximations did not have any effect and the BDDs b_u and b_o returned by $\texttt{f2ApproxBDD}(\psi, p)$ are identical (and thus equal to $\texttt{f2BDD}(\psi)$). In this case, the entire subformula ψ can be *replaced* by $\text{BDD2FORMULA}(b_o)$. To see potential benefit of this, note that ψ might contain quantifiers, but $\text{BDD2FORMULA}(b_o)$ is always quantifier free. The replacement can therefore eliminate quantifiers and make the formula easier for the subsequent solver.

The following two theorems show that the approach is sound, i.e., that the described formula modifications always produce an equivalent formula.

Theorem 2. *Let φ be an arbitrary formula, ψ its subformula, p a precision, and $\texttt{f2ApproxBDD}(\psi, p) = (b_u, b_o)$. Then the formula φ is equivalent to*

$$\varphi\Big[\psi \leftarrow \big((\psi \wedge BDD2FORMULA(b_o)) \vee BDD2FORMULA(b_u)\big)\Big].$$

Proof. The properties of $\texttt{f2ApproxBDD}$ together with Theorem 1 imply that $\text{BDD2FORMULA}(b_u) \models \psi$ and $\psi \models \text{BDD2FORMULA}(b_o)$. The claim then directly follows from the fact that for each three formulas such that $\psi_u \models \psi \models \psi_o$, we have that $\psi \wedge \psi_o \equiv \psi$ and $\psi \vee \psi_u \equiv \psi$.

Theorem 3. *Let φ be an arbitrary formula, ψ its subformula, and p a precision such that $\texttt{f2ApproxBDD}(\psi, p) = (b_u, b_o)$ satisfies $b_u = b_o$. Then the formulas φ and $\varphi[\psi \leftarrow BDD2FORMULA(b_o)]$ are equivalent.*

Proof. Follows from the previous theorem and the fact that in this case,

$$\text{BDD2FORMULA}(b_o) \equiv \text{BDD2FORMULA}(b_u) \equiv \psi.$$

4.1   Overall Algorithm

The resulting algorithm is presented as Algorithm 4. Besides the input formula φ it takes as an input the set of subformulas *toProcess* for which BDD-based approximations should be computed and then a desired precision p that is used for approximating BDDs computation. Note that higher values of p will result in more precise approximations, but can require longer computation times and produce larger formulas.

Additionally, the algorithm takes a Boolean flag *replacePrecise* that determines what happens in the case that the BDD computation produces a precise BDD for the subformula ψ: the algorithm either replaces the subformula ψ by the quantifier-free formula obtained from the BDD or keeps ψ and adds the quantifier-free formula to it. Both options might be helpful in practice. As argued above, the subformula ψ might contain quantifiers that might be difficult for the solver and their removal can improve the solver's performance. On the other hand, it might be easier for the the solver to reason with the original subformula ψ on the word level instead of the formula translated from BDD, because it contains mostly bit-level information.

For effectivity, the algorithm applies simplifications before conversion of ψ to BDD (line 3 of the algorithm). This is motivated by earlier observations from other works that the formula simplifications are crucial for usable conversion of quantified bit-vector formulas to BDDs [10]. Clearly, to ensure the correctness of the algorithm, the applied formula simplifications must be equivalence-preserving.

Algorithm 4 Preprocessing formulas using BDD-based approximations.

1: **procedure** BDDPREPROCESS(φ, *toProcess*, p, *replacePrecise*)
2:     **for all** $\psi \leftarrow$ *toProcess* **do**
3:         $\psi' \leftarrow$ `simplify`(ψ)
4:         $(b_u, b_o) \leftarrow$ `f2ApproxBDD`(ψ', p)
5:         $\psi_u \leftarrow$ BDD2FORMULA(b_u)
6:         $\psi_o \leftarrow$ BDD2FORMULA(b_o)
7:         **if** $b_u = b_o$ **then**
8:             **if** *replacePrecise* $=$ **true then**
9:                 $\varphi \leftarrow \varphi[\psi \leftarrow \psi_o]$ ▷ replace ψ with the precise quantifier elimination
10:            **else**
11:                $\varphi \leftarrow \varphi[\psi \leftarrow \psi \wedge \psi_o]$ ▷ add the BDD-based approximation of ψ
12:            **end if**
13:        **else**
14:            $\varphi \leftarrow \varphi[\psi \leftarrow ((\psi \wedge \psi_o) \vee \psi_u)]$ ▷ add the BDD-based approximation of ψ
15:        **end if**
16:    **end for**
17:    **return** φ
18: **end procedure**

4.2 Time-based Cut-off

In practice, it might be hard to determine the desired precision p in the calls of `f2ApproxBDD` correctly. The precision usually expresses some internal implementation detail of `f2ApproxBDD`, such as the employed effective bit-width or the limit on intermediate BDD sizes. To make the algorithm easier to use, we propose the following modification that instead of the precision works with the *time budget* for the BDD computation.

We modify the algorithm to start with the lowest possible precision p and to gradually increase it and compute increasingly precise BDD approximations. The algorithm finishes either when it computes all the BDDs precisely, or exhausts the time budget. It then substitutes the subformulas $\varphi \in toProcess$ using the most precise computed results.

5   Implementation

We implemented the conversion BDD2FORMULA and Algorithm 4 in a new experimental tool BDDFORMULASIMPLIFIER, which is open source and available on GitHub from

$$\texttt{https://github.com/JakubHorak2003/BDDFormulaSimplifier/}$$

The tool is written in C++ and uses C++ API of the SMT solver Z3 [15] for formula parsing, internal representation, and for manipulations with the formula. It also uses C++ API of the SMT solver Q3B [9] for conversion of quantified bit-vector formulas to BDDs (i.e., `f2ApproxBDD`) and for formula simplifications before the conversion. The simplification passes implemented in Q3B only produce equisatisfiable formulas and are not guaranteed to preserve logical equivalence. We therefore modified some of the provided simplification passes, including simplifications using unconstrained variables [8], to preserve logical equivalence. BDDFORMULASIMPLIFIER uses the SMT-LIB format both for input formulas and as the output format, so that virtually any existing state-of-the-art SMT solver for quantified bit-vectors can be applied to the resulting formula.

In the implementation, we take the parameter *toProcess* of Algorithm 4 to be the set of all *maximal quantified subformulas* of the input formula, denoted $maxQuant(\varphi)$. That is, the algorithm is applied to all subformulas of form $\exists x.\rho$ or $\forall x.\rho$ that are not direct arguments to another quantifier application. We found out by our preliminary experimental evaluation that on one hand this does not entail an overwhelming number of potentially expensive `f2ApproxBDD` calls and on the other hand still provides plenty of opportunities for obtaining useful quantifier-free approximations. Additionally, the tool has an option to include also the entire input formula φ in the set *toProcess*.

The implementation has configurable time budget for formula to BDD conversion, as described in Subsection 4.2. For fairness reasons, all formulas $\psi \in$ *toProcess* are processed *concurrently* in separate threads. This ensures that a single hard subformula cannot exhaust the entire time budget, but all the subformulas get approximately same share of the time budget.

6   Experimental Evaluation

We evaluated the effect of BDDFORMULASIMPLIFIER on three state-of-the-art SMT solvers for quantified bit-vector formulas: Bitwuzla [17], CVC5 [1], and Z3 [15]. We refer to those solvers as *base solvers* in the following. We also refer to BDDFORMULASIMPLIFIER as BFS for brevity. We want to answer the following research questions:

RQ1 What is the performance of the base solver, compared to its performance when it is executed on the formula preprocessed by BFS?
RQ2 How do the different values of parameters of BFS affect its effectivity?
RQ3 How does the pattern detection (Section 3.2) affect the BFS effectivity?
RQ4 BFS uses the SMT solver Q3B for formula to BDD conversion. What is the comparison of running the base solver on the formula processed by BFS, compared to the straightforward combination of the base solver and Q3B, i.e, their parallel portfolio?
RQ5 Does BFS allow deciding satisfiability of some formulas that could not be decided without it?

To answer the research questions, we used all 6185 quantified bit-vector formulas from the SMT-LIB benchmark repository [2]. We executed all three base solvers on all of the formulas. We also processed all formulas by BFS with four different configurations depending on the used parameters:

- BFS with $toProcess = maxQuant(\varphi)$ and $replacePrecise = false$;
- BFS_{rp} with $toProcess = maxQuant(\varphi)$ and $replacePrecise = true$;
- BFS^{φ} with $toProcess = maxQuant(\varphi) \cup \{\varphi\}$ and $replacePrecise = false$;
- $\text{BFS}^{\varphi}_{rp}$ with $toProcess = maxQuant(\varphi) \cup \{\varphi\}$ and $replacePrecise = true$.

Additionally, we ran all the configurations with disabled pattern detection. These configurations are denoted as NP-BFS, with the possible additional subscript and superscript. We then ran all base solvers on all the resulting preprocessed formulas. The results of the *base* solver on the preprocessed formula are denoted BFS→*base*, possibly with a subscript and superscript according to the used configuration of BFS. To answer RQ4, we also executed the SMT solver Q3B on all benchmarks separately and computed virtual-best solvers from various combinations of the base solver, Q3B, and the solvers BFS→*base* in different configurations. In the results, we denote as $solver_1 + solver_2 + \ldots + solver_k$ the virtual-best solver of all solvers $solver_i$.

We ran the evaluation on a machine equipped with two AMD EPYC 7371 16-Core processors and with 1008 GB of RAM. For each *base* solver, we executed each benchmark with the wall time limit of 10 minutes. To obtain comparable execution of BFS→*base*, we ran BFS with the time budget of 1 minute and then the *base* solver with wall time limit of 9 minutes. We also limited BFS to use only a single CPU core in order not to give it an advantage of parallel processing of the subformulas. Detailed experimental results are available from

https://fi.muni.cz/~xjonas/papers/tacas26

Table 1. Numbers of solved formulas by the individual solvers.

$base$ solver	$base$	BFS$\to base$	BFS$^\varphi\to base$	BFS$_{rp}\to base$	BFS$^\varphi_{rp}\to base$
Q3B	5887	—	—	—	—
Bitwuzla	5763	5895	6011	6017	6020
CVC5	5662	5432	5651	5539	5677
Z3	5628	5840	5938	5957	5968

Table 2. Numbers of solved formulas by the individual solvers with and without pattern detection.

$base$	BFS$_{rp}\to base$	BFS$^\varphi_{rp}\to base$	NP-BFS$_{rp}\to base$	NP-BFS$^\varphi_{rp}\to base$
Bitwuzla	6017	6020	6015	6011
CVC5	5539	5677	5408	5678
Z3	5957	5968	5958	5962

6.1   Results

RQ1 and RQ2 The results for RQ1 and RQ2 are presented in Table 1. It can be seen that the usage of BFS before running the base solver dramatically improves the number of formulas solved by Bitwuzla and Z3. On the other hand, the performance of CVC5 is significantly degraded by applying BFS when not applying the processing to the entire input formula φ and only marginally improved when the input formula is processed. We conjecture that the reason for this is that BFS computes formula approximations that mostly express the formulas using the individual bits, while the quantifier instantiation based on invertibility conditions [18], which is used in CVC5, is more dependent on the word-level information in the input formula. For all solvers, both replacing the precise results and processing also the entire input formula φ generally improve the number of solved formulas.

RQ3 Table 2 compares the results of selected configurations that use pattern detection (BFS) and the corresponding configurations without pattern detection (NP-BFS). For brevity, we compare only the configurations that replace the precise results, as it improves the performance (see RQ2). It can be seen that when the whole input formula is also processed, the pattern detection added 9 solved formulas for Bitwuzla, removed 1 solved formula for CVC5, and added 6 solved formulas for Z3. Without processing the whole input formula, the pattern detection added 2 formulas for Bitwuzla, 131 for CVC5, and removed 1 solved formula for Z3. We again conjecture that the biggest effect on CVC5 is due to its usage of invertibility conditions that rely on word-level information in the input formula.

Table 3. Numbers of solved formulas by the individual solvers and the selected virtual-best solvers.

base solver	*base*	$\text{BFS}^{\varphi}_{rp}{\rightarrow}base$	*base*+Q3B	*base*+Q3B+$(\text{BFS}^{\varphi}_{rp}{\rightarrow}base)$
Q3B	5887	—	—	—
Bitwuzla	5763	6020	6052	6070
CVC5	5662	5677	6004	6010
Z3	5628	5968	6024	6041

RQ4 To answer RQ4, Table 3 puts the results of the best-performing configuration $\text{BFS}^{\varphi}_{rp}{\rightarrow}base$ into context of the virtual-best solver of *base* and Q3B, which is used in BFS for formula to BDD conversion. It can be seen that the number of solved formulas by $\text{BFS}^{\varphi}_{rp}{\rightarrow}base$ is usually lower than the number of formulas solved by the straightforward parallel portfolio of the solvers. However, when considering also the virtual-best solver consisting of the base solver, Q3B, and $\text{BFS}^{\varphi}_{rp}{\rightarrow}base$, it can be seen that $\text{BFS}^{\varphi}_{rp}{\rightarrow}base$ can solve several formulas that neither of the two solvers can solve on their own. In particular, $\text{BFS}^{\varphi}_{rp}{\rightarrow}$Bitwuzla solves 18 formulas that can be solved neither by Bitwuzla nor by Q3B. These benchmarks are from 7 different benchmark families (6 from `2020-Preiner-fmcad20`, 5 from `20170501-Heizmann-UltimateAutomizer`, 2 formulas from `2017-Preiner-scholl-smt08`, 2 from `20210301-Alive2`, and 1 from each of `2018-Preiner-cav18`, `20190429-UltimateAutomizerSvcomp2019`, and `20230321-UltimateAutomizerSvcomp2023`). Note that out of the total 6185 formulas, the number of formulas not solved by Bitwuzla nor by Q3B is only 133 and thus $\text{BFS}^{\varphi}_{rp}{\rightarrow}$Bitwuzla additionally solves 13.5 % of the previously unsolved formulas. Similarly, $\text{BFS}^{\varphi}_{rp}{\rightarrow}$CVC5 solves 6 formulas not solved by CVC5 nor Q3B (3.3 % of the 181 unsolved formulas) from 2 benchmark families (5 from `2017-Preiner-scholl-smt08` and 1 from `2017-Preiner-psyco`). Finally, $\text{BFS}^{\varphi}_{rp}{\rightarrow}$Z3 solves 17 formulas not solved by Z3 nor Q3B (10.5 % of the 161 unsolved formulas) from 5 different benchmark families (8 formulas from the family `2020-Preiner-fmcad20`, 4 from `2017-Preiner-scholl-smt08`, 3 benchmarks from `20170501-Heizmann-UltimateAutomizer`, and 1 benchmark from each of `20190429-UltimateAutomizerSvcomp2019` and `llvm13-smtlib`).

RQ5 For RQ5, we note that the virtual-best solver Bitwuzla+CVC5+Q3B+Z3 of all the compared SMT solvers can solve 6073 of the total 6185 considered benchmarks. When also the three solvers that use BDD-based formula approximations, i.e., $\text{BFS}^{\varphi}_{rp}{\rightarrow}$Bitwuzla, $\text{BFS}^{\varphi}_{rp}{\rightarrow}$CVC5, and $\text{BFS}^{\varphi}_{rp}{\rightarrow}$Z3, are considered, the resulting virtual-best solver solves 6082 benchmarks. We thus conclude that the formula approximations enable solving additional 9 formulas that are beyond reach of any compared state-of-the art solver individually. Note that these 9 formulas amount to 8 % of the 112 previously unsolved formulas. These benchmarks come from 3 different benchmark families (6 from

2020-Preiner-fmcad20, 2 benchmarks from 2017-Preiner-scholl-smt08, and 1 from 20210301-Alive2).

Formula Approximation Statistics To give a more nuanced picture of the results, we report some statistics of runs of the best-performing configuration, $\mathrm{BFS}^{\varphi}_{rp}$. From the overall 6185 formulas, the precise BDD for φ was computed in 5114 cases. Of those, the precise BDD was $\boxed{0}$ in 5051 cases, $\boxed{1}$ in 60 cases, and a non-trivial BDD in 3 remaining cases. This is not surprising, as many of the benchmarks are actually not hard to solve: Q3B alone can solve 5518 of the 6185 benchmarks within 1 second and 4748 benchmarks can be solved by *all* the considered solvers within 1 second. Moreover, most of the benchmarks are unsatisfiable.

For the remaining 1071 benchmarks where the precise BDD for φ was not computed, we report the number of patterns that were detected during the conversion of the BDD to formula. The *EqNum* pattern was detected at least once in 649 benchmarks, the *EqVar* pattern in 423 benchmarks, and the *IneqVar* pattern in 605 benchmarks.

7   Conclusions and Future Work

We presented a technique that combines BDD-based solvers for quantified bit-vectors with other solvers by employing the BDD-based solver on subformulas of the problem and adding the obtained information back to the original formula. The technique relies on a preexisting algorithm for computing approximate BDDs from the given quantified bit-vector formula and on a novel algorithm that translates the resulting BDD back to a bit-vector formula while preserving some word-level information. We have implemented the technique and shown that it can improve performance of existing state-of-the-art SMT solvers and can solve satisfiability of some formulas that were beyond reach of all the compared solvers.

In the future, we want to extend the translation of BDDs to formulas with additional patterns to detect even more word-level information. We also want to explore further options of running the approximate BDD to formula conversion beyond the current time-budget-based implementation, possibly with heuristically setting desired precisions for individual subformulas. Going even further, it should be possible to make the integration with the base SMT solver tighter, and increase the precision on demand based on the computation of the base SMT solver and the quantifier instances that it uses.

Data Availability Statement. All scripts used for the experimental evaluation, the obtained data, and additional analyses are available from `https://fi.muni.cz/~xjonas/papers/tacas26`. The implemented tool is available from `https://github.com/JakubHorak2003/BDDFormulaSimplifier`.

References

1. Barbosa, H., Barrett, C.W., Brain, M., Kremer, G., Lachnitt, H., Mann, M., Mohamed, A., Mohamed, M., Niemetz, A., Nötzli, A., Ozdemir, A., Preiner, M., Reynolds, A., Sheng, Y., Tinelli, C., Zohar, Y.: cvc5: A versatile and industrial-strength SMT solver. In: Fisman, D., Rosu, G. (eds.) Tools and Algorithms for the Construction and Analysis of Systems - 28th International Conference, TACAS 2022, Held as Part of the European Joint Conferences on Theory and Practice of Software, ETAPS 2022, Munich, Germany, April 2-7, 2022, Proceedings, Part I. Lecture Notes in Computer Science, vol. 13243, pp. 415–442. Springer (2022). https://doi.org/10.1007/978-3-030-99524-9_24, https://doi.org/10.1007/978-3-030-99524-9_24
2. Barrett, C., Fontaine, P., Tinelli, C.: The Satisfiability Modulo Theories Library (SMT-LIB). www.SMT-LIB.org (2016)
3. Barrett, C.W., Tinelli, C.: Satisfiability Modulo Theories. In: Handbook of Model Checking, pp. 305–343. Springer (2018)
4. Biere, A., Cimatti, A., Clarke, E.M., Zhu, Y.: Symbolic model checking without BDDs. In: TACAS. Lecture Notes in Computer Science, vol. 1579, pp. 193–207. Springer (1999)
5. Bryant, R.E.: Graph-Based Algorithms for Boolean Function Manipulation. IEEE Trans. Comput. **35**(8), 677–691 (1986)
6. Bryant, R.E.: On the complexity of VLSI implementations and graph representations of boolean functions with application to integer multiplication. IEEE Trans. Comput. **40**(2), 205–213 (1991)
7. Cimatti, A., Griggio, A., Mover, S., Tonetta, S.: Infinite-state invariant checking with IC3 and predicate abstraction. Formal Methods Syst. Des. **49**(3), 190–218 (2016)
8. Jonáš, M., Strejček, J.: On simplification of formulas with unconstrained variables and quantifiers. In: Gaspers, S., Walsh, T. (eds.) Theory and Applications of Satisfiability Testing - SAT 2017 - 20th International Conference, Melbourne, VIC, Australia, August 28 - September 1, 2017, Proceedings. Lecture Notes in Computer Science, vol. 10491, pp. 364–379. Springer (2017), https://doi.org/10.1007/978-3-319-66263-3_23
9. Jonáš, M., Strejček, J.: Q3B: An efficient BDD-based SMT solver for quantified bit-vectors. In: Dillig, I., Tasiran, S. (eds.) Computer Aided Verification - 31st International Conference, CAV 2019, New York City, NY, USA, July 15-18, 2019, Proceedings, Part II. Lecture Notes in Computer Science, vol. 11562, pp. 64–73. Springer (2019). https://doi.org/10.1007/978-3-030-25543-5_4, https://doi.org/10.1007/978-3-030-25543-5_4
10. Jonáš, M., Strejček, J.: Solving quantified bit-vector formulas using binary decision diagrams. In: Creignou, N., Berre, D.L. (eds.) Theory and Applications of Satisfiability Testing - SAT 2016 - 19th International Conference, Bordeaux, France, July 5-8, 2016, Proceedings. Lecture Notes in Computer Science, vol. 9710, pp. 267–283. Springer (2016). https://doi.org/10.1007/978-3-319-40970-2_17, https://doi.org/10.1007/978-3-319-40970-2_17
11. Jonáš, M., Strejček, J.: Truncating abstraction of bit-vector operations for bdd-based SMT solvers. Theor. Comput. Sci. **1008**, 114664 (2024). https://doi.org/10.1016/J.TCS.2024.114664, https://doi.org/10.1016/j.tcs.2024.114664
12. King, J.C.: Symbolic execution and program testing. Commun. ACM **19**(7), 385–394 (1976), https://doi.org/10.1145/360248.360252

13. Kovásznai, G., Fröhlich, A., Biere, A.: Complexity of fixed-size bit-vector logics. Theory Comput. Syst. **59**(2), 323–376 (2016)
14. Kroening, D., Lewis, M., Weissenbacher, G.: Under-approximating loops in C programs for fast counterexample detection. In: Computer Aided Verification - 25th International Conference, CAV 2013. LNCS, vol. 8044, pp. 381–396. Springer (2013)
15. de Moura, L.M., Bjørner, N.S.: Z3: An efficient SMT solver. In: Ramakrishnan, C.R., Rehof, J. (eds.) Tools and Algorithms for the Construction and Analysis of Systems, 14th International Conference, TACAS 2008, Held as Part of the Joint European Conferences on Theory and Practice of Software, ETAPS 2008, Budapest, Hungary, March 29-April 6, 2008. Proceedings. Lecture Notes in Computer Science, vol. 4963, pp. 337–340. Springer (2008). `https://doi.org/10.1007/978-3-540-78800-3_24`, `https://doi.org/10.1007/978-3-540-78800-3_24`
16. Mrázek, J., Bauch, P., Lauko, H., Barnat, J.: SymDIVINE: Tool for control-explicit data-symbolic state space exploration. In: Model Checking Software - 23rd International Symposium, SPIN 2016, Co-located with ETAPS 2016, Eindhoven, The Netherlands, April 7-8, 2016, Proceedings. pp. 208–213 (2016)
17. Niemetz, A., Preiner, M.: Bitwuzla. In: Enea, C., Lal, A. (eds.) Computer Aided Verification - 35th International Conference, CAV 2023, Paris, France, July 17-22, 2023, Proceedings, Part II. Lecture Notes in Computer Science, vol. 13965, pp. 3–17. Springer (2023). `https://doi.org/10.1007/978-3-031-37703-7_1`, `https://doi.org/10.1007/978-3-031-37703-7_1`
18. Niemetz, A., Preiner, M., Reynolds, A., Barrett, C., Tinelli, C.: Solving quantified bit-vectors using invertibility conditions. In: Computer Aided Verification - 30th International Conference, CAV 2018, Held as Part of the Federated Logic Conference, FloC 2018, Oxford, UK, July 14-17, 2018, Proceedings, Part II. pp. 236–255 (2018). `https://doi.org/10.1007/978-3-319-96142-2_16`
19. Niemetz, A., Preiner, M., Reynolds, A., Barrett, C.W., Tinelli, C.: Syntax-guided quantifier instantiation. In: Groote, J.F., Larsen, K.G. (eds.) Tools and Algorithms for the Construction and Analysis of Systems - 27th International Conference, TACAS 2021, Held as Part of the European Joint Conferences on Theory and Practice of Software, ETAPS 2021, Luxembourg City, Luxembourg, March 27 - April 1, 2021, Proceedings, Part II. Lecture Notes in Computer Science, vol. 12652, pp. 145–163. Springer (2021). `https://doi.org/10.1007/978-3-030-72013-1_8`, `https://doi.org/10.1007/978-3-030-72013-1_8`
20. Sheeran, M., Singh, S., Stålmarck, G.: Checking safety properties using induction and a SAT-solver. In: FMCAD. Lecture Notes in Computer Science, vol. 1954, pp. 108–125. Springer (2000)
21. Slaby, J., Strejček, J., Trtík, M.: Compact symbolic execution. In: Hung, D.V., Ogawa, M. (eds.) Automated Technology for Verification and Analysis - 11th International Symposium, ATVA 2013, Hanoi, Vietnam, October 15-18, 2013. Proceedings. Lecture Notes in Computer Science, vol. 8172, pp. 193–207. Springer (2013). `https://doi.org/10.1007/978-3-319-02444-8_15`, `https://doi.org/10.1007/978-3-319-02444-8_15`
22. Wintersteiger, C.M., Hamadi, Y., de Moura, L.M.: Efficiently solving quantified bit-vector formulas. Formal Methods in System Design **42**(1), 3–23 (2013). `https://doi.org/10.1007/s10703-012-0156-2`

SMTScope: Automated and Efficient Analysis of SMT Traces

Jonáš Fiala and Peter Müller

Department of Computer Science, ETH Zurich, Zurich, Switzerland
`{jonas.fiala, peter.mueller}@inf.ethz.ch`

Abstract. SMT solvers enable the automated verification of complex software, but they frequently also cause performance problems, proof brittleness, and spurious errors. Debugging such issues is challenging because it is difficult to understand and predict how the solver's complex algorithms and heuristics will interact with a given query.
We present SMTSCOPE, a tool for the automatic analysis and visualisation of z3 executions. It helps detect and explain issues in SMT queries, such as indefinite chains of quantifier instantiations (matching loops), and proliferation of quantifier instantiations. Additionally, it provides a useful interface for other tools. Compared to the existing AXIOM PROFILER, SMTSCOPE offers more effective analyses, novel visualisations of matching loops and proof search, as well as more efficient algorithms, which allow SMTSCOPE to scale to large SMT traces. Our evaluation shows that SMTSCOPE can identify problem behaviours in real-world traces, finding hundreds of unique issues in four state-of-the-art verifiers.

1 Introduction

SMT solvers are powerful and highly optimised tools, often able to handle complex queries efficiently. However, their performance is sometimes slow and unpredictable [20]. Identifying the root cause of these performance issues is very hard, as SMT solvers are essentially a black box for their applications.

The input to SMT solvers is a query consisting of a sequence of variable declarations and first-order logic constraints written as boolean assertions. The solver tries to either find a satisfying assignment to the variables or prove that the constraints are unsatisfiable. Especially in the important application domain of program verification, the constraints may contain quantifiers, enabling complex program semantics to be encoded as axioms. The complicated interactions of these axioms, as well as the sheer size of generated queries, make it infeasible to manually debug their performance. For example, the DAFNY [12] verifier turns a 30-line tutorial program into a 1000-line query with almost 200 quantifiers.

Unfortunately, the quantifiers which are so critical for verification are also a leading cause of performance issues. Their solving is tricky to automate due to their unbounded nature, thus SMT solvers expose a customisable instantiation mechanism via *e-matching* [6]. E-matching requires quantifiers to be annotated with syntactic *patterns* containing all the quantified variables. When the SMT

© The Author(s) 2026
S. Junges and G. Katz (Eds.): TACAS 2026, LNCS 16505, pp. 233–251, 2026.
https://doi.org/10.1007/978-3-032-22752-2_12

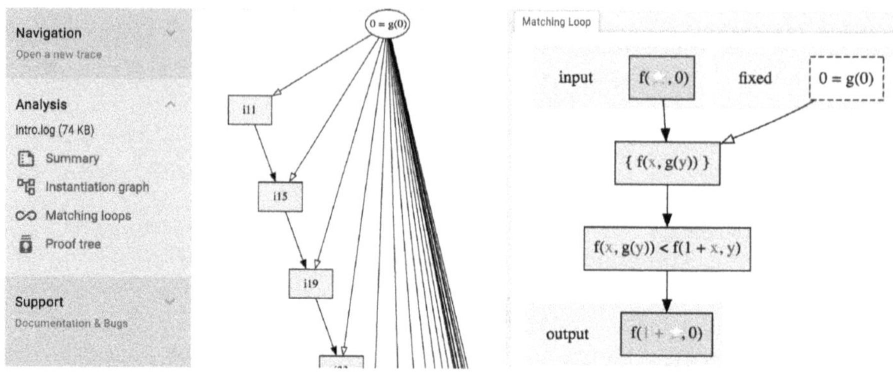

Fig. 1. A screenshot of SmtScope explaining a matching loop. The middle section shows the individual instantiations of the loop (turquoise nodes), how each subsequent one depends on a term produced by the prior (black arrows), and how each depends on `0 = g(0)` (white arrows and node). Our tool automatically finds the loop and generates the explanation graph on the right. It generalises one iteration of the loop: the pattern (top turquoise node) is matched by using the equality `0 = g(0)` to rewrite the ever-growing term `f(☆, 0)`. The resulting instantiation produces a new term (bottom grey node). The ☆ denotes an arbitrary term, with the blue `1+` indicating how it grows.

solver encounters a *ground term* (one with no quantified variables) matching the pattern, it unifies the two and uses the sub-terms that unified with the quantified variables to instantiate the quantifier. Importantly, this matching is not purely syntactic, instead being performed modulo equalities. Thus, understanding and predicting SMT quantifier instantiations is a formidable task [5].

Badly chosen patterns may lead to poor performance. As an extreme case, *matching loops* cause an excessive number of instantiations [15]. They occur when a term causes an instantiation which, in turn, produces a new term matching the same pattern, continuing the loop indefinitely and producing many new terms in the process. Figure 1 describes a non-syntactic matching loop. The quantifier $\forall$`x:Int, y:Int :: {f(x, g(y))}` `f(x,g(y)) < f(1+x,y)`, with its e-matching pattern in the braces, cannot *syntactically* produce a new term matching the pattern. However, in our example, z3 proved `0 = g(0)` which sets off a loop starting with `f(n,0)` and continuing with `f(1+n,0)`, `f(2+n,0)`, ... An equality required for a matching loop may not be proved or even present in all queries, making such loops harder to detect, reproduce, and debug the caused performance problems.

Matching loops are not the only *problem behaviour* that significantly impacts performance. Quantifiers with patterns that can turn a few terms into many instantiations are another common issue. An example of this proliferation of quantifier instantiations is the following axiom expressing transitivity of subtyping:

$\forall$`x:Type, y:Type, z:Type :: {subtype(x, y), subtype(x, z)}`
    `subtype(x, y)` $\wedge$ `subtype(y, z)` $\Rightarrow$ `subtype(x, z)`

Given n terms of the form `subtype(A, `T_i`)`, this quantifier will be instantiated n^2 times with $[x \mapsto A, y \mapsto T_i, z \mapsto T_j]$. Additionally, these instantiations produce n^2 new terms; all combinations of `subtype(`T_i`, `T_j`)`, which in turn cause a further n^3 instantiations. When these problem behaviours are combined, they can exponentially degrade performance.

Understanding SMT behaviour is not only necessary to debug performance bugs, but also to enable useful tool features. Recent work [9,21] analyses successful verification runs to optimise future queries. Both tools use a solver-provided unsatisfiability (UNSAT) core; a minimal subset of the assertions required to logically prove UNSAT. However, Gopinathan et al. [9] found that this core is often not sufficient to replay an SMT proof. They describe the missing key: axioms that are not logically required, but rather, produce terms required for instantiating axioms in the UNSAT core. Finding these *lurking axioms* requires understanding *how* the solver proved UNSAT. These three examples show that understanding and optimising solver behaviour is difficult and requires tool support that scales to the queries produced by modern verification tools.

The current state of the art in troubleshooting Z3 [16] issues with quantifiers is the AXIOM PROFILER [3]. It presents three views: a list of all instantiations, an instantiation dependency graph, and a textual explanation of an instantiation when selected. A variety of filtering operations help find problematic instantiations within the graph. Additionally, it can detect and explain some matching loops, although this is not fully automated as the user must manually identify suspicious chains to analyse. The tool focuses on quantifier instantiations only and does not support any other aspects of SMT execution, thus being ill-suited to precisely find, e.g., lurking axioms. Unfortunately, bad performance and frequent crashes make the tool notoriously cumbersome to use.

This work. We present SMTSCOPE, a novel tool for automated and efficient analysis of Z3 executions. It analyses a Z3 trace and automatically detects and reports the aforementioned quantifier problem behaviours. It also understands other Z3 aspects, such as proof search, enabling it to precisely identify lurking axioms. Integration with existing verifiers is easy, enabling the fully-automatic analysis of a broad set of real-world queries, for instance, in continuous integration. Additionally, SMTSCOPE allows for comprehensive inspection of said executions when problems are detected. It has already helped discover over 300 unique problems in verifier axiomatisations. Compared to prior work, SMTSCOPE can identify more problem behaviours while doing so automatically and without any observed false positives. Our analyses asymptotically outperform those of the AXIOM PROFILER, are more stable, and support all modern versions of Z3 (v4.8.5+).

Our contributions are:

- We develop efficient algorithms for analysing Z3 trace files, including novel matching loop and multiplicative axiom detection.
- We identify a new class of equality-based matching loops and describe how to detect and eliminate them.
- We develop functionality to analyse and visualise the proof search, which can be used to precisely identify lurking axioms.
- We evaluate our tool on the state-of-the-art verifiers DAFNY, F* [19], VERUS [11], and VIPER [17], and find over 300 unique problem behaviours.
- We release SMTSCOPE as open-source, available and runnable online [7].

2   Analysing an SMT Trace

In this section, we present the main features of SMTSCOPE. We describe how it helps pinpoint troublesome axioms and expensive lemmas and how it explains matching loops and multiplicative behaviour. Moreover, we show how our tool visualizes Z3's proof search and how it finds lurking axioms.

We illustrate SMTSCOPE on a simplified extract of a vector axiomatisation, shown in Figure 2. Our vector supports two operations: pop, which removes one element and returns the empty vector if the input was already empty, and trim, which pops N times. The pop-trim axiom equates a pop of a trim with the simpler expression of a one-larger trim. We use a custom uninterpreted add function to get around the fact that Z3 does not allow the built-in + in patterns. The add-lt axiom gives an ordering to this add function. Though this example seems innocuous, it results in both a matching loop and multiplicative behaviour. pop-trim and add-lt are based on axioms from VIPER and F* that exhibit the same problem behaviours—issues which went unnoticed for years, but have now been identified by SMTSCOPE.

2.1   SMT Trace Summary

After opening a trace file, SMTSCOPE presents a summary of each analysis. Figure 3 shows this for the example from Figure 2. This screen consists of three data components: aggregate (highlighted red), quantifier (blue), and proof (omitted in the figure). Each component helps the user identify potential problem areas.

The aggregate data component consists of the two leftmost boxes in Figure 3. The first lists all problem behaviours detected and the axioms involved. The second has the raw totals for a variety of metrics. These totals are useful when comparing traces to quickly see if a change was effective.

The quantifier component helps pinpoint troublesome axioms that should be changed to avoid unnecessary instantiations. It consists of three boxes and a summary graph. The boxes list all quantifiers sorted by: instantiation count,

```
(declare-sort Vec)                              ; vector sort
(declare-const empty Vec)                       ; empty vector
(declare-fun pop (Vec) Vec)                     ; pop one element
(declare-fun trim (Vec Int) Vec)                ; pop N times
(declare-fun add (Int Int) Int)                 ; + (for patterns)
(assert pop(empty) = empty)                     ; pop-empty axiom
(assert trim(empty, 1) = empty)                 ; trim-empty axiom
(assert ∀v:Vec, n:Int :: {pop(trim(v, n))}
  pop(trim(v, n)) = trim(v, add(1, n)))         ; pop-trim axiom
(assert ∀x:Int, y:Int, z:Int :: {add(x, y), add(x, z)}
  add(x, y) < add(x, z) = y < z)                ; add-lt axiom
```

Fig. 2. A simplified encoding of a vector. We use pseudocode based on the SMT-LIB format with presentational liberties.

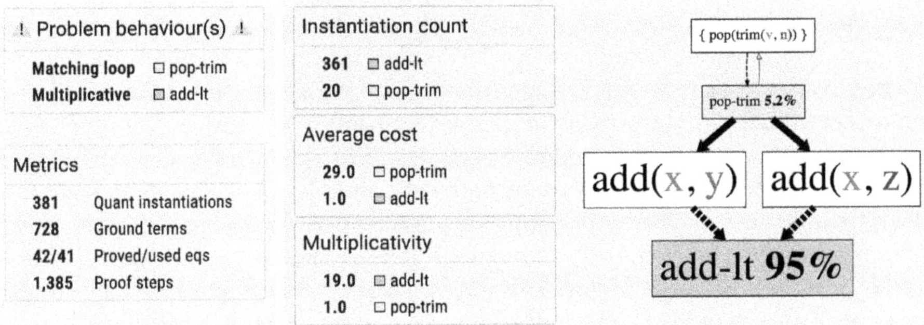

Fig. 3. SMTSCOPE's summary screen for the example from Figure 2. The two leftmost boxes show aggregate data, the middle three and the graph show quantifier data. This toy example has no interesting proof data, thus we have omitted it. In the graph, coloured nodes represent the instantiations of a quantifier. White nodes and dashed arrows represent a matched pattern leading to an instantiation. Solid arrows represent term- or equality-dependencies, denoted by solid or hollow arrowheads respectively. Both nodes and edges are sized according to their percentage contribution to the total instantiation count. This percentage is also listed next to the quantifier name.

average cost, and multiplicativity. An instantiation's cost is based on the number of instantiations directly or transitively caused by this instantiation [3]; a quantifier's cost is the average over all of its instantiations. We say that a child instantiation directly depends on a parent one if the parent produced a term or equality used for matching the child's pattern. Multiplicativity represents a quantifier's ability to turn a few terms into many instantiations. It is calculated per quantifier as the number of unique instantiations divided by the number of terms matched for these instantiations. We call a quantifier *multiplicative* if this value exceeds a threshold (based on our experience, 5).

The list sorted by instantiation count helps compare traces across changes and rule out irrelevant quantifiers. The average cost indicates how effective reducing a quantifier's instantiation count would be. Optimising the top quantifiers in this list is often the most fruitful. In our example, all 381 instantiations depend on the first instantiation of `pop-trim`, contributing to its high average cost.

However, the cost metric can miss problematic multiplicative quantifiers, such as `add-lt` in our example. As we will see in the next subsection, `pop-trim` produces ever larger terms of the form `add(1, add(1, ...))`. These terms match `add-lt`'s pattern pairwise, causing n^2 instantiations from only n terms. None of these instantiations has any children, and thus their cost is 1. Solving the problem of many `add-lt` instantiations by reducing the number of `add` terms (by fixing the `pop-trim` matching loop, which produces these terms) is not always possible. For instance, a user assertion (from the program under verification) could result in the following line being added to the query (with 19 nested `adds`):

`(assert 20 = add(1, add(1, add(1, ...)))))`

In this case, fixing `pop-trim` would not help, as the query itself contains all the `add` terms. Instead, we must identify and fix the problematic `add-lt` itself. Our novel multiplicativity analysis precisely identifies these problematic quantifiers. Concretely, for `add-lt` we calculate 19^2 instantiations/19 terms = 19.

Lastly, SMTSCOPE renders a summary graph to visualise the most important quantifiers (those at the top of the three quantifier lists) and causal relations between them, as seen on the right of Figure 3. The graph provides a visual summary and explanation of the quantifier lists that is faster to comprehend and clearly shows the relative importance of the included quantifiers. For our running example, we see the cyclic dependency of `pop-trim` and its own pattern indicative of a matching loop. Below this, we see how a few `pop-trim` instantiations cause many more `add-lt` instantiations, indicative of high multiplicativity.

The proof component (omitted from Figure 3) provides a list of lemmas z3 proved by contradiction, sorted by proof cost, i.e., the number of proof steps required to reach the contradiction. Lemmas that are proved using axioms purely from a verifier's background theory are particularly interesting, as they indicate missing axioms. Asserting these lemmas directly (e.g., by adding an axiom) is sound w.r.t. the background theory and would potentially speed up the proof search, since z3 could use them directly rather than re-proving them each time.

2.2 Understanding Matching Loops

SMTSCOPE can automatically find all matching loops in the instantiation graph. The *instantiation graph* [3] is a DAG where nodes represent instantiations and edges represent causality (producing a term or equality that a child depends on). A matching loop must be a sequence of one or more quantifiers that repeats down a path of instantiations. Analysing the full graph path-by-path is infeasible, since the number of paths can be exponential. We describe our matching loop detection algorithm, which solves this exponential blow-up, in the next section.

Once a matching loop is identified, SMTSCOPE builds a *generalised iteration graph* to explain it. Figure 4 shows this graph for the `pop-trim` matching loop that the summary warned us about in Figure 3. This graph explains how a group of inputs results in a sequence of instantiations, and how these instantiations lead to outputs that set off the next iteration. In our example, the graph starts with the term (T) `pop(empty)` and the equalities (E) `pop(empty) = empty` and (A) `empty = trim(empty, ⋆)`. z3 rewrites (T) using (A) into the term `pop(trim(empty, ⋆))`. This instantiates `pop-trim` with $[v \mapsto \texttt{empty}, n \mapsto \star]$, yielding the equality (Y) `pop(trim(empty, ⋆)) = trim(empty, add(1, ⋆))`. Using the three equalities we now have, the graph shows that z3 derives the term (B) `empty` $=^E$ `pop(empty)` $=^A$ `pop(trim(empty, ⋆))` $=^Y$ `trim(empty, add(1, ⋆))`. This closes the loop as a new iteration can now start with (T), (E), and (B).

This matching loop is interesting because it is perpetuated by equalities only, while the term used for matching the pattern remains fixed. We are able to identify it as a matching loop due to SMTSCOPE's advanced understanding of z3's equality reasoning, which is described in Subsection 2.3. To our knowledge, such equality-based matching loops have not been described previously, and prior to SMTSCOPE, no tool was able to detect them. Matching loops of this form often happen when two axioms can be used to define the same term.

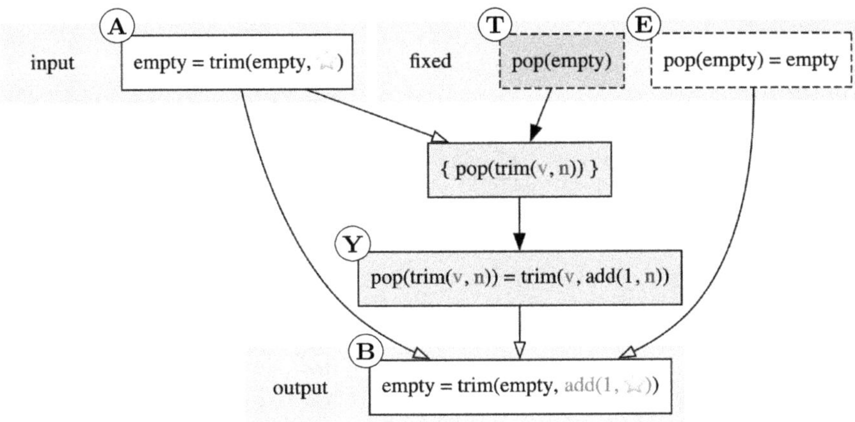

Fig. 4. The generalised iteration graph for the matching loop from Figure 2. The inputs are at the top and are categorised into those that stay fixed (grey background) and those that change (blue). The ones that change are also displayed as outputs at the bottom, closing the loop. The grey nodes are terms, white nodes are proved equalities, and coloured nodes are the pattern and body of the corresponding quantifier (`pop-trim`). Arrows leading to a pattern explain how it is matched, those leading to an equality explain which equalities are transitively combined to derive it. The ✳ denotes the same arbitrary term in the input and output, with the blue text indicating how it grows.

They can be fixed by guarding one of the axioms with a (stronger) implication. Indeed, this also applies to our example; both `pop-empty` and `pop-trim` "define" the term `pop(empty)`. To fix this, we should rewrite the body of `pop-trim` to `trim(v, n)` $\neq$ `empty` $\Rightarrow$ `pop(trim(v, n))` = `trim(v, add(1, n))`. This differs from other matching loops, which are often resolved by changing the pattern.

2.3   Understanding Other Instantiation Behaviours

As explained earlier, the summary screen provides indications for other quantifier behaviours, such as high cost and multiplicativity. To investigate those further, SMTSCOPE offers an instantiation graph view, which displays a raw dependency graph of individual instantiations. Figure 5 shows SMTSCOPE's instantiation graph for our running example. In this subsection, we explain how to use the graph to understand why the `add-lt` axiom is highly multiplicative. We first explain how the terms causing high multiplicativity are produced. Then, we see how the instantiation graph helps us understand the problematic behaviour of `add-lt`. Lastly, we propose a general solution for fixing a class of multiplicative axioms.

In Figure 5, the node $i10$ for an instantiation of `pop-trim` is selected, causing a detailed explanation to appear on the right. There, we see the matched pattern and which term and equalities were used. Importantly, we see all the *new* terms produced by this instantiation, which may be used for further instantiations. Additional relevant graph properties are also shown, such as the fact that $i10$ sets off a chain 39 nodes long—the matching loop explained earlier.

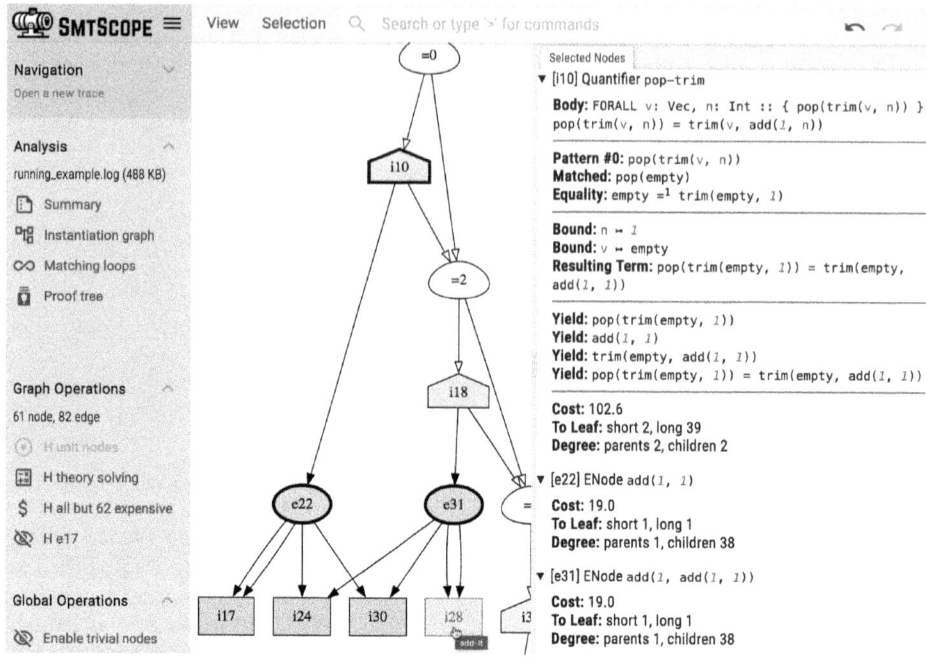

Fig. 5. A screenshot of SMTSCOPE's instantiation graph view for our running example. Instantiation nodes are coloured with the unique colour of their quantifier. Oval nodes represent terms (grey) and equalities (white). Instantiations with hidden parents or children indicate this with a pointy top or bottom, respectively.

Nodes for `add(1, 1)` (*e*22) and `add(1, add(1, 1))` (*e*31) are also selected. Under 'Degree' in the side panel, we see that each directly causes 38 instantiations. Since the overview indicated a high multiplicativity for `add-1t`, the user could select the instantiation nodes corresponding to this quantifier (the blue nodes) and observe that each `add(1, A)` term pairs with any other `add(1, B)` term to cause an instantiation, resulting in the 361 instantiations from only 19 terms. The dependency on the exact terms is visualised in our graph by explicitly representing terms as nodes (here, *e*22 and *e*31).

Our graphs also have explicit nodes for equalities, which are added by reconstructing the transitive equality reasoning that z3 performs. As an ever-larger `empty = trim(empty, N)` (white nodes) is constructed in our example, only two nodes are blamed: the prior equality and the one obtained from `pop-trim` (green nodes) for the step N ↦ `add(1, N)`. Having an explicit representation of equalities results in a repeating pattern that can be detected visually and that our matching loop detection (Section 3) can generalise. Both the term and equality nodes can be disabled when users want to focus on instantiations only.

Since instantiation graphs of realistic examples are very large, SMTSCOPE offers various ways to filter out irrelevant nodes. This filtering is configurable by changing the entries under 'Graph Operations' in the left side panel. When an intermediate node is hidden due to filtering, we add dashed edges to preserve transitive dependencies. Additional filters to pull out useful subgraphs are available under the 'View' and 'Selection' menus at the top. To help navigate the graph, one can use the search bar to find nodes by quantifier or function name.

In our evaluation, we found a common class of multiplicative quantifiers in verifier axiomatisations: ordering axioms. These encode properties such as transitivity of subtyping. We suggest replacing such axioms with z3's built-in decision procedures for various types of ordering, including total and partial orders. The `add-lt` axiom from our example also expresses ordering. In this case, the most complete solution is to rely on z3's native integer reasoning. We can do this by changing the quantifier to:

```
(assert ∀x:Int, y:Int :: {add(x, y)} add(x, y) = x + y)
```

2.4 Understanding the Proof Tree

SMTSCOPE can explain other z3 aspects, aside from e-matching. Understanding z3's proof search and how it proved UNSAT is crucial for identifying missing axioms and finding a precise UNSAT core that includes lurking axioms. SMTSCOPE parses and analyses the proof derivation tree that z3 constructs while trying to prove UNSAT. Each node in the proof tree represents a proof step used to prove a boolean term, and incoming edges represent its prerequisites. The SMT solver reports UNSAT if it proves false. The resulting proof tree contains a `false` node; its ancestors correspond to the UNSAT core, but it does *not* contain lurking axioms. Consequently, the core logically implies false, but might not be sufficient to replay the proof in the SMT solver, as it might not contain all the terms needed to perform necessary quantifier instantiations.

```
(declare-fun non_empty (Vec) Bool)           ; is vector non-empty?
(declare-fun length (Vec) Int)               ; length of vector
(declare-fun append (Vec Vec) Vec)           ; append two vectors
(assert ∀x:Vec :: {non_empty(x)}
   non_empty(x) = 1 ≤ length(x))             ; non_empty-def axiom
(assert ∀x:Vec, y:Vec :: {length(x), length(y)} ; append ax.
   non_empty(append(x, y)) = non_empty(x) || non_empty(y))

(declare-const a Vec) (declare-const b Vec)  ; inputs a and b
(assert non_empty(a) && non_empty(b))        ; precondition
(assert !non_empty(append(a, b)))            ; negated postcondition
(check-sat) (get-unsat-core)
```

Fig. 6. An extension of our vector encoding. The **non_empty-def** axiom defines the **non_empty** function, and the **append** axiom states that the result of appending two vectors is non-empty if and only if at least one of them is non-empty. The remainder simulates verification of a function taking two vectors **a** and **b** as input, with a precondition that both are non-empty and a postcondition that their append is also non-empty. The postcondition is negated, such that its validity is proved by an UNSAT result.

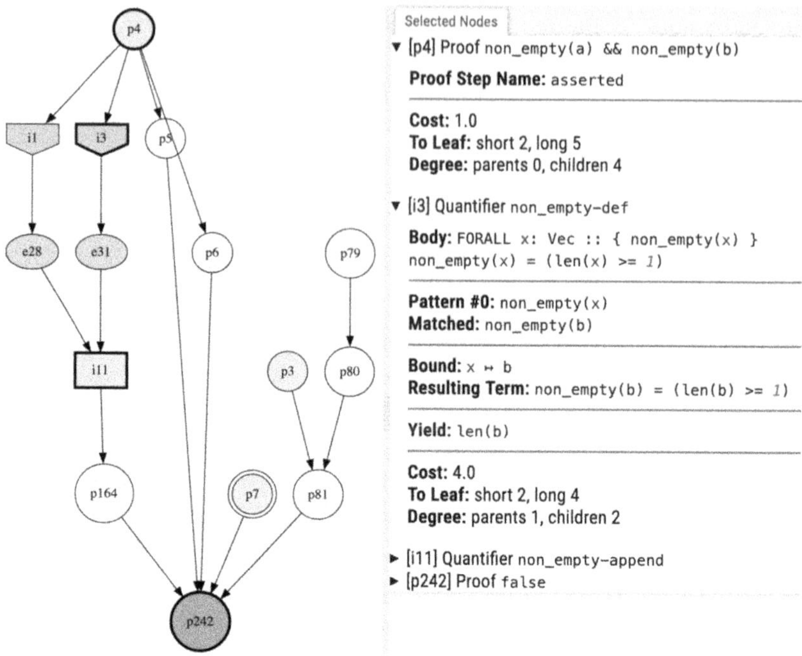

Fig. 7. A screenshot of SMTSCOPE's proof view. The proof node $p164$ representing the instantiation of **append** is linked to the corresponding instantiation node $i11$ in the instantiation graph. The red $p242$ node represents a proof of **false** and the green nodes are the assertions from the query.

Gopinathan et al. [9] solve this problem by using our instantiation graph to extend Z3's UNSAT core with the axioms that any core axiom transitively depends on to get instantiated. However, their approach overapproximates; some instantiations of a core axiom might not be required for the proof, but all their dependencies are included nonetheless. By combining our instantiation graph with the proof tree, we can find a precise extended UNSAT core.

To explain how, we adapt an example from Gopinathan et al. [9] in Figure 6. Here, **non_empty-def** is a lurking axiom: it is not logically required, but it produces the **length** terms required to instantiate **append**. Figure 7 shows the combined proof tree and instantiation graph view, which makes the dependency on **non_empty-def** explicit (instantiations $i1$ and $i3$). Walking over all ancestors of the **false** node, we are able to return the precise extended UNSAT core. It is also available via a non-GUI interface.

Our combined graph is also useful for understanding how, for a particular query, Z3 proved UNSAT or why it failed to do so. Namely, the proof tree often includes lemmas that Z3 proved by contradiction. By inspecting these derived lemmas, one can identify missing axioms that would provide the lemma outright, avoiding the need to prove them. As with the instantiation graph view, filtering operations are available to help focus on interesting parts of the graph.

3   Matching Loop Detection Algorithm

Our novel matching loop detection fundamentally improves on prior work [3] in two ways: (1) the false-positive rate is near-zero, and (2) it is asymptotically faster, enabling automatic analysis of full instantiation graphs for realistic examples. In this section, we explain the insights that enable these improvements and present how they are leveraged in our algorithm.

The key observation is that we need to consider instantiations only *pairwise*, without regard for the path connecting them. Compared to the algorithm of prior work, which is designed to analyse individual paths, our pairwise one asymptotically improves performance, because the number of paths is often exponential in the number of quantifier instantiations, whereas the number of pairs is quadratic. Our observation holds true even for matching loops where multiple quantifiers are instantiated in a single iteration of the loop; the repeating instantiations of each quantifier can be identified and generalised individually, and then later combined to build the generalised iteration graph for the entire matching loop. This pairwise analysis has worst-case quadratic time performance, though in practice it is often linear with the number of instantiations. Therefore, we can analyse full instantiation graphs of real-world queries with hundreds of thousands of instantiations, allowing us to give completeness guarantees.

Our matching loop algorithm is shown in Figure 8. It has two phases: first, a topological walk to perform the pairwise analysis, and second, a pass to collect the full matching loops and construct their generalised iteration graphs.

Phase 1: Identifying Candidate Pairs

We use three filters to identify instantiation pairs that are likely part of a matching loop. Any pair in a matching loop must satisfy these filters, while those not in a loop are very unlikely to do so. The first phase, for each instantiation `inst`, performs the following three steps (each one explains a filter).

Step 1: Root dependencies and ancestors, lines 4–6. We will use $I_0, I_1, I_2, \ldots$ to denote successive instantiations of `pop-trim` in our running example. The first instantiation I_0 depends on the term Ⓣ `pop(empty)` and the equality Ⓐ `empty = trim(empty, 1)` (see Figure 4, the loop starts with $[\star \mapsto 1]$). Both are from the input query; we call these *root dependencies*. The next instantiation I_1 depends on the same term Ⓣ and the equality Ⓑ, thus it transitively depends on Ⓐ, Ⓨ, and Ⓔ. However, since Ⓨ is derived from a prior instantiation and is not from the input query, it is not a root dependency. Therefore, the root dependencies of I_1 are the same two as for I_0 plus the equality Ⓔ. All subsequent `pop-trim` instantiations depend on *the same three* root dependencies.

We can generalise this observation to obtain our first filter: in a matching loop, the set of (transitive) root dependencies cannot change because (1) by definition, the set of root dependencies cannot shrink from parent to child, and (2) it cannot grow in each iteration of a matching loop since the number of root dependencies is bounded by the size of the input query.

We store the set of root dependencies for each instantiation as the union of the direct root dependencies and the root dependencies of all parents. Similarly, we compute the set of ancestors (`get_ancestors`) by taking the union of the **ancestors** of all parents and adding the parents themselves. Next, we iterate over these ancestors to perform the pairwise analysis.

Step 2: Pairwise instantiation signature check, lines 7–10 and 15. In our example, `pop-trim`'s pattern `{pop(trim(v, n))}` successively matches the terms I_0: `pop(trim(empty, 1))`, I_1: `pop(trim(empty, add(1, 1)))`, ... Thus, the quantified variables are successively instantiated with I_0: `[v ↦ empty, n ↦ 1]`, I_1: `[v ↦ empty, n ↦ add(1, 1)]`, I_2: `[v ↦ empty, n ↦ add(1, add(1, 1))]`, and so on. We define the size of a term as the node count of its AST, we then define the *size of an instantiation* as the vector of sizes of each substituted term; in our example, this is I_0: `[1, 1]`, I_1: `[1, 3]`, I_2: `[1, 5]`, and so on. The key

```
1   function find_matching_loops(g: InstGraph)
2       # Phase 1: Pairwise analysis
3       for inst in topological_sort(g):
4           inst.root_deps = direct_root_deps(inst) ∪
5                               parent_root_deps(inst)
6           for anc in get_ancestors(inst):
7               sig_compat = quant(inst) == quant(anc) &&
8                               inst.root_deps == anc.root_deps &&
9                               inst_size(inst) >= inst_size(anc)
10              if sig_compat:
11                  gen = try_generalise(anc, inst)
12                  inst.potential_loop = (anc, gen)
13                  (inst.leaf, anc.leaf) = (true, false)
14              else:
15                  inst.ancestors = inst.ancestors ∪ {anc}
16      # Phase 2: Build generalised iteration graphs
17      for inst in leaf_nodes(g):
18          (prev, gen) = inst.potential_loop
19          if gen.success:
20              others = inst.ancestors \ prev.ancestors
21              fixed = dependencies_of({inst} ∪ others) \
22                          produced_by(others ∪ {prev})
23              graph = build_graph(g, inst, others)
24              matching_loops += (inst, graph)
25          else:
26              suspicious += inst
27      return (matching_loops, suspicious)
```

Fig. 8. Our matching loop detection algorithm. It takes as input the instantiation graph and returns two lists: the identified matching loops (including the generalised iteration graph of each), and the suspicious instantiation chains that we failed to generalise. The $\geq$ on line 9 is shorthand for elementwise comparison of the two vectors.

observation is that in a matching loop, this size cannot decrease between successive instantiations of the same quantifier[1]—our second filter. If it were to decrease, we could use this as a termination measure due to the lower bound to prove the absence of a matching loop.

We call the set of root dependencies and the size vector the *instantiation signature* of a quantifier instantiation. The signatures of an ancestor and descendant instantiation are *compatible* if the instantiated quantifier is the same, the set of root dependencies is equal, and the size vector of the descendant instantiation is elementwise greater than or equal to that of the ancestor.

The first two filters are strong enough to rule out the majority of non-matching loop instantiation pairs: Filter 1 (root dependencies) avoids a class of false positives that prior work suffers from, such as an axiom for lookups in program heaps leading to long chains of instantiations of the same axiom but for different versions of the heap (each version is a new root dependency). Filter 2 (instantiation size) is complementary, avoiding false positives for quantifiers that recursively deconstruct a large term into smaller ones, such as one defining the length of a list with the pattern `{len(cons(x, xs))}`.

Lines 7–9 in Figure 8 check whether `inst`'s instantiation signature is compatible with that of each ancestor `anc`. If they are compatible, we consider the pair as a potential matching loop and proceed to the next step. Otherwise, we save `anc` for comparison with `inst`'s descendants (for loops with multiple quantifiers).

Step 3: Generalised repetition, lines 11–13. At this point, we have identified a pair of instantiations (`anc`, `inst`) that is likely part of a matching loop. In our example, (I_1, I_2) is such a pair (remember that I_0 is not compatible with I_1, since the root dependencies differ). The final key observation is that the term and equality dependencies of such pairs must generalise—our third filter. That is, they either remain the same (fixed inputs) or grow in a systematic way enabling the matching loop to continue indefinitely. The generalisation is done using syntactic anti-unification (from prior work [3,18]), slightly modified to help find the most general result. Applied to our example, where I_1 depends on the equality `empty = trim(empty, add(1, 1))`, while I_2 depends on the equality `empty = trim(empty, add(1, add(1, 1)))`, our anti-unification yields `empty = trim(empty, *)`. The $*$ represents a fresh variable; one that can be substituted to get either input. Next, we try to identify the iteration step. We take the subexpression that the variable replaced in `anc`, `add(1, 1)`, and try to find it in the corresponding subexpression it replaced in `inst`, `add(1, add(1, 1))`. In our example, we successfully identify the iteration step as `[* ↦ add(1, *)]`.

We save the reference to `anc` along with the generalisation: we will use these in Phase 2 of the algorithm to build a generalised iteration graph. Generalisation may fail when the subexpression cannot be found. This was rare during our evaluation; when we inspected such cases, we confirmed that none of them were matching loops. However, due to issues in how z3 logs equality dependencies, it may be possible that an actual matching loop fails to generalise. Therefore, we also keep these failing cases and report them as `suspicious` in the next phase.

---

[1] All terms may remain equal-size due to arithmetic simplification, such as `3+1` to `4`.

Phase 2: Constructing Generalised Iteration Graphs

The pairs identified in Phase 1 form chains of matching loop instantiations. In our example, the pairs (I_1, I_2), (I_2, I_3), ... form the chain $[I_1, I_2, I_3, \ldots]$. Phase 2 combines these *instantiation chains* with other interleaved chains to build generalised iteration graphs, possibly involving multiple quantifiers. For our example, this is trivial as there is only one quantifier involved: the generalised iteration graph in Figure 4 follows directly from the generalisation we just found.

To better illustrate Phase 2, we use a new example matching loop with two quantifiers: q and r, with instantiations $Q_0, Q_1, \ldots$ and $R_0, R_1, \ldots$, respectively. An instantiation of q produces a term matching the pattern of r, which in turn produces a term matching the pattern of q, resulting in a matching loop. The instantiation graph contains the following chain of instantiations: $Q_0 \rightarrow R_0 \rightarrow Q_1 \rightarrow R_1 \rightarrow \ldots$. For this example, Phase 1 identifies two independent chains: $[Q_0, Q_1, \ldots]$ and $[R_0, R_1, \ldots]$. Phase 2 combines these as follows.

Step 1: Identify suspicious chains, lines 17–19 and 26. We iterate over all instantiations marked as a leaf on line 13. Following the ancestor references identifies a chain, and we mark those as suspicious for which generalisation from Step 3 in Phase 1 failed. Otherwise, we proceed to the next step.

Step 2: Identify interleaved chains, lines 20–22. Let R_n (inst) and R_{n-1} (prev) be the last two instantiations of the second chain from the example above. This chain alone is not sufficient to explain the matching loop; each iteration requires one instantiation of r but also one of q. To identify such required interleaved instantiations, we take the set difference of the ancestors of R_n ($\{Q_0, R_0, \ldots, Q_{n-1}, Q_n\}$) and those of R_{n-1} ($\{Q_0, R_0, \ldots, Q_{n-1}\}$). This yields $\{Q_n\}$—all instantiations between R_{n-1} and R_n. The resulting instantiations (stored in **others**) come from an identified chain themselves; these are the other chains required to explain the matching loop. The matching loop may also require fixed dependencies to perpetuate (the nodes with a grey background in the generalised instantiation graph). To identify those, we take the term and equality dependencies of **inst** and **others** that are not produced by any instantiations in **others** or **prev**. Our current example has no fixed dependencies: each new iteration depends entirely on the term produced by the previous iteration.

Step 3: Generalised iteration graph, line 23. Now that we have identified all the instantiations involved in one iteration of the matching loop (**inst** and **others**) and we have their associated generalisations and fixed dependencies, we can build the generalised iteration graph. For each of these instantiations, we create nodes for the quantifier pattern and body in the generalised iteration graph (coloured nodes). We connect these nodes as the instantiations themselves are connected, but replace the term and equality nodes with their generalised forms (unless they are fixed). The result is a generalised iteration graph, which explains the full matching loop (involving both r and q in the example).

The algorithm returns all identified suspicious chains (as the leaf node, from which the chain can be reconstructed) and matching loops (as the leaf node and the generalised iteration graph).

4 Implementation and Evaluation

SMTSCOPE operates on the trace file created by Z3 when run with the trace flag. All of SMTSCOPE's algorithms and analyses are equally applicable to any other SMT solver that uses e-matching (e.g., CVC5 [1]). If these SMT solvers were extended with the same tracing functionality, our tool would work with them as well. Our tool is written in Rust and consists of two crates: a parsing and analysis library (including a command-line interface) and a web-based visualisation frontend. The former allows one to incorporate our analyses into other tools. The latter is compiled to WASM and runs in a static webpage entirely in the user's browser. Such a web-app approach improves portability and ease of use, as the tool works with any OS and requires no installation.

We designed an evaluation to answer the following questions:

(Q1) Can SMTSCOPE identify and explain problem behaviours such as matching loops, is the analysis accurate, and are these problem behaviours important?
(Q2) Is SMTSCOPE fast and stable enough to scale to large real-world examples?

We assembled a test suite of 29,305 Z3 v4.8.7 trace files generated while running the test suites of DAFNY, F*, VERUS, and VIPER, as well as running Z3 on the SMT-COMP 2024 [4] benchmarks (all logics). With the latter, we test that SMTSCOPE does not crash, even when using a wide variety of SMT-LIB features.

Q1: Problem Behaviours. To identify problem behaviours, we ran SMTSCOPE in the command-line mode on each of the trace files. This mode reports the number of matching loops, suspicious chains, and multiplicative behaviours detected, and prints the names of the axioms involved. So that we avoid counting repeated occurrences of the same issue, we recorded the set of names of the axioms involved in each issue. We then counted the number of unique issues for each problem behaviour. The results are summarised in Table 1. Clearly, SMTSCOPE is able to automatically detect a significant number of problem behaviours.

To answer the second part of our question, we chose to focus on VIPER-SE . In the visualisation frontend, we inspected the trace files containing the 15 longest (by iteration count) identified matching loops, all 5 suspicious chains and the 15 most multiplicative quantifiers. Using the matching loop view, we confirmed that all 15 matching loops were identified correctly. The generalised iteration graph helped us quickly understand the loops, and we have successfully implemented a few fixes to the VIPER axioms. Of the 5 suspicious chains, none were matching loops. This indicates that our analysis is accurate and does not misclassify matching loops as mere suspicious chains. We were able to quickly understand all 15 multiplicative behaviours using the instantiation graph view. Interestingly, we noticed that some axioms had non-symmetric patterns such as `{f(x), g(y)}` but were still multiplicative due to a large number of f and g terms.

We then ran the AXIOM PROFILER on all trace files. It supports a very limited automated analysis that searches the longest instantiation chains for matching loops. Only 31 matching loops were reported (compared to 130 with SMTSCOPE), and manual inspection showed that 11 of these were false positives.

For the last part of the question, we compared the proportion of quantifiers we identified as problematic (not including the suspicious ones) to the proportion of total instantiations they caused. We found that only 382 out of $159,031$ (0.24%) quantifiers across our entire test suite were problematic (multiple quantifiers may be involved in a single matching loop). However, these 0.24% of quantifiers caused over 12.2 million out of 47.9 million total instantiations (25.5%). This does not even include other instantiations resulting from the new terms or equalities produced by these 25.5%. Clearly, the two problem behaviours we describe and tackle in this work cause a substantial fraction of all quantifier instantiations, and thus, are likely to degrade the performance of the SMT solver.

Q2: Scalability. To evaluate the stability and performance of SMTSCOPE and to compare it to the AXIOM PROFILER, we timed both while analysing the 29,305 trace files from above. We modified the AXIOM PROFILER to log timing information and added a one-second timeout for parsing each line (when handling some trace lines, it would freeze). We found that SMTSCOPE handily outperforms the AXIOM PROFILER by multiple orders of magnitude, even though it performs a more advanced and complete analysis. For a 200 MB trace file, SMTSCOPE takes around 1 s while the AXIOM PROFILER takes over 40 s. SMTSCOPE's runtime was on average 30% that of the z3 execution which generated the trace file. This means that our tool can be run alongside existing verifier CI pipelines with little overhead.

Regarding stability, we observed that for 25% of the trace files the AXIOM PROFILER either failed to parse the whole file or reported an error during analysis. That is despite using a version of z3 which it officially supports. In contrast, SMTSCOPE successfully parses and analyses all trace files in the benchmark suite and supports all modern versions of z3 (v4.8.5+).

Table 1. Number of problem behaviours detected by SMTSCOPE in each category. We split the VIPER files based on the verification backend: symbolic execution (VIPER-SE) and verification condition generation (VIPER-VCG). A multiplicativity of 5 or more is categorised as a problem behaviour, and between 3 and 5 as suspicious.

Category	Trace files	Matching loops (+sus.)	Multiplicative (+sus.)
DAFNY	13153	45 (+6)	38 (+33)
VIPER-SE	2724	51 (+5)	37 (+60)
VIPER-VCG	4774	17 (+1)	98 (+194)
F*	608	8 (+1)	6 (+6)
VERUS	2581	3 (+0)	0 (+5)
SMT-COMP	5465	6 (+5)	32 (+14)
Total	**29305**	**130 (+18)**	**211 (+312)**

5   Related Work and Conclusion

The AXIOM PROFILER [3] is the most closely related tool; they developed the idea of an instantiation graph, and our summary graphs (in Figure 3) are an extended version of similar graphs implemented by Pit-Claudel for the AXIOM PROFILER. As discussed in Section 1, SMTSCOPE supersedes it in several ways. First, we developed new algorithms to find and explain matching loops and multiplicative quantifiers more accurately and efficiently. Second, our tool is designed from the ground up to scale to large and complex real-world traces, enabling automated testing in verifier CI pipelines. Third, we analyse the proof tree to both provide a precise UNSAT core that includes lurking axioms and to visualise and explain the proof search, something that prior work does not do.

Z3TRACER [2] allows one to parse Z3's trace files and compute high-level per-quantifier metrics, comparable to some of those on our summary screen. However, it reconstructs only a basic picture of e-matching, thus none of the analyses that our tool offers can be implemented on top of it. Further, Z3TRACER does not handle any aspect of proof search.

The challenge of selecting patterns that are neither overly-strict nor overly-permissive has been widely studied [15,13,5], with approaches presented that avoid some simple matching loops [14]. In addition to adjusting patterns, the solutions we propose (correctly conditioning equalities, replacing quantifiers with decision procedures) complement these.

Several techniques [9,20,21] optimise SMT-based verifiers by understanding and analysing successful proof runs to either reduce instability or to minimise future queries for faster proof replay. They can directly benefit from SMTSCOPE.

In summary, SMTSCOPE can automatically, efficiently, and reliably identify many problem behaviours in real-world Z3 traces. Once identified, it effectively explains these behaviours by providing a breadth of visualisations. Additionally, our novel proof tree visualisation shines a light on this important but previously opaque aspect of SMT execution, enabling features such as finding precise UNSAT cores that include lurking axioms.

Acknowledgments. We thank Oskari Jyrkinen for his significant help in developing the initial version of the tool during his bachelor's thesis [10], Alexander J. Summers for helpful discussions, and the anonymous reviewers for their valuable feedback.

Data Availability. The two Rust crates comprising SMTSCOPE, along with instructions to build and run it, are available online [7]. The tool, along with the SMT-LIB query files required to generate the trace files used in the evaluation, and sufficient instructions to reproduce our results are available as an artifact [8].

References

1. Barbosa, H., Barrett, C.W., Brain, M., Kremer, G., Lachnitt, H., Mann, M., Mohamed, A., Mohamed, M., Niemetz, A., Nötzli, A., Ozdemir, A., Preiner, M., Reynolds, A., Sheng, Y., Tinelli, C., Zohar, Y.: CVC5: A versatile and industrial-strength SMT solver. In: TACAS (1). Lecture Notes in Computer Science, vol. 13243, pp. 415–442. Springer (2022)
2. Baudet, M.: z3tracer (October 2021), `https://github.com/facebookarchive/smt2utils/tree/main/z3tracer`, GitHub
3. Becker, N., Müller, P., Summers, A.J.: The axiom profiler: Understanding and debugging SMT quantifier instantiations. In: TACAS (1). Lecture Notes in Computer Science, vol. 11427, pp. 99–116. Springer (2019)
4. Bromberger, M., Bobot, F., Jonáš, M.: SMT-COMP 2024 (July 2024), `https://smt-comp.github.io/2024/`
5. Bugariu, A., Ter-Gabrielyan, A., Müller, P.: Identifying overly restrictive matching patterns in SMT-based program verifiers. In: FM. Lecture Notes in Computer Science, vol. 13047, pp. 273–291. Springer (2021)
6. Detlefs, D., Nelson, G., Saxe, J.B.: Simplify: a theorem prover for program checking. J. ACM **52**(3), 365–473 (2005)
7. Fiala, J., Jyrkinen, O., et al.: SMTScope (October 2025), `https://github.com/viperproject/smt-scope`, GitHub
8. Fiala, J., Müller, P.: Artifact for "SMTScope: Automated and efficient analysis of smt traces" (2025). `https://doi.org/10.5281/zenodo.17491144`, `https://doi.org/10.5281/zenodo.17491144`
9. Gopinathan, K., Spiliopoulos, D., Goyal, V., Müller, P., Püschel, M., Sergey, I.: Accelerating automated program verifiers by automatic proof localization. In: International Conference on Computer Aided Verification. pp. 153–174. Springer (2025)
10. Jyrkinen, O.: Developing Tool Support for Understanding Quantifier Instantiations. Bachelor's thesis, ETH Zurich (2024)
11. Lattuada, A., Hance, T., Cho, C., Brun, M., Subasinghe, I., Zhou, Y., Howell, J., Parno, B., Hawblitzel, C.: Verus: Verifying rust programs using linear ghost types. Proceedings of the ACM on Programming Languages **7**(OOPSLA1), 286–315 (2023)
12. Leino, K.R.M.: Dafny: An automatic program verifier for functional correctness. In: LPAR (Dakar). Lecture Notes in Computer Science, vol. 6355, pp. 348–370. Springer (2010)
13. Leino, K.R.M., Monahan, R.: Reasoning about comprehensions with first-order SMT solvers. In: Proceedings of the 2009 ACM symposium on Applied Computing. pp. 615–622 (2009)
14. Leino, K.R.M., Pit-Claudel, C.: Trigger selection strategies to stabilize program verifiers. In: International Conference on Computer Aided Verification. pp. 361–381. Springer (2016)
15. Moskal, M.: Programming with triggers. In: Proceedings of the 7th International Workshop on Satisfiability Modulo Theories. pp. 20–29 (2009)
16. de Moura, L.M., Bjørner, N.S.: Z3: an efficient SMT solver. In: TACAS. Lecture Notes in Computer Science, vol. 4963, pp. 337–340. Springer (2008)
17. Müller, P., Schwerhoff, M., Summers, A.J.: Viper: A verification infrastructure for permission-based reasoning. In: International conference on verification, model checking, and abstract interpretation. pp. 41–62. Springer (2015)

18. Plotkin, G.D.: A note on inductive generalization. Machine intelligence **5**(1), 153–163 (1970)
19. Swamy, N., Hriţcu, C., Keller, C., Rastogi, A., Delignat-Lavaud, A., Forest, S., Bhargavan, K., Fournet, C., Strub, P.Y., Kohlweiss, M., et al.: Dependent types and multi-monadic effects in F★. In: Proceedings of the 43rd annual ACM SIGPLAN-SIGACT Symposium on Principles of Programming Languages. pp. 256–270 (2016)
20. Zhou, Y., Bosamiya, J., Takashima, Y., Li, J., Heule, M., Parno, B.: Mariposa: Measuring SMT instability in automated program verification. In: 2023 Formal Methods in Computer-Aided Design (FMCAD). pp. 178–188. IEEE (2023)
21. Zhou, Y., Shah, A., Lin, Z., Heule, M., Parno, B.: Cazamariposas: Automated instability debugging in SMT-based program verification. In: Conference on Automated Deduction. vol. 122 (2025)

Proofs and Quantifier Elimination

Hint-Based SMT Proof Reconstruction

Joshua Clune[1] , Haniel Barbosa[2] , and Jeremy Avigad[1]

[1] Carnegie Mellon University, Pittsburgh, PA, USA
[2] Universidade Federal de Minas Gerais, Belo Horizonte, Brazil

Abstract. There are several paradigms for integrating interactive and automated theorem provers, combining the convenience of powerful automation with strong soundness guarantees. We introduce a new approach for reconstructing proofs found by SMT solvers which we intend to be complementary with existing techniques. Rather than verifying or replaying a full proof produced by the SMT solver, or at the other extreme, rediscovering the solver's proof from just the set of premises it uses, we explore an approach which helps guide an interactive theorem prover's internal automation by leveraging derived facts during solving, which we call hints. This makes it possible to extract more information from the SMT solver's proof without the cost of retaining a dependency on the SMT solver itself. We implement a tactic in the Lean proof assistant, called QUERYSMT, which leverages hints from the cvc5 SMT solver to improve existing Lean automation. We evaluate QUERYSMT's performance on relevant Lean benchmarks, compare it to other tools available in Lean relating to SMT solving, and show that the hints generated by cvc5 produce a clear improvement in existing automation's performance.

Keywords: SMT Solving · Interactive Theorem Proving · Lean

1 Introduction

When it comes to formal verification, interactive and automatic theorem provers (ITPs or proof assistants, and ATPs, respectively) have complementary strengths. Proof assistants offer powerful languages for expressing arbitrary mathematical statements and the ability to verify claims down to domain-specific axioms and the rules of the underlying logical foundation, but doing so often requires considerable effort. Automatic provers offer push-button verification but often fail to scale to complex verification tasks and do not provide the same strong guarantees as interactive theorem provers. Proof assistants like Isabelle/HOL [9,10,20,32], Rocq [1,17], and Lean [13,24,26] aim for the best of both worlds by translating goals in a proof assistant to the language of a powerful external prover and then using information from the external prover to reconstruct a proof of the original result that is checked within the ITP. The challenge, then, is to bridge the gap and establish appropriate communication between the two.

There are several existing paradigms for effectively communicating between ATPs and proof assistants. Their approaches to reconstructing ATP proofs vary. One approach, often used for superposition theorem provers such as E [34],

S. Junges and G. Katz (Eds.): TACAS 2026, LNCS 16505, pp. 255–275, 2026.
https://doi.org/10.1007/978-3-032-22752-2_13

`Vampire` [19] and `Zipperposition` [33], is to supply a large number of premises to the ATP, use the ATP's proof to identify a minimal subset of necessary premises, and then supply just those premises to internal ITP automation such as METIS [18]. This has the benefit of entirely removing the call to the external prover, but has the possibility of failure because it ultimately depends on internal automation independently discovering a proof.

SMT solvers [7], which combine generic first-order reasoning with theory-specific decision procedures, generally warrant reconstruction methods which more closely follow the external solver's original proof. Isabelle/HOL relies on internal tactics to replay each step in the certificates from the SMT solvers it supports (`z3` [25], `veriT` [12], and `cvc5` [3]). SMTCoq uses the SMT solver `veriT`, which can produce detailed certificates, and checks its certificates via a formally verified procedure within Rocq. LEAN-SMT uses a mixtures of these two approaches, but mostly proof replay, to reconstruct certificates from `cvc5`.

Our goal in this paper is to explore an alternative approach to proof reconstruction. Instead of reconstructing the SMT solver's proof exactly, retaining a dependency on it, or discarding all information about the solver's proof except the set of premises used, our approach uses the SMT solver's proof to help guide ITP automation by providing *hints*.

We develop a Lean tactic, called QUERYSMT, which uses LEAN-AUTO [29] to export problems from Lean's dependent type theory to the language of an SMT solver. We then instrument `cvc5` to report the preprocessing and theory reasoning performed while solving the translated problem. This is used by QUERYSMT to insert, in the Lean source file, a self-contained proof script for the goal, with Lean formulations of the theory-specific facts formalized as subgoals. The proof script uses GRIND, a built-in Lean tactic inspired by SMT solvers, to supply proofs of those subgoals, and uses a proof-producing superposition prover, DUPER [15], to prove the original goal using those facts. The result is a structured proof that users can inspect, modify, and simplify, if they wish. Notably, the proof does not depend on calling an SMT solver anymore. As in Isabelle's Sledgehammer when not using the `smt` tactic, the call to the external prover disappears.

We believe this approach has complementary strengths to others. SMT solvers are notoriously unstable; small changes in context, even as minor as renaming variables, can cause proofs to break, as well as different solver versions running on the same problem [35]. Therefore, eliminating the SMT call in favor of a modular source-code proof results in a more stable artifact. Additionally, we consider it a benefit that users can inspect and modify the resulting proof script. Powerful automation may be good at finding a proof, but it rarely yields the nicest one.

We demonstrate the method with arithmetic and inductive types, two of the most important and common theories in Lean and other proof assistants, though our approach is not specific to these. We evaluate the approach on relevant benchmark problems from Lean's Init, Batteries, and Mathlib [16] libraries, and compare it to other SMT-related tools available in Lean. We show that although proof reconstruction does not always succeed, incorporating SMT hints significantly improves internal automation's chances of successful reconstruction.

Our contributions are as follows:

- We augment cvc5 with the ability to record data that will be useful for proof reconstruction and report it back to Lean.
- We develop a method of translating statements about natural numbers to SMT queries on the integers.
- We augment our back-end reconstruction, DUPER [15], to implement a set of support strategy [30], improving its ability to incorporate SMT hints.
- We evaluate QUERYSMT's performance on Lean benchmarks, showing that QUERYSMT compares favorably to existing SMT-related Lean automation and that SMT hints produce a clear improvement in DUPER's performance.

2 QUERYSMT Overview

To demonstrate and evaluate our approach, we develop QUERYSMT, a Lean tactic which utilizes hints from the cvc5 SMT solver to suggest a self-contained proof script. The overall structure of QUERYSMT is given in Figure 1.

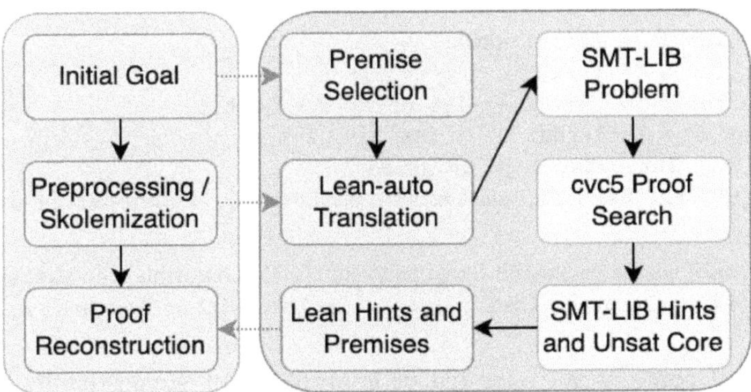

Fig. 1. Overview of the QUERYSMT tactic. Blue boxes indicate Lean stages. Yellow boxes indicate SMT stages. Stages in the green area directly transform the Lean goal and must be replayed in the final suggested proof script. Stages in the purple area do not transform the goal and therefore do not need to be replayed. Red dotted lines indicate information transfer between stages.

QUERYSMT consists of five primary components: preprocessing, translation, hint generation, hint interpretation, and proof reconstruction. Preprocessing transforms the goal into a form that reduces the likelihood of cvc5 producing hints that can't be interpreted or proven. Translation from Lean's dependent type theory [2] to the many-sorted first-order logic used by SMT solvers [5] is handled by LEAN-AUTO [29], with extensions made to LEAN-AUTO's SMT-LIB translation described in Section 4. Hint generation consists of recording facts generated over the course of cvc5's proof search and identifying an unsat core from the given goal and set of premises provided by premise selection. Hint interpretation involves translating cvc5's generated hints into usable Lean expressions. Finally, proof reconstruction accepts cvc5's unsat core and the output of hint interpretation and uses them to suggest a self-contained proof script that the user can examine and modify.

```
example (f : Int → Int) (h1 : ∀ x y, f x = f y → x = y)
  (h2 : ∃ x, ∀ y, f x ≤ f y) : ∃ x, ∀ y, x ≠ y → f x < f y := by
  apply @Classical.byContradiction
  intro negGoal
  skolemizeAll
  have smtLemma0 : (∀ (_i_0 : Int), f sk0 ≤ f _i_0) →
    ∀ (_i_0 : Int), ¬f sk0 + -Int.ofNat 1 * f _i_0 ≥ Int.ofNat 1 :=
    by grind
  have smtLemma1 :
    (∀ (_i : Int),
        have _let_1 := sk1 _i;
        ¬(¬_i = _let_1 → f _i < f _let_1)) →
      ∀ (BOUND_VARIABLE_4962 : Int), f BOUND_VARIABLE_4962 +
    -Int.ofNat 1 * f (sk1 BOUND_VARIABLE_4962) ≥ Int.ofNat 0 :=
    by grind
  have smtLemma2 :
    have _let_1 := f (sk1 sk0);
    have _let_2 := f sk0;
    have _let_3 := _let_2 + -Int.ofNat 1 * _let_1;
    (¬_let_3 ≥ Int.ofNat 0 ∨ _let_2 = _let_1) ∨
    _let_3 ≥ Int.ofNat 1 := by grind
  duper [h1, h2, negGoal, smtLemma0, smtLemma1, smtLemma2] []
```

Fig. 2. A proof script suggested by QUERYSMT. In this example, the `skolemizeAll` call produces (sk0 : Int) and (sk1 : Int → Int) from h2 and `negGoal` respectively.

Figure 2 contains an example of a proof script suggested by QUERYSMT. The first three lines reproduce QUERYSMT's preprocessing and Skolemization, the **have** statements that follow are Lean translations of hints recommended by cvc5, and the final line is a call to DUPER which uses the recommended hints to complete the overall goal. As of Lean version v4.22.0, neither GRIND nor DUPER can prove this example alone, as DUPER cannot verify the hints output by cvc5 and GRIND cannot complete the overall proof even with cvc5's hints. But by using GRIND to reconstruct cvc5's theory reasoning and DUPER to reconstruct cvc5's logical reasoning, QUERYSMT is able to complete the proof.

On a first pass, the proof script in Figure 2 is not very easy to read. QUERYSMT does some work for the user by filtering the set of suggested hints to only include those necessary for DUPER's final proof,[3] but even so, the individual hints can still be unnecessarily verbose. In this example, the hypotheses in `smtLemma0`'s and `smtLemma1`'s implications directly match the statements of h2 and `negGoal`

---

[3] In the example from Figure 2, cvc5 generates 8 hints initially, but QUERYSMT is able to filter them down to 3 for the final proof script.

after the modifications made by `skolemizeAll`, making the hypotheses redundant. The proof script can be made significantly more readable by removing these hypotheses and making some other minor changes, such as renaming `BOUND_VARIABLE_4962` as `z`, performing zeta-reduction to remove unnecessary `let` expressions, and simplifying expressions of the form `-Int.ofNat 1 * e` to `-e`. A simplified version of Figure 2's proof script is shown in Figure 3. QUERYSMT does not currently have a postprocessing module to perform such simplifications automatically, but this would be worth exploring as future work.

```
example (f : Int → Int) (h1 : ∀ x y, f x = f y → x = y)
  (h2 : ∃ x, ∀ y, f x ≤ f y) : ∃ x, ∀ y, x ≠ y → f x < f y := by
  apply @Classical.byContradiction
  intro negGoal
  skolemizeAll
  have smtLemma0 : ∀ (_i_0 : Int), ¬f sk0 - f _i_0 ≥ 1 := by grind
  have smtLemma1 : ∀ (z : Int), f z - f (sk1 z) ≥ 0 := by grind
  have smtLemma2 :
    (¬f sk0 - f (sk1 sk0) ≥ 0 ∨ f sk0 = f (sk1 sk0)) ∨
    f sk0 - f (sk1 sk0) ≥ 1 := by grind
  duper [h1, h2, negGoal, smtLemma0, smtLemma1, smtLemma2] []
```

Fig. 3. A simplified version of the proof script shown in Figure 2.

3   Preprocessing

Preprocessing takes a Lean goal of the form $\Gamma \vdash p :$ Prop and transforms it into a goal of the form $\Gamma' \vdash$ False : Prop where all hypotheses in Γ' are Skolemized and Γ' entails Γ and $\neg p$. This transformation is necessary for two reasons.

First, the hints that `cvc5` generates may depend on the falsity of the initial target p. When this occurs, the generated hints are not entailed by Γ, meaning that any proof automation that attempts to derive the hint from Γ is doomed to fail. By preprocessing the goal into a state where the local context Γ' entails both Γ and $\neg p$, QUERYSMT ensures that when it comes time to prove the hints provided by `cvc5`, all pertinent information is accessible in the local context.

Second, the hints that `cvc5` generates may include constants that do not appear in the original SMT-LIB problem produced by LEAN-AUTO. This occurs when `cvc5` internally Skolemizes existential quantifiers, generating constants of the form `@QUANTIFIERS_SKOLEMIZE_X`.[4] While it is possible to recover the meaning of these constants by following the chain of inferences that were taken to reach `cvc5`'s Skolemization inferences, this approach essentially amounts to partial proof replay, which goes against the intention of QUERYSMT's design.

---

[4] As defined in `https://cvc5.github.io/docs/cvc5-1.3.1/skolem-ids.html`, this constant corresponds to a term resulting from Skolemization, which could be defined e.g. via Hilbert's choice operator if the Skolemized quantifier were given as well. However, this is only done when proofs are generated.

To avoid this issue, QUERYSMT handles Skolemization in Lean prior to calling LEAN-AUTO's translation procedure. We define a tactic called `skolemizeAll` which iterates through every hypothesis in the local context and attempts to remove existential quantifiers and negated universal quantifiers, replacing them with fresh free variables. When no Skolemization is necessary because neither the original context Γ nor the negated target $\neg p$ contain existential quantifiers or negated universal quantifiers, QUERYSMT notes that `skolemizeAll` has no impact on the goal state and omits it from the final proof script suggestion.

We note that because Lean's dependent type theory includes empty types, `skolemizeAll` may fail in cases where it is unable to verify type inhabitation. For example, Skolemizing the hypothesis $h : (\exists x : \alpha, P\ x) \vee$ `True` requires generating a free variable $y : \alpha$ and replacing h with $h' : P\ y \vee$ `True`. However, h alone does not entail that α is inhabited. Unless α is already known to be inhabited, `skolemizeAll` cannot soundly add $y : \alpha$ to the local context. Consequently, there are some theorems that QUERYSMT is fundamentally unable to tackle due to the presence of empty types or possibly empty polymorphic types. This limitation is inherent to approaches translating from Lean's logic to SMT-LIB, and also affects e.g. LEAN-SMT [24, Sec. 3.2], where proof replay may fail when the solver relied on the non-emptiness of a type and that cannot be established by Lean.

4   Translation to SMT-LIB

4.1   LEAN-AUTO

For translation to the many-sorted first-order logic of SMT-LIB, we rely on LEAN-AUTO [29]. LEAN-AUTO normalizes universe levels, monomorphizes definitions, handles definitional equalities, and broadly takes care of the many features that make Lean's type theory complex. When targeting SMT-LIB, LEAN-AUTO attempts to translate Lean types to their closest SMT-LIB analogues. For example, Lean's `Prop` and `Bool` types are both translated to SMT-LIB's `Bool` sort, and Lean's `Int` and `Nat` types are both translated to SMT-LIB's `Int` sort. This ensures that the translation takes full advantage of SMT solvers' theories, but sometimes creates complications for interpreting the SMT hints (see Section 6).

LEAN-AUTO primarily translates essentially higher-order problems in Lean to monomorphic higher-order logic, but also can translate essentially first-order problems in Lean to first-order logic for the purpose of targeting SMT-LIB [15,29]. Although the most recent version of the SMT-LIB standard (Version 2.7) defines an SMT-LIB logic which extends beyond the many-sorted first-order logic adopted by the previous version [6], this SMT-LIB logic is not specifically targeted by LEAN-AUTO. When the upcoming Version 3 of the SMT-LIB standard is released with a higher-order base logic, we expect it will be fruitful to modify LEAN-AUTO so that it uses its primary translation procedure even when targeting SMT-LIB. This would expand the fragment of Lean that can be effectively translated to SMT-LIB, but is beyond the scope of this paper.

4.2 Translating Natural Numbers

Unlike the translation procedures used by SMTCoq [1] or Isabelle's Sledgehammer [22,23,27,28], LEAN-AUTO does not adopt an encoding-based approach to translating natural numbers. Instead, LEAN-AUTO directly translates Lean terms of type `Nat` to SMT-LIB terms of sort `Int` along with assertions of the form `(assert (>= n 0))`. Although this approach is sufficient for many common use cases, it is incomplete and can lead to unsound translations when natural numbers are embedded in larger structures or inductive types. For example, LEAN-AUTO is able to soundly translate `example` $(n : \mathtt{Nat}) : 0 \leq n :=$ ... into an unsatisfiable SMT-LIB problem, but the SMT-LIB problem generated from `example` $(x : \mathtt{Nat} \times \mathtt{Nat}) : 0 \leq x.\mathtt{fst} :=$ ... is satisfiable because LEAN-AUTO fails to assert that both projections of x must be nonnegative.

We extend LEAN-AUTO's procedure by preserving the direct translation from Lean `Nat` terms to SMT-LIB `Int` terms while expanding the set of circumstances in which nonnegativity assertions are made. For every Lean type α which appears in the problem, we define an SMT-LIB predicate $\mathtt{wf}_\alpha : \hat{\alpha} \to \mathtt{Bool}$ where $\hat{\alpha}$ is the SMT-LIB sort corresponding to α. This predicate is meant to encode the fact that the SMT-LIB term it applies to is *well-formed*, meaning it satisfies all of the nonnegativity constraints imposed by the `Nat` type on the Lean term from which it was derived. As a concrete example, if $\alpha = \mathtt{Nat} \times \mathtt{Int}$, then $\mathtt{wf}_\alpha$ asserts that the first projection of the term it applies to is nonnegative.

Definition 1. *The predicate* $\mathtt{wf}_\alpha$ `x` *is defined inductively on* α *as follows:*

- *If* $\alpha = \mathtt{Nat}$ *then:*
    - $\mathtt{wf}_\alpha$ `x = (>= x 0)`
- *If* $\alpha = \alpha_1 \to \alpha_2$ *then:*
    - $\mathtt{wf}_\alpha$ `x = (forall ((y` $\hat{\alpha_1}$`)) (=> (wf`$_{\alpha_1}$ `y) (wf`$_{\alpha_2}$ `(x y))))`
- *If* α *is a structure[5] with projections* $p_1 : \alpha \to \alpha_1, \ldots p_n : \alpha \to \alpha_n$ *then:*
    - $\mathtt{wf}_\alpha$ `x =` $\bigwedge\limits_{i=1}^{n} \mathtt{wf}_{\alpha_i}$ `(`$\hat{p}_i$ `x)`
- *If* α *is an inductive datatype with constructors* $(c_1 : \beta_{1,1} \to \ldots \to \beta_{1,m_1} \to \alpha), \ldots (c_n : \beta_{n,1} \to \ldots \beta_{n,m_n} \to \alpha)$ *and is translated to a datatype with constructors* $\hat{c}_1, \ldots \hat{c}_n$ *and selectors* $s_{i,j} : \hat{\alpha} \to \hat{\beta_{i,j}}$ *then:*
    - $\mathtt{wf}_\alpha$ `x =` $\bigwedge\limits_{i=1}^{n}$ `(=> (x is` $\hat{c}_i$`) (` $\bigwedge\limits_{j=1}^{m_i} \mathtt{wf}_{\beta_{i,j}}$ `(`$s_{i,j}$ `x)))`
- *Otherwise:*
    - $\mathtt{wf}_\alpha$ `x = True`

---

[5] In Lean's type theory, all structures are inductive datatypes, meaning there is no need to distinguish between them [2]. Definition 1's treatment of structures is logically equivalent to its treatment of inductive datatypes with one constructor, so it would be straightforward to eliminate the distinction. We nonetheless distinguish between them because only structures are guaranteed to have projections already defined in Lean. This has consequences for hint interpretation, which are discussed in Section 6.

To ensure that the semantics of the SMT-LIB problem coincide with the semantics of the original Lean goal, `wf` constraints are inserted such that almost all terms which appear in the SMT-LIB problem are provably well-formed. Whenever an SMT-LIB function or constant is declared, an assertion is added to guarantee that it is well-formed. Additionally, whenever an SMT-LIB formula is translated from a Lean proposition, the translation of quantifiers is modified to assert the well-formedness of the introduced variable. Universal quantification over α is translated to `(forall ((x` $\hat{\alpha}$`)) (=> (wf`$_\alpha$ `x) (...)))` and existential quantification over α is translated to `(exists ((x` $\hat{\alpha}$`)) (and (wf`$_\alpha$ `x) (...)))`.

We note that this approach to translating natural numbers appears to coincide with `Trakt`'s methodology for handling partial embeddings on problems that do not involve inductive datatypes [11]. Our approach diverges from `Trakt`'s when inductive datatypes are involved because `Trakt` is intended to provide preprocessing transformations that are independent of the targeted backend while we explicitly aim to take advantage of SMT solvers' built-in datatype support.

Theorem 1. *All terms except datatype selectors[6] which appear in an SMT-LIB problem generated by our procedure are provably well-formed.*

Proof (sketch). Let $t : \hat{\alpha}$ be some term which appears in the generated SMT-LIB problem. The proof proceeds by induction on t. Here, we show one nontrivial case. For a proof sketch which covers more cases, see Appendix A of the extended version of this paper [14].

- If t is an application of of the form $(t_1\ t_2)$, then the Lean term corresponding to t_1 has type $\beta \to \alpha$ and the Lean term corresponding to t_2 has type β.[7] By the inductive hypothesis, t_2 is well-formed and t_1 is either well-formed or a selector function.
  - If t_1 is well-formed, then from the definition of well-formedness on functions, `wf`$_{\beta \to \alpha}$ t_1 `=` `(forall ((y` $\hat{\beta}$`)) (=> (wf`$_\beta$ `y) (wf`$_\alpha$ `(`t_1 `y))))`. From this and `wf`$_\beta$ t_2, it follows that `wf`$_\alpha$ `(`$t_1\ t_2$`)` as desired.
  - If t_1 is a selector function, then β is a structure or inductive datatype and t_1 has some associated constructor $\hat{c}$. From the definition of well-formedness on structures and inductive datatypes, `wf`$_\beta$ t_2 entails `(=> (`t_2 `is` $\hat{c}$`) (wf`$_\alpha$ `(`$t_1\ t_2$`)))`. LEAN-AUTO's translation procedure guarantees that if $(t_1\ t_2)$ appears in the generated SMT-LIB problem, then t_2 satisfies the tester for t_1's constructor, meaning $(t_2$ `is` $\hat{c})$ holds. From this and the implication entailed by `wf`$_\beta$ t_2, it follows that `wf`$_\alpha$ `(`$t_1\ t_2$`)`.

---

[6] Theorem 1 does not assert that datatype selectors are well-formed because in general they aren't. When a selector is passed a well-formed datatype built from the wrong constructor, the resulting application's output is only constrained by its sort (see remark 20 of the SMT-LIB standard [6]). Therefore, the output may fail to satisfy the nonnegativity constraints required by well-formedness.

[7] We can infer the form of the Lean term corresponding to t because Lean-auto's monomorphization procedure preserves term structures during translation.

5   Hint Generation

We have instrumented the cvc5 SMT solver to report hints for external tools (such as QUERYSMT) based on logical consequences derived during proof search from the input formula and the theories supported by the solver.

The hints are collected from the internal proof produced by cvc5 [4], which is then discarded. We consider three kinds of hints: *preprocessing lemmas, theory lemmas,* and *rewrite steps.* We consider them because they each contain theory reasoning performed by the solver while proving the given goal. We restrict ourselves to hints that were *useful* to the solver, i.e., they were used in the final proof. A useful by-product of the search for hints is to also collect an *unsat core* of the input, i.e., the elements of the input that were present in the proof.

Preprocessing is a key element of SMT solving where an input formula is simplified according to a series of preprocessing passes, each potentially modifying the input, be it by replacing the formula with a simplified version or generating new formulas entailed by it. The hints collected are entailments between the input formula and the preprocessed ones. An example of a key preprocessing step performed by cvc5 is the inference and application of a substitution over part of the input to eliminate terms that are definable by others, as per the rest of the input (e.g. if the input contains the equality $x = 5$, a substitution corresponding to $x \mapsto 5$ is applied to the rest of the input to remove x [4, Sect. 5.1]).

Theory lemmas are valid disjunctions of literals from one or more theories. They generally correspond to explanations of why a given assignment of truth values to literals is inconsistent (e.g. assigning True to both $a = b$ and $f(a) \neq f(b)$), and allow the pruning of search space relative to that wrong assignment.

Finally, we also collect intermediate theory reasoning steps applied during preprocessing and during theory lemma generation that correspond to rewrite steps. These are important because they encapsulate key theory reasoning that would be difficult to gauge from just the preprocessing or theory lemmas themselves. An example is how cvc5 reduces all arithmetic terms to sums of monomials. Since the hints will contain only the fully reduced terms, including the intermediate rewrite steps increases the information made available to QUERYSMT.

While the proof contains other elements (besides the justification themselves for those hints), such as the resolution reasoning performed by a SAT solver on the Boolean structure of the formula and its connection with the hints, we do not consider them because this logical reasoning can be performed by DUPER.

Normalization of AC operators. Internally cvc5, as most SMT solvers, represent associative operators not as binary but as n-ary operators, so it is common to apply a "flattening" simplification so that terms such as (* (* x_1 x_2) x_3) and (* x_2 (* x_3 x_1))) are represented as the same term (* x_i x_j x_k). Not only are applications of the operator flattened, but arguments are rearranged according to a canonical order. This normalization is useful for solving, but it complicates proof reconstruction in systems not representing AC operators in a normalized form. Since hints generated by cvc5 refer to the normalized version of a term, and this normalization is not present in the hints (it would only be present in a proper proof), the applicability of the hints by QUERYSMT can be limited unless QUERYSMT can infer the relation between original terms and their normalized versions. A potential solution is to integrate facts pertaining to AC reasoning in QUERYSMT's proof reconstruction, but this has the disadvantage that the extra facts may lead to proof instability and loss of performance. QUERYSMT does not make use of such facts by default, but has an option to enable their inclusion. We discuss the impact of this option in Appendix B of the extended version of this paper [14].

6   Hint Interpretation

For the most part, interpreting cvc5's SMT-LIB hints and translating them into Lean expressions is straightforward. At each stage of LEAN-AUTO's translation pipeline, LEAN-AUTO creates mappings from terms and types in the source language to terms and types in the target language. This is to ensure that when the same term or type appears multiple times in the source problem, each instance of said term or type is translated in the same way. We modified LEAN-AUTO's translation procedure to make each of these mappings reversible, allowing QUERYSMT to translate SMT-LIB symbols and identifiers by simply passing them to the composition of LEAN-AUTO's reversed mappings. Although this is sufficient in most cases, there are two complications which merit further discussion.

Non-injectivity. LEAN-AUTO's mapping from Lean types to SMT-LIB sorts is not injective. LEAN-AUTO translates Lean's `Prop` and `Bool` types to the same SMT-LIB `Bool` sort, and as discussed in Section 4, it also translates Lean's `Int` and `Nat` types into the same SMT-LIB `Int` sort. Consequently, it is possible for cvc5's hints to contain applications which typecheck according to SMT-LIB's semantics but fail to typecheck when naively translated into Lean. For example, if the original Lean goal contains n : `Nat` and x : `Int`, cvc5 may create a hint which involves subtracting $\hat{n}$ from $\hat{x}$, an operation that is unproblematic in SMT-LIB but would fail to typecheck when translated back into Lean.

QUERYSMT's approach to interpreting such hints consists of defaulting to `Prop` and `Int` interpretations of SMT-LIB's `Bool` and `Int` sorts, inserting coercions as needed. There is only one circumstance in which expressions must be coerced to `Bool` or `Nat`, namely, when supplying an argument to a function that takes `Bool` or `Nat` inputs. To give a concrete example, if f : `Nat` $\to$ `Nat`, n : `Nat`, and m : `Nat`, then the SMT-LIB hint (< $\hat{n}$ ($\hat{f}$ (- $\hat{n}$ $\hat{m}$))) would be translated to `Int.ofNat` n < `Int.ofNat` (f (`Int.ofNat` n − `Int.ofNat` m)`.natAbs`). This is more verbose than the seemingly more natural translation $n < f\,(n - m)$, but a faithful interpretation of cvc5's hints requires that all built-in mathematical operations occur on integers rather than naturals.[8]

---

[8] This is particularly relevant when subtraction is involved, as the semantics of subtraction on the naturals differs from the semantics of subtraction on the integers. For example, the SMT-LIB term (+ (- x y) y) always evaluates to x, but the Lean expression $(x - y) + y$ is equal to `Nat.max` $x\,y$ if x and y have type `Nat`.

Note that in the previous example, f is not supplied with the (possibly negative) result of subtracting `Int.ofNat` m from `Int.ofNat` n. Instead, f is supplied with the absolute value of said result. This coercion is needed to make the Lean expression typecheck, but one might reasonably question whether it compromises the faithfulness of the hint's interpretation. To answer this concern, we observe a subtle consequence of Theorem 1.

Corollary 1. *Let P be the SMT-LIB problem obtained by using* LEAN-AUTO *to translate a Lean goal, let f : `Nat` $\to \alpha$ be a Lean function in said goal, and let $\hat{f}$ be the the SMT-LIB translation of f in P. For any SMT-LIB formula F, if F is entailed by P, then $F[(\hat{f} \circ \mathtt{abs})/\hat{f}]$ is also entailed by P.*

Proof (sketch). From Theorem 1, wherever $(\hat{f}\ \mathtt{t})$ appears in the problem generated by LEAN-AUTO, the term `t` is well-formed. Therefore, any nontrivial assertions about the output of $\hat{f}$ which can be derived from the generated problem are conditioned on $\hat{f}$'s input being nonnegative. Since the output of $\hat{f}$ on negative inputs is unconstrained, any derivable fact about $\hat{f}$ also applies to all functions which agree with $\hat{f}$ on nonnegative inputs. $\hat{f} \circ \mathtt{abs}$ agrees with $\hat{f}$ on nonnegative inputs, so any fact that can be derived about $\hat{f}$ also applies to $\hat{f} \circ \mathtt{abs}$.

Non-surjectivity. There are two ways SMT-LIB terms without direct Lean equivalents may appear in `cvc5`'s hints. First, during the course of `cvc5`'s proof search, `cvc5` may apply Skolemization rules to generate constants which lack direct analogues among the expressions that appear in the input goal. This issue is mitigated by the preprocessing discussed in Section 3.

The second way SMT-LIB terms without direct Lean equivalents may appear in `cvc5`'s hints relates to the translation of inductive datatypes. In Lean, a constructor's arguments can be accessed via pattern matching or by invoking a recursor that every inductive type is automatically equipped with. But in SMT-LIB, constructors' arguments are accessed via selector functions whose symbols are given as part of the datatype's declaration. In the special case that the inductive datatype being translated is also a structure, these selector functions can be identified with the projection functions that come with all Lean structures. But when the inductive datatype being translated is not a structure, there is no guarantee that Lean has ready-made analogues for SMT-LIB's selector functions.

In order to interpret hints which refer to selector functions, QUERYSMT adds fresh functions to the local context along with proofs that they satisfy the property that characterizes SMT-LIB's selector functions. The functions themselves are constructed from the inductive datatype's recursor, and the proofs they are paired with assert that if the function is passed the correct constructor, then the resulting application returns the appropriate argument of said constructor.

Figure 4 provides an example showcasing the construction on a goal with lists. When given the wrong constructor, the function returns `default`, an arbitrary element of the appropriate type which is only accessible if said type is `Inhabited`. If typeclass inference cannot prove that the type is `Inhabited`, then it instead uses `sorry`, leaving the proof of type inhabitation as a subgoal for the user.

```
example {α : Type} [Inhabited α] (x y : α) : [x] = [y] ↔ x = y := by
  apply @Classical.byContradiction
  intro negGoal
  obtain ⟨_List.cons_sel0, _List.cons_sel0Fact⟩ :
    ∃ (_List.cons_sel0 : List α → α),
      ∀ (arg0 : α) (arg1 : List α),
        _List.cons_sel0 (arg0 :: arg1) = arg0 := by
    apply
      Exists.intro (List.rec (motive := fun (_ : List α) => α)
        default fun (arg0 : α) (arg1 : List α) (_ : α) => arg0)
    intros
    rfl
  duper [negGoal, _List.cons_sel0Fact] []
```

Fig. 4. A proof script suggested by QUERYSMT showcasing how Lean analogues for SMT-LIB's selector functions are constructed. Only one of the selector functions for lists is reproduced in the proof script because the other selector function (which retrieves the tail of a nonempty list) is not needed for the proof DUPER finds.

7   Proof Reconstruction

The primary goal of QUERYSMT's proof reconstruction is not to produce a complete proof term for the given goal. Instead, the goal of QUERYSMT's proof reconstruction is to suggest a self-contained proof script for the user to examine and potentially modify. All proof scripts suggested by QUERYSMT consist of:

1. A tactic sequence designed to reproduce the effects of QUERYSMT's preprocessing and Skolemization, described in Section 3.
2. A sequence of **obtain** statements which create functions satisfying the properties of SMT-LIB's selectors. The construction of these functions is described in Section 6.
3. A sequence of **have** statements which assert hints output by **cvc5**. These **have** statements are proven with GRIND, a built-in Lean tactic.
4. A final call to DUPER [15], a superposition theorem prover intended to reconstruct the logical component of **cvc5**'s top-level proof.

To minimize the suggested proof script, some sections are omitted if deemed unnecessary. As mentioned in Section 3, **skolemizeAll** is only added to the suggested proof script if Skolemization will change the goal. Additionally, the sequence of **obtain** and **have** statements from steps 2 and 3 are minimized by only including those that are necessary for the proof DUPER finds in step 4.

QUERYSMT's ability to perform this minimization, and therefore suggest a usable proof script, depends on DUPER successfully finding a proof. Although DUPER has been shown to be effective in solving problems previously minimized by other superposition theorem provers [15], its performance degrades significantly when given too many unnecessary or irrelevant premises, and it lacks the theory-specific knowledge leveraged by SMT solvers.

To increase DUPER's effectiveness in reconstructing the logical component of cvc5's proofs, we augment its given clause procedure to implement a variant of the set of support strategy used by Vampire [30]. This set of support strategy is designed to enable reasoning about theory axioms while mitigating the negative impact of their explosive properties. Facts that are included in DUPER's set of support are treated normally, but facts that are excluded from DUPER's set of support are only considered when they can be applied to facts in the set of support. The core idea is to limit theory axioms' explosive behavior by only applying them to facts that directly relate to the original goal.

We initially implemented this set of support strategy to exclude cvc5's hints from the set of support, thinking that cvc5's hints might behave similarly to more general theory axioms. However, experiments described in Appendix B of the extended version of this paper revealed that this was actually detrimental to performance [14]. Instead, the set of support strategy is used to exclude a small set of theory lemmas detailing properties of integers and natural numbers that cvc5's hints aren't expected to capture [14, Appendix C].

8   Evaluation

We evaluate QUERYSMT and existing tools on 9,904 theorems related to integers, natural numbers, and lists taken from Lean's Init, Batteries, and Mathlib [16] libraries. Our evaluation focuses on these domains in particular, rather than randomly selected theorems, because we specifically seek to evaluate whether QUERYSMT benefits from cvc5's domain-specific knowledge. Int theorems are chosen to test QUERYSMT's ability to benefit from hints related to SMT-LIB's LIA logic. Nat theorems are chosen to test whether QUERYSMT can make use of these hints even when it requires encoding Nat goals into Int problems and inferring facts about natural numbers from hints about integers. List theorems are chosen as a proxy for testing QUERYSMT's ability to make use of SMT solvers' built-in support for reasoning about algebraic datatypes.

8.1   Methodology

We perform all experiments on version `leanprover/lean4:v4.22.0` of Lean. The 9,904 theorems used as benchmark problems are obtained by scraping user-defined theorems from `Init.Data.X`, `Batteries.Data.X`, and `Mathlib.Data.X`, where `X` is any file prefixed with `Int`, `Nat`, or `List`. A constant is considered a user-defined theorem if it is marked as a theorem, has an explicit declaration in source code, and is not a projection function. All experiments are performed on an Amazon EC2 `ami-04f167a56786e4b09` instance with 4 virtual CPUs and 16 GiB memory. Each theorem is given a wall clock timeout of 30 seconds and the default Lean heartbeat limit of 200,000. The short timeout is used to reflect the expectation of proof assistant users of having quick results from tactics.

For premise selection, we approximate an ideal premise selector by inspecting the existing proofs of the benchmark theorems and extracting the set of premises

$\mathcal{P}$ used to prove them. We also gather the set of constants $\mathcal{C}$ that are not theorems which appear in `rw` or `simp` calls of tactic proofs. These constants are used to indicate to the relevant automation that said constant should be unfolded, enabling the automation to invoke definitional equalities not otherwise captured by $\mathcal{P}$. Both QUERYSMT and the tools we compare with benefit from receiving these constants, so in the experiments, all tools are given $\mathcal{P} \cup \mathcal{C}$ as input.

Our testing script implements the following procedure:

1. Identify the (theorem, tool) pair to be tested.
2. Create a temporary Lean file which imports the benchmark theorem's original file as well as any files needed to run the tool being evaluated.
3. In the temporary Lean file, define `alias fakeThm := originalThm`.
4. Compile the temporary Lean file and extract the `ConstantInfo` associated with `fakeThm` along with the environment immediately prior to executing the `alias` command.
5. In the environment extracted from the previous step, create a fresh metavariable whose type is determined by the extracted `ConstantInfo` and attempt to instantiate this metavariable with the tool being tested.[9]

We note that the environment in which the tools are run does not perfectly match the original proof's environment. It is infeasible to exactly mimic this environment because among the tools being evaluated, only GRIND (which is built into Lean and requires no special imports) would be callable. The differences between the original environments and the environments used in our experiments are largely benign, but in Section 8.2 we discuss one circumstance where the difference in environments is more impactful.

8.2   Results

Tool Comparison We compare QUERYSMT's performance against other tools available in Lean which either interface with external SMT solvers or implement techniques used by SMT solvers. Descriptions of these tools are included in Figure 5 and their respective performances are shown in Table 1.

In all categories, QUERYSMT performs noticeably better with SMT hints than without. On Int and Nat benchmarks, QUERYSMT only outperforms GRIND with these hints. The impact of hints on QUERYSMT's performance appears to be more significant on Int and Nat benchmarks than on List benchmarks, and not coincidentally, LEAN-AUTO + cvc5 solves a much smaller fraction of List theorems

---

[9] The tool is considered to have succeeded if the variable is instantiated, regardless of whether the instantiation contains `sorry`. When LEAN-AUTO + cvc5 is evaluated, the only proof it produces is `sorry` (indicating that cvc5 found a proof and LEAN-AUTO trusts the result). QUERYSMT also closes goals with `sorry` because QUERYSMT is meant to be replaced with the suggested proof script. Since QUERYSMT only suggests a proof script if DUPER finds a proof that follows from the hints, the suggested script is expected to succeed up to proof reconstruction for the individual hint assertions, for which we have a high success rate.

1. LEAN-AUTO + cvc5: A tactic which uses LEAN-AUTO to translate input problems into the SMT-LIB format and trusts any proofs produced by cvc5. This serves as a theoretical upper bound for both QUERYSMT and LEAN-SMT.
2. QUERYSMT: The default implementation of QUERYSMT. QUERYSMT is considered to succeed if DUPER finds a top level proof of the original goals assuming the hints given by cvc5. This does not necessarily entail that GRIND alone is sufficient to prove all the hints DUPER depends on. GRIND's success rate at proving the hints output by cvc5 is evaluated separately.
3. QUERYSMT−: A modified implementation of QUERYSMT in which DUPER is not provided the hints output by cvc5. QUERYSMT− retains the preprocessing described in Section 3 and still uses cvc5's unsat core to minimize the set of premises provided to DUPER, but does not translate cvc5's hints into Lean subgoals or pass the resulting assertions into DUPER.
4. LEAN-SMT: A tactic that interfaces with cvc5 and performs proof reconstruction via proof replay [24]. At the advice of one of its authors, LEAN-SMT is run with the + mono option which instructs LEAN-SMT to use LEAN-AUTO as a component of its preprocessing.
5. GRIND: A built-in Lean tactic inspired by modern SMT solvers. GRIND does not interface with external SMT solvers, but the inspiration for its underlying design and widespread use make it a helpful point of comparison.

Fig. 5. Descriptions of SMT-related methods

Table 1. Benchmark theorems solved by SMT-related methods

	Int Theorems	Nat Theorems	List Theorems
Total	2058	3270	4576
LEAN-AUTO + cvc5	1137	1486	891
QUERYSMT	840	892	749
QUERYSMT−	472	627	708
LEAN-SMT	333	35	445
GRIND	541	812	-

than Int or Nat theorems. From manual inspection of the theorems involved, we suspect that a significant factor contributing to this discrepancy is that in the List category, there is a significant overlap between the set of theorems for which built-in datatype reasoning would be helpful and the set of theorems for which induction is necessary. cvc5 is not able to solve problems requiring induction by default [31], or to produce proofs for it, so it cannot be used by QUERYSMT in this scenario. We therefore suspect that a smaller fraction of the List theorems being solved by LEAN-AUTO + cvc5 genuinely require theory reasoning.

On problems relating to Ints and Nats, QUERYSMT performs best, followed by GRIND, followed by LEAN-SMT. We note that GRIND has stricter conditions on its input lemmas than QUERYSMT or LEAN-SMT, and also that GRIND benefits from additional hints about how to use its input lemmas (in the form of custom attributes). It may be possible to achieve better performance with GRIND either by tailoring the set of provided premises to better suit GRIND or by manually providing additional hints about how to use the premises it receives.

LEAN-SMT's performance in both the Int and Nat categories is severely diminished by the fact that LEAN-SMT lacks special support for natural numbers. This says more about temporary limitations resulting from LEAN-SMT's current coverage than the theoretical limit of LEAN-SMT's approach. Still, we note that one of the benefits of our method is relative ease of extensionality. It requires much less effort to add support for parsing hints in a new theory than to add full-fledged proof replay for the same theory.

We omit GRIND's performance on List problems in Table 1 because it is significantly impacted by our evaluation methodology. When evaluating GRIND's performance on List problems with the same script used in the other experiments, GRIND succeeds at finding proofs for 1,458 problems. However, upon investigating why GRIND performs so much better than the other tools, we discovered that a nontrivial number of problems are solved by GRIND accessing lemmas it wouldn't have access to in the original environment. In particular, several theorems tagged with GRIND attributes yield benchmark problems that GRIND solves by invoking the original theorem. When we modify the evaluation script to test GRIND in the original theorem's proof environment[10], GRIND only solves 439 problems. The interpretation of these results depends on whether one views the theorems tagged with GRIND attributes as part of GRIND's implementation.

Hint Evaluation As noted in Figure 5, QUERYSMT's success criteria depends on DUPER deriving a proof of the original goal from the hints output by cvc5, but does not depend on GRIND succeeding at proving all of the subgoals generated by assuming these hints. If QUERYSMT finds a proof and successfully outputs a proof script in which GRIND fails to prove one or more of the generated hints, QUERYSMT has still done something valuable in reducing the original goal to a smaller subgoal. Still, QUERYSMT's usefulness is significantly impacted by the frequency with which cvc5's hints can be proven automatically, so we perform an additional evaluation to test how frequently cvc5 produces hints that GRIND can't solve. This evaluation includes not just hints that appear in QUERYSMT's suggestions, but all hints output by cvc5 regardless of whether DUPER succeeds in its proof search, and regardless of whether they would actually appear in the final proof script suggestion.

Of the 9,904 problems tested, 499 produce a set of hints that GRIND fails to certify, approximately 5% of the total. 57 of these failures come from Int problems, 168 of these failures come from Nat problems, and 274 of these failures come from List problems. From manual inspection, we know that many of these failures are false negatives owed to cvc5 producing large sets of hints that can be solved individually by GRIND but collectively cause GRIND to time out[11]. We still register such cases as failures because it is difficult to distinguish this behavior

---

[10] Note that this test is only feasible because GRIND is built into Lean and is therefore accessible in the original proof environment.

[11] As in other experiments, GRIND gets 200,000 heartbeats and 30 seconds per theorem.

from tests in which GRIND genuinely times out on a single hint. Not all failures are false negatives, but anecdotally, the hints GRIND genuinely fails on tend to be easy to discharge manually using some combination of AESOP [21] and DUPER.

We also measure the number of hints generated for problems where QUERYSMT succeeds in suggesting a proof script. Proof scripts with many hints are harder to read, modify, and maintain than proof scripts with just a few hints, so it is preferred for QUERYSMT to include as few hints as possible in the final suggestion.

The average number of hints cvc5 generates on Int, Nat, and List problems that QUERYSMT solves is 3.1, 4.6, and 4.6 respectively. After filtering out hints that are not needed for the final proof, QUERYSMT's final suggestion only includes 0.8, 0.7, and 0.2 hints on average for Int, Nat, and List problems respectively. These averages are brought down by the problems that DUPER can solve without any hints, but even after filtering out all problems in which QUERYSMT produces 0 hints, the average number of hints produced is only 1.5, 1.7, and 1.2 for Int, Nat, and List problems respectively. This does not mitigate all readability concerns, as individual hints can still be unnecessarily verbose, but it does show that QUERYSMT tends to produce suggestions of manageable size.

9   Conclusion

We explored a new hint-based approach to leveraging SMT solvers for ITP automation. We implemented this approach in the Lean proof assistant to create QUERYSMT, a tactic that translates Lean goals to SMT-LIB, extracts the preprocessing and theory reasoning used by cvc5 to solve the translated problem, and uses that information to produce a self-contained proof script for the original goal which does not depend on cvc5. We evaluated QUERYSMT on problems related to its supported theories, showing that QUERYSMT compares favorably to existing SMT-related Lean automation and that the hints extracted from cvc5 produce a clear improvement in the underlying proof automation.

We see several possible directions for future work. One possibility is to implement our approach in other proof assistants or SMT solvers to see whether it can be applied to more than just Lean and cvc5. Another is to add support for more SMT theories to see how our approach generalizes beyond hints relating to integers and algebraic datatypes. A third possibility is to explore ways to gather even more information from cvc5's proofs. For example, collecting instances generated for quantified formulas could lead to DUPER finding proofs more quickly, as was recently done for METIS in Isabelle's Sledgehammer [8]. We also expect that QUERYSMT's reconstruction success rate could be increased with better instrumentation for tracking how cvc5 normalizes AC operators.

Acknowledgements We thank Hanna Lachnitt for discussing the translation described in Section 4.2 and for bringing the Trakt paper [11] to our attention. We also thank the anonymous reviewers for their feedback on this paper. This work was partially supported by funding from AFRL and DARPA under Agreements FA8750-24-9-1000 and FA8750-24-2-1001.

Data-Availability Statement The source code for QUERYSMT is available at `https://github.com/JOSHCLUNE/QuerySMT`. An artifact with the code necessary to replicate our experiments is available at `https://zenodo.org/records/18190143`.

References

1. Armand, M., Faure, G., Grégoire, B., Keller, C., Théry, L., Werner, B.: A Modular Integration of SAT/SMT Solvers to Coq through Proof Witnesses, p. 135–150. Springer Berlin Heidelberg (2011). `https://doi.org/10.1007/978-3-642-25379-9_12`
2. Avigad, J., de Moura, L., Kong, S., Ullrich, S.: Theorem proving in Lean 4, `https://leanprover.github.io/theorem_proving_in_lean4/`
3. Barbosa, H., Barrett, C.W., Brain, M., Kremer, G., Lachnitt, H., Mann, M., Mohamed, A., Mohamed, M., Niemetz, A., Nötzli, A., Ozdemir, A., Preiner, M., Reynolds, A., Sheng, Y., Tinelli, C., Zohar, Y.: cvc5: A versatile and industrial-strength SMT solver. In: Fisman, D., Rosu, G. (eds.) Tools and Algorithms for Construction and Analysis of Systems (TACAS), Part I. Lecture Notes in Computer Science, vol. 13243, pp. 415–442. Springer (2022). `https://doi.org/10.1007/978-3-030-99524-9_24`, `https://doi.org/10.1007/978-3-030-99524-9_24`
4. Barbosa, H., Reynolds, A., Kremer, G., Lachnitt, H., Niemetz, A., Nötzli, A., Ozdemir, A., Preiner, M., Viswanathan, A., Viteri, S., Zohar, Y., Tinelli, C., Barrett, C.W.: Flexible proof production in an industrial-strength SMT solver. In: Blanchette, J., Kovács, L., Pattinson, D. (eds.) International Joint Conference on Automated Reasoning (IJCAR). Lecture Notes in Computer Science, vol. 13385, pp. 15–35. Springer (2022). `https://doi.org/10.1007/978-3-031-10769-6_3`, `https://doi.org/10.1007/978-3-031-10769-6_3`
5. Barrett, C., Fontaine, P., Tinelli, C.: The SMT-LIB Standard: Version 2.6. Tech. rep., Department of Computer Science, The University of Iowa (2017), available at `www.SMT-LIB.org`
6. Barrett, C., Fontaine, P., Tinelli, C.: The SMT-LIB Standard: Version 2.7. Tech. rep., Department of Computer Science, The University of Iowa (2025), available at `www.SMT-LIB.org`
7. Barrett, C.W., Sebastiani, R., Seshia, S.A., Tinelli, C.: Satisfiability modulo theories. In: Biere, A., Heule, M., van Maaren, H., Walsh, T. (eds.) Handbook of Satisfiability - Second Edition, Frontiers in Artificial Intelligence and Applications, vol. 336, pp. 1267–1329. IOS Press (2021). `https://doi.org/10.3233/FAIA201017`, `https://doi.org/10.3233/FAIA201017`
8. Bartl, L., Blanchette, J., Nipkow, T.: Exploiting instantiations from paramodulation proofs in isabelle/hol. In: Barrett, C.W., Waldmann, U. (eds.) Proc. Conference on Automated Deduction (CADE). Lecture Notes in Computer Science, vol. 15943, pp. 573–593. Springer (2025). `https://doi.org/10.1007/978-3-031-99984-0_30`, `https://doi.org/10.1007/978-3-031-99984-0_30`
9. Blanchette, J.C., Böhme, S., Paulson, L.C.: Extending sledgehammer with SMT solvers. In: Bjørner, N.S., Sofronie-Stokkermans, V. (eds.) Automated Deduction - CADE-23 - 23rd International Conference on Automated Deduction, Wroclaw, Poland, July 31 - August 5, 2011. Proceedings. Lecture Notes in Computer Science, vol. 6803, pp. 116–130. Springer (2011). `https://doi.org/10.1007/978-3-642-22438-6_11`, `https://doi.org/10.1007/978-3-642-22438-6_11`

10. Blanchette, J.C., Kaliszyk, C., Paulson, L.C., Urban, J.: Hammering towards QED. J. Formalized Reasoning **9**(1), 101–148 (2016)
11. Blot, V., Cousineau, D., Crance, E., de Prisque, L.D., Keller, C., Mahboubi, A., Vial, P.: Compositional pre-processing for automated reasoning in dependent type theory. In: Proceedings of the 12th ACM SIGPLAN International Conference on Certified Programs and Proofs. p. 63–77. CPP '23, ACM (Jan 2023). `https://doi.org/10.1145/3573105.3575676`
12. Bouton, T., de Oliveira, D.C.B., Déharbe, D., Fontaine, P.: veriT: An Open, Trustable and Efficient SMT-Solver. In: Schmidt, R.A. (ed.) Proc. Conference on Automated Deduction (CADE). Lecture Notes in Computer Science, vol. 5663, pp. 151–156. Springer (2009). `https://doi.org/10.1007/978-3-642-02959-2_12`, `http://dx.doi.org/10.1007/978-3-642-02959-2_12`
13. Böving, H., Bhat, S., Cicolini, L., Keizer, A., Frenot, L., Mohamed, A., Stefanesco, L., Khan, H., Clune, J., Barrett, C., Grosser, T.: Interactive bitvector reasoning using verified bit-blasting. Proceedings of the ACM on Programming Languages **9**(OOPSLA2), 3259–3285 (Oct 2025). `https://doi.org/10.1145/3763167`, `http://dx.doi.org/10.1145/3763167`
14. Clune, J., Barbosa, H., Avigad, J.: Hint-based smt proof reconstruction (2026). `https://doi.org/10.48550/ARXIV.2601.14495`, `https://arxiv.org/abs/2601.14495`
15. Clune, J., Qian, Y., Bentkamp, A., Avigad, J.: Duper: A Proof-Producing Superposition Theorem Prover for Dependent Type Theory. In: Bertot, Y., Kutsia, T., Norrish, M. (eds.) Interactive Theorem Proving (ITP). vol. 309, pp. 10:1–10:20. Schloss Dagstuhl – Leibniz-Zentrum für Informatik, Dagstuhl, Germany (2024). `https://doi.org/10.4230/LIPIcs.ITP.2024.10`
16. mathlib Community, T.: The Lean mathematical library. In: Blanchette, J., Hritcu, C. (eds.) Proceedings of the 9th ACM SIGPLAN International Conference on Certified Programs and Proofs, CPP 2020, New Orleans, LA, USA, January 20-21, 2020. pp. 367–381. ACM (2020). `https://doi.org/10.1145/3372885.3373824`
17. Czajka, L., Kaliszyk, C.: Hammer for coq: Automation for dependent type theory. Journal of Automated Reasoning **61**(1–4), 423–453 (Feb 2018). `https://doi.org/10.1007/s10817-018-9458-4`
18. Hurd, J.: First-order proof tactics in higher-order logic theorem provers. In: Design and Application of Strategies/Tactics in Higher Order Logics (STRATA 2003). pp. 56–68 (2003), `http://www.gilith.com/papers`
19. Kovács, L., Voronkov, A.: First-order theorem proving and vampire. In: Sharygina, N., Veith, H. (eds.) Computer Aided Verification - 25th International Conference, CAV 2013, Saint Petersburg, Russia, July 13-19, 2013. Proceedings. Lecture Notes in Computer Science, vol. 8044, pp. 1–35. Springer (2013). `https://doi.org/10.1007/978-3-642-39799-8_1`
20. Lachnitt, H., Fleury, M., Barbosa, H., Jakpor, J., Andreotti, B., Reynolds, A., Schurr, H., Barrett, C.W., Tinelli, C.: Improving the SMT proof reconstruction pipeline in isabelle/hol. In: Forster, Y., Keller, C. (eds.) Interactive Theorem Proving (ITP). LIPIcs, vol. 352, pp. 26:1–26:22. Schloss Dagstuhl - Leibniz-Zentrum für Informatik (2025). `https://doi.org/10.4230/LIPICS.ITP.2025.26`, `https://doi.org/10.4230/LIPIcs.ITP.2025.26`
21. Limperg, J., From, A.H.: Aesop: White-box best-first proof search for lean. In: Krebbers, R., Traytel, D., Pientka, B., Zdancewic, S. (eds.) Proceedings of the 12th ACM SIGPLAN International Conference on Certified Programs and Proofs, CPP 2023, Boston, MA, USA, January 16-17, 2023. pp. 253–266. ACM (2023). `https://doi.org/10.1145/3573105.3575671`

22. Meng, J., Paulson, L.C.: Translating higher-order clauses to first-order clauses. J. Autom. Reason. **40**(1), 35–60 (2008). https://doi.org/10.1007/S10817-007-9085-Y

23. Meng, J., Paulson, L.C.: Lightweight relevance filtering for machine-generated resolution problems. J. Appl. Log. **7**(1), 41–57 (2009). https://doi.org/10.1016/J.JAL.2007.07.004

24. Mohamed, A., Mascarenhas, T., Khan, H., Barbosa, H., Reynolds, A., Qian, Y., Tinelli, C., Barrett, C.: lean-smt: An SMT Tactic for Discharging Proof Goals in Lean, p. 197–212. Springer Nature Switzerland (2025). https://doi.org/10.1007/978-3-031-98682-6_11, http://dx.doi.org/10.1007/978-3-031-98682-6_11

25. de Moura, L.M., Bjørner, N.: Z3: an efficient SMT solver. In: Ramakrishnan, C.R., Rehof, J. (eds.) Tools and Algorithms for Construction and Analysis of Systems (TACAS). Lecture Notes in Computer Science, vol. 4963, pp. 337–340. Springer (2008). https://doi.org/10.1007/978-3-540-78800-3_24, https://doi.org/10.1007/978-3-540-78800-3_24

26. Norman, C., Avigad, J.: Canonical for automated theorem proving in lean. In: Forster, Y., Keller, C. (eds.) 16th International Conference on Interactive Theorem Proving, ITP 2025, September 28 to October 1, 2025, Reykjavik, Iceland. LIPIcs, vol. 352, pp. 14:1–14:20. Schloss Dagstuhl - Leibniz-Zentrum für Informatik (2025). https://doi.org/10.4230/LIPICS.ITP.2025.14, https://doi.org/10.4230/LIPIcs.ITP.2025.14

27. Paulson, L.C., Blanchette, J.C.: Three years of experience with sledgehammer, a practical link between automatic and interactive theorem provers. In: Sutcliffe, G., Schulz, S., Ternovska, E. (eds.) The 8th International Workshop on the Implementation of Logics, IWIL 2010, Yogyakarta, Indonesia, October 9, 2011. EPiC Series in Computing, vol. 2, pp. 1–11. EasyChair (2010). https://doi.org/10.29007/36DT

28. Paulson, L.C., Susanto, K.W.: Source-level proof reconstruction for interactive theorem proving. In: Schneider, K., Brandt, J. (eds.) Theorem Proving in Higher Order Logics, 20th International Conference, TPHOLs 2007, Kaiserslautern, Germany, September 10-13, 2007, Proceedings. Lecture Notes in Computer Science, vol. 4732, pp. 232–245. Springer (2007). https://doi.org/10.1007/978-3-540-74591-4_18

29. Qian, Y., Clune, J., Barrett, C., Avigad, J.: Lean-Auto: An Interface Between Lean 4 and Automated Theorem Provers, p. 175–196. Springer Nature Switzerland (2025). https://doi.org/10.1007/978-3-031-98682-6_10

30. Reger, G., Suda, M.: Set of support for theory reasoning. In: Eiter, T., Sands, D., Sutcliffe, G., Voronkov, A. (eds.) IWIL Workshop and LPAR Short Presentations. Kalpa Publications in Computing, vol. 1, pp. 124–134. EasyChair (2017). https://doi.org/10.29007/ndjg, /publications/paper/4Sd

31. Reynolds, A., Kuncak, V.: Induction for smt solvers. In: D'Souza, D., Lal, A., Larsen, K. (eds.) Verification, Model Checking, and Abstract Interpretation, Lecture Notes in Computer Science, vol. 8931, pp. 80–98. Springer Berlin Heidelberg (2015). https://doi.org/10.1007/978-3-662-46081-8_5, http://dx.doi.org/10.1007/978-3-662-46081-8_5

32. Schurr, H., Fleury, M., Desharnais, M.: Reliable reconstruction of fine-grained proofs in a proof assistant. In: Platzer, A., Sutcliffe, G. (eds.) Proc. Conference on Automated Deduction (CADE). Lecture Notes in Computer Science, vol. 12699, pp. 450–467. Springer (2021). https://doi.org/10.1007/978-3-030-79876-5_26, https://doi.org/10.1007/978-3-030-79876-5_26

33. Vukmirović, P., Bentkamp, A., Blanchette, J., Cruanes, S., Nummelin, V., Tourret, S.: Making Higher-Order Superposition Work, p. 415–432. Springer International Publishing (2021). https://doi.org/10.1007/978-3-030-79876-5_24

34. Vukmirović, P., Blanchette, J., Schulz, S.: Extending a High-Performance Prover to Higher-Order Logic, p. 111–129. Springer Nature Switzerland (2023). `https://doi.org/10.1007/978-3-031-30820-8_10`, `http://dx.doi.org/10.1007/978-3-031-30820-8_10`
35. Zhou, Y., Bosamiya, J., Takashima, Y., Li, J., Heule, M., Parno, B.: Mariposa: Measuring SMT instability in automated program verification. In: Nadel, A., Rozier, K.Y. (eds.) Formal Methods In Computer-Aided Design (FMCAD). pp. 178–188. IEEE (2023). `https://doi.org/10.34727/2023/ISBN.978-3-85448-060-0_26`, `https://doi.org/10.34727/2023/isbn.978-3-85448-060-0_26`

Incremental Forward Reasoning for White-Box Proof Search

Xavier Généreux and Jannis Limperg

Ludwig-Maximilians-Universität München, Munich, Germany
{xavier.genereux,jannis.limperg}@lmu.de

Abstract Several proof assistants provide automation tactics based on tableau-style tree search, such as Isabelle's and Rocq's auto and Lean's Aesop. In this setting we consider *forward rules*, which apply a given theorem, say, $A \to B \to C$, to any goal containing hypotheses A and B, adding C as a new hypothesis. When treated naively, such rules are tried on every goal encountered during the search, leading to repeated unifications of premises A and B with the hypotheses of each goal. We present an approach to forward rules that avoids some of this repeated work by taking advantage of similarities between successive goals. For each goal, we cache partial applications of forward rules in a custom data structure that enables efficient updates. Our technique is compatible with any search strategy and most logics. It has been implemented in Aesop.

Keywords: Forward Reasoning · Forward Chaining · Tactics · Interactive Theorem Proving

1 Introduction

In many proof assistants, simple "white-box" proof automation tactics based on tableau-style tree search play a substantial role in practice: Isabelle's [ ] and Rocq's [ ] auto [ ], ACL2's 'waterfall' [,], various PVS [,] tactics, Lean's [ ] Aesop [ ], etc. These tactics operate on *goals* $\Gamma \vdash A$, where the *context* Γ is a list of hypotheses and A is the proposition to be proved. Faced with an initial goal, the tactics try various user-specified *rules*, which correspond to admissible inferences in the prover's logic. A successful rule reduces the current goal to zero or more subgoals, which are solved recursively until either a full proof is found or no rule applies to any open goal or the search times out. A typical rule is the $\wedge$-introduction lemma $A \to B \to A \wedge B$, which, when applied backwards, reduces a goal $\Gamma \vdash A \wedge B$ to subgoals $\Gamma \vdash A$ and $\Gamma \vdash B$.

In addition to such *backwards rules*, most search tactics can also use arbitrary tactics as rules. For example, Aesop uses the cases tactic on disjunctive hypotheses, splitting goals of the form $\Gamma, h : A \vee B \vdash C$ into subgoals $\Gamma, h : A \vdash C$ and $\Gamma, h : B \vdash C$. Tactics implement arbitrary inferences; in particular, they can remove any hypothesis and add any provable proposition as a new hypothesis.

ACL2, PVS and Aesop additionally provide special support for *forward reasoning*, also known as *forward chaining*, in the form of *forward rules*. Given, for

© The Author(s) 2026
S. Junges and G. Katz (Eds.): TACAS 2026, LNCS 16505, pp. 276–294, 2026.
https://doi.org/10.1007/978-3-032-22752-2_14

example, the transitivity lemma $\forall x\ y\ z,\ x < y \to y < z \to x < z$, a forward rule run on the goal $h_1 : a < b, h_2 : b < c \vdash A$ produces the single subgoal $h_1 : a < b, h_2 : b < c, h_3 : a < c \vdash A$. Hence, forward rules can be used to establish additional facts that may be relevant for other rules. For example, the Aeneas project [ ] uses a mechanism similar to Aesop's forward rules to establish facts that are later used by an arithmetic decision procedure.

Until recently, Aesop used what we call the *naive algorithm* to apply forward rules. When a forward rule was run on a goal, the rule would search the goal's context for all combinations of hypotheses satisfying its premises. This method is simple but involves much repeated work because in practice, contexts encountered during the search tend to be similar. For example, the $\wedge$-introduction rule, when run on $\Gamma \vdash A \wedge B$, produces subgoals $\Gamma \vdash A$ and $\Gamma \vdash B$, so the naive algorithm runs the same forward rules on the same context Γ three times. More generally, any backwards rule leaves the context unchanged, and many rules that alter the context do so only in limited ways.

In this paper, we present an alternative way to apply forward rules that addresses this issue. The central idea is to remember, for each goal $\Gamma \vdash A$, which forward rules can be partially applied to which sets of hypotheses. When a non-forward rule then generates subgoals $\Delta_1 \vdash A_1, \ldots, \Delta_n \vdash A_n$, the new contexts Δ_i are likely similar to Γ. Hence, it is generally cheaper (and often much cheaper) to start with the partial matches for Γ and update them for each of the Δ_i. The update first deletes partial matches that include hypotheses no longer present in Δ_i. Afterwards it adds new partial matches for the hypotheses that are new in Δ_i, extending the existing partial matches for a rule if the new hypothesis is compatible with them. Whenever this process produces a full match—i.e., all premises of a forward rule are satisfied by a set of hypothesis in Δ_i—the rule is applied and adds a corresponding new hypothesis to Δ_i.

Our main contribution is a data structure, the *forward state*, that organises the partial matches so that updates can be done efficiently. In addition to this *incrementality*, the forward state satisfies two other desiderata:

- It is *persistent*, i.e. forward states for parent and child goals share much of their structure. This is desirable since Aesop supports search strategies other than depth-first search and must therefore keep all goals encountered during the search, along with their forward states, in memory.
- It reduces the number of *unifications* performed when matching hypotheses against rule premises. In dependent type theory, unification happens up to definitional equality, which makes it expensive. We therefore want to avoid redundant unifications.

Our evaluation (Sec. 6) shows that this new implementation of forward reasoning in Aesop substantially outperforms the previous, naive implementation on synthetic benchmarks involving heavy use of forward rules. On a natural benchmark involving primarily light use of forward rules, we still obtain modest speedups. Both implementations are available in recent versions of Aesop; benchmarks and evaluation data are available in the artifact.

2   Preliminaries

We first introduce some terminology for matches and for forward rules (which we identify with their underlying lemmas). We use dependent type theory as a foundation, but our technique generalises to other logics.

Given a lemma $\forall (x_1 : A_1) \ldots (x_n : A_n),\ B$, the x_i are *premises* and B is the lemma's *conclusion*. The type A_i of the ith premise may depend on (i.e., refer to) any premise x_j with $j < i$. Implication $A \to B$ is an abbreviation for $\forall x : A,\ B$ where B does not depend on x. Propositions are (certain) types, and we do not distinguish between the two concepts.

Using somewhat non-standard terminology, we call premises on which a later premise depends *variables*. These are usually terms of non-propositional types, e.g. natural numbers or lists. The non-variable premises, whose types are typically propositions, are called *slots*. For example, the lemma $\forall (x\ y\ z : \mathbb{N}),\ x < y \to y < z \to x < z$ has variables x, y, z and slots of types $x < y$ and $y < z$. If more than two premises depend on a variable (e.g. y), the variable is *shared*. Note that premises on which only the conclusion depends are not considered variables.

If a lemma has n slots, each slot is assigned a unique number between 1 and n, and we identify slots with their numbers. For now, we assume that the slots are numbered consecutively, so in the example above slot 1 has type $x < y$ and slot 2 has type $y < z$. The *shared variables of slot i*, svars(i), are those variables that appear in the type of i and also in at least one type of a slot $j < i$.

If $h : C$ is a hypothesis and C matches the type A of slot i, we say that *h matches i*. Matching induces a substitution σ such that $A[\sigma]$ is definitionally equal to C; we define sub$_i(h) := \sigma$. What 'matching' means is explained in Sec. 5.

A *match m* for a given rule r with n slots is a list containing between one and n hypotheses. We interpret m as a partial map from slots of r to hypotheses, so $\mathrm{dom}(m) = \{i \mid 1 \le i \le |m|\}$ and for each slot $i \in \mathrm{dom}(m)$, $m(i)$ is the hypothesis assigned to i. A match m must additionally satisfy the following requirements:

1. For each slot $i \in \mathrm{dom}(m)$, the hypothesis $m(i)$ matches i.
2. For all slots $i, j \in \mathrm{dom}(m)$, the substitutions sub$_i(m(i))$ and sub$_j(m(j))$ are *compatible*. This means that the substitutions agree on all common variables, i.e. for each variable $x \in \mathrm{dom}(\mathrm{sub}_i(m(i))) \cap \mathrm{dom}(\mathrm{sub}_j(m(j)))$ we have $\mathrm{sub}_i(m(i))(x) = \mathrm{sub}_j(m(j))(x)$.

The *substitution of a match m*, sub(m), is the union of the substitutions induced by the hypotheses in m, i.e. $\mathrm{sub}(m) := \bigcup_{i \in \mathrm{dom}(m)} \mathrm{sub}_i(m(i))$. This is well-defined by requirement 2. The *level of a match m*, lvl(m), is the length of m. A match for rule r is *complete* if $i \in \mathrm{dom}(m)$ for every slot i of r, and *partial* otherwise.

A partial match m for rule r corresponds to a partial application of the rule to the terms given in sub(m). The application is type-correct by requirements 1 and 2. If m is complete, then sub(m) contains a term for every slot and every variable—hence for every premise—of r, and we have a full application.

Note that matches represent only those partial applications where arguments are added without gaps. Hence, for a rule $r : A \to B \to C$, the applications

$r\ a\ \_\ : B \to C$ and $r\ a\ b : C$ for some $a : A$ and $b : B$ correspond to matches, but not $r\ \_\ b : A \to C$. This prevents us from constructing $r\ a\ b$ in two different but ultimately redundant ways.

3   Naive Forward Reasoning

Before this work, Aesop used what we call *naive forward reasoning* [ ]. This approach treats forward rules like any other Aesop rule. Hence, when Aesop selects a forward rule r with n slots of types $A_1, \ldots, A_n$ as the highest-priority rule currently applicable to a goal $\Gamma \vdash T$, we look for all complete matches for r in Γ, using an approach reminiscent of backtracking subsumption algorithms.

More specifically, we first match the type of the last slot, A_n, with each hypothesis $h : B$ (using an imperfect discrimination tree [ ] index to quickly determine potentially matching hypotheses). If successful, this results in a substitution σ_1 containing all variables that occur in A_n. We then match $A_{n-1}[\sigma_1]$ against the type of each hypothesis in the context, yielding a substitution σ_2, and proceed with $A_{n-2}[\sigma_2]$, etc., until we obtain a complete match for r. If a premise $A_{n-i}[\sigma_i]$ does not match any hypothesis type, we backtrack and consider other potential matching hypotheses for A_{n-i+1}. These may lead to a different substitution τ and therefore to different matching hypotheses for $A_{n-i}[\tau]$. For each complete match m with substitution σ found during this process, we add a new hypothesis of type $C[\sigma]$, where C is the conclusion of r.

This approach is efficient when the last slot of a rule does not match any hypothesis in the context since the rule is then usually excluded by indexing and never run. Otherwise, we match large numbers of premises and hypotheses against each other, though this process could likely be sped up heuristically [ ]. Moreover, the whole process is repeated when we proceed to another goal with a similar context. In particular, the contexts of subgoals produced by whatever rule is eventually applied to the current goal are likely to be similar to the current context, but the naive algorithm does not exploit these similarities.

4   Incremental Forward Reasoning

With the weaknesses of the naive approach in mind, we introduce an incremental, stateful solution to the problem of finding complete matches. The main idea is to store, for each goal $\Gamma \vdash A$, the partial matches implied by the hypotheses in Γ, and to reuse these partial matches for subgoals $\Delta \vdash B$. This rests on the assumption that Δ is likely similar to Γ in practice, and that it is therefore cheaper to update the partial matches for Γ than to compute those of Δ from scratch. Our main contribution is a data structure, the *forward state*, that allows us to perform these updates efficiently.

Forward States. We associate with each goal in Aesop's search tree a forward state that reflects the goal's context. Let $\mathcal{S}$ be the set of forward states, $\mathcal{H}$ the set of hypotheses, $\mathcal{R}$ the set of rules, $\mathcal{C}$ the set of complete matches and $\mathcal{P}(X)$ the powerset of X. The forward state's interface then consists of two functions

$$\text{addHyp} : \mathcal{S} \to \mathcal{H} \to \mathcal{S} \times \mathcal{P}(\mathcal{R} \times \mathcal{C}) \qquad \text{delHyp} : \mathcal{S} \to \mathcal{H} \to \mathcal{S}$$

The addHyp function adds a hypothesis to the forward state. Hence, if s is the forward state corresponding to context Γ and $\text{addHyp}(s, h : T) = (s', C)$, then s' is the forward state corresponding to $\Gamma, h : T$. Similarly, if s is the forward state corresponding to $\Gamma, h : T$, then $\text{delHyp}(s, h : T)$ is the forward state corresponding to Γ. The second output of addHyp, C, is a set of pairs (r, m) where r is a rule and m is a complete match for r. These are the matches that were completed by adding $h : T$.

When Aesop is run on an initial goal with context $h_1 : T_1, \ldots, h_n : T_n$, the forward state for it is built by starting with an empty state and applying addHyp to each hypothesis h_i. Afterwards, whenever an Aesop rule is run on a goal with context Γ, producing subgoals with contexts $\Delta_1, \ldots, \Delta_n$, we derive the forward state for each subgoal context Δ_j from the forward state for Γ, in two steps:

1. Apply delHyp once for each hypothesis that was deleted, i.e. that appears in Γ but not in Δ_j.
2. Apply addHyp once for each hypothesis that was added, i.e. that appears in Δ_j but not in Γ.

Changes to a hypothesis (e.g. a change of its type) are treated as a deletion followed by an addition.

Rule States. Partial matches are specific to each rule, so the forward state naturally decomposes into a set of *rule states*, one per rule. Given a goal $\Gamma \vdash A$ and a rule r, the rule state for r contains exactly the partial matches of r in context Γ. A rule state supports addHyp and delHyp methods analogous to those on forward states. Adding a hypothesis to a forward state then amounts to adding it to each rule state (which may yield new complete matches for the rule); deleting a hypothesis amounts to deleting it from each rule state. We initially focus on how to add hypotheses, since this question motivates much of the design of the rule state data structure.

When a hypothesis is added to a rule state, two things can happen. First, the hypothesis may allow us to extend partial matches already present in the state. For instance, consider the rule $r : \forall x,\ P\,x \to Q\,x \to R\,x \to S\,x$ and a rule state containing the partial match $[h_1]$, which assigns some hypothesis $h_1 : P\,a$ to the first slot of type $P\,x$. Adding a new hypothesis $h_2 : Q\,a$ to this rule state means that we should add to the state the extended match $[h_1, h_2]$.

Second, adding a match may trigger the insertion of further matches. Suppose that before adding h_1 and h_2, we had already added a hypothesis $h_0 : R\,a$ to the rule state. Once the partial match $[h_1, h_2]$ arrives, we should recognise that it can be extended with h_0 to obtain the (complete) match $[h_1, h_2, h_0]$.

Variable Indices. Extending the matches above was possible only because all hypotheses are compatible on the shared variable x, i.e. they all instantiate x with the same term a. In general, to extend a match m with a hypothesis $h : T$ at slot i, we need to ensure that the substitution of m, $\mathrm{sub}(m)$, is compatible with the substitution of h, $\mathrm{sub}_i(h)$.

The rule state therefore uses two *variable indices* H and M to index hypotheses and matches by their instantiations for shared variables, allowing us to quickly determine compatible pairs of matches and hypotheses. We could use a substitution tree [ ], but our custom data structure is simpler. The *hypothesis index* H maps each triple (x, i, t) (where $i > 1$ is a slot, $x \in \mathrm{svars}(i)$ a variable and t a term) to a set containing hypotheses h added to the rule state such that h matches i and $\mathrm{sub}_i(h)(x) = t$. In other words, H indexes the known hypotheses by the slots they match and the instantiations of shared variables. Note that hypotheses matching slot 1 are not stored since they can never extend a match.

Similarly, the *match index* M maps each triple (x, i, t) to a set containing partial matches m (that can be derived from the hypotheses added to the rule state) such that $i = \mathrm{lvl}(m)$, $x \in \mathrm{svars}(i + 1)$ and $\mathrm{sub}(m)(x) = t$. Matches for the maximal slot are not stored because, being complete, they never need to be extended. We write $M_x(i, t)$ instead of $M(x, i, t)$ and $H_x(i, t)$ instead of $H(x, i, t)$.

Given a hypothesis $h : T$ that matches slot $i > 1$ with substitution $\sigma = \mathrm{sub}_i(h)$, the partial matches that can be extended by h are those at level $i - 1$ whose substitutions are compatible with σ on the variables $\mathrm{svars}(i)$ (i.e., the variables shared between i and any earlier slot). Assuming for the moment that $\mathrm{svars}(i)$ is non-empty for all slots $i > 1$, these matches are

$$\bigcap_{x \in \mathrm{svars}(i)} M_x(i - 1, \sigma(x))$$

Similarly, given a partial match m at level i with substitution $\sigma = \mathrm{sub}(m)$, the hypotheses that could extend m are

$$\bigcap_{x \in \mathrm{svars}(i+1)} H_x(i + 1, \sigma(x))$$

The number of shared variables tends to be small in practice, so these intersections can be computed efficiently.

From here we can directly derive two procedures for adding hypotheses and matches to the rule state. The procedures maintain the invariants of the variable indices while reporting any complete matches discovered during this process. Specifically, if a rule state for a rule r corresponds to the context Γ—i.e., it contains the hypotheses of Γ and all partial matches of r that can be derived from them—then the rule state obtained from $\mathrm{addHyp}(h : T)$ corresponds to $\Gamma, h : T$.

The rule state's addHyp method (Algorithm 1) adds a hypothesis $h : T$ matching slot i to the rule state. (If a hypothesis matches multiple slots, addHyp is called multiple times.) For $i = 1$, we add the singleton match $[h]$ to the rule state. For $i > 1$, we first insert h into the hypothesis index H. Then we query

Input   : A hypothesis $h : T$
Output : All complete matches of r in context Γ, $h : T$ that contain h
Procedure addHyp($h : T$)
    $completeMs \leftarrow \emptyset$
    for *all slots i of r such that h matches i* **do**
        if $i = 1$ **then**
            $completeMs \leftarrow completeMs \cup$ addMatch($[h]$)
        else
            let $\sigma := \mathrm{sub}_i(h)$
            for x **in** svars(i) **do**
                Insert h into the set $H_x(i, \sigma(x))$
            let $ms := \bigcap_{x \in \mathrm{svars}(i)} M_x(i - 1, \sigma(x))$
            for m **in** ms **do**
                $completeMs \leftarrow completeMs \cup$ addMatch($m \mathbin{++} [h]$)
    return $completeMs$

Algorithm 1: Add a hypothesis to the rule state for a rule r and context Γ

the match index M for matches that can be extended by h and add the extended matches to the rule state. While adding matches, we may discover new complete matches, which are collected and returned.

Input   : A partial match m of r at level i with substitution σ
Output : A set of complete matches of r
Procedure addMatch(m)
    if *m is complete* **then**
        return $\{m\}$
    else
        let $\sigma := \mathrm{sub}(m)$
        for x **in** svars($i + 1$) **do**
            Insert m into the set $M_x(i, \sigma(x))$
        let $hs := \bigcap_{x \in \mathrm{svars}(i+1)} H_x(i + 1, \sigma(x))$
        $completeMs \leftarrow \emptyset$
        for h **in** hs **do**
            $completeMs \leftarrow completeMs \cup$ addMatch($m \mathbin{++} [h]$)
        return $completeMs$

Algorithm 2: Add a match to the rule state for a rule r

The rule state's addMatch method (Algorithm 2) adds a match m with level $i = \mathrm{lvl}(m)$ to the rule state. If m is already complete, it is returned. Otherwise, m is inserted into M and we query H for hypotheses that can extend m. Any extended matches thus produced are added to the rule state recursively.

Variable Clusters. We have so far only considered rules where for each slot $i > 1$, the set of shared variables svars(i) is non-empty, i.e. each slot shares at least one variable with at least one of the previous slots. However, there are also rules such as $\forall x\, y,\ P\, x \to Q\, y \to R\, x\, y$, where slot 2 ($Q\, y$) shares no variables with slot 1 ($P\, x$). In this case, any match at level 1 can be extended with any hypothesis at level 2, since the two slots are independent.

To account for this fact, we partition the set of premises of each rule into maximal subsets of premises connected by shared variables, called *variable clusters*, using the same construction as Aesop's *metavariable clusters* [ ]. The variable clusters share no variables with each other, so each can be treated as a separate rule with its own rule state. Finding a complete match for a rule then amounts to finding one complete match for each of its clusters. The slots within each cluster can be ordered to ensure that each slot shares at least one variable with the previous slots.

Deletion. When a hypothesis h is removed from a goal's context, we must update the forward state accordingly. This means deleting h from any rule state to which it was previously added, i.e. from any rule state for a rule r with a slot i matching h. To facilitate deletion, we cache this information when h is added to the rule state. When h is deleted, we can then efficiently determine the relevant rule states and delete h from the hypothesis index H at slot i and from the match index M at all slots $j \geq i$.

Example 1. As a first example, consider a rule state for the transitivity rule $r_1 : \forall x\, y\, z,\ x \leq y \to y \leq z \to x \leq z$ to which we add, in order, the hypotheses $h_1 : b \leq c$ and $h_2 : a \leq b$. The rule has two slots of types $x \leq y$ and $y \leq z$ which share the variable y.

The hypothesis $h_1 : b \leq c$ unifies with both slots, so we execute the outer loop of Algorithm 1 twice. For slot 1, unification yields the substitution $\{x \mapsto b, y \mapsto c\}$. Since this is the first slot, Algorithm 2 inserts the new partial match $[h_1]$ into the set $M_y(1, c)$. This match cannot be extended since the hypothesis index H does not contain a hypothesis for slot 2.

For slot 2, unification yields the substitution $\sigma := \{y \mapsto b, z \mapsto c\}$, so we insert h_1 into $H_y(2, b)$. No matches at level 1 can be extended by h_1 since

$$\bigcap_{x \in \mathrm{svars}(2)} M_x(1, \sigma(x)) = M_y(1, b) = \emptyset$$

At this point, H and M are in state (1), shown below.

<pre>
                2   1   2   1
                | | / \   / \
(1)   H_y: b   M_y: c   (2) H_y: b   a   M_y: c   b
                | | | | | |
              {h_1}   {[h_1]}   {h_1} {h_2}   {[h_1]} {[h_2]}
</pre>

Now we add $h_2 : a \leq b$, which again unifies with both slots. For slot 1, $\mathrm{sub}_1(h_2)(y) = b$, so we add the match $[h_2]$ to $M_y(1, b)$. We then check for hypotheses in slot 2 that also instantiate y with b, and indeed we find $H_y(2, b) = \{h_1\}$.

Hence, we return the complete match $[h_2, h_1]$, which induces $h_3 : a \leq c$ to be added later. For slot 2, we add h_2 to $H_y(2, a)$. There are no compatible matches at level 1, so we are done with h_2, yielding the final rule state (2).

Example 2. We now consider a rule $r_2 : \forall x\ y,\ A\ x\ y \to B\ x\ y \to C\ x\ y$ with multiple shared variables. We add hypotheses $h_1 : B\ a\ a$, $h_2 : A\ a\ b$ and $h_3 : B\ a\ b$ to the rule state of r_2, starting with h_1, which is added to H with slot 2. There are no matches yet, so there is nothing to extend. We then add $h_2 : A\ a\ b$, which initially generates a match $m = [h_2]$ that is added to M, yielding the following rule state:

$$
\begin{array}{cccc}
\overset{2}{\underset{\{h_1\}}{H_x:\quad a}} &
\overset{2}{\underset{\{h_1\}}{H_y:\quad a}} &
\overset{1}{\underset{\{[h_2]\}}{M_x:\quad a}} &
\overset{1}{\underset{\{[h_2]\}}{M_y:\quad b}}
\end{array}
$$

To find hypotheses compatible with m, we consider the set of variables $\mathrm{svars}(\mathrm{lvl}(m) + 1)$. These are the variables shared between slot $\mathrm{lvl}(m) + 1 = 2$ and all previous slots, i.e. x and y. Hence, the compatible hypotheses are

$$
\bigcap_{x \in \mathrm{svars}(\mathrm{lvl}(m)+1)} H_x(\mathrm{lvl}(m) + 1, \mathrm{sub}(m)(x)) = H_x(2, a) \cap H_y(2, b) = \emptyset
$$

This means the match cannot currently be extended. We now turn to $h_3 : B\ a\ b$, adding it first to H. This yields the following rule state:

$$
\begin{array}{cccc}
\overset{2}{\underset{\{h_1, h_3\}}{H_x:\quad a}} &
\overset{2}{\underset{\{h_1\}\,\{h_3\}}{H_y:\quad a\quad b}} &
\overset{1}{\underset{\{[h_2]\}}{M_x:\quad a}} &
\overset{1}{\underset{\{[h_2]\}}{M_y:\quad b}}
\end{array}
$$

Since h_3 matches slot $i = 2$, the matches that can be extended by h_3 are

$$
\bigcap_{x \in \mathrm{svars}(i)} M_x(i - 1, \mathrm{sub}_i(x)) = M_x(1, a) \cap M_y(1, b) = \{[h_2]\}
$$

This produces the complete match $[h_2, h_3]$, so we can add a new hypothesis of type $C\ a\ b$.

5   Implementation

Implementing the preceding technique efficiently requires some care, particularly in the context of dependent type theory.

Matching. In type theory, types contain programs and matching (or, more generally, unification) is expected to respect definitional equality, i.e. equality up to evaluation. For instance, a theorem with premise $P\ 2$, where P is some predicate, should apply to a hypothesis of type $P\ ((\lambda x.\ x)\ 2)$ since the two types are definitionally equal. As a result, matching premises and hypotheses is arbitrarily expensive in theory and a major cost centre in practice. We therefore seek to avoid redundant invocations of the matching procedure.

To limit the cost of matching, we match with *reducible transparency*. Lean has multiple transparency levels that determine which constants are unfolded. 'Reducible' is the most restrictive of these, so we unfold few (and, in practice, only non-recursive) definitions. Additionally, we use Lean's usual approximation of higher-order matching, which is complete for first-order matching problems and heuristically solves some higher-order problems. Either of these limitations render forward reasoning incomplete, but since the same matching algorithm is used throughout Lean, users are used to this source of incompleteness.

Variable Index Implementation The hypothesis index H and the match index M of a rule state have the same domain and are combined into one map. This map, whose domain is a set of triples (x, i, t), is represented by three nested maps. The first two of these, whose keys are variable names x and slot indices i, are persistent hash maps. The third map, called the *instantiation map*, whose keys are instantiation expressions t, is implemented as a persistent array storing pairs (t, d), where t is the instantiation and d is the associated data.

Keys of the instantiation map are identified up to definitional equality at reducible transparency. This means that insertions and lookups involve one definitional equality check for each element of the map, which is fairly expensive. To reduce the number of such checks, we add an imperfect discrimination tree index that allows us to efficiently determine which keys of the map may match a given expression.

Match Equivalence. Naively, two matches would be considered equal if they contain the same hypotheses. However, consider the rule $r : \forall x\ y,\ P\ x\ y \rightarrow Q\ x\ z \rightarrow R\ x$ and the hypotheses $h_1 : P\ a\ b$, $h_2 : P\ a\ c$, $h_3 : Q\ a\ d$ and $h_4 : Q\ a\ e$. The complete matches $m_1 := [h_1, h_3]$ and $m_1' := [h_1, h_4]$ contain different hypotheses, but the difference does not matter because the applications $r\ h_1\ h_3$ and $r\ h_1\ h_4$ both have type $R\ a$. Generating both m_1 and m_1' would therefore be redundant. Similarly, the partial matches $m_2 := [h_1]$ and $m_2' := [h_2]$ are redundant because the choice between h_1 and h_2 affects neither the type of any eventual application derived from m_2 and m_2' nor the hypotheses that can be used to complete them. Hence, we should store only one of m_2 and m_2' in the rule state of r. Based on these observations, we consider two matches m and m' of a rule r equal if $\mathrm{lvl}(m) = \mathrm{lvl}(m')$ and for each premise x that appears either in the conclusion of r or in the type of a slot i of r with $i > \mathrm{lvl}(m)$ we have $\mathrm{sub}(m)(x) = \mathrm{sub}(m')(x)$.

Redundant Hypotheses. When we find a complete match, we add a new hypothesis of the corresponding type T to the goal, but only if there is no other hypothesis of type T already present. To determine this, we iterate through the hypotheses, comparing their types to T up to definitional equality. While this can be expensive, the local context is generally small and definitional equality comparisons are cached globally.

Beyond preventing redundant hypotheses, this check also allows us to simplify the implementation of match equality. When determining whether matches are redundant, we do not use definitional equality but compare expressions structurally (i.e., up to α-equivalence). As a result, we may fail to identify redundant matches, but these are detected once we check whether the hypotheses generated by them are already present.

Lazy Insertion. Adding a hypothesis to a rule state is cheap, but not free: it involves one unification for each slot that the hypothesis may match, according to a discrimination tree index, followed by several operations on the variable indices. We therefore delay insertions in two ways. First, we observe that complete matches can only be generated once all slots have been filled. Therefore, hypotheses are matched against slots and inserted into the variable indices only once we have found a potentially matching hypothesis for each slot. Second, we observe that the variable indices are only queried for hypotheses at a slot $i > 1$ when a match is added at slot $i - 1$. Hence, we delay the insertion of hypotheses at i until there is at least one match in slot $i - 1$.

Phased Insertion We delay insertions further by taking advantage of Aesop's partitioning of rules into several *phases*. When Aesop tries to solve a goal, it first normalises it, using only rules tagged with the *normalisation* phase. Then it tries to apply rules from the *safe* phase, and only when all of them fail does it consider rules from the *unsafe* phase.

This means that we can delay updates to the rule states of normalisation rules until we start working on the goal; updates to safe rules until normalisation is finished; and updates to unsafe rules until we have applied all the safe rules. Sometimes, this allows us to avoid expensive operations, e.g. when a goal is solved only by safe rules and no unsafe rules need to be considered at all. At other times, we can skip specific updates, for example when a hypothesis is added by a normalisation rule but then immediately removed by another normalisation rule. Phased insertion skips any updates to safe and unsafe rules resulting from the transient hypothesis.

To implement this optimisation, we split insertion into two operations. When a hypothesis is added, it is initially just enqueued in per-slot queues of rule states for which it may be relevant. (The same queues are also used to implement lazy insertion.) Then, once we need to determine which rules of a given phase apply to the goal, we move the hypotheses from the slot queues into the variable indices and construct matches, including, perhaps, complete matches that allow us to apply the rules.

6 Evaluation

There are unfortunately no standard benchmarks for Aesop-like tactics, and forward rules are currently little used by Aesop's main client, the Mathlib library [ ]. We therefore use two complementary evaluation schemes. First, we compare our technique against the previous, naive Aesop implementation on synthetic benchmarks that highlight its advantages and disadvantages. Second, we compare the two implementations on the benchmark used by lean-auto [ ], which runs Aesop on all human-written Mathlib theorems with simulated perfect premise selection. The results shown below were obtained on an m8g.metal-48xlarge AWS instance equipped with 192 Graviton4 processors and 768 GB of RAM.

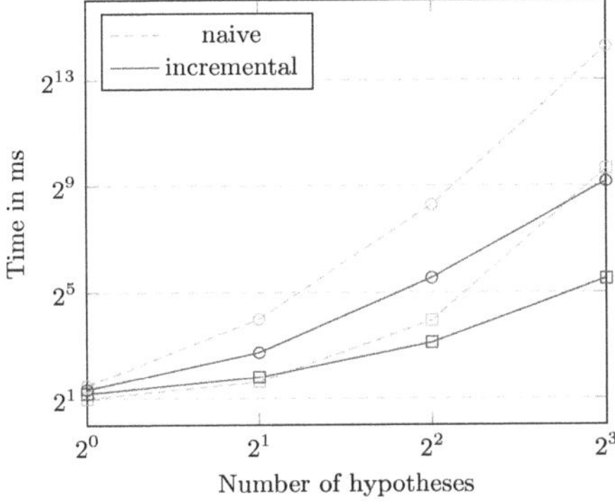

Figure 1: Transitivity benchmark for $a = 0$ ($\square$) and $a = 100$ ($\bigcirc$)

Synthetic Benchmarks. For each benchmark, we set up certain forward rules and a goal with hand-picked hypotheses. We then run the `saturate` tactic, which uses either naive or incremental forward reasoning to exhaustively apply the forward rules. Performing only forward reasoning is the best-case scenario for the incremental algorithm since previous results can be fully reused. When forward reasoning is combined with other rules, we would expect smaller gains, depending on how much reuse the non-forward rules allow.

Instead of the natural numbers from Lean's standard library, which are represented by arbitrary-precision integers, we use a custom type of Peano naturals for the benchmarks. Matching two concrete Peano natural numbers n and m involves comparing $\min(n, m)$ constructors. We can therefore use moderately large numbers to simulate the bigger matching problems that Aesop encounters, for example, in Mathlib's category theory development. All results are averaged over 10 runs per benchmark.

Transitivity Benchmark. Our first benchmark is a scaled-up variant of the transitivity example from Sec. 4. Given some relation $\prec$ on natural numbers, we register the lemma $\forall x\, y,\ x \prec y \to y \prec z \to x \prec z$ as the sole forward rule and set up a goal with hypotheses $h_1 : a \prec a+1, \ldots, h_n : a+n-1 \prec a+n$, where either $a = 0$ (yielding easy unification problems) or $a = 100$. Saturating this goal adds $n(n-1)/2$ hypotheses to the context.

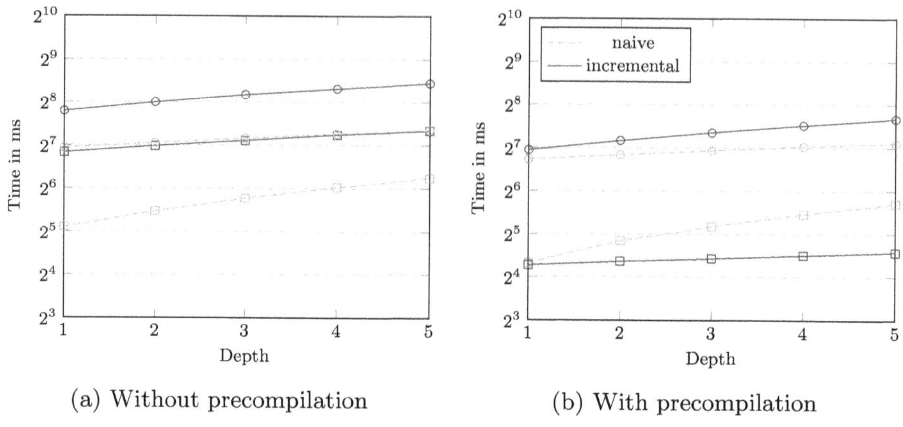

<table>
<tr><td>(a) Without precompilation</td><td>(b) With precompilation</td></tr>
</table>

Figure 2: Results of the depth benchmark for $n = 6$ with precompilation disabled (a) or enabled (b) and with $a = 0$ ($\square$) or $a = 100$ ($\bigcirc$).

In Fig. 1 the incremental algorithm has a sizeable advantage over the naive algorithm. We use a logarithmic scale, with each dotted horizontal line representing a 16-fold increase. Hence, for $2^3 = 8$ hypotheses and $a = 0$, the incremental implementation is over 30 times faster than the naive one. The speedup for $a = 100$ is around 35x, with naive forward reasoning taking over 19 seconds.

These results are largely explained by the number of times either algorithm matches a premise against a hypothesis. The naive algorithm iterates over the context, which initially contains n hypotheses, and compares all hypotheses pairwise. This is repeated approximately for each of the $n(n-1)/2$ added hypotheses, so $\mathcal{O}(n^4)$ match operations are performed. By contrast, the incremental algorithm considers each hypothesis only once, matching it against both slots and then comparing it with at most n other hypotheses. It therefore performs only $\mathcal{O}(n^2)$ match operations.

Both algorithms generate all possible transitivity chains. If only the longest such chain, from a to $a+n$, is desired, the rule can be registered as a *destruct* rule, a special sort of forward rule that removes from the context any hypotheses it is applied to. The incremental algorithm then needs only $\mathcal{O}(n)$ match operations.

Depth Benchmark. Our second benchmark concerns situations where many rules match almost, but not quite. We use 100 copies of a rule $r : \forall x,\ P_1\, x \to \ldots \to P_n\, x \to A$, where the predicates P_i are all distinct and A is an arbitrary proposition. Given a *depth* $k \le n$, the initial goal contains hypotheses of types

$P_i\,a$ for each $i \neq n - k$ with $1 \leq i \leq n$, as well as one hypothesis $P_{n-k}\,(a + 1)$ (with $a = 0$ or $a = 100$). In other words, the hypotheses match all premises with compatible substitutions, except the kth premise from the back. Since the naive algorithm processes the premises from back to front, k determines how many premises the algorithm matches before it notices that the rule cannot be applied. The incremental algorithm would do constant work per hypothesis if not for the lazy insertion optimization, which—combined with a heuristic that reorders slots so later premises come first—has a similar effect.

This setup is challenging for the incremental algorithm because no rule is ever applied, so incrementality does not help. And indeed, Fig. 2a shows that while both approaches slow down for greater k (only slightly as the context contains only $n = 6$ hypotheses), the incremental approach remains slower.

Fig. 2b shows the results of the depth benchmark with *precompilation* enabled. This is a feature of Lean that compiles tactics ahead of time instead of interpreting them. Both implementations benefit from this, but incremental forward reasoning does so disproportionately, perhaps because it uses more custom code that, unlike Lean's built-in routines, is usually interpreted. However, precompilation also substantially increases Aesop's build time, so it is disabled by default.

Mathlib Benchmark. We now use the benchmark introduced by lean-auto [10] to evaluate our forward reasoning technique on 263412 theorems from Mathlib (version 4.27.0-rc1), in two different configurations. In each configuration, the constants that appear in Mathlib's proof of the respective theorem are added as forward rules, simulating perfect premise selection.

In the *Aesop configuration*, Aesop, using naive or incremental forward reasoning, is run on each theorem. An invocation is successful if Aesop proves the theorem. Constants from the theorem's Mathlib proof are added as unsafe forward rules, so they receive a relatively low priority and their application can be backtracked. This configuration yields better results in practice than marking the rules as safe—even though forward rules are conceptually always safe—since it prevents Aesop from applying forward rules in an infinite loop.

In the *saturate configuration*, the `saturate` tactic with naive or incremental forward reasoning is run on each theorem. An invocation is successful if `saturate` generates a hypothesis that matches the theorem statement. The maximum depth of `saturate` is set to 10 to prevent infinite loops.

In either configuration, constants are not added as forward rules if they are private or typeclass instances, or if their types contain only logical symbols. In the Aesop configuration, we also exclude equations used by the simplifier, which Aesop already uses during its search. We use a timeout of 10 s for each tactic invocation, and 1.5 h for each Mathlib module. The module timeout affects 176 modules (out of 7452) where, due to unknown issues, the tactic timeout is not effective.

Each tactic is run three times, and we exclude samples where the minimal and maximal runtime differ by more than 20%. Furthermore, when comparing performance, we only consider theorems where both the naive and the incremental tactic variant succeed. This reduces the likelihood that differences are caused by minor, unintentional changes in behaviour. If the latter restriction is removed, incremental forward reasoning produces an even larger average speedup over naive forward reasoning than that reported below. After these exclusions, the evaluation comprises 53524 Aesop samples and 16452 `saturate` samples.

Aesop is not expected to perform well on this benchmark since it is designed for carefully curated rulesets in which constants are appropriately registered as backward, forward or other types of rules. Nevertheless, the results may be indicative of Aesop's performance on real use cases involving forward rules.

Configuration	Solved	Mean	p1	p10	p25	p50	p75	p90	p99
Aesop naive	55870	146.37	6.70	8.98	11.97	24.05	67.71	235.69	2652.54
Aesop incr.	55394	118.25	6.98	9.29	12.34	25.07	67.96	206.76	1784.33
Aesop speedup		1.24x	0.96x	0.97x	0.97x	0.96x	1.00x	1.14x	1.49x
Saturate naive	17346	71.59	0.91	2.64	4.03	7.69	21.80	76.33	1576.46
Saturate incr.	16995	34.35	0.64	2.22	3.24	6.15	14.38	43.36	523.06
Saturate speedup		2.08x	1.42x	1.19x	1.24x	1.25x	1.52x	1.76x	3.01x

Table 1: Number of problems solved, average elapsed time (in ms) and elapsed time percentiles for the Aesop and `saturate` configuration with naive and incremental forward reasoning. Each speedup is the ratio of naive and incremental time at the respective location of the distribution.

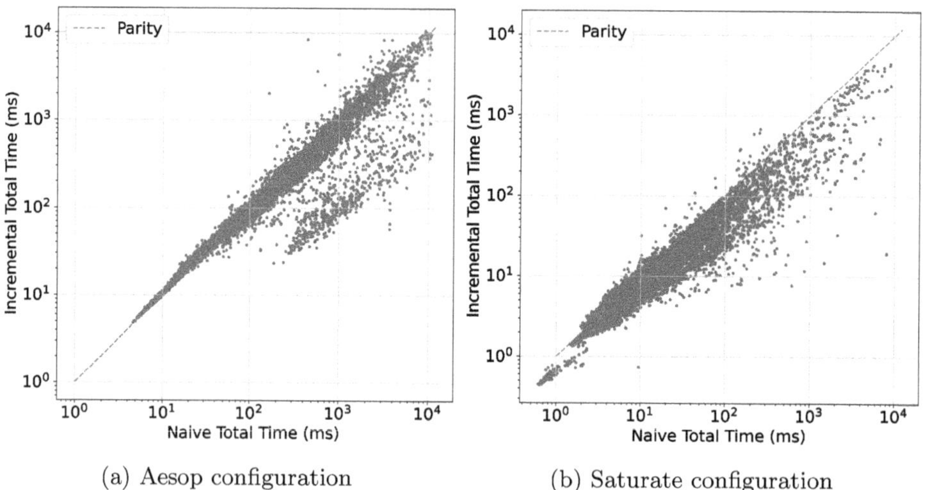

(a) Aesop configuration　　　(b) Saturate configuration

Figure 3: Elapsed time (log scale) per problem with naive and incremental forward reasoning. Points below the parity line indicate a speedup.

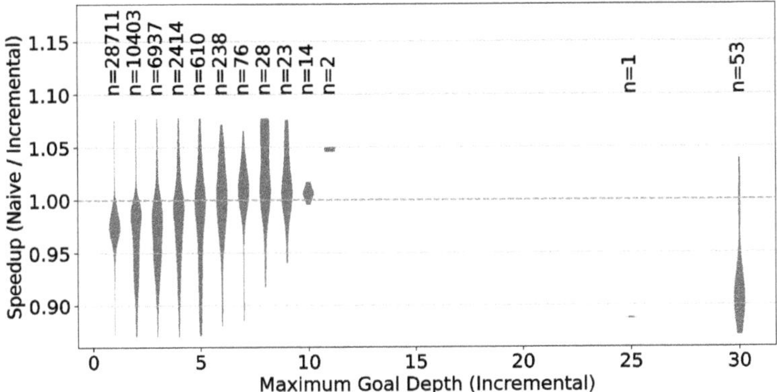

Figure 4: Aesop speedup by maximum goal depth. Problems solved by Aesop are grouped by the maximum depth of any goal in the Aesop search tree. For each depth, n is the number of problems with that maximum depth, and a violin plot shows the distribution of speedups. The whisker indicates the median speedup. We apply the interquartile range method with factor 3 to exclude outliers.

Results. As shown in Table 1, incremental forward reasoning improves the average performance of both Aesop and `saturate`. For `saturate`, we obtain a substantial mean speedup of 2.08x, with incremental forward reasoning outperforming the naive approach at each location of the time distribution. For Aesop, the mean speedup is a more modest 1.24x, and we see slight slowdowns at the lower percentiles, meaning Aesop calls that were already fast become a bit slower. However, we also obtain substantial speedups on problems where Aesop was previously slow, compensating for the slowdowns. Fig. 3 shows a more detailed comparison of running times. Naive and incremental forward reasoning are almost exactly semantically equivalent, so they are expected to solve almost exactly the same number of problems.

A possible explanation for the modest gains in the Aesop configuration is that the vast majority of solved problems require very few rule applications, so the maximum depth of goals in Aesop's search tree is low. As a result, incrementality, which reuses partial matches from parent goals for child goals, does not help much. Fig. 4 shows that with larger maximum depths, we obtain larger speedups (except at Aesop's depth limit of 30; these invocations likely involve looping rules). Combined with our synthetic benchmarks, this indicates that we would see larger gains from incremental forward reasoning with larger-scale Aesop searches.

7   Related Work

White-Box Tactics. Among white-box proof automation tactics, to our knowledge only ACL2's 'waterfall' [7,8] and PVS's various proof search strategies [13,2] have special support for forward reasoning. Both use approaches similar to Aesop's naive algorithm; in particular, the context of each goal is saturated independently. ACL2 additionally allows forward rules to be annotated with *trigger terms*, which cause the rules to be run if the trigger terms are matched anywhere in a goal. Aesop implements a similar mechanism, *rule patterns*, not described here due to space constraints. The auto2 tactic [ ] employs an SMT-like search procedure based on forward reasoning and e-matching [ ]. As such, it does not require incrementality, but it could perhaps benefit from our indexing schemes.

SATCHMO. The SATCHMO first-order theorem prover [ ] uses a search procedure that treats a given set of implications as forward rules and uses a case-splitting rule to perform case analysis on disjunctive hypotheses. SATCHMO-style provers may benefit from our incremental approach if the set of implications is large. However, since unification is comparatively cheap in first-order logic, it is not clear what effect it will have. SATCHMO also employs an optimisation that "focuses" forward reasoning on the hypothesis established by the last case split, providing a different form of incrementality.

Knowledge-Based Systems. Some knowledge-based reasoning systems, e.g. Algernon [ ] and EYE [ ], support combined forward and backward reasoning. However, to our knowledge, no such system allows non-forward rules to change the assumptions available to forward rules, so they do not require incrementality. Nevertheless, our technique bears some resemblance to the RETE algorithm [ ] for forward reasoning in large knowledge bases.

8 Conclusion

We have presented a technique that integrates forward reasoning into a tree-based proof search procedure supporting arbitrary proof rules. We avoid redundant reasoning steps by caching partial forward rule applications in a data structure, the *forward state*, that enables efficient updates. The technique is independent of the search strategy and logic used. Our evaluation shows that the technique outperforms Aesop's previous implementation on both a synthetic and a natural benchmark.

One obvious extension of our method would be to exploit redundancy not just between contexts of parent and child goals, but also between those of siblings or even unrelated goals. This would require no changes to the forward state data structure; we would only need to find pairs of goals that produce small diffs.

Acknowledgements. We thank Jasmin Blanchette, Massin Guerdi and the anonymous reviewers for their very insightful comments on drafts of this paper. Généreux's research was co-funded by the European Union (ERC, 101083038) and by the Fonds de recherche du Québec, 330205. Views and opinions expressed are however those of the authors only and do not necessarily reflect those of the European Union or the European Research Council. Neither the European Union nor the granting authority can be held responsible for them.

Data Availability Statement

The data and software necessary to reproduce our results are available in an artifact at DOI 10.5281/zenodo.18188520. For the purpose of reuse, the artifact's source code is available at https://github.com/JLimperg/artifact-aesop-forward, and Aesop's at https://github.com/leanprover-community/aesop. Aesop's main branch contains the naive and incremental implementations of forward reasoning.

References

1. Crawford, J.M., Kuipers, B.J.: Algernon—a tractable system for knowledge-representation. SIGART Bull. **2**(3), 35–44 (1991). https://doi.org/10.1145/122296.122302
2. Crow, J., Owre, S., Rushby, J., Shankar, N., Srivas, M.: A tutorial introduction to PVS. In: Workshop on Industrial-Strength Formal Specification Techniques (1995), http://www.csl.sri.com/papers/wift-tutorial/
3. Detlefs, D., Nelson, G., Saxe, J.B.: Simplify: A theorem prover for program checking. J. ACM **52**(3), 365–473 (2005). https://doi.org/10.1145/1066100.1066102
4. Forgy, C.L.: RETE: A fast algorithm for the many pattern/many object pattern match problem. In: Mylopolous, J., Brodie, M. (eds.) Readings in Artificial Intelligence and Databases, pp. 547–559. Morgan Kaufmann (1989). https://doi.org/10.1016/B978-0-934613-53-8.50041-8
5. Graf, P.: Substitution tree indexing. In: Rewriting Techniques and Applications (1995). https://doi.org/10.1007/3-540-59200-8_52
6. Ho, S., Protzenko, J.: Aeneas: Rust verification by functional translation. In: ICFP (2022). https://doi.org/10.1145/3547647
7. Kaufmann, M., Strother Moore, J.: ACL2: An industrial strength version of Nqthm. In: COMPASS (1996). https://doi.org/10.1109/CMPASS.1996.507872
8. Kaufmann, M., Manolios, P., Strother Moore, J.: Computer-Aided Reasoning: An Approach. Springer (2000)
9. Limperg, J., From, A.H.: Aesop: White-box best-first proof search for Lean. In: CPP (2023). https://doi.org/10.1145/3573105.3575671
10. Manthey, R., Bry, F.: SATCHMO: A theorem prover implemented in Prolog. In: CADE (1988). https://doi.org/10.1007/BFb0012847
11. McCune, W.: Experiments with discrimination-tree indexing and path indexing for term retrieval. Journal of Automated Reasoning **9**(2), 147–167 (1992). https://doi.org/10.1007/BF00245458
12. de Moura, L., Ullrich, S.: The Lean 4 theorem prover and programming language. In: CADE (2021). https://doi.org/10.1007/978-3-030-79876-5_37
13. Owre, S., Rushby, J.M., Shankar, N.: PVS: A prototype verification system. In: CADE (1992). https://doi.org/10.1007/3-540-55602-8_217
14. Paulson, L.C.: Generic automatic proof tools. Tech. Rep. UCAM-CL-TR-396, University of Cambridge (1996). https://doi.org/10.48456/tr-396
15. Paulson, L.C., Nipkow, T., Wenzel, M.: From LCF to Isabelle/HOL. Formal Aspects of Computing **31**(6) (2019). https://doi.org/10.1007/s00165-019-00492-1
16. Qian, Y., Clune, J., Barrett, C.: Lean-Auto: An Interface Between Lean 4 and Automated Theorem Provers, pp. 175–196 (07 2025). https://doi.org/10.1007/978-3-031-98682-6_10

17. Tammet, T.: Towards efficient subsumption. In: CADE (1998). https://doi.org/10.1007/BFb0054276
18. The Coq development team: The Coq proof assistant (2024). https://doi.org/10.5281/zenodo.1003420
19. The Mathlib community: The Lean mathematical library. In: CPP (2020). https://doi.org/10.1145/3372885.3373824
20. Verborgh, R., De Roo, J.: Drawing conclusions from linked data on the web: The EYE reasoner. IEEE Software **32**(3), 23–27 (2015). https://doi.org/10.1109/MS.2015.63
21. Zhan, B.: AUTO2, a saturation-based heuristic prover for higher-order logic. In: ITP (2016). https://doi.org/10.1007/978-3-319-43144-4_27

Enumerating Choice Terms in Model-Based Quantifier Instantiation

Lydia Kondylidou[1], Andrew Reynolds[2],
Jasmin Blanchette[1], and Cesare Tinelli[2]

[1] Ludwig-Maximilians-Universität München, Munich, Germany
l.kondylidou@lmu.de, jasmin.blanchette@lmu.de
[2] The University of Iowa, Iowa City, United States
andrew-reynolds@uiowa.edu, cesare-tinelli@uiowa.edu

Abstract. Satisfiability modulo theories (SMT) solvers are widely used for determining the satisfiability of logical formulas with respect to background theories. SMT solvers are traditionally based on first-order logic, but some also support higher-order logic. Recently, Kondylidou et al. introduced model-based quantifier instantiation with fast enumeration (MBQI-Enum), a quantifier instantiation strategy that works for both logics. A weakness of MBQI-Enum is that it does not find refutations when Hilbert choice terms are necessary. In this work, we present an extension of MBQI-Enum that enables it to reason effectively about Hilbert's choice operator. The extended strategy substantially increases the success rate of the SMT solver cvc5 on higher-order benchmarks.

1 Introduction

Satisfiability modulo theories (SMT) solvers combine a Boolean satisfiability (SAT) solver with decision procedures for interpreted theories. They work by refutation: They assume the negation of the conjecture as an axiom and try to establish the unsatisfiability (i.e., provability) of the input problem. Several SMT solvers, including Bitwuzla [25], Boolector [26], CVC4 [5], cvc5 [3], veriT [8], and Z3 [23], support quantifiers via Skolemization and instantiation.

Most SMT solvers are based on first-order logic, but a few support higher-order logic. Specifically, CVC4, its successor cvc5, and a prototype version of veriT have been extended to parse and solve higher-order problems [4]. In principle, higher-order logic is often more convenient than first-order logic for expressing problems, particularly those involving binders (e.g., λx, $\sum_i$, $\prod_i$, $\int_x$).

A crucial aspect of higher-order SMT solvers is their use of quantifier instantiation strategies. Barbosa et al. [4] partly extended the first-order E-matching strategy [22] to a higher-order setting. Recently, Kondylidou et al. [19] introduced model-based quantifier instantiation with fast enumeration (MBQI-Enum), a strategy that extends model-based quantifier instantiation (MBQI) [15] with syntax-guided synthesis (SyGuS) [27] techniques. While traditional MBQI relies only on ground terms from the MBQI model to instantiate quantified variables, MBQI-Enum broadens this approach by generating a wider range of candidate

S. Junges and G. Katz (Eds.): TACAS 2026, LNCS 16505, pp. 295–314, 2026.
https://doi.org/10.1007/978-3-032-22752-2_15

instantiations. It does so by enumerating terms guided by a SyGuS grammar, which enables it to construct more complex instantiations involving, for instance, identity functions and uninterpreted symbols. MBQI-Enum was found to be the most successful strategy [19, Sect. 5] for solving higher-order problems from the TPTP [39] library.

A weakness of MBQI-Enum is that it does not attempt instantiations containing Hilbert's choice operator. A Hilbert choice expression has the form $\varepsilon x.\ \varphi$, where variable x is bound in formula φ. The entire expression denotes some value of x that satisfies φ, if such a value exists; otherwise, it denotes an arbitrary value from the type of x. Sometimes the ε operator occurs in the input problem, in which case the SMT solver must reason about it. Even if ε is absent, an ε term might be useful in quantifier instantiations. The ε operator is reputed to be difficult to reason about because it is characterized by a higher-order axiom.

In this paper, we extend MBQI-Enum so that it instantiates quantifiers with terms that include Hilbert's choice operator. This extension requires three main modifications to MBQI-Enum. First, we augment the SyGuS grammar to include ε terms. Second, we introduce fresh Skolem symbols that represent these ε terms, since this is simpler than implementing ε terms throughout the SMT solver. Finally, we generate lemmas corresponding to instances of ε's characteristic axiom and add them to the solver.

Example 1. We compare our extended MBQI-Enum with the original on TPTP benchmark SEV431^1. Let u be an uninterpreted sort, and let f be an uninterpreted symbol of type $u \to u$. Consider the second-order problem consisting of the injectivity axiom $\forall x, y.\ \mathsf{f}\ x = \mathsf{f}\ y \implies x = y$ for f and the negated conjecture $\forall g.\ \exists z.\ g\ (\mathsf{f}\ z) \neq z$, where g has type $u \to u$ and x, y, z have type u. MBQI-Enum generates the instantiations $\lambda y.\ y,\ \lambda y.\ \mathsf{f}\ y,\ \lambda y.\ \mathsf{f}\ (\mathsf{f}\ y),\ \ldots$ for g. As a result, the SMT solver does not terminate. By contrast, our strategy instantiates g with the term $\lambda y.\ \varepsilon x.\ y = \mathsf{f}\ x$ using the grammar. This term denotes the left inverse of f. Then the strategy introduces a fresh Skolem symbol h that represents this term. The lemma $\forall y.\ \neg\,(\exists x.\ y = \mathsf{f}\ x) \vee y = \mathsf{f}\ (\mathsf{h}\ y)$ characterizing h is added to the problem. After instantiating g with h, the solver can derive a contradiction with the injectivity axiom. This implies that the unnegated conjecture $\exists g.\ \forall z.\ g\ (\mathsf{f}\ z) = z$ is entailed by the axiom. ∎

We implemented the extended MBQI-Enum strategy in the cvc5 solver. We evaluated it on the higher-order benchmarks of the TPTP library [39]. The results show that Hilbert's choice is often useful for establishing the unsatisfiability of an input problem without introducing much overhead in problems where it is not needed. Remarkably, our extension solves a strict superset of the problems solved by the original MBQI-Enum.

We also compare our approach with other cvc5 strategies and find that it outperforms them. Finally, we compare cvc5 equipped with our strategy with the provers Satallax [10], Vampire [7], and Zipperposition [40], representing the state of the art in higher-order automated theorem proving, and find that it is highly competitive. The raw evaluation data are available online [21]. Our source code, along with instructions for reproducing the experiments, is also available online [20].

2 Preliminaries

Our approach builds on higher-order logic with Hilbert's choice, SMT with quantifiers, and MBQI-Enum. Below, we briefly introduce these concepts.

Higher-Order Logic with Hilbert's Choice. Monomorphic higher-order logic [1, 16], also called simple type theory [11], generalizes classical first-order logic by allowing quantification over functions. The syntax distinguishes between types and terms. Types τ are either base types, or sorts, κ or applications of the function type constructor $\rightarrow$ to two types: $\tau_1 \rightarrow \tau_2$. The type of Booleans is denoted by o.

The term language is based on the simply typed λ-calculus, where terms $t, e, \ldots$ are inductively defined as variables $g, x, y, z, \ldots$, symbols $\mathsf{a}, \mathsf{b}, \mathsf{f}, \mathsf{h}, \mathsf{p}, \mathsf{r} \ldots$ (possibly of function type), term applications $t \ t'$, and λ-abstractions $\lambda x.\ t$, where x is the bound variable and t is the abstraction's body. A variable is free in a term if it is not bound by an enclosing λ-abstraction. Terms are syntactically equal modulo α-, β-, and η-conversion, meaning, for example, that $(\lambda x.\ \mathsf{f}\ x\ x)\ \mathsf{c}$ is syntactically equal to $\mathsf{f}\ \mathsf{c}\ \mathsf{c}$. Terms of type $\tau_1 \rightarrow \cdots \rightarrow \tau_n \rightarrow o$ are called predicates. A term of type o is called a formula.

A common extension of higher-order logic is *Hilbert's choice operator* ε [17,18, 37]: If x is a variable of type τ and φ is a formula that contains x, then $\varepsilon\ (\lambda x.\ \varphi)$, abbreviated as $\varepsilon x.\ \varphi$, is a term of type τ. Intuitively, the term $\varepsilon x.\ \varphi$ denotes *some* element x of type τ for which the formula φ holds if such an element exists. If no such element exists, it denotes an arbitrary element of type τ. Unlike existential quantification, which only asserts the existence of such an element, the choice operator yields the element. Hilbert's choice operator is characterized by the higher-order axiom $\forall y.\ (\exists x.\ y\ x) \implies y\ (\varepsilon x.\ y\ x)$. The operator makes it possible to denote functions that exist according to the standard semantics of higher-order logic but that otherwise cannot be expressed (cf. Example 1). Some treatments of Hilbert's choice include an axiom $\forall y, z.\ y = z \implies (\varepsilon x.\ y\ x) = (\varepsilon x.\ z\ x)$, but this is a special case of congruence, which is built into higher-order logic.

Quantifier Instantiation in SMT. To reason about the satisfiability of quantified formulas, SMT solvers typically rely on a combination of Skolemization and heuristic instantiation: Universal quantifiers occurring positively in a formula are instantiated, while those occurring negatively are Skolemized. Dually, existential quantifiers occurring positively are Skolemized, whereas those occurring negatively are instantiated.

Let $\mathcal{T}$ be a theory, or combination of theories, over a set of interpreted symbols, and let F be a (conjunctively understood) set of formulas, or *problem*, over the signature of $\mathcal{T}$. To determine the satisfiability of F in $\mathcal{T}$, typical SMT solvers rely on a *quantifier-free subsolver* for reasoning about quantifier-free formulas and an *instantiation module* for reasoning about quantified formulas. The former, which combines a SAT solver and a specialized solver for the theory $\mathcal{T}$, enumerates potential models of an abstraction of F in which quantified subformulas are treated as propositional variables. The SAT solver proposes candidate models for F at the propositional level—truth assignments to atomic formulas in F that propositionally satisfy F—while the theory solvers check these models for theory-specific conflicts. If all candidate models generate conflicts, F is declared unsatisfiable. Otherwise, the instantiation module handles the quantified subformulas in F by generating selected instances of them and adding them to F. The added instances preserve the satisfiability of F. Instances with quantifiers will be possibly instantiated further, whereas those with no quantifiers will be directly processed by the quantified-free subsolver.

Instantiation is performed following user-selectable strategies that compute substitutions σ for the top-level variables in quantified formulas of F, mapping those variables to ground (i.e., variable-free) terms. More precisely, for selected quantified formulas q of the form $\forall x_1, \ldots, x_n.\ \psi$ in F and selected substitutions σ that map each variable x_i to a ground term t_i, the instantiation module produces *lemmas* of the form $q \implies \psi\{x_1 \mapsto t_1, \ldots, x_n \mapsto t_n\}$ that are then added to the set F. Existentially quantified formulas in F are instantiated by Skolemization: for each selected formula q of the form $\exists x_1, \ldots, x_n.\ \psi$ in F, n fresh Skolem symbols $\mathsf{sk}_1, \ldots, \mathsf{sk}_n$ are introduced and a corresponding lemma of the form $q \implies \psi\{x_1 \mapsto \mathsf{sk}_1, \ldots, x_n \mapsto \mathsf{sk}_n\}$ is added to F. The main SMT loop is then reentered with the new F.

This iterative process continues until the SMT solver finds a model for F with respect to $\mathcal{T}$ (which is itself a difficult task given the presence in F of quantified formulas [14, 15, 32, 34]) or the quantifier-free subsolver determines F to be unsatisfiable in $\mathcal{T}$. Of course, at any point, the SMT solver may run out of time or memory.

To generate relevant ground terms for instantiating universal quantifiers, SMT solvers rely on *instantiation strategies*. For first-order logic with theories, some strategies are refutationally complete and enable SMT solvers to offer semi-decision procedures: They will find a proof of unsatisfiability if one exists, but they may not terminate otherwise. Higher-order logic—which allows terms to include functions as arguments, λ-abstractions, and partial applications—remains semidecidable under Henkin semantics but is more challenging to support in practice than first-order logic. The strategies implemented in CVC4, cvc5, and veriT are pragmatic and do not seek refutational completeness [4, 19].

For higher-order logic, cvc5 initially supported only an extension of the E-matching [22] instantiation strategy. New strategies that also partly work on higher-order problems were later added to the solver. Specifically, MBQI [15] is a strategy that iteratively refines a candidate model constructed from the quantifier-free part of the problem and then attempts to refute the model by generating ground instances of the quantified formulas that may be falsified by the model. It has been used on higher-order benchmarks and has proved somewhat effective on these [19, Sect. 5]. Common techniques such as conflict-guided instantiation [35], enumerative instantiation [30], and counterexample-guided instantiation [33] can also be used on higher-order problems, but they have generally proved less effective [19, Sect. 5], which is unsurprising given that they were originally designed for first-order reasoning. SyQI [27], a syntax-guided synthesis approach, works well on some higher-order problems since it can generate terms by synthesizing candidate expressions with the help of a grammar [19, Sect. 5].

MBQI-Enum. MBQI-Enum [19] is a recent addition to cvc5 that integrates a SyGuS-based enumerator directly into MBQI. For each quantified variable in the formula, MBQI-Enum first constructs a grammar. It then iteratively enumerates candidate terms generated from the grammar and checks each resulting instance against the current model. If one instance refutes the current model, the strategy builds a substitution by mapping the quantified variable to the current enumerated term. If the instance fails to refute the model, the enumerator proceeds to the next candidate term. If all candidates are exhausted without success, the strategy reverts to standard MBQI. This fallback mechanism guarantees that MBQI-Enum can, in principle, solve any problem that MBQI can solve.

A key aspect of MBQI-Enum is the construction of the SyGuS grammar that guides the enumeration. The grammar is created from a set of symbols including uninterpreted symbols extracted from the entire formula and bound variables that have not yet been instantiated. For higher-order variables, the grammar incorporates rules for generating λ-abstractions. The enumerator then systematically constructs λ-expressions by generating terms over the abstractions' argument variables.

Example 2. We consider a modified version of the TPTP benchmark SYO288^5, which is over the theory $\mathcal{T}$ of equality with uninterpreted sorts and functions. Let u be an uninterpreted sort. Let f be a function symbol $f : u \to u$ and consider the second-order conjecture $\exists y.\ \forall z.\ y\ z = f\ z$, where y is a variable of type $u \to u$ and z is a variable of type u. To prove its validity in $\mathcal{T}$, we ask the SMT solver to prove the unsatisfiability of its negation, or, equivalently, of the input problem:

$$F = \{\forall y.\ \exists z.\ y\ z \neq f\ z\}$$

MBQI-Enum first constructs a SyGuS grammar for y to guide the enumeration process. The set of symbols is empty. The grammar consists of the rules

$$g_0 ::= \lambda x.\ g_1$$
$$g_1 ::= x \mid f\ g_1 \mid \text{ite}(g_2, g_1, g_1)$$
$$g_2 ::= \text{true} \mid \text{false} \mid g_1 = g_1 \mid \neg g_2 \mid g_2 \wedge g_2 \mid g_2 \vee g_2$$

In the first iteration, MBQI-Enum enumerates terms generated by the grammar and tries them in sequence. When the enumeration reaches the term $\lambda x.\ x$, MBQI-Enum generates the substitution $\sigma = \{y \mapsto \lambda x.\ x\}$. The strategy then determines whether the instantiation of the quantified formula, obtained by applying σ to the subformula $\exists z.\ y\ z \neq f\ z$, refutes the current model. This is achieved by checking whether the negation of that subformula, under the current substitution σ, is $\mathcal{T}$-satisfiable. Now, if we negate the subformula, instantiate y with $\lambda x.\ x$ in it and β-reduce, we obtain a formula equivalent to $\forall z.\ z = f\ z$, which is satisfiable in $\mathcal{T}$ since in that theory the symbol f can be interpreted as the identity function. The substitution σ is then returned.

Back in the SMT loop, the instantiation lemma $(\forall y.\ \exists z.\ y\ z \neq f\ z) \implies \exists z.\ z \neq f\ z$ is then added to F. In essence, this causes the solver to also add the propositionally entailed formula $\exists z.\ z \neq f\ z$ to F. Since that formula has an existential quantifier prefix, it is Skolemized into $sk_1 \neq f\ sk_1$ where sk_1 is a fresh symbol of type u. Then, the Skolemization lemma $(\exists z.\ z \neq f\ z) \implies sk_1 \neq f\ sk_1$ added to F.

In the next iteration, MBQI-Enum tries the term $\lambda x.\ f\ x$ generated by the grammar and produces the substitution $\sigma = \{y \mapsto \lambda x.\ f\ x\}$, leading to the addition of the instantiation lemma $(\forall y.\ \exists z.\ y\ z \neq f\ z) \implies \exists z.\ f\ z \neq f\ z$ to F. Then, the formula $\exists z.\ f\ z \neq f\ z$ is Skolemized, with variable z replaced by a fresh Skolem symbol sk_2, and the Skolemization lemma $(\exists z.\ f\ z \neq f\ z) \implies f\ sk_2 \neq f\ sk_2$ is added to F. Now, from the formulas $\forall y.\ \exists z.\ y\ z \neq f\ z$, $(\forall y.\ \exists z.\ y\ z \neq f\ z) \implies \exists z.\ f\ z \neq f\ z$, and $(\exists z.\ f\ z \neq f\ z) \implies f\ sk_2 \neq f\ sk_2$ in F, the quantifier-free subsolver deduces the propositionally entailed formula $f\ sk_2 \neq f\ sk_2$, which it then determines to be unsatisfiable. The SMT solver then concludes that the original F is unsatisfiable in $\mathcal{T}$, and hence that the conjecture is valid.   ■

3   The Extended Strategy

Our strategy is based on MBQI-Enum, which has proved effective for higher-order reasoning. It adds three main ingredients:

- the grammar guiding the enumeration is augmented to include ε terms;
- fresh Skolem symbols are introduced to represent these terms; and
- term filtering is applied to eliminate redundant or invalid candidate terms during enumeration.

In addition to these extensions, our strategy generalizes MBQI-Enum by returning not only a substitution but also a set of lemmas. These lemmas are added to the input problem F, extending it iteratively.

The generalized strategy is detailed in Algorithm 3. It takes as input a quantified formula q of the form $\forall y_1, \ldots, y_m.\ \psi$ occurring in F, where ψ does not start with a universal quantifier. It starts by computing an initial substitution σ from the model (line 3). If no such substitution exists, it returns the empty set, indicating that no instantiation could be found.

After computing σ, the strategy iterates over the quantified variables $y_1, \ldots, y_m$ in the formula q to instantiate. For each y_i where $i \in \{1, \ldots, m\}$, it constructs a SyGuS grammar G_i based on uninterpreted symbols appearing in the entire input formula (line 7). The grammar is further augmented to include terms of the form $\varepsilon x.\ \varphi$, where x is a variable whose type is the return type of y_i and φ is a formula over x and other free variables and symbols from the formula q.

Algorithm 3 Generalized MBQI-Enum

1: **function** MBQI_ENUM_WITH_CHOICE(q)
2:     **assume** q is $\forall y_1, \ldots, y_n.\ \psi$
3:     **let** $\sigma \leftarrow$ INSTS_MBQI(q)
4:     **if** σ does not exist **then**
5:         **return** $\emptyset$
6:     **for each** $i \in \{1, \ldots, n\}$ **do**
7:         **let** $G_i \leftarrow$ MAKE_GRAMMAR(q, y_i)
8:         **for each** $j \in \{1, 2, \ldots\}$ **do**
9:             **let** $e \leftarrow$ GET_ENUM_TERM(G_i, j)
10:             **if** e does not exist **then**
11:                 **break**
12:             $\sigma' \leftarrow \sigma[y_i \mapsto e]$
13:             **if** $\neg\psi\sigma'$ is satisfiable **then**
14:                 $\sigma \leftarrow \sigma'$
15:                 **break**
16:     **return** GET_LEMMAS(σ)

This grammar guides the enumeration of candidate terms that may be used to instantiate y_i. As a result, the SyGuS enumerator generates both ε and non-ε terms as potential substitutions for y_i.

For each candidate term e generated by the enumerator, a new substitution σ' is formed by mapping y_i to the current term e in the initial substitution σ (line 12). The strategy then checks whether the negation of the body of the quantified formula under σ' is satisfiable in the current model (line 13). This satisfiability check serves as a semantic filter, pruning out terms that do not yield counterexamples. If the check succeeds, σ is updated and the enumeration process proceeds to the next quantified variable. Otherwise, it continues with the next candidate term. Once all quantified variables have been considered, our strategy returns both the final substitution σ and a set of lemmas, which include those introduced during the handling of ε terms and quantifier instantiations. These lemmas are subsequently added to the input formula F, extending it iteratively.

Augmented Grammar. Our strategy augments the base grammar used for term enumeration in MBQI-Enum by incorporating ε terms, allowing the generation of arbitrary formulas. Our approach is detailed in Algorithm 4.

MBQI-Enum constructs a base grammar for each universally quantified variable y_i in the formula q using a set of symbols S from the entire input formula, such as uninterpreted symbols and bound variables (line 4). A grammar G is a triple (g_0, G, R_G), where g_0 is the initial symbol, G is a set of nonterminal symbols with $g_0 \in G$, and R_G is a set of production rules. Each rule has the form $g ::= t$, where $g \in G$ and t is a term built from symbols in the set S, nonterminals in G, free variables, and symbols from the signature of a background theory $\mathcal{T}$. The symbols in S, along with the free variables and the theory symbols from $\mathcal{T}$, act as terminal symbols in the grammar. Each grammar generates

---

Algorithm 4 Augmented grammar

1: **function** MAKE_GRAMMAR(q, y_i)
2:     **let** F be the input formula
3:     $S \leftarrow \text{symbols}(F) \cup \text{symbols}(q) \cup \{y_{i+1}, \ldots, y_n\}$
4:     **let** $(g_0, G, R_G) \leftarrow$ MAKE_BASE_GRAMMAR(S, y_i)
5:     **if** choice is enabled **then**
6:         **let** x be a variable of type τ
7:         $(p_0, P, R_P) \leftarrow$ MAKE_PREDICATE_GRAMMAR(S, x, y_i)
8:         **extend** $G \leftarrow G \cup P$
9:         **extend** $R_G \leftarrow \{g_0 \leftarrow \varepsilon x.\, p_0\} \cup R_G \cup R_P$
10:     **return** (g_0, G, R_G)
11: **function** MAKE_PREDICATE_GRAMMAR(S, x, y_i)
12:     $S \leftarrow S \cup \{x\}$
13:     **let** $\bar{z} \leftarrow$ bound variables in y_i
14:     **define** p_0 nonterminals
15:     **let** $P \leftarrow \{\bar{z}\} \cup S \cup \{\text{true}, \text{false}, =, \neg, \wedge\}$
16:     **define** $R_P \leftarrow$ production rules
17:     **return** (p_0, P, R_P)

---

terms whose type matches the return type τ of y_i. For higher-order variables, the grammars include rules for generating λ-abstractions. In this case, the initial symbol g_0 expands to λ-terms. Whereas earlier versions of MBQI-Enum considered only terms in η-long β-normal form [19], the current cvc5 implementation allows partial application. The variables bound by λ-abstractions are terminal symbols in the grammar that generates the abstraction's body. For example, if y_i is a function variable of arity n whose arguments and result are all of the same type, the grammar includes rules such as

$$g_0 ::= \lambda x_1, \ldots, x_n.\, g_1 \qquad\qquad g_1 ::= x_1 \mid \cdots \mid x_n$$

To include ε terms of the form $\varepsilon x.\, \varphi$, our strategy extends the grammar as follows. For the nonterminal g_1 in the base grammar corresponding to y_i's return type τ, a variable x of type τ is introduced (line 6) and added to the symbol set S (line 12). A new grammar is then built to generate Boolean formulas over the extended symbol set $S \cup \{x\}$ (line 7). This predicate grammar is defined as the triple (p_0, P, R_P), where p_0 is the initial nonterminal symbols and P is a set of nonterminal symbols that includes p_0. The set R_P contains production rules of the form $p ::= t$, where $p \in P$ and t is a term. Each term t is built from symbols in S, nonterminals in P, variables that were bound in y_i but now appear free, and symbols from the signature of the Boolean background theory (line 15). These elements act as terminal symbols in the grammar. The new grammar includes the rules

$$p_0 ::= \text{true} \mid \text{false} \mid p_1 = p_1 \mid \neg p_0 \mid p_0 \wedge p_0 \qquad p_1 ::= x_1 \mid \cdots \mid x_n \mid x$$

The nonterminal p_0 directly defines the body of the ε term. We define a new production rule of the form $g_1 ::= \varepsilon x.\, p_0$. The resulting grammar is constructed by extending the base grammar (g_0, G, R_G) with the predicate grammar (p_0, P, R_P) and the new production rule (lines 8–9). The final grammar is defined as $(p_0, G \cup P, \{g_1 ::= \varepsilon x.\ p_0\} \cup R_G \cup R_P)$. It can be used to enumerate both ε and non-ε terms and is thus more expressive than the original grammar. For our example, the final grammar consists of the rules

$$g_0 ::= \lambda x_1, \ldots, x_n.\ g_1 \qquad\qquad g_1 ::= \varepsilon x.\ p_0 \mid x_1 \mid \cdots \mid x_n$$

$$p_0 ::= \mathsf{true} \mid \mathsf{false} \mid p_1 = p_1 \mid \neg\, p_0 \mid p_0 \wedge p_0 \qquad p_1 ::= x_1 \mid \cdots \mid x_n \mid x$$

Skolem Symbols. The most important part of the strategy is where we take formulas containing ε terms generated by the grammar, abstract these terms into fresh Skolem symbols, and generate corresponding lemmas with triggers to guide efficient higher-order quantifier instantiation. Our approach is detailed in Algorithm 5.

Algorithm 5 Lemmas for Skolem symbols

1: **function** GET_LEMMAS(σ)
2:     **let** $L \leftarrow \emptyset$
3:     **let** $\psi' \leftarrow \psi$
4:     **for all** $i \in \{1, \ldots, m\}$ **do**
5:         **assume** $y_i\sigma = \lambda(x_1, \ldots, x_n).\ t$ $\triangleright$ y_i is the variable being instantiated
6:         **let** $t' \leftarrow t$
7:         **for all** subterms e of t of the form $\varepsilon x : \tau.\ \varphi(\bar{z}, x)$ **do**
8:             **let** $\bar{z} = (z_1 : \tau_1, \ldots, z_k : \tau_k) \subseteq \{x_1, \ldots, x_n\}$ be φ's free variables
9:             **let** $h : (\tau_1, \ldots, \tau_k) \rightarrow \tau$ be a fresh Skolem symbol
10:             **let** $lemma \leftarrow \forall \bar{z}.\ \neg\,(\exists x.\ \varphi(\bar{z}, x)) \vee \varphi(\bar{z}, \mathsf{h}\ \bar{z})$
11:             **extend** $L \leftarrow L \cup \{lemma\}$
12:             **replace** e **in** t' **with** $\mathsf{h}\ \bar{z}$
13:         $\psi' \leftarrow \psi'\{y_i \mapsto \lambda(x_1, \ldots, x_n).\ t'\}$
14:     **let** $inst\_lemma \leftarrow (\forall y_1, \ldots, y_m.\ \psi) \implies \psi'$
15:     **extend** $L \leftarrow L \cup \{inst\_lemma\}$
16:     **return** L

Our strategy generalizes MBQI-Enum by iterating over the variables in $\forall y_1, \ldots, y_m.\ \psi$ and incrementally building a fully instantiated formula before generating the instantiation lemmas. It then returns the set of generated lemmas L instead of only the substitutions.

Given a substitution $\sigma = \{y_i \mapsto \lambda x_1, \ldots, x_n.\ t\}$ for each variable y_i, consider any subterm e of t of the form $\varepsilon x : \tau.\ \varphi(\bar{z}, x)$, where $\bar{z} = (z_1 : \tau_1, \ldots, z_k : \tau_k)$, the free variables of e, are included in $\{x_1, \ldots, x_n\}$. We replace all occurrences of e in t with an application of a fresh Skolem symbol h to the variables $\bar{z}$ (lines 5–10). In other words, the subterm $\varepsilon x.\ \varphi(\bar{z}, x)$ is converted to $\mathsf{h}\ \bar{z}$, where h has type $\tau_1 \rightarrow \cdots \rightarrow \tau_k \rightarrow \tau$. The introduction of these Skolems abstracts the ε binder into symbols understood by the rest of the SMT solver. Our strategy constructs the lemma $\forall \bar{z}.\ \neg\,(\exists x.\ \varphi(\bar{z}, x)) \vee \varphi(\bar{z}, \mathsf{h}\ \bar{z})$ (line 10) and adds it to the lemma set L. When later added to the set F, this lemma makes the strategy less incomplete while preserving F's satisfiability. It guarantees that if there exists an x satisfying $\varphi(\bar{z}, x)$, then $\mathsf{h}\,\bar{z}$ satisfies φ as well.

Additionally, we mark the Skolem application $\mathsf{h}\,\bar{z}$ as a *trigger* [12,13] in the lemma. This trigger guides E-matching, ensuring that instantiations are driven by terms that match the structure of the Skolem application, which is applied to exactly the same set of variables as in the original quantified formula.

After all ε-subterms in t have been abstracted, the modified substitution $y_i \mapsto \lambda x_1, \ldots, x_n.\, t'$, where t' is obtained by replacing the ε-subterms of t with the corresponding Skolem applications $\mathsf{h}\,\bar{z}$ (line 12), is applied to the partially instantiated body ψ of the formula q (line 13). This procedure is repeated for each variable y_i, yielding a fully instantiated formula ψ' in which all substitutions have been applied to the universally quantified variables and all Skolem symbols have been introduced. Finally, the instantiation lemma $(\forall y_1, \ldots, y_m.\, \psi) \implies \psi'$ is generated (line 14) and added to the lemma set L. The complete set L is eventually returned and merged with the current set F.

Filtering. To avoid redundant instantiations, term filtering is applied during enumeration. Enumerated terms already present in the set of candidate terms are discarded, ensuring that terms equivalent under rewriting are considered only once. For terms of the form $\varepsilon x.\, \varphi$, the bound variable x must occur in the body φ. Terms in which x does not occur are excluded, to prevent the introduction of trivial instantiations. Since cvc5 already performs extensive theory-specific filtering by default, no additional filtering is required in our setting.

Example 6. We return to Example 1 and present it in more detail. Let $\mathcal{T}$ be the same theory as in the previous examples. Let u be an uninterpreted sort and let f be an uninterpreted function of type $u \to u$. Consider the conjecture

$$(\forall x, y.\ \mathsf{f}\,x = \mathsf{f}\,y \implies x = y) \implies \exists g.\ \forall z.\ g\,(\mathsf{f}\,z) = z$$

where g has type $u \to u$ and x, y, z have type u. The formula states that if f is injective, then it has a left inverse. We prove that the formula holds in $\mathcal{T}$ by contradiction. That is, we negate it, obtaining the following input problem

$$F = \{\forall x, y.\ \mathsf{f}\,x = \mathsf{f}\,y \implies x = y,\ \forall g.\ \exists z.\ g\,(\mathsf{f}\,z) \neq z\}\,,$$

and prove that F is unsatisfiable in $\mathcal{T}$.

MBQI-Enum generates a grammar for g using the set of symbols $S = \{\mathsf{f}\}$. The grammar consists of the rules

$$g_0 ::= \lambda y.\ g_1 \qquad\qquad g_1 ::= y \mid \mathsf{f}\ g_1$$

Based on this grammar, MBQI-Enum generates the substitutions $\{g \mapsto \lambda y.\ y\}$, $\{g \mapsto \lambda y.\ \mathsf{f}\ y\}$, $\{g \mapsto \lambda y.\ \mathsf{f}\ (\mathsf{f}\ y)\}$, $\ldots$ for g. Since this enumeration does not capture inverse functions, the SMT solver does not terminate.

Our strategy addresses this challenge by constructing a richer grammar. We introduce a variable x of type u and extend the symbol set to $S \cup \{x\}$. We then define the following grammar:

$$p_0 ::= \text{true} \mid \text{false} \mid p_1 = p_1 \mid \neg\, p_0 \mid p_0 \wedge p_0 \qquad p_1 ::= y \mid x \mid \text{f } p_1$$

We extend the MBQI-Enum grammar by adding a rule to produce $\varepsilon x.\ p_0$. The result consists of the rules for p_0 and p_1 above and the following rules:

$$g_0 ::= \lambda y.\ g_1 \qquad\qquad g_1 ::= \varepsilon x.\ p_0 \mid y \mid \text{f } g_1$$

Using this grammar, our strategy generates the term $\lambda y.\ \varepsilon x.\ y = \text{f } x$, which denotes a left inverse of f, leading to the substitution $\{g \mapsto \lambda y.\ \varepsilon x.\ y = \text{f } x\}$.

Corresponding to this term, we introduce a fresh Skolem symbol $\text{h} : u \to u$. Our strategy asserts the following lemma:

$$\forall y.\ \neg\,(\exists x.\ y = \text{f } x) \vee y = \text{f } (\text{h } y) \qquad\qquad (\ell_1)$$

The lemma states that for any y, if there exists an x such that $y = \text{f } x$ (i.e., y is in the image of f), then applying f to h y must yield y. The original enumerated term $\lambda y.\ \varepsilon x.\ y = \text{f } x$ is thus rewritten to the term $\lambda y.\ \text{h } y$. The substitution $\sigma = \{g \mapsto \lambda y.\ \text{h } y\}$ is considered. Next, the instantiation lemma

$$(\forall g.\ \exists z.\ g\ (\text{f } z) \neq z) \implies \exists z.\ \text{h } (\text{f } z) \neq z \qquad\qquad (\ell_2)$$

is generated by applying the substitution σ followed by β-reduction. The set of lemmas $L = \{(\ell_1), (\ell_2)\}$ is constructed. Each lemma in L is then added to set F. After that, Skolemization introduces a fresh symbol sk corresponding to the existentially quantified variable z. The lemma

$$(\exists z.\ \text{h } (\text{f } z) \neq z) \implies \text{h } (\text{f sk}) \neq \text{sk} \qquad\qquad (\ell_3)$$

is also added to F.

The strategy proceeds to instantiate the universally quantified formulas in F. Quantified variables of type u are instantiated using terms from F. First, the strategy instantiates x and y in $\forall x, y.\ \text{f } x = \text{f } y \implies x = y$ with sk and h (f sk), respectively. Then it instantiates x and y in the lemma $\forall y.\ \neg\,(\exists x.\ y = \text{f } x) \vee y = \text{f } (\text{h } y)$ with sk and f sk, respectively. These instantiations arise from E-matching, which matches each lemma's pattern against the terms already present in the equivalence classes maintained by the SMT solver. The instantiation lemmas

$$(\forall y.\ \neg\,(\exists x.\ y = \text{f } x) \vee y = \text{f } (\text{h } y)) \implies \text{f sk} \neq \text{f sk} \vee \text{f sk} = \text{f } (\text{h } (\text{f sk})) \qquad (\ell_4)$$
$$(\forall x, y.\ \text{f } x = \text{f } y \implies x = y) \implies \text{f sk} \neq \text{f } (\text{h } (\text{f sk})) \vee \text{sk} = \text{h } (\text{f sk}) \qquad (\ell_5)$$

are then added to F. At this point, the quantifier-free subsolver finds F unsatisfiable in $\mathcal{T}$ by determining that the conclusions of the lemmas ℓ_3, ℓ_4, and ℓ_5 are jointly unsatisfiable in $\mathcal{T}$. This implies that the conjecture is valid. ∎

Example 7. We consider a simplified version of TPTP benchmark SYO268^5. Let u_1, u_2 be uninterpreted sorts, and let r be a function symbol of type $u_1 \to u_2 \to o$. Consider the conjecture

$$(\forall x. \, \exists y. \, \mathsf{r} \, x \, y) \implies \exists g. \, \forall x. \, \mathsf{r} \, x \, (g \, x)$$

where g has type $u_1 \to u_2$, x has type u_1, and y has type u_2. The formula states that for every total relation r on $u_1 \times u_2$, there exists a corresponding function from u_1 to u_2. To prove the formula by contradiction, we negate it and obtain the input problem $F = \{\forall x. \, \exists y. \, \mathsf{r} \, x \, y, \, \forall g. \, \exists x. \, \neg \mathsf{r} \, x \, (g \, x)\}$.

MBQI-Enum generates a grammar for g using the set of symbols $S = \{\mathsf{r}\}$. The grammar consists of the rules

$$g_0 ::= \lambda y. \, g_1 \qquad\qquad\qquad g_1 ::= t$$

Based on this grammar, MBQI-Enum generates the substitution $\{g \mapsto \lambda y. \, t\}$, where t is a ground term of type u_2. As a result, the SMT solver terminates with an unknown status.

By contrast, with our extension, the solver behaves as follows. Let x be a variable of type u_2. We extend the symbol set to $S \cup \{x\}$. Consider the rules

$$p_0 ::= \mathsf{true} \mid \mathsf{false} \mid p_1 = p_1 \mid p_2 = p_2 \mid \mathsf{r} \, p_1 \, p_2 \mid \neg p_2 \mid p_2 \wedge p_2$$
$$p_1 ::= y$$
$$p_2 ::= x$$

We augment the MBQI-Enum grammar by adding a rule to produce $\varepsilon x. \, p_0$. The resulting grammar consists of the rules for p_0, p_1, and p_2 above together with

$$g_0 ::= \lambda y. \, g_1 \qquad\qquad\qquad g_1 ::= \varepsilon x. \, p_0 \mid t$$

Using this grammar, our strategy generates the term $\lambda y. \, \varepsilon x. \, \mathsf{r} \, y \, x$, leading to the substitution $\{g \mapsto \lambda y. \, \varepsilon x. \, \mathsf{r} \, y \, x\}$.

Corresponding to this term, we introduce a fresh Skolem symbol h $: u_1 \to u_2$. Our strategy asserts the following lemma:

$$\forall y. \, \neg \, (\exists x. \, \mathsf{r} \, y \, x) \vee \mathsf{r} \, y \, (\mathsf{h} \, y) \tag{ℓ_1}$$

The original enumerated term $\lambda y. \, \varepsilon x. \, \mathsf{r} \, y \, x$ is thus rewritten to the term $\lambda y. \, \mathsf{h} \, y$. The substitution $\sigma = \{y \mapsto \lambda y. \, \mathsf{h} \, y\}$ is considered. Next, the instantiation lemma

$$(\forall g. \, \exists x. \, \neg \mathsf{r} \, x \, (g \, x)) \implies \exists x. \, \neg \mathsf{r} \, x \, (\mathsf{h} \, x) \tag{ℓ_2}$$

is generated by applying the substitution σ followed by β-reduction. The set of lemmas $L = \{(\ell_1), (\ell_2)\}$ is constructed and then merged with F. Afterward, Skolemization introduces a fresh symbol sk corresponding to the existentially quantified variable x. The lemma

$$(\exists x. \, \neg \mathsf{r} \, x \, (\mathsf{h} \, x)) \implies \neg \mathsf{r} \, \mathsf{sk} \, (\mathsf{h} \, \mathsf{sk}) \tag{ℓ_3}$$

is added to F.

The strategy proceeds to instantiate the universally quantified formulas of F. Quantified variables of nonfunction type are instantiated using terms from F. First, the strategy instantiates x and y in the lemma $\forall y. \neg (\exists x.\ \mathsf{r}\ y\ x) \vee \mathsf{r}\ y\ (\mathsf{h}\ y)$ with $\mathsf{h}\ \mathsf{sk}$ and sk, respectively. Then it instantiates x and y in the axiom $\forall x.\ \exists y.\ \mathsf{r}\ x\ y$ with sk, and $\mathsf{h}\ \mathsf{sk}$, respectively. These instantiations arise from E-matching, which matches each lemma's pattern against the terms already present in the equivalence classes maintained by the solver. The instantiation lemmas

$$(\forall y. \neg (\exists x.\ \mathsf{r}\ y\ x) \vee \mathsf{r}\ y\ (\mathsf{h}\ y)) \implies \neg\, \mathsf{r}\ \mathsf{sk}\ (\mathsf{h}\ \mathsf{sk}) \vee \mathsf{r}\ \mathsf{sk}\ (\mathsf{h}\ \mathsf{sk}) \qquad (\ell_4)$$

$$(\forall x.\ \exists y.\ \mathsf{r}\ x\ y) \implies \mathsf{r}\ \mathsf{sk}\ (\mathsf{h}\ \mathsf{sk}) \qquad (\ell_5)$$

are added to F. At this point, the quantifier-free subsolver finds F unsatisfiable. Hence the conjecture is valid. ∎

4   Implementation

We developed our strategy as an extension of cvc5's implementation of MBQI-Enum. Our extension refines the selection of grammars for term enumeration, introduces a mechanism for managing choice terms generated by these grammars, and incorporates a filtering step to discard redundant or unsuitable terms.

For each quantified variable, MBQI-Enum constructs a SyGuS grammar that specifies the space of candidate instantiations (Algorithm 4, line 4). Our implementation augments these grammars with terminal rules for generating choice terms. Specifically, for each nonterminal type that qualifies, we add a corresponding expression of the form $\varepsilon x.\ \varphi$, which selects a value satisfying a predicate over that type (lines 5–9). This allows the enumerator to synthesize Skolem-style instantiations directly from the grammar.

We use the existing implementation of the fast SyGuS-based enumerator for term generation. This enumerator considers only terms that are unique up to rewriting [31]. During the enumeration process, ε terms are constructed within cvc5's internal abstract syntax tree representation, thereby exploiting cvc5's built-in rewriter. For example, $\varepsilon x.\ x = t$, where x does not occur free in t, is rewritten to t.

Beyond these rewrite-based simplifications, our implementation applies additional heuristics for filtering ε terms. In particular, it explicitly discards any term of the form $\varepsilon x.\ \varphi$, where x does not occur free in φ. These heuristics are implemented via a callback from the SyGuS enumerator.

The enumerator constructs ε terms that are immediately purified by our implementation. Recall that each ε term is replaced with a fresh Skolem symbol, and an accompanying lemma is generated to relate the Skolem to the original ε term (Algorithm 5, lines 6–10). For example, given a term $\varepsilon x.\ \varphi$, the procedure introduces a fresh Skolem h and asserts that either $\varphi(\mathsf{h})$ holds or the quantified condition that motivated the ε term is already satisfied. An important heuristic is that our approach designates the Skolem application itself as a trigger for the generated quantified formula, thereby ensuring that instantiations during solving are guided by the intended terms.

During instantiation, terms containing ε terms are first normalized through the purification and filtering procedures described above before being considered as candidate substitutions. The generalized strategy, shown in Algorithm 3, iteratively builds substitutions by enumerating terms from the augmented grammars (lines 6–12), tests them in the current model (line 13), and commits suitable assignments (line 14). Notably, unlike the standard MBQI-Enum procedure, our strategy returns not only substitutions but also auxiliary lemmas (line 16).

5   Evaluation

We extensively evaluated our cvc5 implementation of the extended MBQI-Enum on higher-order benchmarks.

Since the publication of Kondylidou et al. [19], MBQI-Enum has been developed further independently of our work on choice. In our evaluation, by "original MBQI-Enum" we mean the most recent version of the strategy excluding our modifications related to ε. This strategy includes the following enhancements over Kondylidou et al.:

- MBQI-Enum now supports partial applications, allowing the strategy to consider candidate terms that partially apply functions during enumeration.

- Timeouts have been added to subsolver invocations used for checking candidate instantiations, preventing individual candidates from stalling the overall SMT loop. In addition, there is an option that completely prohibits nested MBQI calls, which avoids potential nontermination caused by nested subsolver invocations.

- MBQI-Enum now incorporates a guess-and-test loop with a progress-aware instantiation cache: When a proposed instantiation fails to refute the current model, it is cached to avoid rechecking the same substitution later, thereby ensuring that the strategy always makes progress.

- We now incorporate a lookahead approach that preemptively considers Skolem symbols for quantified formulas that are not introduced during preprocessing. These symbols are incorporated into the SyGuS grammars, thus enriching the set of terms we consider for instantiation with MBQI-Enum.

Setup. We denote our configuration of MBQI-Enum extended with choice by cvc5[C]. We compare our strategy against several established quantifier instantiation strategies in cvc5: cvc5[s], which uses SyQI [27]; cvc5[m], which implements MBQI [15]; cvc5[M], which implements the original MBQI-Enum [19]; cvc5[hoelim], which eagerly rewrites higher-order constraints into first-order form and applies full quantifier saturation; and cvc5[foinst], which relies on exhaustive first-order-style instantiation and axiomatic handling of higher-order applications.

Table 1. Extended MBQI-Enum vs. other provers on TPTP TH0 benchmarks

	Satallax	Vampire	Zipperposition	cvc5[C]
Satisfiable	196	14	0	**204**
Unsatisfiable	2162	**2303**	2083	2178
Total	2358	2317	2083	**2382**
Unknown	15	16	0	154
Timeouts	1384	1424	1674	1221

We also include a comparison with the state-of-the-art provers Satallax [10], Vampire [7], and Zipperposition [40]. Satallax was run with its default settings. Vampire was run in portfolio mode, as its higher-order reasoning configuration automatically enables this mode and disabling it makes the prover much less competitive. For Zipperposition, we enabled several options that were extensively evaluated by Bozec and Blanchette [9] and shown to achieve the best overall performance on higher-order benchmarks.

All experiments were conducted on a machine with a 40-core Intel Xeon Silver 4114 CPU running at 2.20 GHz, equipped with 192 GB of RAM and running Debian 12 (Bookworm). Each benchmark was executed with a timeout of 60 seconds.

Benchmarks. The experiments were carried out on monomorphic higher-order problems (TH0) from version 9.1.0 of the TPTP library [39]. The benchmark set consists of 3757 problems. From the 3962 TH0 problems, we excluded 205 benchmarks that one or more systems could not parse (e.g., because of the use of interpreted arithmetic).

To support reasoning with choice, we implemented external parser support for the TPTP operators for ε and the definite description operator ι. Although the TPTP library contains very few problems with ε and ι, they might arise in users' problems.

Results. The results are shown in Tables 1 and 2, where bold indicates the most successful system. Notably, our approach achieves the highest total count of solved benchmarks, surpassing the nearest competitor by 24 solved problems and the baseline MBQI-Enum by 23.

Table 1 compares our strategy (cvc5[C]) with external state-of-the-art provers. Our approach achieves the highest total number of solved benchmarks, with 2382 problems, surpassing Satallax, Vampire, and Zipperposition. It outperforms the nearest competitor by 24 benchmarks. In particular, our strategy solves 204 satisfiable problems, while Satallax solves 196, Vampire solves 14, and Zipperposition solves none. For unsatisfiable problems, Vampire performs the best, solving 2303 benchmarks, whereas our strategy solves 2178, Satallax 2162, and Zipperposition 2083. Overall, our strategy demonstrates strong performance across

Table 2. Extended MBQI-Enum vs. other cvc5 strategies on TPTP TH0 benchmarks

	cvc5[hoelim]	cvc5[foinst]	cvc5[s]	cvc5[m]	cvc5[M]	cvc5[C]
Satisfiable	14	37	88	188	204	**204**
Unsatisfiable	2082	2126	1657	2074	2155	**2178**
Total	2096	2163	1745	2262	2359	**2382**
Unknown	0	125	45	289	158	154
Timeouts	1661	1469	1967	1206	1240	1221

both satisfiable and unsatisfiable problems compared with the state-of-the-art provers.

Table 2 compares cvc5[C] with other cvc5 quantifier instantiation strategies. Our configuration solves 23 unsatisfiable benchmarks that the baseline MBQI-Enum cannot, with no benchmarks lost, while solving the same number of satisfiable problems (204). This shows that extending MBQI-Enum with choice consistently improves solver performance. Overall, when compared against all other available quantifier instantiation strategies, our strategy achieves the strongest performance, demonstrating that it is considerably more effective on higher-order benchmarks than any other individual technique in cvc5. It may seem as though 23 additional benchmarks are not that many; however, we should bear in mind that the vast majority of higher-order TPTP benchmarks do not contain choice and can likely be solved without reasoning about choice.

In addition, our technique solves several problems not solved by its competitors: 143 problems not solved by Vampire, 296 not solved by Zipperposition, 235 not solved by Satallax, and 21 not solved by any other cvc5 strategy. When considering all systems, cvc5[C] solves exactly one benchmark that no other system can solve.

6   Related Work

Besides MBQI-Enum, other quantifier instantiation strategies work on higher-order problems, notably E-matching, MBQI, and SyQI. In higher-order E-matching, quantified variables are instantiated by matching their patterns against ground terms available in the current context—that is, the set of ground terms introduced during proof search. This technique has been extended to support higher-order features, such as functional arguments [3]. Higher-order MBQI constructs candidate models that provide interpretations for functions. This enables the solver to generate ground instantiations of quantified formulas in an attempt to refute the current model [15]. Higher-order SyQI further improves the instantiation process by selecting candidate terms using syntactic templates and heuristics derived from the problem's structure, guided by a fixed grammar [27]. None of these approaches provides special support for Hilbert's choice.

Other higher-order provers support Hilbert's choice in various ways. Satallax implements specialized tableau inference rules that directly reason about ε

terms in a sound and refutationally complete way [2]. Leo-III integrates ε into its extensional higher-order paramodulation calculus and supports Henkin semantics with choice [38]. Zipperposition includes a dedicated choice axiom within its higher-order superposition calculus, allowing it to reason about ε terms as needed [6]. Vampire supports Hilbert's choice either through a Leo-III-style inference or by introducing the choice axiom [7].

Hilbert's choice is also present in proof assistants such as Isabelle/HOL [28], Lean [24], and Rocq [36] (formerly known as Coq). In Isabelle/HOL, the choice operator is introduced as an axiom as part of the system's core libraries. In systems based on dependent type theory, such as Lean and Rocq, choice is introduced via classical axioms, which should be avoided in constructive definitions and proofs. Even in Isabelle/HOL, some users, such as Paulson [29], prefer to avoid choice:

> Pragmatists may argue that in verification nobody cares whether choice is used or not. However, pragmatists should be concerned that reasoning about ε-terms is tricky.

Reasoning about choice is indeed tricky, but cvc5 can do it reasonably well now.

7   Conclusion

We presented an SMT quantifier instantiation strategy that extends the MBQI-Enum strategy so as to reason natively about Hilbert's choice operator. It can be used to solve problems that contain Hilbert's choice but also problems that do not (cf. Example 1). We implemented the approach in the SMT solver cvc5. The empirical results on higher-order TPTP benchmarks show that our strategy is clearly superior to the original MBQI-Enum.

We believe there is potential for further improving the strategy. We noticed that the ε terms we need often occur too late in the term enumeration (which is by increasing term size), since they tend to be relatively complex. Better term enumeration heuristics and term filtering could help the SMT solver generate the desired terms earlier—before the timeout.

Acknowledgments. We thank Mark Summerfield and the anonymous reviewers for their helpful comments. We also thank Haniel Barbosa, who provided many comments on an earlier draft.

This research was cofunded by the European Union (ERC, Nekoka, 101083038). Views and opinions expressed are however those of the authors only and do not necessarily reflect those of the European Union or the European Research Council. Neither the European Union nor the granting authority can be held responsible for them.

This research was also partially funded by the Defense Advanced Research Projects Agency (DARPA) under contract FA8750-24-2-1001. Any opinions, findings, and conclusions or recommendations expressed here are those of the authors and do not necessarily reflect the views of DARPA.

Data-Availability Statement. The artifact associated with this paper, including the software and scripts used for experiments, is publicly available on Zenodo [20]. The raw evaluation data are also available on Zenodo [21]. The instructions on the first Zenodo page [20] explain how to reproduce the experimental evaluation.

References

1. Andrews, B.: An Introduction to Mathematical Logic and Type Theory: To Truth Through Proof, APLS, vol. 27. Springer (2022)
2. Backes, J., Brown, C.E.: Analytic tableaux for higher-order logic with choice. Journal of Automated Reasoning **47**, 451–479 (2011)
3. Barbosa, H., Barrett, C., Brain, M., Kremer, G., Lachnitt, H., Mann, M., Mohamed, A., Mohamed, M., Niemetz, A., Nötzli, A., Ozdemir, A., Preiner, M., Reynolds, A., Sheng, Y., Tinelli, C., Zohar, Y.: cvc5: A versatile and industrial-strength SMT solver. In: Fishman, D., Rosu, G. (eds.) TACAS 2022. LNCS, vol. 13243, pp. 415–442. Springer (2022)
4. Barbosa, H., Reynolds, A., Ouraoui, D.E., Tinelli, C., Barrett, C.: Extending SMT solvers to higher-order logic. In: Fontaine, P. (ed.) CADE 2019. LNCS, vol. 11716, pp. 35–54. Springer (2019)
5. Barrett, C.W., Conway, C.L., Deters, M., Hadarean, L., Jovanovic, D., King, T., Reynolds, A., Tinelli, C.: CVC4. In: Gopalakrishnan, G., Qadeer, S. (eds.) CAV 2011. LNCS, vol. 6806, pp. 171–177. Springer (2011)
6. Bentkamp, A., Blanchette, J., Tourret, S., Vukmirović, P.: Superposition for higher-order logic. Journal of Automated Reasoning **67** (2023)
7. Bhayat, A., Suda, M.: A higher-order Vampire (short paper). In: Benzmüller, C., Heule, M.J.H., Schmidt, R.A. (eds.) IJCAR 2024. LNCS, vol. 14739, pp. 75–85. Springer (2024)
8. Bouton, T., de Oliveira, D.C.B., Déharbe, D., Fontaine, P.: veriT: An open, trustable and efficient SMT-solver. In: Schmidt, R.A. (ed.) CADE 2009. LNCS, vol. 5663, pp. 151–156. Springer (2009)
9. Bozec, T., Blanchette, J.: Iterative monomorphisation. In: Thiemann, R., Weidenbach, C. (eds.) FroCoS 2025. LNCS, vol. 15979, pp. 269–286. Springer (2025)
10. Brown, C.E.: Satallax: An automatic higher-order prover. Journal of Automated Reasoning **7364**, 111–117 (2012)
11. Church, A.: A formulation of the simple theory of types. Journal of Symbolic Logic **5**, 56–68 (1940)
12. Detlefs, D., Nelson, G., Saxe, J.B.: Simplify: A theorem prover for program checking. Journal of the ACM **52**(3), 365–473 (2005)
13. Dross, C., Conchon, S., Paskevic, A.: Reasoning with triggers. In: Fontaine, P., Goel, A. (eds.) SMT 2012. EPiC Series in Computing, vol. 20, pp. 22–31 (2012)
14. Ge, Y., Barrett, C.W., Tinelli, C.: Solving quantified verification conditions using satisfiability modulo theories. Annals of Mathematics and Artificial Intelligence **55**(1-2), 101–122 (2009)
15. Ge, Y., de Moura, L.: Complete instantiation for quantified formulas in satisfiabiliby modulo theories. In: Bouajjani, A., Maler, O. (eds.) CAV 2009. LNCS, vol. 5643, pp. 306–320. Springer (2009)
16. Gordon, M.J.C.: Introduction to the HOL system. In: Archer, M., Joyce, J.J., Levitt, K.N., Windley, P.J. (eds.) HOL 1991. pp. 2–3. IEEE (1991)

17. Hilbert, D., Ackermann, W.: Grundzüge der Theoretischen Logik, Grundlehren der mathematischen Wissenschaften, vol. 27. Springer (1928)
18. Hilbert, D., Bernays, P.: Grundlagen der Mathematik I, Grundlehren der mathematischen Wissenschaften, vol. 40. Springer (1934)
19. Kondylidou, L., Reynolds, A., Blanchette, J.: Augmenting model-based instantiation with fast enumeration. In: Gurfinkel, A., Heule, M. (eds.) TACAS 2025. LNCS, vol. 15696, pp. 85–103. Springer (2025)
20. Kondylidou, L., Reynolds, A., Blanchette, J., Tinelli, C.: Artifact for paper "Enumerating choice terms in model-based quantifier instantiation". In: TACAS 2026. Zenodo (2026), https://doi.org/10.5281/zenodo.18304537
21. Kondylidou, L., Reynolds, A., Blanchette, J., Tinelli, C.: Enumerating choice terms in model-based quantifier instantiation [data set]. In: TACAS 2026. Zenodo (2026), https://doi.org/10.5281/zenodo.18212605
22. de Moura, L., Bjørner, N.: Efficient E-matching for SMT solvers. In: Pfenning, F. (ed.) CADE 2007. LNCS, vol. 4603, pp. 183–198. Springer (2007)
23. de Moura, L., Bjørner, N.: Z3: An efficient SMT solver. In: Ramakrishnan, C.R., Rehof, J. (eds.) TACAS 2008. LNCS, vol. 4963, pp. 337–340. Springer (2008)
24. de Moura, L., Ullrich, S.: The Lean 4 theorem prover and programming language. In: Platzer, A., Sutcliffe, G. (eds.) CADE 2021. LNCS, vol. 12699, pp. 625–635. Springer (2021)
25. Niemetz, A., Preiner, M.: Bitwuzla. In: Enea, C., Lal, A. (eds.) CAV 2023. LNCS, vol. 13965, pp. 3–17. Springer (2023)
26. Niemetz, A., Preiner, M., Biere, A.: Boolector 2.0. Journal on Satisfiability, Boolean Modeling and Computation **9**, 53–58 (2014)
27. Niemetz, A., Preiner, M., Reynolds, A., Barrett, C., Tinelli, C.: Syntax-guided quantifier instantiation. In: Groote, J.F., Larsen, K.G. (eds.) TACAS 2021. LNCS, vol. 12652, pp. 145–163. Springer (2021)
28. Nipkow, T., Paulson, L.C., Wenzel, M.: Isabelle/HOL: A Proof Assistant for Higher-Order Logic, LNCS, vol. 2283. Springer (2002)
29. Paulson, L.C.: Defining functions on equivalence classes. In: Guruswami, V., Glazener, T. (eds.) CoRR 2019. vol. 7, pp. 658–675. Association for Computing Machinery (2019)
30. Reynolds, A., Barbosa, H., Fontaine, P.: Revisiting enumerative instantiation. In: Beyer, D. (ed.) TACAS 2018. LNCS, vol. 10806, pp. 112–131. Springer (2018)
31. Reynolds, A., Barbosa, H., NÖtzli, A., Barrett, C.W., Tinelli, C.: cvc4sy: Smart and fast term enumeration for syntax-guided synthesis. In: Dillig, I., Tasiran, S. (eds.) CAV 2019, Part II. LNCS, vol. 11562, pp. 74–83. Springer (2019)
32. Reynolds, A., Blanchette, J.C., Cruanes, S., Tinelli, C.: Model finding for recursive functions in SMT. In: Olivetti, N., Tiwari, A. (eds.) IJCAR 2016. LNCS, vol. 9706, pp. 133–151. Springer (2016)
33. Reynolds, A., Deters, M., Kuncak, V., Tinelli, C., Barrett, C.: Counterexample-guided quantifier instantiation for synthesis in SMT. In: Kroening, D., Păsăreanu, C.S. (eds.) CAV 2015. LNCS, vol. 9207, pp. 198–216. Springer (2015)
34. Reynolds, A., Tinelli, C., Goel, A., Krstić, S.: Finite model finding in SMT. In: Sharygina, N., Veith, H. (eds.) CAV 2013. LNCS, vol. 8044, pp. 640–655. Springer (2013)
35. Reynolds, A., Tinelli, C., de Moura, L.: Finding conflicting instances of quantified formulas in SMT. In: FMCAD 2014. pp. 195–202. IEEE (2014)
36. Rocq Development Team: Rocq Prover. https://zenodo.org/records/15149629 (2025), Zenodo

37. Simpson, S.G.: The epsilon calculus and conservative extensions. Notre Dame Journal of Formal Logic **25**(3), 193–202 (1984)
38. Steen, A.: Extensional Paramodulation for Higher-Order Logic and its Effective Implementation Leo-III. Ph.D. thesis, Freie Universität Berlin (2020)
39. Sutcliffe, G.: The TPTP problem library and associated infrastructure—from CNF to TH0, TPTP v6.4.0. Journal of Automated Reasoning **59**, 483–502 (2017)
40. Vukmirović, P., Bentkamp, A., Blanchette, J., Cruanes, S., Nummelin, V., Tourret, S.: Making higher-order superposition work. Journal of Automated Reasoning **66**, 541–564 (2022)

Fast Ramsey Quantifier Elimination in LIRA
(with applications to liveness checking)

Kilian Lichtner[1], Pascal Bergsträßer[1]✉,
Moses Ganardi[1], Anthony W. Lin[1,2],
and Georg Zetzsche[2]

[1] RPTU University Kaiserslautern-Landau
`{lichtner,pbergstr,moses.ganardi}@rptu.de`
[2] Max Planck Institute for Software Systems (MPI-SWS)
`{awlin,georg}@mpi-sws.org`

Abstract. Ramsey quantifiers have recently been proposed as a unified framework for handling properties of interests in program verification involving proofs in the form of infinite cliques, which are not expressible in first-order logic. Among others, these include liveness verification and monadic decomposability. We present the tool REAL, which implements an efficient elimination of Ramsey quantifiers in existential linear arithmetic theories over integers (LIA), reals (LRA), and the mixed case (LIRA). The tool supports a convenient input format, which is an extension of SMT-LIB over the aforementioned theories with Ramsey quantifiers. We also demonstrate a substantial speedup from the original prototype. As an application, we provide an automatic translation from FASTer (a tool for verifying reachability over infinite-state systems) output format to our extension of SMT-LIB and show how our tool extends FASTer to liveness checking.

Keywords: Satisfiability Modulo Theories · Linear Arithmetics · Quantifier Elimination · Infinite-State Verification

1 Introduction

Satisfiability Modulo Theories (SMT) (cf. [7]) is a highly successful automated reasoning framework that is based on first-order theorem proving. In particular, building on the success of propositional SAT-solvers, SMT-solvers support numerous first-order theories including linear arithmetics, array theory, string theory, bitvector theory, and Equality logic with Uninterpreted Functions (EUF), to name a few. The SMT framework is also suitable for reasoning about programs with respect to safety properties, e.g., using Constraint Horn Clauses [6,11]. Proving liveness (e.g. termination), however, typically requires an extension of the SMT framework with reasoning about well-foundedness, which is not first-order definable even with the help of recursive predicates (equivalently, second-order quantifiers).

S. Junges and G. Katz (Eds.): TACAS 2026, LNCS 16505, pp. 315–323, 2026.
https://doi.org/10.1007/978-3-032-22752-2_16

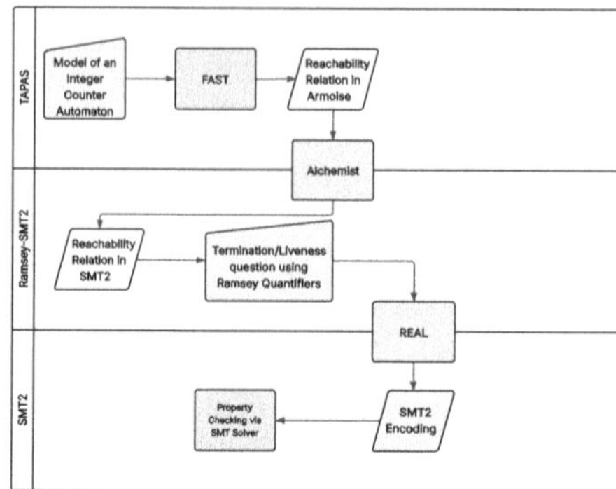

Fig. 1: Toolchain

In recent years, Ramsey quantifiers have been proposed [4,5] as a uniform framework for handling properties of interests in program verification involving infinite *cliques*. These include, among others, liveness [4,16,17] and monadic decomposability [18]. In essence, we extend an SMT with formulas of the form

$$\psi(\boldsymbol{z}) := \exists^{\mathrm{ram}}\boldsymbol{x}, \boldsymbol{y} \colon \varphi(\boldsymbol{x}, \boldsymbol{y}, \boldsymbol{z}) \tag{1}$$

with $|\boldsymbol{x}| = |\boldsymbol{y}|$ and with the semantics that it is true under the valuation $\boldsymbol{z} \mapsto \boldsymbol{c}$ iff the graph $\varphi(\boldsymbol{x}, \boldsymbol{y}, \boldsymbol{c})$ has an infinite directed clique, i.e., there is an infinite sequence $\boldsymbol{a}_1, \boldsymbol{a}_2, \ldots$ of pairwise distinct vectors such that $\varphi(\boldsymbol{a}_i, \boldsymbol{a}_j, \boldsymbol{c})$ holds for all $1 \leq i < j$. To see how Ramsey quantifiers can be used to encode liveness properties, assume that $R \subseteq \mathbb{R}^k \times \mathbb{R}^k$ is the reachability relation (i.e. transitive closure) of some transition relation $T \subseteq \mathbb{R}^k \times \mathbb{R}^k$. Then T terminates iff both $\exists \boldsymbol{z} \colon Start(\boldsymbol{z}) \wedge \exists^{\mathrm{ram}}\boldsymbol{x}, \boldsymbol{y} \colon R(\boldsymbol{z}, \boldsymbol{x}) \wedge R(\boldsymbol{x}, \boldsymbol{y})$ and $\exists \boldsymbol{x}, \boldsymbol{y} \colon Start(\boldsymbol{x}) \wedge R(\boldsymbol{x}, \boldsymbol{y}) \wedge R(\boldsymbol{y}, \boldsymbol{y})$ are not satisfied.

It was shown in [5] that Ramsey quantifiers can be eliminated in polynomial time for the existential fragments of LIA (Linear Integer Arithmetic), LRA (Linear Real Arithmetic) and LIRA (Linear Integer Real Arithmetic). Despite this, only a very prototypical implementation of the algorithms [5] exists for LIA and LRA, and no complete implementation so far exists for LIRA. In particular, scalability test was done only on a small micro-benchmark. Furthermore, the current implementation depends very much on the Z3 Python API, and the user cannot simply specify the constraint in an SMT-LIB-like format, which can be reduced to any SMT-solver.

Contributions. In this paper, we present REAL — Ramsey Elimination for Arithmetic Logic — a solver-agnostic elimination procedure for Ramsey quantifiers. REAL allows constraints to be specified in an extension of SMT-LIB with Ramsey quantifiers and significantly improves elimination speeds. REAL also improves on resulting formula sizes and solving times (see Fig. 4). Finally, REAL outputs the resulting formula as an SMT-LIB file, which can then be solved by any SMT-solver supporting LIA, LRA, and LIRA.

To demonstrate efficacy of the tool, we apply REAL to liveness verification. More precisely, we use FAST(er) [2] — which uses the Talence Presburger Arithmetic Suite (TaPAS) [12] — to compute the reachability relations of *integer counter systems* in Armoise, a language for Presburger-definable sets of integer vectors (equivalently, relations over numbers). In particular, numerous benchmarks are available, which encode parameterized distributed protocols. We implemented *Alchemist*, which transpiles such relations into SMT-LIB [3]. Combined with REAL, we successfully verify liveness over parameterized distributed protocols (using the toolchain described in Fig. 1), for which FAST(er) successfully computes reachability relations, including McCarthy91. See Fig. 2.

Illustrating example. We illustrate on a simple example how REAL can be used to prove termination. More involved examples can be found in Section 3 and [5]. The following program has two integer variables x_1, x_2 and as long as both have values greater 0, the program nondeterministically decrements one of them.

Algorithm 1: Example of a terminating program

---

1 **int** $x_1 \leftarrow$ input-int();
2 **int** $x_2 \leftarrow$ input-int();
3 **while** $x_1 > 0 \wedge x_2 > 0$ **do**
4 | **either** $x_1 \leftarrow x_1 - 1$ **or** $x_2 \leftarrow x_2 - 1$
5 **end**

We observe that an overapproximation of the reachability relation after at least one iteration of the while loop can be expressed by the LIA formula

$$\varphi := [(y_1 < x_1 \wedge y_2 \leq x_2) \vee (y_1 \leq x_1 \wedge y_2 < x_2)] \wedge y_1 \geq 0 \wedge y_2 \geq 0$$

where y_1, y_2 are the new values of x_1, x_2. Now, REAL in combination with an SMT-solver can be used to verify the absence of both an infinite clique and a loop in φ, which proves termination of the program.

2 Implementation

2.1 Alchemist

Alchemist is a transpiler for the output of FASTer, which is a subset of Armoise, to SMT-LIB. We refer to the full version [13] for an Armoise example and its transpiled version.

Armoise is designed to describe semilinear sets and common operations on them, such as union, intersection, and complement. It also supports set comprehensions with arbitrary Presburger guards.

The translation from Armoise to SMT-LIB reduces to the standard translation from semilinear sets to Presburger arithmetic [10], together with the elimination of any existential quantifiers introduced in the process, which requires inlining all identifier definitions.

2.2   REAL

The algorithm presented in [5] takes a formula ψ as in Eq. (1), where φ is an existential formula in LIRA, and computes a formula equivalent to ψ that only contains existential quantifiers, i.e., where the Ramsey quantifier is eliminated. To this end, the existentially quantified variables in φ are first replaced with additional Ramsey quantified variables. Then [5] identifies sufficient and necessary conditions that can be formulated in existential LIRA for the existence of an infinite clique. For example, let

$$\varphi(\boldsymbol{x}, \boldsymbol{y}, z) := y_1 > x_1 \wedge x_1 + x_2 < z$$

be a formula in LIA. One can observe that $\exists^{\mathrm{ram}}\boldsymbol{x}, \boldsymbol{y}\colon \varphi(\boldsymbol{x}, \boldsymbol{y}, z)$ is equivalent to the existence of a sequence $\boldsymbol{a}, \boldsymbol{a} + \boldsymbol{b}, \boldsymbol{a} + 2\boldsymbol{b}, \ldots$ such that $a_1 + a_2 < z$, $b_1 > 0$, and $b_1 + b_2 \leq 0$, which can be stated by the existential LIA formula

$$\exists \boldsymbol{x}, \boldsymbol{y}\colon x_1 + x_2 < z \wedge y_1 > 0 \wedge y_1 + y_2 \leq 0.$$

Clearly, any such sequence $\boldsymbol{a}, \boldsymbol{a} + \boldsymbol{b}, \boldsymbol{a} + 2\boldsymbol{b}, \ldots$ is also an infinite clique of φ. For the converse, let $\boldsymbol{a}_1, \boldsymbol{a}_2, \ldots$ be an infinite clique of φ for the valuation $z \mapsto c$. Let $\boldsymbol{a}_i = (a_{i,1}, a_{i,2})$. Since $a_{i,1} + a_{i,2} < c$ and $a_{i,1}, a_{i,2}$ are integers for all $i \geq 1$, there is $k \geq 1$ such that $a_{k,1} + a_{k,2} \geq a_{j,1} + a_{j,2}$ for all $j \geq 1$. Thus, if we define $\boldsymbol{a} := \boldsymbol{a}_k$ and $\boldsymbol{b} := \boldsymbol{a}_{k+1} - \boldsymbol{a}_k$, we have that $a_1 + a_2 < c$, $b_1 > 0$, and $b_1 + b_2 \leq 0$ as required.

REAL improves the prototype implementation in three main categories:

(i) Enabling input formulas from a convenient extension of SMT-LIB (removing previous strict restrictions) and producing formulas in SMT-LIB format,

(ii) Using more efficient data structures and procedures to speed up the elimination process (e.g. caching and sharing (sub)formulas, more efficient atom shape normalization, combining duplicate tree walks),

(iii) Producing more compact and structured formulas, e.g., by handling integer equalities and non-strict real inequalities directly, sharing common subexpressions in the Boolean abstraction, and replacing unnecessary theory variables with Boolean variables where possible.

For (i), REAL extends PySMT's [9] abstract syntax tree with the Ramsey quantifier, enabling both parsing from and exporting to an *extended SMT-LIB syntax*. We extend the SMT-LIB grammar (following the conventions in [3]) as follows, where ... denotes existing production rules:

$$\langle \text{term} \rangle ::= \ldots$$

$$| \ (\textbf{ramsey}\ (\langle \text{sorted\_var} \rangle^{+})\ (\langle \text{sorted\_var} \rangle^{+})\ \langle \text{term} \rangle)$$

$$| \ (\textbf{ramsey}\ \langle \text{sort} \rangle\ (\langle \text{symbol} \rangle^{+})\ (\langle \text{symbol} \rangle^{+})\ \langle \text{term} \rangle)$$

Here, symbols enclosed by $\langle . \rangle$ are non-terminals. The first rule is for mixed quantifiers, and the second offers a shorthand for integer or real-only quantifiers. The new symbol **ramsey** has the semantics of $\exists^{\mathrm{ram}}$ as defined above.

Benchmark	FAST	Alchemist	REAL Solving		SAT
sliding_window	421.67ms	0.164s	0.076s	82.61ms	True
lamport_bakery	1.83s	9.505s	18.629s	6.23s	True
mccarthy91	145.29ms	2.282s	7.834s	853.53ms	False
Berkley	191.99ms	0.002s	0.003s	13.88ms	False
DRAGON	2.07s	0.457s	0.276s	23.71ms	False
futurbus	125.95s	16.972s	28.570s	1.46s	False
MOESI	409.04ms	0.103s	0.052s	18.04ms	False
SYNAPSE	78.53ms	0.017s	0.016s	13.05ms	False

Benchmark	Armoise Formula	SMT Pre-elimination	SMT Post-elimination
sliding_window	5795	82254	18825
lamport_bakery	54348	25120657	5150912
mccarthy91	3385	3984717	1701846
Berkley	98	35	397
DRAGON	20318	186122	44126
futurbus	83510	27605000	5433832
MOESI	5941	21606	9125
SYNAPSE	946	2285	2709

Fig. 2: Liveness verification results with execution times (left) and formula sizes measured in tree nodes (right)

3 Benchmarks and Experiments

Experiments were performed on an Arch Linux machine (AMD Ryzen 7 2700X, 32 GiB RAM). Satisfiability was checked using Z3 v4.15.1, while FASTer utilized the PresTAF solver. Tool timings were recorded via the time command. While REAL and Alchemist use the inbuilt timing reports.

3.1 Case Studies

We evaluated our verification pipeline on a selection of both classical and practical examples, chosen to represent a broad range of system behaviors.

McCarthy 91 Function [15]: The McCarthy 91 function is a classical example in program verification defined as:

$$M(n) = \begin{cases} n - 10 & \text{if } n > 100 \\ M(M(n + 11)) & \text{if } n \leq 100 \end{cases}$$

We verify the first part of the termination condition, namely the absence of an infinite clique, for $n \geq 0$. We refer to the full version [13] for more details.

Sliding Window Protocol: We verify liveness of a TCP-like protocol (with window size 3) to ensure continuous progress.

Lamport's Bakery Algorithm [8]: A two-process mutual exclusion model. Verifying absence of an infinite clique starving one process fails without fairness assumptions.

Cache Coherence: We verify the convergence to a coherent state for five protocols, including SYNAPSE, Berkeley, and Dragon [1]. As well as versions of futurbus and MOESI.

Fig. 2 shows our pipeline efficiently handles liveness questions, producing concise SMT encodings and enabling practical verification. The original prototype lacks SMT-LIB support, so direct comparison with REAL is not possible, we compare them on different benchmarks below.

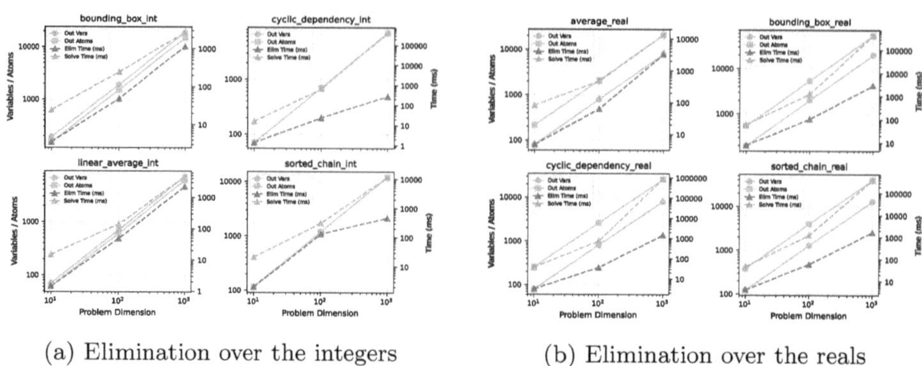

(a) Elimination over the integers   (b) Elimination over the reals

Fig. 3: Experimental results of REAL on parameterized benchmarks (see [13] for the data)

3.2   Elimination

We evaluate the performance of REAL on the following parameterized benchmarks. Let $x, y \in \mathbb{K}^D$ with $\mathbb{K} \in \{\mathbb{Z}, \mathbb{R}\}$.

$$
\begin{aligned}
\text{Sorted Chain:} \quad & \exists^{\text{ram}} x, y : \bigwedge_{i=0}^{D-1}(y_i > x_i) \wedge \bigwedge_{i=0}^{D-2}(y_i < y_{i+1}) \\
\text{Average:} \quad & \exists^{\text{ram}} x, y : \bigwedge_{i=0}^{D-1}\left(D \cdot y_i > \sum_{j=0}^{D-1} x_j\right) \\
\text{Cyclic Dependency:} \quad & \exists^{\text{ram}} x, y : (y_0 > y_{D-1}) \wedge \bigwedge_{i=1}^{D-1}(y_i > x_i + y_{i-1}) \\
\text{Bounding Box:} \quad & \exists z_1, z_2 : \exists^{\text{ram}} x, y : \bigwedge_{i=0}^{D-1}(x_i < z_{1,i} < y_i < z_{2,i})
\end{aligned}
$$

The results in Figs. 3a and 3b highlight two key trends. First, elimination scales almost linearly with the problem dimension across all benchmark families and is consistently dominated by solving times. Even formulas with thousands of atoms and variables complete in the sub-second to low-second range.

3.3   Comparison

To evaluate performance improvements over the original prototype (prot), we ran additional benchmarks using a modified version of the Average benchmark for $D = 100$.

- Real case: $\exists^{\text{ram}} x, y : \bigwedge_{i=0}^{D-1}\left(D \cdot y_i \geq \sum_{j=0}^{D-1} x_j\right)$
- Integer case: $\exists^{\text{ram}} x, y : \bigwedge_{i=0}^{D-1}\left(D \cdot y_i = \sum_{j=0}^{D-1} x_j\right)$

The results in Fig. 4 show that the new elimination method outperforms the previous implementation in both elimination and solving times by several magnitudes. In the integer case, the generated output is so simple and easy to prove unsatisfiable that the solver is faster than our elimination procedure. However, as demonstrated above, the typical trend is that elimination time is dominated by solving time.

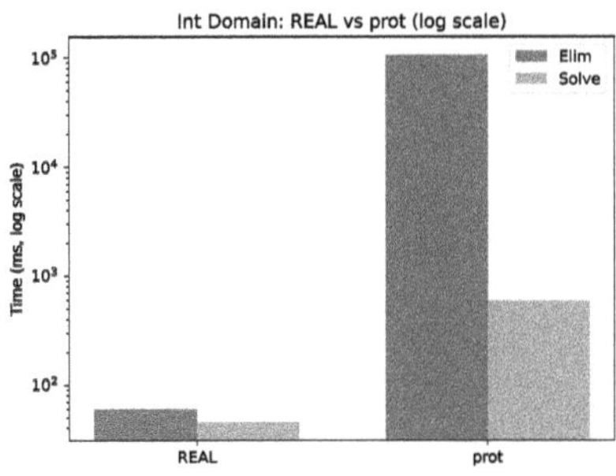

(a) Elimination over the integers

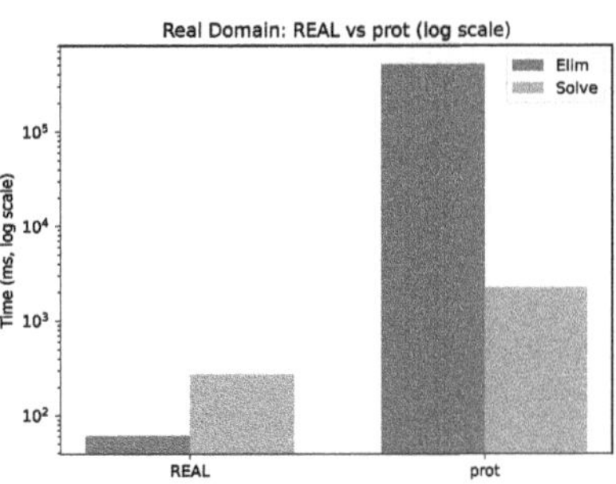

(b) Elimination over the reals

Fig. 4: Comparison of REAL and the prototype in terms of elimination and solving times (see [13] for the data)

4   Conclusion and Future Work

We presented a modular verification pipeline that combines Armoise specifications, the Alchemist transpiler, and REAL. Benchmarks on classical and practical examples demonstrate that the approach efficiently handles infinite-state systems.

The case of mixed linear integer real arithmetic still leaves room for improvement, as the overhead compared to pure LIA and LRA remains substantial, due to the separation of integer and real variables in the current approach. Moreover, replacing FASTer with a tool that directly targets reachability relations, or streamlining FASTer's ergonomics, could significantly reduce the size and redundancy of SMT encodings. Finally, we propose to extend the pipeline to counter systems over the reals (and the mixed case).

Acknowledgments. We thank anonymous reviewers for their helpful feedback.

Funded by the Deutsche Forschungsgemeinschaft (DFG, German Research Foundation) – 522843867.

Data-Availability Statement. The experimental results of this paper may be reproduced using the artifact on Zenodo [14]. For reuse of our tools, we refer to the GitHub repositories of Alchemist and REAL.

References

1. Archibald, J.K., Baer, J.: Cache coherence protocols: Evaluation using a multiprocessor simulation model. ACM Trans. Comput. Syst. **4**(4), 273–298 (1986). https://doi.org/10.1145/6513.6514
2. Bardin, S., Finkel, A., Leroux, J.: Faster acceleration of counter automata in practice. In: Jensen, K., Podelski, A. (eds.) Tools and Algorithms for the Construction and Analysis of Systems, 10th International Conference, TACAS 2004,

Held as Part of the Joint European Conferences on Theory and Practice of Software, ETAPS 2004, Barcelona, Spain, March 29 - April 2, 2004, Proceedings. Lecture Notes in Computer Science, vol. 2988, pp. 576–590. Springer (2004). https://doi.org/10.1007/978-3-540-24730-2_42

3. Barrett, C., Fontaine, P., Tinelli, C.: The SMT-LIB Standard: Version 2.7. Tech. rep., Department of Computer Science, The University of Iowa (2025), available at www.SMT-LIB.org

4. Bergsträßer, P., Ganardi, M., Lin, A.W., Zetzsche, G.: Ramsey quantifiers over automatic structures: Complexity and applications to verification. In: Baier, C., Fisman, D. (eds.) LICS '22: 37th Annual ACM/IEEE Symposium on Logic in Computer Science, Haifa, Israel, August 2 - 5, 2022. pp. 28:1–28:14. ACM (2022). https://doi.org/10.1145/3531130.3533346

5. Bergsträßer, P., Ganardi, M., Lin, A.W., Zetzsche, G.: Ramsey quantifiers in linear arithmetics. Proc. ACM Program. Lang. **8**(POPL), 1–32 (2024). https://doi.org/10.1145/3632843

6. Bjørner, N.S., McMillan, K.L., Rybalchenko, A.: Program verification as satisfiability modulo theories. In: Fontaine, P., Goel, A. (eds.) 10th International Workshop on Satisfiability Modulo Theories, SMT 2012, Manchester, UK, June 30 - July 1, 2012. EPiC Series in Computing, vol. 20, pp. 3–11. EasyChair (2012). https://doi.org/10.29007/1L7F

7. De Moura, L., Bjørner, N.: Satisfiability modulo theories: introduction and applications. Commun. ACM **54**(9), 69–77 (Sep 2011). https://doi.org/10.1145/1995376.1995394

8. Dijkstra, E.W.: Solution of a problem in concurrent programming control. Commun. ACM **8**(9), 569 (Sep 1965). https://doi.org/10.1145/365559.365617

9. Gario, M., Micheli, A.: Pysmt: a solver-agnostic library for fast prototyping of smt-based algorithms. In: SMT Workshop 2015 (2015)

10. Ginsburg, S., Spanier, E.: Semigroups, presburger formulas, and languages. Pacific journal of mathematics **16**(2), 285–296 (1966). https://doi.org/10.2140/pjm.1966.16.285

11. Grebenshchikov, S., Lopes, N.P., Popeea, C., Rybalchenko, A.: Synthesizing software verifiers from proof rules. In: Proceedings of the 33rd ACM SIGPLAN Conference on Programming Language Design and Implementation. p. 405–416. PLDI '12, Association for Computing Machinery, New York, NY, USA (2012). https://doi.org/10.1145/2254064.2254112

12. Leroux, J., Point, G.: Tapas: The talence presburger arithmetic suite. In: Kowalewski, S., Philippou, A. (eds.) Tools and Algorithms for the Construction and Analysis of Systems, 15th International Conference, TACAS 2009, Held as Part of the Joint European Conferences on Theory and Practice of Software, ETAPS 2009, York, UK, March 22-29, 2009. Proceedings. Lecture Notes in Computer Science, vol. 5505, pp. 182–185. Springer (2009). https://doi.org/10.1007/978-3-642-00768-2_18

13. Lichtner, K., Bergsträßer, P., Ganardi, M., Lin, A.W., Zetzsche, G.: Fast ramsey quantifier elimination in LIRA (with applications to liveness checking). CoRR **abs/2511.05323** (2025). https://doi.org/10.48550/ARXIV.2511.05323

14. Lichtner, K., Bergsträßer, P., Ganardi, M., Lin, A.W., Zetzsche, G.: TACAS2026 AE Artifacts for "Fast Ramsey Quantifier Elimination in LIRA" (2026). https://doi.org/10.5281/zenodo.18311746

15. Manna, Z., Pnueli, A.: Formalization of properties of functional programs. J. ACM **17**(3), 555–569 (Jul 1970). https://doi.org/10.1145/321592.321606

16. To, A.W., Libkin, L.: Recurrent reachability analysis in regular model checking. In: Cervesato, I., Veith, H., Voronkov, A. (eds.) Logic for Programming, Artificial Intelligence, and Reasoning, 15th International Conference, LPAR 2008, Doha, Qatar, November 22-27, 2008. Proceedings. Lecture Notes in Computer Science, vol. 5330, pp. 198–213. Springer (2008). https://doi.org/10.1007/978-3-540-89439-1_15
17. To, A.W., Libkin, L.: Algorithmic metatheorems for decidable LTL model checking over infinite systems. In: Ong, C.L. (ed.) Foundations of Software Science and Computational Structures, 13th International Conference, FOSSACS 2010, Held as Part of the Joint European Conferences on Theory and Practice of Software, ETAPS 2010, Paphos, Cyprus, March 20-28, 2010. Proceedings. Lecture Notes in Computer Science, vol. 6014, pp. 221–236. Springer (2010). https://doi.org/10.1007/978-3-642-12032-9_16
18. Veanes, M., Bjørner, N.S., Nachmanson, L., Bereg, S.: Monadic decomposition. J. ACM **64**(2), 14:1–14:28 (2017). https://doi.org/10.1145/3040488

QSOLE: Automatic QBF Equivalence Checking [*]

Peter Pfeiffer[1,2], Mark Peyrer[1],
Daniel Große[2], and Martina Seidl[1]

[1] Institute for Symbolic Artificial Intelligence, JKU Linz, Austria
[2] Institute for Complex Systems, JKU Linz, Austria

{peter.pfeiffer, mark.peyrer, daniel.große, martina.seidl}@jku.at

Abstract. Quantified Boolean Formulas (QBFs) extend propositional logic with existential and universal quantifiers, making their decision problem PSPACE-hard. Recent advances in QBF solvers have established QBFs as an attractive framework for encoding PSPACE-hard problems across domains such as formal verification, synthesis, and symbolic AI. Despite progress in solving techniques, less attention has been given to the infrastructure for constructing correct and efficient QBF encodings. For instance, it is often unclear whether two QBFs that encode the same problem in different ways yield the same solutions. Traditional QBF equivalence checking focuses only on free variables, yet in many cases, the quantified variables must also be considered.

In this paper, we present QSOLE, the first fully automatic checker for solution-based QBF equivalence. Based on a recently introduced approach, QSOLE decomposes equivalence checks into smaller entailment computations and is capable of generating witnesses for detected inequivalences, which can be used to debug encodings. Furthermore, it allows for explicit exclusion of variables from equivalence checks enabling comparison of formulas using different local auxiliary variables.

Keywords: QBF · QBF Solutions · Equivalence Checking.

1 Introduction

Quantified Boolean formulas (QBFs) [1,4] extend propositional logic with existential and universal quantifiers, thereby representing PSPACE-complete problems. QBFs play a key role in areas such as formal verification, reactive synthesis and planning [11]. Solutions to QBFs are functions that capture the dependencies between the different types of variables. These functions describe, for example, winning strategies in encodings of two-player games or automatically generated programs in encodings of synthesis problems.

Traditionally, QBF equivalence has been evaluated through satisfiability comparison over free variables [5,6]. Given two QBFs that are defined over the same

---

[*] Supported by the LIT AI Lab and the LIT Secure and Correct Systems Lab funded by the state of Upper Austria and by the Austrian Science Fund (FWF) [10.55776/COE12].

S. Junges and G. Katz (Eds.): TACAS 2026, LNCS 16505, pp. 324–332, 2026.
https://doi.org/10.1007/978-3-032-22752-2_17

set of free variables, it is checked if for all assignments of the free variables, the two formulas have the same truth value. This is a rather restricted notion of equivalence checking, because the quantified variables are not taken into account. In recent work [8] we introduced solution-based notions of equivalence grounded in Skolem and Herbrand functions, a well-explored way of expressing QBF solutions. With this, we obtain a more expressive notion of equivalence. If two QBFs are solution equivalent, on the one hand, they evaluate to the same truth value, on the other hand they also have the same set of solutions. If, for example, the second formula should be an optimized encoding of the first formula, it can be shown that the optimization did not change the set of solutions. This is valuable for debugging and validating practical encodings. Moreover, two formulas generated through completely different encodings can be compared to ensure correctness of encoding techniques.

The first practical approach to compare individual solutions of two QBFs was presented by Shaik et al. [10]. This approach is an interactive approach, i.e., manual intervention is necessary. To the best of our knowledge, so far there is no tool that offers automatic solution-based QBF equivalence checking.

In this work, we present QSOLE, an automatic checker for solution-based QBF equivalence notions as defined in [8]. Our tool QSOLE is implemented in C++, uses the QBF solver DEPQBF [7] as a reasoning backend and allows for witness extraction of inequivalences using the SAT solver CADICAL [2]. We propose a flexible QBF encoding that supports the exclusion of auxiliary variables from equivalence checks and introduce the first equivalence-specific solving techniques, including substitution-based encoding optimization for formulas with shared clauses. To the best of our knowledge, QSOLE is the first practical framework for automated reasoning about semantic QBF equivalence. Our tool QSOLE is openly available at `https://doi.org/10.5281/zenodo.17356608`.

2 Preliminaries

A *Boolean formula* is built from a set of Boolean variables V and the logical connectives $\{\neg, \wedge, \vee, \rightarrow, \leftrightarrow\}$. The set of variables occurring in a formula φ is denoted by $var(\varphi)$. An *assignment* $\sigma : V' \rightarrow \{\mathbf{1}, \mathbf{0}\}$ maps variables $V' \subseteq V$ to $\mathbf{1}$ and $\mathbf{0}$. By $[\varphi]_\sigma$ we denote the formula obtained from φ by setting all variables $v \in V'$ in to $\sigma(v)$ and simplifying the formula according to standard semantics. An assignment σ is a model of φ iff $[\varphi]_\sigma = \mathbf{1}$. If $[\varphi]_\sigma = \mathbf{0}$, it is a *counter-model*. A Boolean formula is in *Conjunctive Normal Form (CNF)* if it is a conjunction of disjunctions (clauses), where negation applies only to Boolean variables.

Quantified Boolean Formulas (QBFs) [1,4] extend Boolean formulas with *quantifiers* $\mathcal{Q} = \{\forall, \exists\}$ that bind variables in subformulas, which may themselves contain quantifiers. A QBF $\forall v : \Phi$ is true iff both $([\Phi]_{\{v=1\}})$ and $([\Phi]_{\{v=0\}})$ are true. Dually, a QBF $\exists v : \Phi$ is true iff $([\Phi]_{\{v=1\}})$ or $([\Phi]_{\{v=0\}})$ is true. Quantification over multiple variables $V = v_1, \ldots, v_n$ is abbreviated as $\mathcal{Q}V = \mathcal{Q}v_1 \ldots \mathcal{Q}v_n$. A sequence $P = \mathcal{Q}_1 v_1 \ldots \mathcal{Q}_n v_n$ of quantifiers is called a *prefix*, and $\overline{P}$ denotes its dual where all quantifiers are flipped. A QBF is in *Prenex Conjunctive Normal*

Form (PCNF) if it has the structure $P : \varphi$, where P is a prefix and φ (the *matrix*) is in CNF. Variables bound in P are denoted by $var(P)$. *Free variables* $free(\Phi) = var(\varphi) \setminus var(P)$ are not bound by a quantifier in a QBF $\Phi = P : \varphi$. A QBF without free variables is *closed*.

Given a QBF $\Phi = \mathcal{Q}_1 v_1 \ldots \mathcal{Q}_n v_n : \varphi$, consider an assignment tree whose internal nodes correspond to variables v_i, where edges assign truth values $\{\mathbf{1}, \mathbf{0}\}$, and each path from the root to a leaf represents an assignment σ with leaf label $[\varphi]_\sigma$. A model of a true QBF is a subtree of the assignment tree such that existential nodes have one child, universal nodes have two, and all leaves are $\mathbf{1}$. Dually, a counter-model of a false QBF requires one child for universal nodes, two for existential nodes, and all leaves to be $\mathbf{0}$. We denote the sets of models and counter-models of Φ as $\mathbb{S}_\exists(\Phi)$ and $\mathbb{S}_\forall(\Phi)$ respectively. Classically, two QBFs Φ and Ψ are said to be (satisfiability-)equivalent if they evaluate to the same truth value under all (resp. some) assignment(s) to their common free variables [5,6]. Solution-based notions of entailment and equivalence have been introduced in [8] and are defined as follows: Given two true QBFs with the same prefix P. Then Φ Skolem-entails Ψ, denoted by $\Phi \models_{\mathsf{Sk}} \Psi$ iff $\mathbb{S}_\exists(\Phi) \subseteq \mathbb{S}_\exists(\Psi)$. Skolem equivalence $\Phi \Leftrightarrow_{\mathsf{Sk}} \Psi$ holds if $\mathbb{S}_\exists(\Phi) = \mathbb{S}_\exists(\Psi)$. In a dual manner, Herbrand entailment and Herbrand equivalence is defined for false formulas. Solution equivalence $\Phi \Leftrightarrow_{\mathsf{Sol}} \Psi$ holds iff Φ and Ψ are Skolem equivalent or Herbrand equivalent. Note that Herbrand equivalence checking can be reduced to Skolem equivalence checking by negating the formulas.

3   Solution-Based QBF Equivalence Checking

We introduce QSOLE, an automatic checker for solution-based notions of QBF equivalence. It works for true and for false formulas in a similar manner. Our tool takes two input formulas in QDIMACS format and can determine whether they are Skolem entailed, Skolem equivalent, or solution equivalent. Additionally, it requires a mandatory numeric parameter `PCOUNT` to denote the length of the quantifier prefix used for comparison. To compute equivalence wrt. the full prefix this value has to be set to $|var(P)|$. In the next section, we explain what happens if not the full quantifier prefix is considered.

Figure 1 illustrates how QSOLE checks whether two QBFs Φ and Ψ are solution equivalent. For this, it first evaluates the truth value of Φ (purple). If Φ evaluates to true, i.e., $\mathbb{S}_\forall(\Phi) = \emptyset$, Skolem entailment needs to checked in both directions (blue part of Figure 1). If $\Phi \models_{\mathsf{Sk}} \Psi$ holds, it follows that Ψ is true as well. Analogously, if Φ is false (yellow), then QSOLE instead checks for Skolem equivalence of the negated formulas $\neg\Phi \models_{\mathsf{Sk}} \neg\Psi$ and $\neg\Psi \models_{\mathsf{Sk}} \neg\Phi$ (red). If any Skolem entailment check fails during this process, $\Phi \Leftrightarrow_{\mathsf{Sol}} \Psi$ does not hold. Then a witness can be generated that is part of the solution of one formula but not of the other.

QSOLE computes Skolem entailment $\Phi \models_{\mathsf{Sk}} \Psi$ checks based on the QBF encoding presented in [8]. The Plaisted-Greenbaum transformation [9] is applied to obtain a PCNF representation of this formula, which is subsequently solved

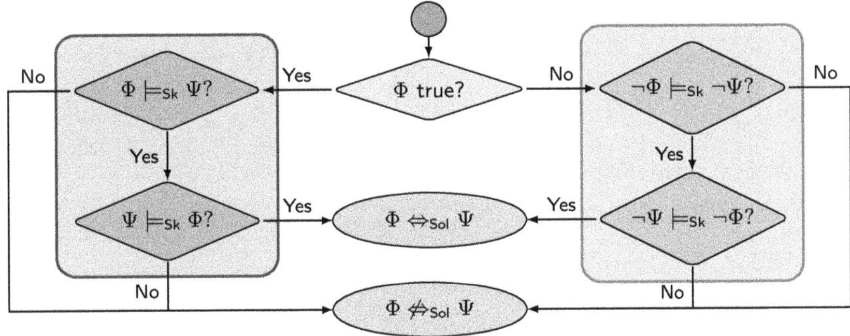

Fig. 1: Solution equivalence $\Phi \Leftrightarrow_{\mathsf{Sol}} \Psi$ check in QSOLE.

using the QBF solver DEPQBF. A counter-model to $\Phi \models_{\mathsf{Sk}} \Psi$ represents a model of Φ, which does not satisfy Ψ, indicated by a propositional countermodel for ψ, which we refer to as a *witness*. If the `--models` flag is set, QSOLE generates witnesses for failed Skolem entailment checks. They are constructed from the terminating assignment of DEPQBF using the SAT solver CADICAL.

We demonstrate this solving process on an example: Consider the two QBFs

$$\Phi = P : \varphi = \forall a \exists b \exists c : (a \lor c) \land (\neg a \lor \neg c) \land (b \lor c) \land (\neg b \lor \neg c)$$

$$\Psi = P : \psi = \forall a \exists b \exists c : (a \lor \neg b) \land (\neg a \lor b) \land (a \lor c)$$

Suppose it is claimed that Ψ encodes the same problem as Φ, i.e., that $\Phi \Leftrightarrow_{\mathsf{Sol}} \Psi$ holds. Figure 2 shows the input formulas Φ (left) and Ψ (center) in QDIMACS format. The quantified variables a, b, and c correspond to QDIMACS variables **1**, **2**, and **3**, respectively. The assignment tree (right) represents the propositional models of Φ and Ψ simultaneously. The leaves are labeled by φ/ψ where φ (resp., ψ) represents the truth value of Φ (resp., Ψ) under the assignment on the path to the root of the tree. The highlighted (yellow) subgraph marks a model of Φ, which is not a model for Ψ as indicated by a propositional counter-model for ψ (red). This refutes the claim that $\Phi \Leftrightarrow_{\mathsf{Sol}} \Psi$.

Listing 1 illustrates how QSOLE can be used to automatically show that the two formulas do not have the same solutions. In a first call, it checks solution equivalence (parameter `--check psole`). The prefix length is set to 3 to compare over the full quantifier prefix $P = \forall a \exists b \exists c$. QSOLE first calculates the value of Φ, which evaluates to true. Given this information, it proceeds with a Skolem equivalence check for $\Phi \models_{\mathsf{Sk}} \Psi$. Since this check also succeeds, QSOLE has to check $\Psi \models_{\mathsf{Sk}} \Phi$. However, this check fails, ultimately refuting the solution equivalence. To generate a witness, we invoke QSOLE again with the option `--models`. We only rerun the check $\Psi \models_{\mathsf{Sk}} \Phi$ (parameter `--check skent`) which previously returned false. QSOLE reports the witness `"v 1 2 3 0"` assigning all variables to **1**. This corresponds directly to the counter-model (red) for ψ in the binary tree of Figure 2.

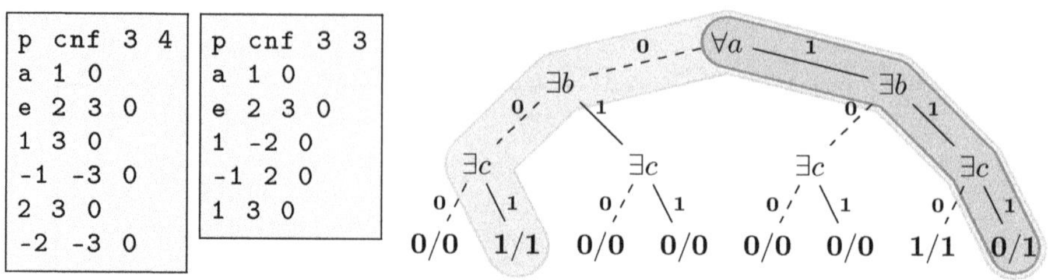

Fig. 2: Φ (left) and Ψ (center) in QDIMACS format next to assignment tree (right) on variables $V = \{a, b, c\}$ with leaf labels φ/ψ and model of Ψ (yellow) containing counter-model for φ (red).

4   Auxiliary Variables

Some PCNF encodings, such as efficient normal form transformation [12,9] of formulas, require that auxiliary variables are added to the formula. For example, consider the QBF $\Phi = \forall a \exists b \exists c : (a \vee c) \wedge (\neg a \vee \neg c) \wedge (b \vee c) \wedge (\neg b \vee \neg c)$ from before. The variable c indirectly enforces $(a \leftrightarrow b)$ through $(a \not\leftrightarrow c) \wedge (b \not\leftrightarrow c)$. Suppose we wanted to disregard the semantics of c and only focus on the relation between a and b enforced through it. Figure 3 illustrates this idea: The full assignment tree for Ψ (left) is pruned after b (right), whereas leaves correspond to the evaluation of the subformula that was eliminated. The outer leaves of the pruned tree represent $(a \leftrightarrow b)$ and are, therefore, labeled with **1**, whereas the inner leaves denote $a \not\leftrightarrow b$ and are labeled with **0**. The same relation between a and b is also present in $\Psi = \forall a \exists b \exists c : (a \vee \neg b) \wedge (\neg a \vee b) \wedge (a \vee c)$. To verify this, we can separate the outer prefix $P = \forall a \exists b$ from the auxiliary variable c, which is treated as local to each formula (with $P_1 = \exists c$ and $P_2 = \exists c'$), to obtain $\Phi = P : P_1 : \varphi$ and $\Psi = P : P_2 : \psi$ and compare them based on P. QSOLE allows restriction to a common outer prefix with the parameter PCOUNT. In this case, we can set

```
> qsole phi.qdimacs psi.qdimacs 3 --check psole --info
[QSOLE] [INF] Polarity check of f1 resulted in 10
[QSOLE] [INF] Skolem Entailment f1 |=SK f2 resulted in 10
[QSOLE] [INF] Skolem Entailment f2 |=SK f1 resulted in 20
[QSOLE] [INF] Polarity Solution Equivalence (f1 <->PSOL f2)
    resulted in 20
> qsole psi.qdimacs phi.qdimacs 3 --check skent --models
c f1 |=SK f2
v 1 2 3 0
```

Listing 1: QSOLE check for $\Phi \Leftrightarrow_{\mathsf{Sol}} \Psi$ with PCOUNT $= 3$ and witness generation

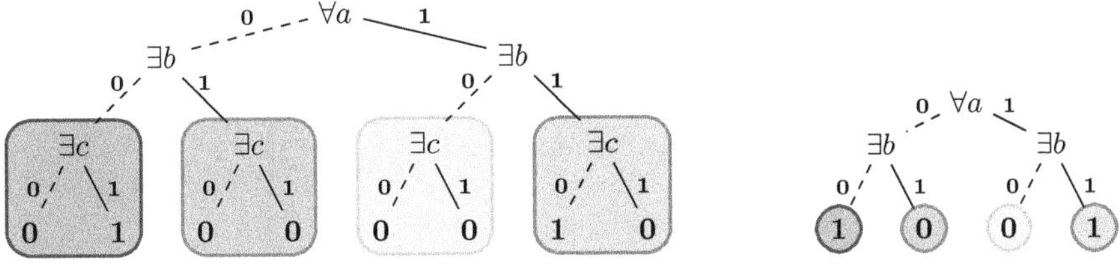

Fig. 3: Left: Assignment tree of Ψ. Right: Pruned assignment tree with $P = \forall a \exists b$. Subformulas with prefix $\exists c$ are replaced with leaves indicating their truth value.

$\texttt{PCOUNT} = 2$ resulting in Φ and Ψ being solution equivalent wrt. $P = \forall a \exists b$. We confirm this with QSOLE in Listing 2.

```
> qsole  phi.qdimacs psi.qdimacs  2 --check psole  --info
[QSOLE] [INF] Polarity check of f1 resulted in 10
[QSOLE] [INF] Skolem Entailment f1 |=SK f2 resulted in 10
[QSOLE] [INF] Skolem Entailment f2 |=SK f1 resulted in 10
[QSOLE] [INF] Polarity Solution Equivalence (f1 <->PSOL f2)
    resulted in 10
```

Listing 2: QSOLE check for $\Phi \Leftrightarrow_{\mathsf{Sol}} \Psi$ with $\texttt{PCOUNT} = 2$

The encoding used by QSOLE to compute whether $\Phi \models_{\mathsf{Sk}} \Psi$ holds for some QBFs $\Phi = P : \varphi$ and $\Psi = P : \psi$ requires the negation of ψ. This introduces at least one additional auxiliary variable per clause, leading to a large overhead. To mitigate this, QSOLE can perform *subsumption* of clauses in ψ with clauses of φ before applying negation in the encoding. Since the Skolem entailment check looks for a model of Φ that includes a counter-model of ψ, all clauses in φ must be satisfied. Therefore, any clause in ψ that is subsumed by a clause in φ cannot refute ψ. Thus, any such clause can be removed from ψ for the check. This can considerably reduce the number of auxiliary variables, particularly when φ and ψ share many clauses. This optimization is available in QSOLE via the flag `--subsumption`.

5   Evaluation

We tested QSOLE on two sets of synthetic benchmarks derived from pseudo-Boolean constraints: For "equals-k" constraints exactly k out of n variables must be true. We used PySAT [3] to generate two different standard encodings, namely `seqcounter` and `kmtotalizer`, and added a randomly generated quantifier prefix containing u universal quantifiers over the common n variables. Auxiliary variables are existentially quantified. This construction yields pairs of formulas that are guaranteed to be solution equivalent wrt. their n common variables. Analogously, we used "at-least-k" constraints (at least k of n variables must be

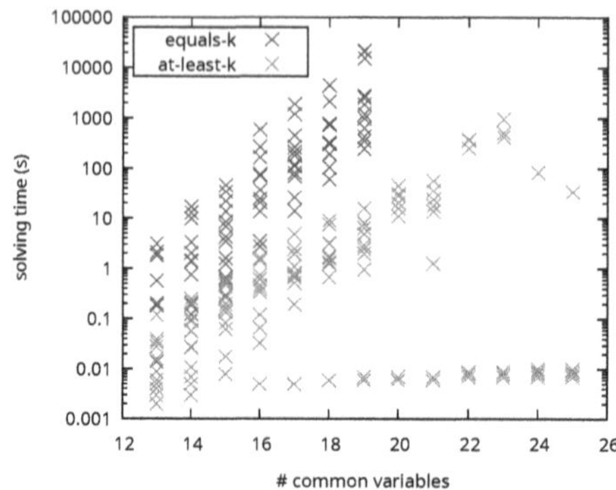

Fig. 4: QSOLE Solution Equivalence checking on synthetic benchmarks equals-k (blue) and atleast-k (red); x-axis: number of common variables; y-axis: time in seconds.

true) to generate pairs of formulas that are not solution equivalent. Any model for a larger bound k is also a model for a smaller bound, but not vice versa. This holds inversely for counter-models in false formulas. This setup can be scaled along several dimensions: total number of variables, the bounds k, the encoding type, and both the ratio and ordering of universal vs. existential variables in the prefix. However, the lift to QBF is conducted with random prefixes and these benchmarks may, therefore, not be reliable performance indicators for concrete QBF applications.

We computed solution equivalence for one test case per combination of $k \in \{8, 10, 12\}$ and $u \in \{8, 10, 12, 14\}$ with $n \in \{13, \ldots, 19\}$ for equals-k and $n \in \{13, \ldots, 25\}$ for at-least-k. Quantifier prefixes were generated independently for each test case. Our experiments were run on an AMD Ryzen Threadripper PRO 5955WX with 16-Cores and 248Gi RAM. Figure 4 shows the result grouped by the number of common variables. The performance gap within at-least-k benchmarks can be attributed to early returns in cases where the first Skolem entailment check yields a refutation.

6   Conclusion and Future Work

In this paper, we introduced QSOLE, which automatically checks if two QBFs have the same set of solutions. The approach is implemented for true and for false formulas based on the encoding presented in [8]. We extended the encoding to handle local auxiliary variables that are at the end of the quantifier prefix. In future work, we plan to lift this restriction and allow for local variables at arbitrary positions in the quantifier prefix. Furthermore, we plan to improve on the user interface to facilitate the development and the debugging of QBF encodings.

Data Availability Statement The QSOLE artifact containing the tool implementation, benchmarks, and scripts required to reproduce the experiments presented in this paper is openly available at `https://doi.org/10.5281/zenodo.18590551`.

References

1. Beyersdorff, O., Janota, M., Lonsing, F., Seidl, M.: Quantified boolean formulas. In: Handbook of Satisfiability - Second Edition, Frontiers in Artificial Intelligence and Applications, vol. 336, pp. 1177–1221. IOS Press (2021)
2. Biere, A., Faller, T., Fazekas, K., Fleury, M., Froleyks, N., Pollitt, F.: Cadical 2.0. In: Gurfinkel, A., Ganesh, V. (eds.) 36th International Conference on Computer Aided Verification (CAV). pp. 133–152. Springer Nature Switzerland, Cham (2024)
3. Ignatiev, A., Tan, Z.L., Karamanos, C.: Towards Universally Accessible SAT Technology. In: 27th International Conference on Theory and Applications of Satisfiability Testing (SAT). pp. 4:1–4:11 (2024). `https://doi.org/10.4230/LIPICS.SAT.2024.16`, `https://doi.org/10.4230/LIPIcs.SAT.2024.16`
4. Kleine Büning, H., Bubeck, U.: Theory of quantified boolean formulas. In: Handbook of Satisfiability - Second Edition, Frontiers in Artificial Intelligence and Applications, vol. 336, pp. 1131–1156. IOS Press (2021)
5. Kleine Büning, H., Lettmann, T.: Aussagenlogik – Deduktion und Algorithmen. Teubner (1994)
6. Kleine Büning, H., Zhao, X.: Equivalence models for quantified boolean formulas. In: 7th International Conference on Theory and Applications of Satisfiability Testing (SAT). Lecture Notes in Computer Science, vol. 3542, pp. 224–234. Springer (2004)
7. Lonsing, F., Egly, U.: Depqbf 6.0: A Search-Based QBF Solver Beyond Traditional QCDCL. In: de Moura, L. (ed.) 26th International Conference on Automated Deduction (CADE). pp. 371–384. Springer International Publishing, Cham (2017)
8. Pfeiffer, P., Große, D., Seidl, M.: Refined Notions of QBF Equivalences. In: 19th European Conference on Logics in Artificial Intelligence (JELIA). p. 159–165. Springer-Verlag, Berlin, Heidelberg (2025). `https://doi.org/10.1007/978-3-032-04590-4_11`
9. Plaisted, D.A., Greenbaum, S.: A Structure-preserving Clause Form Translation. Journal of Symbolic Computation **2**(3), 293–304 (1986). `https://doi.org/https://doi.org/10.1016/S0747-7171(86)80028-1`
10. Shaik, I., Heisinger, M., Seidl, M., van de Pol, J.: Validation of QBF Encodings with Winning Strategies. In: 26th International Conference on Theory and Applications of Satisfiability Testing (SAT). Leibniz International Proceedings in Informatics (LIPIcs), vol. 271, pp. 24:1–24:10. Schloss Dagstuhl – Leibniz-Zentrum für Informatik (2023)
11. Shukla, A., Biere, A., Pulina, L., Seidl, M.: A Survey on Applications of Quantified Boolean Formulas. In: 31st International Conference on Tools with Artificial Intelligence (ICTAI). pp. 78–84. IEEE (2019)
12. Tseitin, G.S.: On the Complexity of Derivation in Propositional Calculus, pp. 466–483. Springer Berlin Heidelberg, Berlin, Heidelberg (1983)

Real-time Proof Checking for Distributed Incremental SAT Solving

Dominik Schreiber[1], Mathias Fleury[2], Katalin Fazekas[3], and Armin Biere[2]

[1] Karlsruhe Institute of Technology, Germany
`dominik.schreiber@kit.edu`
[2] University of Freiburg, Germany
[3] TU Wien, Austria

Abstract. Distributed clause-sharing SAT solvers are powerful automated reasoning tools capable of rapidly solving many difficult instances. Users of SAT solving often rely on incremental SAT solving, i.e., interactive solve calls over an evolving formula. We present the first approach to distributed incremental SAT solving that grants full confidence in the obtained result. Specifically, we extend a recent distributed real-time proof checking approach with an incremental proof interface. Our approach offers great flexibility in that it supports dynamic re-scheduling of computational resources and enables safely sharing clauses across tasks that operate on deviating assumptions and formula increments. We further add on-the-fly clause compression to checkers in order to reduce memory consumption. Experiments with the distributed solver MallobSat on up to 1216 cores show that our trusted solving approach checks incremental SAT tasks with small mean overhead ($< 33\%$) over unchecked solving.

Keywords: Propositional satisfiability · Distributed computing · Proofs.

1 Introduction

Propositional satisfiability (SAT) solving is an essential tool at the core of automated reasoning and symbolic AI [13]. In recent years, parallel (multi-core) and distributed (multi-node) approaches to SAT solving have gained traction and are now capable of solving many challenging instances hundreds of times faster than the best available sequential (single-core) solvers [37,38]. Moreover, recent works have brought the efficient generation and validation of *proofs of unsatisfiability* to large-scale SAT solvers [23,24,31]. Proofs of unsatisfiability [17,18] are artifacts that allow to validate a solver's claim of a formula's unsatisfiability with simple, independent, and even formally verified checker programs [8,22].

Modern use cases of SAT solving often require a mode of operation named *incremental SAT solving*. Rather than encoding and solving a single propositional formula, incremental SAT solving allows for interactive and interrelated solving calls on an evolving formula while preserving the SAT solver's knowledge base gathered thus far. While such interaction schemes are essential for many important application domains such as verification, electronic design automation, or

© The Author(s) 2026
S. Junges and G. Katz (Eds.): TACAS 2026, LNCS 16505, pp. 333–352, 2026.
https://doi.org/10.1007/978-3-032-22752-2_18

scheduling, a first proof format for (sequential) incremental SAT solving has been proposed only recently [11]. Parallel and distributed SAT solvers that operate incrementally [32] do not support proof production and checking yet. As such, challenging incremental problems for which proof checking is desired have to be solved sequentially or must be broken down into sequences of non-incremental SAT instances, both of which can drastically impact performance.

In this work, we propose the first approach to proof checking for (parallel and) distributed incremental SAT solving. We build upon a recently proposed, bottleneck-free approach that checks proofs *in real time* during solving and validates results of (un)satisfiability as soon as a solver emits it [31]. This immediate proof checking is highly natural for incremental SAT solving (see also [11]), more so than post-mortem checking of a monolithic proof produced during solving, since solving already has an interactive on-demand nature and a user may want to have full confidence in a result before proceeding with the next solving call. The downsides of real-time proof checking are that no persistent proof is generated – i.e., trust in a result cannot be easily transferred to other parties – and that distributed real-time checking relies on hash-based *fingerprints* to ensure the integrity of messages across trusted checker programs. While these particularities reduce confidence compared to conventional proof checking to some degree, real-time checking can still be a highly appealing method, e.g., for software verification in continuous integration workflows [7], for debugging purposes [26], or whenever persistent proof logging is infeasible due to time or space restrictions.

Our contributions are as follows: We significantly expand on the prior real-time checking framework ImpCheck [30] by transferring aspects of the incremental (sequential) LIDRUP format [11]. Our framework allows to check a distributed *incremental* clause-sharing solver's reasoning even if its solver units operate on deviating assumptions and/or increments of the problem. This allows our approach to support flexible (re-)scheduling of workers [27] and checked clause sharing *across* distinct tasks that operate on related problems (cf. [34]).

We formalize our approach and implemented it in a small (< 2000 effective lines of code) toolchain, connected to the distributed platform Mallob [30] as a first major use case. Evaluations at up to 1216 cores confirm that our real-time checking approach incurs little mean overhead ($< 33\%$) over un-checked solving, less than prior results for non-incremental real-time proof checking [31]. Lastly, we extend our checkers by simple and effective clause compression techniques that reduce the main memory overhead of proof checking from 45% to 32%.

2   Incremental SAT Solving

We consider *incremental SAT solving under assumptions* [9] – adjusting the formalism by Fazekas et al. [11] to allow flexible incremental interactions.

An incremental SAT task $P = (F, Q)$ consists of a *sequence of clauses* $F = \langle c_1, c_2, \ldots \rangle$ and a sequence of *queries* $Q = \langle q_1, q_2, \ldots \rangle$, where each $q_i = (e_i, A_i)$ features a *clause index* e_i and a set of *assumption literals* A_i. We define $F_e :=$ $\bigcup_{i=1}^{e} \{c_i\}$ as the *prefix* of formula F that includes its first e clauses.

A query $q = (e, A)$ is *satisfiable* if and only if the clause set $F_e \cup \bigcup_{a \in A}\{a\}$ (which consists of $e + |A|$ clauses) is satisfiable. We assume queries to be ordered w.r.t. the formula prefix, i.e., for any q_i, q_j with $i < j$, we have $e_i \le e_j$.

Consider $F = \langle a \vee b, a \vee \neg b, \neg b \rangle$ and $Q = \langle (2, \{a, b\}), (2, \{\neg a\}), (3, \emptyset) \rangle$ as an example: q_1 features clause set $F_2 = \{a \vee b, a \vee \neg b\}$ and assumes $a = b = 1$, which satisfies F_2; q_2 also features F_2, assumes $a = 0$ and is unsatisfiable; q_3 features $F_3 = F_2 \cup \{\neg b\}$, makes no assumptions and is satisfiable ($a = 1$, $b = 0$).

The incremental LIDRUP proof format [11] allows to log and validate incremental reasoning. It extends the non-incremental LRUP proof format [26]. An LRUP proof is a sequence of clause derivations and deletions, where each clause (original or learned) has a unique identifier (ID) and each derivation of a learned clause c involves a list of prior clause IDs. These *dependencies*, or *prerequisites*, indicate how to efficiently check that c is entailed, using the so-called *Reverse Unit Propagation* (RUP) criterion [40]. An LRUP proof of unsatisfiability ends with the derivation of the *empty clause*, which implies unsatisfiability.

In contrast to LRUP proofs, a LIDRUP proof begins with explicitly listing the (initial) input clauses. It also features statements that mark the beginning of a solving query with according assumption literals. Subsequent learned and deleted clauses are stated as in LRUP. The end of each query is marked by a result statement (SAT, UNSAT, or UNKNOWN), potentially with the found satisfying assignment or the *core* clause (corresponding to *failed* assumptions) that renders the query unsatisfiable. After the result line(s), input clauses can be added once again and another query can begin. LIDRUP also supports advanced features that we do not consider in this work, such as assumption-like *constraint clauses* [14] and interactions with IPASIR-UP style *user propagators* [10].

3   Proof-Producing Clause-Sharing Solving

In parallel *clause-sharing SAT solving* [2,38], many sequential SAT solver threads are run in parallel, all on the original input formula, and occasionally exchange *learned conflict clauses* among each another. Careful clause sharing grants significant scalability up to thousands of cores [38], even if individual solver threads run (almost) the same solver program [36]. The distributed SAT solver MallobSat [38] is the first such system that supports incremental SAT solving [32]. MallobSat is integrated in the distributed framework Mallob, which allows for *flexible multi-tasking*, i.e., to process SAT tasks on-demand while continuously balancing the available workers among all active tasks. Mallob's flexible multi-tasking of incremental SAT tasks is being exploited for distributed MaxSAT solving [34] and for massively parallel bit-precise verification (SMT) [35].

As of now, there are two viable proof checking methods in parallel and distributed clause-sharing solving. Both approaches are limited to RUP proof steps and to sequential solver backends that support LRUP proof logging.[4]

---

[4] Authors often simplifyingly state that they use/support the *LRAT* [8] format while they focus exclusively on its *LRUP* feature subset [23,24,26,31].

First, Michaelson et al. [23,24] proposed to (re-)construct a global proof by logging all solver threads' proof information during solving and then performing a post-solving parallel backwards traversal over the transitive prerequisites of the found empty clause [23]. While this approach outputs a plain LRUP proof file like a sequential solver, funnelling all required proof steps into a single file constitutes an I/O bottleneck, and the proof's potentially huge set of active clauses can cause main memory shortage during checking [24].

Second, we introduced *ImpCheck* [31] (Immediate Massively Parallel Propositional Proof Checking) – a framework where the parallel / distributed solver's reasoning is checked *in real time* during solving. ImpCheck consists of three small sequential executables that are run as a part of the solving procedure and whose output ensures correctness. First, a *parser* process parses the input formula and returns the read clauses. Second, for each solver thread during solving, a dedicated *checker* process is executed and receives the parsed formula. Each solver thread uses inter-process communication to send its proof steps to its checker, which checks them in real-time. After checking, the learned clauses can be shared between solver threads. If a solver thread imports such a shared clause c, it also forwards c to its checker, which accepts c *without* checking – note that the dependencies of c are unknown and might not be present locally.

This approach alone would not yet offer particularly high confidence since the information transfer between trusted executables is untrusted and may corrupt or fabricate clauses. For this reason, we introduced formula and clause *fingerprints* (based on keyed pseudo-random functions [1]) that only the trusted executables are able to compute. Specifically, each ImpCheck process outputs a fingerprint together with each formula / clause it outputs and, in turn, expects a valid fingerprint for each incoming piece of information from another process. This scheme establishes trustworthy communication channels across the trusted executables that do not depend on the employed technology (shared-memory synchronization, distributed message passing, parallel file systems, etc.).

Lastly, a *confirmer* executable can be used to validate a fingerprint that a checker has output when it concluded the problem's (un)satisfiability.

While the ImpCheck approach does not yield a persistent proof, it is substantially more scalable than monolithic proof production and checking, only incurring a mean overhead of $\leq 42\%$ over a distributed solver's running time [31].

4   Distributed Incremental Real-time Checking

We extend the distributed real-time checking method ImpCheck [31] (Section 3) to support a significant subset of the incremental LIDRUP proof format [11], including *incremental addition of input clauses* with corresponding fingerprints, *incremental queries* with *assumption literals*, and the validation of (un)satisfiability results against (failed) assumption literals, with the following main challenges:

- We need to ensure that all p interacting checker instances in a setup operate on a *consistent set of input clauses*, i.e., that, given some $e \geq 1$, F_e involves exactly the same clauses across all checkers.

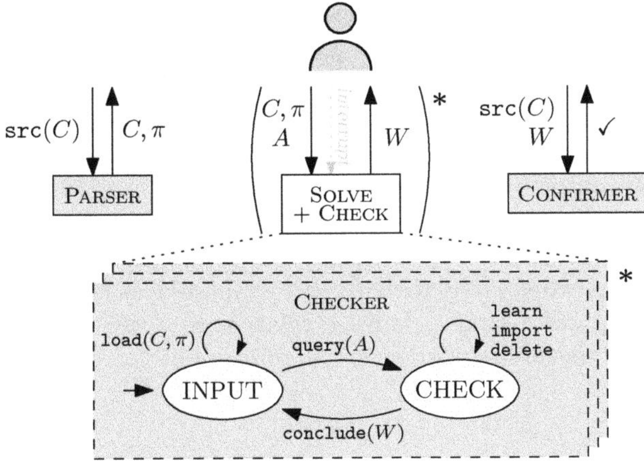

Fig. 1. Top: Possible user interactions with our system, on clauses C, fingerprints π, assumptions A and witnesses W. Bottom: Internal state machine of a checker unit. Trusted modules of the procedure are colored in green. All interactions are repeatable loops, e.g., the user can obtain growing prefixes of F by querying the parser incrementally many times over with an updated clause source. The parser and confirmer modules are considered singletons whereas multiple distinct "Solve + Check" (S+C) interactions can co-exist. In turn, each S+C procedure can entail many incarnations of the displayed checker module, each of which is controlled by the surrounding solver program. Lastly, all checker modules across *all* of the user's concurrent S+C procedures can interact with each another by sharing learned fingerprinted clauses.

- Since checker instances are not necessarily strictly synchronized, we need to ensure that learned clauses can *never travel back in time*, i.e., a clause derived from formula F_e must never be shared with a checker that currently operates on some $F_{e'}$ with $e' < e$.
- We require a *globally consistent allocation* of IDs for original clauses as well as learned clauses from all increments and across all solver units.

Our approach, illustrated in Fig. 1, offers a generic and flexible interface for trusted distributed incremental SAT. We first define the required types of fingerprints, then describe the interface of the three types of trusted modules (parser, checker, confirmer), and finally touch on strategies to assign clause IDs.

4.1   Fingerprints

In our setting, a number of individually trusted checker instances run in parallel, potentially distributed across different compute nodes. These checkers will need to exchange information such as, e.g., a certain clause being entailed by the problem. In order to trust the overall procedure, we have to either let the checkers share the full reasoning behind every result they share (e.g., dependencies of learned clauses) or establish a means of *trusted communication* between checkers.

Given that the former option is prohibitive in practice, the real-time checking approach ImpCheck established *fingerprints*[5] as an efficient, environment-independent, and highly trustworthy mechanism of establishing such trusted communication. We adopt and extend this method to our incremental setting.

As in original ImpCheck, we define fingerprinting function f using an underlying checksum or hashing algorithm $H_K : \{0,1\}^* \to \{0,1\}^\ell$, where ℓ is the bitlength of each fingerprint (e.g., 64 or 128 bits) and the output is influenced by a global *key* K. This key K is private to all trusted modules.[6] The outer function $f(\cdot) := f_K(\cdot)$ is parametrized with K and evaluated in three different contexts: on a formula F_e, on a single clause c relative to a certain increment, and to certify a query's unsatisfiability or satisfiability. Let "$\circ$" denote concatenation.

$$f_K(F_e) \quad := H_K(F_e) \tag{1}$$

$$f_K^{F_e}(c) \quad := H_K(id(c) \circ c \circ f_K(F_e)) \tag{2}$$

$$f_K^{F_e}(\top, A) := H_K(10 \circ f_K(F_e) \circ A) \tag{3}$$

$$f_K^{F_e}(\bot, \phi) := H_K(20 \circ f_K(F_e) \circ \phi) \tag{4}$$

Defining each clause signature $f_K^{F_e}(c)$ relative to F_e (2) ensures that receiving checkers can confirm the *no back-in-time* property of shared clauses. A fingerprint representing satisfiability (3) is based on all of the current query's assumptions A, thus ensuring that all assumptions have been checked to be satisfied by the found model. Similarly, a fingerprint representing unsatisfiability (4) must be relative to the set of *failed assumptions* $\phi \subseteq A$ that render the query unsatisfiable – otherwise, a fingerprint representing unsatisfiability w.r.t. some non-empty ϕ could be misinterpreted to represent the formula's overall unsatisfiability.

We ensure that all definitions have disjoint inputs to prevent ambiguities (cf. [31]) by prepending 10 or 20 to $f_K(F_e)$ as a single byte and by padding each clause ID with two zero-bytes, while F_e consists of a multiple of four bytes.

4.2   Trusted Modules

We now detail our changes and extensions to each of the three trusted modules of ImpCheck (see Section 3), as shown in Fig. 1.

We extend ImpCheck's **parser** to successively parse F and output a corresponding sequence $\langle (F_e, f_K(F_e)), (F_{e'} \setminus F_e, f_K(F_{e'})), (F_{e''} \setminus F_{e'}, f_K(F_{e''})), \ldots \rangle$ (where $e \leq e' \leq e'' \leq \ldots$) via a series of incremental calls. To match the incremental nature of our approach, our parser also works incrementally; a single parser execution spans an entire incremental SAT task P, where formula increments can be provided via a static or a successively updated input source (see

---

[5] ImpCheck's fingerprints are called *signatures* [31], which we renamed following a remark by David Basin that *signatures* have a deviating meaning in cryptography.

[6] In ImpCheck's current implementation, each trusted module computes K based on (i) some internal "salt" in the source code, (ii) compile-time system randomness compiled into the executables, and (iii) a seed provided as command-line argument.

```
state == INPUT
load(clauses: ClauseList, f: Fingerprint) → bool

oldstate == INPUT && state == CHECK
query_sat(asmpt: LiteralList) → bool

oldstate == CHECK && state == CHECK
learn(id: ID, lits: LiteralList, hints: IDList, share: bool)
   → (bool, Fingerprint?, u32?)

oldstate == CHECK && state == CHECK
import(id: ID, lits: LiteralList, fp: Fingerprint, cidx: u32) → bool

oldstate == CHECK && state == CHECK
delete(ids: IDList) → bool

oldstate == CHECK && state == INPUT
conclude_sat(M: Model) → (bool, Fingerprint?)
conclude_unsat(id: ID, failed: LiteralList) → (bool, Fingerprint?)
conclude_unknown() → bool

Terminates checker module from any state, returns acknowledgment
terminate() → bool
```

Fig. 2. Abstract checker interface with basic state invariants. Each method, if used from the wrong state or with invalid or unsound arguments, can bring the checker into an INVALID state in which all subsequent calls will return **false**.

Section 7 for details). Assumptions can either be provided with the input, in which case the parser forwards them as well, or can be introduced by the user at a later point, since assumptions are not subject to fingerprinting at this point.

The **confirmer** executable operates in an analogous fashion to the parser, the only difference being that the confirmer additionally takes a *witness* $W = (e, s, \pi, w)$ for each incremental call, where $s \in \{0, 10, 20\}$ is a result code, π is a fingerprint, and w is a (possibly empty) sequence of assumption literals. The confirmer then explicitly checks the validity of each witness W, i.e., that $\pi = f_K^{F_e}(\top, w)$ if $s = 10$ ("satisfiable") and that $\pi = f_K^{F_e}(\bot, w)$ if $s = 20$ ("unsatisfiable"). For the case $s = 0$ ("unknown"), π and w can be empty.

ImpCheck's **checker** features an initial *input* stage of loading the formula and then a subsequent *checking* stage until, at some point, the checker is terminated. We replace this linear program flow by a loop, alternating between the *input* and *check* states. Transitioning from *input* to *check* requires a **query_sat** call with a set of assumptions A. Transitioning from *check* to *input* requires a **conclude** call with a SAT, UNSAT, or no (UNKNOWN) result. Fig. 1 (bottom) shows an according state transition graph whereas Fig. 2 shows the full checker interface.

When a **learned** clause is checked, its fingerprint is output together with the current e. When **importing** an external clause c, the according e must be provided. The receiving checker then uses $f_K(F_e)$ to recompute and thus validate the fingerprint $f_K^{F_e}(c)$. In other words, the receiver must check that its current F_e entails the clauses entailing c. In particular, this ensures that the message did not travel back in time from a "future" formula $F_{e'}$, $e' > e$. On a practical note, supplying each clause with its index of origin increases the metadata to be carried with during clause sharing, e.g., from 24 to 28 bytes for 32-bit indices. Additionally, each checker must remember $f_K(F_e)$ for all e.

For any set A of assumptions, validating a satisfiability result (`conclude_sat`) entails checking the supplied model against each assumption in A and the original problem clauses (which must be kept by the checker). Conversely, validating an unsatisfiability result (`conclude_unsat`) involves a set of failed assumptions ϕ, which the checker makes sure to be part of the queried assumptions A, and a reference to a previously added *conclusion clause* $\hat{c}$, which must be (a subset of) the negation of ϕ. Thus $\hat{c}$ confirms that the provided failed assumptions in conjunction are unsatisfiable. It is important to note that the solver learns clauses that are entailed by the formula and independent of the assumptions; as such, sharing clauses is independent of the sender's and the receiver's assumptions.

The LIDRUP format tracks clause *weakening* and *restoring* in a solver [11]. For our checkers, this would mean to store active and inactive clauses separately or to supply each clause with a flag indicating whether it is active. This added effort comes at no benefit because our checker never needs to iterate over all active clauses (exploiting ID hints instead). As such, we decided to ignore weakening and restore operations, with the consequence that our checker tolerates if a solver uses a clause that it internally considers "inactive". Note that the correctness of an unsatisfiability result solely depends on each individual clause being entailed by the formula, and for satisfiable problems, the witness assignment is a model for the entire original formula. As such, (not) tracking weakened clauses is inconsequential for correctness. Lifting this restriction and extending our approach to stronger forms of learning [12] is left for future work.

4.3   Clause ID Domains

In single-threaded proof production, clause (LRAT/LRUP) IDs are commonly assigned based on a single integer counter. To obtain globally unique IDs in distributed settings, non-incremental ImpCheck requires that the first o IDs are reserved for the o original problem clauses and that producing solver thread i (out of p) should only assign new clause IDs of the shape $i + k \cdot p$ ($k \in \mathbb{N}$).[7]

In our distributed and incremental setting, we have no prior knowledge of how many clauses will be learned and shared in the scope of a single increment. Moreover, we want to support flexible modes of parallelism, where SAT solving processes can be added or removed *during* an ongoing solving procedure [27,38]. New solver-checking units joining an existing solve procedure thus also need to operate on "fresh" ID domains without interfering with existing ones.

At an abstract level, we consider each clause ID not as a plain number but as a pair (i, x), where i indicates the clause's *origin* ($i = 0$ for original input clauses and the globally unique index $i > 0$ of the producing solver-checker unit

---

[7] In the original ImpCheck [31], assigned clause IDs have the shape $o + 1 + i + k \cdot p$ ($k \in \mathbb{N}_0$) if there are o original input clauses (cf. [23]). Later versions use $i + k \cdot p$, which simplifies arithmetic on clause IDs and makes them independent of o.

otherwise) and x is the unit's local clause counter. There are many possibilities to encode this information into a single unsigned integer, including algebras with which we can uniquely express arbitrarily large i and x given sufficiently large IDs [4,6]. As a more pragmatic alternative, we can reserve the first O clause IDs for *all* original clauses across all increments, for some conservatively chosen O (e.g., $O = 2^{32} \approx 4.3$ billion), and then employ modulus arithmetic as in earlier works [23,31] to encode i. Specifically, each ID assigned by the i-th solver-checker unit satisfies ID $\equiv i \mod p^*$, where p^* is an upper bound for the number of solver-checker units that may be initialized in the scope of the entire procedure.

In all instances where our approach expects clause IDs to be restricted to certain domains, any violation will be noticed by a checker unit *if it results in an unsound proof.* Each checker, at any point in time, internally maps each known ID to exactly one clause. Upon receiving a clause with an already known ID, the checker raises an unrecoverable error. Similarly, an error is raised if a derivation uses a clause ID in a context that does not fit the local clause known under this ID. If a checker raises no such error, then each of its clauses has (had) a unique ID in the scope of its life time. Even if a clause ID is reused after its original clause was deleted, there is a straightforward way of renaming conflicting clause IDs that results in a sound global proof.

5   Correctness

We now prove the correctness of our approach. We first introduce an abstract solving model, determine that it is sound and then show how our real-time distributed incremental proof checking approach implements this model.

At an intuitive level, our abstract model captures two kinds of clause sets. First, there is a *local* clause database C_i for each solver/checker unit i, which contains the problem clauses of i as well as its learned and imported clauses. Second, for each increment index e there is a *global* clause database B_e that contains all clauses exported by units that operated on F_e at that point in time.

Formally, we establish clause sets $B := \langle B_1, B_2, \ldots \rangle$ and $C := \langle C_1, C_2, \ldots \rangle$ and perform a sequence of *actions*: (i) $\mathtt{read}(i)$ reads a single input clause from some external source and adds it to C_i; (ii) $\mathtt{learn}(i)$ learns a RUP clause c from clauses in C_i and inserts c to C_i; (iii) $\mathtt{push}(i, e)$ exports a clause from C_i to B_e; (iv) $\mathtt{fetch}(e, i)$ imports a clause from B_e to C_i.

For any i, we define η_i as the number of $\mathtt{read}(i)$ actions performed thus far. Given formula F, we define the following *conditions* for the above procedure:

C1 All clause sets are initially empty and modified only by the above actions.
C2 For any e and i, the first e $\mathtt{read}(i)$ actions together yield a prefix F_e of F.
C3 For any i, any action $\mathtt{push}(i, e)$ satisfies $e = \eta_i$ and any action $\mathtt{fetch}(e, i)$ satisfies $e \leq \eta_i$ at the point of their respective execution.

For example, consider $F = \{a \vee b, a \vee \neg b, \neg a\}$ and actions $\mathcal{A} := \langle \mathtt{read}(0),$ $\mathtt{read}(0), \mathtt{learn}(0), \mathtt{push}(0, 2), \mathtt{read}(1), \mathtt{read}(1), \mathtt{read}(1), \mathtt{fetch}(2, 1), \mathtt{learn}(1) \rangle$. Instance $i = 0$ reads the first two clauses of F, learns a clause (unit clause a), and writes this clause to B_2 (since $\eta_0 = 2$ at that point). Instance $i = 1$ reads all three clauses of F, fetches clause a from B_2 (which is valid since $2 \leq \eta_1 = 3$), and can now learn the empty clause. In the end, we have $C_0 = \{a \vee b, a \vee \neg b, a\}$ and $C_1 = \{a \vee b, a \vee \neg b, \neg a, a, \bot\}$. Note that the actions of $i = 0$ and of $i = 1$ could be interleaved arbitrarily in $\mathcal{A}$ as long as $\texttt{push}(0, 2) \prec \texttt{fetch}(2, 1)$.

Theorem 1 (Soundness). *Assume a sequence of n actions that satisfies C1–C3. For any $e \geq 1$, each $c \in B_e \cup \{C_i : \eta_i \leq e\}$ is entailed by F_e.*

Proof. We show the claim via induction over n. After $n = 0$ actions, all clause sets are empty (C1). Next, given that the claim holds after n actions, action $n + 1$ preserves it: Action $\texttt{read}(i)$ increments η_i and subsequently adds the η_i-th clause of F (C2), which is trivially entailed by F_{η_i}, to C_i. Action $\texttt{learn}(i)$ learns a clause c from clauses inductively entailed by F_{η_i} and adds it to C_i. Action $\texttt{push}(i, e)$, for $e = \eta_i$ (C3), adds a clause inductively entailed by F_{η_i} to B_{η_i}. Action $\texttt{fetch}(e, i)$, for $e \leq \eta_i$ (C3), adds a clause inductively entailed by F_{η_i} to C_i. In all cases, the action preserves the claimed property. $\square$

Note how this model, *by design*, rules out cyclic clause dependencies. The induction over the linear action sequence shows that the distributed proof remains a DAG at all times and that no action can ever induce a dependency loop.

As the next step, we correspond the above abstract model to our checking approach. For this means, consider assumption **A1**: Fingerprints provide **perfect authenticity**, i.e., each string s that constitutes a valid fingerprint for object x originates from trusted code explicitly computing s as the fingerprint of x.

Note that (A1) rules out fingerprints $f(x)$ with a *second preimage* $x' \neq x$ such that $f(x) = f(x')$: Any such $f(x')$ is a valid fingerprint for x but was not computed as the fingerprint of x. We discuss the validity of (A1) after the proof.

Theorem 2. *Consider our distributed incremental checking under assumption (A1) with a parser that emits fingerprints for formula F. This approach implements the above abstract procedure for F while satisfying conditions C1–C3.*

Proof. We first establish a mapping between the abstract model and our concrete checking approach. Each C_i corresponds to the i-th checker's clause database in our approach. Each $\texttt{load}(i)$ corresponds to checker i loading its next input clause and validating it against a provided fingerprint, and each $\texttt{learn}(i)$ corresponds to checker i adding a *confirmed* RUP clause to its clause database. We define the clause sets B virtually: We consider clause c to be part of B_e if and only if fingerprint $f_K^{F_e}(c)$ has been emitted by some checker. As such, each $\texttt{push}(i, e)$ corresponds to checker i emitting a fingerprint for a clause entailed by F_e, and each $\texttt{fetch}(e, i)$ corresponds to checker i importing a clause with a valid fingerprint for an index $e \leq \eta_i$. In practice, some actions can occur in parallel and thus do not constitute a single linear sequence, which is required for the clause derivations' acyclicity and soundness (Theorem 1). However, any actions applicable in parallel are functionally independent and can thus always be ordered into such a sequence. Lastly, if a checker i receives an invalid or erroneous input, it terminates – leaving C_i in its last, valid state and not modifying B any further. As such, we can equivalently assume that no such errors occur.

Under the described correspondence, our setup satisfies C1 because a clause can only enter a checker's database via `read`, `learn`, or `fetch`; no clause fingerprints exist initially (A1); and only `push` actions emit a clause fingerprint (A1). Condition C2 is met because fingerprints ensure that any participating checker i with $\eta_i = e$ operates on the intended formula F_e (A1). If we consider a checker x that operates not on F but on formula $F' \neq F$ (with accordingly different fingerprints), then all outputs of x are invalid inputs to checkers operating on F; therefore x is, functionally, not part of the procedure. Lastly, a checker only emits $f_K^{F_e}(c)$ if $\eta_i = e$ and it only imports incoming clauses c with fingerprint $f_K^{F_e}(c)$ if $e \leq \eta_i$, which satisfies C3. $\qquad\square$

Note that we abstracted away clause deletions in the above proof. Deleted clauses (for LIDRUP) can be modelled as *inactive* parts of the C_i that are no longer used in derivations and exports. Original clauses from F_e are never deleted by checkers that are configured to check satisfying assignments.

Finally, we obtain an end-to-end correctness result, also when considering assumptions of individual queries and including the confirmer module.

Theorem 3. *Assume* (A1). *Consider a parser executable that successively emits pairs $(F_e, f_K(F_e))$ of an incremental SAT task $P = (F, Q)$. If a confirmer executed on F accepts a witness $W = (e, s, \pi, w)$, then for any query $q = (e, A) \in Q$, q is satisfiable if $s = 10 \land w = A$ and unsatisfiable if $s = 20 \land w \subseteq A$.*

Proof. Since the confirmer accepts W, π represents the (un)satisfiability of the corresponding F_e with (failed) assumptions w. Due to (A1), such a fingerprint can only originate from a checker i with $\eta_i = e$ producing this result. For $s = 10$ (SAT), we have $\pi = f_K^{F_e}(\top, w)$ with $w = A$, which signifies that the checker checked a model against F_e and, additionally, against each literal in A. As such, q is satisfiable. For $s = 20$ (UNSAT), $\pi = f_K^{F_e}(\bot, w)$ signifies that the checker confirmed that the entailed clause $\neg w$ is part of its database. Due to Theorem 2, $F_e \land w$ is unsatisfiable. Due to $w \subseteq A$, the query $q = (e, A)$ is unsatisfiable. $\qquad\square$

Note that our argument leaves the number of actors open and (largely) how they interact. A direct consequence is that any set of incremental SAT tasks can *freely share clauses* derived at F_e if the receiver operates on a later $F_{e'}$. For singular queries without assumptions, our proof provides a more formal argument of correctness for non-incremental ImpCheck than originally [31].

We ensure (A1) in practice by choosing a high-quality 128-bit keyed hash function [1] that rules out spurious valid fingerprints and coincidental second preimages beyond any reasonable doubt. Assuming a non-adversarial environment,[8] this hashing in fingerprints is part of our approach's *trusted core*, which,

---

[8] A non-adversarial environment is an implicit assumption in all widespread propositional proof checking approaches, including formally verified ones. As an example, an adversary to a verified sequential proof checker (e.g., [8]) could manipulate the formula file (while it is being parsed) or the underlying filesystem.

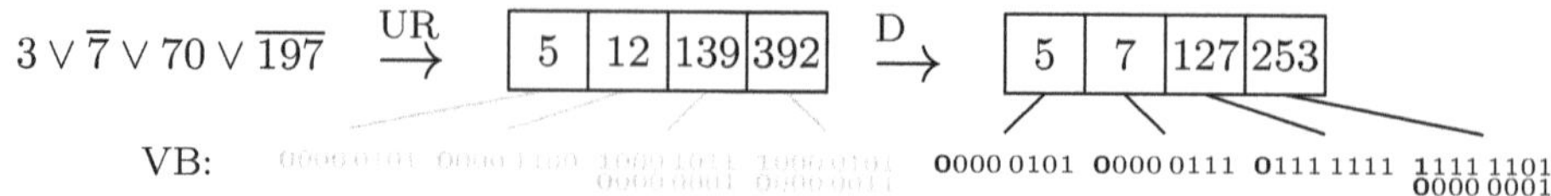

Fig. 3. Compression of a clause whose unsigned representation (UR) would, naïvely, take $4 \times 4 = 16$ bytes to store. Immediately applying variable-bytelength (VB) results in six bytes whereas first employing a differential encoding (D) results in five bytes.

as usual in proof checking, already includes the trusted executables and other aspects like file I/O (for parsing F) and integrity of main memory.

6 Reducing Memory Requirements

Real-time checking requires significant amounts of main memory since each clause is present once in the solver thread and once in the checker process [31]. As a (partial) mitigation, we introduce clause compression to the checker units.

Firstly, we compress clauses based on a *differential coding* (Fig. 3). Given a clause $c = l_1 \vee \cdots \vee l_k$, where $l_1 < \cdots < l_k$ in terms of the literals' unsigned integer representation, we store c as sequence $S_c = \langle l_1, l_2 - l_1, \ldots, l_k - l_{k-1} \rangle$. Due to the literals being sorted, all elements of S_c are positive. We then encode S_c with *variable bytelength*, where one bit per byte signifies whether a number ends at this byte (cf. [16]). Applying this encoding to differences between neighbored literals, we expect most individual values to only take a small number of bytes.

Secondly, we employ *bit-stuffing* for small clauses to avoid some memory (de)allocations. Whenever a clause's literals, after compression, take up ≤ 7 bytes, we store them directly in the 64-bit pointer field rather than pointing to a separate chunk of memory. The eighth byte of the repurposed pointer field is masked in a way that unambiguously marks the pointer as repurposed.

With our compression, fetching a prerequisite clause for checking a derivation incurs added work: The clause's literals are decompressed on-the-fly by reversing the compression steps. We refrained from compressing clauses at bit rather than byte granularity since this would introduce further complexity and overhead.

7 Implementation

We implemented our real-time checking applications (available online [33]) in C99, building upon the ImpCheck codebase [31]. Our project is now comprised of roughly 1800 effective lines of code (including some non-essential logging and debugging functionality), uses plain file I/O on *named pipes* for inter-process communication, and relies only on the C standard library.

The provided *source* from which the trusted parser reads F is a single file path across all incremental calls. If a set of input clauses resides in the user's main memory (e.g., after an internal encoding procedure), the clauses can be written to a named pipe that is treated as the parser's input. With each call, the parser continues to read the source from where it last left off up until a termination character. This allows us to input clauses reactively based on the last solve call's outcome. As a slight deviation from our formalism, our framework also allows the solver to parse and load *batches* of $x > 1$ input clauses with a single fingerprint – skipping $x - 1$ intermediate fingerprints if they are never needed (after loading).

As a first major use case, we integrated our approach in Mallob [27] and its distributed incremental SAT solver MallobSat [30,32] (see Section 3). We use CaDiCaL [5] as MallobSat's currently only LIDRUP producing solver backend and modified its internal LIDRUP interface analogous to the original ImpCheck approach [31]: each proof line is forwarded to MallobSat, where dedicated threads write proof lines to checker processes and read their responses. Since solver threads wait for a checker confirmation before reporting a result, the user does not need to screen for potential checker errors but can consider each returned result as checked (and run the confirmer on returned fingerprints for full confidence). Our incremental checking already proved valuable during development, revealing several logical errors and bugs in early versions of our integration.

As sequential baseline approach, we run a stand-alone (C++) executable that reads and solves an incremental SAT input using CaDiCaL [5] as a library. CaDiCaL writes its LIDRUP reasoning to a named pipe while a separate process running `lidrup-check` [11] reads and validates this information in real time.

8   Experimental Setup

Throughout all experiments, we use the HPC cluster HoreKa [21] with 76-core nodes (two sockets with 38 cores each) connected by fast InfiniBand interconnect. We further use Mallob's CaDiCaL [5] backend for all experiments.

Tab. 1 lists all benchmark sets used. In terms of non-incremental SAT solving, we include the 400 instances from the 2024 International SAT Competition [20]. For incremental solving, benchmark problems are more scattered and less accessible, and consequently we hand-crafted a number of benchmarks from different application domains. First, we use incremental SAT tasks emitted by SMT solver

Table 1. Instance sets used in our evaluation. For each set we indicate whether it features incremental SAT solving ("incr.") and/or flexible scheduling of multiple, related sub-tasks with clause sharing across them ("multi"), as well as the general domain, the employed system, the origin of instances, and the number of "top level" tasks.

incr.	multi	Domain	System	Instances	#
✗	✗	Generic SAT	N/A	SAT Comp. 2024	400
✓	✗	SMT	Bitwuzla	SMT-LIB: non-inc. QF_BV	389
✓	✗	BMC	2LS	SV-Comp 2024	415
✓	✗	Planning	Lilotane	IPC 2023	537
✓	✓	EDA	Mallob C&C	28- to 32-bit `cruxmiter`	4

Bitwuzla [25] when run on SMT-LIB's `QF_BV` instances (quantifier-free bit vectors) without *incremental SMT* calls. Mathias Preiner provided this selection of instances, sampled by difficulty as in ref. [35]. Our second benchmark set was provided by Oguz Mutlu and is based on problems from the C program verification track of SV-Comp 2024, processed with the model checker 2LS [28]. The set features an incremental SAT instance for each checked property in each problem taking 2LS between 60 s and 900 s. Thirdly, we include incremental SAT instances extracted from the SAT-based hierarchical planner Lilotane [29], using problems from the International Planning Competition [3]. These were already used for Schreiber's initial study on distributed incremental SAT solving [32].

Lastly, as a proof of concept for settings with multiple solving tasks on deviating assumptions, we run a simple Cube & Conquer (C&C) setup [19] in Mallob ($\approx$ 300 lines of code) on a few *miter* instances from electronic design that were used before to assess distributed C&C [15]. The formula is split up into a fixed number of sub-problems (*cubes*) using CaDiCaL's built-in, look-ahead based cubing method. Each cube is represented as a set of assumption literals, which allows for clause sharing across solving tasks that solve different cubes.

The developed software and gathered data is available online [33].

9   Results

First, we examine the slowdown for *non-incremental* solving incurred by our proof checking, i.e., when used just like non-incremental ImpCheck [31]. Fig. 4 shows results at 16 nodes (1216 cores). Here and in the following, we compare our trusted setup with a run of MallobSat where proof logging is disabled entirely, which we refer to as *unchecked solving*. Remarkably, we measured a mean slowdown of only 25.3% over unchecked solving – much less than the 37.7% reported

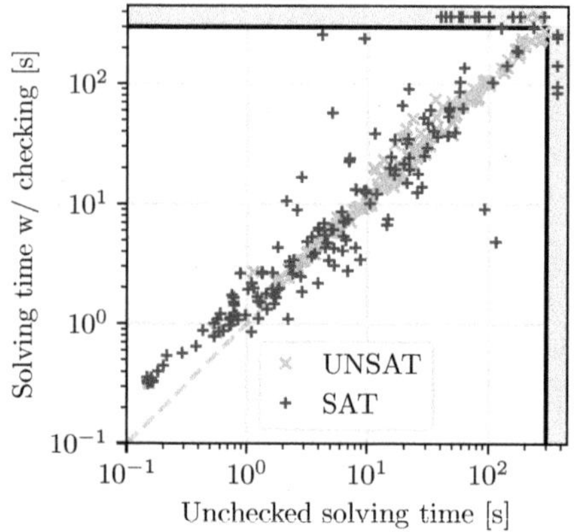

	all		sat.		unsat.	
	#	PAR	#	PAR	#	PAR
Unchecked	339	92.3	163	129.4	176	110.8
Checked	330	105.8	157	151.4	173	119.8

Fig. 4. Performance with vs. without checking at 16 nodes for non-incremental (SAT Comp. 2024) benchmarks – by-instance comparison (left) and summary (right), showing solved instances (#) and a Penalized Average Runtime (PAR, in seconds) that attributes a running time of twice the time limit ($2 \times 300\,\text{s} = 600\,\text{s}$) to each timeout.

Table 2. Basic performance metrics for incremental benchmarks: Number of solved instances and Penalized Average Runtime (PAR-2, in wallclock seconds), which attributes twice the time limit ($2 \times 300\,\text{s} = 600\,\text{s}$) to each unsolved instance.

Approach	SMT (#389)		BMC (#415)		Plan (#537)	
	#	PAR	#	PAR	#	PAR
CaDiCaL+lc	383	11.2	285	374.2	516	44.0
Unchecked 1x76	388	4.5	409	93.5	528	18.3
Unchecked 4x76	388	4.3	408	85.5	528	17.7
Unchecked 16x76	388	4.0	397	98.6	529	15.8
Checked 1x76	387	5.6	362	172.2	526	20.9
Checked 4x76	387	5.7	382	137.3	527	19.9
Checked 16x76	388	4.2	371	147.6	530	15.8

for original ImpCheck at the same scale [31]. Possible reasons are (a) deviating benchmarks, (b) MallobSat's latest configuration sharing fewer clauses [36], and (c) low-level optimizations we introduced to proof checking. Ignoring trivial solving times (below $1\,\text{s}$), our checking incurs an overhead of only 21.3% (29.2% for satisfiable, 15.5% for unsatisfiable inputs). As such, the experiment confirms that our checking approach comes with little added cost in non-incremental settings.

Next, we proceed with the results obtained on incremental instances. Tab. 2 shows performance results for the sequential baseline as well as checked and unchecked MallobSat at 1, 4, and 16 nodes (76, 304, and 1216 cores). While the scalability of incremental SAT solving with MallobSat is not the focus of this work, we note that not all of the tested incremental benchmarks were able to profit from large-scale parallelism. While the planning and SMT benchmarks yield mostly consistent scaling behavior, the BMC benchmark actually reveals deteriorating performance when increasing the scale of computing from 4 to 16 nodes. This regression is caused by the very large number of incremental SAT calls per instance (on average 2619 calls per instance compared to 11.5 and 3.2 calls p.i. for Planning and SMT respectively), almost all of which are trivial.

The relative slowdown incurred by our checking approach is shown in Fig. 5. The boxplots confirm that the slowdown remains constant regardless of the scale of solving – as for non-incremental ImpCheck [31] – and stay below 33% for the median input. As Fig. 5 (right) shows, overheads are more erratic and often higher than average for BMC inputs, which, again, we attribute to the high number of trivial increments in this benchmark. In particular, a solver thread that solved a certain increment needs to block and wait for its checker's confirmation of the obtained result before it can report the result, which occasionally takes an additional few milliseconds compared to an unchecked setup.

Next, we assess our approach's memory usage. To discern meaningful differences in RAM usage, we measured each execution's global RAM usage after $30\,\text{s}$ of elapsed wallclock time. Given a pair of runs, we compute a memory ratio for each input where both runs reached $30\,\text{s}$. At 48 cores, our checking *without* com-

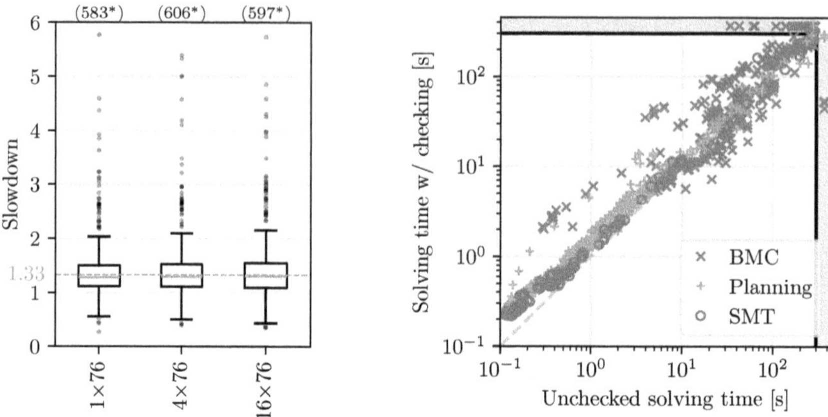

Fig. 5. Results on incremental benchmarks (planning, BMC, SMT). Left: Distribution over the relative overhead incurred by real-time proof checking compared to unchecked solving, at 1/4/16 compute nodes and over instances that took sequential CaDiCaL at least 1 s to solve. The numbers at the top denote the total number of data points used for each box plot, of which some outliers at the top have been cut off (*). Right: Per-instance comparison of running times with vs. without proof checking at 16 nodes.

pression increases memory usage by 45.2% (geom. mean) over unchecked Mallob-Sat. Our compression reduces this overhead to 31.7%. Overall, distributed solving with compressing checkers uses 9.5% less memory than with naïve checkers. The compression's impact on performance is negligible (<1% mean deviation).

Lastly, we consider a more complex use case, using a setup with 16×4 processes à 19 cores. A single-threaded Cube&Conquer controller generates 1024 cubes and then runs 19 distributed incremental SAT solving engines, initially

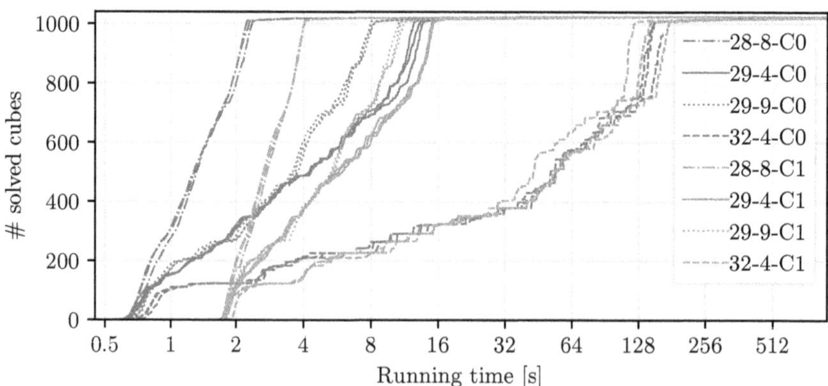

Fig. 6. Cube & Conquer experiment with (C1) and without checking (C0) on four different SAT instances `cruxmiter(`*bit-width*`)seed(`*seed*`).cnf` with several runs each.

queried on the first 19 cubes. Whenever a SAT query returns, the controller sends back the next unsolved cube as the next SAT query, until all cubes are processed or the time limit of 900 s is reached. Clauses are exchanged within and across the co-existing distributed SAT solvers, checked by our checking approach.

Fig. 6 shows the number of solved cubes over solving time for our checked vs. unchecked setup. Initially, the checked setup incurs more than one second of additional upstart overhead due to initializing many trusted checker processes. Despite this initial bottleneck, the checked runs' relative slowdowns quickly diminish, e.g., down to about 22% for 29-4, where all cubes are solved after 343 vs. 281 seconds (on average). After about eight seconds, the checked runs on the hardest instance (32-4) become difficult to discern from the unchecked runs: Significant random deviations in cube solving times cause the overall system states to increasingly diverge over time, thus causing high variances.

To summarize, our evaluations show that reliably checking the reasoning of a distributed incremental clause-sharing SAT solver in real-time is not only possible and viable but also incurs little overhead in terms of running times and memory usage. Moreover, this checking can be employed even in complex setups featuring multiple deviating incremental SAT solving tasks running in parallel, operating on different assumptions, and sharing clauses among each another.

10   Conclusion

The work at hand presents the first proof checking approach for distributed incremental SAT solving. Our real-time proof checking model covers advanced aspects like flexible re-scheduling, asynchronous and diverging solver units, and deviating assumptions. Experiments with a state-of-the-art distributed incremental solver show that a small and self-contained implementation of our checking incurs running time overhead over unchecked solving of about 33%. Optional compression techniques in our checkers reduce the main memory overhead from 45% to 32%.

Concerning future work, we aim to devise a formally verified implementation of our approach (e.g., via CakeML [39]). In the longer term, we are interested to further extend our solving and checking model towards settings where not only assumptions but also permanent clauses may deviate and clauses can still be shared under certain conditions, e.g., when all solver units operate on subsets of a common base formula (as done for example by Schreiber at al. [34]).

Acknowledgments. This work was performed on the HoreKa supercomputer funded by the Ministry of Science, Research and the Arts Baden-Württemberg and by the Federal Ministry of Education and Research (Germany). We further acknowledge support by an Amazon Research Award (Fall 2023). The authors wish to thank Yong Kiam Tan for his idea of introducing a "virtual" clause database that is defined to contain all fingerprinted clauses. The authors also thank Florian Pollitt for helpful insights on CaDiCaL's LIDRUP backend, Mathias Preiner and Oguz Mutlu for providing SMT and BMC benchmarks, and David Basin for helpful remarks on ImpCheck.

Data Availability Statement. The artifact accompanying this paper is archived and available in the Zenodo repository at https://zenodo.org/records/18330440.

References

1. Aumasson, J.P., Bernstein, D.J.: SipHash: a fast short-input PRF. In: International Conference on Cryptology in India. pp. 489–508. Springer (2012). https://doi.org/10.1007/978-3-642-34931-7_28
2. Balyo, T., Sinz, C.: Parallel satisfiability. In: Hamadi, Y., Sais, L. (eds.) Handbook of Parallel Constraint Reasoning. Springer (2018). https://doi.org/10.1007/978-3-319-63516-3_1
3. Behnke, G., Höller, D., Bercher, P. (eds.): Proceedings of the 10th International Planning Competition: Planner and Domain Abstracts – Hierarchical Task Network (HTN) Planning Track (IPC 2020) (2021), https://ipc2020.hierarchical-task.net/publications/IPC2020Booklet.pdf
4. Berners-Lee, T., Fielding, R., Masinter, L.: Uniform resource identifier (uri): Generic syntax. Tech. rep. (2005). https://doi.org/10.17487/rfc3986
5. Biere, A., Faller, T., Fazekas, K., Fleury, M., Froleyks, N., Pollitt, F.: CaDiCaL 2.0. In: International Conference on Computer Aided Verification. pp. 133–152. Springer (2024). https://doi.org/10.1007/978-3-031-65627-9_7
6. Cantor, G.: Ein Beitrag zur Mannigfaltigkeitslehre. Journal für die reine und angewandte Mathematik (Crelles Journal) **1878**(84), 242–258 (1878). https://doi.org/10.1515/crelle-1878-18788413
7. Chong, N., Cook, B., Kallas, K., Khazem, K., Monteiro, F.R., Schwartz-Narbonne, D., Tasiran, S., Tautschnig, M., Tuttle, M.R.: Code-level model checking in the software development workflow. In: Proceedings of the ACM/IEEE 42nd International Conference on Software Engineering: Software Engineering in Practice. p. 11–20. ICSE-SEIP '20 (2020). https://doi.org/10.1145/3377813.3381347
8. Cruz-Filipe, L., Heule, M.J.H., Hunt, Warren A., J., Kaufmann, M., Schneider-Kamp, P.: Efficient certified RAT verification. In: de Moura, L. (ed.) Proc. CADE. Lecture Notes in Computer Science, vol. 10395, pp. 220–236 (2017). https://doi.org/10.1007/978-3-319-63046-5_14
9. Eén, N., Sörensson, N.: Temporal induction by incremental SAT solving. Electronic Notes in Theoretical Computer Science **89**(4), 543–560 (2003). https://doi.org/10.1016/s1571-0661(05)82542-3
10. Fazekas, K., Niemetz, A., Preiner, M., Kirchweger, M., Szeider, S., Biere, A.: Satisfiability modulo user propagators. Journal of Artificial Intelligence Research **81**, 989–1017 (2024). https://doi.org/10.1613/jair.1.16163
11. Fazekas, K., Pollitt, F., Fleury, M., Biere, A.: Certifying incremental SAT solving. In: Conference on Logic for Programming, Artificial Intelligence and Reasoning (LPAR). vol. 100, pp. 321–340 (2024). https://doi.org/10.29007/pdcc
12. Fazekas, K., Pollitt, F., Fleury, M., Biere, A.: Incremental inprocessing rules beyond resolution. In: Hoenicke, J., Janota, M., Niemetz, A., Tourret, S. (eds.) Proceedings 16'th Pragmatics of SAT International Workshop (POS'25). pp. 190–200. No. 4008 in CEUR Workshop Proceedings (2025), https://ceur-ws.org/Vol-4008
13. Fichte, J.K., Le Berre, D., Hecher, M., Szeider, S.: The silent (r)evolution of SAT. Comm. ACM **66**(6), 64–72 (2023). https://doi.org/10.1145/3560469
14. Froleyks, N., Biere, A.: Single clause assumption without activation literals to speed-up IC3. In: Formal Methods in Computer Aided Design (FMCAD). pp. 72–76. IEEE (2021). https://doi.org/10.34727/2021/isbn.978-3-85448-046-4_15

15. Heisinger, M., Fleury, M., Biere, A.: Distributed cube and conquer with Paracooba. In: Theory and Applications of Satisfiability Testing (SAT). pp. 114–122. Springer (2020). https://doi.org/10.1007/978-3-030-51825-7_9

16. Heule, M.J.H.: The DRAT format and DRAT-trim checker. CoRR **abs/1610.06229** (2016)

17. Heule, M.J.H.: Proofs of unsatisfiability. In: Biere, A., Heule, M., van Maaren, H., Walsh, T. (eds.) Handbook of Satisfiability - Second Edition, Frontiers in Artificial Intelligence and Applications, vol. 336, pp. 635–668. IOS Press (2021). https://doi.org/10.3233/FAIA200998

18. Heule, M.J.H., Biere, A.: Proofs for satisfiability problems. In: All about Proofs, Proofs for All (APPA), Math. Logic and Foundations, vol. 55. College Pub. (2015)

19. Heule, M.J.H., Kullmann, O., Wieringa, S., Biere, A.: Cube and conquer: Guiding CDCL SAT solvers by lookaheads. In: Haifa Verification Conference. pp. 50–65. Springer (2011). https://doi.org/10.1007/978-3-642-34188-5_8

20. Heule, M.J., Iser, M., Järvisalo, M., Suda, M.: Proceedings of SAT Competition 2024: Solver, benchmark and proof checker descriptions (2024), https://researchportal.helsinki.fi/files/324666039/sc2024-proceedings.pdf

21. Hardware overview of HoreKa (2026), https://www.nhr.kit.edu/userdocs/horeka/hardware/

22. Lammich, P.: Efficient verified (UN)SAT certificate checking. J. Autom. Reason. **64**(3), 513–532 (2020). https://doi.org/10.1007/s10817-019-09525-z

23. Michaelson, D., Schreiber, D., Heule, M.J.H., Kiesl-Reiter, B., Whalen, M.W.: Unsatisfiability proofs for distributed clause-sharing SAT solvers. In: Tools and Algorithms for the Construction and Analysis of Systems (TACAS). pp. 348–366. Springer (2023). https://doi.org/10.1007/978-3-031-30823-9_18

24. Michaelson, D., Schreiber, D., Heule, M.J., Kiesl-Reiter, B., Whalen, M.W.: Producing proofs of unsatisfiability with distributed clause-sharing SAT solvers. Journal of Automated Reasoning **69**(2), 12 (2025). https://doi.org/10.1007/s10817-025-09725-w

25. Niemetz, A., Preiner, M.: Bitwuzla. In: International Conference on Computer Aided Verification (CAV). vol. 13965, pp. 3–17. Springer (2023). https://doi.org/10.1007/978-3-031-37703-7_1

26. Pollitt, F., Fleury, M., Biere, A.: Faster LRAT checking than solving with CaDiCaL. In: Theory and Applications of Satisfiability Testing (SAT). Schloss Dagstuhl – Leibniz-Zentrum für Informatik (2023). https://doi.org/10.4230/LIPIcs.SAT.2023.21

27. Sanders, P., Schreiber, D.: Decentralized online scheduling of malleable NP-hard jobs. In: Euro-Par 2022: Parallel Processing. pp. 119–135. Springer (2022). https://doi.org/10.1007/978-3-031-12597-3_8

28. Schrammel, P., Kroening, D.: 2LS for program analysis - (competition contribution). In: Tools and Algorithms for the Construction and Analysis of Systems (TACAS). vol. 9636, pp. 905–907. Springer (2016). https://doi.org/10.1007/978-3-662-49674-9_56

29. Schreiber, D.: Lilotane: A lifted SAT-based approach to hierarchical planning. JAIR **70**, 1117–1181 (2021). https://doi.org/10.1613/jair.1.12520

30. Schreiber, D.: MallobSat and MallobSat-ImpCheck in the SAT Competition 2024. In: SAT Competition 2024: Solver, Benchmark and Proof Checker Descriptions. pp. 21–22 (2024)

31. Schreiber, D.: Trusted scalable SAT solving with on-the-fly LRAT checking. In: Theory and Applications of Satisfiability Testing (SAT). pp. 25:1–25:19.

Schloss Dagstuhl – Leibniz-Zentrum für Informatik (2024). https://doi.org/10.4230/LIPIcs.SAT.2024.25

32. Schreiber, D.: Distributed incremental SAT solving with Mallob: Report and case study with hierarchical planning. https://arxiv.org/abs/2505.18836 (2025)

33. Schreiber, D., Fleury, M., Fazekas, K., Biere, A.: Experimental data of TACAS 2026 publication "Real-time Proof Checking for Distributed Incremental SAT Solving". Zenodo Dataset (2026). https://doi.org/10.5281/zenodo.18330440

34. Schreiber, D., Jabs, C., Berg, J.: From scalable SAT to MaxSAT: Massively parallel solution improving search. In: Symposium on Combinatorial Search (SoCS) (2025). https://doi.org/10.1609/socs.v18i1.35984

35. Schreiber, D., Niemetz, A., Preiner, M.: Massively parallel bit-precise verification with Bitwuzla and Mallob. In: Tools and Algorithms for the Construction and Analysis of Systems (TACAS) (2026), to appear

36. Schreiber, D., Rigi-Luperti, N., Biere, A.: Streamlining distributed SAT solver design. Theory and Applications of Satisfiability Testing (SAT) **23**, 1–23 (2025). https://doi.org/10.4230/LIPIcs.SAT.2025.27

37. Schreiber, D., Sanders, P.: Scalable SAT solving in the cloud. In: Theory and Applications of Satisfiability Testing (SAT). pp. 518–534. Springer (2021). https://doi.org/10.1007/978-3-030-80223-3_35

38. Schreiber, D., Sanders, P.: MallobSat: Scalable SAT solving by clause sharing. Journal of Artificial Intelligence Research **80**, 1437–1495 (2024). https://doi.org/10.1613/jair.1.15827

39. Tan, Y.K., Heule, M.J.H., Myreen, M.O.: cake_lpr: Verified propagation redundancy checking in CakeML. In: Tools and Algorithms for the Construction and Analysis of Systems (TACAS). pp. 223–241. Springer (2021). https://doi.org/10.1007/978-3-030-72013-1_12

40. Van Gelder, A.: Verifying RUP proofs of propositional unsatisfiability. In: International Symposium on Artificial Intelligence and Mathematics (ISAIM) (2008), http://isaim2008.unl.edu/PAPERS/TechnicalProgram/ISAIM2008_0008_60a1f9b2fd607a61ec9e0feac3f438f8.pdf

Quantifier Elimination Meets Treewidth

Hao Wu[*,1,2], Jiyu Zhu[*,1,2], Amir Kafshdar Goharshady[3],
Jie An[4,2], Bican Xia[5], and Naijun Zhan[6,7]($\boxtimes$)

[1] KLSS, Institute of Software, Chinese Academy of Sciences, China
[2] University of Chinese Academy of Sciences, China
[3] University of Oxford, United Kingdom
[4] National Key Laboratory of Space Integrated Information System,
Institute of Software, Chinese Academy of Sciences, China
[5] School of Mathematical Sciences, Peking University, China
[6] School of Computer Science, Peking University, China
[7] Zhongguancun Laboratory, China
{wuhao, zhujy}@ios.ac.cn   amir.goharshady@cs.ox.ac.uk
anjie@iscas.ac.cn   xbc@math.pku.edu.cn   njzhan@pku.edu.cn

Abstract. In this paper, we address the complexity barrier inherent in Fourier-Motzkin elimination (FME) and cylindrical algebraic decomposition (CAD) when eliminating a block of (existential) quantifiers. To mitigate this, we propose exploiting structural sparsity in the variable dependency graph of quantified formulas. Utilizing tools from parameterized algorithms, we investigate the role of *treewidth*, a parameter that measures the graph's tree-likeness, in the process of quantifier elimination. A novel dynamic programming framework, structured over a tree decomposition of the dependency graph, is developed for applying FME and CAD, and is also extensible to general quantifier elimination procedures. Crucially, we prove that when the treewidth is a constant, the framework achieves a significant exponential complexity improvement for both FME and CAD, reducing the worst-case complexity bound from doubly exponential to single exponential. Preliminary experiments on sparse linear real arithmetic (LRA) and nonlinear real arithmetic (NRA) benchmarks confirm that our algorithm outperforms the existing popular heuristic-based approaches on instances exhibiting low treewidth.

Keywords: Quantifier Elimination · Fourier-Motzkin Elimination · Cylindrical Algebraic Decomposition · Parameterized Algorithms · Treewidth

1 Introduction

Quantifier elimination (QE) is a fundamental technique in mathematical logic that transforms a first-order formula containing existential ($\exists$) and universal ($\forall$) quantifiers into an equivalent quantifier-free formula. A theory that admits a

---

The first two authors marked with $\star$ contributed equally to this work and should be considered co-first authors. A longer version with appendices is available at [74].

S. Junges and G. Katz (Eds.): TACAS 2026, LNCS 16505, pp. 353–373, 2026.
https://doi.org/10.1007/978-3-032-22752-2_19

quantifier elimination procedure is highly desirable, as its decidability immediately reduces to the decidability of its quantifier-free fragment. This theoretical significance strongly motivates researchers in mathematics and computer science to investigate various theories that admit quantifier elimination procedures. This paper primarily focuses on quantifier elimination within two central theories over the real numbers: *linear real arithmetic* (LRA), where atomic formulas are defined by strictly linear constraints, and *nonlinear real arithmetic* (NRA), which permits general polynomial constraints.

For LRA, the *Fourier-Motzkin elimination* (FME) algorithm is the first quantifier elimination procedure, originally proposed by Fourier [33] and rediscovered by Motzkin [61]. This algorithm can be understood as reducing a system of linear inequalities by removing variables one by one. Its importance primarily stems from its geometric interpretation, which corresponds to the projection of a polyhedron (described by linear inequalities) onto lower-dimensional subspaces [68, Sect. 12.2]. However, a significant challenge of applying the FME algorithm is its high worst-case complexity, which is doubly exponential in the number of quantified variables. This high complexity results from the rapid, often redundant, proliferation of new constraints during the elimination steps [43,44,51,47]. For eliminating a block of existential quantifiers, recent works [62,63] provide a divide-and-conquer approach to improve the complexity to single exponential.

For NRA, the first quantifier elimination procedure was developed around the 1930s by Tarski in his seminal work [73]. While Tarski's procedure is not elementary recursive, the first elementary recursive quantifier elimination procedure was developed by Collins in 1975 [20], known as *cylindrical algebraic decomposition* (CAD). The CAD algorithm marks a milestone in real algebraic geometry and a comprehensive survey can be found in [16]. Ever since its origin, the CAD algorithm, as well as its various variants [60,39,21,13,18,40,15,38,69,10,37], has remained the most authoritative procedure for NRA. It has found broad application in critical domains, including formal verification [50,66,55,34,1], control synthesis [28,49,41], and hybrid system analysis [2,70]. Similar to the FME algorithm, the CAD algorithm also suffers from a worst-case doubly exponential complexity, but in the number of *all* occurring variables [23]. Besides the complexity of internal algebraic operations, it is well known that the order of variables to be eliminated, called *variable elimination ordering*, has a huge impact on the practical performance when eliminating a block of existential quantifiers. Therefore, many heuristics based on sophisticated structural analysis [14,26,11,54] and machine learning techniques have been applied to this task [42,31,19,46].

While existing works mostly focus on improving FME and CAD for general inputs, a natural but unexplored (up to our knowledge) problem is: **Can we design strategies for certain classes of inputs with better worst-case complexity upper bounds?** Specifically, in this paper, we consider posing restrictions on the structural complexity of the dependency relationship of variables. This relationship is typically represented by a graph, precisely the *primal graph*, whose nodes correspond to variables of the input formula, and two variables are linked if and only if they both occur in an atomic formula. To study this problem, we utilize tools coming from *parameterized algorithms*.

The study of parameterized algorithms offers a fine-grained analytical framework for tackling computationally hard problems by introducing a secondary measurement, k, known as the parameter [29,22]. For example, a problem is classified as *fixed-parameter tractable* (FPT) if it admits an algorithm with a time complexity of $O(f(k) \cdot n^c)$, where n is the input size, f is a computable function depending solely on k, and c is a constant independent of n. In general, the goal of parameterized complexity is to conduct a finer-grained analysis of complexity by isolating the combinatorial explosion to a specific parameter.

When the input is a graph, *treewidth* is one of the most important parameters to measure its inherent complexity. Intuitively, treewidth quantifies how "tree-like" a graph is: a smaller treewidth value indicates a greater sparsity in the graph structure. The main advantage of treewidth is that a bounded treewidth allows a vast collection of classical NP-hard problems to become fixed-parameter tractable [65,8,22]. This tractability is fundamentally realized by employing *dynamic programming* (DP) techniques executed over a tree structure related to the graph, called a *tree decomposition* [6]. For constraint satisfiability problems, treewidth measures the structural complexity of variable dependencies and has been extensively studied [71,58,32,27,35,56]. However, the role of treewidth in the quantifier elimination of first-order logic theories is largely untouched, possibly due to the inherent high complexity of these procedures.

Contributions. In this paper, we develop a novel framework to exploit the treewidth sparsity pattern in the process of applying quantifier elimination procedures to eliminate a block of (existential) quantifiers. Here, the treewidth sparsity pattern means that the primal graph of the input formula has a small treewidth. The primary contributions include:

- We propose a dynamic programming algorithm for applying FME and CAD to eliminate a block of quantifiers. It is executed over a tree decomposition of the formula's primal graph, where the treewidth of the graph determines the structure of this decomposition. We prove its correctness and demonstrate its extensibility to general quantifier elimination procedures.
- We prove that, when the treewidth is a constant, the worst-time complexity of FME and CAD can be *exponentially improved* from doubly exponential to single exponential in the number of *eliminated* variables and *all occurring* variables, respectively. The core idea is the utilization of a special tree decomposition structure, called *balanced tree decompositions* [17].
- We conduct experiments on randomly generated LRA and NRA benchmarks exhibiting sparse patterns. Experimental results indicate that our algorithm outperforms other popular heuristics on problem instances with low treewidth.

Our starting point is a parameterized algorithmic perspective, a methodology that is orthogonal to most existing techniques. The most closely related work is [54], which exploits the chordal structure of the primal graph to guide the variable elimination ordering in CAD. Since chordal graphs and tree decompositions are two sides of one coin [25, Sec. 12.3], our algorithm in Sect. 3 can be viewed as a dual version of theirs. Nevertheless, utilizing treewidth offers significant algorithmic advantages. Specifically, it enables a dynamic programming framework that is more comprehensible and, by drawing upon concepts from parameterized complexity theory, a more fine-grained analysis of the complexity issues involved.

Outline. The rest of this paper is organized as follows: Sect. 2 introduces necessary concepts. Sect. 3 presents the dynamic programming algorithm for FME and presents how to extend it to CAD and general quantifier elimination procedures. Sect. 4 analyzes the complexity of our framework for FME and CAD under the assumption that the treewidth is a constant. Sect. 5 reports the experimental results and Sect. 6 finally concludes the paper.

2   Preliminaries

Let $\mathbb{R}$ and $\mathbb{N}$ denote the set of real numbers and natural numbers, respectively. A vector of n real variables is denoted by $(x_1, \ldots, x_n) \in \mathbb{R}^n$, also written as $\mathbf{x}$ for short. We denote by $\langle x_{\sigma(1)}, \ldots, x_{\sigma(n)} \rangle$ a linear ordering among these variables, where σ is from the permutation group of size n. For example, $\langle x_1, \ldots, x_n \rangle$ denotes the natural order from x_1 to x_n. We assume readers are familiar with first-order logic and recommend the book [12] for reference. For a set C of atomic formulas, we denote by $\bigwedge C$ the conjunction of all atomic formulas in C.

2.1   LRA, NRA, and Quantifier Elimination

Quantifier Elimination (QE). We say a first-order theory $\mathcal{T}$ admits *quantifier elimination* if there exists an algorithm, called a quantifier elimination procedure, that transforms a given quantified $\mathcal{T}$-formula into an equivalent formula without quantifiers. Formally, w.l.o.g., we consider the input formula Φ to be a conjunction of atomic formulas that is existentially quantified:

$$\Phi \triangleq \exists x_m, \ldots, \exists x_1. \bigwedge_i \varphi_i(x_1, \ldots, x_n), \tag{1}$$

where $m, n \in \mathbb{N}$, $m \leq n$, and each φ_i is an atomic $\mathcal{T}$-formula. The output of the quantifier elimination procedure is a quantifier-free formula in variables $x_{m+1}, \ldots, x_n$ that is equivalent to Φ. For formulas with quantifier alternations (e.g., $\forall x_2 \exists x_1$), we eliminate quantifiers from inside out, eliminating a block of quantifiers of the same type at each step. In what follows, we primarily focus on the FME algorithm for LRA and on the CAD algorithm for NRA.

Linear Real Arithmetic (LRA). LRA refers to the first-order theory with signature $\{0, 1, +, <\}$ and domain $\mathbb{R}$. Given variables $(x_1, \ldots, x_n) \in \mathbb{R}^n$ and real constants $(a_1, \ldots, a_n, b) \in \mathbb{R}^{n+1}$, an LRA atomic formula is of the form

$a_1 x_1 + \cdots + a_n x_n - b \bowtie 0$, where the relation symbol $\bowtie \in \{<, >, =, \leq, \geq\}$. The semantics of LRA is interpreted in the standard way.

Fourier-Motzkin Elimination (FME). The FME algorithm takes a pair (C, x_r) as input, where C is a set of LRA atomic formulas and x_r is a variable occurring in these constraints, and proceeds one of the following two steps:

(I) If x_r appears in an equality constraint of the form $\sum_{j=1}^n a_{i,j} \cdot x_j - b_i = 0$ with $a_{i,r} \neq 0$, the procedure removes this constraint from C and outputs C by replacing every occurrence of x_r with $\frac{b_i}{a_{i,r}} - \sum_{j=1}^{r-1} \frac{a_{i,j}}{a_{i,r}} \cdot x_j - \sum_{j=r+1}^n \frac{a_{i,j}}{a_{i,r}} \cdot x_j$.

(II) If x_r only appears in inequality constraints of the form $\sum_{j=1}^n a_{i,j} \cdot x_j - b_i \bowtie 0$, where $\bowtie$ is not $=$ and $a_{i,r} \neq 0$, for each of such constraints we derive a term $\frac{b_i}{a_{i,r}} - \sum_{j=1}^{r-1} \frac{a_{i,j}}{a_{i,r}} \cdot x_j - \sum_{j=r+1}^n \frac{a_{i,j}}{a_{i,r}} \cdot x_j$ that is called a *bound* of x_r. Moreover, the bound is called an upper bound if $a_{i,r} > 0$ and a lower bound if $a_{i,r} < 0$. In either case, it is called strict if $\bowtie \in \{<, >\}$. Let U_r and L_r denote the set of upper bounds and lower bounds of x_r, respectively. Then, the procedure outputs the set of constraints $\{l \lhd u \mid l \in L_r, u \in U_r\}$, where $\lhd$ is $<$ if both u and l are strict and is $\leq$ otherwise.

We denote the output by $\mathsf{FME}(C, x_r)$, which is a set of atomic formulas without x_r. If C is taken to be the set of atomic formulas of an LRA formula Φ of the form Eq. (1), then Φ is equivalent to the following quantifier-free formula $\bigwedge \mathsf{FME}(C, \langle x_1, \ldots, x_m \rangle)$, where $\mathsf{FME}(C, \langle x_1, \ldots, x_m \rangle)$ denotes the output of recursively applying FME procedure on C w.r.t. the ordering from x_1 to x_m. For a more detailed description of the algorithm, please refer to [53, Sec. 5.4].

Nonlinear Real Arithmetic (NRA). NRA refers to the first-order theory with signature $\{0, 1, +, \cdot, <\}$ and domain $\mathbb{R}$. A monomial is a product of powers of variables with nonnegative integer exponents, denoted by $\mathbf{x}^\alpha = x_1^{\alpha_1} \ldots x_n^{\alpha_n}$ for some $\alpha \in \mathbb{N}^n$. A polynomial is a finite summation of monomials $\sum_\alpha c_\alpha \mathbf{x}^\alpha$, where $c_\alpha \in \mathbb{R}$ are called coefficients. The set of polynomials in variables $\mathbf{x}$ with real coefficients is denoted by $\mathbb{R}[\mathbf{x}]$. An NRA atomic formula is of the form $f(\mathbf{x}) \bowtie 0$, where $f(\mathbf{x}) \in \mathbb{R}[\mathbf{x}]$ and $\bowtie \in \{<, >, =, \leq, \geq\}$. It is clear that an LRA constraint is a special case of an NRA constraint where the polynomial f is linear, i.e., of degree 1. The semantics of NRA are also interpreted in the standard way.

Cylindrical Algebraic Decomposition (CAD). Given an NRA formula Φ of the form Eq. (1) and letting $P \subset \mathbb{R}[x_1, \ldots, x_n]$ denote the set of polynomials occurring in Φ, the key idea underlying CAD is to decompose the state space $\mathbb{R}^n$ into a finite number of regions called *cells*. This decomposition satisfies two primary properties: (i) in each cell each polynomial in P remains a constant sign, and (ii) the boundary of each cell can be derived from polynomials in P. Due to the first property, the sign of a polynomial in P over a cell can be determined by a single sample point within that cell. Consequently, a finite set of sample points from the decomposition is sufficient to determine in which cells the conjunction of atomic formulas in Φ evaluates to true. Finally, by utilizing the formulas that define these cells, we can construct a quantifier-free formula equivalent to Φ.

The CAD algorithm consists of two phases, *projection* and *lifting*, while in this paper, *we solely focus on the projection phase*. The projection phase takes a variable ordering, say $\langle x_1, x_2 \ldots, x_n \rangle$, where quantified variables precede free variables, and constructs a sequence of polynomial sets

$$\{P_1(= P), P_2, \ldots, P_n\} \text{ with } P_i \subset \mathbb{R}[x_i, \ldots, x_n] \tag{2}$$

through the iterative application of a projection operator Proj. Each subsequent set $P_{i+1} = \mathsf{Proj}(P_i, x_i)$ is defined in a lower-dimensional space by removing the variable x_i and carries enough information about P_i. There exist several different definitions of the projection operator, and in our analysis, we use McCallum's projection operator [60]. After the projection phase, the lifting phase then constructs the sign-invariant cells from 1-dimension to higher dimensions. We provide a more detailed description of the CAD algorithm [4,48,67] in [74, Appendix A.1], which may not affect the understanding of this paper.

2.2   Treewidth and Tree Decomposition

In this part, we introduce basic concepts related to the sparsity of graphs. We recommend referring to [22, Ch. 7] for an in-depth investigation of this topic.

Graph and Primal Graph. We use $G = (V, E)$ to denote an undirected graph, where V is a finite set of vertices and $E \subset V \times V$ is the set of edges. The size of a graph, denoted $|G|$, is the cardinality of V. A clique in a graph is a subset of mutually adjacent vertices. Given a formula Φ in the form of Eq. (1), the *primal graph* $G_\Phi = (V_\Phi, E_\Phi)$ is a graph associated to Φ such that $V_\Phi = \{x_1, \ldots, x_m\}$ is the collection of *(existentially) quantified variables* and $(x_{j_1}, x_{j_2}) \in E_\Phi$ if and only if both $a_{i,j_1} \neq 0$ and $a_{i,j_2} \neq 0$ for some index i of atomic formulas, i.e., x_{j_1}, x_{j_2} occur simultaneously in an atomic formula. Throughout this paper, we will always assume the primal graphs are connected; otherwise, each connected component can be processed separately.

Example 1 (Running Example). Consider an LRA formula Φ of the form Eq. (1) and contains existentially quantified variables $(x_1, \ldots, x_8)$. The portion of Φ related to x_1 is displayed in Fig. 1; the complete formula containing 20 atomic formulas is in the full version [74, Appendix A.2]. The atomic formulas in Φ display a certain "sparsity" pattern—each variable only occurs in a small portion of atomic formulas. For example, variable x_1 only occurs in three atomic formulas, namely $x_1 + 2x_2 + 3x_3 \leq 20$, $x_1 - x_2 + 2x_3 \geq -5$, and $x_1 - 4x_2 \leq 0$. The primal graph of Φ is shown in Fig. 2.

Tree. A tree $T = (V, E)$ is an undirected graph that contains no cycles, i.e., there is only one unique path between any two vertices. For clarity, the vertices of a tree will be called *nodes*. We always assume that a tree under consideration is *rooted*, i.e., a node $r \in V$ is designated as the root. The *level* of a node $v \in V$, denoted $\mathsf{Lv}(v)$, is the length of the simple path from r to v. The *height* of a tree is the maximum level among all nodes. The *parent* of a node v is the node

$\Phi \doteq \exists x_1, \ldots, x_8.$

$$\begin{pmatrix} x_1 + 2x_2 + 3x_3 \le 20 \\ \wedge\ x_1 - x_2 + 2x_3 \ge -5 \\ \wedge\ x_1 - 4x_2 \le 0 \\ \wedge\ \ldots (\text{constraints without } x_1) \end{pmatrix}$$

Fig. 1: An LRA formula Φ

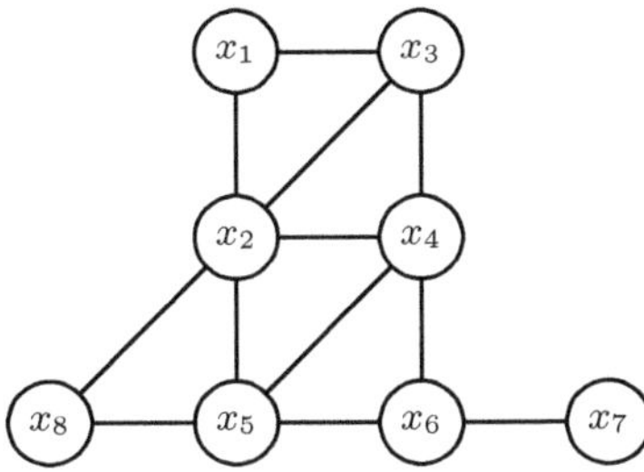

Fig. 2: The primal graph of Φ

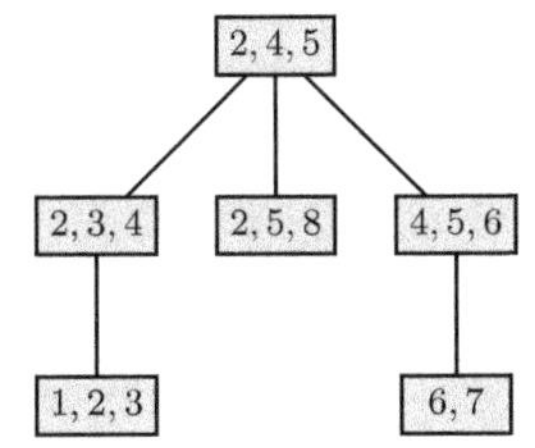

Fig. 3: A tree decomposition of Fig. 2

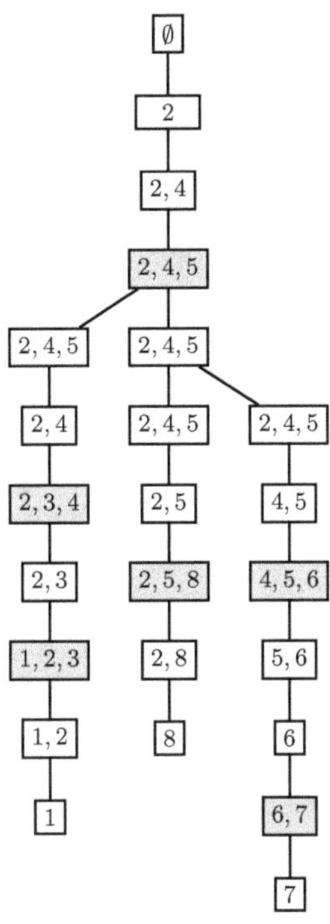

Fig. 4: The nice tree decomposition of Fig. 3. Gray nodes correspond to the nodes in Fig. 3

connected to v on the path to the root, and a child of a node v is a node of which v is the parent. A *leaf* is a node with no children. A tree is called *binary* if each node has at most two children. For each node v in T, we denote by T_v the subtree rooted at v; the nodes in T_v (excluding v itself) are called the *descendants* of v.

Tree Decomposition and Treewidth [36,64,65]. Given an undirected graph $G = (V, E)$, a *tree decomposition* of G is a tree $T = (\mathcal{B}, E_T)$ satisfying the following conditions: (1) Each node $b \in \mathcal{B}$ of T, also called a *bag*, is associated to a subset of the vertex set $V_b \subseteq V$; (2) The bags cover the entire vertex set V of G, i.e., $\bigcup_{b \in \mathcal{B}} V_b = V$; (3) For every edge $e = (u, v) \in E$, there exists a bag b such that both $u \in V_b$ and $v \in V_b$; and (4) For every three bags $b_1, b_2, b_3 \in \mathcal{B}$, if b_3 is on the path from b_1 to b_2 in T, then $V_{b_1} \cap V_{b_2} \subseteq V_{b_3}$ (equivalently, every vertex $v \in V$ appears in a connected subtree of T).

The *width* of a tree decomposition T, denoted by $w(T)$, is defined to be the size of the largest bag minus one, i.e., $w(T) = \max_{b \in \mathcal{B}} |V_b| - 1$. The *treewidth* of the graph G, denoted by $tw(G)$, is defined to be the minimum width among all possible tree decompositions of G. A tree decomposition with width $tw(G)$ is called *optimal*. For example, Fig. 3 presents an optimal tree decomposition of the primal graph in Exmp. 1 of width 2. The numbers in the labels refer to the variable indexes, for instance, the node labeled $\{1, 2, 3\}$ in Fig. 3 represents the bag $\{x_1, x_2, x_3\}$. For a primal graph G_Φ, since every clique is contained in at least one bag in its tree decomposition [22], the largest number of quantified variables in an atomic formula gives a lower bound for $tw(G_\Phi)$.

A smaller treewidth indicates a greater sparsity. In general, it is NP-complete to determine whether a given graph G has treewidth at most a given variable k [3]. However, Bodlaender showed that when k is fixed, there exists a linear-time algorithm to test whether G has treewidth at most k, and if so, to construct an optimal tree-decomposition with $O(n)$ nodes [7]. In this paper, we rely on an external algorithm [72] to compute tree decompositions. There are also many other well-optimized tools, see [24] for a survey.

Nice Tree Decomposition [52]. A tree decomposition $T = (\mathcal{B}, E_T)$ of a graph G is *nice* if T is rooted at a bag $r \in \mathcal{B}$ with $V_r = \emptyset$ and each bag of T is of one of the following four types: (1) *leaf* bag is a bag b having no children and $|V_b| = 1$; (2) A *join* bag is a bag b having exactly two children b_1 and b_2 such that $V_b = V_{b_1} = V_{b_2}$; (3) An *introduce* bag is a bag b having exactly one child b' such that $|V_b| = |V_{b'}| + 1$ and $V_{b'} \subseteq V_b$; (4) A *forget* bag is a bag b having exactly one child b' such that $|V_b| = |V_{b'}| - 1$ and $V_b \subseteq V_{b'}$. As an example, Fig. 4 gives a nice tree decomposition based on the tree decomposition in Fig. 3.

The concept of nice tree decomposition is introduced as a canonical form for representing tree decompositions. When the treewidth is a constant, a tree decomposition can be transformed into a nice tree decomposition in linear time, with the same width but a linear increase in size [22, Lem. 7.4], which helps design dynamic programming algorithms and conduct computational analysis.

3 Exploiting Treewidth Sparsity in Quantifier Elimination

Now we show how to exploit the treewidth sparsity of the primal graph in quantifier elimination. In Sect. 3.1, we explain our main idea using Exmp. 1 and present our dynamic programming framework for FME based on tree decomposition. Then we extend the framework to CAD and the general quantifier elimination procedures in Sect. 3.2. The formal analysis of the complexity improvement brought by the treewidth sparsity will be presented in Sect. 4.

3.1 A Dynamic Programming Framework for FME

To exploit the sparsity pattern within the primal graph, we begin by showing that the FME algorithm can be understood as a vertex elimination operation. Let us consider applying the FME algorithm to our running example Exmp. 1 to eliminate the variable x_1. We first rewrite the three atomic formulas containing x_1 into the following forms, separating x_1 from other terms: $x_1 \leq 20 - 2x_2 - 3x_3 \wedge -5 + x_2 - 2x_3 \leq x_1 \wedge x_1 \leq 4x_2$, which give upper bounds and lower bounds for x_1. Then, the FME algorithm removes x_1 by requiring that each lower bound is less than each upper bound. This results in two atomic formulas

$-5 + x_2 - 2x_3 \leq 20 - 2x_2 - 3x_3 \wedge -5 + x_2 - 2x_3 \leq 4x_2$, which only involve x_2 and x_3. Here, a straightforward yet important observation is that the FME algorithm is performed *locally*—when a variable is eliminated (e.g., x_1), the variables in the newly introduced atomic formulas will be exactly its neighbors in the primal graph (e.g., x_2 and x_3). In other words, eliminating variables from a formula corresponds to removing vertices from the primal graph, accompanied by the introduction of new atomic formulas about the neighbor.

Using tree decompositions, we can re-explain the process of eliminating x_1 in a tree-like manner. Consider the nice tree decomposition presented in Fig. 4, the process of eliminating x_1 consists of two steps. In the first step, we assign each atomic formula of Φ to a bag in the nice tree decomposition depending on the involved variables. This is described by the initialization of a function $\mathcal{I}$ that maps each bag to a set of atomic formulas. For example, for the three bags located at the left-most branch of the nice tree decomposition in Fig. 4, we set $\mathcal{I}(\{x_1\}) \leftarrow \{\}$ (meaning there are no atomic formulas containing only x_1), $\mathcal{I}(\{x_1, x_2\}) \leftarrow \{x_1 - 4x_2 \leq 0\}$, and $\mathcal{I}(\{x_1, x_2, x_3\}) \leftarrow \{x_1 - x_2 + 2x_3 \geq -5, x_1 + 2x_2 + 3x_3 \leq 20\}$. Note that the atomic formula $x_1 - 4x_2 \leq 0$ can also be assigned to $\mathcal{I}(\{x_1, x_2, x_3\})$ without affecting the result.

In the second step, we propagate the atomic formulas stored in $\mathcal{I}$ from bottom up, by recursively computing another function $\mathcal{V}$. For example, for the leaf bag $\{x_1\}$, we set $\mathcal{V}(\{x_1\}) = \mathcal{I}(\{x_1\}) = \{\}$. For the introduce bag $\{x_1, x_2\}$, we set $\mathcal{V}(\{x_1, x_2\}) \leftarrow \mathcal{I}(\{x_1, x_2\}) \cup \mathcal{V}(\{x_1\}) = \{x_1 - 4x_2 \leq 0\}$. The computation of $\mathcal{V}(\{x_1, x_2, x_3\})$ is similar. When the forget bag $\{x_2, x_3\}$ is reached, we set $\mathcal{V}(\{x_2, x_3\}) \leftarrow \mathcal{I}(\{x_2, x_3\}) \cup \mathsf{FME}(\bigwedge \mathcal{V}(\{x_1, x_2, x_3\}), x_1)$, which corresponds an application of the FME algorithm w.r.t. the variable removed at this bag.

By repeating the above operations, the execution of the FME algorithm can be described through a dynamic programming framework, as shown in Alg. 1, which consists of three steps.

Step 1: Constructing a nice tree decomposition (Line 1–3). To exploit the sparsity of the input formula, the algorithm first computes a tree decomposition of the formula's primal graph, by invoking some external tree decomposition algorithms. Different choices of the algorithms lead to different tree decompositions and hence impact the overall computational complexity, which will be detailed later in Sect. 4 and Sect. 5. Nevertheless, our framework works as long as $T = (\mathcal{B}, E_T)$ in Line 2 is a nice tree decomposition.

Step 2: Initialization (Line 4–17). Based on the nice tree decomposition T, we can perform the FME algorithm in a dynamic programming style. To achieve this, we define two value functions, $\mathcal{I}$ and $\mathcal{V}$, that map bags in T into sets of atomic formulas. In this step, the value function $\mathcal{I}$ is initialized from top down: when a bag $b \in T$ is visited, all atomic formulas φ with $\mathsf{var}(\varphi) \subseteq b$ are collected in $\mathcal{I}(b)$ and removed from C. According to the definition of tree decompositions, it is straightforward to see that the following properties hold: Each atomic formula $\varphi \in C$ is assigned to a bag b such that $\mathsf{var}(\varphi) \subseteq b$ and $\mathsf{Lv}(b)$ is minimized. We note that, when adding the children of a bag b into the queue in Line 10, we can break ties with any user-specified heuristics. The selection

---

Algorithm 1: A Dynamic Programming Framework for FME

Input : a LRA formula Φ of the form Eq. (1);
Output: a quantifier-free formula equivalent to Φ

```
1  ▷ Invoke external algorithms to compute nice tree decompositions.
2  Construct the primal graph G_Φ = (V_Φ, E_Φ) of Φ;
3  Compute a nice tree decomposition T = (B, E_T) of G_Φ;
4  ▷ Initialize I from top down.
5  C ← atomic formulas in Φ;
6  Initialize an empty queue of bags q = ⟨⟩;
7  q.enqueue(r_T) ;                        // add to the end of the queue
8  while q is not empty do
9  |   b ← q.dequeue() ;                   // remove from the front of the queue
10 |   q.enqueue(b.children);              // break ties with any heuristics
11 |   if b.type = leaf then
12 |   |   I(b) ← {} ;                     // if b is a leaf bag
13 |   else
14 |   |   I(b) ← {φ ∈ C | var(φ) ⊆ b} ;  // if b is of other types
15 |   |   C ← C \ I(b);
16 |   end
17 end
18 ▷ Recursively compute V from bottom up.
19 q.enqueue(B.leaves) ;
20 while q is not empty do
21 |   b ← q.dequeue();
22 |   q.enqueue(b.parent);
23 |   Compute V(b) according to Eq. (3);
24 end
25 return ⋀ V(r_T)
```

---

of the heuristics impacts the overall efficiency in the practical implementation, which will be detailed in Sect. 5.

Step 3: Recursion (Line 18–25). The value function $\mathcal{V}$ is then updated from bottom up, i.e., $\mathcal{V}(b)$ is updated after the values for all b's children have been updated. Let us denote by $b.\texttt{(left/right)child}$ the (left/right) child of a (join) bag b, by $b.\texttt{children}$ the collection of all children of a bag b, and by $b.\texttt{forget}$ the removed variable at a forget bag b. At each step, $\mathcal{V}(b)$ is updated according to the type of the bag $b \in T$:

$$\mathcal{V}(b) \leftarrow \begin{cases} \mathcal{I}(b) \cup \mathcal{V}(b.\texttt{leftchild}) \cup \mathcal{V}(b.\texttt{rightchild}) & \text{if } b \text{ is a join bag} \\ \mathcal{I}(b) \cup \mathcal{V}(b.\texttt{children}) & \text{if } b \text{ is an introduce bag} \\ \mathcal{I}(b) \cup \mathsf{FME}(\bigwedge \mathcal{V}(b.\texttt{children}), b.\texttt{forget}) & \text{if } b \text{ is a forget bag} \\ \mathcal{I}(b) & \text{if } b \text{ is a leaf bag} \end{cases}$$

$$(3)$$

Finally, the algorithm outputs the conjunction of all atomic formulas stored in $\mathcal{V}(r_T)$.

Theorem 1 (Correctness). *The formula $\bigwedge \mathcal{V}(r_T)$ is equivalent to Φ.*

Proof. Let $T_b = (\mathcal{B}_b, E_{T_b})$ denote the sub-tree rooted at a bag b. We denote by $\mathsf{ElimVar}(T_b) \triangleq \left(\bigcup_{b' \in T_b} b' \right) \setminus b$ the set of removed variables at forget bags in T_b. In this proof, we prove a stronger result by showing that, for each bag $b \in \mathcal{B}$, $\bigwedge \mathcal{V}(b) \equiv \exists \mathsf{ElimVar}(T_b). \bigwedge_{b' \in \mathcal{B}_b} \mathcal{I}(b')$. Therefore, the original statement is a special case when b is the root r of T, by noting that $\Phi = \exists x_m, \ldots, \exists x_1. \bigwedge_{b \in \mathcal{B}} \mathcal{I}(b)$.

The proof is done by induction on the structure of the nice tree decomposition T. Suppose the above property holds for every descendant of a bag b, we shall prove that the property still holds for b, depending on the type of b. When b is a join, introduce, or leaf bag, the proof is straightforward by the definition of $\mathcal{V}$. When b is a forget bag, we have

$$
\begin{aligned}
\bigwedge \mathcal{V}(b) &= \bigwedge \left(\mathcal{I}(b) \cup \mathsf{FME}(\bigwedge \mathcal{V}(b.\mathtt{children}), b.\mathtt{forget}) \right) \\
&\equiv \bigwedge \mathcal{I}(b) \wedge \bigwedge \mathsf{FME}(\exists \mathsf{ElimVar}(T_{b.\mathtt{children}}). \bigwedge_{b' \in \mathcal{B}_{b.\mathtt{children}}} \mathcal{I}(b'), b.\mathtt{forget}) \\
&\equiv \bigwedge \mathcal{I}(b) \wedge \left(\exists \mathsf{ElimVar}(T_{b.\mathtt{children}}) \exists b.\mathtt{forget}. \bigwedge_{b' \in \mathcal{B}_{b.\mathtt{children}}} \mathcal{I}(b') \right) \\
&\equiv \exists \mathsf{ElimVar}(T_b). \bigwedge \mathcal{I}(b) \wedge \bigwedge_{b' \in \mathcal{B}_{b.\mathtt{children}}} \mathcal{I}(b') \equiv \exists \mathsf{ElimVar}(T_b). \bigwedge_{b' \in \mathcal{B}_b} \mathcal{I}(b'),
\end{aligned}
$$

where the second line is obtained by applying the induction hypothesis, and the last line is correct because variables in $\mathsf{ElimVar}(T_b)$ do not occur in $\mathcal{I}(b)$. $\square$

3.2 Extending to CAD and General QE

Extending to CAD's projection phase. The framework Alg. 1 can be utilized in CAD's projection phase with only minor modifications. We present the whole algorithm in the full version [74, Appendix A.3] and here only explain the differences: (i) The two value functions $\mathcal{I}$ and $\mathcal{V}$ are defined as mappings from bags in T to set of polynomials in $\mathbb{R}[x_1, \ldots, x_n]$, instead of atomic formulas; (ii) In the recursion step, for a forget bag b, we compute $\mathcal{V}(b)$ via $\mathcal{V}(b) \leftarrow \mathcal{I}(b) \cup \mathsf{Proj}(\mathcal{V}(b.\mathtt{children}), b.\mathtt{forget})$, while for other types of bags, the computation of $\mathcal{V}(b)$ remains the same as in Alg. 1; and (iii) Finally, after applying the projection operation for all quantified variables, the CAD algorithm continues the projection phases for free variables, after which the lifting phase can start. The correctness of the framework follows from the fact that the algebraic operations in the projection operator (presented in [74, Appendix A.1]) preserve locality, i.e., will not introduce new variables.

We shall note here that we *cannot* simply replace the invocation of the FME algorithm in Alg. 1 by the CAD algorithm, i.e., the projection phase and lifting phase of CAD must be separated. This is because the lifting phase produces a formula in disjunction normal form, on which we can not directly apply the dynamic programming framework.

Extending to general quantifier elimination algorithms. We now extend our framework to an arbitrary logic theory $\mathcal{T}$ that admits quantifier elimination. This is achieved by extracting a variable elimination order from the tree decomposition, which involves the following steps: (1) Construct a nice tree decomposition T of the input $\mathcal{T}$-formula's primal graph; (2) Traverse T from top to bottom to obtain an ordering of the eliminated variables corresponding to the forget bags; and (3) Finally, reverse the ordering and use it as the variable elimination order in any quantifier elimination procedure for theory $\mathcal{T}$. The pseudo-code description of the algorithm is presented in [74, Appendix A.3]. The correctness of the algorithm is straightforward, as the change of variable order will not affect the correctness of a quantifier elimination algorithm.

In fact, the variable ordering extracted via the above algorithm can be shown to be a *perfect elimination ordering*[1], say $(1, 3, 8, 7, 6, 5, 4, 2)$ for our running example. Hence, it is possible that our variable ordering coincides with the one extracted from a chordal extension graph [54]. However, since we have exploited the sparsity information in building the tree decompositions, our variable orderings are usually superior for performing quantifier elimination on sparse problem instances. This will be further evidenced by our experimental results in Sect. 5. Moreover, our framework is stated for general quantifier elimination procedures and enables a fine-grained complexity analysis, explained in the following Sect. 4.

4   Complexity Analysis

In this section, we analyze the worst-case complexity of our framework in Sect. 3. The core idea is to combine the standard analysis with a special kind of tree decomposition, called *balanced tree-decomposition*. We prove that when the treewidth is constant, a nice and balanced tree-decomposition with logarithmic height in the number of variables can be found in sub-polynomial time. By working on this tree decomposition, our dynamic programming framework can achieve exponential improvement in the worst-case complexity for both FME and CAD. To our knowledge, this gives the first complexity result of FME and CAD directly related to treewidth sparsity.

Balanced tree-decomposition. The concept of (β, γ)-*balanced tree decompositions* [17] generalizes the notion of balanced tree decompositions that arise in the analysis of the space complexity of tree decomposition algorithms [9,30]. Informally, a (β, γ)-balanced tree-decomposition requires, for each bag b, the size of subtree T_b decreases proportionally as $\mathsf{Lv}(b)$ increases.

Definition 1 ((β, γ)-Balanced Tree Decomposition). *For constants $0 < \beta < 1$ and $\gamma \in \mathbb{N}_{>0}$, a binary tree-decomposition T is called (β, γ)-balanced if, for every bag b, every descendant b' of b with $\mathsf{Lv}(b') - \mathsf{Lv}(b) = \gamma$ satisfies that $|T_{b'}| \leq \beta \cdot |T_b|$.*

---

[1] In graph theory, a perfect elimination ordering of a graph G is an ordering of its vertices such that for every vertex v, the set consisting of v and its neighbors that come after v in the ordering forms a clique in G.

The construction of a (β, γ)-balanced tree decomposition is elucidated in [17, Sec. 3], which gives the following theorem.

Theorem 2 ([17, Thm. 3.1]). *Given a graph G with n vertices and of constant treewidth k. For any fixed $\delta > 0$ and $\lambda \in \mathbb{N}$ with $\lambda \geq 2$, a binary (β, γ)-balanced tree-decomposition T with $\beta = (\frac{1+\delta}{2})^{\lambda-1}$ and $\gamma = \lambda$ can be constructed in $O(n \cdot \log n)$ time and $O(n)$ space. Moreover, the tree decomposition T has $O(n)$ bags and width $\frac{6\lambda}{\delta} \cdot (k+1) - 1$ at most.*

Relying on the above theorem, we can construct a nice tree decomposition with logarithmic height, as stated below.

Proposition 1. *Given a graph G with n vertices and of constant treewidth k, a nice tree decomposition T of height $O(\log n)$ and constant width can be constructed in $O(n \log n)$ time.*

Proof. Take $\delta = 1/2$ and $\lambda = 2$ in Thm. 2, then a $(3/4, 2)$-balanced tree decomposition $T = (\mathcal{B}, E_T)$ of width at most $24(k+1) - 1$ can be constructed in $O(n \cdot \log n)$ time. Because of the $(3/4, 2)$-balancing, we have in every 2-levels of T a decrease of at least $3/4$ in the size of the bags. Therefore, the height of T is $2 \log_{\frac{3}{4}} n$, which is $O(\log n)$. Then, we extend T into a nice tree decomposition, which involves the following steps:

Step 1: reroot. Choose an arbitrary bag $r \in \mathcal{B}$ of T to be its current root. We first construct a new bag r' such that $V_{r'} = \emptyset$ as the new root of the nice tree decomposition. Then, a sequence of forget bags is introduced to remove the variables in V_r one by one until reaching r'. This step takes $O(k)$ time and increases the height of T by k at most.

Step 2: ensure join bags have identical children. For each bag b that has two children, we construct two more bags that are identical to b and insert them between b and its two children, respectively. This step takes $O(n)$ time and will double the height at most.

Step 3: create introduce and forget chains. After the previous steps, for each edge (b_1, b_2) in T, the bags V_{b_1} and V_{b_2} may still differ by more than one variables. So we insert between b_1 and b_2 a chain of introduce and forget bags to make sure that every consecutive pair of bags differ in at most one variable. This step takes $O(kn)$ time and increases the height by up to k times at most.

To conclude, when k is a constant, we can obtain a nice tree decomposition of height $O(\log n)$ in $O(n)$ time. Hence, the total time cost remains $O(n \log n)$ as in Thm. 2. $\qquad\square$

In the following, we analyze the complexity of our frameworks for FME and CAD in Sect. 3 under the assumption that k is a constant. For consistency[2], we assume that $m = n$ in the input formula Eq. (1), i.e., there are no free variables.

Complexity analysis for FME. The complexity of the FME algorithm can be measured by the number of atomic formulas produced in the elimination process.

---

[2] Recall that the CAD's projection phase requires performing the projection operation for all variables, including the quantifier-free ones.

Assume that there are s atomic formulas in the input formula Eq. (1). Then, after eliminating the variable x_r, the number of atomic formulas in the output depends on the number of lower/upper bounds, which is at most $|L_r| \cdot |U_r| \leq \frac{s^2}{4}$. Therefore, the complexity of eliminating n variables is at most $O(s^{2^n})$.

By combining the standard analysis with the nice tree decomposition obtained in Prop. 1, we show that a single exponential complexity upper bound w.r.t. n can be achieved when the treewidth is a constant.

Theorem 3. *If the primal graph of an LRA formula Φ in Eq. (1) has constant treewidth and includes s atomic formulas, the number of atomic formulas in the output of Alg. 1 is $s^{O(n)}$ at most.*

Proof. Let T be the nice tree decomposition given by Prop. 1 with height h. In the following, we count the atomic formulas stored in $\mathcal{V}(b)$ for each bag b in T. For a bag b with $\mathsf{Lv}(b) = h$, which must be a leaf bag, we have $\mathcal{V}(b) = \mathcal{I}(b) \leq s$. Consider going one step up, for a bag b with $\mathsf{Lv}(b) = h-1$: if b is a join, introduce, or leaf bag, we have $\mathcal{V}(b) \leq 3s$ according to the definition of $\mathcal{V}$; if b is a forget bag, we apply the one-step analysis for FME and have $\mathcal{V}(b) \leq s + \frac{s^2}{4}$. Since the height h is bounded by $O(\log n)$ according to Prop. 1, for the root r, we have $\mathcal{V}(r) = O(s^{2^{O(\log n)}}) = s^{O(n)}$. $\qquad\square$

Complexity analysis for CAD. The CAD complexity is usually measured by the number of sign-invariant cells. Our analysis uses a similar approach as [54] but provides an improved bound based on the assumption of constant treewidth and the structure of balanced tree decompositions.

Before presenting the results, we introduce some tools to estimate the growth of the size of the polynomials in the projection phase. For a set of polynomials $P \subset \mathbb{R}[\mathbf{x}]$, we define the *combined degree* [59] of P to be $\max_{1 \leq i \leq n} \deg_{x_i}(\prod_{p \in P} p)$, where $\deg_{x_i}(\cdot)$ denotes the degree of a polynomial in a single variable x_i. A set of polynomials has the (m, d)-property if it can be partitioned into m sets, such that each set has maximum combined degree d [10, Def. 7]. It has been shown in [10, Lem. 11] that for a set $P \subset \mathbb{R}[\mathbf{x}]$ with the (m, d)-property, the set $\mathsf{Proj}(P, x_i)$ after projection has the $(M, 2d^2)$-property with $M = \lfloor \frac{(m+1)^2}{2} \rfloor$ for any $x_i \in \mathbf{x}$.

Proposition 2. *If the primal graph of an NRA formula Φ in Eq. (1) has constant treewidth and the corresponding polynomial set has the (m, d)-property, the number of cells in the CAD algorithm can be made $m^{O(n)}(2Md)^{O(n \log n)}$ at most.*

Proof. The proof is inspired by the proof of [54, Thm. 11, Thm. 12]. Here we explain the main idea.

We first analyze the increase in the number of polynomials in the projection phase. Let T be the nice tree decomposition given by Prop. 1 with height h. By assumption, for each leaf bag b with $\mathsf{Lv}(b) = h$, the polynomial set $\mathcal{V}(b)$ has the (m, d)-property. Following a similar argument in the proof of Thm. 3, we can show that for each bag b with $\mathsf{Lv}(b) \leq h - 1$, the polynomial set $\mathcal{V}(b)$ has the $(3^{2^{l_b}-1}M^{2^{l_b-1}}, 2^{2^{l_b}-1}d^{2^{l_b}})$-property with $l_b = h - 1 - \mathsf{Lv}(b)$.

Then we analyze the lifting phase. Note that, for a polynomial set P, the real roots of the product $\prod_{p \in P} p$ include all real roots of each individual polynomial in P. Hence, if a univariate polynomial set P has the (m, d)-property, the number of real roots in P is at most md, and the number of the corresponding sets in $\mathbb{R}^1$ is at most $2md + 1$. The total number of cells produced in the lifting phase is bounded by the product of all $\mathbb{R}^1$-cells corresponding to each bag b, i.e. $\prod_{b \in \mathcal{B}}(2K_b + 1)$, where

$$K_b = \begin{cases} md, & \text{if } \mathsf{Lv}(b) = h, \text{ i.e., } l_b \text{ undefined;} \\ 3^{2^{l_b}-1} M^{2^{l_b}-1} 2^{2^{l_b}-1} d^{2^{l_b}}, & \text{if } h - 1 \geq \mathsf{Lv}(b) \geq 0, \text{ i.e., } 0 \leq l_b \leq h - 1. \end{cases}$$

Since T is a binary tree, the number of bags on each level is bounded by $2^{\mathsf{Lv}(b)}$. Therefore, we have

$$\prod_{b \in \mathcal{B}}(2K_b + 1) \leq (md)^{2^h} \prod_{0 \leq l_b \leq h-1} \left(3^{2^{l_b}-1} M^{2^{l_b}-1} 2^{2^{l_b}-1} d^{2^{l_b}}\right)^{2^{h-1-l_b}}$$

$$\leq m^{2^h} 6^{(h-2)2^{h-1}+1} M^{h2^{h-2}} d^{(h+2)2^{h-1}} = O(m^{2^h} 6^{h2^{h-1}} M^{h2^{h-2}} d^{h2^{h-1}})$$

$$= m^{O(n)}(2Md)^{O(n \log n)}$$

where the final step is obtained by using $h = O(\log n)$. $\square$

5 Implementation and Experiments

In this section, we explain our implementation details and present the experimental results. We aim to answer the following research question: Compared with the existing heuristics for deciding the variable elimination ordering, *how does our tree-decomposition-based algorithm perform on the QE problems of LRA and NRA instances with relatively small treewidth?*

Computation Environment. We use the tool from [72] to compute tree decompositions, which are then processed by Python scripts. For LRA, we compare different heuristics based on a naive FME implementation in Python, while for NRA, we work on CAD implemented in MATHEMATICA [45]. All experiments were conducted on a Windows PC with i7-13700 CPU and 32GB RAM.

Existing Heuristics. For comparison, we briefly explain the most frequently used heuristic strategies for selecting the variable elimination ordering in FME and CAD. For FME, the baseline Random strategy makes $N = 5$ trials according to different orderings that are sampled randomly and records the best result; the Greedy strategy chooses the next variable to be eliminated by minimizing the number of generated constraints. For CAD, the Brown's heuristic, denoted Brown [14], chooses the next eliminated variable that has the lowest maximum degree across all polynomials in which it appears (and breaks ties with addition rules); the PEO strategy [54] extracts a perfect elimination ordering from the chordal extension of the primal graph; and we also compare with the default strategy in MAPLE [57] to suggest variable ordering, denoted SVO.

Table 1: FME performance on randomly generated LRA instances

ID	Instance Set (10 instances per set)		Random	Greedy	Ours
1	#var=15 #ineq=75	Ave. ineq. count	51,608.4	**4,404.7**	4,841.3
	#elim=5 #tw=2	Ave. run Time(s)	0.21	**0.018**	**0.018**
2	#var=15 #ineq=75	Ave. ineq. count	>10,000,000	28,362.3	**28,244.8**
	#elim=5 #tw=4	Ave. run Time(s)	NA	**0.17**	**0.17**
3	#var=20 #ineq=100	Ave. ineq. count	>10,000,000	290,597.8	**194,645.3**
	#elim=10 #tw=2	Ave. run Time(s)	NA	2.0	**1.1**
4	#var=20 #ineq=100	Ave. ineq. count	>10,000,000	**313,584.0**	313,585.9
	#elim=6 #tw=4	Ave. run Time(s)	NA	2.6	**2.4**
5	#var=30 #ineq=150	Ave. ineq. count	>10,000,000	343,705.4	**110,304.9**
	#elim=12 #tw=3	Ave. run Time(s)	NA	3.7	**1.2**
6	#var=30 #ineq=150	Ave. ineq. count	>10,000,000	**974,233.4**	**974,233.4**
	#elim=5 #tw=8	Ave. run Time(s)	NA	14.9	**14.4**

Our Implementation. In our practical implementation, we elected not to construct a balanced tree decomposition as described in Sect. 4. While the main advantage of the balanced tree decomposition lies in estimating the asymptotic complexity, it often performs suboptimally on problems of relatively small scale. Instead, we work with the tree decomposition computed by [72] and follow the approach detailed in Sect. 3.2 to extract the elimination order[3]. When traversing from top to bottom, we break ties using the aforementioned Greedy and Brown heuristics for FME and CAD, respectively.

Benchmarks. As our algorithm targets dealing with LRA and NRA problems that are *small enough* to do quantifier elimination but also *have low treewidth*. This requirement rules out most existing standard benchmarks (an analysis on SMT-LIB benchmarks [5] can be found in the full version [74, Appendix A.4]). Hence, for comparison, we generated a set of benchmarks with treewidth sparsity as follows: We construct benchmark inequality systems from graphs of prescribed treewidth k by a two-stage procedure. We first generate a graph of treewidth k by iteratively attaching nodes to a $(k+1)$-clique. Then, for each bag, we enumerate all monomials of total degree not exceeding the maximum degree (1 for LRA), select at least one highest-degree monomial, and randomly include other monomials with a probability ranging from 0.05 to 0.15, while ensuring that every scoped variable appears. For each set of hyperparameters, we randomly generated 10 examples for LRA and 1 example for NRA, because the randomly selected monomials significantly impact the CAD efficiency, and the average runtime is usually dominated by the worst instance.

Results. Table 1 and Table 2 present the results of FME and CAD, respectively. On LRA benchmarks, our strategy consistently yielded the lowest average inequality count and average runtime, achieving the best result in 4 out of 6 sets.

---

[3] In our non-parallel setting, using the elimination order is functionally equivalent to running the dynamic programming framework, without the explicit computation of the value functions.

Table 2: CAD performance on randomly generated NRA instances

ID	Instance		SVO	Brown	PEO	Ours
7	#var=6 #ineq=6	Cells	1,133,532	271,120	274,724	**110,828**
	#max_deg=2 #tw=2	Time(s)	640.3	307.0	114.7	**40.5**
8	#var=7 #ineq=4	Cells	126,328	89,804	89,804	**49,108**
	#max_deg=3 #tw=3	Time(s)	42.1	34.5	29.0	**11.6**
9	#var=7 #ineq=5	Cells	2,020,378	1,926,208	740,380	**181,090**
	#max_deg=2 #tw=2	Time(s)	702.0	416.2	96.1	**84.1**
10	#var=8 #ineq=5	Cells	3,721,372	3,721,372	**984,008**	2,155,132
	#max_deg=4 #tw=2	Time(s)	1843.8	1718.2	**567.7**	1090.3
11	#var=8 #ineq=6	Cells	**38,212**	69,748	69,748	**38,212**
	#max_deg=2 #tw=3	Time(s)	**42.0**	633.3	427.9	**42.0**
12	#var=9 #ineq=10	Cells	1,804,224	1,804,224	954,432	**52,992**
	#max_deg=2 #tw=3	Time(s)	742.3	746.7	156.7	**83.3**

The Greedy strategy showed a very similar performance with the runtime difference being negligible, but was significantly slower on ID 3 and 5. The Random strategy performed poorly, generating an extremely high number of inequalities, often exceeding 10^7 for most instances. On NRA benchmarks, our strategy also demonstrates superior performance in all but one benchmark, in terms of both the number of cells generated and the runtime. For benchmark ID 9 and ID 12, it significantly outperforms all other methods. The only instance where our strategy did not have the lowest cell count was ID 10, where PEO was superior. The results answer our research question affirmatively, indicating that *our proposed strategy is effective and more efficient in dealing with problems with low treewidth*, compared to the existing heuristics. More experiments on benchmarks from [54] are available at [74, Appendix A.5].

6 Conclusion

This paper introduces a high-level, treewidth-aware approach to reduce the computational burden of quantifier elimination procedures, especially FME and CAD, for problems with treewidth sparsity. By leveraging parameterized algorithm tools, our method establishes an improved complexity upper bound, thus offering novel insights into mitigating the inherent complexity of quantifier elimination. Future work will focus on combining this treewidth-aware method with existing heuristics and exploring its application in various practical scenarios.

Acknowledgments. We thank the anonymous reviewers for their valuable comments and helpful suggestions. This work has been partially funded by the National Key R&D Program of China under grant No. 2022YFA1005101 and 2022YFA1005102, the National NSF of China under grant No.62192732 and W2511064, the ERC Starting Grant 101222524 (SPES), and the Ethereum Foundation Research Grant FY24-1793.

Data Availability Statement. The code for our experiments is available at `https://doi.org/10.5281/zenodo.18150640`.

References

1. An, J., Zhan, N., Li, X., Zhang, M., Yi, W.: Model checking bounded continuous-time extended linear duration invariants. In: HSCC. pp. 81–90 (2018)
2. Anai, H., Weispfenning, V.: Reach set computations using real quantifier elimination. In: HSCC. pp. 63–76 (2001)
3. Arnborg, S., Corneil, D.G., Proskurowski, A.: Complexity of finding embeddings in a k-tree. SIAM J. Algebraic Discrete Methods **8**(2), 277–284 (1987)
4. Arnon, D.S., Collins, G.E., McCallum, S.: Cylindrical algebraic decomposition I: the basic algorithm. SIAM J. Comput. **13**(4), 865–877 (1984)
5. Barrett, C., Fontaine, P., Tinelli, C.: The Satisfiability Modulo Theories Library (SMT-LIB). www.SMT-LIB.org (2016)
6. Bodlaender, H.L.: Dynamic programming on graphs with bounded treewidth. In: ICALP. pp. 105–118 (1988)
7. Bodlaender, H.L.: A linear-time algorithm for finding tree-decompositions of small treewidth. SIAM J. Comput. **25**(6), 1305–1317 (1996)
8. Bodlaender, H.L.: Treewidth: Algorithmic techniques and results. In: MFCS. pp. 19–36 (1997)
9. Bodlaender, H.L., Hagerup, T.: Parallel algorithms with optimal speedup for bounded treewidth. SIAM J. Comput. **27**(6), 1725–1746 (1998)
10. Bradford, R.J., Davenport, J.H., England, M., McCallum, S., Wilson, D.J.: Truth table invariant cylindrical algebraic decomposition. J. Symb. Comput. **76**, 1–35 (2016)
11. Bradford, R.J., Davenport, J.H., England, M., Wilson, D.J.: Optimising problem formulation for cylindrical algebraic decomposition. In: CICM. pp. 19–34 (2013)
12. Bradley, A.R., Manna, Z.: The calculus of computation - decision procedures with applications to verification. Springer (2007)
13. Brown, C.W.: Improved projection for cylindrical algebraic decomposition. J. Symb. Comput. **32**(5), 447–465 (2001)
14. Brown, C.W.: Companion to the tutorial presented at issac'04: Cylindrical algebraic decomposition. In: ISSAC, tutorial (2004), https://www.usna.edu/Users/cs/wcbrown/research/ISSAC04/handout.pdf
15. Brown, C.W.: Open non-uniform cylindrical algebraic decompositions. In: ISSAC. pp. 85–92 (2015)
16. Caviness, B.F., Johnson, J.R.: Quantifier Elimination and Cylindrical Algebraic Decomposition. Texts and Monographs in Symbolic Computation (1998)
17. Chatterjee, K., Ibsen-Jensen, R., Goharshady, A.K., Pavlogiannis, A.: Algorithms for algebraic path properties in concurrent systems of constant treewidth components. ACM Trans. Program. Lang. Syst. **40**(3), 9:1–9:43 (2018)
18. Chen, C., Maza, M.M., Xia, B., Yang, L.: Computing cylindrical algebraic decomposition via triangular decomposition. In: ISSAC. pp. 95–102 (2009)
19. Chen, C., Zhu, Z., Chi, H.: Variable ordering selection for cylindrical algebraic decomposition with artificial neural networks. In: International Congress on Mathematical Software. pp. 281–291 (2020)
20. Collins, G.E.: Quantifier elimination for real closed fields by cylindrical algebraic decompostion. In: Automata Theory and Formal Languages, 2nd GI Conference. pp. 134–183. Springer (1975)
21. Collins, G.E., Hong, H.: Partial cylindrical algebraic decomposition for quantifier elimination. J. Symb. Comput. **12**(3), 299–328 (1991)

22. Cygan, M., Fomin, F.V., Kowalik, Ł., Lokshtanov, D., Marx, D., Pilipczuk, M., Pilipczuk, M., Saurabh, S.: Parameterized algorithms. Springer (2015)
23. Davenport, J.H., Heintz, J.: Real quantifier elimination is doubly exponential. Journal of Symbolic Computation **5**(1-2), 29–35 (1988)
24. Dell, H., Komusiewicz, C., Talmon, N., Weller, M.: The PACE 2017 Parameterized Algorithms and Computational Experiments Challenge: The Second Iteration. In: IPEC (2017)
25. Diestel, R.: Graph Theory (2nd ed.). Springer (2000)
26. Dolzmann, A., Seidl, A., Sturm, T.: Efficient projection orders for CAD. In: ISSAC. pp. 111–118 (2004)
27. Dong, S., Lee, Y.T., Ye, G.: A nearly-linear time algorithm for linear programs with small treewidth: a multiscale representation of robust central path. In: STOC. pp. 1784–1797 (2021)
28. Dorato, P., Yang, W., Abdallah, C.T.: Robust multi-objective feedback design by quantifier elimination. J. Symb. Comput. **24**(2), 153–159 (1997)
29. Downey, R.G., Fellows, M.R.: Parameterized complexity. Springer (2012)
30. Elberfeld, M., Jakoby, A., Tantau, T.: Logspace versions of the theorems of bodlaender and courcelle. In: FOCS. pp. 143–152 (2010)
31. England, M., Florescu, D.: Comparing machine learning models to choose the variable ordering for cylindrical algebraic decomposition. In: CICM. pp. 93–108 (2019)
32. Fichte, J.K., Hecher, M., Kieler, M.F.I.: Treewidth-aware quantifier elimination and expansion for QCSP. In: CP. pp. 248–266 (2020)
33. Fourier, J.B.J.: Analyse des travaux de l'Academie Royale des Sciences, pendant l'année 1827. Partie mathématique (1826)
34. Gan, T., Chen, M., Li, Y., Xia, B., Zhan, N.: Reachability analysis for solvable dynamical systems. IEEE Trans. Autom. Control. **63**(7), 2003–2018 (2018)
35. Gu, Y., Song, Z.: A faster small treewidth sdp solver (2022), `https://arxiv.org/abs/2211.06033`
36. Halin, R.: S-functions for graphs. Journal of geometry **8**, 171–186 (1976)
37. Han, J., Dai, L., Hong, H., Xia, B.: Open weak CAD and its applications. J. Symb. Comput. **80**, 785–816 (2017)
38. Han, J., Jin, Z., Xia, B.: Proving inequalities and solving global optimization problems via simplified CAD projection. J. Symb. Comput. **72**, 206–230 (2016)
39. Hong, H.: An improvement of the projection operator in cylindrical algebraic decomposition. In: ISSAC. pp. 261–264 (1990)
40. Hong, H., Din, M.S.E.: Variant quantifier elimination. J. Symb. Comput. **47**(7), 883–901 (2012)
41. Hong, H., Liska, R., Steinberg, S.L.: Testing stability by quantifier elimination. J. Symb. Comput. **24**(2), 161–187 (1997)
42. Huang, Z., England, M., Wilson, D.J., Davenport, J.H., Paulson, L.C., Bridge, J.P.: Applying machine learning to the problem of choosing a heuristic to select the variable ordering for cylindrical algebraic decomposition. In: CICM. pp. 92–107 (2014)
43. Imbert, J.: About redundant inequalities generated by fourier's algorithm. In: AIMSA. pp. 117–127 (1990)
44. Imbert, J.: Fourier's elimination: Which to choose? In: PPCP. pp. 117–129 (1993)
45. Inc., W.R.: Mathematica, Version 14.3, `https://www.wolfram.com/mathematica`, champaign, IL, 2025

46. Jia, F., Dong, Y., Liu, M., Huang, P., Ma, F., Zhang, J.: Suggesting variable order for cylindrical algebraic decomposition via reinforcement learning. NeurIPS **36**, 76098–76119 (2023)
47. Jing, R., Maza, M.M., Talaashrafi, D.: Complexity estimates for fourier-motzkin elimination. In: CASC. pp. 282–306 (2020)
48. Jirstrand, M.: Cylindrical algebraic decomposition-an introduction. Technical Report, Linköping University (1995)
49. Jirstrand, M.: Nonlinear control system design by quantifier elimination. J. Symb. Comput. **24**(2), 137–152 (1997)
50. Kapur, D.: A quantifier-elimination based heuristic for automatically generating inductive assertions for programs. Journal of Systems Science and Complexity **19**, 307–330 (2006)
51. Khachiyan, L.: Fourier-motzkin elimination method. In: Encyclopedia of Optimization, pp. 1074–1077. Springer (2009)
52. Kloks, T.: Treewidth, Computations and Approximations. Springer (1994)
53. Kroening, D., Strichman, O.: Decision Procedures: An Algorithmic Point of View. Springer Publishing Company, Incorporated (2008)
54. Li, H., Xia, B., Zhang, H., Zheng, T.: Choosing better variable orderings for cylindrical algebraic decomposition via exploiting chordal structure. J. Symb. Comput. **116**, 324–344 (2023)
55. Liu, J., Zhan, N., Zhao, H.: Computing semi-algebraic invariants for polynomial dynamical systems. EMSOFT pp. 97–106 (2011)
56. Mallach, S.: On integer linear programs for treewidth based on perfect elimination orderings (extended version). Acta Informatica **62**(3), 34 (2025)
57. Maplesoft, a division of Waterloo Maple Inc..: Maple, `https://hadoop.apache.org`, waterloo, Ontario, 2019
58. Marx, D.: Can you beat treewidth? Theory Comput. **6**(1), 85–112 (2010)
59. McCallum, S.: An improved projection operation for cylindrical algebraic decomposition. Phd thesis (computer sciences tech. rep. 578), Univ. Wisconsin–Madison. (1985)
60. McCallum, S.: An improved projection operation for cylindrical algebraic decomposition of three-dimensional space. J. Symb. Comput. **5**(1/2), 141–161 (1988)
61. Motzkin, T.S.: Beiträge zur theorie der linearen ungleichungen. Azriel (1936)
62. Promies, V., Ábrahám, E.: A divide-and-conquer approach to variable elimination in linear real arithmetic. In: FM (1). pp. 131–148 (2024)
63. Promies, V., Nalbach, J., Ábrahám, E., Kobialka, P.: Fmplex: Exploring a bridge between fourier-motzkin and simplex. Log. Methods Comput. Sci. **21**(2) (2025)
64. Robertson, N., Seymour, P.D.: Graph minors. iii. planar tree-width. Journal of Combinatorial Theory, Series B **36**(1), 49–64 (1984)
65. Robertson, N., Seymour, P.D.: Graph minors. II. algorithmic aspects of tree-width. J. Algorithms **7**(3), 309–322 (1986)
66. Rodríguez-carbonell, E., Kapur, D.: Automatic generation of polynomial loop invariants: Algebraic foundations. In: ISSAC. pp. 266–273 (2004)
67. Saugata Basu, Richard Pollack, M.F.R.: Algorithms in Real Algebraic Geometry. Springer Berlin, Heidelberg (2006)
68. Schrijver, A.: Theory of linear and integer programming. John Wiley & Sons (1998)
69. Strzebonski, A.W.: Cylindrical algebraic decomposition using local projections. J. Symb. Comput. **76**, 36–64 (2016)
70. Sturm, T., Tiwari, A.: Verification and synthesis using real quantifier elimination. In: ISSAC. pp. 329–336. ACM (2011)

71. Szeider, S.: Finding paths in graphs avoiding forbidden transitions. Discret. Appl. Math. **126**(2-3), 261–273 (2003)
72. Tamaki, H.: Positive-instance driven dynamic programming for treewidth. J. Comb. Optim. **37**(4), 1283–1311 (2019)
73. Tarski, A.: The Completeness of Elementary Algebra and Geometry. Reprinted in 1967 by CNRS, Institute Blaise Pascal, Paris (1930)
74. Wu, H., Zhu, J., Goharshady, A.K., An, J., Xia, B., Zhan, N.: Quantifier elimination meets treewidth (2026), https://arxiv.org/abs/2601.00312

Automata

Concurrent Permissive Strategy Templates*

Ashwani Anand[1], Christel Baier[2], Calvin Chau[2], Sascha Klüppelholz[2],
Ali Mirzaei**, Satya Prakash Nayak[1], and Anne-Kathrin Schmuck[1]

[1] Max Planck Institute for Software Systems, Kaiserslautern, Germany
{ashwani,sanayak,akschmuck}@mpi-sws.org
[2] Technische Universität Dresden, Germany
{christel.baier,calvin.chau,sasha.klueppelholz}@tu-dresden.de

Abstract Two-player games on finite graphs provide a rigorous foundation for modeling the strategic interaction between reactive systems and their environment. While concurrent game semantics naturally capture the synchronous interactions characteristic of many cyber-physical systems (CPS), their adoption in CPS design remains limited. Building on the concept of permissive strategy templates (PeSTels) for turn-based games, we introduce concurrent (permissive) strategy templates (ConS-Tels) – a novel representation for sets of randomized winning strategies in concurrent games with Safety, Büchi, and Co-Büchi objectives. ConS-Tels compactly encode infinite families of strategies, thereby supporting both offline and online adaptation. Offline, we exploit compositionality to enable incremental synthesis: combining ConSTels for simpler objectives into non-conflicting templates for more complex combined objectives. Online, we demonstrate how ConSTels facilitate runtime adaptation, adjusting action probabilities in response to observed opponent behavior to optimize performance while preserving correctness. We implemented ConSTel synthesis and adaptation in a prototype tool and experimentally show its potential.

Keywords: Concurrent Games · Permissive Strategies · Strategy Adaptation.

1 Introduction

Two player games on finite graphs [18] provide a powerful abstraction for modeling the strategic interactions between reactive systems and their environment.

* Authors are ordered alphabetically. All authors are supported by the DFG project 389792660 TRR 248-CPEC. Additionally A.-K. Schmuck is supported by the DFG project SCHM 3541/1-1. C. Baier, C. Chau, and S. Klüppelholz are supported by the German Federal Ministry of Research, Technology and Space within the project SEMECO Q1 (03ZU1210AG) and funded by the German Research Foundation (DFG, Deutsche Forschungsgemeinschaft) as part of Germany's Excellence Strategy - EXC 2050/2 - Project ID 390696704 - Cluster of Excellence "Centre for Tactile Internet with Human-in-the-Loop" (CeTI) of Technische Universität Dresden.

** This research was conducted while Ali Mirzaei was interning at MPI-SWS, Germany (ali.mirzaei78@sharif.edu).

S. Junges and G. Katz (Eds.): TACAS 2026, LNCS 16505, pp. 377–397, 2026.
https://doi.org/10.1007/978-3-032-22752-2_20

As such, they have been successfully applied to both software [21,19] and cyber-physical system (or component) design [33,24,36] to ensure that interactions adhere to stringed correctness requirements. Such requirements are typically temporal – modeling the correct interaction of processes over time – and can be formalized in temporal logic or, more generally, as an ω-regular language.

Depending on the mode of interaction between systems (resp. components) the interaction semantics of players in the resulting game differ. Asynchronous interactions result in *turn-based* games [31,16], where in each round only one of the two players can choose among several moves. On the other hand, synchronous interactions lead to *concurrent* games [2,1,14], where in each round both players can choose simultaneously and independently among several moves.

In fact, many strategic interactions of reactive systems are naturally synchronous – especially in the context of cyber-physical system design. Multiple robots are moving into different regions of the states space concurrently and do not wait for each other to complete a motion. Similarly, human-robot cooperation in unstructured environments, e.g. emptying a dishwasher, are only truly helpful to the human if both work alongside (synchronously) and are not forced to take turns (as in structured environments like manufacturing lines). Finally, physical conditions are also typically changing synchronously to the system's actions, e.g. wind conditions might become challenging *while* a drone is landing – not 'waiting' for the drone to land before causing turbulence.

Despite these natural synchronous strategic interactions of technological systems with their environment, almost all existing work – especially in the context of strategic control for CPS – focuses on the use of turn-based game semantics to abstract system interaction (see [24,36] for overviews). While traditional approaches typically use games-based synthesis as a black-box in CPS design, a recent line of work introduced *permissive strategy templates* (PeSTels) [7,8,9] as a new concise data structure which captures an infinite number of winning strategies in turn-based graph games. This *permissiveness* allows for the adaptation of strategies both *offline*, e.g., for incremental or distributed synthesis [8,10,28] and *online*, e.g., to handle actuation faults or enable dynamic multi-layered control [27] of CPS. While the work in [30] extends templates to almost sure winning in stochastic parity games, it does not consider the concurrent setting.

Concurrent games on the other hand, were first considered by Shapley [32] and have been studied since [17,2,1,14]. For a detailed historical account, see [18]. In particular, the work of [1] provides algorithms for solving concurrent ω-regular games. It has been shown that – in contrast to turn-based games – concurrent games might require players to use *randomization* over their strategic choices to win. This makes the corresponding solution algorithms strictly more complex than existing algorithms for turn-based games.

While concurrent games are theoretically well-studied, tool support for ω-regular objectives is scarce. The MOCHA tool [5] considers concurrent systems in the form of reactive modules [3] and supports Alternating Temporal Logic (ATL), but appears to be no longer available. The GAVS+ platform [15] only handles concurrent reachability games. PRISM-games [25] support concurrent stochastic games, but not Büchi or Co-Büchi conditions. PRALINE [13] can check the existence of *pure* (i.e. no randomization) strategy Nash equilibria. MCMAS [26] and EVE [20] also check pure Nash equilibria. This limited support for richer property classes, such as ω-regular objectives, additionally hinders the adaptation of concurrent games as abstractions for CPS design, despite their natural semantic fit.

Contribution. Based on the success of PeSTels for CPS design and the observation that most of their interactions are synchronous, this paper develops *concurrent strategy templates* (ConSTels) for Safety, Büchi and Co-Büchi objectives. We further present a prototype tool `ConSTel` which automatically computes ConSTels for these games. We exploit the advantages of ConSTels over (classical) winning strategies in concurrent games w.r.t. both the (i) *offline* and (ii) *online* adaptation of strategies, respectively.

(i) *Offline adaptation:* We formalize incremental synthesis, i.e., the combination of ConSTels computed for individual Büchi or Co-Büchi objectives into a new ConSTel for the combined objective, which are strictly more complex than both individually. Our techniques allow to compute winning strategies for these multi-dimensional objectives if the resulting ConSTels are non-conflicting. While this approach is necessarily incomplete, we show experimentally, that it is successful on several examples adapted from the SYNTCOMP benchmark suite [22] (see Fig. 3). This is particularly interesting, as there is currently no other tool support for concurrent parity games.

(ii) *Online adaptation:* We experimentally showcase the potential of our templates for the purpose of runtime optimization. As ConSTels capture an infinite set of randomized strategies, we can adapt the probability distributions over actions for a certain state during runtime. Given an opponent with a fixed but unknown action distribution, ConSTels allow to infer this distribution at runtime and adapt strategies accordingly. This enables efficient satisfaction of objectives (see Fig. 4). While this experiment solely serves as a proof-of-concept, we note that it shows the potential of ConSTels to integrate matrix games [29] per state to resolve local dependencies of action probabilities among agents within a strategic, long-term game. We leave this exploration for future work.

While there exists limited work on concurrent games in robotic planning [34], multi-agent learning [12] and collective strategy synthesis in multi-agent systems [35] via ATL [4,5], to the best of our knowledge, we present the first approach to permissive strategies for concurrent games motivated by CPS applications.

All proofs and additional information about the experiments can be found in the extended version paper [6].

2   Preliminaries

This section recalls all necessary preliminaries on concurrent games from [1] and strategy templates from [8].

Notation. For a finite alphabet Σ, we use Σ^*, Σ^+, and Σ^ω to denote the set of all finite, non-empty finite, and infinite words over Σ, respectively. We define

$\Sigma^\infty := \Sigma^* \cup \Sigma^\omega$ and for any word $\omega \in \Sigma^\infty$, ω_i denotes the i-th symbol in ω and $\omega_{\leq i} := \omega_1 \omega_2 \ldots \omega_i$. A *probability distribution* on a finite set A is a function $p : A \to [0,1]$ s.t. $\sum_{a \in A} p(a) = 1$. The set of all probability distributions on A is denoted by $\mathcal{D}(A)$. The *support* of a probability distribution p on set A is defined by $\mathsf{supp}(p) := \{a \in A \mid p(a) > 0\}$. For $B \subseteq A$, we define $p(B) := \sum_{b \in B} p(b)$.

Concurrent Game Graphs. A *two-player concurrent game graph* is a tuple $G = (V, \Gamma_1, \Gamma_2, \delta)$ where V is a finite set of states, Γ_1 and Γ_2 are finite sets of actions for Player 1 and Player 2, respectively, and $\delta : V \times \Gamma_1 \times \Gamma_2 \to V$ is a transition function. At every state $v \in V$, we denote all possible actions for player i by $\Gamma_i(v) \subseteq \Gamma_i$ and, Player 1 chooses an action $a \in \Gamma_1(v)$ and simultaneously and independently Player 2 chooses an action $b \in \Gamma_2(v)$. Then the game proceeds to a state $v' \in V$ such that $\delta(v, a, b) = v'$. A *play* from a state v_0 is a finite or infinite sequence of states $\rho \in V^\infty$ such that $\rho_0 = v_0$ and for every $0 \leq i \leq |\rho|$, there are actions $a_i \in \Gamma_1(\rho_i)$ and $b_i \in \Gamma_2(\rho_i)$, such that $\delta(\rho_i, a_i, b_i) = \rho_{i+1}$. We write $\mathsf{inf}(\rho)$ to denote the set of all states that appear infinitely often in ρ.

Strategies. A *(randomized) strategy* for player $i \in \{1, 2\}$ over a concurrent game graph G is a function $\pi_i : V^+ \to \mathcal{D}(\Gamma_i)$ such that for all $\rho v \in V^+$, it holds that $\mathsf{supp}(\pi_i(\rho v)) \subseteq \Gamma_i(v)$. We collect all player i strategies over G in the set Π_i. A strategy π is *deterministic* (or pure) if for every *play* ρ, the distribution $\pi(\rho)$ assigns probability 1 to a single action, and *randomized* otherwise. A strategy π is *memoryless* if for all $\rho v, \rho' v \in V^+$, it holds that $\pi(\rho v) = \pi(\rho' v)$. An *infinite play* $\rho \in V^\omega$ is *compliant* with a Player 1 strategy π_1 if for every $i \in \mathbb{N}$ there exist actions $a \in \Gamma_1(\rho_i)$ and $b \in \Gamma_2(\rho_i)$ s.t. $\delta(\rho_i, a, b) = \rho_{i+1}$ and $a \in \mathsf{supp}(\pi_1(\rho_{\leq i}))$, i.e. $\pi_1(\rho_{\leq i})(a) > 0$. A strategy for Player 2 is defined analogously. We refer to a play compliant with π_i and a play compliant with both π_1 and π_2 as a π_i-*play* and a $\pi_1 \pi_2$-*play*, respectively and collect all π_i-plays in the set $\mathsf{plays}(\pi)$.

Winning Conditions. We consider safety, Büchi and co-Büchi winning conditions over *infinite* plays. Given a set of safe states $I \subseteq V$, an infinite play $\rho \in V^\omega$ over G is winning in the *concurrent safety game* $(G, \Box I)$ iff for all $i \in \mathbb{N}$ holds $\rho(i) \in I$. Given a set of Büchi states $T \subseteq V$, an infinite play $\rho \in V^\omega$ over G is winning in the *concurrent Büchi game* $(G, \Box \Diamond T)$ iff for all $i \in \mathbb{N}$ exists $j \geq i$ s.t. $\rho(j) \in T$. Given a set of co-Büchi states $\overline{T} \subset V$ with $T = V \setminus \overline{T}$, an infinite play $\rho \in V^\omega$ over G is winning in the *concurrent co-Büchi game* $(G, \Diamond \Box T)$ iff there exists $i \in \mathbb{N}$ s.t. for all $j \geq i$ holds $\rho(j) \notin \overline{T}$. We write (G, Φ) with $\Phi \in \{\Box I, \Box \Diamond I, \Diamond \Box I\}$ s.t. $I \subseteq V$ to denote any concurrent game and denote by $\mathcal{L}(\Phi)$ the corresponding set of winning plays.

Almost-Sure Winning. We consider almost-sure winning in concurrent games. A strategy π for Player 1 is *almost-sure winning* (winning for short) from v in (G, Φ) if $\mathrm{Pr}_v^\pi(\mathcal{L}(\Phi)) = 1$, where $\mathrm{Pr}_v^{\pi_i}(X)$ denotes the probability that a π_i-play starting from v belongs to X. The *almost sure winning region* (winning region for short) for Player 1 in the concurrent game (G, Φ) is the set $\mathcal{W}_i(\Phi) \subseteq V$ of states from which Player 1 has a strategy to win. A strategy π is a *winning strategy* for Player 1 in (G, Φ), if it is winning from every $v \in \mathcal{W}_i(\Phi)$.

Strategy Templates. Formally, a strategy template Λ is a (possibly infinite) set of Player 1 strategies, i.e. $\Lambda \subseteq \Pi_1$. Then, a Player 1 strategy π_1 is said to *follow* the template Λ, if $\pi_1 \in \Lambda$. We say a strategy template Λ is *winning from a state v* in a game (G, Φ), if every Player 1 strategy following the template Λ is winning in (G, Φ) from v. Moreover, we say a strategy template Λ is *winning*, if it is winning from every state in $\mathcal{W}_1$. In addition, we call Λ *maximally permissive* for $\mathcal{G}$, if every Player 1 strategy π which is winning in $\mathcal{G}$ also follows Λ.

3   Overview and Problem Statement

As formalized in the previous section, winning strategy templates directly generalize from turn-based to concurrent games, due to their simple definition as sets of strategies. Their main advantage over classical winning strategies, however, is rooted in a simple and local data structure which concisely describes these strategy sets. Concretely, for turn-based (parity) games, it is shown in [8] that winning strategy templates can be defined as conjunctions of three simple types of Player 1 edges conditions, namely (i) *unsafe edges*: edges that Player 1 should never take, (ii) *co-live edges*: edges that may only be taken by Player 1 finitely many times along a play, and (iii) *live-groups*: sets of edges such that, if the source state of some live edges is visited infinitely often, Player 1 must take at least one edge from the set infinitely often. In particular, these conditions can be extracted by careful bookkeeping during the solution (i.e., the winning region computation) of a safety, Büchi and co-Büchi game, respectively.

The main contribution of this paper is the automatic extraction of a similarly concise data structure to capture a permissive set of winning strategies in concurrent safety, Büchi and co-Büchi games. Due to the synchronous game semantics, the need for randomized strategies, and the substantially different solution algorithms for concurrent games, the formalization and the computation of these edge conditions is substantially different from the turn-based case.

We use an example to outline the general construction of concurrent strategy templates which allows us to illustrate their advantages over classical strategies. In addition, we use this example to outline the remaining structure of this paper which formalizes all concepts previewed in this example.

Modeling Strategic Interaction as a Concurrent Game. We consider two robots – a controlled robot R_C and an environment robot R_E – in the very simple grid world depicted in Fig. 1a where R_C must enter a green region *alone* in order to fulfill a particular task. Both robots can move either clockwise or anti-clockwise through the grid.

This strategic interaction can be modeled as a concurrent game between R_C as Player 1 and R_E as Player 2 over the game graph G depicted in Fig. 1b. The game has four states, distinguishing all relevant configurations of robot positions in the workspace. The initial state S_0 represents the configurations where both robots are in diagonally opposite white corners of the grid. The state S_1 (resp. S_2) represents the configurations, where both robots are in a green cell (resp. a white cell) together. Finally, the escape state S_e represents the configurations where R_C is in a green cell and R_E is in a white cell. In every state, both players can choose to move clockwise ($\circlearrowright$) or anti-clockwise ($\circlearrowleft$) to the adjacent cell. To

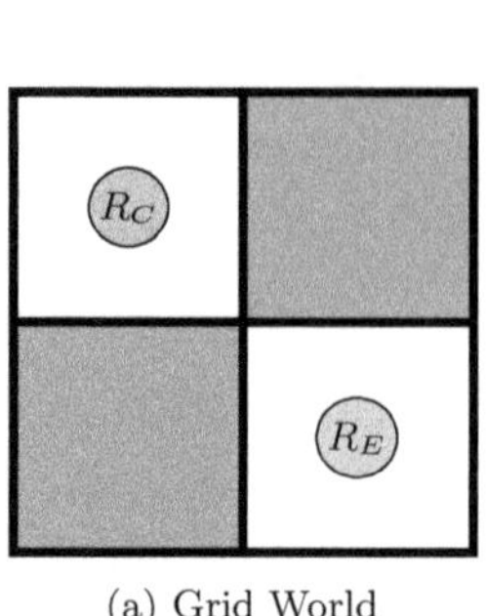

(a) Grid World

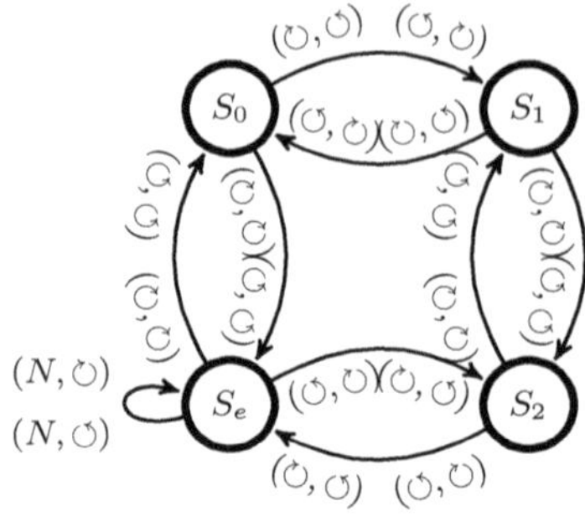

(b) Concurrent Game Graph

Figure 1: Motivating Example. Left: Two robots, R_C and R_E, moving in a grid world. R_C must enter a green region *alone* to fulfill a task. Both robots can move either clockwise ($\circlearrowright$) or anti-clockwise ($\circlearrowleft$). Right: Concurrent game graph capturing the synchronous strategic interaction of R_C and R_E.

simplify the resulting game, we assume for illustration purposes, that within the escape state S_e, Player 1 (the robot R_C) can choose to stay (N) in the cell and then, irrespective of the Player 2's action, the robots remain in S_e.

Safety Templates. Let us first consider a very simple safety game where both robots start in S_e and R_C must ensure that the play stays in S_e. Here, the winning region is $\mathcal{W}_1(\square S_e) = \{S_e\}$ and R_C must never choose actions from the set $\{\circlearrowright, \circlearrowleft\}$ to win from states in $\mathcal{W}_1$. This is modeled by a safety template which allows all strategies which do not assign positive probability to actions specified by the safety function $\mathsf{S}(S_e) = \{\circlearrowright, \circlearrowleft\}$, see Section 4.2 for details.

Live-Group Templates. Let us now consider the Büchi game $(G, \square\lozenge\{S_e\})$. Note that, in this game, the robot R_C can not win from the initial configuration S_0 by choosing moves deterministically in every state. For every deterministic choice of R_C in states $\{S_0, S_2\}$, R_E can choose an action which prevents reaching S_e. Therefore, R_C must choose both actions with positive probability in states $\{S_0, S_2\}$ to ensure that, irrespective of R_E's strategy, the game will reach S_e with probability 1. In this case, however, we have $\mathcal{W}_1(\square\lozenge S_e) = V$ and a winning strategy template for R_C in this game would ask to assign positive probability to both moves $\{\circlearrowright, \circlearrowleft\}$ in every state $\{S_0, S_2\}$, while in states $\{S_e, S_1\}$, the strategy template would not restrict R_C's moves to remain permissive.

Formally, we encode this strategy template as a live-group template $\Lambda_1 = \Lambda_{\mathrm{LIVE}}(\mathsf{H}, \mathsf{P})$, where H is a function that maps every state to a set of action sets such that each action set needs to be assigned positive probability, and P allows to have multiple liveness constraints from different states to ensure permissiveness. In this example, with the above intuition, we have $\mathsf{H}(S_0) = \mathsf{H}(S_2) = \{\{\circlearrowright\}, \{\circlearrowleft\}\}$, and $\mathsf{H}(S_e) = \{\Gamma_1(S_e)\}$, $\mathsf{H}(S_1) = \{\Gamma_1(S_1)\}$. However, we actually do not need to satisfy the liveness constraints from both S_1 *and* S_2, but only from one of them (along with the liveness constraints of state S_1) to guarantee reaching state S_e. This is captured by combining S_1 and S_2 into the same *live group*, leading to $\mathsf{P} = \{\{S_0, S_2\}, \{S_1\}\}$. The resulting live group template only requires a following strategy to assign positive probability to either $\mathsf{H}(S_1)$ or $\mathsf{H}(S_2)$ to be a winning strategy for R_C. In the general setting where $\mathcal{W}_1(\Box\Diamond S_e) \subsetneq V$, we additionally need a safety template to prevent strategies to leave $\mathcal{W}_1$, as a live-group template for Büchi games is only defined over winning states. We discuss live-group templates formally in Section 4.3.

Co-Live Templates. Now, let us consider a co-Büchi game $(G, \Diamond\Box\{S_1, S_2, S_e\})$. We observe that R_C cannot ensure not visiting the initial state S_0 from states $\{S_1, S_2\}$. Hence, the only way for R_C to win this game is to ensure that (i) it always eventually reaches S_e and (ii) from some point onward, it always stays in the escape state S_e. A permissive template is therefore composed of two parts. To realize (i) it requires the live-group template $\Lambda_{\mathrm{LIVE}}(\mathsf{H}, \mathsf{P})$ computed for the Büchi game $(G, \Box\Diamond\{S_e\})$. To realize (ii), within state S_e, from some point onwards, a winning strategy must assign probability 0 to both moves $\{\circlearrowright, \circlearrowleft\}$. This can be encoded as a co-liveness template via a co-live function which maps a state to all actions whose accumulated probability must be bounded over time, so that it is eventually not taken again. In this example, we have $\mathsf{C}(S_e) = \{\{\circlearrowright\}, \{\circlearrowleft\}\}$, and for every other state s, $\mathsf{C}(s) = \emptyset$. Again, if the winning region does not span the entire states pace, an additional safety template is required. In addition, co-Büchi games might require a more complex combination of co-live and live-group templates in the general case, leading to a more involved extraction algorithm. We discuss co-live templates formally in Section 4.4.

Offline Adaptability. One major advantage of the permissiveness of ConSTels is their induced offline adaptability. As an example, consider a game with the conjunction of the above discussed Büchi and co-Büchi winning conditions, i.e., $\Phi = \Box\Diamond\{S_e\} \wedge \Diamond\Box\{S_1, S_2, S_e\}$. In this case, we can compose the constraints of the two strategy templates by taking their intersection, which simply coincides with the template for the co-Büchi objective for this example. In general, such a composition leads to a winning strategy templates for the combined objective, if no conflict arises between templates, e.g., the only remaining live action set of a state contains a co-live action. We formalize this notion in Section 5-Section 6. We empirically demonstrate in Section 7 that such conflicts are rare in practice, and composition is possible in a large number of cases.

Online Adaptability. Due to their permissive structure, strategy templates are useful for optimizing the robot's behavior based on additional information available at runtime. To illustrate this, assume that R_E has a randomized strategy in the game which uses a fixed probability distribution over actions. While this probability distribution is not known to R_C, R_C can observe the actions chosen by R_E *at runtime*. R_C can therefore "estimate" R_E's action distribution and adapt its own action distribution *online* s.t. it is still following the strategy template but also optimizing its action choices to reach S_e efficiently. This idea was implemented in our prototype tool for the robot example in Fig. 1a and the experimental results are depicted in Fig. 4. We see that R_C reaches S_e much faster when adapting its strategy.

4   Computing Winning Strategy Templates

This section contains the main contribution of this paper which is the formalization and construction of *concurrent* safety templates (Section 4.2), live-group templates (Section 4.3) and co-live templates (Section 4.4). Similar to the construction of these templates for turn-based games, we extract them from the symbolic computation of the winning region for concurrent safety, Büchi and co-Büchi games, respectively. To formalize this extraction, we present additional preliminaries in Section 4.1.

4.1   Preliminaries

Observing space constrains, we refer the reader to [23] for an introduction to μ-calculus, and to [7] for its particular use in the context of template computations. To ensure a minimum level of self-containedness, this section recalls the set-transformers needed to define the symbolic fixed-point algorithms for concurrent safety, Büchi and co-Büchi games from [1].

Given a concurrent game (G, Φ), a state $v \in V$ and transition distributions $d_i \in \mathcal{D}(\Gamma_i(v))$ for players $i \in \{1, 2\}$, the one-round probability of reaching a set $X \subseteq V$ from v is defined by

$$\mathrm{Pr}_v^{d_1, d_2}(X) := \sum_{a \in \Gamma_1(v)} \sum_{b \in \Gamma_2(v)} \sum_{\{v' \in X \mid \delta(v, a, b) = v'\}} d_1(a) d_2(b).$$

Then we define three types of *predecessor operators*:

- $\mathsf{pre}_1 : 2^V \to 2^V$ s.t. $v \in \mathsf{pre}_1(X)$ if

$$\exists d_1 \in \mathcal{D}(\Gamma_1(v)).\forall d_2 \in \mathcal{D}(\Gamma_2(v)).\, \mathrm{Pr}_v^{d_1, d_2}(X) = 1.$$

- $\mathsf{Apre}_1 : 2^V \times 2^V \to 2^V$ s.t. $v \in \mathsf{Apre}_1(Y, X)$ if

$$\exists d_1 \in \mathcal{D}(\Gamma_1(v)).\forall d_2 \in \mathcal{D}(\Gamma_2(v)).\, \left[\mathrm{Pr}_v^{d_1, d_2}(Y) = 1 \wedge \mathrm{Pr}_v^{d_1, d_2}(X) > 0 \right]$$

- $\mathsf{AFpre}_1 : 2^V \times 2^V \times 2^V \to 2^V$ s.t. $v \in \mathsf{AFpre}_1(Z, Y, X)$ if for some $\beta > 0$,

$$\exists d_1 \in \mathcal{D}(\Gamma_1(v)).\forall d_2 \in \mathcal{D}(\Gamma_2(v)).\, \begin{pmatrix} \mathrm{Pr}_v^{d_1, d_2}(Z) = 1 \\ \wedge\, \mathrm{Pr}_v^{d_1, d_2}(X) \geq \beta \, \mathrm{Pr}_v^{d_1, d_2}(\neg Y) \geq 0 \end{pmatrix}$$

The predecessor operator $\mathsf{pre}_1(X)$ computes the set of states from which Player 1 can ensure reaching X with probability 1. The predecessor operator $\mathsf{Apre}_1(Y, X)$ computes the set of states from which Player 1 can ensure to stay in Y almost surely and reach X with positive probability. Finally, the predecessor operator $\mathsf{AFpre}_1(Z, Y, X)$ computes the set of states from which Player 1 can ensure to stay in Z almost surely and if it can leave Y with positive probability, then it should also reach X with some positive probability.

In addition, we utilize two action-set functions from [1, Sec.6], namely $\mathsf{A}_Y^v : 2^{\Gamma_2(v)} \to 2^{\Gamma_1(v)}$ and $\mathsf{B}_X^v : 2^{\Gamma_1(v)} \to 2^{\Gamma_2(v)}$ defined s.t.

$$\mathsf{A}_Y^v(\gamma_2) := \{a \in \Gamma_1(v) \mid \forall b \in \Gamma_2(v) \, . \, \delta(v, a, b) \notin Y \Rightarrow b \in \gamma_2\}, \tag{1}$$

$$\mathsf{B}_X^v(\gamma_1) := \{b \in \Gamma_2(v) \mid \exists a \in \gamma_1 \cdot \delta(v, a, b) \in X\} \tag{2}$$

Intuitively, the set $\mathsf{A}_Y^v(\gamma_2)$ captures the set of actions for Player 1 at state v which are guaranteed to lead to a state in $Y \subseteq V$, under the assumption that Player 2 avoids the actions in γ_2. The set $\mathsf{B}_X^v(\gamma_1)$ captures the set of actions for Player 2 at state v for which Player 1 can ensure reaching a state in $X \subseteq V$ with positive probability. It follows from [1, Sec.6] that AFpre can be computed via the equivalence $v \in \mathsf{AFpre}_1(Z, Y, X) \iff \nu\gamma.(\mathsf{A}_Z^v(\emptyset) \cap \mathsf{A}_Y^v(\mathsf{B}_X^v(\gamma))) \neq \emptyset$.

4.2   Concurrent Safety Templates

This section introduces (maximally permissive) safety templates for concurrent games in direct analogy to safety templates for turn-based games.

Template Formalization. As illustrated in Section 3 and similar to their turn-based counterparts, concurrent safety templates are defined via a function $\mathsf{S} : V \to 2^{\Gamma_1(V)}$ specifying a set of *unsafe actions* for Player 1 at each state and collecting all strategies which avoid actions in S. I.e., their support[1] never contains unsafe actions, as formalized next.

Definition 1. *Let G be a concurrent game graph. Given a function $\mathsf{S} : V \to 2^{\Gamma_1(V)}$, the* concurrent safety template $\Lambda_{\mathrm{UNSAFE}}(\mathsf{S})$ *is defined by*

$$\Lambda_{\mathrm{UNSAFE}}(\mathsf{S}) := \{\pi_1 \mid \forall\rho \in \mathit{plays}(\pi_1) \cdot \forall i \geq 0 \cdot \mathit{supp}(\pi_1(\rho_{\leq i})) \cap \mathsf{S}(\rho_i) = \emptyset\}. \quad (3)$$

The remainder of this section shows how S can be computed s.t. $\Lambda_{\mathrm{UNSAFE}}$ is (almost surely) winning in a safety game $(G, \square I)$, and therefore sound.

Template Computation. It is shown in [1] that the (almost sure) wining region for Player 1 in a concurrent safety game $(G, \square I)$ can be computed by a symbolic fixed-point formula which is identical to the fixed-point formula for *turn-based* safety games, i.e. $\mathcal{W}_1(\square I) = \nu X. (\mathsf{pre}_1(X) \cap I)$. We use $\textsc{AlmostSafe}(G, I)$ to denote the algorithm which implements this formula.

Now recall the action set function $\mathsf{A}_Y^v : 2^{\Gamma_2(v)} \to 2^{\Gamma_1(v)}$ from Eq. (1) which captures the set of actions for Player 1 at state v which are guaranteed to lead to a state in $Y \subseteq V$, under the assumption that Player 2 avoids the actions in γ_2. As γ_2 is the only actions which Player 2 could play to avoid remaining in the *safe* set Y, we can set $\gamma_2 = \emptyset$ and $Y = \mathcal{W}_1(\square I)$ in (1) to obtain the set of actions for Player 1 which ensure that the play stays within $\mathcal{W}_1(\square I)$ against all possible actions of Player 2. With this, we obtain the following construction.

Theorem 1. *Let $(G, \square I)$ be a concurrent safety game with $\mathcal{W}_1 = \mathcal{W}_1(\square I)$ and*

$$S(v) := \begin{cases} \Gamma_1(v) \setminus \mathsf{A}_{\mathcal{W}_1}^v(\emptyset) & \text{if } v \in \mathcal{W}_1, \\ \emptyset & \text{if } v \notin \mathcal{W}_1 \end{cases}. \quad (4)$$

Then $\Lambda_{\mathrm{UNSAFE}}(\mathsf{S})$ is (almost surely) winning in $(G, \square I)$ and maximally permissive.

We call S the *safety function* and refer to its computation via $\textsc{SafetyTemp}(G, I)$.

---

[1] Concurrent safety games allow deterministic strategies. We still define safety templates over randomized strategies to ease their combination with other templates.

4.3   Concurrent Live-Group Templates

This section introduces liveness templates for concurrent games in direct analogy to liveness templates for turn-based games. In turn-based games, Anand et al. [8] formalize a template for liveness via live groups, each containing a set H of Player 1 edges. Whenever Player 1's strategy ensures that at least one edge from a group H is taken infinitely often if one source state $\mathbf{src}(H)$ is seen infinitely often along a play, progress towards a goal state is guaranteed always again. The computation of live groups for turn-based games follows the steps of a classical fixed-point algorithm for Büchi games. Intuitively, in each iteration i of the fixed-point algorithm, all edges that Player 1 needs to "actively" choose to make progress to states added in earlier iterations, form one live group H.

While conceptually similar, the data structure needed to realize the same idea in concurrent games is more complicated and its extraction from the corresponding fixed-point algorithm for concurrent Büchi games from [1] more intricate.

Template Formalization. There are two main reasons why a different data structure is needed to formalize concurrent liveness templates. First, we observe that due to the action-based semantics of concurrent games, we can not indirectly define the set of source states $\mathbf{src}(H)$ via an edge set H. We therefore keep a separate list of source states P and live actions H. A second, more intricate, difference lies in the definition of H. Due to the synchronous semantics of concurrent games, progress can only be ensured by a randomized strategy which assigns a positive probability to all actions of Player 1 that might lead to progress in case Player 2 chooses the 'right' action. We therefore need to remember sets of Player 1 actions per 'progress enabling' Player 2 action in every state $v \in V$, leading to a function $\mathsf{H} : V \to 2^{2^{\Gamma_1(V)}}$.

Intuitively, a concurrent liveness template must then ensure that for each state v and for every opponent's action $b \in \Gamma_2(v)$ s.t. progress might be made, a positive probability is assigned to all actions $\gamma^b \subseteq \Gamma_1(v)$ which would enable this progress. Unfortunately, however, it is not sufficient for Player 1 to assign a positive probability to these subsets. It must also be ensured that the probability of taking this action does not vanish over time, to enable infinitely many visits to the target set. This is formalized below.

Definition 2. *Let G be a concurrent game. Given a function $\mathsf{H} : V \to 2^{2^{\Gamma_1(V)}}$ and a partition $\mathsf{P} \subseteq 2^V$, the concurrent live-group template $\Lambda_{LIVE}(\mathsf{H}, \mathsf{P})$ is defined s.t. $\pi_1 \in \Lambda_{LIVE}(\mathsf{H}, \mathsf{P})$ iff for all $\rho \in plays(\pi_1)$ and for all $U \in \mathsf{P}$ it holds that*

$$(U \cap inf(\rho) \neq \emptyset) \Rightarrow \left(\sum\nolimits_{\{i \mid \rho_i \in U\}} minProb_{\pi_1(\rho_{\leq i})}(\mathsf{H}(\rho_i)) = \infty \right), \tag{5}$$

$$\text{where } minProb_p(X) := \min\nolimits_{\gamma \in X} p(\gamma). \tag{6}$$

Intuitively, $\mathsf{H}(\rho_i)$ is a set of Player 1 action sets and (5) ensures that a strategy can only follow $\Lambda_{LIVE}(\mathsf{H}, \mathsf{P})$ if the minimum probability it assigns to all the live action sets in $\mathsf{H}(\rho_i)$ add up to infinity. This ensures that the corresponding actions are indeed taken infinitely often in expectation (if the corresponding live state is seen infinitely often). The remainder of this section shows how H and P can be computed s.t. $\Lambda_{\text{LIVE}}(\mathsf{H},\mathsf{P})$ is (almost surely) winning from all states in the winning region of a Büchi game $(G, \square I)$, and therefore sound.

Template Computation. Following [1] the (almost sure) winning region of Player 1 in a concurrent Büchi game $(G, \square\Diamond I)$ can be computed by the symbolic fixed-point formula $\mathcal{W}_1(\square\Diamond I) = \nu Y.\mu X.((\neg I \cap \mathsf{Apre}_1(Y, X))) \cup (I \cap \mathsf{pre}_1(Y))))$, and $\text{AlmostBüchi}\,(G, I)$ denotes the algorithm which implements this formula.

As commonly done for strategy extraction, we consider the last iteration of $\text{AlmostBüchi}\,(G, I)$ (which computes $Y = \mathcal{W}_1$), and define the sets of states $X_0 \subseteq X_1 \subseteq \ldots X_k = X_{k+1} = \mathcal{W}_1$ s.t. $X_1 = I \cap \mathsf{pre}_1(\mathcal{W}_1)$ and $X_{i+1} = (\neg I \cap \mathsf{Apre}_1(\mathcal{W}_1, X_i)) \cup X_1$ for $i \geq 1$. We further define $I_i := X_i \setminus X_{i-1}$ for $i \geq 1$. Now, we intuitively define H and P s.t. whenever some $v \in I_i$ has been seen infinitely often in the *play* ρ, then Player 1 should assign probabilities in a way, to be able to reach I_{i-1} infinitely many times. Formally, given the above definitions, we define $\mathsf{P} := \{I_1, I_2, \ldots I_k\}$, and for $v \in I_i$ we have

$$\mathsf{H}(v) := \{\mathsf{H}^b(v)\}_{b \in \Gamma_2(v)} \quad \text{s.t. } \mathsf{H}^b(v) := \{a \in \Gamma_1(v) \setminus \mathsf{S}(v) \mid \delta(v, a, b) \in X_{i-1}\},$$

where $\mathsf{S}(v)$ is defined as in (3), but w.r.t. $\mathcal{W}_1 = \mathcal{W}_1(\square\Diamond I)$. We call (H, P) the *live-group function* and refer to their outlined computation via $\text{LivenTemp}(G, I)$.

Soundness. Following [8], we show that concurrent liveness templates computed for concurrent Büchi games are indeed sound. Intuitively, every winning strategy in such a game must (i) ensure that the play always stays in the winning region and (ii) always makes progress towards the Büchi states. While (i) can be ensured by concurrent safety templates, (ii) is ensured by concurrent liveness templates. This is formalized by the following theorem (see [6, Appendix A] for the full algorithm).

Theorem 2. *Let* $(G, \square\Diamond I)$ *be a* concurrent Büchi game *with winning region* $\mathcal{W}_1$, *safety function* $\mathsf{S} = \text{SafetyTemp}(G, \mathcal{W}_1)$ *and live-group functions* $(\mathsf{H}, \mathsf{P}) = \text{LivenTemp}(G, I)$, *then* $\Lambda = \Lambda_{\text{UNSAFE}}(\mathsf{S}) \cap \Lambda_{\text{LIVE}}(\mathsf{H}, \mathsf{P})$ *is a winning strategy template for* $(G, \square\Diamond I)$.

We will show in Corollary 1 that the template $\Lambda = \Lambda_{\text{UNSAFE}}(\mathsf{S}) \cap \Lambda_{\text{LIVE}}(\mathsf{H}, \mathsf{P})$ is complete, i.e., if there exists a winning strategy for Player 1 in the game $\mathcal{G} = (G, \square\Diamond I)$, then there exists a strategy that follows the template Λ. However, the template is not maximally permissive, i.e., there may exist winning strategies for Player 1 that do not follow the template (see [6, Appendix D] for an example).

4.4   Concurrent Co-Live Templates

This section introduces co-live templates for concurrent games in direct analogy to co-live templates for turn-based games. While the intuition behind their definition directly carries over as expected, the extraction of *sound* co-live templates from the fixed-point computation of the winning region of a concurrent co-Büchi game is unfortunately not as straightforward. Before we discuss this challenge in more detail, we formalize co-live templates.

Algorithm 1 COBÜCHITEMP(G, I)

Input: A game graph G, and a subset of states I
Output: A safety function S and a liveness tuple (H, P) and a co-live tuple (C)
 1: $Z \leftarrow$ ALMOSTCO-BÜCHI (G, I); $\mathsf{S} \leftarrow$ SAFETYTEMP(G, Z);
 2: $X \leftarrow$ ALMOSTSAFE(G, I); $\mathsf{C} \leftarrow$ SAFETYTEMP(G, X);
 3: **for** $v \in X \cup (V \setminus Z)$ **do** $\mathsf{H}(v) \leftarrow \{\Gamma_1(v) \setminus \mathsf{S}(v)\}$;
 4: **while** *True* **do**
 5:     $Y' \leftarrow V$;
 6:     **repeat**
 7:         $Y \leftarrow Y'$; $Y' \leftarrow (I \cap \mathsf{AFpre}_1(Z, Y, X)) \cup (\neg I \cap \mathsf{Apre}_1(Z, X))$;
 8:     **until** $Y' == Y$
 9:     **if** $X == Y$ **then break**
10:     **for** $v \in Y \setminus X$ **do**
11:         $\mathsf{H}(v) \leftarrow \emptyset$;
12:         **for** $b \in \Gamma_2(v)$ **do** $\mathsf{H}(v) \leftarrow \mathsf{H}(v) \cup \{\{a \in \Gamma_1(v) \setminus \mathsf{S}(v) \mid \delta(v, a, b) \in X\}\}$;
13:     **if** $Y \setminus X \neq \emptyset$ **then** $\mathsf{P} \leftarrow \mathsf{P} \cup \{Y \setminus X\}$;
14:     $X \leftarrow Y$;
15: **return** $(\mathsf{S}, (\mathsf{H}, \mathsf{P}), \mathsf{C})$

Template Formalization. As illustrated in Section 3 and similar to their turn-based counterparts, concurrent co-live templates are defined via a co-live function $\mathsf{C} : V \to 2^{\Gamma_1(V)}$ specifying the set of actions that Player 1 is only allowed to take finitely often in v. To ensure that all strategies π_1 which follow a co-live template take such actions only a *finite* number of times, the sum of probabilities associated to these actions via π_1 over time must be bounded.

Definition 3. *Let G be a concurrent game graph. Given a co-live function $\mathsf{C} : V \to 2^{\Gamma_1(V)}$, the concurrent co-live template $\Lambda_{COLIVE}(\mathsf{C})$ is defined s.t. $\pi_1 \in \Lambda_{COLIVE}(\mathsf{C})$ iff for all $\rho \in plays(\pi_1)$ holds that*

$$v \in \mathit{inf}(\rho) \Rightarrow \sum\nolimits_{\{i \mid \rho_i = v\}} \pi_1(\rho_{\leq i})(\mathsf{C}(\rho_i)) \neq \infty. \tag{7}$$

Template Computation. Following [1], the (almost sure) winning region of Player 1 in a concurrent co-Büchi game $(G, \Diamond \Box I)$ can be computed by the symbolic fixed-point formula

$$\mathcal{W}_1(\Diamond \Box I) = \nu Z. \mu X. \nu Y. \left((I \cap \mathsf{AFpre}_1(Z, Y, X)) \cup (\neg I \cap \mathsf{Apre}_1(Z, X)) \right), \tag{8}$$

where ALMOSTCO-BÜCHI (G, I) denotes the algorithm implementing this function. It is interesting to note that (8) is a three-nested fixed-point formula, while the computation of $\mathcal{W}_1(\Diamond \Box I)$ in a turn-based game only requires two nestings.

As in the Büchi case, we can extract a winning strategy template from the last iteration of ALMOSTCO-BÜCHI (G, I) (computing $Z^* = \mathcal{W}_1$) as detailed in Algorithm 1. As before, we first compute the winning region $Z^* = \mathcal{W}_1$ and ensure that the play stays in this set via a safety function S (line 1).

In order to understand line 2 of Algorithm 1, recall that Z^* can be written as an increasing sequence of sets $X_1 \subset X_2 \subset X_3 \subset \dots \subset X_k = X_{k+1} = Z^* = \mathcal{W}_1$. It can now be shown that it follows from the definition of AFpre in Section 4.1 that $\mathsf{AFpre}_1(Z^*, Y, \emptyset)$ reduces to $\mathsf{pre}_1(Y)$ while it directly follows that $\mathsf{Apre}_1(Z^*, \emptyset) = \emptyset$ for all $Y \subseteq V$. We can therefore conclude that $X_1 = Y^* = \nu Y. [I \cap \mathsf{pre}_1(Y)] = \mathcal{W}_1(\Box I) = \textsc{AlmostSafe}(G, I)$. I.e., X_1 are the states from which Player 1 has a strategy to keep the game in I indefinitely. However, due to the definition of Z^*, Player 1 is allowed to leave X_1 a finite number of times into Z^*, as AFpre ensures that the play can be forced to again make progress towards X_1 almost surely. We therefore collect all actions leaving X_1 into Z^* into the co-live function C (line 2 in Algorithm 1).

Finally, to ensure the discussed progress towards X_1, we additionally need a live-group template (H, P). This construction is very similar to the Büchi case, but using the particular fixed point in (8) (line 4-19 in Algorithm 1).

In conclusion, a winning strategy template for concurrent co-Büchi games consists of a safety template (to avoid leaving winning region), a co-live template (to avoid leaving X_1 infinitely many times), and a live-group template (to ensure reaching X_1 eventually). This is formalized in the following theorem.

Theorem 3. *Let* $(G, \Diamond\Box I)$ *be a* concurrent co-Büchi game *with winning region* $\mathcal{W}_1$, *if* $(\mathsf{S}, (\mathsf{H}, \mathsf{P}), \mathsf{C}) = co\textsc{Büchi}\textsc{Temp}(G, I)$, *then* $\Lambda = \Lambda_{\textsc{unsafe}}(\mathsf{S}) \cap \Lambda_{\textsc{live}}(\mathsf{H}, \mathsf{P}) \cap \Lambda_{\textsc{colive}}(\mathsf{C})$ *is a* winning strategy template *for* $(G, \Diamond\Box I)$.

While we will show in Corollary 1 that the template $\Lambda = \Lambda_{\textsc{unsafe}}(\mathsf{S}) \cap \Lambda_{\textsc{live}}(\mathsf{H}, \mathsf{P}) \cap \Lambda_{\textsc{colive}}(\mathsf{C})$ is complete for the game $\mathcal{G} = (G, \Diamond\Box I)$, the template is not maximally permissive (see [6, Appendix D] for an example).

Remark 1. We remark that winning strategy templates in turn-based co-Büchi games can be expressed solely by safety and co-liveness templates. This is due to the fact that live-group templates which are needed to ensure progress towards the safe invariant set can be translated into co-live templates for turn-based co-Büchi games, as progress needs to be made only over a *finite* time horizon. For concurrent games, this is unfortunately not possible, as the concurrent versions of live-group and co-live templates are not dual in this case.

5   Conflict-freeness and Strategy Extraction

This section discusses how to efficiently extract a strategy that follows a given strategy template. Although in many cases, as discussed in Section 3, one can easily construct a strategy that follows a given strategy template. However, it is not always the case that a strategy following a given strategy template even exists. For example, consider a strategy template $\Lambda_{\textsc{unsafe}}(\mathsf{S})$ that disallow all the available actions from a state v, i.e., $\mathsf{S}(v) = \Gamma_1(v)$. In this case, there is no strategy that follows the template. We call situations like this *conflicts* in the strategy template. To formalize this notion, we adapt the concept of *conflict-freeness* of strategy templates from [8] to concurrent games.

Definition 4. *Given a game graph* $G = (V, \Gamma_1, \Gamma_2, \delta)$, *a strategy template* $\Lambda = \Lambda_{UNSAFE}(S) \cap \Lambda_{LIVE}(H, P) \cap \Lambda_{COLIVE}(C)$ *is* conflict-free *if the following conditions hold for every state* $v \in V$: *(i)* $\Gamma_1(v) \not\subseteq S(v) \cup C(v)$, *and (ii) for every* $\gamma \in H(v)$, $\gamma \not\subseteq S(v) \cup C(v)$.

Intuitively, condition (i) ensures that there is at least one action available at every state v that is not disallowed by the safety or co-liveness templates. Condition (ii) ensures that even without the unsafe and co-live actions, liveness template can still be satisfied, i.e., for every opponent's action, there is at least one live action available at v that is not disallowed by the safety or co-liveness templates.

With the above intuition, one easy way to extract a memoryless strategy that follows a given conflict-free strategy template is the following: for every state, remove all unsafe and co-live actions, and then, assign positive probabilities to the remaining actions. This strategy is well-defined as condition (i) of Definition 4 ensures that there is at least one action available at every state after removing unsafe and co-live actions. Trivially, this strategy follows the safety and co-liveness templates. Moreover, this strategy also follows the liveness template as condition (ii) of Definition 4 ensures that for every opponent's action, at least one live action has been assigned a positive probability. Hence, the strategy indeed follows the strategy template, giving us the following result.

Theorem 4. *Given a game graph* $G = (V, \Gamma_1, \Gamma_2, \delta)$ *and a conflict-free strategy template* Λ, *one can extract a memoryless strategy that follows the template in time* $\mathcal{O}(|V| \cdot |\Gamma_1| \cdot |\Gamma_2|)$.

Similar to [8], we can also show that all the algorithms we presented in Section 4 produce conflict-free strategy templates.

Theorem 5. *The procedures* SAFETYTEMP, BÜCHITEMP, *and* COBÜCHITEMP *always return conflict-free strategy templates.*

As a consequence of Theorem 5, we also get the completeness of our algorithms in Section 4, i.e., for every state in the winning region, we can extract a winning strategy that follows the computed strategy template.

Corollary 1. *Given the premises of Theorem 2 (resp. Theorem 3), for every state* $v \in \mathcal{W}_1$, *there exists a winning strategy* π_1 *for Player 1 from* v *that follows the strategy template* Λ *computed by* LIVENTEMP *(resp.* COBÜCHITEMP*).*

6   Composition of Strategy Templates

With the conflict-freeness property, we can also now combine different strategy templates by intersecting them, and still be assured that there exists a strategy that follows the combined template. This is particularly useful when we want to combine multiple objectives, as we can compute the strategy template for each objective separately, and then intersect them to get a combined strategy template. Let us start by defining the combination of two strategy templates.

Definition 5. *For a game graph $G = (V, \Gamma_1, \Gamma_2, \delta)$, the combination of strategy templates $\Lambda_i = \Lambda_{UNSAFE}(S_i) \cap \Lambda_{LIVE}(H_i, P_i) \cap \Lambda_{COLIVE}(C_i)$ for $i \in \{1,2\}$, is defined as the strategy template $\Lambda_1 \cap \Lambda_2 = \Lambda_{UNSAFE}(S) \cap \Lambda_{LIVE}(H, P_1 \cup P_2) \cap \Lambda_{COLIVE}(C)$ with $S(v) = S_1(v) \cup S_2(v)$, $H(v) = H_1(v) \cup H_2(v)$, and $C(v) = C_1(v) \cup C_2(v)$.*

Intuitively, the combined strategy template marks an action as unsafe if it is unsafe in either of the individual templates, and similarly for co-live actions. For live actions, the combined template adds all the groups of live actions from both templates and also considers both partitions of the individual templates. This ensures that a strategy follows the combined template if and only if it follows both individual templates. With this definition, whenever the combined strategy template is conflict-free, we can be assured that there exists a strategy that follows both individual templates, leading to the following result.

Theorem 6. *Let (G, Φ_1) and (G, Φ_2) be concurrent games with corresponding winning regions $\mathcal{W}_1$ and $\mathcal{W}_2$, and winning strategy templates Λ_1 and Λ_2. If the combined strategy template $\Lambda_1 \cap \Lambda_2$ is conflict-free, then it is a winning strategy template for the game $(G, \Phi_1 \wedge \Phi_2)$ with winning region $\mathcal{W}_1 \cap \mathcal{W}_2$.*

Note that, in general, the winning region of the game $(G, \Phi_1 \wedge \Phi_2)$ is not necessarily equal to $\mathcal{W}_1 \cap \mathcal{W}_2$. However, if the combined strategy template is conflict-free, then the winning region of the conjoined game is indeed $\mathcal{W}_1 \cap \mathcal{W}_2$.

7 Experiments

Implementation and Setup. Our algorithms are implemented in a Python tool, called `ConSTel`, capable of handling Büchi and co-Büchi games, hence Parity games with two colors. We are unaware of large-scale benchmarks for *concurrent* games. Thus, we converted *turn-based* Parity games from the SYNTCOMP benchmarks [22] to concurrent games for evaluation purposes. Specifically, we considered smaller models which are alternating (i.e. Player 1 states are always followed by Player 2 states and vice versa) and can be converted to Büchi (resp. co-Büchi) games. Our conversion first merges each Player 1 transition with the transitions of the respective successor Player 2 state. Afterwards, it removes all Player 2 states and turns the transition-based into state-based winning conditions[2]. In total we converted 171 games. All experiments were run on a machine with Ubuntu 22.04, an Intel i7-1165G7 CPU and 32GB RAM. Our implementation and experimental data are available in [11].

We compared our prototypical implementation with `PeSTel` [8], a tool for computing strategy templates in *turn-based* games. The results are given in [6, Appendix E] and indicate that `ConSTel` is noticeably slower. We attribute the slower performance to programming language differences and the inherent difficulty of solving concurrent games, and leave engineering improvements open

---

[2] We note that the resulting concurrent game does not capture the same interaction dynamics as the original turn-based game. The conversion procedure and considered models are described in more detail in [6, Appendix E]

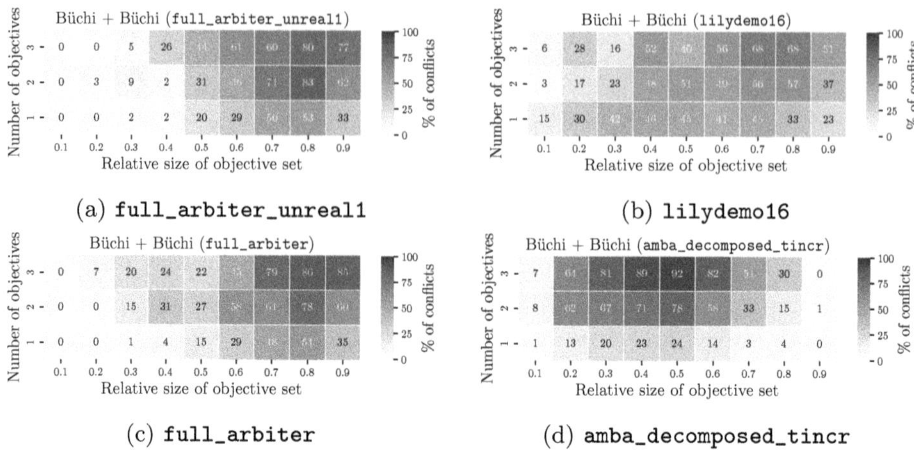

(a) `full_arbiter_unreal1`

(b) `lilydemo16`

(c) `full_arbiter`

(d) `amba_decomposed_tincr`

Figure 2: Conflict analysis for Büchi + Büchi on `full_arbiter_unreal1`.

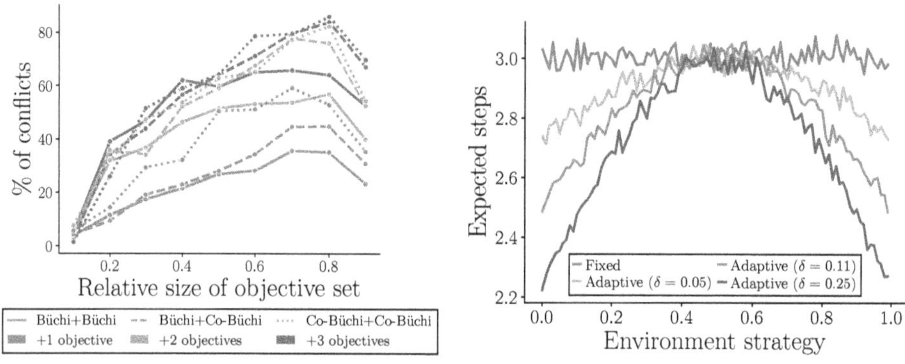

Figure 3: Conflict analysis.

Figure 4: Expected steps to reach S_e.

for future work. For the remainder, we investigate the efficacy of our templates in incremental synthesis and optimizing strategies at runtime.

Incremental Synthesis. We study the ability of our approach to handle newly arriving objectives. Starting with a template for an initial objective, we are interested in the amount of conflicts that occur when combining the existing template with templates of new objectives. We selected four converted games with at least 20 states and for which the winning regions of the initial objectives are non-empty, i.e. (i) `full_arbiter_unreal1`: 55 state and 731 transitions; (ii) `lilydemo16`: 28 state and 1228 transitions; (iii) `full_arbiter`: 55 state and 731 transitions; (iv) `amba_decomposed_tincr`: 26 state and 289 transitions.

For each game, we introduced $k \in \{1, 2, 3\}$ different additional objectives of the same type (Büchi or co-Büchi), each of size $s \in \{10\%, 20\%, \ldots, 90\%\}$ (relative to the number of states). For every configuration (s, k) we considered 100 random samples and reported the relative number of conflicts when combining the existing template with the templates of the new objectives. In Fig. 3 we have aggregated the data over all four selected models while Fig. 2 reports detailed results for model (i) and the Büchi-Büchi case only. Here, each cell (s, k) in the heatmaps corresponds to the percentage of conflicts that occurred when adding k objectives of size s. In Fig. 3 the number of additional objectives k is indicated by colors and the objective types by line styles.

As expected, more conflicts occur as the number of additional objectives increases. Most conflicts occur for larger objective sets (60% to 80%). Intuitively, small sets result in smaller winning regions and thus fewer states where conflicts can potentially occur. Less conflicts arise for the largest set, since the objectives become easier to satisfy. Remarkably, regardless of the objective size, we can *often add additional Büchi templates* to an existing Büchi template without conflicts ($\leq 36\%$ conflicts for +1 objective). Conflicts are more prevalent when co-Büchi objectives are involved, but remain reasonable for smaller objectives. We provide more details and plots in [6, Appendix E].

Runtime Optimization. Finally, we showcase the application of our templates in runtime strategy optimization on the robot example (Fig. 1). The robot R_C reaches a green cell alone almost surely when assigning positive probabilities to actions that lead to green cells, as prescribed by our strategy template. Observe that strategies can differ in the *expected time* it takes for the robot to reach S_e. Conceptually, the template enables the robot to *change its strategy at runtime*, while ensuring it reaches S_e almost surely. Using this flexibility, the robot can adapt its strategy, among the ones prescribed by the template, to minimize the expected time. Assuming a fixed environment strategy, we consider a simple adaptive approach that updates the robot's strategy based on the observed environment actions. Initially, the robot assigns equal probability to both actions leading to the green cells. As the game progresses, the robot observes the environment actions and adjusts the probabilities by δ to favour actions that are more likely to succeed, while ensuring that the template is still followed.

We simulated the approach 10000 times for different environment strategies and values for δ. The results are shown in Fig. 4. The x-axis corresponds to environment strategies and shows the probability of the environment choosing the *clockwise* move. The y-axis depicts the expected time for the robot to reach S_e. The fixed strategy assigns equal probability to both actions and generally requires three steps to reach S_e. Depending on δ and the environment strategy, the robot noticeably reduces the number of steps in the adaptive approach.

While this example is small, we strongly believe that the shown adaptation can be similarly applied in larger instances as it only uses *local information for adaptation*. While ConSTel synthesis is performed over the entire graph – where we discussed scalability before – this last experiment shows ConSTels main potential to make dynamic strategy adaptations local and therefore scalable.

Data Availability Statement. The artefact containing the models, experimental data, implementation, and scripts for reproducing the experiments can be found at `https://doi.org/10.5281/zenodo.18187322`. The latest version of the artefact can be found at `https://doi.org/10.5281/zenodo.17357028` [11].

References

1. de Alfaro, L., Henzinger, T.: Concurrent omega-regular games. In: Proceedings Fifteenth Annual IEEE Symposium on Logic in Computer Science (Cat. No.99CB36332). pp. 141–154 (2000). https://doi.org/10.1109/LICS.2000.855763

2. de Alfaro, L., Henzinger, T.A., Kupferman, O.: Concurrent reachability games. In: 39th Annual Symposium on Foundations of Computer Science, FOCS 1998, Palo Alto, California, USA, November 8-11, 1998. pp. 564–575. IEEE Computer Society (1998). https://doi.org/10.1109/SFCS.1998.743507, https://doi.org/10.1109/SFCS.1998.743507

3. Alur, R., Henzinger, T.A.: Reactive modules. In: Proceedings, 11th Annual IEEE Symposium on Logic in Computer Science, New Brunswick, New Jersey, USA, July 27-30, 1996. pp. 207–218. IEEE Computer Society (1996). https://doi.org/10.1109/LICS.1996.561320, https://doi.org/10.1109/LICS.1996.561320

4. Alur, R., Henzinger, T.A., Kupferman, O.: Alternating-time temporal logic. J. ACM **49**(5), 672–713 (2002). https://doi.org/10.1145/585265.585270, https://doi.org/10.1145/585265.585270

5. Alur, R., Henzinger, T.A., Mang, F.Y.C., Qadeer, S., Rajamani, S.K., Tasiran, S.: MOCHA: modularity in model checking. In: Hu, A.J., Vardi, M.Y. (eds.) Computer Aided Verification, 10th International Conference, CAV '98, Vancouver, BC, Canada, June 28 - July 2, 1998, Proceedings. Lecture Notes in Computer Science, vol. 1427, pp. 521–525. Springer (1998). https://doi.org/10.1007/BFB0028774, https://doi.org/10.1007/BFb0028774

6. Anand, A., Baier, C., Chau, C., Klüppelholz, S., Mirzaei, A., Nayak, S.P., Schmuck, A.K.: Concurrent permissive strategy templates (extended version) (2026), https://arxiv.org/abs/2601.13500

7. Anand, A., Mallik, K., Nayak, S.P., Schmuck, A.: Computing adequately permissive assumptions for synthesis. In: Sankaranarayanan, S., Sharygina, N. (eds.) Tools and Algorithms for the Construction and Analysis of Systems - 29th International Conference, TACAS 2023, Held as Part of the European Joint Conferences on Theory and Practice of Software, ETAPS 2022, Paris, France, April 22-27, 2023, Proceedings, Part II. Lecture Notes in Computer Science, vol. 13994, pp. 211–228. Springer (2023). https://doi.org/10.1007/978-3-031-30820-8_15, https://doi.org/10.1007/978-3-031-30820-8_15

8. Anand, A., Nayak, S.P., Schmuck, A.K.: Synthesizing permissive winning strategy templates for parity games. In: Enea, C., Lal, A. (eds.) Computer Aided Verification. pp. 436–458. Springer Nature Switzerland, Cham (2023)

9. Anand, A., Nayak, S.P., Schmuck, A.: Strategy templates - robust certified interfaces for interacting systems. In: Akshay, S., Niemetz, A., Sankaranarayanan, S. (eds.) Automated Technology for Verification and Analysis - 22nd International Symposium, ATVA 2024, Kyoto, Japan, October 21-25, 2024, Proceedings, Part I. Lecture Notes in Computer Science, vol. 15054, pp. 22–41. Springer (2024). https://doi.org/10.1007/978-3-031-78709-6_2, https://doi.org/10.1007/978-3-031-78709-6_2

10. Anand, A., Schmuck, A.K., Prakash Nayak, S.: Contract-based distributed logical controller synthesis. In: Proceedings of the 27th ACM International Conference on Hybrid Systems: Computation and Control. HSCC '24, Association for Computing Machinery, New York, NY, USA (2024). https://doi.org/10.1145/3641513.3650123, https://doi.org/10.1145/3641513.3650123

11. Anonymous: Artefact for tacas 2026 (Oct 2025). https://doi.org/10.5281/zenodo.17357028, https://doi.org/10.5281/zenodo.17357028

12. Bowling, M.H., Veloso, M.M.: Simultaneous adversarial multi-robot learning. In: Gottlob, G., Walsh, T. (eds.) IJCAI-03, Proceedings of the Eighteenth International Joint Conference on Artificial Intelligence, Acapulco, Mexico, August 9-15, 2003. pp. 699–704. Morgan Kaufmann (2003), http://ijcai.org/Proceedings/03/Papers/102.pdf

13. Brenguier, R.: PRALINE: A tool for computing nash equilibria in concurrent games. In: Sharygina, N., Veith, H. (eds.) Computer Aided Verification - 25th International Conference, CAV 2013, Saint Petersburg, Russia, July 13-19, 2013. Proceedings. Lecture Notes in Computer Science, vol. 8044, pp. 890–895. Springer (2013). https://doi.org/10.1007/978-3-642-39799-8_63, https://doi.org/10.1007/978-3-642-39799-8_63

14. Chatterjee, K.: Concurrent games with tail objectives. Theor. Comput. Sci. **388**(1-3), 181–198 (2007). https://doi.org/10.1016/J.TCS.2007.07.047, https://doi.org/10.1016/j.tcs.2007.07.047

15. Cheng, C., Knoll, A.C., Luttenberger, M., Buckl, C.: GAVS+: an open platform for the research of algorithmic game solving. In: Abdulla, P.A., Leino, K.R.M. (eds.) Tools and Algorithms for the Construction and Analysis of Systems - 17th International Conference, TACAS 2011, Held as Part of the Joint European Conferences on Theory and Practice of Software, ETAPS 2011, Saarbrücken, Germany, March 26-April 3, 2011. Proceedings. Lecture Notes in Computer Science, vol. 6605, pp. 258–261. Springer (2011). https://doi.org/10.1007/978-3-642-19835-9_22, https://doi.org/10.1007/978-3-642-19835-9_22

16. Emerson, E.A., Jutla, C.S.: Tree automata, mu-calculus and determinacy. In: FOCS'91. pp. 368–377 (1991)

17. Etessami, K., Yannakakis, M.: On the complexity of nash equilibria and other fixed points. SIAM J. Comput. **39**(6), 2531–2597 (2010). https://doi.org/10.1137/080720826, https://doi.org/10.1137/080720826

18. Fijalkow, N., Aiswarya, C., Avni, G., Bertrand, N., Bouyer, P., Brenguier, R., Carayol, A., Casares, A., Fearnley, J., Gastin, P., Gimbert, H., Henzinger, T.A., Horn, F., Ibsen-Jensen, R., Markey, N., Monmege, B., Novotný, P., Ohlmann, P., Randour, M., Sankur, O., Schmitz, S., Serre, O., Skomra, M., Sznajder, N., Vandenhove, P.: Games on Graphs: From Logic and Automata to Algorithms. Online (2025)

19. Finkbeiner, B.: Synthesis of reactive systems. In: Dependable Software Systems Engineering, pp. 72–98. IOS Press (2016)

20. Gutierrez, J., Najib, M., Perelli, G., Wooldridge, M.J.: EVE: A tool for temporal equilibrium analysis. In: Lahiri, S.K., Wang, C. (eds.) Automated Technology for Verification and Analysis - 16th International Symposium, ATVA 2018, Los Angeles, CA, USA, October 7-10, 2018, Proceedings. Lecture Notes in Computer Science, vol. 11138, pp. 551–557. Springer (2018). https://doi.org/10.1007/978-3-030-01090-4_35, https://doi.org/10.1007/978-3-030-01090-4_35

21. Henzinger, T.A.: Games in system design and verification. In: Proceedings of the 10th Conference on Theoretical Aspects of Rationality and Knowledge. p. 1–4. TARK '05, National University of Singapore, SGP (2005)

22. Jacobs, S., Pérez, G.A., Abraham, R., Bruyère, V., Cadilhac, M., Colange, M., Delfosse, C., van Dijk, T., Duret-Lutz, A., Faymonville, P., Finkbeiner, B., Khalimov, A., Klein, F., Luttenberger, M., Meyer, K.J., Michaud, T., Pommellet, A., Renkin, F., Schlehuber-Caissier, P., Sakr, M., Sickert, S., Staquet,

G., Tamines, C., Tentrup, L., Walker, A.: The reactive synthesis competition (SYNTCOMP): 2018-2021. Int. J. Softw. Tools Technol. Transf. **26**(5), 551–567 (2024). https://doi.org/10.1007/S10009-024-00754-1, https://doi.org/10.1007/s10009-024-00754-1

23. Kozen, D.: Results on the propositional μ-calculus. Theoretical computer science **27**(3), 333–354 (1983)

24. Kress-Gazit, H., Lahijanian, M., Raman, V.: Synthesis for robots: Guarantees and feedback for robot behavior. Annual Review of Control, Robotics, and Autonomous Systems **1**(1), 211–236 (2018)

25. Kwiatkowska, M., Norman, G., Parker, D., Santos, G.: Prism-games 3.0: Stochastic game verification with concurrency, equilibria and time. In: Lahiri, S.K., Wang, C. (eds.) Computer Aided Verification. pp. 475–487. Springer International Publishing, Cham (2020)

26. Lomuscio, A., Qu, H., Raimondi, F.: MCMAS: an open-source model checker for the verification of multi-agent systems. Int. J. Softw. Tools Technol. Transf. **19**(1), 9–30 (2017). https://doi.org/10.1007/S10009-015-0378-X, https://doi.org/10.1007/s10009-015-0378-x

27. Nayak, S.P., Egidio, L.N., Della Rossa, M., Schmuck, A.K., Jungers, R.M.: Context-triggered abstraction-based control design. IEEE Open Journal of Control Systems **2**, 277–296 (2023)

28. Nayak, S.P., Schmuck, A.K.: Most general winning secure equilibria synthesis in graph games. In: Finkbeiner, B., Kovács, L. (eds.) Tools and Algorithms for the Construction and Analysis of Systems. pp. 173–193. Springer Nature Switzerland, Cham (2024)

29. Nisan, N., Roughgarden, T., Éva Tardos, Vazirani, V.V. (eds.): Algorithmic Game Theory. Cambridge University Press (2007). https://doi.org/10.1017/CB09780511800481, https://doi.org/10.1017/CB09780511800481

30. Phalakarn, K., Pruekprasert, S., Hasuo, I.: Winning strategy templates for stochastic parity games towards permissive and resilient control. In: Anutariya, C., Bonsangue, M.M. (eds.) Theoretical Aspects of Computing – ICTAC 2024. pp. 197–214. Springer Nature Switzerland, Cham (2025)

31. Pnueli, A., Rosner, R.: On the synthesis of a reactive module. In: Proceedings of the 16th ACM SIGPLAN-SIGACT symposium on Principles of programming languages. pp. 179–190 (1989)

32. Shapley, L.S.: Stochastic games. Proceedings of the national academy of sciences **39**(10), 1095–1100 (1953)

33. Tabuada, P.: Verification and control of hybrid systems: a symbolic approach. Springer (2009)

34. Wang, Y., Dantam, N.T., Chaudhuri, S., Kavraki, L.E.: Task and motion policy synthesis as liveness games. In: Coles, A.J., Coles, A., Edelkamp, S., Magazzeni, D., Sanner, S. (eds.) Proceedings of the Twenty-Sixth International Conference on Automated Planning and Scheduling, ICAPS 2016, London, UK, June 12-17, 2016. p. 536. AAAI Press (2016), http://www.aaai.org/ocs/index.php/ICAPS/ICAPS16/paper/view/13146

35. Xiong, L., Liu, Y.: Strategy representation and reasoning for incomplete information concurrent games in the situation calculus. In: Kambhampati, S. (ed.) Proceedings of the Twenty-Fifth International Joint Conference on Artificial Intelligence, IJCAI 2016, New York, NY, USA, 9-15 July 2016. pp. 1322–1329. IJCAI/AAAI Press (2016), http://www.ijcai.org/Abstract/16/191

36. Yin, X., Gao, B., Yu, X.: Formal synthesis of controllers for safety-critical autonomous systems: Developments and challenges. Annual Reviews in Control **57**, 100940 (2024). https://doi.org/https://doi.org/10.1016/j.arcontrol.2024.100940

Modular Attractor Acceleration
in Infinite-State Games

Philippe Heim  and Rayna Dimitrova 

CISPA Helmholtz Center for Information Security, Saarbrücken, Germany
{philippe.heim, dimitrova}@cispa.de

Abstract. Infinite-state games provide a framework for the synthesis of reactive systems with unbounded data domains. Solving such games typically relies on computing symbolic fixpoints, particularly symbolic attractors. However, these computations may not terminate, and while recent acceleration techniques have been proposed to address this issue, they often rely on acceleration arguments of limited expressiveness.

In this work, we propose an approach for the modular computation of acceleration arguments. It enables the construction of complex acceleration arguments by composing simpler ones, thereby improving both scalability and flexibility. In addition, we introduce a summarization technique that generalizes discovered acceleration arguments, allowing them to be efficiently reused across multiple contexts. Together, these contributions improve the efficiency of solving infinite-state games in reactive synthesis, as demonstrated by our experimental evaluation.

Keywords: Reactive Synthesis · Infinite-State Games · Acceleration.

1 Introduction

Two-player infinite-duration graph games are a standard formalism used for synthesis of correct-by-construction reactive systems. Synthesizing such a system reduces to computing a winning strategy for the system player against an adversarial environment. Finite-state games are well-established, and efficient techniques and tools are available. However, many systems operate over unbounded data domains, motivating interest in infinite-state games. Solving such games is undecidable, and recent works explored several incomplete methods. Abstraction-based methods [6, 20, 26, 27, 24, 1, 25] reduce the problem to the finite case. Their effectiveness depends on the abstraction domain's precision and the ability to discover relevant properties when refining the abstraction. Constraint-based methods [9, 8, 29, 21, 13] operate directly on symbolic representations of the infinite state space. The main challenge for these is taming the divergence of the computations.

As many game-solving algorithms rely on (nested) fixpoint computations, one line of recent work [13, 30, 14] has focused on *accelerating* these computations, especially *accelerating attractor computations* which are the main driver of those fixpoint-based algorithms. Intuitively, an attractor is the set of states

S. Junges and G. Katz (Eds.): TACAS 2026, LNCS 16505, pp. 398–418, 2026.
https://doi.org/10.1007/978-3-032-22752-2_21

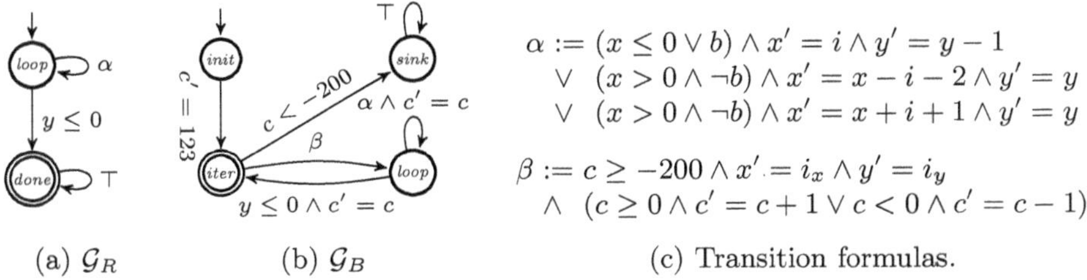

$$\alpha := (x \le 0 \vee b) \wedge x' = i \wedge y' = y - 1$$
$$\vee \ (x > 0 \wedge \neg b) \wedge x' = x - i - 2 \wedge y' = y$$
$$\vee \ (x > 0 \wedge \neg b) \wedge x' = x + i + 1 \wedge y' = y$$

$$\beta := c \ge -200 \wedge x' = i_x \wedge y' = i_y$$
$$\wedge \ (c \ge 0 \wedge c' = c + 1 \vee c < 0 \wedge c' = c - 1)$$

(a) $\mathcal{G}_R$ (b) $\mathcal{G}_B$ (c) Transition formulas.

Fig. 1: Symbolic games $\mathcal{G}_R$ and $\mathcal{G}_B$ for the motivating examples. In both games, x and y are integer state variables, and i and b are input variables with integer and Boolean types, respectively. Additionally, the Büchi game $\mathcal{G}_B$ has an integer state variable c and input variables i_x and i_y, which are also integers.

in the game from which a given player has a strategy to reach a given target set of states, regardless of the opponent's behavior. A key notion in [13, 30, 14] is that of *acceleration lemmas*, which help to establish the existence of strategies for infinite subsets of the attractor, by capturing the effect of an infinite number of computation steps into a single one. Finding acceleration lemmas is challenging, as it requires proving that an acceleration property can be enforced against any adversarial behavior. [13] computes acceleration lemmas by representing candidates for them as uninterpreted functions and by using symbolic game solving to generate constraints on those. However, the resulting constraint systems can become prohibitively large in complex games. The burden of finding acceleration lemmas is then shifted entirely to the SMT solver. Subsequent methods, such as [30] have improved this computation but have not departed conceptually from the original idea. Overall, despite promising results, existing methods often struggle when complex acceleration lemmas are required.

In this work, we investigate methods for efficiently constructing complex acceleration lemmas by systematically composing them from simpler ones, which allows us to conduct a dedicated search for lemmas. In addition, we explore how acceleration arguments can be reused through appropriate generalization. The following examples motivate these ideas.

Example 1. Figure 1a depicts a game $\mathcal{G}_R$, in which the system player must ensure reaching location *done* against all possible behaviors of the environment. The game starts in location *loop* with arbitrary initial values of the state variables x and y. The system controls x and y, subject to the transition formulas labeling the game's edges. In each step, the environment first chooses values for the input variables i and b, after which the system selects a successor location and state consistent with the corresponding transition formula. For example, from location *loop*, the system may remain in *loop* and choose x and y satisfying the transition formula α shown in Figure 1c. Concretely, it may set x to i and decrement y when $x \le 0 \vee b$ holds, or otherwise update x in one of two ways while keeping y unchanged. To show that the system wins, one must establish a strategy that, for any initial values of x and y and any sequence of inputs i and b

chosen by the environment, eventually reaches *done*. This amounts to enforcing a state $(loop, v_x, v_y)$ with $v_y \leq 0$. Such a strategy exists: When $x > 0 \wedge \neg b$ holds, the system can update x depending on i to ensure that x decreases. Hence, while $x > 0$ and the environment keeps b false, the system can reduce x, eventually enabling the disjunct that decrements y. When y is decremented, the environment picks a new value i for x, and the process repeats. Because y never increases, the first disjunct can only be applied finitely many times with $y > 0$, i.e., the system can enforce progress toward *done*. Establishing this formally requires finding a correct strategy (i.e., the system program) and the corresponding acceleration argument.

The reasoning above relies on establishing a lexicographic acceleration argument together with a strategy for the system player that enforces it. The argument is that either y decreases, in which case it does not matter how the value of x changes, or the value of y remains unchanged and the value of x decreases. The latter case relies on the system correctly selecting the update to x based on the current input i provided by the environment.

Although this argument is conceptually simple, the automatic synthesis of such acceleration lemmas is challenging for existing methods. Current tools for solving infinite-state games fail on this example due to the vast search space of potential acceleration arguments and strategies. In this paper, we address this challenge by introducing a modular approach for constructing such a witness. The key idea is to define *composition operations that build up more complex acceleration lemmas from simpler ones*. This enables a structured navigation of the search space, leading to the discovery of powerful acceleration lemmas beyond the reach of existing techniques. However, scalability remains a challenge, particularly when solving complex games that require generating multiple acceleration lemmas. The following example illustrates this issue.

Example 2. Figure 1b depicts a game $\mathcal{G}_B$ with a Büchi winning condition requiring that location *iter* be visited infinitely often. The game contains a sub-game (locations *iter* and *loop*) structurally similar to $\mathcal{G}_R$ from Example 1, extended with a state variable c that remains unchanged by the transitions originating in *loop*. As argued in Example 1, location *iter* can always be reached from *loop* for any initial values of x and y. To ensure that the loop between *iter* and *loop* executes infinitely often, the state variable c must remain at least -200. Inspecting the transition formula β shown in Figure 1c, we see that starting from any non-negative value of c, this is indeed possible. Therefore, the system player has a winning strategy, since the transition from the initial location *init* to *iter* initializes c to 123. However, applying the symbolic method for solving infinite-state Büchi games from [13] requires establishing acceleration arguments for multiple state sets: $c \geq -200$, $c \geq -199$, $c \geq -198$, and so on – until reaching the fixpoint $c \geq 0$. Although the reasoning in each case is identical, this repetition introduces substantial computational overhead. To address this inefficiency, we introduce the notion of *enforcement summaries*, which are witnesses "parameterized" by the target set that a player can enforce reaching. Once computed, an enforcement summary can be applied multiple times during the game's solving by checking lightweight applicability conditions. This is especially helpful when solving Büchi games like $\mathcal{G}_B$, where for each iteration of the outer fixpoint computation, we need to apply acceleration to enforce convergence of the inner fixpoint computation. Using enforcement summaries, each of the remaining 200 inner fixpoints collapses into a single computation step, thereby improving efficiency.

To compute these parameterized summaries, our method uses generic templates with parameters that describe a general set of multiple possible target sets that the player can enforce. Applying the summaries reduces to instantiating those parameters. The key is to ensure that the templates are sufficiently general.

Related work. Recent years have seen significant progress in the synthesis of infinite-state reactive systems, particularly in solving infinite-state games. For comprehensive overviews, we refer the reader to [13, 14]. In this paper, we introduce a novel framework and techniques for attractor acceleration, building upon the symbolic methods developed in [13]. These methods have proven effective for solving games that require reasoning about unbounded loops, where a player must make strategic decisions in response to the opponent. To improve scalability, [30] employs strategy templates in finite abstractions to identify smaller sub-games, which helps solve the overall game. This approach hinges on balancing abstraction size and the usefulness of the sub-games' results. The tool in [14] builds on the methods and ideas in [13, 30] and implements further techniques for acceleration lemma computation. In contrast to abstraction-based approaches [6, 20, 26, 27, 24, 1, 25], which treat finite-state synthesis as a black box, symbolic methods such as those in [13, 14] enable tight integration of game solving and constraint solving, allowing reasoning about data directly within the game-solving procedure.

The synthesis of ranking functions [7, 2, 19, 34, 5, 10, 35] has been extensively studied in software verification and termination analysis, and loop acceleration techniques [3, 4, 18, 17, 12, 11] have been successfully applied to prove termination or non-termination of numerical programs. Synthesizing acceleration lemmas for system synthesis differs fundamentally from these verification settings. While verification techniques reason about a given program, synthesis requires existential quantification over possible implementations. In other words, verification witnesses describe properties of all behaviors of a *given program* (possibly via overapproximation), whereas synthesis witnesses must establish the *existence of a program* that enforces a desired property. Summaries have also been employed to improve verification efficiency [31, 32, 23]. Our enforcement summaries, however, serve a distinct purpose: rather than summarizing the behavior of a program, they capture a *set of properties that can be enforced* by a player in the game, corresponding to families of strategies for that player. A majority of the methods and tools in verification generate ranking functions within a specific class, for example, (combinations of) linear ranking functions, possibly utilizing general templates or grammars [7, 19, 10]. Similarly, our methods generate acceleration lemmas constructed from building blocks that are linear inequalities, and we use linear templates as the base for our enforcement summaries. However, our methods for computing them are based on symbolic game solving.

Contributions. We generalize *acceleration lemmas* [13] to enable their modular construction from simple lemmas via *composition operations* such as intersection, lexicographic combination, and chaining. We present a method for generating those integrated into symbolic game-solving procedures. In contrast to previous work, this method includes a dedicated lemma search procedure that enables more targeted generation of acceleration lemmas. We further extend these procedures with the *computation and application of enforcement summaries* to prevent the repeated computation of similar acceleration lemmas. We implemented our methods on top of the open-source tool `Issy` [14]. Our extensive experimental evaluation demonstrates that the proposed techniques can solve games beyond the reach of current tools while remaining competitive with the state of the art.

2   Preliminaries

First-order logic. We consider a set *Vars* of all variables. For $X \subseteq Vars$, an *assignment to* X is a function $\nu : X \to \mathcal{V}$ where $\mathcal{V}$ is the set of all values. We define $Assignments(X)$ to be the assignments to X. $\nu_1 \uplus \nu_2$ denotes the combination of two assignments ν_1, ν_2 to disjoint variables. X' is the *primed version of* X such that $X' := \{x' \mid x \in X\} \subseteq Vars \setminus X$. If $\nu \in Assignments(X)$, we define $\nu' \in Assignments(X')$ as $\nu'(x') = \nu(x)$ for all $x \in X$. Given $\nu_1, \nu_2 \in Assignments(X)$, we define $\langle \nu_1, \nu_2 \rangle := \nu_1 \uplus \nu_2'$. Let FOL and QF be the sets of first-order and quantifier-free formulas, respectively. For $\alpha \in FOL$ and $X = \{x_1, \ldots, x_n\} \subseteq Vars$, we write $\alpha(X)$ when the free variables of α are a subset of X. We denote with $FOL(X)$ ($QF(X)$) the formulas (quantifier-free formulas) whose free variables belong to X. We use $QX.\alpha$ as a shortcut for $Qx_1 \ldots Qx_n.\alpha$ for $Q \in \{\exists, \forall\}$. The formula $\alpha[x_1 \mapsto y_1, \ldots, x_n \mapsto y_n]$ is obtained from α by replacing all x_i simultaneously by variables y_i. We denote by $\nu \models_T \alpha$ entailment of α by ν in the first-order theory T for $\alpha \in FOL(X)$ and $\nu \in Assignments(X)$. We assume a fixed theory T and define $[\![\alpha(X)]\!] := \{\nu \in Assignments(X) \mid \nu \models_T \alpha\}$. Independent of the theory, we use uninterpreted functions as syntactic placeholders. In their presence entailment is undefined. We call them uninterpreted constants if they have arity zero. $\alpha[c_1 \mapsto x_1, \ldots, c_n \mapsto x_n]$ is obtained from α by replacing all uninterpreted constant symbols c_i simultaneously by x_i. For variables $Y = \{y_1, \ldots, y_m\}$, uninterpreted functions symbols f_i with arity m over Y, and terms θ_i over Y, $\alpha(\!(f_1 \mapsto \theta_1, \ldots, f_n \mapsto \theta_n)\!)$ is obtained by replacing all instances $f_i(t_1, \ldots, t_m)$ in α by θ_i where all variables y_j are replaced by t_j.

Two-Player Turn-Based Games. An *arena* is a tuple $G = (V, V_{Env}, V_{Sys}, \tau)$ where $V = V_{Env} \uplus V_{Sys}$ are the vertices, partitioned between the environment (*Env*) and the system player (*Sys*), and $\tau \subseteq (V_{Env} \times V_{Sys}) \cup (V_{Sys} \times V_{Env})$ is the transition relation. A *play* in G is a sequence $\xi \in V^\omega$ where $(\xi[i], \xi[i+1]) \in \tau$ for all $i \in \mathbb{N}$. A *strategy for player* p is a function $\sigma : V^* V_p \to V$ where $\sigma(\xi \cdot v) = v'$

implies $(v, v') \in \tau$. $Strat_p(G)$ are the strategies for p in G. A play ξ is consistent with σ if $\xi[i+1] = \sigma(\xi[0, i])$ for every $i \in \mathbb{N}$ where $\xi[i] \in V_p$. $Plays_G(v, \sigma)$ is the set of all plays in G starting in v and consistent with σ. The pair (G, Ω) is a *two-player turn-based game* where $\Omega \subseteq V^\omega$ is called the *winning condition* for *Sys*. A sequence $\xi \in V^\omega$ is *winning for Sys* if and only if $\xi \in \Omega$, and is *winning for Env* otherwise. A strategy σ of player p is *winning for p from v* if every play in $Plays_G(v, \sigma)$ is winning for player p.

2.1 Representation and Methods for Solving Infinite-State Games

We follow the formalization in [15] and represent infinite arenas with *symbolic game structures*. Those describe the interaction between an environment selecting values for the input variables $\mathbb{I}$ and a reactive system controlling the program variables $\mathbb{X}$. Formally, a *symbolic game structure* is a tuple $(L, l_{init}, \mathbb{I}, \mathbb{X}, dom, \delta)$ where L is a finite set of *locations*, $l_{init} \in L$ is the *initial location*, $\mathbb{I} \subseteq Vars$ is a finite set of *input variables*, $\mathbb{X} \subseteq Vars$ is a finite set of *program variables*, $dom : L \mapsto QF(\mathbb{X})$ is the *domain of the states*, and $\delta : L \times L \mapsto QF(\mathbb{X} \cup \mathbb{I} \cup \mathbb{X}')$ is the *transition relation*. For $l \in L$ and $\mathbf{x} \in Assignments(\mathbb{X})$ with $\mathbf{x} \models_T dom(l)$, $\mathbf{i} \in Assignments(\mathbb{I})$ is a *valid input* if there exists some $l' \in L$ and $\mathbf{x}' \in Assignments(\mathbb{X}')$ such that $\mathbf{x}' \models_T dom(l')$ and $\mathbf{x} \uplus \mathbf{i} \uplus \mathbf{x}' \models_T \delta(l, l')$. δ is required to be *non-blocking*, i.e., for all $l \in L$ and $\mathbf{x} \in Assignments(\mathbb{X})$ with $\mathbf{x} \models_T dom(l)$ there exists some valid input.

Semantics. A symbolic game structure $\mathcal{G}$ represents a possibly infinite arena $\llbracket \mathcal{G} \rrbracket = (\mathcal{S}, \mathcal{S}_{Env}, \mathcal{S}_{Sys}, \tau)$. $\mathcal{S}_{Env}$ consists of pairs $(l, \mathbf{x})$ of location $l \in L$ and assignment to the program variables $\mathbf{x} \in Assignments(\mathbb{X})$ such that the assignment $\mathbf{x}$ satisfies the condition $dom(l)$, i.e. $\mathcal{S}_{Env} := \{(l, \mathbf{x}) \in L \times Assignments(\mathbb{X}) \mid \mathbf{x} \models_T dom(l)\}$. Those vertices are also called *states*. From such a state, *Env* selects a valid input $\mathbf{i} \in Assignments(\mathbb{I})$. Hence, $\mathcal{S}_{Sys}$ are pairs of states and respective valid inputs, i.e. $\mathcal{S}_{Sys} := \{((l, \mathbf{x}), \mathbf{i}) \in \mathcal{S}_{Env} \times Assignments(\mathbb{I}) \mid ValidIn(l, \mathbf{x}, \mathbf{i})\}$. Then, *Sys* selects a next state $(l', \mathbf{x}')$ with a new assignment to the program variables and next location $l' \in L$ such that $\mathbf{x}' \models_T dom(l')$ and $\mathbf{x} \uplus \mathbf{i} \uplus \mathbf{v}' \models_T \delta(l, l')$. The transition relation $\tau \subseteq (\mathcal{S}_{Env} \times \mathcal{S}_{Sys}) \cup (\mathcal{S}_{Sys} \times \mathcal{S}_{Env})$ describes these interactions. Formally, τ is the largest relation such that $(((l, \mathbf{x}), \mathbf{i}), (l', \mathbf{v})) \in \tau$ implies that $\mathbf{x} \uplus \mathbf{i} \uplus \mathbf{v}' \models_T \delta(l, l')$ holds.

Winning Condition, Realizability and Synthesis Problem. We consider so called location-based winning conditions defined in terms of the infinite sequence of locations $\Lambda \subseteq L^\omega$ visited in a play. Concretely, we consider location-based parity conditions defined by a coloring function $\lambda : L \to \mathbb{N}$ that consist of $l_0 l_1 \ldots \in L^\omega$ where the largest number occurring infinitely often in $\lambda(l_0)\lambda(l_1)$ is odd. These are sufficient to describe all ω-regular temporal properties. The *realizability problem* is to compute whether there exists a strategy σ for *Sys* such that for all $\mathbf{x} \models_T dom(l_{init})$, σ is winning for *Sys* from $(l_{init}, \mathbf{x})$. The *synthesis problem* is to additionally compute some representation for σ.

Algorithm 1: Attractor Computation with Acceleration from [13].

---

1 **function** $\textsc{AttractorAccel}(\ \mathcal{G},\ p \in \{Sys, Env\},\ target \in \mathcal{D})$

3    $\quad a^0 := \lambda l.\ \bot;\ a^1 := target$

5    $\quad$ **for** $n = 1, 2, \ldots$ **do**

7    $\quad\quad$ **if** $a^n \equiv_T a^{n-1}$ **then return** a^n

8    $\quad\quad a^n(l_a) := a^n(l_a) \vee \textsc{Accelerate}(\mathcal{G}, p, a^n, l_a)$ for some $l_a \in L$

9    $\quad\quad a^{n+1} := a^n \vee CPre_{\mathcal{G},p}(a^n)$

Attractors. A key operation for solving symbolic games is *symbolic attractor computation* which is leveraged to solve general symbolic games [13]. Hence, we focus on the **problem of computing attractors in symbolic games**. Intuitively, an attractor is the set of states from which a given player p can enforce reaching a set of target states no matter what the other player does. Formally, the *player-p attractor for $R \subseteq \mathcal{S}$* in a symbolic game structure $\mathcal{G}$ is $Attr_{\mathcal{G},p}(R) := \{s \in \mathcal{S} \mid \exists \sigma \in Strat_p(\llbracket \mathcal{G} \rrbracket).\forall \pi \in Plays_{\llbracket \mathcal{G} \rrbracket}(s, \sigma).\exists n.\ \pi_n \in R\}$. We represent infinite sets of states using the *symbolic states* $\mathcal{D} : L \to FOL(\mathbb{X})$. For $d \in \mathcal{D}$, the concrete states of d are $\llbracket d \rrbracket := \{(l, \mathbf{x}) \mid \mathbf{x} \models_T d(l) \wedge \mathbf{x} \models_T dom(l)\}$. Symbolic attractors are computed using the *symbolic enforceable predecessor operator* $CPre_{\mathcal{G},p} : \mathcal{D} \to \mathcal{D}$. $CPre_{\mathcal{G},p}(d)$ represents the states from which player p can enforce reaching $\llbracket d \rrbracket$ in one step in $\mathcal{G}$ (i.e. one move by each player). Formally,

$$CPre_{\mathcal{G},Sys}(d)(l) := \ dom(l) \wedge \forall \mathbb{I}.\,ValidIn(l) \to \exists \mathbb{X}'.\textstyle\bigvee_{l' \in L} \delta(l, l') \wedge \circ dom(l') \wedge \circ d(l')$$
$$CPre_{\mathcal{G},Env}(d)(l) := \ dom(l) \wedge \exists \mathbb{I}.\,ValidIn(l) \wedge \forall \mathbb{X}'.\textstyle\bigwedge_{l' \in L} \delta(l, l') \wedge \circ dom(l') \to \circ d(l')$$

where $\circ\varphi := \varphi[\mathbb{X} \mapsto \mathbb{X}']$ and $ValidIn(l) := \exists \mathbb{X}' \bigvee_{l' \in L} .\delta(l, l') \wedge \circ dom(l')$.

Using $CPre_{\mathcal{G},p}$, the player-p attractor can be computed as a fixpoint as shown in Algorithm 1. For games with infinite state-spaces, an iterative attractor computation might not terminate. Therefore, [13] introduced *attractor acceleration*, which extends the computed attractor to help finding the fixpoint as shown in Algorithm 1. We explain how attractor acceleration works in the next section.

Theories. The above notions are independent of the theory T. The game-solving methods rely on satisfiability and, sometimes, quantifier elimination, although the latter can often be approximated soundly with the former. In practice, quantifier elimination is crucial to simplify terms. We focus on linear arithmetic.

3   Generalized Acceleration Lemmas

The iterative symbolic computation of attractors in infinite-state games is not guaranteed to terminate. As discussed in Section 1, [13] introduced a method that aims to alleviate this by *accelerating the attractor computation*. This is done by computing a form of inductive statements that establish for some (infinite) set of states the existence of a strategy for a player to enforce reachability of a given target. In [13], these inductive statements are formalized using the notion of *acceleration lemmas*, which intuitively state that: *"If starting from a set of conclusion states, a player can always enforce some step relation between states, then eventually some base set is reached.".* [13] computes acceleration lemmas by representing them via uninterpreted functions that are used in the symbolic computation. In the process, a set of constraints over these functions is constructed and must be solved to determine if acceleration can be applied and derive the respective strategy. A constraint solver then searches for an applicable acceleration lemma. As the constraints encode the existence of a strategy in the game, they quickly get quite complex, leading to scalability issues.

In this paper, we propose a new approach for computing acceleration arguments. In contrast to the "one-shot" approach of [13], our method constructs such arguments in a modular fashion by composing them from simple ones and performs the search for the argument itself. To enable composition, we introduce a novel notion, called *generalized acceleration lemmas (GALs)*, extending acceleration lemmas. Intuitively, a GAL states that *"If starting from a set of conclusion states, a player can **infinitely-often** enforce some step relation between states **and otherwise not lose progress**, then eventually some base set is reached."* Lifting the condition that the step relation is always enforced is crucial for combining arguments. It allows making progress in one part of the argument without having to make progress in another part (while not losing progress there). This is useful, for instance, for lexicographic arguments like the one in Example 1, where y remains the same while x decreases.

A GAL, formally introduced below, is a tuple $(base, stay, step, conc)$ of *FOL* formulas. The *base condition base* characterizes a set of target states. The *step relation step* and the *stay relation* are relations between states. The *conclusion conc* characterizes states from which every sequence of states in which each pair of consecutive states conforms to either *step* or *stay* will necessarily reach the target set *base*, if it conforms to *step* infinitely often. Thus, the relation *step* captures a ranking argument for establishing the reachability of *base* starting from *conc*, while *stay* captures preservation of progress. As a simple example, consider the GAL $(y \leq 0, y' \leq y, y' < y, \top)$ where y is an integer variable, which captures the fact that any sequence where y decreases infinitely often and otherwise does not increase must eventually reach a state where y is non-positive.

Definition 1 (Generalized Acceleration Lemma). *A generalized acceleration lemma (GAL) is a tuple $(base, stay, step, conc)$ of first-order formulas $base, conc \in FOL(V)$ and $stay, step \in FOL(V \cup V')$ for some $V \subseteq Vars$, where*

(I) For every sequence $\alpha \in Assignments(V)^{\omega}$, if $\alpha[0] \models_T conc$, and
  (a) for all $i \in \mathbb{N}$, $\langle \alpha[i], \alpha[i+1] \rangle \models_T step \vee stay$ and
  (b) for all $i \in \mathbb{N}$ there exists $j \geq i$ such that $\langle \alpha[j], \alpha[j+1] \rangle \models_T step$,
  then there exists some $k \in \mathbb{N}$ such that $\alpha[k] \models_T base$,
(II) and, for all $\nu, \nu' \in Assignments(V)$ with $\nu \models_T conc$ and $\langle \nu, \nu' \rangle \models_T step \vee stay$ we have that $\nu' \models_T conc$ holds.

3.1 Using (Generalized) Acceleration Lemmas (adapted from [13])

Before we present our novel method for the computation of GALs, we first explain how (generalized) acceleration lemmas are used to accelerate attractor computation. In Algorithm 2, we re-frame the procedure from [13], in that we clearly distinguish the two parts of the lemma computation: (1) the construction of a candidate lemma in line 2 of the algorithm, and (2) checking that the step of the lemma can actually be enforced by the respective player in the game, expressed using the condition constructed in line 3.

In [13], the two aspects are heavily intertwined. There, PICK simply introduces uninterpreted functions representing the lemma that is passed to the symbolic procedure for generating and verifying the applicability conditions. If the latter requires acceleration, further lemmas and constraints are accumulated.

In contrast, the approach we describe in Section 3.2 and Section 3.3 analyzes the target of the acceleration and the game to construct a concrete GAL on which the enforcement condition is then checked. An important feature of our GAL construction is that it uses the structure of the target and the game's transition relation to derive complex GALs from simpler ones using the composition operations presented in Section 3.2. As we demonstrate in Section 5, this significantly improves performance when complex acceleration arguments are needed.

In more detail, Algorithm 2 shows how acceleration is computed. The procedure accelerates iterative attractor computations based on sub-games that contain a loop at a location l in the respective location graph. A lemma must satisfy two conditions: First, $base$ should be part of the target player p tries to enforce (first conjunct in line 4). The second conjunct in line 4 requires that every state s that satisfies $conc \wedge \neg base$ also satisfies the loop-step condition ψ in 3, meaning that it should be possible to enforce from s in location l to come back to l with a state s' such that s and s' satisfy $step$. This condition is computed by LOOPSTEP.

First, LOOPSTEP constructs a so-called *loop game* [13] from location l to a copy of itself, obtained by "braking" the loop in l. LoopGame$(\mathcal{G}, l, l_{End})$ is the symbolic game structure obtained by adding a new location l_{End} and redirecting all edges in $\mathcal{G}$ with target location l to the new location l_{End}. We provide an adapted version of the definition from [13] in the full version of this paper [16].

Then, LOOPSTEP computes the attractor (or an under-approximation of it) to reach $step$ (with swapped variables, since we are doing backward computation) in the copied location of the loop game (or reach $target$ directly). For more intuition, we refer the reader to Example 7.5 from [13].

3.2 Composition Operations for Generalized Acceleration Lemmas

We now turn to the first key ingredient of our method for the synthesis of GALs, the operations for composing simpler GALs into more complex ones. The proofs of all statements in the rest of the section can be found in the full paper [16].

Two key composition operators are *intersection* and *lexicographic union*. The first one allows for reasoning about progress towards conjunctions of targets in a modular way. As established in the next lemma, if we start in the intersection of the conclusions of two GALs, we can reach the intersection of the respective bases by making progress in one of the GALs while not losing progress in the other one.

Lemma 1 (Intersection of GALs). *Let* $(base_0, stay_0, step_0, conc_0)$ *and* $(base_1, stay_1, step_1, conc_1)$ *be GALs over the same variables* V. *Then, for*

Algorithm 2: Acceleration procedure re-framed from [13].

---

1 function $\textsc{Accelerate}(\,\mathcal{G},\,p \in \{Sys, Env\},\, target \in \mathcal{D},\, l \in L)$
2 $\quad$ $\textsc{pick}\ (base, stay, step, conc) \in GALs$
3 $\quad$ $\psi := \textsc{LoopStep}(\mathcal{G}, p, target, l, step)$
4 $\quad$ **if** $(\forall \mathbb{X}.\ base \wedge dom(l) \to target(l))$ **and** $(\forall \mathbb{X}.\ conc \wedge \neg base \wedge dom(l) \to \psi)$
$\quad\quad$ **then return** $conc \wedge dom(l)$
5 $\quad$ **return** $\bot$

6 function $\textsc{LoopStep}(\,\mathcal{G},\,p \in \{Sys, Env\},\, target \in \mathcal{D},\, l \in L,\, step \in FOL(\mathbb{X}))$
7 $\quad$ $\mathcal{G}_{Loop} := \textsf{LoopGame}(\mathcal{G}, l, l_{End})$ for $l_{End} \notin L$
8 $\quad$ Let $E := \{e_x \mid x \in \mathbb{X}\}$ be fresh uninterpreted constants
9 $\quad$ $target_{loop} := \lambda l'.\textsc{if}\ l' = l_{End}\ \textsc{then}\ step[\mathbb{X} \mapsto E, \mathbb{X}' \mapsto \mathbb{X}]\ \textsc{else}\ target(l')$
10 $\quad$ $d_{Loop} := \textsc{Attractor}(\mathcal{G}_{Loop}, p, target_{loop})$ /* can under-approximate */
12 $\quad$ **return** $d_{Loop}(l)[E \mapsto \mathbb{X}]$

$step := stayBase \wedge \bigvee_{i \in \{0,1\}}(step_i \wedge \neg base_i \wedge stay_{1-i})$ and
$stayBase := \bigwedge_{i \in \{0,1\}}((base_i \wedge \neg base_{1-i}) \to base_i[\mathbb{X} \mapsto \mathbb{X}'])$, the tuple
$(base_0 \wedge base_1, stay_0 \wedge stay_1 \wedge stayBase, step, conc_0 \wedge conc_1)$ is also a GAL.

Note that $step$ ensures that we do not stop making progress in one of the GALs after reaching the base of the other, by excluding the bases from doing a step.

The second combination, akin to lexicographic combinations of ranking functions, allows us to combine two GALs via union. The union combination is lexicographic, i.e. if we make progress on the first GAL, this is fine regardless of the other one. If instead we only progress on the second one, we should not lose progress in the first one. The last condition ensures that it is not possible to jump back and forth between the two GALs to cancel out the progress made.

Lemma 2 (Lexicographic-Union of GALs). *Let* $(base_0, stay_0, step_0, conc_0)$ *and* $(base_1, stay_1, step_1, conc_1)$ *be GALs over the same variables* V. *Then, for* $step := (conc_0 \wedge step_0) \vee (conc_1 \wedge step_1 \wedge stay_0)$, *the tuple* $(base_0 \vee base_1, stay_0 \wedge stay_1, step, conc_0 \vee conc_1)$ *is also a GAL.*

Example 3. These two operations allow us to build up the enforcement argument for Example 1 from individual ones for each of the two variables. The intersection $lem_{x,y}$ of $(y \leq 0, y' \leq y, y' < y, \top)$ and $(x \leq 0, x' \leq x, x' < x, \top)$ ensures that $y \leq 0 \wedge x \leq 0$ is reached if each of x and y can be decreased while the other one is not increasing. However, this cannot be enforced in the game in Figure 1a, since by always setting b to true in *loop* and picking larger and larger values for i, the environment can prevent progress on x. If, however, we take the lexicographic union with first element $lem_y := (y \leq 0, y' \leq y, y' < y, \top)$ and second element $lem_{x,y}$ we obtain a GAL that states that $y \leq 0 \vee (y \leq 0 \wedge x \leq 0)$ can be reached from any state if the lexicographic step relation $(y' < y) \vee (step_{x,y} \wedge y' \leq y)$ can be enforced. This is indeed possible, as explained informally in Example 1. This GAL is the one automatically constructed by our implementation and is sufficient for accelerating the attractor computation for the game in Figure 1a.

The GAL constructed in the previous example requires the introduction of the sub-lemma about x, which enables the main argument on y. It is sometimes easier to find such arguments in the form of a "chain" of two GALs by analysis of the transition relations in the game structure. More concretely, we can chain two GALs by extending the step relation of the first GAL by the possibility to perform the step of the second GAL until it reaches its base. This can then be used as an additional condition enabling a step in the first GAL. However, theoretically this is subsumed by applying Lemmas 1 and 2 to $\varphi \equiv \varphi \vee (\varphi \wedge \psi)$.

Lemma 3 (Chaining of GALs). *Let $(base_0, stay_0, step_0, conc_0)$ and $(base_1, stay_1, step_1, conc_1)$ be GALs over the same variables V. Then for $step := step_0 \vee (conc_1 \wedge \neg base_1 \wedge step_1 \wedge stay_0)$ and $stay := stay_0 \wedge stay_1 \wedge (base_1 \to base_1[\mathbb{X} \mapsto \mathbb{X}'])$ the tuple $(base_0, stay, step, conc_0)$ is also a GAL.*

In complex games, it is useful to restrict a GAL to only take effect in a specific sub-part of the state space by adding an invariant as follows.

Lemma 4 (Invariant Strengthening of GALs (extended from [13])). *Let $(base, stay, step, conc)$ be a GAL over V and $inv \in FOL(V)$. Then for $inv' := inv[V \mapsto V']$, $(base \wedge inv, stay \wedge inv', step \wedge inv', conc \wedge inv)$ is also a GAL.*

3.3   Computation of Generalized Acceleration Lemmas

In the rest of this section, we present our method for computing GALs that are possibly useful to reach a given $target \in \mathcal{D}$ in a location $l \in L$. We use the operations from the previous subsection to compose GALs as the building blocks forming the base layer for applying the combinations. We use GALs whose components are inequalities between affine terms, as formalized in the next lemma.

Lemma 5 (Inequality Base GALs). *Let t be a linear term over numeric variables V and let $a \in \mathbb{R} \cup \{-\infty\}$, $b \in \mathbb{R} \cup \{\infty\}$ with $a \leq b$ be bounds. Then, $(base, stay, step, conc)$ is a GAL for $t' := t[V \mapsto V']$ and $\epsilon > 0$,*

- *$base := a \leq t \leq b$, $conc := \top$,*
- *$stay := (a \leq t' \leq b) \vee (t < a \wedge t \leq t' \leq b) \vee (t > b \wedge t \geq t' \geq a)$, and*
- *$step := (a \leq t' \leq b) \vee (t < a \wedge t + \epsilon \leq t' \leq b) \vee (t > b \wedge t - \epsilon \geq t' \geq a)$.*

Note that there also exist variants of the above GAL with strict inequalities, but we omit those for the brevity of the presentation. Also, Lemma 5 is specific to linear arithmetic, and other theories would need analogous lemmas.

Starting from inequality base GALs, our method proceeds in two phases. First, we consider the formula $target(l)$ in order to derive suitable base GALs, strengthen them with invariants, and build combinations thereof. Next, we consider the given game structure $\mathcal{G}$ and the conditions that need to be satisfied to enforce the step relation in $\mathcal{G}$. We now describe the two phases in detail.

We begin by rewriting $target(l)$ into a disjunction of polyhedra conjuncted with (non-linear) terms (which is always possible), i.e., into the form $target(l) \equiv \bigvee_{i=1,...,n} A_i \mathbf{x} \leq c_i \wedge \psi_i(\mathbb{X})$ for matrices A_i, constant vectors c_i, a vector $\mathbf{x}$ for the numeric variables in $\mathbb{X}$ and remaining constraints ψ_i for all variables. For each disjunct, we select a subset of the inequalities of the polyhedra to get GALs by Lemma 5, which we combine using Lemma 1. We then add the remaining inequalities and the non-linear terms as invariants using Lemma 4. The disjuncts (or a subset of those) can then be combined in different orders by Lemma 2. These steps are carried out in line 2 of our method for constructing GALs shown in Algorithm 3. As there are multiple combinations, this provides a well-defined space of lemmas to search through based on the $target(l)$ that we want to reach.

Example 4. Suppose that $target(l) = (q \wedge 3x + 2y \leq z \wedge z \leq 4x \vee \neg q \wedge 2x = y)$ for Boolean input q and numerical variables x, y and z. One option is to pick $3x + 2y \leq z$ from the first disjunctct and $y \leq 2x$ from the second one, and use each of them as the *base* for a base GAL as per Lemma 5. After that, applying Lemma 4, we strengthen each of them with an invariant consisting of the Boolean term and the remaining inequality from the respective disjunct. Finally, we can combine the resulting GALs using Lemma 2.

Next, we account for the need to enforce the step relation in the game, which also allows us to generate sub-arguments for chain combinations via Lemma 3. To this end, in Algorithm 3 we consider the *enforcement condition for acceleration* lemmas as computed by LoopStep (shown in Algorithm 2) and use it to generate the intermediate arguments. More precisely, *pre* in line 4 is the condition that enables player p to enforce the step relation *once*. If this condition is not implied by the GAL's precondition (that is, the check in line 5 fails), we attempt to fulfill it by either making it an invariant or by computing a sub-lemma that establishes this condition as a sub-argument. Note that we might want to iterate this process, as, e.g., strengthening the lemma with an invariant makes the step condition harder to apply and might need even a stronger invariant. While this process is not guaranteed to succeed with an applicable lemma, it provides a robust method for computing GALs, as demonstrated by our experimental evaluation.

Note that Recurse? and Iterate? are heuristics that determine the space of GALs we search through. In practice, we found it effective to start with a few iterations and recursions, gradually increasing them if acceleration fails.

4   Enforcement Summaries

In this section, we define enforcement summaries and demonstrate their use and computation. Intuitively, an enforcement summary is a *parametrized formula* φ that states that player p can enforce to reach a symbolic state d starting from a location l_s and assignment for $\mathbb{X}$ that φ describes when its parameters are instantiated by d. To insert values of a symbolic state into a formula, we represent the parameters as uninterpreted function symbols. However, those are merely syntactic placeholders, and we perform no computation on them. In most cases, it is not possible to fully characterize in FOL all states from which any arbitrary symbolic state d is enforceable by a given player. Hence, enforcement

---

Algorithm 3: Computation of generalized acceleration lemmas.

```
1  function GETGAL( G, p ∈ {Sys, Env}, l ∈ L, target ∈ D)
2  |    (base, stay, step, conc) := Get lemma from target using Lemmas 5, 4, 2, 1
3  |    while ITERATE? do
4  |    |    pre := LOOPSTEP(G, p, target, l, step)
5  |    |    if ∀X. conc ∧ ¬base ∧ dom(l) → pre then
6  |    |    |    return (base, stay, step, conc)
7  |    |    if RECURSE? then
8  |    |    |    subGAL := GETGAL(G, p, l, λl'.IF l = l' THEN pre ELSE ⊥)
9  |    |    |    Chain subGAL to (base, stay, step, conc) using Lemma 3
10 |    |    else
11 |    |    |    Add pre as invariant to (base, stay, step, conc) with Lemma 4
```

---

summaries have the following characteristics: First, they can *under-approximate* the starting set from which d is enforceable. Second, they do not apply to all possible d but can be *restricted to a subset* of $\mathcal{D}$. Formally, that is:

Definition 2 (Enforcement Summary). *Let $\mathcal{G} = (L, l_{init}, \mathbb{I}, \mathbb{X}, dom, \delta)$ be a symbolic game structure. An* enforcement summary *in $\mathcal{G}$ is a tuple (p, l_s, φ, D) where $p \in \{Env, Sys\}$, $l_s \in L$ is the support location, $D \subseteq \mathcal{D}$ is the support set, and $\varphi \in FOL(\mathbb{X})$ is the summary statement with uninterpreted function symbols $next_l$ over $\mathbb{X}$ for all $l \in L$ such that for every $d \in D$ we have*

$$[\![\varphi(next_l \mapsto d(l) \mid l \in L)]\!] \subseteq Attr_{\mathcal{G},p}([\![d]\!])(l_s).$$

For a finite characterization of D, we use template formulas over state and *meta-variables*. Those describe all symbolic states for which meta-values exist such that the template is a subset of the symbolic state. More precisely, a *set of meta-variables $Meta \subseteq Vars \setminus \mathbb{X}$* and a template $\tau : L \to FOL(\mathbb{X} \cup Meta)$ define the support set $D = \{d \in \mathcal{D} \mid \exists Meta.\forall l \in L.\forall \mathbb{X}.\tau(l) \to d(l) \text{ holds}\}$.

Usage. The application of enforcement summaries follows Definition 2. During attractor computation for player p in $\mathcal{G}$, if for a summary (p, l_s, φ, D) the current attractor a is in D, we extend $a(l_s)$ by φ with the uninterpreted functions substituted by the current values of a. By Definition 2, we have that the added set is indeed subset of $Attr_{\mathcal{G},p}([\![target]\!])(l_s)$. Algorithm 4 formalizes this.

Example 5. Recall Example 2. The enforcement summary for the system player described informally there has support location *loop*. The summary statement is $\varphi := \exists m_c, m_y.((c = m_c \land y = m_y) \to next_{loop}(x, y, c)) \land c = m_c$. If we apply this for attractor a with $a(loop) = (c \geq -199) \land y \leq 0$, we get $\exists m_c, m_y.((c = m_c \land y = m_y) \to (c \geq -199 \land y \leq 0)) \land c = m_c$ which simplifies to $c \geq -199$. Hence, we set $a(loop) := (c \geq -199)$ and reach a fixpoint in *loop* after a single step.

Algorithm 4: Attractor computation using summaries.

---

1 function $\textsc{AttractorSumm}($ $\mathcal{G}$, $p \in \{Sys, Env\}$, $target \in \mathcal{D}$, $Summaries)$

2 $\quad$ . . .

7 $\quad$ **if** $a^n \equiv_T a^{n-1}$ **then return** a^n

8 $\quad$ **foreach** $(p, l_s, \varphi, D) \in Summaries$ *for* $\mathcal{G}$ **do**

9 $\quad\quad$ **if** $a^n \in D$ /* Checked by validity query for representation.   */

10 $\quad\quad$ **then**

11 $\quad\quad\quad$ $a^n(l_s) := a^n(l_s) \ \vee \ \varphi(\!|next_l \mapsto a^n(l) \mid l \in L|\!)$

12 $\quad$ . . .

4.1   Computation of Enforcement Summaries

Our game-solving method computes enforcement summaries for a given location based on a template characterization of D. It does so by performing attractor computation on the template, keeping the meta-variables constant. The later is done by *lifting* $\mathcal{G} = (L, l_{init}, \mathbb{I}, \mathbb{X}, dom, \delta)$ by meta-variables $Meta \subseteq Vars$ to the symbolic game structure $\mathcal{G} \uparrow Meta = (L, l_{init}, \mathbb{I}, \mathbb{X} \cup Meta, dom, \delta_C)$ with $\delta_C(l, l') := \delta(l, l') \wedge \bigwedge_{m \in Meta} m = m'$. The result of this attractor computation in the aforementioned location is then the summary statement, which is formally stated in the next lemma.

Lemma 6. *Let $\mathcal{G}$ be a symbolic game structure as above, $Meta \subseteq Vars$ meta-variables, and $\tau : L \to FOL(\mathbb{X} \cup Meta)$ a template. Note that τ is an element of the symbolic states of $\mathcal{G} \uparrow Meta$. If for $p \in \{Env, Sys\}$ and $l_s \in L$, $[\![\psi]\!] \subseteq Attr_{\mathcal{G} \uparrow Meta, p}([\![\tau]\!])(l_s)$ holds with $\psi \in FOL(\mathbb{X} \cup Meta)$, then (p, l_s, φ, D) with $\varphi := \exists Meta.\, \psi \wedge \bigwedge_{l \in L} \forall \mathbb{X}.\, (\tau(l) \to next_l)$ is an enforcement summary in $\mathcal{G}$.*

When applying φ by replacing $next_l$ with some actual symbolic state, it is helpful to apply quantifier elimination. As ψ can be an under-approximation of the attractor to the template, we can do the summary computation as an anytime computation. That is, within a given budget, we try to get as good a summary as possible, and we restrict the computation to a part of the overall game. Furthermore, as the computation reduces to a normal symbolic attractor computation, we can use all available acceleration techniques. Additionally, this makes summary computation very amenable to being done on demand as needed. Next, we describe how we utilize this approach to compute the templates.

Template Computation. For a support location l_s and a current attractor subset $a \in \mathcal{D}$, we compute a template by generalizing a. This helps with obtaining summaries that are more broadly applicable. To this end, we analyze the game around l_s to identify variables $G \subseteq \mathbb{X}$, over which to generalize. For a location subset $L_S \subseteq L$, variables $G \subseteq \mathbb{X}$, and current attractor subset $a \in \mathcal{D}$ we derive a template as follows. We introduce one meta-variable per location in $L_S \setminus \{l_s\}$ and variable in G, i.e. $Meta := \{m_x^l \mid l \in L_S \setminus \{l_s\}, x \in G\}$, and define τ for all $l \in L$:

$$\tau(l) := \text{IF } l \in L_S \setminus \{l_s\} \text{ THEN } \text{QELIM}(\exists G.a(l)) \wedge \left(\bigwedge_{x \in G} (x = m_x^l) \right) \text{ ELSE } \bot.$$

The first conjunct[1] states the most general condition for the variables $\mathbb{X} \setminus G$, such that we can still apply the template in a. The second part characterizes (parameterized) assignments for the variables in G. Summaries where individual assignments can be enforced are easy to apply generally.

To select L_S, we start with the support location l_s in question and add more locations reachable from it, starting with smaller (local) sets then moving to more global ones. We select the variables for G, according to a novel notion of *point-enforceable variables*. Intuitively, a variable x is point-enforceable if player p can, for some states, enforce for x to reach any specific value. Formally, $x \in \mathbb{X}$ is point-enforceable by player p in $L_S \subseteq L$, if for all $l \in L_S$ the following is true

$$\exists \mathbb{X} \setminus \{x\}. \forall c. \exists x. CPre_{\mathcal{G}\uparrow\{c\},p}(\lambda l'. \text{ IF } l' \in Successor_{\mathcal{G}}(l) \text{ THEN } x = c \text{ ELSE } \bot)$$

where c is a fresh variable and $Successor_{\mathcal{G}}(l) \subseteq L$ are the successors of l.

These variables are useful for generalization, as they allow us to propagate equalities in the proposed templates, and with this, generalize over arbitrary conditions on those variables. This notion is more general than that of *independent variables* (i.e., variables that do not change) from [30].

Remark 1. Unlike the precomputed attractor acceleration caches in [30], our enforcement summaries are computed during the actual game-solving. As a consequence, the result is in general better suited for subsequent applications. Also, note that enforcement summaries are conceptually more general than attractor acceleration caches and are computed differently.

Example 6. In our example, for $l_s = loop$ and a with $a(iter) = \top$ we select $L_S = \{loop, iter\}$ and $G = \{c\}$ and obtain a template where $\tau(iter) = (c = m_c^{iter}) \wedge (x = m_x^{iter}) \wedge (y = m_y^{iter})$. The computation in the game $\mathcal{G} \uparrow Meta$ results in attractor mapping $loop$ to $c = m_c^{iter}$, from which we obtain the summary statement shown in Example 5.

5   Implementation and Experimental Evaluation

We implemented[2] our acceleration method in the open-source tool `Issy` [14]. `Issy` implements different symbolic solving methods and versions of attractor acceleration and allows writing benchmarks as temporal logic formulas and games.

We compare our method (with and without summaries) against the standard version of `Issy`, `Issy` without acceleration, `sweap` [1], `Syntheos` [25], and

---

[1] QELIM($\cdot$) is the result of quantifier elimination applied to the argument.

[2] The implementation, all benchmarks, the data of the results, and the competing tools are available in the artifact at https://doi.org/10.5281/zenodo.18163658.

MuVal [33]. The last three solve LTL objectives over program arenas, $LTL^{\mathcal{T}}$, and fixpoint equations, respectively. As [14], we do not use [9, 28, 6, 29, 26, 27, 24] as their prototypes are unavailable, not usable, or are outperformed by the state-of-the-art. We also do not include the prototypes from [13, 30, 15] as those are integrated in Issy. We also omit [20] as it does not have any acceleration techniques and Issy outperforms it [14].

Benchmarks. We use 76 rpg benchmarks from [22, 13, 30], 56 tslmt benchmarks from [22, 20, 15], 22 prog benchmarks from [22, 1], 41 $LTL^{\mathcal{T}}$ benchmarks from [26, 25], and 81 issy benchmarks from [14]. As the tools use different formalisms and formats, we implemented automatic encodings and used those if a tool does not accept the native benchmark. This includes translations from $LTL^{\mathcal{T}}$ to issy, prog to issy, and from each of rpg, tslmt, and issy to each of prog, $LTL^{\mathcal{T}}$, and hes, where hes is the format for MuVal. We discarded manually translated benchmarks used in other works[3] as we found that some of those contain serious mistakes, e.g., introducing falsity in the assumptions.

However, to be semantic preserving, the automatic encoding is sometimes fairly elaborate. In particular, since sweap's formalism does not support unbounded inputs or outputs (such as integers), those have to be modeled as multi-step inputs or outputs, resulting in overhead that can affect performance. It was sometimes unclear what some of the tools accept, with errors occurring late at runtime. Also, some benchmarks from [1] are not well-defined according to their semantics, and we choose an interpretation that seems to be different from sweap. Nevertheless, an automatic encoding is the better scientific choice.

We created new benchmarks for which we expected that more complicated acceleration arguments would be needed than in the existing ones. Some are abstract and conceptual, while others are application-inspired, and they are both temporal formulas and games. We also adapted verification examples from [19].

Results. We ran all experiments on an AMD EPYC processor with 1 core, 6GB of memory, and a 20-minute wall-clock time-out per run. Figure 2 and Table 1 show the results on the literature benchmarks. We did not use enforcement summaries there, as they would introduce additional overhead. However, they are not required for those benchmarks that are already handled well by existing techniques. Table 2 shows the results on the new benchmarks. If not stated otherwise, we ran the tools (if possible) to check realizability. We do not distinguish between runtime errors and out-of-memory errors for technical reasons.

Discussion. Overall, the results indicate that our new technique for composing acceleration arguments broadens the range of solvable problems while remaining competitive with the state of the art. Table 1 shows that from the literature benchmarks, it has the most unique solves. In Figure 2 we see that the overall performance on these benchmarks is comparable to the state-of-the-art tool Issy. The results on new benchmarks reported in Table 2 show that our tool

---

[3] This is why some results in the literature might look fairly different.

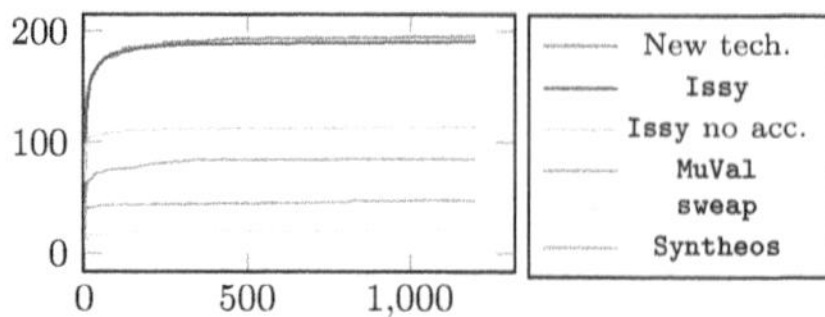

Name	Tot	Sol	Un	TO	NR
New tech.	239	195	13	40	4
Issy	239	191	3	32	16
Issy no acc.	239	113	1	71	55
sweap	206	20	6	59	127
MuVal	239	84	4	80	75
Syntheos	180	47	0	37	96

Fig. 2: Solved literature benchmarks (out of 239) within time in seconds. The new technique is without summaries.

Table 1: On 239 literature benchmarks, **Tot**al applicable, **Sol**ved, **Un**iquely solved (full list in [16]), **T**ime**O**ut, **N**o**R**esult (MO/err.)

Name	W	NT	SU	I	A	W	Y	M	NT-S	SU-S
buchi	R	**63**	T	T	T	T	N	T	95	T
buchi-simple	R	**19**	T	T	T	N	T	T	38	T
choice-3-actions	R	**1**	2	4	T	T	N	T	213	N
choice-4-actions	R	**1**	2	9	T	T	N	T	N	T
choice-actions-i	R	**16**	T	T	T	T	N	T	599	T
equal-mod2-real	R	**1**	T	2	T	N	T	T	4	T
fault-tolerance	R	**4**	T	T	T	N	-	T	T	T
lemma-chain-control	R	**1**	2	T	T	N	-	T	T	N
lemma-chain	R	**1**	2	T	T	N	-	T	73	T
nested-x-y-z	R	**39**	42	T	T	N	N	T	T	T
nondet-exit-swap-in	R	**1**	2	3	T	T	-	T	485	N
nondet-exit-swap	R	**1**	2	3	T	T	-	T	5	T
prevent-zeno	R	**3**	12	N	T	-	N	N	N	T
ranking-choice-2	R	**4**	T	T	T	T	N	T	78	T
ranking-choice-3	R	**26**	T	T	T	T	N	T	327	T
ranking-choice-4	R	**507**	T	T	T	T	N	T	T	T
transfer-lin-constr.	R	**1**	T	T	T	-	N	N	T	T
uav-chaotic-unreal	U	**5**	7	T	T	-	N	N	-	-
bu-hard-loop-200	U	282	62	T	T	N	-	**24**	-	-
bu-hard-loop-400	U	784	121	T	T	N	-	**14**	-	-
bu-hard-loop-800	U	T	241	T	T	N	-	**29**	-	-
equal-mod2-unreal	U	T	T	T	T	N	N	**39**	-	-
inequality-assump.	R	15	T	**5**	T	T	N	T	41	T
prio-tasks-real-100	R	T	1125	**378**	T	T	N	T	T	T
prio-tasks-real-200	R	T	T	**758**	T	T	N	T	T	T
prio-tasks-unre-100	U	58	8	**2**	T	T	N	288	-	-
rect-patrol-buchi	R	T	T	N	**29**	-	N	N	T	T
service-2	R	14	T	**11**	T	N	N	T	73	T
service-4	R	77	T	**24**	T	N	N	N	480	T

Name	W	NT	SU	I	A	W	Y	M	NT-S	SU-S
service-8	R	1160	T	**45**	T	N	N	N	T	T
service-bounds-10	R	167	T	**19**	T	N	N	T	609	T
service-bounds-20	R	166	T	**19**	T	N	N	T	608	T
double	R	T	T	T	T	N	N	T	T	T
equality-assump.	R	T	T	T	T	T	N	T	T	T
nested-x-y-z-u	R	T	T	T	T	N	N	T	T	T
nested-x-y-z-u-v	R	T	T	T	T	N	T	T	T	T
service-10	R	T	T	T	T	N	N	N	T	T
bu-loop-200	R	96	**55**	T	T	N	-	T	111	68
bu-loop-400	R	190	**108**	T	T	N	-	T	218	126
bu-loop-800	R	381	**216**	T	T	N	-	T	430	248
bu-loop-chain-200	R	813	**55**	T	T	T	-	T	1133	N
bu-loop-chain-400	R	T	**108**	T	T	N	-	T	T	N
bu-loop-chain-800	R	T	**215**	T	T	N	-	T	T	N
bu-loop-swap-200	R	512	**55**	709	T	T	-	T	T	N
bu-loop-swap-400	R	1014	**111**	T	T	T	-	T	T	N
bu-loop-swap-800	R	T	**220**	T	T	T	-	T	T	N
reach-either-or	R	**1**	**1**	T	T	N	-	T	2	N
torus-game	R	21	**19**	92	T	-	N	N	N	T
uav-chaotic	R	T	**38**	T	T	-	N	N	T	N
ex-2-05 (*adapted*	R	**1**	2	2	T	N	T	T	2	N
ex-4-06 *from*	R	**1**	2	**1**	T	N	T	T	6	N
ex-4-11 [19])	R	**1**	T	4	T	N	T	T	T	T
ex-4-12	U	T	T	T	T	T	T	**98**	-	-
ex-4-13	R	T	T	T	T	T	N	T	T	T
ex-4-15	R	T	T	T	T	T	N	T	T	T
ex-4-18	R	**1**	2	T	T	N	-	T	353	356
ex-4-21	R	**1**	32	**1**	T	N	-	T	4	T
ex-5-01	R	**110**	115	T	T	N	N	T	T	N

Table 2: Run on new benchmarks which are **R**ealizable or **U**nrealizable of the **N**ew **T**echnique, new technique with **SU**mmaries, **Issy**, **Issy** without **A**cceleration, s**W**eap, **SY**ntheos, **MuVal**, and synthesis variants (*-**S**), depicting resulting runtime in seconds, **T**imeout, **N**o result, or not applicable (-). The runs were grouped retrospectively.

can discover complex acceleration arguments and solve games that other tools fail to handle. The closest competitor, **Issy**, can in some cases find simple arguments where the GAL search explores unfruitful parts of the lemma space. As expected, the use of summaries provides notable performance benefits on benchmarks where similar GALs are otherwise computed over and over again, such as most of the Büchi game benchmarks. However, summary computation can introduce significant overhead, as our implementation allocates a lot of time for computing summaries and blocks the remaining computation. This could be mitigated by interleaving summary computation with the main analysis.

In the future, we plan to address the observed performance drawbacks in the current GAL computation. We aim to develop better strategies for guiding the GAL search, for example, by applying data-flow analysis to the symbolic game. Other scalability challenges (e.g., for synthesis) stem from the complexity of generated terms and the current limitations of **Issy**'s term simplification mechanism. We believe incorporating abstraction techniques can be fruitful there.

Data Availability Statement. The software generated during and analysed during the current study, as well as the associated data and benchmarks, is available in the Zenodo repository https://doi.org/10.5281/zenodo.18163658. A full version of this paper is available through arXiv [16].

Disclosure of Interests. The authors have no competing interests to declare that are relevant to the content of this article.

References

1. Azzopardi, S., Stefano, L.D., Piterman, N., Schneider, G.: Full LTL synthesis over infinite-state arenas. In: Piskac, R., Rakamaric, Z. (eds.) Computer Aided Verification - 37th International Conference, CAV 2025, Zagreb, Croatia, July 23-25, 2025, Proceedings, Part IV. Lecture Notes in Computer Science, vol. 15934, pp. 274–297. Springer (2025). https://doi.org/10.1007/978-3-031-98685-7_13, https://doi.org/10.1007/978-3-031-98685-7_13
2. Bagnara, R., Mesnard, F., Pescetti, A., Zaffanella, E.: A new look at the automatic synthesis of linear ranking functions. Inf. Comput. **215**, 47–67 (2012). https://doi.org/10.1016/J.IC.2012.03.003, https://doi.org/10.1016/j.ic.2012.03.003
3. Bardin, S., Finkel, A., Leroux, J., Petrucci, L.: FAST: fast acceleration of symbolic transition systems. In: Jr., W.A.H., Somenzi, F. (eds.) Computer Aided Verification, 15th International Conference, CAV 2003. LNCS, vol. 2725, pp. 118–121. Springer (2003). https://doi.org/10.1007/978-3-540-45069-6_12
4. Bardin, S., Finkel, A., Leroux, J., Schnoebelen, P.: Flat acceleration in symbolic model checking. In: Peled, D.A., Tsay, Y. (eds.) Automated Technology for Verification and Analysis, Third International Symposium, ATVA 2005. LNCS, vol. 3707, pp. 474–488. Springer (2005). https://doi.org/10.1007/11562948_35
5. Borralleras, C., Brockschmidt, M., Larraz, D., Oliveras, A., Rodríguez-Carbonell, E., Rubio, A.: Proving termination through conditional termination. In: Legay, A., Margaria, T. (eds.) Tools and Algorithms for the Construction and Analysis of Systems - 23rd International Conference, TACAS 2017, Held as Part of the European Joint Conferences on Theory and Practice of Software, ETAPS 2017, Uppsala, Sweden, April 22-29, 2017, Proceedings, Part I. Lecture Notes in Computer Science, vol. 10205, pp. 99–117 (2017). https://doi.org/10.1007/978-3-662-54577-5_6, https://doi.org/10.1007/978-3-662-54577-5_6
6. Choi, W., Finkbeiner, B., Piskac, R., Santolucito, M.: Can reactive synthesis and syntax-guided synthesis be friends? In: Jhala, R., Dillig, I. (eds.) PLDI '22: 43rd ACM SIGPLAN International Conference on Programming Language Design and Implementation, 2022. pp. 229–243. ACM (2022). https://doi.org/10.1145/3519939.3523429
7. Colón, M., Sipma, H.: Synthesis of linear ranking functions. In: Margaria, T., Yi, W. (eds.) Tools and Algorithms for the Construction and Analysis of Systems, 7th International Conference, TACAS 2001 Held as Part of the Joint European Conferences on Theory and Practice of Software, ETAPS 2001 Genova, Italy, April 2-6, 2001, Proceedings. Lecture Notes in Computer Science, vol. 2031, pp. 67–81. Springer (2001). https://doi.org/10.1007/3-540-45319-9_6, https://doi.org/10.1007/3-540-45319-9_6

8. Faella, M., Parlato, G.: Reachability games modulo theories with a bounded safety player. In: Proceedings of the Thirty-Seventh AAAI Conference on Artificial Intelligence and Thirty-Fifth Conference on Innovative Applications of Artificial Intelligence and Thirteenth Symposium on Educational Advances in Artificial Intelligence. AAAI Press (2023). https://doi.org/10.1609/aaai.v37i5.25779
9. Farzan, A., Kincaid, Z.: Strategy synthesis for linear arithmetic games. Proc. ACM Program. Lang. **2**(POPL), 61:1–61:30 (2018). https://doi.org/10.1145/3158149
10. Fedyukovich, G., Zhang, Y., Gupta, A.: Syntax-guided termination analysis. In: Chockler, H., Weissenbacher, G. (eds.) Computer Aided Verification - 30th International Conference, CAV 2018, Held as Part of the Federated Logic Conference, FloC 2018, Oxford, UK, July 14-17, 2018, Proceedings, Part I. Lecture Notes in Computer Science, vol. 10981, pp. 124–143. Springer (2018). https://doi.org/10.1007/978-3-319-96145-3_7, https://doi.org/10.1007/978-3-319-96145-3_7
11. Frohn, F.: A calculus for modular loop acceleration. In: Biere, A., Parker, D. (eds.) Tools and Algorithms for the Construction and Analysis of Systems - 26th International Conference, TACAS 2020, Held as Part of the European Joint Conferences on Theory and Practice of Software, ETAPS 2020, Dublin, Ireland, April 25-30, 2020, Proceedings, Part I. Lecture Notes in Computer Science, vol. 12078, pp. 58–76. Springer (2020). https://doi.org/10.1007/978-3-030-45190-5_4, https://doi.org/10.1007/978-3-030-45190-5_4
12. Frohn, F., Giesl, J.: Proving non-termination via loop acceleration. In: Barrett, C.W., Yang, J. (eds.) 2019 Formal Methods in Computer Aided Design, FMCAD 2019, San Jose, CA, USA, October 22-25, 2019. pp. 221–230. IEEE (2019). https://doi.org/10.23919/FMCAD.2019.8894271, https://doi.org/10.23919/FMCAD.2019.8894271
13. Heim, P., Dimitrova, R.: Solving infinite-state games via acceleration. Proc. ACM Program. Lang. **8**(POPL), 1696–1726 (2024). https://doi.org/10.1145/3632899
14. Heim, P., Dimitrova, R.: Issy: A comprehensive tool for specification and synthesis of infinite-state reactive systems. In: Piskac, R., Rakamaric, Z. (eds.) Computer Aided Verification - 37th International Conference, CAV 2025, Zagreb, Croatia, July 23-25, 2025, Proceedings, Part IV. Lecture Notes in Computer Science, vol. 15934, pp. 298–312. Springer (2025). https://doi.org/10.1007/978-3-031-98685-7_14, https://doi.org/10.1007/978-3-031-98685-7_14
15. Heim, P., Dimitrova, R.: Translation of temporal logic for efficient infinite-state reactive synthesis. Proc. ACM Program. Lang. **9**(POPL), 1536–1567 (2025). https://doi.org/10.1145/3704888
16. Heim, P., Dimitrova, R.: Modular attractor acceleration in infinite-state games (full version) (2026). https://doi.org/10.48550/arXiv.2601.14068
17. Kincaid, Z., Breck, J., Cyphert, J., Reps, T.W.: Closed forms for numerical loops. Proc. ACM Program. Lang. **3**(POPL), 55:1–55:29 (2019). https://doi.org/10.1145/3290368, https://doi.org/10.1145/3290368
18. Kroening, D., Sharygina, N., Tonetta, S., Tsitovich, A., Wintersteiger, C.M.: Loop summarization using state and transition invariants. Formal Methods Syst. Des. **42**(3), 221–261 (2013). https://doi.org/10.1007/s10703-012-0176-y
19. Leike, J., Heizmann, M.: Ranking templates for linear loops. Log. Methods Comput. Sci. **11**(1) (2015). https://doi.org/10.2168/LMCS-11(1:16)2015, https://doi.org/10.2168/LMCS-11(1:16)2015
20. Maderbacher, B., Bloem, R.: Reactive synthesis modulo theories using abstraction refinement. In: Griggio, A., Rungta, N. (eds.) 22nd Formal Meth-

ods in Computer-Aided Design, FMCAD 2022. pp. 315–324. IEEE (2022). https://doi.org/10.34727/2022/ISBN.978-3-85448-053-2_38
21. Maderbacher, B., Windisch, F., Bloem, R.: Synthesis from infinite-state generalized reactivity(1) specifications. In: Margaria, T., Steffen, B. (eds.) Leveraging Applications of Formal Methods, Verification and Validation. Software Engineering Methodologies - 12th International Symposium, ISoLA 2024. LNCS, vol. 15222, pp. 281–301. Springer (2024). https://doi.org/10.1007/978-3-031-75387-9_17
22. Neider, D., Topcu, U.: An automaton learning approach to solving safety games over infinite graphs. In: Chechik, M., Raskin, J. (eds.) Tools and Algorithms for the Construction and Analysis of Systems - 22nd International Conference, TACAS 2016. LNCS, vol. 9636, pp. 204–221. Springer (2016). https://doi.org/10.1007/978-3-662-49674-9_12
23. Pimpalkhare, N., Kincaid, Z.: Monotone procedure summarization via vector addition systems and inductive potentials. Proc. ACM Program. Lang. **8**(OOPSLA2), 1873–1899 (2024). https://doi.org/10.1145/3689777, https://doi.org/10.1145/3689777
24. Rodríguez, A., Gorostiaga, F., Sánchez, C.: Predictable and performant reactive synthesis modulo theories via functional synthesis. In: Akshay, S., Niemetz, A., Sankaranarayanan, S. (eds.) Automated Technology for Verification and Analysis - 22nd International Symposium, ATVA 2024. LNCS, vol. 15055, pp. 28–50. Springer (2024). https://doi.org/10.1007/978-3-031-78750-8_2
25. Rodríguez, A., Gorostiaga, F., Sánchez, C.: Counter example guided reactive synthesis for LTL modulo theories[*]. In: Piskac, R., Rakamaric, Z. (eds.) Computer Aided Verification - 37th International Conference, CAV 2025, Zagreb, Croatia, July 23-25, 2025, Proceedings, Part IV. Lecture Notes in Computer Science, vol. 15934, pp. 224–248. Springer (2025). https://doi.org/10.1007/978-3-031-98685-7_11, https://doi.org/10.1007/978-3-031-98685-7_11
26. Rodríguez, A., Sánchez, C.: Boolean abstractions for realizability modulo theories. In: Enea, C., Lal, A. (eds.) Computer Aided Verification - 35th International Conference, CAV 2023. LNCS, vol. 13966, pp. 305–328. Springer (2023). https://doi.org/10.1007/978-3-031-37709-9_15
27. Rodríguez, A., Sánchez, C.: Adaptive reactive synthesis for LTL and LTLf modulo theories. In: Wooldridge, M.J., Dy, J.G., Natarajan, S. (eds.) Thirty-Eighth AAAI Conference on Artificial Intelligence, AAAI 2024, Thirty-Sixth Conference on Innovative Applications of Artificial Intelligence, IAAI 2024, Fourteenth Symposium on Educational Advances in Artificial Intelligence, EAAI 2024. pp. 10679–10686. AAAI Press (2024). https://doi.org/10.1609/AAAI.V38I9.28939
28. Samuel, S., D'Souza, D., Komondoor, R.: Gensys: a scalable fixed-point engine for maximal controller synthesis over infinite state spaces. In: Spinellis, D., Gousios, G., Chechik, M., Penta, M.D. (eds.) ESEC/FSE '21: 29th ACM Joint European Software Engineering Conference and Symposium on the Foundations of Software Engineering. pp. 1585–1589. ACM (2021). https://doi.org/10.1145/3468264.3473126
29. Samuel, S., D'Souza, D., Komondoor, R.: Symbolic fixpoint algorithms for logical LTL games. In: 38th IEEE/ACM International Conference on Automated Software Engineering, ASE 2023. pp. 698–709. IEEE (2023). https://doi.org/10.1109/ASE56229.2023.00212
30. Schmuck, A., Heim, P., Dimitrova, R., Nayak, S.P.: Localized attractor computations for infinite-state games. In: Gurfinkel, A., Ganesh, V. (eds.) Computer Aided Verification - 36th International Conference, CAV 2024. LNCS, vol. 14683, pp. 135–158. Springer (2024). https://doi.org/10.1007/978-3-031-65633-0_7

31. Sery, O., Fedyukovich, G., Sharygina, N.: Interpolation-based function summaries in bounded model checking. In: Eder, K., Lourenço, J., Shehory, O. (eds.) Hardware and Software: Verification and Testing - 7th International Haifa Verification Conference, HVC 2011, Haifa, Israel, December 6-8, 2011, Revised Selected Papers. Lecture Notes in Computer Science, vol. 7261, pp. 160–175. Springer (2011). https://doi.org/10.1007/978-3-642-34188-5_15, https://doi.org/10.1007/978-3-642-34188-5_15
32. Solanki, M., Chatterjee, P., Lal, A., Roy, S.: Accelerated bounded model checking using interpolation based summaries. In: Finkbeiner, B., Kovács, L. (eds.) Tools and Algorithms for the Construction and Analysis of Systems - 30th International Conference, TACAS 2024, Held as Part of the European Joint Conferences on Theory and Practice of Software, ETAPS 2024, Luxembourg City, Luxembourg, April 6-11, 2024, Proceedings, Part II. Lecture Notes in Computer Science, vol. 14571, pp. 155–174. Springer (2024). https://doi.org/10.1007/978-3-031-57249-4_8, https://doi.org/10.1007/978-3-031-57249-4_8
33. Unno, H., Terauchi, T., Gu, Y., Koskinen, E.: Modular primal-dual fixpoint logic solving for temporal verification. Proc. ACM Program. Lang. **7**(POPL), 2111–2140 (2023). https://doi.org/10.1145/3571265
34. Urban, C., Gurfinkel, A., Kahsai, T.: Synthesizing ranking functions from bits and pieces. In: Chechik, M., Raskin, J. (eds.) Tools and Algorithms for the Construction and Analysis of Systems - 22nd International Conference, TACAS 2016, Held as Part of the European Joint Conferences on Theory and Practice of Software, ETAPS 2016, Eindhoven, The Netherlands, April 2-8, 2016, Proceedings. Lecture Notes in Computer Science, vol. 9636, pp. 54–70. Springer (2016). https://doi.org/10.1007/978-3-662-49674-9_4, https://doi.org/10.1007/978-3-662-49674-9_4
35. Zhu, S., Kincaid, Z.: Breaking the mold: Nonlinear ranking function synthesis without templates. In: Gurfinkel, A., Ganesh, V. (eds.) Computer Aided Verification - 36th International Conference, CAV 2024, Montreal, QC, Canada, July 24-27, 2024, Proceedings, Part I. Lecture Notes in Computer Science, vol. 14681, pp. 431–452. Springer (2024). https://doi.org/10.1007/978-3-031-65627-9_21, https://doi.org/10.1007/978-3-031-65627-9_21

A Myhill-Nerode Characterization and Active Learning for One-Clock Timed Automata

Kyveli Doveri[1] , Pierre Ganty[2] , and

B. Srivathsan[3,4]

[1] Unaffiliated `kyv_4@hotmail.com`
[2] IMDEA Software Institute, Madrid, Spain `pierre.ganty@imdea.org`
[3] Chennai Mathematical Institute, Chennai, India `sri@cmi.ac.in`
[4] CNRS IRL 2000, ReLaX, Chennai, India

Abstract. We present a Myhill-Nerode style characterization for languages recognized by one-clock deterministic timed automata (1-DTA). Although there is only one clock, distinct automata may reset it differently along the same word. This adds a significant challenge in the search for a canonical automaton. Our characterization is based on a new perspective of 1-DTAs in terms of "half-integral" words that they accept, along with the reset information encoded by them. We apply our results to develop L^* style algorithms that learn the canonical 1-DTA.

Keywords: Timed languages, Deterministic Timed automata, Canonical representation, Myhill-Nerode equivalence, Active Learning

1   Introduction

One of the most fundamental results in the theory of finite automata is the Myhill-Nerode theorem, which gives a characterization of regular languages in terms of the so-called Nerode equivalence. The Nerode equivalence is key to defining a canonical representation for regular languages given by their corresponding minimal deterministic finite automata.

Given a regular language L, the Nerode equivalence relation $\sim_L$ partitions the set of all words such that two words u and v are equivalent ($u \sim_L v$) if and only if, for all continuations w, $uw \in L$ if and only if $vw \in L$. Moreover, the Nerode equivalence is the coarsest among all equivalences $\sim$ that satisfy two properties: $u \sim v$ implies $ua \sim va$ for all letters a, and $u \sim v$ implies $u \in L$ iff $v \in L$. From there, the Myhill-Nerode theorem states that L is regular if and only if $\sim_L$ has finitely many equivalence classes. The Nerode equivalence provides a deep insight into the structure of regular languages and enables the definition of a canonical representation for regular languages by associating to each regular language a deterministic finite automaton (DFA) as follows. Each state uniquely corresponds to a Nerode equivalence class. Furthermore, the defined automaton is minimal since the Nerode equivalence is the coarsest among all equivalences

S. Junges and G. Katz (Eds.): TACAS 2026, LNCS 16505, pp. 419–437, 2026.
https://doi.org/10.1007/978-3-032-22752-2_22

induced by DFAs for the language. The Nerode equivalence also plays a key role in the active learning of regular languages like Angluin's L* algorithm [6].

Our focus in this paper is on developing a Myhill-Nerode characterization, a canonical representation and, finally, an active learning algorithm for 1-clock deterministic timed automata. The model of timed automata [1] provides a de facto automaton model for real-time systems. Verification of timed automata has been extensively studied, with industry-strength tools [7]. Results about canonical representations or active learning algorithms have been more elusive. However, there has been a flurry of recent activity on active learning algorithms [3,16,15,9,10] where the main challenge revolves around identifying the guards and resets of the transitions in the timed automaton. Short of solving the problem, research works have considered restricted versions of timed automata.

The most common restriction is to look at automaton models with *input-driven resets*: the clock values are determined by the timed word, and not by the automaton. In Event-Recording Automata (ERA) [2], there is a clock x_a attached to every letter a in the alphabet. There are no other clocks. Clock x_a records the time since the last occurrence of a. For instance, on reading a timed word $(2 \cdot a)(1.3 \cdot b)$ (where 1.3 is the time between a and b), we will have $x_a = 1.3$ and $x_b = 0$, no matter which ERA reads it. An L*-like algorithm for learning ERAs was first proposed in 2010 [12].

In the model of integer reset timed automata (IRTA) [14], clocks can be arbitrary. However, every transition that resets a clock, say x, must have a guard of the form $x = c$, where c is a natural number. Therefore, every reset occurs at an integer time point. Hence, the fractional values of all clocks are equal. This makes it possible to reduce every IRTA to a language equivalent single-clock IRTA. It still does not (yet) induce an input-driven reset. However, the work of Bhave et al. [8] tells us that we can assume, without loss of generality, a transition with a guard of the form $x = c$ necessarily resets the clock. Such a model is referred to as strict 1-IRTA. Hence, if we know the maximum constant K used in the automaton, and if we assume the automaton is complete with guards of the form $x = 0$, $0 < x < 1$, $x = 1$, ..., $x = K$, $K < x$, the resets becomes input-driven. Using these properties, a Myhill-Nerode characterization and an L* algorithm for strict 1-IRTAs was first formulated in 2024 [10].

In real-time automata, there is a single clock which is reset in every transition. Hence, on reading a timed word $(t_1 \cdot a_1)(t_2 \cdot a_2) \cdots (t_n \cdot a_n)$, the value of the clock is 0, and while executing the transition corresponding to a_i, the clock value is t_i (time between a_{i-1} and a_i). This property has been used to give a Myhill-Nerode characterization and an L* algorithm [4,5].

A second type of restriction that appears in the literature on timed automata learning is to consider one-clock deterministic timed automata (1-DTA). Here, the clock resets are not determined by the word and instead depend on the automaton. This makes the search for canonicity and Myhill-Nerode style characterizations particularly challenging. To the best of our knowledge, no Nerode equivalences or Myhill-Nerode characterizations exist for 1-DTAs. On the other hand, active learning algorithms for 1-DTAs have been studied without going via the Nerode equivalence route. As there is no notion of a canonical 1-DTA for a language, the learning algorithms may produce different automata in different runs. Two L*-like algorithms for 1-DTAs were presented in 2020 [3].

More recently [16], in an exceptional result which considers no restriction on the model, a Myhill-Nerode characterization and an L*-like algorithm for deterministic timed automata (DTA) has been proposed. The algorithm considers *elementary languages*, which are sets of timed words, as the basis for the equivalence. For example $\{(t_0 \cdot a)(t_1 \cdot b) \mid t_0 + t_1 = 1\}$ is an elementary language. The paper proposes a Nerode equivalence over elementary languages and proves that for deterministic timed languages, this equivalence induces finitely many classes. Using a monoid-based representation of deterministic timed languages [13], a deterministic timed automaton is constructed. However, there is no counterpart to the segment of the classical Myhill-Nerode theorem which says that the Nerode equivalence is the coarsest among all equivalences induced by DFAs. Hence there is no concept of a canonical deterministic timed automaton for a language.

In an orthogonal line of work, timers have been considered in the place of clocks [15,9]. A timer can be set to an integer value in a transition, and its value decreases along with time. The associated *timeout* is observable by a series of experiments. This facilitates a learning algorithm. We are not aware of any Myhill-Nerode theorems or notions of canonicity for this model.

Our contributions. In the works presented above [16,3,15,9], several models are on one-clock (or one-timer) automata. Hence, this restriction to a single clock assumes substantial significance in practice. In this work, we study 1-DTAs and provide a fresh perspective which leads to a Myhill-Nerode characterization, a canonical 1-DTA and a novel L* algorithm to learn the canonical 1-DTA. The first and foremost technical challenge lies in handling the clock resets. We propose an automaton-independent way of viewing resets as *reset functions* and identify a canonical reset function for each language. A second key idea is to restrict attention to *half-integral words* inside a language. These are timed words where the delays are of the form $\frac{n}{2}$ for some natural number n. We show that 1-DTA languages are determined by the half-integral words that they accept and the canonical reset function. Equipped with these new fundamental insights, we develop technical machinery for the Myhill-Nerode characterization and extend it to a learning algorithm.

2   Background

Words and Languages. An *alphabet* is a finite set of *letters* which we typically denote by Σ. An *untimed word* is a finite sequence $a_1 \cdots a_n$ of letters $a_i \in \Sigma$. As usual, we denote the empty word by ϵ. We denote by Σ^* the set of untimed words over Σ. An *untimed language* is a subset of Σ^*. We denote non-negative reals by $\mathbb{R}_{\geq 0}$ and the set of all finite sequences of these numbers by $\mathbb{T}$. A *timed word* is a finite sequence $(t_1 \cdot a_1) \cdots (t_n \cdot a_n)$ where $a_1 \cdots a_n \in \Sigma^*$ and $t_1 \cdots t_n \in \mathbb{T}$. The value t_i denotes the delay between a_{i-1} and a_i, for $i > 1$. We denote the set of timed words by $\mathbb{T}\Sigma^*$. A *timed language* is a set of timed words.

The *residual language* of a (un)timed language L with regard to a (un)timed word u is defined as $u^{-1}L = \{w \mid uw \in L\}$. In particular $\epsilon^{-1}L = L$ for every (un)timed language L. Timed automata are recognizers of timed languages [1]. We focus on one-clock timed automata subclasses in this work. Hence we present a modified definition suitable for our work.

One-Clock Timed Automata. We assume the presence of a single clock x. A *One-clock Timed Automaton* (1-TA) over Σ is a tuple $\mathcal{A} = (Q, q_I, T, F)$ where Q is a finite set of states, $q_I \in Q$ is the initial state, $F \subseteq Q$ is the set of final states and $T \subseteq Q \times Q \times \Sigma \times \Phi \times \{0,1\}$ is a finite set of transitions where Φ is the set of clock constraints given by

$$\phi ::= c < x \quad | \quad x = c \quad | \quad x < c \quad | \quad \phi \wedge \phi \;, \text{ where } c \in \mathbb{N} \text{ (natural numbers) .}$$

For a clock constraint ϕ, we write $[\![\phi]\!]$ for the set of values of x that satisfies the constraint. In our syntax, a transition looks like (q, q', a, ϕ, r) where ϕ is a clock constraint called the *guard* of the transition and $r \in \{0,1\}$ denotes whether the single clock x is *reset* in the transition: 0 denotes that it is reset, whereas 1 denotes otherwise. The idea for this notation is that on reading the transition, the value of the clock is multiplied with r. When depicting 1-TA (as in Section 4), we use dashed edges for resetting transitions.

We say that a 1-TA with transitions T is *deterministic* whenever for every pair $\theta = (q, q', a, \phi, r)$ and $\theta_1 = (q_1, q_1', a_1, \phi_1, r_1)$ of transitions in T such that $\theta \neq \theta_1$ we have that either $q \neq q_1$, $a \neq a_1$ or $[\![\phi]\!] \cap [\![\phi_1]\!] = \emptyset$. We write 1-DTA for a one-clock deterministic timed automaton.

A *run* e of $\mathcal{A}$ on a timed word $(t_1 \cdot a_1) \ldots (t_k \cdot a_k) \in \mathbb{T}\Sigma^*$ is a finite sequence

$$e = (q_0, \nu_0) \xrightarrow{t_1, \theta_1} (q_1, \nu_1) \xrightarrow{t_2, \theta_2} \cdots \xrightarrow{t_k, \theta_k} (q_k, \nu_k) \;,$$

where $q_j \in Q$, $\nu_j \in \mathbb{R}_{\geq 0}$ for all $j \in \{0, \ldots, k\}$ and, for each $i \in \{1, \ldots, k\}$ the following hold: (i) $\theta_i = (q_{i-1}, q_i, a_i, \phi_i, r_i) \in T$, (ii) $\nu_{i-1} + t_i \in [\![\phi_i]\!]$, and (iii) $\nu_i = (\nu_{i-1} + t_i) \times r_i$. Therefore if $r_i = 0$, we have $\nu_i = 0$ and if $r_i = 1$ we have $\nu_i = \nu_{i-1} + t_i$. A pair $(q, \nu) \in Q \times \mathbb{R}_{\geq 0}$ like the ones occurring in the run e is called a *configuration* of $\mathcal{A}$ and the configuration $(q_I, 0)$ is called *initial*. The run e is deemed *accepting* if $q_k \in F$. For $w \in \mathbb{T}\Sigma^*$ we write $(q, \nu) \rightsquigarrow^w (q', \nu')$ if there is a run of $\mathcal{A}$ on w from (q, ν) to (q', ν'). When $\mathcal{A}$ is deterministic we note that every timed word has at most one run starting from the initial configuration. We say that $\mathcal{A}$ is *complete* when it has exactly one run for every timed word. Assuming $\mathcal{A}$ is complete and deterministic, given a timed word u denote by $\mathcal{A}(u)$ the unique state reached by the one run of $\mathcal{A}$ on u from the initial configuration.

Finally, given a configuration (q, ν), define $\mathcal{L}(q, \nu) = \{w \in \mathbb{T}\Sigma^* \mid (q, \nu) \rightsquigarrow^w (q', \nu'), q' \in F, \nu' \in \mathbb{R}_{\geq 0}\}$. We write $\mathcal{L}(\mathcal{A})$ for $\mathcal{L}(q_I, 0)$. We say that a language L is 1-DTA recognizable if $L = \mathcal{L}(\mathcal{A})$ for some 1-DTA $\mathcal{A}$.

Equivalence Relation. A binary relation $\sim \subseteq S \times S$ on a set S is an *equivalence* if it is reflexive (i.e. $y \sim y$), transitive (i.e. $y \sim z \wedge z \sim z' \implies y \sim z'$) and symmetric (i.e. $y \sim z \implies z \sim y$). The equivalence class of $s \in S$ w.r.t. $\sim$ is the subset $[s]_\sim = \{s' \in S \mid s \sim s'\}$. A *representative* of the class $[s]_\sim$ is any element $s' \in [s]_\sim$. Given a subset D of S we define $[D]_\sim = \{[d]_\sim \mid d \in D\}$. We say that $\sim$ has *finite index* when $[S]_\sim$ is a finite set.

Region Equivalence for one clock. An important technical tool in the analysis of timed automata is the *region equivalence* [1]. We recall this equivalence in the setting of 1-TAs. Define the equivalence $\equiv \; \subseteq \mathbb{R}_{\geq 0} \times \mathbb{R}_{\geq 0}$ by

$$y \equiv z \iff \lfloor y \rfloor = \lfloor z \rfloor \wedge (\{y\} = 0 \Leftrightarrow \{z\} = 0) \; ,$$

where given $y \in \mathbb{R}_{\geq 0}$, $\lfloor y \rfloor$ denotes its *integral part* and $\{y\}$ its *fractional part* so that $y = \lfloor y \rfloor + \{y\}$. [5]

Given a constant $K \in \mathbb{N}$ define the equivalence $\equiv^K \; \subseteq \mathbb{R}_{\geq 0} \times \mathbb{R}_{\geq 0}$ by

$$y \equiv^K z \iff (y \equiv z) \vee (y > K \wedge z > K) \; .$$

The equivalence $\equiv^K$ is called the *region equivalence w.r.t constant K* and its classes are called K-*regions* (or regions when K is clear from the context).

Assumption 1. *Without loss of generality, we assume that guards of a 1-TA are of the form $x = c$ for $c \in \{0, \ldots, K\}$, $c < x < c+1$ for $c \in \{0, \ldots, K-1\}$, or $K < x$, where K is the largest constant appearing in the transitions of the automaton (in other words, every guard ϕ is such that $[\![\phi]\!]$ is a K-region).*

Building on the above assumption, we introduce a notation that is useful for defining 1-TA. Given $t \in \mathbb{R}_{\geq 0}$ and $K \in \mathbb{N}$ define the clock constraint $\phi_K(t)$ as:

$$\phi_K(t) = \begin{cases} x = t & \text{if } t \leq K \wedge \{t\} = 0 \; , \\ \lfloor t \rfloor < x < \lceil t \rceil & \text{if } t \leq K \wedge \{t\} \neq 0 \; , \\ K < x & \text{else (i.e. } K < t) \; . \end{cases}$$

3 Reset Functions

As said before, our goal in this work is to determine a machine-independent characterization for 1-DTA languages. A key challenge is to determine how the clock should be reset. Different automata for the same language L may reset the clock differently along the same word. In this section, we first abstract away from the underlying automaton and consider resets as a function from words to reals. Then, we propose the *syntactic reset function* which relies solely on the structure of L, and is independent of any particular automaton.

A *reset function* is a function $R : \mathbb{T}\Sigma^* \to \mathbb{R}_{\geq 0}$ such that for every $u \in \mathbb{T}\Sigma^*, t \in \mathbb{R}_{\geq 0}$ and $a \in \Sigma$, we have $R(\epsilon) = 0$ and $R(u(t \cdot a))$ is either 0 or $R(u) + t$. As its name suggests, a reset function prescribes how resets occur along a word: $R(u(t \cdot a)) = 0$ corresponds to resetting after reading $u(t \cdot a)$ whereas $R(u(t \cdot a)) = R(u) + t$ corresponds to not resetting. Every (complete) 1-DTA $\mathcal{A}$ induces a reset function $R^{\mathcal{A}}$ defined as $R^{\mathcal{A}}(u) = y$ if $(q_I, 0) \rightsquigarrow^u (q, y)$. $R^{\mathcal{A}}(u)$ gives the value of the clock in $\mathcal{A}$ after reading u.

---

[5] Besides the floor function ($\lfloor y \rfloor$), we use the ceiling notation ($\lceil y \rceil$) for convenience.

3.1 Syntactic Reset Function

Given any arbitrary language L, we want to define a machine-independent reset function $\mathbf{R}^L : \mathbb{T}\Sigma^* \to \mathbb{R}_{\geq 0}$ capturing the "resetting behaviour" of L. The main idea for defining $\mathbf{R}^L$ is that resets are determined by the residual languages of words. Assume that L is 1-DTA recognizable and fix a 1-DTA $\mathcal{A}$ accepting it. If, after reading a word u, $\mathcal{A}$ resets the clock, then the residual language $u^{-1}L$ is also recognized by a 1-DTA: namely, by the same automaton $\mathcal{A}$ with the initial state replaced by the state reached after reading u. Thus, resetting implies that $u^{-1}L$ is 1-DTA recognizable. What about the converse? That is, is there a 1-DTA accepting L that resets after every word whose residual is 1-DTA recognizable? The answer is yes (our main result, Theorem 4). We define $\mathbf{R}^L$ so that for every word u, $\mathbf{R}^L(u) = 0$ iff $u^{-1}L$ is 1-DTA recognizable, whenever L is.

Formally, we define $\mathbf{R}^L$ inductively, prefix by prefix, starting from ϵ as given next. We set $\mathbf{R}^L(\epsilon) = 0$, even when L is not 1-DTA recognizable, since this definition is tailored to capture the behavior of 1-DTA languages.

Definition 2 (Syntactic reset function). *Given a language $L \subseteq \mathbb{T}\Sigma^*$ we define the reset function $\mathbf{R}^L : \mathbb{T}\Sigma^* \to \mathbb{R}_{\geq 0}$ inductively: $\mathbf{R}^L(\epsilon) = 0$ and*

$$\mathbf{R}^L(u(t \cdot a)) = \begin{cases} 0 & \text{if } (u(t \cdot a))^{-1}L \text{ is a 1-DTA recognizable language,} \\ \mathbf{R}^L(u) + t & \text{otherwise.} \end{cases}$$

Example 3. Let $L = \{(t_1 \cdot a)(t_2 \cdot b) \mid 0 < t_1 < 1, t_1 + t_2 = 2\}$. Consider the word $(0 \cdot a)$. Notice that $\mathbf{R}^L(0 \cdot a)$ must be zero since the word $(0 \cdot a)$ has delay zero, and every reset function returns 0 on this word. For $1 \leq t_1$, $\mathbf{R}^L(t_1 \cdot a) = 0$ since $(t_1 \cdot a)^{-1}L = \emptyset$ is a 1-DTA recognizable language and similarly $\mathbf{R}^L(u) = 0$ if u is prefix of no word in L. For $0 < t_1 < 1$, $(t_1 \cdot a)^{-1}L = \{(t_2 \cdot b) \mid t_1 + t_2 = 2\}$ cannot be recognized using a clock initialized to zero, thus $\mathbf{R}^L(t_1 \cdot a) = t_1$. For $u \in L$, $\mathbf{R}^L(u) = 0$ because $u^{-1}L = \{\epsilon\}$ is 1-DTA recognizable.

We now state our main theorem of this section which says that a 1-DTA inducing the syntactic reset function $\mathbf{R}^L$ can in fact be computed starting from any 1-DTA recognizing L. Along with it, we make another observation: the range of the syntactic reset function is bounded by a constant K_L, and moreover, within this interval $[0, K_L]$, the range does not take any integral value other than 0. Denoting by $\mathbb{N}_{>0}$, the set of natural numbers strictly bigger than 0, we can summarize the range of $\mathbf{R}^L$ as $[0, K_L] \setminus \mathbb{N}_{>0}$. Interestingly, this constant K_L turns out to be the smallest constant needed for any 1-DTA to accept L.

Theorem 4.

- *Given a 1-DTA for L, we can compute an equivalent 1-DTA with the same constant such that it induces the syntactic reset function $\mathbf{R}^L$.*
- *If L is a 1-DTA recognizable language then for every timed word u, $\mathbf{R}^L(u) \in [0, K_L] \setminus \mathbb{N}_{>0}$ where K_L is the smallest constant K such that there exists a 1-DTA with maximum constant K that accepts L.*

4   1-DTAs in Terms of Reset Functions and Half-Integral Words

For our next step, we want to view 1-DTA recognizable languages in terms of special discrete words. In the untimed world, each run of a deterministic automaton corresponds to a unique word. This correspondence does not hold for 1-DTAs. In the automaton $\mathcal{A}_s$ below all timed words of the form $(t_1 \cdot a)(t_2 \cdot b)$ such that $0 < t_1 < 1$ and $0 < t_1 + t_2 < 1$ follow exactly the same run.

$$\mathcal{A}_s \longrightarrow \bigcirc \xrightarrow{a,\, 0 < x < 1,\, 1} \bigcirc \dashrightarrow{b,\, 0 < x < 1,\, 0} \circledcirc$$

To address this, some approaches use symbolic words [16,12], where each letter represents a region and each word represents a set of timed words. We introduce *half-integral words* which are viewed as a canonical choice of a concrete timed word within a symbolic word. The half-integral word accepted by $\mathcal{A}_s$ is $(\frac{1}{2}\cdot a)(0\cdot b)$.

Half-integral words. A timed word $(t_1 \cdot a_1)(t_2 \cdot a_2)\ldots(t_n \cdot a_n)$ is *half-integral* if each t_i $(1 \leq i \leq n)$ is of the form $t_i = \frac{m}{2}$ for some $m \in \mathbb{N}$, that is, the fractional part $\{t_i\}$ is either 0 or $\frac{1}{2}$. Also the empty word ϵ is a half-integral word. For a language L, we write $\mathcal{HI}(L)$ for the set of all half-integral words in L. For brevity, we write $\mathcal{HI}$ instead of $\mathcal{HI}(\mathbb{T}\Sigma^*)$.

We observe an intriguing fact: a 1-DTA language is almost entirely determined by the subset of its half-integral words. We illustrate this with an example. Consider the 1-DTA $\mathcal{A}_s$ above and the following 1-DTA $\mathcal{A}_q$:

$$\mathcal{A}_q \longrightarrow \bigcirc \dashrightarrow{a,\, 0 < x < 1,\, 0} \bigcirc \dashrightarrow{b,\, x = 0,\, 0} \circledcirc$$

The language $\mathcal{L}(\mathcal{A}_s)$ equals $\{(t_1 \cdot a)(t_2 \cdot b) \mid 0 < t_1 < 1 \text{ and } 0 < t_1 + t_2 < 1\}$ while $\mathcal{L}(\mathcal{A}_q)$ equals $\{(t_1 \cdot a)(t_2 \cdot b) \mid 0 < t_1 < 1 \text{ and } t_2 = 0\}$. Clearly, the two languages do not coincide. However, they coincide when restricted to half-integral words as $\mathcal{HI}(\mathcal{L}(\mathcal{A}_s)) = \mathcal{HI}(\mathcal{L}(\mathcal{A}_q)) = \{(\frac{1}{2} \cdot a)(0 \cdot b)\}$. The difference stems from the resets: $\mathcal{A}_s$ does not reset its clock after a, whereas $\mathcal{A}_q$ resets it after a.

This example illustrates our main observation: every 1-DTA language L is uniquely determined by the set of its half-integral words $\mathcal{HI}(L)$ *and* the syntactic reset function $\mathbf{R}^L$. Therefore, if we are given that $\mathcal{HI}(L) = \{(\frac{1}{2} \cdot a)(0 \cdot b)\}$ and $\mathbf{R}^L$ does not reset after a, then $L = \mathcal{L}(\mathcal{A}_s)$, whereas for the same $\mathcal{HI}(L)$, if $\mathbf{R}^L$ does reset after a, then $L = \mathcal{L}(\mathcal{A}_q)$. To formalize this idea, we first define a map from timed words to half-integral words using a reset function.

From timed words to half-integral words, through a reset function. We now relate half-integral words and reset functions: given a reset function, we associate each timed word to a unique half-integral word such that every 1-DTA conforming to the reset function has both the original word and the half-integral word thereof visit the same states along the exact same path.

Given a reset function R, the *normal form* $N^R(u)$ of an arbitrary timed word $u \in \mathbb{T}\Sigma^*$ is a half-integral word with the same untimed part as u and with shifted delays. Given $x \in \mathbb{R}_{\geq 0}$ let $hi(x)$ denote the unique half-integral value such that $hi(x) = x$ if $\{x\} = 0$ and, $hi(x) = \lfloor x \rfloor + \frac{1}{2}$ if $\{x\} \neq 0$. For example, $hi(2.7) = 2.5$, $hi(1.2) = 1.5$, etc. Notice that $hi(x)$ is the unique half-integral value such that $x \equiv hi(x)$. We extend the function hi to sets as expected. Building upon the function hi we define the normal form by induction on the length of words: $N^R(\epsilon) = \epsilon$ and $N^R(u(t \cdot a)) = N^R(u)(t' \cdot a)$ where $t' = \frac{n}{2}$ for some $n \in \mathbb{N}$ such that $R(u) + t \equiv hi(R(u)) + t'$. For instance, if $R((0.3 \cdot a)) = 0$, then $N^R((0.3 \cdot a)(1.9 \cdot b)) = (0.5 \cdot a)(1.5 \cdot b)$; whereas if $R((0.3 \cdot a)) = 0.3$, then $N^R((0.3 \cdot a)(1.9 \cdot b)) = (0.5 \cdot a)(2 \cdot b)$.

Remark 5. For $w \in \mathcal{HI}$ we have $N^R(w) = w$.

Proposition 6. *If R is the reset function of a 1-DTA $\mathcal{A}$, then for every word u, the runs of u and $N^R(u)$ in $\mathcal{A}$ follow the same sequence of transitions. In particular, $u \in L(\mathcal{A})$ iff $N^R(u) \in L(\mathcal{A})$.*

We now obtain the characterization previously announced: a 1-DTA recognizable language is entirely determined by its half-integral words together with its syntactic reset function.

Theorem 7. *If L_1 and L_2 are 1-DTA recognizable languages then $L_1 = L_2$ iff $\mathcal{HI}(L_1) = \mathcal{HI}(L_2)$ and $\mathbf{R}^{L_1} = \mathbf{R}^{L_2}$.*

Proof. The left-to-right implication is immediate. Assume the right-hand side and let $R = \mathbf{R}^{L_1} = \mathbf{R}^{L_2}$. By Theorem 4 there is a 1-DTA accepting L_1 whose reset function is R, and the analogue holds for L_2. By Proposition 6 for every word u we have $u \in L_1 \iff N^R(u) \in L_1$ and $u \in L_2 \iff N^R(u) \in L_2$. Since $\mathcal{HI}(L_1) = \mathcal{HI}(L_2)$ we have $N^R(u) \in L_1 \iff N^R(u) \in L_2$. Hence, $u \in L_1 \iff u \in L_2$. $\square$

5 Equivalences on Half-Integral Words

Here, we aim to further decompose our understanding of 1-DTA recognizable languages. As seen in the previous section, a 1-DTA language is determined by a reset function together with a set of half-integral words. We now focus on understanding the structure of this set of half-integral words, examining how a 1-DTA organizes them. We would like to describe this set based on an equivalence on half-integral words, in a similar way as the classical DFA case, where words are identified to be equivalent when they reach the same state. Here, however, states are not enough to capture the future of words since this future also depends on the clock value the words reach. Here is an example that illustrates this aspect. Let L be the language recognized by the following 1-DTA.

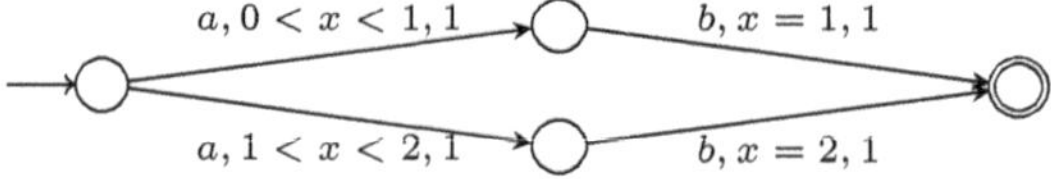

Consider the half-integral words $u = (0.5, a)$ and $v = (1.5, a)$. Their residuals are the same: $u^{-1}L = v^{-1}L = \{(0.5, b)\}$. However, if u and v go to the same state in a 1-DTA, then the extension $(1.5, b)$ would also be possible from u. Thus, even though the residuals coincide, they need not go to the same state in a 1-DTA. Hence residuals do not identify states. Here is the plan for this section.

1. Following a similar reasoning on a subclass of 1-DTAs called integer reset timed automata [10], we consider 1-DTAs with a special syntax, which we call K-acceptors: every state is associated to a K-region and all words landing in the state end up with a clock value in this region.
2. On the algebraic perspective, we consider a combination of equivalences over half-integral words and a reset function. We call this pair a *profile*.

The main contribution of this section is in showing a correspondence between K-acceptors and profiles. In the integer reset subclass [10], the clock resets were input-determined, that is, each word determined exactly when to reset. For 1-DTAs this is no longer the case, which is why we consider reset functions in addition to equivalences. The presence of reset functions also adds new challenges in proving the correspondence between acceptors and profiles.

K-acceptors. A *K-acceptor* is a complete 1-DTA with maximum constant K such that each state q is associated with a unique K-region, denoted *region(q)*. Every timed word u that reaches q arrives with a clock value inside *region(q)*: $[R(u)]_{\equiv_K} = region(q)$ where R is the reset function of the acceptor. Syntactically, this means the following: if some incoming transition to q resets the clock, then every incoming transition resets it and *region(q)* = $\{0\}$; else, every incoming transition has a guard ϕ such that $[\![\phi]\!] = region(q)$.

Lemma 8. *Given a 1-DTA of constant K we can compute an equivalent K-acceptor with the same reset function.*

Profiles. A *profile* is a pair $(R, \approx)$ where R is a reset function, and $\approx \subseteq \mathcal{HI} \times \mathcal{HI}$ is an equivalence relation on half-integral words.

Every acceptor $\mathcal{A}$ induces a natural equivalence on half-integral words: $u \approx^{\mathcal{A}} v$ if $\mathcal{A}(u) = \mathcal{A}(v)$. In other words, two half-integral words are equivalent whenever they lead to the same control state from the initial configuration. The pair $(R^{\mathcal{A}}, \approx^{\mathcal{A}})$ thus forms a profile. But, what additional properties does $(R^{\mathcal{A}}, \approx^{\mathcal{A}})$ satisfy? This will help us understand the other direction: given an arbitrary profile $(R, \approx)$ when does it reflect an acceptor, in other words, when is there an acceptor $\mathcal{A}$ such that $(R^{\mathcal{A}}, \approx^{\mathcal{A}})$ equals $(R, \approx)$?

The first step is to determine the maximum constant of an acceptor associated with $(R, \approx)$. To do so, we associate to $(R, \approx)$ a constant $K_{(R,\approx)} \in \mathbb{N} \cup \{\infty\}$ defined as follows. Let $C(K)$ be the following proposition $\forall u \in \mathcal{HI}$, $\forall a \in \Sigma$ and $\forall n \in \mathbb{N}$, $R(u) + \frac{n}{2} > K \implies u(\frac{n}{2} \cdot a) \approx u(K + \frac{1}{2} \cdot a)$. Intuitively, $C(K)$ says, the profile identifies $u(\frac{n}{2} \cdot a)$ and $u(K + \frac{1}{2} \cdot a)$ if after elapsing a delay $\frac{n}{2}$ from $R(u)$ the clock goes above K. Then $K_{(R,\approx)} = \inf\{K \in \mathbb{N} \mid C(K) \text{ holds}\}$ if this infimum is defined and $K_{(R,\approx)} = \infty$ otherwise. As expected, for $(R, \approx)$ to define an acceptor, $K_{(R,\approx)}$ must be finite. Next we give the extra conditions required.

Definition 9 (monotonic, L-preserving). *A profile $(R, \approx)$ is L-preserving when for all $u, v \in \mathcal{HI}$, $u \approx v \implies (u \in L \iff v \in L)$ and for all $w \in \mathbb{T}\Sigma^*$, we have $w \in L$ iff $N^R(w) \in L$. It is said to have* finite index *when $\approx$ has finite index and $K_{(R,\approx)} < \infty$. A profile $(R, \approx)$ is* monotonic *if for every $u, v \in \mathcal{HI}$,*

$u \approx v$ *implies* (a) $R(u) \equiv^{K_{(R,\approx)}} R(v)$ *and* (b) $\forall n \in \mathbb{N}, \forall a \in \Sigma$, $u(\frac{n}{2} \cdot a) \approx v(\frac{n}{2} \cdot a)$ *and, the reset function* R *satisfies* (c) $R(u) \equiv R(N^R(u))$ *for all* $u \in \mathbb{T}\Sigma^*$.

Proposition 10. *For an acceptor* $\mathcal{A}$, *the profile* $(R^{\mathcal{A}}, \approx^{\mathcal{A}})$ *is monotonic,* $\mathcal{L}(\mathcal{A})$-*preserving and has finite index.*

For the converse, suppose $(R, \approx)$ is monotonic, L-preserving (for some L) and has finite index. We construct an acceptor $\mathcal{A}_{(R,\approx)}$ of constant $K_{(R,\approx)}$ and prove that its language is L. The acceptor $\mathcal{A}_{(R,\approx)}$ has states $\{[u]_\approx \mid u \in \mathcal{HI}\}$. The initial state is $[\epsilon]_\approx$. Final states are $\{[u]_\approx \mid u \in L \cap \mathcal{HI}\}$. There is a transition $([u]_\approx, [v]_\approx, a, g, s)$ in $\mathcal{A}_{(R,\approx)}$ if there exists $n \in \mathbb{N}$ such that: $u(\frac{n}{2} \cdot a) \approx v$, and $g = \phi_K(R(u) + \frac{n}{2})$, and $s = 0$ if $R(v) = 0$ and $s = 1$ otherwise. Next we establish the correspondence between acceptors and profiles.

Proposition 11. *Let* $(R, \approx)$ *be an* L-*preserving, monotonic profile with finite index. Then* $\mathcal{A}_{(R,\approx)}$ *is a acceptor of profile* $(R, \approx)$ *such that* $\mathcal{L}(\mathcal{A}_{(R,\approx)}) = L$.

6   Myhill-Nerode Style Characterization

In this section, given a language L, we define the *syntactic profile* of L, which is a machine-independent profile based on the syntactic reset function $\mathbf{R}^L$. Using the syntactic profile and together with the results of the previous section, we obtain a Myhill-Nerode style characterization of 1-DTA recognizable languages.

Syntactic Profile. The syntactic profile of L is $(\mathbf{R}^L, \approx^L)$ where $\mathbf{R}^L$ is the syntactic reset function of L and $\approx^L \subseteq \mathcal{HI} \times \mathcal{HI}$ is the equivalence that identifies two half-integral words whenever their $\mathbf{R}^L$ values are equal and their residual languages are the same. Formally, we define

$$u \approx^L v \iff \mathbf{R}^L(u) = \mathbf{R}^L(v) \text{ and } u^{-1}L = v^{-1}L .$$

As shown next, when L is a 1-DTA recognizable language $(\mathbf{R}^L, \approx^L)$ satisfies all the conditions of Definition 9. We are thus in position to define the *canonical acceptor* of L as $\mathcal{A}_{(\mathbf{R}^L, \approx^L)}$. Moreover, the maximum constant of $\mathcal{A}_{(\mathbf{R}^L, \approx^L)}$ is K_L where we recall that K_L is the smallest constant K such that there exists a 1-DTA with maximum constant K that accepts L.

Proposition 12. *If* L *is a 1-DTA recognizable language then* $(\mathbf{R}^L, \approx^L)$ *is* L-*preserving, monotonic and has finite index and* $K_{(\mathbf{R}^L, \approx^L)} = K_L$.

From Proposition 12 together with the results of Section 3.1 we get the first part of the Myhill-Nerode style characterization: L is 1-DTA recognizable if and only if $(\mathbf{R}^L, \approx^L)$ is L-preserving, monotonic and has finite index.

The second part of a Myhill-Nerode style characterization concerns "minimality" of $\mathcal{A}_{(\mathbf{R}^L, \approx^L)}$. Here, minimality refers to the number of states and the value of the maximum constant. While the minimality of the constant is achieved by K_L, minimality w.r.t. states is more involved. To resolve this, we need to analyze the syntactic reset function $\mathbf{R}^L$ more closely which we proceed to do now.

Strictness. We single out a subclass of acceptors to which $\mathcal{A}_{(\mathbf{R}^L, \approx^L)}$ belongs called *strict* acceptors. Strict acceptors are a syntactic restriction of acceptors, analogous to the *strict IRTAs* [8] class: every transition with an equality guard, i.e. a guard of the form "$x = n$" for some $n \in \mathbb{N}$, resets the clock. Restricting to strict acceptors does not reduce expressiveness as shown next.

Lemma 13. *Given a K-acceptor we can compute a language equivalent strict K'-acceptor with $K' \leq K$.*

The next proposition shows that $\mathcal{A}_{(\mathbf{R}^L, \approx^L)}$ achieves minimality within the class of strict acceptors. We showed in the long version [11] that $\mathcal{A}_{(\mathbf{R}^L, \approx^L)}$ is not necessarily minimal among all acceptors.

Proposition 14. *If L is a 1-DTA recognizable language then $\mathcal{A}_{(\mathbf{R}^L, \approx^L)}$ is a strict K_L-acceptor with reset function $\mathbf{R}^L$. Moreover, no strict acceptor for L has fewer states than $\mathcal{A}_{(\mathbf{R}^L, \approx^L)}$.*

Combining the results of Section 3.1, Proposition 12 and 14 we finally get:

Theorem 15 (Myhill-Nerode style characterization for 1-DTA).
For a language $L \subseteq \mathbb{T}\Sigma^*$ the following statements hold:

(a) *L is 1-DTA recognizable if and only if $(\mathbf{R}^L, \approx^L)$ is L-preserving, monotonic and has finite index.*

(b) *No strict acceptor for L has fewer states or smaller constant than $\mathcal{A}_{(\mathbf{R}^L, \approx^L)}$.*

Computing the canonical acceptor. Given a 1-DTA $\mathcal{A}$ for L, we compute the canonical acceptor $\mathcal{A}_{(\mathbf{R}^L, \approx^L)}$ as follows. By applying Theorem 4, we transform $\mathcal{A}$ into a 1-DTA whose reset function is $\mathbf{R}^L$. We then transform this 1-DTA into an acceptor $\mathcal{A}_{\mathbf{R}^L}$. This preserves the reset function so that the reset function of $\mathcal{A}_{\mathbf{R}^L}$ is also $\mathbf{R}^L$. However, the equivalence on half-integral words induced by $\mathcal{A}_{\mathbf{R}^L}$ need not coincide with $\approx^L$: there may be two half-integral words u and u' such that $u \approx^L u'$ but $u \not\approx^{\mathcal{A}_{\mathbf{R}^L}} u'$. Since $u \approx^L u'$ we have that $\mathbf{R}^L(u) = \mathbf{R}^L(u')$ and $u^{-1}L = u'^{-1}L$. Let $\frac{n}{2} = \mathbf{R}^L(u)$, $q = \mathcal{A}_{\mathbf{R}^L}(u)$ and $q' = \mathcal{A}_{\mathbf{R}^L}(u')$. Then $region(q) = region(q')$ and $\mathcal{L}(q, \frac{n}{2}) = \mathcal{L}(q', \frac{n}{2})$. Conversely, if two states q and q' of $\mathcal{A}_{\mathbf{R}^L}$ have the same region and the same language when evaluated at the half-integral value of their region, this witnesses the existence of two half-integral words for which $\approx^L$ and $\approx^{\mathcal{A}_{\mathbf{R}^L}}$ disagree. Hence, to transform $\mathcal{A}_{\mathbf{R}^L}$ into an acceptor whose equivalence is $\approx^L$ we apply on $\mathcal{A}_{\mathbf{R}^L}$ the following state merging algorithm. For every pair of states q and q' such that $region(q) = region(q')$ let $\frac{n}{2}$ be the unique half-integral value in $region(q)$. If $\mathcal{L}(q, \frac{n}{2}) = \mathcal{L}(q', \frac{n}{2})$, we merge q and q' by keeping one of them, say q, redirecting all transitions entering q' to q and then deleting q' together with all its transitions. Firstly notice that this modification preserves the set of half-integral words that are accepted. Secondly, the redirection does not change the reset function, hence the modified automaton still implements $\mathbf{R}^L$. Hence, from Theorem 7 the automaton obtained by merging the states still accepts the same language. Deciding $\mathcal{L}(q, \frac{n}{2}) = \mathcal{L}(q', \frac{n}{2})$ reduces to deciding equivalence of 1-DTAs as explained in the long version [11].

After merging all states that can be merged the resulting acceptor $\mathcal{B}$ has profile $(\mathbf{R}^L, \approx^L)$. However, its constant may still be higher than K_L. The final step, is thus to adjust the constant.

Let K be the constant of $\mathcal{B}$ and, T its set of transitions. For a state q and a letter $a \in \Sigma$ define q_a to be the target state of the transition with label a and guard "$x > K$". Let $C_\mathcal{B}(m)$ be the proposition "for every state q and every letter a, all a-labelled transitions from q requiring the clock to be strictly above m go to state q_a". Formally, $C_\mathcal{B}(m) : \forall (q, q', a, \phi_K(t), r) \in T, t > m \implies q' = q_a$.

Lemma 16. $C_\mathcal{B}(K_L)$ *holds.*

Due to Lemma 16 for every state q we group together all transitions of the form $(q, q_a, a, \phi_K(t), 0)$ with $t > K_L$ (all these transitions are necessarily resetting since $region(q_a) = \{0\}$) into one transition $(q, q_a, a, x > K_L, 0)$. The constant of the automaton thereof is K_L. We finish with examples related to Theorem 15.

Example 17.

1. The language $L = \{(t \cdot a) \mid t \in \mathbb{N}\}$ is not 1-DTA recognizable. For every K we have $(K + 1 \cdot a) \in L$ but $(K + \frac{1}{2} \cdot a) \notin L$. Thus, $K_{(\mathbf{R}^L, \approx^L)} = \infty$.
2. The language $L = \{(t_1 \cdot a)(t_2 \cdot b) \mid t_1 \in (0,1) \setminus \{\frac{1}{2}\}, t_1 + t_2 < 1\} \cup \{(\frac{1}{2} \cdot a)(0 \cdot b)\}$ is not 1-DTA recognizable as its syntactic profile is not monotonic due to condition (c) of Definition 9. We have $R^L(0.1 \cdot a) = 0.1$ and $R^L(\frac{1}{2} \cdot a) = 0$.
3. Consider the language $L = \{(t_1 \cdot a) \ldots (t_n \cdot a) \mid \exists i \leq j, t_i + \cdots + t_j = 1\}$ of all timed words over the alphabet $\Sigma = \{a\}$. The residual $(0.3 \cdot a)^{-1}L$ is equal to the union of L and the language comprising all words whose delays add up to 0.7. It cannot be recognized using a clock initialized to zero thus, $\mathbf{R}^L(0.3 \cdot a) = 0.3$. Hence, $N^{\mathbf{R}^L}((0.3 \cdot a)(1.2 \cdot a)) = (\frac{1}{2} \cdot a)(1 \cdot a)$. Since $(\frac{1}{2} \cdot a)(1 \cdot a) \in L$ and $(0.3 \cdot a)(1.2 \cdot a) \notin L$ the syntactic profile of L is not L-preserving. Thus, L is not 1-DTA recognizable.

7   Learning the Canonical Acceptor

In this section, we apply our Myhill-Nerode characterization for active learning of 1-DTA languages. We present our Angluin-style L* [6] algorithms for learning the canonical acceptor $\mathcal{A}_{(\mathbf{R}^L, \approx^L)}$ defined in Section 6. In this setting, a Learner aims to learn an unknown language L from a Teacher through *membership* and *equivalence* queries. In a membership query, the Learner gives a word w to the Teacher, who responds saying whether $w \in L$ or not. In an equivalence query, the Learner gives a candidate automaton (a *conjecture*) to the Teacher. If the automaton accepts L, the Teacher responds with a Yes, else the Teacher gives a counterexample to the conjecture. All the information obtained using the queries is maintained by the Learner as an *observation table*.

We first adapt observation tables to our setting, and then present two algorithms, in the same spirit as in the work of An et al. [3] on 1-DTA learning. However, our objective is to learn the canonical acceptor and this is the new challenge which is not tackled by An et al. [3]. In our first algorithm, we assume a

Smart Teacher who can inform the Learner about the $\mathbf{R}^L$ function. In this case, the task of the Learner lies in identifying $\approx^L$. The algorithm is almost similar to the classical L^*, except that now we need to also identify the unknown constant K. In the second algorithm, we remove the Smart Teacher assumption and use a technique, partly inspired by the approach of An et al. [3], that guesses all possible resets and converges to a strict acceptor for the language. We show that using some additional equivalence queries, we can derive the canonical acceptor.

Observation tables. Given a finite subset $S \subseteq \mathcal{HI}$ of half-integral words we define the "one letter" extensions of S to be the words in $S\Sigma_K$, where $\Sigma_K = hi([0, K+1)) \times \Sigma$. Recall that $hi([0, K+1])$ stands for the set $\{0, 0.5, \ldots, K, K + 0.5\}$. An *Observation Table (OT)* is a tuple $\mathcal{T} = (K, S, E, T)$ where $K \in \mathbb{N}$ is called *the constant of* $\mathcal{T}$, $S \subseteq \mathcal{HI}$ is a prefix-closed finite subset of half-integral words, $E \subseteq \mathcal{HI}$ is a suffix-closed finite subset of half-integral words and $T : (S \cup S\Sigma_K) \times E \to \{0, 1\} \times hi(\mathbb{R}_{\geq 0} \setminus \mathbb{N}_{>0})$. [6]

The *reset assignment* of $\mathcal{T}$ is the function $r : (S \cup S\Sigma_K) \times E \to hi(\mathbb{R}_{\geq 0} \setminus \mathbb{N}_{>0})$ defined by $r(s, e) = T(s, e)(2)$ where $T(s, e)(i)$ denotes the i-th component of $T(s, e)$. We abuse notations and write $r(s)$ for $r(s, \epsilon)$.

Intuitively, if L is the unknown language, we will compute OTs such that $T(s, e)(1) = 1$ iff $se \in L$ and $T(s, e)(2)$ is a guess for $\mathbf{R}^L(se)$.

We view $\mathcal{T}$ as a table of entries $(x, y) \in \{0, 1\} \times hi(\mathbb{R}_{\geq 0} \setminus \mathbb{N}_{>0})$ with rows $S \cup S\Sigma_K$ and columns E labeled by half-integral words. We write $row(s)$ for the row vector in $\mathcal{T}$ indexed by s and, $row(s)(e)$ for the entry $T(s, e)$. For $i \in \{1, 2\}$, $row(s)(e)(i) = T(s, e)(i)$. Table 1 shows examples of OTs. In the OT $\mathcal{T}_0'$, the entry $(0, \frac{1}{2})$ for the word $u = (\frac{1}{2} \cdot a) \cdot \epsilon$ says that $u \notin L$ and the value of the clock on reading u is $\frac{1}{2}$. In the OT $\mathcal{T}_0''$, $row((\frac{1}{2} \cdot a)(1 + \frac{1}{2} \cdot a)) = ((1, 0))$.

Definition 18. *An OT $\mathcal{T}$ of constant K is* valid *when its reset assignment has range included in $[0, K] \setminus \mathbb{N}_{>0}$. It is* closed *if for every $w \in S\Sigma_K$ there is $s \in S$ such that $row(w) = row(s)$. We say that $\mathcal{T}$ is* consistent *if*

(a) *for every $s_1, s_2 \in S$ if the equality $row(s_1) = row(s_2)$ holds then we find that $row(s_1(t \cdot a)) = row(s_2(t \cdot a))$ for every $(t \cdot a) \in \Sigma_K$.*
(b) *for every $s(t \cdot a) \in S \cup S\Sigma_K$ if the inequality $r(s) + t > K$ holds then $row(s(t \cdot a)) = row(s(K + \frac{1}{2} \cdot a))$.*

Conjecture of an OT. A closed, consistent and valid OT $\mathcal{T}$ of constant K induces a strict K-acceptor $\mathcal{A}_{\mathcal{T}}$. The automaton $\mathcal{A}_{\mathcal{T}}$ has states $\{row(s) \mid s \in S\}$. The initial state is $row(\epsilon)$ and a state $row(s)$ is final if $row(s)(\epsilon)(1) = 1$. There is a transition $(row(s), row(s'), a, g, d)$ if there exists $(t \cdot a) \in \Sigma_K$ such that: $row(s(t \cdot a)) = row(s')$, $g = \phi_K(r(s) + t)$ and $d = 0$ if $r(s') = 0$ and, $d = 1$ otherwise. Since the range of the reset assignments in an OT exclude $\mathbb{N}_{>0}$, the resulting acceptor will in fact be strict, leading us to state this proposition.

---

[6] $\mathbb{R}_{\geq 0} \setminus \mathbb{N}_{>0}$ is the set of real numbers minus the set of strictly positive integers.

Proposition 19. *If $\mathcal{T}$ is closed, consistent and valid, and has constant K then $\mathcal{A}_{\mathcal{T}}$ is a strict K-acceptor such that $R^{\mathcal{A}_{\mathcal{T}}} : \mathbb{R}_{\geq 0} \to [0, K] \setminus \mathbb{N}_{>0}$. Moreover, for every $s \in S$, $(row(\epsilon), 0) \rightsquigarrow^s (row(s), r(s))$*

Table 1: Examples of Observation Tables

(a) Initial with $K = 0$

$\mathcal{T}_0, K = 0$	ϵ
ϵ	$(0, 0)$
$(0 \cdot a)$	$(0, 0)$
$(\frac{1}{2} \cdot a)$	$(0, \frac{1}{2})$

(b) With $K = 1$

$\mathcal{T}_0', K = 1$	ϵ
ϵ	$(0, 0)$
$(0 \cdot a)$	$(0, 0)$
$(\frac{1}{2} \cdot a)$	$(0, \frac{1}{2})$
$(1 \cdot a)$	$(0, 0)$
$(1 + \frac{1}{2} \cdot a)$	$(0, 0)$

(c) With $K = 1$

$\mathcal{T}_0'', K = 1$	ϵ
ϵ	$(0, 0)$
$(\frac{1}{2} \cdot a)$	$(0, \frac{1}{2})$
$(0 \cdot a)$	$(0, 0)$
$(1 \cdot a)$	$(0, 0)$
$(1 + \frac{1}{2} \cdot a)$	$(0, 0)$
$(\frac{1}{2} \cdot a)(\{0, \frac{1}{2}, 1\} \cdot a)$	$(0, 0)$
$(\frac{1}{2} \cdot a)(1 + \frac{1}{2} \cdot a)$	$(1, 0)$

Learning with a Smart Teacher. Our first learning algorithm, the *Smart Teacher algorithm*, works under the assumption that the Teacher provides reset information. More precisely, we assume that for every word $u \in \mathbb{T}\Sigma^*$ the Teacher provides the value $\mathbf{R}^L(u)$. Hence, in all the OTs computed the reset assignment corresponds to $\mathbf{R}^L$ that is for every row s and column e, $r(s, e) = \mathbf{R}^L(s \cdot e)$.

The algorithm proceeds as follows. The Learner starts with the OT $\mathcal{T}_0 = (0, \{\epsilon\}, \{\epsilon\}, T_0)$ like the one shown in Table 1. At each moment the Learner maintains an OT $\mathcal{T}$ and executes the following main loop. This loop uses the two auxiliary procedures $Process(\mathcal{T})$ and $Refine(\mathcal{T}, w)$ where $\mathcal{T}$ is an OT and $w \in \mathbb{T}\Sigma^*$. Both procedures return an OT and are described after the main loop.

- if $\mathcal{T}$ is not closed or not consistent or not valid then $\mathcal{T} \leftarrow Process(\mathcal{T})$.
- if $\mathcal{T}$ is closed, consistent and valid the Learner conjectures $\mathcal{A}_{\mathcal{T}}$ and asks the Teacher whether the equivalence $L(\mathcal{A}_{\mathcal{T}}) = L$ holds.
  - If $L(\mathcal{A}_{\mathcal{T}}) = L$ holds the algorithm terminates and returns $\mathcal{A}_{\mathcal{T}}$.
  - Else, Teacher gives a counterexample $w \in \mathbb{T}\Sigma^*$ and $\mathcal{T} \leftarrow Refine(\mathcal{T}, w)$.

Processing $\mathcal{T}$. Given an OT $\mathcal{T} = (K, S, E, T)$, $Process(\mathcal{T})$ outputs a closed, consistent valid OT of constant $K' \geq K$. It consists of applying the following *four actions* until none of them is applicable.

1. If for $w \in S\Sigma_K$ $row(w) = row(s)$ for no $s \in S$, move w from $S\Sigma_K$ to S.
2. If for $s_1, s_2 \in S$, $row(s_1) = row(s_2)$ but $row(s_1(t \cdot a))(e) \neq row(s_2(t \cdot a))(e)$ for some $e \in E$, add $(t \cdot a)e$ to E.
3. If $\mathcal{T}$ is not consistent w.r.t. item (b) in Definition 18, increase K by one.
4. If for $s \in S \cup S\Sigma_K$ and $e \in E$, $r(s, e) > K$, increase K by one.

Action 1 corresponds to "closing" $\mathcal{T}$, action 2 and 3 correspond to "making $\mathcal{T}$ consistent" and action 4 to "making it valid". Notice that adding $(t \cdot a)e$ to E adds new entries that need to be filled using additional membership queries. Similarly, incrementing K enlarges Σ_K, and hence $S\Sigma_K$. Once again, new entries are created which need to filled using membership queries.

Refining $\mathcal{T}$ with w. Given an OT $\mathcal{T}$ and a word $w \in \mathbb{T}\Sigma^*$ (which may not be a half-integral word), $Refine(\mathcal{T}, w)$ computes its normal form $N^{\mathbf{R}^L}(w)$ and then adds it along with its prefixes to S. Notice that if $w \in \mathcal{HI}$ then $N^{\mathbf{R}^L}(w) = w$ (Remark 5) and that if $w \notin \mathcal{HI}$, $N^{\mathbf{R}^L}(w)$ is computable from the values $\mathbf{R}^L(w')$ for every prefix w' of w, which the Teacher provides.

Proposition 20. *Smart Teacher algorithm terminates and returns $\mathcal{A}_{(\mathbf{R}^L, \approx^K)}$. Moreover, the algorithm processes at most $K_L + n$ OTs and the number of membership queries is $O(mn^2 K_L |\Sigma|)$ where n is the number of equivalence classes for $\approx^L$ and m the length of the longest counterexample.*

Learning with a Normal Teacher. We now consider an algorithm, with no assumption on the Teacher. The idea is similar to the Normal teacher algorithm of An et al. [3], but now, we are able to give minimality guarantees. Since we do not have the reset information upfront, we need to guess all possible ways to reset the clock. However, going down a wrong reset branch may not ensure termination. Hence we need to explore a tree of OTs in a lock-step fashion, extending each leaf by one step. The branch with the reset assignment corresponding to $\mathbf{R}^L$ produces a valid conjecture, and once we reach this node in the exploration tree, the algorithm terminates.

At each moment i the Learner keeps a pool P_i of OTs starting with the pool $P_0 = \{\mathcal{T}_0, \ldots, \mathcal{T}_n\}$ where all the $\mathcal{T}_i$'s are defined for $K = 0$, only contain the word ϵ and differ from each other on the reset assignments such that all the possible reset assignments for the extensions of ϵ appear in P_0. Given a pool P_i of OTs the Learner picks (and removes) one OT $\mathcal{T} \in P_i$ and applies exactly *one step* of the Smart Teacher algorithm: if $\mathcal{T}$ is not closed or is inconsistent or is not valid, a single action among 1–4 of the procedure $Process(\mathcal{T})$ is applied; if $\mathcal{T}$ is closed, consistent and valid, the Learner makes a conjecture and processes the counterexample if one is returned, as explained next.

Processing counterexamples. The difference from the Smart Teacher algorithm is that if the Teacher returns a counterexample w that is not a half-integral word we do not know the values $\mathbf{R}^L(w')$ for the prefixes w' of w and thus cannot compute $N^{\mathbf{R}^L}(w)$. Instead, the Learner computes all possible normal forms of w and adds them, along with all their prefixes, to the OT. For example for $w = (0.2 \cdot a)(1.3 \cdot a)$ there are two possible normal forms $N_1(w) = (\frac{1}{2} \cdot a)(1 + \frac{1}{2} \cdot a)$ and $N_2(w) = (\frac{1}{2} \cdot a)(1 \cdot a)$.

Applying a single step of the Smart Teacher algorithm results in an extended OT, adding new entries — either new row words (from action 1 or from processing a counterexample), new suffix words (from action 2), or new extensions from increasing the constant (action 3 and 4). For these new entries, the Learner must assign reset values. To do so, it generates all possible reset assignments extending the assignment of $\mathcal{T}$. We require a possible reset assignment to satisfy $r(\epsilon) = r(\epsilon, \epsilon) = 0$, for every $s(t \cdot a) \in S \cup S\Sigma_K$, $r(s(t \cdot a)) \in \{r(s) + t, 0\}$ and, for every $u_1, u_2 \in S \cup S\Sigma_K$ and every $v_1, v_2 \in E$ if $u_1 v_1 = u_2 v_2$ then we require that $r(u_1, v_1) = r(u_2, v_2)$.

Each such assignment yields a distinct OT; The Learner adds all these OTs to P_{i+1} and moves on to the next OT from P_i. Once all the OTs in P_i have been processed, P_i becomes empty and the new pool is P_{i+1}. Termination follows from the termination of the Smart Teacher algorithm and the fact that one of the branches corresponds to the execution of the Smart Teacher algorithm.

Theorem 21. *The Normal Teacher algorithm terminates and returns a strict acceptor for L of constant $K \geq K_L$ and reset function $R : \mathbb{R}_{\geq 0} \to [0, K] \setminus \mathbb{N}_{>0}$. Moreover, the algorithm processes $O(2^{H^3 m 2^m |\Sigma|} H)$ observation tables and performs $O(2^{H^3 m 2^m |\Sigma|} H^3 m 2^m |\Sigma|)$ membership queries where $H = K_L + n$, n is the number of equivalence classes for $\approx^L$ and m the length of the longest counterexample.*

Obtaining the canonical acceptor. Let $\mathcal{T}$ be the final OT returned by the Normal Teacher algorithm and $(R, \approx)$ be the profile of $\mathcal{A}_{\mathcal{T}}$. A priori, the reset function R may differ from $\mathbf{R}^L$. Consequently, $\mathcal{A}_{\mathcal{T}}$ need not be isomorphic to $\mathcal{A}_{(\mathbf{R}^L, \approx^L)}$. We show next how to learn $\mathcal{A}_{(\mathbf{R}^L, \approx^L)}$ from $\mathcal{A}_{\mathcal{T}}$ using only equivalence queries. We do it in two steps. From $\mathcal{A}_{\mathcal{T}}$ we build a language equivalent acceptor $\mathcal{A}_{\mathbf{R}^L}$ whose reset function is $\mathbf{R}^L$, using Algorithm 1. Secondly, from $\mathcal{A}_{\mathbf{R}}^L$ we perform a state merging to obtain the automaton which induces $\approx^L$ by the method explained in the subsection on computing canonical acceptor in Section 6. They key point is that deciding whether q and q' should be merged can be implemented by doing the merge and then checking whether the resulting automaton has an equivalent language, through an equivalence query to the Teacher.

We now explain Algorithm 1. Given a strict acceptor $\mathcal{A}$ for L Algorithm 1 modifies one by one every state q at which the reset function of $\mathcal{A}$ differs from $\mathbf{R}^L$ i.e., $q = \mathcal{A}(u)$ for some $u \in \mathbb{T}\Sigma^*$ and $R^{\mathcal{A}}(u) \neq \mathbf{R}^L(u)$. Notice that necessarily $region(q) \neq \{0\}$. The acceptor returned at the end has no such states, thus its reset function is $\mathbf{R}^L$. The condition $R^{\mathcal{A}}(u) \neq \mathbf{R}^L(u)$ is checked by the equivalence query $\mathcal{L}(\mathcal{A}_q) = L$ where $\mathcal{A}_q$ is a modification of the automaton which only affects transitions and the region of state q. This region now becomes $\{0\}$. As a result, the number of states at which the reset function differs from $\mathbf{R}^L$ strictly decreases.

Given a strict K-acceptor $\mathcal{A}$, and a state q such that $region(q) \neq \{0\}$, we define the strict acceptor $\mathcal{A}_q$ obtained by modifying $\mathcal{A}$ as follows:

- Replace every transition $(q', q, a, \phi, 1)$ with $q' \neq q$ in $\mathcal{A}$ (there are no transitions incoming to q where clock is reset) by the transition $(q', q, a, \phi, 0)$ (clock is necessarily reset).
- Remove all transitions whose source is q.

– Add a transition $(q, q_a, a, 0 \leq x, 0)$, where q_a is the state corresponding to the transition $(q, q_a, a, x = K, 0)$ in $\mathcal{A}$.

Algorithm 1: Learning a acceptor with reset function $\mathbf{R}^L$

Input: A strict acceptor $\mathcal{A}$ for L
Output: An acceptor with reset function $\mathbf{R}^L$
1 **foreach** *state q in $\mathcal{A}$ with region$(q) \neq \{0\}$* **do**
2   **if** *Teacher confirms $\mathcal{L}(\mathcal{A}_q) = L$* **then** change $\mathcal{A}$ to $\mathcal{A}_q$;
3 **return** $\mathcal{A}$;

Correctness of Algorithm 1 is given in the long version [11].

For the complexity: Algorithm 1 requires a number of equivalence queries equal at most to the number of states of $\mathcal{A}_\mathcal{T}$ which is bounded by $Hm2^m$ (by proof Theorem 21). Minimization of $\mathcal{A}_{\mathbf{R}^L}$ uses at most $(Hm2^m)^2$ equivalence queries.

8 Conclusion

We have presented a Myhill-Nerode characterization for languages recognized by 1-DTAs. Theoretically, this is appealing since we are now able to identify a canonical automaton for a 1-DTA language L and are also able to learn it. Moreover, the canonical automaton has the minimal number of states among all strict acceptors for L. The work [16] on the full class of deterministic timed automata presents one aspect of a Myhill-Nerode characterization: a language L is recognized by a DTA iff a certain equivalence has finite index. It does not go on to identify canonical candidate automata. One interesting future direction is to examine their results specifically for 1-DTAs, equipped with our new insights. From a practical perspective, the algorithms for 1-DTA learning [3] were enhanced [17] using satisfiability solvers to encode the guesses for the resets. Since we work with strict acceptors, resets are fixed at transitions with guards $x = c$. This means that, in principle, we need fewer guesses. A comprehensive optimization of our learning algorithm based on techniques from DFA learning, implementing and comparing to existing tools on 1-DTA learning, is an interesting direction for future work.

References

1. Alur, R., Dill, D.L.: A theory of timed automata. Theoretical Computer Science **126**(2), 183–235 (1994). https://doi.org/10.1016/0304-3975(94)90010-8
2. Alur, R., Fix, L., Henzinger, T.A.: Event-clock automata: A determinizable class of timed automata. Theor. Comput. Sci. **211**(1-2), 253–273 (1999). https://doi.org/10.1016/S0304-3975(97)00173-4

3. An, J., Chen, M., Zhan, B., Zhan, N., Zhang, M.: Learning one-clock timed automata. In: Tools and Algorithms for the Construction and Analysis of Systems - 26th International Conference, TACAS 2020, Held as Part of the European Joint Conferences on Theory and Practice of Software, ETAPS 2020, Proceedings, Part I. Lecture Notes in Computer Science, vol. 12078, pp. 444–462. Springer (2020). https://doi.org/10.1007/978-3-030-45190-5_25

4. An, J., Wang, L., Zhan, B., Zhan, N., Zhang, M.: Learning real-time automata. Sci. China Inf. Sci. **64**(9) (2021). https://doi.org/10.1007/S11432-019-2767-4

5. An, J., Zhan, B., Zhan, N., Zhang, M.: Learning Nondeterministic Real-Time Automata. ACM Transactions on Embedded Computing Systems **20**(5s), 1–26 (2021). https://doi.org/10.1145/3477030

6. Angluin, D.: Learning regular sets from queries and counterexamples. Inf. Comput. **75**(2), 87–106 (1987). https://doi.org/10.1016/0890-5401(87)90052-6

7. Behrmann, G., David, A., Larsen, K.G.: A tutorial on uppaal. In: Formal Methods for the Design of Real-Time Systems, International School on Formal Methods for the Design of Computer, Communication and Software Systems, SFM-RT 2004, Revised Lectures. Lecture Notes in Computer Science, vol. 3185, pp. 200–236. Springer (2004). https://doi.org/10.1007/978-3-540-30080-9_7

8. Bhave, D., Guha, S.: Adding Dense-Timed Stack to Integer Reset Timed Automata. In: RP'17: Proc. 11th International Conference on Reachability Problems. LNCS, vol. 10506, pp. 9–25. Springer (2017). https://doi.org/10.1007/978-3-319-67089-8_2

9. Bruyère, V., Garhewal, B., Pérez, G.A., Staquet, G., Vaandrager, F.W.: Active learning of mealy machines with timers. CoRR **abs/2403.02019** (2024). https://doi.org/10.48550/ARXIV.2403.02019

10. Doveri, K., Ganty, P., Srivathsan, B.: A Myhill-Nerode style characterization for timed automata with integer resets. In: 44th IARCS Annual Conference on Foundations of Software Technology and Theoretical Computer Science, FSTTCS 2024. LIPIcs, vol. 323, pp. 21:1–21:18. Schloss Dagstuhl - Leibniz-Zentrum für Informatik (2024). https://doi.org/10.4230/LIPICS.FSTTCS.2024.21

11. Doveri, K., Ganty, P., Srivathsan, B.: A Myhill-Nerode characterization and active learning for one-clock timed automata (2026), https://arxiv.org/abs/2601.15104

12. Grinchtein, O., Jonsson, B., Leucker, M.: Learning of event-recording automata. Theoretical Computer Science **411**(47), 4029–4054 (2010). https://doi.org/10.1016/j.tcs.2010.07.008

13. Maler, O., Pnueli, A.: On Recognizable Timed Languages. In: FoSSaCS'04: Proc. of the Int. Conf. on Foundations of Software Science and Computation Structures. LNCS, vol. 2987, pp. 348–362. Springer (2004). https://doi.org/10.1007/978-3-540-24727-2_25

14. Suman, P.V., Pandya, P.K., Krishna, S.N., Manasa, L.: Timed Automata with Integer Resets: Language Inclusion and Expressiveness. In: FORMATS'08: Proc. of the Int. Conf. on Formal Modeling and Analysis of Timed Systems. vol. 5215, pp. 78–92. Springer (2008). https://doi.org/10.1007/978-3-540-85778-5_7

15. Vaandrager, F.W., Ebrahimi, M., Bloem, R.: Learning mealy machines with one timer. Inf. Comput. **295**(Part A), 105013 (2023). https://doi.org/10.1016/J.IC.2023.105013

16. Waga, M.: Active Learning of Deterministic Timed Automata with Myhill-Nerode Style Characterization. In: CAV'23: Proc. of the 35th Int. Conf. on Computer Aided Verification. LNCS, vol. 13964, pp. 3–26. Springer (2023). https://doi.org/10.1007/978-3-031-37706-8_1

17. Xu, R., An, J., Zhan, B.: Active learning of one-clock timed automata using constraint solving. In: Automated Technology for Verification and Analysis - 20th International Symposium, ATVA 2022, Virtual Event, October 25-28, 2022, Proceedings. Lecture Notes in Computer Science, vol. 13505, pp. 249–265. Springer (2022). https://doi.org/10.1007/978-3-031-19992-9_16

Faster Signature Refinement for Branching Bisimilarity Minimization

Jan Martens[1] and Maurice Laveaux[2]

[1] Leiden Institute of Advanced Computer Science, The Netherlands
[2] Eindhoven University of Technology, The Netherlands
j.j.m.martens@liacs.leidenuniv.nl, m.laveaux@tue.nl

Abstract. We present a new algorithm to efficiently minimize state spaces with respect to branching bisimilarity. Our approach combines signature-based refinement with Hopcroft's "process-the-smaller-half" optimization to avoid unnecessary computation. This combination results in a conceptually simpler and empirically faster algorithm for state space minimization modulo branching bisimilarity. While the theoretical worst-case complexity is slightly worse than existing algorithms, empirical evaluations on benchmarks demonstrate significantly better performance.

1   Introduction

Deciding behavioural equivalences for state spaces is an important instrument for analysing and verifying state-based systems [12]. Intricate models often contain abstractions in the form of silent actions. A rich theory of equivalences that give semantics to these silent actions has arisen [22]. Branching bisimilarity is one of these equivalences and is widely used for various reasons: (1) It maintains the branching structure of the process with respect to silent actions, (2) it is efficiently computable, and (3) it is a coarse equivalence that can be used as preprocessing step in computing many other equivalences, for example weak bisimulation [19].

Most algorithms that decide bisimulation relations are so-called *partition refinement* algorithms. A partition refinement algorithm works by maintaining a partition that represents the equivalence relation identified so far. Initially all states are considered equivalent. The algorithm then incrementally refines the partition by separating states that witness distinct behaviour with respect to the current partition. These algorithms work for many different settings, deterministic, probabilistic, weighted, timed, etc [5,21,25].

Within this partition refinement paradigm there are two main styles of algorithms to decide branching bisimilarity: Hopcroft-style algorithms [15,13], and so-called signature refinement algorithms [6,7]. Signature refinement algorithms iteratively group states with identical behaviour with respect to the current partition. Hopcroft-style algorithms refine the partition by separating states based on individual behavioural properties, working in the opposite direction as signature refinement. Signature refinement algorithms work surprisingly well

S. Junges and G. Katz (Eds.): TACAS 2026, LNCS 16505, pp. 438–456, 2026.
https://doi.org/10.1007/978-3-032-22752-2_23

in practice. However, they inspect more transitions than necessary and have a worse theoretical runtime complexity. In practice, it can be seen that for certain systems signature refinement scales significantly worse than the Hopcroft-style algorithms.

Recently, Jacobs and Wißmann [14] proposed an algorithm that combines advantages from both styles of partition refinement algorithms. This algorithm works for a wide range of (coalgebraic) equivalences without silent actions. The proposed algorithm uses signature refinement but incorporates the Hopcroft's "process-the-small-half" optimization. Their benchmarks empirically show that this method improves on the performance of these algorithms. However, the algorithm does not work for deciding behavioural equivalences with silent transitions like branching bisimulation.

In this paper, we propose an algorithm that minimizes states spaces modulo branching bisimilarity based on the ideas of [14]. We use a modified version of inductive signatures [7] and carefully process the states in the right order. This combination guarantees succinct signatures while avoiding unnecessary work. Our empirical evaluation shows that our algorithm is significantly faster than other algorithms.

Structure. The remainder of this paper is structured as follows. First, we introduce the necessary preliminaries and definitions in Section 2. In Section 3 we present our new algorithm for branching bisimilarity minimization. We start by giving a high level overview of the algorithm, and finish the chapter with pseudocode and data structures. Section 4 contains an analysis of the algorithms correctness and runtime complexity. In Section 5 we empirically compare our implementation with other tools. Additionally, we provide families of systems to illustrate the gap between the theoretical worst-case time complexities of our algorithm and the other algorithms. Finally, in Section 6 we provide concluding remarks and directions for future work.

2   Preliminaries

In this section we define branching bisimulation and explain the algorithmic framework of signature refinement.

Definition 1. A labelled transition system (LTS) M is a triple $M = (S, Act_\tau, \rightarrow)$ consisting of:

- a finite set of states S,
- a finite set of action labels Act_τ containing the silent action $\tau \in Act_\tau$,
- a transition function $\rightarrow \subseteq S \times Act_\tau \times S$.

We write a transition $(s, a, s') \in \; \rightarrow$ as $s \xrightarrow{a} s'$. With $Act = Act_\tau \setminus \{\tau\}$ we denote the set of all non-silent action labels. We write $\twoheadrightarrow = \{ (s, s') \mid s \xrightarrow{\tau} \cdots \xrightarrow{\tau} s' \}$ for the transitive and reflexive closure of all τ-transitions.

Definition 2. Let M be an LTS. A symmetric relation $R : S \times S$ is called a *branching bisimulation* relation if and only if for all $(s, t) \in R$ and $s \xrightarrow{a} s'$ either:

- $a = \tau$ and $(s', t) \in R$, or
- there are t', t'' such that $t \twoheadrightarrow t' \xrightarrow{a} t''$, $(s, t') \in R$, and $(s', t'') \in R$.

The largest branching bisimulation relation, denoted $\underline{\leftrightarrow}_b$, is called branching *bisimilarity*.

Given an LTS $M = (S, Act_\tau, \rightarrow)$, we define the pre-order $\preccurlyeq_\tau$ defining reachability under τ-transitions. More formally, $s \preccurlyeq_\tau t$ if and only if there is a path of τ transitions from s to t, i.e. $s \twoheadrightarrow t$. This order induces a *topological sort*, which can be computed in linear time. The topological order with respect to silent actions is relevant for our algorithm.

An important property of branching bisimilarity is the so-called *stuttering* property.

Lemma 3. (Stuttering Lemma cf. [23, Lem. 2.5]) Let $M = (S, Act_\tau, \rightarrow)$ be an LTS, then for all $s, t, u \in S$ such that $s \underline{\leftrightarrow}_b t$ it holds that:

$$s \preccurlyeq_\tau u \text{ and } u \preccurlyeq_\tau t \implies u \underline{\leftrightarrow}_b s.$$

A direct consequence of this lemma is that if two states s and t are on the same τ-cycle, then they are branching bisimilar. More precisely,

$$s \preccurlyeq_\tau t \text{ and } t \preccurlyeq_\tau s \implies s \underline{\leftrightarrow}_b t.$$

It is convenient and common to preprocess a given LTS into one that is free of τ-cycles. This can be done by computing the strongly connected components under τ-transitions, and replacing each strongly connected component by a single state. This decomposition can be computed in linear time with Tarjan's algorithm [20].

2.1   Signature refinement and Hopcroft's trick

A *partition* π of a set of states S is a disjoint cover of S, i.e., a collection of non-empty sets of states $B_1, \ldots, B_k \subseteq S$ such that $\bigcup_{i \in [1,k]} B_i = S$ and $B_i \cap B_j = \emptyset$ for all $i \neq j$. We refer to an element $B \in \pi$ as a *block*. We see a partition $\pi = \{B_1, \ldots, B_k\}$ as a function $\pi : S \mapsto [1, k]$, such that for every state $s \in S$, $\pi(s) = i$ if and only if $s \in B_i$. A partition π naturally induces an equivalence relation where the blocks of π are the equivalence classes.

The signature refinement framework iteratively characterizes the behaviour of states. A specific behavioural equivalence defines what is considered the behaviour of a state. We define the *successors* to capture all behaviour from a given LTS. For instance, given an LTS M, the successors of s without taking into account silent actions are given as set $\{(a, s) \mid s \xrightarrow{a} s'\}$. For branching bisimilarity the successors are defined as map $c : S \rightarrow 2^{S \times Act_\tau \times S}$,

$$c(s) = \{(s', a, s'') \mid s \twoheadrightarrow s' \text{ and, either } s' \xrightarrow{a} s'' \text{ or } a = \tau \wedge s' = s''\}.$$

A *signature function* is obtained by substituting states with π equivalence classes in the successor structure c. This yields a function $sig_\pi^{\leftrightarrow b}$, where each state s is associated with a set of behaviours. This characterizes the behaviour of a state with respect to the current partition. Formally, for branching bisimulation,

$$sig_\pi^{\leftrightarrow b}(s) = \{\, (\pi(s'), a, \pi(s'')) \mid (s', a, s'') \in c(s) \,\}.$$

We claim without proof that the equivalence relation induced by π is a branching bisimulation relation if and only if for all states s and t it holds that $\pi(s) = \pi(t) \iff sig_\pi^{\leftrightarrow b}(s) = sig_\pi^{\leftrightarrow b}(t)$. The process of defining the successor relations explicitly can be seen as a τ-saturated system, which is often used to reason about weak bisimilarity [4, Section 3.2.5]. For branching bisimulation this was also noticed in [11, Section 5.3].

Signature refinement is the process of iteratively classifying distinct signatures until a fixed point is reached. The naive algorithm starts with a partition with only one block, i.e. all states are related. Then it iteratively groups all states with equal signatures until a fixed point is reached. The limitation of this naive approach is that it recomputes the signature of every state in each iteration, even when the signature remains unchanged.

The main algorithmic improvement of [14] addresses this limitation and only recomputes a state's signature if there is a reason to. This is done by maintaining a set of so-called *dirty* states of which the signature is necessarily different from the signature last computed. A state is marked dirty if one of the successors is in a new block in the previous iteration.

By reusing the old block for the largest block in a split, each state is only part of a *new* block at most logarithmic number of times. Hence, every state has their predecessors marked at most a logarithmic time. Algorithm 1 contains a sketch of this signature refinement framework.

Algorithm 1 Faster signature refinement [14].

Input: An LTS $M = (S, Act, \rightarrow)$ where $S = \{s_1, \ldots, s_n\}$.
Output: The largest partition π that expresses the behavioural equivalence of sig.
    Initialize $\pi := \{S\}$
    Mark all states dirty.
    while there are dirty states **do**
        Pick $B \in \pi$ that contains dirty states.
        Refine B into sig equivalence classes $B_1, \ldots, B_k$.
        Let $B_{max} \in \{B_1, \ldots, B_k\}$ be the largest block, i.e. $|B_{max}| \geq |B_i|$ for all $i \in [1, k]$.
        Replace B with B_{max} in π.
        Add the new blocks $B_i \neq B_{max}$ to π.
        for each new block B_i **do**
            Mark s_p dirty if there is a $s \in B_i$ that occurs in $c(s_p)$ (e.g. $s_p \xrightarrow{a} s$ for strong bisimilarity).

We note that this signature refinement framework works for many different behavioural equivalences. More signature functions for other equivalences with

τ-transitions are given in [24, Section 3]. Our presentation differs from these signatures in the fact that we define the successors separately and independent from the partition. Conceptually these successor structures fit directly in the coalgebraic framework of [14].

Main challenges for branching bisimulation The algorithm introduced in [14] works generically for a wide range of state-based systems. However, it does not work efficiently for equivalences that have silent actions. The main reason is that it relies on a (local) successor structure that captures the behaviour of the states. Implementing the successor structure is not obvious for an equivalence like branching bisimulation since the behaviour of a state also contains τ-paths of arbitrary lengths. Including all these paths in the signature would make signatures unnecessarily large.

In order to employ the ideas of [14], we use the notion of inductive signatures [7], and rely on properties of branching bisimulation with respect to the topological sort of states under silent transitions.

3   Algorithm

In this section we describe the algorithm that reduces an LTS without τ-cycles modulo branching bisimilarity. First, we define the signature the algorithm uses in Section 3.1. Then in Section 3.2 we give an overview of the main ideas of the algorithm. After that, we provide details for the data structures, and procedures necessary for an efficient implementation.

3.1   Signatures

The notion of inductive signatures was first defined in [7]. The main advantage of using inductive signatures over traditional signatures is that all behaviour over silent paths is not part of the signature, but can be inferred inductively from the local signature. This causes the size of a signature to be bounded by the out-degree of a state. In the signature a fresh symbol $\dot{\tau} \notin Act_\tau$ is used to represent silent actions that *may* be an inert transition, i.e. a silent transition $s \xrightarrow{\tau} s'$ where s and s' remain related in the next partition. We define two signature functions, the local $\mathtt{PreSig}_\pi$ and the inductive $\mathtt{Sig}_\pi$. The main difference with respect to [7, Def. 10] is that these signature functions are defined with respect to arbitrary partitions.

Definition 4 (Signature). Let $M = (S, Act_\tau, \rightarrow)$ be an LTS without τ-cycles, π a partition, and $h : \mathcal{I}m(\mathtt{Sig}_\pi) \rightarrow \mathbb{N}$ an isomorphism. We define for all $s \in S$ the local and inductive signature:

$$\mathtt{PreSig}_\pi(s) = \{(a, \pi(s')) \mid s \xrightarrow{a} s' \text{ and either } a \neq \tau \text{ or } \pi(s) \neq \pi(s')\}$$
$$\cup \{(\dot{\tau}, h(\mathtt{Sig}_\pi(s'))) \mid s \xrightarrow{\tau} s' \text{ and } \pi(s) = \pi(s')\}$$

$$\mathtt{Sig}_\pi(s) = \begin{cases} \mathtt{Sig}_\pi(s') & \text{if } s \xrightarrow{\tau} s' \text{ such that } \pi(s) = \pi(s'), \text{and} \\ & \quad \mathtt{PreSig}_\pi(s) \subseteq \mathtt{Sig}_\pi(s') \cup \{(\dot{\tau}, h(\mathtt{Sig}_\pi(s')))\} \\ \mathtt{PreSig}_\pi(s) & \text{otherwise} \end{cases}$$

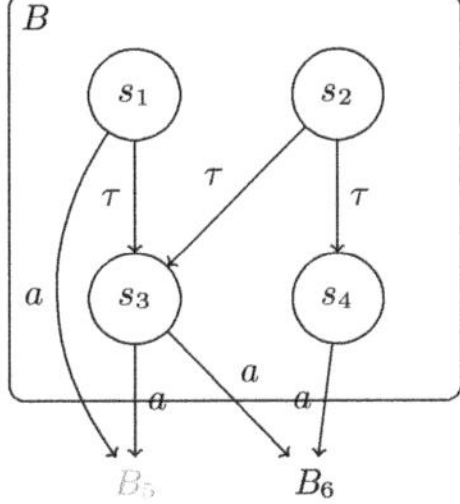

	s_3	s_4	s_1	s_2
$\texttt{PreSig}_\pi$	$\{(a,5),(a,6)\}$	$\{(a,6)\}$	$\{(a,5),(\dot\tau,1)\}$	$\{(\dot\tau,2),(\dot\tau,1)\}$
$\texttt{Sig}_\pi$	$\{(a,5),(a,6)\}$	$\{(a,6)\}$	$\{(a,5),(a,6)\}$	$\{(\dot\tau,2),(\dot\tau,1)\}$
$\texttt{state2sig}$	1	2	1	3

$\texttt{sigs} = [\{(a,5),(a,6)\},\{(a,6)\},\{(a,5),(\dot\tau,1)\},\{(\dot\tau,2),(\dot\tau,1)\}]$

Fig. 1. Example of inductive signatures, where $B = \{s_1, s_2, s_3, s_4\}$.

Note that this definition is not circular because the LTS M does not contain τ-cycles.

The isomorphism h acts as numbering function assigning to each distinct signature a distinct number. This function exists since the set of all signatures with respect to π is finite. As is noted in [14] it is possible to implement such a morphism in linear time in size of the signatures. In practice we implement this using a hash table, and maintaining an array $\texttt{state2sig}$ that represents the function $s \mapsto h(\texttt{Sig}_\pi(s))$.

To confirm that this notion of signature correctly captures branching bisimilarity, we state the following two properties.

Lemma 5. Let $L = (S, Act_\tau, \rightarrow)$ be an LTS without τ-cycles and π a partition such that $\underline{\leftrightarrow}_b \subseteq \sim_\pi$. The following two properties hold:

- for all pairs $s, t \in S$ we have, $s \underline{\leftrightarrow}_b t \implies \texttt{Sig}_\pi(s) = \texttt{Sig}_\pi(t)$, and
- if for all $s \sim_\pi t$: $\texttt{Sig}_\pi(s) = \texttt{Sig}_\pi(t)$ then $\sim_\pi = \underline{\leftrightarrow}_b$.

These properties and their proofs are in the same spirit as for inductive signatures defined earlier [7, Lemma 14 and Lemma 16]. The main difference in this definition of inductive signatures takes into account arbitrary partitions π and thus is more flexible. For completeness a proof is included in Appendix A of the full version of this paper.

3.2   Algorithm outline

Now we explain the main structure of the program, which is one iteration of the **while**-loop from Algorithm 2. We assume that the input LTS is preprocessed such that it does not contain τ-cycles. We maintain a set of *dirty* states as $\mathcal{X} \subseteq S$. The other states $S \setminus \mathcal{X}$ are then naturally referred to as clean states. Given an LTS $M = (S, Act_\tau, \rightarrow)$, the algorithm starts with the initial partition $\pi_0 = \{S\}$, and every state is dirty, i.e. $\mathcal{X}_0 = S$. Now at some point in the execution, given the partition π and set of dirty states $\mathcal{X}$, the process performs the following steps.

1. Pick a block $B \in \pi$ that contains at least one dirty state, i.e. $(B \cap \mathcal{X} \neq \emptyset)$.

2. Compute the backwards transitive closure of inert paths of dirty states, i.e. $B_{dirty} = \{s \in B \mid s \twoheadrightarrow s' \text{ and } s' \in B \cap \mathcal{X}\}$.
3. Compute the signatures $\mathtt{Sig}_\pi(s)$ of all dirty states $s \in B_{dirty}$.
4. Split the block B in the clean states $B_{cl} = B \setminus B_{dirty}$ and $\mathtt{Sig}_\pi$ equivalence classes:

$$B \mapsto \{B_{cl}\} \cup \{\, \{s' \in B_{dirty} \mid \mathtt{Sig}_\pi(s) = \mathtt{Sig}_\pi(s')\} \mid s \in B_{dirty}\}\,.$$

5. Replace B in π with the largest block and add all other blocks as new blocks $\mathtt{new\_blocks}$.
6. Update the dirty states $\mathcal{X}$. First remove the states B_{dirty} from $\mathcal{X}$. After that, add all the predecessors $\mathtt{Pred}(\cup_{B_i \in \mathtt{new\_blocks}} B_i)$ of all newly added blocks to $\mathcal{X}$. Here, we define predecessors as function $\mathtt{Pred}$ for a set $U \subseteq S$,

$$\mathtt{Pred}(U) = \{s_p \mid \exists s \in U \text{ s.t. } s_p \xrightarrow{a} s \text{ and } a = \tau \Rightarrow s_p \notin U\}.$$

Now $\mathtt{Pred}(U)$ contains all states s such that the signature $\mathtt{PreSig}_\pi(s)$ contains a non-inert element corresponding to a state in U. Here we mean non-inert with respect to U, since τ-transitions between two states in U are already handled in the signature.

Algorithm 2 The signature refinement algorithm for branching bisimulation.

---

procedure BRANCHINGBISIM
    $B_0 := (0, 0, N)$
    $worklist := [B_0]$
    while $worklist$ is not empty and $B := worklist.pop()$ **do**
        Clear hash map h.
        $B_{dirty} = $ SORTEDCLOSURE(B)
        Initialise the array $\mathtt{state2sig} : B_{dirty} \to \mathbb{N}$.
        for each $s \in B_{dirty}$ **do**
            ▷ Importantly B_{dirty} is topologically sorted.
            Compute $sig = \mathtt{PreSig}_\pi(s, \mathtt{state2sig})$.
            if $sig \subseteq h^{-1}(c) \cup \{(\dot\tau, c)\}$ for some $(\dot\tau, c) \in sig$ **then**
                $\mathtt{state2sig}[s] = c$
            else
                $\mathtt{state2sig}[s] = h(sig)$
        $\mathtt{new_blocks} := $ SPLIT$(B, \mathtt{state2sig})$
        $U_{new} := \bigcup_{B' \in \mathtt{new\_blocks}} B'$
        for $s_p \in \mathtt{Pred}(U_{new})$ **do**
            MARKDIRTY(s_p)

This procedure only splits states with a distinct signature. If two states in the same block have a distinct signature, then at least one of the states is marked dirty. Once a fixed point is reached the paritition π is equal to branching bisimilarity.

3.3 Data structures

Given an input LTS $M = (S, Act_\tau, \rightarrow)$, with $n = |S|$ states and $m = |\rightarrow|$ transitions. The states are represented as integers $\{0, \ldots, |S| - 1\}$. The partition $\pi = \{B_1, \ldots, B_k\}$ is represented in an array `state2block` with $|S|$ elements that maps states to the indices of the blocks `state2bloc`$[s] = \pi(s)$. We maintain the following data structures to represent the LTS.

- The array `transitions` of length m with pairs (a, t) for a transition $\overset{a}{\rightarrow} t$, and
- `states`, an array of tuples $(start\_out, end\_out)$ of length n. For each state index s, `states`$[s] = (start\_out, end\_out)$ means that the outgoing transitions for s are located in `transitions`$[start\_out, \ldots, end\_out - 1]$.

We maintain an additional copy of the LTS $M^{-1} = (S, Act_\tau, \rightarrow^{-1})$ for incoming transitions, $\rightarrow^{-1} = \{(s', a, s) \mid s \overset{a}{\rightarrow} s'\}$. This is necessary to access incoming transitions in constant time.

Additionally, we maintain a refinable partition data structure [14,21]. The set of states S are represented as natural numbers $\{0, \ldots, |S| - 1\}$ in an array `loc2state`. The location of a state is the position in this array, and are also maintained in the array `state2loc`. Blocks are tuples $(start, marked\_split, end)$ that indicate a range in this array from $start \ldots end$ that contain the states of the block. The clean states of the block are located in $start \ldots marked\_split - 1$, and the dirty states in $marked\_split \ldots end$.

- `loc2state` An array that maps locations to their corresponding states.
- `state2loc` An array that maps states to their corresponding locations.
- `state2block` An array that maps states to the block they are currently in.
- `blocks` a vector that contains all blocks currently in the partition.
- `worklist` a stack containing all blocks that have dirty states.

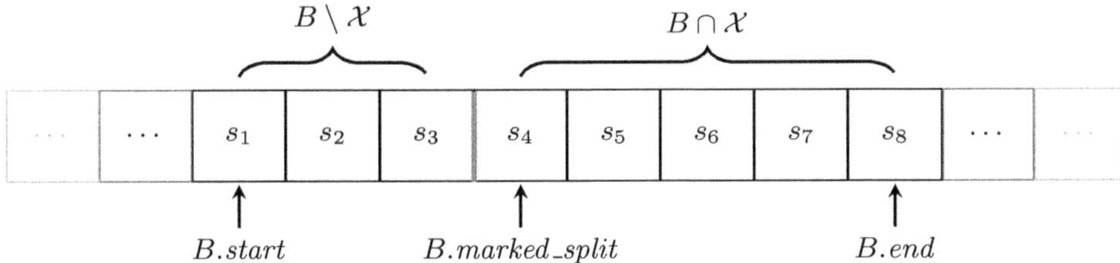

Fig. 2. Example of the block $B = \{s_1, \ldots, s_8\}$ represented in the array `loc2state` in the refineable partition data structure, here the dirty states are $B \cap \mathcal{X} = \{s_4, \ldots, s_8\}$.

This refinable partition data structure is illustrated in Figure 2 and enable the marking of dirty states in constant time. This is done by swapping the state with the last clean state in the block, and updating the block's *marked-split* variable. This is shown in the Procedure MARKDIRTY listed in Algorithm 3. Marking a state clean is done analogously. We can also iterate over marked states of one block in linear time, and access all transitions in and out of s in time proportional to the out-degree and in-degree of s.

Algorithm 3 Procedures for marking a state dirty and splitting states according to signatures represented in `state2sig`.

---

procedure MARKDIRTY(s)
   $B :=$ `state2block`$[s]$
   if s not marked dirty **then**
      if B contains no dirty states yet **then**
         $worklist.push(B)$
      Swap s with $B.marked\_split - 1$
      $B.marked\_split := B.marked\_split - 1$
procedure SPLIT$(B,\ state2sig\colon B_{dirty} \to \mathbb{N})$
   Initialize new_blocks
   if $B \setminus B_{dirty} \neq \emptyset$ **then**
      $new\_blocks.push(B \setminus B_{dirty})$ ▷ The untouched clean states.
   for $b \in \{state2sig[s] \mid s \in B_{dirty}\}$ **do**
      $new\_blocks.push(\{s \mid s \in B_{dirty}$ and $state2sig[s] = b\})$
   $B_{max} := max(new\_blocks)$
   In π replace B with B_{max}
   Add $new\_blocks \setminus \{B_{max}\}$ to π as new blocks.
   return $new\_blocks \setminus \{B_{max}\}$

Moreover, this partition data structure allows us to split a block B into subblocks according to the signatures in time linear in the size of B. This is done by iterating over all states in B and grouping them according to their signature. This is shown in Algorithm 3 in the SPLIT procedure, or more detailed in [14, Algorithm. 5].

3.4   Silent closure & topological sort

Before processing the dirty states of a block B, we compute the backwards closure. Additionally, we sort this closure in order to guarantee the states are in topological order before processing. This can be done in time linear in the size of the marked states and transitions. An example that illustrates the functionality of this function is shown in Figure 3.

The procedure SORTEDCLOSURE(B) implements this functionality. The function consists of two distinct passes of all states two phases backwards closure, and topological sort. This is analogous to the normal methods of topologically sorting graphs [16, Section 2.2.3].

Algorithm 4 Procedure that marks the backwards closure of the dirty states of B and guarantees marked elements are topologically sorted.

---

procedure SORTEDCLOSURE(B)
    for $i := B.end - 1;\ i \geq B.marked\_split;\ i{-}{-}$ **do**
        $s := \texttt{loc2state}[i]$
        for each $s' \xrightarrow{\tau} s$ such that $s' \in B \setminus \mathcal{X}$ **do**
            MARKDIRTY(s').
    return $\texttt{TopoSort}(\texttt{loc2state}[B.marked\_split \ldots B.end])$

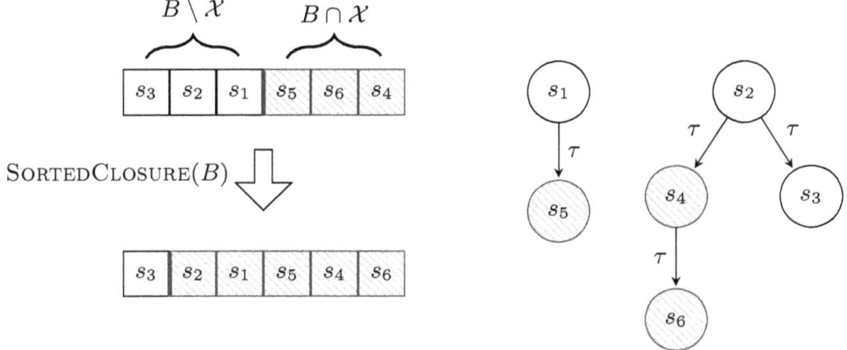

Fig. 3. Illustration of the SORTEDCLOSURE function, where the highlighted states at the right were initially marked dirty.

3.5 Signature Computation

The signature of the behaviour with respect to the current partition is computed in arrays. All states are processed in the topological order, and the signatures of all states are dynamically allocated. This ensures that for any inert outgoing transition the signatures of the target state are already computed.

The procedure $\texttt{PreSig}_\pi$ in Algorithm 5, builds a sorted array that represents the signature $\texttt{PreSig}_\pi(s)$ of a state s in the current partition π. Since the signatures are typically small, we found that using sorting performed better than a hash table. To achieve the theoretical complexity a radix sort could be used.

4 Correctness & complexity

In this section we evaluate the algorithm. First, we establish the correctness of the algorithm. After that we analyse the theoretical complexity.

4.1 Correctness

To establish the correctness of the algorithm, we show that the algorithm correctly identifies states as dirty states. More precisely, it must be shown that if two states in a processed block are not touched, then the signatures are equal.

Algorithm 5 Computing a signature.

---

procedure $\textsc{PreSig}_\pi(s, \texttt{state2sig} : B_{dirty} \to \mathbb{N})$
    Initialize sig
    for each $s \xrightarrow{a} s'$ **do**
        if $a \neq \tau$ or $s' \notin B_{dirty}$ **then**
            $sig.push(\langle a, \pi(s) \rangle)$
        else
            $sig.push(\langle \dot\tau, \texttt{state2sig}[s'] \rangle)$ $\triangleright$ $\texttt{state2sig}[s']$ exists since $s' \preccurlyeq_\tau s$.
    $\textsc{Sort}(sig)$
    $\textsc{RemoveDuplicates}(sig)$
    return sig

Lemma 6. Let $L = (S, Act_\tau, \to)$ be an LTS without τ-cycles. Consider a run of Algorithm 2, where π is the partition before an arbitrary iteration of the **while**-loop, and B_{dirty} the set of dirty states after the $\textsc{SortedClosure}$-call. If two states $s, t \in B \setminus B_{dirty}$, then $\texttt{Sig}_\pi(s) = \texttt{Sig}_\pi(t)$.

Proof. Since s and t are initially marked dirty, there was a most recent iteration where s and t are processed and marked clean. Let π' be the partition just before this iteration and thus $\texttt{Sig}_{\pi'}(s) = \texttt{Sig}_{\pi'}(t)$, such that s, t are now marked clean. Since neither state is marked dirty since, we know that all behaviour is *old*. We make this formal by using the way we number blocks in the partition. Let $c_{max} = \max_{s \in S} \pi'(s)$, the largest number of a block in π'. Now all blocks in π with identifier $c \leq c_{max}$ are considered old blocks and clean states only have outgoing transitions to old blocks.

Now we assume that t is a so-called *bottom state*, i.e. $\{t \xrightarrow{\tau} t' \mid t \sim_{\pi'} t'\} = \emptyset$. Using this assumption, we prove $\texttt{Sig}_\pi(s) = \texttt{Sig}_\pi(t)$ by induction on the well-order $\preccurlyeq_\tau$. Note that the order $\preccurlyeq_\tau$ is a well-order, and that each block B has a bottom state, since S is finite and there are no τ- cycles in L. The correctness of the lemma follows by transitivity.

In the base case s is a bottom state, and we know that $\texttt{Sig}_\pi(s) = \texttt{PreSig}_\pi(s)$. Assume $(a, c) \in \texttt{PreSig}_\pi(s)$, then since s is not marked dirty, $c \leq c_{max}$ which is an old block in π'. This means there is a transition $s \xrightarrow{a} s'$ such that $\pi(s') = \pi'(s') = c$. Since $\texttt{Sig}_{\pi'}(s) = \texttt{Sig}_{\pi'}(t)$ and we assumed that t is a bottom state it holds that $\texttt{Sig}_{\pi'}(t) = \texttt{PreSig}_{\pi'}(t)$, and thus $t \xrightarrow{a} t'$ such that $\pi'(t') = c$. Because t is also not marked dirty we know that $\pi(t') = \pi'(t') = c$. This means that $(a, c) \in \texttt{PreSig}_\pi(t)$, and in particular $\texttt{PreSig}_\pi(s) \subseteq \texttt{PreSig}_\pi(t)$. The symmetric case is the same and we conclude $\texttt{PreSig}_\pi(s) = \texttt{PreSig}_\pi(t)$.

In the inductive case there is a $s \xrightarrow{\tau} s'$ such that $s' \in B$. Since $s \notin \{u_p \mid u_p \twoheadrightarrow u, u \in \mathcal{X} \cap B\} = B_{dirty}$ it holds in particular that $s' \notin \{u_p \mid u_p \twoheadrightarrow u, u \in \mathcal{X} \cap B\}$ and hence s' is not dirty $s' \in B \setminus B_{dirty}$. By induction it holds that $\texttt{Sig}_\pi(s') = \texttt{Sig}_\pi(t)$. The proof is completed by showing that in this case $\texttt{Sig}_\pi(s) = \texttt{Sig}_{\pi'}(s')$ because $\texttt{PreSig}_\pi(s) \subseteq \texttt{Sig}_\pi(s') \cup \{(\dot\tau, h(\texttt{Sig}(s')))\}$. $\qquad\square$

The contrapositive of the above lemma guarantees that whenever there is a block in the partition that contains states with distinct signatures, then the block is in the worklist and at least one of the states is contained in B_{dirty}. Together with the properties from Lemma 5 this proves the correctness of the algorithm.

Theorem 7. *Algorithm 2 computes branching bisimilarity.*

4.2 Complexity analysis

In this section we analyse the algorithm for a τ-cycle free LTS $M = (S, Act_\tau, \rightarrow)$, where we write $n = |S|$ for the number of states and $m = |\rightarrow|$ for the number of transitions. Furthermore, we write c for the maximum out-degree of M and d the length of the longest τ-path.

First, we argue that the worst-case complexity of this algorithm is in $O(mn)$, the complexity of [7]. This uses a similar argument as used in [18], and boils down to the fact that a processed block is only processed again if at least one split occured. Since the number of blocks is bounded by n this bounds the number of iterations at $2n$.

Now we analyse the algorithm in a more fine-grained way and provide a better understanding of the performance, and the worst-case scenario. We count the number of times a `PreSig` is computed. This number dominates the complexity.

For each state s the `PreSig` is computed once in the beginning and for each time it was marked as dirty again. Let $B_{new} = \bigcup_{B_i \in \texttt{new\_blocks}} B_i$ be the set of all states in the new blocks. A state $s \in S$ is in B_{dirty} when either:

1. $s \in \mathrm{Pred}(B_{new})$, or
2. $s \twoheadrightarrow s'$ such that $s \sim_\pi s'$ and $s' \in \mathrm{Pred}(B_{new})$.

Since `new_blocks` does not contain the largest block of a split, Hopcroft's reasoning gives us that a state s is contained at most $\log n$ times in `new_blocks`. A state s is in $\mathrm{Pred}(B_{new})$ for at most $\log n$ times for each out going transition.

Lemma 8. For each state $s \in S$ it holds that $s \in \mathrm{Pred}(B_{new})$ at most $c \log n$ times.

This puts a bound on case 1. In the other case, a state is marked dirty because there is an inert path to a state which is marked dirty. We analyse the number of times this could happen, using the bound from previous lemma.

Lemma 9. A state $s \in S$ is in B_{dirty} at most $d + cd \log n$ times, where d is the length of the largest τ-path.

Proof sketch. We write $\#(s)$ for the largest number of times the state s is in B_{dirty}. We prove the statement by induction on the order $\preccurlyeq_\tau$. If s is the smallest element, it does not contain any silent outgoing transitions, and hence by 8 $\#(s) \leq c \log n$.

For the induction case assume that $U = \{s' \mid s \xrightarrow{\tau} s' \text{ and } s \sim_\pi s'\}$. An important observation is that for any pair $s', s'' \in U$, it can only happen once that only one of s', and s'' is in B_{dirty}. Since in this scenario these states are split in that iteration. Hence, the number of times s is in B_{dirty} indirectly by a τ transition is:

$$\max_{s' \in U} \#(s') + 1$$

Let the longest silent path from s be $d' + 1$, then by our induction hypothesis for every $s' \in U$ it holds that $\#(s') \leq cd' \log n + 1$. By Lemma 8 s is only in $\mathtt{Pred}(U)$ at most $c \log n$ times and thus $\#(s) = cd' \log n + c \log n + d' + 1$. $\quad\square$

This automatically gives us a bound on the number of times $\mathtt{PreSig}$ is computed.

Lemma 10. The $\mathtt{PreSig}$ function is computed at most $O(cdn \log n + dn)$ times, where c is the maximum out-degree and d the length of the longest τ path.

Since we only use local signatures in our computations we know that the size of each signature is bounded by c. This means that using the right datastructures the computing time per $\mathtt{PreSig}$ call is bounded by c.

Theorem 11. *Algorithm 2 has worst-case runtime complexity* $O(c^2 d\, n \log n + cdn)$.

For families of LTSs where $c, d \in \Omega(n)$ this is worse than the $O(m \log n)$ from [13]. In particular we consider the factor d troublesome. We note however that in practice this factor d seems often low. Additionally, it is not trivial to find families of LTSs that showcase this worst-case runtime complexity.

Techniques from $O(m \log n)$ algorithms [13,15] might be able to improve on this second term in the complexity. The idea would be to keep track of the bottom states in the partition structure. This can be used to derive information about large groups of states that reach these bottom states without explicitly inspecting them. We believe that such a change would make the algorithm much more complicated and negatively impact the practical performance of the algorithm.

5 Experimental results

In this section we empirically evaluate a Rust implementation [17] of our algorithm. The algorithm is also implemented within the Merc toolset [3]. We compare our implementation (**our**) with different algorithms and tools. The first tool we compare it to is the **mCRL2** toolset [9]. The fastest results in the current **mCRL2** toolset which implements the algorithm [13] which currently claims to be the best tool for deciding branching bisimilarity. The **ltsmin** tool [8] uses signature refinement based on inductive signatures by Blom and van der Pol [7]. We show the average run-times of five runs of each algorithm. They were executed on a machine with a Intel Xeon Gold 6136 CPU with 3TB of main memory.

Benchmark	Size (x1000)		Variables		Total time (s)			Reduction time (s)		
	#states	#trans	%τ	τ-path	mCRL2	ltsmin	our	mCRL2	ltsmin	our
3_Ideal_trace.exp	28	52	0%	0	0.1	1.2	**0.0**	**0.0**	1.2	**0.0**
vasy_40_60	40	60	33%	2	0.0	5.4	**0.0**	0.0	5.4	**0.0**
vasy_65_2621	65	2 621	0%	0	4.0	1.3	**1.0**	2.0	0.2	**0.1**
vasy_164_1619	164	1 619	7%	1	1.9	0.6	**0.6**	0.9	**0.2**	0.2
domineering	455	2 062	0%	0	4.0	4.1	**1.3**	2.3	3.4	**0.6**
cwi_566_3984	566	3984	92%	31	4.3	1.7	**1.3**	2.8	0.2	**0.2**
vasy_574_13561	574	13 561	0%	0	13.7	4.4	**4.0**	8.8	2.7	**1.1**
clobber	600	2 221	0%	0	4.7	5.4	**1.8**	2.9	4.6	**1.0**
3_Regular.exp	951	2 023	0%	0	2.9	6.7	**1.1**	1.9	6.4	**0.6**
3_Mute_follower.exp	994	2 080	0%	0	3.2	9	**1.2**	2.1	8.6	**0.6**
3_Mute_leader.exp	1 000	2 091	0%	0	3.2	11.5	**1.2**	2.2	11.1	**0.7**
vasy_1112_5290	1 112	5 290	0%	0	7.6	**1.7**	2.5	4.9	**0.9**	1.2
cwi_2165_8723	2 165	8723	44%	54	14.2	5.3	**3.7**	10.6	1.3	**1.1**
cwi_2416_17605	2 416	17 605	99%	53	19.2	7.7	**5.2**	12.5	0.5	**0.4**
vasy_2581_11442	2 581	11 442	22%	7	18.2	9.7	**7.0**	12.5	4.0	**3.0**
vasy_4220_13944	4 220	13 944	18%	7	23.0	16.1	**7.9**	16.0	8.4	**2.8**
vasy_4338_15666	4 338	15 666	20%	7	24.6	13.6	**8.8**	17.2	5.6	**3.8**
vasy_6020_19353	6 020	19 353	91%	7	9.7	7.6	**4.4**	2.2	**0.1**	0.2
vasy_6120_11031	6 120	11 031	29%	4	16.5	8.6	**5.6**	12.4	3.1	**2.3**
cwi_7838_59101	7 838	59 101	39%	170	103.2	51.9	**26.6**	72.4	21.4	**7.9**
vasy_8082_42933	8 082	42 933	6%	2	52.6	28.6	**15.7**	35.6	8.8	**3.9**
vasy_11026_24660	11 026	24 660	11%	5	47.5	41.0	**15.3**	37.3	27.9	**7.7**
vasy_12323_27667	12 323	27 667	11%	5	55.5	42.1	**17.5**	44.3	27.3	**8.9**
cwi_33949_165318	33 949	165 318	45%	77	354.9	115.8	**77.4**	285.0	30.4	**25.6**

Table 1. Average running times of computing branching bisimilarity. The column '%τ' contains the percentage of the τ-transitions and 'τ-path' the length of the longest τ-path in the benchmark.

Benchmarks. The first benchmark we use is the *VLTS benchmark suite*[1] [1] which consists of a collection of very large transition systems derived from both industrial applications and academic examples. These benchmarks are widely used to evaluate the performance of algorithms for minimizing state spaces and deciding (branching) bisimilarity. Additionally, we include LTSs that can be feasibly generated from examples contained in the mCRL2 toolset [2]. We only show results for benchmarks in which at least one of the algorithms takes more than 1 second.

We also evaluate the performance of our algorithm on some constructed hard cases for signature refinement algorithms. These examples give some intuition in the differences of the worst case behaviour of both algorithms.

First we define Fibonacci automata. We believe this example is insightful because these simple deterministic LTSs with only a few outgoing transitions. In particular, an LTS from this family with N states has a unique partition refinement sequence of length N, which means that in each of the N iterations there is exactly one block which splits in two.

---

[1] https://cadp.inria.fr/resources/vlts/

Fibonacci automata. We consider the example of LTSs that represent Fibonacci automata [10]. We define the finite Fibonacci words $w_n \in \{0, 1\}^*$ for every $n \in \mathbb{N}$ inductively as $w_0 = 0, w_1 = 01, w_{i+1} = w_{i-1} \cdot w_i$. For every $n \geq 0$, we define the LTS $Fib_n = (S, \{a, b\}, \rightarrow)$ where the set of states $S = \{1, \ldots, |w_n|\}$ and the transition relation is

$$\begin{aligned}
\rightarrow = \; &\{(i, a, i + 1) \mid i \in [1, n - 1]\} \\
&\cup \{(n, a, 1)\} \\
&\cup \{(i, b, i) \mid i \in S \text{ and } w_n[i] = 1\}.
\end{aligned}$$

The LTS Fib_n contains $N = |w_n| = F_{n+1}$ states, where F_i is the i-th fibonacci number, and $F_{n+1} + F_{n-1} \leq 2N$ transitions.

Next, we present a second family of LTSs on which the **ltsmin** toolset scales bad due to an unbounded fan out. This showcases that our algorithm does not share this weakness.

Unbounded fan-out. For every $n \geq 2$, we define $\mathcal{A}_n = (S, \{a, b\}, \rightarrow)$ where the set of states $S = \{1, \ldots, n\}$ and the transition relation is

$$\begin{aligned}
\rightarrow = \; &\{(i, b, i + 1) \mid i \in [1, n-1]\} \\
&\cup \{(1, a, i) \mid i \in S\} \\
&\cup \{(2, a, i) \mid i \in S\}.
\end{aligned}$$

The LTS $\mathcal{A}_n$ contains n states and $3n - 1$ transitions. From states 1 and 2 there is an outgoing a-transition to every state $i \in S$ and additionially there is a long path of b-transitions connecting $i \xrightarrow{b} i+1$ for every $i \in [1, n-1]$. The LTS $\mathcal{A}_5$ is pictured in Figure 4.

Hard example for improved signature refinement. The last family of LTSs is similar to the previous one, but it contains many states with large fan out. On this family of LTSs we observe the worse theoretical run-time of our signature refinement algorithm. For every $n \in \mathbb{N}$, we define $\mathcal{B}_n = (S, \{a\}, \rightarrow)$ where the set of states $S = \{1, \ldots n\}$ and the transition relation is

$$\rightarrow = \{(i, a, j) \mid i, j \in S \text{ and } i < j\}$$

For a state with number i, the transition relation for a actions reaches all states which are larger than i. The LTS $\mathcal{B}_5$ is pictured in Figure 4. Experimental results of the different algorithms on this example are found in Table 2. This family of LTSs does not use silent actions and hence can also be seen as a bottleneck example for the algorithm in [14].

Results. The results of the experiments on the VLTS benchmark suite are presented in Table 1. The results of the tools on all the hard examples are found in Table 2.

We see that the total time of our implementation is consistently faster than both mCRL2 and ltsmin. The reduction time of our implementation is on average 8 times faster than the mCRL2 toolset and 2.5 times faster than ltsmin. On some

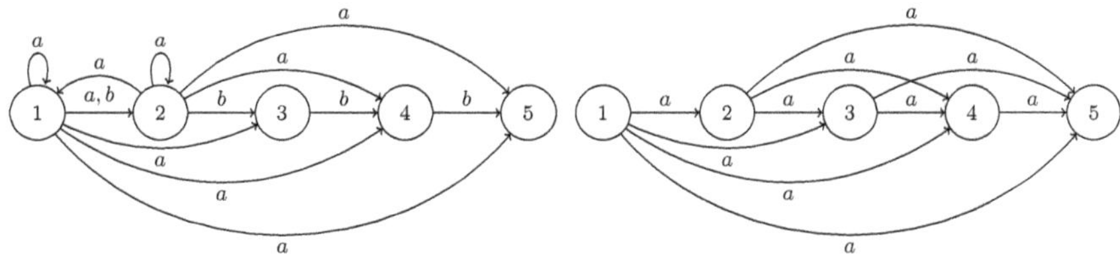

Fig. 4. The LTS $\mathcal{A}_5$ (left), and $\mathcal{B}_5$ (right).

instances the reduction time of ltsmin and our implementation is comparable, which can be explained by the fact that in these cases there is not much redundant work. We note the existence of cases that do have this redundant work and in which the ltsmin tool scales badly. For example 'vasy_40_60' and '3_Mut_leader' where our reduction is orders of magnitude faster.

On the generated hard examples, we see that on the families Fib_n and $\mathcal{A}_n$ our tool scales similar to the algorithm of mCRL2. On the last example the family $\mathcal{B}_n$ which has a large number of states with a growing fan-out our tools scales worse than mCRL2. Despite our efforts, we were not able to find a family in which the algorithm scales worse by long paths of silent τ transitions. Even though our analysis shows this can be a bottleneck, we believe that this is not likely to present itself in practical use cases.

	#States	#Transitions	mCRL2(s)	ltsmin(s)	our(s)
Fib_{22}	29k	39k	0.0	15.4	**0.0**
Fib_{26}	196k	271k	0.7	T/O	**0.2**
Fib_{30}	1.3M	1.9M	8.4	T/O	**3.1**
Fib_{34}	9.2M	13M	100.1	T/O	**34.2**
$\mathcal{A}_{20k}$	20k	60k	**0.0**	10.5	**0.0**
$\mathcal{A}_{30k}$	30k	90k	**0.0**	23.6	**0.0**
$\mathcal{A}_{40k}$	40k	120k	0.1	42.8	**0.0**
$\mathcal{A}_{50k}$	50k	150k	0.1	66.8	**0.0**
$\mathcal{B}_{1500}$	1.5k	1.1M	**0.4**	15.0	10.1
$\mathcal{B}_{2000}$	2k	2M	**1.0**	35.7	24.6
$\mathcal{B}_{2500}$	2.5k	3M	**1.8**	69.6	49.2
$\mathcal{B}_{3000}$	3k	4.5M	**2.6**	118.9	85.9

Table 2. Reduction time on the hard example Fib_n, $\mathcal{A}_n$, and $\mathcal{B}_n$.

6   Conclusion

In this paper, we presented a new algorithm for minimizing state spaces with respect to branching bisimilarity. Our approach translates ideas of the generic coalgebraic algorithm [14] to branching bisimulation. This results in a conceptually simpler and empirically faster algorithm. Experimental results on the VLTS benchmark suite and other examples show that our algorithm significantly outperforms existing tools.

Future work includes exploring extensions for other behavioural equivalences in the van Glabbeek spectrum [22]. The main challenge here is to create efficient signature functions for equivalences like weak bisimulation. Naive signatures for several behavioural equivalences are given in [24, Section 3.]. It would be interesting to see if implementing these naive signature functions in this framework would result in a competitive tool. Preliminary work of this is already available within the Merc Toolset [3]. An interesting question is whether for other equivalences an efficient signature functions exists similar to inductive signatures for branching bisimulation.

Acknowledgements. The authors would like to thank Jules Jacobs and Thorsten Wißmann for providing implementation details of their algorithm. Furthermore we thank Jan Friso Groote, Anton Wijs, and the anonymous reviewers for providing useful feedback on the manuscript.

Data-Availability Statement The code used to obtain the results in this paper and instructions on how to obtain the used benchmarks are available in the accompanying artifact `https://doi.org/10.5281/zenodo.17858373`[17].

Disclosure of Interests. The authors have no competing interests to declare that are of relevance to the contents of this paper.

References

1. VLTS benchmark suite, 2018. URL: `https://cadp.inria.fr/resources/vlts/`, `doi:10.18709/PERSCIDO.2017.11.DS100`.
2. mCRL2 Toolset, 2025. URL: `https://github.com/mCRL2org/mCRL2`, `doi:10.5281/zenodo.17278624`.
3. Merc Toolset, 2025. URL: `https://github.com/mercOrg/merc`, `doi:10.5281/zenodo.18244742`.
4. L. Aceto, A. Ingolfsdottir, and J. Srba. The algorithmics of bisimilarity. *Advanced Topics in Bisimulation and Coinduction*, 52:100–172, 2012.
5. C. Baier. Polynomial time algorithms for testing probabilistic bisimulation and simulation. In *Computer Aided Verification: 8th International Conference, CAV'96 New Brunswick, NJ, USA, July 31–August 3, 1996 Proceedings 8*, pages 50–61. Springer, 1996.
6. S.C.C. Blom and S. Orzan. Distributed branching bisimulation reduction of state spaces. In *Proc. of PDMC 2003*, volume 89 of *ENTCS*, pages 99–113. Elsevier, 2003. `doi:10.1016/S1571-0661(05)80099-4`.
7. S.C.C. Blom and J.C. van de Pol. Distributed branching bisimulation minimization by inductive signatures. In L. Brim and J.C. van de Pol, editors, *Proc. of PDMC 2009*, volume 14 of *EPTCS*, pages 32–46, 2009. `doi:10.4204/EPTCS.14.3`.

8. S.C.C. Blom, J.C. van de Pol, and M. Weber. LTSmin: Distributed and symbolic reachability. In *Proc. of CAV 2010*, pages 354–359. Springer, 2010. `doi:10.1007/978-3-642-14295-6_31`.

9. O. Bunte, J.F. Groote, J.J.A. Keiren, M. Laveaux, T. Neele, E.P. de Vink, A. Wijs, J.W. Wesselink, and T.A.C. Willemse. The mCRL2 toolset for analysing concurrent systems. In T. Vojnar and L. Zhang, editors, *Proc. of TACAS 2019*, pages 21–39. LNCS 11428, 2019. `doi:10.1007/978-3-030-17465-1_2`.

10. G. Castiglione, A. Restivo, and M. Sciortino. Hopcroft's algorithm and cyclic automata. In C. Martín-Vide, F. Otto, and H. Fernau, editors, *Proc. of LATA 2008*, volume 5196 of *LNCS*, pages 172–183. Springer, 2008. `doi:10.1007/978-3-540-88282-4_17`.

11. R. Erkens, J. Rot, and B. Luttik. Up-to techniques for branching bisimilarity. In *International Conference on Current Trends in Theory and Practice of Informatics*, pages 285–297. Springer, 2020. `doi:10.1007/978-3-030-38919-2_24`.

12. H. Garavel and F. Lang. Equivalence checking 40 years after: A review of bisimulation tools. *A Journey from Process Algebra via Timed Automata to Model Learning: Essays Dedicated to Frits Vaandrager on the Occasion of His 60th Birthday*, pages 213–265, 2022.

13. J.F. Groote and D.N. Jansen. A state-based O (m log n) partitioning algorithm for branching bisimilarity. In *Proc. of CONCUR 2025*, pages 18–1. Schloss Dagstuhl–Leibniz-Zentrum für Informatik, 2025. `doi:10.4230/LIPIcs.CONCUR.2025.18`.

14. J. Jacobs and T. Wißmann. Fast coalgebraic bisimilarity minimization. *Proc. ACM Program. Lang.*, 7(POPL), January 2023. `doi:10.1145/3571245`.

15. D.N. Jansen, J.F. Groote, J.J.A. Keiren, and A. Wijs. An $O(m \log n)$ algorithm for branching bisimilarity on labelled transition systems. In A. Biere and D. Parker, editors, *Proc. of TACAS 2020*, volume 12079 of *LNCS*, pages 3–20. Springer, 2020. `doi:10.1007/978-3-030-45237-7_1`.

16. D. E. Knuth. *The Art of Computer Programming, Vol. 1: Fundamental Algorithms*. Addison-Wesley, third edition, 1997.

17. M. Laveaux and J.J.M. Martens. Artifact for faster signature refinement for branching bisimilarity minimization, 2025. `doi:10.5281/zenodo.17858373`.

18. J.J.M. Martens, J.F. Groote, L.B. van den Haak, H.P. Hijma, and A.J. Wijs. Linear parallel algorithms to compute strong and branching bisimilarity. *Software and Systems Modeling*, 22(2):521–545, 2023. `doi:10.1007/s10270-022-01060-7`.

19. R. Milner. *A Calculus of Communicating Systems*, volume 92 of *Lecture Notes in Computer Science*. Springer, Cham, 1980. `doi:10.1007/3-540-10235-3`.

20. R.E. Tarjan. Depth-first search and linear graph algorithms. *SIAM journal on computing*, 1(2):146–160, 1972.

21. A. Valmari. Simple bisimilarity minimization in $O(m \log n)$ time. *Fundamenta Informaticae*, 105(3):319–339, 2010. `doi:10.3233/FI-2010-369`.

22. R. J. van Glabbeek. The linear time — branching time spectrum II. In E. Best, editor, *Proc. of CONCUR 1993*, pages 66–81. Springer, 1993. `doi:10.1007/3-540-57208-2_6`.

23. R. J. van Glabbeek and W. P. Weijland. Branching time and abstraction in bisimulation semantics. *J. ACM*, 43(3):555–600, May 1996. `doi:10.1145/233551.233556`.

24. R. Wimmer, M. Herbstritt, H. Hermanns, K. Strampp, and B. Becker. Sigref—a symbolic bisimulation tool box. In *International Symposium on Automated Technology for Verification and Analysis*, pages 477–492. Springer, 2006. `doi:10.1007/11901914_35`.

25. T. Wißmann, U. Dorsch, S. Milius, and L. Schröder. Efficient and modular coalgebraic partition refinement. *Logical Methods in Computer Science*, 16, 2020.

MIGHTYPPL: Model Checking MITL with Past and Pnueli Modalities

Hsi-Ming Ho[1], Shankara Narayanan Krishna[2], Khushraj Madnani[3],
Rupak Majumdar[4], and Paritosh Pandya[2]

[1] University of Sussex, Brighton, United Kingdom
[2] Indian Institute of Technology Bombay, Mumbai, India
[3] Indian Institute of Technology Guwahati, Guwahati, India
[4] Max Planck Institute for Software Systems (MPI-SWS), Kaiserslautern, Germany

Abstract. *Metric Interval Temporal Logic* (MITL) is a popular formalism for specifying properties of reactive systems with timing constraints. Existing approaches to using MITL in verification tasks, however, have notable drawbacks: they either support only limited fragments of the logic (the future only fragment MITL[Fut]) or allow for only incomplete verification. This paper introduces MIGHTYPPL, a new tool for translating formulae in *Metric Interval Temporal Logic with Past and Pnueli modalities* (MITPPL) over the pointwise semantics into timed automata, enabling *satisfiability* and *model checking* of this expressive specification logic over both finite and infinite timed words. MIGHTYPPL optimises performance via specialised constructions for simple cases, a novel symbolic transition encoding, and a symmetry reduction technique that yields an exponential improvement in reachable discrete states. The tool generates language-equivalent automata compatible with back-ends such as UPPAAL, TCHECKER, and LTSMIN. Our evaluation demonstrates that MIGHTYPPL significantly outperforms the state-of-the-art tool MIGHTYL on future-only fragments and across various benchmarks.

1 Introduction

Real-time logics provide a formal framework for specifying and reasoning about time-dependent behaviours of reactive systems (see, e.g., [12, 13, 41, 21, 24]). *Metric Temporal Logic* (MTL) [54] and its non-singular counterpart *Metric Interval Temporal Logic* (MITL) [11] are prominent real-time logics extending *Linear Temporal Logic* (LTL) [70] with constructs that associate *time intervals* with temporal operators. For example, the property *each request is followed by an ack within 5 seconds* is written in MTL (and MITL) as $\Box(req \implies \Diamond_{[0,5]} ack)$. Thanks to their familiar LTL-like syntax that appeals to practitioners, logic MTL is now widely used in the design and analysis of cyber-physical systems (CPSs) in various safety-critical application domains such as automotives [51, 32], robotics [73], medical monitoring [77], smart grids [16] and so on.

Timed logics have two semantics: *continuous* where it is represented as a signal (i.e, as a function from non-negative real numbers to a set of events),

S. Junges and G. Katz (Eds.): TACAS 2026, LNCS 16505, pp. 457–479, 2026.
https://doi.org/10.1007/978-3-032-22752-2_24

and *pointwise*, where it is represented as a timed word (a sequence of (event, timestamp) pairs). MITL under the continuous semantics is also known as *Signal Temporal Logic* (STL) [57]. The satisfiability problem is undecidable [13] for the future only fragment of MTL (MTL[Fut]) under the continuous semantics as well as in the pointwise semantics over infinite words [67]. When one restricts to finite timed words over the pointwise semantics, MTL is decidable and Ackermann-complete [66]. For MITL, satisfiability and model checking are both decidable (EXPSPACE- or PSPACE-complete, depending on the timing constraints allowed in formulae [11, 75, 41]) under both semantics. However, despite numerous advances in *incomplete* verification methods such as *monitoring* [34, 65] and *falsification* [14, 5, 80], *complete* verification methods are often overlooked in practice due to lack of tool support. In this paper, we focus only on the pointwise interpretation of timed logics.

Logics MTL and MITL cannot express some natural properties; one such is the 'counting' property 'p must occur at least twice within the next 10 time units'. This is expressible in the decidable real-time logic Q2MLO [47] but not in MTL [13, 22, 46, 68]. An extension of MITL is proposed in [45, 46] by adding counting modalities (or Pnueli modalities) to MITL. This logic, called *Metric Interval Temporal Logic with Past and Pnueli Modalities* (MITPPL) is capable of expressing this property, while having the same complexity as MITL (EXPSPACE-complete) [72] for satisfiability. MITPPL is *expressively complete* for many other proposals of strong decidable real-time logics, including Q2MLO [47].

Pnueli modalities are written as $\mathbf{Pn}_J(\varphi_1, \ldots, \varphi_k)$ where J is an interval of the form $[0, u\rangle$, and $\varphi_1, \ldots, \varphi_n$ are MITPPL formulae. Such a formula, when asserted at a time point t, specifies that a sequence of events in the interval $t + J$ must satisfy $\varphi_1, \ldots, \varphi_k$ in the given order. For instance, $\mathbf{Pn}_{[0,10]}(p, p)$ at t specifies that there are two occurrences of p in the interval $t + [0, 10] = [t, t + 10]$. To highlight their practical utility, we now consider an example.

Consider a city with three eateries: a pizzeria (serving pizzas, denoted by P), a burger joint (serving burgers, B), and a cafe (serving coffees, C). Locations $L1$ and $L2$, represent the origin points for customer orders. The delivery driver starts at a designated initial location $L0$. See Fig. 1 for a map where $L0$ is the leftmost location. We write $K{:}L$ (where $K \in \{P, B, C\}$ and $L \in \{L1, L2\}$) for an order from location L for item K. For example, $P{:}L1$ denotes

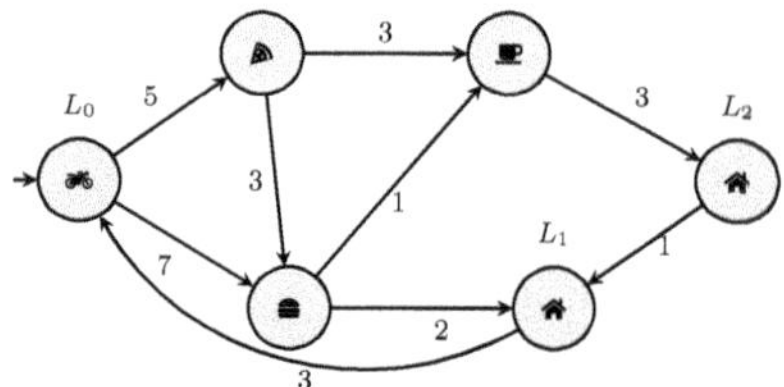

Fig. 1: City map with eateries (pizzeria, burger, cafe), driver start, and customer homes. Edges show travel times.

that $L1$ has ordered a pizza. The property 'once $K{:}L$ occurs, the driver should pick up item K and deliver it to L within the next 15 mins' is written as $\Box(K{:}L \implies \mathbf{Pn}_{[0,15]}(K, L))$.

In this paper, we consider the satisfiability and model-checking problem for MITPPL. For example, the property 'each acknowledgement is preceded by a request at most 5 seconds ago and followed by a three-step locking process in the next 10 seconds' can be written using past and Pnueli modalities as $\Box\left(ack \implies \overleftarrow{\Diamond}_{[0,5]}\, req \land \mathbf{Pn}_{[0,10]}(lock_1, lock_2, lock_3)\right)$. We propose a construction from MITPPL formulae into language-equivalent *timed automata* (TAs) over *timed words*, which can be analysed by a number of existing TA-based tools, including LTSMIN [52], UPPAAL [17] and TCHECKER [44]. On a high level, our fully compositional construction is based on translating subformulae into *tester automata* [53, 71], which can be combined into a single monolithic TA with the standard product construction, if required. While our approach also extends to past and Pnueli modalities, it is instructive to first focus on understanding and improving the treatment of future modalities.

Revisiting the construction for MITL *future modalities.* In MITL, modalities annotated with unilateral time intervals (e.g., $\langle l, \infty)$ or $[0, u\rangle$) can be translated into tester automata relatively easily [75, 37]. In contrast, general intervals $\langle l, u\rangle$ are often required in practice [15], but their automata constructions are substantially more involved due to the need to manage a potentially unbounded number of *obligations*—assertions about future or past events. For instance, if an automaton guesses that $\Diamond_{[10,20]}\, q$ holds at two points $t_1 < t_2$, it must ensure q occurs in both $[t_1 + 10, t_1 + 20]$ and $[t_2 + 10, t_2 + 20]$. From a theoretical standpoint, there is also a strict expressiveness gap: MITL *formulae with general intervals cannot, in general, be rewritten using only unilateral intervals over timed words* [43, 74]. Specific automata constructions for general intervals were developed in [25, 26] which were improved and implemented in MⅠGHTYL [27]. The central idea in MⅠGHTYL is to maintain an abstraction of overlapping obligations using boundedly many clocks. This abstraction, however, incurs an exponential blow-up in the discrete state space, and empirical results with MⅠGHTYL indicate that even limited use of general intervals are infeasible.

Obligations and sequentialisation. We propose a more modular and scalable construction for MITL modalities with general intervals. Building on a surprising connection between Pnueli modalities with unilateral intervals and MITL modalities with general intervals (Lemma 3), we introduce an abstraction where (i) overlapping obligations are merged so that they do not overlap with others, and, (ii) all obligations share a uniform structure and satisfaction mechanism. Each obligation is verified by a dedicated component automaton, avoiding intricate clock manipulations such as shifting or renaming [58, 8]. To curb the combinatorial explosion that arises from composing multiple components, we adopt a sequentialisation scheme: obligations are processed in a fixed order, akin to strategies used in concurrent software verification [56, 36, 30]. This ensures that the product of all component automata—language-equivalent to a monolithic tester automaton for the same subformula—has size polynomial in the bounds of $\langle l, u\rangle$. Experimental evaluation on MITL[Fut] formulae shows that MⅠGHTYPPL is several times faster in magnitude than MⅠGHTYL.

Handling past and Pnueli modalities. Exploiting the fundamental symmetry between the past and the future, we propose a novel approach based on the key property that *timed regular languages are closed under reversal*. This property enables a unified and modular treatment of both temporal directions in our framework, which we formalise and prove in Lemma 1. We then show that the tester automaton for a future / past Pnueli modality $\mathbf{Pn}_I(\varphi_1, \ldots, \varphi_n)$ is obtained as a composition of n component TAs, each having 1 clock each and at most $n + 2$ locations. Overall, for any MITL modality over a general interval $\langle l, u \rangle$, we obtain equivalent timed automata with linearly many clocks and quadratic number of locations in $n = \lceil \frac{l}{u-l} \rceil + 1$.

Summary. We outline our key contributions.

- We propose a fully compositional construction from MITPPL, one of the most expressive decidable real-time logics, to timed automata. The construction supports both the future and past variants of MITL modalities and Pnueli modalities in a uniform manner.
- We propose a new abstraction for handling obligations in the tester automata for MITL modalities associated with intervals of the form $\langle l, u \rangle$. In particular, the obligations can be handled by a bounded number of *identical* simple component automata, and a novel sequentialisation technique is applied to achieve an exponential improvement in the number of reachable locations over the state-of-the-art approach implemented in MIGHTYL.
- We present a complete implementation of the discussed construction in the tool MIGHTYPPL and present comprehensive experimental results, which shows the efficiency of our approach.

Related work. Timed temporal logics such as MTL [54] and TCTL [9] were introduced in the early 1990s. The fragment MITL [11] achieves decidability by forbidding punctual intervals but cannot express counting properties; moreover, its past modalities add expressive power [22]. Extensions such as Q2MLO [47] and MITL with counting modalities [50] address these limitations but have only incomplete bounded-checking procedures [20]. Our logic MITPPL subsumes these. In parallel, automata-based verification has advanced via efficient zone abstractions [23], implemented in tools such as UPPAAL [18], LTSMIN, and TCHECKER [44], though these support only restricted TCTL fragments. Several translations from MITL to timed automata have been proposed [11, 59, 64, 35] under continuous semantics, but none have been implemented. The state-of-the-art tool MIGHTYL [27] works in the pointwise semantics, but it is limited to the future MITL fragment and subject to exponential blow-up in discrete state space. Another approach using generalized timed automata [7, 8] has been implemented very recently in the TEMPORA tool [6, 3], but its reliance on *future clocks* restricts its compatibility with existing tools. In contrast, MIGHTYPPL outputs standard timed automata, ensuring seamless integration with TA-based model checkers.

Full version. More extensive technical details and additional experimental evaluations can be found in the full version of this paper [48].

2 Preliminaries

Let $\mathbb{R}_{\geq 0}$ and $\mathbb{N}$ respectively represent the set of non-negative reals and naturals (including 0). Let $\langle$ denote left open '(' or left closed '[', and $\rangle$ denote right open ')' or right closed ']'. Let $\mathbb{I}$ denote the set of all intervals $\langle l, u \rangle$ for $l \leq u$, $l \in \mathbb{N}$, $u \in \mathbb{N} \cup \{\infty\}$, and $\mathbb{I}_0$ the set of all intervals $[0, u\rangle$ for $0 \leq u$, $u \in \mathbb{N}$. Let AP be a finite set of atomic propositions, and let $\Sigma_{\mathsf{AP}} = 2^{\mathsf{AP}}$ be the finite alphabet that contains all the subsets of AP. An infinite (resp. finite) *timed word* ρ over Σ_{AP} is an infinite (resp. finite) sequence of *events* (pairs of letters and *timestamps*) $\rho = (\sigma_1, \tau_1)(\sigma_2, \tau_2) \ldots$ where $\sigma_i \in \Sigma_{\mathsf{AP}}, \tau_i \in \mathbb{R}_{\geq 0}$, $\tau_1 = 0^5$, and $\tau_i \leq \tau_{i+1}$ for all *positions* $i > 0$. For example, $(\{p, q\}, 0)(\emptyset, 1.1)(\{p\}, 2.1)(\{q\}, 2.1)$ is a finite timed word over the set of atomic propositions $\mathsf{AP} = \{p, q\}$. The set of all infinite (resp. finite) timed words over Σ is denoted $T\Sigma^\omega$ (resp. $T\Sigma^*$).

An infinite timed word is called *Zeno* if the sequence $(\tau_i)_{i \geq 0}$ converges, and non-Zeno otherwise. We restrict ourselves to non-Zeno infinite timed words.

Metric Temporal Logic with Past and Pnueli modalities (MTLPPL). Logic MTLPPL is an extension of the classical *Metric Temporal Logic* (MTL) [54] with past and Pnueli modalities [72]. Formulae of MTLPPL over a set of atomic propositions AP are defined as follows:

$$\varphi := \top \mid p \mid \neg\varphi \mid \varphi_1 \wedge \varphi_2 \mid \varphi_1 \mathbf{U}_I \varphi_2 \mid \varphi_1 \mathbf{S}_I \varphi_2 \mid \mathbf{Pn}_J(\varphi_1, \ldots, \varphi_k) \mid \overleftarrow{\mathbf{Pn}}_J(\varphi_1, \ldots, \varphi_k)$$

where $p \in \mathsf{AP}$, I is an interval in $\mathbb{I}$, and J is an interval in $\mathbb{I}_0$. We define the *size* $|\varphi|$ of an MTLPPL formula φ as $M + \sum_N \log(N)$ where M is the number of modalities and $N \in \mathbb{N}$ is a constant in φ. Given a timed word $\rho = (\sigma_1, \tau_1)(\sigma_2, \tau_2) \ldots$ over Σ_{AP} and a *position* $i \in \mathbb{N}_{>0}$, we define the *pointwise semantics* of MTLPPL formulae inductively as follows:

(i) $\rho, i \models \top$; (ii) $\rho, i \models p$ iff $p \in \sigma_i$; (iii) $\rho, i \models \neg\varphi$ iff $\rho, i \not\models \varphi$;

(iv) $\rho, i \models \varphi_1 \wedge \varphi_2$ iff $\rho, i \models \varphi_1$ and $\rho, i \models \varphi_2$;

(v) $\rho, i \models \varphi_1 \mathbf{U}_I \varphi_2$ iff $\exists j > i$ s.t. $\tau_j - \tau_i \in I$, $\rho, j \models \varphi_2$, and $\forall i < k < j, \rho, k \models \varphi_1$;

(vi) $\rho, i \models \varphi_1 \mathbf{S}_I \varphi_2$ iff $\exists j < i$ s.t. $\tau_i - \tau_j \in I$, $\rho, j \models \varphi_2$, and $\forall j < k < i, \rho, k \models \varphi_1$;

(vii) $\rho, j \models \mathbf{Pn}_J(\varphi_1, \ldots \varphi_k)$ iff $\exists i_k > \ldots > i_1 > j$ s.t. $\forall 1 \leq n \leq k, \tau_{i_n} - \tau_j \in J, \rho, i_n \models \varphi_n$;

(viii) $\rho, j \models \overleftarrow{\mathbf{Pn}}_J(\varphi_1, \ldots \varphi_k)$ iff $\exists i_k < \ldots < i_1 < j$ s.t. $\forall 1 \leq n \leq k, \tau_j - \tau_{i_n} \in J, \rho, i_n \models \varphi_n$.

We define the *timed language* of φ as $[\![\varphi]\!] = \{\rho | \rho, 1 \models \varphi\}$. Derived operators $\Diamond_I$ (eventually), $\Box_I$ (globally), $\overleftarrow{\Diamond}_I$ (past), $\overleftarrow{\Box}_I$ (globally in the past), $\bigcirc$ (next) and $\overleftarrow{\bigcirc}$ (previous) are defined in terms of $\mathbf{U}$ and $\mathbf{S}$ in the usual way, for instance, $\bigcirc \varphi \equiv \bot \mathbf{U} \varphi$. We also define some additional dual operators as follows.

$$\varphi_1 \mathbf{R}_I \varphi_2 \equiv \neg((\neg\varphi_1) \mathbf{U}_I (\neg\varphi_2)), \qquad \varphi_1 \mathbf{T}_I \varphi_2 \equiv \neg((\neg\varphi_1) \mathbf{S}_I (\neg\varphi_2)),$$

$$\mathbf{Pn}_J^\sim(\varphi_1, \varphi_2, \ldots) \equiv \neg\,\mathbf{Pn}_J(\neg\varphi_1, \neg\varphi_2, \ldots), \quad \overleftarrow{\mathbf{Pn}}_J^\sim(\varphi_1, \varphi_2, \ldots) \equiv \neg\,\overleftarrow{\mathbf{Pn}}_J(\neg\varphi_1, \neg\varphi_2, \ldots)$$

The subclass *Metric Interval Temporal Logic with Past and Pnueli modalities*, written MITPPL, consists of all MTLPPL formulae where all intervals I are non-singular (i.e., of the form $\langle l, u \rangle$, where $l < u$). *Metric Temporal Logic* (MTL) [54]

---

[5] the semantics of logics we discuss depend solely on the relative distances between timestamps, it is wlg to assume that every timed word begins with $\tau_1 = 0$. This normalisation, also employed in [81], simplifies the presentation.

and *Metric Interval Temporal Logic* (MITL) [11] can be seen as fragments of MTLPPL (resp., MITPPL) without Pnueli modalities $\mathbf{Pn}_J$ and $\overleftarrow{\mathbf{Pn}}_J$. The *unilateral* fragment of all these logics consist of the fragment in which all intervals I are either of the form $[0, u\rangle$ or $\langle l, \infty)$.

Example 1. Let $\varphi = \mathbf{Pn}_{[0,2)}(p, q, r)$. We have $\rho, 1 \models \varphi$ for

$$\rho = (\{p\}, 0)(\{p\}, 0.5)(\emptyset, 0.9)(\{q, r\}, 1.1)(\{p, q, r\}, 1.8)\ldots$$

since $\tau_5 - \tau_1, \tau_4 - \tau_1, \tau_2 - \tau_1 \in (0, 2)$ and $\rho, 2 \models p$, $\rho, 4 \models q$ and $\rho, 5 \models r$. However, $\rho', 1 \not\models \varphi$ for $\rho' = (\{p\}, 0)(\{r\}, 0.1)(\{q\}, 1.1)(\{p, q\}, 1.9)(\emptyset, 2)\ldots$

Timed Automata (TA). Let X be a finite set of *clocks*; a *valuation* ν for X maps each clock $x \in X$ to a value in $\mathbb{R}_{\geq 0}$. $\mathbf{0}$ denotes the valuation that maps every clock to 0. The set $\mathcal{G}(X)$ of *clock constraints* g over X is generated by $g := \top \mid g \wedge g \mid x \bowtie c$, where $\bowtie \in \{\leq, <, \geq, >\}$, $x \in X$, and $c \in \mathbb{N}$. The satisfaction relation $\nu \models g$ is defined in the usual way. For $t \in \mathbb{R}_{\geq 0}$, let $\nu + t$ be the valuation defined by $(\nu + t)(x) = \nu(x) + t$ for all $x \in X$. For $\lambda \subseteq X$, let $v[\lambda \leftarrow 0]$ be the valuation defined by $(\nu[\lambda \leftarrow 0])(x) = 0$ if $x \in \lambda$, and $(\nu[\lambda \leftarrow 0])(x) = \nu(x)$ otherwise. A *timed automaton* (TA) over a finite alphabet Σ is a tuple $\mathcal{A} = \langle \Sigma, S, s_0, X, \Delta, \mathcal{F} \rangle$ where S is a finite set of locations, $s_0 \in S$ is the initial location, X is a finite set of clocks, $\Delta \subseteq S \times \Sigma \times \mathcal{G}(X) \times 2^X \times S$ is the transition relation, and $\mathcal{F} = \{F_1, \ldots, F_n\}$, with $F_i \subseteq S$ for all i, $1 \leq i \leq n$, is a *generalised Büchi acceptance condition*, i.e. a set of sets of final locations.

A run of $\mathcal{A}$ on a timed word $(\sigma_1, \tau_1)(\sigma_2, \tau_2) \cdots$ is an alternating sequence of states (s_i, ν_i) such that $\nu_0 = \mathbf{0}$ and each transition $(s_i, \sigma_{i+1}, g_{i+1}, \lambda_{i+1}, s_{i+1})$ satisfies $\nu_i + (\tau_{i+1} - \tau_i) \models g_{i+1}$ and $\nu_{i+1} = (\nu_i + (\tau_{i+1} - \tau_i))[\lambda_{i+1} \leftarrow 0]$. A run is accepting if the set of locations visited infinitely often intersects every F_i. The accepted timed language $[\![\mathcal{A}]\!]$ is *timed regular*; finite-word acceptance is defined analogously. For TAs $\mathcal{A}^1, \mathcal{A}^2$ over Σ, the synchronous product $\mathcal{A}^1 \times \mathcal{A}^2$ combines states, clocks and transitions symbolwise, conjoins guards and unions resets, and has acceptance sets defined componentwise. Then $[\![\mathcal{A}^1 \times \mathcal{A}^2]\!] = [\![\mathcal{A}^1]\!] \cap [\![\mathcal{A}^2]\!]$.

Compositional translation from temporal logics to automata. Temporal logics such as LTL and MITL offer a concise, declarative way to express (timed) requirements, while automata-based models are better suited for algorithmic verification tasks such as model checking and satisfiability. Translating formulae into TAs enables the use of established automata-theoretic techniques and tools such as UP-PAAL [17] and TCHECKER [44]. We recall the translation from Brihaye et al. [27], which maps future MITL (restricted to $\mathbf{U}_I$) into a network of TAs, reminiscent of the *stratification* method for untimed temporal logics [60, 28, 31, 53].

Let φ be an MITL formula in negation normal form, that is, negations applied only to atomic propositions. Let Ψ denote the set of temporal subformulae of φ whose outermost operator is a temporal modality ∇_I—specifically, either $\square_I$, $\lozenge_I$, $\mathbf{U}_I$, or $\mathbf{R}_I$. For instance, if $\varphi = \left(p\,\mathbf{U}_{[0,2)}\left((q\,\mathbf{U}_{[3,5]}r) \wedge s\right)\right)$, then $\Psi = \{\varphi, \kappa\}$ where $\kappa = (q\,\mathbf{U}_{[3,5]}r)$. For each $\psi \in \Psi$, introduce a fresh atomic proposition p_ψ

(called its *trigger*), and define $\mathsf{AP}_\Psi = \{p_\psi \mid \psi \in \Psi\}$. Replacing each *top-level* temporal subformula in φ by its trigger yields the *propositional skeleton* $\overline{\varphi}$. Then $\overline{\varphi} = p_\varphi$, $\overline{\left((q\,\mathbf{U}_{[3,5]}\,r) \wedge s\right)} = p_\kappa \wedge s$, and $\overline{\kappa} = p_\kappa$.

We then construct a formula $\varphi' = \overline{\varphi} \wedge \bigwedge_{\psi \in \Psi} \Box(p_\psi \Rightarrow \nabla_I(\overline{\phi_1}, \ldots, \overline{\phi_n}))$ equisatisfiable with φ over the extended set of propositions $\mathsf{AP} \cup \mathsf{AP}_\Psi$. For each conjunct, we build a *tester automaton* $\mathcal{C}_\psi$ [71] such that $[\![\mathcal{C}_\psi]\!] = [\![\Box(p_\psi \Rightarrow \nabla_I(\ldots))]\!]$, which checks, at every point where p_ψ holds, whether the subformula is satisfied. A simple automaton $\mathcal{C}_{\overline{\varphi}}$ enforces $\overline{\varphi}$ at the initial instant. The final automaton is obtained compositionally as $\mathcal{C}_{\varphi'} = \mathcal{C}_{\overline{\varphi}} \times \left(\times_{\psi \in \Psi}\mathcal{C}_\psi\right)$, which accepts $[\![\varphi']\!]$ and is therefore equisatisfiable with φ.

3 Unilateral Intervals

We extend the translation of future MITL formulae [27] to past and Pnueli modalities with *unilateral* intervals, taking the view that *past and future are reflections of each other*. In general, for any temporal operator ∇_I, if for each subformula $\psi = \nabla_I(\phi_1, \ldots, \phi_n)$ of φ we can construct a tester automaton $\mathcal{C}_\psi$ accepting $[\![\mathcal{C}_\psi]\!] = [\![\Box(p_\psi \Rightarrow \nabla_I(\overline{\phi_1}, \ldots, \overline{\phi_n}))]\!]$, then the compositional construction applies. We focus below on past MITL and Pnueli modalities.

3.1 Reversing Finite-Word Timed Languages

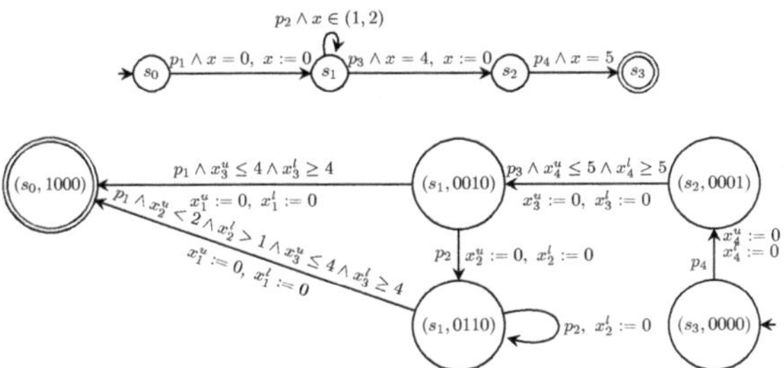

Intuitively, tester automata for past MITL modalities need only track the prefix of a timed word till the current point and 'output' accordingly. For past MITL modalities with unilateral intervals this is simple: e.g., for $p\mathbf{S}_{[0,2]}q$, a clock is reset on each q-event, and $p\,\mathbf{S}_{[0,2]}\,q$ holds until either $\neg p$ or

Fig. 2: A TA with finite-word acceptance condition (above) and its corresponding reversed TA (below). The upper TA has one clock x and 4 transitions; the reversed one introduces clocks x_i^u, x_i^ℓ for $1 \le i \le 4$, and bit-vectors of length 4 at each location.

the clock exceeds 2. More generally, constructing testers for sophisticated past modalities relies on our observation that *finite-word timed regular languages are closed under reversal*. Reversing a finite timed word $\rho = (\sigma_1, \tau_1) \ldots (\sigma_n, \tau_n)$ yields $\rho^R = (\sigma_n, 0)(\sigma_{n-1}, \tau_n - \tau_{n-1}) \ldots (\sigma_1, \tau_n - \tau_1)$, and similarly, $L^R = \{\rho^R \mid \rho \in L\}$.

Let φ be a MITPPL formula and Ψ its temporal subformulae. Let $\rho = (\sigma'_1, \tau_1) \ldots (\sigma'_i, \tau_i) \ldots$ be an infinite timed word over the alphabet $\Sigma_{\mathsf{AP} \cup \mathsf{AP}_\Psi}$. For a past subformula $\psi = \overleftarrow{\nabla}_I(\phi_1, \ldots, \phi_n)$, its satisfaction at position i of a timed word

ρ implies that the finite-word future counterpart $\vec{\triangledown}_I\,(\overline{\phi_1}, \ldots, \overline{\phi_n})$ holds on the reverse of the prefix read till that point, that is, $(\sigma_1', \tau_1) \ldots (\sigma_i', \tau_i)$ and vice versa. Consequently, the tester TA for $\overleftarrow{\triangledown}_I\,(\overline{\phi_1}, \ldots, \overline{\phi_n})$ can be obtained by reversing the corresponding finite-word future tester: $[\![\mathcal{C}_\psi]\!] = [\![\Box(p_\psi \Rightarrow \vec{\triangledown}_I\,(\overline{\phi_1}, \ldots, \overline{\phi_n}))]\!]$[6] More generally, we have Lemma 1 which states that this is always possible for any TA over finite timed words (see Fig. 2 for an example).

Lemma 1. *Finite-word timed regular languages are closed under reversal.*

Proof (sketch). Let $\mathcal{A}$ be a TA with clocks X, locations S, and transitions Δ. The reversed automaton $\mathcal{B}$ swaps initial and final locations and tracks which guards have been visited. Each location of $\mathcal{B}$ has the form $(s, \mathbf{b})$, where $s \in S$ and $\mathbf{b}$ is a zero-initialised bit-array indexed by (x, δ) for $x \in X$, $\delta \in \Delta$. For each $\delta = (s, \sigma, g, \lambda, t) \in \Delta$ and each $\mathbf{b}$, $\mathcal{B}$ has a reversed transition $\delta_{\mathbf{b}}^{\mathrm{R}} = ((t, \mathbf{b}), \sigma, g^{\mathrm{R}}, \lambda^{\mathrm{R}}, (s, \mathbf{b}'))$ with $\mathbf{b}'[x, \delta] = 1$ for all $x \in g$. For every $x \in g$, $\mathcal{B}$ introduces clocks x_δ^u and x_δ^l recording the upper and lower bounds of $g(x)$, respectively; x_δ^u is reset upon the first traversal of $\delta_{\mathbf{b}}^{\mathrm{R}}$, and x_δ^l on each traversal. For each $x \in \lambda$, $\delta_{\mathbf{b}}^{\mathrm{R}}$ checks the 'accumulated' guards encoded by $\mathbf{b}$ and resets $\mathbf{b}'[x, \delta'] = 0$ for all $\delta' \neq \delta$, and also $\mathbf{b}'[x, \delta] = 0$ if $x \notin g$.

While the above construction is generic to TAs over finite timed words, for our purpose it suffices to handle past modalities. Testers TAs for these can be built with sizes comparable to (or smaller than) their future counterparts due to simpler acceptance conditions. For instance, Fig. 3(a) shows the tester for $\phi_1 \, \mathbf{U}_{\geq l} \, \phi_2$ *for finite timed words*, where the running obligation is "ϕ_1 holds continuously and once $x \geq l$, eventually ϕ_2 holds." Here, TA resets x and moves from s_0 to s_1 when the trigger p_ψ first becomes true; while in s_1, x is reset whenever p_ψ is true, ensuring $\overline{\phi_1}$ holds continuously until the obligation is met $(\neg p_\psi \wedge \overline{\phi_2} \wedge x \geq l)$. Since $[l, \infty)$ is unilateral, only *one* obligation is maintained, with x reset on each trigger p_ψ. The tester for $\phi_1 \, \mathbf{S}_{\geq l} \, \phi_2$ (Fig. 3(b)) is symmetric, obtained by reversing transitions and swapping clock constraints / resets. A bit-array is unnecessary to record if x has been reset before as $x \geq l$ can only follow $x := 0$. Other past MITL tester TAs can be found in [48].

3.2   Tester Automata for Pnueli Modalities

We now describe how to handle Pnueli modalities and their past counterparts. On an example, consider $\psi = \mathbf{Pn}_{<10}(p_1, p_2)$ and the timed word
$\rho = (\{p_\psi, p_5\}, \tau_1)(\{p_1, p_4\}, \tau_2)(\{p_\psi\}, \tau_3)(\{p_1\}, \tau_4)(\{p_\psi\}, \tau_5)(\emptyset, \tau_6)(\{p_2\}, \tau_7)(\{p_1\}, \tau_8)(\{p_2\}, \tau_9) \ldots$
A tester TA $\mathcal{C}_\psi$ for ψ is triggered at positions with p_ψ (times τ_1, τ_3, τ_5). Assume $\tau_7 < \tau_1 + 10 < \tau_9 < \tau_3 + 10$. To accept ρ, $\mathcal{C}_\psi$ may non-deterministically *merge* the first two obligations—witnessed by $(\{p_1\}, \tau_4)$ and $(\{p_2\}, \tau_7)$—validating $\tau_7 < \tau_1 + 10$. The third obligation (from τ_5) is separate, witnessed by $(\{p_1\}, \tau_8)$ and $(\{p_2\}, \tau_9)$, requiring $\tau_9 < \tau_5 + 10$. Alternatively, it may merge the second and

---

[6] For past modalities $\overleftarrow{\triangledown}_I$, the finite-word future tester TAs for $\vec{\triangledown}_I$ is derived from the infinite-word version with only minor changes to acceptance conditions.

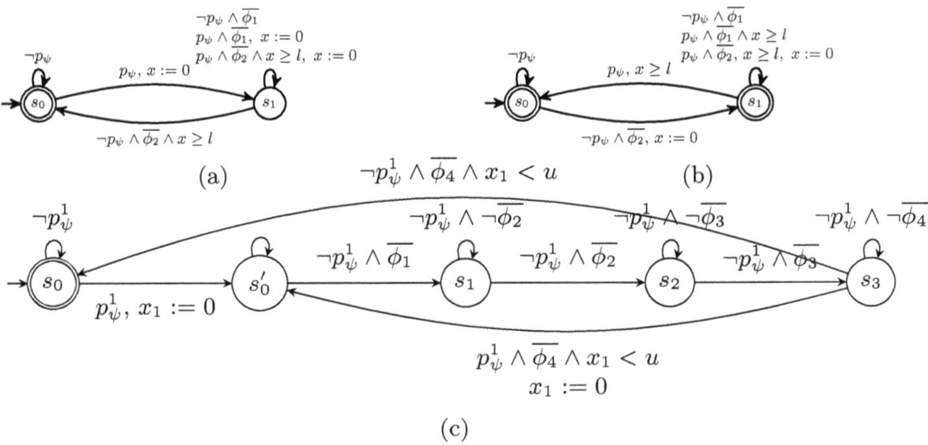

Fig. 3: Tester TA: (a) $\phi_1 \, \mathbf{U}_{\geq l} \, \phi_2$, (b) $\phi_1 \, \mathbf{S}_{\geq l} \, \phi_2$, (c) $\mathbf{Pn}_{<u}(\phi_1, \phi_2, \phi_3, \phi_4)$.

third obligations. In all cases, $\mathcal{C}_\psi$ requires 2 clocks. In general, it can be argued that a tester TA for $\mathbf{Pn}_{<u}(\phi_1, \ldots, \phi_n)$ needs exactly n clocks; similar arguments hold for other types of intervals J and $\mathbf{Pn}_{\widetilde{J}}(\phi_1, \ldots, \phi_n)$.

A tester TA for $\mathbf{Pn}_{<u}(\phi_1, \ldots, \phi_n)$ maintains n obligation types: the first expects $\phi_1, \ldots, \phi_n$, the second $\phi_2, \ldots, \phi_n$, and so on. Since $[0, u)$ is unilateral, at most one obligation per type suffices, i.e., at most n obligations in total. We construct the tester TA as the synchronous product of n component TAs, each tracking one obligation with its own clock. The trigger p_ψ is split into individual triggers $p_\psi^1, \ldots, p_\psi^n$ where exactly one is triggered when ψ must hold. For example, with $n = 4$, a component TA for $\mathbf{Pn}_{<u}(\phi_1, \ldots, \phi_4)$ is shown in Fig. 3(c). Components differ only in their triggers and each tracks one obligation type: s_0', s_1, s_2, s_3 correspond to the four obligation types. After p_ψ^1 is triggered, the component waits at s_0' to capture as many obligations as possible before reading $\overline{\phi_1}$, after which p_ψ^1 is no longer accepted. The correctness of the tester TA for Pnueli modalities is stated in Lemma 2.

Lemma 2. *For* $\psi = \mathbf{Pn}_{<u}(\phi_1, \ldots, \phi_n)$ *over* AP *and component TAs* $\mathcal{C}_\psi^1, \ldots, \mathcal{C}_\psi^n$ *where* $\mathcal{C}_\psi^i$ *is the i-th component TA (over* $\Sigma_{\mathsf{AP} \cup \mathsf{AP}_\Psi}$ *where* $p_\psi^1, \ldots, p_\psi^n \in \mathsf{AP}_\Psi$) *as discussed above and depicted in Fig. 3(c) (for $n = 4$),*

1. $[\![\mathcal{C}_\psi^1 \times \cdots \times \mathcal{C}_\psi^n]\!] \subseteq [\![\Box(p_\psi^1 \vee \cdots \vee p_\psi^n \implies \mathbf{Pn}_{<u}(\overline{\phi_1}, \ldots, \overline{\phi_n}))]\!]$.
2. *For any* $\rho \in [\![\Box(p_\psi^1 \vee \cdots \vee p_\psi^n \implies \mathbf{Pn}_{<u}(\overline{\phi_1}, \ldots, \overline{\phi_n}))]\!]$ *there is a* $\rho' \in [\![\mathcal{C}_\psi^1 \times \cdots \times \mathcal{C}_\psi^n]\!]$ *where*

   − $\rho, i \models p \iff \rho', i \models p$ *for all $i > 0$, $p \notin \{p_\psi^1, \ldots, p_\psi^n\}$, $p \in \mathsf{AP} \cup \mathsf{AP}_\Psi$ and*
   − $\rho, i \models p_\psi^1 \vee \cdots \vee p_\psi^n \iff \rho', i \models p_\psi^1 \vee \cdots \vee p_\psi^n$ *for all $i > 0$.*

As with past MITL modalities, the tester TA for $\overleftarrow{\mathbf{Pn}}_{<u}(\phi_1, \ldots, \phi_n)$ is obtained by reversing transitions and swapping clock constraints / resets, exploiting the simple TA structure and the fact that interval $[0, u)$ is unilateral.

Model checking unilateral MITL *with past and Pnueli modalities.* We now claim that the number of tester/component TAs needed for a *unilateral* MITPPL formula φ is at most polynomial in $|\varphi|$. In particular, for $\phi_1 \triangledown_I \phi_2$ with $\triangledown \in \{\mathbf{U}, \mathbf{S}, \mathbf{R}, \mathbf{T}\}$ and unilateral I, we can construct a one clock tester TA with at most 3 locations; for $\mathbf{Pn}_J(\phi_1, \ldots, \phi_n)$ as well as $\overleftarrow{\mathbf{Pn}}_J(\phi_1, \ldots, \phi_n)$ or $\overleftarrow{\mathbf{Pn}}_{\tilde{J}}(\phi_1, \ldots, \phi_n)$, we can construct n one clock component TAs (of the tester TA), each with $n+1$ locations. Since the product of these TAs and the system $\mathcal{M}$ (modelled as a TA) can be checked for emptiness on-the-fly in PSPACE [10], the satisfiability and model-checking problems for unilateral MITPPL are in PSPACE. In the next section, we will see that this fragment is actually already expressively complete for full MITPPL.

Theorem 1. *The satisfiability and model-checking problems for unilateral* MITPPL *are* PSPACE-*complete.*

4   General Intervals and Sequentialisation

We construct tester TAs for MITL formulae with general intervals (e.g., $\phi_1 \mathbf{U}_{[9,10]} \phi_2$) by using the same idea as for Pnueli modalities: each obligation is tracked by an identical component TA, with a bound on the number of simultaneous obligations. The tester TA is then a product of these components, which is simpler and easier to implement than monolithic constructions [27, 8]. To avoid unnecessary interleavings, we introduce a sequentialisation technique, yielding an exponential reduction in the number of reachable locations.

4.1   Expressing General Interval MITL in Pnueli Modalities

Over timed words, MITL modalities with intervals $\langle l, u \rangle$ cannot be expressed in unilateral MITL [76, 74]. We present simple and non-inductive equivalence rules that express past/future modalities with general intervals directly in terms of Pnueli modalities and modalities with unilateral intervals for which the tester TAs are fairly simple (as discussed in the last section) and helps achieve compositionality. This also shows that the unilateral fragment of MITPPL (Theorem 1) is already expressively complete for full MITPPL. We consider equivalences of $\mathbf{U}, \mathbf{S}, \mathbf{R}, \mathbf{T}$ with intervals $(k, k+1)$ for $k > 0$; these generalise to arbitrary intervals $I = \langle l, u \rangle$. Recall from Sect. 2 that $\overline{\phi}$ is obtained from ϕ by replacing its temporal subformulae by the corresponding triggers. Lemma 3 proves the equivalence $\mathbf{U}_{(k,k+1)}$ in terms of $\mathbf{U}_{(k,\infty)}$ and Pnueli modalities (similar lemmas for $\mathbf{R}, \mathbf{S}, \mathbf{T}$ can be found in [48]).

Lemma 3. *Let* $\psi = \phi_1 \mathbf{U}_{(k,k+1)} \phi_2$ *be a subformula of the* MITPPL *formula* φ, *and* Ψ *be the set of all temporal subformulae of* φ. *For all timed words* ρ *over* $\Sigma_{\mathsf{AP} \cup \mathsf{AP}_\Psi}$, *positions* $i \geq 1$, *and* $\phi^{\geq 1} \equiv \overline{\phi_2} \wedge (\neg \overline{\phi_2} \, \mathbf{U}_{\geq 1} \, \overline{\phi_2})$, *we have*

$$\rho, i \models \overline{\phi_1} \, \mathbf{U}_{(k,k+1)} \, \overline{\phi_2} \Leftrightarrow \rho, i \models \overline{\phi_1} \, \mathbf{U}_{>k} \, \overline{\phi_2} \wedge$$

$$\bigvee_{\ell=0}^{k+1} \left(\mathbf{Pn}_{<k+1}(\underbrace{\phi^{\geq 1}, \ldots, \phi^{\geq 1}}_{\ell}, \overline{\phi_2}) \wedge \neg \, \mathbf{Pn}_{\leq k}(\underbrace{\phi^{\geq 1}, \ldots, \phi^{\geq 1}}_{\ell}) \right)$$

Proof (sketch). If $\overline{\phi_1}\,\mathbf{U}_{>k}\,\overline{\phi_2}$ and $\overline{\phi_2}$ occurs in $\tau_i + [0, k+1)$, then there are two possible cases: (1) $\phi^{\geq 1}$ never occurs in $\tau_i + [0, k]$—in other words, the occurrences of $\overline{\phi_2}$ are all closely adjacent to each other—we are guaranteed to have $\overline{\phi_2}$ in $\tau_i + (k, k+1)$. (2) There are large gaps between the occurrences of $\overline{\phi_2}$ (where $\phi^{\geq 1}$ holds), but the number of such gaps are bounded—we can write each case as a disjunct.

4.2   Tester Automata for MITL Modalities with General Intervals

At this point we may just use Lemma 3 (and similar lemmas for other types of operators) to rewrite all MITL modalities with $\langle l, u \rangle$ and use the tester TA constructions described in the previous section. This is not ideal, as there are $\approx 2 \cdot \lfloor \frac{l}{u-l} \rfloor$ occurrences of Pnueli or dual Pnueli modalities in each of these lemmas. Each occurrence of Pnueli or dual Pnueli modalities with n arguments needs n component TAs and n clocks, giving $2 \cdot \lfloor \frac{l}{u-l} \rfloor \cdot n$ clocks in total (where n again can be as large as $\lfloor \frac{l}{u-l} \rfloor + 1$). Significant simplifications can be achieved, however, by working directly with component TAs instead of with formulae. We now present two such simplifications with Lemma 3; the argument for other modalities are similar.

Reducing the number of component TAs and clocks. We observe that

- The structures of the component TAs for $\mathbf{Pn}_{<k+1}(\underbrace{\phi^{\geq 1}, \ldots, \phi^{\geq 1}}_{\ell}, \overline{\phi_2})$ and

  $\neg\,\mathbf{Pn}_{\leq k}(\underbrace{\phi^{\geq 1}, \ldots, \phi^{\geq 1}}_{\ell})$ are similar and the conjunction, in effect, specifies that

  $\phi^{\geq 1}$ occurs exactly ℓ times before $\tau_i + k$.
- The first ℓ arguments are the same, and thus we only need to maintain $k + 2$ obligations (recall that $\ell \in \{0, \ldots, k+1\}$) at any time across all the disjuncts.

We only need $k + 2$ component TAs to 'implement' the whole disjunct; each such component TA uses two clocks, x and y (x is reset when the trigger p_ψ for $\overline{\phi_1}\,\mathbf{U}_{(k,k+1)}\,\overline{\phi_2}$ first holds; y is reset when p_ψ holds later each time) to keep track of an obligation, which may correspond to any of the disjuncts.

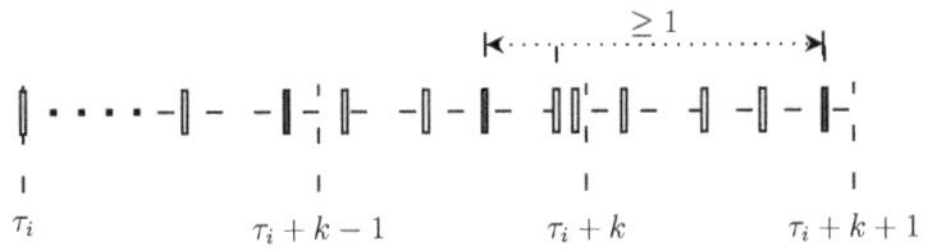

Fig. 4: Case (1). Blue boxes are $\overline{\phi_2}$-events.   **Fig. 5:** Case (2). Blue boxes are $\overline{\phi_2}$-events.

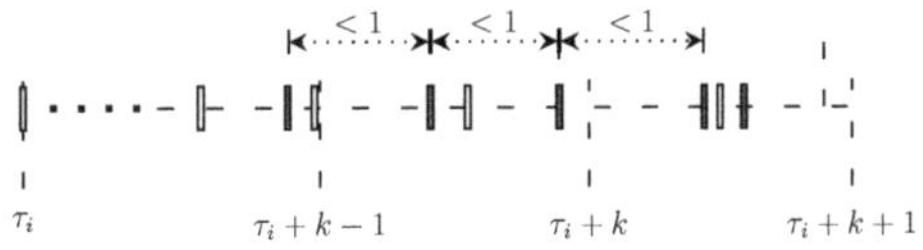

Simplifying individual component automata. The whole purpose of the large disjunction in Lemma 3 is to 'locate' the last event where $\phi^{\geq 1}$ holds in $\tau_i + [0, k]$ and ensure either of the following is true.

1. The next $\overline{\phi_2}$ is just in $\tau_i + (k, k+1)$ (see Fig. 4). This corresponds to $y > k$ being true when the component TA reads that $\overline{\phi_2}$.

2. The next $\overline{\phi_2}$ is still in $\tau_i + [0, k]$. If $y \leq k$, then this $\overline{\phi_2}$ satisfies the first and possibly some of the earlier obligations but not all of them, in particular not the latest one (triggered at position i). This is so since we have been resetting y on each instance of the trigger p_ψ, $y \leq k$ does not contradict with the possibility that some of the earlier positions j where y has been reset are now $> k$ away, but for the latest p_ψ (say at i), the time elapse is $\leq k$. For each such older occurrence of $\overline{\phi_2}$, we enforce $\neg\phi^{\geq 1}$ holds until a later event where $y > k$ and $\overline{\phi_2}$ both hold. Such a sequence of $\overline{\phi_2}$-events satisfies all the intermediate obligations (since we enforce a later one where $y > k$ and $\overline{\phi_2}$) and in particular the last one satisfies the latest obligation.

But, probably a bit surprisingly, a component TA can *guess* the beginning of such a sequence, i.e. an event where $x < k + 1$ and $\overline{\phi_2}$ holds! This leads to drastically simpler component TAs whose number of locations is independent of $\lfloor\frac{l}{u-l}\rfloor$.

4.3   Sequentialisation

The simplified tester TA construction is correct by Lemma 3, the other lemmas (in [48]), and the discussion above. However, it allows for arbitrary interleavings of obligations, which can cause an exponential blow-up in the number of locations. For example, if there are n component TAs and n obligations, then there are $n!$ ways to allocate these obligations to the component TAs. To avoid this exponential blow-up, we *sequentialise* the obligations by introducing new atomic propositions; our approach is inspired by [56, 36, 30] and shares conceptual similarities with *partial-order methods* [78, 38, 49, 39, 79, 69]. We relegate the technical details of how we implement sequentialisation to [48]. In effect, we enforce a first-in-first-out queueing discipline for obligations: (i) they are allocated to the component TAs in a sequential order, (ii) they are satisfied in the same order, (iii) $p_\psi^1, \ldots, p_\psi^n$ are never overlapping, (iv) $q_\psi^1, \ldots, q_\psi^n$ are never overlapping, where $q_\psi^1, \ldots, q_\psi^n$, marks the ends of obligations (symmetric to $p_\psi^1, \ldots, p_\psi^n$). This gives Theorem 2.

Theorem 2. *For a subformula of the form $\phi_1 \nabla_I \phi_2$ with $I = \langle l, u \rangle$ where $n = \lceil\frac{l}{u-l}\rceil + 1$, and $\nabla \in \{\mathbf{U}, \mathbf{R}, \mathbf{S}, \mathbf{T}\}$, we can construct a tester TA with at most $\mathcal{O}(n^2)$ locations and $2n$ clocks.*

Comparison with MIGHTYL. The constructions in [25, 26] encode merged obligations via clock values, using $\approx 4n$ clocks ($n = \lfloor\frac{u}{u-l}\rfloor + 2$). MIGHTYL [27] lowers this to $\approx 2n$ clocks by distinguishing obligation types through location encoding, causing an exponential blow-up in n. Both handle only the future fragment. Unlike them, where each obligation is discharged by a single $\overline{\phi_2}$-event, ours allows one or more consecutive $\overline{\phi_2}$-events, enabling uniform and independent treatment. With sequentialisation, we retain the same clock count but achieve exponentially fewer reachable locations.

Comparison with other constructions. The classical construction for $\phi_1 \, \mathbf{U}_{\langle l,u \rangle}$ ϕ_2 [11] and its timed-signal-transducer reformulation [59] rely on *guessing* the exact instants when $\overline{\phi_2}$ starts or ends. Such guessing is not supported by standard timed automata (without ϵ-transitions [19]), which can reset clocks only on events. The approach of [8], expressed via *generalized timed automata* (GTAs) [7], preserves this idea using *future clocks* to emulate the missing feature. In contrast, our construction uses standard TAs and avoids this dependency; by Lemma 1, it can be viewed as a compositional 'reverse' of [58]. Also, as we will see in Sect. 5, the practical benefit offered by GTAs over TAs for MITL satisfiability or model checking is unclear—especially given the maturity of TA-based tools.

5   Implementation and Experiments

Overview. MightyPPL is a command-line program written in C++17. Given an MITPPL formula, MightyPPL can output in TChecker or Uppaal format, enabling satisfiability and model checking of MITPPL using these tools as the back-ends (Uppaal files can be used with LTSmin for multi-core model checking [55]), or the user can use a built-in implementation of the standard backward (nested) fixpoint algorithm [42] (based on MoniTAal [40] and PARDIBAAL [2]) for satisfiability and model checking. In addition to the optimisations found in MightyL and a more modular architecture with broader back-end compatibility, MightyPPL uses *symbolic values* to synchronise transitions labelled by Boolean formulae, can construct products of tester automata directly (and only for the forward- and backward-reachable parts), and uses specialised constructions for modalities that are *existentially quantified*, e.g., only in the scope of $\mathbf{U}$ or $\mathbf{S}$.

Experimental setup. All the experiments were conducted on a machine with an Intel i9-13900K CPU and 64GB memory. For experiments that involve LTSmin, we run it on a single thread for a consistent comparison with the other back-end tools (Uppaal and TChecker), which are single-threaded. In the tables, we use the following notations: 'noflat' means generating individual tester TAs and individual component TAs; 'compflat' means generating individual tester TAs and *synchronous products of component* TAs (for Pnueli modalties or MITL modalities with general intervals); 'flat' means generating *synchronous products of all tester and component* TAs; 'verifyta' means using Uppaal for finite-word satisfiability; '-b' or '-d' means using breadth-first or depth-first search orders, respectively; 'opaal_ltsmin' means using LTSmin (with the opaal front-end) for infinite-word satisfiability; 'fp' means using the built-in backward fixpoint algorithm; 'tck --inf' or 'tck --fin' means using TChecker as the back-end tool for infinite- and finite-word satisfiability, respectively. To ease the reading of the tables, we highlight the runtime for infinite- and finite-word satisfiability in blue and yellow , respectively. For benchmarks that involve only future MITL formulae, we also compare with MightyL [1]. A separate paragraph dedicated to a comparison with Tempora [3] can be found at the end of this section.

Benchmarks. We consider the following set of benchmark categories, spanning both satisfiability and model-checking of MITPPL formulae. More benchmarks can be found in [48].

- Benchmarks from MIGHTYL [1].
- Benchmarks adapted from the LTL formulae in Acacia-Bonsai [29].
- A set of benchmarks [33] for debugging MITL specs of cyber-physical systems.
- A set of real-world specifications used in robotic missions [63, 61, 62].
- A food delivery timed path-planning, formulated as MITPPL model checking.

MIGHTYL **benchmarks.** We consider the finite- and infinite-word satisfiability of formulae from MIGHTYL. The results are listed in Table 1 and plotted in Figs. 6 to 8 (all satisfiable). Table 1 uses the notations : $F(k, I) = \bigwedge_{i=1}^{k} \Diamond_I p_i$, $G(k, I) = \bigwedge_{i=1}^{k} \Box_I p_i$, $U(k, I) = (\cdots (p_1 \mathbf{U}_I p_2) \mathbf{U}_I \cdots) \mathbf{U}_I p_k$, $R(k, I) = (\cdots (p_1 \mathbf{R}_I p_2) \mathbf{R}_I \cdots) \mathbf{R}_I p_k$, $\mu(k) = \bigwedge_{i=1}^{k} \Diamond_{[3(i-1),3i]} t_i \wedge \Box(\neg p)$, $\theta(k) = \neg(\bigwedge_{i=1}^{k} \Box \Diamond p_i \implies \Box(q \implies \Diamond_{[100,1000]} r))$. MIGHTYPPL clearly performs much better than MIGHTYL on most benchmarks on both back-ends.

Table 1: Execution times on the MIGHTYL benchmarks. Times are in seconds. 'TO' indicates timeouts (300s) and 'ERR' means out-of-memory errors.

Formula	MIGHTYL opaal_ltsmin	MIGHTYL verifyta -b	MIGHTYL verifyta -d	MIGHTYPPL opaal_ltsmin compflat	MIGHTYPPL verifyta -b compflat	MIGHTYPPL verifyta -d compflat
$F(2, [1, 2])$	76.575	0.949	0.929	0.335	0.015	0.014
$F(3, [1, 2])$	122.174	1.754	1.502	0.359	0.021	0.020
$F(5, [1, 2])$	225.575	11.001	5.604	0.493	0.110	0.034
$F(5, [3, 8])$	220.238	10.577	5.548	0.488	0.109	0.034
$G(2, [1, 2])$	4.442	0.015	0.014	0.347	0.009	0.008
$G(3, [1, 2])$	1.196	0.023	0.021	0.381	0.010	0.010
$G(5, [1, 2])$	3.460	0.096	0.071	0.430	0.017	0.016
$G(5, [3, 8])$	3.426	0.091	0.070	0.430	0.017	0.016
$U(2, [1, 2])$	37.204	0.481	0.471	0.312	0.009	0.009
$U(3, [1, 2])$	80.216	0.986	2.242	5.119	0.179	0.180
$U(5, [1, 2])$	171.445	7.440	TO	17.326	0.519	0.515
$U(5, [3, 8])$	169.950	6.773	TO	17.300	0.522	0.519
$R(2, [1, 2])$	0.545	0.009	0.008	0.331	0.009	0.008
$R(3, [1, 2])$	0.879	0.015	0.015	0.379	0.056	0.053
$R(5, [1, 2])$	2.249	0.064	0.043	0.470	0.156	0.152
$R(5, [3, 8])$	2.223	0.061	0.044	0.468	0.166	0.151
$\mu(1)$	-	0.003	0.003	-	0.008	0.007
$\mu(2)$	-	0.518	0.479	-	0.012	0.011
$\mu(3)$	-	2.261	1.649	-	0.026	0.017
$\mu(4)$	-	55.616	11.338	-	0.118	0.025
$\theta(1, [100, 1000])$	0.807	-	-	0.370	-	-
$\theta(2, [100, 1000])$	2.215	-	-	0.425	-	-
$\theta(3, [100, 1000])$	ERR	-	-	0.920	-	-
$\theta(4, [100, 1000])$	ERR	-	-	11.727	-	-

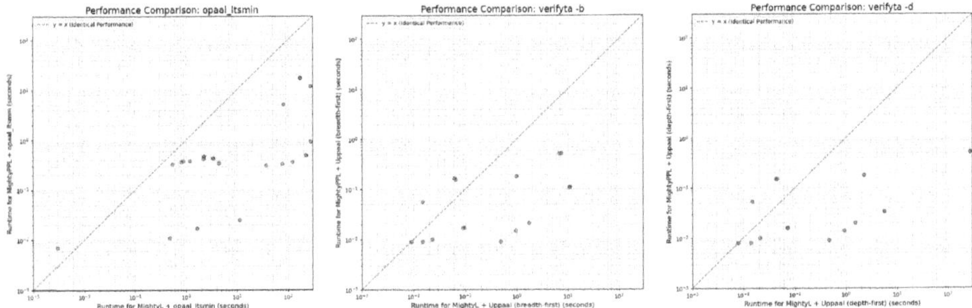

Fig. 6: MightyL benchmarks with `opaal_ltsmin` as the back-end.

Fig. 7: MightyL benchmarks with `verifyta -b` as the back-end.

Fig. 8: MightyL benchmarks with `verifyta -d` as the back-end.

Acacia-Bonsai benchmarks. This set of benchmarks is taken from Acacia-Bonsai [29], and it is also part of the SYNTCOMP 2021 LTL competition suite. We consider the infinite-word satisfiability of 5 formulae $\varphi_1 \ldots \varphi_6$ chosen from this set and modified by adding time intervals:

$$\varphi_1 = (((\square(\lozenge_{[1,2]}\, p)) \vee (\square(\lozenge_{[1,2]}\, q)) \vee (\square(\lozenge_{[1,2]}\, r))) \wedge (\square(\lozenge(a)))) \vee$$
$$(\neg((\square(\lozenge_{[1,2]}\, p)) \vee (\square(\lozenge_{[1,2]}\, q)) \vee (\square(\lozenge_{[1,2]}\, r))) \wedge \neg(\square(\lozenge(a)))) \,,$$

$$\varphi_2 = (\square(((p\, \mathbf{U}_{[1,2]}\, q)\, \mathbf{U}_{[1,2]}\, (\neg p))\, \mathbf{U}_{[1,2]}\, (\neg r)) \wedge \square(\lozenge(a))) \vee$$
$$(\neg(\square(((p\, \mathbf{U}_{[1,2]}\, q)\, \mathbf{U}_{[1,2]}\, (\neg p))\, \mathbf{U}_{[1,2]}\, (\neg r))) \wedge \neg(\square(\lozenge(a)))) \,,$$

$$\varphi_3 = (((\square(\neg p \vee (\lozenge_{[0,2]}\, q))) \wedge (\square(p \vee (\lozenge_{[0,4]}(\neg q))))) \wedge (\square(\lozenge a))) \wedge$$
$$(\neg((\square(\neg p \vee (\lozenge_{[0,2]}\, q))) \wedge (\square(p \vee (\lozenge_{[0,4]}(\neg q))))) \wedge \neg(\square(\lozenge a))) \,,$$

$$\varphi_4 = (((\square(\lozenge_{[2,4]}\, p)) \wedge (\square(\lozenge_{[2,4]}\, q)) \wedge (\square(\lozenge_{[2,4]}\, r)) \wedge (\square(\lozenge_{[2,4]}\, s)) \wedge (\square(\lozenge_{[2,4]}\, u))) \wedge (\square(\lozenge(a)))) \vee$$
$$(\neg((\square(\lozenge_{[2,4]}\, p)) \wedge (\square(\lozenge_{[2,4]}\, q)) \wedge (\square(\lozenge_{[2,4]}\, r)) \wedge (\square(\lozenge_{[2,4]}\, s)) \wedge (\square(\lozenge_{[2,4]}\, u))) \wedge \neg(\square(\lozenge(a)))) \,,$$

$$\varphi_5 = ((\square_{[0,2]}\, r) \wedge (\square_{[0,2]}(\neg p \vee (\lozenge_{[1,2]}\, q))) \wedge (\square_{[0,2]}(\neg q \vee (\lozenge_{[1,2]}\, r)))) \wedge (\square(\lozenge(a)))) \vee$$
$$(\neg((\square_{[0,2]}\, r) \wedge (\square_{[0,2]}(\neg p || (\lozenge_{[1,2]}\, q))) \wedge (\square_{[0,2]}(\neg q \vee (\lozenge_{[1,2]}\, r)))) \wedge \neg(\square(\lozenge(a)))) \,.$$

The results are listed in Table 2. For satisfiable formulae, MightyPPL in the 'noflat' mode is generally the fastest approach with TChecker. We also note that for this set of benchmarks, TChecker performs better than LTSmin.

Table 2: Execution times on the Acacia benchmarks. Times are in seconds. 'TO' indicates timeouts (300s) and 'ERR' means out-of-memory errors.

φ	Sat?	MightyL opaal_ltsmin	MightyPPL opaal_ltsmin noflat	MightyPPL opaal_ltsmin compflat	MightyPPL tck --inf noflat	MightyPPL tck --inf compflat	MightyPPL tck --inf flat	MightyPPL fp --inf
φ_1	✓	TO	TO	TO	0.126	1.407	170.040	TO
φ_2	✓	TO	TO	TO	0.097	1.261	TO	TO
φ_3	✗	ERR	TO	TO	0.531	0.533	4.443	2.381
φ_4	✓	TO	TO	TO	0.582	7.548	TO	TO
φ_5	✓	TO	TO	TO	0.077	0.788	TO	TO

472   H.-M. Ho et al.

Table 3: Execution times on the specification debugging benchmarks. Times are in seconds. 'TO' indicates timeouts (300s).

Formula	MIGHTYPPL tck --inf noflat	MIGHTYPPL tck --inf compflat	MIGHTYPPL tck --inf flat	MIGHTYPPL fp --inf	MIGHTYPPL tck --fin noflat	MIGHTYPPL tck --fin compflat	MIGHTYPPL tck --fin flat	MIGHTYPPL fp --fin
φ_1'	0.019	0.013	0.021	0.015	0.015	0.009	0.012	0.006
φ_2'	3.230	2.232	0.737	0.807	0.055	0.053	0.122	0.100
φ_3'	0.011	0.010	0.051	0.053	0.010	0.010	0.024	0.016
$\Diamond\,past(\varphi_1')$	1.520	1.517	0.431	0.189	0.043	0.046	0.106	0.056
$\Diamond\,past(\varphi_2')$	TO	TO	43.686	3.718	0.945	0.941	2.439	0.652
$\Diamond\,past(\varphi_3')$	0.179	0.179	0.230	0.112	0.043	0.042	0.079	0.041

Table 4: Execution times on the robotic missions benchmarks. Times are in seconds. 'TO' indicates timeouts (300s).

Pattern	Formula	Sat?	MIGHTYPPL tck --inf noflat	MIGHTYPPL tck --inf compflat	MIGHTYPPL tck --inf flat	MIGHTYPPL fp --inf
TPA	φ_1''	✓	0.007	0.007	0.013	0.008
TSV	φ_2''	✓	0.008	0.007	0.010	0.007
TSP	φ_3''	✓	0.024	0.035	0.055	0.044
TSV, TPA	φ_4''	✗	0.031	0.032	0.106	0.061

Table 5: Execution times on the food delivery benchmarks. Times are in seconds. 'TO' indicates timeouts (300s).

K	L	(l, u)	Hold?	MIGHTYPPL tck --fin noflat	MIGHTYPPL tck --fin compflat	MIGHTYPPL tck --fin flat	MIGHTYPPL fp --fin
P	$L1$	$(15, 20)$	✗	2.327	0.447	2.065	104.157
B	$L2$	$(3, 5)$	✗	5.304	1.864	2.633	6.509
C	$L1$	$(10, 12)$	✗	1.400	0.520	1.733	212.396

Debugging specifications for cyber-physical systems. [33] introduces the *debugging* problem of formal specifications written as MITL formulae. We consider the finite- and infinite-word satisfiability of the formulae below:

$$\varphi_1' = (p_2 \vee \Diamond_{[0,40]}\, p_2) \wedge \left(\Diamond_{[0,40]}(p_1 \wedge \Box_{[0,30]}\, p_1)\right) \wedge \neg\left((p_1 \vee p_3) \vee \Diamond_{[0,40]}(p_1 \vee p_3)\right),$$

$$\varphi_2' = \Diamond_{[10,40]}\left((p_1 \vee p_3 \implies \Diamond_{[0,20]}\, p_2) \wedge p_1 \wedge \Box_{[0,30]}\, p_1\right)$$
$$\wedge \neg\Diamond_{[10,40]}\left((p_1 \vee \bot \implies \Diamond_{[0,20]}\, p_2) \wedge p_1 \wedge \Box_{[0,30]}\, p_1\right),$$

$$\varphi_3' = \neg\left((p \wedge \Box_{[0,40]}\, p \wedge \Diamond_{[20,40]}\, \top) \implies ((p \vee \Diamond_{[0,20]}\, p) \wedge \Box_{[0,20]}(p \vee \Diamond_{[0,20]}\, p))\right).$$

For each of them, we also consider a modified version, where $past(\varphi)$ is obtained by replacing all the future modalities with their past counterparts in φ. The results are listed in Table 3 (all unsatisfiable).

Robotic missions. This set of benchmarks is adapted from [63, 61, 62]:

$$\varphi_1'' = \Box(l_1 \implies \overleftarrow{\Diamond}_{[0,2]}\, l_2) \wedge \Box(l_3 \implies \overleftarrow{\Diamond}_{[0,2]}\, l_4),$$

$$\varphi_2'' = \mathbf{Pn}_{[0,2]}(p_1, p_2, p_3, p_4, p_5, p_6, p_7)\,,$$
$$\varphi_3'' = \Box\,\mathbf{Pn}_{[0,1]}(p_1, p_2, p_3)\,,$$
$$\varphi_4'' = \mathbf{Pn}_{[0,1]}(p_1, p_2, p_3) \wedge \Box(p_2 \implies \neg\overleftarrow{\Diamond}_{[0,1]}\, p_1) \wedge \Box(p_3 \implies \neg\overleftarrow{\Diamond}_{[0,1]}\, p_2)\,.$$

The results are listed in Table 4.

Food delivery. Consider a food delivery scenario (Sect. 1) where deliveries must be quick (≤ 15 minutes of order) and fresh (≤ 10 minutes of pickup), captured by $\phi'(K, L) = \mathbf{Pn}_{[0,15]}(K \wedge \Diamond_{[0,10]}\, L, L)$. Given a city map (Fig. 1) and order patterns, the planning problem—can a driver satisfy these constraints?—is formulated as model checking over the TA $\mathcal{M}$. We check $\mathcal{M}$ against $\pi(K, L, (l, u)) \to \Diamond(K{:}L \wedge \neg\phi'(K, L))$ where $\pi(K, L, (l, u)) = \Diamond_{[0,1]}(K{:}L) \wedge \Box_{[0,50]}(K{:}L \to ((\neg K{:}L)\, \mathbf{U}_{[l,\infty)}\, K{:}L) \wedge ((\neg K{:}L)\, \mathbf{U}_{[0,u]}\, K{:}L))$. The results are listed in Table 5. TChecker performs similarly with MightyPPL in both the 'compflat' and 'flat' modes, significantly outperforming the backward fixpoint algorithm.

Comparison with Tempora. We consider the infinite-word satisfiability of some simple MITL formulae, some formulae from the Acacia-Bonsai benchmarks $(\varphi_1, \ldots, \varphi_5)$, and some formulae from the specification debugging benchmarks $(\varphi_1', \ldots, \varphi_3')$ and compare with Tempora [3]. The results are listed in Table 6. MightyPPL performs better on most instances, although there are some exceptions (φ_3 and φ_5). We also note that in some cases Tempora produced wrong results. Consequently, this comparison is best viewed as a preliminary evaluation of Tempora's efficiency rather than a definitive assessment of its reliability.

Table 6: Times are in seconds; TO = 300s. Superscripts * and ** denote incorrect results by Tempora in the Docker image version and the project repository version, respectively. All reported times (including TO) are from the Docker image version.

| | | | MightyPPL |
| | | Tempora [3] | tck --inf |
φ	Sat?		compflat
$\Diamond((p\,\mathbf{U}_{[1,2]}\, q) \wedge \neg(p\,\mathbf{U}_{[0,3]}\, q))$	✗	0.066^{*}	0.008
$\Diamond((p\,\mathbf{S}_{[1,2]}\, q) \wedge \neg(p\,\mathbf{S}_{[1,3]}\, q))$	✗	0.017^{*}	0.007
$\Diamond((p\,\mathbf{S}_{[1,5]}\, (\Diamond_{[2,3]}\, q)) \wedge \neg(\top\,\mathbf{S}\, q))$	✓	TO^{**}	0.001
$\Diamond((\Diamond_{[2,3]}(p\,\mathbf{S}_{[1,5]}\, q)) \wedge \neg(\top\,\mathbf{S}\, q))$	✓	TO^{**}	0.001
φ_1	✓	TO	1.407
φ_2	✓	TO	1.261
φ_3	✗	0.050	0.533
φ_4	✓	TO	7.548
φ_5	✓	0.011	0.788
φ_1'	✗	0.080	0.013
φ_2'	✗	TO	2.232
φ_3'	✗	0.011	0.010

Data availability statement. The models, tools, and scripts to reproduce our experimental evaluation are available at [4].

References

[1] MIGHTYL virtual machine. https://verif.ulb.ac.be/mightyl/ (2025)

[2] PARDIBAAL library. https://github.com/DEIS-Tools/PARDIBAAL (2025)

[3] TEMPORA Docker image (October 2025) and project repository (March 2026), howpublished = "https://doi.org/10.6084/m9.figshare.30490967.v1 and https://github.com/EQuaVe/TEMPORA/tree/1ba0bad25a9015a077f5990b93954bc2157f0186", year = 2025

[4] MIGHTYPPL project repository. https://github.com/hsimho/MightyPPL (2026)

[5] Abbas, H., Fainekos, G., Sankaranarayanan, S., Ivančić, F., Gupta, A.: Probabilistic temporal logic falsification of cyber-physical systems. ACM Transactions on Embedded Computing Systems (TECS) **12**(2s), 1–30 (2013)

[6] Akshay, S., Contractor, P., Gastin, P., Govind, R., Srivathsan, B.: Efficient verification of metric temporal properties with past in pointwise semantics. arXiv preprint arXiv:2510.14699 (2025), URL https://arxiv.org/abs/2510.14699

[7] Akshay, S., Gastin, P., Govind, R., Joshi, A.R., Srivathsan, B.: A unified model for real-time systems: Symbolic techniques and implementation. In: International Conference on Computer Aided Verification, pp. 266–288, Springer (2023)

[8] Akshay, S., Gastin, P., Govind, R., Srivathsan, B.: MITL model checking via generalized timed automata and a new liveness algorithm. In: CONCUR (2024)

[9] Alur, R., Courcoubetis, C., Dill, D.: Model-checking in dense real-time. Information and computation **104**(1), 2–34 (1993)

[10] Alur, R., Dill, D.L.: A theory of timed automata. Theor. Comput. Sci. **126**(2), 183–235 (1994), https://doi.org/10.1016/0304-3975(94)90010-8, URL http://dx.doi.org/10.1016/0304-3975(94)90010-8

[11] Alur, R., Feder, T., Henzinger, T.: The benefits of relaxing punctuality. J.ACM **43(1)**, 116–146 (1996)

[12] Alur, R., Henzinger, T.A.: Logics and models of real time: A survey. In: REX, LNCS, vol. 600, pp. 74–106, Springer-Verlag (1992)

[13] Alur, R., Henzinger, T.A.: Real-time logics: Complexity and expressiveness. Inf. Comput. **104**(1), 35–77 (1993), https://doi.org/10.1006/inco.1993.1025, URL http://dx.doi.org/10.1006/inco.1993.1025

[14] Annpureddy, Y., Liu, C., Fainekos, G., Sankaranarayanan, S.: S-taliro: A tool for temporal logic falsification for hybrid systems. In: International Conference on Tools and Algorithms for the Construction and Analysis of Systems, pp. 254–257, Springer (2011)

[15] Bae, K., Lee, J.: Bounded model checking of signal temporal logic properties using syntactic separation. Proceedings of the ACM on Programming Languages **3**(POPL), 1–30 (2019)

[16] Beg, O.A., Nguyen, L.V., Johnson, T.T., Davoudi, A.: Signal temporal logic-based attack detection in dc microgrids. IEEE Transactions on Smart Grid **10**(4), 3585–3595 (2018)

[17] Behrmann, G., Cougnard, A., David, A., Fleury, E., Larsen, K.G., Lime, D.: Uppaal-tiga: Time for playing games! In: International Conference on Computer Aided Verification, pp. 121–125, Springer (2007)

[18] Behrmann, G., David, A., Larsen, K.G., Håkansson, J., Pettersson, P., Yi, W., Hendriks, M.: Uppaal 4.0. In: QEST, pp. 125–126, IEEE (2006)

[19] Bérard, B., Petit, A., Diekert, V., Gastin, P.: Characterization of the expressive power of silent transitions in timed automata. Fundamenta Informaticae **36**(2-3), 145–182 (1998)

[20] Bersani, M.M., Rossi, M., San Pietro, P.: A tool for deciding the satisfiability of continuous-time metric temporal logic. Acta Informatica **53**(2), 171–206 (2016)

[21] Bouyer, P.: Model-checking timed temporal logics. Electronic notes in theoretical computer science **231**, 323–341 (2009)

[22] Bouyer, P., Chevalier, F., Markey, N.: On the expressiveness of tptl and mtl. Information and Computation **208**(2), 97–116 (2010)

[23] Bouyer, P., Gastin, P., Herbreteau, F., Sankur, O., Srivathsan, B.: Zone-based verification of timed automata: extrapolations, simulations and what next? In: International Conference on Formal Modeling and Analysis of Timed Systems, pp. 16–42, Springer (2022)

[24] Bouyer, P., Laroussinie, F., Markey, N., Ouaknine, J., Worrell, J.: Timed temporal logics. Models, Algorithms, Logics and Tools: Essays Dedicated to Kim Guldstrand Larsen on the Occasion of His 60th Birthday pp. 211–230 (2017)

[25] Brihaye, T., Estiévenart, M., Geeraerts, G.: On MITL and alternating timed automata. In: Formal Modeling and Analysis of Timed Systems: 11th International Conference, FORMATS 2013, Buenos Aires, Argentina, August 29-31, 2013. Proceedings 11, pp. 47–61, Springer (2013)

[26] Brihaye, T., Estiévenart, M., Geeraerts, G.: On MITL and alternating timed automata over infinite words. In: Formal Modeling and Analysis of Timed Systems: 12th International Conference, FORMATS 2014, Florence, Italy, September 8-10, 2014. Proceedings 12, pp. 69–84, Springer (2014)

[27] Brihaye, T., Geeraerts, G., Ho, H., Monmege, B.: Mightyl: A compositional translation from MITL to timed automata. In: Majumdar, R., Kuncak, V. (eds.) Computer Aided Verification - 29th International Conference, CAV 2017, Heidelberg, Germany, July 24-28, 2017, Proceedings, Part I, Lecture Notes in Computer Science, vol. 10426, pp. 421–440, Springer (2017), `https://doi.org/10.1007/978-3-319-63387-9_21`, URL `https://doi.org/10.1007/978-3-319-63387-9_21`

[28] Burch, J.R., Clarke, E.M., McMillan, K.L., Dill, D.L., Hwang, L.J.: Symbolic model checking: 1020 states and beyond. Information and computation **98**(2), 142–170 (1992)

[29] Cadilhac, M., Pérez, G.A.: Acacia-bonsai: A modern implementation of downset-based LTL realizability. In: Sankaranarayanan, S., Sharygina, N. (eds.) Tools and Algorithms for the Construction and Analysis of Systems - 29th International Conference, TACAS 2023, Held as Part of the European Joint Conferences on Theory and Practice of Software, ETAPS 2022, Paris, France, April 22-27, 2023, Proceedings, Part II, Lecture Notes in Computer Science, vol. 13994, pp. 192–207, Springer (2023), `https://doi.org/10.1007/978-3-031-30820-8_14`, URL `https://doi.org/10.1007/978-3-031-30820-8_14`

[30] Chaki, S., Gurfinkel, A., Strichman, O.: Time-bounded analysis of real-time systems. In: FMCAD, pp. 72–80, IEEE (2011)

[31] Clarke, E., Grumberg, O., Hamaguchi, K.: Another look at ltl model checking. In: Computer Aided Verification: 6th International Conference, CAV'94 Stanford, California, USA, June 21–23, 1994 Proceedings 6, pp. 415–427, Springer (1994)

[32] Deshmukh, J.V., Donzé, A., Ghosh, S., Jin, X., Juniwal, G., Seshia, S.A.: Robust online monitoring of signal temporal logic. Formal Methods in System Design **51**, 5–30 (2017)

[33] Dokhanchi, A., Hoxha, B., Fainekos, G.: Formal requirement debugging for testing and verification of cyber-physical systems. ACM Transactions on Embedded Computing Systems (TECS) **17**(2), 1–26 (2017)

[34] Donzé, A., Ferrere, T., Maler, O.: Efficient robust monitoring for stl. In: International conference on computer aided verification, pp. 264–279, Springer (2013)

[35] D'Souza, D., Matteplackel, R.M.: A clock-optimal hierarchical monitoring automaton for MITL. ICLA 2021 Proceedings p. 83 (2021)

[36] Fischer, B., Inverso, O., Parlato, G.: Cseq: A concurrency pre-processor for sequential c verification tools. In: 2013 28th IEEE/ACM International Conference on Automated Software Engineering (ASE), pp. 710–713, IEEE (2013)

[37] Geilen, M.: An improved on-the-fly tableau construction for a real-time temporal logic. In: Computer Aided Verification: 15th International Conference, CAV 2003, Boulder, CO, USA, July 8-12, 2003. Proceedings 15, pp. 394–406, Springer (2003)

[38] Godefroid, P.: Using partial orders to improve automatic verification methods. In: International Conference on Computer Aided Verification, pp. 176–185, Springer (1990)

[39] Godefroid, P., Wolper, P.: A partial approach to model checking. Information and Computation **110**(2), 305–326 (1994)

[40] Grosen, T.M.: The MONITAAL tool. https://github.com/DEIS-Tools/MoniTAal (2025)

[41] Henzinger, T.A.: It's about time: Real-time logics reviewed. In: Sangiorgi, D., de Simone, R. (eds.) CONCUR'98 Concurrency Theory, pp. 439–454, Springer Berlin Heidelberg, Berlin, Heidelberg (1998), ISBN 978-3-540-68455-8

[42] Henzinger, T.A., Nicollin, X., Sifakis, J., Yovine, S.: Symbolic model checking for real-time systems. Information and computation **111**(2), 193–244 (1994)

[43] Henzinger, T.A., Raskin, J., Schobbens, P.: The regular real-time languages. In: Larsen, K.G., Skyum, S., Winskel, G. (eds.) Automata, Languages and Programming, 25th International Colloquium, ICALP'98, Aalborg, Denmark, July 13-17, 1998, Proceedings, Lecture Notes in Computer Science, vol. 1443, pp. 580–591, Springer (1998), https://doi.org/10.1007/BFb0055086, URL https://doi.org/10.1007/BFb0055086

[44] Herbreteau, F., Point, G.: The tchecker tool and libraries. https://github.com/ticktac-project/tchecker (2019)

[45] Hirshfeld, Y., Rabinovich, A.: An expressive temporal logic for real time. In: MFCS, pp. 492–504 (2006)

[46] Hirshfeld, Y., Rabinovich, A.: Expressiveness of metric modalities for continuous time. Logical Methods in Computer Science **3**(1), 1–11 (2007)

[47] Hirshfeld, Y., Rabinovich, A.M.: Logics for real time: Decidability and complexity. Fundamenta Informaticae **62**(1), 1–28 (2004)

[48] Ho, H.M., Krishna, S.N., Madnani, K., Majumdar, R., Pandya, P.: Mightyppl: Verification of mitl with past and pnueli modalities. arXiv preprint arXiv:2510.01490 (2025), URL https://arxiv.org/abs/2510.01490

[49] Holzmann, G.J., Godefroid, P., Pirottin, D.: Coverage preserving reduction strategies for reachability analysis. In: Protocol Specification, Testing and Verification, XII, pp. 349–363, Elsevier (1992)

[50] Hunter, P.: When is metric temporal logic expressively complete? In: CSL, pp. 380–394 (2013)

[51] Jin, X., Deshmukh, J.V., Kapinski, J., Ueda, K., Butts, K.: Powertrain control verification benchmark. In: Proceedings of the 17th international conference on Hybrid systems: computation and control, pp. 253–262 (2014)

[52] Kant, G., Laarman, A., Meijer, J., van de Pol, J., Blom, S., van Dijk, T.: LTSmin: High-performance language-independent model checking. In: TACAS, LNCS, vol. 9035, pp. 692–707, Springer (2015)

[53] Kesten, Y., Pnueli, A., Raviv, L.o.: Algorithmic verification of linear temporal logic specifications. In: Automata, Languages and Programming: 25th International

Colloquium, ICALP'98 Aalborg, Denmark, July 13–17, 1998 Proceedings 25, pp. 1–16, Springer (1998)

[54] Koymans, R.: Specifying real-time properties with metric temporal logic. Real Time Syst. **2**(4), 255–299 (1990), https://doi.org/10.1007/BF01995674, URL https://doi.org/10.1007/BF01995674

[55] Laarman, A., Olesen, M.C., Dalsgaard, A.E., Larsen, K.G., Van De Pol, J.: Multicore emptiness checking of timed büchi automata using inclusion abstraction. In: Computer Aided Verification: 25th International Conference, CAV 2013, Saint Petersburg, Russia, July 13-19, 2013. Proceedings 25, pp. 968–983, Springer (2013)

[56] Lal, A., Reps, T.: Reducing concurrent analysis under a context bound to sequential analysis. Formal Methods in System Design **35**, 73–97 (2009)

[57] Maler, O., Nickovic, D.: Monitoring temporal properties of continuous signals. In: International Symposium on Formal Techniques in Real-Time and Fault-Tolerant Systems, pp. 152–166, Springer (2004)

[58] Maler, O., Nickovic, D., Pnueli, A.: Real time temporal logic: Past, present, future. In: International conference on formal modeling and analysis of timed systems, pp. 2–16, Springer (2005)

[59] Maler, O., Nickovic, D., Pnueli, A.: From MITL to timed automata. In: Formal Modeling and Analysis of Timed Systems: 4th International Conference, FORMATS 2006, Paris, France, September 25-27, 2006. Proceedings 4, pp. 274–289, Springer (2006)

[60] Manna, Z., Pnueli, A.: Completing the temporal picture. In: International Colloquium on Automata, Languages, and Programming, pp. 534–558, Springer (1989)

[61] Menghi, C., Tsigkanos, C., Berger, T., Pelliccione, P.: Psalm: specification of dependable robotic missions. In: Proceedings of the 41st International Conference on Software Engineering: Companion Proceedings, p. 99–102, ICSE '19, IEEE Press (2019), https://doi.org/10.1109/ICSE-Companion.2019.00048, URL https://doi.org/10.1109/ICSE-Companion.2019.00048

[62] Menghi, C., Tsigkanos, C., Berger, T., Pelliccione, P., Ghezzi, C.: Poster: Property specification patterns for robotic missions. In: 2018 IEEE/ACM 40th International Conference on Software Engineering: Companion (ICSE-Companion), pp. 434–435 (2018)

[63] Menghi, C., Tsigkanos, C., Pelliccione, P., Ghezzi, C., Berger, T.: Specification patterns for robotic missions. IEEE Transactions on Software Engineering **47**(10), 2208–2224 (2021), https://doi.org/10.1109/TSE.2019.2945329

[64] Ničković, D., Piterman, N.: From mtl to deterministic timed automata. In: International Conference on Formal Modeling and Analysis of Timed Systems, pp. 152–167, Springer (2010)

[65] Ničković, D., Yamaguchi, T.: Rtamt: Online robustness monitors from stl. In: International Symposium on Automated Technology for Verification and Analysis, pp. 564–571, Springer (2020)

[66] Ouaknine, J., Worrell, J.: On the decidability of metric temporal logic. In: LICS, pp. 188–197 (2005)

[67] Ouaknine, J., Worrell, J.: On metric temporal logic and faulty turing machines. In: Aceto, L., Ingólfsdóttir, A. (eds.) Foundations of Software Science and Computation Structures, 9th International Conference, FOSSACS 2006, Held as Part of the Joint European Conferences on Theory and Practice of Software, ETAPS 2006, Vienna, Austria, March 25-31, 2006, Proceedings, Lecture Notes in Computer Science, vol. 3921, pp. 217–230, Springer (2006), https://doi.org/10.1007/11690634_15, URL https://doi.org/10.1007/11690634_15

[68] Pandya, P.K., Shah, S.: On expressive powers of timed logics: Comparing bounded-ness, non-punctuality, and deterministic freezing. In: CONCUR, pp. 60–75 (2011)

[69] Peled, D.: All from one, one for all: on model checking using representatives. In: International Conference on Computer Aided Verification, pp. 409–423, Springer (1993)

[70] Pnueli, A.: The temporal logic of programs. In: 18th Annual Symposium on Foundations of Computer Science (sfcs 1977), pp. 46–57 (1977), https://doi.org/10.1109/SFCS.1977.32

[71] Pnueli, A., Zaks, A.: On the merits of temporal testers. In: 25 Years of Model Checking: History, Achievements, Perspectives, pp. 172–195, Springer (2008)

[72] Rabinovich, A.: Complexity of metric temporal logics with counting and the pnueli modalities. Theor. Comput. Sci. **411**(22-24), 2331–2342 (2010), https://doi.org/10.1016/j.tcs.2010.03.017, URL https://doi.org/10.1016/j.tcs.2010.03.017

[73] Raman, V., Maasoumy, M., Donzé, A.: Model predictive control from signal temporal logic specifications: A case study. In: Proceedings of the 4th ACM SIGBED International Workshop on Design, Modeling, and Evaluation of Cyber-Physical Systems, pp. 52–55 (2014)

[74] Raskin, J.F.: Logics, Automata and Classical Theories for Deciding Real Time. Ph.D. thesis, Université de Namur (1999)

[75] Raskin, J.F., Schobbens, P.Y.: State clock logic: A decidable real-time logic. In: International Workshop on Hybrid and Real-Time Systems, pp. 33–47, Springer (1997)

[76] Raskin, J.F., Schobbens, P.Y.: The logic of event clocks - decidability, complexity and expressiveness. Journal of Automata, Languages and Combinatorics **4**(3), 247–286 (1999)

[77] Roohi, N., Kaur, R., Weimer, J., Sokolsky, O., Lee, I.: Parameter invariant monitoring for signal temporal logic. In: Proceedings of the 21st International Conference on Hybrid Systems: Computation and Control (part of CPS Week), pp. 187–196 (2018)

[78] Valmari, A.: A stubborn attack on state explosion. In: International Conference on Computer Aided Verification, pp. 156–165, Springer (1990)

[79] Valmari, A.: On-the-fly verification with stubborn sets. In: International Conference on Computer Aided Verification, pp. 397–408, Springer (1993)

[80] Waga, M.: Falsification of cyber-physical systems with robustness-guided black-box checking. In: Proceedings of the 23rd International Conference on Hybrid Systems: Computation and Control, pp. 1–13 (2020)

[81] Wilke, T.: Specifying timed state sequences in powerful decidable logics and timed automata. In: Formal Techniques in Real-Time and Fault-Tolerant Systems, Third International Symposium Organized Jointly with the Working Group Provably Correct Systems - ProCoS, Lübeck, Germany, September 19-23, Proceedings, pp. 694–715 (1994), https://doi.org/10.1007/3-540-58468-4_191, URL https://doi.org/10.1007/3-540-58468-4_191

LTL$_f$ Learning Meets Boolean Set Cover*

Gabriel Bathie[1,2], Nathanaël Fijalkow[1],
Théo Matricon[1,3], Baptiste Mouillon[1],
and Pierre Vandenhove[1,4]

[1] LaBRI, CNRS, Université de Bordeaux, France
[2] DIENS, Paris, France
[3] Univ Rennes, CNRS, Inria, IRISA, Rennes, France
[4] UMONS – Université de Mons, Belgium

Abstract. Learning formulas in Linear Temporal Logic (**LTL**$_f$) from finite traces is a fundamental research problem which has found applications in artificial intelligence, software engineering, programming languages, formal methods, control of cyber-physical systems, and robotics. We implement a new CPU tool called Bolt improving over the state of the art by learning formulas more than 100x faster over 70% of the benchmarks, with smaller or equal formulas in 98% of the cases. Our key insight is to leverage a problem called *Boolean Set Cover* as a subroutine to combine existing formulas using Boolean connectives. Thanks to the Boolean Set Cover component, our approach offers a novel trade-off between efficiency and formula size.

Keywords: Linear Temporal Logic · Finite Traces · Specification Mining · Boolean Set Cover

1 Introduction

Linear Temporal Logic (**LTL**) [45] is a prominent logic for specifying temporal properties over infinite traces; in this paper, we consider **LTL** on finite traces [27], abbreviated **LTL**$_f$. The fundamental problem we study is to learn **LTL**$_f$ formulas from traces: given a set of positive and negative traces, find an **LTL**$_f$ formula separating positive from negative ones. **LTL**$_f$ learning spans different research communities, each contributing applications, approaches, and viewpoints on this problem. We give below a cursory cross-sectional survey of motivations and applications of **LTL**$_f$ learning in three communities.

* This work was partially supported by the SAIF project, funded by the "France 2030" government investment plan managed by the French National Research Agency, under the reference ANR-23-PEIA-0006. Pierre Vandenhove was funded by ANR project G4S (ANR-21-CE48-0010-01). Experiments presented in this paper were carried out using the Grid'5000 testbed, supported by a scientific interest group hosted by Inria and including CNRS, RENATER and several Universities as well as other organizations (see `https://www.grid5000.fr/`).

S. Junges and G. Katz (Eds.): TACAS 2026, LNCS 16505, pp. 480–501, 2026.
https://doi.org/10.1007/978-3-032-22752-2_25

Software Engineering, Programming Languages, Formal Methods. **LTL**$_f$ learning is an instantiation of specification mining, which is an active area of research devoted to discovering formal specifications of code. Already back in the 1970s, Wegbreit [53] and Caplain [14] propose frameworks to automatically generate properties of code. At this point, it is important to distinguish between the dynamic and the static setting: in this paper, we are interested in the *dynamic* setting where we observe program executions (also called *traces*) to infer properties of the code. The term *specification mining* was coined by Ammons, Bodík, and Larus [1] in a seminal paper where finite-state machines capture both temporal and data dependencies. Zeller [57] contributed a roadmap to mining specifications in 2010, highlighting its potential for software engineering. A few years later, Rozier [49] shaped an entire research program revolving around ***LTL Genesis***, motivating and introducing the **LTL** learning problem as we study it here. Early works focused on mining simple temporal properties [22]. In particular, Perracotta [56] and Javert [25] focus on patterns of the form $(ab)^*$ and $(ab^*c)^*$. The first tool supporting all **LTL**$_f$ formulas is called Texada, and was created in 2015 [38,37]. Following Texada, a line of work focuses on scaling **LTL**$_f$ learning to industrial sizes, conjuring different approaches. We mention here the state-of-the-art **LTL**$_f$ learning tools: Scarlet, based on combinatorial search [46], and a GPU-accelerated algorithm (later referred to as *VFB algorithm* given its authors Valizadeh, Fijalkow, and Berger) [52]. Applications of mining specifications for software include detecting malicious behaviors [17] or violations [40] and are already widely adopted in software engineering: for instance, the ARSENAL and ARSENAL2 projects [26] have been successful in constructing **LTL**$_f$ formulas inferred from natural language requirements, and the FRET project generates **LTL**$_f$ from trace descriptions [28]. We refer to the textbook [41] and the PhD thesis of Li [39] for comprehensive presentation of specification mining for software, and its relationship to data mining.

Control of Cyber-Physical Systems and Robotics. **LTL**$_f$ learning is extensively studied in a second area of research with different goals and very different methods: to capture properties of trajectories in models and systems. Given its quantitative nature, Signal Temporal Logic (**STL**) is preferred over **LTL**$_f$ since it involves numerical constants and can thus capture real-valued and time-varying behaviors. In particular, temporal logics allow reasoning about robustness [5] and anomaly detection [34,36]. There is a vast body of work on learning temporal logics in control and robotics, which can be divided into two: techniques aiming at fitting parameters of a fixed assumed **STL** formula [4,55,33], and approaches searching for both formulas and parameters [33,7]. This led to many case studies: automobile transmission controller and engine airpath control [55], assisted ventilation in intensive care patients [10], anomaly detection in a maritime environment [7], demonstrations in robotics [15], detection of attention loss in pilots [42], and analysis of computer games [29].

Artificial Intelligence. The field of AI has contributed to **LTL**$_f$ learning a number of applications, but also a wealth of techniques. The overarching philosophy

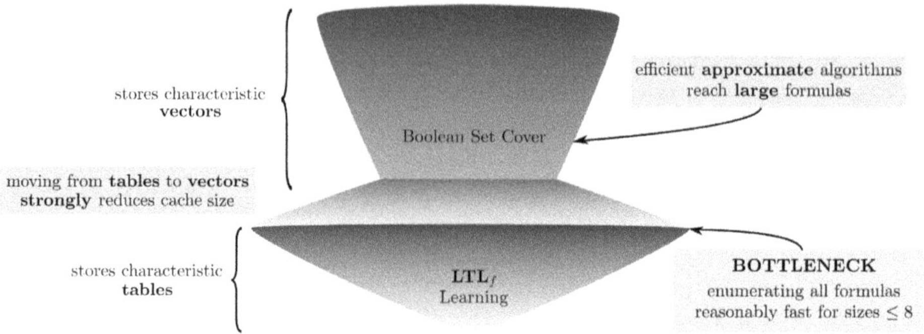

Fig. 1. Overview of $\mathbf{LTL}_f$ Learning with Boolean Set Cover

of $\mathbf{LTL}_f$ learning in AI is that $\mathbf{LTL}_f$ forms a natural and explainable formalism [13] for specifying objectives [30] in various machine learning contexts. For instance, in the context of reinforcement learning, $\mathbf{LTL}_f$ formulas have been used to either guide [11,9] or constrain policies [31,12]. Another recent application aims to speed up synthesis by separating data and control [44].

SOTA on $\mathbf{LTL}_f$ Learning. Since learning temporal logics is computationally hard[5], different approaches have been explored. The state-of-the-art tool is Scarlet, which is based on specifically tailored fragments of $\mathbf{LTL}_f$ [46,47]. A GPU-accelerated algorithm was published in 2024 [52], yielding an improved state of the art in a different category. Scarlet cannot reliably learn formulas of size greater than 15, which is less than ideal: we aim to change this.

Boolean Set Cover. Our key insight in this work, and what we believe is the key to scaling $\mathbf{LTL}_f$ learning to industrial sizes, is to treat Boolean operators differently from temporal operators. To address the former, we leverage a novel solution to a problem we call *Boolean Set Cover* [46,48]. When enumerating $\mathbf{LTL}_f$ formulas, we quickly hit a wall because of the exponential number of formulas. Let us say that at this point, we have enumerated the formulas $\varphi_1, \ldots, \varphi_k$ but have not found a solution. Instead of giving up, Boolean Set Cover looks for solutions in the form of Boolean combinations of the formulas $\varphi_1, \ldots, \varphi_k$, allowing us to generate much larger and more expressive formulas.

Boolean Set Cover is a fundamental problem which has been studied under different names. In the 80s, when key concepts from learning theory emerged, it was known as *Boolean Concept learning* [50,2] (see also the textbook [3]). In logic, it has been extensively studied as *extending partially defined Boolean functions*; see, e.g., [18]. The name *Boolean Set Cover* was introduced in [46] in the context of $\mathbf{LTL}_f$ learning, highlighting that it extends the classical *Set Cover* problem. For consistency in this line of work, we adhere to this terminology.

The **key finding** of this work is that the Boolean Set Cover problem can be solved *in an approximate way* very efficiently, which can then be leveraged to

---

[5] It is NP-complete, even for restricted fragments of $\mathbf{LTL}_f$ [23,43].

learn **LTL**$_f$ formulas of size beyond the reach of existing tools. An overview of our general approach is depicted in Figure 1.

Our Contributions. Our contributions can be summarized as follows:

- We propose a framework to combine **LTL**$_f$ learning with Boolean Set Cover.
- We implement our algorithms in a new tool called BOLT.
- We consolidate a benchmark suite for **LTL**$_f$ learning with over 15,000 tasks.
- We show through experiments that BOLT significantly improves over the state of the art, both in terms of wall-clock time and size of learned formulas.

We believe Boolean Set Cover is a fundamental problem of independent interest, which has a lot of potential applications beyond **LTL**$_f$ learning. We leave as future work to explore them; we discuss perspectives in Section 6.

Code Availability. BOLT's code is available at `https://github.com/Synthesis Lab/Bolt`. The **LTL**$_f$-learning benchmarks used for the evaluation of our tool are available at `https://github.com/SynthesisLab/LTLf_Learning_Benchm arks`.

Extended Version. Due to a lack of space, some proofs and details are omitted from this version. They can be found in the extended version [6], along with additional details and examples.

2   LTL$_f$ Learning

2.1   Problem Definition

One of the reasons for the success of *Linear Temporal Logic* (**LTL**$_f$) as a logical formalism for temporal reasoning on traces is that its semantics can be conveyed using a single picture:

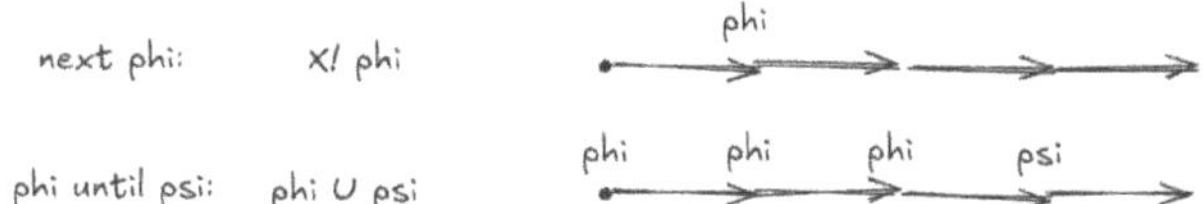

The syntax of **LTL**$_f$ is particularly simple (no variables and no quantifiers), it uses only the classical *Boolean operators* and two *temporal operators*: **X!**, called *Strong Next*, and **U**, called *Until*.[6] Informally, **X!** φ holds if φ holds starting from the next position, and φ **U** ψ holds if there exists a later position such that ψ holds, and φ holds in the meantime.

Formally, let us fix a finite set of *atomic propositions* AP. A (finite) trace is a (non-empty) sequence where each position holds a subset of atomic propositions; for instance, with AP = $\{p, q\}$:

---

[6] The temporal operators **F** and **G** will be derived from **U**.

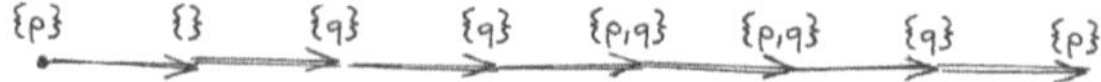

We index traces from position 1 (not 0) and the letter at position i in the trace w is written $w(i)$, so $w = w(1) \ldots w(\ell)$ where ℓ is the length of w, written $|w| = \ell$. We write $w[k \ldots] = w(k) \ldots w(\ell)$. We only consider non-empty traces.

The syntax of *Linear Temporal Logic* ($\mathbf{LTL}_f$) includes atomic propositions $c \in \mathsf{AP}$ as well as $\top$ and $\bot$, the Boolean operators $\neg$, $\wedge$, and $\vee$, and the *temporal operators* $\mathbf{X}!$ and $\mathbf{U}$. The semantics of $\mathbf{LTL}_f$ are defined inductively, through the notation $w \models \varphi$ where w is a non-empty trace and φ is an $\mathbf{LTL}_f$ formula. The definition is given below for the atomic propositions and temporal operators $\mathbf{X}!$ and $\mathbf{U}$, with Boolean operators interpreted as usual. For w of length ℓ:

- $w \models \top$ and $w \not\models \bot$.
- $w \models c$, with $c \in \mathsf{AP}$, if $c \in w(1)$.
- $w \models \mathbf{X}! \varphi$ if $\ell > 1$ and $w[2 \ldots] \models \varphi$ (*strong next*).
- $w \models \varphi \mathbf{U} \psi$ if there is $i \in [1, \ell]$ such that for $j \in [1, i-1]$ we have $w[j \ldots] \models \varphi$, and $w[i \ldots] \models \psi$ (*until*).

We say that w *satisfies* φ if $w \models \varphi$. We define the *size* of an $\mathbf{LTL}_f$ formula φ as the number of nodes in its syntactic tree.

As customary, we include some additional temporal operators: $\mathbf{X} \varphi$ is "weak next φ", it is a shortcut for $\neg \mathbf{X}! \neg \varphi$; $\mathbf{F} \varphi$ is "eventually φ", it is a shortcut for $\top \mathbf{U} \varphi$; $\mathbf{G} \varphi$ is "globally φ", it is a shortcut for $\neg \mathbf{F} \neg \varphi$; $\varphi \mathbf{R} \psi$ is "release φ", it is a shortcut for $\neg \psi \mathbf{U} \neg \varphi$.

The $\mathbf{LTL}_f$ learning problem is defined as follows:

INPUT: two disjoint finite sets of traces P and N
OUTPUT: an $\mathbf{LTL}_f$ formula φ of minimal size such that all of P satisfies φ and none of N satisfies φ

The minimality of a formula depends on the set of operators considered (both Boolean and temporal). The set of operators we consider is standard for $\mathbf{LTL}_f$.

2.2   The VFB Algorithm

Our first baseline for $\mathbf{LTL}_f$ learning is an optimized enumerative algorithm from Valizadeh, Fijalkow, and Berger [52]; we call it the *VFB algorithm*. Simply put:

$$\text{VFB algorithm} =$$
$$\text{combinatorial search} + \text{fast evaluation} + \text{observational equivalence}.$$

Combinatorial Search. The core algorithm is a bottom-up enumeration of $\mathbf{LTL}_f$ formulas by size. First, the set of formulas of size 1 contains all atomic propositions. At step k, we generate all formulas of size $k + 1$. In order to do this, for each operator, we take arguments such that the sum of sizes of arguments is equal to k; this way, the generated formula will have size $k + 1$ by combining it with the selected operator. This algorithm is agnostic to the operators: it can be adapted to any fragment or be augmented with other operators, as long as we can easily compute inductively whether a trace satisfies a formula.

Fast Evaluation. The key idea is to represent the semantics of **LTL**$_f$ formulas on input traces using so-called "characteristic tables":

- The *characteristic sequence (CS)* of a formula φ on a trace w is the bit vector $v \in \{0, 1\}^{|w|}$ such that $w[i \ldots] \models \varphi$ if and only if $v(i) = 1$;
- The *characteristic table (CT)* of a formula φ over the traces P and N is a sequence t such that $t(i)$ is the CS of φ on the ith trace of $P \cup N$.

We give an example of characteristic sequences and table in Figure 2.

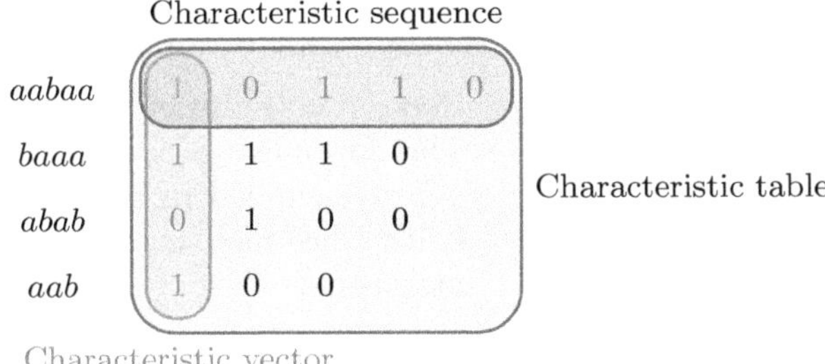

Fig. 2. Characteristic *sequences* and *table* of $\varphi = \mathbf{X!}\, a$ with $P = \{aabaa, baaa\}$ and $N = \{abab, aab\}$. We also use *characteristic vector* for the vector of first bits of the characteristic sequences. Looking at the characteristic vector suffices to check whether φ is a solution: it must have 1's (resp. 0's) at all positions of P (resp. N). Yet, we need to keep in memory the whole characteristic table to check for observational equivalence.

With these objects, one can compute inductively the characteristic sequences and tables of formulas with only a few bitwise operations. For instance, the semantic of the strong next operator **X!** is simply a "left shift" on characteristic sequences. This idea originates from [52]. The brief Python code to compute efficiently the characteristic sequences of **LTL**$_f$ formulas is recalled in [6, Appendix A].

Observational Equivalence. A second idea to tackle the combinatorial explosion of the number of formulas is to consider only "semantically unique" formulas. *Observational equivalence* is an idea from program synthesis [24]; in our context, two formulas are *observationally equivalent* on (P, N) if they generate the same characteristic table. When enumerating formulas, we may keep a single representative for each equivalence class without losing completeness.

Scaling Issues. Despite these improvements to a simple exhaustive search, the scaling of the problem is enormous. We identified two problems.

The first issue, of course, is the exponential blow-up due to the number of increasingly large formulas. The second issue is the memory used to store the evaluation of $\mathbf{LTL}_f$ formulas in the form of characteristic tables, which is necessary to check for observational equivalence. The more input traces there are, the larger the characteristic tables are; the longer the traces are, the wider the tables are. When tables have more elements, observational equivalence is also less likely to occur.

3   Boolean Set Cover

Let us define *Boolean Set Cover*. Let X be a finite set partitioned into positive and negative elements: $X = P \cup N$. We are given a (potentially large) set of atomic formulas $\varphi_1, \ldots, \varphi_k$ over X. The goal is to construct a formula separating P from N using conjunctions and disjunctions of the atomic formulas.

As an example, consider the following instance (adapted from [46, Fig. 1]).

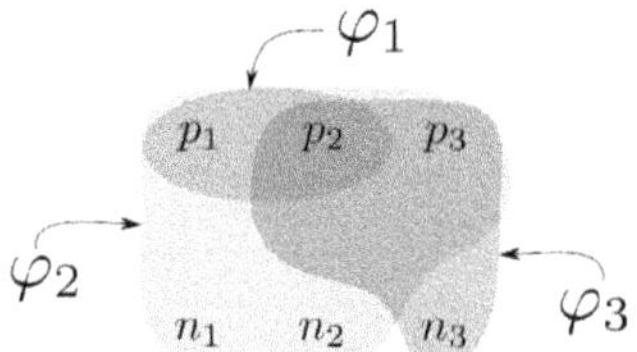

Here, $P = \{p_1, p_2, p_3\}$ and $N = \{n_1, n_2, n_3\}$. The formulas φ_1, φ_2, and φ_3 satisfy the points encircled in the corresponding area. In this instance, $\varphi_1 \vee (\varphi_2 \wedge \varphi_3)$ is a (minimal) solution.

Our idea to tackle these scaling issues is to use the VFB algorithm on the full $\mathbf{LTL}_f$ only up to a fixed formula size, chosen based on a memory or time threshold. Since the exponential blow-up does not allow to go much further beyond size 8, we then restrict our focus to the fragment of $\mathbf{LTL}_f$ with only $\wedge$ and $\vee$ to move forward. In other words, we keep all formulas we have generated and then only combine them with $\wedge$ or $\vee$. This restricted problem is an instance of *Boolean Set Cover*, that is solved as a subroutine in our $\mathbf{LTL}_f$ learning algorithms.

A high-level view of the procedure is in Algorithm 1. In this algorithm, VFB-BOUNDED is a variant of VFB which only computes $\mathbf{LTL}_f$ formulas up to some fixed size using operators from sets of unary and binary operators O_1 and O_2. This fixed size is a hyperparameter called LTL2BS-switch. Algorithm VFB-BOUNDED returns two objects: a solution to the $\mathbf{LTL}_f$ learning instance (or $\bot$ if it has not found a solution), and a set $\mathcal{F}$ containing all generated formulas up to size LTL2BS-switch. If no solution was found, the generated formulas are fed to a Boolean Set Cover solver called BS-SOLVER. From the point of view of the Boolean Set Cover solver, the $\mathbf{LTL}_f$ formulas are letters of a new alphabet, each being associated with a positive integer called *weight* (which is in practice the size of the $\mathbf{LTL}_f$ formula).

When we send the generated formulas to a Boolean Set Cover solver, two kinds of collapses occur (represented in Algorithm 1 with function COLLAPSE).

First, once we restrict our focus to operators $\wedge$ and $\vee$, two formulas can be assumed to be observationally equivalent if and only if they have the same *first*

Algorithm 1 VFB algorithm with Boolean Set Cover solver

Hyperparameter: LTL2BS-switch (below, k), the maximal size of **LTL**$_f$ formulas to enumerate before switching to Boolean Set Cover.

1: **procedure** SEARCH($\mathsf{AP}, O_1, O_2, P, N, k$)
2:     $S, \mathcal{F} \leftarrow$ VFB-BOUNDED(AP, O_1, O_2, k)
3:     **if** $S \neq \perp$ **then return** S ▷ If the VFB algorithm found a solution
4:     **else**
5:         $\mathcal{F}' \leftarrow$ COLLAPSE($\mathcal{F}$)
6:         **return** BS-SOLVER($\mathcal{F}', P, N$)

---

bit for each row of their characteristic table. Indeed, as there is no more "temporal phenomenon", this is a sufficient information to determine whether a given trace satisfies a Boolean combination of (already evaluated) **LTL**$_f$ formulas. In other words, we move from the computation of *tables* to *vectors* (the vectors of first bits; see Figure 2), which produces many collisions and reduces the number of formulas to consider. We quantified this collapse in practice over a small set of tasks chosen randomly. Let $\mathcal{F}$ denote the set of observationally non-equivalent **LTL**$_f$ formulas of size at most 8, and $\mathcal{F}' = $ COLLAPSE($\mathcal{F}$) denote the set of formulas with a distinct first column in the characteristic table. On average over 780 tasks, the ratio $|\mathcal{F}|/|\mathcal{F}'|$ is 3.54, with a minimum of 1.09, a maximum of 48.22, and a standard deviation of 5.46.

Second, storing vectors instead of tables is a massive gain: both space-wise, as storing the evaluation of a formula is a bit vector of size $|P| + |N|$ instead of $\ell \cdot (|P| + |N|)$, where ℓ is the total number of bits in an input trace, and time-wise, as new formulas can be evaluated faster. This enables exploring much larger formulas (though in an incomplete way, as some operators are missing) at a reduced space and time cost.

3.1   Definition and Properties of Boolean Set Cover

Let P and N be two disjoint finite sets. Let $\mathcal{F}$ be a family of sets with $F \subseteq P \cup N$ for all $F \in \mathcal{F}$. We assume that a *weight* $\mathsf{weight}(F) \geq 1$ is associated with each set $F \in \mathcal{F}$ (which is unrelated to the cardinality of F).

We define *positive Boolean formulas* and their weights inductively:

- $\emptyset$ is a formula of weight 0;
- $F \in \mathcal{F}$ is a formula of weight $\mathsf{weight}(F)$;
- if θ_1 and θ_2 are positive Boolean formulas, then so are $\theta_1 \cup \theta_2$ and $\theta_1 \cap \theta_2$, both of weight $1 + \mathsf{weight}(\theta_1) + \mathsf{weight}(\theta_2)$.

The interpretation $[\![\theta]\!]$ of a positive Boolean formula θ is simply the set it describes. We adjust observational equivalence: two formulas θ and θ' are observationally equivalent if $[\![\theta]\!] = [\![\theta']\!]$. The Boolean Set Cover problem is then:

> **INPUT:**   two disjoint finite sets P, N and a family $\mathcal{F}$ of weighted subsets of $P \cup N$
>
> **OUTPUT:** a positive Boolean formula θ of minimal weight such that $[\![\theta]\!] = P$ (i.e., it contains all elements of P but none of N)

The Boolean Set Cover problem can be seen as a restriction of $\mathbf{LTL}_f$ learning to a subset of the operators, namely $\wedge$ and $\vee$. The Boolean Set Cover problem was briefly considered in [46] (under the name *Boolean Subset Cover*). We will compare our algorithm to theirs in Section 5.

Polynomial Criterion for a Solution of Arbitrary Weight. We show that we can check whether there exists a formula θ (*of arbitrary weight*) such that $[\![\theta]\!] = P$ in polynomial time, just by evaluating a specific formula of length $\mathcal{O}(|P| \cdot |\mathcal{F}|)$. This allows to quickly decide the nonexistence of a solution, and when a solution exists, it gives a polynomial upper bound on the weight of formulas to consider (proof in [6, Section 3]).

Lemma 1 (Existence of a solution). *Let P, N, $\mathcal{F}$ be an instance of Boolean Set Cover. There exists a positive Boolean formula θ such that $[\![\theta]\!] = P$ if and only if for all $p \in P$, $n \in N$, there is $F \in \mathcal{F}$ such that $p \in F$ and $n \notin F$. Moreover, when it exists, there is such a formula of size $\mathcal{O}(|\mathcal{F}| \cdot |P|)$.*

Complexity. Boolean Set Cover is a generalization of the NP-complete *set cover* problem [35]: an instance of the set cover problem corresponds to an instance of Boolean Set Cover with $N = \emptyset$ (in which case using $\cap$ is futile, and minimal formulas can be obtained only using $\cup$). This proves NP-hardness of the decision problem for Boolean Set Cover. Since there are short solutions by Lemma 1, and since computing the set described by a Boolean formula is polynomial in its length, Boolean Set Cover is NP-complete.

3.2   Domination for positive Boolean Formulas

In this section, we describe *domination*, a generalization of observational equivalence that identifies even more redundant objects than observational equivalence.

Intuitively, we say that a formula θ_1 *dominates* a formula θ_2 if θ_2 can be replaced with θ_1 in any formula without increasing its weight or decreasing its "quality". More formally, let $\mathsf{sat}(\theta)$ be the subset of elements of $P \cup N$ that θ classifies correctly, i.e., $\mathsf{sat}(\theta) = ([\![\theta]\!] \cap P) \cup (N \setminus [\![\theta]\!])$. The goal of Boolean Set Cover can then be rephrased as finding a formula θ such that $\mathsf{sat}(\theta) = P \cup N$.

Definition 1. *A formula θ_2 is* dominated *by a formula θ_1, denoted $\theta_2 \preceq \theta_1$, if* $\mathsf{weight}(\theta_1) \leq \mathsf{weight}(\theta_2)$ *and* $\mathsf{sat}(\theta_2) \subseteq \mathsf{sat}(\theta_1)$.

We claim that this notion corresponds to the above intuition. Formally, for a positive Boolean formula θ, let $\theta[\theta_2 \leftarrow \theta_1]$ denote the formula obtained by replacing any occurrence of θ_2 in θ by θ_1; this operation is defined inductively:

$$F_i[\theta_2 \leftarrow \theta_1] = \begin{cases} \theta_1 & \text{if } F_i = \theta_2 \\ F_i & \text{otherwise,} \end{cases}$$

$$\theta_2[\theta_2 \leftarrow \theta_1] = \theta_1,$$
$$(\theta \cap \theta')[\theta_2 \leftarrow \theta_1] = \theta[\theta_2 \leftarrow \theta_1] \cap \theta'[\theta_2 \leftarrow \theta_1],$$
$$\text{and } (\theta \cup \theta')[\theta_2 \leftarrow \theta_1] = \theta[\theta_2 \leftarrow \theta_1] \cup \theta'[\theta_2 \leftarrow \theta_1].$$

Any occurrence of a dominated formula can be replaced with its dominating formula (proof in [6, Section 3]).

Lemma 2. *Let θ, θ_1, and θ_2 be positive Boolean formulas. If $\theta_2 \preceq \theta_1$, then $\theta \preceq \theta[\theta_2 \leftarrow \theta_1]$.*

Domination can be thought of as a variation on *Property dependence* (see Theorem 6 in [20]), used to prune **LTL**$_f$ formulas for efficient model-checking.

Further Reducing the Input Set. Lemma 2 implies that we can preprocess $\mathcal{F}$ to only keep maximal elements for $\preceq$ (transforming the input into an *antichain* for $\preceq$). By encoding the characteristic vectors of formulas in bits of integers, testing whether θ_1 dominates θ_2 can be implemented efficiently using bitwise operations. Our algorithms for Boolean Set Cover start by reducing $\mathcal{F}$ in this way.

The Need for a Heuristic. We argue that the existence of a subquadratic algorithm to completely reduce a set $\mathcal{F}$ with domination is unlikely. The obvious algorithm to find whether a given formula $\theta \in \mathcal{F}$ is dominated by a formula $\theta' \in \mathcal{F}$ is to go through every formula in $\mathcal{F}$ and check whether it dominates θ. This takes linear time, and when there are $O(n)$ formulas θ and θ', this approach takes quadratic time. We do not expect a faster algorithm: the *Orthogonal Vectors problem* [54] can be reduced to whether there exists a formula $\theta_1 \in A$ that dominates a formula $\theta_2 \in B$ where A, B are sets of n formulas, and a strongly subquadratic algorithm for Orthogonal Vectors would imply that the Strong Exponential Time Hypothesis is false. The reduction between our problem and the Orthogonal Vectors problem is presented in [8].

Fast Approximate Domination. Yet, a quadratic running time is prohibitive in our application where we need to test domination for millions of Boolean formulas: we therefore propose a heuristic that drastically speeds up the search of a dominating formula while allowing for some false negatives.

Instead of searching through all of $\mathcal{F}$ for dominating formulas, we restrict the search to a small subset of candidates with a high likelihood of dominating other formulas. For a given weight value w and an integer k, let $\mathcal{T}(w, k)$ denote the k formulas θ that maximize $|\mathsf{sat}(\theta)|$ among formulas of weight w in $\mathcal{F}$. Our heuristic searches for a formula θ that dominates θ' in the sets $\mathcal{T}(w, k)$ for

$w \leq \mathsf{weight}(\theta')$. The value chosen for k controls the trade-off between speed and accuracy of the technique. We illustrate the gain in practice over a small set of tasks chosen randomly, which is substantial even for small values of k. Let $\mathcal{F}'$ be as in Algorithm 1, and $\mathcal{F}'' = \textsc{FastNonDominated}(\mathcal{F}', k)$ be the result of the shrinkage of $\mathcal{F}'$ by the above approximate algorithm. On average, over 780 tasks, the ratio $|\mathcal{F}'|/|\mathcal{F}''|$ is 3.45 for $k = 3$, 4.07 for $k = 5$, 4.97 for $k = 10$, 5.94 for $k = 25$, and 6.60 for $k = 50$.

3.3 Divide and Conquer

Before describing our algorithms, we show a general procedure to extend any solver for Boolean Set Cover to mitigate its inability to find a valid solution (due to time, space, or incompleteness of the algorithm). The general idea is part of the $\mathbf{LTL}_f$ learning algorithm from [52]. It is an application of *divide and conquer*: when a Boolean Set Cover solver fails to find a solution, divide P or N in two smaller subsets, solve the two subproblems, and combine them into a solution. See [6, Section 3] for the complete pseudocode.

The meta-algorithm first calls a Boolean Set Cover solver; we assume that this algorithm always returns a formula, but which may not be a valid solution. In case no solution is found, the problem is broken into two subproblems. If $|P| \geq |N|$, then P is randomly split into two subsets P_1, P_2 of roughly equal cardinality. From this, we consider two smaller instances of Boolean Set Cover: $(P_1, N, \mathcal{F}_{\restriction P_1 \cup N})$ and $(P_2, N, \mathcal{F}_{\restriction P_2 \cup N})$, where $\mathcal{F}_{\restriction U} = \{F \cap U \mid F \in \mathcal{F}\}$. The two subproblems are solved recursively, yielding respectively solutions θ_1 and θ_2; observe that $\theta = \theta_1 \cup \theta_2$ is a solution to the original problem. If $|N| > |P|$, we split N and the arguments are symmetrical.

Importantly, this algorithm *always finds a solution if there exists one*, no matter how the Boolean Set Cover solver is implemented. Indeed, if the Boolean Set Cover solver never returns a valid solution, we end up in the base case for divide and conquer, where both P and N contain a single element — assume $P = \{p\}$ and $N = \{n\}$. Per Lemma 1, an F such that $p \in F$ and $n \in F$ necessarily exists if there is a solution, and failure to exist immediately indicates that there is no solution to the Boolean Set Cover problem. This shows that the algorithm always returns a valid solution if there exists one, no matter how the Boolean Set Cover solver is implemented. However, there is no guarantee of minimality.

Although the idea of this algorithm originated from [52] for $\mathbf{LTL}_f$ learning, we introduce two optimizations. The first is to use the solution from the first subproblems to simplify the second subproblems further; if θ_1 is the returned solution to the problem instance $(P_1, N, \mathcal{F}_{\restriction P_1 \cup N})$, it may already contain elements of P_2. It therefore suffices to solve the instance $(P_2 \setminus [\![\theta_1]\!], N, \mathcal{F}_{\restriction (P_2 \setminus [\![\theta_1]\!]) \cup N})$ for the second subproblem. This optimization means that the solution may depend on the order in which we solve the two subproblems. The second is related to Boolean Set Cover: the divide and conquer only combines existing formulas with operators $\cup$ and $\cap$, and can thus be seen as a Boolean Set Cover algorithm.

Hence, once it is called, the other optimizations for Boolean Set Cover (reducing evaluations from tables to vectors, stronger collapse due to observational equivalence, domination reduction) can be applied.

4   Algorithm for Boolean Set Cover

To solve Boolean Set Cover, we propose a greedy algorithm based on *beam search*. The gist is to enumerate formulas in order of their weight, but only keep a fixed number of "best" formulas of each weight. The notion of "best" is again based on the cardinality of $\mathsf{sat}(\theta)$, below called *score*. The number of formulas to keep for each weight is a hyperparameter beam-width, and the parameter D&C-switch is the depth at which we stop exploring and simplify the problem using divide-and-conquer.

We provide the full pseudocode of Beam Search in Algorithm 2. For each weight, a "min" priority queue pq stores the (at most) beam-width formulas of this weight with the largest score, where the priority queue allows for an efficient query of the stored formula with the lowest score. Formulas are added to the queue using the procedure ADDBOUNDED, which ensures that the queue never exceeds size beam-width.

Algorithm 2 Beam search algorithm for Boolean Set Cover

Hyperparameters: D&C-switch (not shown below), the weight up to which to enumerate before splitting with DIVCONQ, and beam-width (below, b), the maximal number of formulas to store for each weight.

1: **procedure** BEAMSEARCH($P, N, \mathcal{F}, b$)
2:     $\mathsf{pq}_1, \ldots, \mathsf{pq}_{\max_{F \in \mathcal{F}} \mathsf{weight}(F)} \leftarrow$ empty priority queues
3:     **for** $F \in \mathcal{F}$ **do**
4:         ADDBOUNDED($F, P, N, \mathsf{pq}_{\mathsf{weight}(F)}, b$)

5:     $k \leftarrow 2$
6:     $\mathcal{M} \leftarrow \mathsf{pq}_1 \cup \mathsf{pq}_2$
7:     **while** True **do**
8:         **for** $i, j \geq 1, i + j = k$ **do**
9:             **for** $\theta_1 \in \mathsf{pq}_i, \theta_2 \in \mathsf{pq}_j, \mathsf{op} \in \{\cup, \cap\}$ **do**
10:                $\theta \leftarrow \theta_1 \mathsf{\ op\ } \theta_2$ $\triangleright$ θ has weight $k + 1$
11:                **if** there is $\theta' \in \mathcal{M}$ s.t. θ' and θ are obs. equivalent **then continue**
12:                **if** there is $\theta' \in \mathcal{M}$ s.t. $\theta \preceq \theta'$ **then continue**
13:                **if** $\llbracket \theta \rrbracket = P$ **then return** θ
14:                ADDBOUNDED($\theta, P, N, \mathsf{pq}_{k+1}, b$)

15:        $\mathcal{M} \leftarrow \mathcal{M} \cup \mathsf{pq}_{k+1}$
16:        $k \leftarrow k + 1$

---

	solved tasks (TO 60 s)		avg. time (s)		avg. size ratio	
	Scarlet	BOLT	Scarlet	BOLT	Scarlet	BOLT
All benchmarks	11468 / 15595	14374 / 15595	4.21	2.05	1.15	1.01
Fixed formulas	74 / 81	81 / 81	1.83	0.00	1.19	1.00
Ordered Sequence	1188 / 2160	2160 / 2160	7.16	0.28	1.70	1.00
Subword	532 / 1256	1182 / 1256	5.86	8.56	1.43	1.01
Subset	1304 / 1800	1082 / 1800	10.58	3.69	1.17	1.00
Hamming	3 / 500	304 / 500	42.90	5.93	1.65	1.16
Single counter	17 / 46	22 / 46	7.79	1.38	1.40	1.05
Double counter	7 / 18	7 / 18	0.39	0.00	1.09	1.00
Nim	23 / 63	22 / 63	2.16	0.00	1.15	1.00
Random conjuncts	7549 / 8172	8074 / 8172	2.13	0.35	1.06	1.00
Random Boolean combinations	771 / 1499	1440 / 1499	8.21	7.04	1.24	1.08

Table 1. Number of tasks solved by BOLT and Scarlet [47] per benchmark family. For each algorithm and benchmark, we also report the average time (using *arithmetic mean*) and average size ratio (using *geometric mean*) on tasks that do not time out. BOLT is faster and returns smaller formulas on average, even as we average over the 2906 tasks for which BOLT returns a formula but Scarlet does not.

5   Experiments

We perform experiments to address the following questions:

1. What is BOLT's performance against the state of the art?
2. How is BOLT's performance impacted by the switch to the Boolean Set Cover problem? Is it better than simply enumerating all LTL formulas?

For each question, there are two (independent) metrics: wall-clock time and formula size.

5.1   Benchmarks and State of the Art

As discussed in Section 1, many tools have been constructed recently for $\mathbf{LTL}_f$ learning. As an independent contribution, we propose a consolidated benchmark suite of over 15,000 $\mathbf{LTL}_f$ learning tasks with difficulty ranging from very easy (solved by most existing tools) to very hard (not solved by any tool). Our benchmark suite includes 10 families (detailed in [6, Section 5]), encompassing all publicly available benchmarks for $\mathbf{LTL}_f$ learning we are aware of. All but one family are inspired by existing benchmarks either directly for $\mathbf{LTL}_f$ learning, or for related problems on $\mathbf{LTL}_f$: in particular, we take advantage of SYNTCOMP's extensive collection of $\mathbf{LTL}_f$ formulas [32]. The benchmark suite is available at `https://github.com/SynthesisLab/LTLf_Learning_Benchmarks`.

   Each of the 10 families consists of two scripts: (*i*) a *formula-generating script* for generating $\mathbf{LTL}_f$ formulas, and (*ii*) a *task-generating script* for generating positive and negative traces for a formula in the family. Following [46], we implement a generic task-generating script based on compiling the $\mathbf{LTL}_f$ formulas

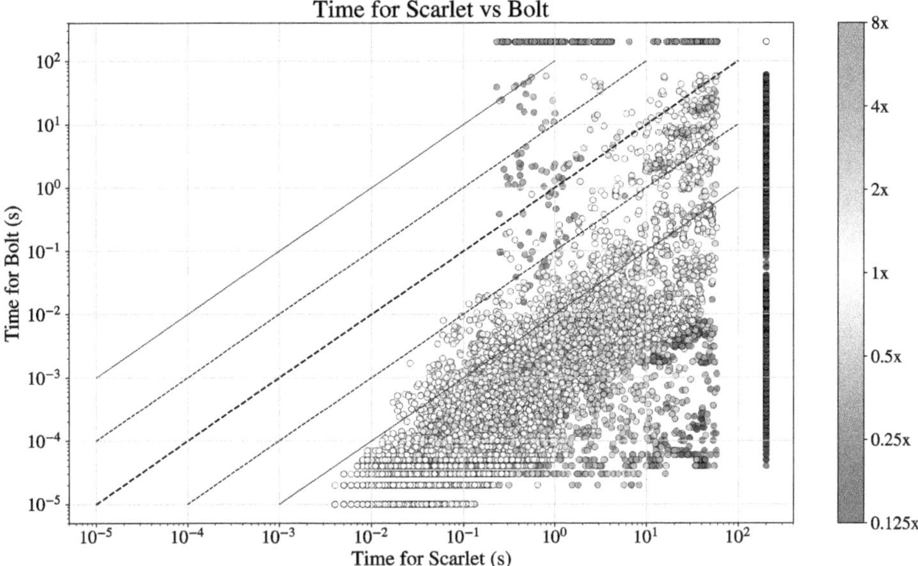

Fig. 3. Comparison of running times (logarithmic axes) between Scarlet [47] and Bolt. The diagonal lines represent ratios of time between the two tools: from bottom to top, Bolt is 100x faster, 10x faster, equal, 10x slower, and 100x slower than Scarlet. Tasks that time out are assumed to be 200 s so that they are apart in the plot. The timeout used in practice is 60 s. The color represents the ratio of the size of the formula returned by Bolt against the size of the formula returned by Scarlet.

into deterministic automata (using the tool *Spot* [21]) and sampling accepting and rejecting runs of a given length. For some families, dedicated task-generating scripts yield finer and more challenging tasks.

Both scripts can be either deterministic or stochastic[7], and use four parameters: trace length, number of atomic propositions, number of positive traces, and number of negative traces. For generating the benchmark suite, we fixed trace lengths to be in $\{16, 32, 64\}$, and numbers of positive and negative traces to be in $\{5, 20, 100\}$. As we will see, this produces challenging benchmarks — should future progress move so far as to solve them all efficiently, changing these parameters will yield even harder benchmarks.

5.2 Experiments

Comparison with Scarlet. Since Scarlet [46,47] is a CPU algorithm which improved over its competitors by a large margin, we take it as a reference point for the state of the art. Scarlet is an "anytime" algorithm, meaning that it outputs a stream of formulas, each of them solutions for the task but of decreasing size,

---

[7] In case of stochastic scripts, they are seeded for reproducibility.

and it guarantees that the final output is minimal (within the targeted "directed fragment of $\mathbf{LTL}_f$") upon termination. When reporting on time for Scarlet, we report how long it took to output the last formula, and *not* termination time, which is typically a lot longer.

Below, "BOLT" refers to our VFB algorithm implementation with *beam search* as a Boolean Set Cover solver, with LTL2BS-switch = 8, beam-width = 100, and D&C-switch = 70.[8] The most critical hyperparameter is LTL2BS-switch, for which 8 appears to achieve the best trade-off between running time and size ratio. Higher values of LTL2BS-switch lead to more timeouts: more time is spent enumerating small $\mathbf{LTL}_f$ formulas, but less time is spent exploring large formulas with a Boolean Set Cover solver. With smaller values, about the same number of benchmarks are solved, but the Boolean Set Cover phase has access to fewer $\mathbf{LTL}_f$ formulas, leading to longer solves and formulas of much larger sizes.

When comparing formula size, we use *size ratio*, which is the ratio between the size of the returned formula and the shortest formula found by all our runs using Scarlet, Bolt, and the GPU algorithm (with a few combinations of hyperparameters). We use size ratio instead of formula size to have a uniform measure over all tasks, as different tasks may admit minimal formulas of widely different sizes. No algorithm uses randomization and we observe negligible performance shifts on runs over the same tasks.

BOLT has been implemented in Rust using standard libraries (in particular, no parallel architectures). Our implementation includes two other Boolean Set Cover solvers, but we do not report on them here as they do not yield better results than the beam-search algorithm we described. The experiments were conducted on identical nodes of the *Grid'5000* cluster, running Debian GNU/Linux 5.10.0-34-amd64. The hardware configuration includes an Intel(R) Xeon(R) Gold 5320 CPU @ 2.20GHz and 384GB of RAM. BOLT is implemented in the Rust programming language. Our code was compiled in `release` mode, using the `rustc` Rust compiler, version 1.87.0 (`17067e9ac`, 2025-05-09).

We compare BOLT against Scarlet [46] in Table 1 and Figure 3. In Table 1, we see that, except for the *Subset* family (where one could argue that the formulas used to generate traces correspond to the fragment of formulas manipulated by Scarlet) and the small *Nim* family, BOLT performs better on all benchmarks families: it returns a solution for more tasks, with a better average running time and smaller average size ratio. Figure 3 illustrates that BOLT returns solutions more than 100x faster over 70% of the benchmarks, with formulas of smaller or equal size in 98% of the cases (most of the formulas in the remaining 2% are in the *Subset* family).

Comparison with the GPU algorithm. In 2024, article [52] targeted a new category: GPU-based tools, meaning that the implementation specifically takes advantage of the specificities of GPUs (mainly, massively parallel computations).

---

[8] We have performed experiments on a small training set (containing 20% of the data) to determine good hyperparameters; we do not include these experiments here.

	solved tasks (TO 60 s)		avg. time (s)		avg. size ratio	
	GPU	BOLT	GPU	BOLT	GPU	BOLT
All benchmarks	10948 / 11038	10259 / 11038	2.48	2.56	1.09	1.02
Fixed formulas	54 / 54	54 / 54	0.78	0.00	1.06	1.00
Ordered Sequence	1440 / 1440	1440 / 1440	0.84	0.40	1.04	1.00
Subword	1242 / 1256	1182 / 1256	8.91	8.56	1.29	1.01
Subset	1174 / 1200	710 / 1200	2.06	3.71	1.10	1.00
Hamming	308 / 320	284 / 320	12.83	6.15	1.16	1.17
Single counter	22 / 31	15 / 31	7.62	2.01	1.22	1.07
Double counter	12 / 12	5 / 12	5.47	0.00	1.03	1.00
Nim	28 / 42	15 / 42	1.67	0.00	1.06	1.00
Random conjuncts	5442 / 5448	5366 / 5448	0.80	0.42	1.04	1.00
Random Boolean combinations	1226 / 1235	1188 / 1235	3.14	7.47	1.17	1.09

Table 2. Number of tasks solved by BOLT and the GPU algorithm [52], per benchmark family. We omit in this comparison the 4557 tasks that the GPU algorithm cannot handle due to technical constraints (trace lengths of size ≥ 64). See Table 1 for an explanation of the columns. The GPU algorithm returns formulas for more tasks, but BOLT is competitive in terms of time and size ratio over tasks solved by both algorithms.

We provide a brief comparison with the GPU-based algorithm of [52] in Table 2. A few details make this comparison difficult: (i) the GPU implementation is obviously highly parallelized, which is not the case for our CPU implementation BOLT; (ii) the current version of the GPU algorithm has technical limitations, such as not being able to handle tasks where the trace length is ≥ 64, which prevents us from running it on 4557 of our new benchmark tasks; (iii) the GPU algorithm always requires about 0.75 s to start, which means that BOLT is much faster on small tasks (such as the *Fixed formulas* benchmarks); (iv) the set of **LTL**$_f$ operators used by the GPU implementation is smaller than the one we use, which means that comparing the size of formulas makes little sense.

Ablation Study. To evaluate the impact of Boolean Set Cover, we compare BOLT with the raw VFB algorithm (i.e., BOLT without Boolean Set Cover) in Figure 4. The raw VFB algorithm solves fewer tasks, which shows that switching to Boolean Set Cover helps solve more hard tasks, while sacrificing little w.r.t. the size of the formulas. Observe in the right plot that the raw VFB algorithm either finds a minimal formula or times out, as expected.

6 Perspectives

The first contribution of this paper is a framework for combining **LTL**$_f$ learning with Boolean Set Cover. We proposed a new algorithm for Boolean Set Cover and, through experimental analyses, we showed that our new tool BOLT greatly improves over the state of the art for CPU algorithms.

These results yield evidence toward our main thesis: Boolean Set Cover is a fundamental problem of independent interest, which has a lot of potential

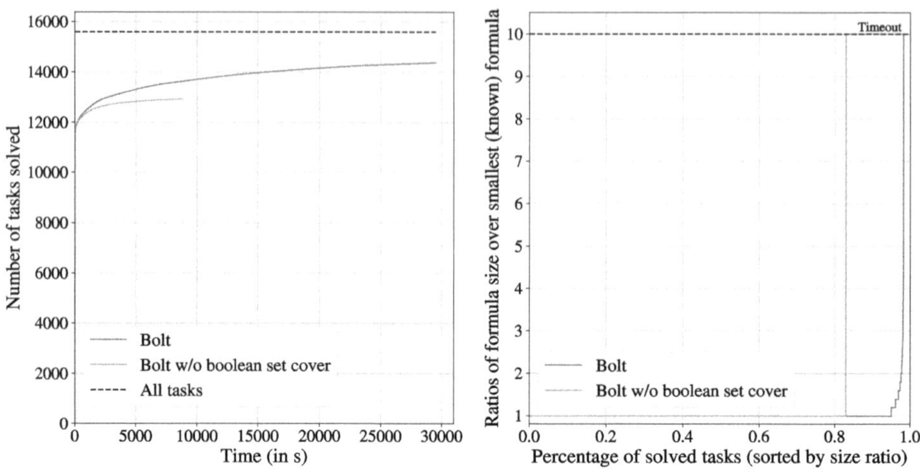

Fig. 4. Ablation study: removing Boolean Set Cover.

applications beyond $\mathbf{LTL}_f$ learning. Our framework is generic; for instance, our tool (through the VFB algorithm) can be adapted to any kind of temporal operators, and Boolean Set Cover can be used for any logic or specification language with disjunctions and conjunctions. Natural candidates include regular expressions [51], Boolean circuits [16], and Bit-vector programs [19].

Our paper provides a first step toward efficiently and approximately solving Boolean Set Cover. We believe there are algorithms that achieve better trade-offs between compute time and size of learned formulas. In particular, we expect our algorithms to be highly parallelizable; we leave for future work an implementation of our framework for GPUs and a comparison with the CPU implementation. We also contributed a large consolidated benchmark suite, much needed to push further the theory and practice of $\mathbf{LTL}_f$ learning and Boolean Set Cover.

Data-Availability Statement. An artifact with all the code, dataset, and additional scripts to reproduce our experiments is available at `https://doi.org/10.5281/zenodo.18175020`. BOLT's code is also available at `https://github.com/SynthesisLab/Bolt`. The $\mathbf{LTL}_f$-learning benchmarks used for the evaluation of our tool are available at `https://github.com/SynthesisLab/LTLf_Learning_Benchmarks`.

References

1. Ammons, G., Bodík, R., Larus, J.R.: Mining specifications. In: ACM SIGPLAN-SIGACT Symposium on Principles of Programming Languages. pp. 4–16. POPL'02, Association for Computing Machinery (2002). `https://doi.org/10.1145/503272.503275`
2. Angluin, D.: Queries and concept learning. Machine Learning **2**(4), 319–342 (1988). `https://doi.org/10.1023/a:1022821128753`

3. Anthony, M., Biggs, N.: Computational Learning Theory. Cambridge Tracts in Theoretical Computer Science, Cambridge University Press (1997)
4. Asarin, E., Donzé, A., Maler, O., Nickovic, D.: Parametric identification of temporal properties. In: Khurshid, S., Sen, K. (eds.) Runtime Verification. pp. 147–160. Springer Berlin Heidelberg (2012). https://doi.org/10.1007/978-3-642-29860-8_12
5. Bartocci, E., Bortolussi, L., Nenzi, L., Sanguinetti, G.: System design of stochastic models using robustness of temporal properties. Theoretical Computer Science **587**, 3–25 (2015). https://doi.org/10.1016/J.TCS.2015.02.046
6. Bathie, G., Fijalkow, N., Matricon, T., Mouillon, B., Vandenhove, P.: LTL$_f$ learning meets boolean set cover. CoRR **abs/2509.24616** (2025). https://doi.org/10.48550/arXiv.2509.24616
7. Bombara, G., Vasile, C.I., Penedo Alvarez, F., Yasuoka, H., Belta, C.: A decision tree approach to data classification using signal temporal logic. In: Hybrid Systems: Computation and Control. HSCC'16 (2016). https://doi.org/10.1145/2883817.2883843
8. Borassi, M., Crescenzi, P., Habib, M.: Into the square: On the complexity of some quadratic-time solvable problems. In: Crescenzi, P., Loreti, M. (eds.) Proceedings of the 16th Italian Conference on Theoretical Computer Science, ICTCS 2015. Electronic Notes in Theoretical Computer Science, vol. 322, pp. 51–67. Elsevier (2015). https://doi.org/10.1016/J.ENTCS.2016.03.005
9. Brafman, R.I., Giacomo, G.D., Patrizi, F.: LTLf/LDLf non-Markovian rewards. In: McIlraith, S.A., Weinberger, K.Q. (eds.) AAAI Conference on Artificial Intelligence. pp. 1771–1778. AAAI Press (2018). https://doi.org/10.1609/AAAI.V32I1.11572
10. Bufo, S., Bartocci, E., Sanguinetti, G., Borelli, M., Lucangelo, U., Bortolussi, L.: Temporal logic based monitoring of assisted ventilation in intensive care patients. In: Margaria, T., Steffen, B. (eds.) International Symposium on Leveraging Applications of Formal Methods, Verification and Validation. Specialized Techniques and Applications. Lecture Notes in Computer Science, vol. 8803, pp. 391–403. Springer (2014). https://doi.org/10.1007/978-3-662-45231-8_30
11. Camacho, A., Chen, O., Sanner, S., McIlraith, S.A.: Non-Markovian rewards expressed in LTL: Guiding search via reward shaping. In: Fukunaga, A., Kishimoto, A. (eds.) International Symposium on Combinatorial Search. pp. 159–160. AAAI Press (2017). https://doi.org/10.1609/SOCS.V8I1.18421
12. Camacho, A., Icarte, R.T., Klassen, T.Q., Valenzano, R.A., McIlraith, S.A.: LTL and beyond: Formal languages for reward function specification in reinforcement learning. In: Kraus, S. (ed.) International Joint Conference on Artificial Intelligence. pp. 6065–6073. ijcai.org (2019). https://doi.org/10.24963/IJCAI.2019/840
13. Camacho, A., McIlraith, S.A.: Learning interpretable models expressed in linear temporal logic. International Conference on Automated Planning and Scheduling **29** (2019). https://doi.org/10.1609/icaps.v29i1.3529
14. Caplain, M.: Finding invariant assertions for proving programs. In: Shooman, M.L., Yeh, R.T. (eds.) International Conference on Reliable Software 1975. pp. 165–171. ACM (1975). https://doi.org/10.1145/800027.808436
15. Chou, G., Ozay, N., Berenson, D.: Explaining multi-stage tasks by learning temporal logic formulas from suboptimal demonstrations. In: Toussaint, M., Bicchi, A., Hermans, T. (eds.) Robotics: Science and Systems XVI (2020). https://doi.org/10.15607/RSS.2020.XVI.097

16. Chowdhury, A.B., Romanelli, M., Tan, B., Karri, R., Garg, S.: Retrieval-guided reinforcement learning for Boolean circuit minimization. In: International Conference on Learning Representations, ICLR. OpenReview.net (2024)
17. Christodorescu, M., Jha, S., Kruegel, C.: Mining specifications of malicious behavior. In: Crnkovic, I., Bertolino, A. (eds.) Joint meeting of the European Software Engineering Conference and the ACM SIGSOFT International Symposium on Foundations of Software Engineering. pp. 5–14. ACM (2007). `https://doi.org/10.1145/1287624.1287628`
18. Crama, Y., Hammer, P.L., Ibaraki, T.: Cause-effect relationships and partially defined Boolean functions. Annals of Operations Research **16**(1), 299–325 (1988). `https://doi.org/10.1007/bf02283750`
19. Ding, Y., Qiu, X.: Enhanced enumeration techniques for syntax-guided synthesis of bit-vector manipulations. Proceedings of the ACM on Programming Languages **8**(POPL), 2129–2159 (2024). `https://doi.org/10.1145/3632913`
20. Dureja, R., Rozier, K.Y.: More scalable LTL model checking via discovering design-space dependencies (D^3). In: International Conference on Tools and Algorithms for the Construction and Analysis of Systems, TACAS. Lecture Notes in Computer Science, vol. 10805, pp. 309–327. Springer (2018). `https://doi.org/10.1007/978-3-319-89960-2_17`
21. Duret-Lutz, A., Renault, E., Colange, M., Renkin, F., Aisse, A.G., Schlehuber-Caissier, P., Medioni, T., Martin, A., Dubois, J., Gillard, C., Lauko, H.: From Spot 2.0 to Spot 2.10: What's new? In: Shoham, S., Vizel, Y. (eds.) Computer Aided Verification – 34th International Conference, CAV 2022, Proceedings, Part II. Lecture Notes in Computer Science, vol. 13372, pp. 174–187. Springer (2022). `https://doi.org/10.1007/978-3-031-13188-2_9`
22. Engler, D.R., Chen, D.Y., Chou, A.: Bugs as deviant behavior: A general approach to inferring errors in systems code. In: Marzullo, K., Satyanarayanan, M. (eds.) ACM Symposium on Operating System Principles. pp. 57–72. ACM (2001). `https://doi.org/10.1145/502034.502041`
23. Fijalkow, N., Lagarde, G.: The complexity of learning linear temporal formulas from examples. In: International Conference on Grammatical Inference. ICGI'21, vol. 153, pp. 237–250. Proceedings of Machine Learning Research (2021)
24. Gabbrielli, M., Levi, G., Meo, M.C.: Observational equivalences for logic programs. In: Joint International Conference and Symposium on Logic Programming. pp. 131–145 (1992)
25. Gabel, M., Su, Z.: Javert: Fully automatic mining of general temporal properties from dynamic traces. In: ACM SIGSOFT International Symposium on Foundations of Software Engineering. pp. 339–349. FSE'08, Association for Computing Machinery, New York, NY, USA (2008). `https://doi.org/10.1145/1453101.1453150`
26. Ghosh, S., Elenius, D., Li, W., Lincoln, P., Shankar, N., Steiner, W.: ARSENAL: Automatic requirements specification extraction from natural language. In: Rayadurgam, S., Tkachuk, O. (eds.) International Symposium on NASA Formal Methods. Lecture Notes in Computer Science, vol. 9690, pp. 41–46. Springer (2016). `https://doi.org/10.1007/978-3-319-40648-0_4`
27. Giacomo, G.D., Vardi, M.Y.: Linear temporal logic and linear dynamic logic on finite traces. In: Rossi, F. (ed.) International Joint Conference on Artificial Intelligence. pp. 854–860. IJCAI'13, IJCAI/AAAI (2013)
28. Giannakopoulou, D., Pressburger, T., Mavridou, A., Rhein, J., Schumann, J., Shi, N.: Formal requirements elicitation with FRET. In: International Conference on Requirements Engineering: Foundation for Software Quality. CEUR Workshop Proceedings, vol. 2584. CEUR-WS.org (2020)

29. Gutiérrez-Sánchez, P., Pérez-Liébana, D., Gaina, R.D.: Explaining and clustering playtraces using temporal logics. In: Proceedings of the 20th International Conference on the Foundations of Digital Games. pp. 1–10. FDG'25, ACM (2025). https://doi.org/10.1145/3723498.3723719

30. Icarte, R.T., Klassen, T.Q., Valenzano, R.A., McIlraith, S.A.: Teaching multiple tasks to an RL agent using LTL. In: André, E., Koenig, S., Dastani, M., Sukthankar, G. (eds.) International Conference on Autonomous Agents and MultiAgent Systems. pp. 452–461. International Foundation for Autonomous Agents and Multiagent Systems Richland, SC, USA / ACM (2018)

31. Icarte, R.T., Klassen, T.Q., Valenzano, R.A., McIlraith, S.A.: Using reward machines for high-level task specification and decomposition in reinforcement learning. In: Dy, J.G., Krause, A. (eds.) International Conference on Machine Learning. Proceedings of Machine Learning Research, vol. 80, pp. 2112–2121. PMLR (2018)

32. Jacobs, S., Pérez, G.A., Abraham, R., Bruyère, V., Cadilhac, M., Colange, M., Delfosse, C., van Dijk, T., Duret-Lutz, A., Faymonville, P., Finkbeiner, B., Khalimov, A., Klein, F., Luttenberger, M., Meyer, K.J., Michaud, T., Pommellet, A., Renkin, F., Schlehuber-Caissier, P., Sakr, M., Sickert, S., Staquet, G., Tamines, C., Tentrup, L., Walker, A.: The reactive synthesis competition (SYNTCOMP): 2018-2021. International Journal on Software Tools for Technology Transfer **26**(5), 551–567 (2024). https://doi.org/10.1007/S10009-024-00754-1

33. Jin, X., Donzé, A., Deshmukh, J.V., Seshia, S.A.: Mining requirements from closed-loop control models. IEEE Transactions on Computer-Aided Design of Integrated Circuits and Systems **34**(11), 1704–1717 (2015). https://doi.org/10.1109/TCAD.2015.2421907

34. Jones, A., Kong, Z., Belta, C.: Anomaly detection in cyber-physical systems: A formal methods approach. In: IEEE Conference on Decision and Control. pp. 848–853. IEEE (2014). https://doi.org/10.1109/CDC.2014.7039487

35. Karp, R.M.: Reducibility among combinatorial problems. In: Miller, R.E., Thatcher, J.W. (eds.) Symposium on the Complexity of Computer Computations. pp. 85–103. The IBM Research Symposia Series, Plenum Press, New York (1972). https://doi.org/10.1007/978-1-4684-2001-2_9

36. Kong, Z., Jones, A., Belta, C.: Temporal logics for learning and detection of anomalous behavior. IEEE Transactions on Automatic Control **62**(3), 1210–1222 (2017). https://doi.org/10.1109/TAC.2016.2585083

37. Lemieux, C., Beschastnikh, I.: Investigating program behavior using the Texada LTL specifications miner. In: IEEE/ACM International Conference on Automated Software Engineering. pp. 870–875. ASE'15, IEEE Computer Society (2015). https://doi.org/10.1109/ASE.2015.94

38. Lemieux, C., Park, D., Beschastnikh, I.: General LTL specification mining. In: IEEE/ACM International Conference on Automated Software Engineering. pp. 81–92. ASE'15, IEEE Computer Society (2015). https://doi.org/10.1109/ASE.2015.71

39. Li, W.: Specification Mining: New Formalisms, Algorithms and Applications. Ph.D. thesis, University of California, Berkeley, USA (2013)

40. Li, Z., Zhou, Y.: PR-Miner: automatically extracting implicit programming rules and detecting violations in large software code. In: Wermelinger, M., Gall, H.C. (eds.) European Software Engineering Conference held jointly with 13th ACM SIGSOFT International Symposium on Foundations of Software Engineering. pp. 306–315. ACM (2005). https://doi.org/10.1145/1081706.1081755

41. Lo, D., Khoo, S.C., Han, J., Liu, C.: Mining Software Specifications: Methodologies and Applications. CRC Press, Inc., USA, 1st edn. (2017). https://doi.org/10.1201/b10928
42. Lyu, M., Li, F., Lee, C.H., Chen, C.H.: VALIO: Visual attention-based linear temporal logic method for explainable out-of-the-loop identification. Knowledge-Based Systems **299**, 112086 (2024). https://doi.org/10.1016/j.knosys.2024.112086
43. Mascle, C., Fijalkow, N., Lagarde, G.: Learning temporal formulas from examples is hard. CoRR **abs/2312.16336** (2023). https://doi.org/10.48550/arXiv.2312.16336
44. Murphy, W., Holzer, N., Koenig, N., Cui, L., Rothkopf, R., Qiao, F., Santolucito, M.: Guiding LLM temporal logic generation with explicit separation of data and control. CoRR **abs/2406.07400** (2024). https://doi.org/10.48550/arXiv.2406.07400
45. Pnueli, A.: The temporal logic of programs. In: Symposium on Foundations of Computer Science. SFCS'77 (1977). https://doi.org/10.1109/SFCS.1977.32
46. Raha, R., Roy, R., Fijalkow, N., Neider, D.: Scalable anytime algorithms for learning fragments of linear temporal logic. In: International Conference on Tools and Algorithms for the Construction and Analysis of Systems. TACAS'22, vol. 13243, pp. 263–280. Springer (2022). https://doi.org/10.1007/978-3-030-99524-9_14
47. Raha, R., Roy, R., Fijalkow, N., Neider, D.: Scarlet: Scalable anytime algorithms for learning fragments of linear temporal logic. Journal of Open Source Software (2024). https://doi.org/10.21105/joss.05052
48. Roy, R., Pote, Y., Parker, D., Kwiatkowska, M.: Learning probabilistic temporal logic specifications for stochastic systems
49. Rozier, K.Y.: Specification: The biggest bottleneck in formal methods and autonomy. In: Blazy, S., Chechik, M. (eds.) International Conference on Verified Software. Theories, Tools, and Experiments. Lecture Notes in Computer Science, vol. 9971, pp. 8–26 (2016). https://doi.org/10.1007/978-3-319-48869-1_2
50. Valiant, L.G.: A theory of the learnable. Communications of the ACM **27**(11), 1134–1142 (1984). https://doi.org/10.1145/1968.1972
51. Valizadeh, M., Berger, M.: Search-based regular expression inference on a GPU. Proceedings of the ACM on Programming Languages **7**(PLDI), 1317–1339 (2023). https://doi.org/10.1145/3591274
52. Valizadeh, M., Fijalkow, N., Berger, M.: LTL learning on GPUs. In: International Conference on Computer Aided Verification, CAV. Lecture Notes in Computer Science, vol. 14683, pp. 209–231. Springer (2024). https://doi.org/10.1007/978-3-031-65633-0_10
53. Wegbreit, B.: The synthesis of loop predicates. Communications of the ACM **17**(2), 102–112 (1974). https://doi.org/10.1145/360827.360850
54. Williams, R.: A new algorithm for optimal 2-constraint satisfaction and its implications. Theoretical Computer Science **348**(2-3), 357–365 (2005). https://doi.org/10.1016/j.tcs.2005.09.023
55. Yang, H., Hoxha, B., Fainekos, G.E.: Querying parametric temporal logic properties on embedded systems. In: Nielsen, B., Weise, C. (eds.) IFIP International Conference on Testing Software and Systems. Lecture Notes in Computer Science, vol. 7641, pp. 136–151. Springer (2012). https://doi.org/10.1007/978-3-642-34691-0_11
56. Yang, J., Evans, D., Bhardwaj, D., Bhat, T., Das, M.: Perracotta: Mining temporal API rules from imperfect traces. In: International Conference on Software Engineering. pp. 282–291. ICSE'06, Association for Computing Machinery (2006). https://doi.org/10.1145/1134285.1134325

57. Zeller, A.: Mining specifications: A roadmap. In: Nanz, S. (ed.) The Future of Software Engineering. pp. 173–182. Springer (2010). https://doi.org/10.1007/978-3-642-15187-3_13

Verification of Probabilistic Systems

Robust Verification of
Concurrent Stochastic Games

Angel Y. He and David Parker

Department of Computer Science, University of Oxford, Oxford OX1 2JD, UK
`angel.he@balliol.ox.ac.uk, david.parker@cs.ox.ac.uk`

Abstract. Autonomous systems often operate in multi-agent settings and need to make concurrent, strategic decisions, typically in uncertain environments. Verification and control problems for these systems can be tackled with concurrent stochastic games (CSGs), but this model requires transition probabilities to be precisely specified — an unrealistic requirement in many real-world settings. We introduce *robust CSGs* and their subclass *interval CSGs* (ICSGs), which capture epistemic uncertainty about transition probabilities in CSGs. We propose a novel framework for *robust* verification of these models under worst-case assumptions about transition uncertainty. Specifically, we develop the underlying theoretical foundations and efficient algorithms, for finite- and infinite-horizon objectives in both zero-sum and nonzero-sum settings, the latter based on (social-welfare optimal) Nash equilibria. We build an implementation in the PRISM-games model checker and demonstrate the feasibility of robust verification of ICSGs across a selection of large benchmarks.

Keywords: Robust quantitative verification · Probabilistic model checking · Concurrent stochastic games · Epistemic uncertainty.

1 Introduction

Autonomous and intelligent systems are increasingly deployed in environments that are *nondeterministic*, *stochastic* and *concurrent*, such as autonomous vehicle coordination, robotic exploration and networked market interactions. In these settings, decision-making involves simultaneous strategic interactions between multiple agents, often within uncertain and dynamic environments.

Concurrent stochastic games (CSGs) [47], also known as *Markov games*, provide a powerful framework for modelling such multi-agent systems. Unlike the simpler model of *turn-based* stochastic games (TSGs) [15], CSGs allow players to select their actions simultaneously, without knowledge of each other's choices. The outcomes depend probabilistically on the players' joint actions.

Formal verification techniques for CSGs provide a means to establish quantitative guarantees on the behaviour of these stochastic multi-agent systems, e.g., ensuring that "a drone can safely reach its target with at least 95% probability, regardless of the actions of other aircraft". They can also be used to automatically synthesise controllers or strategies that achieve these guarantees. Early

© The Author(s) 2026
S. Junges and G. Katz (Eds.): TACAS 2026, LNCS 16505, pp. 505–525, 2026.
https://doi.org/10.1007/978-3-032-22752-2_26

work on these models focused on the zero-sum setting (e.g., [9, 17, 18]), whilst more recent work has added support for various temporal logics and the use of nonzero-sum game-theory solution concepts such as Nash equilibria (NE) and their variants [34, 35], along with widely used tool support [31].

Despite their modelling effectiveness, a limitation of CSGs is that they assume transition probabilities are *precisely known*. In reality, system dynamics are often only partially known due to abstraction, modelling inaccuracies, noise, or limited data in learned statistical models. This is particularly evident in data-driven contexts like (model-based) reinforcement learning (RL), where transition probabilities are estimated from data. These issues limit the reliability of guarantees from verification and can make synthesised strategies sub-optimal.

In recent years, there has been growing interest in principled approaches to reasoning about *epistemic uncertainty* in probabilistic models for verification [3]. For the simpler, single-agent setting, where decision making is performed using Markov decision processes (MDPs), a well studied approach is *robust MDPs* (RMDPs) [28, 41, 54], which capture model uncertainty via a set of possible transition probability functions. A common subclass is *interval MDPs* (IMDPs) [22], where transition probabilities are bounded within intervals. Verification techniques then provide guarantees or synthesise optimal controllers in a *robust* manner, i.e., making *worst-case* assumptions about model uncertainty.

However, analogous frameworks for stochastic multi-agent systems remain underdeveloped. In this paper, we address that gap and propose *robust concurrent stochastic games* (RCSGs), a novel verification framework that augments CSGs with transition uncertainty and robust solution concepts. In fact, RMDPs already have a link to stochastic games: they can be interpreted as a *zero-sum TSG* between the agent and an adversarial *nature* player that resolves uncertain transition probabilities; this view underlies many algorithms for solving RMDPs [10, 28, 39, 41]. However, extending this framework to *multi-agent*, and especially *concurrent* settings, is non-trivial, as the interplay between transition uncertainty and simultaneous player actions significantly complicates both the reasoning and the very definition of robustness.

Contributions and challenges. In this work, we develop a framework for robust verification of CSGs under adversarial transition uncertainty, covering both zero-sum and nonzero-sum settings with finite- and infinite-horizon objectives. We focus primarily on the subclass of interval CSGs (ICSGs) characterised by transition probability intervals. Extending robustness from MDPs to concurrent multi-agent games introduces fundamental challenges: optimality requires mixed strategies; equilibria definitions must incorporate uncertainty resolutions; and, in the nonzero-sum case, the adversarial role of nature differs from standard best-response reasoning. To address these, we: introduce robust equilibrium notions; establish theoretical results, e.g., on value preservation under player/nature action ordering; and present novel reductions from ICSGs to (non-robust) CSGs by adding an adversarial nature player. The latter yields a 2-player game in the zero-sum case, and a more subtle 3-player construction in the nonzero-sum case where nature minimises social welfare. Building on these results, we derive tractable algorithms for solving ICSGs and implement them in PRISM-games [31]. We show their practicality via empirical evaluations on a set of large benchmarks: verification for zero-sum ICSGs performs comparably to CSGs, while nonzero-sum methods scale effectively but also provide insights into the intrinsic challenges of robust multi-agent reasoning.

Related work. In the *single-agent* setting, RMDPs are solvable via robust dynamic programming (RDP) [28, 41, 54]. Recent work develops generic algorithms for polytopic [10, 53] and more general RMDPs with constant support (e.g., [39]) via reduction to TSGs. Robust methods for multi-agent settings are more limited, restricted to *turn-based* polytopal stochastic games [8], *qualitative* verification [5]; or *sampling-based*, learning-driven algorithms (e.g., [19, 45, 48]) for the similar problem of distributionally *robust Markov games* [21, 37, 47] in RL, without model-checking capabilities or verification guarantees.

2   Preliminaries

Let $\mathcal{D}(X)$ denote the set of discrete probability distributions over a finite set X, and let $\mathbb{1}[A]$ be the indicator function that equals 1 if A holds and 0 otherwise.

2.1   Robust Markov Decision Processes

A core model for verification and control tasks in the context of uncertainty is *Markov decision processes (MDPs)* [4, 27].

Definition 1 (MDP). *A Markov decision process (MDP) is a tuple $M = (S, \bar{s}, A, P)$, where S is a finite set of states with initial state $\bar{s} \in S$; A is a finite set of actions; and $P : S \times A \rightharpoonup \mathcal{D}(S)$ is a probabilistic transition function.*

$A(s)$ denotes the enabled actions in state s. We write $P_{sa} = P(s, a)$ for the next-state distribution at s under action a and $P_{sas'} = P_{sa}(s')$ for the corresponding transition probability to s'. A *path* is a finite or infinite sequence $\pi = s_0 \xrightarrow{a_0} s_1 \xrightarrow{a_1} \ldots$ such that $s_0 = \bar{s}$, $a_i \in A(s_i)$ and $P_{s_i a_i s_{i+1}} > 0$ for all i. We write $\pi(i) = s_i$, $\pi[i] = a_i$, and let $FPaths_M$ and $IPaths_M$ be the sets of finite and infinite paths in M, respectively.

A *strategy* (or policy) of M is a function $\sigma : FPaths_M \to \mathcal{D}(A)$ that resolves the choices of action in each state. Typically, we aim to find an optimal strategy for an MDP, e.g., one that maximises the probability of a target state set being reached or the expected value of some reward function.

In order to reason about MDPs *robustly* in the context of (epistemic) uncertainty about the model itself, we can use *robust MDPs*.

Definition 2 (RMDP). *A robust MDP (RMDP) is a tuple $M_R = (S, \bar{s}, A, \mathcal{P})$, where S, $\bar{s}$ and A are as for MDPs (Definition 1), and $\mathcal{P} : S \times A \rightharpoonup 2^{\mathcal{D}(S)}$ is an uncertain probabilistic transition function.*

Intuitively, an RMDP captures unknown transition dynamics: for each state s and action $a \in A(s)$, the *uncertainty set* $\mathcal{P}_{sa} = \mathcal{P}(s, a)$ represents the *set* of possible next-state distributions. Selecting a single $P_{sa} \in \mathcal{P}_{sa}$ for each (s, a) yields a probabilistic transition function $P : S \times A \to \mathcal{D}(S)$, giving a specific MDP. Abusing notation slightly, we also treat P as a set and write $P \in \mathcal{P}$, referring to each P as an *uncertainty resolution*. Typically, we aim to find a *robust optimal* strategy, i.e., one that is optimal against the worst-case uncertainty resolution.

An RMDP M_R can be viewed as a zero-sum TSG, i.e., a game which alternates between an agent choosing an $a \in A(s)$ in each state s and then an adversarial player *nature* resolving the choices $P_{sa} \in \mathcal{P}_{sa}$. Assumptions or restrictions on the strategies for nature dictate the kind of uncertainty considered: 1) *rectangularity* [28, 41], i.e., whether transition uncertainty is resolved independently across different states (*s-rectangular*) or state-action pairs (*(s, a)-rectangular*); 2) *static (stationary)* vs. *dynamic (time-varying)* semantics [28, 41], i.e., whether nature follows a *memoryless* strategy that has to make consistent choices at each (s, a) over time. We can also restrict the nature of the uncertainty sets $\mathcal{P}_{sa}$, notably whether they are polytopic, i.e., next-state distributions in $\mathcal{P}_{sa}$ form a polytope. In this work, we focus on (s, a)-rectangular, polytopic uncertainty. This setting includes the well-studied class of IMDPs [22, 41], where each $\mathcal{P}_{sa}$ is defined by independent intervals over transition probabilities.

2.2   Concurrent Stochastic Games

CSGs [47] provide the semantic basis for the class of games we introduce.

Definition 3 (CSG). *An (n-player) concurrent stochastic game (CSG) is a tuple* $\mathcal{G} = (N, S, \bar{s}, A, \Delta, P)$ *where* $N = \{1, \dots, n\}$ *is a finite set of players;* S, $\bar{s} \in S$ *and* $P : S \times A \to \mathcal{D}(S)$ *are as defined for an MDP (Definition 1);* $A = \times_{i \in N}(A_i \cup \{\bot\})$ *where* A_i *is the set of actions for player* i *and* $\bot$ *is an idle action disjoint from* $\cup_{i \in N} A_i$; $\Delta : S \to 2^{\cup_{i \in N} A_i}$ *is an action assignment function.*

A CSG $\mathcal{G}$ begins in the initial state $\bar{s}$. At each state $s \in S$, each player $i \in N$ simultaneously selects an action $a_i \in A_i(s)$, where $A_i(s) = \Delta(s) \cap A_i$ if $\Delta(s) \cap A_i \neq \emptyset$ and $A_i(s) = \{\bot\}$ otherwise. The game then transitions to state s' following the distribution P_{sa}, where $a = (a_1, \dots, a_n) \in A(s) := \times_{i \in N} A_i(s)$.

To allow quantitative analysis of $\mathcal{G}$, we augment CSGs with *reward structures*.

Definition 4 (Reward structure). *A reward structure for a CSG $\mathcal{G}$ is a tuple* $r = (r_A, r_S)$ *where* $r_A : S \times A \to \mathbb{R}$ *is the* action reward *function, and* $r_S : S \to \mathbb{R}$ *is the* state reward *function. We denote the total reward associated with a state-action pair (s, a) as* $r_{sa} = r(s, a) := r_A(s, a) + r_S(s)$.

A *strategy* for player i is a function $\sigma_i : FPaths_{\mathcal{G}} \to \mathcal{D}(A_i)$ mapping finite histories to distributions over actions. A *strategy profile* (or just *profile*) is a tuple of strategies for each player, denoted $\sigma = (\sigma_1, \dots, \sigma_n) \in \Sigma := \times_{i \in N} \Sigma_i$. An *objective* (or utility function) of player i is a random variable $X_i : IPaths_{\mathcal{G}} \to \mathbb{R}$. In a *zero-sum* game, which is 2-player by definition, players have directly opposing objectives, i.e., $X_1 = -X_2$. In this case, we will represent their objectives using a single variable $X := X_1$, so that $X_2 = -X$. In the *nonzero-sum* (or *general-sum*) case, we write $X = (X_1, \ldots, X_n)$ for the tuple of all player objectives.

In this paper we focus on the four common objectives below, two of which are finite-horizon and two infinite-horizon. We assume a set of target states $T \subseteq S$ and, for the finite-horizon case, a time horizon $k \in \mathbb{N}$.

- *Bounded probabilistic reachability*: $X(\pi) = \mathbb{1}\left[\exists j \leq k.\ \pi(j) \in T\right]$;
- *Bounded cumulative reward*: $X(\pi) = \sum_{i=0}^{k-1} r(\pi(i), \pi[i])$;
- *Probabilistic reachability*: $X(\pi) = \mathbb{1}\left[\exists j \in \mathbb{N}.\ \pi(j) \in T\right]$; and
- *Reachability reward*: $X(\pi) = \sum_{i=0}^{k_{\min}-1} r(\pi(i), \pi[i])$ if $\exists j \in \mathbb{N}.\ \pi(j) \in T$ and $X(\pi) = \infty$ otherwise, where $k_{\min} = \min\left\{j \in \mathbb{N} \mid \pi(j) \in T\right\}$.

We denote the *expected utility* of player i from state s under profile σ in $\mathcal{G}$ as $u_i(\sigma \mid s, X) := V_{\mathcal{G}}^i(s \mid \sigma, X) := \mathbb{E}_{\mathcal{G},s}^{\sigma}[X_i]$, with the index i omitted in the zero-sum case. In zero-sum games, the *value* of $\mathcal{G}$ with respect to X exists if the game is *determined*, i.e., the maximum payoff that player 1 can guarantee equals the minimum payoff player 2 can enforce; the corresponding strategies are said to be *optimal*. For nonzero-sum games where players may cooperate or compete, we use the concept of a *Nash equilibrium* (NE): a profile in which no player can improve their utility by unilaterally deviating. A *social-welfare optimal NE* (SWNE) [34] refers to an NE that also maximises the players' total utility.

A special, degenerate "one-shot" case of a CSG is a *normal form game* (NFG), which consists of a single state and a single decision round. Thus, an NFG can be represented as a simplified tuple $\mathcal{Z} = (N, A, u)$, where N and A are as defined for a CSG, and $u = (u_1, \ldots, u_n)$ with $u_i : A \to \mathbb{R}$ defining player i's utility for each joint action. A 2-player NFG can be represented as a *bimatrix game*, defined by two matrices $\mathcal{Z}_1, \mathcal{Z}_2 \in \mathbb{R}^{l \times m}$ with entries $z_{ij}^1 = u_1(a_i, b_j)$ and $z_{ij}^2 = u_2(a_i, b_j)$, where $A_1 = \{a_1, \ldots, a_l\}$ and $A_2 = \{b_1, \ldots, b_m\}$. The game is called *zero-sum* if $\forall a \in A.\ u_1(a) + u_2(a) = 0$, in which case we can represent it as a single *matrix game* $\mathcal{Z} \in \mathbb{R}^{l \times m}$ with $z_{ij} = u_1(a_i, b_j) = -u_2(a_i, b_j)$, i.e., $\mathcal{Z} = \mathcal{Z}_1 = -\mathcal{Z}_2$.

3 Robust Concurrent Stochastic Games

We now propose the model of *robust CSGs* (RCSGs), which unifies the notions of *robustness* from RMDPs and *concurrent* decision-making from CSGs.

Definition 5 (RCSG). *A robust CSG (RCSG) is a tuple* $\mathcal{G} = (N, S, \bar{s}, A, \Delta, \mathcal{P})$ *where* $\mathcal{P}$ *is an* uncertain *transition function defined as for RMDPs in Definition 2, and all other components are as defined for CSGs in Definition 3.*

Similar to the way that fixing the transition function in an RMDP induces an MDP, fixing the transition function in an RCSG to a particular $P \in \mathcal{P}$ induces a CSG $\mathcal{G}_P = (N, S, \bar{s}, A, \Delta, P)$. We parametrise the corresponding notation with P. Notably, for a state s of $\mathcal{G}$ and a strategy profile σ (defined as for CSGs), we write $u_i(\sigma, P \mid s, X) := \mathbb{E}_{\mathcal{G},s}^{\sigma,P}[X]^1$ for the expected value of an objective X under σ applied to $\mathcal{G}_P$.

---

[1] We use these interchangeably and omit parameters that are clear from the context.

By contrast to the uncertainty semantics in RMDPs (see Section 2.1), multi-player RCSGs introduce an additional dimension: whether uncertainty is resolved *adversarially* or is *controlled* by players [8]. In the adversarial case, nature resolves uncertainty against the players: in zero-sum games, where players have directly opposing objectives, nature aligns with one player to minimise the other's payoff; in nonzero-sum games, it acts against both by minimising a joint objective such as social welfare or cost.

The controlled case assumes that one or more players resolve uncertainty to optimise their own objectives. This corresponds to optimistic reasoning in single-agent or zero-sum settings and can be seen as the dual of the adversarial case. However, in nonzero-sum games, assigning control to a single player can undermine fairness by attributing uncertainty to that player's decisions, while shared control would require principled coordination among players. We therefore focus on the adversarial resolution in both zero- and nonzero-sum games.

Next, we define the *robust* analogue of several game-theoretic concepts in the context of RCSGs. In general, we enforce that their defining properties hold under every $P \in \mathcal{P}$, or equivalently under the worst case $P^* := \arg\min_{P \in \mathcal{P}} \mathbb{E}_{\mathcal{G},s}^{\sigma,P}[X]$.

Zero-sum RCSGs. We first adapt classical minimax concepts for (2-player) zero-sum games, assuming that player 1 maximises an objective X.

Definition 6 (Robust determinacy and optimality). *A zero-sum RCSG $\mathcal{G}$ is robustly determined with respect to an objective X, if for any state $s \in S$:*

$$\sup_{\sigma_1 \in \Sigma_1} \inf_{\sigma_2 \in \Sigma_2} \inf_{P \in \mathcal{P}} \mathbb{E}_{\mathcal{G},s}^{(\sigma_1,\sigma_2),P}[X] = \inf_{\sigma_2 \in \Sigma_2} \sup_{\sigma_1 \in \Sigma_1} \inf_{P \in \mathcal{P}} \mathbb{E}_{\mathcal{G},s}^{(\sigma_1,\sigma_2),P}[X] =: V_{\mathcal{G}}(s, X)$$

where we call $V_{\mathcal{G}}(s, X)$ the robust value of $\mathcal{G}$ in s with respect to X. Also, $\sigma_1^* \in \Sigma_1$ is a robust optimal strategy of player 1 with respect to X if $\mathbb{E}_{\mathcal{G},s}^{(\sigma_1^*,\sigma_2),P}[X] \geq V_{\mathcal{G}}(s, X)$ for all $s \in S, \sigma_2 \in \Sigma_2, P \in \mathcal{P}$; similarly $\sigma_2^* \in \Sigma_2$ is a robust optimal strategy of player 2 if $\mathbb{E}_{\mathcal{G},s}^{(\sigma_1,\sigma_2^*),P}[X] \leq V_{\mathcal{G}}(s, X)$ for all $s \in S, \sigma_1 \in \Sigma_1, P \in \mathcal{P}$.

Nonzero-sum RCSGs. In the nonzero-sum case, each player $i \in N$ has a distinct objective X_i. For this setting, we adopt the concept of a *robust Nash equilibrium* (RNE) [1, 30, 43], which refers to a profile σ^* that remains a Nash equilibrium under any uncertainty resolution. Note that, in the zero-sum case, RNE coincide with the notion of robust optimal strategies.

As is common for CSGs, we use *subgame-perfect* NE [42], which require equilibrium behaviour in every state of the game, not just the initial one. We call these *subgame-perfect RNE* but, for brevity, often refer to them simply as RNE. In standard CSGs with infinite-horizon objectives, NE may not exist [6], but ε-NE do exist for any $\varepsilon > 0$ under the objectives we consider. We therefore work with *subgame-perfect ε-RNE* for infinite-horizon properties.

Definition 7 (Subgame-perfect ε-RNE). *A profile σ^* is a subgame-perfect robust ε-NE (ε-RNE) iff $\varepsilon + \inf_{P \in \mathcal{P}} \left[u_i(\sigma_{-i}^*[\sigma_i^*], P) - u_i(\sigma_{-i}^*[\sigma_i], P) \right] \geq 0$ for all $\sigma_i \in \Sigma_i, i \in N$ at every state $s \in S$. We define $\langle \inf_{P \in \mathcal{P}} u_i(\sigma^*, P) \rangle_{i \in N}$ as the corresponding ε-RNE values. A subgame-perfect robust NE (RNE) is an ε-RNE* *with $\varepsilon = 0$. We write $\Sigma_{\varepsilon\text{-}RNE}$ for the set of all ε-RNE and Σ_{RNE} for the set of all RNE.*

Even if all induced CSGs $\mathcal{G}_P$ of an RCSG $\mathcal{G}$ have an NE (ε-NE), there may not exist an RNE (ε-RNE). This is because a profile that is an NE in one induced CSG may not be an NE across all others. See the extended version of this paper [24] for an illustration.

Next, we propose the robust counterparts of SWNE [34, 46] as RNE that maximise the robust (worst-case) total utility of the players, denoted $u_+(\sigma, P) := \sum_{i \in N} u_i(\sigma, P)$ for a given profile $\sigma \in \Sigma$ and $P \in \mathcal{P}$.

Definition 8 (RSWNE). *An RNE σ^* of $\mathcal{G}$ is a* robust social-welfare optimal NE *(RSWNE) if it maximises the* robust social welfare *amongst all RNE, i.e., $\sigma^* \in \arg\max_{\sigma \in \Sigma_{RNE}} u_+(\sigma, P_\sigma^*)$ where $P_\sigma^* := \arg\inf_{P \in \mathcal{P}} u_+(\sigma, P)$. We define $\langle u_i(\sigma^*, P_{\sigma^*}^*)\rangle_{i \in N}$ as the corresponding RSWNE values.*

Like RMDPs, various uncertainty models are applicable in RCSGs, such as those characterised by L^p-balls [26, 49] and non-rectangular sets. However, value computation is often computationally intractable under these models, even in single-agent settings [54]. By contrast, *interval* uncertainty yields convex uncertainty sets, enabling tractable computation while effectively capturing bounded but unstructured estimation errors, e.g., those derived from confidence intervals [50]. Hence, for the remainder of the paper we focus on *interval CSGs*, as a natural and scalable foundation for incorporating robustness into CSGs.

Definition 9 (ICSG). *An interval CSG (ICSG) is a tuple $\mathcal{G} = (N, S, \bar{s}, A, \Delta, \check{P}, \hat{P})$ where $\check{P}, \hat{P} : S \times A \times S \rightharpoonup [0, 1]$ are partial functions that assign lower and upper bounds, respectively, to transition probabilities, such that $\check{P}_{sas'} \leq \hat{P}_{sas'}$. All other components are defined as for CSGs (Definition 3).*

An ICSG is an RCSG where $\mathcal{P}_{sa} = \{P_{sa} \in \mathcal{D}(S) \mid \forall s' \in S.\ P_{sas'} \in [\check{P}_{sas'}, \hat{P}_{sas'}]\}$. We also require that $\check{P}_{sas'} = 0 \iff \hat{P}_{sas'} = 0$, i.e., each transition is either excluded or assigned a non-degenerate interval with a strictly positive lower bound. This enables the standard *graph preservation* constraint [12, 39], which requires that all $P \in \mathcal{P}$ share the same support. This property is essential for ensuring the tractability of RDP [28, 41] over (s, a)-rectangular uncertainty models.

4 Zero-sum ICSGs

We now establish the theoretical foundations for robust verification of ICSGs, starting with the *zero-sum* case. We fix an ICSG $\mathcal{G} = (N, S, \bar{s}, A, \Delta, \check{P}, \hat{P})$ where $N = \{1, 2\}$ and in which player 1 maximises an objective X. For now, we assume that X is infinite-horizon: either probabilistic/reward reachability.

At a high level, analogously to the stochastic game view of an RMDP, we will reduce ICSG $\mathcal{G}$ to a CSG $\mathcal{G}^A$ extended with a third player, *nature*, who resolves transition uncertainty adversarially against player 1. Since player 2 and 3 (nature) share the same objective, they can be merged into a single coalition, making $\mathcal{G}^{\mathcal{A}}$ a 2-player CSG between coalitions $\{1\}$ and $\{2,3\}$. We refer to $\mathcal{G}^{\mathcal{A}}$ as the *adversarial expansion* of $\mathcal{G}$. We will establish a one-to-one correspondence between optimal values and strategies in $\mathcal{G}^{\mathcal{A}}$ and their robust counterparts in $\mathcal{G}$, allowing us to reduce robust verification of zero-sum ICSGs to solution of zero-sum CSGs. The latter can be performed with value iteration [34] although, as for RMDPs, explicit construction of the full CSG $\mathcal{G}^{\mathcal{A}}$ is not required.

Player-first vs. nature-first semantics. In the CSG reduction, a natural question to consider is the order in which uncertainty is resolved relative to players' moves. Under the *player-first* semantics, nature acts *after* both players have chosen their actions. While this aligns closely with the adversarial interpretation of robustness (see Definition 6), it requires nature's minimisation problem (against player 1's objective) to be solved separately for every player profile $\sigma \in \Sigma$, which is computationally demanding. By contrast, the *nature-first* semantics assumes that nature first commits to a realisation of $\mathcal{P}$ *before* any player acts, thereby inducing a fixed CSG upfront. This formulation allows the use of efficient dynamic programming techniques, such as *robust value iteration* (RVI) [28, 41], which we adopt for solving these games.

This distinction corresponds to the difference between *agent first* and *nature first* semantics for robust partially observable MDPs in [7]. While in general this assumption can affect the game value, we establish in Theorem 1 that both semantics yield the same value in our setting (finitely-branching zero-sum ICSGs).

Theorem 1 (Player/nature-first Value Equivalence). *From any $s \in S$, $V_{\mathcal{G}}(s)$ is invariant under the player-first or nature-first semantics:*

$$\sup_{\sigma_1 \in \Sigma_1} \inf_{\sigma_2 \in \Sigma_2} \inf_{P \in \mathcal{P}} \mathbb{E}_{\mathcal{G},s}^{(\sigma_1,\sigma_2),P}[X] = \inf_{P \in \mathcal{P}} \sup_{\sigma_1 \in \Sigma_1} \inf_{\sigma_2 \in \Sigma_2} \mathbb{E}_{\mathcal{G},s}^{(\sigma_1,\sigma_2),P}[X].$$

Proof (Sketch). We prove the result top-down via construction of the *adversarial expansion* $\mathcal{G}^{\mathcal{A}}$ (Definition 10) and subsequent determinacy and value preservation results (Corollary 1) established in this section. Specifically, determinacy of the finite CSG $\mathcal{G}^{\mathcal{A}}$ justifies exchanging the order of optimisation between players and nature without changing the game value. Full proof in [24].   □

This value equivalence justifies using the nature-first semantics in implementations, so that nature's minimisation problem is solved only *once* per step, after which player strategies are derived from the minimising distributions P_{sa}^*. Henceforth, without loss of generality, we focus on the player-first semantics.

We next observe that optimal strategies for ICSGs with infinite-horizon objectives admit a memoryless form, which allows the game to be analysed via fixed-point equations over the state space.

Lemma 1 (Strategy class sufficient for optimality). *Given an* infinite-horizon *objective X for $\mathcal{G}$, each player has a* memoryless *robust optimal strategy, and nature has a* deterministic memoryless *optimal strategy.*

Proof (Sketch). Under (s,a)-rectangularity, nature's optimal resolution and players' continuation values depend only on the current state, so histories ending in the same state can be collapsed. Further, nature's independent choices across state–action pairs define a single transition function, so nature *deterministically* commits to one such function. Full proof in [24]. $\qquad\square$

Henceforth in the zero-sum setting, we let Σ_i denote the set of *memoryless* strategies for each player $i \in \{1, 2\}$, and interpret $\mathcal{P}$ as the set of transition functions resulting from *memoryless* nature strategies.

Using also the (s, a)-rectangularity of ICSGs, the *robust Bellman equation* for $\mathcal{G}$ (proved in [24]) is given by:

$$V(s) = \sup_{\sigma_1 \in \mathcal{D}(A_1(s))} \inf_{\sigma_2 \in \mathcal{D}(A_2(s))} \left\{ r_s^\sigma + \sum_{a \in A(s)} \sigma_{sa} \inf_{P_{sa} \in \mathcal{P}_{sa}} \sum_{s' \in S} P_{sas'} \cdot V(s') \right\} \quad (1)$$

where $\sigma_{sa} = \sigma_1(s, a_1)\sigma_2(s, a_2)$ with $a = (a_1, a_2)$ and $r_s^\sigma = \sum_{a \in A(s)} \sigma_{sa} r_{sa}$.

This characterises the fixed-point that our game solving algorithms will later compute iteratively. We remark that, unlike the standard Bellman equation for CSGs, Equation (1) includes nature's *inner problem* $\inf_{P_{sa} \in \mathcal{P}_{sa}}$, which captures transition uncertainty and is solved using a greedy algorithm adapted from the IMDP setting [41]; details are provided in [24]. Furthermore, whereas the Bellman equations for TSGs and RMDPs [28, 41] optimise over *deterministic* player strategies by selecting pure actions, here we optimise over *randomised* (memoryless) strategies, i.e., distributions over actions. This reflects the added complexity of concurrent multi-agent interaction.

The CSG reduction. We now formally define the *adversarial expansion* $\mathcal{G}^{\mathcal{A}}$ for ICSG $\mathcal{G}$, which is a CSG containing intermediate states representing state–action pairs of $\mathcal{G}$. In the following, we use the operator $\cdot^{\mathcal{A}}$ to denote a structure associated with $\mathcal{G}^{\mathcal{A}}$. We write $\mathbb{V}(K)$ for the vertices of a polytope K and use notation such as "$s^{\mathcal{A}} = s \in S$" as shorthand for "$\exists s \in S.\, s^{\mathcal{A}} = s$".

Definition 10 (Adversarial expansion). *We define the* adversarial expansion *of ICSG $\mathcal{G}$ as a 2-player CSG $\mathcal{G}^{\mathcal{A}} = (\{1, 2\}, S^{\mathcal{A}}, \bar{s}, A^{\mathcal{A}}, \Delta^{\mathcal{A}}, P^{\mathcal{A}})$ where:*

- *$S^{\mathcal{A}} = S \cup S'$, with $S' = \{(s, a) \mid s \in S, a \in A\}$;*
- *$A^{\mathcal{A}} = (A_1^{\mathcal{A}} \cup \{\bot\}) \times (A_2^{\mathcal{A}} \cup \{\bot\})$, with $A_1^{\mathcal{A}} = A_1$, $A_2^{\mathcal{A}} = A_2 \cup \left(\bigcup_{s \in S, a \in A} \mathbb{V}[\mathcal{P}_{sa}] \right)$;*
- *$\Delta^{\mathcal{A}} : S^{\mathcal{A}} \to 2^{A_1^{\mathcal{A}} \cup A_2^{\mathcal{A}}}$, such that if $s^{\mathcal{A}} = s \in S$ then $\Delta^{\mathcal{A}}(s^{\mathcal{A}}) = \Delta(s)$, else if $s^{\mathcal{A}} = (s, a) \in S'$ then $\Delta^{\mathcal{A}}(s^{\mathcal{A}}) = \mathbb{V}[\mathcal{P}_{sa}]$, else $\Delta^{\mathcal{A}}(s^{\mathcal{A}}) = \emptyset$;*
- *$P^{\mathcal{A}} : S^{\mathcal{A}} \times A^{\mathcal{A}} \to \mathcal{D}(S^{\mathcal{A}})$ such that if $s^{\mathcal{A}} = s \in S \wedge s' = (s, a) \in S'$ then $P^{\mathcal{A}}(s^{\mathcal{A}}, a^{\mathcal{A}}, s') = 1$, else if $s^{\mathcal{A}} = (s, a) \in S' \wedge a^{\mathcal{A}} = (\bot, P_{sa}) \wedge s' \in S$ then $P^{\mathcal{A}}(s^{\mathcal{A}}, a^{\mathcal{A}}, s') = P_{sas'}$, and $P^{\mathcal{A}}(s^{\mathcal{A}}, a^{\mathcal{A}}, s') = 0$ otherwise.*

As discussed earlier, player 2 in $\mathcal{G}^{\mathcal{A}}$ acts as a coalition of nature and player 2 in $\mathcal{G}$, such that the original player 2 acts at the S-states and nature moves at the S'-states. Given a choice $P_{sa} \in \mathcal{P}_{sa}$ of nature, a $\mathcal{G}$-transition $s \xrightarrow{a} s'$ corresponds to the two-step $\mathcal{G}^{\mathcal{A}}$-transition $s \xrightarrow{a} (s, a) \xrightarrow{(\bot, P_{sa})} s'$, and vice versa. In essence, the dynamics at S-states are unchanged. At an auxiliary state $(s, a) \in S'$, both players receive zero reward; and player 1 stays idle whilst player 2 deterministically selects a next-state distribution $P_{sa} \in \mathcal{P}_{sa}$, with P_{sa}^* being an optimal such choice as characterised by Lemma 1. The notion of adversarial expansion naturally extends to strategies, paths, rewards, and objectives (see [24]).

We highlight that $\mathcal{G}^{\mathcal{A}}$ is a finite-state, *finite-action* CSG. As formalised in [24], since an ICSG is polytopic, we can restrict player 2's actions to the vertices of the polytope $\mathcal{P}_{sa}$ at each S'-state without loss of optimality. The following results formalise the relationship between $\mathcal{G}$ and $\mathcal{G}^{\mathcal{A}}$.

Lemma 2 (Utility-preserving strategy bijection). *For any $\mathcal{G}$-profile $\sigma = (\sigma_1, \sigma_2)$, there exists a corresponding $\mathcal{G}^{\mathcal{A}}$-profile $\sigma^{\mathcal{A}} = (\sigma_1^{\mathcal{A}}, \sigma_2^{\mathcal{A}})$ and vice versa, such that $\inf_{P \in \mathcal{P}} u_1(\sigma, P) = u_1^{\mathcal{A}}(\sigma^{\mathcal{A}})$ and $\sup_{P \in \mathcal{P}} u_2(\sigma, P) = u_2^{\mathcal{A}}(\sigma^{\mathcal{A}})$, where $u_i^{\mathcal{A}}(\sigma^{\mathcal{A}})$ denotes player i's expected utility in $\mathcal{G}^{\mathcal{A}}$ under $\sigma^{\mathcal{A}}$.*

Proof. As shown in [24], $\mathcal{G}^{\mathcal{A}}$ preserves the set of possible paths, their probabilities and objective values. It follows directly that:

$$u_1(\sigma, P) = \sum_{\pi \in IPaths_{\mathcal{G},s}} \mathbb{P}^{\sigma}(\pi) \cdot X(\pi) = \sum_{\pi^{\mathcal{A}} \in IPaths_{\mathcal{G}^{\mathcal{A}},s}} \mathbb{P}^{\sigma}(\pi^{\mathcal{A}}) \cdot X^{\mathcal{A}}(\pi^{\mathcal{A}}) = u_1^{\mathcal{A}}(\sigma^{\mathcal{A}})$$

where $\mathbb{P}^{\sigma}$ is the path probability function under profile σ. Then by the zero-sum structure: $\sup_P u_2(\sigma, P) = u_2(\sigma, P^*) = -u_1(\sigma, P^*) = -u_1^{\mathcal{A}}(\sigma^{\mathcal{A}}) = u_2^{\mathcal{A}}(\sigma^{\mathcal{A}})$. $\square$

Corollary 1 (Determinacy and Value Preservation). *$\mathcal{G}$ is determined iff $\mathcal{G}^{\mathcal{A}}$ is determined. Further, if both games are determined, then the robust value of $\mathcal{G}$ is equal to the value of $\mathcal{G}^{\mathcal{A}}$, i.e., $V_{\mathcal{G}}(s, X) = V_{\mathcal{G}^{\mathcal{A}}}(s, X^{\mathcal{A}})$.*   (Proof in [24])

Theorem 2 ($\mathrm{RNE}_{\mathcal{G}} \Leftrightarrow \mathrm{NE}_{\mathcal{G}^{\mathcal{A}}}$). *In a determined zero-sum ICSG $\mathcal{G}$, for any $\mathcal{G}$-profile $\sigma \in \Sigma$, σ is an RNE in $\mathcal{G}$ with value $V_{\mathcal{G}}(s, X)$ iff $\sigma^{\mathcal{A}}$ is an NE in $\mathcal{G}^{\mathcal{A}}$ with value $V_{\mathcal{G}^{\mathcal{A}}}(s, X^{\mathcal{A}}) = V_{\mathcal{G}}(s, X)$.*

Proof (Sketch). Both directions follow from Definition 7 of RNE. The forward case additionally uses utility preservation (Lemma 2); the reverse relies on Definition 6 of the game value and value preservation (Corollary 1). Full proof in [24]. $\square$

Solving zero-sum ICSGs. Finally, combining the above results, since $\mathcal{G}^{\mathcal{A}}$ is finite-state and finitely-branching, it is determined for all the objectives we consider [38]. By Corollary 1, the original game $\mathcal{G}$ is therefore also robustly determined with the same value. Moreover, since $\mathcal{G}$ is zero-sum, any RNE profile and its value coincides with an optimal profile and the game value.

Hence, by Theorem 2, we can perform robust verification of an ICSG $\mathcal{G}$ by solving the 2-player CSG $\mathcal{G}^{\mathcal{A}}$, e.g, with the value iteration approach from [34]. In fact, we do not need to explicitly construct $\mathcal{G}^{\mathcal{A}}$, nor its auxiliary states S' corresponding to the possible (s, a) pairs. Instead, for each state s, we first solve an inner optimisation problem over uncertainty set $\mathcal{P}_{sa}$ for each joint action a, and then solve a linear programming (LP) problem of size $|A|$ using the resulting values. We discuss this further in Section 6 and give full details in [24].

Finite-horizon properties. When X is a *bounded* probabilistic reachability or cumulative reward objective, the previous results still hold under two changes: 1) Robust optimal strategies are now *time-varying*, i.e., with the extended signature $\sigma : S \times H \rightharpoonup A$ and $P^* : S \times A \times H \rightharpoonup \mathcal{D}(S)$, where H represents *finite-memory* used to track the time-step. Accordingly, we extend $\mathcal{G}^{\mathcal{A}}$ with time-augmented states. 2) Finite-horizon objectives are evaluated over $k < \infty$ steps, thus *exact* game values can be computed via *robust backward induction* (RBI) [28,41], noting that $\mathcal{G}$ is always determined due to the finite game tree. We provide the detailed construction of $\mathcal{G}^{\mathcal{A}}$ in this setting in [24].

5   Nonzero-sum ICSGs

Next, we consider *nonzero-sum* 2-player ICSGs, where each player i maximises a distinct objective X_i, assuming for now that both objectives are infinite-horizon.[2] As in the zero-sum case, we continue to focus on player-first semantics and memoryless strategies, as both Theorem 1 and Lemma 1 extend to the nonzero-sum setting (see proofs in [24]).

We again reduce a 2-player ICSG $\mathcal{G}$ to its *adversarial expansion* $\mathcal{G}^{\mathcal{A}}$, which is a 3-player CSG, but in which the *nature* player now acts adversarially against both other players, aiming to minimise their social welfare. The reduction is more complex than the zero-sum case and requires an additional *filtering* step per iteration to identify robust equilibria. This reduction again allows us to build on standard CSG solution methods [34].

Our goal for nonzero-sum ICSGs is to find subgame-perfect ε-RNE (Definition 7), and more specifically, ε-RSWNE (Definition 8), which consider the *sum* of the utilities for the two players. We add a subscript $+$ to the relevant game notation (e.g., r, u, X, V) to indicate this. The *robust Bellman equation* is:

$$V_+(s) = \sup_{\sigma \in \Sigma_{\varepsilon\text{-RNE}}} \inf_{P \in \mathcal{P}} \mathbb{E}^{\sigma,P}_{\mathcal{G},s}[X_+] = \sup_{\sigma \in \Sigma_{\varepsilon\text{-RNE}}} \left[r_+(s,\sigma) + \sum_{a \in A} \inf_{P_{sa} \in \mathcal{P}_{sa}} f^{\sigma,P}_{sa} \right] \quad (2)$$

where $f^{\sigma,P}_{sa} := \sigma_{sa} \sum_{s' \in S} P_{sas'} V_+(s')$ and $\Sigma_{\varepsilon\text{-RNE}}$ denotes the set of *one-shot ε-RNE*. The second equality follows from a similar proof to the zero-sum case (see [24]). In this formulation, nature's inner problem is now to minimise the social welfare $u_+ := u_1 + u_2$, while each player $i \in \{1,2\}$ maximises their individual expected payoff u_i. Consequently, we maximise over the set of ε-RNE, capturing equilibrium behaviour under worst-case uncertainty.

The adversarial expansion $\mathcal{G}^{\mathcal{A}}$ of ICSG $\mathcal{G}$ for the nonzero-sum case follows a similar construction to the zero-sum setting (Definition 10), but now models nature as an explicit third player distinct from player 2. Henceforth, if $a = (a_1, a_2)$, let $*a$ denote the flattened tuple a_1, a_2.

Definition 11 (Adversarial expansion). *We define the* adversarial expansion *of $\mathcal{G}$ as a 3-player CSG $\mathcal{G}^{\mathcal{A}} = (N^{\mathcal{A}}, S^{\mathcal{A}}, \bar{s}, A^{\mathcal{A}}, \Delta^{\mathcal{A}}, P^{\mathcal{A}})$ where:*

---

[2] Following the usual approach for nonzero-sum CSGs [34], we focus on ICSGs that can be seen as a variant of *stopping games* [14], where each player's target set is reached with probability 1 from all states under all profiles.

- $N^{\mathcal{A}} = \{1, 2, 3\}$, *with player 3 representing* nature;
- $S^{\mathcal{A}} = S \cup S'$, *with* $S' = \{(s, a) \mid s \in S, a \in A\}$;
- $A^{\mathcal{A}} = \times_{l=1}^{3}(A_l^{\mathcal{A}} \cup \{\perp\})$ *where* $A_1^{\mathcal{A}} = A_1$, $A_2^{\mathcal{A}} = A_2$ *and* $A_3^{\mathcal{A}} = \cup_{s \in S, a \in A} \mathbb{V}[\mathcal{P}_{sa}]$;
- $\Delta^{\mathcal{A}} : S^{\mathcal{A}} \to 2^{\cup_{i=1}^{3} A_i^{\mathcal{A}}}$, *such that if* $s^{\mathcal{A}} = s \in S$ *then* $\Delta^{\mathcal{A}}(s^{\mathcal{A}}) = \Delta(s)$, *else if* $s^{\mathcal{A}} = (s, a) \in S'$ *then* $\Delta^{\mathcal{A}}(s^{\mathcal{A}}) = \mathbb{V}[\mathcal{P}_{sa}]$ *and* $\emptyset$ *otherwise.*
- $P^{\mathcal{A}} : S^{\mathcal{A}} \times A^{\mathcal{A}} \to \mathcal{D}(S^{\mathcal{A}})$, *such that if* $s^{\mathcal{A}} = s \in S \wedge a^{\mathcal{A}} = (*a, \perp) \wedge s' = (s, a) \in S'$ *then* $P^{\mathcal{A}}(s^{\mathcal{A}}, a^{\mathcal{A}}, s') = 1$, *else if* $s^{\mathcal{A}} = (s, a) \in S' \wedge a^{\mathcal{A}} = (\perp, \perp, P_{sa}) \wedge s' \in S$ *then* $P^{\mathcal{A}}(s^{\mathcal{A}}, a^{\mathcal{A}}, s') = P_{sas'}$, *and* $P^{\mathcal{A}}(s^{\mathcal{A}}, a^{\mathcal{A}}, s') = 0$ *otherwise.*

Under this definition of $\mathcal{G}^{\mathcal{A}}$, a $\mathcal{G}$-transition $s \xrightarrow{(a_1, a_2)} s'$ corresponds to a two-step $\mathcal{G}^{\mathcal{A}}$-transition $s \xrightarrow{(a_1, a_2, \perp)} (s, (a_1, a_2)) \xrightarrow{(\perp, \perp, P_{s(a_1, a_2)})} s'$. Adversarial expansions of paths, strategies, rewards and objectives follow analogously to the zero-sum case, and are formalised in [24]. The following results relate $\mathcal{G}$ and $\mathcal{G}^{\mathcal{A}}$. Their proofs mirror the zero-sum case, with adaptations to the nonzero-sum definition of $\mathcal{G}^{\mathcal{A}}$.

Lemma 3 (Utility-preserving strategy bijection).   *For any $\mathcal{G}$-profile σ under nature's choice of $P \in \mathcal{P}$, there exists a corresponding $\mathcal{G}^{\mathcal{A}}$-profile $\sigma^{\mathcal{A},P}$ and vice versa such that $u_i(\sigma, P) = u_i^{\mathcal{A}}(\sigma^{\mathcal{A},P})$ for $i \in \{1, 2\}$. Further, for any $\sigma \in \Sigma$, there exists a corresponding $\sigma^{\mathcal{A}} \in \Sigma^{\mathcal{A}}$ and vice versa such that $\inf_{P \in \mathcal{P}} u_+(\sigma, P) = u_+^{\mathcal{A}}(\sigma^{\mathcal{A}}) = u_1^{\mathcal{A}}(\sigma^{\mathcal{A}}) + u_2^{\mathcal{A}}(\sigma^{\mathcal{A}})$.*

Lemma 4 (ε-RNE$_{\mathcal{G}} \Rightarrow \varepsilon$-NE$_{\mathcal{G}^{\mathcal{A}}}$).   *For any $\mathcal{G}$-profile $\sigma \in \Sigma$, if σ is an ε-RNE in $\mathcal{G}$ then $\sigma^{\mathcal{A}} \in \Sigma^{\mathcal{A}}$ is an ε-NE in $\mathcal{G}^{\mathcal{A}}$.*   (Proof in [24])

Unlike the zero-sum setting, for Lemma 4 the converse does *not* necessarily hold: if $\sigma^{\mathcal{A}}$ is an ε-NE in $\mathcal{G}^{\mathcal{A}}$, σ need not be an ε-RNE in $\mathcal{G}$. This is because $\sigma_3^{\mathcal{A}}$ selects a transition function P^* that minimises the *total* utility of player 1 and 2, rather than each player's utility individually as required by the ε-RNE condition (see Definition 7). Therefore, any ICSG where nature's minimisation of the sum induces asymmetric incentives suffices as an example (see [24]).

Consequently, before identifying the RSWNE, for each state $s \in S$ we filter the set of ε-NE in $\mathcal{G}^{\mathcal{A}}$ to retain only those that correspond to an ε-RNE in $\mathcal{G}$, i.e., $\Sigma_{\varepsilon\text{-RNE}}^{\mathcal{A}} := \{\sigma^{\mathcal{A}} \in \Sigma^{\mathcal{A}} \mid \sigma \in \Sigma_{\varepsilon\text{-RNE}}\}$. Note that filtering is applied separately at each state since we construct subgame-perfect equilibria.

Filtering $\Sigma_{\varepsilon\text{-NE}}^{\mathcal{A}}$ for $\Sigma_{\varepsilon\text{-RNE}}$.   Our method of filtering is based on a notion of *deviations* made by players. In this section, we fix a state $s \in S$ and candidate ε-RNE profile $\sigma \in \Sigma$. We designate player i as the *deviator*, whose strategy deviations $\sigma_i' \in \Sigma_i$ from σ will be evaluated. Further, we define the *deviation gain* of player i under its deviation σ_i' and nature's choice of $P \in \mathcal{P}$ as:

$$u_i^{\Delta}(\sigma_i', P) := u_i(\sigma_{-i}[\sigma_i'], P) - u_i(\sigma, P). \tag{3}$$

Lemma 5 (ε-RNE condition over pure deviations).   *Let Σ_i^{det} denote the set of (memoryless) deterministic strategies for player $i \in N = \{1, 2\}$. A profile $\sigma \in \Sigma$ is an ε-RNE iff the following condition holds:*

$$\overline{V}_{i,\sigma} := \sup_{P \in \mathcal{P}} \sup_{\sigma_i' \in \Sigma_i^{det}} u_i^{\Delta}(\sigma_i', P) \leq \varepsilon \quad \forall i \in N.$$

Proof (Sketch). The ε-RNE condition for σ (Definition 7) can be rewritten as $\sup_P \sup_{\sigma'_i \in \Sigma_i} u_i^{\Delta}(\sigma'_i, P) \leq \varepsilon$. Since the expected utility (from any state s) is linear in the deviation σ'_i, the maximal gain is attained by a deterministic deviation. So it suffices to consider pure deviations. Full proof in [24]. $\qquad\square$

Observe that $\overline{V}_{i,\sigma}$ corresponds exactly to the *optimistic value* of an IMDP $\mathcal{G}_{i,\sigma}^{\mathcal{D}}$ in which player i acts as the agent. We refer to this IMDP as the *deviation IMDP* and formalise it in [24]. The value correspondence relies on the IMDP's construction whereby, given state space $S^{\mathcal{A}} = S \cup S'$ of $\mathcal{G}^{\mathcal{A}}$, transitions from states in S to S' depend exclusively on the fixed player's strategy, whilst those from S' to S are governed by nature's choice of $P \in \mathcal{P}$. Further, the reward assigned to each state $s \in S$ corresponds to the expected reward gain at s if player i deviates from σ_i to σ'_i.

Therefore, following Lemma 5, if the deviation IMDP has optimistic value $\overline{V}_{i,\sigma} \leq \varepsilon$ for both players $i \in \{1, 2\}$, then the candidate profile σ constitutes an ε-RNE profile of $\mathcal{G}$. We can thus characterise our goal in solving $\mathcal{G}$ as identifying:

$$\Sigma_{\varepsilon\text{-RNE}} = \left\{ \sigma \in \Sigma \mid \sigma^{\mathcal{A}} \in \Sigma_{\varepsilon\text{-NE}}^{\mathcal{A}} \ \wedge \ \forall i \in \{1, 2\}. \overline{V}_{i,\sigma} \leq \varepsilon \right\}. \tag{4}$$

Solving nonzero-sum ICSGs. Altogether, a profile $\sigma \in \Sigma$ is an ε-RSWNE in $\mathcal{G}$ iff its corresponding $\sigma^{\mathcal{A}} \in \Sigma_{\varepsilon\text{-RNE}}^{\mathcal{A}}$ maximises $u_+^{\mathcal{A}}$ in $\mathcal{G}^{\mathcal{A}}$. Hence, computing ε-RSWNE in the 2-player ICSG $\mathcal{G}$ reduces to finding SWNE in the 3-player CSG $\mathcal{G}^{\mathcal{A}}$ over $\Sigma_{\varepsilon\text{-RNE}}^{\mathcal{A}}$. While this would in principle require a general 3-player CSG solver (e.g., [33]), such algorithms rely on nonlinear programming and are computationally expensive. However, by exploiting the zero-sum coalitional structure of $\mathcal{G}^{\mathcal{A}}$, the *trimatrix* game at each state $s \in S$ can be reduced to a *bimatrix* game (see [24]). This can thus be solved more efficiently using the 2-player nonzero-sum CSG solution approach from [34], together with the inner-problem solution algorithm in [24] to ensure robustness. As in the zero-sum case, this computation does not require explicit construction of $\mathcal{G}^{\mathcal{A}}$.

Once we have the set of one-shot ε-NE of $\mathcal{G}^{\mathcal{A}}$ at each $s \in S$, we filter for the ε-RNE equivalents: for each profile $\sigma^{\mathcal{A}} \in \Sigma_{\varepsilon\text{-NE}}^{\mathcal{A}}$, we: 1) compute $\overline{V}_{i,\sigma}$ for each player $i \in \{1, 2\}$ on the deviation IMDP $\mathcal{G}_{i,\sigma}^{\mathcal{D}}$; and 2) retain σ if all $\overline{V}_{i,\sigma} \leq \varepsilon$. The resulting profiles correspond to the ε-RNE in $\mathcal{G}$, from which we select the one maximising u_+. This gives an ε-RSWNE profile and values in $\mathcal{G}$ (by Lemma 3).

Finite- and mixed-horizon properties. Since players' objectives are distinct, they may differ in time horizon. If both X_1 and X_2 are finite-horizon, then we define the analysis horizon as the maximum of the two, i.e., $k := \max(k_1, k_2)$. In mixed-horizon cases, where one objective is finite-horizon and the other infinite-horizon, we transform the game into an equivalent one with two infinite-horizon objectives on an augmented model, following [32]. Thus, we focus on cases where both objectives are either finite- or infinite-horizon.

The infinite-horizon framework generalises to finite-horizon objectives in a similar way to the zero-sum setting. Additionally, we consider exact RNE and RSWNE (i.e., $\varepsilon = 0$), and account for potentially different player horizons by labelling time-augmented states that record when each player's target is reached within their respective horizon. The full construction is detailed in [24].

6   Value Computation for Two-player ICSGs

Sections 4 and 5 have presented the theoretical foundations for solving zero-sum and non-zero sum ICSGs, respectively, and described how a reduction to an *adversarial expansion* CSG provides the basis for iterative solution methods. In this section, we present some additional implementation details and discuss correctness and complexity. Full details are provided in [24].

Both approaches use elements of robust dynamic programming for RMDPs, i.e, robust value iteration (RVI) for infinite-horizon properties and robust backward induction (RBI) for finite-horizon properties, and of value iteration based methods for CSGs [34]. For both zero-sum and nonzero-sum objectives, the procedure performed per iteration for each state $s \in S$ is:

Algorithm 1 RVI/RBI update for state $s \in S$ in $\mathcal{G} = (N, S, \bar{s}, A, \Delta, \check{P}, \hat{P})$

1: **for all** $a \in A(s)$ **do**
2:     $P^*_{sa} \leftarrow \text{SolveInnerProblem}(s, a, V_{prev}, \check{P}, \hat{P})$ ▷ see [24]
3: **end for**
4: $\mathcal{Z} \leftarrow \text{ConstructNFG}(P^*_s, V_{prev})$ ▷ see [24]
5: $V_{next}[s] \leftarrow \text{SolveNFG}(\mathcal{Z})$

The SolveInnerProblem function (line 2) uses an algorithm adapted from a greedy method for IMDPs [41], which we detail in [24]. At line 4, we build a normal form game: for zero-sum ICSGs this a *matrix* game, reusing the zero-sum CSG algorithms in [34]; for nonzero-sum ICSGs, we build a (general-sum) *bimatrix* game using multi-player CSG algorithms in [33], which coincide with those for nonzero-sum 2-player CSGs in [34]. Our derivations appear in [24], where we demonstrate how to directly compute values of $\mathcal{G}$ without explicit construction of $\mathcal{G}^A$.

At line 5, SolveNFG computes the matrix game value via an LP formulation [40, 52] in the zero-sum case. For nonzero-sum ICSGs, this is a multi-step procedure which involves: 1) enumerating NE for bimatrix games, using e.g., the *Lemke-Howson algorithm* [36]; and 2) filtering these for RNE as outlined in Section 5 using deviation IMDPs. The latter can be done using IMDP verification algorithms already supported in PRISM-games [31]. If no profiles remain, our algorithm terminates early; otherwise the value of state s is updated to the RSWNE value of $\mathcal{Z}$.

Correctness.   This relies on the reduction of solving an ICSG $\mathcal{G}$ to solving a standard CSG $\mathcal{G}^A$, whose correctness is established in Section 4 (zero-sum) and 5 (nonzero-sum). Correctness of the underlying CSG algorithm over $\mathcal{G}^A$ is inherited from [33, 34], which relies on classical results, e.g., correctness of value iteration and backward induction [44] and solution of matrix games [40, 52]. Robustness is ensured by solving the inner problem, for which the correctness of our adapted algorithm in [24] follows from [41].

Complexity. Runtime depends on the number of iterations and per-iteration cost, both of which are dependent on game size. Finite-horizon objectives require exactly k iterations, while infinite-horizon ones iterate until convergence, which may be exponential in $|A|$ in the worst case [11] (even for MDPs [23]). Since line 2 takes $O(|S| \log |S|)$ time per execution, the per-iteration cost for zero-sum ICSGs is $O\left(|S|^2 |A| \log |S| + |S| L_{|A|}\right)$, where $L_{|A|}$ is the cost of solving an LP problem of size $|A|$. This is polynomial in $|S|$ and $|A|$ with e.g., Karmarkar's algorithm [29]; or exponential under the simplex algorithm [16], which is PSPACE-complete in the worst case [20] but performs well on average [51]. For nonzero-sum ICSGs, each iteration takes worst-case exponential time due to NE enumeration [2].

Strategy synthesis. At each state, solving the NFG yields both the value(s) and optimal player strategies, while nature's optimal strategy is given by the returned values of SOLVEINNERPROBLEM (line 2 of Algorithm 1). These are memoryless and taken from the final RVI iteration for infinite-horizon objectives; but time-varying and taken from each RBI step for finite-horizon objectives.

7   Tool support and Experimentation

We extended PRISM-games [31] to support modelling and solution of 2-player ICSGs, building on its existing functionality for CSGs and IMDPs. The tool and case studies are available at [25].

Experimental setup. We evaluate the efficiency and scalability of our techniques, comparing, as a point of reference, to standard (non-robust) CSG solution from PRISM-games.[3] We use the benchmarks from [34], obtaining ICSGs by perturbing all non-0/1 probability CSG transitions with a two-sided uncertainty $\pm\epsilon$. This includes a combination of finite-, infinite- and mixed-horizon properties specified in the logic rPATL [13,34]. All experiments were run on a 3.2 GHz Apple M1 with 16 GB memory. Further statistics for benchmark models and an extended set of results can be found in [24].

Q1. How does verification time for ICSGs compare to CSGs? Results for solving CSGs and ICSGs under adversarial uncertainty, completed within a 2-hour time limit, are shown in Table 1 for zero-sum games and Table 2 for nonzero-sum games. Overall, the increase in verification time when moving from CSGs to ICSGs is significantly more pronounced in the nonzero-sum setting, highlighting the added complexity introduced by the nonzero-sum formulation.

Across all benchmarks, verification times for zero-sum ICSGs remained within a factor of two of their CSG counterparts (see Table 1), with all test instances (except for *User-centric network* with $K > 4$) solved within 2 hours. These include models with over 2 million states and 10 million transitions. By contrast, for nonzero-sum ICSGs, verification completes within 2 hours for models up to 0.4 million states and 1.3 million transitions. This aligns with the underlying reduction framework: in the zero-sum setting, the problem reduces to a 2-player game, whereas in the nonzero-sum case it is a more complex 3-player game.

---

[3] Due to improvements in PRISM-games, some statistics differ slightly from [34].

Table 1: Zero-sum verification results, with full statistics in [24].

Case study: [params], ϵ Property	Param. values	Avg # actions	States	Val. Iters CSG	Val. Iters ICSG	Verif. time (s) CSG	Verif. time (s) ICSG	Value CSG	Value ICSG
Robot coordination: $[l]$, 0.01 $\langle\!\langle rbt_1 \rangle\!\rangle \mathrm{R}_{\min=?}[\mathrm{F}\, g_1]$	4	2.07,2.07	226	19	18	0.15	0.27	4.55	4.39
	8	2.52,2.52	3,970	29	29	2.50	3.61	8.89	8.63
	12	2.68,2.68	20,450	39	37	16.22	31.73	13.15	12.84
User centric network: $[K]$, 0.01; $\langle\!\langle usr \rangle\!\rangle \mathrm{R}_{\min=?}[\mathrm{F}\, f]$	3	2.11,1.91	32,214	60	59	789.66	834.92	0.04	0.03
	4	2.31,1.92	104,897	81	81	3525.67	3729.40	4.00	4.00
Aloha: $[b_{\max}]$, 1/257 $\langle\!\langle u_2, u_3 \rangle\!\rangle \mathrm{R}_{\min=?}[\mathrm{F}\, s_{2,3}]$	2	1.00120,1.00274	14,230	105	103	5.31	5.61	4.34	4.28
	3	1.00023,1.00054	72,566	128	125	18.50	26.39	4.54	4.46
	4	1.00004,1.00009	413,035	195	190	225.69	291.72	4.62	4.53
	5	1.00001,1.00002	2,237,981	343	327	4669.54	4260.59	4.65	4.54
Jamming radio systems: $[chans, slots]$, 0.01 $\langle\!\langle u \rangle\!\rangle \mathrm{P}_{\max=?}[\mathrm{F}\,(sent \geq slots/2)]$	4,6	2.17,2.17	531	7	7	0.32	0.46	0.84	0.80
	4,12	2.49,2.49	1,623	13	13	1.39	2.94	0.77	0.71
	6,6	2.17,2.17	531	7	7	0.25	0.45	0.84	0.80
	6,12	2.49,2.49	1,623	13	13	1.46	2.37	0.77	0.71

Table 2: Nonzero-sum verification results, with full statistics in [24].

Case study: [params], ϵ Property	Param. values	Avg # actions	States	Val. Iters CSG	Val. Iters ICSG	Verif. time (s) CSG	Verif. time (s) ICSG	Value CSG	Value ICSG
Robot coordination: $[l, k]$, 0.01 $\langle\!\langle r_1 : r_2 \rangle\!\rangle_{\max=?} \left(\mathrm{P}[\neg c\ \mathrm{U}^{\leq k} g_1] + \mathrm{P}[\neg c\ \mathrm{U}^{\leq k} g_2]\right)$	4,4	2.07,2.07	226	4	4	0.26	0.60	1.55	1.50
	8,8	2.52,2.52	3,970	8	8	1.03	54.74	0.92	0.84
	12,12	2.68,2.68	20,450	12	12	8.55	2895.60	0.49	0.40
Robot coordination: $[l, k]$, 0.01 $\langle\!\langle r_1 : r_2 \rangle\!\rangle_{\max=?} \left(\mathrm{P}[\neg c\ \mathrm{U}^{\leq k} g_1] + \mathrm{P}[\neg c\ \mathrm{U}\, g_2]\right)$	4,8	2.10,2.04	226	14	14	1.22	17.54	2.00	2.00
	4,16	2.12,2.05	3,970	14	11	2.08	75.23	2.00	2.00
Aloha (deadline): $[b_{\max}, D]$, 1/257 $\langle\!\langle u_1 : u_2, u_3 \rangle\!\rangle_{\max=?} \left(\mathrm{P}[\mathrm{F}\, s_1] + \mathrm{P}[\mathrm{F}\, s_{2,3}]\right)$	1,8	1.0048,1.0111	14,230	23	23	0.45	5.13	1.99	1.99
	2,8	1.0012,1.0027	72,566	23	23	1.17	107.63	1.98	1.97
	3,8	1.0002,1.0005	413,035	22	22	3.96	3306.24	1.97	1.97
Medium access: $[e_{\max}, k_1, k_2]$, 0.01 $\langle\!\langle p_1 : p_2, p_3 \rangle\!\rangle_{\max=?} \left(\mathrm{R}[\mathrm{C}^{\leq k_1}] + \mathrm{R}[\mathrm{C}^{\leq k_2}]\right)$	10,20,25	1.91,3.63	10,591	25	25	577.60	614.46	26.10	25.88
	15,20,25	1.94,3.75	33,886	25	25	1148.02	6109.14	34.35	34.06

While the main overhead arises from solving the inner problem at each iteration, in the zero-sum setting this is often offset by faster RVI convergence. For example, in the *Aloha* model with $b_{\max} = 5$, ICSG verification outperformed CSGs in runtime and required noticeably fewer iterations to converge. Additionally, consistent with [34], for both zero- and nonzero-sum CSGs and ICSGs, verification time appears to depend more on the number of actions per player/coalition than the number of states. For example, the minimally branched *Aloha* instances (averaging close to one action per coalition) are verified relatively efficiently compared to other games with similarly sized state spaces.

Q2. How does ϵ affect verification time? Interestingly, as shown in Figure 1, verification times are often the lowest when ϵ is very small or close to its maximum value, while intermediate ϵ values tend to be slower. This non-monotonic behaviour again reflects the trade-off due to uncertainty: larger ϵ increases the per-iteration cost by giving nature more choices, but also accelerates convergence by flattening the value landscape [41], thus reducing the number of iterations required until convergence. Thus ϵ can be tuned to balance robustness and efficiency. However, the net effect of ϵ on verification time is model-specific: e.g., in the *Robot Coordination* case with $l = 12$ from Table 1, ICSG verification required fewer iterations but still resulted in a longer overall verification time.

Q3. How does ϵ influence the computed value? Increasing ϵ yields more conservative results, as shown in Figure 2. This is to be expected, as expanding the

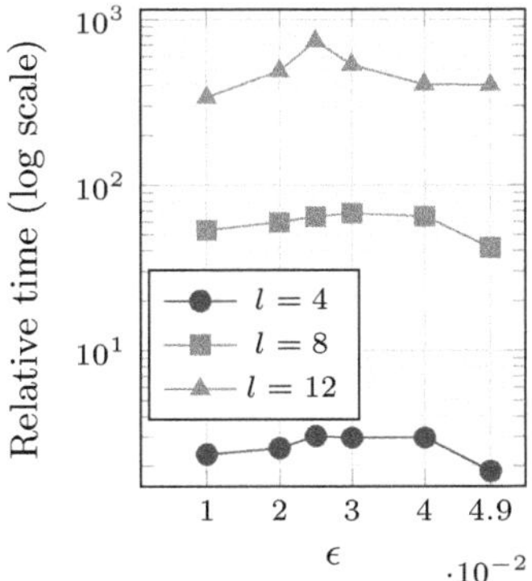

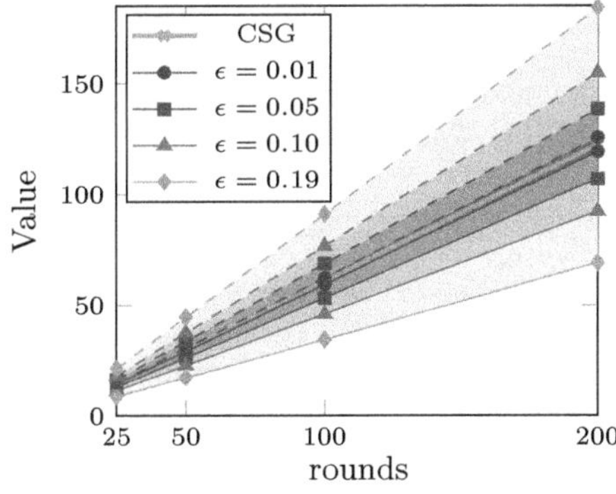

Fig. 1: Total verification time relative to CSG baseline in the first nonzero-sum *Robot coordination* case study, which requires $\epsilon < 0.05$.

Fig. 2: ICSG values over game size in the *Intrusion Detection* case study, under two resolutions of uncertainty: *adversarial* (solid lines) and *controlled* by coalition 1 (dashed).

uncertainty set enables nature to select "worse" transitions that reduce the game value. The effect is amplified in larger, more connected models, in which pessimistic transitions propagate over longer paths [54]. Figure 2 also illustrates a practical use of ICSG verification in computing two-sided, ϵ-parametrised bounds on verification results, which can be interpreted as confidence intervals under transition uncertainty. This is useful in safety-critical and performance-sensitive settings, where robustness must be ensured against worst-case security attacks, while enabling estimation of, e.g., optimistic operational performance.

8   Conclusion

We have introduced robust CSGs, an extension of classical CSGs with transition uncertainty that enables principled analysis of multi-agent, concurrent stochastic systems with imprecise dynamics. Focusing on interval uncertainty, i.e., ICSGs, we developed verification algorithms for the 2-player setting, for both finite- and infinite-horizon objectives. Our approach relies on a value-preserving reduction of ICSGs to standard CSGs, thereby allowing reuse of elements of the solution methods for both CSGs and RMDPs, plus custom adaptations and filtering. Our implementation in PRISM-games shows that solution in the zero-sum case scales comparably to standard CSGs, with runtime increases below a factor of two. In the nonzero-sum case, computational demands are higher but we still scale successfully to large CSGs. Future work could explore RCSGs with richer uncertainty models and/or alternative solution concepts (e.g., robust correlated equilibria), and consider objectives with more general temporal specifications.

Data Availability Statement. The models, tools, and scripts to reproduce our experimental evaluation are archived and available at [25].

Acknowledgments. Supported by the EPSRC Centre for Doctoral Training no. EP/Y035070/1 and the UKRI AI Hub on Mathematical Foundations of AI.

References

1. Aghassi, M., Bertsimas, D.: Robust game theory. Mathematical programming **107(1)**, 231–273 (2006)
2. Avis, D., Rosenberg, G.D., Savani, R., Von Stengel, B.: Enumeration of nash equilibria for two-player games. Economic theory **42(1)**, 9–37 (2010)
3. Badings, T., Simao, T.D., Suilen, M., Jansen, N.: Decision-making under uncertainty: beyond probabilities: Challenges and perspectives. International Journal on Software Tools for Technology Transfer **25(3)**, 375–391 (2023)
4. Bellman, R.: Dynamic programming. science **153(3731)**, 34–37 (1966)
5. Berthon, R., Katoen, J.P., Mittelmann, M., Murano, A.: Robust strategies for stochastic multi-agent systems. In: Proceedings of the 24th International Conference on Autonomous Agents and Multiagent Systems. p. 2437–2439. AAMAS '25, International Foundation for Autonomous Agents and Multiagent Systems, Richland, SC (2025)
6. Bouyer, P., Markey, N., Stan, D.: Mixed nash equilibria in concurrent terminal-reward games. In: FSTTCS 2014 (2014)
7. Bovy, E.M., Suilen, M., Junges, S., Jansen, N.: Imprecise probabilities meet partial observability: Game semantics for robust POMDPs. In: Proceedings of the Thirty-Third International Joint Conference on Artificial Intelligence, IJCAI-24. pp. 6697–6706 (8 2024), main Track
8. Castro, P.F., D'Argenio, P.: Polytopal stochastic games. In: Principles of Verification: Cycling the Probabilistic Landscape: Essays Dedicated to Joost-Pieter Katoen on the Occasion of His 60th Birthday, pp. 99—-117. Springer (2024)
9. Chatterjee, K., De Alfaro, L., Henzinger, T.A.: Strategy improvement for concurrent reachability and turn-based stochastic safety games. Journal of computer and system sciences **79(5)**, 640–657 (2013)
10. Chatterjee, K., Goharshady, E.K., Karrabi, M., Novotný, P., Žikelić, u.: Solving long-run average reward robust MDPs via stochastic games. In: Proceedings of the Thirty-Third International Joint Conference on Artificial Intelligence. IJCAI '24 (2024)
11. Chatterjee, K., Henzinger, T.A.: A survey of stochastic ω-regular games. Journal of Computer and System Sciences **78(2)**, 394–413 (2012)
12. Chatterjee, K., Sen, K., Henzinger, T.A.: Model-checking ω-regular properties of interval Markov chains. In: International Conference on Foundations of Software Science and Computational Structures. pp. 302–317. Springer (2008)
13. Chen, T., Forejt, V., Kwiatkowska, M., Parker, D., Simaitis, A.: Automatic verification of competitive stochastic systems. Formal Methods in System Design **43**, 61–92 (2013)
14. Chen, T., Han, T., Kwiatkowska, M.: On the complexity of model checking interval-valued discrete time Markov chains. Information Processing Letters **113(7)**, 210–216 (2013)
15. Condon, A.: The complexity of stochastic games. Information and Computation **96(2)**, 203–224 (1992)
16. Dantzig, G.B.: Programming of interdependent activities: Ii mathematical model. Econometrica, Journal of the Econometric Society pp. 200–211 (1949)
17. De Alfaro, L., Henzinger, T.A., Kupferman, O.: Concurrent reachability games. Theoretical computer science **386(3)**, 188–217 (2007)
18. De Alfaro, L., Majumdar, R.: Quantitative solution of omega-regular games. In: Proceedings of the thirty-third annual ACM symposium on Theory of computing. pp. 675–683 (2001)

19. Farhat, Z.U., Ghosh, D., Atia, G.K., Wang, Y.: Online robust multi-agent reinforcement learning under model uncertainties (2025), https://arxiv.org/abs/2508.02948
20. Fearnley, J., Savani, R.: The complexity of the simplex method. In: Proceedings of the forty-seventh annual ACM symposium on Theory of computing. pp. 201–208 (2015)
21. Filar, J., Vrieze, K.: Competitive Markov decision processes. Springer Science & Business Media (2012)
22. Givan, R., Leach, S., Dean, T.: Bounded-parameter Markov decision processes. Artificial Intelligence **122(1-2)**, 71–109 (2000)
23. Hansen, K.A., Ibsen-Jensen, R., Miltersen, P.B.: The complexity of solving reachability games using value and strategy iteration. In: International Computer Science Symposium in Russia. pp. 77–90. Springer (2011)
24. He, A.Y., Parker, D.: Robust verification of concurrent stochastic games under interval uncertainty. Extended Version (2026), https://arxiv.org/abs/2601.12003, extended version of the TACAS 2026 paper
25. He, A.Y., Parker, D.: Artifact for "Robust verification of concurrent stochastic games" (2026). https://doi.org/10.5281/zenodo.18189280
26. Ho, C.P., Petrik, M., Wiesemann, W.: Fast bellman updates for robust MDPs. In: International Conference on Machine Learning. pp. 1979–1988. PMLR (2018)
27. Howard, R.A.: Dynamic Programming and Markov Processes. John Wiley & Sons, New York (1960)
28. Iyengar, G.N.: Robust dynamic programming. Mathematics of Operations Research **30(2)**, 257–280 (2005)
29. Karmarkar, N.: A new polynomial-time algorithm for linear programming. In: Proceedings of the sixteenth annual ACM symposium on Theory of computing. pp. 302–311 (1984)
30. Klibano, P.: Uncertainty, decision, and normal form games,". Journal of Economic Theory, forthcoming (1993)
31. Kwiatkowska, M., Norman, G., Parker, D., Santos, G.: PRISM-games 3.0: Stochastic game verification with concurrency, equilibria and time. In: Proc. 32nd International Conference on Computer Aided Verification (CAV'20). LNCS, vol. 12225, pp. 475–487. Springer (2020)
32. Kwiatkowska, M., Norman, G., Parker, D., Santos, G.: Equilibria-based probabilistic model checking for concurrent stochastic games. In: International Symposium on Formal Methods. pp. 298–315. Springer (2019)
33. Kwiatkowska, M., Norman, G., Parker, D., Santos, G.: Multi-player equilibria verification for concurrent stochastic games. In: International Conference on Quantitative Evaluation of Systems. pp. 74–95. Springer (2020)
34. Kwiatkowska, M., Norman, G., Parker, D., Santos, G.: Automatic verification of concurrent stochastic systems. Formal Methods in System Design **58(1)**, 188–250 (2021)
35. Kwiatkowska, M., Norman, G., Parker, D., Santos, G.: Correlated equilibria and fairness in concurrent stochastic games. In: International Conference on Tools and Algorithms for the Construction and Analysis of Systems. pp. 60–78. Springer (2022)
36. Lemke, C.E., Howson, Jr, J.T.: Equilibrium points of bimatrix games. Journal of the Society for industrial and Applied Mathematics **12(2)**, 413–423 (1964)
37. Littman, M.L.: Markov games as a framework for multi-agent reinforcement learning. In: Machine learning proceedings 1994, pp. 157–163. Elsevier (1994)
38. Martin, D.A.: The determinacy of blackwell games. The Journal of Symbolic Logic **63(4)**, 1565–1581 (1998)

39. Meggendorfer, T., Weininger, M., Wienhöft, P.: Solving robust Markov decision processes: Generic, reliable, efficient. In: Proceedings of the AAAI Conference on Artificial Intelligence. vol. 39(25), pp. 26631–26641 (2025)
40. v. Neumann, J.: Zur theorie der gesellschaftsspiele. Mathematische annalen **100(1)**, 295–320 (1928)
41. Nilim, A., El Ghaoui, L.: Robust control of Markov decision processes with uncertain transition matrices. Operations Research **53(5)**, 780–798 (2005)
42. Osborne, M.J., et al.: An introduction to game theory, vol. 3(3). Springer (2004)
43. Perchet, V.: Finding robust nash equilibria. In: Algorithmic Learning Theory. pp. 725–751. PMLR (2020)
44. Raghavan, T., Filar, J.A.: Algorithms for stochastic games—a survey. Zeitschrift für Operations Research **35(6)**, 437–472 (1991)
45. Roch, Z., Wang, Y.: Distributionally robust Markov games with average reward (2025), https://arxiv.org/abs/2508.03136
46. Roughgarden, T.: Algorithmic game theory. Communications of the ACM **53(7)**, 78–86 (2010)
47. Shapley, L.S.: Stochastic games. Proceedings of the national academy of sciences **39(10)**, 1095–1100 (1953)
48. Shi, L., Mazumdar, E., Chi, Y., Wierman, A.: Sample-efficient robust multi-agent reinforcement learning in the face of environmental uncertainty. arXiv preprint arXiv:2404.18909 (2024)
49. Strehl, A.L., Littman, M.L.: An empirical evaluation of interval estimation for Markov decision processes. In: 16th IEEE International Conference on Tools with Artificial Intelligence. pp. 128–135. IEEE (2004)
50. Strehl, A.L., Littman, M.L.: A theoretical analysis of model-based interval estimation. In: Raedt, L.D., Wrobel, S. (eds.) Machine Learning, Proceedings of the Twenty-Second International Conference (ICML 2005). pp. 856–863. ACM (2005)
51. Todd, M.J.: The many facets of linear programming. Mathematical programming **91(3)**, 417–436 (2002)
52. Von Neumann, J., Morgenstern, O.: Theory of games and economic behavior, princeton (1944)
53. Wang, Y., Velasquez, A., Atia, G., Prater-Bennette, A., Zou, S.: Robust average-reward Markov decision processes. In: Proceedings of the AAAI Conference on Artificial Intelligence. vol. 37(12), pp. 15215–15223 (2023)
54. Wiesemann, W., Kuhn, D., Rustem, B.: Robust Markov decision processes. Mathematics of Operations Research **38(1)**, 153–183 (2013)

Multiple Long-Run and ω-Regular Objectives in MDPs*

Julius Ide, Joost-Pieter Katoen,
Hannah Mertens, and Tim Quatmann

RWTH Aachen University, Aachen, Germany
✉ tim.quatmann@cs.rwth-aachen.de

Abstract. We consider Markov decision processes (MDPs) with three types of objectives: (1) the probability of satisfying an ω-regular objective, (2) the expected long-run average (LRA) reward, and (3) the probability that the long-run average reward exceeds a given threshold. All types of objectives address infinite system behavior. The challenge lies in capturing all possible trade-offs between satisfiable LTL formulas and achievable LRA rewards inside the end components (ECs) of the MDP. Our approach translates LTL to Rabin objectives and then splits ECs into various sub-components in which (a subset of) the Rabin objectives are satisfied. LRA expectation and threshold satisfaction objectives are then optimized in those sub-components independently, where we exploit iterative techniques for multiple expected LRA reward objectives. We realized the approach into the STORM model checker and empirically show feasibility of verification of large models with more than half a million states—outperforming a reference implementation based on linear programming by several orders of magnitude.

1 Introduction

Markov decision processes (MDPs) [33] are a well-established model for analyzing systems that combine probabilistic and nondeterministic behavior. Applications such as planning [6,18] and scheduling [28] often require optimizing multiple objectives simultaneously. Multi-objective verification asks whether there is *one* strategy (aka policy or scheduler) under which a series of quantitative objectives achieve sufficiently high values. We study three different types of objectives:

1. the probability of satisfying a linear time logic (LTL) [32] formula, which express temporal requirements over infinite executions—e.g., whenever a process requests a resource, it is granted within k steps,
2. the expected long-run average (LRA) reward [33], which capture the expected average performance of a system over an infinite time horizon—e.g., the long-run average throughput of a communication channel, and

---

* This work has been partially funded by the KI-Starter Project 'Verifying AI Systems under Partial Observability' of the Ministry of Culture and Science of the German State of North Rhine-Westphalia. Experiments were performed with computing resources granted by RWTH Aachen University under project rwth1632.

S. Junges and G. Katz (Eds.): TACAS 2026, LNCS 16505, pp. 526–546, 2026.
https://doi.org/10.1007/978-3-032-22752-2_27

3. the probability that the LRA reward satisfies a given threshold [7]—e.g., the probability that on average at least m packages per time step are delivered.

Prior work has addressed the combination of an LTL objective with multiple LRA expectation objectives using linear programming (LP) [29], implemented in the tool MULTIGAIN 2.0 [5]. The approach is restricted to a single LTL formula that is translated into a limit-deterministic Büchi automaton using the construction of [37]. Multiple LRA threshold satisfaction objectives (also referred to as percentile queries) have been considered in [7,36,11,3]—again relying on LP encodings. Several works [17,2,35,24] have pointed out scalability issues of LP-based solution methods for single-objective and multi-objective MDP model checking. [17,35] avoid LP by reducing the multi-objective query to a series of single-objective queries that are solved using standard methods such as value iteration [33]. Our techniques build upon the existing works for MDPs with multiple LTL and LRA reward objectives while avoiding large LP encodings. Our main contributions are as follows.

- *Multiple LTL objectives via deterministic Rabin automata and demerging of end components.* Our approach is compatible with a broad set of LTL translation algorithms and tools—including SPOT [15]. The construction yields an equivalent multi-objective query on a modified MDP with LRA and total reward objectives that can be model checked efficiently via [35].
- *An iterative approach for LRA threshold satisfaction objectives.* We exploit a connection to expected LRA reward objectives for strongly-connected MDPs and embed this into the framework of [35]—enabling arbitrary mixtures of all three types of objectives.
- *A prototypical implementation in STORM and an empirical evaluation.* Our implementation outperforms an LP-based reference implementation in MULTI-GAIN 2.0 [5] on almost all case studies and scales to large MDPs with more than half a million states.

Related Work. MDPs with multiple linear-time (ω-regular or LTL) objectives and multi-dimensional reachability are examined in [16]. The work has been extended towards total reward objectives in [20]. [21] presents an approach based on value iteration instead of linear programming. [12] considers LTL objectives for stochastic games. In [40], the authors examined the combination of an LTL and a steady-state objective, which is a special case of an LRA objective. However, only deterministic finite-memory strategies were considered. [22] also studied the restriction to finite-memory strategies for the combination of a single LTL and a single LRA objective.

As an extension of [14,39,13], Svoreňová et al. [38] consider almost-sure satisfaction of an LTL specification (represented as a DRA) in an MDP, while simultaneously minimizing the expected average cost between successive visits to designated surveillance states. Surveillance is encoded directly into the LTL specification which avoids conflicts between the objectives.

Regarding objectives that concern the probability of achieving multiple LRA constraints, existing works [19,7,11,36,3] have primarily relied on LP. The approach of Randour et al. [36], building on [19,7], requires solving several LP encodings—one for each maximal end component—followed by an additional program to combine the partial results. In contrast, [11] proposes a unified method that reduces the entire problem to a single LP. [3] presents (mixed-integer) LP-based techniques to obtain certificates and witnessing subsystems for LRA threshold satisfaction objectives and includes an empirical evaluation using a prototype implementation.

Paper overview. Section 2 introduces preliminaries and formally states the multi-objective model checking problem. Section 3 handles combinations of LTL and LRA reward objectives via a reduction to total rewards. Section 4 discusses LRA threshold satisfaction objectives and their connection to LRA expectation objectives. Section 5 presents our implementation and the experimental evaluation.

2 Preliminaries

$\mathbb{N}$ and $\mathbb{R}$ denote the sets of non-negative integers and real numbers, respectively. The i-th component of a vector $\boldsymbol{v} \in \mathbb{R}^n$ with $1 \leq i \leq n \in \mathbb{N}$ is denoted as v_i. For $\boldsymbol{v}, \boldsymbol{w} \in \mathbb{R}^n$ we write $\boldsymbol{v} \cdot \boldsymbol{w} = \sum_{i=1}^{n} v_i \cdot w_i$ for the *dot product* and $\boldsymbol{v} \geq \boldsymbol{w}$ if $v_i \geq w_i$ for all $1 \leq i \leq n$. For sets A and B, $f \colon A \hookrightarrow B$ denotes a *partial function* from A to B with domain $dom(f) \subseteq A$. The set of *distributions* over countable set A is $Dist(A) = \{\mu \colon A \to [0,1] \mid \sum_{a \in A} \mu(a) = 1\}$. We define the *support* of a distribution $\mu \in Dist(A)$ as $supp(\mu) = \{a \in A \mid \mu(a) > 0\}$. *Iverson brackets* $\left[\, expression \,\right]$ evaluate to 1 if the Boolean *expression* is true and to 0 otherwise.

Definition 1. *A* Markov decision process (MDP) *is a tuple* $\mathcal{M} = (S, Act, \mathbf{P}, s^I)$, *where* S *is a finite set of states with initial state* $s^I \in S$, Act *is a finite set of actions, and* $\mathbf{P} \colon S \times Act \hookrightarrow Dist(S)$ *is a (partial) probabilistic transition function.*

We fix an MDP $\mathcal{M} = (S, Act, \mathbf{P}, s^I)$ and provide basic definitions. See [33,4] for further details. For $s \in S$, let $Act(s) = \{a \in Act \mid (s,a) \in dom(\mathbf{P})\}$ denote the set of *enabled actions*. We assume $Act(s) \neq \emptyset$ for all $s \in S$. A *transition* from $s \in S$ via $a \in Act(s)$ to $s' \in supp(\mathbf{P}(s,a))$ is denoted by $s \xrightarrow{a} s'$. A *path* in $\mathcal{M}$ is an infinite sequence $\rho = s_0 a_0 s_1 a_1 s_2 a_2 \cdots \in (SA)^\omega$ where $s_i \xrightarrow{a_i} s_{i+1}$ for all $i \in \mathbb{N}$. A finite path $\pi \in (SA)^n S$ of length $|\pi| = n$ is a prefix $\pi = s_0 a_0 \ldots s_{n-1} a_{n-1} s_n$ of a path. We set $\pi[i] = s_i$ for all $0 \leq i \leq n$ and $last(\pi) = s_n$. $Paths_{\mathcal{M}}$ and $Paths^*_{\mathcal{M}}$ denote the set of all paths and all finite paths in $\mathcal{M}$, respectively. An *end component (EC)* of $\mathcal{M}$ is a non-empty set $\mathcal{E} \subseteq dom(\mathbf{P})$ such that—using $states(\mathcal{E}) = \{s \in S \mid (s,a) \in \mathcal{E}$ for some $a \in Act(s)\}$: $(s,a) \in \mathcal{E}$ implies $supp(\mathbf{P}(s,a)) \subseteq states(\mathcal{E})$ and for $s, s' \in states(\mathcal{E})$ exists $s_0 a_0 \ldots a_{n-1} s_n \in Paths_{\mathcal{M}}$ such that $s_0 = s$, $s_n = s'$, and $(s_i, a_i) \in \mathcal{E}$ for all $0 \leq i < n$. A *maximal EC (MEC)* is an EC that is not a subset of another EC. $Mecs_{\mathcal{M}}$ is the set of MECs of $\mathcal{M}$.

Example 1. Consider the MDP $\mathcal{M}$ depicted in Figure 1. The depicted transitions are annotated with an action a or b, and have a probability of 1. The MDP has three ECs: $\{s_0, s_1\}, \{s_2, s_3\}$, and $\{s_0, s_1, s_2, s_3\}$, where the latter one is a MEC.

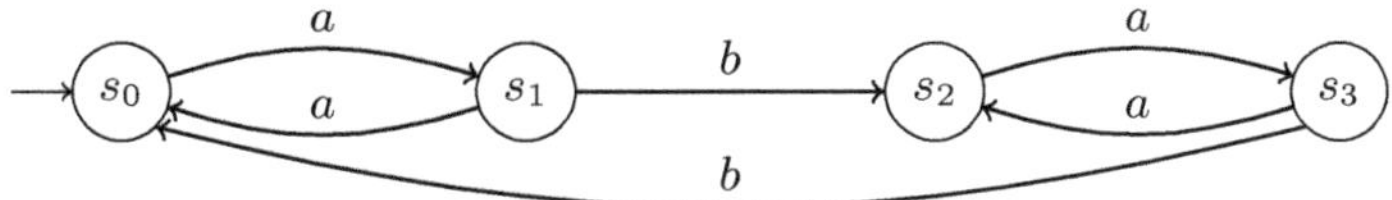

Fig. 1: Example MDP $\mathcal{M}$.

Definition 2. *A* strategy *for MDP $\mathcal{M}$ is a function $\sigma\colon Paths^*_{\mathcal{M}} \to Dist(Act)$ such that $\sigma(\pi) \in Dist(Act(last(\pi)))$ for any $\pi \in Paths^*_{\mathcal{M}}$.*

The set of all strategies for $\mathcal{M}$ is given by $Str_{\mathcal{M}}$. Let $\sigma \in Str_{\mathcal{M}}$. Intuitively, after observing finite path π, $\sigma(\pi)$ yields a probability distribution over the possible actions at $last(\pi)$. Strategy σ is *pure* (or deterministic) if $|supp(\sigma(\pi))| = 1$ for all $\pi \in Paths^*_{\mathcal{M}}$ and *memoryless* if it depends only on the current state, i.e., $\sigma(\pi) = \sigma(\pi')$ holds for all $\pi, \pi' \in Paths^*_{\mathcal{M}}$ with $last(\pi) = last(\pi')$. A *finite-memory* strategy is described by a finite-state Mealy machine that takes MDP paths as input and outputs distributions over available actions. Using a standard cylinder set construction, MDP $\mathcal{M}$ and strategy $\sigma \in Str_{\mathcal{M}}$ induce a *probability measure* $\mathrm{Pr}^{\sigma}_{\mathcal{M}}$ on measurable sets of infinite paths. Intuitively, given $\pi \in Paths^*_{\mathcal{M}}$ with $last(\pi) = s$, the transition $s \xrightarrow{a} s'$ is taken with probability $\sigma(\pi)(a) \cdot \mathbf{P}(s,a)(s')$.

In the following, we use $\overline{\mathbb{R}} = \mathbb{R} \cup \{-\infty, +\infty\}$ for the set of extended real numbers.

Definition 3. *An* objective *for MDP $\mathcal{M}$ is a function $f\colon Paths_{\mathcal{M}} \to \overline{\mathbb{R}}$. The* value *of f induced by $\sigma \in Str_{\mathcal{M}}$ is the expected value of f with respect to $\mathrm{Pr}^{\sigma}_{\mathcal{M}}$, formally given by the Lebesgue integral $\mathrm{Ex}^{\sigma}_{\mathcal{M}}(f) = \int_{\rho} f(\rho)\, d\mathrm{Pr}^{\sigma}_{\mathcal{M}}(\rho)$.*[1]

We refer to objectives $f\colon Paths_{\mathcal{M}} \to \{0,1\}$ as *probability objectives*: their expected value equals the probability $\mathrm{Pr}^{\sigma}_{\mathcal{M}}(\{\rho \in Paths_{\mathcal{M}} \mid f(\rho) = 1\})$. To formalize objectives that refer to quantities such as energy consumption or delivered packages, the MDP can be annotated using a *reward function rew*$\colon S \times Act \to \mathbb{R}$.

Definition 4. *Let rew be a reward function for $\mathcal{M}$. The* total reward objective *for rew is given by $tot(rew)\colon Paths_{\mathcal{M}} \to \overline{\mathbb{R}}$, where for $\rho = s_0 a_0 s_1 a_1 \cdots \in Paths_{\mathcal{M}}$ we set $tot(rew)(\rho) = \liminf_{n\to\infty} \sum_{i=0}^{n} rew(s_i, a_i)$. The* long-run average *(LRA) objective for rew is given by $lra(rew)\colon Paths_{\mathcal{M}} \to \mathbb{R}$, where for $\rho = s_0 a_0 s_1 a_1 \cdots \in Paths_{\mathcal{M}}$ we set $lra(rew)(\rho) = \liminf_{n\to\infty} \frac{1}{n} \sum_{i=0}^{n-1} rew(s_i, a_i)$.*

For objectives $f_1, \ldots, f_n\colon Paths_{\mathcal{M}} \to \overline{\mathbb{R}}$, we call $\mathfrak{MO} = (f_1, \ldots, f_n)$ a multi-objective query (mo-query) and lift the notation for expected value to tuples: $\mathrm{Ex}^{\sigma}_{\mathcal{M}}(\mathfrak{MO}) = (\mathrm{Ex}^{\sigma}_{\mathcal{M}}(f_1), \ldots, \mathrm{Ex}^{\sigma}_{\mathcal{M}}(f_n)) \in \overline{\mathbb{R}}^n$. We say that $\sigma \in Str_{\mathcal{M}}$ achieves a threshold point $\boldsymbol{p} \in \mathbb{R}^n$ if $\mathrm{Ex}^{\sigma}_{\mathcal{M}}(\mathfrak{MO}) \geq \boldsymbol{p}$ and call $Ach_{\mathcal{M}}(\mathfrak{MO}) = \{\boldsymbol{p} \in \mathbb{R}^n \mid$

---

[1] We only consider objectives whose expected value is always well-defined. This is not the case if objective values $-\infty$ and $+\infty$ both occur with positive probability.

$\exists \sigma \in Str_{\mathcal{M}}: Ex^{\sigma}_{\mathcal{M}}(\mathfrak{MO}) \geq \boldsymbol{p}\}$ the set of *achievable* points.[2] We formalize our main problem statement.

Problem 1: Multi-Objective Achievability

Given an MDP $\mathcal{M}$, mo-query $\mathfrak{MO} = (f_1, \ldots, f_n)$, and thresholds $\boldsymbol{p} = (p_1, \ldots, p_n) \in \mathbb{R}^n$, decide if $\boldsymbol{p} \in Ach_{\mathcal{M}}(\mathfrak{MO})$, i.e., if

$$\left(Ex^{\sigma}_{\mathcal{M}}(f_1), \ldots, Ex^{\sigma}_{\mathcal{M}}(f_n)\right) \geq \boldsymbol{p} \text{ for some strategy } \sigma \in Str_{\mathcal{M}}.$$

Related works [21,35,5]—and our experiments in Section 5—also consider *multi-objective Pareto queries* that ask for (an approximation of) the complete set of achievable points $Ach_{\mathcal{M}}(\mathfrak{MO})$ as well as variations where a threshold $\geq p_i$ is only imposed on a subset of the objectives. [35] presents an efficient procedure to answer multi-objective queries for arbitrary combinations of total reward and LRA objectives which we take as a basis for our techniques.

Example 2. Reconsider the MDP $\mathcal{M}$ depicted in Figure 1. Let *rew* be a reward function given by $rew(s_i, a) = 0$ and $rew(s_i, b) = 100$, for $i \in \{0, 1, 2, 3\}$. Consider the mo-query $\mathfrak{MO} = (f_1, lra(rew))$, where the probability query f_1 is given by $f_1(\rho) = \left[\text{"either } s_1 \text{ or } s_2 \text{ is visited finitely often on } \rho\text{"}\right]$. Threshold point $\boldsymbol{p} = (0.5, 50)$ is not achievable as there is no strategy σ such that $Ex^{\sigma}_{\mathcal{M}}(\mathfrak{MO}) \geq (0.5, 50)$. The maximum achievable LRA reward is 50, obtained by the strategy σ that cycles through the MDP, alternating between the actions a and b. In this case, both s_1 and s_2 are visited infinitely often and consequently, the first objective evaluates to 0. On the other hand, the finite-memory strategy σ' that with 50% probability always chooses action a and otherwise alternates between a and b achieves the point $\boldsymbol{p}' = (0.5, 25)$.

3   Combining Rabin and Long-run Average Objectives

Let $Inf(\rho)$ denote the set of states visited infinitely often along $\rho \in Paths_{\mathcal{M}}$.

Definition 5. *A* Rabin condition *is a set* $rab = \{(L_1, K_1), \ldots, (L_m, K_m)\}$ *of Rabin pairs with* $L_i, K_i \subseteq S$ *for all* $1 \leq i \leq m$. *A path* $\rho \in Paths_{\mathcal{M}}$ *is winning for rab if there is a Rabin pair* $(L, K) \in rab$ *with* $Inf(\rho) \cap L = \emptyset$ *and* $Inf(\rho) \cap K \neq \emptyset$. *The* Rabin probability objective *is given by* $acc(rab): Paths_{\mathcal{M}} \to \{0, 1\}$ *with* $acc(rab)(\rho) = \left[\rho \text{ is winning for rab}\right]$.

Verifying Rabin objectives is usually done via a reachability analysis of *accepting ECs* of the MDP [4, Ch. 10]; an EC $\mathcal{E}$ of an MDP is *accepting* w.r.t. *rab* if there exists some $(L, K) \in rab$ such that $states(\mathcal{E}) \cap L = \emptyset$ and $states(\mathcal{E}) \cap K \neq \emptyset$. A *maximal accepting EC (MAC)* is an accepting EC that is not a subset of another accepting EC. $Macs_{\mathcal{M}, rab}$ is the set of MACs of $\mathcal{M}$ w.r.t. *rab*.

---

[2] For simplicity, we restrict to lower bounds $Ex^{\sigma}_{\mathcal{M}}(f_i) \geq p_i$ for all $1 \leq i \leq n$. Upper bounds can be converted to lower bounds by negating the objective $f'_i = -f_i$.

Example 3. The objective f_1 from Example 2 can be rephrased as Rabin objective $acc(rab)$ for $rab = \{(\{s_1\}, \emptyset), (\{s_2\}, \emptyset)\}$. The corresponding MACs are $\mathcal{C}_1 = \{s_0, s_1\}$ and $\mathcal{C}_2 = \{s_2, s_3\}$.

Remark 1 (LTL Objectives).   Every LTL formula can be translated into an equivalent deterministic Rabin automaton (DRA) $\mathcal{A}$. Forming the synchronous product of the MDP $\mathcal{M}$ and the DRA $\mathcal{A}$ yields a new MDP whose paths are winning for a Rabin condition rab iff the original execution of $\mathcal{M}$ satisfies the LTL formula. Thus model checking an LTL specification is reduced to verifying a Rabin objective on the product MDP [4, Ch. 10]. Throughout the remainder of this paper we therefore focus exclusively on Rabin objectives, noting that all results carry over to LTL objectives.

We tackle the multi-objective achievability problem for queries containing Rabin and LRA objectives. This is a challenging problem: First, strategies with *unbounded* memory might be required, see [29, Example 2]. Second, Rabin acceptance may require visiting certain sets of states only finitely often which potentially conflicts with LRA-optimal strategies, as shown in Example 2. The latter challenge is avoided in [29] by translating LTL formulas to limit-deterministic *Büchi* automata (LDBA)—following [37]. While this yields a complete procedure, it prohibits the use of LTL-to-DRA translations. Additionally, it relies on a specific class of LDBA that satisfy additional structural conditions (see [37, Sec. 8]) and is therefore not applicable to arbitrary LTL-to-LDBA translations.

In contrast, our approach is formulated for Rabin objectives, which strictly subsume Büchi objectives. This allows us to either employ standard LTL-to-DRA translations together with the conventional MDP–DRA product construction, or to instantiate our framework using the same MDP–LDBA product as in [29]. Existing experiments [37, Sec. 9] indicate that, depending on the LTL formula, either an LDBA or a DRA representation may be smaller in practice, even though both constructions have doubly exponential worst-case size. Moreover, Rabin automata benefit from broader tool support; for instance, SPOT version 2.14.3 [15] does not currently provide an LTL-to-LDBA translation.

The key idea of our approach is to reduce the Rabin objectives to total reward objectives. We first consider multi-objective queries with a single Rabin objective and generalize to arbitrary numbers of objectives afterwards.

3.1   Single Rabin Objective

Let $\mathfrak{MO} = (acc(rab), lra(\mathbf{rew}))$ be a multi-objective query, where we use the shorthand $lra(\mathbf{rew}) = lra(rew_1), \ldots, lra(rew_n)$. We show that the verification of $\mathfrak{MO}$ can be reduced to analyzing a multi-objective query in which the Rabin objective is replaced by a total reward objective $(tot(rew_{rab}), lra(\mathbf{rew}))$ for a modified MDP $\mathcal{M}[\![Macs_{\mathcal{M},rab}]\!]$. As shown in Example 2, an EC containing an MAC may admit an LRA-optimal strategy that leaves the MAC. Strategies must choose between Rabin satisfaction and LRA optimization. The MDP $\mathcal{M}[\![Macs_{\mathcal{M},rab}]\!]$—obtained via *demerging*—encodes this trade-off between Rabin

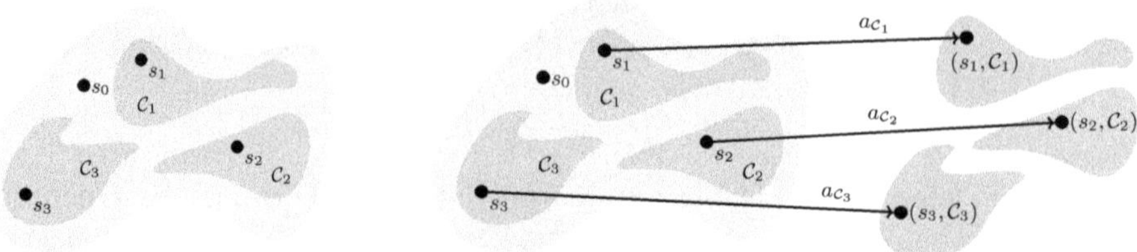

Fig. 2: Visualization of an EC before (left) and after (right) demerging.

satisfaction and LRA optimization by making the choice explicit. Figure 2 illustrates the construction for an MDP with three MACs $Macs_{\mathcal{M},rab} = \{\mathcal{C}_1, \mathcal{C}_2, \mathcal{C}_3\}$. From each MAC $\mathcal{C}_i$, a strategy can either continue staying in the original MDP or move to a copy of $\mathcal{C}_i$ via a new action $a_{\mathcal{C}_i}$. This way, $\mathcal{M}[\![Macs_{\mathcal{M},rab}]\!]$ directly encodes the choice between staying inside a particular MAC to satisfy the Rabin objective by picking $a_{\mathcal{C}_i}$ and purely optimizing only the LRA objectives.

Definition 6 (Demerged MDP). *Let $\mathcal{M}$ be an MDP with set G of ECs. The demerged MDP is defined as $\mathcal{M}[\![G]\!] = (S_{\text{dem}}, Act_{\text{dem}}, \mathbf{P}_{\text{dem}}, s^I)$, where $S_{\text{dem}} = S \cup \{(s, \mathcal{C}) \mid \mathcal{C} \in G, s \in states(\mathcal{C})\}$, $Act_{\text{dem}} = Act \cup \{a_{\mathcal{C}} \mid \mathcal{C} \in G\}$, and $\mathbf{P}_{\text{dem}} \colon S_{\text{dem}} \times Act_{\text{dem}} \to [0,1]$ such that*

- *$\mathbf{P}_{\text{dem}}(s, a)(s') = \mathbf{P}(s, a)(s')$ for all $(s, a) \in dom(\mathbf{P})$, $s' \in S$,*
- *$\mathbf{P}_{\text{dem}}((s, \mathcal{C}), a)((s', \mathcal{C})) = \mathbf{P}(s, a)(s')$ for all $\mathcal{C} \in G, (s, a) \in \mathcal{C}, s' \in S$, and*
- *$\mathbf{P}_{\text{dem}}(s, a_{\mathcal{C}})((s, \mathcal{C})) = 1$ for all $\mathcal{C} \in G, s \in states(\mathcal{C})$.*

We show that the Rabin objective of an MDP $\mathcal{M}$ can equivalently be expressed as a total reward objective over its demerged MDP. To this end, we lift each reward function rew_i on $\mathcal{M}$ to the demerged MDP $\mathcal{M}[\![G]\!]$ by preserving the original reward values within each MAC-copy. Given a reward function rew_i for $\mathcal{M}$, the lifted reward function $rew_i[\![G]\!]$ for $\mathcal{M}[\![G]\!]$ is given by

$$rew_i[\![G]\!](s, a) = \begin{cases} rew_i(s, a) & \text{if } s \in S, a \in Act \\ rew_i(s', a) & \text{if } s = (s', \mathcal{C}), (s', a) \in \mathcal{C} \text{ for some } \mathcal{C} \in G \\ 0 & \text{otherwise.} \end{cases}$$

Additionally, for Rabin condition rab, let rew_{rab} be a reward function with

$$rew_{rab}(s, a) = \big[\, a = a_{\mathcal{C}} \text{ for some } \mathcal{C} \in G \text{ accepting w.r.t. } rab \,\big].$$

Theorem 1. *Let $\boldsymbol{p} \in \mathbb{R}^{n+1}$. Using $G = Macs_{\mathcal{M},rab}$, we have*

$$\exists \sigma \in Str_{\mathcal{M}} : \mathrm{Ex}^{\sigma}_{\mathcal{M}}(acc(rab), lra(\mathbf{rew})) \geq \boldsymbol{p}$$

$$iff \quad \exists \sigma \in Str_{\mathcal{M}[\![G]\!]} : \mathrm{Ex}^{\sigma}_{\mathcal{M}[\![G]\!]}(tot(rew_{rab}), lra(\mathbf{rew}[\![G]\!])) \geq \boldsymbol{p}.$$

Proof (sketch). " $\Longrightarrow$ ": Let $\sigma \in Str_{\mathcal{M}}$ such that $\mathrm{Ex}_{\mathcal{M}}^{\sigma}(acc(rab), lra(\mathbf{rew})) \geq \boldsymbol{p}$. We show that there is a (finite memory) strategy $\widehat{\sigma}_{\epsilon}$ of $\mathcal{M}[\![G]\!]$ for every $\epsilon > 0$ such that $\mathrm{Ex}_{\mathcal{M}[\![G]\!]}^{\widehat{\sigma}_{\epsilon}}(tot(rew_{rab}), lra(\mathbf{rew}[\![G]\!])) \geq \boldsymbol{p} - \epsilon$. As the set of achievable points is closed[3], there must exist a strategy $\widehat{\sigma}$ of $\mathcal{M}[\![G]\!]$ for which we have $\mathrm{Ex}_{\mathcal{M}[\![G]\!]}^{\widehat{\sigma}}(tot(rew_{rab}), lra(\mathbf{rew}[\![G]\!])) \geq \boldsymbol{p}$. We construct $\widehat{\sigma}_{\epsilon}$ similar to the proof of [20, Proposition 5]. By [29, Theorem 1], for every $\delta > 0$, there exists a finite-memory strategy that δ-precisely satisfies any combination of LTL and LRA objectives. Their proof proceeds via the LDBA-product construction, which introduces only a finite amount of additional memory. As Rabin objectives are expressible in LTL, it follows that a finite memory strategy σ_{ϵ} of $\mathcal{M}[\![G]\!]$ satisfying $\mathrm{Ex}_{\mathcal{M}[\![G]\!]}^{\sigma_{\epsilon}}(acc(rab), lra(\mathbf{rew}[\![G]\!])) \geq \boldsymbol{p} - \epsilon$ exists. The strategy $\widehat{\sigma}_{\epsilon}$ of $\mathcal{M}[\![G]\!]$ mimics σ_{ϵ} until a finite prefix π is reached such that all paths extending π are either

(a) winning for *rab*: there is a corresponding MAC for $\mathcal{C} \in Macs_{\mathcal{M},rab}$ that is never left again, and $\widehat{\sigma}_{\epsilon}$ jumps to the corresponding $\mathcal{C}$-copy via $a_{\mathcal{C}}$, after which it continues to mimic σ_{ϵ} forever.
(b) not winning for *rab*: $\widehat{\sigma}_{\epsilon}$ mimics σ_{ϵ} forever.

Every path almost surely has such a prefix π: As σ_{ϵ} only uses finite memory, the corresponding paths in the (finite) Markov chain induced by $\mathcal{M}$ and σ_{ϵ} almost surely reach a bottom SCC which coincides with an (a) accepting or (b) not accepting EC of $\mathcal{M}$.

" $\Longleftarrow$ ": Let $\sigma \in Str_{\mathcal{M}[\![G]\!]}$ satisfying $\mathrm{Ex}_{\mathcal{M}[\![G]\!]}^{\sigma}(tot(rew_{rab}), lra(\mathbf{rew}[\![G]\!])) \geq \boldsymbol{p}$. We construct $\widehat{\sigma} \in Str_{\mathcal{M}}$ as follows:

- $\widehat{\sigma}$ mimics σ until a jump action $a_{\mathcal{C}}$ into an MAC-copy is taken.
- After the jump, it reproduces σ's behavior and it visits all states of the MAC once every i steps, where i gradually increases over time. In the limit, this preserves the expected LRA rewards while ensuring that every state in the MAC-copy is visited infinitely often, satisfying the Rabin condition.

The lifting of the reward function rew_i on $\mathcal{M}$ to $\mathcal{M}[\![G]\!]$ ensures that the rewards in an MAC in $\mathcal{M}$ and the MAC-copy in $\mathcal{M}[\![G]\!]$ coincide. The reward function rew_{rab} guarantees that a reward is gained when an MAC-copy is entered via $a_{\mathcal{C}}$ reflecting that the Rabin condition is satisfied in $\mathcal{M}$. $\qquad\square$

We note that for overlapping MACs—i.e., distinct MACs $\mathcal{C}_1, \mathcal{C}_2 \in Macs_{\mathcal{M},rab}$ with $\mathcal{C}_1 \cap \mathcal{C}_2 \neq \emptyset$—the created copies in $\mathcal{M}[\![Macs_{\mathcal{M},rab}]\!]$ do not overlap. This might blow up the size of the demerged MDP. For an MDP and a single Rabin objective with m pairs, the demerging yields an MDP with at most $|S| \cdot (m+1)$ states, because for each Rabin pair a state can belong to at most one maximal accepting end component. Similar blow-ups appear when considering LDBAs as they require a non-deterministic guess of the "right" accepting component [37].

---

[3] This is a consequence of the linear program characterization of [29].

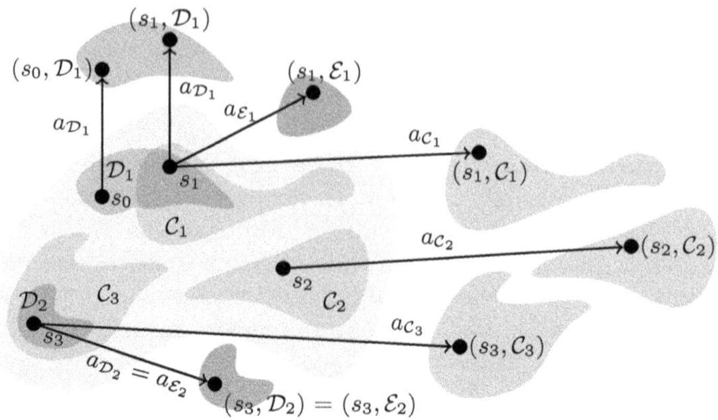

Fig. 3: Visualization of an EC after demerging for two Rabin conditions rab_1 and rab_2. The MACs w.r.t. rab_1 are C_1, C_2, C_3, MACs w.r.t. rab_2 are D_1, D_2, and MACs w.r.t. their conjunction $rab_1 \wedge rab_2$ are $\mathcal{E}_1, \mathcal{E}_2$, where $\mathcal{E}_1 \subsetneq C_1 \cap D_1$.

3.2   Multiple Rabin Objectives

We now consider *multiple* Rabin and LRA objectives, i.e., we consider a multi-objective query $\mathfrak{MO} = (acc(rab_1), \ldots, acc(rab_k), lra(\mathbf{rew}))$, for $k > 1$ and $lra(\mathbf{rew}) = lra(rew_1), \ldots, lra(rew_n)$. To answer our achievability problem, we generalize the single Rabin reduction from above to the case of multiple Rabin objectives.

The idea is to consider each possible conjunction of the Rabin objectives: For a conjunction $\bigwedge_{rab \in R} rab$ with $R \subseteq \{rab_1, \ldots, rab_k\}$, we proceed as in the single-Rabin case: We create copies of the relevant MACs, and transitions into these MAC copies yield a reward of 1 for the Rabin objectives that are satisfied within the MAC. To compute the MACs for a conjunction of Rabin pairs, we rewrite the conjunction of Rabin objectives—a conjunction of disjunctions of Rabin pairs—into a disjunction of conjunctions of Rabin pairs. For each conjunction, we identify the MECs that (i) exclude any states that should be visited only finitely often, and (ii) include at least one state from each Rabin pair that must be visited infinitely often.

Figure 3 depicts an EC demerged w.r.t. $G = Macs_{\mathcal{M}, rab_1} \cup Macs_{\mathcal{M}, rab_2} \cup Macs_{\mathcal{M}, rab_1 \wedge rab_2}$, which contains a copy of each MAC C_1, C_2, C_3 and D_1, D_2 for the single Rabin condition rab_1 and rab_2, respectively and, additionally, a copy of $\mathcal{E}_1$—an MAC for the conjunction $rab_1 \wedge rab_2$ of both Rabin conditions. Note that a MAC for the conjunction $rab_1 \wedge rab_2$ is (a possibly proper) subset of the intersection of MACs for rab_1 and rab_2. When MACs corresponding to different Rabin conditions coincide—for example, $D_2 \in Macs_{\mathcal{M}, rab_2}$ and $\mathcal{E}_2 \in Macs_{\mathcal{M}, rab_1 \wedge rab_2}$—the demerged MDP contains only a single copy. Recall from Section 3.1 that demerging with respect to a single Rabin objective yields at most $|S| \cdot (m + 1)$ states. For an MDP with $k > 1$ Rabin objectives with $m_1, \ldots, m_k$ acceptance pairs, respectively, the demerging construction yields at most $|S| \cdot \prod_{i=1}^{k}(m_i + 1)$ states.

Theorem 2. *Let $p \in \mathbb{R}^{k+n}$. Using $G = \bigcup_{R \subseteq \{rab_1,\dots,rab_k\}} Macs_{\mathcal{M},R_\wedge}$, where $R_\wedge = \bigwedge_{rab \in R} rab$, we have*

$$\exists \sigma \in Str_{\mathcal{M}} : \mathrm{Ex}_{\mathcal{M}}^{\sigma}(acc(rab_1),\dots,acc(rab_k), lra(\mathbf{rew})) \geq p$$

iff $\exists \sigma \in Str_{\mathcal{M}\llbracket G \rrbracket} : \mathrm{Ex}_{\mathcal{M}\llbracket G \rrbracket}^{\sigma}((tot(rew_{rab_1}),\dots,tot(rew_{rab_k}), lra(\mathbf{rew}\llbracket G \rrbracket)) \geq p.$

Proof (sketch). The proof is similar to that of Theorem 1. The only difference arises when constructing $\widehat{\sigma} \in Str_{\mathcal{M}\llbracket G \rrbracket}$ from $\sigma \in Str_{\mathcal{M}}$. If multiple Rabin conditions are satisfied almost surely, then several MACs may be available to jump to. In this case, $\widehat{\sigma}$ is defined to take the jump action $a_{\mathcal{C}}$ into the MAC $\mathcal{C}$ that satisfies the largest number of Rabin conditions (equivalently, the most specific or "smallest" such MAC). $\square$

Theorem 2 establishes that Rabin objectives can be expressed as total reward objectives in the demerged MDP. This reduction allows us to apply existing techniques—e.g. [35]—for multi-objective optimization over combinations of LRA and total reward objectives.

Remark 2 (Qualitative Rabin objectives). Multi-objective queries that require one or more Rabin objectives to hold almost-surely (i.e., with probability 1) can be treated more efficiently. First, when finding MACs, it suffices to consider conjunctions where all such objectives are true. Second, MECs that do not contain any accepting MAC, as well as transitions that lead to such MECs with positive probability can safely be removed from the MDP as they are never reachable under an achieving strategy.

4 Long-run Average Satisfaction Objectives

We now consider objectives that impose constraints on the probability of achieving a given long-run average reward—following [7,11,36].

Definition 7. *The* long-run average threshold satisfaction objective *for a reward function rew and a threshold $\lambda \in \mathbb{R}$ is defined as $lrasat(rew, \lambda)\colon Paths_{\mathcal{M}} \to \mathbb{R}$, where for $\pi \in Paths_{\mathcal{M}}$:*

$$lrasat(rew, \lambda)(\pi) = \begin{cases} 1 & \text{if } lra(rew)(\pi) \geq \lambda \\ 0 & \text{otherwise.} \end{cases}$$

LRA satisfaction objectives complement both expected LRA objectives and Rabin objectives. The former only considers the expected value of the LRA reward, which might yield solutions with high variance. The latter does not quantify the expected frequency with which "good" states are visited. Achievability with multiple LRA satisfaction objectives requires infinite memory [7,36].

Example 4. Consider the MDP $\mathcal{M}$ from Figure 4 and two reward functions rew_0 and rew_1, where $rew_i(s_i, a) = 1$ for $i = 0,1$ and all other rewards are 0. We consider the objectives $\mathfrak{MO} = (lrasat(rew_0, 0.5), lrasat(rew_1, 0.5))$. Both probability objectives can be achieved with value 1, i.e., $p = (1,1) \in Ach_{\mathcal{M}}(\mathfrak{MO})$. However, an unbounded memory strategy is required that infinitely often but with decreasing frequency switches between s_0 and s_1 using action b.

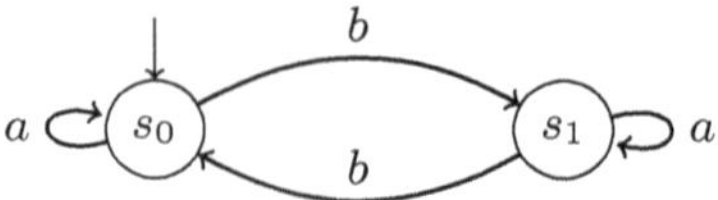

Fig. 4: Example MDP $\mathcal{M}$

4.1   Deciding Achievability through Weighted Sum Optimization

Algorithms for multiple LRA satisfaction objectives based on linear programming exist. Our goal is to instead lift the approach of [21,35] to enable computations based on more practical, iterative solution methods. The approach relies on optimizing weighted sums of objectives. Specifically, given an MDP $\mathcal{M}$, an mo-query $\mathfrak{MO} = (f_1, \ldots, f_n)$, and weights $\boldsymbol{w} = (w_1, \ldots, w_n) \in [0,1]^n$ with $\sum_{i=1}^{n} w_i = 1$, the *weighted optimization problem (WSO)* refers to finding a point $\boldsymbol{p_w} \in \mathbb{R}^n$ such that for some $\sigma_{\boldsymbol{w}} \in Str_{\mathcal{M}}$:

$$\boldsymbol{p_w} = \mathrm{Ex}_{\mathcal{M}}^{\sigma_{\boldsymbol{w}}}(f_1, \ldots, f_n) \quad \text{and} \quad \boldsymbol{w} \cdot \boldsymbol{p_w} = \sup_{\sigma} \boldsymbol{w} \cdot \mathrm{Ex}_{\mathcal{M}}^{\sigma}(f_1, \ldots, f_n) \tag{1}$$

We briefly outline a procedure for WSO (i.e., computing $\boldsymbol{p_w}$ as in Equation (1)) under LRA objectives $\mathfrak{MO} = (lra(rew_1), \ldots, lra(rew_n))$ and sketch an algorithm for multi-objective achievability (Problem 1) that uses the WSO procedure as a sub-routine. See [21,35,34] for further details. Let $\boldsymbol{w} = (w_1, \ldots, w_n) \in [0,1]^n$ with $\sum_{i=1}^{n} w_i = 1$. The supremum in Equation (1) can be restated as a single-objective expected LRA reward query:

$$\sup_{\sigma \in Str_{\mathcal{M}}} \boldsymbol{w} \cdot \mathrm{Ex}_{\mathcal{M}}^{\sigma}(lra(rew_1), \ldots, lra(rew_n)) = \sup_{\sigma \in Str_{\mathcal{M}}} \mathrm{Ex}_{\mathcal{M}}^{\sigma}(lra(rew_{\boldsymbol{w}}))$$

with $rew_{\boldsymbol{w}}(s,a) = \sum_{i=1}^{n} w_i \cdot rew_i(s,a)$. Consequently, a pure memoryless strategy $\sigma_{\boldsymbol{w}} \in \arg\max_{\sigma \in Str_{\mathcal{M}}} \mathrm{Ex}_{\mathcal{M}}^{\sigma}(lra(rew_{\boldsymbol{w}}))$ attaining the supremum can be computed using standard methods such as value iteration [2,10]. Evaluating the individual objectives w.r.t. $\sigma_{\boldsymbol{w}}$—again using single-objective methods on the induced Markov chain—yields a point $\boldsymbol{p_w} = \left(\mathrm{Ex}_{\mathcal{M}}^{\sigma_{\boldsymbol{w}}}(lra(rew_1)), \ldots, \mathrm{Ex}_{\mathcal{M}}^{\sigma_{\boldsymbol{w}}}(lra(rew_n))\right)$ as in Equation (1). In particular, we derive that $\boldsymbol{p_w}$ is achievable and all achievable points $\boldsymbol{q}$ satisfy $\boldsymbol{w} \cdot \boldsymbol{q} \leq \boldsymbol{w} \cdot \boldsymbol{p_w}$. We can decide Problem 1 by solving WSO (i.e. computing points $\boldsymbol{p_{w_i}}$ as in Equation (1)) for an increasing number of weight vectors $\boldsymbol{w}_1, \boldsymbol{w}_2, \ldots$. The convexity of the set of achievable points yields the following approximation of $Ach_{\mathcal{M}}(\mathfrak{MO})$:

$$DownConv\left(\bigcup_{0 < i \leq n} \{\boldsymbol{p_{w_i}}\}\right) \subseteq Ach_{\mathcal{M}}(\mathfrak{MO}) \subseteq \bigcap_{0 < i \leq n} \{\boldsymbol{q} \in \mathbb{R}^n \mid \boldsymbol{w}_i \cdot \boldsymbol{q} \leq \boldsymbol{w}_i \cdot \boldsymbol{p_{w_i}}\},$$

where $DownConv(P) = \{\boldsymbol{p} \in \mathbb{R}^n \mid \exists \mu \in Dist(P): \boldsymbol{p} \leq \sum_{\boldsymbol{q} \in P} \mu(\boldsymbol{q}) \cdot \boldsymbol{q}\}$ is the downward closure of the convex hull of $P \subseteq \mathbb{R}^n$. Under certain assumptions on the selection of weight vectors, the approximation becomes tight after analyzing finitely many weight vectors and we can decide whether $\boldsymbol{p} \in Ach_{\mathcal{M}}(\mathfrak{MO})$ for a given threshold value point $\boldsymbol{p}$. The number of weight vectors necessary to compute $Ach_\mathcal{M}(\mathfrak{MO})$ exactly can be exponential in the size of the MDP. However, the experiments in, e.g., [21,35,34] and in Section 5 indicate that only a small number of weight vectors suffice to obtain good approximations of $Ach_\mathcal{M}(\mathfrak{MO})$ — commonly outperforming procedures based on linear programming (LP) by several orders of magnitude.

4.2   Reduction to Expected LRA Reward Objectives

For simplicity, we first assume a *weakly communicating* MDP $\mathcal{M}$ with a single maximal end component, i.e., $|Mecs_\mathcal{M}| = 1$. Remark 3 lifts this assumption. We consider n reward functions $rew_1, \ldots, rew_n$ with corresponding expected LRA objectives $\mathfrak{MO}_{lra} = (lra(rew_1), \ldots, lra(rew_n))$ and LRA satisfaction objectives $\mathfrak{MO}^{\boldsymbol{\lambda}}_{lrasat} = (lrasat(rew_1, \lambda_1), \ldots, lrasat(rew_n, \lambda_n))$ parameterized by threshold values $\boldsymbol{\lambda} = (\lambda_1, \ldots, \lambda_n) \in \mathbb{R}^n$. The following results connect achievability of expected LRA rewards and almost-sure LRA satisfaction objectives.

Lemma 1 ([7, Section 5]). *Assume* $|Mecs_\mathcal{M}| = 1$. *For* $\boldsymbol{p} = (p_1, \ldots, p_n) \in \mathbb{R}^n$ *we have*

$$\exists \sigma \in Str_\mathcal{M}: \ \mathrm{Ex}^\sigma_\mathcal{M}(\mathfrak{MO}_{lra}) \geq \boldsymbol{p} \quad \textit{iff} \quad \exists \sigma \in Str_\mathcal{M}: \ \mathrm{Ex}^\sigma_\mathcal{M}(\mathfrak{MO}^{\boldsymbol{p}}_{lrasat}) = 1.$$

Proof (sketch). The claim is shown in [7, Section 5], as a consequence of their Proposition 5.1. $\qquad\square$

Theorem 3. *If* $|Mecs_\mathcal{M}| = 1$, *then* $DownConv(B) = Ach_\mathcal{M}(\mathfrak{MO}^{\boldsymbol{\lambda}}_{lrasat})$ *for*

$$B = \{([\![p_i \geq \lambda_i]\!])_{1 \leq i \leq n} \mid \boldsymbol{p} \in Ach_\mathcal{M}(\mathfrak{MO}_{lra})\} \subseteq \{0,1\}^n.$$

Proof. "$\subseteq$": We show $B \subseteq Ach_\mathcal{M}(\mathfrak{MO}^{\boldsymbol{\lambda}}_{lrasat})$. Containment of $DownConv(B)$ holds because achievable points are downward closed and convex [34, Chapter 3]. Let $\boldsymbol{b} = ([\![p_i \geq \lambda_i]\!])_{1 \leq i \leq n} \in B$ for appropriate $\boldsymbol{p} \in Ach_\mathcal{M}(\mathfrak{MO}_{lra})$. Consider the indices $\{i_1, \ldots, i_k\} = \{i \in \{1, \ldots, n\} \mid b_i = 1\}$ for which $\boldsymbol{b}$ is 1. When restricting to those k objectives, Lemma 1 yields

$$1 \in Ach_\mathcal{M}(lrasat(rew_{i_1}, p_{i_1}), \ldots, lrasat(rew_{i_k}, p_{i_k})).$$

Inserting the remaining objectives yields $b \in Ach_\mathcal{M}(\mathfrak{MO}^{\boldsymbol{\lambda}}_{lrasat})$.

"$\supseteq$": Assume a point $\boldsymbol{p} \in Ach_\mathcal{M}(\mathfrak{MO}^{\boldsymbol{\lambda}}_{lrasat})$ and an achieving strategy $\sigma \in Str_\mathcal{M}$. Consider the distribution $\mu \in Dist(\{0,1\}^n)$, where for $\boldsymbol{b} \in \{0,1\}^n$

$$\mu(\boldsymbol{b}) = \mathrm{Pr}^\sigma_\mathcal{M}\Big(\bigwedge_{1 \leq i \leq n} b_i = 1 \text{ iff } lra(rew_i) \geq \lambda_i\Big).$$

For $1 \leq i \leq n$, we get

$$p_i \leq \mathrm{Ex}^\sigma_\mathcal{M}(lrasat(rew_i, \lambda_i)) = \mathrm{Pr}^\sigma_\mathcal{M}(lra(rew_i) \geq \lambda_i) = \sum_{b \in \{0,1\}^n} b_i \cdot \mu(\boldsymbol{b}),$$

> **Input**   : MDP $\mathcal{M}$ with $|Mecs_{\mathcal{M}}| = 1$, objectives $\mathfrak{MO}^{\lambda}_{lrasat}$ and weights $\boldsymbol{w}$
> **Output** : A point $\boldsymbol{p_w}$ as in Equation (1)
>
> **1** $P \leftarrow \emptyset$ *// Collects achievable points found so far.*
> **2** $H \leftarrow \emptyset$ *// Collects halfspaces that contain all achievable points.*
> **3** $q \leftarrow \boldsymbol{0}$ *// Current candidate point, initialized arbitrarily.*
> **4** **while** there are weights $\boldsymbol{w}'$ such that $\forall \boldsymbol{p} \in P : \boldsymbol{w}' \cdot \boldsymbol{p} < \boldsymbol{w}' \cdot \boldsymbol{q}$ **do**
> **5** $\boldsymbol{p}' \leftarrow \mathsf{WSO}(\mathcal{M}, \mathfrak{MO}_{lra}, \boldsymbol{w}')$ *// Answer WSO for exp. LRA query.*
> **6** $P \leftarrow P \cup \{\boldsymbol{p}'\}$; $H \leftarrow H \cup \{(\boldsymbol{w}', \boldsymbol{w}' \cdot \boldsymbol{p}')\}$ *// Refine approximation.*
> **7** $\boldsymbol{q} \leftarrow \arg\max_{\boldsymbol{p} \in A} \sum_{1 \le i \le n} w_i \cdot \lceil p_i \ge \lambda_i \rceil$ *// Update candidate point.*
> **8**   using $A = \bigcap_{(\boldsymbol{w}', c) \in H} \{\boldsymbol{p} \in \mathbb{R}^n \mid \boldsymbol{w}' \cdot \boldsymbol{p} \le c\}$
>
> **9** **return** $\boldsymbol{p_w} = (\lceil q_i \ge \lambda_i \rceil)_{1 \le i \le n}$

Algorithm 1: Answering WSO Queries for Weakly Communicating MDPs

where the last equality is valid as we split the event "$lra(rew_i) \ge \lambda_i$" into disjoint subsets. Lifting to the n-dimensional case yields $\boldsymbol{p} \le \sum_{\boldsymbol{b} \in \{0,1\}^n} \mu(\boldsymbol{b}) \cdot \boldsymbol{b}$. To finally prove $\boldsymbol{p} \in DownConv(B)$, it remains to show that $supp(\mu) \subseteq B$. To this end, assume $\mu(\boldsymbol{b}) > 0$. Intuitively, the strategy σ reaches (with positive probability) an EC in which the corresponding LRA rewards are collected. Since $\mathcal{M}$ only has a single MEC, we can also reach such an EC almost surely, implying that there is a strategy $\sigma_{\boldsymbol{b}}$ with $\mathrm{Pr}^{\sigma_{\boldsymbol{b}}}_{\mathcal{M}} \big(\bigwedge_{1 \le i \le n} b_i = 1 \text{ iff } lra(rew_i) \ge \lambda_i \big) = 1$. See [7, Proposition 5.1] for a more formal proof of this claim. For all $1 \le i \le n$, we get $b_i = \mathrm{Pr}^{\sigma_{\boldsymbol{b}}}_{\mathcal{M}}(lra(rew_i) \ge \lambda_i) \in \{0, 1\}$ and therefore $\mathrm{Ex}^{\sigma_{\boldsymbol{b}}}_{\mathcal{M}}(lra(rew_i)) \ge \lambda$ iff $b_i = 1$. The strategy $\sigma_{\boldsymbol{b}}$ thus achieves a point $\boldsymbol{q} \in Ach_{\mathcal{M}}(\mathfrak{MO}_{lra})$ with $\boldsymbol{b} = (\lceil q_i \ge \lambda_i \rceil)_{1 \le i \le n}$, yielding $\boldsymbol{b} \in B$. $\square$

Algorithm 1 outlines our procedure for WSO—i.e. for computing $\boldsymbol{p_w}$ as in Equation (1)—with LRA satisfaction objectives in MDPs with a single MEC. The approach is to approximate $Ach_{\mathcal{M}}(\mathfrak{MO}_{lra})$ and apply Theorem 3 to translate that to an approximation of the set $Ach_{\mathcal{M}}(\mathfrak{MO}^{\lambda}_{lrasat})$. The algorithm maintains a set of points P and a set of halfspaces H that represent an approximation of $Ach_{\mathcal{M}}(\mathfrak{MO}_{lra})$ as explained in Section 4.1. In addition, we consider a point $\boldsymbol{q}$ that—at the end of the loop body—maximizes the weighted sum $\sum_{1 \le i \le n} w_i \cdot \lceil q_i \ge \lambda_i \rceil$ among all points in the set A from Line 8. Since $Ach_{\mathcal{M}}(\mathfrak{MO}_{lra}) \subseteq A$, Theorem 3 yields that $\boldsymbol{w} \cdot \boldsymbol{p_w} \ge \sup_{\sigma} \boldsymbol{w} \cdot \mathrm{Ex}^{\sigma}_{\mathcal{M}}(\mathfrak{MO}^{\lambda}_{lrasat})$ for the returned point $\boldsymbol{p_w}$. Achievability of $\boldsymbol{p_w}$ is ensured by the termination criterion in Line 4. More precisely, we check whether there is a halfspace $\{\boldsymbol{p} \in \mathbb{R}^n \mid \boldsymbol{w}' \cdot \boldsymbol{p} \le c\}$ that (i) contains all achievable points collected in the set P so far but (ii) does not contain the current candidate point $\boldsymbol{q}$. If no such halfspace exists, we know that $\boldsymbol{q} \in DownConv(P) \subseteq Ach_{\mathcal{M}}(\mathfrak{MO}_{lra})$ by the *separating hyperplane theorem* [21, Proposition 3]. Otherwise, we can use its normal vector $\boldsymbol{w}'$ as a new weight vector to refine the approximation. The computations in Lines 4, 7 and 8 can be implemented using (mixed integer) linear programming. Algorithm 1 is guaranteed to terminate provided that the WSO instances in

Line 5 are solved exactly and that the weight vectors $\boldsymbol{w}$ are selected according to suitable heuristics [21,35].

Remark 3 (General MDPs). The lifting of our approach to MDPs with more than one MEC (multichain MDPs) is analogous to the approach for expected LRA reward objectives outlined in [35, Section 4.3]. Given an MDP $\mathcal{M}$ with LRA satisfaction objectives $\mathfrak{MO}_{lrasat}$ and weights $\boldsymbol{w}$, we solve the corresponding instance for WSO as follows.

- For each MEC $\mathcal{E} \in Mecs_{\mathcal{M}}$ apply Algorithm 1 to the restricted MDP $\mathcal{M}_{\mathcal{E}}$, yielding a point $\boldsymbol{p}_{w}^{\mathcal{E}}$.
- Construct the MEC quotient $\mathcal{M}'$ obtained by collapsing each MEC $\mathcal{E}$ of $\mathcal{M}$ into a single state $s^{\mathcal{E}}$ and introducing a new transition $s^{\mathcal{E}} \xrightarrow{\perp} s^{\perp}$ to a fresh bottom state $s^{\perp}$.
- Answer WSO on the MEC quotient $\mathcal{M}'$, using weights $\boldsymbol{w}$ and total reward objectives $(tot(rew'_1), \ldots, tot(rew'_n))$ for the reward functions $rew'_i(s, a) = \left[\exists \mathcal{E} \in Mecs_{\mathcal{M}} \colon s = s^{\mathcal{E}} \text{ and } a = \perp \right] \cdot (\boldsymbol{p}_{w}^{\mathcal{E}})_i$.

Further details are provided in [35], which also handles combinations of expected LRA and total reward objectives.

In summary, multi-objective achievability (Problem 1) and Pareto queries with arbitrary mixtures of total reward, LTL, expected LRA, and LRA satisfaction objectives are solved as follows:

- Reduce LTL objectives to total reward objectives as discussed in Section 3.
- Employ the approach of [35] for total reward and LRA objectives.
- When analyzing MECs (as part of the approach of [35]), apply Algorithm 1 for handling LRA satisfaction objectives.

Our procedures compute finite-memory strategies which—based on Theorem 1, Lemma 1, and related works [20,29,7]—can be lifted to infinite-memory strategies that ensure achievability.

5   Experimental Evaluation

Implementation details. We extend the implementation of [35] for multiple LRA expectation and total reward objectives in the STORM model checker [26], building on top of version 1.11. Our implementation uses explicit data structures such as matrices and vectors. The MDP can be given in the PRISM [30] or JANI [9] modeling formats. Following Remark 1, we first translate LTL formulas to deterministic generalized Rabin automata using SPOT version 2.14.1 [15] and build a standard product MDP with Rabin objectives [4]. Then, we apply demerging of MECs as outlined in Section 3 to obtain an MDP with total reward objectives. Finally, STORM applies collapsing of 0-ECs in which no total reward is collected. See [35] for details. Qualitative LTL objectives are treated as a special case as outlined in Remark 2. Towards LRA satisfaction objectives, we use

Table 1: Results for Mixture of LTL and LRA Expectation Objectives

Benchmark			Data						Runtime	
Model	Par.	#lra/ltl	$|S_{in}|$	$|S_{dem}|$	$|\mathbf{P}_{dem}|$	$|Mecs|$	$|S_{mec}|$	#iter	STORM	MG2
csnfail	3	1-1	605	1605	3427	112	1000	4	<1	10.3
csnfail	4	1-1	3439	9277	$2 \cdot 10^4$	526	5838	4	1.43	TO
csnfail	5	1-1	$2 \cdot 10^4$	$5 \cdot 10^4$	$1 \cdot 10^5$	2344	$3 \cdot 10^4$	4	56.2	TO
grid-det	128	3-1	$2 \cdot 10^4$	$3 \cdot 10^4$	$1 \cdot 10^5$	1	$2 \cdot 10^4$	1	<1	103
grid-det	128	3-1	$2 \cdot 10^4$	$5 \cdot 10^4$	$2 \cdot 10^5$	3	$3 \cdot 10^4$	4	<1	NS
grid-det	128	3-1	$2 \cdot 10^4$	$5 \cdot 10^4$	$2 \cdot 10^5$	2	$3 \cdot 10^4$	4	<1	59.4
grid-det	128	3-1	$3 \cdot 10^4$	$7 \cdot 10^4$	$3 \cdot 10^5$	5	$4 \cdot 10^4$	4	1.45	1282
grid-rnd	64	3-1	7143	$1 \cdot 10^4$	$4 \cdot 10^4$	1	4096	1	<1	<1
grid-rnd	64	3-1	4096	$1 \cdot 10^4$	$5 \cdot 10^4$	2	8192	6	441	2.4
grid-rnd	64	3-1	$1 \cdot 10^4$	$2 \cdot 10^4$	$7 \cdot 10^4$	2	8192	?	TO	6.03
grid-rnd	64	3-1	$1 \cdot 10^4$	$2 \cdot 10^4$	$7 \cdot 10^4$	2	8192	?	TO	21.8
mer	3	1-1	$2 \cdot 10^4$	$3 \cdot 10^4$	$8 \cdot 10^4$	9451	$1 \cdot 10^4$	1	<1	132
mer	4	1-1	$1 \cdot 10^5$	$2 \cdot 10^5$	$8 \cdot 10^5$	$7 \cdot 10^4$	$1 \cdot 10^5$	1	1.83	MO
mer	5	1-1	?	?	?	?	?	?	MO	MO
phil	3	1-1	1602	2716	7560	3	1114	4	<1	<1
phil	3	1-3	8526	$2 \cdot 10^4$	$4 \cdot 10^4$	27	7432	23	9.16	NS
phil	4	1-1	$2 \cdot 10^4$	$4 \cdot 10^4$	$1 \cdot 10^5$	3	$2 \cdot 10^4$	4	1.4	40.8
phil	4	1-4	$2 \cdot 10^5$	$4 \cdot 10^5$	$1 \cdot 10^6$	81	$2 \cdot 10^5$	?	TO	NS
phil	5	1-1	$2 \cdot 10^5$	$4 \cdot 10^5$	$2 \cdot 10^6$	3	$2 \cdot 10^5$	4	42.9	MO
phil	5	1-1	?	?	?	?	?	?	MO	NS
resources	3-3	2-1	587	1048	3182	1	461	5	<1	NS
resources	5-5	2-1	2618	4323	$1 \cdot 10^4$	1	1705	5	<1	NS
resources	10-10	2-1	$4 \cdot 10^4$	$6 \cdot 10^4$	$2 \cdot 10^5$	1	$2 \cdot 10^4$	9	69.6	NS
resources	15-15	2-1	$2 \cdot 10^5$	$3 \cdot 10^5$	$1 \cdot 10^6$	1	$1 \cdot 10^5$	7	1212	MO
resources	20-20	2-1	?	?	?	?	?	?	?	MO
sensors	2	1-1	7860	9093	$3 \cdot 10^4$	8	1233	3	<1	2.84
sensors	3	1-1	$8 \cdot 10^4$	$9 \cdot 10^4$	$4 \cdot 10^5$	38	8977	4	2.6	470

weighted sum optimization as in Algorithm 1 to obtain the achievable trade-offs in each MEC $\mathcal{E}$. We cache the obtained sets (P, H) for each MEC to speed up invocations for different weights $\boldsymbol{w}$. Single-objective expected long-run average reward computations within MECs are conducted using value iteration [2,10]. Single-objective expected total rewards are computed using optimistic value iteration [25]. For both, we use STORM's default precision parameter $\varepsilon = 10^{-6}$. Similarly, for approximations of achievable points (e.g. Pareto curves), we used STORM's default precision of $\eta = 10^{-4}$.

Benchmarks We consider 7 benchmark MDP models from the literature: csnfail (client-server mutual exclusion protocol [28]), grid-det (grid world with deterministic transitions [5,40]), grid-rnd (grid world with random transitions [5,40]), mer (resource arbiter for mars exploration rover [17,1]), phil (randomized dining philosophers [30]), resources (resource gathering grid world [6,35]), and sensors (sensor network [28]). Each model is instantiated with different parameters, yielding a total of 18 concrete MDPs. For the multi-objective queries, we consider combinations of LTL and LRA expectation or satisfaction objectives that either already appear in related works [8,35,1,5] or—if that was not applicable—were formulated by us. In contrast to Problem 1, our queries only specify a threshold value p_i for a strict, potentially empty, subset of the objectives and ask for

Table 2: Results for Mixtures of all Objectives

Benchmark			Data						Runtime
Model	Par.	#lra/ltl/lrs	$|S_{in}|$	$|S_{dem}|$	$|\mathbf{P}_{dem}|$	$|Mecs|$	$|S_{mec}|$	#iter	STORM
csnfail	3	0-0-3	184	177	427	38	158	13	3.73
csnfail	4	0-0-4	960	945	2753	176	880	38	557
csnfail	5	0-0-5	4864	4833	$2 \cdot 10^4$	782	4622	?	TO
mer	3	1-0-2	$2 \cdot 10^4$	$2 \cdot 10^4$	$6 \cdot 10^4$	9451	$1 \cdot 10^4$	9	496
mer	4	1-0-2	$1 \cdot 10^5$	$1 \cdot 10^5$	$5 \cdot 10^5$	$7 \cdot 10^4$	$1 \cdot 10^5$	9	2354
mer	5	1-0-2	$8 \cdot 10^5$	$8 \cdot 10^5$	$4 \cdot 10^6$	$5 \cdot 10^5$	$8 \cdot 10^5$	?	TO
phil	3	0-1-1	1602	2716	7560	3	1114	3	< 1
phil	4	0-1-1	$2 \cdot 10^4$	$4 \cdot 10^4$	$1 \cdot 10^5$	3	$2 \cdot 10^4$	3	1.02
phil	5	0-1-1	$2 \cdot 10^5$	$4 \cdot 10^5$	$2 \cdot 10^6$	3	$2 \cdot 10^5$	3	31
resources	3–3	2-0-2	587	587	1890	1	587	13	< 1
resources	3–3	2-1-2	587	1635	5073	2	1048	33	48.9
resources	5–5	2-0-2	2618	2618	8577	1	2618	39	13.9
resources	5–5	2-1-2	2618	6941	$2 \cdot 10^4$	2	4323	86	6239
resources	10–10	2-0-2	$4 \cdot 10^4$	$4 \cdot 10^4$	$1 \cdot 10^5$	1	$4 \cdot 10^4$	13	9.63
resources	10–10	2-1-2	$4 \cdot 10^4$	$1 \cdot 10^5$	$3 \cdot 10^5$	2	$6 \cdot 10^4$	24	113
resources	15–15	2-0-2	$2 \cdot 10^5$	$2 \cdot 10^5$	$7 \cdot 10^5$	1	$2 \cdot 10^5$	5	2182
resources	15–15	2-1-2	$2 \cdot 10^5$	$5 \cdot 10^5$	$2 \cdot 10^6$	2	$3 \cdot 10^5$	10	4975
resources	20–20	2-0-2	$8 \cdot 10^5$	$8 \cdot 10^5$	$2 \cdot 10^6$	1	$8 \cdot 10^5$	9	661
sensors	2	0-0-3	7860	7855	$2 \cdot 10^4$	3996	6105	13	158
sensors	3	0-0-3	$8 \cdot 10^4$	$8 \cdot 10^4$	$3 \cdot 10^5$	$5 \cdot 10^4$	$7 \cdot 10^4$	13	1971

(Pareto-)optimal achievable values for the remaining objectives. A complete list of the exercised multi-objective queries is given in [27].

Experimental set-up. We compare our implementation in STORM with a reference implementation of the linear-programming-based approach of [29] in MULTI-GAIN 2.0 [5] using GUROBI [23]. Both implementations are invoked with a PRISM description of the input MDP and a multi-objective query. We measure the wall-time it takes for the tool to solve the query (excluding model construction times[4]). Executions are aborted after 2h or when they require more than 32 GB of memory. All experiments were run on a ROCKY Linux 9.6 system using 8 cores of an Intel Xeon 8468 Sapphire (2.1 GHz) CPU.

Results. Tables 1 and 2 summarize our results. Table 1 focuses on combinations of LTL and expected LRA reward objectives and a comparison with MULTI-GAIN 2.0. Table 2 also considers LRA satisfaction objectives which are not supported in MULTIGAIN 2.0. The first three columns of each table depict the benchmark instance given by model name, parameters, and the number of involved expected LRA reward, LTL, and LRA satisfaction objectives. The next five columns provide additional data for the benchmark instance, consisting of the number of states of the input model after applying the translation from LTL to Rabin objectives (Remark 1) as well as the number of states, enabled state-action pairs, MECs, and states inside MECs of the demerged MDP (Definition 6). The latter indicates how many states are relevant for LRA reward analysis. We then provide for STORM the number of instances of Equation (1)

---

[4] Excluded model construction time refers to translating the PRISM model into an explicit MDP; reported times include building the product with the automaton.

that were checked to solve the respective queries as well as the wall-clock time for solving the query. The last column of Table 1 shows the model checking time of MULTIGAIN 2.0. TO and MO indicate situations where the computation required more than 2 hours of time and more than 32 GB of memory, respectively. MULTIGAIN 2.0 did not support some instances (indicated by NS): (i) for grid-det, an SCC decomposition triggered a stack overflow, (ii) for phil, the instances with more than one LTL objective were not supported, and (iii) for resources an error[5] was thrown.

Discussion. STORM produces results for large instances with hundreds of thousands of states and two to five objectives. In most cases, our iterative approach required only a handful iterations and outperformed the LP-based approach by at least one order of magnitude. The grid-rnd benchmarks made an exception: we noticed that the value iteration-based procedures of STORM converged very slowly, likely because of the cyclic structure of the model. For the instances we tested, demerging increases the number of states of the model by a factor of approximately 2 to 3.

6 Conclusion

We presented a framework for verifying MDPs against combinations of ω-regular objectives—represented as Rabin objectives—and LRA objectives. The core idea is to *demerge* accepting end components and encode Rabin satisfaction as total-reward objectives on the resulting demerged MDP. This reduction allows us to use iterative solution methods for LRA/total-reward objectives instead of LP encodings. For LRA *satisfaction* queries, we present an approach based on weighted-sum optimization, which permits solving multi-objective achievability problems by a sequence of single-objective iterative solves (e.g., value iteration). Our implementation scales to models with several hundred thousand states and typically outperforms an LP-based reference implementation, while also supporting LRA satisfaction queries. Future work is to investigate practical representations of the resulting (potentially infinite-memory) strategies and their approximation by finite-memory strategies. Further directions include empirically comparing with LDBA-based LTL translations (thus avoiding demerging) within STORM and exploring possible applications such as assume-guarantee reasoning [31].

Data availability statement. The artifact [27] contains all model files, multi-objective queries, logfiles, our implementation in STORM, and scripts to reproduce the experiments. It is available at DOI 10.5281/zenodo.18194070.

References

1. Andriushchenko, R., Bork, A., Budde, C.E., Ceska, M., Grover, K., Hahn, E.M., Hartmanns, A., Israelsen, B., Jansen, N., Jeppson, J., Junges, S., Köhl, M.A.,

---

[5] The error message was `GRBException: Unable to retrieve attribute 'X'.`

Könighofer, B., Křetínský, J., Meggendorfer, T., Parker, D., Pranger, S., Quatmann, T., Ruijters, E., Taylor, L., Volk, M., Weininger, M., Zhang, Z.: Tools at the frontiers of quantitative verification - QComp 2023 competition report. In: TOOLympics@ETAPS. Lecture Notes in Computer Science, vol. 14550, pp. 90–146. Springer (2023). `https://doi.org/10.1007/978-3-031-67695-6_4`

2. Ashok, P., Chatterjee, K., Daca, P., Kretínský, J., Meggendorfer, T.: Value iteration for long-run average reward in Markov decision processes. In: Majumdar, R., Kuncak, V. (eds.) Computer Aided Verification - 29th International Conference, CAV 2017, Heidelberg, Germany, July 24-28, 2017, Proceedings, Part I. Lecture Notes in Computer Science, vol. 10426, pp. 201–221. Springer (2017). `https://doi.org/10.1007/978-3-319-63387-9_10`

3. Baier, C., Chau, C., Klüppelholz, S.: Certificates and witnesses for multi-objective queries in Markov decision processes. Perform. Evaluation **168**, 102482 (2025). `https://doi.org/10.1016/J.PEVA.2025.102482`

4. Baier, C., Katoen, J.: Principles of model checking. MIT Press (2008)

5. Bals, S., Evangelidis, A., Kretínský, J., Waibel, J.: MULTIGAIN 2.0: MDP controller synthesis for multiple mean-payoff, LTL and steady-state constraints. In: Ábrahám, E., Jr., M.M. (eds.) Proceedings of the 27th ACM International Conference on Hybrid Systems: Computation and Control, HSCC 2024, Hong Kong SAR, China, May 14-16, 2024. pp. 24:1–24:7. ACM (2024). `https://doi.org/10.1145/3641513.3650135`

6. Barrett, L., Narayanan, S.: Learning all optimal policies with multiple criteria. In: ICML. ACM International Conference Proceeding Series, vol. 307, pp. 41–47. ACM (2008). `https://doi.org/10.1145/1390156.1390162`

7. Brázdil, T., Brozek, V., Chatterjee, K., Forejt, V., Kucera, A.: Markov decision processes with multiple long-run average objectives. Log. Methods Comput. Sci. **10**(1) (2014). `https://doi.org/10.2168/LMCS-10(1:13)2014`

8. Brázdil, T., Chatterjee, K., Forejt, V., Kucera, A.: MultiGain: A controller synthesis tool for MDPs with multiple mean-payoff objectives. In: TACAS. Lecture Notes in Computer Science, vol. 9035, pp. 181–187. Springer (2015). `https://doi.org/10.1007/978-3-662-46681-0_12`

9. Budde, C.E., Dehnert, C., Hahn, E.M., Hartmanns, A., Junges, S., Turrini, A.: JANI: quantitative model and tool interaction. In: TACAS (2). Lecture Notes in Computer Science, vol. 10206, pp. 151–168 (2017). `https://doi.org/10.1007/978-3-662-54580-5_9`

10. Butkova, Y., Wimmer, R., Hermanns, H.: Long-run rewards for Markov automata. In: TACAS (2). Lecture Notes in Computer Science, vol. 10206, pp. 188–203 (2017). `https://doi.org/10.1007/978-3-662-54580-5_11`

11. Chatterjee, K., Kretínská, Z., Kretínský, J.: Unifying two views on multiple mean-payoff objectives in Markov decision processes. Log. Methods Comput. Sci. **13**(2) (2017). `https://doi.org/10.23638/LMCS-13(2:15)2017`

12. Chen, T., Kwiatkowska, M.Z., Simaitis, A., Wiltsche, C.: Synthesis for multi-objective stochastic games: An application to autonomous urban driving. In: Joshi, K.R., Siegle, M., Stoelinga, M., D'Argenio, P.R. (eds.) Quantitative Evaluation of Systems - 10th International Conference, QEST 2013, Buenos Aires, Argentina, August 27-30, 2013. Proceedings. Lecture Notes in Computer Science, vol. 8054, pp. 322–337. Springer (2013). `https://doi.org/10.1007/978-3-642-40196-1_28`

13. Chen, Y., Tumova, J., Belta, C.: LTL robot motion control based on automata learning of environmental dynamics. In: IEEE International Conference on Robotics and Automation, ICRA 2012, 14-18 May, 2012, St. Paul, Minnesota, USA. pp. 5177–5182. IEEE (2012). `https://doi.org/10.1109/ICRA.2012.6225075`

14. Ding, X.C., Smith, S.L., Belta, C., Rus, D.: MDP optimal control under temporal logic constraints. In: 50th IEEE Conference on Decision and Control and European Control Conference, 11th European Control Conference, CDC/ECC 2011, Orlando, FL, USA, December 12-15, 2011. pp. 532–538. IEEE (2011). https://doi.org/10.1109/CDC.2011.6161122
15. Duret-Lutz, A., Renault, E., Colange, M., Renkin, F., Aisse, A.G., Schlehuber-Caissier, P., Medioni, T., Martin, A., Dubois, J., Gillard, C., Lauko, H.: From spot 2.0 to spot 2.10: What's new? In: CAV (2). Lecture Notes in Computer Science, vol. 13372, pp. 174–187. Springer (2022). https://doi.org/10.1007/978-3-031-13188-2_9
16. Etessami, K., Kwiatkowska, M.Z., Vardi, M.Y., Yannakakis, M.: Multi-objective model checking of Markov decision processes. Log. Methods Comput. Sci. 4(4) (2008). https://doi.org/10.2168/LMCS-4(4:8)2008
17. Feng, L., Kwiatkowska, M.Z., Parker, D.: Automated learning of probabilistic assumptions for compositional reasoning. In: FASE. Lecture Notes in Computer Science, vol. 6603, pp. 2–17. Springer (2011). https://doi.org/10.1007/978-3-642-19811-3_2
18. Feng, L., Wiltsche, C., Humphrey, L.R., Topcu, U.: Controller synthesis for autonomous systems interacting with human operators. In: ICCPS. pp. 70–79. ACM (2015). https://doi.org/10.1145/2735960.2735973
19. Filar, J.A., Krass, D., Ross, K.: Percentile performance criteria for limiting average Markov decision processes. IEEE Trans. Autom. Control. 40(1), 2–10 (1995). https://doi.org/10.1109/9.362904
20. Forejt, V., Kwiatkowska, M.Z., Norman, G., Parker, D., Qu, H.: Quantitative multi-objective verification for probabilistic systems. In: Abdulla, P.A., Leino, K.R.M. (eds.) Tools and Algorithms for the Construction and Analysis of Systems - 17th International Conference, TACAS 2011, Held as Part of the Joint European Conferences on Theory and Practice of Software, ETAPS 2011, Saarbrücken, Germany, March 26-April 3, 2011. Proceedings. Lecture Notes in Computer Science, vol. 6605, pp. 112–127. Springer (2011). https://doi.org/10.1007/978-3-642-19835-9_11
21. Forejt, V., Kwiatkowska, M.Z., Parker, D.: Pareto curves for probabilistic model checking. In: Chakraborty, S., Mukund, M. (eds.) Automated Technology for Verification and Analysis - 10th International Symposium, ATVA 2012, Thiruvananthapuram, India, October 3-6, 2012. Proceedings. Lecture Notes in Computer Science, vol. 7561, pp. 317–332. Springer (2012). https://doi.org/10.1007/978-3-642-33386-6_25
22. Guo, M., Zavlanos, M.M.: Probabilistic motion planning under temporal tasks and soft constraints. IEEE Trans. Autom. Control. 63(12), 4051–4066 (2018). https://doi.org/10.1109/TAC.2018.2799561
23. Gurobi Optimization, LLC: Gurobi Optimizer Reference Manual (2025), https://www.gurobi.com
24. Hartmanns, A., Junges, S., Quatmann, T., Weininger, M.: A practitioner's guide to MDP model checking algorithms. In: TACAS (1). Lecture Notes in Computer Science, vol. 13993, pp. 469–488. Springer (2023). https://doi.org/10.1007/978-3-031-30823-9_24
25. Hartmanns, A., Kaminski, B.L.: Optimistic value iteration. In: CAV (2). Lecture Notes in Computer Science, vol. 12225, pp. 488–511. Springer (2020). https://doi.org/10.1007/978-3-030-53291-8_26
26. Hensel, C., Junges, S., Katoen, J., Quatmann, T., Volk, M.: The probabilistic model checker Storm. Int. J. Softw. Tools Technol. Transf. 24(4), 589–610 (2022). https://doi.org/10.1007/S10009-021-00633-Z

27. Ide, J., Katoen, J.P., Mertens, H., Quatmann, T.: Artifact for paper: Multiple long-run and omega-regular objectives in MDPs. Zenodo (2026). `https://doi.org/10.5281/zenodo.18194069`

28. Komuravelli, A., Pasareanu, C.S., Clarke, E.M.: Assume-guarantee abstraction refinement for probabilistic systems. In: CAV. Lecture Notes in Computer Science, vol. 7358, pp. 310–326. Springer (2012). `https://doi.org/10.1007/978-3-642-31424-7_25`

29. Kretínský, J.: LTL-constrained steady-state policy synthesis. In: Zhou, Z. (ed.) Proceedings of the Thirtieth International Joint Conference on Artificial Intelligence, IJCAI 2021, Virtual Event / Montreal, Canada, 19-27 August 2021. pp. 4104–4111. ijcai.org (2021). `https://doi.org/10.24963/IJCAI.2021/565`

30. Kwiatkowska, M.Z., Norman, G., Parker, D.: PRISM 4.0: Verification of probabilistic real-time systems. In: CAV. Lecture Notes in Computer Science, vol. 6806, pp. 585–591. Springer (2011). `https://doi.org/10.1007/978-3-642-22110-1_47`

31. Kwiatkowska, M.Z., Norman, G., Parker, D., Qu, H.: Assume-guarantee verification for probabilistic systems. In: TACAS. Lecture Notes in Computer Science, vol. 6015, pp. 23–37. Springer (2010). `https://doi.org/10.1007/978-3-642-12002-2_3`

32. Pnueli, A.: The temporal logic of programs. In: FOCS. pp. 46–57. IEEE Computer Society (1977). `https://doi.org/10.1109/SFCS.1977.32`

33. Puterman, M.L.: Markov Decision Processes: Discrete Stochastic Dynamic Programming. Wiley Series in Probability and Statistics, Wiley (1994). `https://doi.org/10.1002/9780470316887`

34. Quatmann, T.: Verification of multi-objective Markov models. Ph.D. thesis, RWTH Aachen University, Germany (2023), `https://publications.rwth-aachen.de/record/971553`

35. Quatmann, T., Katoen, J.: Multi-objective optimization of long-run average and total rewards. In: Groote, J.F., Larsen, K.G. (eds.) Tools and Algorithms for the Construction and Analysis of Systems - 27th International Conference, TACAS 2021, Held as Part of the European Joint Conferences on Theory and Practice of Software, ETAPS 2021, Luxembourg City, Luxembourg, March 27 - April 1, 2021, Proceedings, Part I. Lecture Notes in Computer Science, vol. 12651, pp. 230–249. Springer (2021). `https://doi.org/10.1007/978-3-030-72016-2_13`

36. Randour, M., Raskin, J., Sankur, O.: Percentile queries in multi-dimensional Markov decision processes. Formal Methods Syst. Des. **50**(2-3), 207–248 (2017). `https://doi.org/10.1007/S10703-016-0262-7`

37. Sickert, S., Esparza, J., Jaax, S., Kretínský, J.: Limit-deterministic Büchi automata for linear temporal logic. In: Chaudhuri, S., Farzan, A. (eds.) Computer Aided Verification - 28th International Conference, CAV 2016, Toronto, ON, Canada, July 17-23, 2016, Proceedings, Part II. Lecture Notes in Computer Science, vol. 9780, pp. 312–332. Springer (2016). `https://doi.org/10.1007/978-3-319-41540-6_17`

38. Svorenová, M., Cerna, I., Belta, C.: Optimal control of MDPs with temporal logic constraints. In: Proceedings of the 52nd IEEE Conference on Decision and Control, CDC 2013, Florence, Italy, December 10-13, 2013. pp. 3938–3943. IEEE (2013). `https://doi.org/10.1109/CDC.2013.6760491`

39. Svoreňová, M., Cerná, I., Belta, C.: Optimal receding horizon control for finite deterministic systems with temporal logic constraints. In: American Control Conference, ACC 2013, Washington, DC, USA, June 17-19, 2013. pp. 4399–4404. IEEE (2013). `https://doi.org/10.1109/ACC.2013.6580517`

40. Velasquez, A., Alkhouri, I., Beckus, A., Trivedi, A., Atia, G.K.: Controller synthesis for omega-regular and steady-state specifications. In: AAMAS. pp. 1310–1318. International Foundation for Autonomous Agents and Multiagent Systems (IFAAMAS) (2022). https://doi.org/10.5555/3535850.3535996

Computing Fixpoints of Learned Functions: Chaotic Iteration and Simple Stochastic Games

Paolo Baldan[1], Sebastian Gurke[2], Barbara König[2], and Florian Wittbold[2]

[1] Department of Mathematics, University of Padua, Italy
`baldan@math.unipd.it`
[2] Universität Duisburg-Essen
`{sebastian.gurke,barbara_koenig,florian.wittbold}@uni-due.de`

Abstract. The problem of determining the (least) fixpoint of (higher-dimensional) functions over the non-negative reals frequently occurs when dealing with systems endowed with a quantitative semantics. We focus on the situation in which the functions of interest are not known precisely but can only be approximated. As a first contribution we generalize an iteration scheme called dampened Mann iteration, recently introduced in the literature. The improved scheme relaxes previous constraints on parameter sequences, allowing learning rates to converge to zero or not converge at all. While seemingly minor, this flexibility is essential to enable the implementation of chaotic iterations, where only a subset of components is updated in each step, allowing to tackle higher-dimensional problems. Additionally, by allowing learning rates to converge to zero, we can relax conditions on the convergence speed of function approximations, making the method more adaptable to various scenarios. We also show that dampened Mann iteration applies immediately to compute the expected payoff in various probabilistic models, including simple stochastic games, not covered by previous work.

1   Introduction

This paper focuses on the problem of identifying fixpoint iteration schemes for determining the (least) fixpoint of a d-dimensional function f on the reals in scenarios where this function is not known precisely, but can only be approximated. Concretely, we assume to be able to construct a sequence of approximating functions $f_1, f_2, f_3, \ldots$ that converges to f. The problem is non-trivial for a number of reasons, starting from the fact that the least fixpoint operator is not necessarily continuous and hence the sequence of least fixpoints of the functions f_n does not always converge to the least fixpoint of f.

This task can be seen as an abstract formulation of the problem that occurs in reinforcement learning, where a Markov Decision Process (MDP) – a transition system based on probabilistic and non-deterministic branching as well as rewards – is given and the aim is to determine the expected return and the optimal strategy to achieve it. In a real-world scenario the probabilities (and possibly

S. Junges and G. Katz (Eds.): TACAS 2026, LNCS 16505, pp. 547–565, 2026.
https://doi.org/10.1007/978-3-032-22752-2_28

the rewards) of such MDPs are often not known, but can only be determined by exploring the MDP and sampling. Reinforcement learning algorithms such as Q-learning [22], SARSA [17] or Dyna-Q [18,19,12] typically proceed by interleaving exploration of the MDP and strategy computation. These algorithms can be classified as model-based (e.g., Dyna-Q) – where the (approximated) MDP is explicitly computed – and model-free (e.g., SARSA, Q-learning) – where updates are not dependent on the estimated probabilities, but on the current sample.

Indeed, the expected return of a (finite state) MDP can be characterized as the least fixpoint of a function based on the Bellman equation. This function is monotone with respect to the pointwise order on tuples and non-expansive (1-Lipschitz) with respect to the supremum metric, i.e., function application does not increase the distance of two points in the space. The fact that the same happens for a number of other fixpoint equations of interest (e.g., for computing payoffs for simple stochastic games [8] and for behavioural metrics [1]) leads us to develop our theory for monotone and non-expansive functions.

In [3], we proposed a solution to this problem: instead of computing fixpoints via Kleene iteration – as common for such models – the idea is to perform a so-called dampened Mann iteration that adds a dampening factor to the well-known Mann iteration [6]. Concretely the following iteration schema is proposed:

$$x_{n+1} = (1 - \beta_n) \cdot (x_n + \alpha_n \cdot (f_n(x_n) - x_n))$$

The parameter α_n, often referred to as the learning rate, is used to take a weighted sum between the previous value and the value obtained by applying the n-th approximated function, making the iteration more robust with respect to perturbations. A central ingredient is the dampening factor $1 - \beta_n$, inspired by [14]. Its purpose is to decrease a value that for some reasons might over-estimate the least fixpoint. This is essential when the function of interest admits more than one fixpoint and the iteration in early phases can get stuck at a fixpoint that is not the least. According to [3], the parameters α_n, β_n have to be chosen such that α_n converges to 1 (the iteration scheme converges to a Kleene iteration) and β_n converges to 0 (the dampening is vanishing over time). For most results the first condition can be relaxed to α_n converging to some $\alpha > 0$.

Then, the sequence x_n generated by the above iteration scheme is guaranteed to converge to the least fixpoint of f in a number of situations: when the function f is a (power) contraction, when the the sequence (f_n) converges monotonically to f and when (f_n) converges normally. The latter means that $\sum_n \|f - f_n\| < \infty$ (where $\| \cdot \|$ is the supremum norm), a condition which can always be enforced by "speeding" up the iteration and determining a function g such that $f_{g(i)}$ converges fast enough and thus normally. For instance, consider the sequence of functions $f_n(x) = 1/n + (1 - 1/n) \cdot x$ converging to the identity $f(x) = x$. It can be seen that (f_n) does not converge normally as $\|f_n - f\| = 1/n$ and, indeed, the dampened Mann iteration scheme from [3] fails. However, normal convergence can be enforced by considering a subsequence $f_{g(n)}$ with $g(n) = n^2$. Whenever approximations are realized by means of samplings, this speedup can be obtained by increasing the number of samplings performed between two iterations.

Interestingly, the mentioned paper also shows that, in the case of MDPs, approximations obtained by sampling always guarantee convergence of the dampened Mann iteration scheme, independently of the speed of convergence.

The solution in [3] has some drawbacks. A relevant issue resides in the fact that it implicitly assumes that all components are updated at each iteration. Clearly, in applications such as reinforcement learning where large models can produce functions working in dimensions of several thousands, this becomes impractical if not impossible. Chaotic iterations [11] instead offer a scalable alternative where only a subset (possibly only one) of the components are updated at each iteration. The components to be updated might be chosen, for example, to be the ones that seem statistically more relevant to the goal (such as states that are visited more often in sampled runs of a Markov decision process) or that are dependent on components that were previously updated. Using chaotic strategies can often result in less computation and while not necessarily so, its faster update cycle can give better insight into the convergence behaviour at runtime or even produce approximations where full updates are infeasible.

While this might look like a minor implementation aspect, one can see that generalizing to chaotic iteration requires quite a radical change to the theory. The parameters α_n and β_n have to become dependent on the dimension (the state), i.e., they become themselves vectors. If we write $z(i)$ for the i-th component of a vector z, the iteration schemes becomes of the following form, where setting $\alpha_n(i) = \beta_n(i) = 0$ we ensure that component i is not updated at step n:

$$x_{n+1}(i) = (1 - \beta_n(i)) \cdot (x_n(i) + \alpha_n(i) \cdot (f_n(x_n) - x_n)(i))$$

Since in a proper chaotic iteration, components may not be updated infinitely often, parameters $\alpha_n(i)$ must be allowed to be 0 infinitely often, which means that they either converge to 0 or do not converge at all. This deeply deviates from the theory in [3], which heavily relies on the learning rate sequence α_n converging to 1 or at least to a value strictly larger than 0.

In this paper, we will indeed show that the iteration scheme can work with more general parameter sequences, where the learning rate can converge to 0 or is even allowed not to converge. This relaxation of the condition on the parameters requires a substantial change in the proof techniques.

Besides enabling chaotic iteration, the additional flexibility for the parameter sequences allows one to treat different components of the system in a different way. If the value of some components is known to be close to the solution, the corresponding $\beta_n(i)$ and $\alpha_n(i)$ should be chosen close to zero. For components where little information is available and and further correction of a potential over-approximation is needed, the parameters should be chosen away from 0.

The more general schema allows us to match it with the practice of a number of model-based reinforcement learning techniques. For instance, Dyna-Q, a model-based extension of Q-learning, uses chaotic iteration and considers a learning rate α_n converging to 0. More generally, the present work might be a useful step also towards the development of a theory encompassing model-free reinforcement learning techniques. In fact, in a model-free approach, such as

Q-learning [22], the update is based on the current sample and not on the estimated probabilities and rewards. Hence, in order to converge to the solution, the learning rate α_n must converge to 0, giving more and more weight to the previous estimate rather than to the result of applying the function, otherwise the iteration would oscillate (due to the varying samples) rather than converge. Existing convergence results (e.g., [7,22]) for these algorithms typically assume functions with unique fixpoints (as is the case for discounted problems or systems with some termination guarantees) or convergence to some fixpoint, while the case of convergence to the least fixpoint is not treated.

Finally, the possibility of setting a learning rate α_n converging to 0 also offers the potential to relax the condition on the speed of convergence of the sequence f_n. While we required in [3] that f_n converges normally to f, i.e., $\sum_n \|f - f_n\| < \infty$, here we can relax the condition to $\sum_n \alpha_n \|f - f_n\| < \infty$, which is easier to satisfy when α_n tends to 0 and thus the iteration relies less and less on the approximations.

Another relevant question – unanswered in [3] – is whether dampened Mann iteration works – out of the box – for simple stochastic games (SSGs). The mentioned paper only offers a solution, sketched above, involving a speedup of the sampling process for ensuring normal convergence. However, this is costly since it requires to obtain many samples before being able to do the next iteration and obtain the next estimate of the solution. Even worse, the periods until the next estimate are getting longer and longer since the number of needed samples might increase non-linearly. The question of whether one can instead directly apply dampened Mann iteration to SSGs was thus relevant and still open.

The results from [3] cannot be easily adapted to handle SSGs. The proof strategy was to first show that dampened Mann iteration works in the exact case and for the case of power contractions. From there one is able to derive other results, for instance for MDPs (where the fact is exploited that the Bellman equations of MDPs without end components result in fixpoint functions that are power contractions). Including SSGs in the picture and accomodating for the generalized parameter sequences, requires completely new proofs. We prove convergence of dampened Mann iteration for sequences of functions converging monotonically and generalize the result for power contractions to the case of Picard operators. Together with the fact that the least fixpoint operator is continuous for Markov Chains and for SSGs, these results allow us to conclude that dampened Mann iteration works for both MDPs and SSGs. For MDPs the novelty lies in the new types of parameters, while for SSGs this result was completely open in [3].

Being able to treat SSGs also allows us to solve (least) fixpoint equations for behavioural metrics [20,21], another important application area. In [13,10], it was observed that a small perturbation of the transition probabilities in a model can drastically change the distance and the authors suggest an alternative, more robust, notion of distance. With our results it is now also possible to keep the original notion of pseudometric and use dampened Mann iteration with increasingly better approximations to converge to the true distance.

In summary, our main contribution is a generalisation of the dampened Mann iteration scheme proposed in previous work for approximating fixpoints of functions arising from quantitative models. More precisely

- We allow the learning rate to converge to 0 or not converge at all, enabling better adaptation to different convergence rates of function approximations.
- We introduce a generalized dampened Mann iteration where the learning rate and dampening parameters can vary across dimensions, allowing for chaotic iteration strategies.
- We establish convergence of the introduced schemes for simple stochastic games and their sampled approximations.

Full proofs for all results can be found in [5].

2   Preliminaries and Notation

We denote by $\mathbb{R} = (-\infty, \infty)$ the set of real numbers, by $\mathbb{R}_+ = [0, \infty)$ the set of non-negative reals, by $\overline{\mathbb{R}} = [-\infty, \infty]$ and $\overline{\mathbb{R}}_+ = [0, \infty]$ the sets of (non-negative) real numbers including infinity, and by $\mathbb{N}_0$ and $\mathbb{N}$ the set of natural numbers with and without 0, respectively.

For sets X, Y, we will denote by Y^X the set of functions $f \colon X \to Y$. If X is finite, we will identify Y^X with the set of vectors $Y^{|X|}$. A sequence in X is denoted by $(x_n)_{n \in \mathbb{N}_0}$ or simply by (x_n) when the index is clear from the context. For $x \in \mathbb{R}^d$ and $i \in \{1, \ldots, d\}$, we will write $x(i) \in \mathbb{R}$ to denote its i-th component and, if clear from the context, we will sometimes identify $x \in \mathbb{R}$ with the vector $(x, \ldots, x) \in \mathbb{R}^d$. For $x, y \in \mathbb{R}^d$, $x \cdot y = (x(1)y(1), \ldots, x(d)y(d)) \in \mathbb{R}^d$ will denote their component-wise product.

For $x, y \in \overline{\mathbb{R}}^d$, we write $x \leq y$ for the pointwise (partial) order, i.e., $x(i) \leq y(i)$ for all $i \in \{1, \ldots, d\}$. A function $f \in Y^X$, where $X, Y \subseteq \overline{\mathbb{R}}^d$, is monotone if, for all $x, y \in X$, we have that $x \leq y$ implies $f(x) \leq f(y)$. It is called ω-continuous if, for all $(x_n) \subseteq X$ with $x_1 \leq x_2 \leq \ldots$ and $x = \sup_{n \in \mathbb{N}} x_n \in X$, we have $f(x) = \sup_{n \in \mathbb{N}} f(x_n)$. Note that any ω-continuous function is monotone.

We equip $\mathbb{R}^d$ with the *supremum norm* defined as $\|x\| = \sup\{x(i) \mid i \in \{1, \ldots, d\}\}$ for $x \in \mathbb{R}^d$ and extended to functions $f \in Y^X$, where $X, Y \subseteq \mathbb{R}^d$, by $\|f\| = \sup_{x \in X} \|f(x)\| \in [0, \infty]$. A function $f \in Y^X$ is L-Lipschitz for a constant $L \in \mathbb{R}_+$ if, for all $x, y \in X$, $\|f(x) - f(y)\| \leq L\|x - y\|$. It is non-expansive if it is 1-Lipschitz. It is a contraction if it is q-Lipschitz for contraction factor $q < 1$.

A fixpoint of $f \colon X \to X, X \subseteq \mathbb{R}_+^d$, is $x \in X$ such that $f(x) = x$. We denote the set of fixpoints of f by $\mathrm{Fix}(f)$ and, in case it exists, the *least fixpoint* of f by μf. We will be interested in approximating least fixpoints of non-expansive and monotone functions $f \colon X \to X$ where X is a *0-box*, i.e. a set of the form

$$X = \{x \in \mathbb{R}_+^d \mid x \leq x^*\} \qquad \text{for some } x^* \in \overline{\mathbb{R}}_+^d. \qquad (1)$$

Each such function f extends to an ω-continuous function $\overline{f} \colon \overline{\mathbb{R}}_+^d \to \overline{\mathbb{R}}_+^d$ given by $\overline{f}(x) = \sup\{f(y) \mid y \leq x\}$. Using Kleene's fixpoint theorem, $\overline{f}$ has a least fixpoint and $\text{Fix}(f) \neq \emptyset$ iff $\mu\overline{f} \in X$ in which case $\mu f = \mu\overline{f}$. Abusing the notation, we will write μf for $\mu\overline{f} \in \overline{\mathbb{R}}_+^d$. A function $f\colon X \to X$ is a power contraction if the k-fold iteration f^k is a contraction for some $k \in \mathbb{N}$. The map f is a Picard operator if it has a unique fixpoint $x^* \in X$ and the sequence $(f^n(x))$ converges to x^* for all $x \in X$. If $f\colon X \to X$ is a contraction on a closed (hence complete) set $X \subseteq \mathbb{R}_+^d$, then, by Banach's theorem, it is a Picard operator.

Dampened Mann iteration. For the rest of the paper, we will be interested in approximating least fixpoints of non-expansive and monotone functions $f\colon X \to X$, where X is a 0-box, given only approximations $f_n\colon X \to X$ of f. In [3], we suggested the use of a dampened Mann iteration, which is a variation of Mann iteration scheme with the addition of dampening factor.

Definition 2.1 (Mann scheme). *A (dampened) Mann scheme $\mathcal{S}$ is a pair $((\alpha_n), (\beta_n))$ of parameter sequences in $[0,1)$, referred to as* learning rates *and* dampening factors, *respectively, such that*

$$\lim_{n \to \infty} \beta_n = 0, \tag{2}$$

$$\sum_{n \in \mathbb{N}_0} \beta_n = \infty \quad \left(\text{or equivalently,} \prod_{n \in \mathbb{N}_0} (1 - \beta_n) = 0\right). \tag{3}$$

Given a 0-box $X \subseteq \mathbb{R}_+^d$ and a sequence (f_n) of functions $f_n\colon X \to X$, a Mann scheme $\mathcal{S}$ generates a class of sequences (x_n) with $x_0 \in X$ chosen aritrarily and

$$x_{n+1} = (1 - \beta_n) \cdot (x_n + \alpha_n \cdot (f_n(x_n) - x_n)) \tag{4}$$

A Mann scheme $\mathcal{S}$ is exact *if for all monotone and non-expansive $f\colon X \to X$, setting $f_n = f$ for all n, the sequences (x_n) generated by $\mathcal{S}$ converge to μf.*

Intuitively, the learning rates determine to what extent the update $f(x_n) - x_n$ is applied to the current guess x_n, ranging from a full Kleene update ($\alpha_n = 1$, implying $x_{n+1} = (1 - \beta_n)f_n(x_n)$) to no update at all ($\alpha_n = 0$, implying $x_{n+1} = (1 - \beta_n)x_n$). The dampening factors ensure that over-approximations of μf introduced by starting from x_0 instead of 0 and using f_n instead of f, and which would lead to possible divergence of a Kleene iteration, can be dampened. Condition (2) ensures that dampening eventually reduces – meaning that, in the long run, when we are close to the least fixpoint of f, we stay close to it. On the other hand, Condition (3) guarantees that at any stage there is still enough "dampening power" left to correct possible over-approximations.

In [3], we showed several convergence results for *Mann-Kleene schemes*, i.e., Mann schemes such that $\lim_{n \to \infty} \alpha_n = 1$ and *relaxed Mann-Kleene schemes* where $\lim_{n \to \infty} \alpha_n > 0$.[3] More precisely, it shows that (relaxed) Mann-Kleene schemes are exact and it proves convergence in the "approximated case", i.e., when we use at each iteration approximations from a sequence (f_n) converging to f, with conditions on the target functions f (power contraction) or on the mode of convergence of the sequence (f_n) (monotone or normal convergence).

---

[3] Note that in [3] α_n is replaced with $1 - \alpha_n$. Here, we chose this notation instead as it better reflects the widespread interpretation of α_n as a learning rate.

3   Generalizing Dampened Mann Iteration

In this section we generalize the convergence results for Mann schemes from [3]. First, in §3.1 we overcome the restriction to Mann-Kleene schemes, and show convergence results for learning rates which are allowed to converge to 0 or to not converge at all. Relying on this, in §3.2 we further generalize the scheme by allowing the parameter values α_n, β_n to depend on the dimension, thus, in particular, enabling a chaotic iteration. While the results for chaotic iteration in §3.2 are for the exact case, i.e., the function f is known and used at each iteration, the extension to the case in which f can be only approximated via a sequence (f_n) is described in §3.3.

3.1   Schemes With Non-Converging Learning Rates

We start by lifting the restriction to *(relaxed) Mann-Kleene* schemes, showing that convergence can be guaranteed also when the learning rate does not converge or converges to zero. In addition, while [3] restricts to functions $f\colon X \to X$ with $\mu f < \infty$, here we allow the fixpoint to be infinite in some (or all) dimensions.

Definition 3.1 (Progressing scheme). *A Mann scheme* $\mathcal{S} = ((\alpha_n), (\beta_n))$ *is called* progressing *if, assuming* $^0\!/_0 = 0$ *and* $^x\!/_0 = \infty$ *for* $x > 0$, *it holds*

$$\lim_{n\to\infty} \beta_n/\alpha_n = 0. \tag{5}$$

Intuitively, Condition (5) ensures that the scheme eventually prioritizes updates over dampening. Also, Condition (2) of Definition 2.1, i.e., $\lim_{n\to\infty} \beta_n = 0$, is implied by Condition (5) above, since $\beta_n/\alpha_n \geq \beta_n$. Note also that there is no convergence requirement on α_n and thus, in particular, α_n is allowed to tend to 0.

Canonical choices of the parameters are $\beta_n = 1/n$ and either $\alpha_n = 1$ (Kleene updates at every step) or $\alpha_n = 1/n^\varepsilon$ with $0 < \varepsilon < 1$ (decreasing learning rates).

We first show that, when the exact function f is known and can be used at each iteration, progressing schemes ensure convergence to the least fixpoint.

Theorem 3.2 (Progressing is exact). *Progressing Mann schemes are exact.*

When f can only be approximated, the following generalisation of [3, Theorem 4.4.2] shows the benefits of using decreasing learning rates.

Corollary 3.3 (Approximated function). *Let* $\mathcal{S}$ *be a progressing Mann scheme,* $f\colon X \to X$ *a monotone and non-expansive map over a 0-box* $X \subseteq \mathbb{R}_+^d$, *and* (f_n) *a sequence of maps* $f_n\colon X \to X$ *such that* $\sum \alpha_n \|f - f_n\| < \infty$. *Then the sequences* (x_n) *generated by* $\mathcal{S}$ *on* (f_n) *satisfy* $x_n \to \mu f$.

This significantly improves [3, Theorem 4.6] which requires $\sum \|f - f_n\| < \infty$, since when $\alpha_n \to 0$, then $\sum \alpha_n \|f - f_n\|$ is, of course, more likely to be bounded. Indeed, for any sequence (f_n) converging to f it can be shown that there is a progressing Mann scheme working for any starting point.

Example 3.4. Consider the identity $f\colon [0,1] \to [0,1]$ and a sequence of approximating functions $f_n\colon [0,1] \to [0,1]$ defined by $f_n(x) = (1 - 1/n)x + 1/n$. Then one can see that any sequence (x_n) generated, starting from $x_0 = 1$, by a relaxed Mann-Kleene scheme with dampening factors $\beta_n = 1/n$ does not converge to the least fixpoint $\mu f = 0$, for any choice of the learning rates α_n. Instead, by Corollary 3.3, for any $0 < \epsilon < 1$ the sequence obtained with learning rates $\alpha_n := 1/n^\epsilon$ converges to μf.

3.2 Chaotic Dampened-Mann Iteration

We now generalize Mann schemes by allowing parameters α_n, β_n to depend not only on the step, but also on the dimensions. This establishes the basis for performing chaotic iteration to approximate the least fixpoint.

The formal switch is, again, apparently minor: dampening and learning parameters become vectors instead of scalars.

Definition 3.5 (Generalized Mann scheme). *A generalized (dampened) Mann scheme $\mathcal{S} = ((\alpha_n), (\beta_n))$ is a pair of parameter sequences where the learning rates (α_n) and dampening factors (β_n) are sequences of vectors in $[0,1)^d$, such that conditions (2) $\lim_{n\to\infty} \beta_n = 0$ and (3) $\sum_{n\in\mathbb{N}_0} \beta_n = \infty$ of Definition 2.1 hold pointwise.*

Notions introduced for Mann schemes naturally extend to generalized ones. The sequence generated by a generalized scheme $\mathcal{S}$ is still defined by (4), but interpreted pointwise. Similarly, the notion of *exactness* naturally extends to generalized Mann schemes.

One might think that in order to ensure convergence one could just extend the notion of progressing schemes to the generalized case by interpreting Condition (5) pointwise. The next example shows that this does not work in general.

Example 3.6. Consider $f\colon [0,1]^2 \to [0,1]^2$ with $f(x,y) = (\max(x,y), \max(x,y))$ and the (vector-)sequences $(\alpha_n), (\beta_n)$ with $\alpha_n = (1,1)$ and

$$\beta_n(1) = \begin{cases} 1/(n+2) & \text{if } n \text{ is even} \\ 1/(n+2)^2 & \text{if } n \text{ is odd} \end{cases} \qquad \beta_n(2) = \begin{cases} 1/(n+2)^2 & \text{if } n \text{ is even} \\ 1/(n+2) & \text{if } n \text{ is odd} \end{cases}$$

Clearly, $\mu f = (0,0)$, but it is easy to see that the sequence (x_n) generated by dampened Kleene Iteration with these parameters from the starting point $(1,1)$ will not converge to $(0,0)$, because the positive number $\prod_{n=2}^{\infty}(1 - 1/n^2)$ is a lower bound for at least one component of all x_n.

The crux is that we need sufficiently strong dampening, uniformly across all components. Otherwise, thinking of applications to state-based systems, it might happen that two states *convince each other* of a too large value by passing it on between each other and, at each step, one of them preserves the over-approximation while the other one gets dampened.

For this reasons, we extend the notion of progressing schemes as follows:

Definition 3.7 (Progressing generalized Mann scheme). *A generalized Mann scheme* $\mathcal{S} = ((\alpha_n), (\beta_n))$ *is* progressing *if condition below holds pointwise*

$$\lim_{n \to \infty} \beta_n / \alpha_n = 0 \tag{6}$$

and there exists a strictly increasing sequence (m_k) *such that, for all* $k \in \mathbb{N}_0$ *and* $i \in \{1, \ldots, d\}$, $U_k(i) := \{\ell \in \{m_k, \ldots, m_{k+1} - 1\} \mid \alpha_\ell(i) > 0\} \neq \emptyset$ *and, letting* $\ell_k(i) := \max U_k(i)$, *we have*

$$\sum_k \min\{\beta_{\ell_k(i)}(i) \mid i = 1, \ldots, d\} = \infty \tag{7}$$

Intuitively, $U_k(i)$ is the set of steps in $\{m_k, \ldots, m_{k+1} - 1\}$ in which component i has been updated and $\ell_k(i)$ is the last update in the interval. Hence Condition (7) requires that the dampening factors in each component decrease in some sense fairly: There is a sequence of time steps such that in between any two subsequent time steps, each component is updated at least once and, considering only the last updates in each component, the worst dampening factors still sum up to infinity. This is a natural extension of the non-generalized case: a (non-generalized) progressing scheme using the same parameter sequences in each component fulfills (7) for the sequence $m_k = k$.

Our first main result is the convergence of generalized dampened Mann iteration to the least fixpoint of f when the exact function f is known.

Main Theorem 3.8 (Exact Case). *Progressing generalized Mann schemes are exact.*

Proof (sketch). The statement is shown in two parts:

- First we show that $\limsup_{n \to \infty} x_n \leq \mu f$. This is done by comparing (x_n) to a sequence (y_n) that is generated with the same parameters but starts from the bottom element $y_n = 0$. It is clear that (y_n) always stays below the least fixpoint of f and one can show that the distance $\|x_n - y_n\|$ between the two sequences converges to zero. Here we need our additional assumption that the dampening is uniform over all components.
- In the more interesting part of the proof we show that $\limsup_{n \to \infty} x_n \geq \mu f$. To this end we construct, by transfinite induction, a sequence (t_α) of *stepping stones* below μf with the property that (x_n) is eventually above t_α. One might hope that (t_α) is monotonically increasing and converges to μf. We do not achieve monotonicity in the proof but we show that the sequence can be constructed in a way that the sequence of sums $t_\alpha(1) + \cdots + t_\alpha(d)$ is strictly increasing. That means, even if we loose progress towards μf in one dimension, the overall progress in the other components still makes up for it. For this we need the property that the dampening factors decrease more rapidly than the learning-rates. The fact that there is always an overall gain in the sum of the components of t_α (together with the first part of the proof) allows us to conclude that the sequence (x_n) converges to μf. $\qquad\square$

Dampened Mann iteration admits chaotic iteration as a special case.

Definition 3.9 (Chaotic iteration). *Let $\mathcal{S} = ((\alpha_n), (\beta_n))$ be a generalized Mann scheme and let (f_n) be a sequence of monotone and non-expansive maps over a 0-box $X \subseteq \mathbb{R}_+^d$. A chaotic iteration on $\mathcal{S}$ based on a sequence of index sets (I_n), $I_n \subseteq \{1, \ldots, d\}$, is defined as below, with $x_0 \in X$ arbitrary, and*

$$\begin{cases} x_{n+1}(i) = (1 - \beta_n(i))(x_n(i) + \alpha_n(i)(f_n(x_n) - x_n)(i)) & \text{for } i \in I_n \\ x_{n+1}(j) = x_n(j) & \text{for } j \notin I_n \end{cases} \tag{8}$$

The results for generalized dampened Mann iterations immediately imply analogous results for chaotic dampened Mann iterations. Here, assuming (β_n) pointwise monotonically decreasing, the somewhat technical condition in Theorem 3.8 translates to the intuitive requirement that the time interval between two complete sweeps should not become arbitrary large.

Corollary 3.10 (Chaotic iteration). *Let $\mathcal{S} = ((\alpha_n), (\beta_n))$ be a generalized Mann scheme with (β_n) pointwise monotonically decreasing. Let (f_n) be a sequence of monotone and non-expansive maps on a 0-box $X \subseteq \mathbb{R}_+^d$, converging to f. Let (I_n) be a sequence of set of indices and inductively define (m_k) by $m_0 = 0$ and m_{k+1} the least $m \in \mathbb{N}$ such that $\bigcup_{n=m_k}^{m-1} I_n = \{1, \ldots, d\}$. If*

$$\sum_{k \in \mathbb{N}} \min_i \beta_{m_k}(i) = \infty \tag{9}$$

then the sequences (x_n) generated by chaotic iteration converge to μf.

Given a (non-generalized) Mann scheme, a simple way of applying the scheme in a chaotic fashion consists in associating to each component a local copy of the parameters and then updating at each step a single (independently) randomly chosen state, letting the parameters progress to the next value only for this state. It can be proved that, in this way, starting from a progressing scheme, the generated sequence converges almost surely to the fixpoint. This will be used in the numerical experiments in §5.

3.3 Working with Approximations

Theorem 3.8 assumes that the monotone and non-expansive function f of interest is known exactly. The benefits of the (generalized) dampened Mann iteration, however, lie in the case where f can only be approximated by a sequence (f_n) of monotone and non-expansive approximations.

The main result of this section is the following result that gives an essential sufficient criterion for convergence.

Main Theorem 3.11 (Approximated Case). *Let $\mathcal{S} = ((\alpha_n), (\beta_n))$ be a progressing Mann scheme, $X \subseteq \mathbb{R}_+^d$ a 0-box, and let (f_n) be a sequence of monotone and non-expansive functions $f_n \colon X \to X$, pointwise converging to $f \colon X \to X$. Then, the sequence (x_n) generated by $\mathcal{S}$ fulfills*

1. $\liminf_{n\to\infty} x_n \geq \mu f$

2. if $\lim_{n\to\infty} \mu(\sup_{k\geq n} f_k) = \mu f,$ *then* $\lim_{n\to\infty} x_n = \mu f$

This result, in particular, implies convergence to the least fixpoint if (f_n) converges monotonically and $\mu f_n \to \mu f$, thus generalizing [3, Theorem 4.6.1]. Instead, in general, the fact $\mu f_n \to \mu f$ is not sufficient to have convergence, as shown by the example below, inspired by [3, Example 4.4].

Example 3.12. Consider the function $f(x,y) = (y,x)$ and the sequence of approximations (f_n) given by

$$f_n(x,y) = \begin{cases} (y,x) & \text{if } n \text{ even} \\ (y \ominus 2/n, x \oplus 2/n) & \text{if } n \text{ uneven} \end{cases}$$

Despite μf_n converging to $\mu f = (0,0)$, it can be seen that dampened Mann iteration does not converge in general. Indeed, the hypotheses of Theorem 3.11(2) are violated, since the supremum $F_n = \sup_{k\geq n} f_k$ is always of the form $F_n(x,y) = (y, x+\varepsilon)$ for some $\varepsilon > 0$, thus having fixpoint $\mu F_n = (\infty, \infty) \not\to (0,0)$.

By relying on Theorem 3.11 one can also prove convergence in the approximated case when the limit function f is sufficiently well-behaved (without assumptions on the mode of convergence).

Theorem 3.13 (Convergence for Picard limit functions). *Let (f_n) be a sequence of monotone and non-expansive functions $f_n \colon X \to X$ with X a 0-box, converging pointwise to a Picard operator $f \colon X \to X$. Then, we have*

$$\lim_{n\to\infty} \mu(\sup_{k\geq n} f_k) = \mu f.$$

As a consequence, for any progressing Mann scheme $\mathcal{S}$, the sequence (x_n) generated by $\mathcal{S}$ on (f_n) converges to μf.

Note that this result implies convergence, in particular, for cases where the limit function is contractive or power contractive, thus generalizing both [4, Theorem 4.3 and Theorem B.3].

4   Applications to State-based Systems

We treat the convergence of dampened Mann iterations for piecewise linear functions such as those arising when dealing with optimal returns and optimal policies in zero-sum two-player (turn-based) stochastic games. These results generalize those in [3] which are limited to MDPs, with proofs relying on techniques specifically designed for this setting, like collapsing end-components, making it difficult to generalize them to other function classes. Furthermore, we lift the requirement that the least fixpoint, i.e., the expected return is finite for all states. Finally, in [3], we showed convergence only for Mann-Kleene schemes, while here we consider generalized Mann schemes which allow also for asynchronous iteration.

4.1   Simple Stochastic Games

We will be working with the following definition of simple stochastic games.

Definition 4.1 (Simple stochastic game). *A zero-sum two-player (turn-based) stochastic game $\mathcal{G}$ (short: simple stochastic game or SSG) is a tuple $(S, A, T, R, S_{\max}, S_{\min})$ where*

- *S is a (finite) set of states*
- *$(A(s))_{s \in S}$ is a family of (finite) sets of actions $A(s)$ enabled in state s, and, by abuse of notation, we write $A := \bigcup_{s \in S} A(s)$;*
- *$T \colon S \times A \times S \to [0, 1], (s, a, s') \mapsto T_a(s, s')$ is a transition function fulfilling;*

$$T_a(s) := \sum_{s' \in S} T_a(s, s') \in [0, 1] \quad \text{for all } s \in S, a \in A$$

- *$R \colon S \times A \to \mathbb{R}_+, (s, a) \mapsto R_a(s)$ is a reward function;*
- *$S_{\max} \cup S_{\min} = S$ are a partition of S where $S_{\max}$ and $S_{\min}$ are states controlled by the max- and min-player, respectively.*

We write $F = F(\mathcal{G}) := \{s \in S \mid A(s) = \emptyset\}$ for the set of final states.

Intuitively, an SSG is a probabilistic state-based system where, in a given non-final state $s \in S \setminus F$, one of two external agents (the max-player if $s \in S_{\max}$ or min-player if $s \in S_{\min}$) chooses one of the actions $a \in A(s)$ enabled in said state after which the system emits a reward $R_a(s)$ and transitions to a new state $s' \in S$ with probability $T_a(s, s')$ (or terminates with probability $1 - T_a(s)$). The goal of the two players is to choose actions in order to maximize (max-player) or minimize (min-player) the total expected reward.

As we allow $T_a(s) < 1$, this definition also encompasses systems with a discount factor. Furthermore, it comprises as special cases also Markov chains (where $|A(s)| \leq 1$ for all $s \in S$), (maximizing) Markov decision processes (MDPs; where $|A(s)| \leq 1$ for all $s \in S_{\min}$), and minimizing Markov decision processes (Min-MDPs; where $|A(s)| \leq 1$ for all $s \in S_{\max}$).

Policies, as defined below, resolve the non-determinism present in SSGs by fixing the agents' behaviour.

Definition 4.2 (Policy). *Let $(S, A, T, R, S_{\max}, S_{\min})$ be a SSG. A (memoryless and deterministic) policy on a set $S' \subseteq S \setminus F$ is a map $\pi \colon S' \to A$ with $\pi(s) \in A(s)$ for $s \in S'$. Given an SSG $\mathcal{G} = (S, A, T, R, S_{\max}, S_{\min})$ and a policy $\pi \colon S' \to A$, we write $\mathcal{G}^\pi = (S, A^\pi, T, R, S_{\max}, S_{\min})$ for the SSG where, for $s \in S$*

$$A^\pi(s) = \begin{cases} \{\pi(s)\} & \text{if } s \in S' \\ A(s) & \text{otherwise} \end{cases}$$

Note that, when $\pi_{\min} \colon S_{\min} \setminus F \to A$ and $\pi_{\max} \colon S_{\max} \setminus F \to A$ are policies of the min- and max-player, respectively, we have that $\mathcal{G}^{\pi_{\min}}$ is a (Max-)MDP, $\mathcal{G}^{\pi_{\max}}$ is a Min-MDP, and $\mathcal{G}^{(\pi_{\min}, \pi_{\max})}$ is a Markov chain (where $(\pi_{\min}, \pi_{\max})$ denotes the combined policy for both players).

The expected total reward for each starting state s in $\mathcal{G}$, assuming that both players act optimally, can be characterized as the least fixpoint (in $\overline{\mathbb{R}}_+^S$) of the so-called Bellman operator $f_{\mathcal{G}} \colon \mathbb{R}_+^S \to \mathbb{R}_+^S$ given by

$$f_{\mathcal{G}}(v)(s) = \begin{cases} \max_{a \in A(s)} (R_a(s) + \sum_{s' \in S} T_a(s, s') v(s')) & \text{if } s \in S_{\max} \\ \min_{a \in A(s)} (R_a(s) + \sum_{s' \in S} T_a(s, s') v(s')) & \text{if } s \in S_{\min} \end{cases}$$

Note that the expected total reward might be infinite.

For finite-state SSGs, it is known that memoryless policies such as the ones described above are sufficient to act optimally (see, e.g., [8]) whence we have

$$\mu f_{\mathcal{G}} = \mu f_{\mathcal{G}^{\pi_{\min}^*}} = \mu f_{\mathcal{G}^{\pi_{\max}^*}} = \mu f_{\mathcal{G}^{\pi_{\max}^*, \pi_{\min}^*}} \tag{10}$$

for some (optimal) policies $\pi_{\min} \colon S_{\min} \setminus F \to A$ and $\pi_{\max} \colon S_{\max} \setminus F \to A$.

Before we give convergence proofs, we end this subsection by giving a definition of a sampled SSG:

Definition 4.3 (Sampling). *Given an SSG* $\mathcal{G} = (S, A, T, R, S_{\max}, S_{\min})$, *a sequence* $(\mathcal{G}_n)$ *of SSGs* $\mathcal{G}_n = (S, A, T_n, R_n, S_{\max}, S_{\min})$ *is a sampling of* $\mathcal{G}$ *if*

- *$T_n \to T$ and $R_n \to R$ for $n \to \infty$.*
- *For $s, s' \in S, a \in A$, if $T_a(s, s') = 0$, then $(T_n)_a(s, s') = 0$ for all $n \in \mathbb{N}$, i.e., a non-existing transition can never be sampled.*
- *For $s \in S, a \in A$, if $R_a(s) = 0$, then $(R_n)_a(s) = 0$ for all $n \in \mathbb{N}$, i.e., a non-existing reward can never be sampled.*
- *For $s \in S, a \in A$, if $T_a(s) = 1$, then $(T_n)_a(s) = 1$ for all $n \in \mathbb{N}$, i.e., a non-terminating action can never be sampled as terminating.*

4.2 Convergence for Simple Stochastic Games

The proof of convergence of the dampened Mann iteration for SSGs will mainly be based on the technical convergence criterion given by Theorem 3.11.

To be precise, we will show that the sequences of Bellman operators (f_n) of sampled SSGs fulfill the condition

$$\lim_{n \to \infty} \mu(\sup_{k \geq n} f_k) = \mu(\lim_{n \to \infty} f_n). \tag{11}$$

This will be done by first reducing the problem to MDPs which, in turn, depends on results for Markov chains, using (10). In fact, we use the following result for the optimal values of Markov chains.

Lemma 4.4. *Given a sampling* $\mathcal{M} = (M_n)$ *of a Markov chain M, we have* $\mu f_M = \lim_{n \to \infty} \mu f_{M_n}$.

We proved such a result already in [3], yet some extra work has to be done to adapt to the new setting, allowing for approximated rewards and infinite values. The idea is that states with zero or infinite value are determined by the underlying structure of the Markov chain (in terms of Definition 4.3), whereas on the 'non-trivial' states, the Bellman operator enjoys a power contraction property ensuring convergence to the (unique) fixpoint.

Using this result for Markov chains, it is easy to generalize to SSGs using (10).

Corollary 4.5 (Sampling-continuity of least-fixpoint operator). *Given a sampling $\mathcal{G} = (G_n)$ of an SSG G, we have $\mu f_G = \lim_{n\to\infty} \mu f_{G_n}$.*

We continue by showing Condition (11) for MDPs and derive the following.

Theorem 4.6 (Convergence for MDPs). *Given a sampling $\mathcal{M} = (M_n)$ of an MDP M, we have $\lim_{n\to\infty} \mu(\sup_{k\geq n} f_{M_k}) = \mu f_M$. Therefore for any progressing Mann scheme $\mathcal{S}$, the sequence (x_n) generated by $\mathcal{S}$ on (f_{M_n}) converges to μf_M.*

Proof (sketch). The main idea used to prove this statement is that the supremum of Bellman operators of arbitrary many MDPs of the same underlying structure (in the sense of Definition 4.3) is itself a Bellman operator of an MDP with the 'same' structure (although with potentially many more actions) as long as all transition probabilities and rewards are close enough. Using this, Condition (11) can be shown to break down to continuity of the least fixpoint operator for a 'sampling' sequence. $\qquad\square$

Using the validity of Condition (11) for MDPs, we can derive the same result for SSGs using (10) and an optimal min-player strategy.

Corollary 4.7. *Given a sampling $\mathcal{G} = (G_n)$ of an SSG G, we have that $\lim_{n\to\infty} \mu(\sup_{k\geq n} f_{G_k}) = \mu f_G$. As a consequence, for any progressing Mann scheme $\mathcal{S}$, the sequence (x_n) generated by $\mathcal{S}$ on (f_{G_n}) converges to μf_G.*

Remark 4.8. This result can be used to show convergence for a wider range of 'sampled' piecewise linear functions by making use of the fact that convergence of progressing generalized schemes for a sampled SSG (f_{M_n}) directly implies convergence for the sequences $(f_{M_n}^k)_n$ for any fixed $k > 1$ (k-step Bellman operators). The result can also be used to obtain a direct proof of convergence for state-action-value Bellman operators, where rewards are given to transitions.

5   Numerical Experiments

In this section we illustrate a number of experiments comparing the convergence behaviour of (relaxed) Mann-Kleene schemes as presented in [3] with schemes working with vanishing or divergent learning rates as well as chaotic schemes. The aim of these experiments is to provide some insights on how the generalisations to dampened Mann iteration in the paper affect the convergence speed when using a randomized strategy for chaotic updates. In particular, we cannot expect an improvement in efficiency that, instead, could potentially be obtained using more informed heuristics for choosing which components to update.

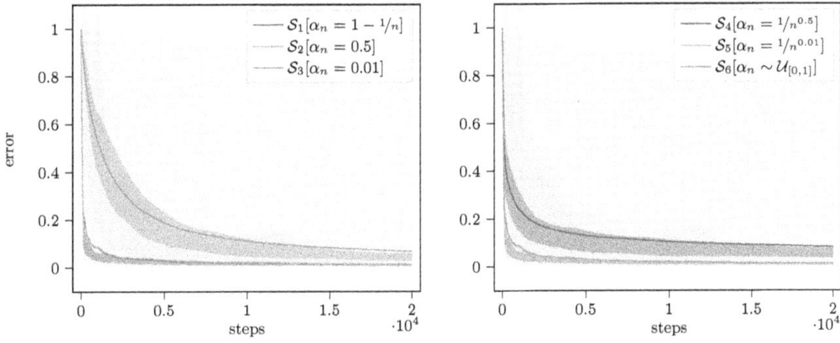

Fig. 1: Results for the experiments of non-chaotic iterations on 50 randomly generated SSGs. Lines denote the mean error, the half-opaque area the 25th to 75th percentile, the weakly visible area the minimum to maximum area. Results for $\mathcal{S}_1$ and $\mathcal{S}_4$ are only barely visible as they are almost identical to the ones from $\mathcal{S}_2$ and $\mathcal{S}_6$, respectively.

We tested all iteration schemes on the same set of 50 randomly generated SSGs G with 15 min- and 15 max-player states, at most 5 actions per state, each of them with a normalized value $\|\mu f_G\| = 1$ and for which the Kleene iteration on f_G 'converges' in at most 10000 steps (we assume convergence when changes are below 10^{-8}).

Vanishing and diverging learning rates. To test the influence of vanishing or diverging learning rates on the convergence rate, we compared the performance of the six iteration schemes shown in Table 1. The scheme $\mathcal{S}_1$ is a Mann-Kleene scheme, while $\mathcal{S}_2$ and $\mathcal{S}_3$ are relaxed Mann-Kleene schemes. Instead $\mathcal{S}_4$ and $\mathcal{S}_5$ have vanishing learning rate and $\mathcal{S}_6$ chooses a random learning rate at each step independently w.r.t. a uniform distribution, and thus the sequence of learning rates is almost surely non-converging. Note that convergence for the first three schemes (at least for MDPs) is covered by the results in [3] while the last three require the results in the present paper.

In the experiments, before each Mann iteration step, the SSGs $\mathcal{G}$ are sampled by performing 30 model steps for randomly chosen state-action pairs.

$\mathcal{S}$	$\mathcal{S}_1$	$\mathcal{S}_2$	$\mathcal{S}_3$	$\mathcal{S}_4$	$\mathcal{S}_5$	$\mathcal{S}_6$
α_n	$1 - 1/n$	0.5	0.01	$1/n^{0.5}$	$1/n^{0.01}$	$\sim \mathcal{U}_{[0,1]}$
β_n	$1/n$	$1/n$	$1/n$	$1/n$	$1/n$	$1/n$

Table 1: Dampened Mann Schemes used in the experiments.

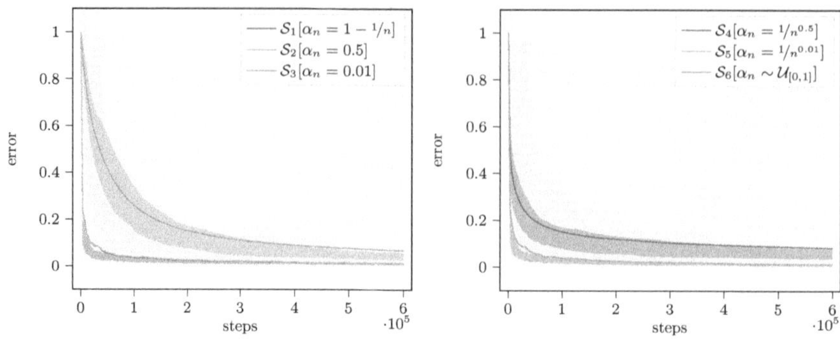

Fig. 2: Results for the experiments of chaotic iterations on 50 randomly generated SSGs. Again, the results for $\mathcal{S}_1$ and $\mathcal{S}_4$ are only barely visible as they are almost identical to the ones from $\mathcal{S}_2$ and $\mathcal{S}_6$, respectively.

The results of these experiments are in Figure 1. Observe that both vanishing and random (diverging) learning rates yield similar results as (relaxed) Mann-Kleene parameters.

Also, the schemes that keep having a higher learning rate (for longer) perform better (higher constant learning rates or lower exponent α for learning rates of the form $1/n^\alpha$). This is expected since we are dealing with faultless sampling of SSGs and the advantage of lower learning rates does not lie in faster convergence but in higher robustness to 'irregular' approximations (see Example 3.4).

Chaotic iteration. To test the influence of chaotic updates on the convergence rate, we repeated the experiments with chaotic variants of the above iteration schemes. As outline at the end of §3.2, at each step, the chaotic iteration performs an update for one single (independently) randomly chosen state, updating the learning rate (and dampening factor) only for this state. Thus, to have a 'full sweep' over the states, the chaotic variants need (at least) 30 steps (while the non-chaotic variants above perform 30 updates in one step). To have a fair comparison to the non-chaotic variants, the sampling $\mathcal{G}$ only simulates a single model step for a randomly chosen state-action pair before each iteration step. In total, after 30 steps, the chaotic schemes thus have the same information and the same number of updates (thus, the same amount of computation) as a single step of the non-chaotic variants, while allowing for intermediate results.

The results of these experiments are in Figure 2. It can be seen directly that the schemes all have almost the same convergence speed as the non-chaotic variants (keeping in mind that the non-chaotic variants perform 30 updates per step), even if we use a random non-informed choice of components to update in each step. As a consequence, the experiments suggest that performing a chaotic iteration (randomly) comes at no additional cost while allowing for intermediate results even when the computation with non-chaotic variants would be infeasible. It should further be noted that, in most practical use cases, the components to update might be chosen in a more informed manner, e.g., by taking into account which components had been updated, which might result in faster convergence.

6   Conclusion

Mann iteration is a classical technique for generating a sequence which, under suitable hypotheses, converges to a fixpoint of a continuous function starting from any initial state [6]. Dampened versions are considered in [14,23] where convergence to a fixpoint is shown in a uniformly smooth Banach space and Hilbert spaces, under suitable assumptions on the parameter sequences. In [3], we proposed the use of dampened Mann iteration for dealing with functions which can only be approximated. This work sensibly deviates from [14,23] as the intended applications, for approximating fixpoints of functions arising from quantitative models like MDPs and SSGs, lead to focus on the case of monotone non-expansive functions in (finite-dimensional) Banach spaces with the supremum norm, which are neither uniformly smooth nor Hilbert spaces.

Our paper takes the same setting as [3] and generalizes its results. The generalisations include the possibility of having learning rates converging to 0 or not converge at all, the possibility of varying parameters across dimensions, thus enabling chaotic iteration and the proof of convergence of these schemes for simple stochastic games approximated via sampling.

We provided some numerical results, showing that the chaotic iteration (with random choice of updated component) yields almost identical results in terms of convergence of standard dampened Mann iteration, while giving more flexibility, e.g., opening the way to parallel and distributed implementations. We plan a further exploration of effective chaotic iteration strategies, including data-driven approaches to select the components to update at each step based on statistical properties of the model, possibly tuning the learning rate and dampening parameters based on observed convergence behaviour during execution.

We furthermore plan to investigate applications of our results to the computation of behavioural metrics, in particular probabilistic bisimilarity distances. In fact, [2] shows how to reduce this problem to the solution of a simple stochastic game. Computing behavioural metrics in the approximated setting is also discussed [13,10] where the authors observe that a small perturbation of the transition probabilities can drastically change the distance apparently hindering the possibility of properly approximating the distance when such probabilities can be only estimated. Our results suggest that, instead, one can use dampened Mann iteration for obtaining increasingly better approximations of the distance.

We are also interested in considering the problem of approximating the least fixpoint in scenarios, where the functions do not necessarily converge, but converge in the limit-average, providing a close match with reinforcement learning algorithms such as Q-learning [22]. For this one might be able to draw inspiration from theory of stochastic approximation [7,9,15], going back to [16] that deals with the case where a function contains an error term with expected value zero.

References

1. Giorgio Bacci, Giovanni Bacci, Kim G. Larsen, and Radu Mardare. On-the-fly exact computation of bisimilarity distances. *Logical Methods in Computer Science*, 13(2:13):1–25, 2017.
2. Giorgio Bacci, Giovanni Bacci, Kim G. Larsen, Radu Mardare, Qiyi Tang, and Franck van Breugel. Computing probabilistic bisimilarity distances for probabilistic automata. *Logical Methods in Computer Science*, 17(1), 2021.
3. Paolo Baldan, Sebastian Gurke, Barbara König, Tommaso Padoan, and Florian Wittbold. Approximating fixpoints of approximated functions. In Ruzica Piskac and Zvonimir Rakamaric, editors, *Proc. of CAV 2025 – Part II*, pages 193–215. Springer, 2025. LNCS 15932.
4. Paolo Baldan, Sebastian Gurke, Barbara König, Tommaso Padoan, and Florian Wittbold. Approximating fixpoints of approximated functions, 2025. arXiv:2501.08950.
5. Paolo Baldan, Sebastian Gurke, Barbara König, and Florian Wittbold. Computing fixpoints of learned functions: Chaotic iteration and simple stochastic games, 2026. arXiv:2601.16142.
6. Vasile Berinde. *Iterative Approximation of Fixed Points*, volume 1912 of *Lecture Notes in Mathematics*. Springer, 2007.
7. Dimitri P. Bertsekas and John N. Tsitsiklis. *Neuro-Dynamic Programming*. Athena Scientific, Belmont, Massachusetts, 1996.
8. Anne Condon. The complexity of stochastic games. *Information and Computation*, 96(2):203–224, 1992.
9. Marie Duflo. *Random Iterative Models*. Number 34 in Applications of Mathematics – Stochastic Modelling and Applied Probability. Springer, 1991. Translated by Stephen S. Wilson.
10. Syyeda Zainab Fatmi, Stefan Kiefer, David Parker, and Franck van Breugel. Robust probabilistic bisimilarity for labelled markov chains. In Ruzica Piskac and Zvonimir Rakamarić, editors, *Proceedings of CAV'2025*, pages 254–275. Springer, 2025.
11. Andreas Frommer and Daniel B. Szyld. On asynchronous iterations. *Journal of Computational and Applied Mathematics*, 123(1):201–216, 2000. Numerical Analysis 2000. Vol. III: Linear Algebra.
12. Leslie Pack Kaelbling, Michael L Littman, and Andrew W Moore. Reinforcement learning: A survey. *Journal of artificial intelligence research*, 4:237–285, 1996.
13. Stefan Kiefer and Qiyi Tang. Approximate bisimulation minimisation. In *Proc. of FSTTCS '21*, volume 213 of *LIPIcs*, pages 48:1–48:16. Schloss Dagstuhl – Leibniz-Zentrum für Informatik, 2021.
14. Tae-Hwa Kim and Hong-Kun Xu. Strong convergence of modified Mann iterations. *Nonlinear Analysis: Theory, Methods & Applications*, 61(1):51–60, 2005.
15. Harold J. Kushner and Dean S. Clark. *Stochastic Approximation Methods for Constrained and Unconstrained Systems*. Number 26 in Applied Mathematical Sciences. Springer, 1978.
16. H. Robbins and S. Monro. A stochastic approximation method. *The Annals of Mathematical Statistics*, 22(3):400–407, 1951.
17. Gavin A Rummery and Mahesan Niranjan. *On-line Q-learning using connectionist systems*, volume 37. University of Cambridge, Department of Engineering Cambridge, UK, 1994.
18. Richard S. Sutton. Dyna, an integrated architecture for learning, planning, and reacting. *SIGART Bulletin*, 2(4):160–163, 1991.

19. Richard S. Sutton. Planning by incremental dynamic programming. In *Proc. of ML '91 (Conference on Machine Learning)*, pages 353–357. Morgan Kaufmann, 1991.
20. Franck van Breugel. Probabilistic bisimilarity distances. *ACM SIGLOG News*, 4(4):33–51, 2017.
21. Franck van Breugel and James Worrell. The complexity of computing a bisimilarity pseudometric on probabilistic automata. In *Horizons of the Mind. A Tribute to Prakash Panangaden – Essays Dedicated to Prakash Panangaden on the Occasion of His 60th Birthday*, pages 191–213. Springer, 2014. LNCS 8464.
22. Christopher J. C. H. Watkins and Peter Dayan. Q-learning. *Machine Learning*, 8:279–292, 1992.
23. Yonghong Yao, Haiyun Zhou, and Yeong-Cheng Liou. Strong convergence of a modified Krasnoselski-Mann iterative algorithm for non-expansive mappings. *Journal of Applied Mathematics and Computing*, 29:383–389, 2008.

DeGAS: Gradient-Based Optimization of Probabilistic Programs without Sampling

Francesca Randone[1] , Romina Doz[2] ,
Mirco Tribastone[3] , and Luca
Bortolussi[2]

[1] TU Wien, Wien, Austria `francesca.randone@tuwien.ac.at`
[2] University of Trieste, Trieste, Italy
[3] IMT School for Advanced Studies Lucca, Lucca, Italy

Abstract. We present DeGAS, a differentiable Gaussian approximate semantics for loopless probabilistic programs that enables sample-free, gradient-based optimization in models with both continuous and discrete components. DeGAS evaluates programs under a Gaussian-mixture semantics and replaces measure-zero predicates and discrete branches with a vanishing smoothing, yielding closed-form expressions for posterior and path probabilities. We prove differentiability of these quantities with respect to program parameters, enabling end-to-end optimization via standard automatic differentiation, without Monte Carlo estimators. On thirteen benchmark programs, DeGAS achieves accuracy and runtime competitive with variational inference and MCMC. Importantly, it reliably tackles optimization problems where sampling-based baselines fail to converge due to conditioning involving continuous variables.

Keywords: Probabilistic Programming · Gaussian Mixtures · Differentiable Semantics · Sample-Free Optimization

1 Introduction

Probabilistic programming languages (PPLs) extend general-purpose languages with probabilistic primitives. In recent years they have received significant attention, motivated by their ability to model and analyze inherently stochastic systems such as randomized algorithms [18], probabilistic cyber-physical systems [23], and machine-learning models [8].

Probabilistic programs (PPs) typically expose parameters that must be tuned to meet goals: maximize likelihood [10, 5], satisfy safety constraints [31], calibrate uncertainty [13], or optimize bespoke utilities [29]. Current practice relies on sampling—either Markov chain Monte Carlo (MCMC) [2] or variational inference (VI) [7]. While often effective, these methods can exhibit high-variance gradient estimates and brittle behavior on discontinuous objectives induced by branching and hard conditioning, frequently necessitating problem-specific reparameterization tricks [34, 28, 1, 14, 26].

S. Junges and G. Katz (Eds.): TACAS 2026, LNCS 16505, pp. 566–585, 2026.
https://doi.org/10.1007/978-3-032-22752-2_29

This paper asks the following: *Can we obtain gradients for PP objectives without sampling?* We answer affirmatively by introducing DeGAS, a differentiable Gaussian-mixture approximate semantics that renders end-to-end evaluation differentiable, enabling optimization with off-the-shelf automatic differentiation (AD) and *without* Monte Carlo estimators. The key idea is a principled, vanishing smoothing of discrete and measure-zero constructs (e.g., point masses and Boolean predicates), which yields differentiable densities and path probabilities throughout a program's execution. This delivers deterministic objective values and gradients with respect to the program parameters.

DeGAS builds on the SOGA (second-order Gaussian approximation) semantics for a class of loop-free probabilistic programs [30]. With SOGA, each program state is represented as a Gaussian mixture (GM) and program constructs update mixtures analytically (affine transforms, products, and conditioning via truncation) to approximate the posterior over program variables. DeGAS smooths the discontinuities that arise under branching and conditioning by injecting small Gaussian noise where needed and relaxing predicates accordingly, while preserving closure under mixture operations. We prove differentiability of posterior distributions and path probabilities with respect to parameters, and we show that as the smoothing parameter tends to zero, the differentiable semantics converges to the unsmoothed SOGA semantics under mild regularity conditions.

We implement DeGAS in PyTorch leveraging its AD capabilities to provide a sample-free gradient-based optimizer. Numerical experiments show that, on thirteen benchmark programs, DeGAS achieves accuracy and runtime competitive with VI and MCMC. More important, we show DeGAS is able to solve instances of optimization problems for which sampling baselines fail to converge due to the presence of constructs such as conditional statements depending on continuous variables.

Structure of the paper. Section 2 reviews related work. Section 3 presents the syntax and defines the differentiable semantics. Section 4 states and proves our main properties (differentiability and convergence). Section 5 reports the experimental results. Section 6 concludes.

2 Related Work

To the best of our knowledge, this is the first work that computes gradients of probabilistic programs without sampling. For deterministic programs, the idea of smoothing to achieve sample-free optimization via gradient-free methods has been explored in [11, 12], and successively adapted for automatic differentiation in [20]. However, as will be shown in Section 4, the smoothing of deterministic programs does not trivially carry over to PPs.

An attempt was made to extend the smoothing to PPs in Leios [22]. Leios takes as input a discrete or hybrid discrete-continuous PP and approximates it with a fully continuous one using smoothing. The authors notice that the relaxation parameters must be tuned to avoid collapsing any probability event to zero. For example, a variable initially distributed as a Bernoulli after smoothing becomes distributed as a mixture of two components, with means in 0 and 1 and small standard deviations. This implies that the probability of the event $x == 0$ passes from 0.5 to 0. To avoid this, Leios solves an optimization problem to replace all Booleans predicate depending on smoothed variables. Conceptually, we are close in spirit in that we tackle discontinuities by controlled smoothing. However, the goal is fundamentally different: similarly to the previously mentioned works, Leios aids sampling-based inference; instead, we enable sample-free optimization.

For PPs, most of the work has focused on coupling AD with sampling-based inference, designing gradient estimators for discontinuous programs—either to improve MCMC and VI globally [34, 28, 1, 14, 26] or only on the discontinuous parts [35, 21, 24]. These approaches still estimate gradients via sampling and are used to run inference faster or more stably. In contrast, we compute deterministic gradients by evaluating a differentiable program semantics; no Monte Carlo appears in the optimization loop. This lets us optimize likelihood and non-likelihood probabilistic objectives directly (such as reachability), not just expected values under a sampler.

Some methods start from an input program and compute a second program, whose expected return value is the derivative of the input program's expected return value [3, 27]; the new program can then be sampled to obtain gradient estimations. We differ in both goal (optimization rather than derivative-estimation for inference) and mechanism: for our smoothing, we leverage the analytical properties of the SOGA/GM semantics [30], that yield closed-form truncated moments and CDFs for every node, which we then backpropagate through analytically.

3   Syntax and Semantics

SOGA was introduced in [30] as a semantics for a loop-free PPL that manipulates input variables distributed as GMs. SOGA makes the language closed under GMs, providing an analytical representation of the posterior that enables efficient computation of moments, cumulative distribution functions (CDFs), and probability density functions (PDFs). This semantics is the second-order approximation of a family of approximate semantics based on Gaussian Mixtures, guaranteed to convergence to the true one, and demonstrated high accuracy across a variety of programs. Here, we add the possibility of specifying parameters to be used for optimization.

Notation. For a distribution D, let f_D denote its pdf. A normal random variable with mean μ and covariance matrix Σ is denoted by $\mathcal{N}(\mu, \Sigma)$. A GM is a weighted sum of Gaussians, $G_{\pi,\mu,\Sigma} = \sum_{i=1}^{c} \pi_i \mathcal{N}(\mu_i, \Sigma_i)$ where c is the number of *components* and $(\pi_i)_{\{i=1,...,c\}}$ is the vector of *weights* satisfying $0 \leq \pi_i \leq 1$ and $\sum_{i=1}^{c} \pi_i = 1$. A Dirac delta centered on x_0 is denoted by δ_{x_0}. Let $x[x_i \to e]$ denote the vector with e as i-th component, and every other component equal to x_j. Let $\mathrm{Marg}_y(D)$ denote the marginal of distribution D with respect to sub-vector y. We denote with $\mathbf{I}_n$ the identity matrix of dimension n and with $\mathbb{I}_A$ the characteristic function of set A. We use $\otimes$ for the product of probability measures: if D_1, D_2 are distributions on $\mathbb{R}$, $D_1 \otimes D_2$ is a distribution on $\mathbb{R}^2$ whose marginal on the first coordinate is D_1 and the marginal on the second coordinate is D_2. For a predicate b, $P_D(b)$ denotes the probability of b under distribution D. $D_{|b}$ denotes distribution D conditioned to b.

3.1 Syntax

Variables. We consider programs defined over a vector of real variables $x = (x_1, \ldots, x_n)$ and a set Θ of parameters, $\Theta = \{\theta_i = d_i\}_{i=1,\ldots,p}$ where θ_i is the name of the parameter and $d_i \in \mathbb{R}$ is an initial value. In addition, for each parameter an interval domain is specified. For instance, we can specify a standard deviation (std) as a parameter called σ, with initial value 1, and interval domain $(0, +\infty)$.

Expressions. Expressions over program variables can either be products between two variables or linear expressions on program variables, where the coefficients of the variables or the zero-th order term can either be constants or parameters:

$$\mathbb{E} = \{x_i x_j \mid i, j = 1 \ldots n\} \cup \{c_1 x_1 + \ldots + c_n x_n + c_0 \mid c_i \in \mathbb{R} \cup \Theta\} \; .$$

Boolean predicates. Boolean predicates are *true* or *false*, or inequalities between a variable and a real number, which can either be a constant or a parameter:

$$\mathbb{B} = \{true, false\} \cup \{x_i \bowtie c \mid c \in \mathbb{R} \cup \Theta, \bowtie \in \{<, \leq, ==, \geq, >\}\}$$

Boolean predicates in the guards of conditional (if) statements are restricted to $\mathbb{B}_{\mathrm{if}}$ with $\bowtie \in \{<, \leq, \geq, >\}$.

The restrictions on expressions and Boolean predicates are inherited by SOGA and are motivated by the need to preserve closure of the Gaussian-mixture semantics under the supported operations. However, our grammar is expressive enough to encode general polynomial assignments and guards.

Language. Our syntax uses the primitive $x \sim gm(\pi, \mu, \sigma)$ for random assignments with GMs, where $\pi = (\pi_1, \ldots, \pi_c)$, $\mu = (\mu_1, \ldots, \mu_c)$, $\sigma = (\sigma_1, \ldots, \sigma_c)$ are vectors of weights, means and standard deviations, respectively, and π_i, μ_i, σ_i can either be real constants or real parameters, with the restriction that $\pi_i, \sigma_i \geq 0$ and $\sum_i \pi_i = 1$. The complete grammar of our programming language is:

$$
\begin{array}{lll}
P ::= & \texttt{skip} \mid x \texttt{ := } e & \text{(deterministic assignments)} \\
& x \sim gm(\pi, \mu, \sigma) & \text{(random assignment)} \\
& \texttt{if } b \texttt{ \{ } P \texttt{ \} else \{ } P \texttt{ \}} & \text{(test)} \\
& \texttt{observe } b & \text{(observe)} \\
& P; \; P & \text{(sequential composition)}
\end{array}
$$

The $\texttt{observe } b$ construct represents a hard observe, which conditions the program's distribution on the event specified by b, effectively truncating the support of the resulting distribution to the states satisfying b.

3.2   Semantics

We denote with $\llbracket \cdot \rrbracket$ the operator for the *exact semantics* of the program,intended in the classic sense of Kozen's Semantics 2 [19]; instead, $\llbracket \cdot \rrbracket^S$ denotes the *Second Order Gaussian Approximation (SOGA) semantics operator* as defined in [30] (both reported in Appedix A for completeness), which closes the language under GMs. The closure is realized by replacing every distribution that would not be a GM in the exact semantics (for instance, when conditioning due to a branch) with a GM. The substitution is performed by a dedicated operator called *the moment-matching operator*, denoted by $\mathcal{T}_{\mathrm{gm}}$, which approximates a density function with a GM by matching its first two moments. In particular, when $\mathcal{T}_{\mathrm{gm}}$ acts on a mixture, it acts on every component; when it acts on a single-component mixture, it maps it to a Gaussian having mean and covariance matrix matching the original distribution, denoted by μ_D, Σ_D. Formally:

$$
\mathcal{T}_{\mathrm{gm}}(D) = \begin{cases} \pi_1 \mathcal{T}_{\mathrm{gm}}(D_1) + \ldots + \pi_c \mathcal{T}_{\mathrm{gm}}(D_c) & \text{if } D = \sum_{i=1}^{c} \pi_i D_i \\ \mathcal{N}(\mu_D, \Sigma_D) & \text{else.} \end{cases}
\tag{1}
$$

Notably, when acting on Gaussian mixtures, $\mathcal{T}_{\mathrm{gm}}$ leaves them unaltered [30].

Non-differentiability of SOGA semantics. By closing the semantics with respect to GMs, the general pdf of the distribution yielded by a program dependent on parameters Θ can be shown to take the general form

$$
f_\Theta(x) = \sum_{i=1}^{C} \frac{\pi_i(\Theta)}{(2\pi)^{n/2} |\Sigma_i(\Theta)|^{1/2}} \exp\left(-\frac{1}{2}(x - \mu_i(\Theta))^T \Sigma_i^{-1}(\Theta)(x - \mu_i(\Theta)) \right).
$$

Assuming that $\pi(\Theta), \mu(\Theta)$ and $\Sigma(\Theta)$ are differentiable in Θ, f_Θ can only be nondifferentiable in Θ if a covariance matrix is singular, i.e., $|\Sigma_i(\Theta)| = 0$.

Figure 1 shows four minimal examples in which this may occur. In Figure 1a, y is assigned a constant value c, setting its variance to 0; in Figure 1b, y is assigned with a discrete (Bernoulli) distribution, yielding again 0 variance; in Figure 1c, y is assigned a deterministic function of x, so the distribution of y is completely determined by that of x; reflected in the singularity of the covariance matrix. In Figure 1d, y is observed to take on a real value, having an effect analogous to a constant assignment.

In order to deal with such cases consistently, we smooth the semantics. Smoothing will depend on a hyper-parameter $\epsilon > 0$ that we assume fixed for the rest of this section. Intuitively, ϵ represents the amount of smoothing applied to the program and corresponds to the standard deviation of the Gaussian perturbation applied to smoothed variables.

Next, we discuss how we smooth Boolean predicates and the whole semantics separately. Throughout the section, we let V denote the set of program variables that have been smoothed.

```
x = gm([1.], [0], [1]);
y = c;
```

$$\pi = 1, \quad \mu = \begin{bmatrix} 0 \\ c \end{bmatrix}, \quad \Sigma = \begin{bmatrix} 1 & 0 \\ 0 & 0 \end{bmatrix}$$

(a) Assignment with a constant.

```
x = gm([1.], [0], [1]);
y = gm([0.5, 0.5], [0, 1], [0, 0]);
```

$$\pi_1 = 0.5, \ \mu_1 = \begin{bmatrix} 0 \\ 0 \end{bmatrix}, \ \Sigma_1 = \begin{bmatrix} 1 & 0 \\ 0 & 0 \end{bmatrix}$$

$$\pi_2 = 0.5, \ \mu_2 = \begin{bmatrix} 0 \\ 1 \end{bmatrix}, \ \Sigma_2 = \begin{bmatrix} 1 & 0 \\ 0 & 0 \end{bmatrix}$$

(b) Assignment with a discrete distribution.

```
x = gm([1.], [0], [1]);
y = x + 1;
```

$$\pi = 1, \quad \mu = \begin{bmatrix} 0 \\ 1 \end{bmatrix}, \quad \Sigma = \begin{bmatrix} 1 & 1 \\ 1 & 1 \end{bmatrix}$$

(c) Deterministic function.

```
x = gm([1.], [0], [1]);
y = gm([1.], [0], [1]);
observe(y == 0.5);
```

$$\pi = 1, \quad \mu = \begin{bmatrix} 0 \\ 0.5 \end{bmatrix}, \quad \Sigma = \begin{bmatrix} 1 & 0 \\ 0 & 0 \end{bmatrix}$$

(d) Observation of a constant value.

Fig. 1: Nondifferentiability of SOGA semantics. Examples yielding singular covariance matrices.

Smoothing operator for Boolean predicates. We define the following smoothing operator for Boolean predicates, that takes as input a predicate b and a set of smoothed variables V and returns a new predicate.

$$\mathcal{B}_\epsilon(x \bowtie c, V) = \begin{cases} x > c + \delta_\epsilon & \text{if } \bowtie \text{ is } >, x \in V \\ x > c - \delta_\epsilon & \text{if } \bowtie \text{ is } \geq, x \in V \\ x < c + \delta_\epsilon & \text{if } \bowtie \text{ is } \leq, x \in V \\ x < c - \delta_\epsilon & \text{if } \bowtie \text{ is } <, x \in V \\ (x > c - \delta_\epsilon) \wedge (x < c + \delta_\epsilon) & \text{if } \bowtie \text{ is } == t, x \in V \\ x \bowtie c & \text{else} \end{cases} \tag{2}$$

For now we allow δ_ϵ to vary with ϵ under the only assumption that $\lim_{\epsilon \to 0} \delta_\epsilon = 0$. In the next section we will introduce an additional restriction to guarantee convergence to the SOGA semantics.

DeGAS. As in [30], we introduce the semantics in terms of the program's control flow graph (cfg). Each node in the graph represents a program instruction. We consider six node types: *entry, det, rnd, test, observe* and *exit* and use the notation $v: type$ to denote that v is of type *type*. Nodes of type *det* are labelled by `skip` or by a deterministic assignment $x_i := e$. Nodes of type *rnd* are labelled by a random assignment $x_i \sim gm(\pi, \mu, \sigma)$. Nodes of type *test* are labelled by a Boolean predicate in $\mathbb{B}_{if}$, while *observe* node are labelled by a Boolean predicate in $\mathbb{B}$. A function *arg* is defined on all labelled nodes v, returning the label of v. In addition, a function *cond* is defined on the set of *det* and *rnd* nodes, returning either *true, false* or *none* and such that $cond(v) = none$ if and only if the parent of v is not a *test* node. Arithmetic expressions and Boolean predicates are interpreted in the standard way. An expression $e \in \mathbb{E}$ denotes a mapping $e \colon \mathbb{R}^n \to \mathbb{R}$. A Boolean predicate $b \in \mathbb{B}$ denotes the set of vectors $x \in \mathbb{R}^n$ that satisfy the predicate.

For a program P we let Ω^P denote the set of paths in its cfg. For each path $\omega \in \Omega^P$ the function $s_\omega(v)$ associates $v \in \omega$ with its succcessor in ω. The semantics of path ω, denoted by $[\![\omega]\!]^{\Delta,\epsilon}$ is defined as a function taking no input and returning a pair (p, D) where $p \in \mathbb{R}_{\geq 0}$ and D is a GM on $\mathbb{R}^n$. The semantics of a path $\omega = v_0..v_n$ is defined as the composition of the semantics of each node in the path: $[\![\omega]\!]^{\Delta,\epsilon} = [\![v_n]\!]_\omega^{\Delta,\epsilon} \circ \ldots \circ [\![v_0]\!]_\omega^{\Delta,\epsilon}$.

As noted earlier, when computing the semantics of a node, in addition to p and D, we need to keep track of the smoothed variables, so we augment the semantics with a set V, containing the variables that would be discrete in the exact semantics. The semantics of a node v is a function taking as input a triple (p, D, V), and returning a triple (p', D', V') of the same type. The only exceptions are the *entry* node which takes no input and the *exit* node which just outputs the pair (p, D) The semantics of each node type is defined separately.

- If v: *entry*, then $[\![v]\!]_\omega^{\Delta,\epsilon} = (1, \mathcal{N}(0, \mathbb{I}_n), \emptyset)$.
- If v: *det*, let D' denote the distribution of $x[x_i \to e]$ and D^ϵ denote the distribution of $x[x_i \to e + z]$, where z is a fresh program variable with distribution $\mathcal{N}(0, \epsilon)$. Let V' be $V \cup \{x_i\}$ if all variables in e are in V and $V' = V$ else. Then:

$$
[\![v]\!]_\omega^{\Delta,\epsilon}(p, D, V) = \begin{cases} (p, D, V) & arg(v) = \texttt{skip} \\ (p, D^\epsilon, V \cup \{x_i\}) & arg(v) = x_i := c \\ (p, D^\epsilon, V') & arg(v) = x_i := e, e \text{ linear}, x_i \text{ not in } e \\ (p, \mathcal{T}_{\text{gm}}(D'), V') & \text{else.} \end{cases}
$$

- If v: *rnd* and $arg(v) = x_i \sim gm(\pi, \mu, \sigma)$, let σ' be the vector with $\sigma'_j = \sigma_j$ if $\sigma_j \neq 0$ and $\sigma'_j = \epsilon$ else. Then:

$$
[\![v]\!]_\omega^{\Delta,\epsilon}(p, D, V) = \begin{cases} (p, \text{Marg}_{x \setminus x_i}(D) \otimes G_{\pi,\mu,\sigma'}, V \cup \{x_i\}) & \sigma_j = 0 \text{ for some } j \\ (p, \text{Marg}_{x \setminus x_i}(D) \otimes G_{\pi,\mu,\sigma}, V) & \text{else.} \end{cases}
$$

- If v: *test*, letting $arg(v) = b$ and $b' = \mathcal{B}_\epsilon(b, V)$:

$$
[\![v]\!]_\omega^{\Delta,\epsilon}(p, D, V) = \begin{cases} (p \cdot P_D(b'), \mathcal{T}_{\text{gm}}(D_{|b'}), V) & cond(s_\omega(v)) = true \\ (p \cdot P_D(\neg b'), \mathcal{T}_{\text{gm}}(D_{|\neg b'}), V) & cond(s_\omega(v)) = false. \end{cases}
$$

- If v: *observe*, letting $arg(v) = b$, $I = \int_{\mathbb{R}^{n-1}} f_D(x[x_i \to c])d(x \setminus x_i)$ and $b' = \mathcal{B}_\epsilon(b, V)$:

$$\llbracket v \rrbracket_\omega^{\Delta,\epsilon}(p, D, V) = \begin{cases} (p \cdot I, \mathrm{Marg}_{x \setminus x_i}(D_{|b}) \otimes \mathcal{N}(c, \epsilon), V \cup \{x_i\}) & \\ \qquad\qquad\qquad\qquad b \text{ is } x_i == c, x_i \notin V \\ (p \cdot P_D(b'), \mathcal{T}_{\mathrm{gm}}(D_{|b'}), V) & \text{else} \end{cases}$$

- If v: *exit*, $\llbracket v \rrbracket_\omega^{\Delta,\epsilon}(p, D, V) = (p, D)$.

A program P is called *valid* if for at least a path $\omega \in \Omega^P$ $\llbracket \omega \rrbracket = (p, D)$ with $p > 0$. The semantics of a valid program P is then defined as a mixture of the semantics of its path:

$$\llbracket P \rrbracket^{\Delta,\epsilon} = \sum_{\substack{\omega \in \Omega^P \\ \llbracket \omega \rrbracket^{\Delta,\epsilon} = (p,D)}} \frac{p \cdot D}{\sum_{\substack{\omega' \in \Omega^P \\ \llbracket \omega' \rrbracket^{\Delta,\epsilon} = (p',D')}} p'}.$$

Let us go back to Figure 1, to briefly discuss how $\llbracket \cdot \rrbracket^{\Delta,\epsilon}$ avoids the discontinuities. For the program in Figure 1a, $\llbracket \cdot \rrbracket^{\Delta,\epsilon}$ effectively assigns y with $c + z$, where z is a freshly defined variable, Gaussianly distributed with mean 0 and std ϵ. This is equivalent to assigning y with $\mathcal{N}(c, \epsilon)$, and yields a non-degenerate covariance matrix $\Sigma = \begin{bmatrix} 1 & 0 \\ 0 & \epsilon^2 \end{bmatrix}$. For the program in Figure 1b, $\llbracket \cdot \rrbracket^{\Delta,\epsilon}$ replaces components with zero std with non-degenerate components with std ϵ. Therefore the assignment effectivaly performed would be $y = gm([0.5, 0.5], [0, 1], [\epsilon, \epsilon])$, yielding $\Sigma_1 = \Sigma_2 = \begin{bmatrix} 1 & 0 \\ 0 & \epsilon^2 \end{bmatrix}$. For the program in Figure 1c, $\llbracket \cdot \rrbracket^{\Delta,\epsilon}$ acts similarly as in the first case, y is a assigned with $x + 1 + z$, with z fresh Gaussian variable with mean 0 and std ϵ. The covariance matrix then becomes $\Sigma = \begin{bmatrix} 1 & 1 \\ 1 & 1 + \epsilon^2 \end{bmatrix}$. Finally, for the program in Figure 1d, the variance of y after the observation is corrected and put equal to ϵ, yielding $\Sigma = \begin{bmatrix} 1 & 0 \\ 0 & \epsilon^2 \end{bmatrix}$.

To avoid unwanted changes in the behaviour of the probability mass due to the smoothing, $\llbracket \cdot \rrbracket^{\Delta,\epsilon}$ uses the operator $\mathcal{B}_\epsilon$ to interpret differently Boolean predicates when they involve smoothed variables, as reflected in the definition of the semantics of *test* and *observe* nodes. This has the effect of avoiding conditioning to zero probability events, since $\llbracket \cdot \rrbracket^{\Delta,\epsilon}$ always acts on non-degenerate distributions and $\mathcal{B}_\epsilon(b, V)$ always returns open sets.

In the next section, we will prove that the semantics computed by $\llbracket \cdot \rrbracket^{\Delta,\epsilon}$ is indeed differentiable in the program parameters and that by suitably choosing the value of δ_ϵ when applying $\mathcal{B}_\epsilon$ $\llbracket \cdot \rrbracket^{\Delta,\epsilon}$ will converge to to $\llbracket \cdot \rrbracket^S$.

Example 1. Consider the program P and its cfg in Fig. 2, where θ and σ are parameters with $\theta \in (-\infty, +\infty)$ and $\sigma \in (0, +\infty)$. The exact semantics is:

$$\llbracket P \rrbracket = \Phi(\theta/\sigma) \cdot (\mathcal{N}(0, \sigma)_{|x<\theta} \otimes \delta_{-1}) + (1 - \Phi(\theta/\sigma)) \cdot (\mathcal{N}(0, \sigma)_{|x \geq \theta} \otimes \delta_1)$$

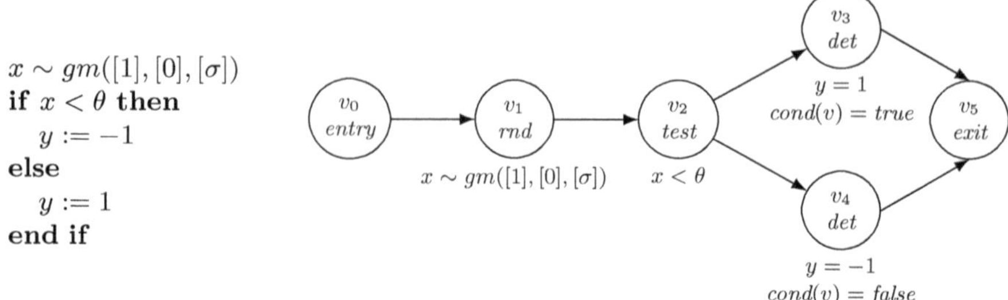

Fig. 2: Example program P (left) and its cfg (right).

In particular, the exact marginal over y is a discrete distribution putting $\Phi(\theta/\sigma)$ probability mass on -1 and $1 - \Phi(\theta/\sigma)$ on 1. Therefore, the exact marginal over y is nondifferentiable (in fact, discontinuous) in the parameters.

Using the SOGA semantics, closed with respect to GMs, yields:

$$[\![P]\!]^S = \Phi(\theta/\sigma) \cdot \mathcal{T}_{\mathrm{gm}}(\mathcal{N}(0,\sigma)_{|x<\theta} \otimes \delta_{-1}) + (1 - \Phi(\theta/\sigma)) \cdot \mathcal{T}_{\mathrm{gm}}(\mathcal{N}(0,\sigma)_{|x\geq\theta} \otimes \delta_1)$$

However, the marginal over y remains unchanged, and therefore still nondifferentiable. When computing the differentiable semantics, not only is the moment-matching operator applied to close the semantics with respect to GMs, degeneracies are avoided by smoothing the assignments of y. This yields:

$$[\![P]\!]^{\Delta,\epsilon} = \Phi(\theta/\sigma) \cdot \mathcal{T}_{\mathrm{gm}}(\mathcal{N}(0,\sigma)_{|x<\theta} \otimes \mathcal{N}(-1,\epsilon)) +$$
$$+ (1 - \Phi(\theta/\sigma)) \cdot \mathcal{T}_{\mathrm{gm}}(\mathcal{N}(0,\sigma)_{|x\geq\theta} \otimes \mathcal{N}(1,\epsilon))$$

For any $\sigma \in (0, +\infty)$, the differentiable marginal over y is given by

$$\Phi(\theta/\sigma) \cdot \mathcal{N}(-1,\epsilon) + (1 - \Phi(\theta/\sigma)) \cdot \mathcal{N}(1,\epsilon).$$

The marginal densities of the three semantics, computed for $\sigma = 1$ and $\theta = 0$ are represented in Fig. 3, where the densities of the components of the mixtures are highlighted in orange and for DeGAS we fixed $\epsilon = 0.05$.

4   Properties of $[\![\cdot]\!]^{\Delta,\epsilon}$

In this section we prove two properties of the DeGAS semantics operator $[\![\cdot]\!]^{\Delta,\epsilon}$, namely differentiability of $[\![P]\!]^{\Delta,\epsilon}$ with respect to the parameters and convergence of $[\![P]\!]^{\Delta,\epsilon}$ to $[\![P]\!]^S$ as $\epsilon \to 0$.

Differentiability. First, we focus on the differentiability of the DeGAS semantics with respect to Θ. For this reason, in this subsection we make the dependence of the programs on the parameters explicit, using the notation $P(\Theta)$. For instance, program P from Example 1 would be denoted as $P(\theta, \sigma)$. We assume that the parameters come with assigned initial values and interval domains and that

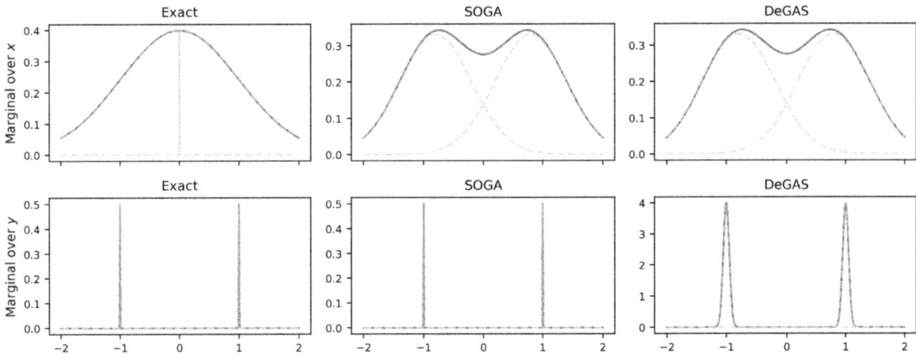

Fig. 3: Marginal posterior densities of program P under different semantics. The orange lines highlight the different components of the mixtures.

they always take values in the interval domains. For instance, for $P(\theta, \sigma)$ we could specify the initial values $d_\theta = 0$ and $d_\sigma = 1$ and the interval domains $\theta \in (-\infty, +\infty)$, $\sigma \in (0, +\infty)$. We say that a distribution $D(\Theta)$ is differentiable in Θ if its pdf is. For example, if $D(\Theta)$ is a GM, $D(\Theta)$ is differentiable in Θ if, for $i = 1, \ldots, c$ (i) $\pi_i(\Theta)$, $\mu_i(\Theta)$ and $\Sigma_i(\Theta)$ are differentiable in Θ; (ii) $\Sigma_i(\Theta)$ is non-singular for every value of Θ that satisfies the constraints.

Theorem 1. *For any valid program $P(\Theta)$, $[\![P(\Theta)]\!]^{\Delta, \epsilon}$ returns $(p'(\Theta), D'(\Theta), V')$ such that $p'(\Theta)$ and $D'(\Theta)$ are differentiable in Θ.*

This is the core theoretical result of the paper (proved in the Appendix), because it allows for a safe application of gradient-based optimization methods to PPs.

Convergence. DeGAS adds an additional layer of approximation, through the Gaussian perturbation, to the already approximated semantics of SOGA $[\![\cdot]\!]^S$. We prove that this additional approximation tends to disappear when the perturbation becomes very small, i.e. in the limit for $\epsilon \to 0$. Coupled with SOGA's convergence result to the true semantics $[\![\cdot]\!]$, this offers a principled way of obtaining sample-free gradients for a class of PPs.

DeGAS' convergence proof (provided in the Appendix) is surprisingly subtle and deserves an intuitive explanation. When smoothing the predicates, the dependence of δ_ϵ on ϵ can jeopardize the convergence. The following example motivates the introduction of an additional requirement, called *consistency*, that is needed to guarantee convergence.

Example 1. We consider two example programs:

$$P_1 \colon x := 0; y \sim gm([1.], [0.], [1.]); \texttt{observe } x \geq 0,$$
$$P_2 \colon x := 0; y \sim gm([1.], [0.], [1.]); \texttt{observe } x > 0.$$

In SOGA we have $[\![P_1]\!]^S = (1, \delta_0 \times \mathcal{N}(0,1))$ and $[\![P_2]\!]^S = (0, \delta_0 \times \mathcal{N}(0,1))$. In DeGAS, before the observe statement for both programs we have the output triple $(1, D_\epsilon, \{x\})$ where $D_\epsilon = \mathcal{N}(0,\epsilon) \times \mathcal{N}(0,1)$. However, the predicates of the observe node are smoothed differently:

$$\mathcal{B}_\epsilon(x \geq 0, \{x\}) = x > -\delta_\epsilon, \qquad \mathcal{B}_\epsilon(x > 0, \{x\}) = x > \delta_\epsilon.$$

Consider P_1. To compute the differentiable semantics of the observe node we need to compute $P_{D_\epsilon}(x > -\delta_\epsilon)$ and the moments of $(D_\epsilon)_{|x>\delta_\epsilon}$, and we want them to tend to 1 and to the moments of $\delta_0 \times \mathcal{N}(0,1)$, respectively. Here, we focus on the probabilities, since the convergence of the moments are proved using similar arguments. Letting $\varPhi$ denote the cdf of the standard Gaussian, then $P_{D_\epsilon}(x > -\delta_\epsilon) = 1 - \varPhi\left(-\frac{\delta_\epsilon}{\epsilon}\right)$. For this quantity to tend to 1 we need $\frac{\delta_\epsilon}{\epsilon} \to \infty$. Intuitively, this limit forces δ_ϵ to decrease slower than the variance of x (in this case ϵ), so that as ϵ tends to 0 more and more of the probability mass of D_ϵ is inside $\{x > -\delta_\epsilon\}$. Moreover, it is clear that if δ_ϵ is a linear function of ϵ or if it decreases faster than it, the limit cannot hold.

Analogously consider P_2 for which $P_{D_\epsilon}(x > \delta_\epsilon) = 1 - \varPhi(\frac{\delta_\epsilon}{\epsilon})$. For it to tend to 0 we need again $\frac{\delta_\epsilon}{\epsilon} \to \infty$. This time the slower convergence of δ_ϵ to 0 allows a larger part of the probability mass of D_ϵ to remain outside $\{x > \delta_\epsilon\}$.

The previous example leads us to the following definition and theorem (we report the full proof in the Appendix).

Definition 1. *The operator $\mathcal{B}_\epsilon$ is applied* consistently *if for every test and observe node with $\arg(v) = x_i \bowtie c$ when $\mathcal{B}_\epsilon$ is applied to compute $[\![v]\!]^{\Delta,\epsilon}(p, D, V)$ and $x_i \in V$, δ is chosen such that:*

$$\lim_{\epsilon \to 0} \delta_\epsilon(\epsilon) = 0 \qquad and \qquad \lim_{\epsilon \to 0} \frac{\delta_\epsilon(\epsilon)}{\sqrt{\Sigma_{x_i, x_i}(\epsilon)}} = +\infty$$

for every $\Sigma(\epsilon)$ covariance matrix of a component of D. The dependence of Σ from ϵ is guaranteed by the fact that $x_i \in V$.

Theorem 2. *Suppose P is a valid program and $\mathcal{B}_\epsilon$ is applied consinstently when computing $[\![P]\!]^{\Delta,\epsilon}$. Then $\lim_{\epsilon \to 0} [\![P]\!]^{\Delta,\epsilon} = [\![P]\!]^S$ (where convergence for the distributions is intended in the sense of convergence in distribution).*

We remark that, while in theory it is possible to let ϵ tend to 0 to make the additional error vanish, in practice we want to use a value of ϵ large enough to enable efficient gradient-based optimization, as will be discussed next.

5　Experimental Evaluation

Setup. We evaluate DeGAS along two axes: (i) we optimize parameters of benchmark probabilistic programs taken from the literature comparing with Variational Inference (VI) and Markov Chain Monte Carlo (MCMC); (ii) we evaluate

DeGAS on programs with discontinuities related to continuous variables, which, as we will show, make standard optimization methods inapplicable. In this case we consider classic models of cyber-physical systems (CPS), whose parameters are synthesized to optimize trajectory likelihoods or reachability properties.

We implemented DeGAS in Pytorch, leveraging automatic differentiation for the gradient computation (cf. Appendix C) and employing Adam as optimizer. For all the experiments we set $\delta_\epsilon = \sqrt{\epsilon}$ and report the results for $\epsilon = 0.001$. The choice of δ_ϵ is coherent for the consistency assumptions. Furthermore, we did not observe significant accuracy changes with respect to the SOGA approximation when varying ϵ, as long as it stays below 0.1, as reported in Appendix D.1. This is further confirmed by the results reported in Appendix D.6, pointing to the fact that the main source of error is that induced by SOGA, while ϵ has a negligible empirical effect for the considered values. For a dedicated analysis of the SOGA error for inference tasks, including discussion on increasing the Gaussian approximation order, we refer the reader to [30]. We run all the experiments on a machine equipped with an Apple M2 processor with 8 cores running at 3.49 GHz and 8 GB RAM. For all the experiments we set a time-out threshold of 600s.

Comparison with VI and MCMC. We start by comparing DeGAS with Variational Inference (VI) and Markov Chain Monte Carlo (MCMC) as implemented in Pyro [5] on a set of 13 case studies taken from the PPL literature ([10, 15, 16]). As a standard benchmark optimization task, we also consider a Proportional Integral Derivative (PID) controller, described in Appendix D.2.

For each case study, some of the significant variables are set as optimizable parameters while others as observables. For the observables a dataset D of size $N = 1000$ is generated for the true value of the parameters. For the PID case study, data correspond to idealized representations of stable dynamics, maintaining the system at its equilibrium point. For each program, the posterior density computed by DeGAS is used to compute the negative log-likelihood $l(\Theta) = -\log f_\Theta(x)$ of the dataset D; then, we optimize to find $\Theta^* = \mathrm{argmin}_\Theta l(\Theta)$.

For both VI and DeGAS, we report the results for the value of the learning rate chosen among $\{0.001, 0.005, 0.01, 0.05, 0.1, 0.2\}$ that achieves the minimum error. The optimization is stopped upon convergence within a tolerance of 10^{-8} with a patience of 30 iterations, with a maximum of 500 steps for DeGAS (except 1000 for the PID model) and 1000 for VI. For VI, we use the `Trace_ELBO` loss[4]. For MCMC, we run the NUTS kernel with 4 chains, initially running inference with 500 samples and 50 warm-up steps. If $\hat{R}$ exceeds 1.05, the procedure is repeated, increasing the number of samples by 500 and the warm-up steps by 50 when the total number of steps is between 2000 and 5000, and by 100 thereafter, up to a maximum of 6000 total steps. All hyperparameter values are reported in Appendix D.3.

Table 1 collects the results, where 'time' refers to the average runtimes (in s) out of 10 executions and 'error' refers to the average relative difference between the optimized value and the real value across all the optimizable parameters of

---

[4] https://docs.pyro.ai/en/dev/inference_algos.html

Model	# Par.	# Var.	VI		MCMC		DeGAS	
			Time	Error	Time	Error	Time	Error
Bernoulli	1	2	0.204	0.024	10.968	0.023	1.986	0.001
Burglary	2	7	3.244	0.913	13.014	0.141	14.347	1.686
ClickGraph	1	6	1.635	0.376	62.546	0.096	21.600	0.086
ClinicalTrial	3	6	1.055	1.980	120.492	2.536	17.070	0.657
Grass	4	6	3.077	0.306	58.151	0.015	317.582	0.036
MurderMistery	1	1	0.792	8.015	14.036	2.303	2.508	0.203
SurveyUnbiased	2	2	0.794	0.013	17.030	0.013	11.570	0.008
TrueSkills	3	6	2.056	0.003	t.o.	t.o.	1.664	0.003
TwoCoins	2	1	0.095	0.864	49.120	0.873	3.410	0.688
AlterMu	3	5	1.007	1.043	t.o.	t.o.	0.640	0.312
AlterMu2	2	3	0.718	0.556	384.730	0.139	0.618	0.096
NormalMixtures	3	3	1.061	0.909	345.409	0.053	2.941	0.386
PID	2	55	10.778	–	nc	nc	213	–

Table 1: Comparison of inference methods across models. Models highlighted in gray indicate cases where DeGAS outperformed both other methods in either accuracy or execution time. For the last model, PID, we are not able to quantify the error, as the true parameters are unknown, but we show the result of the optimization in Figure 7. MCMC fails to converge for this case study ($\hat{R} \gg 1$.)

the program. As the table shows, our approach generally achieves performance comparable to the baseline methods, and in several benchmarks it outperforms them in terms of accuracy. Two models particularly challenging for DeGAS are Grass and Burglary. Both models contain a large number of nested if statements, that give rise to a high number of components in the GM approximation. This problem is also known for SOGA and can be mitigated using a pruning strategy [30], whose tuning is outside the scope of this paper.

Many benchmark programs include conditional statements with Boolean guards over discrete variables. When these conditions are enumerable, both VI MCMC can correctly perform inference through enumeration.[5] However, when the condition depends on continuous variables, the resulting model becomes discontinuous and nondifferentiable, breaking the smoothness assumptions of gradient-based VI and affecting the convergence of MCMC. This behavior is clearly visible in the program on the right inset adapted from [25], where μ_1 and μ_2 are optimizable parameters and whose true value is 0.5 and 1. Fig-

$$v \sim gm([1], [\mu_1], [5])$$
if $v > 0$ **then**
$\quad y \sim gm([1], [\mu_2], [1])$
else
$\quad y \sim gm([1], [-2], [1])$
end if

ure 4 shows that VI has oscillatory loss values (similarly, MCMC does not reach a value of $\hat{R} < 1.05$, indicating nonconvergence), while DeGAS optimizes successfully. This highlights the complementarity of DeGAS with existing methods:

---

[5] https://pyro.ai/examples/enumeration.html

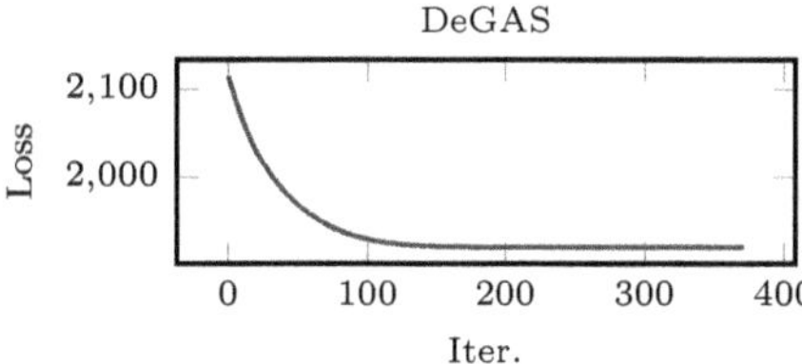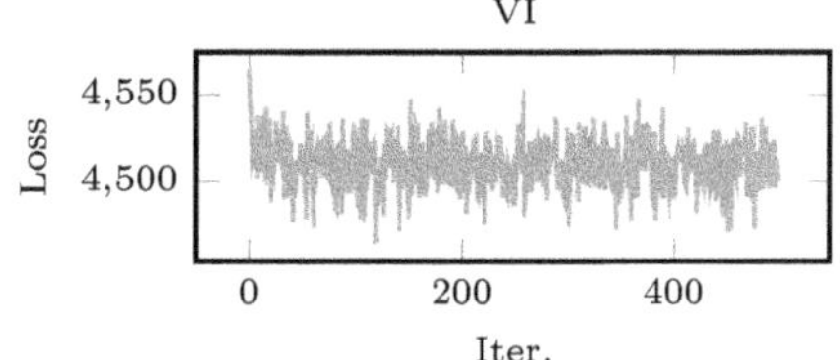

Fig. 4: Comparison of DeGAS and VI loss curves for the program in Section 5.

while it may incur longer runtimes on some benchmarks, it can also enable efficient optimization in challenging discontinuous settings, where VI and MCMC are known to struggle.

Parameter synthesis for cyberphysical systems. We now consider models of cyberphysical systems (CPS) where control-flow branches depend on continuous random variables such that the previously described nondifferentiability issue arises. DeGAS, instead, provides an analytic form for the loss functions: we show examples of both data likelihoods and complex reachability objectives. We consider the following models taken from [32, 11] and fully described in Appendix D.4:

1. **Thermostat** represents a thermostat maintaining fixed temperature by switching an heater on or off when the temperature crosses the thresholds t_{on} and t_{off} (optimizable parameters). The temperature evolves according to a first-order decay process with an added heating term when the heater is active and stochastic fluctuations due to noise.
2. **Gearbox** represents a car's transmission system. We consider a model with three gears. The controller determines when to shift from one gear to the next, allowing only consecutive transitions. The thresholds s_i (optimizable parameters) specify the velocity at which gear i is released and gear $i + 1$ engages. Additionally, gear shifts are not instantaneous: in our model, each transition lasts 0.3 seconds, during which the gearbox remains disengaged. The velocity grows linearly when the gear is engaged and decreases quadratically when disengaged. In both cases it is subject to stochastic fluctuations.
3. **Controlled Bouncing Ball** represents a ball dropped onto a platform with a spring and damper. The spring pushes the ball back with a force determined by the compliance C, and the damper slows the ball according to the coefficient R (both are optimizable parameters). When the ball reaches the platform, the system transitions to a reflection mode, returning to free fall once the height is positive.

Parameter synthesis by data likelihoods. As in the previous case studies, the goal of the optimization is to maximize the negative log-likelihood with respect to a set of 100 trajectories generated from the models using the true parameter values. Table 2 and Figure 5 show that DeGAS consistently recovers parameter values close to the ground truth. The optimized mean trajectories (in red) accurately

Table 2: Results for the CPS optimization from trajectories

Case Study	Params	lr	Steps	Time	Init	Target	Result
Thermostat	t_{ON}, t_{OFF}	0.1	40	61.964	$(15, 22)$	$(17, 20)$	$(16.78, 19.97)$
Gearbox	s_1, s_2	0.15	200	167.643	$(8, 12)$	$(10, 20)$	$(8.69, 19.24)$
Bouncing Ball	$R, 1/C$	0.8	100	500.621	$(-1, 450)$	$(7, 400)$	$(5.27, 408.99)$

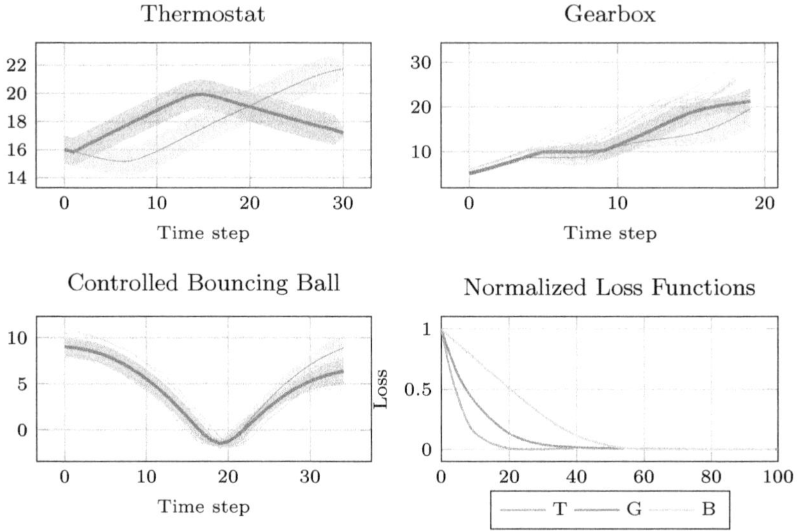

Fig. 5: Mean trajectories with one standard deviation (red) obtained using optimized parameters, compared to trajectories generated with initial parameters (blue). The gray trajectories represent the samples used for optimization.

capture the behavior of the stochastic simulations (in grey), even when the initial trajectories (in blue) are far from the correct one. The normalized loss curves confirm convergence in all three cases.

Synthesis by reachability A complementary synthesis objective consists in optimizing the parameters of the CPS to maximize the probability of reaching specific target states or satisfying certain behavioral constraints. We consider three such cases. Thermostat: the goal is to maximize the probability of reaching the region $T(t) \in [T_{min}, T_{max}] = [19.9, 20.1]$ in mode "ON" at various time points ($\tau_1 = 0.6, \tau_2 = 1.8$ and $\tau_3 = 2.4$); gearbox: we maximize the probability of maintaining velocity below 16 across the whole trajectory; bouncing ball: we want to maximize the probability that the ball reaches $H \geq 7$ when falling after making one bounce. The optimizable parameters are the same as the ones in the previous section.

Table 3: Results for the CPS optimization from reachability properties

Case Study	lr	Steps	Time(s)	Init	Init Loss	Result	Fin. Loss
Thermostat	0.1	100	2770	$(16.5, 22)$	$-2e^{-12}$	$(19.04, 21.30)$	-5695
1Gearbox	0.5	40	52.642	$(10, 20)$	1.000	$(1.92, -1.57)$	0.966
Bounc. Ball	0.2	50	184.264	$(7, 200)$	-0.002	$(-3.87, 210.14)$	-0.979

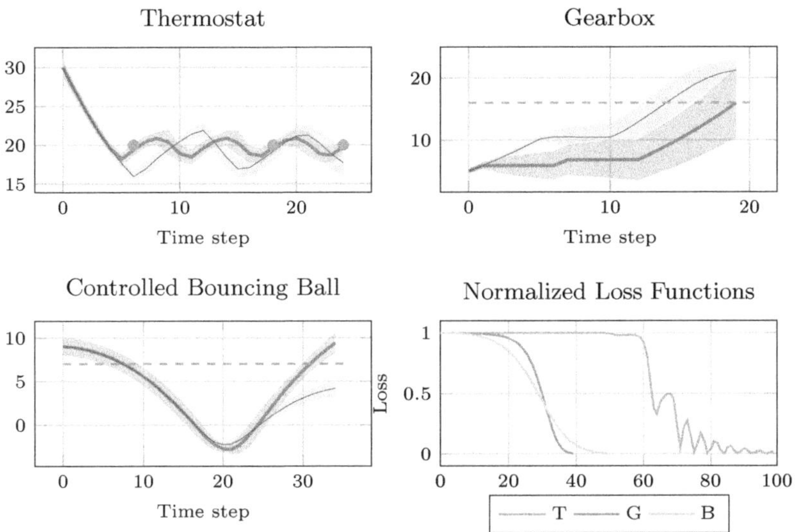

Fig. 6: Mean trajectories with one standard deviation (red) obtained by optimizing the target represented in gray are compared with initial trajectories (blue)

We report the results in Table 3 and Figure 6. The table reports the initial and final loss values, since the true optimal parameters are unknown. As shown in the figure, for all models the optimized trajectories (in red) satisfy the desired behavioral constraints, unlike the initial trajectories (in blue). The optimization curves further confirm convergence across all three models.

6   Conclusions

We introduced DeGAS, a method to enable sample-free optimization of probabilistic programs via a differentiable program semantics. DeGAS smoothens SOGA, a semantics which represents a program evolution through Gaussian-mixture updates (affine maps, products, and truncated moments) that enable an analytic—but, in general, discontinuous, representation of the posterior distribution. We demonstrated the potential of DeGAS in tackling synthesis tasks that cannot be directly solved through classic optimization methods such as variational inference and Markov chain Monte Carlo, due to the presence of discontinuities hindering convergence.

In principle, the main ideas behind DeGAS can be applied to any semantics that (i) represents program states in a tractable form, (ii) supports closed-form (or deterministic-quadrature) updates for transforms and conditioning, and (iii) admits a smooth relaxation of discrete or measure-zero constructs whose parameter $\varepsilon \to 0$ recovers the original semantics. We conjecture that under these conditions, all statements about differentiability hold for $\varepsilon > 0$, and convergence back to the unsmoothed semantics follows by similar arguments as for SOGA. Thus, an interesting direction for future work is to study other semantics such as probabilistic circuits, mixture of exponentials or general symbolic PPs that provide analytic or semi-analytic representations of distributions.

Data Availability Statement

DeGAS is publicly available on Github at https://github.com/frarandone/DeGAS. This paper was accompanied by an artifact for the replication of the experimental results which can be found at: https://zenodo.org/records/18197807.

Acknowledgements

This project has received funding from the European Union's Horizon 2020 research and innovation programme under the Marie Skłodowska Curie grant agreement No 101205923 (MSCA Post-doctoral Fellowship EMBEr).

References

1. Afshar, H.M., Domke, J.: Reflection, refraction, and hamiltonian monte carlo. In: Cortes, C., Lawrence, N.D., Lee, D.D., Sugiyama, M., Garnett, R. (eds.) Advances in Neural Information Processing Systems 28: Annual Conference on Neural Information Processing Systems 2015, December 7-12, 2015, Montreal, Quebec, Canada. pp. 3007–3015 (2015)
2. Andrieu, C., De Freitas, N., Doucet, A., Jordan, M.I.: An introduction to mcmc for machine learning. Machine learning **50**(1), 5–43 (2003)
3. Arya, G., Schauer, M., Schäfer, F., Rackauckas, C.: Automatic differentiation of programs with discrete randomness. In: Koyejo, S., Mohamed, S., Agarwal, A., Belgrave, D., Cho, K., Oh, A. (eds.) Advances in Neural Information Processing Systems 35: Annual Conference on Neural Information Processing Systems 2022, NeurIPS 2022, New Orleans, LA, USA, November 28 - December 9, 2022 (2022)
4. Billingsley, P.: Convergence of probability measures. John Wiley & Sons (2013)
5. Bingham, E., Chen, J.P., Jankowiak, M., Obermeyer, F., Pradhan, N., Karaletsos, T., Singh, R., Szerlip, P., Horsfall, P., Goodman, N.D.: Pyro: Deep universal probabilistic programming. Journal of machine learning research **20**(28), 1–6 (2019)
6. Bishop, C.M., Nasrabadi, N.M.: Pattern recognition and machine learning, vol. 4. Springer (2006)

7. Blei, D.M., Kucukelbir, A., McAuliffe, J.D.: Variational inference: A review for statisticians. Journal of the American statistical Association **112**(518), 859–877 (2017)
8. Borgström, J., Gordon, A.D., Greenberg, M., Margetson, J., Van Gael, J.: Measure transformer semantics for bayesian machine learning. In: European symposium on programming. pp. 77–96. Springer (2011)
9. Boyd, S.P., Vandenberghe, L.: Convex optimization. Cambridge university press (2004)
10. Carpenter, B., Gelman, A., Hoffman, M.D., Lee, D., Goodrich, B., Betancourt, M., Brubaker, M., Guo, J., Li, P., Riddell, A.: Stan: A probabilistic programming language. Journal of statistical software **76**, 1–32 (2017)
11. Chaudhuri, S., Solar-Lezama, A.: Smooth interpretation. ACM Sigplan Notices **45**(6), 279–291 (2010)
12. Chaudhuri, S., Solar-Lezama, A.: Smoothing a program soundly and robustly. In: International Conference on Computer Aided Verification. pp. 277–292. Springer (2011)
13. Chong, A., Menberg, K.: Guidelines for the bayesian calibration of building energy models. Energy and Buildings **174**, 527–547 (2018)
14. Dinh, V., Bilge, A., Zhang, C., IV, F.A.M.: Probabilistic path hamiltonian monte carlo. In: Precup, D., Teh, Y.W. (eds.) Proceedings of the 34th International Conference on Machine Learning, ICML 2017, Sydney, NSW, Australia, 6-11 August 2017. Proceedings of Machine Learning Research, vol. 70, pp. 1009–1018. PMLR (2017), http://proceedings.mlr.press/v70/dinh17a.html
15. Gehr, T., Misailovic, S., Vechev, M.: Psi: Exact symbolic inference for probabilistic programs. In: International Conference on Computer Aided Verification. pp. 62–83. Springer (2016)
16. Huang, Z., Dutta, S., Misailovic, S.: Aqua: Automated quantized inference for probabilistic programs. In: International Symposium on Automated Technology for Verification and Analysis. pp. 229–246. Springer (2021)
17. Kan, R., Robotti, C.: On moments of folded and truncated multivariate normal distributions. Journal of Computational and Graphical Statistics **26**(4), 930–934 (2017)
18. Karp, R.M.: An introduction to randomized algorithms. Discrete Applied Mathematics **34**(1-3), 165–201 (1991)
19. Kozen, D.: Semantics of probabilistic programs. In: 20th Annual Symposium on Foundations of Computer Science (sfcs 1979). pp. 101–114. IEEE (1979)
20. Kreikemeyer, J.N., Andelfinger, P.: Smoothing methods for automatic differentiation across conditional branches. IEEE Access **11**, 143190–143211 (2023)
21. van Krieken, E., Tomczak, J.M., ten Teije, A.: Storchastic: A framework for general stochastic automatic differentiation. In: Ranzato, M., Beygelzimer, A., Dauphin, Y.N., Liang, P., Vaughan, J.W. (eds.) Advances in Neural Information Processing Systems 34: Annual Conference on Neural Information Processing Systems 2021, NeurIPS 2021, December 6-14, 2021, virtual. pp. 7574–7587 (2021)
22. Laurel, J., Misailovic, S.: Continualization of probabilistic programs with correction. In: Müller, P. (ed.) Programming Languages and Systems - 29th European Symposium on Programming, ESOP 2020, Held as Part of the European Joint Conferences on Theory and Practice of Software, ETAPS 2020, Dublin, Ireland, April 25-30, 2020, Proceedings. Lecture Notes in Computer Science, vol. 12075, pp. 366–393. Springer (2020). https://doi.org/10.1007/978-3-030-44914-8_14, https://doi.org/10.1007/978-3-030-44914-8_14

23. Lee, E.A., Seshia, S.A.: Introduction to embedded systems: A cyber-physical systems approach. MIT press (2016)
24. Lee, W., Rival, X., Yang, H.: Smoothness analysis for probabilistic programs with application to optimised variational inference. Proc. ACM Program. Lang. **7**(POPL), 335–366 (2023). https://doi.org/10.1145/3571205, https://doi.org/10.1145/3571205
25. Lee, W., Yu, H., Rival, X., Yang, H.: Towards verified stochastic variational inference for probabilistic programs. Proceedings of the ACM on Programming Languages **4**(POPL), 1–33 (2019)
26. Lee, W., Yu, H., Yang, H.: Reparameterization gradient for non-differentiable models. Advances in Neural Information Processing Systems **31** (2018)
27. Lew, A.K., Huot, M., Staton, S., Mansinghka, V.K.: ADEV: sound automatic differentiation of expected values of probabilistic programs. Proc. ACM Program. Lang. **7**(POPL), 121–153 (2023). https://doi.org/10.1145/3571198, https://doi.org/10.1145/3571198
28. Pakman, A., Paninski, L.: Auxiliary-variable exact hamiltonian monte carlo samplers for binary distributions. In: Burges, C.J.C., Bottou, L., Ghahramani, Z., Weinberger, K.Q. (eds.) Advances in Neural Information Processing Systems 26: 27th Annual Conference on Neural Information Processing Systems 2013. Proceedings of a meeting held December 5-8, 2013, Lake Tahoe, Nevada, United States. pp. 2490–2498 (2013)
29. Rainforth, T., Le, T.A., van de Meent, J.W., Osborne, M.A., Wood, F.: Bayesian optimization for probabilistic programs. Advances in Neural Information Processing Systems **29** (2016)
30. Randone, F., Bortolussi, L., Incerto, E., Tribastone, M.: Inference of probabilistic programs with moment-matching gaussian mixtures. Proc. ACM Program. Lang. **8**(POPL), 1882–1912 (2024). https://doi.org/10.1145/3632905, https://doi.org/10.1145/3632905
31. Sato, T., Aguirre, A., Barthe, G., Gaboardi, M., Garg, D., Hsu, J.: Formal verification of higher-order probabilistic programs: reasoning about approximation, convergence, bayesian inference, and optimization. Proceedings of the ACM on Programming Languages **3**(POPL), 1–30 (2019)
32. Shmarov, F., Zuliani, P.: Probreach: Verified probabilistic delta-reachability for stochastic hybrid systems (2015), https://arxiv.org/abs/1410.8060
33. Wick, G.C.: The evaluation of the collision matrix. Physical review **80**(2), 268 (1950)
34. Zhang, Y., Sutton, C., Storkey, A.J., Ghahramani, Z.: Continuous relaxations for discrete hamiltonian monte carlo. In: Bartlett, P.L., Pereira, F.C.N., Burges, C.J.C., Bottou, L., Weinberger, K.Q. (eds.) Advances in Neural Information Processing Systems 25: 26th Annual Conference on Neural Information Processing Systems 2012. Proceedings of a meeting held December 3-6, 2012, Lake Tahoe, Nevada, United States. pp. 3203–3211 (2012)
35. Zhou, Y., Gram-Hansen, B.J., Kohn, T., Rainforth, T., Yang, H., Wood, F.: LF-PPL: A low-level first order probabilistic programming language for non-differentiable models. In: Chaudhuri, K., Sugiyama, M. (eds.) The 22nd International Conference on Artificial Intelligence and Statistics, AISTATS 2019, 16-18 April 2019, Naha, Okinawa, Japan. Proceedings of Machine Learning Research, vol. 89, pp. 148–157. PMLR (2019), http://proceedings.mlr.press/v89/zhou19b.html

AKR: A Model Checker for an Adaptive Probabilistic Knowing-How Logic

Valentin Cassano[1,2,3], Pablo F. Castro[1,3], Pedro R. D'Argenio[1,2], and Raul Fervari[1,2,4]

[1] Consejo Nacional de Investigaciones Científicas y Técnicas (CONICET), Argentina
[2] Universidad Nacional de Córdoba (UNC), Argentina
[3] Universidad Nacional de Río Cuarto (UNRC), Argentina
[4] Université Paris-Saclay, CNRS, ENS Paris-Saclay, LMF, France

Abstract. We present AKR, a model checking tool for an adaptive probabilistic knowing-how epistemic logic. The tool takes as input the specification of a scenario modeled via a probabilistic LTS (in PRISM notation), a collection of regular expressions acting as agent's perception, a knowing-how property, and checks whether the formula holds in the model under the given perception. The tool combines automata-based techniques with calls to the PRISM tool to compute the result. AKR is a publicly available, open-source tool entirely programmed in Python. We describe the tool's architecture and illustrate its use via some examples.

1 Introduction

Knowing-how modal logics [5] are epistemic logics designed to reason about an agent's ability to achieve specific goals. They have found important applications in artificial intelligence, particularly in planning [11], where the central task is to identify sequences of actions (plans) that enable an agent to accomplish a desired objective. Such planning techniques are widely used in areas including robotics, autonomous vehicles, and conversational agents. Thus, knowing-how logics provide a formal foundation for reasoning about these scenarios. In these logics, modalities of the form $\mathsf{Kh}(\varphi, \psi)$ express that an agent knows the existence of a plan whose execution, starting from any state satisfying φ, guarantees the achievement of the goal ψ (see, e.g., [8,7,6,10,9]). The semantics of these logics are typically given in terms of Labeled Transition Systems (LTSs), which model the actions available to an agent and their possible effects.

Recent extensions of knowing-how logics [1,2] enrich the framework with indistinguishability relations between plans, allowing the formal representation of situations in which multiple plans are perceived as equally effective from the agent's perspective. Particularly interesting here is the extension proposed in [4], which introduces a probabilistic version of knowing-how logics. This framework enables us to reason about scenarios in which the result of executing an action may exhibit a stochastic behavior. As a simple example, consider a robot navigating a corridor with dynamic obstacles (e.g., human beings). In this scenario,

© The Author(s) 2026
S. Junges and G. Katz (Eds.): TACAS 2026, LNCS 16505, pp. 586–593, 2026.
https://doi.org/10.1007/978-3-032-22752-2_30

there is a certain probability that the robot gets stuck at some location, which must be taken into account when computing its plans. Among the logics investigated in [4], one stands out that concentrates on *adaptative plans*, that is, the choice of a plan may change following the outcomes of the probabilistic actions.

Model checking procedures for knowing-logics provide an automated method for verifying the existence of plans reaching a certain goal on a given scenario. The model checking problem for the adaptative probabilistic logic from [4] can be solved in polynomial time: a description of the agent's perception given by a deterministic automaton is synchronized with a description of the domain via a probabilistic automaton, then checking the knowing-how property can be reduced to verifying a *minimum reachability property* over the obtained structure.

In this paper we present AKR, a model checker for the adaptative probabilistic knowing-how logic from [4]. The tool takes as input a PRISM model describing the domain of the problem, a collection of regular expressions representing an agent's perception, and a knowing-how formula. From this input the tool constructs the corresponding automata and synchronizes them with the probabilistic automaton describing the domain. Interestingly, this product differs from the synchronization mechanism provided by PRISM. Finally, the reachability property is verified using the PRISM tool over the resulting model.

The rest of the paper is structured as follows. In Sec. 2, we provide a high-level presentation of the logic. In Sec. 3, we introduce the architecture of the tool and its usage. Sec. 4 describes results obtained with some experiments.

2   Adaptative Probabilistic Knowing How

In this section, we briefly overview the syntax and semantics of the adaptative probabilistic knowing-how logic $\mathcal{L}_{\mathsf{Kh}^q}^{\mathrm{A}}$. A detailed introduction can be found in [4].

Syntax. The formulas of $\mathcal{L}_{\mathsf{Kh}^q}^{\mathrm{A}}$ are constructed from a set Prop of propositional symbols following the grammar: $\varphi, \psi ::= p \mid \neg\varphi \mid \varphi \vee \psi \mid \mathsf{Kh}^q(\varphi, \psi)$, where $p \in$ Prop and $q \in (0, 1]$. Formulas $\mathsf{Kh}^q(\varphi, \psi)$ are intuitively read as *"the agent knows how to achieve a goal ψ given that φ holds, with probability at least q"*.

Semantics. The semantics of $\mathcal{L}_{\mathsf{Kh}^q}^{\mathrm{A}}$ is defined with respect to *uncertainty-based probabilistic labeled transition systems (PLTSU)*. In brief, a PLTSU extends a probabilistic LTS (see, e.g., Fig. 2) with a *perception* set U, whose elements are a non-empty pairwise-disjoint members of $\mathscr{P}(\mathsf{Act}^*) \setminus \emptyset$. Here, Act^* is the set of all sequences of actions, or *plans*, available to the agent and each $\Pi \in$ U is a set of plans the agent "perceives" as equally suitable for achieving a goal [1,2].

The semantics of the Boolean fragment is defined in the standard way. In turn, we say that $\mathsf{Kh}^q(\varphi, \psi)$ holds *everywhere* (respectively, *nowhere*) in a PLTSU iff there exists (respectively, does not exist) a set of plans $\Pi \in$ U such that, for every state satisfying φ, any strategy σ *compatible* with Π ensures a probability of at least q of reaching a state where ψ holds. A strategy σ is compatible with Π if every finite sequence of actions prescribed by σ is a prefix of some plan in Π. We refer to the logic as being *adaptative* because the agent can dynamically decide whether to continue with one plan or switch to another plan within Π, depending on the random outcomes of actions.

Model Checking. The model-checking problem for $\mathcal{L}_{\mathsf{Kh}^q}^{\mathsf{A}}$ consists of, given a PLTSU $\mathfrak{M}$ and an arbitrary formula φ, deciding whether φ holds in $\mathfrak{M}$. This problem is decidable in polynomial time if every $\Pi \in \mathsf{U}$ is recognized by a deterministic finite automaton (DFA). The algorithm is presented in Fig. 1 (see [4] for details). Therein, the family $\{\mathfrak{D}_i \mid i \in I\}$ represents the perception U. Finally, notice that $(\inf_\sigma \mathbb{P}_{s_A}^\sigma(\mathrm{Reach}(G \times F_i)))$ computes the minimum probability of reaching a "goal state", represented in the product automaton as a pair whose first component is a state of the original PLTSU satisfying the post-condition χ, and the second component is a final state of the DFA $\mathfrak{D}_i$ under consideration.

```
fun Check(𝔐: PLTSU, φ: formula) is
  S ← ∅;
  switch φ do
    case p ∈ Prop do S ← p-labeled states of 𝔐;
    case φ = ¬ψ do
      S ← states of 𝔐 not in Check(ψ);
    case φ = ψ ∨ χ do S ← Check(ψ) ∪ Check(χ);
    case φ = Khq(ψ, χ) do
      A, G ← Check(ψ), Check(χ);
      foreach i ∈ I do
        compute the PLTSU product of 𝔐 with 𝔇i,
        extended with a fresh state sA and
        τ-transitions
        sA → s for all s ∈ A;
        if (infσ Pσ_sA(Reach(G×Fi))) ≥ q then
          S ← the set of states of 𝔐
  return S;
```

require: perception set U in $\mathfrak{M}$ represented as a family $\{\mathfrak{D}_i \mid i \in I\}$ of live DFAs;
ensure: Check$(\mathfrak{M}, \varphi)$=the states of $\mathfrak{M}$ where φ holds.

Fig. 1: A Model Checking Algorithm.

Example. We conclude this section with an example illustrating the syntax and the semantics of $\mathcal{L}_{\mathsf{Kh}^q}^{\mathsf{A}}$. Consider a cleaning robot (named Tango) tasked with servicing an even number of hotel rooms arranged in pairs along both sides of a hallway, with even room numbers on one side, and odd numbers on the opposite side. The robot succeeds if it services more than a required number of rooms on a floor before moving on to the next one.

The robot travels only in a grid-like fashion: it moves forward or backward along the hallway, and laterally across to the opposite side. Upon reaching a room, the robot tries to service it. Since it must avoid disturbing guests, it services only rooms without a "do not disturb" sign. The presence of these signs is determined probabilistically. We assume that once a room has been visited, its status becomes fixed: either serviced or not. Repeated visits do not change this status, and once a room is cleaned, it remains clean, i.e., repeated cleaning counts only once toward the total.

Such scenarios can be naturally modeled with a probabilistic LTS. Fig. 2 shows part of the model for a six hotel rooms in PRISM notation. In this case, Tango is required to clean at least two rooms. Variable s indicates the room the robot is currently located, while variables vi, for i = 1,..,6, keep track of the rooms visited by the robot. The variable c counts the number of rooms that have been cleaned. Actions are expressed in probabilistic guard-command form, following standard PRISM conventions. For instance, action:

```
[one](s=0)->0.5:(s'=1)&(c'=min(6,c+(1-v1)))&(v1'=1)+0.5:(s'=1)&(v1'=1);
```

specifies that when the robot is in the initial state ($s=0$), it moves to room 1 with probability 0.5 and successfully cleans it, or moves to the same room with probability 0.5 but fails to clean it. The probability is determined by presence of the "do not disturb" sign. In this setting, perceptions arise from the different itineraries the robot may consider while cleaning. For instance, it may regard the zig-zag pattern $1, 2, 4, 3, 5, 6$ as indistinguishable from $2, 1, 3, 4, 5, 6$. Likewise, it may treat the circular pattern $1, 3, 5, 6, 4, 2$ as indistinguishable from $3, 5, 6, 4, 2, 1$, and so on. Patterns of this kind can be naturally characterized by regular expressions (which can be translated to DFAs). For instance, the regular expression `((one+two).(three+four).(five+six))*` could be one of them. Note that the notation used for regular expressions is standard, i.e., we use the following operators: + (union), . (concatenation), and * (Kleene closure).

In this setting, the formula `Kh(launch,complete) >= 0.25` expresses that the robot can complete its task with probability greater or equal than 0.25 (where `complete` is a variable that holds true whenever a certain given number of rooms have been cleaned).

3 The Tool AKR

AKR is a publicly-available open-source tool implemented in Python[5]. The tool uses the Lark library [12] to parse an input specification and generate an abstract syntax tree (AST) capturing its main structural components. An input specification consists of three parts: (i) a PRISM model describing the domain, (ii) a collection of regular expressions representing the agent's perception, and (iii) the property to be verified. Each regular expression is translated into an NFA, which is then determinized and transformed into a live automaton, i.e., a deterministic automaton in which every state has at least one path leading to an accepting state. Subsequently, the PRISM domain model is synchronized with these deterministic live automata, implementing the algorithm of Fig. 1. Finally, the resulting synchronized model is analyzed using the PRISM model checker to verify the probability of the specified reachability property.

3.1 Tool Architecture

The architecture of the tool is described in Fig. 3. Its key components are:

Preprocessing: It performs basic syntactic analysis over the input models and produces ASTs describing the inputs. The library Lark is used to automatically generate the parser from a grammar describing the modeling language.

NFA Module: The regular expressions obtained from the input are translated into NFAs, which in turn are converted into live DFAs, as required by the model checking procedure.

PLTS Description: The domain described as a PRISM model is translated to a representation with suitable data structures to facilitate its manipulation.

---

[5] https://github.com/pablofcastro/AKR

```
plts:
formula launch = (s=0) & (c=0) & (v1=0) & (v2=0) & (v3=0) & (v4=0) & (v5=0) & (v6=0);
formula complete = (c>=2);
module plts
s : [0..6]; c : [0..6];
v1 : [0..1]; v2 : [0..1]; v3 : [0..1]; v4 : [0..1]; v5 : [0..1]; v6 : [0..1];
[one]   (s=0) -> 0.5:(s'=1)&(c'=min(6,c+(1-v1)))&(v1'=1) + 0.5:(s'=1)&(v1'=1);
[two]   (s=0) -> 0.5:(s'=2)&(c'=min(6,c+(1-v2)))&(v2'=1) + 0.5:(s'=2)&(v2'=1);
[two]   (s=1) -> 0.5:(s'=2)&(c'=min(6,c+(1-v2)))&(v2'=1) + 0.5:(s'=2)&(v2'=1);
[three] (s=1) -> 0.5:(s'=3)&(c'=min(6,c+(1-v3)))&(v3'=1) + 0.5:(s'=3)&(v3'=1);
// more actions follow

endmodule
endplts
perception : ((one+two).(three+four).(five+six))*
endperception
property : Kh(launch,complete) >= 0.25
endproperty
```

Fig. 2: Fragment of an AKR Specification.

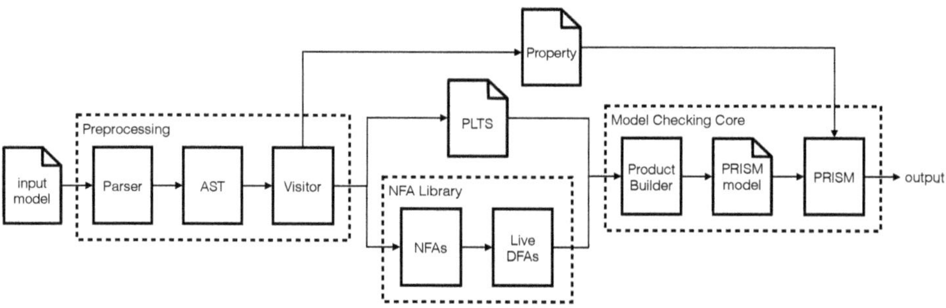

Fig. 3: Architecture of the Tool.

Model Checking Core: It implements the recursive procedure in Fig. 1. To this end, it constructs a product using each live DFA and the input property. The reachability property is checked by calling the PRISM tool.

3.2   Usage

The standard command to execute AKR in a Unix-like operating system is:

```
python akr.py -i <file> <options>
```

Here, `<file>` is the path to a file containing the model, the perception, and the property to be checked. The tool returns whether the property holds in the given model taking into account the given perception, together with the time taken for the verification, and the maximum number of states and transitions of the models created during the verification. Note that every set of indistinguishable plans (given at this stage, as a DFA) is composed with the PRISM model, hence several probabilistic automata are constructed. The available `<options>` are as follows. The flag `-v <level>`, where `<level>` is a number between 1 and 5, controls the

```
Property checked: Kh(launch,complete)>=0.25
The property is: true
Maximum number of states: 20
Maximum number of trans: 36
the witness is :(((one + two) . (three + four)) . (five + six))*
The compatible strategy is:
['accept=0','s=3','c=0', 'v1=1','v2=0','v3=1','v4=0','v5=0','v6=0','action=five']
['accept=0','s=3','c=1','v1=1','v2=0','v3=1','v4=0','v5=0','v6=0','action=five']
['accept=0','s=0','c=0','v1=0','v2=0','v3=0','v4=0','v5=0','v6=0','action=one']
['accept=1','s=0','c=0','v1=0','v2=0','v3=0','v4=0','v5=0','v6=0','action=one']
['accept=0','s=1','c=0','v1=1','v2=0','v3=0','v4=0','v5=0','v6=0','action=three']
...
```

Fig. 4: Example of the tool's output.

verbosity level of the output. For example, `-v 5` displays the synchronized models generated during verification, along with additional debugging information. The `-strat` option instructs AKR to return a strategy compatible with the given plans satisfying the property within the specified probability threshold, provided that the formula holds (the strategy is only displayed if a single Kh(A,B)>=q expression is checked). Finally, the flag `-pp <PRISMPATH>` specifies the path to the executable file of the PRISM model checker.

As an example, Fig. 4 shows an excerpt of the output obtained for the specification of Fig. 2. Note that in the displayed strategy, the variable `accept` is used to mark whether the live automaton is in an accepting state or not.

4   Experimental Results

In this section, we report some experiments performed over several instances of our running example. We considered scenarios with n rooms, with n an even number in the range $[4, 100]$. The robot is required to clean at least half of the rooms on the floor. We incorporated three modes into the robot: *Milonga*, *Salon*, and *Canyengue*. Each of them is described by a corresponding regular expression, capturing alternative perceptions. For instance, for four rooms, *Milonga* yields `(one.two.four.three)+(two.one.three.four)`, while *Salon* yields `(one.three.four.two)*+(two.four.three.one)*`, and *Canyengue* yields `(one.two.one.two)^k.(three.four.three.four)^k` (where `R^k` means `R` concatenated k times). These patterns are straightforwardly extended to scenarios with more rooms. Note that *Salon* uses the star operator while *Milonga* does not. This enables us to contrast the results obtained for both case studies to see if the star operator has some impact in the performance of the procedure. Furthermore, note that *Canyengue* allows us to evaluate how increasing k may affect the performance of the tool. Notice that for each configuration, we play with distinct parameters to evaluate our tool.

Fig. 5 shows the time the tool took to verify each instance, as well as the number of states of the obtained model and the different probabilities. The tool behaves reasonably well even in cases of thousands of states. Note that the variance of probabilities does not seem to affect the tool's performance. Interestingly,

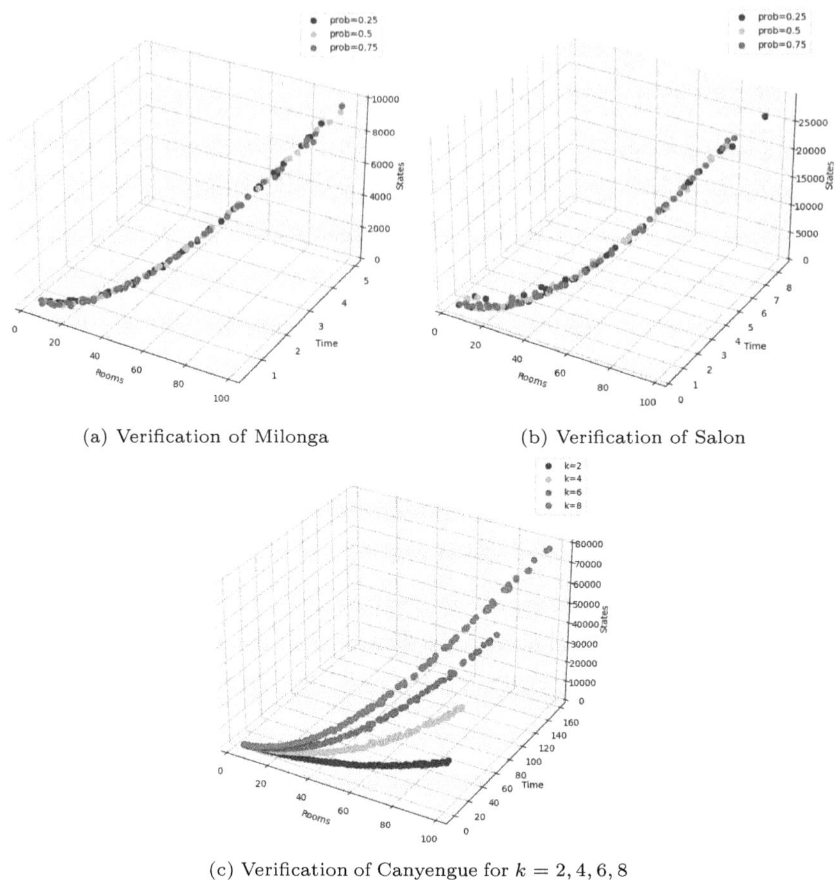

(a) Verification of Milonga

(b) Verification of Salon

(c) Verification of Canyengue for $k = 2, 4, 6, 8$

Fig. 5: Results for Milonga, Salon, and Canyengue modes.

the star operator seems to have only a minor impact on the number of states and the verification time, by comparing *Milonga* and *Salon* configurations. On the other hand, the length of regular expressions has a stronger impact on both the number of states and the verification time, as demonstrated by the *Canyengue* case, where different values of k are plotted.

We ran our experiments on an M2 processor MacBook with 16GB of RAM. The case studies for reproducing the results are available in the tool's repository.

Acknowledgments. This work was supported by Agencia I+D+i grant PICT 2021-00400, the EU H2020 programme under the MSC grant agreement 101008233 (MIS-SION), the IRP SINFIN, SeCyT-UNC grants 33620230100384CB (MECANO) and 33620230100178CB, and as part of France 2030 program ANR-11-IDEX-0003.

Data Availability Statement. The tool's source code and data used for the experimental evaluation in the current paper are available at [3].

References

1. Areces, C., Fervari, R., Saravia, A.R., Velázquez-Quesada, F.R.: Uncertainty-based semantics for multi-agent knowing how logics. In: 18th Conference on Theoretical Aspects of Rationality and Knowledge (TARK 2021). EPTCS, vol. 335, pp. 23–37. Open Publishing Association (2021)
2. Areces, C., Fervari, R., Saravia, A.R., Velázquez-Quesada, F.R.: Uncertainty-based knowing how logic. Journal of Logic and Computation **35**(1), 1–35 (2025)
3. Cassano, V., Castro, P.F., D'Argenio, P.R., Fervari, R.: AKR: a model checker for an adaptative knowing-how probabilistic logic with regular expression perceptions (Oct 2025). `https://doi.org/10.5281/zenodo.17465089`
4. Castro, P.F., D'Argenio, P.R., Fervari, R.: How lucky are you to know your way? a probabilistic approach to knowing how logics. In: IJCAI (ed.) Proceedings of the Twenty Second International Conference, KR 2025. pp. 229–239. ijcai.org (2025)
5. Fantl, J.: Knowing-how and knowing-that. Philosophy Compass **3**(3), 451–470 (2008)
6. Fervari, R., Herzig, A., Li, Y., Wang, Y.: Strategically knowing how. In: 26th International Joint Conference on Artificial Intelligence (IJCAI 2017). pp. 1031–1038. International Joint Conferences on Artificial Intelligence (2017)
7. Li, Y.: Stopping means achieving: A weaker logic of knowing how. Studies in Logic **9**(4), 34–54 (2017)
8. Li, Y., Wang, Y.: Achieving while maintaining: A logic of knowing how with intermediate constraints. In: 7th Indian Conference on Logic and Its Applications (ICLA 2017). pp. 154–167. LNCS, Springer (2017)
9. Naumov, P., Tao, J.: Together we know how to achieve: An epistemic logic of know-how. Artificial Intelligence **262**, 279–300 (2018)
10. Naumov, P., Tao, J.: Knowing-how under uncertainty. Artificial Intelligence **276**, 41–56 (2019). `https://doi.org/10.1016/j.artint.2019.06.007`, `https://doi.org/10.1016/j.artint.2019.06.007`
11. Russell, S., Norvig, P.: Artificial Intelligence: A Modern Approach. Pearson, 4th edn. (2020), `http://aima.cs.berkeley.edu/`
12. Shinan, E.: Lark: a parsing toolkit for Python (2024), `https://github.com/lark-parser/lark`

Cyber-Physical Systems

Driving by Disproof: A Practical Model Checking Approach to Fleet Coordination

Lukas König[1]([✉]) [iD], Christian Schildwächter[1] [iD], Michaela Klauck[1] [iD], and Christian Heinzemann[1] [iD]

Robert Bosch GmbH, 70465 Stuttgart, Germany
{lukas.koenig, christian.schildwaechter, michaela.klauck,
christian.heinzemann}@de.bosch.com

Abstract. A model checker automatically verifies whether a formal model satisfies a given specification or produces a counterexample showing how it fails. We present a new way of using the counterexample to actively control a group of autonomous vehicles online in traffic. Each vehicle provides its own set of driving rules (requirements) about how it wants to traverse through traffic. The model checker is asked to prove the *wrong* specification that there are *no* trajectories such that the requirements of all vehicles are obeyed. Thus, we provoke a counterexample to the negated statement of what we are actually interested in, a solution to the driving task of the whole group. The resulting behavior is white-box, provably correct, and directly emerges from the requirements shared by the vehicles, without the need for an explicit implementation layer. Initial experiments with an open-source HighwayEnv implementation using the nuXmv model checker indicate that small fleets could be guided in real-time, and we see great potential for performance improvements by customizing the model checker for this task.

Keywords: Automated Driving · Fleet Control · Model Checking · Industry Application

1 Introduction

The advent of *automated and autonomous driving (AD)* represents a transformative shift in the landscape of transportation, promising to enhance road safety, improve traffic efficiency, and reduce environmental impact. With recent advancements in AI, *machine learning (ML)*, and sensor technologies, operating effectively even in complex urban environments is becoming increasingly feasible. However, ensuring safety of the driving functions remains one of the most challenging and widely open issues [64].

It is currently common practice to equip each individual *automated vehicle (AV)* with a self-reliant software stack which incorporates explicit instructions on how to behave in traffic. Classical approaches often implement the "sense-plan-act" paradigm for this purpose [56], while AI-based solutions replace parts of this paradigm with trained models, up to full-fledged end-to-end approaches which map directly from sensors to actuators via AI. In any case, the logic for

S. Junges and G. Katz (Eds.): TACAS 2026, LNCS 16505, pp. 597–619, 2026.
https://doi.org/10.1007/978-3-032-22752-2_31

steering the vehicle ("ego") is hard-coded on-board of the AV. This general idea is currently broadly applied, and with increasing success.

Given its obvious benefits and undeniable effectiveness, there are still drawbacks inherent to this approach. One is the necessity for an *explicit controller implementation* which is highly safety-relevant and requires great efforts for *verification and validation (V&V)* [50, 38, 29, 51]. For level 3 driving functions and higher, car manufacturers need to show that their AVs obey strict safety regulations in their respective operational domains (acc. to standard SAE J3016 [11]). Another drawback is the decoupling of the AV's behavior from the requirements towards safety, comfort etc., as requested by OEMs and customers. Firstly, the V&V process has to constantly ensure the synchronization and inter-linkage between requirements and controller implementation during development, which, in practice, demands a great chunk of the overall development costs. Secondly, when requirements change, this requires a re-implementation of the controller, either via human programming or by re-training of the model, which is expensive in both cases. This poses a recurring issue even during the development of a single AD product. From a more general perspective, applying such an "ego-centric" approach makes the problem of steering a whole group of AVs safely through traffic much harder, because each AV comes with its own set of requirements (matching their individual brand identities, e. g., more "sportive," more "conservative" etc.) for which it provides its own individual implementation, but none can reliably take into account the behavior of the others. Abandoning the ego-centric view opens up a space for new solutions to these problems.

We start from an already published *model checking (MC)* approach for verification of an (ego-centric) driving function by analyzing its behavior within a vast set of traffic scenarios [38, 39]. The non-ego traffic is controlled by an *environment model (EM)* which comprises degrees of freedom for each car in each step, limited only by physics and the constraint to avoid collisions. The general idea is, now, to not have a dedicated ego vehicle but to consider all cars in the scene equally, ending up with a general traffic progression model which contains a notion of "every possible vehicle behavior on a given road topology." From a practical point of view, we imagine a central MC entity (e. g., on a radio tower in the middle of a crossing) which observes traffic flow within a designated area and maintains a communication channel to the involved cars, cf. Figure 1. The traffic observer continuously updates the EM with the current states of the cars. This includes a set of formal requirements, sent by each car upon entering the scene, which precisely formulate safety, comfort and other constraints to obey, as well as the desired target to exit the scene from. Given this, a negated specification is generated, which effectively states: *In this traffic situation, there exists no progression of all cars in the scene such that all the requirements are obeyed.* Assuming "sound" requirements and a "reasonable" street topology, we expect this specification to be *false* in "almost all" real traffic situations (the quotes denoting open points which we start answering in this paper). Therefore, running the MC will provoke a *counterexample (CEX)*. This CEX includes trajectories for each car to drive on such that the requirements are (provably!) *not* violated, which is a solution to the given driving problem.

Attempts to solve the planning and/or fleet control problem with formal methods have yielded a range of theoretical frameworks, cf. Section 2. We see our main contribution in bridging the gap towards application from the practical side. The presented approach comes with no obvious insuperable hurdles towards practice (such as runtime). It emerged from the Automated Driving Alliance, a big industrial AD project between Bosch and Cariad, with an actual application in mind. On the other hand, this comes, for now, with a concession towards the provability claim, which we soften on the path to a practical implementation.

The remainder of this paper, therefore, intends to shed light on the theoretical, and mid-term practical feasibility of such an approach. In Section 2, we analyze the current state of the art before describing the theoretical foundations of our approach in Section 3. In Section 4, we introduce a prototypical open-source implementation with HighwayEnv [44], present and discuss the results of first experiments and comment on remaining open points towards an adoption in practice. Section 5 concludes the paper.

2 State of the Art

Our contributions relate to different areas of research, most notably to approaches for coordinating multiple vehicles, formal methods used for behavior verification, safe-by-design behavior construction, and symbolic planning approaches. We discuss related approaches in this order in the following.

There exists different strategies aimed at coordinating multiple autonomous vehicles to achieve further objectives such as safety, efficiency, and scalability. The literature can be broadly categorized into formation control [57], multi-agent coordination [48], cooperative multi-agent planning [58], cooperative decision-making [31] and reinforcement learning-based methods for multi-agent systems [65, 17]. We refer to the cited surveys for a general overview on these fields.

Formation control emphasizes structured formations, notably vehicle platooning, where AVs maintain close proximity to enhance traffic flow and reduce fuel consumption. Formation control techniques are classified into leader-follower models, virtual structures, consensus algorithms, and behavior-based methods, highlighting challenges like communication delays and dynamic reconfiguration. Being fairly well understood and reasonably controllable, these coordination techniques mostly rely on rather rigid geometric structures or role assignments and provide limited degrees of freedom for the individual cars [57].

A specific variant of such systems is *Cooperative Adaptive Cruise Control (CACC)*, which incorporates *vehicle-to-vehicle (V2V)* communication, enabling vehicles to share information such as speed, acceleration, and intended maneuvers. This allows for tighter vehicle spacing, improved traffic flow, and enhanced safety [62, 61]. CACC has been integrated with higher-level cooperative maneuvers (e. g., lane changes, merging), often using hybrid systems modeling or reinforcement learning for decision making [8, 45]. There is also growing interest in using formal methods for verification of CACC algorithms, especially in the context of ISO 26262 safety standards [63, 67, 49]. Our approach, in contrast, aims at providing more flexible coordination of diverting traffic flows.

Multi-agent coordination targets decentralized coordination of multiple agents in dynamic environments. Taxonomies for coordination problems have been proposed, addressing areas like intersection management and cooperative lane changes. They categorize coordination strategies based on autonomy levels, communication requirements, and decision-making architectures [48]. In addition, the concept of a control center for automated vehicle fleet orchestration, similar to the tower in flight control, has already been discussed for, among others, emergency, fleet, or teleoperation services [22], of which the latter is the most complicated one and closest to our method. The approach named *SOTA* provides a framework for goal-oriented requirements engineering, context-aware systems, and dynamical systems modeling of vehicle collectives [1]. SOTA is well-suited as umbrella framework for our approach, both in identifying how knowledge needs to be distributed between components (AVs and central MC instance), and w.r.t. assessing formal properties of requirements, such as mutual compatibility. Indeed, the authors suggest to assess requirements via MC techniques [2].

Verification and testing approaches aim at guaranteeing correctness and safety for multi-agent systems [5]. We specifically focus on *formal verification (FV)* techniques that hold great promise for enhancing safety in AD, particularly in planning functions [53, 47, 46]. MC [4] systematically explores all possible behaviors of a system to uncover edge cases that violate specifications. For example, NuSMV has been applied to MATLAB/Simulink models for features like cruise control, lane change, gap maintenance, and obstacle avoidance, using *linear temporal logic (LTL)* to formalize environment transitions [51]. In another case, a Stateflow model of a tactical planner was translated into Promela and verified using Spin [42]. However, this method required frequent updates to keep pace with changes in the planner [41]. Other efforts include verifying MATLAB implementations of motion planning post-development [55], which avoids model-code mismatch but delays bug detection. These examples show the difficulties of integrating MC into fast-paced development workflows like industrial contexts [69].

A key barrier to broader adoption of MC is the limited expressiveness of model checker input languages, which often lack features like object orientation and dynamic data structures [28, 6, 7, 43, 16]. To address this, many domains use higher-level modeling languages with automated translation to MC tools [54, 15, 24, 26]. Such approaches are often impractical since the driving function logic exists only as source code in some higher language like C++. Manual translation, as used in some industrial contexts [35, 23], is also unsuitable during early development stages, where both code and interfaces change frequently. Another practical hurdle is runtime, MC being prone to hardly predictable state explosion events [38].

To the best of our knowledge, MC has so far always been applied primarily to verify the behavior of a single ego vehicle, not to coordinate freely moving fleets in an ego-less setup. The closest work to ours is investigating communication between AVs modeled using timed automata [3], focusing on the impact of various types of communications on vehicles' safety and traffic fluidity to evaluate the quality of a given AV's decision policy. In contrast, we consider the behavior of the whole fleet at once, not only of one car, and not only focusing on the effect of communication, but on behavior planning. All other works are on FV of AV platooning [60] and on verifying convoy behavior based on predefined platooning protocols [18]. One such approach combines system model and agent code verification [34], while another formalizes various control strategies in higher-order logic, verifying stability using multivariate calculus and Laplace transforms, with a focus on ISO 26262 compliance [52].

A different line of research for achieving robot executions satisfying a formal specification is temporal-logic-based synthesis of controllers [21, 40]. Here, the locations that a robot shall visit and all safety-related side conditions are encoded as a temporal logic formula and a satisfying control automaton is synthesized from the formula, if it exists. There exist extensions to settings with sensor errors [32], actuation errors [33], runtime conflict resolution [66], and interaction with humans in a probabilistic setting [14]. In contrast to these approaches, we only require a single execution path for the situation at hand, not a generalized automaton being able to handle all situations as the latter would be hard to obtain via formal synthesis due to the size of the *environment model (EM)* and the complexity of the overall safety specification. In [20] MC is used as an online monitor for the feedback-controller of a single drone by looking ahead to predict possible outcomes and then safeguard the controller decisions by handing back and forth between the controller and the model checker. In contrast, our approach is used to get a fully safe driving plan for the whole fleet of cars upfront for which we assume that a controller is able to drive it.

There also exists a rich body of literature on symbolic planning techniques that rely on formal solvers for obtaining a sequence of actions, i.e. a *plan*, that brings a system into a target state with guarantees on the success. Examples include solvers based on PDDL [25] such as fast downward [27], approaches based on Answer-Set Programming [59], and approaches using MC [10, 9]. These approaches, if not explicitly mentioned before, focus on planning for a single system, whereas our approach considers collective planning.

3   Foundations

We propose a framework derived from existing work on MC of driving functions for AD [38]. Throughout the paper, we make the (bold) assumption that all cars within the traffic scenario of interest are fully controlled by MC or fully predictable. This being arguably hard to achieve in practice from today's standpoint, we imagine as possible first adopter, for example, closed corporate facilities, or a single crossing which allows only participating cars to enter, while regular traffic needs to take another route. Note that, in the following, the nuXmv symbolic model checker [7] is mainly discussed as possible solver for the core MC problem, because it has been used as base for the existing EM in the earlier work. Nonetheless, other model checkers are suitable for this task, as well.

Basic Principle of the Proposed Approach.   Overall, the fleet control process consists of a closed feedback loop where requirements and physical states of cars within a traffic scene are submitted to a central MC instance which solves the driving problem posed by this information, and transmits driving instructions back to the cars in the scene. Figure 1 shows an overview of the process, which can be compared to Figure 2 in the original paper [38]. There, the task was to formally verify safety-relevant properties of a *Behavior Planner (BP)*, i. e., it was an intrinsically ego-centric approach. From a MC perspective, the new approach introduces two key differences: ⟨1⟩ The whole "Behavior Planner" part of the input towards the model checker (1, 2, in the original paper) is missing here since we are not interested in analyzing a specific driving function. Rather, we rely on the EM (3) to provide *all drivable maneuvers* of all the cars in the scene. Particularly, this means that there is no distinguished ego vehicle anymore. ⟨2⟩ Specification and initial state of the EM are no longer fixed, but need to be adjusted before each MC run to reflect the current observed traffic scene and the requirements passed on by the cars. Therefore, items (1) and (2) of the input now represent requirements and physical features of the cars in traffic.

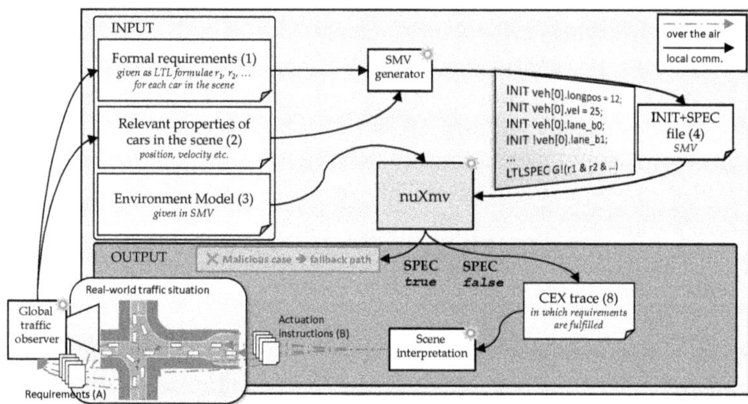

Fig. 1: Overview of the proposed process. For each car i, a requirements formula r_i (A), as well as physical features are derived as input for the MC process (1), (2). The specification is defined as the negation of all the r_i being *true* at once. The expected outcome is a CEX (8) containing trajectories for all cars such that the requirements are fulfilled; these are sent back to the cars.

The requirements of the n cars in the scene are given as formulas $r_1, \ldots, r_n$ (1). In general, this can be LTL formulas [30] in nuXmv (although we only use non-temporal invariants in the experiments). The actual specification for MC is defined as: $G! \bigwedge_{i=1}^{n} r_i$. This formula is *true* if and only if there is no possibility that all r_i become *true* at once within the space of all traffic situations spanned by the EM. Given a sufficiently general EM, and sound r_i, this formula is expected to be *false*, as long as the presented scene is not malicious by itself (see below).

The physical properties of the cars in the scene (2) are translated into *initial constraints* for the model checker, in the nuXmv case by using the SMV language. Given this input, the overall control loop consists of the following steps:

1. Generate a model based on initial constraints, specification and the EM.
2. Run nuXmv on this model, with the expectation to receive a CEX as result.
3. Translate the CEX into driving instructions for the individual cars.
4. Transmit these instructions to the cars in the scene, thus closing the loop.

Under "ideal" conditions, the unexpected case that the specification is *true*, and thus the requirements actually *cannot* be fulfilled, should not happen. For these ideal conditions it is necessary[1] that $\langle 1 \rangle$ the requirements are pairwise non-conflicting, $\langle 2 \rangle$ the current traffic scene is not a "dead end" from the start, i. e., it does not by itself prevent some required property from being fulfilled (e. g., by implying an inevitable crash), and $\langle 3 \rangle$ the requirements make statements about the *whole time* a car spends in the MC-controlled road section. (The latter is a rather technical constraint which prevents the MC trajectories from ending prematurely if all requirements are fulfilled before the car's departure, giving no guarantee for a solution for the remainder of the way. This property can be accomplished fairly easily, e. g., by requesting a desired exit from the scene.)

$\langle 1 \rangle$ and $\langle 3 \rangle$ are fundamental constraints that can be claimed automatically. Regarding $\langle 2 \rangle$, we can never fully eliminate the possibility of situations evolving into "dead ends," solely from imprecisions of sensors and actuators. This alone requires a fallback path in practice, should MC provide no solution. From a logical point of view (assuming perfect sensing and actuation), we can demand to start with a "benign" initial traffic situation, for example, one that contains no cars at all, and then assume that all subsequent situations have evolved through MC control. Were there only cars *within the scene* to consider, it could now be reasoned that all requirements will always be satisfiable, since transitions from one iteration to the next provably obey the requirements, and, through $\langle 3 \rangle$, the requirements always apply to the whole traversal of the cars through the scene.

However, when assuming that cars can enter or leave the scene, we need to consider these events as additional cases with specific constraints. Firstly, an entering car must not render its own or others' requirements unsatisfiable (e. g., by driving too fast). This could be established by a "safety zone" before the actual entrance to the scene. Within it, a car could already request a takeover by the MC system and submit its desired requirements, but not be guaranteed to actually be taken over from the start. Should there be trajectories satisfying all requirements *including* the ones from the newly entering car, it can be led directly into the scene. Otherwise, the car could be requested to adjust its parameters, possibly up to a full stop, until entering becomes possible with all requirements

---

[1] We do not prove that the above conditions are also sufficient to avoid the malicious case. This requires a more formal definition of the system and is left for future work. Intuitively, they cover the three mentioned aspects as argued in the main text.

obeyed. Leaving the scene is not problematic by itself, the trajectory problem becomes only simpler with fewer cars. However, some peculiar requirements of the remaining cars might become unsatisfiable on participants leaving. E. g., a request for following another specific car (platoon driving), could become invalid when this car leaves the scene. This type of requirements has to be rejected.

Conflicting requirements can be filtered out automatically by including the exiting and entering events into the MC process, and for a new requirement beforehand performing an offline check if it is satisfiable for all expected situations (i. e., all except dead-end situations emerging from imperfect control).

Model Checking.   The system under analysis is derived from the EM code and additional code snippets, representing the current traffic situation and the specification to check. It is finally represented as a symbolic transition system $S = \langle X, I, T \rangle$, expressed using quantifier-free formulas in first-order logic modulo theories. Here, X is a set of state variables, $I(X)$ is a formula representing the initial states, and $T(X, X')$ is a formula representing the transitions, with X' denoting the set of variables which represent the next state of the system (cf. [4]). We work in the setting of many-sorted first-order logic, and we assume the usual first-order notions of interpretation, satisfiability, validity, logical consequence, and theory, as given, e. g., in [19]. A *state* s of S is an assignment to the state variables X; a *path (trace)* π of S is a sequence $\pi := (s_0, s_1, \ldots, s_i, \ldots)$ of states s_i such that $I(X)$ is *true* under the assignment s_0, and $T(X, X')$ is *true* under the assignment s_{i-1}, s'_i for all $i > 0$ in π, where s' is the assignment obtained by replacing each $x \in X$ with the corresponding $x' \in X'$. A state s is *reachable* in S if and only if there exists a path π of S such that $s \in \pi$. Given a formula $P(X)$ over the variables X, the *invariant verification problem (IVP)* for S and P is the problem of checking if all the reachable states of S satisfy the formula P, i. e., S satisfies P. For this work, we solve the IVP and thereby make use of nuXmv's feature to provide a CEX in the case of an unsatisfied P, which is a path towards a state which does not satisfy P. We use the *bounded model checking (BMC)* mode which has the additional property of providing a shortest-possible CEX, i. e., the resulting trajectories are as short as possible for the stated problem.

4   Experiments

Our goal is to (begin to) answer the following crucial questions which need to be affirmed for the approach to be applicable in practice:

1. Can the MC simulation be aligned to a realistic driving model such that the MC-provided trajectories can actually be driven in simulation (and later in real traffic) as intended in a majority of cases?
2. Are solutions (i. e., CEXs) provided in a majority of cases, rather than ending up in dead-end states which require special treatment?
3. Is MC sufficiently efficient to provide solutions online for a fast-evolving traffic scene?

These questions are not sufficient for an exhaustive investigation of the approach in practice (e. g., missing the issue of imperfect control), but they provide a good base for a discussion and an extendable foundation for a more comprehensive evaluation in future (cf. Section 4.4).

4.1   Implementation

As a *proof of concept (POC)* we present an implementation of the proposed approach based on the HighwayEnv simulation [44] and the nuXmv model checker, available as artifact on Zenodo or on github (release 0.9.5). For this first POC, we choose a preferably simple setting, sufficient to preliminarily investigate the above questions, by not overly predetermining directions of future research. We see this implementation as a first proposal to experiment with and further build upon. We focus on an open-end highway setting because of the simplicity of implementation, compared to more complex road topologies. We, thus, accept the discrepancy to the "closed area" proposal in the theoretical framework (cf. Section 3). It is not expected that the whole highway can be controlled by MC in practice, but we deem the presented results fairly well transferable to moderately complex closed-area topologies, such as urban crossings (cf. Section 4.4).

In a possible future real-world setting, the interface between MC and perception and actuation of the cars needs to be perfectly aligned. This assimilation is not pushed to perfection here, we accept the following differences for now:

1. *Lateral (lat)* control: MC provides requests for *lane keeping* or *changing towards the left or right neighboring lane.* In HighwayEnv, these are executed using a *pure pursuit* implementation [13], based on floating-point variables; on the MC side, the car jumps laterally in half-lane steps. Lane change completion time, as well as, lateral positioning of the cars on MC side, have been assimilated by trial-and-error, using heading and velocity as parameters.

2. *Longitudinal (long)* control: MC provides target accelerations for each car, which is, apart from low-level dynamics, exactly matched on HighwayEnv side. However, cars in HighwayEnv have a heading, therefore, long deviations are expected when lane changes are executed. Also, HighwayEnv uses floating-point values for velocities, which are rounded to $1\,\mathrm{m\,s^{-1}}$ on MC side.

In the beginning of a run, the cars are placed randomly, according to HighwayEnv's built-in `reset` function, and the initial velocity is randomized uniformly between a minimum and a maximum. In each "`policy`" step of HighwayEnv, MC is run once, providing instructions for HighwayEnv for the remainder of the "`simulation`" iterations. Perception is modeled with perfect vision towards front and rear. Further details can be found in the official documentation. The MC simulation is implemented within the EM and described in detail in the extended version of the previous paper [38]. Figure 2 shows a traffic scene as visualized by HighwayEnv, and, in comparison, the corresponding MC view.

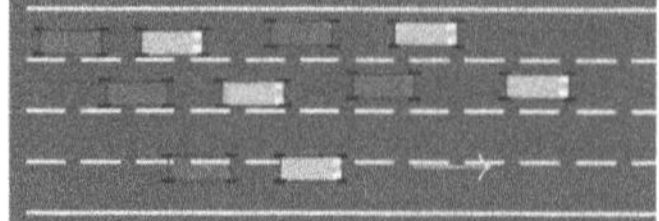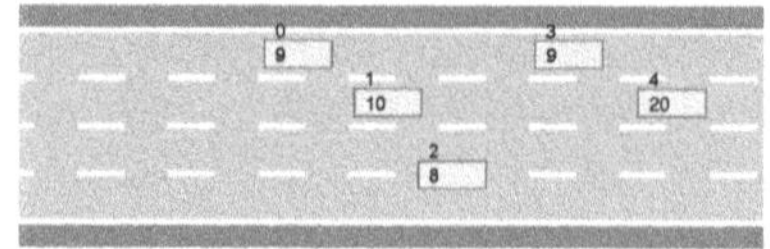

Fig. 2: Snapshot from experiments. 5 cars on 4-lane highway in HighwayEnv (left), as seen by MC (right); blue numbers: car IDs, black: velocities in $\mathrm{m\,s^{-1}}$. (Grey boxes on the left are past positions which HighwayEnv draws by default).

4.2 Experimental Setup

We investigate five driving tasks. Three have a focus on either long (tasks 0, 1) or lat (task 2) control only, these have been used for calibration and benchmarking. The remaining two (3, 4) have been designed to be more complex than typical highway driving, having the actual target usecase of a closed urban area in mind, where more dynamic control is required than typical for the highway.

Task 0 (long only)[2]: all cars decelerate to zero (to an accuracy of $1\,\mathrm{m\,s^{-1}}$). **Task 1 (long only)**[3]: all cars accelerate to $50\,\mathrm{m\,s^{-1}}$ (to an accuracy of $1\,\mathrm{m\,s^{-1}}$). **Task 2 (lat only)**[4]: all cars must be pair-wise at most one lane width apart. **Task 3 (lat/long)**[5]: all cars must eventually (re-)take their original (long) ordering while being not more than $20\,\mathrm{m}$ apart, four cars drive not faster than $10\,\mathrm{m\,s^{-1}}$, and one (the foremost) drives not slower than $20\,\mathrm{m\,s^{-1}}$; this dynamic specification can only be satisfied for a short amount of time: one car needs to fall behind and then overtake with exact timing to achieve the correct position and speed (Figure 2 depicts such a situation). **Task 4 (lat/long)**[6]: all cars invert their (long) ordering.

Note that these specifications denote the expected final goal of each task only; they are disproven once, meaning that their negation holds in the last state of the calculated CEX trace. To provide a complete task, the initial state has to be set up accordingly (e. g., for task 4, the cars must initially be sorted in the opposite way as in the end), such that a succession of states is needed to accomplish the task. Furthermore, not only physics and driving behavior, but also basic safety properties are intrinsically provided by the EM (e. g., exclusion of collisions; cf. artifact). "Unsafe" states are, thus, excluded by design, and do not need to be explicitly handled by the specifications. Invariant specifications suffice to express the described tasks here since progression of time is simply introduced by the relation between the initial state and the expected property. Nonetheless, nuXmv allows to define LTL specifications, as well, which are suited to express more complex temporal relations.

The setting is a 4-lane highway with 5 cars (i. e., task 4 can never be accomplished without lane changes, task 3 rarely), velocity ranges from 0 to $70\,\mathrm{m\,s^{-1}}$

---

[2] SPEC: `!(veh0.v=0 & veh1.v=0 & veh2.v=0 & veh3.v=0 & veh4.v=0)`

[3] SPEC: `!(veh0.v=50 & veh1.v=50 & veh2.v=50 & veh3.v=50 & veh4.v=50)`

[4] SPEC: `!(veh0.onlane=veh1.onlane & veh1.onlane=veh2.onlane & ...)`

[5] SPEC: *Too long, refer to the artifact for this spec and other details (cf. Section 6).*

[6] SPEC: `!(veh0.pos-veh4.pos<50 & veh0.pos>veh1.pos & veh1.pos>veh2.pos & ...)`

(initially randomized between 20 and $30\,\mathrm{m\,s}^{-1}$), acceleration ranges from -6 to $6\,\mathrm{m\,s}^{-2}$. The *policy frequency* is $2\,\mathrm{Hz}$, i. e., the MC is executed twice per second, the *simulation frequency* is $60\,\mathrm{Hz}$ (see HighwayEnv documentation). nuXmv has been run in BMC mode with a bound of 100 (which could be further reduced since the longest traces had 17 steps, see Section 4.3). Since it is a property of the BMC mode to retrieve shortest-possible traces, the MC-proposed solutions are implicitly as short as the respective task in the given situation allows.

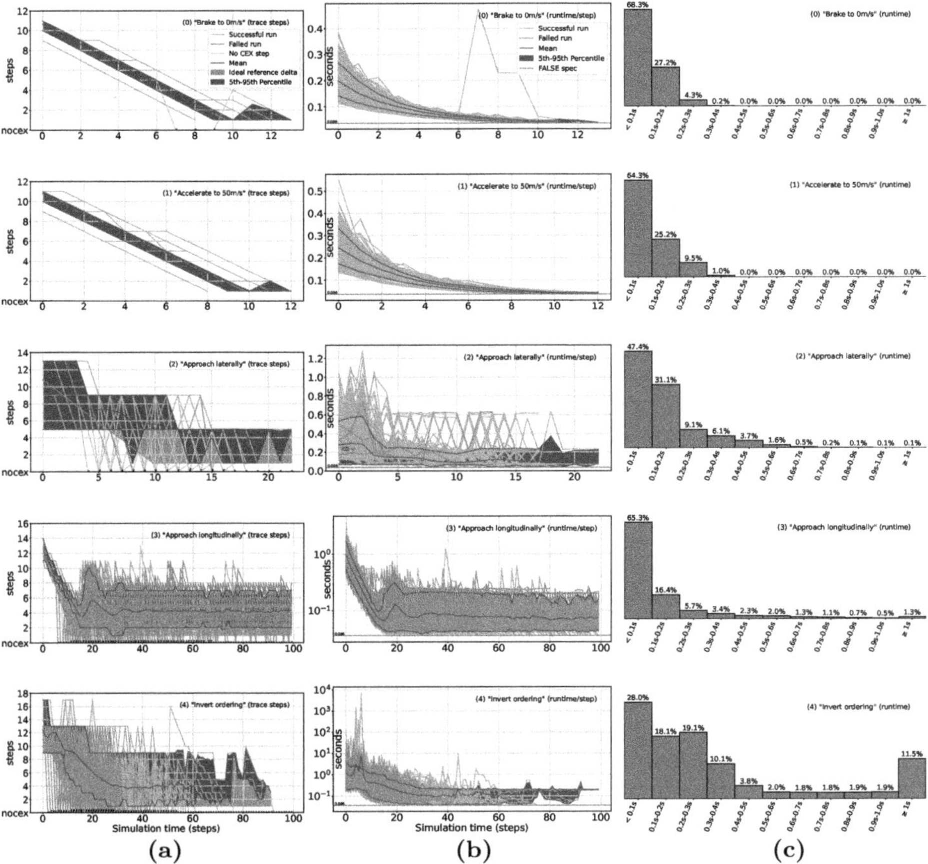

Fig. 3: **CEX trace length in steps (a), time of MC run/step (b) over sim. time; aggregated run times (c).** Individual runs painted as thin grey/red/yellow lines, mean in blue. (a) Light-red area: delta to hypothetical ideal gradient; tiny numbers near horiz. axis: "no CEX" events/step. (b) Green line: ref. time of FALSE spec ($\approx$ init. time); (3)/(4) in log scale, due to outliers.

Each of the five tasks is executed 1000 times, each run lasting for 100 simulation steps, i. e., $50\,\mathrm{s}$ of simulation time. In case of a dead end situation (no CEX provided), there is no explicit fallback path, but MC continues in the next step trying to re-take control. No-CEX events can happen when HighwayEnv and MC simulation drift apart leading to unforeseen situations (e. g., a collision becomes seemingly inevitable). However, the no-CEX event itself can be based on a mis-interpretation, as well, such that MC can in some cases re-take control in the next step. In such "blind" iterations, HighwayEnv continues simulating by finalizing ongoing lane changes, and keeping formerly chosen target velocities.

All experimental runs have been conducted on an Ubuntu workstation with 12th Gen Intel Core i9-12900K 5200 MHz CPUs and 128 GB of RAM. The experiments ran sequentially and had at all time one full physical CPU at disposal.

4.3 Results

Figure 3 provides a summary of the experimental data and serves as foundation for our analysis. Videos of all runs, as well as, detailed data for each step of each run, can be downloaded as supplementary material from Zenodo.

Success Rates. A run is counted as *generally successful* if the task has been accomplished within the given time frame and no crash has occurred. (I. e., this includes runs containing "blind" iterations.) The success rates of the tasks were: **task 0 − 100%, task 1 − 100%, task 2 − 98.2%** *(99.7%)*, **task 3 − 73.1%, task 4 − 62.7%** *(66.4%)*. (In brackets: success rate when counting accomplished tasks even after a crash occurred; HighwayEnv stops cars shorty after a crash.)

In addition to the pure success rate, we measure two more fine-granular indicators of correct steering of the fleet. Apart from being successful, a perfect run should evolve as predicted by MC and finish after the number of steps given in the first CEX. I. e., the pursued regular case should be that the earlier suggestion only needs to be re-confirmed (making in practice a new MC run possibly even unnecessary). Thus, a simulation step in which the trace length is not reduced by exactly one indicates a readjustment caused by a mis-alignment between the MC prediction and the HighwayEnv simulation. We first measure the actual number of steps of successful runs compared to the number predicted in the first step. Secondly, we measure the rate of "no-CEX" events per run, which can be seen as a particularly severe case of mis-alignment.

The long-only runs were almost perfect in these indicators. Of the 2000 runs of experiments (0) and (1), all of which were generally successful, only one run involved no-CEX events (in three of its 13 steps, showing up in plot (0a) and as outliers in plot (0b), steps 7-9), and 97.3% of the runs finished in the ideal time as predicted by MC from the start. On average, the runs were 0.0305 steps longer than the theoretical ideal (which has been 10.738, on average). *Ideal gradients* can, thus, be observed for most of the runs in plots (0a) and (1a) as straight lines, starting at $(0, l)$ for some initial trace length l, and ending in $(l − 1, 1)$ (since a CEX includes the initial situation, and thus requires only $l − 1$ iterations).

In Figure 3 (a), this notion is generalized to account for deviations from the ideal by a *series* of plots. There, the light-red area indicates the deviation of the mean curve from a hypothetical *mean ideal*, starting at the origin of the respective mean curve and representing how the gradient would have evolved, were there only perfect runs. Note that a deviation is also possible in the shorter direction, typically occurring when the lat movement is faster than predicted.

The latter can be observed in plot (2a) where in many cases the number of CEX steps is reduced by more than one in one simulation step, or where runs finish before reaching the 1-step mark. Overall, this has happened in 228 of the 1000 runs, with these runs being on average 1.79 steps shorter than predicted. Nonetheless, all runs overall were 0.82 steps longer than predicted (which was on average 10.82 steps). 140 runs finished in the MC-predicted number of steps. The deviation in both directions indicates that these errors might be inherent to the differing calculation of lat movement on MC and HighwayEnv side. 784 of these runs were successful without encountering a no-CEX event.

Of the runs for the dynamic tasks 3 and 4 which combine lat and long control, none finished in the initially predicted number of steps. For task 3, the runs were 26.64 steps longer than predicted (on average 12.57 steps), for task 4, 20.16 steps longer than predicted (on average 12.35 steps). Both of these sets of experiments suffer from the imprecise emulation of lat control on MC side, which we deem the most important issue to improve in future. Task 3 additionally challenges long control to a high degree due to the very small window where the exact velocity and positional constraints have to hold. For this task, the fleet typically needed several attempts of the foremost car falling back and accelerating, trying to meet the desired constraints. Nonetheless, the traffic situation evolved fairly rarely into a critical state. 587 runs were successful without encountering a no-CEX event. Unsuccessful runs could in many cases be attributed to simulation time exceeding the 100 step limit (105 runs), while crashes were the reason in 164 runs. In contrast, for task 4, 369 runs were unsuccessful due to crashes, while in only 4 runs the reason was an exceeded time limit; only 53 runs were successful without encountering at least one no-CEX event. One aggravating factor for this task was nuXmv's property of delivering a shortest-possible solution, which required the cars to approach each other closely, both during the complex choreography of simultaneous overtakes and then in the end when taking close-by final positions. A possible countermeasure for practice could be to explicitly demand solutions which obey minimal distances between the cars, a property which seems wise to incorporate in early adoptions of the approach, anyway.

Although tasks 3 and 4 fairly often did not succeed, and provable compliance to requirements was even less frequently continuously traceable throughout whole runs, we still consider these preliminary results overall promising. Firstly, because the tasks were generally solvable by MC, while reflecting a complexity which seems realistic for real-world usecases, and with runtimes close to practical applicability (see below), and secondly, because the identified countermeasures, improving lat control and explicit safety distances, hold a prospect of significant further improvements with little additional risk (cf. discussion in Section 4.4).

Runtimes. Overall, MC was executed $10,668 + 10,869 + 11,896 + 55,752 + 55,857 = 145,042$ times for the five tasks. As Figure 3 (c) shows, most of these executions (54.66%) took less than 0.1 s, which is a typical threshold in the automotive industry below which the high-level reactivity of an AV is considered sufficient (for example by the J3131 norm [12]). However, the remaining, longer-lasting executions are in general too long and need to be further examined. We observe that long execution times tend to occur in the beginning of runs, while later, when approaching a solution, execution times decrease. In theory, the first execution of each run is the most important, since, in ideal runs, the remaining executions could be replaced by mere re-confirmations of the original prediction. On the other hand, the first executions can take considerably longer than the 0.1 s threshold, particularly for the most complex task 4. Here, the mean time in the beginning was 1.22 s with the 95-th percentile starting at 3.19 s, and runtimes up to 10 s occurred occasionally[7]; the fastest run in the first iteration was still at 0.17 s. These runtimes seem overall too high for an immediate adoption in practice. However, we use a very naïve setup where a single nuXmv instance is called from scratch in every iteration. We, therefore, nonetheless, consider these runtimes promising, as argued in the discussion below.

4.4   Discussion

As the data suggests, the final answer to questions 1. and 2. (above) will mainly depend on the effects of improving lat control on MC side. While the long control benchmark tasks (0, 1) have been accomplished almost perfectly, the discrepancy between HighwayEnv and nuXmv on the lat movement in the current implementation becomes apparent already for task 2, and we consider it the crucial factor for "critical" failures of tasks 3 and 4 (see comment below on criticality). Overall, we consider both the success rates for the dynamic tasks 3 and 4, and the runtimes (question 3.) promising, given the current simplified lat control implementation and the naïve MC integration.

Runtime.   Having the model checker running continuously would immediately eliminate the initialization time, which we estimated to ≈ 0.036 s (by executing 1000 calls with specification *FALSE*; cf. dashed green lines in Figure 3 (b)). Far greater potential is to be expected, though, if the model checker could build up an ever growing state space over time, instead of starting over for each call. Over time, runtime could, thus, drastically decrease down to acceptable levels (≈ 0.1 s). This we consider the strongest instrument of runtime reduction in practice. For simpler cases, it could even be possible to pre-compute the full state space, and only query it based on the traffic situation at hand. A pre-computation of only the "entering" events could also significantly reduce the computational load. Other than that, faster CPUs could directly improve runtime, and parallel calls to different MC instances with slightly varying EMs could reduce the risk of outliers and also improve runtime. This all being subject to further research, we expect that runtimes within acceptable ranges can be reached in practice for the tasks presented here. On the other hand, it needs to be considered that $\langle 1 \rangle$ the experiments incorporated (only) 5 cars, $\langle 2 \rangle$ the street topology was simple, and $\langle 3 \rangle$ the requirements might in reality become significantly more complex

---

[7] Only 35 calls over all runs of all tasks took longer than 10 s. We do not comment on crass outliers which took up to several hours for one single MC call; their rare occurrence is well-known, and in practice runs need to be cut off when lasting longer than some acknowledged threshold (possibly 0.1 s).

than the artificial tasks inspected here. Of these issues, we consider $\langle 1 \rangle$ to be the most crucial. It is likely that fleets of 10 cars or more are to be controlled at once, and it is up for future work to explore how well the approach scales with the number of cars. Generally, runtime is exponential in the number of vehicles, which probably cannot be avoided. However, we have not performed any tailored optimization in this direction so far, for example, exploitation of symmetries specific to traffic situations. The fleet control system is currently fixed to exactly five cars, which we considered a reasonable number for a first evaluation, and enough to regard the solutions non-trivial and beneficial in practice. Experiments with 15 and more vehicles in somewhat different settings have been conducted (and ran considerably longer, but without "hitting the exponential wall"), but transferability of these results is limited. Regarding $\langle 2 \rangle$, we expect that the EM can usually be optimized well for a given delimited road topology, such as a medium-sized crossing or roundabout. Regarding $\langle 3 \rangle$, the formulas can be optimized beforehand, and since they do not contribute to the state space size, the suggested measures w. r. t. online built-up and offline pre-computation of the search space should still apply. Investigating these topics more closely is left for future work.

Criticality.   To measure the performance in a more fine-granular way, dividing the requirements into "critical" and "non-critical" seems useful. For example in task 3, many runs have not actually finally failed to solve the task but were cut off due to the simulation time limit. For these runs, the MC-predicted trajectories could not be followed precisely, i. e., a traceable provable correctness of the behavior was not given, but no critical incident (crash, in this case) happened. In reality, such a distinction could be necessary, as well, since physics cannot be mimicked exactly, and poor predictions by MC can never be ruled out completely. Then, the most important aspect is to remain in "safe" states, even if the property of provably obeying all requirements is momentarily lost. One solution could be to provide a set of critical requirements for all participants to obey, and allow only non-critical requirements to be claimed by individual agents.

Concurrency and Timing.   In the presented implementation, the HighwayEnv simulation stops while MC is running, which over-simplifies the alignment between the two simulations. In reality, the input for MC needs to be a prediction of the future state expected when the MC run is finished. For this, a guarantee of maximum runtime is necessary, which MC by itself cannot deliver. Therefore, runs exceeding a given threshold (e. g., 0.1 s) need to be cut off and in this case a fallback mechanism needs to take over control for one iteration. Such a mechanism is necessary for no-CEX events, as well. The prediction itself should then be easily feasible, as long as the threshold time is sufficiently low. Note that pausing the simulation during the MC run is not per se unrealistic. In a state-of-the-art automated car the planner receives environment updates every 100 ms, which can be seen as the world "pausing," as well. Another related constraint is the planning frequency which has been adjusted here to 2 Hz, but possibly needs to be re-adapted for other topologies and tasks.

Mapping from CEX to Actuation Instructions.   The CEX provides all object positions, velocities etc. for all time steps up to a solution of the task. These signals already sufficiently describe the trajectories to be followed. However, to follow them precisely, the controllers need to provide an interface which makes it possible to implement the exact actuation instructions coming from the MC. This can be done by aligning the MC simulation to the car dynamics (as has been mostly done for the implementation in this paper) or by providing high-level maneuver blocks on the car side which mimic the MC simulation.

Constraint about Controllability of Moving Objects.   The trajectory problem is greatly simplified if all movements are under control or at least fully predictable by MC. In general, MC can only be used as solver if all non-deterministic degrees of freedom are controllable. To assure this, it might be necessary to narrow down the operational design domain to streets which are structurally separated from non-MC-managed parts of the road network. For some specific situations it can be feasible to only require a limited subset of traffic participants to be cooperative, and assume that the others are "shielded" from direct interaction. For example, when entering a highway and searching for a gap, it may suffice to only cooperate with one car next to us such that a gap is opened by braking, while cars further behind are implicitly determined to cooperate, as well (see [68] for further examples). On the other hand, this constraint may be loosened if good predictions are available which essentially eliminate remaining degrees of freedom. It then depends on the situation (type and number of uncontrolled objects), how much harder the problem gets and "how much" of the *provability* property is lost. Pedestrians or cyclists, for example, are way harder to predict than cars.

Ensuring Sound, Non-Conflicting Requirements.   To prevent conflicts between the requirements, an automatic check can be performed. For this, a full (unbounded) MC run can be performed in the following setting. The initial traffic situation is completely empty, cars can enter and leave via corresponding events modeled in the EM. For all requirements r_i (high-level or individual), the specification to check is the CTL formula: $EG \bigwedge_i r_i$. Note, however, that a useful "entering event" may be the challenging part to establish here, since unpredictable non-determinism seems to be inevitable at the inflow from the free road network. Furthermore, the state space size may become a limiting factor for this automatic check.

Introduction into Real Road Networks.   Introducing the system in practice is challenging primarily due to the demand of full control over the vehicles. A feasible setting for early adoption could be a structurally separated crossing which allows only registered participants to enter. In addition to cars fully implementing the system, non-controlled cars could be included if they give guarantees about their behavior, which do not create conflicts. One central station is needed to gather all necessary information and to run the model checker. There are different ways to observe the current traffic situation and control the involved vehicles. $\langle 1 \rangle$ Complex infrastructure case: the infrastructure has sensors to detect all relevant vehicles and does all the planning centrally, just the low level control commands are sent to the vehicles to execute. This case is comparable to already existing systems such as the Automated Valet Parking service by Bosch and Mercedes. $\langle 2 \rangle$ Complex vehicles case: the vehicles are able to precisely localize and maybe also detect other vehicles. This information is sent to a central station which combines information from all vehicles, does the high level planning and sends full trajectories to the vehicles to do the low level trajectory control. $\langle 3 \rangle$ A combination of the above, e. g., it may be beneficial to sense the vehicles with infrastructure sensors but to send complete trajectories to the vehicles to improve latencies and robustness. With modern self-driving vehicles this is becoming more and more feasible and can enable a safer, more efficient and more comfortable behavior.

5   Conclusion

We introduced a novel MC-based method for coordinating fleets of autonomous vehicles in an ego-less, requirement-driven setup. By framing the driving task as a falsification problem, our approach leverages the CEX trace of a disproved specification to generate provably correct and interpretable driving trajectories for the entire fleet. This shifts the paradigm from handcrafted ego-centric planning to a centralized, requirement-centric control logic that is inherently aligned with safety and formal correctness.

Our prototypical implementation using the nuXmv model checker and the HighwayEnv simulator indicates that small fleets can be effectively coordinated in real-time. This underscores the potential of using formal methods not only for verification but as an integral part of the driving logic itself. The approach offers transparent, white-box behavior and reduces the burden of implementing and validating complex control code for each vehicle individually. The proposed method offers several key benefits: it is provably correct by construction, transparent in its decision-making, and does not require hand-crafted control algorithms for individual agents, reducing industrial development time significantly.

To realize this vision on real roads, challenges remain, such as handling timing constraints, ensuring compatibility with existing vehicle controllers, and managing scenes with partially equipped vehicles. Yet, with modern vehicles already capable of low-level trajectory following, and communication infrastructure evolving rapidly, this work provides a concrete starting point to rethink fleet control from a formal and centralized perspective. Looking ahead, future work will focus on improving scalability through tailored optimizations in the model checker, extending the approach to more complex traffic scenarios, and exploring integration into the early stages of development pipelines for AD systems.

As a call to action, we invite researchers and industry stakeholders to further explore the scalability, infrastructure requirements, and regulatory frameworks needed to bring this model-checking-driven fleet coordination into operational domains. With targeted refinement, this approach has the potential to transform traffic orchestration in structured environments, such as smart intersections, campus shuttles, or automated valet parking zones, safely and by construction.

6   Data-Availability Statement

The experimental data including videos of all runs is available as supplementary material on Zenodo [36]. A complementary artifact on Zenodo can be used to reproduce the results, and re-used for conducting new research [37].

References

1. Abeywickrama, D.B., Mamei, M., Zambonelli, F.: Engineering collectives of self-driving vehicles: The sota approach. In: Leveraging Applications of Formal Methods, Verification and Validation. Distributed Systems: 8th International Symposium, ISoLA 2018, Limassol, Cyprus, November 5-9, 2018, Proceedings, Part III 8. pp. 79–93. Springer (2018)
2. Abeywickrama, D.B., Zambonelli, F.: Model checking goal-oriented requirements for self-adaptive systems. In: 2012 IEEE 19th International Conference and Workshops on Engineering of Computer-Based Systems. pp. 33–42 (2012). https://doi.org/10.1109/ECBS.2012.30
3. Arcile, J., Devillers, R.R., Klaudel, H.: Verifcar: a framework for modeling and model checking communicating autonomous vehicles. Auton. Agents Multi Agent Syst. **33**(3), 353–381 (2019). https://doi.org/10.1007/S10458-019-09409-X, https://doi.org/10.1007/s10458-019-09409-x
4. Baier, C., Katoen, J.P.: Principles of Model Checking. MIT Press, Cambridge, MA, USA (2008)
5. Bakar, N.A., Selamat, A.: Agent systems verification: systematic literature review and mapping. Applied Intelligence **48**(5), 1251–1274 (May 2018). https://doi.org/10.1007/s10489-017-1112-z, https://doi.org/10.1007/s10489-017-1112-z
6. Behrmann, G., David, A., Larsen, K.G., Pettersson, P., Yi, W., Hendriks, M.: Uppaal 4.0. In: Proceedings of the 3rd International Conference on the Quantitative Evaluation of Systems. pp. 125–126. QEST 2006, IEEE Computer Society, Los Alamitos, CA, USA (Sep 2006). https://doi.org/10.1109/QEST.2006.59
7. Cavada, R., Cimatti, A., Dorigatti, M., Griggio, A., Mariotti, A., Micheli, A., Mover, S., Roveri, M., Tonetta, S.: The nuXmv Symbolic Model Checker. In: Computer Aided Verification. CAV 2014 (2014)
8. Chu, T., Kalabić, U.: Model-based deep reinforcement learning for cacc in mixed-autonomy vehicle platoon. In: 2019 IEEE 58th Conference on Decision and Control (CDC). pp. 4079–4084. IEEE (2019)
9. Cimatti, A., Pistore, M., Roveri, M., Traverso, P.: Weak, strong, and strong cyclic planning via symbolic model checking. Artificial Intelligence **147**(1), 35–84 (2003). https://doi.org/https://doi.org/10.1016/S0004-3702(02)00374-0, https://www.sciencedirect.com/science/article/pii/S0004370202003740, planning with Uncertainty and Incomplete Information
10. Cimatti, A., Roveri, M.: Conformant planning via symbolic model checking. J. Artif. Int. Res. **13**(1), 305–338 (Dec 2000)
11. Committee, O.R.A.D.: Taxonomy and definitions for terms related to driving automation systems for on-road motor vehicles (2021), https://doi.org/10.4271/J3016_202104, accessed: 2026-02-28
12. Committee, O.R.A.D.O.: Definitions for Terms Related to Automated Driving Systems Reference Architecture, Fig. 1 (Mar 2022). https://doi.org/https://doi.org/10.4271/J3131_202203

13. Coulter, C.: Implementation of the pure pursuit path tracking algorithm. Tech. rep., Robotics Institute Carnegie Mellon University (1992), https://api.semanticscholar.org/CorpusID:62550799

14. Cubuktepe, M., Jansen, N., Alshiekh, M., Topcu, U.: Synthesis of provably correct autonomy protocols for shared control. IEEE Transactions on Automatic Control **66**(7), 3251–3258 (Jul 2021). https://doi.org/10.1109/TAC.2020.3018029

15. Daw, Z., Cleaveland, R., Vetter, M.: Integrating model checking and uml based model-driven development for embedded systems. In: Automated Verification of Critical Systems 2013. Electronic Communications of the EASST, vol. 66 (2013). https://doi.org/10.14279/tuj.eceasst.66.888

16. Dehnert, C., Junges, S., Katoen, J.P., Volk, M.: A storm is coming: A modern probabilistic model checker. In: Majumdar, R., Kunčak, V. (eds.) Computer Aided Verification. pp. 592–600. Springer International Publishing, Cham (2017)

17. Dinneweth, J., Boubezoul, A., Mandiau, R., Espié, S.: Multi-agent reinforcement learning for autonomous vehicles: A survey. Autonomous Intelligent Systems **2**(1), 27 (2022)

18. Eckardt, T., Heinzemann, C., Henkler, S., Hirsch, M., Priesterjahn, C., Schäfer, W.: Modeling and verifying dynamic communication structures based on graph transformations. Computer Science - Research and Development **28**(1), 3–22 (Feb 2013). https://doi.org/10.1007/s00450-011-0184-y, published online July 2011

19. Enderton, H.B.: "A Mathematical Introduction to Logic". Academic Press, Boston, MA, USA, 2. edn. (2001)

20. Etigowni, S., Hossain-McKenzie, S., Kazerooni, M., Davis, K., Zonouz, S.: Crystal (ball): I look at physics and predict control flow! just-ahead-of-time controller recovery. In: Proceedings of the 34th Annual Computer Security Applications Conference. p. 553–565. ACSAC '18, Association for Computing Machinery, New York, NY, USA (2018). https://doi.org/10.1145/3274694.3274724, https://doi.org/10.1145/3274694.3274724

21. Fainekos, G.E., Girard, A., Kress-Gazit, H., Pappas, G.J.: Temporal logic motion planning for dynamic robots. Automatica **45**(2), 343 – 352 (2009). https://doi.org/http://dx.doi.org/10.1016/j.automatica.2008.08.008

22. Feiler, J., Hoffmann, S., Diermeyer, F.: Concept of a control center for an automated vehicle fleet. In: 2020 IEEE 23rd international conference on intelligent transportation systems (ITSC). pp. 1–6. IEEE (2020)

23. Gardner, R.W., Genin, D., McDowell, R., Rouff, C., Saksena, A., Schmidt, A.: Probabilistic model checking of the next-generation airborne collision avoidance system. In: 2016 IEEE/AIAA 35th Digital Avionics Systems Conference (DASC). pp. 1–10 (2016). https://doi.org/10.1109/DASC.2016.7777963

24. Gerking, C., Dziwok, S., Heinzemann, C., Schäfer, W.: Domain-specific model checking for cyber-physical systems. In: 12th Workshop on Model-Driven Engineering, Verification and Validation. pp. 18–27. MoDeVVa 2015, CEUR-WS.org Vol-1514, Ottawa (Sep 2015)

25. Haslum, P., Lipovetzky, N., Magazzeni, D., Muise, C.: An Introduction to the Planning Domain Definition Language. Springer Cham, 1st edn. (2019). https://doi.org/10.1007/978-3-031-01584-7

26. Heinzemann, C., Lange, R.: vTSL – a formally verifiable dsl for specifying robot tasks. In: 2018 IEEE/RSJ International Conference on Intelligent Robots and Systems (IROS). pp. 8308–8314. IROS'18, IEEE Computer Society, Madrid, Spain (2018). https://doi.org/10.1109/IROS.2018.8593559

27. Helmert, M.: The fast downward planning system. Journal Artificial Intelligence Research (JAIR) **26**, 191–246 (2006). https://doi.org/10.1613/jair.1705

28. Holzmann, G.J.: The model checker spin. Software Engineering, IEEE Transactions on **23**(5), 279 –295 (may 1997). https://doi.org/10.1109/32.588521
29. Huang, Z., Li, B., Du, D., Li, Q.: A model checking based approach to detect safety-critical adversarial examples on autonomous driving systems. In: Seidl, H., Liu, Z., Pasareanu, C.S. (eds.) Theoretical Aspects of Computing – ICTAC 2022. pp. 238–254. Springer International Publishing, Cham (2022)
30. Huth, M., Ryan, M.: Logic in Computer Science: Modelling and Reasoning about Systems. Cambridge University Press, USA (2004), page 175
31. Jin, W., Du, H., Zhao, B., Tian, X., Shi, B., Yang, G.: A comprehensive survey on multi-agent cooperative decision-making: Scenarios, approaches, challenges and perspectives (2025), https://arxiv.org/abs/2503.13415
32. Johnson, B., Kress-Gazit, H.: Probabilistic guarantees for high-level robot behavior in the presence of sensor error. Autonomous Robots **33**(3), 309–321 (Oct 2012). https://doi.org/10.1007/s10514-012-9301-4
33. Johnson, B., Kress-Gazit, H.: Analyzing and revising high-level robot behaviors under actuator error. In: IEEE/RSJ International Conference on Intelligent Robots and Systems. pp. 741–748. IROS'13, IEEE Computer Society (Nov 2013). https://doi.org/10.1109/IROS.2013.6696434
34. Kamali, M., Dennis, L.A., McAree, O., Fisher, M., Veres, S.M.: Formal verification of autonomous vehicle platooning. Science of computer programming **148**, 88–106 (2017)
35. Keating, D., McInnes, A., Hayes, M.: An industrial application of model checking to a vessel control system. In: 2011 Sixth IEEE International Symposium on Electronic Design, Test and Application. pp. 83–88 (2011). https://doi.org/10.1109/DELTA.2011.24
36. König, L., Heinzemann, C.: Supplementary material for "driving by disproof: A model checking approach to fleet coordination" (Aug 2025). https://doi.org/10.5281/zenodo.16738026
37. König, L., Heinzemann, C.: Artifact for "driving by disproof: A model checking approach to fleet coordination" (Jan 2026). https://doi.org/10.5281/zenodo.18171064
38. König, L., Heinzemann, C., Griggio, A., Klauck, M., Cimatti, A., Henze, F., Tonetta, S., Küperkoch, S., Fassbender, D., Hanselmann, M.: Towards safe autonomous driving: Model checking a behavior planner during development. In: Finkbeiner, B., Kovács, L. (eds.) Tools and Algorithms for the Construction and Analysis of Systems. pp. 44–65. Springer Nature Switzerland, Cham (2024)
39. König, L., Henze, F., Klauck, M., Heinzemann, C., Griggio, A., Cimatti, A., Tonetta, S.: Formally verifying a behavior planner: Balancing efficiency and precision. IEEE Transactions on Intelligent Vehicles **Under Review**(x), xx–yy (2025). https://doi.org/xxdoixx
40. Kress-Gazit, H., Fainekos, G.E., Pappas, G.J.: Temporal-logic-based reactive mission and motion planning. IEEE Transactions on Robotics **25**(6), 1370–1381 (Dec 2009). https://doi.org/10.1109/TRO.2009.2030225
41. Krook, J., Kianfar, R., Fabian, M.: Formal synthesis of safe stop tactical planners for an automated vehicle. IFAC-PapersOnLine **53**(4), 445–452 (2020). https://doi.org/https://doi.org/10.1016/j.ifacol.2021.04.059, 15th IFAC Workshop on Discrete Event Systems WODES 2020 – Rio de Janeiro, Brazil, 11-13 November 2020
42. Krook, J., Svensson, L., Li, Y., Feng, L., Fabian, M.: Design and formal verification of a safe stop supervisor for an automated vehicle. In: 2019 International Conference on Robotics and Automation (ICRA). pp. 5607–5613 (2019). https://doi.org/10.1109/ICRA.2019.8793636

43. Kwiatkowska, M., Norman, G., Parker, D.: PRISM 4.0: Verification of probabilistic real-time systems. In: Gopalakrishnan, G., Qadeer, S. (eds.) Proc. 23rd International Conference on Computer Aided Verification (CAV'11). LNCS, vol. 6806, pp. 585–591. Springer (2011)
44. Leurent, E.: An environment for autonomous driving decision-making. https://github.com/eleurent/highway-env (2018)
45. Liu, J., Wang, Z., Hang, P., Sun, J.: Delay-aware multi-agent reinforcement learning for cooperative adaptive cruise control with model-based stability enhancement. arXiv preprint arXiv:2404.15696 (2024)
46. Luckcuck, M., Farrell, M., Dennis, L.A., Dixon, C., Fisher, M.: Formal specification and verification of autonomous robotic systems: A survey. ACM Comput. Surv. **52**(5) (2019). https://doi.org/10.1145/3342355, https://doi.org/10.1145/3342355
47. Ma, Y., Sun, C., Chen, J., Cao, D., Xiong, L.: Verification and validation methods for decision-making and planning of automated vehicles: A review. IEEE Transactions on Intelligent Vehicles **7**(3), 480–498 (2022). https://doi.org/10.1109/TIV.2022.3196396
48. Mariani, S., Cabri, G., Zambonelli, F.: Coordination of autonomous vehicles: taxonomy and survey. ACM Computing Surveys (CSUR) **54**(1), 1–33 (2021)
49. Mehdipour, N., Althoff, M., Tebbens, R.D., Belta, C.: Formal methods to comply with rules of the road in autonomous driving: State of the art and grand challenges. Automatica **152** (2023). https://doi.org/10.1016/j.automatica.2022.110692
50. Provan, G.: Formal methods for autonomous vehicles. IT Professional **26**(1), 50–56 (2024)
51. Rao, A., Wang, Y.: Formal verification of autonomous vehicles: Bridging the gap between model-based design and model checking. SAE Int. J. Adv. & Curr. Prac. in Mobility **6**(2), 814–826 (2024). https://doi.org/10.4271/2023-01-0116
52. Rashid, A., Siddique, U., Hasan, O.: Formal verification of platoon control strategies. In: Johnsen, E.B., Schaefer, I. (eds.) Software Engineering and Formal Methods - 16th International Conference, SEFM 2018, Held as Part of STAF 2018, Toulouse, France, June 27-29, 2018, Proceedings. Lecture Notes in Computer Science, vol. 10886, pp. 223–238. Springer (2018). https://doi.org/10.1007/978-3-319-92970-5_14, https://doi.org/10.1007/978-3-319-92970-5_14
53. Riedmaier, S., Ponn, T., Ludwig, D., Schick, B., Diermeyer, F.: Survey on scenario-based safety assessment of automated vehicles. IEEE Access **8**, 87456–87477 (2020). https://doi.org/10.1109/ACCESS.2020.2993730
54. Schmidt, Á., Varró, D.: Checkvml: A tool for model checking visual modeling languages. In: Stevens, P., Whittle, J., Booch, G. (eds.) UML 2003 - The Unified Modeling Language. Modeling Languages and Applications, Lecture Notes in Computer Science, vol. 2863, pp. 92–95. Springer Berlin Heidelberg (Oct 2003). https://doi.org/10.1007/978-3-540-45221-8_8
55. Selvaraj, Y., Ahrendt, W., Fabian, M.: Verification of decision making software in an autonomous vehicle: An industrial case study. In: Larsen, K.G., Willemse, T. (eds.) Formal Methods for Industrial Critical Systems. pp. 143–159. Springer International Publishing, Cham (2019)
56. Siegel, M.: The sense-think-act paradigm revisited. In: 1st International Workshop on Robotic Sensing, 2003. ROSE'03. pp. 5–pp. IEEE (2003)
57. Soni, A., Hu, H.: Formation control for a fleet of autonomous ground vehicles: A survey. Robotics **7**(4), 67 (2018)
58. Torreño, A., Onaindia, E., Komenda, A., Štolba, M.: Cooperative multi-agent planning: A survey. ACM Comput. Surv. **50**(6) (Nov 2017). https://doi.org/10.1145/3128584, https://doi.org/10.1145/3128584

59. Tran, S.C., Pontelli, E., Balduccini, M., Schaub, T.: Answer set planning: A survey. Theory and Practice of Logic Programming **23**(1), 226–298 (2023). https://doi.org/10.1017/S1471068422000072

60. Van, T.N., Geihs, K.: Formal verification of multi-agent plans for vehicle platooning. In: Vinh, P.C., Rakib, A. (eds.) Context-Aware Systems and Applications, and Nature of Computation and Communication - 9th EAI International Conference, ICCASA 2020, and 6th EAI International Conference, ICTCC 2020, Thai Nguyen, Vietnam, November 26-27, 2020, Proceedings. Lecture Notes of the Institute for Computer Sciences, Social Informatics and Telecommunications Engineering, vol. 343, pp. 3–15. Springer (2020). https://doi.org/10.1007/978-3-030-67101-3_1, https://doi.org/10.1007/978-3-030-67101-3_1

61. Van Arem, B., Van Driel, C.J., Visser, R.: The impact of cooperative adaptive cruise control on traffic-flow characteristics. IEEE Transactions on intelligent transportation systems **7**(4), 429–436 (2006)

62. Wang, Z., Wu, G., Barth, M.J.: A review on cooperative adaptive cruise control (cacc) systems: Architectures, controls, and applications. In: 2018 21st International Conference on Intelligent Transportation Systems (ITSC). pp. 2884–2891. IEEE (2018)

63. Waqas, M., Murtaza, M.A., Nuzzo, P., Ioannou, P.: Correct-by-construction design of adaptive cruise control with control barrier functions under safety and regulatory constraints. In: 2022 American Control Conference (ACC). pp. 5140–5146. IEEE (2022)

64. Werling, M., Faller, R., Betz, W., Straub, D.: Safety integrity framework for automated driving (2025), https://arxiv.org/abs/2503.20544

65. Wesselhöft, M., Hinckeldeyn, J., Kreutzfeldt, J.: Controlling fleets of autonomous mobile robots with reinforcement learning: a brief survey. Robotics **11**(5), 85 (2022)

66. Wong, K.W., Ehlers, R., Kress-Gazit, H.: Resilient, provably-correct, and high-level robot behaviors. IEEE Transactions on Robotics **34**(4), 936–952 (Aug 2018). https://doi.org/10.1109/TRO.2018.2830353

67. Xu, X., Grizzle, J.W., Tabuada, P., Ames, A.D.: Correctness guarantees for the composition of lane keeping and adaptive cruise control. IEEE Transactions on Automation Science and Engineering **15**(3), 1216–1229 (2017)

68. Yan, S., König, L., Burgard, W.: Agent-agnostic centralized training for decentralized multi-agent cooperative driving (2024), https://arxiv.org/abs/2403.11914

69. Zita, A., Mohajerani, S., Fabian, M.: Application of formal verification to the lane change module of an autonomous vehicle. In: 2017 13th IEEE Conference on Automation Science and Engineering (CASE). pp. 932–937 (2017). https://doi.org/10.1109/COASE.2017.8256223

VERILHYS: a Framework for LTL Specification and Verification of Hybrid Systems

Ludovico Battista, Stefano Tonetta,
and Gianni Zampedri

Fondazione Bruno Kessler, Trento 38123, Italy

Abstract. The automated verification of Linear Temporal Logic (LTL) properties over hybrid systems is an important challenge in formal methods. While numerous tools exist for checking safety and reachability, no framework currently provides a concrete language and algorithm for the full verification of LTL on hybrid models that combine discrete and continuous dynamics described in terms of differential equations. We present VERILHYS, the first tool that enables the specification and automated verification of LTL properties for hybrid automata. The framework integrates continuous analysis techniques with symbolic model checking, leveraging Lyapunov-like, descent, and barrier certificates, as well as reachability set overapproximations, to derive sound LTL constraints on the system abstraction. These constraints are then checked using symbolic LTL model checking, ensuring correctness of the verified property on the original hybrid system. VERILHYS supports both linear and non-linear dynamics and is built on top of existing engines such as CORA, NUXMV, and SMT solvers. Our experiments show that it can handle complex hybrid benchmarks that go beyond the reach of existing tools.

1 Introduction

The verification of liveness properties in hybrid systems is a highly challenging problem. While safety and reachability properties have received significant attention, with mature tools and techniques available (see, e.g., [22,17,4,9,31]), the automated verification of liveness properties - such as recurrence, responsiveness, and region stability - has been tackled only for specific types of discrete or continuous evolutions [5,18] or properties [15,28,33,25,11], and remains a hard challenge in general. These properties, often expressed in Linear Temporal Logic (LTL) [29], are crucial for reasoning about the long-term behavior of systems.

In this paper, we present VERILHYS, a fully automated tool for VERIfying LTL properties of HYbrid Systems. The tool takes advantage of continuous analysis techniques and discrete-time model checking. It constructs a coarse discrete abstraction of the hybrid system and makes use of synthesized certificate functions (e.g., Lyapunov-like, descent, and barrier functions) and reachability set overapproximation (RSO) to derive a set of LTL constraints that are provably satisfied by the discrete system; it then uses symbolic model checking to verify

S. Junges and G. Katz (Eds.): TACAS 2026, LNCS 16505, pp. 620–639, 2026.
https://doi.org/10.1007/978-3-032-22752-2_32

the desired property on the abstraction. Theoretical arguments show that this ensures that the property holds on the original hybrid system.

After a recap of the formal problem and the algorithmic solution presented in [13], the paper provides a detailed description of the architecture of VERILHYS. The architecture specifies the software components of the framework together with their inputs and outputs. We then move to the input language of the tool, which extends the standard SPACEEX format [22] to allow the specification of LTL properties for hybrid systems. Then, specific parts of the verification algorithm that make VERILHYS fully automated are detailed: (i) the synthesis of certificate functions, including Lyapunov-like, descent, and barrier certificates, obtained through LMI- and SMT-based techniques; (ii) the generation of semialgebraic regions by means of a heuristic combination of the regions appearing in the input (initial conditions and property) with sublevel sets derived from the synthesized Lyapunov-like functions; and (iii) the construction of the finite discrete abstraction used for symbolic model checking with an ALLSMT procedure [32] strengthened by valid constraints on the Boolean variables representing the regions statically learned by checking intersection or containment of the corresponding semialgebraic sets.

VERILHYS is implemented by integrating several existing tools: CORA [4] for reachability analysis, NUXMV [16] for symbolic model checking, numerical solvers (YALMIP [26], MOSEK [7]) for synthesis of candidate certificate functions, and SMT solvers for certificate validation and abstraction synthesis. The tool supports both linear and nonlinear (polynomial) dynamics and scales to systems with large discrete structures and complex behaviors.

We demonstrate the effectiveness of VERILHYS on a series of benchmarks, including systems with switching logic and nonlinear flows. The tool can automatically generate and handle hundreds of regions and constraints, proving properties that are currently out of reach for other verification frameworks. The tool and benchmarks are available at https://es-static.fbk.eu/tools/verilhys.

The rest of the paper is organized as follows. Sec. 2 discusses related work and tools. Sec. 3 establishes the formal Background for our work, defining Hybrid Automata and the LTL properties, and summarizing the verification approach that VERILHYS implements. Sec. 4 presents the Architectural Design, detailing the structure of the tool and the integration of external engines. Sec. 5 describes the Input Language used by VERILHYS, focusing on the syntax for specifying the hybrid automaton and the LTL properties. Sec. 6 focuses on the implementation and details three key aspects: the synthesis of the certificates, the synthesis of the regions and the computation of the abstraction. Sec. 7 presents the Experimental Evaluation using a variety of complex benchmarks. Finally, Sec. 8 summarizes our contributions and discusses future work.

2   Related works

A wide range of abstraction and verification techniques have been developed for hybrid systems (see, e.g., [3]), typically under specific assumptions on the dynamics. For linear or rectangular hybrid automata, predicate abstraction and CEGAR approaches have proved effective for verifying safety properties [6], while liveness-related properties have been tackled only under restrictive conditions (see, e.g., [30,15,28,33,25,12]). Complete discrete abstractions are known to exist only for particular classes of continuous or discrete evolutions [5], and SMT-based model checking has been successfully applied to rectangular hybrid automata [18]. In contrast, VERILHYS builds a simple but general abstraction that can handle arbitrary polynomial dynamics and supports the verification of full LTL properties.

Several tools address hybrid system verification, such as SPACEEX [22], FLOW* [17], CORA [4], HYLAA [9], and HYPRO [31], focusing primarily on reachability and verification of safety properties. These methods are highly effective for bounded-time verification but do not provide algorithms to prove temporal or liveness properties beyond safety. KEYMAERAX [23] is a deductive framework that provides an interactive environment for proving temporal properties using differential dynamic logic, but the automated proof strategy for LTL verification is very limited. Some works have approached the verification of liveness properties, using Lyapunov-like functions as certificates for the validity of temporal properties [25], and, in the context of non-linear systems, to invalidate substrings to prove general LTL properties implied by safety properties [33]. However, no implemented tools exist for these methods.

To the best of our knowledge, VERILHYS is the first tool that provides a concrete specification language and a fully automated algorithm for verifying generic LTL formulas on hybrid systems governed by ordinary differential equations. It integrates continuous analysis (via certificate and reachability computations) with symbolic model checking into a unified and sound workflow. Moreover, the benchmark specification format adopted by VERILHYS —an extension of the SPACEEX language to include LTL properties—ensures compatibility with existing hybrid system models and encourages the development of future tools supporting temporal logic verification, e.g., within the ARCH competition [2].

3   Background

In this section we briefly recollect the main definitions and concepts used in the paper. We refer to [13] for more details.

3.1   Hybrid Automata and Hybrid Traces

A *Hybrid Automaton* is given as a tuple
$H = (X, Q, q_0, E, init, flow, inv, guard, jump)$, where:
  - X is a finite set of real-valued variables $x_1, \ldots, x_n$;
  - Q is a finite collection of discrete states (also called locations);
  - $q_0 \in Q$ denotes the initial location;
  - $E \subseteq Q \times Q$ is the set of discrete transitions;
  - $init \subseteq \mathbb{R}^n$ specifies the set of initial continuous states;

- $inv : Q \to 2^{\mathbb{R}^n}$ assigns to each location q an invariant $inv(q)$, describing the set of continuous states in which the system may remain while in q;
- $flow : Q \times \mathbb{R}^n \to \mathbb{R}^n$ is a (possibly partial) function that determines the continuous evolution in each location $q \in Q$ via a system of differential equations;
- $guard : E \to 2^{\mathbb{R}^n}$ assigns to each edge a guard condition, specifying when the transition (q, q') is enabled depending on the current continuous state;
- $jump : E \to 2^{\mathbb{R}^n \times \mathbb{R}^n}$ assigns to each transition a relation describing the possible resets (jumps) of the continuous variables.

In this paper, we focus on hybrid automata where invariants, flows, guards, and jumps are described by (boolean combinations of) polynomials.

A *hybrid trace* for a hybrid automaton H is an infinite sequence

$$\sigma = \langle f_0, I_0, q_0 \rangle, \langle f_1, I_1, q_1 \rangle, \ldots$$

where for each $i \geq 0$:
- $q_i \in Q$ is a location,
- $I_i \subseteq \mathbb{R}_{\geq 0}$ is a (possibly unbounded) interval, with $l(I_{i+1}) = u(I_i)$,
- The intervals I_i cover $\mathbb{R}_{\geq 0}$.
- $f_i : I_i \to \mathbb{R}^n$ is analytic.

Given an interval $I \subseteq \mathbb{R}$, let $l(I)$ and $u(I)$ be its extremal points. A hybrid trace is a *trajectory* (also called a *run* or a *solution*) of H if:
- the image of f_i is contained in $inv(q_i)$.
- if $l(I_i) \neq u(I_i)$, then $\frac{df_i}{dt}(t) = flow(q_i)(f_i(t))$ for all $t \in I_i$;
- if $q_i = q_{i+1}$, then $f_i \cup f_{i+1}$ is well defined and analytic on $I_i \cup I_{i+1}$. In particular, either I_i is right-closed or I_{i+1} is left-closed;
- if $q_i \neq q_{i+1}$, then I_i is right-closed, I_{i+1} is left-closed, $e = (q_i, q_{i+1}) \in E$, $f_i(u(I_i)) \in guard(e)$, and $(f_i(u(I_i)), f_{i+1}(l(I_{i+1}))) \models jump(e)$.

3.2   LTL

We use the standard syntax of LTL and the semantics over hybrid traces as defined in [19]. We adopt the variant HLTL defined in [13] where the propositions of LTL can be either a discrete location $q \in Q$ or a region predicate $R \subseteq \mathbb{R}^n$ over the continuous variables. For simplicity, we use LTL throughout this paper to refer to this hybrid variant.

Let $Expr(X)$ denote the set of Boolean combinations of polynomial constraints over X (called *regions*). The syntax of LTL formulas is given by:

$$\varphi ::= q \mid R \mid \varphi \vee \varphi \mid \neg \varphi \mid \varphi U \varphi$$

where $q \in Q$ and $R \in Expr(X)$. We use standard abbreviations: $\varphi \wedge \psi := \neg(\neg\varphi \vee \neg\psi)$, $\varphi \to \psi := \neg\varphi \vee \psi$, $F\varphi := \top U \varphi$, $G\varphi := \neg F \neg\varphi$. In the rest of the paper, we often refer to *local regions* $Z = (R_Z, Q_Z)$: they can be thought as formulas of the form $R_Z \wedge (\bigvee_{q \in Q_Z} q)$: they represent regions that can be reached only in certain locations.

Given a hybrid trace $\sigma = \langle f_0, I_0, q_0 \rangle, \langle f_1, I_1, q_1 \rangle, \ldots$ and an LTL formula φ, the satisfaction relation $\sigma, i \models \varphi$ (at position i) is defined inductively as:

- $\sigma, i \models q$ iff $q_i = q$,
- $\sigma, i \models R$ iff for all $t \in I_i$, $f_i(t) \models R$,
- $\sigma, i \models \varphi_1 \vee \varphi_2$ iff $\sigma, i \models \varphi_1$ or $\sigma, i \models \varphi_2$,
- $\sigma, i \models \neg\varphi$ iff $\sigma, i \not\models \varphi$,
- $\sigma, i \models \varphi_1 U \varphi_2$ iff there exists $k \geq i$ such that $\sigma, k \models \varphi_2$ and for all j with $i \leq j < k$, $\sigma, j \models \varphi_1$.

We write $\sigma \models \varphi$ if $\sigma, 0 \models \varphi$.

Given a hybrid automaton H and an LTL formula φ over Q and X, we write $H \models \varphi$ if for all hybrid traces σ that satisfy initial conditions (*i.e.*, the starting location is q_0 and $f_0(0)$ is in *init*) that are *ground* for φ (*i.e.*, the truth of each region predicate is constant over each interval I_i), it holds that $\sigma \models \varphi$.

3.3   Certificate functions and RSO

We use mainly two methods to get information on the behaviour of the system: (i) *certificate functions* and (ii) *Reachability Set Over-approximation (RSO)*. We briefly recall these two concepts and refer to [13, Section 2.4] for more details.

Certificate functions   Certificate functions are real-valued functions defined over a subset of $X \times Q$. They are used to prove properties about the system's behavior, such as safety, stability, and progress. In VERILHYS, we use three types of certificate functions: Lyapunov-like functions, Descent functions, and Barrier functions.

- *Lyapunov-like functions* help establish stability, even when the system does not converge to a single equilibrium. They consist in non-negative functions that tend to zero along trajectories within designated locations.
- *Descent functions* are similar in spirit but strictly decrease (with temporal derivative $< -\varepsilon$) along trajectories within designated locations. They are useful for proving progress properties.
- *Barrier functions* are used to certify safety. They ensure that trajectories starting in a safe region (where the barrier function is non-positive) cannot cross into unsafe regions (where the function becomes positive), provided the system remains within a specified subset of locations.

Each certificate function F is defined as a pair (F_f, F_Q), where $F_Q \subseteq Q$ is the set of locations where the function's conditions hold, and F_f is a scalar function from $X \times F_Q$ to $\mathbb{R}$. We use these functions to derive LTL constraints that are guaranteed to hold on the original hybrid system.

Reachability Set Over-approximation (RSO)   Reachable Set Overapproximations (*RSO*) are a powerful tool for analyzing the behavior of hybrid systems by estimating where the system can evolve over time. Given a hybrid system H, an initial region R, and a starting location q, an RSO with granularity τ up to time T is a finite collection of triples (Y_i, J_i, p_i), where: Y_i is a region in the state space, $J_i = [l_i\tau, u_i\tau]$ is a time interval, and $p_i \in Q$ is a system location, such that for every run $\sigma = \langle f_j, I_j, q_j \rangle$ with $f_0(0) \in R$ and $q_0 = q$, for every $0 \leq t \leq T$ and every j such that $t \in \mathrm{Dom}\, f_j$, the point $f_j(t)$ is inside $\bigcup_{i \;|\; t \in J_i, p_i = q_j} Y_i$.

Object	Property	Type
Lyapunov-like Function	$G(F(G(\neg Z) \vee (\neg q)))$	Liveness
Descent Function	$G(F(G(\neg Z) \vee (\neg q)))$	Liveness
Barrier Function	$G((\bigvee Z_1) \to (G(\neg((\bigvee Z_2))W(\neg q)))$	Safety
Reachable Set Overapproximation	$R_1 \wedge (Z_1 U(Z_2 \wedge Z_2 U(Z_3 \wedge Z_3 U \dots)))$	Liveness

Table 1. Summary of the form of LTL properties generated from each analysis technique. Z_i represents regions and q represents a location.

Informally, the RSO captures all possible positions the system may occupy at any time t within $[0, T]$, given its initial condition, by covering them with a union of regions indexed by time and location.

3.4   Algorithm

The algorithm implemented in VERILHYS is described in [13], we briefly summarize it here. It takes as input: a hybrid system H as defined in Definition 3.1, an LTL formula φ, and (optionally) a set of user-defined local regions $\mathcal{Z}_{add}$, and performs the following steps:

1. it extracts the initial set of local regions $\mathcal{Z}_{in}$ from φ and the initial condition;
2. it synthesizes and validates Lyapunov-like $\mathcal{L}$ and descent functions $\mathcal{D}$;
3. it synthesizes additional local regions $\mathcal{Z}_{Lyap}$ to be used in the abstraction. Let $\mathcal{Z} = \mathcal{Z}_{in} \cup \mathcal{Z}_{Lyap} \cup \mathcal{Z}_{add}$;
4. it computes the barrier functions $\mathcal{B}$. Let $\mathcal{F}$ be $\mathcal{L} \cup \mathcal{D} \cup \mathcal{B}$;
5. it computes an LTL formula γ_f over $\mathcal{Z}$ and Q for each $f \in \mathcal{F}$;
6. it performs RSO for each local region $(R_Z, Q_Z) \in \mathcal{Z}$ and each $q \in Q_Z$ and computes the LTL formula $\gamma_{Z,q}$ over $\mathcal{Z}$ and Q (the granularity τ and time T are fixed parameters of the algorithm).
7. it computes the discrete abstraction D_H, which has a variable v_Z for each local region $(R_Z, Q_Z) \in \mathcal{Z}$ and a variable v_q for each location $q \in Q$;
8. it transforms φ and each generated γ_i into LTL properties $\widehat{\varphi}$ and $\widehat{\gamma_i}$ substituting Z with v_Z and q with v_q;
9. if $D_H \models (\bigwedge_{f \in \mathcal{F}} \widehat{\gamma_f} \wedge \bigwedge_{Z \in \mathcal{Z}, q \in Q_Z} \widehat{\gamma_{Z,q}}) \to \widehat{\varphi}$, then it returns $True$;
10. else it returns $Unknown$.

The correctness of the algorithm is given by [13, Theorems 1 - ... - 5].

LTL constraints In Table 1 we summarize the form of the LTL constraints that are obtained via the steps 5 and 6 above. Lyapunov-like and Descent functions capture progress properties: they ensure that regions that assume values bounded from zero (or from $-\infty$ for descent functions) are eventually left (if the systems stays in the valid locations of the function). Barrier functions capture safety properties: they ensure that the system cannot pass from a region that assumes only non-negative values to a region that assumes only positive values (if the systems stays in the valid locations of the function). Finally, RSO constraints

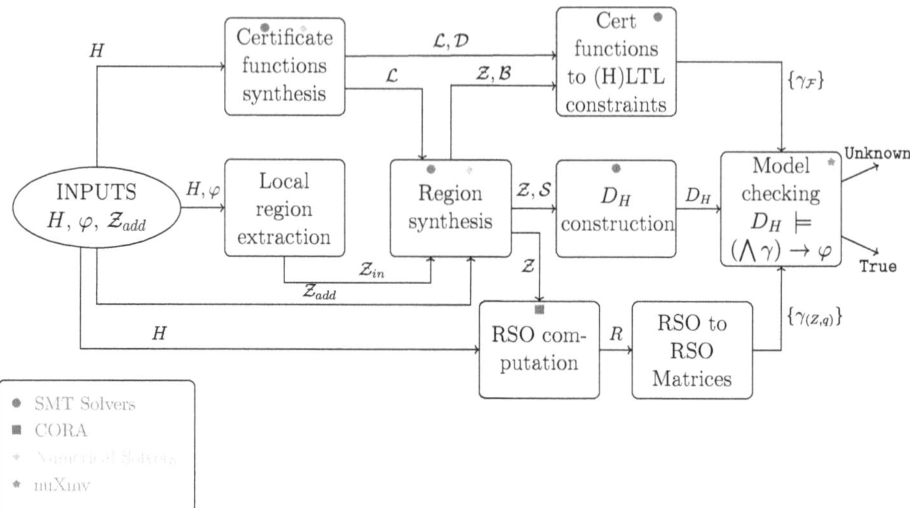

Fig. 1. Architecture of the tool.

give information on the evolution of the system: if the RSO tells us that we go from R_1 to R_2 without passing to R_3, this is implied by the LTL constraint given in the table.

4   Design

4.1   High-level architecture

VERILHYS implements the algorithm described in Section 3.4 and is structured according to the main phases of the algorithm. Figure 1 shows the high-level functional architecture of the tool, detailing the software components in term of input and output. These correspond to the main phases of the algorithm:

1. **Local region extraction.** Reads the hybrid automaton H and the property φ and extracts local regions of interest $\mathcal{Z}_{\text{in}}$.
2. **Certificate functions synthesis.** Synthesizes and validates Lyapunov-like and descent functions using (a) SOS/LMI-based numerical synthesis followed by SMT validation, or (b) direct SMT-based synthesis.
3. **Regions synthesis.** From Lyapunov-like functions it generates sublevel-set regions and (optionally) their images through admissible jumps. It employs numerical optimization followed by SMT validation to compute maxima and minima of functions; the image is computed by finding the inverse of the reset map when possible and considering resets. For each generated sublevel set it also produces the associated barrier function.
4. D_H **construction.** Constructs the finite transition system (FTS) D_H with Boolean variables for locations and (local) regions, encoding geometric properties of the system (as adjacency of regions, possible transitions allowed by

jumps, and non-empty combinations) in invariant and transition constraints. Such constraints are computed using ALLSMT queries to SMT solvers.

5. **Cert functions to LTL constraints.** Converts certificate functions into LTL constraints $\gamma_{\mathcal{F}}$.
6. **RSO computation.** Computes Reachable Set Overapproximations (RSO) for pairs (Z, q) up to horizon T with granularity τ using CORA.
7. **RSO to RSO Matrices.** Converts RSOs into matrices that captures the reachability information on the abstracted system (see [13] for details). These are readily converted into LTL constraints $\gamma_{Z,q}$.
8. **Model Checking** $D_H \models (\bigwedge \gamma) \rightarrow \varphi$. Checks whether $D_H \models (\bigwedge \gamma_f \wedge \gamma_{Z,q}) \rightarrow \varphi$ via symbolic LTL model checking using NUXMV.

Implementation bindings As shown in Figure 1, we use the following tools: SOStools for numerical synthesis of certificate functions; CORA (MATLAB) for RSO; Z3 and CVC5 for ALLSMT checks and certificate synthesis and validation; PYVMT and PYSMT for model construction and manipulation of formulas; NUXMV for LTL model checking.

5   Input details

VERILHYS takes in input a hybrid automaton and an LTL property. These are specified in an extension of the modeling language employed by SPACEEX [22].

Formally, the input format is defined by a grammar expressed in Compact RelaxNG format, which builds upon the original schema of the SPACEEX language. The grammar introduces the following additions:

InitialLocation An optional element that specifies the initial location of the system. The value must correspond to a location defined within the model's location list. For example,

```
<initial_location>1</initial_location>
```

InitialRegion An optional element used to define the initial region of the system's state space. For example,

```
<initial_region>x &gt; 0 &amp; x &lt; 51/5</initial_region>
```

Invar, Reach and LTLProp These elements allow the specification of invariants (Gp), reachability (Fp), and general LTL formulas, respectively, which are used during system analysis. For example,

```
<invariant>x &gt;= 0</invariant>
<reach>(x == 1)</reach>
<ltl-property> (F (G ( x &lt; 1)) ) &amp;&amp; y </ltl-property>
```

Invar, Reach and LTLProp elements must contain syntactically valid LTL expressions, which conform to the following grammar:

```
<ltl_expr> :: basic_expr
           | X <ltl_expr>
           | G <ltl_expr>
           | F <ltl_expr>
           | <ltl_expr> U <ltl_expr>
           | <ltl_expr> R <ltl_expr>
```

`ltl_expr` expressions can be composed using standard logical operators and can also incorporate `basic_expr` expressions, which support classical arithmetic operations and functions over reals.

In contrast to the assumptions made by the native SPACEEX language, VERILHYS enforces syntactic and semantic validation of expressions embedded within the standard tags `flow`, `guard` and `reset-relation`.

Additionally, VERILHYS supports the specification of auxiliary regions via a dedicated parameter. This parameter must reference an external file that conforms to the following syntax:

```
<?xml version="1.0" encoding="UTF-8"?>
   <additional-regions version="0.1">
      <region>
         <polynomial-constraints>
         (x1_sp &gt;= 19/20) &amp; (x2_sp &gt;= 1/20)
         </polynomial-constraints>
         <valid-locations>
             <loc>all</loc>
         </valid-locations>
      </region>
      <region>
      ...
      </region>
   </additional-regions>
```

6   Implementation details

Key aspects of VERILHYS proofs are the synthesis of the certificate functions, the synthesis of regions, and the construction of the discrete abstraction. In this section, we detail some heuristics used to make these phases more effective.

6.1   Certificate synthesis

VERILHYS implements the algorithm described in [13] to synthesize the certificate functions. Two implementation synthesis strategies are used to find Lyapunov-like and Descent functions: (i) numerical synthesis using Sum-of-Squares (SOS), followed by SMT-based validation, and (ii) direct SMT-based synthesis. The resulting functions are validated to ensure they satisfy the required conditions on flows and jumps. These certificates will later be used to derive LTL constraints.

Based on several tests, we noticed that strategy (i) was more effective for Lyapunov-like functions, while strategy (ii) was more effective for Descent functions. In particular, the non-existence of a quadratic Lyapuov-like function took a long time to be proved by SMT solvers, while numerical solvers were not effective in finding Descent functions. For this reason, we implemented strategy (i) for Lyapunov-like functions and strategy (ii) for Descent functions.

6.2   Region synthesis

The local regions used for abstraction come from three sources: (i) the initial set of regions $\mathcal{Z}_{in}$ extracted from the property φ and the initial condition; (ii) user-defined regions $\mathcal{Z}_{add}$; (iii) regions $\mathcal{Z}_{Lyap}$ generated as sublevel sets of the synthesized Lyapunov-like functions. The union of these three sets forms the complete set of local regions $\mathcal{Z}$ used for abstraction.

The regions in $\mathcal{Z}_{in}$ consist in the local region $(init, \{q_i\})$ and $(\psi, \{q_i\}_{i \in I})$ given by the subtrees of the DAG representation of φ of the form $(\psi(X) \wedge \bigvee_{i \in I} q_i)$, where ψ is a semialgebraic formula over the continuous variables X and q_i are locations; more details on this can be found in the extended version [14].

The regions in $\mathcal{Z}_{add}$ are given to the tool as input by the user. As already mentioned, we have defined a simple grammar for specifying them.

The regions in $\mathcal{Z}_{Lyap}$ are synthesised using Lyapunov-like functions. From each validated Lyapunov-like function (L_f, L_Q), the tool generates a set of sublevel-set regions of the form $(L_f \leq a, L_Q)$, where a ranges over a set of critical values computed from the regions in $\mathcal{Z}_{in} \cup \mathcal{Z}_{add}$.

Critical values computation The constants that define the sublevel sets of Lyapunov-like functions are critical to ensure that the sublevel sets are meaningful and interact appropriately with the information abstracted in the discrete system. We compute these constants a for each Lyapunov-like function based on the minimum and maximum values that the Lyapunov functions attain over existing regions.

In particular, for each Lyapunov function (L_f, L_Q), we:

1. identify the local regions $(R_Z, Q_Z) \in \mathcal{Z}_{in} \cup \mathcal{Z}_{add}$ such that $C \cap Q_Z \neq \emptyset$;
2. for each such local region (R_{Z_i}, Q_{Z_i}), compute the minimum and maximum values of L_f over the polynomial constraints defining R_i:

$$k^{(i)}_{\min} = \min_{x \in R_{Z_i}} L_f(x), \quad k^{(i)}_{\max} = \max_{x \in R_{Z_i}} L_f(x).$$

   This is done using numerical optimization techniques, followed by SMT-based validation to ensure correctness. When the validation fails, we proceed by increasing (resp. decreasing) slightly the candidate maximum (resp. minimum) value and re-validate; if this fails after a fixed number of attempts, we discard the value;
3. collect all critical values $\{a_i\}$: the value zero and all minima and maxima from step 2;

4. sort the critical values in ascending order, compute intermediate values between each consecutive pair a_i, a_{i+1}, and add them to the set $\{a_i\}$; we sort again the set of constants $\{a_i\}$ including these intermediate values; we also remove duplicates.

5. for each constant a_i, define a new local region as: $(\{x \in \mathbb{R}^n \mid L_f(x) \leq a_i\}, L_Q)$.

This procedure aims to ensure that the sublevel sets are constructed using meaningful thresholds derived from the behavior of the Lyapunov function over known regions. By including intermediate values, we increase the granularity of the abstraction, aiming to capture more behaviours. Finally, for every generated sublevel set, the associated barrier function $(L_f - a, L_Q)$ is added to the set of certificates.

Images through jumps To keep some information on the behaviour of the system after jumps, we generate additional local regions by considering the images through admissible jumps of the synthesized sublevel sets.

To compute these images, for each $(q_1, q_2) \in E$ such that $q_1 \in L_Q$, we compute the intersection of the sublevel set with the guard $L_f \leq a \cap guard((q_1, q_2))$, and we compute its image through the reset map $jump((q_1, q_2))$. In general, the computation of the image of a semialgebraic set through a polynomial map is can be tackled using quantifier elimination techniques. However, these techniques are often impractical. In our tool, we compute these images only in the case the reset map is invertible, is a projection, or is a combination of these two. In these cases the explicit computation of the image is straightforward.

6.3   SMT-based computation of the discrete abstraction

The computation of the abstract FTS D_H, as described in [13, Definition 14], is achieved with a series of quantifier elimination queries computed with an ALLSMT procedure (see, e.g., [32]). The FTS is built using PYVMT [1] and PYSMT [24] libraries. The ALLSMT is performed using Z3 [27] and CVC5 [10] solvers. An important optimization that we implemented is inspired by standard static learning techniques in SMT (see, e.g., [8]) and precomputes a set of valid constraints to simplify the ALLSMT queries.

Static learning While synthesizing the regions given by sublevels of Lyapunov-like functions, we save a set of propositions that come naturally from the definitions of the synthesized regions. Given a Lyapunov-like function (L_f, L_Q), let $Z_{a_1}, \ldots, Z_{a_k}$ be the local regions generated as sublevel sets of L_f; suppose that $a_1 < a_2 < \ldots < a_k$. We consider two types of propositions that can be learned statically:

- *Type-1 static learnt propositions.* Clearly, the sublevel sets are nested: therefore, for every $i < j$, the following implication holds: $v_{Z_{a_i}} \to v_{Z_{a_j}}$.

Benchmark	dim	$|Q|$	flow	$|\mathcal{Z}_{in}|$	$|\mathcal{Z}_{add}|$	LTL properties tested
Linear Overtake	4	3	Lin	2	0	$G(q_1 \to ((\neg(B))Uq_3))$, $G(F(q_1)), G(\neg B)$
Multiple choice example	2	$2+2n$	Lin	2	0	$F(G(Z_{target}))$
Navigation Benchmark	4	25	Lin	1	14	$G(F(Z_0))$
Non-linear circular	2	1	Nonlin	2	11	$G(F(R_{0,\alpha})), G(\neg B)$
Multilayer control lin	3	n	Lin	2	0	$G(q_i \to (\neg q_J W q_K)) \to (G(\neg B))$, $G(G(q_1) \to F(G(Z_0)))$
Multilayer control nonlin	3	n	Nonlin	2	0	$G(q_i \to (\neg q_J W q_K)) \to (G(\neg B))$, $G(G(q_1) \to F(G(Z_0)))$
Bball	2	1	Lin	2	0	$G(F(v \le 1))$
Circle	2	2	Lin	2	0	$G(Z_0 \to F(Z_1))$
Drivetrain	10	4	Lin	1	0	$G(q_1 \wedge (F\neg(q_2)) \to F(\neg(q_3)))$
Rendezvous	4	1 to 3	Nonlin	1	0	$F(G(q_{final}))$

Table 2. Characteristics of the benchmarks. When $|\mathcal{Z}_{add}| = 0$, we did not need any additional handcrafted region to prove the properties. Some information on the LTL properties can be found in the description of the benchmarks, here they are presented to show the diversity of the properties verified.

- *Type-2 static learnt propositions.* During the generation of sublevel sets, we have associated to each Lyapunov-like function (L_f, L_Q) and each local region Z in $\mathcal{Z}_{in} \cup \mathcal{Z}_{add}$ the maximum M_{Z,L_f} and the minimum m_{Z,L_f} of L_f on Z. Whenever $M_{Z,L_f} < a_i$, the following implication holds: $v_Z \to v_{Z_{a_i}}$, and whenever $m_{Z,L_f} > a_i$, the following implication holds: $v_{Z_{a_i}} \to (\neg v_Z)$.

We call $\mathcal{S}$ the conjunction of all such implications for all Lyapunov-like functions. The actual ALLSMT queries are then performed on the formula $\lambda \wedge \mathcal{S}$, which is equisatisfiable to λ but is simpler to solve, as it contains additional information that the solver can exploit.

7   Experimental evaluation

7.1   Benchmarks

We evaluate the effectiveness and robustness of our tool in proving LTL properties of hybrid systems across several benchmarks:

- Linear Overtake [13]: A 4-dimensional linear hybrid system modeling overtaking behavior of a vehicle. Here, q_1 represents the initial phase of the overtake and q_3 the final phase; B is the region occupied by the overtaken vehicle.
- Multiple Choice [13]: A scalable 2D benchmark with discrete jumps. The system passes through several locations before reaching a final location with converging dynamics. Z_{target} is a small region around the target point.

- Navigation Benchmark [21]: A 4D system (space and velocity variables) with linear dynamics and 25 locations. Here we prove that the system always eventually returns to a specific region Z_0.
- Non-linear Circular [13]: A 2D system with non-linear dynamics converging to the unit circle. We prove that the system always returns to the starting region $R_{0,\alpha}$ (that changes based on α) avoiding an obstacle B.
- Multilayer Control (Linear and Nonlinear) [13]: A scalable 3D system with multiple locations converging (with linear or nonlinear dynamics) to different points in the space. We prove that if the switching takes place only among contiguous locations, then the system always avoids an obstacle B, and that if the system stays in location q_1, it eventually converges to a region Z_0.
- Bball [4]: 2D linear systems representing a bouncing ball. We prove that the velocity v of the ball is always eventually less than a threshold.
- Circle [4]: A 2D linear system with two locations representing circular motion. We prove a reactive property.
- Drivetrain [4]: A 10D linear system modeling a vehicle's drivetrain. Available in 2 different versions. We prove a property on the possible evolution of locations.
- Rendezvous [4,2]: A 4D nonlinear system modeling a spacecraft rendezvous maneuver. Available in 6 different versions. We prove that the system eventually reaches the final location.

The properties of these benchmarks are presented in Table 2. We test four configurations of our algorithm: with/without images through jumps (as explained in Section 6.2) and with/without stabilizing constraints [20]. In particular, CF1 is without both, CF2 is without stabilizing constraints but with images, CF3 is without images but with stabilizing constraints, and CF4 is with both. For systems that admit several configurations, we report the entry *Param* that identifies the specific version of the model.

Metrics. We collect execution times (in seconds) for key components:
- T_{TOT}: total time.
- T_{Lyap}: Lyapunov-like function synthesis.
- $T_{ASJump}, T_{ASReg}, T_{AdReg}$: AllSMT-based abstractions.
- T_{RSO}, T_{RSOMat}: RSO and reachability matrix computation.
- T_{p_i}: time for solving the model checking problem for property i.
  We also report:
- N_{LTL}: number of synthesized LTL constraints.
- $|\mathcal{Z}|$: number of regions.
- md_{RSO}, ms_{RSO}: average temporal depth and size of LTL properties coming from RSO.
- ms_{bar}: average size of LTL properties coming from barrier functions.

We do not show depths and sizes of other LTL constraints since they are fixed (see Table 1). The parameters T and τ are used by CORA in the computation of RSO. We set $T = 10$ and $\tau = 0.1$ for all benchmarks, and we changed τ to 0.01 when we were not able to prove the properties. We run benchmarks with

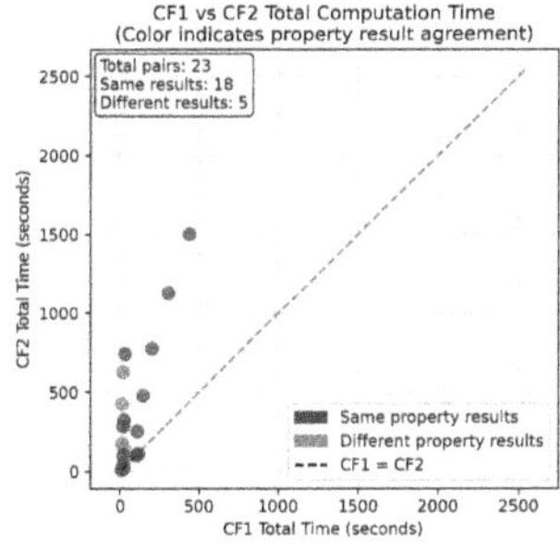

Fig. 2. Comparison of properties proved under CF1 and CF2 configurations across all benchmarks.

1h timeout. Navigation benchmark was particularly challenging, and we set a timeout of 10h for it.

Experiments were run on a 12-core 3.5 GHz machine with 32 GB RAM. Full logs and additional details are available in the extended version [14].

7.2 Results

We here recollect some key observations from our experiments, and we refer the reader to the extended version [14] for the tables of all the results.

Effectiveness Our approach is effective in proving a variety of LTL properties on all the benchmarks considered, as shown in Table 2. All the shown properties were proved in at least one configuration (we refer again to the extended version [14] for more details).

In Figure 2 we compare the total time when using CF1 and CF2 (resp. without and with considering images through jumps in the abstraction), underlining the cases where we have obtained different results in terms of properties proved. In particular, it is expected that CF2 is more effective than CF1, at cost of a higher execution time. This is confirmed by the results, and paves the way to understanding when the use of images is more beneficial.

As explained in Section 4, the tool creates two families of contraints (one coming from certificate functions and one coming from RSO). Interestingly, the benchmarks show that the two families are complementary to prove the original LTL properties: in some cases (*e.g.* Linear Overtake, Multilayer Control) the tool needs both parts, in some cases (*e.g.* Navigation, Non-linear circular) RSOs suffice, in others (*e.g.* Multiple Choice) certificate functions suffice. In general, it is not straightforward to decide in advance which type of constraints is needed for a given benchmark.

Scalability We evaluate the scalability of our approach on the Multiple Choice benchmark and the Multilayer Control benchmarks, which are both parametric

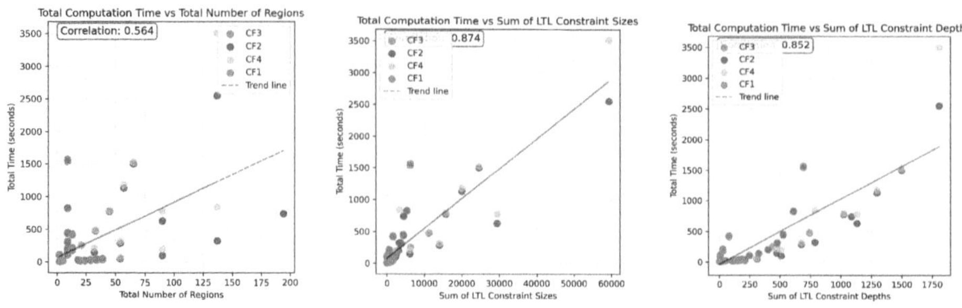

Fig. 3. Total execution time as a function of (a) number of regions, (b) LTL property size, and (c) LTL property temporal depth, across all benchmarks.

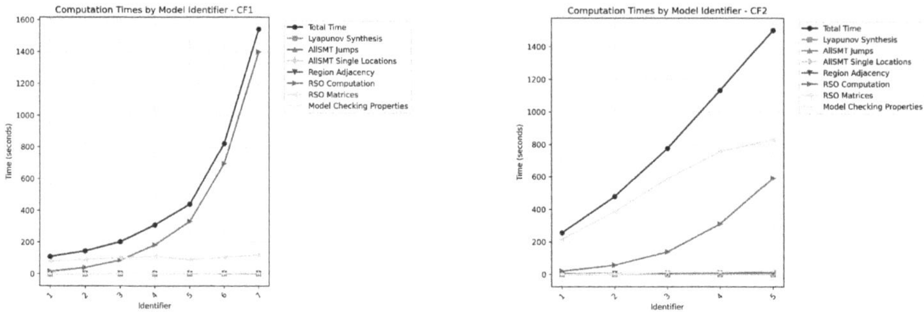

Fig. 4. Execution times for the Multiple Choice benchmark with increasing locations, under CF1 and CF2 configurations. The Identifier represents the number of intermediate layers between initial and final locations.

in the number of locations. Results are shown in Figure 4 and Figure 5, respectively. They confirm a sustainable scalabitility of our approach, which is further confirmed by the results on the other benchmarks, with particular reference to the Navigation benchmark (see Table 3), where we manage 222 LTL constraints and 37 regions.

We also present in Figure 3 a comparison of total execution time against three metrics across all benchmarks: number of regions, LTL property size, and LTL property temporal depth. To improve readability, we excluded Navigation benchmark that was run with a different timeout. We notice that the conncection with the complexity at level of LTL contraints complexity appears stronger than the one at level of number of regions, suggesting a possible improvement of the tool via better ways to handle such constraints.

7.3   Limitations

We only reported the cases of successful verification to showcase the applicability and scalability of the tool and give some insights on the results. As the general

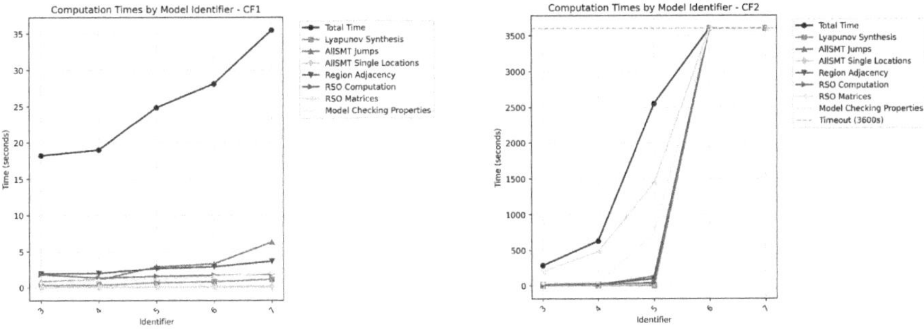

Fig. 5. Execution times for the Multilayer Control linear benchmark with increasing polytope vertices and sides. The Identifier represents the amount of locations of the system.

T_{TOT}	Config	T_{Lyap}	T_{ASJump}	T_{ASReg}	T_{AdReg}	T_{RSO}	T_{RSOMat}	$T\varphi_1$	Res φ_1	md_{RSO}	ms_{RSO}	ms_{bar}	N_{LTL}	$|\mathcal{Z}|$
24459.45	CF1	5.92	9.65	1.22	23.12	22.24	263.15	23915.48	True	35.33	2256.00	148.64	222	37

Table 3. Computation times and statistics for model *navigation* with $\tau = 0.01$ and $T = 10$.

problem of LTL verification for hybrid systems is undecidable, the VERILHYS framework is not guaranteed to terminate successfully for all inputs and in many cases it may instead return 'Unknown' or time out. These unresolved cases generally occur when the continuous analysis phase fails to yield sufficiently tight sound overapproximations. For instance, the certificate synthesis may fail to find suitable Lyapunov-like functions to define significant regions for the abstraction: this is often the case when VERILHYS deals with high-dimensional systems (*e.g.*, no valid Lyapunov-like function was synthesized for the *Drivetrain* benchmark). Another possible issue is given by the RSO computation, that may produce very coarse bounds due to high-dimensional state space or prolonged time horizons, leading to ambiguous LTL constraints. This could in principle take advantage of the automatic tuning of CORA, but we currently do not exploit this feature. All benchmark results, including the cases that currently return 'Unknown' or time out, are publicly available on the project website as open challenges.

8   Conclusions and Future Works

In this paper, we presented VERILHYS, a novel framework that addresses the automated verification of Linear Temporal Logic (LTL) properties over hybrid systems with the continuous dynamics expressed in terms of differential equations. While existing tools primarily focus on restricted properties like safety and reachability, VERILHYS is the first tool to provide a concrete language and algorithm for specifying and verifying full LTL specifications on this types of hybrid automata.

Our approach integrates techniques from both continuous and discrete verification domains. By leveraging Lyapunov-like, descent, and barrier certificates, alongside Reachability Set Overapproximations computed by engines like CORA, VERILHYS is able to derive sound, guaranteed LTL constraints that hold on the original hybrid system. These constraints are then encoded as assumption on a finite system abstraction using the NUXMV symbolic model checker to prove more general LTL properties. The experimental results demonstrate that VERILHYS is practical and scalable, capable of handling complex hybrid benchmarks with both linear and non-linear dynamics that are beyond the range of current verification tools.

Future work will focus on enhancing the precision and scope of the framework. Specifically, we plan to investigate methods to improve the quality of the synthesized regions, which should help minimize the number of 'Unknown' verification results. Furthermore, we intend to explore extensions of the framework to richer properties with metric operators.

Data-Availability Statement The data presented in this paper was obtained using files available at the link https://zenodo.org/records/17628465. The tool VERILHYS can be found at https://es-static.fbk.eu/tools/verilhys/.

References

1. PyVmt: a python library to interact with transition systems. `https://github.com/pyvmt/pyvmt` (2022), [Github repository]
2. Abate, A., Althoff, M., Bu, L., Ernst, G., Frehse, G., Geretti, L., Johnson, T.T., Menghi, C., Mitsch, S., Schupp, S., Soudjani, S.: The ARCH-COMP Friendly Verification Competition for Continuous and Hybrid Systems. In: TOOLympics@ETAPS. Lecture Notes in Computer Science, vol. 14550, pp. 1–37. Springer (2023)
3. Abate, A., Giacobbe, M., Roy, D., Schnitzer, Y.: Model Checking and Strategy Synthesis with Abstractions and Certificates, pp. 360–391. Springer Nature Switzerland, Cham (2025). `https://doi.org/10.1007/978-3-031-75775-4_16`
4. Althoff, M.: An introduction to CORA 2015. In: Proc. of the 1st and 2nd Workshop on Applied Verification for Continuous and Hybrid Systems. pp. 120–151. EasyChair (December 2015). `https://doi.org/10.29007/zbkv`, `https://easychair.org/publications/paper/xMm`
5. Alur, R., Henzinger, T., Lafferriere, G., Pappas, G.: Discrete abstractions of hybrid systems. Proceedings of the IEEE **88**(7), 971–984 (2000). `https://doi.org/10.1109/5.871304`
6. Alur, R., Dang, T., Ivančić, F.: Counterexample-guided predicate abstraction of hybrid systems. Theoretical Computer Science **354**(2), 250–271 (2006). `https://doi.org/10.1016/j.tcs.2005.11.026`, `https://www.sciencedirect.com/science/article/pii/S0304397505008662`, tools and Algorithms for the Construction and Analysis of Systems (TACAS 2003)
7. ApS, M.: Mosek. `https://www.mosek.com/` (2026)
8. Audemard, G., Bertoli, P., Cimatti, A., Kornilowicz, A., Sebastiani, R.: Integrating Boolean and Mathematical Solving: Foundations, Basic Algorithms, and Requirements. In: AISC. Lecture Notes in Computer Science, vol. 2385, pp. 231–245. Springer (2002)
9. Bak, S., Duggirala, P.S.: HyLAA: A Tool for Computing Simulation-Equivalent Reachability for Linear Systems. In: HSCC. pp. 173–178. ACM (2017)
10. Barbosa, H., Barrett, C.W., Brain, M., Kremer, G., Lachnitt, H., Mann, M., Mohamed, A., Mohamed, M., Niemetz, A., Nötzli, A., Ozdemir, A., Preiner, M., Reynolds, A., Sheng, Y., Tinelli, C., Zohar, Y.: cvc5: A versatile and industrial-strength SMT solver. In: TACAS (1). Lecture Notes in Computer Science, vol. 13243, pp. 415–442. Springer (2022)
11. Basagiannis, S., Battista, L., Becchi, A., Cimatti, A., Giantamidis, G., Mover, S., Tacchella, A., Tonetta, S., Tsachouridis, V.: SMT-based stability verification of an industrial switched PI control systems. In: 2023 53rd Annual IEEE/IFIP International Conference on Dependable Systems and Networks Workshops (DSN-W). pp. 243–250 (2023). `https://doi.org/10.1109/DSN-W58399.2023.00063`
12. Battista, L., Tonetta, S.: Formal verification of stability for parametric affine switched systems. IFAC-PapersOnLine **58**(11), 37–42 (2024). `https://doi.org/10.1016/j.ifacol.2024.07.422`, `https://www.sciencedirect.com/science/article/pii/S2405896324005214`
13. Battista, L., Tonetta, S.: Deriving liveness properties of hybrid systems from reachable sets and Lyapunov-like certificates. In: D´Souza, M., Komondoor, R., Srivathsan, B. (eds.) Automated Technology for Verification and Analysis. pp. 363–386. Springer Nature Switzerland, Cham (2026). `https://doi.org/10.1007/978-3-032-08707-2_17`

14. Battista, L., Tonetta, S., Zampedri, G.: Extended version, https://es-static.fbk.eu/people/lbattista/pages/verilhys_tool.html

15. Carter, R., Navarro-López, E.M.: Dynamically-driven timed automaton abstractions for proving liveness of continuous systems. In: Jurdzinski, M., Nickovic, D. (eds.) Formal Modeling and Analysis of Timed Systems - 10th International Conference, FORMATS 2012, London, UK, September 18-20, 2012. Proceedings. Lecture Notes in Computer Science, vol. 7595, pp. 59–74. Springer (2012). https://doi.org/10.1007/978-3-642-33365-1_6

16. Cavada, R., Cimatti, A., Dorigatti, M., Griggio, A., Mariotti, A., Micheli, A., Mover, S., Roveri, M., Tonetta, S.: The nuXmv symbolic model checker. In: Biere, A., Bloem, R. (eds.) CAV. Lecture Notes in Computer Science, vol. 8559, pp. 334–342. Springer (2014)

17. Chen, X., Ábrahám, E., Sankaranarayanan, S.: Flow*: An Analyzer for Non-linear Hybrid Systems. In: CAV. Lecture Notes in Computer Science, vol. 8044, pp. 258–263. Springer (2013)

18. Cimatti, A., Griggio, A., Mover, S., Tonetta, S.: Verifying LTL Properties of Hybrid Systems with K-Liveness. In: CAV. Lecture Notes in Computer Science, vol. 8559, pp. 424–440. Springer (2014)

19. Cimatti, A., Roveri, M., Tonetta, S.: Requirements validation for hybrid systems. In: Bouajjani, A., Maler, O. (eds.) Computer Aided Verification. pp. 188–203. Springer Berlin Heidelberg, Berlin, Heidelberg (2009)

20. Claessen, K., Sörensson, N.: A liveness checking algorithm that counts. In: FMCAD. pp. 52–59. IEEE (2012)

21. Fehnker, A., Ivančić, F.: Benchmarks for hybrid systems verification. In: Alur, R., Pappas, G.J. (eds.) Hybrid Systems: Computation and Control. pp. 326–341. Springer Berlin Heidelberg, Berlin, Heidelberg (2004)

22. Frehse, G., Guernic, C.L., Donzé, A., Cotton, S., Ray, R., Lebeltel, O., Ripado, R., Girard, A., Dang, T., Maler, O.: SpaceEx: Scalable Verification of Hybrid Systems. In: CAV. Lecture Notes in Computer Science, vol. 6806, pp. 379–395. Springer (2011)

23. Fulton, N., Mitsch, S., Quesel, J.D., Völp, M., Platzer, A.: KeYmaera X: An axiomatic tactical theorem prover for hybrid systems. In: Felty, A.P., Middeldorp, A. (eds.) CADE. LNCS, vol. 9195, pp. 527–538. Springer (2015). https://doi.org/10.1007/978-3-319-21401-6_36

24. Gario, M., Micheli, A.: Pysmt: a solver-agnostic library for fast prototyping of smt-based algorithms. In: SMT Workshop 2015 (2015)

25. Han, H., Sanfelice, R.G.: Linear temporal logic for hybrid dynamical systems: Characterizations and sufficient conditions. Nonlinear Analysis: Hybrid Systems **36**, 100865 (2020). https://doi.org/10.1016/j.nahs.2020.100865, https://www.sciencedirect.com/science/article/pii/S1751570X20300121

26. Löfberg, J.: Yalmip : A toolbox for modeling and optimization in matlab. In: In Proceedings of the CACSD Conference. Taipei, Taiwan (2004)

27. de Moura, L.M., Bjørner, N.S.: Z3: an efficient SMT solver. In: TACAS. Lecture Notes in Computer Science, vol. 4963, pp. 337–340. Springer (2008). https://doi.org/10.1007/978-3-540-78800-3_24

28. Plaku, E., Kavraki, L.E., Vardi, M.Y.: Falsification of LTL safety properties in hybrid systems. Int. J. Softw. Tools Technol. Transf. **15**(4), 305–320 (2013)

29. Pnueli, A.: The Temporal Logic of Programs. In: FOCS. pp. 46–57. IEEE Computer Society (1977)

30. Podelski, A., Wagner, S.: Model Checking of Hybrid Systems: From Reachability Towards Stability. In: HSCC. Lecture Notes in Computer Science, vol. 3927, pp. 507–521. Springer (2006)
31. Schupp, S., Ábrahám, E., Makhlouf, I.B., Kowalewski, S.: HyPro: A C++ Library of State Set Representations for Hybrid Systems Reachability Analysis. In: NFM. Lecture Notes in Computer Science, vol. 10227, pp. 288–294 (2017)
32. Spallitta, G., Sebastiani, R., Biere, A.: Disjoint projected enumeration for SAT and SMT without blocking clauses. Artificial Intelligence **345**, 104346 (2025)
33. Wongpiromsarn, T., Topcu, U., Lamperski, A.G.: Automata theory meets barrier certificates: Temporal logic verification of nonlinear systems. IEEE Transactions on Automatic Control **61**, 3344–3355 (2014), `https://api.semanticscholar.org/CorpusID:17453206`

TEMPORA: Efficient Verification of Metric Temporal Properties with Past in Pointwise Semantics [*]

S Akshay[1] , Prerak Contractor[1],
Paul Gastin[2,5], R Govind[3][**], and
B Srivathsan[4,5]

[1] Indian Institute of Technology Bombay, India
akshayss@cse.iitb.ac.in, prerakcontractor24@gmail.com
[2] Université Paris-Saclay, CNRS, ENS Paris-Saclay, LMF, France gastin@lmf.cnrs.fr
[3] Institute of Mathematical Sciences, Chennai, India   govind@imsc.res.in
[4] Chennai Mathematical Institute, India   sri@cmi.ac.in
[5] CNRS, ReLaX, IRL 2000, Siruseri, India

Abstract. Model checking of real-time systems is a well-studied topic, with Metric Interval Temporal Logic (MITL) playing a key role in expressing timed properties. We present TEMPORA, a new tool for MITL model checking under pointwise semantics, that integrates both past and future modalities. TEMPORA is based on a recent translation from MITL to the model of Generalized Timed Automata (GTA) [3] and the zone-based algorithms for reachability and liveness in GTA [2,3]. A straightforward implementation of the construction proposed in [3] falls short of state-of-the-art performance. Through a series of conceptual and engineering optimizations, we significantly improve its scalability and obtain a tool that outperforms existing approaches. In this work, we present the key techniques underlying these improvements and introduce our tool.

1   Introduction

A central ingredient in the model-checking approach is a translation from logic to automata. In the classical setting, Linear Temporal Logic (LTL) is a standard specification formalism and the study of algorithmic techniques to optimize LTL-to-automata translations spans almost four decades – see [41] for a recent survey of this topic. Many of the theoretical techniques have also been incorporated in practical model-checking tools [27,17,21,40,28]. For model-checking systems with timing constraints, the de-facto automaton model would be *timed automata* (TA) [6,5]. State-of-the-art timed automata tools [30,25,40,28] implement analysis methods for models represented as (networks of) timed automata. Typical properties allowed by these verification tools include reachability, liveness, fragments of

---

[*] This work was largely completed while R. Govind was a postdoctoral researcher at Uppsala University.

[**] Corresponding author

© The Author(s) 2026
S. Junges and G. Katz (Eds.): TACAS 2026, LNCS 16505, pp. 640–659, 2026.
https://doi.org/10.1007/978-3-032-22752-2_33

timed CTL [30] or (untimed) LTL. In this work, we are interested in an end-to-end tool to check Metric Interval Temporal Logic (MITL) properties on timed models.

MITL is an extension of LTL where the temporal operators are equipped with a time interval (for instance $F_{[a,b]}\,p$ means p becomes true within a time in the interval $[a, b]$). The foundations for MITL-to-TA have been laid out in [7]. Broadly, there are two ways to interpret MITL formulae: over continuous (dense/super-dense) timed signals [7,33] or pointwise timed words [8,43,15]. In *continuous (state-based) semantics*, the formula is interpreted over *signals*, which are functions that associate the valuation of the propositions to *all* timestamps in $\mathbb{R}_+$. Over the *pointwise semantics*, the formula is interpreted over sequences of events (timed words), each consisting of a timestamp and a set of propositions. Thus, in the continuous semantics, the system is under observation at all times, while in the pointwise semantics, it is observed only when it executes a discrete transition. However, as noted by Ferrére et al. [22], in the continuous semantics, arbitrary MITL formulae can be simplified to the $[0, \infty)$ fragment (the intervals in the temporal operators have either 0 or ∞), while as pointed out in [3], this simplification is not possible in the pointwise semantics. In this work, *we only consider pointwise semantics* as our focus is on models represented in tools like UPPAAL, PAT, and TChecker where behaviours are given as timed words, as in the classical timed automata model of Alur and Dill [6].

The classical approach for model checking MITL involves translating MITL formula into timed automata (TA) and then using state-of-the-art TA tools. The best known tool that accomplishes this translation in the pointwise semantics, called MIGHTYL [15], goes via alternating 1-clock automata and compiles to timed automata. An extension of timed automata called *generalized timed automata* (GTA) was introduced in [2]. GTA are equipped with richer features than TA, and enable a different translation from MITL to GTA, which can then be analyzed using a GTA analysis tool from [2]. The theoretical foundations for such an MITL-to-GTA translation which goes via transducers was presented in [3], where it was argued that the MITL-to-GTA translation has clear theoretical benefits over the MITL to 1-clock Alternating Timed Automata translation [13,14] on which MIGHTYL is based on. However, the approach in [3] was not implemented. Moreover, neither of these approaches considered Past modalities, and were restricted only to Future.

Our Contributions. In this work, we start from the basic MITL-to-GTA translation of [3], incorporate past modalities to the construction and study various optimizations that substantially improve the construction in practice resulting in a new tool TEMPORA. To strike an analogy, consider the influential work [23] on LTL which starts with a classical LTL-to-automata construction [42] as a basis and investigates simplifications inside the construction, resulting in a remarkable gain in the performance. At a high level, this is the same spirit in TEMPORA: we start from the theoretical MITL-to-GTA translation [3], and study optimizations that can result in visible gains in practice. Figure 1 gives a schema of our steps in the theory-to-tool journey. In this paper, our goal is to focus on

MITL-TO-GTA [3] $\longrightarrow$ **GTA networks** $\longrightarrow$ detMITL^{+p} $\longrightarrow$ **SCC-based liveness** $\longrightarrow$ TEMPORA

Fig. 1. From theory [3] to tool TEMPORA

the key insights and challenges in the optimizations, and present our tool. The underlying theoretical developments and formal proofs appear in [1].

GTA networks. The MITL-to-GTA construction of [3] constructs one GTA (with outputs) for every subformula of an MITL formula. Each automaton reads the outputs of its subformulae-automata, processes it and sends it to its parent. All of this processing and communication happens instantaneously with no time delay. In the construction of [3], each automaton had its own local clocks. Our first goal was to share information among these sub-formula automata, as far as possible. In order to do so, we need a clear notion of a synchronization between components in a network. The definitions known for networks of timed automata are not sufficient: in a timed automaton, transitions contain a guard and a reset, whereas in a GTA, each transition contains a *sequence* of tests and updates. Therefore when different GTA of a network synchronize, questions on handling *shared variables* arise, when there is an update of a variable in one component and a test in another. Our first contribution is a formal definition of a network of timed systems whose transitions are instantaneous programs, and not just guard-reset pairs (Section 2).

detMITL^{+p}. Our second objective lies in getting determinism as far as possible in the resulting formulae automata. When we compose a non-deterministic automaton $\mathcal{B}$ with a model $\mathcal{A}$, each branch of $\mathcal{A}$ can potentially explode into multiple branches in the product $\mathcal{A} \times \mathcal{B}$, whereas if $\mathcal{B}$ had been deterministic, this multiplication does not occur. The advantage of more determinism in LTL-to-automata translations has been comprehensively studied in [39], and even in the timed setting under the continuous signal semantics [35]. For the pointwise semantics, we identify a fragment of the more general Metric Temporal Logic (MTL) with past and future, for which we provide a linear time translation to synchronous networks of *deterministic* timed automata. In this fragment, that we call detMITL^{+p}, the outermost temporal modalities are future (Next, Until, eventually, always) and can even have punctual intervals, while inner temporal modalities should be past: Yesterday or Since with non-punctual interval. This fragment already subsumes many safety properties, extending e.g., the G(pLTL) fragment defined in [9]. We present the syntax of detMITL^{+p} in Section 3. Since detMITL^{+p} allows past operators, we adapted the construction of [3] to past operators. Section 4 presents an overview of the construction along with a full example. As mentioned earlier, the constructions for the continuous semantics [35] cannot be directly applied in the pointwise semantics.

MITL^{+p} *and GTA liveness.* We extend this algorithm (with shared clocks and information) to handle future modalities obtaining a translation from general MITL^{+p} (with Future and Past, allowing punctual intervals at the outermost level) to networks of GTA with shared variables (extending the model from [2]). While non-determinism cannot be avoided here, we reduce non-deterministic branching by *sharing clocks and predictions* in the GTA. Section 5 presents a brief overview of this approach. Finally, since our model checking approach ultimately reduces to checking reachability and liveness for GTAs, we integrate the liveness-checking algorithm from [3] with Couvreur's SCC algorithm [20] (which is the state-of-the-art for TA) in the setting of GTAs.

Remark 1. Although $\mathsf{detMITL}^{+p}$ is presented first as a distinguished fragment, our approach implements a *single* translation algorithm for full MITL^{+p}. Simply, when the input formula belongs to $\mathsf{detMITL}^{+p}$, the algorithm produces a deterministic network, yielding better performance.

TEMPORA. Our key contribution is an implementation of our algorithms in a prototype tool, called TEMPORA, built on top of the open-source timed automata library TCHECKER. TEMPORA supports satisfiability and model checking for $\mathsf{detMITL}^{+p}$ and general MITL^{+p}, for both finite and infinite words, in the pointwise semantics. We compare against MIGHTYL which translates MITL formula to TA (and uses UPPAAL to check satisfiability for finite words and OPAAL for infinite words). Our comparison on a suite of 72 benchmarks (22 new and 50 taken from the literature) shows that our pipeline (TEMPORA+TCHECKER) outperforms MIGHTYL pipeline; it is faster in all benchmarks for finite words and all but 2 for infinite words, and most often explores a smaller state space (in zones). As a baseline, we also implement the translation to GTA presented in [3] and demonstrate an order of magnitude improvement. Finally, we implement an end-to-end model checking algorithm for MITL^{+p} over the pointwise semantics and evaluate it on two classical benchmarks: Fischer's mutual exclusion algorithm and the Dining Philosophers problem.

Related work. In [7] that introduced MITL, the authors propose the first such translation, which is known to be notoriously complicated, and acknowledged to be difficult in the follow-up works by different authors [33]. The current state-of-the-art for MITL model checking in pointwise semantics was proposed by Brihaye et al. in [15]. Their procedure and the associated tool, called MIGHTYL [15] is based on a series of works that translate MITL to timed automata [13,14], via alternating timed automata [36]. We became aware of an extension of MIGHTYL [26] only very recently. As it was developed independently and concurrent to our work, we do not make a direct comparison. Moreover, at the time of writing of this document, we could not access the link to the tool of [26].

We already discussed several works in the *signal semantics* that build networks of TA for various fragments of MITL with and without past including [22,32,33]. These often employ compositional testers or transducers for timed modalities, but do not focus on sharing e.g., of networks and subformula. A different logic based approach in [34], translates MITL in signal semantics to an intermediate logical language, and encodes it into an SMT solver. This also included synchronization primitives and was implemented in a Java tool. Several tools support MITL model checking under continuous semantics, including [29,18,19,38,31,34], but under pointwise semantics, to the best of our knowledge, MightyL [15] is the only tool that can handle the full future fragment of MITL (even if it only solves satisfiability and does not handle past operators). The other works (to our knowledge) that offer tool support are for restricted fragments such as $\mathsf{MITL}_{(0.\infty)}$ [16], or MITL over untimed words [44].

2 Synchronous network of TA with shared variables

We formally define the notion of a network of timed systems that we use in this paper. To focus on the network part, we consider automata with the usual kind of clocks as in a timed automaton. The presentation is different from previous works [10,12,24,3], and is geared towards providing a clean and concise explanation of our logic-to-automata translation. At a high level, each component in our network is a timed automaton with shared variables and the semantics of the network is *synchronous*: either time elapses in all components of the network (all clocks are increased by the same amount), or all components execute simultaneously an instantaneous transition. The components of the system communicate via *shared variables* (clocks, states, Boolean variables, ...). The paradigm is concurrent-read owner-write (CROW). Hence, each variable is *owned* by a unique component of the system.

A *timed automaton with shared variables* is a tuple $\mathcal{A} = (Q, X, V, \Delta, \mathsf{init})$ where $\mathcal{A}$ is the name, Q is a finite set of locations over which ranges the *state variable* $\mathcal{A}.\mathsf{st}$, X is a finite set of clock variables *owned* by $\mathcal{A}$, V is a finite set of Boolean variables owned by $\mathcal{A}$, Δ is the finite set of transitions, and init is an initial condition for the variables owned by $\mathcal{A}$. A transition is a triple $(\ell, \mathsf{prog}, \ell')$ where $\ell, \ell' \in Q$ are locations and prog is an *instantaneous program*. A program is a sequence of *tests* and *updates*. For instance, if x, y are clocks owned by $\mathcal{A}$ and out is a Boolean variable owned by $\mathcal{A}$, then a purely local program could be $\mathcal{A}.x \in (3, 5]; \mathcal{A}.y := 2; \mathcal{A}.\mathsf{out} := 0$ where $\mathcal{A}.x \in (3, 5]$ is a test which succeeds if the current value of clock x is within the interval, and $\mathcal{A}.y := 2$ and $\mathcal{A}.\mathsf{out} := 0$ are updates. Tests may also use variables owned by other components.

An atomic update for a Boolean variable $v \in V$ owned by $\mathcal{A}$ has the form $\mathcal{A}.v := c$ (or simply $v := c$ when $\mathcal{A}$ is clear from the context) with $c \in \{0, 1\}$. An atomic update for a clock variable $x \in X$ owned by $\mathcal{A}$ has the form $\mathcal{A}.x := c$ (or simply $x := c$) with $c \in \overline{\mathbb{N}} = \mathbb{N} \cup \{+\infty\}$. We assume that each variable is updated at most once in a program. An atomic test for a clock variable $x \in X$ owned by $\mathcal{A}$ has the form $\mathcal{A}.x \in I$ (or simply $x \in I$) where I is an integer bounded interval whose end points come from $\overline{\mathbb{N}}$ (e.g., $[0, 3)$ or $[2, +\infty)$ or $(2, 5]$, etc). $\mathcal{A}$ may also test a clock variable owned by another component with $\mathcal{N}.x \in I$ or $\mathcal{N}.x^\bullet \in I$ where $\mathcal{N}$ is a name and I is an integer bounded interval. Similarly, an atomic test for a Boolean variable b owned by $\mathcal{A}$ has the form $b = 0$ or $b = 1$ (also written b and $\neg b$) and if the variable is not owned by $\mathcal{A}$ we use $\mathcal{N}.b$ or $\mathcal{N}.b^\bullet$. We write $\mathcal{N}.\mathsf{st} = \ell$, $\mathcal{N}.\mathsf{st} \neq \ell$, $\mathcal{N}.\mathsf{st}^\bullet = \ell$ and $\mathcal{N}.\mathsf{st}^\bullet \neq \ell$ for testing whether component $\mathcal{N}$ is in location ℓ or not. Finally, a test in a program is a Boolean combination of atomic tests. The initialisation init of $\mathcal{A}$ is a conjunction of atomic tests, one for each variable of $\mathcal{A}$, including the state variable. For instance, init could be $\mathsf{st} = \ell_0 \wedge y = +\infty \wedge \mathsf{out} = 0$. By default, a variable such as $\mathcal{A}.x$ or $\mathcal{B}.z$ used in a

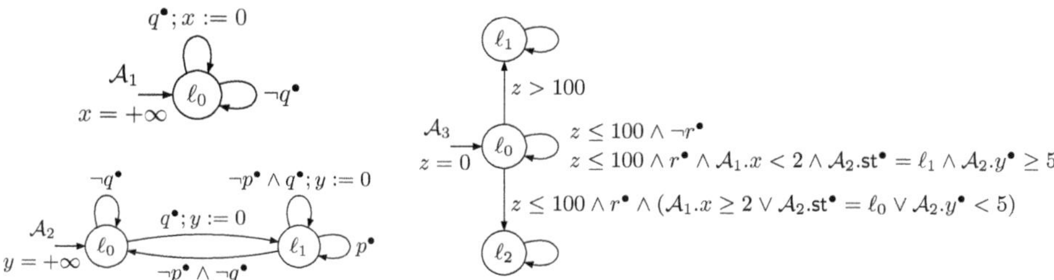

Fig. 2. Synchronous Network of timed automata with shared variables implementing specification of Example 3, where we simply write $p^\bullet$, $q^\bullet$ and $r^\bullet$ instead of $\mathcal{M}.p^\bullet$, $\mathcal{M}.q^\bullet$ and $\mathcal{M}.r^\bullet$. Names, initial conditions are depicted with an incoming arrow to a location.

test refers to the value of the variable *before* the synchronous transition is taken. It is sometimes convenient to refer to the value a variable will have *after* the synchronous transition is taken. We do so by writing $\mathcal{B}.\mathsf{out}^\bullet$ or $\mathcal{B}.\mathsf{st}^\bullet$.

For example, consider two components $\mathcal{A}$ and $\mathcal{B}$ where $\mathcal{B}$ owns clock x and a transition where the component $\mathcal{B}$ updates its clock x. Then a program of $\mathcal{A}$ of the form $\mathcal{B}.x^\bullet \in [2,5]$ is evaluated by checking the value of clock x *after* $\mathcal{B}$ takes its transition. In other words, the transition is taken if the value of x is updated to a value in the interval $[2,5]$ by $\mathcal{B}$'s transition, otherwise it is not taken. Thus, post-transition clock tests constrain admissible successor configurations rather than predicting future values.

We now provide the formal syntax and semantics for our model of networks.

Definition 2 (Synchronous network of timed automata). *A network is a tuple $\overline{\mathcal{A}} = (\mathcal{A}_1, \ldots, \mathcal{A}_n)$ where each $\mathcal{A}_i = (Q_i, X_i, V_i, \Delta_i, \mathsf{init}_i)$ is a timed automaton with shared variables. The network is* closed *if the references to external variables in programs are all of the form $\mathcal{A}_i.\mathsf{st}$ or $\mathcal{A}_i.\mathsf{st}^\bullet$, $\mathcal{A}_i.x$ or $\mathcal{A}_i.x^\bullet$ with $x \in X_i$, $\mathcal{A}_i.v$ or $\mathcal{A}_i.v^\bullet$ with $v \in V_i$, for some $1 \le i \le n$. The network is* partially ordered *if there is a partial order $\preceq$ on its components such that whenever component $\mathcal{A}$ refers to a variable owned by component $\mathcal{B}$, we have $\mathcal{B} \preceq \mathcal{A}$. In this paper, we will only use partially ordered networks.*

We describe now the semantics of a network. A *configuration* C of $\overline{\mathcal{A}}$ is a valuation of all variables of the network: for all $1 \le i \le n$, we have $C(\mathcal{A}_i.\mathsf{st}) \in Q_i$, $C(\mathcal{A}_i.x) \in \overline{\mathbb{R}}_+ = \mathbb{R}_+ \cup \{+\infty\}$ for $x \in X_i$, and $C(\mathcal{A}_i.v) \in \{0,1\}$ for $v \in V_i$. A configuration is *initial* if it satisfies all initial conditions of its components. For instance, if init_2 is $\mathsf{st} = \ell_0 \wedge y = +\infty \wedge \mathsf{out} = 0$, then it is satisfied at C if $C(\mathcal{A}_2.\mathsf{st}) = \ell_0$, $C(\mathcal{A}_2.y) = +\infty$ and $C(\mathcal{A}_2.\mathsf{out}) = 0$.

The network is *synchronous*, i.e., all components move simultaneously, and has two types of transitions: time elapse and discrete. A *time elapse* by some non-negative real number $\delta \ge 0$ is written $C \xrightarrow{\delta} C'$ where C' coincides with C on all variables other than clocks, and the value of each clock is advanced by the same quantity δ: $C'(\mathcal{A}_i.x) = C(\mathcal{A}_i.x) + \delta$ for all $1 \le i \le n$ and $x \in X_i$ (with $+\infty + \delta = +\infty$). A *discrete* transition occurs in the network when each component executes simultaneously a transition. Let $\bar{t} = (t_1, \ldots, t_n)$ with $t_i = (\ell_i, \mathsf{prog}_i, \ell_i') \in \Delta_i$ for all $1 \leq i \leq n$. Let C, C' be two configurations. There is a discrete transition $C \xrightarrow{\bar{t}} C'$ if the following holds:

- $C(\mathcal{A}_i.\mathsf{st}) = \ell_i$ and $C'(\mathcal{A}_i.\mathsf{st}) = \ell_i'$ for all $1 \leq i \leq n$,
- for all i and $x \in X_i \cup V_i$, we have $C'(\mathcal{A}_i.x) = c$ if prog_i contains an update $\mathcal{A}_i.x := c$ and $C'(\mathcal{A}_i.x) = C(\mathcal{A}_i.x)$ otherwise (recall that each variable is updated at most once),
- all tests occurring in the programs evaluate to true:
- for all i and clock $x \in X_i$ and integer bounded interval I, an atomic test $\mathcal{A}_i.x \in I$ (resp. $\mathcal{A}_i.x^\bullet \in I$) evaluates to true if $C(\mathcal{A}_i.x) \in I$ (resp. $C'(\mathcal{A}_i.x) \in I$),
- for all i, Boolean variables $v \in V_i$ and $c \in \{0, 1\}$, an atomic test $\mathcal{A}_i.v = c$ (resp. $\mathcal{A}_i.v^\bullet = c$) evaluates to true if $C(\mathcal{A}_i.v) = c$ (resp. $C'(\mathcal{A}_i.v) = c$),
- for all i, an atomic test $\mathcal{A}_i.\mathsf{st} = \ell$ (resp. $\mathcal{A}_i.\mathsf{st}^\bullet = \ell$) evaluates to true if $C(\mathcal{A}_i.\mathsf{st}) = \ell$ (resp. $C'(\mathcal{A}_i.\mathsf{st}) = \ell$).

Example 3. We consider the specification given by the sentence $\Phi = \mathsf{G}_{\leq 100}\,(r \longrightarrow (\mathsf{YP}_{<2}\, q \wedge p\,\mathsf{S}_{\geq 5}\, q))$. Assume that model $\mathcal{M}$ owns the Boolean variables $\mathsf{Prop} = \{p, q, r\}$, also called atomic propositions. Sentence Φ says that during the first 100 units of time, whenever an event satisfies r (i.e., $\mathcal{M}$ sets r to true, or r was true and is not updated by $\mathcal{M}$) then some event less than 2 time units in the strict past satisfies q (written $\mathsf{YP}_{<2}\, q$), and some other event at least 5 time units in the past satisfies q and since then all events satisfy p (written $p\,\mathsf{S}_{\geq 5}\, q$).

Figure 2 is a network of timed automata which implements the specification Φ. Component $\mathcal{A}_1$ records with clock x the time elapsed since the latest q event occurred. Clock x is initialized to $+\infty$ and remains so until the first q event is seen. Then it is reset to 0 whenever a q event occurs. Component $\mathcal{A}_2$ is in location ℓ_1 iff p since q holds (there is a q event in the past such that since then all events satisfy p). When $\mathcal{A}_2$ is in location ℓ_1, clock y records the time elapsed since the earliest *witness* of $p\,\mathsf{S}\, q$, i.e., the earliest q event such that since then all events satisfy p. Finally, $\mathcal{A}_3$ is in location ℓ_2 if the sequence of events seen so far violates Φ: within the first 100 time units, there is an r event such that the closest q event is at least 2 time units in the strict past $(\mathcal{A}_1.x \geq 2)$ or $p\,\mathsf{S}\, q$ does not hold $(\mathcal{A}_2.\mathsf{st}^\bullet = \ell_0)$ or the earliest witness of $p\,\mathsf{S}\, q$ is less than 5 time units in the past. Component $\mathcal{A}_3$ is in location ℓ_1 if Φ is definitely satisfied, more than 100 time units has elapsed without violating the property. Finally, $\mathcal{A}_3$ stays in location ℓ_0 if the sequence of events seen so far satisfies Φ and at most 100 time units has elapsed. $\square$

The model checking problem. Given a model $\mathcal{M}$ owning a set Prop of atomic propositions, and a specification Φ on Prop, do all behaviours of $\mathcal{M}$ satisfy Φ. Behaviours of a model are formalized as *timed words* over sets of atomic propositions. The alphabet Σ is 2^{Prop}, the set of subsets of Prop. A timed word over Σ, denoted by $w \in (\Sigma \times \mathbb{R})^\infty$, is an *infinite* sequence of pairs of letter and timestamp of the form $(a_0, \tau_0)(a_1, \tau_1)(a_2, \tau_2) \ldots$, where each a_i is a (possibly empty) subset of Prop and τ_i is the timestamp of the i-th letter; timestamps are assumed to be non-decreasing, i.e., $0 \leq \tau_0 \leq \tau_1 \leq \tau_2 \cdots$. It is *non-Zeno* if the sequence $\tau_0, \tau_1, \ldots$ is diverging. A run ρ of the model $\mathcal{M}$ is an infinite alternating sequence of delay and discrete transitions, starting from an initial configuration: $\rho := C_0 \xrightarrow{\delta_0} C_0' \xrightarrow{\bar{t}_0} C_1 \xrightarrow{\delta_1} C_1' \xrightarrow{\bar{t}_1} C_2 \cdots$ where C_0 is an initial configuration, each $\delta_i \geq 0$ is a time delay, and each $\bar{t}_i$ is a tuple of transitions (one from each component of the model), such that each step respects the semantics of time elapse and discrete transitions. The timed word $w_\rho = (a_0, \tau_0)(a_1, \tau_1) \cdots$ associated to the above run ρ is given as follows: for all $i \geq 0$ (1) $\tau_i = \delta_0 + \delta_1 + \cdots + \delta_i$ (the timestamp of occurrence of $\bar{t}_i$) and (2) a_i is the set of atomic propositions p such that $C_{i+1}(p) = 1$ (the propositions that are true *after* executing $\bar{t}_i$). The *model checking problem* asks whether all (infinite, non-Zeno) behaviours generated by all possible runs of the model $\mathcal{M}$ satisfy a given specification Φ, written as $\mathcal{M} \models \Phi$. To solve the model checking problem, we construct from the specification Φ a network of timed automata $\mathcal{A} = (\mathcal{A}_1, \ldots, \mathcal{A}_n)$, and check if some (bad) cycle can be iterated infinitely often in the *closed* network $(\mathcal{M}, \mathcal{A})$. For instance, to check whether a given model $\mathcal{M}$ satisfies the specification Φ from Example 3, we consider the *closed* network $\mathcal{N} = (\mathcal{M}, \mathcal{A}_1, \mathcal{A}_2, \mathcal{A}_3)$ where the automata $\mathcal{A}_1, \mathcal{A}_2, \mathcal{A}_3$ are given in Figure 2. Then, $\mathcal{M} \not\models \Phi$ iff a configuration C of $\mathcal{N}$ where $\mathcal{A}_3$ is in location ℓ_2 is visited infinitely often.

3   The detMITL$^{+\mathsf{p}}$ fragment

We present a fragment of MTL for which we can construct a network $(\mathcal{A}_1, \ldots, \mathcal{A}_n)$ such that each $\mathcal{A}_i$ is deterministic. For the formula in Example 3, the automata $\mathcal{A}_1, \mathcal{A}_2$ and $\mathcal{A}_3$ shown in Figure 2 are deterministic. The set of MTL formulae over the atomic propositions Prop is defined as

$$\varphi := p \mid \varphi \wedge \varphi \mid \neg\varphi \mid \mathsf{Y}_I\,\varphi \mid \mathsf{X}_I\,\varphi \mid \varphi\,\mathsf{U}_I\,\varphi \mid \varphi\,\mathsf{S}_I\,\varphi$$

where $p \in \mathsf{Prop}$, and I is an interval with end-points from $\overline{\mathbb{N}} = \mathbb{N} \cup \{\infty\}$. Note that, our definition of MTL is with both past and future modalities. The *pointwise semantics* of MTL formulae is defined inductively as follows. A timed word $w = (a_0, \tau_0)(a_1, \tau_1)(a_2, \tau_2) \cdots$ is said to satisfy the MTL formula φ at position $i \geq 0$, denoted as $(w, i) \models \varphi$ if (omitting the classical Boolean connectives)

- $(w, i) \models p$ if $p \in a_i$
- $(w, i) \models \mathsf{Y}_I\,\varphi$ if $i > 0$, $(w, i - 1) \models \varphi$ and $\tau_i - \tau_{i-1} \in I$.
- $(w, i) \models \mathsf{X}_I\,\varphi$ if $(w, i + 1) \models \varphi$ and $\tau_{i+1} - \tau_i \in I$.
- $(w, i) \models \varphi_1\,\mathsf{U}_I\,\varphi_2$ if there exists $j \geq i$ s.t. $(w, j) \models \varphi_2$, $\tau_j - \tau_i \in I$ and $(w, k) \models \varphi_1$ for all $i \leq k < j$.
- $(w, i) \models \varphi_1\,\mathsf{S}_I\,\varphi_2$ if there exists $0 \leq j \leq i$ s.t. $(w, j) \models \varphi_2$, $\tau_i - \tau_j \in I$ and $(w, k) \models \varphi_1$ for all $j < k \leq i$.

A word w *initially* satisfies φ, written as $w \models \varphi$ if $(w, 0) \models \varphi$. Finally, a model $\mathcal{M}$ satisfies MTL formula φ, denoted as $\mathcal{M} \models \varphi$ if $w_\rho \models \varphi$ for every run ρ of $\mathcal{M}$. We rewrite the derived operators $\mathsf{G}, \mathsf{F}, \mathsf{P}, \mathsf{H}$ in terms of U or S, in the standard manner: $\mathsf{F}_I\,\varphi = \mathsf{true}\,\mathsf{U}_I\,\varphi$, $\mathsf{G}_I\,\varphi = \neg\mathsf{F}_I\,\neg\varphi$, $\mathsf{P}_I\,\varphi = \mathsf{true}\,\mathsf{S}_I\,\varphi$ and $\mathsf{H}_I\,\varphi = \neg\mathsf{P}_I\,\neg\varphi$.

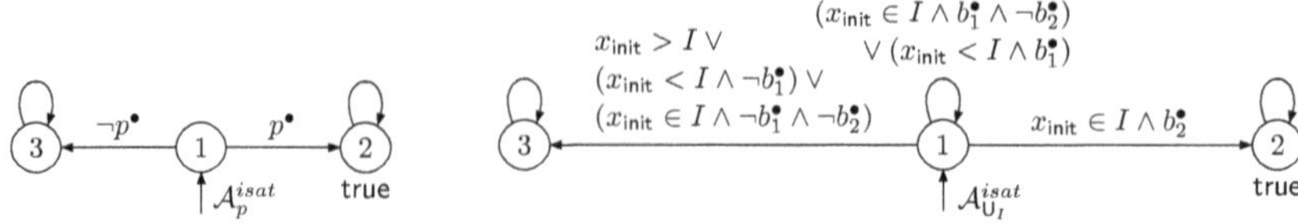

Fig. 3. Left: Automaton $\mathcal{A}_p^{isat}$.   Right: Automaton $\mathcal{A}_{\mathsf{U}_I}^{isat}$ for the initial satisfiability for $b_1 \, \mathsf{U}_I \, b_2$ (with $I \neq \emptyset$). The Boolean variables b_1, b_2 are not owned by $\mathcal{A}_{\mathsf{U}_I}^{isat}$ and stand for the left and right arguments of U_I. The automaton is deterministic and complete. We write $x_{\mathsf{init}} < I$ (resp. $x_{\mathsf{init}} > I$) to state that x_{init} is smaller (resp. larger) than all values in I. For instance, if $I = [b, c)$ with $b < c$ then $x_{\mathsf{init}} < I$ means $x_{\mathsf{init}} < b$ and $x_{\mathsf{init}} > I$ means $x_{\mathsf{init}} \geq c$. If a run reaches state 2 (resp. 3) then we know for sure that $b_1 \, \mathsf{U}_I \, b_2$ was initially true (resp. false). State 1 means we still do not know whether $b_1 \, \mathsf{U}_I \, b_2$ was initially true. If the run stays forever in state 1, $b_1 \, \mathsf{U}_I \, b_2$ was initially false.

Definition 4 (detMITL$^{+\mathsf{P}}$). *The fragment* detMITL$^{+\mathsf{P}}$ *consists of formulae where the outermost temporal operators are future operators* X_I, U_I *and may use arbitrary intervals* I, *while all inner temporal operators are restricted to past operators. Inner* Since *operators must use non-punctual intervals (either* $[0,0]$ *or non-singleton intervals). Formally, formulae are built as follows:*

$$(\textit{Sentences}) \quad \Phi := p \mid \Phi \wedge \Phi \mid \neg \Phi \mid \mathsf{X}_I \, \varphi \mid \varphi \, \mathsf{U}_I \, \varphi$$
$$(\textit{Point-formulae}) \quad \varphi := p \mid \varphi \wedge \varphi \mid \neg \varphi \mid \mathsf{Y}_I \, \varphi \mid \varphi \, \mathsf{S}_{I'} \, \varphi$$

where I, I' *are intervals, and* I' *is either* $[0,0]$ *or a non-singleton interval.*

Sentences are evaluated at the first position $(w, 0)$ of a word w, whereas point-formulae can be checked anywhere in the word. The formula in Example 3 is a sentence in the detMITL$^{+\mathsf{P}}$ fragment: the derived G_I operator induces an outer U_I formula, and all the inner operators are past. The formula $\mathsf{YP}_{<2} \, q$ can be rewritten as $\mathsf{P}_{(0,2)} \, q \vee \mathsf{Y}_{[0,0]} \, \mathsf{P}_{[0,0]} \, q$.

4   From detMITL$^{+\mathsf{P}}$ to Network of Deterministic TA

The construction in [3] does not consider the past operators. For the future U_I operator, the construction produces a non-deterministic automaton which at every point in the word predicts whether the Until formula holds, and verifies it later. However, in the detMITL$^{+\mathsf{P}}$ fragment the future formulae appear only at the top level. Our goal in this section is to fill the gap about past formulae, and present customised automata for the future operators that appear at the top level. For a detMITL$^{+\mathsf{P}}$ sentence Φ we build a deterministic network $\mathcal{N}_\Phi$ and specify a set Bad$_\Phi$ of bad configurations. Our objective is to achieve a construction that entails the following theorem for detMITL$^{+\mathsf{P}}$ sentences.

Theorem 5. *Let* Φ *be a* detMITL$^{+\mathsf{P}}$ *sentence and* $\mathcal{M}$ *a timed model. Then:* $\mathcal{M} \not\models \Phi$ *iff there exists an infinite run of the closed network* $(\mathcal{M}, \mathcal{N}_\Phi)$ *which eventually remains in bad configurations.*

Initial satisfiability. For a sentence Φ, we start with three deterministic automata $\mathcal{A}_p^{isat}$, $\mathcal{A}_{\mathsf{X}_I}^{isat}$, $\mathcal{A}_{\mathsf{U}_I}^{isat}$, corresponding respectively to every atomic proposition $p \in$ Prop that is not under the scope of a temporal operator, and every subformula X_I and U_I appearing in the sentence. They are called *initial satisfiability automata*, and superscripted with an *isat*. Apart from these, we have $\mathcal{A}_{\mathsf{init}}$ which resets a clock x_{init} at the first action. All the *isat* automata make use of this single clock x_{init} in their tests, and do not own any other clocks. Figure 3 depicts the automaton $\mathcal{A}_p^{isat}$ which takes as input the atomic proposition p, and has the property that $w \models p$ iff for all configurations obtained after taking the first transition, $\mathcal{A}_p^{isat}$ is in state 2. Figure 4 describes $\mathcal{A}_{\mathsf{init}}$ and $\mathcal{A}_{\mathsf{X}_I}^{isat}$, where $\mathcal{A}_{\mathsf{X}_I}^{isat}$ takes as input the Boolean variable b_1 corresponding to the argument of X_I. The invariant satisfied by $\mathcal{A}_{\mathsf{X}_I}^{isat}$ is explained in the caption of Figure 4 - essentially, for every word w, $(\mathcal{A}_{\mathsf{init}}, \mathcal{A}_{\mathsf{X}_I}^{isat})$ has a unique run, and $w \models \mathsf{X}_I b_1$ iff for all configurations obtained after taking the second transition, $\mathcal{A}_{\mathsf{X}_I}^{isat}$ is in state 3. Finally, Figure 3 gives the deterministic automaton for the initial satisfiability of U_I, where $\mathcal{A}_{\mathsf{U}_I}^{isat}$ takes two Boolean variables b_1, b_2 as inputs corresponding to the first and second arguments of U_I. It can be shown that $w \models b_1 \, \mathsf{U}_I \, b_2$ iff there exists an $i \geq 1$ s.t. for all configurations obtained after taking the first i transitions, $\mathcal{A}_{\mathsf{U}_I}^{isat}$ is in state 2.

Past operators. For every temporal point-formula φ in a subformula of Φ, we build a deterministic automaton $\mathcal{A}_\varphi$. For these point-formula automata we also allow for sharing of clocks. The Y automaton, depicted in Figure 5 (left), has two states ℓ_0 and ℓ_1. The states remember if the argument b_1 of Y was true or not at the previous letter: all transitions reading a b_1 enter ℓ_1, and the ones that read $\neg b_1$ go to ℓ_0. To incorporate the timing constraint, we use a single state automaton $\mathcal{A}_{\mathsf{last}}$, depicted in Figure 5 (right), which resets a clock x_{last} in every step. Now, for an arbitrary interval constraint I, the current position satisfies $\mathsf{Y}_I b_1$ if the previous letter had a b_1 and the value of clock x_{last} (which was reset at the previous position) when the current position is read falls in the interval I. The construction for the Since operator S_I is provided in [1].

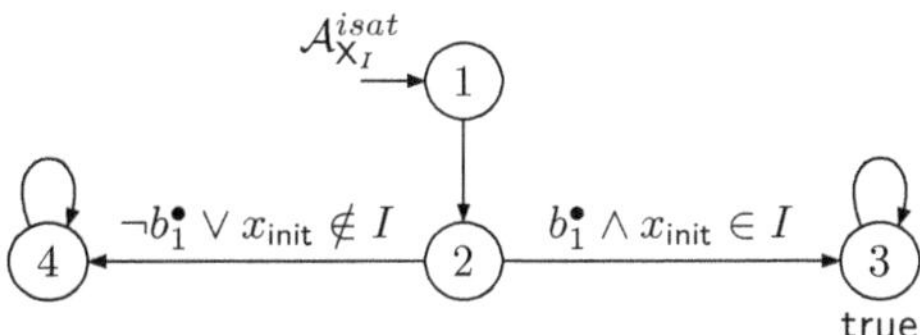

Fig. 4. Left: Clock x_{init} is reset on the first event and measures time elapsed for all the initial satisfiability automata ($\mathcal{A}_{\mathsf{X}_I}^{isat}$ and $\mathcal{A}_{\mathsf{U}_I}^{isat}$).

Right: Automaton $\mathcal{A}_{\mathsf{X}_I}^{isat}$ for initial satisfiability for $\mathsf{X}_I b_1$. The Boolean variable b_1 is not owned by $\mathcal{A}_{\mathsf{X}_I}^{isat}$ and stands for the argument of X_I. In $\mathcal{A}_{\mathsf{X}_I}^{isat}$, we simply write x_{init} instead of $\mathcal{A}_{\mathsf{init}}.x_{\mathsf{init}}$. The automaton is deterministic and complete. If a run reaches state 3 (resp. 4) then $\mathsf{X}_I b_1$ was initially true (resp. false).

Fig. 5. Left: Automaton $\mathcal{A}_{\mathsf{Y}}$ for the untimed Yesterday operator $\mathsf{Y}\, b_1$. The Boolean variable b_1 is not owned by $\mathcal{A}_{\mathsf{Y}}$ and stands for the argument of Y.   Right: Sharer automaton $\mathcal{A}_{\mathsf{last}}$ with clock x_{last} used by all Yesterday operators.

Bad configurations. The collection of all the *isat* automata, $\mathcal{A}_{\mathsf{init}}$ and the temporal point-formula automata for Φ form the network $\mathcal{N}_\Phi$, which along with the model $\mathcal{M}$ will become a closed network. Now, states of each of the *isat* automata will be marked either true or false. A configuration C of $\mathcal{N}_\Phi$ is bad if Φ evaluates to false when we replace every outermost p, and operators X_I, U_I of Φ by the truth value of the state the corresponding *isat* automata are in. For example if $\Phi = p \wedge \mathsf{X}_I\, q$, a configuration C_1 where $\mathcal{A}_p^{isat} = $ true and $\mathcal{A}_{\mathsf{X}_I q}^{isat} = $ true is *not bad*, whereas C_2 with $\mathcal{A}_p^{isat} = $ false will be bad. The set of bad configurations of Φ will be called Bad_Φ. This notion naturally extends to the product $(\mathcal{M}, \mathcal{N}_\Phi)$: a configuration of the product is bad if its projection to $\mathcal{N}_\Phi$ evaluates to false.

4.1   A full example

We explain the construction of a network $\mathcal{N}_\Phi$ associated with a sentence Φ on an example. We use the template automata defined in the previous sections. We instantiate the formal arguments b_1, b_2 of these template automata with actual test formulae. For instance, $\mathcal{A}_{\mathsf{Y}}[b_1^\bullet/(\neg p^\bullet \wedge q^\bullet)]$ denotes a copy of the automaton $\mathcal{A}_{\mathsf{Y}}$ from Figure 5 (left) in which we substitute the test $\neg p^\bullet \wedge q^\bullet$ for the formal argument $b_1^\bullet$. We consider the sentence $\Phi = (\Phi_1 \wedge \Phi_2) \to \Phi_3$ where $\Phi_1 = r$ and

$$\Phi_2 = \mathsf{F}_{I_6}(p \wedge \varphi_4) = \mathsf{true}\ \mathsf{U}_{I_6}\ (p \wedge \varphi_4) \qquad \Phi_3 = \mathsf{F}_{I_7}(\varphi_3 \wedge \varphi_5) = \mathsf{true}\ \mathsf{U}_{I_7}\ (\varphi_3 \wedge \varphi_5)$$

$$\varphi_4 = (p \vee q)\, \mathsf{S}_{I_4}\, \varphi_3 \qquad\qquad\qquad \varphi_5 = (\varphi_1 \vee \varphi_2)\, \mathsf{S}_{I_5}\, (q \vee \varphi_3)$$

$$\varphi_1 = \mathsf{Y}_{I_1}(\neg p \wedge q) \qquad \varphi_2 = \mathsf{Y}_{I_2}(\neg p \wedge q) \qquad \varphi_3 = \mathsf{Y}_{I_3}\, r$$

with $I_4 = [0, c_4)$ an upper bound and $I_5 = [c_5, +\infty)$ a lower bound constraint.

Recall that the network $\mathcal{N}_\Phi$ does not contain automata for the Boolean connectives. We illustrate below how we use the power of tests in automata, which allow arbitrary Boolean combinations of atomic tests. The temporal subformulae (atomic proposition or a formula with outermost connective being temporal) of the sentence Φ are the atomic propositions p, q, r, the point formulae $\varphi_1, \dots, \varphi_5$ and the sentences Φ_2, Φ_3. Also, $\mathcal{N}_\Phi$ does not need automata for the atomic propositions since they are owned by the model $\mathcal{M}$. For each temporal subformula, we add to the network the automata required to determine the truth value of the subformula, as described earlier. For instance, the temporal subformula φ_4 requires a copy of the automata for Since ($\mathcal{A}_{\mathsf{S}}$ and $\mathcal{A}_{\mathsf{S}}^{\mathsf{last}}$ from Figure 6 in [1]), with suitable substitutions of the formal arguments.

Thus, for the sentence $\Phi = (\Phi_1 \wedge \Phi_2) \to \Phi_3$, we construct the network

$$\mathcal{N}_\Phi = (\mathcal{B}_0, \mathcal{B}_1, \mathcal{B}_2, \mathcal{B}_3, \mathcal{B}_4, \mathcal{B}_5, \mathcal{B}_6, \mathcal{B}_7, \mathcal{A}_1, \mathcal{A}_2, \mathcal{A}_3) \quad \text{where}$$

$$\mathcal{B}_1 := \mathcal{A}_{\mathsf{last}} \qquad\qquad \mathcal{B}_2 := \mathcal{A}_{\mathsf{Y}}[b_1^\bullet/(\neg p^\bullet \wedge q^\bullet)]$$

$$\mathsf{out}_1 = (\mathcal{B}_2.\mathsf{st} = \ell_1 \wedge \mathcal{B}_1.x_{\mathsf{last}} \in I_1)\mathsf{out}_2 = (\mathcal{B}_2.\mathsf{st} = \ell_1 \wedge \mathcal{B}_1.x_{\mathsf{last}} \in I_2)$$

$$\mathcal{B}_3 := \mathcal{A}_{\mathsf{Y}}[b_1^\bullet/r^\bullet] \qquad\qquad \mathsf{out}_3 = (\mathcal{B}_3.\mathsf{st} = \ell_1 \wedge \mathcal{B}_1.x_{\mathsf{last}} \in I_3)$$

$$\mathcal{B}_4 := \mathcal{A}_{\mathsf{S}}[b_1^\bullet/(p^\bullet \vee q^\bullet), b_2^\bullet/\mathsf{out}_3] \qquad\qquad \mathcal{B}_5 := \mathcal{A}_{\mathsf{S}}^{\mathsf{last}}[b_2^\bullet/\mathsf{out}_3]$$

$$\mathcal{B}_6 := \mathcal{A}_{\mathsf{S}}[b_1^\bullet/(\mathsf{out}_1 \vee \mathsf{out}_2), b_2^\bullet/(q^\bullet \vee \mathsf{out}_3)]$$

$$\mathcal{B}_7 := \mathcal{A}_{\mathsf{S}}^{\mathsf{first}}[b_1^\bullet/(\mathsf{out}_1 \vee \mathsf{out}_2), b_2^\bullet/(q^\bullet \vee \mathsf{out}_3)]$$

$$\mathsf{out}_4 = (\mathcal{B}_4.\mathsf{st}^\bullet = \ell_1 \wedge \mathcal{B}_5.x^\bullet \in I_4) \qquad\qquad \mathsf{out}_5 = (\mathcal{B}_6.\mathsf{st}^\bullet = \ell_1 \wedge \mathcal{B}_7.y^\bullet \in I_5)$$

$$\mathcal{B}_0 := \mathcal{A}_{\mathsf{init}} \qquad\qquad \mathcal{A}_1 := \mathcal{A}_r^{isat}$$

$$\mathcal{A}_2 := \mathcal{A}_{\mathsf{U}_{I_6}}^{isat}[b_1^\bullet/\mathsf{true}, b_2^\bullet/(p^\bullet \wedge \mathsf{out}_4)] \qquad\qquad \mathcal{A}_3 := \mathcal{A}_{\mathsf{U}_{I_7}}^{isat}[b_1^\bullet/\mathsf{true}, b_2^\bullet/(\mathsf{out}_3 \wedge \mathsf{out}_5)]$$

In the automata above, we use ghost variables $(\mathsf{out}_i)_{1 \leq i \leq 5}$ to make the definitions easier to read. When we expand these definitions, we get for instance

$$\mathcal{B}_4 = \mathcal{A}_{\mathsf{S}}[b_1^\bullet/(p^\bullet \vee q^\bullet), b_2^\bullet/(\mathcal{B}_3.\mathsf{st} = \ell_1 \wedge \mathcal{B}_1.x_{\mathsf{last}} \in I_3)]$$

$$\mathcal{A}_2 := \mathcal{A}_{\mathsf{U}_{I_6}}^{isat}[b_1^\bullet/\mathsf{true}, b_2^\bullet/(p^\bullet \wedge (\mathcal{B}_4.\mathsf{st}^\bullet = \ell_1 \wedge \mathcal{B}_5.x^\bullet \in I_4))]$$

Notice that the automaton $\mathcal{B}_2$ is shared: it is used in $\mathsf{out}_1, \mathsf{out}_2$. Similarly, $\mathcal{B}_0$ and $\mathcal{B}_1$ are shared. It remains to define the set Bad_Φ of *bad* configurations for the sentence Φ. A configuration C is bad if Φ evaluates to false at C. Hence, Bad_Φ is the set of configurations C which satisfy $\mathcal{A}_1.\mathsf{st} = 2 \wedge \mathcal{A}_2.\mathsf{st} = 2 \wedge \neg(\mathcal{A}_3.\mathsf{st} = 2)$ (i.e., $\Phi_1 \wedge \Phi_2 \wedge \neg\Phi_3$).

5   Integrating the Future

As our final objective, we want to include future modalities X_I and $\mathsf{U}_{I'}$ in the inner operators (point-formulae) of $\mathsf{detMITL}^{+\mathsf{p}}$ from Definition 4. This results in a restriction of MTL in which, except in the topmost level, the intervals in Since and Until are restricted to be $[0, 0]$ or non-singleton, and we denote this as $\mathsf{MITL}^{+\mathsf{p}}$. We can no longer guarantee a deterministic network for this class. Moreover, for this class, we make use of the full power of Generalized Timed Automata. In particular, we use *future clocks* in our constructions. Briefly: future clocks can be *released* (in other words, re-initialized)

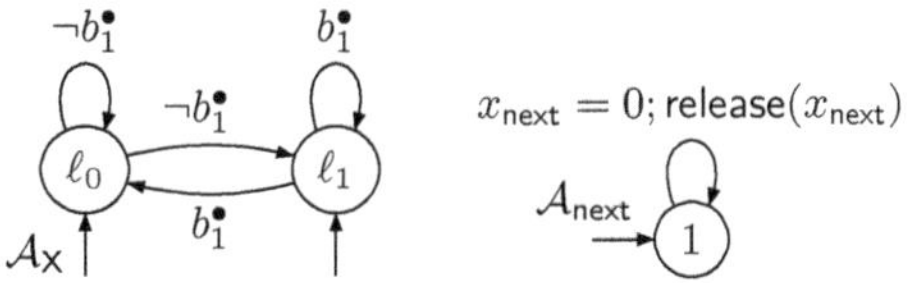

Fig. 6. Left: Automaton $\mathcal{A}_{\mathsf{X}}$ for the untimed Next operator $\mathsf{X}\, b_1$. The Boolean variable b_1 is not owned by $\mathcal{A}_{\mathsf{X}}$ and stands for the argument of X.   Right: Automaton $\mathcal{A}_{\mathsf{next}}$ with clock x_{next} used (shared) by all Next operators. Recall that when x_{next} is released, it is non-deterministically assigned a non-positive value.

to a value ≤ 0 and they increase along with time until they hit 0. When a future clock hits 0 time cannot progress anymore, unless there is a transition that re-initializes it to a different value. For the inner X_I and U_I formulae, we use the construction from [3], but thanks to our new formulation as a network of automata, we can additionally allow for sharing of clocks.

We leave the technical details and the formal proof to the full version at [1], which extends ideas from [3]. We highlight below one novelty. Our *networks of GTA with shared variables* for each future modality allow sharing of clocks and automata (compared e.g., to using combined transducers as done in [3]). For instance, for any occurrence of the Next operator X_I, we have an automaton depicted in Figure 6 (left), which has two states ℓ_0 and ℓ_1 and captures the *untimed semantics* of Next. Then, we use a single state automaton $\mathcal{A}_{\mathsf{next}}$, depicted in Figure 6 (right), which releases clock x_{next} whenever it reaches 0. Thus, it always predicts the time to the next event and is shared across all occurrences of Next in the entire network, to check all the timing constraints. For an Until formula $b_1 \, U_I \, b_2$, by using different automata we can share not only clocks but even the prediction of the earliest witness without insisting to share the latest witness at a point. This results in increased sharing and thus decreased non-deterministic branching. Our experimental results in Section 6 validate these theoretical insights.

Remark 6. Note that Theorem 5, and its counterpart for the general case containing future operators in point formulae, can be extended to the case of finite words, where we want to reach a bad configuration instead of eventually remaining in bad configurations.

6   Implementation and Experimental evaluation

In this section, we present an experimental evaluation of our prototype implementation tool TEMPORA for satisfiability and model checking for $\mathsf{MITL}^{+\mathsf{p}}$ formulae. The tool contains two modules: (i) **MITL2GTA** that implements our optimized translation from $\mathsf{detMITL}^{+\mathsf{p}}$ to networks of deterministic timed automata (from Section 4) and the optimized translation from $\mathsf{MITL}^{+\mathsf{p}}$ to networks of GTA (from Section 5) and (ii) **LiveRGTA** that implements reachability and liveness algorithms for GTA. For reachability, we use an enhanced version of the GTA reachability algorithm from [2], built on top of the open source tool Tchecker [25]. For liveness, we implement an adaptation of the decision procedure for liveness for safe GTA from [3, Theorem 11], which relies on a finiteness test based on simulations [4], to the well-studied framework of Couvreur's Strongly Connected Component (SCC) algorithm [20]. More details of our liveness procedure, along with the pseudocode, are provided in [1]. Combining these modules, we obtain the new pipeline **Tempora** (MITL2GTA + LiveRGTA). Checking satisfiability over finite timed words reduces to checking reachability in the corresponding GTA, while over infinite timed words, it reduces to checking liveness (Büchi acceptance). Our tool, along with the benchmarks used in this paper, is available

Formula	Tempora	
	Stored nodes	Time in ms.
$F_{[0,20]}(Y_{[2,3]}\, p_1 \vee Y_{[4,5]}\, p_2) \vee Y_{[6,7]}\, p_3)$	287	1.5
$G_{[0,20]}(Y_{[2,3]}\, p_1 \vee Y_{[4,5]}\, p_2) \vee Y_{[6,7]}\, p_3)$	262	3.1
$F(p\, S_{[1,2]}\, (p\, S_{[1,2]}\, (p\, S_{[1,2]}\, q)))$	1,303	29.9
$F(p\, S_{[1,\infty)}\, (p\, S_{[1,\infty)}\, (p\, S_{[1,\infty)}\, q)))$	66	0.5
$F(p\, S_{[1,2]}\, q \wedge p\, S_{[2,3]}\, q \wedge p\, S_{[3,4]}\, q \wedge p\, S_{[4,5]}\, q)$	1,571	50.9
$F(p\, S_{[1,\infty)}\, q \wedge p\, S_{[2,\infty)}\, q \wedge p\, S_{[3,\infty)}\, q \wedge p\, S_{[4,\infty)}\, q)$	68	0.8
$F(p\, S_{[1,2]}\, q \wedge p\, S_{[2,3]}\, q \wedge p\, S_{[3,4]}\, q \wedge p\, S_{[4,5]}\, q \wedge p\, S_{[5,6]}\, q)$	27,737	1,762.1
$F(p\, S_{[1,2]}\, q \wedge p\, S_{[2,3]}\, q \wedge p\, S_{[3,4]}\, q \wedge p\, S_{[4,5]}\, q \wedge p\, S_{[5,6]}\, q \wedge p\, S_{[6,7]}\, q)$	167,077	21,490.5
$G(\neg p_1 \vee (a_1\, S_{[0,2]}\, b_1)) \wedge (\neg p_2 \vee (a_2\, S_{[0,2]}\, b_2)) \wedge (\neg p_3 \vee (a_3\, S_{[0,2]}\, b_3)) \wedge (\neg p_4 \vee (a_4\, S_{[0,2]}\, b_4)) \wedge G(p_1 \vee p_2 \vee p_3 \vee p_4)$	186	1.67

Table 1. Results of Tempora for satisfiability of detMITL^{+p} formulae over finite timed words. Timeout is set to 300s.

and can be downloaded from `https://github.com/EQuaVe/TEMPORA`. Further details of our implementation, including the various engineering optimisations, are discussed in [1].

We organize our evaluation into three parts as follows:

- First, we evaluate Tempora for detMITL^{+p} formulae including both standalone past modalities and combinations with future modalities.
- Next, we compare Tempora against two existing approaches in the pointwise semantics, namely: MightyL [15], a state-of-the-art tool that translates MITL to networks of timed automata. The resulting automata are analyzed using UPPAAL [30] (for finite words) and OPAAL [28] (for infinite words); *Baseline GTA Translation*, an implementation of the translation in [3].
- Finally, to demonstrate the full scope of our implementation, we use Tempora for model-checking two classical examples, namely Fischer and Dining Philosophers with MITL^{+p} formulae capturing some standard properties.

Benchmarks. We conduct our experiments on a suite of 72 benchmarks, which we have grouped into three groups: (1) 22 benchmarks designed to demonstrate past operators (alongside future modalities), (2) 33 benchmarks from MightyL [15] that are themselves based on examples from [23,37], and (3) 17 benchmarks from Acacia synthesis tool's benchmark suite [11]. The complete list of all 72 benchmark formulae are given in Tables A and B of the full version [1], where we also describe each group in detail. All experiments were run on an Ubuntu 18.04 machine with an Intel i7 3.40GHz processor and 32 GB RAM. We now discuss our experimental results.

Satisfiability for the past fragment of detMITL^{+p}. The first set of experiments, presented in Table 1, evaluates the performance of our tool Tempora on detMITL^{+p}. The last but two formulae are specifically designed to stress-test the handling of multiple nested past operators. Tempora processes each of them efficiently, storing only a small number of nodes and completing each run in under 30 seconds. The final formula in this set is more complex, combining several past operators with a conjunction of future modalities. Here too, Tempora performs efficiently, requiring only 186 nodes and less than

2 ms to check satisfiability. Further, if we consider, for instance, the formula $F(p\,U_{[1,2]}\,q \wedge p\,U_{[2,3]}\,q \wedge p\,U_{[3,4]}\,q \wedge p\,U_{[4,5]}\,q)$, obtained by replacing the past operator S with the future operator U in the 5th entry TEMPORA solves this by generating 28,030 nodes in 784 ms. In the nested formula $F(p\,U_{[1,2]}\,(p\,U_{[1,2]}\,(p\,U_{[1,2]}\,q)))$ which results in 299,130 nodes and takes 9 seconds, compared to the past version $F(p\,S_{[1,2]}\,(p\,S_{[1,2]}\,(p\,S_{[1,2]}\,q)))$ which generates only 1,303 nodes in 29.9 milliseconds. *These results demonstrate effectiveness of our deterministic translation, avoiding the exponential blowup typically associated with non-deterministic approaches and enables scalable analysis even for complicated formulae.*

Satisfiability for full MITL^{+p} and comparisons. For the second set of experiments, we evaluate the performance of TEMPORA on the satisfiability problem for MITL^{+p} formulae over both finite and infinite timed words. We compare our tool against MIGHTYL and the baseline translation proposed in [3]. For finite timed words, we compare against MIGHTYL using UPPAAL's reachability analysis; for infinite we use MIGHTYL with OPAAL's liveness checking algorithm. Figure 7(left) compares the performance of our tool and the MIGHTYL pipeline on all 72 benchmarks for finite timed words, and Figure 7(right) presents the same comparison for infinite words. We report the time after the translation (to TA in case of MIGHTYL and GTA for TEMPORA), that is, the time for zone graph exploration. This is because, the time for the translation itself is rather small in most cases (of the order of 3-4ms). For OPAAL, we report the sum of time taken by OPAAL to generate C++ code, the **g++** compiler to compile

Formula	Baseline		MIGHTYL+ OPAAL		TEMPORA	
	Stored nodes	Time in ms.	Stored nodes	Time in ms.	Stored nodes	Time in ms.
$F(5, [2, \infty))$	-	TO	3069	$373 + 820 + 85$	200	2.38
$F(5, [0, 2])$	952	5.99	2693	$214 + 702 + 82$	68	0.49
$U(5, [2, \infty))$	567,192	5,404	9,383	$382 + 960 + 114$	4,075	32.70
$U(5, [1, 2])$	-	TO	-	TO	465,185	8,750
$\mu(2)$	953,492	24,977	964	$68,462 + 20,584 + 103$	158	0.90
$\mu(3)$	-	TO	-	TO	315	3.34
$\theta(3)$	-	TO	42,804	$836 + 1,057 + 225$	330,044	2977
$G(5, [0, 2])$	4,793	34.6	5,913	$257 + 760 + 101$	224	1.45
$G(5, [1, 2])$	-	TO	-	TO	225	2.45
$R(5, [2, \infty))$	29,685	278.3	1,059	$231 + 726 + 77$	3,119	27.75
$R(5, [1, 2])$	-	TO	-	TO	1,093,187	23,474
$p\,U_{[11,12]}\,q$	1,484	53	-	TO	220	1.37
$Req - grant$	-	TO	-	TO	444	4.00
$Spot - ex$	117,319	1,141	7,921	$74,585 + 20,184 + 238$	504	3.50
$\eta(4)$	-	TO	-	NA	249	1.49
$\rho(4)$	-	TO	-	TO	1933	15.93
Acacia$_1$	-	TO	4,943	$258 + 755 + 96$	390	2.54
Acacia$_2$	-	TO	742,427	$426 + 949 + 1,683$	231	1.94
Acacia$_3$	-	TO	7,271,276	$611 + 1,143 + 21,349$	918	7.41
Acacia$_4$	-	TO	-	TO	4,159	55.71

Table 2. Selected set of results of TEMPORA, MIGHTYL and, the baseline implementation of [3] for satisfiability over infinite traces. Timeout is set to 300s. The rows corresponding to formulae belonging to the **detMITL^{+p}** fragment are highlighted in green. The complete table is available in Table 8 in [1].

the generated code and LTSMIN to check liveness. We note that OPAAL is a multi-core tool and uses 8 cores on our machine. On 10 of the benchmarks, OPAAL gave a segmentation fault (which we mark as timeout) and UPPAAL reported an overflow error on the output generated by MIGHTYL for 2 benchmarks. Table 2 presents selected results reporting the number of nodes stored and time taken by each tool to check satisfiability over infinite words, with full results in [1].

As can be seen from Figure 7, for finite timed words, TEMPORA is always faster than MIGHTYL + UPPAAL and for benchmarks where both tools take more than 1s, it is significantly faster, as the plot is in *log-scale*. Further, UPPAAL times out in several cases, while we never do so on the benchmarks tested. For the infinite case, except for 2 formulae we are always faster. The plot is only on the 63 benchmarks on which all three tools work, and therefore, we exclude the formulae containing past operators. Further, out of these 63 benchmarks, OPAAL timed out or seg-faulted on 18 benchmarks whereas we timeout on only 4 benchmarks (of which OPAAL also times out/segfaults on 3). Finally, Table 2 (and the extended tables in [1]) show that TEMPORA is also significantly better than the Baseline (in fact the MIGHTYL pipeline also outperforms Baseline significantly on most benchmarks) on all benchmarks.

In summary, both for finite words and infinite words over the pointwise semantics, TEMPORA significantly outperforms MIGHTYL and the baseline for checking satisfiability, both in terms of time taken and size of stored nodes.

Model checking. Finally, beyond satisfiability, we evaluate our model-checking pipeline on a set of MITL^{+p} formulae using two classical benchmarks: Fischer's mutual exclusion algorithm and the Dining Philosophers problem. The pipeline, implemented in TEMPORA with TChecker for zone graph exploration, is - to

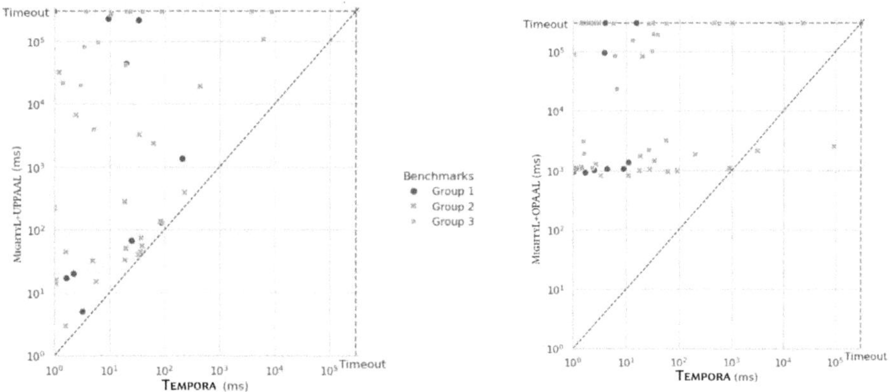

Fig. 7. Log-scale plot MIGHTYL vs TEMPORA comparison for time taken to check satisfiability on finite (left) and infinite (right) timed words, after the translation. Group 1 refers to our benchmarks, while Group 2 are MIGHTYL benchmarks [15] are Group 3 benchmarks derived from Acacia [11]. Timeout set to 300s.

Sl. No.	Models	Formula	TEMPORA	
			Stored nodes	Time (ms)
1	Fischer (3)	$G(\neg req_1 \vee F_{[0,20]}\, wait_1)$	32,817	221.3
2	Fischer (4)	$G(\neg req_1 \vee F_{[0,20]}\, wait_1)$	449,108	5,723
3	Fischer (6)	$G(\neg req_1 \vee F_{[0,5]}\, wait_1)$	362	4.6
4	Fischer (7)	$G(\neg req_1 \vee F_{[0,5]}\, wait_1)$	391	5.3
5	Fischer (3)	$G(\neg req_1 \vee F_{[0,20]}\, cs)$	33,918	209.69
6	Fischer (4)	$G(\neg req_1 \vee F_{[0,20]}\, cs)$	352,774	3,749.6
7	Fischer (5)	$G(\neg((cs_1 \wedge (cs_2 \vee cs_3 \vee cs_4 \vee cs_5)) \vee$ $(cs_2 \wedge (cs_1 \vee cs_3 \vee cs_4 \vee cs_5)) \vee (cs_3 \wedge (cs_1 \vee cs_2 \vee cs_4 \vee cs_5)) \vee$ $(cs_4 \wedge (cs_1 \vee cs_2 \vee cs_3 \vee cs_5)) \vee (cs_5 \wedge (cs_1 \vee cs_2 \vee cs_3 \vee cs_4))))$	527,829	15,514
8	Din-Phil(8, 10, 3, 1)	$F_{[0,20]}(eating_1 \vee eating_2 \vee eating_3 \vee eating_4$ $\vee eating_5 \vee eating_6 \vee eating_7 \vee eating_8)$	371	5.8
9	Din-Phil(2, 10, 3, 1)	$G_{[10,\infty)}(F_{[0,30]}(eating) \wedge F_{[0,30]}(eating_2))$	4,904	31.35

Table 3. Results obtained by running TEMPORA for model checking. The numbers in the parentheses in the models represent parameterization: for Fischer's it is no. of processes and for Dining Philosophers, it is respectively, the no. of philosophers, timeout before releasing fork, time to eat and delay time to release fork.

the best of our knowledge - the first to support complete model checking under pointwise semantics for a model and an $MITL^{+P}$ formula. As no existing tools (UPPAAL, MIGHTYL, OPAAL) offer comparable functionality, we are unable to provide comparisons, but we present our results as a proof of concept in Table 3.

For Fischer's algorithm, we analyze models with 3-7 processes and verify several properties: (i) whether the first process eventually enters the waiting state after making a request, (ii) whether it eventually enters the critical section, and (iii) the classical safety property ensuring that no two processes are simultaneously in the critical section. Our results show that $G(req_1 \rightarrow F_{[0,5]}\, wait_1)$ can be checked to hold in 4.6 ms for 6 processes, and 5.3 ms for 7 processes. The mutual exclusion property is seen to hold for 5 processes in 15.51s. For the Dining Philosophers problem, we analyze models with 2 and 8 philosophers and verify properties such as (i) whether at least one philosopher eventually eats, and (ii) whether both are guaranteed to eat within a specified time window. For the 8-philosopher model, the property $F_{[0,20]}(\vee_{i=1}^{8}\, eating_i)$ is falsified within 0.01 seconds, indicating that not all philosophers can eat simultaneously, and with 2-philosophers, the property (ii) is falsified within 0.03s. *These results demonstrate that our model-checking pipeline efficiently verifies $MITL^{+P}$ properties on such models, highlighting its applicability for timed-systems verification.* Additional results, including ablation studies, are presented in [1].

7   Conclusion

We presented TEMPORA, a model checker for timed systems for $MITL^{+P}$ properties and indicated our challenges and solutions while transforming [3] into an implementation that outperforms the state-of-the-art. Our general theme has been to make the construction "more deterministic" and allow sharing of information between components corresponding to subformulae. As future work, two natural directions would be monitoring of $MITL^{+P}$ properties in the pointwise semantics, and extending our approach to the signal/continuous semantics.

Data-Availability Statement. All data and software required to reproduce the experiments are publicly available. Our implementation, benchmarks, and scripts are available at `https://github.com/EQuaVe/TEMPORA`, with a version of the artifact at `https://figshare.com/articles/software/Tempora/30490967?file=59187428`.

The experimental comparison involves third-party tools that are not redistributed with our artifacts. To reproduce the comparison results with MightyL, we refer to the virtual machine provided by its developers at `https://amubox.univ-amu.fr/s/HiyAc3YzTF6eWQ3`. Additionally, for experiments on finite words (Table A), UPPAAL is required and can be obtained under an academic license from the UPPAAL website. For experiments on infinite words (Table B), OPAAL (within LTSMin) is required and can be downloaded from `https://opaal-modelchecker.com/opaal-ltsmin/`

References

1. Akshay, S., Contractor, P., Gastin, P., Govind, R., Srivathsan, B.: Efficient verification of metric temporal properties with past in pointwise semantics (2025), `https://arxiv.org/abs/2510.14699`
2. Akshay, S., Gastin, P., Govind, R., Joshi, A.R., Srivathsan, B.: A unified model for real-time systems: Symbolic techniques and implementation. In: CAV (1). Lecture Notes in Computer Science, vol. 13964, pp. 266–288. Springer (2023)
3. Akshay, S., Gastin, P., Govind, R., Srivathsan, B.: MITL model checking via generalized timed automata and a new liveness algorithm. In: CONCUR. LIPIcs, vol. 311, pp. 5:1–5:19. Schloss Dagstuhl - Leibniz-Zentrum für Informatik (2024)
4. Akshay, S., Gastin, P., Govind, R., Srivathsan, B.: Simulations for event-clock automata. Log. Methods Comput. Sci. **20**(3) (2024)
5. Alur, R., Dill, D.L.: Automata for modeling real-time systems. In: ICALP. LNCS, vol. 443, pp. 322–335. Springer (1990)
6. Alur, R., Dill, D.L.: A theory of timed automata. Theoretical Computer Science **126**, 183–235 (1994)
7. Alur, R., Feder, T., Henzinger, T.A.: The benefits of relaxing punctuality. J. ACM **43**(1), 116–146 (1996)
8. Alur, R., Henzinger, T.A.: Real-time logics: Complexity and expressiveness. In: LICS. pp. 390–401. IEEE Computer Society (1990)
9. Artale, A., Geatti, L., Gigante, N., Mazzullo, A., Montanari, A.: Complexity of safety and cosafety fragments of linear temporal logic. In: AAAI. pp. 6236–6244. AAAI Press (2023)
10. Behrmann, G., David, A., Larsen, K.G.: A tutorial on UPPAAL. In: SFM. Lecture Notes in Computer Science, vol. 3185, pp. 200–236. Springer (2004)
11. Bohy, A., Bruyère, V., Filiot, E., Jin, N., Raskin, J.: Acacia+, a tool for LTL synthesis. In: CAV. Lecture Notes in Computer Science, vol. 7358, pp. 652–657. Springer (2012)
12. Bouyer, P., Haddad, S., Reynier, P.: Timed unfoldings for networks of timed automata. In: ATVA. Lecture Notes in Computer Science, vol. 4218, pp. 292–306. Springer (2006)
13. Brihaye, T., Estiévenart, M., Geeraerts, G.: On MITL and alternating timed automata. In: FORMATS. LNCS, vol. 8053, pp. 47–61. Springer (2013)

14. Brihaye, T., Estiévenart, M., Geeraerts, G.: On MITL and alternating timed automata over infinite words. In: FORMATS. LNCS, vol. 8711, pp. 69–84. Springer (2014)
15. Brihaye, T., Geeraerts, G., Ho, H., Monmege, B.: MightyL: A compositional translation from MITL to timed automata. In: CAV (1). Lecture Notes in Computer Science, vol. 10426, pp. 421–440. Springer (2017)
16. Bulychev, P.E., David, A., Larsen, K.G., Li, G.: Efficient controller synthesis for a fragment of $MTL_{0,\infty}$. Acta Informatica **51**(3-4), 165–192 (2014)
17. Cimatti, A., Clarke, E.M., Giunchiglia, F., Roveri, M.: NUSMV: A new symbolic model verifier. In: CAV. LNCS, vol. 1633, pp. 495–499. Springer (1999)
18. Cimatti, A., Griggio, A., Magnago, E., Roveri, M., Tonetta, S.: Extending nuXmv with timed transition systems and timed temporal properties. In: CAV (1). Lecture Notes in Computer Science, vol. 11561, pp. 376–386. Springer (2019)
19. Cimatti, A., Griggio, A., Magnago, E., Roveri, M., Tonetta, S.: SMT-based satisfiability of first-order LTL with event freezing functions and metric operators. Inf. Comput. **272**, 104502 (2020)
20. Couvreur, J.: On-the-fly verification of linear temporal logic. In: World Congress on Formal Methods. Lecture Notes in Computer Science, vol. 1708, pp. 253–271. Springer (1999)
21. Duret-Lutz, A., Lewkowicz, A., Fauchille, A., Michaud, T., Renault, E., Xu, L.: Spot 2.0 - A framework for LTL and ω-automata manipulation. In: ATVA. LNCS, vol. 9938, pp. 122–129 (2016)
22. Ferrère, T., Maler, O., Nickovic, D., Pnueli, A.: From real-time logic to timed automata. J. ACM **66**(3), 19:1–19:31 (2019)
23. Gastin, P., Oddoux, D.: Fast LTL to Büchi automata translation. In: CAV. LNCS, vol. 2102, pp. 53–65. Springer (2001)
24. Govind, R., Herbreteau, F., Srivathsan, B., Walukiewicz, I.: Revisiting local time semantics for networks of timed automata. In: CONCUR. LIPIcs, vol. 140, pp. 16:1–16:15. Schloss Dagstuhl - Leibniz-Zentrum für Informatik (2019)
25. Herbreteau, F., Point, G., Sankur, O.: TChecker. `https://github.com/ticktac-project/tchecker` (v08 - September 2023)
26. Ho, H.M., Krishna, S.N., Madnani, K., Majumdar, R., Pandya, P.: MightyPPL: Verification of MITL with past and pnueli modalities (2025), `https://arxiv.org/abs/2510.01490`
27. Holzmann, G.J.: The model checker SPIN. IEEE Trans. Software Eng. **23**(5), 279–295 (1997)
28. Kant, G., Laarman, A., Meijer, J., van de Pol, J., Blom, S., van Dijk, T.: LTSmin: High-performance language-independent model checking. In: TACAS. Lecture Notes in Computer Science, vol. 9035, pp. 692–707. Springer (2015)
29. Kindermann, R., Junttila, T.A., Niemelä, I.: Bounded model checking of an MITL fragment for timed automata. In: ACSD. pp. 216–225. IEEE Computer Society (2013)
30. Larsen, K.G., Pettersson, P., Yi, W.: UPPAAL in a nutshell. STTT **1**(1-2), 134–152 (1997)
31. Lee, J., Yu, G., Bae, K.: Efficient SMT-based model checking for signal temporal logic. In: ASE. pp. 343–354. IEEE (2021)
32. Maler, O., Nickovic, D., Pnueli, A.: Real time temporal logic: Past, present, future. In: FORMATS. Lecture Notes in Computer Science, vol. 3829, pp. 2–16. Springer (2005)
33. Maler, O., Nickovic, D., Pnueli, A.: From MITL to timed automata. In: FORMATS. LNCS, vol. 4202, pp. 274–289. Springer (2006)

34. Menghi, C., Bersani, M.M., Rossi, M., San Pietro, P.: Model checking MITL formulae on timed automata: A logic-based approach. ACM Trans. Comput. Log. **21**(3), 26:1–26:44 (2020). `https://doi.org/10.1145/3383687`, `https://doi.org/10.1145/3383687`

35. Nickovic, D., Piterman, N.: From mtl to deterministic timed automata. In: FORMATS. Lecture Notes in Computer Science, vol. 6246, pp. 152–167. Springer (2010)

36. Ouaknine, J., Worrell, J.: On metric temporal logic and faulty turing machines. In: FoSSaCS. LNCS, vol. 3921, pp. 217–230. Springer (2006)

37. Plaku, E., Karaman, S.: Motion planning with temporal-logic specifications: Progress and challenges. Artificial Intelligence **232**, 1–20 (2015)

38. Pradella, M.: A user's guide to Zot. CoRR **abs/0912.5014** (2009)

39. Sebastiani, R., Tonetta, S.: "More Deterministic" vs. "Smaller" büchi automata for efficient LTL model checking. In: Proceedings of the 12th Advanced Research Working Conference on Correct Hardware Design and Verification Methods (CHARME 2003). pp. 126–140 (2003)

40. Sun, J., Liu, Y., Dong, J.S., Pang, J.: PAT: Towards flexible verification under fairness. LNCS, vol. 5643, pp. 709–714. Springer (2009)

41. Tsay, Y.K., Vardi, M.Y.: From linear temporal logics to büchi automata: The early and simple principle. In: Proceedings of the 2021 International Conference on Model Checking Software (SPIN 2021). pp. 8–40 (2021)

42. Vardi, M.Y.: An automata-theoretic approach to linear temporal logic. LNCS **1043**, 238–266 (1996)

43. Wilke, T.: Specifying timed state sequences in powerful decidable logics and timed automata. In: FTRTFT. LNCS, vol. 863, pp. 694–715. Springer (1994)

44. Zhou, Y., Maity, D., Baras, J.S.: Timed automata approach for motion planning using metric interval temporal logic. In: ECC. pp. 690–695. IEEE (2016)

Trace Repair for Temporal Behavior Trees

Sebastian Schirmer[1] , Philipp Schitz[1], Johann C. Dauer[1],
Bernd Finkbeiner[3], and Sriram Sankaranarayanan[2]

[1] DLR German Aerospace Center, Institute of Flight Systems, Braunschweig,
Germany, {sebastian.schirmer, philipp.schitz, johann.dauer}@dlr.de
[2] University of Colorado Boulder, Boulder, USA, srirams@colorado.edu
[3] CISPA Helmholtz Center for Information Security, Saarbrücken, Germany,
finkbeiner@cispa.de

Abstract. We present methods for repairing traces against specifications given as temporal behavior trees (TBT). TBT are a specification formalism for action sequences in robotics and cyber-physical systems, where specifications of sub-behaviors, given in signal temporal logic, are composed using operators for sequential and parallel composition, fallbacks, and repetition. Trace repairs are useful to explain failures and as training examples that avoid the observed problems. In principle, repairs can be obtained via mixed-integer linear programming (MILP), but this is far too expensive for practical applications. We present two practical repair strategies: (1) incremental repair, which reduces the MILP by splitting the trace into segments, and (2) landmark-based repair, which solves the repair problem iteratively using TBT's robust semantics as a heuristic that approximates MILP with more efficient linear programming. In our experiments, we were able to repair traces with more than 25 000 entries in under ten minutes, while MILP runs out of memory.

1 Introduction

We study the problem of trace repair for temporal behavior tree specifications. Behavior trees specify complex sequences of actions for applications in robotics and cyber-physical systems (CPS) using operators for sequential composition, fallbacks, repetitions, and parallel executions. Specification formalisms based on behavior trees have been widely studied for applications such as runtime monitoring of CPS [2,19,9,11,24,13]. *Temporal behavior trees* (TBTs) are one such formalism based on behavior trees [21]. TBTs combine formulas in Signal Temporal Logic (STL) using the operators defined by behavior trees. They have been shown to be strictly more powerful than linear temporal logic and equivalent to formalisms such as regular temporal logic [16]. Previous work has studied the construction of monitors that check whether a given trace satisfies a TBT specification, and provides *quantitative robustness semantics* that measures the distance between a trace and a TBT [21]. Furthermore, the monitor is able to split the input trace into segments while mapping each segment to a subtree of the TBT specification, where the STL formulas at the leaf nodes represent

© The Author(s) 2026
S. Junges and G. Katz (Eds.): TACAS 2026, LNCS 16505, pp. 660–679, 2026.
https://doi.org/10.1007/978-3-032-22752-2_34

the finest level of granularity. Given such a segmentation, the overall Boolean verdict of the monitor can be justified.

In this paper, we study the case that the observed behavior does *not* satisfy the specification. We are interested in solving the *trace repair* problem: given a violating trace and a specification, compute a trace that satisfies the specification while minimally modifying the original trace. The repaired trace can be used as a modified plan that corrects the output of an untrusted planner based on a correctness specification. Furthermore, it provides valuable information about what went wrong in the violating trace. For systems that involve a machine-learned component (or a human operator), they are also useful as training examples to avoid the problem in the future.

Figure 1a shows an excerpt of a TBT that specifies an automated landing maneuver of an unmanned aerial vehicle (UAV) on a ship. The TBT decomposes the maneuver into two parts before descending: first, the UAV moves to a position diagonally behind the ship and holds there for five seconds; second, the UAV transitions above the touchdown point while aligning its heading with the heading of the ship. Typically, the TBT would include other fallback maneuvers, such as approaching the ship from behind or from the side, which we omit here for brevity. The formulas at the TBT's leaf nodes specify the successful execution of the various actions. For instance, the UAV reaching and holding a diagonal position behind the ship is expressed by the STL formula $\Diamond \Box_{[0,5]} \, diagonalBehind$. Figure 1b shows a plot of a landing maneuver. While the UAV seems to reach the dotted line representing the correct diagonal position, it is actually slightly off and therefore violates the STL specification. Finding such minor deviations is challenging but correcting them is even more difficult with system dynamics involved. Here, the minimal trace repair highlights this by adjusting the UAV's position closer to the dotted line while keeping the rest of the trace unchanged.

In theory, the repair problem could be solved using mixed-integer linear programming (MILP), where the system model, the trace, and the relevant parts of the TBT specification are encoded as constraints. To compute an "optimal repair" we impose a cost function, such as the L_1 norm, that penalizes deviation of the repaired trace states from the original trace states. Since the size of the MILP grows with the length of the trace, the overall complexity of solving the MILP is exponential in the size of the trace. As a result, the MILP encoding approach does not scale.

We address this problem with two complementary repair strategies. The first strategy, *incremental repair*, uses the segmentation provided by the TBT monitor to avoid encoding the entire trace. Instead, it locally repairs segments, starting with leaf nodes, i.e., STL formulas, and incrementally moving up the TBT only if necessary. Note that the segmentation serves as a heuristic, which may be off for repair, e.g., due to constraints imposed by the system model. In our experiments, for a landing depicted in Figure 1b with a trace length of 1014, this approach successfully repairs within 30 s, whereas the straightforward MILP encoding takes over 2000 s. The second strategy, *landmark-based repair*, is an iterative approach that identifies candidate landmarks within the trace for the

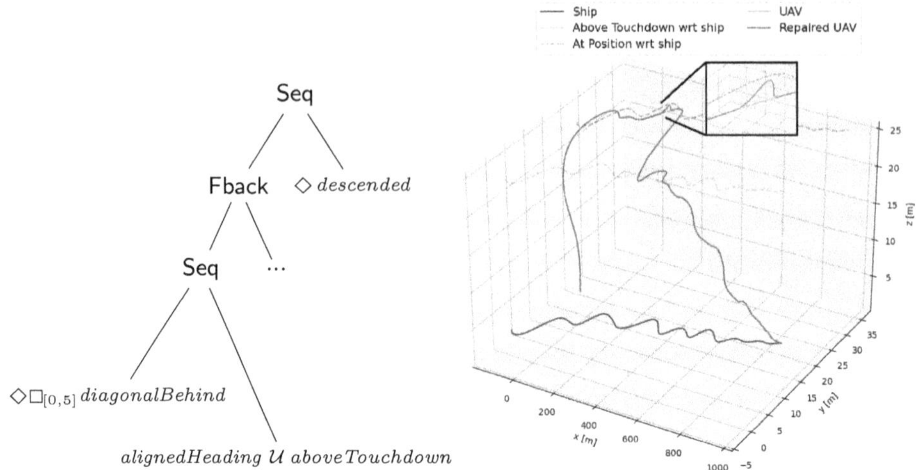

(a) Excerpt from a TBT specifying a UAV landing maneuver on a ship.

(b) Trace repair of an execution of the landing maneuver against the TBT in Figure 1a.

Fig. 1: Repair of a UAV ship landing maneuver [21] against a TBT specification.

repair. If a repaired trace is found that satisfies the landmark, then its satisfaction guarantees the satisfaction of the TBT specification. Given the abundance of candidates, we use the robust semantics of TBTs as a heuristic to find good candidates. This approach entirely avoids the integer and binary variables introduced by the TBT encoding, enabling the problem to be solved as a linear program (LP) instead. As a result, landmark-based repair successfully finds a solution for a trace with over 25 000 entries in under ten minutes, where approaches that fully encode the TBT run out of memory.

The remainder of the paper is structured as follows: Section 3 provides background on system models and TBTs, then Section 4 introduces the repair strategies, finally Section 5 demonstrates experimental results.

2   Related Work

Trace repair was first introduced as correction for regular languages by Wagner [27], and was later referred to as regular repair of specification [6]. Both works investigate the repair in terms of sequences of a finite alphabet, i.e., words. They showed that the problem is decidable using distance automata, but becomes PSPACE when the target language is specified in LTL. To the best of our knowledge, we are the first to extend the notion of repair to traces of CPS, where traces consist of sequences of numerical events, including sensor readings and actuator commands, instead of words. Because CPS traces involve numerical values and must respect the system's dynamics, simple symbolic edits such as changing a single symbol are insufficient. This makes automata-based approaches not applicable. Instead, we formulate the repair problem as MILP, which naturally handles numerical constraints.

STL is widely used as a specification language for controlling system behaviors. In [17], STL formulas are transformed into a MILP for model-predictive control. However, the NP-HARD complexity of MILP limits this approach, especially with nested formulas or longer trajectories, making it unsuitable for long-horizon trajectory planning. [14] addresses this by structurally decomposing STL formulas to then incrementally solving them. However, their decomposition does not handle disjunctions, whereas our repair does.

Landmarks have been studied for strategy solving [4] and planning [12] as key features that must be true on any solution. In this work, we adopt a similar conceptual role but with a distinct technical use. Here, a landmark serves as a sufficient feature that guarantees the satisfaction of a TBT specification. This enables a more efficient LP encoding, significantly extending the capability to handle longer traces.

Falsification [3] tries to find traces that "falsify" a given specification by using stochastic optimization to minimize its robustness. Trace synthesis [18], on the other hand, generates traces that satisfy the specification. In contrast, this work addresses the problem of trace repair: given a violating trace, we minimally modify it so that the resulting trace satisfies the specification. Our approach avoids stochastic optimization and uses a MILP formulation that ensures specification satisfaction while minimizing changes to the violating trace.

Repairing specification has been studied [7,8,10]. In [10], a user can modify the specification online to "repair" a robot's execution when it no longer matches their intent. In this work, we keep the specification fixed and focus on repairing traces. Similar to our work, [25] repairs traces directly, but within an online runtime enforcer setting. There, the goal is to prevent imminent safety violations over short horizons, i.e., short traces, rather than repairing long traces corresponding to an entire task as in our setting.

3 Preliminaries

We revisit the definition of a system model and temporal behavior trees.

3.1 System Model

We consider discrete-time systems with linear dynamics, represented by

$$X_{t+1} = A \cdot X_t + B \cdot U_t, \tag{1}$$

where $X_t \in \mathbb{X} \subseteq \mathbb{R}^n$ is the state at time step t with n variables, $u_t \in \mathbb{U} \subseteq \mathbb{R}^m$ is the control input at time t. A is an $n \times n$ while B is a $n \times m$ matrix [5].

Example 1. Consider a one-dimensional integrator system with position p and velocity v as states, i.e., $X = [p, v]^T$, and an acceleration command as the input U. For a sampling time t_s, the system is described as

$$\begin{bmatrix} p_{t+1} \\ v_{t+1} \end{bmatrix} = \begin{bmatrix} 1 & t_s \\ 0 & 1 \end{bmatrix} \begin{bmatrix} p_t \\ v_t \end{bmatrix} + \begin{bmatrix} t_s^2/2 \\ t_s \end{bmatrix} U_t.$$

The execution of a system provides a *trace* σ that is a finite sequence of states $\sigma(1), \ldots, \sigma(N)$, where $\sigma(i)$ represents the state of the model and the control input at timesteps $i \in \{1, \ldots, N\}$, i.e., $[X_{i-1}, U_{i-1}]^T$. To access the state of the model X_{i-1} at timestep i we define a projection operation π_X that extracts this state from $\sigma(i)$: $\pi_X(\sigma(i)) = X_{i-1}$. The length of a trace is denoted as $|\sigma|$, with $|\sigma| = 0$ indicating an *empty trace*. Given a trace σ, the expression $\sigma[l : u]$ retrieves a slice of the trace from offsets l to u with $l, u \in \mathbb{N}_0$:

$$\sigma[l : u] ::= \begin{cases} \sigma(l+1), \cdots, \sigma(\min(u+1, N)), & \text{if } l \leq u \text{ and } l < N \\ \text{empty trace} & \text{otherwise} \end{cases}$$

For convenience, let $\sigma[l :] = \sigma[l : N - 1]$ and $\sigma[: u] = \sigma[0 : u]$.

Example 2. Consider the system described in Example 1. Let $t_s = 1\text{s}$, $X_0 = [0, 1]^T$ and $U_t = 0$ for all timesteps t. Executing the system for three timesteps yields $X_1 = [1, 1]^T$, $X_2 = [2, 1]^T$, and $X_3 = [3, 1]^T$. The corresponding trace has a length of four where $\sigma(1) = [0, 1, 0]^T$, $\sigma(2) = [1, 1, 0]^T$, $\sigma(3) = [2, 1, 0]^T$, and $\sigma(4) = [3, 1, 0]^T$. To exclude the first trace entry, slicing can be applied: $\sigma[1 :] = \sigma(2), \sigma(3), \sigma(4)$. Similarily, $\sigma[3 : 3] = \sigma(4)$ only accesses the last entry.

3.2 Temporal Behavior Trees

Temporal Behavior Trees (TBTs) [21] extend behavior trees [2,19,9,11,24], as commonly used in robotics, with temporal formulas at the leaf nodes of the trees.

Definition 1 (Syntax of Temporal Behavior Trees [21]). *We construct a temporal behavior tree $\mathcal{T}$ using the following syntax:*

$$\begin{aligned} \mathcal{T} ::= \; & \mathsf{Fback}([\mathcal{T}, \ldots, \mathcal{T}]), && \leftarrow \textit{Fallback node} \\ & | \; \mathsf{Par}_M([\mathcal{T}, \ldots, \mathcal{T}]), M \in \mathbb{N} && \leftarrow \textit{Parallel node} \\ & | \; \mathsf{Seq}([\mathcal{T}, \mathcal{T}]), && \leftarrow \textit{Sequence node} \\ & | \; \mathsf{Leaf}(\varphi), && \leftarrow \textit{Leaf node} \end{aligned}$$

where φ is a local property expressed in a temporal language. Note that we restrict our focus to a selected subset of TBT operators for brevity and clarity.

Informally, $\mathsf{Fback}([\mathcal{T}_1, \ldots, \mathcal{T}_n])$ mimics the semantics of a "fallback" node in a behavior tree: at least one of the subtrees $\mathcal{T}_1, \ldots, \mathcal{T}_n$ must eventually be satisfied by the trace. $\mathsf{Par}_M([\mathcal{T}_1, \ldots, \mathcal{T}_n])$ denotes a parallel operator that specifies that at least M distinct subtrees must be satisfied simultaneously by the trace σ. $\mathsf{Seq}([\mathcal{T}_1, \mathcal{T}_2])$ is a sequential node that denotes that σ must be partitioned into two parts $\sigma_1; \sigma_2$ such that $\sigma_1 \models \mathcal{T}_1$ and $\sigma_2 \models \mathcal{T}_2$. For convenience, we rewrite $\mathsf{Seq}([\mathcal{T}_1, (\mathsf{Seq}([\mathcal{T}_2, \cdots, \mathsf{Seq}([\mathcal{T}_{n-1}, \mathcal{T}_n])]))))$ for $n \geq 2$ as $\mathsf{Seq}([\mathcal{T}_1, \ldots, \mathcal{T}_n])$. Finally, a local formula at a leaf specifies that the corresponding trace segment must satisfy the formula. For brevity, we occasionally omit $\mathsf{Leaf}(\varphi)$ and write φ.

Local properties are specified using Signal Temporal Logic (STL), a prominent specification language for CPS. STL is defined recursively as follows:

$$\varphi ::= \mathrm{AP} \mid \neg\varphi \mid \varphi \wedge \varphi \mid \varphi \vee \varphi \mid \Diamond_{[l,u]}(\varphi) \mid \Box_{[l,u]}(\varphi) \mid \varphi\, \mathcal{U}_{[l,u]}\, \varphi$$

with an interval $[l, u]$ wherein $0 \leq l \leq u \leq \infty$. Note that $\bigcirc(\varphi)$ is a shorthand for $\Diamond_{[1,1]}$ as is $\Diamond(\varphi)$ for $\Diamond_{[0,\infty)}$. Similar conventions apply for $\Box(\varphi)$ and $\varphi_1 \mathcal{U} \varphi_2$. The set of *atomic propositions* is $\mathrm{AP} \in \{p_1, \ldots, p_m\}$, with each p_i associated with a function f_i that maps states to a real number. In this work, f_i is restricted to be a linear function A trace σ satisfies p_i if and only if $f_i(\sigma(1)) \geq 0$. Informally, STL extends propositional logic by temporal operators, where $\Diamond_{[l,u]}(\varphi)$ requires φ to be satisfied eventually at some point between l and u steps, $\Box_{[l,u]}(\varphi)$ requires φ to be satisfied at every step between l and u, and $\varphi_1\, \mathcal{U}_{[l,u]}\, \varphi_2$ requires φ_1 to hold *until* φ_2 is eventually satisfied at some point between l and u steps. Next, we formally define the satisfaction of a TBT specification that uses STL as specification language for its leaf nodes.

Definition 2 (Boolean Semantics of Temporal Behavior Trees [21]).
We write $\sigma \models \mathcal{T}$ to denote that trace σ satisfies the TBT $\mathcal{T}$, defined as follows:

$$\sigma \models \mathsf{Fback}([\mathcal{T}_1, \ldots, \mathcal{T}_n]) \iff \exists j \in [1, n], \exists i \in [0, |\sigma| - 1], \sigma[i :] \models \mathcal{T}_j$$

$$\sigma \models \mathsf{Par}_M([\mathcal{T}_1, \ldots, \mathcal{T}_n]) \iff \exists I \subseteq [1, n], |I| \geq M \wedge \forall i \in I, \sigma \models \mathcal{T}_i$$

$$\sigma \models \mathsf{Seq}([\mathcal{T}_1, \mathcal{T}_2]) \iff \exists i \in [0, |\sigma| - 1], \sigma[: i] \models \mathcal{T}_1 \wedge \sigma[i + 1 :] \models \mathcal{T}_2$$

$$\sigma \models \mathsf{Leaf}(\varphi) \iff \sigma \models \varphi$$

$$\sigma \models p_i \iff f_i(\sigma(1)) \geq 0 \text{ if } |\sigma| > 0 \text{ else } \mathbf{false}$$

$$\sigma \models \neg\varphi \iff \sigma \not\models \varphi$$

$$\sigma \models \varphi_1 \wedge \varphi_2 \iff \sigma \models \varphi_1 \wedge \sigma \models \varphi_2$$

$$\sigma \models \varphi_1 \vee \varphi_2 \iff \sigma \models \varphi_1 \vee \sigma \models \varphi_2$$

$$\sigma \models \Diamond_{[l,u]}(\varphi) \iff \exists\, i \in [l, u],\, \sigma[i :] \models \varphi$$

$$\sigma \models \Box_{[l,u]}(\varphi) \iff \forall\, i \in [l, u],\, \sigma[i :] \models \varphi$$

$$\sigma \models \varphi_1\, \mathcal{U}_{[l,u]}\, \varphi_2 \iff \exists i \in [l, u], (\forall j \in [0, i - 1],\, \sigma[j :] \models \varphi_1) \wedge \sigma[i :] \models \varphi_2$$

Note that by Definition 2, the formula $\neg \bigcirc true$ is true only in the last state of a finite trace. We abbreviate this formula by $\bullet$.

Example 3. Consider a robot tasked with searching for objects, specifically apples and oranges[4], while avoiding certain areas. Assume there are three known locations, L_1, L_2, and L_3, where these objects are most likely to be found. The robot needs to search these locations in some order and discover either an apple or an orange in each location within a specified time limit. We can encode this search task using a TBT, as shown in Figure 2. The APs *found* 🍎 and *found* 🍊 return 1 if the robots reports finding an apple or an orange, respectively; otherwise, they return -1. The APs atL_1, atL_2, and atL_3 denote that the robot is

---

[4] https://robohub.org/introduction-to-behavior-trees/

at positions L_1, L_2, and L_3, respectively. Similar, the AP *avoidArea* is satisfied iff the robot is outside the areas. Note that according to the TBT, the order in which the robot finds an apple, an orange, or both is not relevant for successfully completing the task.

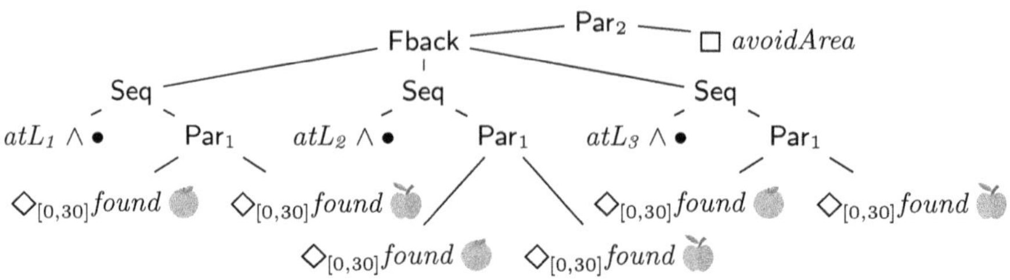

Fig. 2: TBT to search for at least an apple or an orange at different locations.

TBTs also provide a robust semantics yielding a numerical value [21]. Intuitively, a positive value indicates that the specification is satisfied, while a negative value corresponds to a violation. Additionally, the magnitude of the numerical value reflects the degree to which the specification is satisfied or violated. In essence, we obtain the robust semantics by replacing all instances of $\exists$ and $\vee$ by max and all instances of $\forall$ and $\wedge$ by min in Definition 2. This semantics was used to compute a segmentation of a trace [21]. A segmentation assigns segments of the trace to TBT $\mathcal{T}$ nodes. It is represented as a graph that consists of a set of vertices $V = \{(\hat{\mathcal{T}}, i, j) \mid \hat{\mathcal{T}}$ is a subtree of $\mathcal{T}$, $0 \leq i \leq j \leq |\sigma| - 1\}$ that capture the assignment. Figure 3 provides a segmentation for a trace of length 100 using the TBT specification depicted in Figure 2. The segmentation shows that the robot moves to location L_2 and then searches an orange.

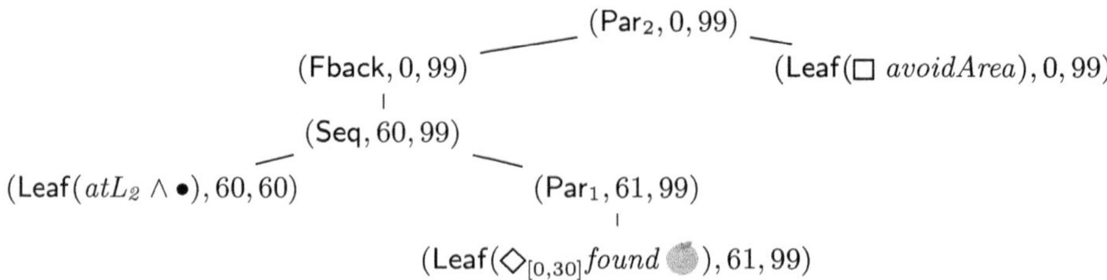

Fig. 3: Segmentation graph for the TBT in Fig. 2, numbers indicate segments.

4 Repairing Traces

Given a system model M, a TBT specification $\mathcal{T}$, and a trace σ with $\sigma \not\models \mathcal{T}$, we construct a repaired trace σ_R that satisfies $\mathcal{T}$ with $|\sigma_R| = |\sigma|$, denoted by $\mathsf{repair}_{\sigma_R}(\mathcal{T}, M, \sigma, \xi)$, as follows:

$$\left.\begin{array}{ll}\arg\min_{\sigma_R} J(\sigma, \sigma_R) & \leftarrow \text{Minimize cost function} \\ \quad s.t.\ \sigma_R \models \mathsf{encode}_{\sigma_R}(M) & \leftarrow \text{Trace follows system model} \\ \quad\ \ \sigma_R \models \mathsf{encode}_{\sigma_R}(\mathcal{T}) & \leftarrow \text{Trace satisfies TBT} \\ \quad\ \ \sigma_R \models \xi & \leftarrow \text{Additional constraints, cf. Section 4.1}\end{array}\right\} \tag{2}$$

Note that $\mathsf{repair}_{\sigma_R}$ does not change the length of the trace: each state of the repaired trace is a one to one correspondent to a state of the original trace. A repair problem can be infeasible. For instance, one may need a strictly longer trace σ_R to satisfy $\mathcal{T}$. In this case, $\mathsf{repair}_{\sigma_R}$ returns none. In the following, we introduce $\mathsf{encode}_{\sigma_R}(M)$, $\mathsf{encode}_{\sigma_R}(\mathcal{T})$, and present different cost functions J. We then present complementary repair strategies. We encode σ and σ_R using $2 \cdot |\sigma|$ continuous variables with $|\sigma|$ constraints for the original trace.

Encoding of the System Model. Since we consider discrete-time systems with linear dynamics, Equation (1) can be directly encoded as a MILP with X_t being the states of the repaired trace σ_R. In this way we ensure that σ_R follows the dynamics. We furthermore introduce lower and upper bounds for each control input in U_t. We denote this encoding by $\mathsf{encode}_{\sigma_R}(M)$. The encoding $\mathsf{encode}_{\sigma_R}(M)$ adds $3 \cdot |\sigma_R|$ constraints. These constraints include the system model itself, a lower bound on the inputs, and an upper bound on the inputs. Since A and B are constants, the encoding adds $|\sigma|$ continuous variables for U.

Encoding of the Temporal Behavior Tree. Since the length of the trace is known, the satisfaction of a trace with respect to a TBT specification, as defined in Definition 2, can be encoded in a MILP by extending the MILP encoding for STL to TBT. For a detailed explanation for STL, we refer to [17]. Next, we provide a summary of the STL encoding before extending it to TBTs.

For each STL (sub)formula ψ, and for a trace σ_R with $|\sigma_R| = N$, we introduce a binary variable z_t^ψ for each trace position $0 \leq t < N$. The variable $z_t^\psi = 1$ if and only if ψ is satisfied at position t in the trace. Since the length of the trace is known, existential quantifiers $\exists j \in [1, \ldots, N]$ and universal quantifiers $\forall j \in [1, \ldots, N]$ are encoded by $\bigvee_{j=1}^{N}$ and $\bigwedge_{j=1}^{N}$, respectively. Thus, the remaining task is to encode $\vee$ and $\wedge$ using a Pseudo-Boolean encoding [1,17] (see Section A.2).

To extend the encoding to TBTs $\mathcal{T}$, we introduce binary variables that account for the current segment: $z_{[t_1:t_2]}^{\mathcal{T}}$. The encoding is as follows:

$$\begin{array}{ll}\mathcal{T} = \mathsf{Leaf}(\varphi) & : z_{[t_1:t_2]}^{\mathcal{T}} = z_{[t_1:t_2]}^{\varphi} \\[4pt] \mathcal{T} = \mathsf{Fback}([\mathcal{T}_1, \ldots, \mathcal{T}_n]) & : z_{[t_1:t_2]}^{\mathcal{T}} = \bigvee_{j=1}^{n} \bigvee_{i=t_1}^{t_2} z_{[i:t_2]}^{\mathcal{T}_j} \\[4pt] \mathcal{T} = \mathsf{Par}_M([\mathcal{T}_1, \ldots, \mathcal{T}_n]) & : z_{[t_1:t_2]}^{\mathcal{T}} = (\sum_{j=1}^{n} z_{[t_1:t_2]}^{\mathcal{T}_j}) \geq M \\[4pt] \mathcal{T} = \mathsf{Seq}([\mathcal{T}_1, \mathcal{T}_2]) & : z_{[t_1:t_2]}^{\mathcal{T}} = \bigvee_{i=t_1}^{t_2-1} (z_{[t_1:i]}^{\mathcal{T}_1} \wedge z_{[i+1:t_2]}^{\mathcal{T}_2})\end{array} \tag{3}$$

We denote this encoding by $\mathsf{encode}_\sigma(\mathcal{T})$. A trace σ satisfies a specification $\mathcal{T}$ iff $z^{\mathcal{T}}_{[0:N-1]} = 1$. Let $|\varphi|$ represent the size of the temporal formula. Unlike the previous STL encoding, which introduces $(|\text{AP}| + |\varphi|) \cdot N$ binary variables, this encoding requires $(|\text{AP}| + |\mathcal{T}|) \cdot N^2$ binary variables to account for the different segments with the same number of constraints that track their satisfaction.

Encoding of Cost Functions. The cost function in Equation (2) ensures that the repaired trace σ_R is *similar* to the original trace σ, thereby providing a clear and intuitive explanation of *what should have been done differently* to satisfy the TBT $\mathcal{T}$ specification. We consider the following cost functions:

- *L1-Distance* $L1(\sigma, \sigma_R) = \sum_{i=1}^{|\sigma|} \|\pi_X(\sigma(i)) - \pi_X(\sigma_R(i))\|_1$
  This metric computes the point-wise distance between both trajectories.
- *Hamming-Distance* $H(\sigma, \sigma_R) = \sum_{i=1}^{|\sigma|} \begin{cases} 1 & , \pi_X(\sigma(i)) \neq \pi_X(\sigma_R(i)) \\ 0 & , \text{otherwise.} \end{cases}$
  This metrics counts the changes necessary to the original trajectory.

We also consider the robust semantics of TBTs as cost function to maximize "satisfaction" and introduce a weighted combination $W(\sigma, \sigma_R)$, which integrates multiple objectives and constraints into the repair strategy: $\tau_{L1} \cdot L1(\sigma, \sigma_R) + \tau_H \cdot H(\sigma, \sigma_R) + \tau_R \cdot R(\sigma_r)$ where τ_{L1}, τ_H, and τ_R are positive weights that sum up to one. Note that we can encode $|x|$ using linear constraints within the cost function by defining an auxiliary variable $a = |x| : a \geq x \wedge a \geq -x$ or using the Big-M method [28]. For brevity, the paper focuses on cost functions that are intuitive for pilots and control engineers. Other cost functions that find repairs using shorter traces will be explored in future.

4.1 Repair Strategies

Equation (2) provides an optimal repair, but for long traces and complex specifications, the solution quickly becomes impractical, as indicated by the reported number of variables. We introduce two repair strategies, to address two distinct scalability concerns. The first strategy is an incremental approach, enabling local repairs of violating trace segments, which avoids encoding the full trace. The second strategy uses landmarks to resolve choices introduced by disjunctions in the specification. This reduces the MILP encoding to a LP, which allows for more efficient optimization algorithms, such as the simplex algorithm [26]. The strategies can be applied both in isolation and in combination with each other.

(1) Incremental Repair Strategy The incremental repair strategy uses information provided by a segmentation. Recall that a segmentation of a trace w.r.t. a TBT $\mathcal{T}$ divides the trace σ into multiple subtraces of the form $\sigma[i : j]$ and assigns a (sub)tree to each of them. By induction on the structure of the TBT and matching the semantics of TBTs (Def. 2) against the definition of a segmentation (Def. 4 in Section A.1), the satisfaction of a TBT can be reduced to checking the temporal formulas at its leaf nodes under the given segmentation: $\sigma \models_G \mathcal{T}$ if and only if for all $(\mathsf{Leaf}(\varphi), i, j) \in V, \sigma[i:j] \models \varphi$. However, an "optimal" segmentation can be defined and computed even for violating traces, i.e., a subtrace violates its assigned subtree. Although segmentation matches only leaf formulas at the most granular level, it still provides useful clues for repairing the trace.

Example 4. We now evaluate the segmentation depicted in Figure 3, assuming all leaves satisfy their STL formula with respect to their respective segment, except $\mathsf{Leaf}(\square \; avoidArea)$. Since $((\mathsf{Par}_1, 61, 99), (\mathsf{Leaf}(\lozenge_{[0,30]} found \; \text{⬤}), 61, 99))$ is an edge and the leaf is satisfied, it follows that $(\mathsf{Par}_1, 61, 99)$ is satisfied. The same holds for $(\mathsf{Seq}, 60, 99)$ and $(\mathsf{Fback}, 0, 99)$: both are satisfied. However, since $(\mathsf{Leaf}(\square \; avoidArea), 0, 99)$ is not satisfied, $(\mathsf{Par}_2, 0, 99)$ is also not satisfied. Ideally, we only need to repair $\mathsf{Leaf}(\square \; avoidArea)$ to satisfy the TBT specification.

Incremental repair is based on this idea. The strategy first attempts to repair violating segments *locally* w.r.t. their respective leaf nodes, i.e., temporal formulas. In doing so, it may need to ensure that a valid transition exists from the end states of the repaired trace segments to the states of the original trace, allowing the repaired segment to be substituted into the original trace. If this local repair fails, it incrementally widens the scope of the repair, first allowing changes in end states (later referred to as *loose*), then adjusting segment boundaries, and moving up to the parent node only in the worst case. The approach aims to avoid the costly search for boundaries during optimization using the guidance provided by a segmentation. We define the local repair strategy as follows.

Definition 3 (Local Repair). *Let M be a system model, σ be a trace, $G = (V, E)$ be a segmentation graph with $V' \subseteq V$, $f \in \{valid, loose\}$ indicate whether a valid transition to the next segment is required, and let $validTransition_M(\sigma, \sigma_R)$ be a function that checks for a valid transition from the repaired trace segment to the original trace. We repair a trace locally, denoted $local(M, \sigma, V', f)$, as follows:*

$$\bigoplus_{(\mathcal{T},i,j)\in V'} repair_{\sigma_R}(\mathcal{T}, M, \sigma[i:j], validTransition_M(\sigma, \sigma_R) \vee f = loose)$$

where $\bigoplus$ merges the models, enforcing all constraints while minimizing the sum of the individual costs. Note that $repair_{\sigma_R}$ is defined in Equation (2).

If no leaf node segments overlap, an efficient approach is to locally repair each leaf node. However, for more complex cases like the segmentation graph in Figure 3 this is insufficient. Locally repairing $(\mathsf{Leaf}(\square \; avoidArea), 0, 99)$ may affect the satisfaction of other leaf nodes, since the segment spans the entire trace. The incremental repair strategy handles this. It is shown below as Algorithm 1. It initializes two sets: C for the repaired segments (Line 1) and L for the segments to be repaired (Line 2). Initially, L contains all leaves in G that violate its segment. Since segmentation may have overlapping violating segments that must be repaired together to avoid side effects, $\mathsf{mergeOverlap}_G(L)$ merges

---

Algorithm 1 The incremental$_G(M, \sigma)$ repair strategy.

Require: Segmentation $G = (V, E)$, a system model M, and trace σ
Ensure: Repaired trace σ_R or none
1: $C \leftarrow \{\}$ $\triangleright$ Successful repairs
2: $L \leftarrow \{\{v | v \in V \wedge v = (\mathsf{Leaf}(\varphi), i, j) \wedge \sigma[i : j] \not\models \varphi\}\}$ $\triangleright$ Start with violating leaves
3: $L \leftarrow \mathsf{mergeOverlap}_G(L)$ $\triangleright$ Groups overlapping leaves into one set
4: **while** $L \neq \emptyset$ **do**
5:      $l \leftarrow L.pop()$ $\triangleright$ Set of nodes in V that must be repaired
6:      $\sigma_R \leftarrow \mathsf{local}(M, \sigma, l, valid)$ $\triangleright$ If successful, it avoids affecting other leaves
7:      **if** $\sigma_R = $ none **then**
8:          $\sigma_R \leftarrow \mathsf{local}(M, \sigma, l, loose)$ $\triangleright$ Could affect transitions to other leaves
9:      **end if**
10:     **if** $\sigma_R \neq $ none **then** $\triangleright$ There is a repair
11:          affected $\leftarrow \mathsf{affectedLeaves}(\sigma, \sigma_R, V)$ $\triangleright$ Tracks leaf changes due to $\sigma_R \neq \sigma$
12:          **if** affected $\setminus l = \emptyset$ **then**
13:              $C \leftarrow C \cup (l, \sigma_R)$ $\triangleright$ Successful repair!
14:          **else**
15:              $L = L \cup$ affected $\triangleright$ Accounts for affected leaves
16:          **end if**
17:      **else** $\triangleright$ There is no repair, therefore we need to move up the TBT
18:          $L \leftarrow L \cup \mathsf{getCommonAncestor}_G(l)$
19:      **end if**
20:      $L \leftarrow \mathsf{mergeOverlap}_G(L)$
21: **end while**
22: **return** $\mathsf{compose}(C, \sigma)$

---

these overlapping sets in L and removes entries if an ancestor node is already in the set. Afterwards, one set is removed from L (Line 5). Next, Line 6 tries to find a repair in which the end states of the segment remain unchanged, i.e., ensuring a valid transition. Then, in Line 8, the repair allows changes to these states, which may in turn affect other segments. If there is an existing repair (Line 10), then $\mathsf{affectedLeaves}(\sigma, \sigma_R, V)$ checks if other leaves are affected by changes of σ_R. For instance consider Example 4, in the beginning the set L is $\{\{(\mathsf{Leaf}(\square\ avoidArea), 0, 99)\}\}$ and if $\sigma_R[61 : 99] \neq \sigma[61 : 99]$ then the evaluation of $(\mathsf{Leaf}(\Diamond_{[0,30]} found\ \text{⬤}), 61, 99)$ might change. A repair is considered successful if only the leaves in l are affected (Line 13). Otherwise, a subsequent local repair must account for the affected leaves in the next iteration (Line 15). If the local repairs were not successful (Line 18), then the repair moves to its next common ancestor w.r.t. the elements in l. Finally, if there are no open repairs, i.e., $L = \emptyset$, we can read off σ_R using the set C (Line 22).

The incremental repair leverages information from the segmentation graph to avoid a costly exploration within the optimization model. Note, however, that a segmentation omits the different choices for a Fback node, which also means that the incremental repair does not take these into account. Fortunately, the approach presented in [21], which utilizes dynamic programming, provides "alternative segmentations" for every choice of a Fback node by simply "reading off" the table entries. We denote the set of segmentations that contains all choices of Fback nodes in a TBT $\mathcal{T}$ as $\hat{G}$.

Proposition 1. *If for all $G \in \hat{G}$, incremental$_G(M, \sigma) =$ none then there is no σ_R with $|\sigma_R| = |\sigma|$ for which $\sigma_R \models \mathcal{T}$.*

Theorem 1. *The incremental repair strategy is sound w.r.t. a segmentation and terminates (see Section A.3 for the proof).*

(2) Landmark-Based Repair Strategy The incremental repair strategy can be complemented by an approach that deals with the disjunctive constraints encountered in the encoding of the repair problem (3). These constraints arise, for instance, when a fallback operator is encoded, or at a leaf node with a $\Diamond$ formula. Given a disjunctive formula $\bigvee_{j=1}^{m} \psi_j$, the landmark based strategy uses information from the original trace to select a candidate ψ_j that will be satisfied.

Formally, a candidate for a landmark is a minimal set of propositions that is sufficient to satisfy the TBT specification. This simplifies the optimization problem to a LP for the L_1 and Hamming distance, as it no longer requires integer or binary variables, and only linear constraints remain[5]. Outside the optimization problem, the robust semantics of TBTs can be used to rank candidates in a heuristic manner. In Section 5, we will see that this strategy provides a fast solution and improves upon that, similar to an anytime algorithm.

Example 5. Given a leaf node $\Diamond_{[0,10]} atL_1$ with $f_{atL_1}(x) = x - 2.5$, encode$_{\sigma_R}(\mathcal{T})$ unfolds into a disjunction of atL_1 at the next positions. The trace shown in Figure 4 violates the property because there is no value of x at any position i in the trace where $f_{atL_1}(x)$ yields a positive value. Landmark-based repair will pick a candidate to solve the disjunction. Here, eleven candidates for landmarks exist. The best candidate w.r.t. the robustness value of atL_1 is at position $i = 7$ with value close to -0.5. The landmark is encoded by $\sigma_R(8) \models atL_1$.

Algorithm 2 provides an iterative repair strategy based on landmarks. The repair receives a segmentation, a system model, and the violating trace. In Line 3, the set of candidates is computed and ordered. It then takes the most promising candidate (Line 5), sets an upper bound on the repair cost (Line 6), encodes the repair (Line 7), and checks if the current landmark returns a better repair (Line 8). Note that the constraints on the system model and cost function remain unchanged throughout the iteration (Line 4). Therefore, the LP can be efficiently

---

[5] Using the robust semantics of TBTs requires the Big-M encoding of the absolute value function, which in turn adds binary variables.

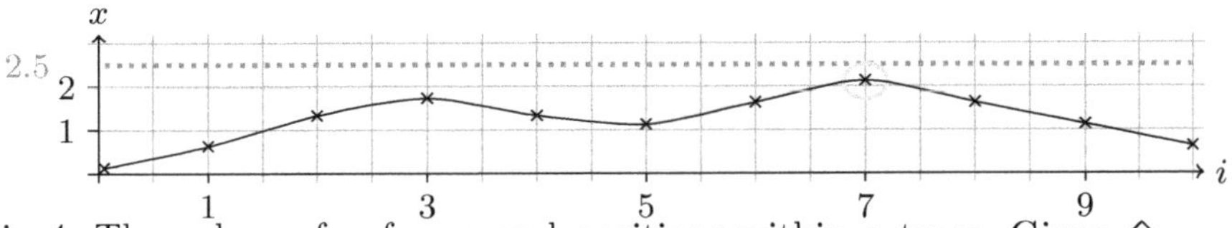

Fig. 4: The values of x for several positions within a trace. Given $\Diamond_{[0,10]} atL_1$ with $f_{atL_1}(x) = x - 2.5$, position $i = 7$ is a good candidate for a landmark.

updated by simply removing the previous landmark and adding the next one, avoiding the need to rebuild the LP from scratch. For the experiments, two optimizations were implemented but are omitted here for brevity. First, candidates are computed on-the-fly instead of upfront as robustness maximizes. Second, candidates are ranked by robustness and explored while maintaining a minimum distance w.r.t. the position of previously tested candidates. This distance starts large and gradually decreases whenever no candidates are left within this distance. Once the distance reaches 1 and no further candidates are available, the repair terminates. For instance, considering Example 5 where position $i = 7$ is chosen as first landmark, a distance of two excludes Positions $5, 6, 8, 9$ and allows to explore Position 3 next. So far, the correct distance and its rate of decrease are user-defined parameters.

Algorithm 2 The landmark-based$_G(M, \sigma)$ repair strategy.

Require: A segmentation G, a system model M, and trace σ
Ensure: Repaired trace σ_R or none
  1: $\sigma_R \leftarrow$ none
  2: $J_{upper} \leftarrow \infty$
  3: $candidates \leftarrow$ computeCandidates(G, σ) ▷ List of landmarks ordered by heuristic
  4: **while** $candidates \neq \emptyset$ **do**
  5:     $landmark \leftarrow candidates.\text{pop}()$
  6:     $improve \leftarrow J(\sigma, \sigma_R) < J_{upper}$ ▷ Upper bound on the cost of the repair
  7:     $\sigma'_R \leftarrow$ repair$_{\sigma_R}$(**true**, $M, \sigma, landmark \wedge improve$)   ▷ *landmark* replaces TBT
  8:     **if** $\sigma'_R \neq$ none **then**   ▷ If there is a repair, it must be better
  9:         $\sigma_R \leftarrow \sigma'_R$
 10:         $J_{upper} \leftarrow J(\sigma, \sigma'_R)$
 11:     **end if**
 12: **end while**
 13: **return** σ_R

Discussion. Both strategies can be combined to solve complex repairs. The incremental repair allows to divide the trace into smaller segments, each of which can be repaired locally. When a local property contains multiple disjunctions, e.g., when using an unbounded $\Diamond$, the optimization becomes more challenging. In such cases, we can use the landmark-based repair. If the combination of both strategies fails, refining the TBT specification is a viable option.

The closer the violating trace is to satisfying the specification, the more effective segmentation and landmarks are as starting points for the repair. In contrast, if the TBT consists of a sequence of two nodes, with the segmentation assigning a very short segment to the first node – potentially too short for a repair – and the remainder of the trace to the second node, incremental repair will converge to the full encoding. In such cases, starting with the full encoding or even finding a new unrelated trace can be faster.

5   Empirical Evaluation and Case-Studies

This section presents two case studies: the robot search task shown in Figure 2 and the automated landing of a UAV on a ship. The first case study illustrates the impact of different cost functions, while the second showcases incremental repair and compares it to landmark-based repair. All experiments were run on a single 16-core machine with a 2.50 GHz 11th Gen Intel(R) Core(TM) i7-11850H processor with 32 GB RAM. The algorithms are implemented in Python using Gurobi[6] as optimizer. Segmentations were obtained using the approach from [20].

5.1   Robot Search Task

Using the robot search task introduced in Example 2, we demonstrate two different cost functions using incremental repair. The trace we used has a best segmentation in which both the location and one of the fruits were narrowly missed. Also, the restricted area that was meant to be avoided was breached. The original trace, consisting of 540 entries, was reduced to 68 entries through subsampling by [20], which computed the best segmentation in under a second. Figure 5 depicts the results of the incremental repair: on the left, using $L1$ as cost function, and on the right, using a weighted combination W of $L1$ and robustness R with weights 0.01 and 0.99, respectively. It took 6 s to repair using $L1$ and 21 s using W. Both repairs reach the location $L2$ and find a fruit (top left). Note that the repair using W provides larger separation from the restricted area compared to $L1$ but still resembles the original trace. The runtime of the repair is mostly impacted by $\square$ $avoidArea$, as it relies on the whole trace. Also, AP $avoidArea$ adds constraints to keep points outside the region and maintain a minimum distance to the corners of the restricted areas. This can be avoided by a syntactic reformulation of the TBT, optimizing it to provide segmentation graphs that are easier to repair. For instance, by moving the $\square$ $avoidArea$ invariant into the individual leaf nodes. Yet, this is not the scope of this paper.

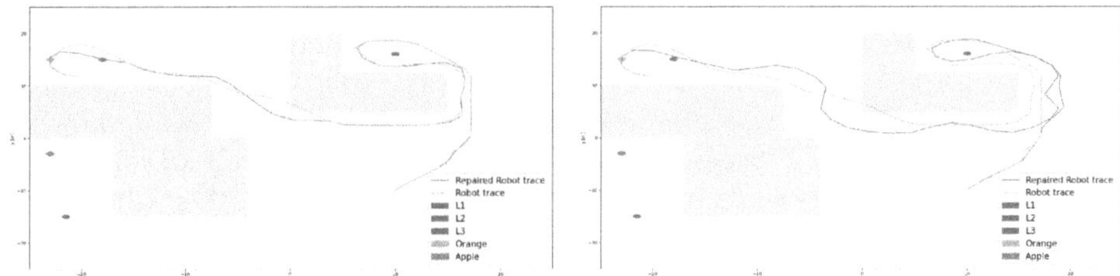

Fig. 5: Repair using different cost functions: on the left using $L1$ and on the right using combination W with weights ($L1 : 0.01, R : 0.99$).

---

[6] https://www.gurobi.com/: Gurobi Optimizer version 11.0.0 build v11.0.0rc2

5.2 Automated Ship Deck Landing

Landing on a ship is a challenging task, wherein various landing aids and maneuvers need to be carefully selected [22,23]. The benefits of TBTs for an automated lander are discussed in [21]. The TBT in Figure 1a is a simplified version of the TBT $\mathcal{T}$, where all landing maneuvers are used in the fallback node: *Straight-in*, *Lateral*, *45-Degree*, and *Oblique*. Each of them is represented by a sequence node. Here, we consider the *45-Degree* sequence: $\mathsf{Seq}([\mathsf{Leaf}(\Diamond\ diagonalBehind(s)), \mathsf{Leaf}(\Box_{[0,5]}\ (diagonalBehind(s)\ \wedge\ alignedHeading(s))), \mathsf{Leaf}(alignedHeading(s)\ \mathcal{U}\ aboveTouchdown(s) \wedge \bullet)])$ where s contains the position, velocity, and heading of the ship and the UAV. We abbreviate this sequence by $\mathsf{Seq}([\mathcal{T}_1, \mathcal{T}_2, \mathcal{T}_3])$, e.g., $\mathcal{T}_1 = \mathsf{Leaf}(\Diamond\ diagonalBehind(s))$. The AP *diagonalBehind* represents that the UAV is diagonally behind the ship, *alignedHeading* ensures that the UAV has a heading that is aligned with the ship heading, *aboveTouchdown* represents that the UAV is above the touchdown point of the ship. The other sequence nodes beneath the fallback are similar, only the target position and the prescribed heading change. The final leaf node also given in Figure 1a is common for all behaviors and specifies the descend property $\mathsf{Leaf}(\Diamond\ descended(s))$, where $descended(s)$ states that the UAV landed on the touchdown point. We abbreviate this node by $\mathcal{T}_4$. The repair only impacts the UAV's states.

Incremental Repair. All segmentations were computed in under 30 s. The original trace had a mission-time of 126 s and a length of 25 349, subsampled to 1014 by the segmentation. Nonlinear helicopter dynamics were simplified into four independent integrator chains similar to Example 1: one for each of the three inertial axes (x, y, z) and one for the heading [15]. The repair works on the subsampled trace using $L1$ as the cost function. The segments of the leaf nodes are: $(\mathcal{T}_1, 0, 265)$, $(\mathcal{T}_2, 266, 306)$, $(\mathcal{T}_3, 307, 581)$, and $(\mathcal{T}_4, 582, 1013)$. Segments $\mathcal{T}_1, \mathcal{T}_2$, and $\mathcal{T}_3$ are violating. As a reference for a full MILP encoding of the entire trace, we encoded a simplified landing as $\mathsf{Leaf}(land)$ using the formula $land = \Diamond(diagonalBehind(s) \wedge \bigcirc(\Box_{[0,5]} stayPos \wedge \Diamond_{[6,\infty]}(alignedHeading(s) \wedge aboveTouchdown(s) \wedge \Diamond descended(s))))$, i.e., we replaced $\mathcal{U}$ with $\Diamond$ by omitting the left side. We chose $\mathsf{Leaf}(land)$ because a full MILP encoding, i.e., directly solving the root node, caused an out-of-memory error. Note that this allows a baseline comparison to standard approximations techniques supported by the optimizer. We use Gurobi with its default parameters, which include features such as root relaxation and presolve. Experimental results in Table 1 show that the reference full MILP repair of $\mathsf{Leaf}(land)$ does not scale well for longer trace – it took over 2000 s – while incremental repair took less than 60 s. The detailed steps of the incremental repair show that ensuring *valid* transitions did not save time for Steps 1, 4, and 6 (8.87 s were unnecessary spend), but Step 3 saved presumably around 11 s. The reason for this is that the last state of the segment must change too radically to satisfy the specification and only when both leaf nodes are encoded (Step 3), a matching state can be found. The evaluation shows that getCommonAncestor (Line 18 in Algorithm 1) was never invoked; only the affected leaves needed to be accounted for. This avoided the need for a costly repair. The result of the repair is shown in Figure 1a (see Section A.4 for the

Formula	L	Time (s)
Leaf($land$)	$\{\{(\mathsf{Leaf}(land), 0, 1013)\}\}$	2200.40
$\mathcal{T}$	$\{\{(\mathcal{T}_1, 0, 265)\}, \{(\mathcal{T}_2, 266, 306)\}, \{(\mathcal{T}_3, 307, 581)\}\}$	**29.62**
Step 1	$l = \{(\mathcal{T}_3, 307, 581)\}, f = valid$	*3.72* ✗
Step 2	$l = \{(\mathcal{T}_3, 307, 581)\}, f = loose$	*3.86* ✓
	$\{\{(\mathcal{T}_1, 0, 265)\}, \{(\mathcal{T}_2, 266, 306)\}, \{(\mathcal{T}_3, 307, 581), (\mathcal{T}_4, 582, 1013)\}\}$	
Step 3	$l = \{\{(\mathcal{T}_3, 307, 581), (\mathcal{T}_4, 582, 1013)\}\}, f = valid$	*10.93* ✓
	$\{\{(\mathcal{T}_1, 0, 265)\}, \{(\mathcal{T}_2, 266, 306)\}\}$	
Step 4	$l = \{(\mathcal{T}_2, 266, 306)\}, f = valid$	*0.60* ✗
Step 5	$l = \{(\mathcal{T}_2, 266, 306)\}, f = loose$	*0.85* ✓
	$\{\{(\mathcal{T}_1, 0, 265), (\mathcal{T}_2, 266, 306)\}\}$	
Step 6	$l = \{(\mathcal{T}_1, 0, 265), (\mathcal{T}_2, 266, 306)\}, f = valid$	*4.55* ✗
Step 7	$l = \{(\mathcal{T}_1, 0, 265), (\mathcal{T}_2, 266, 306)\}, f = loose$	*5.11* ✓

Table 1: Trace repair results with intermediate steps of the incremental repair. The Time column includes setting up the model and solving it. The results show that incrementally repairing $\mathcal{T}$ is more efficient than the reference repair of Leaf($land$). ✗ represents infeasible runs whereas ✓ represents successful runs.

required heading changes). It shows that a segmentation can be a good heuristic to decompose the specification.

Landmark-based Repair. To illustrate the impact of disjunctions, we use incremental repair while omitting • from the last leaf node of the *45-Degree* sequence node. Specifically, we consider Leaf($alignedHeading(s)$ $\mathcal{U}$ $aboveTouchdown(s)$) instead of Leaf($alignedHeading(s)$ $\mathcal{U}$ $aboveTouchdown(s) \wedge$ •). Therefore, the optimizer must determine the optimal position to satisfy $aboveTouchdown(s)$, while • constrains it to the last position of this segment. As a result, the computation time increases from 29.62 s as in Table 1 to 278.32 s using incremental repair. Figure 6 illustrates this effect, comparing it to the results from the iterative landmark-based repair, where dots represent when solutions were found. The time limit was set to 300 s. The landmark-based repair finds its first solution after just 12 s and continues to improve upon it. Within approximately 40 s, a repair is achieved that is comparable to the one found by the incremental repair while saving 235 s. Figure 7 shows the important excerpt of the repair (see Section A.5 for the full plot). Note that, without the •, the leaf node $\mathcal{T}_3$, which contains the $aboveTouchdown$ propo-

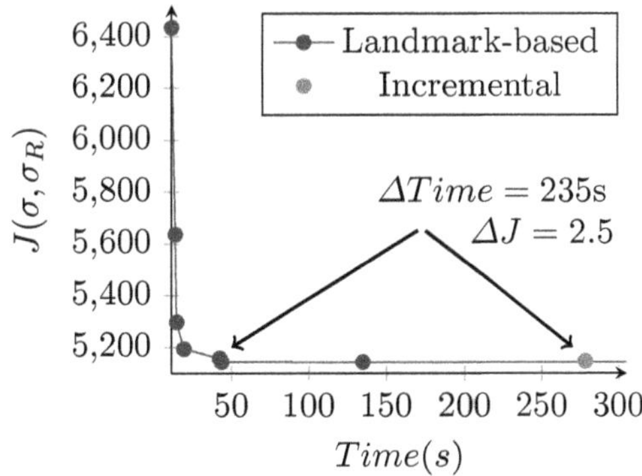

Fig. 6: Comparison of repair strategies.

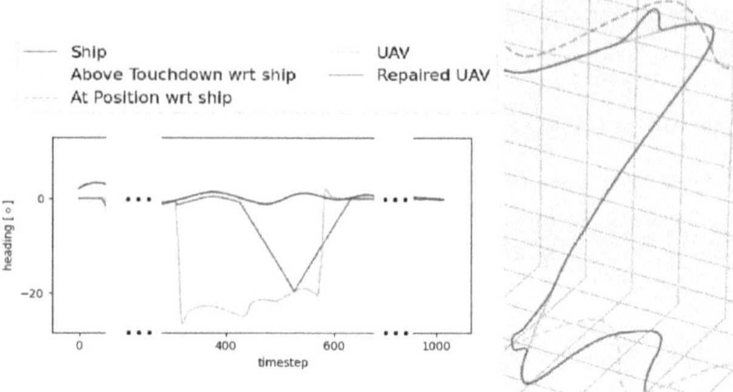

Fig. 7: The repair chooses an earlier *aboveTouchdown* when omitting •.

sition, can be satisfied earlier (around Timestep 450), thereby preventing the need of repairing heading thereafter. Further, the repair chooses the same position to repair the *diagonalBehind* proposition in $\mathcal{T}_1$ as in Figure 1b. Next, we applied the same TBT specification, but instead of using the subsampled trace, we encoded the full original trace that contains 25 348 entries. We were able to successfully identify a repair within 362 s.

6   Conclusions

We have presented methods for repairing traces of CPS that violate a given TBT specification. While a MILP could theoretically solve the problem, our experiments show that this is too expensive in practice. To address this, we introduced an incremental repair strategy that uses the segmentation information from a TBT monitor to repair violating segments locally. Additionally, we presented a landmark-based repair strategy, an iterative approach that avoids MILP encoding of the TBT by using landmarks. The landmarks allow us to formulate the repair as a linear program. Our experiments demonstrate that the two strategies make it possible to repair traces of more than 25 000 entries in under ten minutes, while the full MILP runs out of memory. Future work will explore the use of trace repair for reinforcement learning, focusing on situations where agents fail their task and need assistance.

Acknowledgments. This work was supported by the German federal aviation research program (LuFo VI-2, ID: 20D2111C), the DFG grant 389792660 as part of TRR 248 - CPEC, the European Union through ERC Grant HYPER (No. 101055412), and the US National Science Foundation (NSF) under award number 1836900. Views and opinions expressed are however those of the authors only and do not necessarily reflect those of the European Union or the European Research Council Executive Agency. Neither the European Union nor the granting authority can be held responsible for them. S. Schirmer carried out this work as a member of the Saarbrücken Graduate School of Computer Science.

References

1. Aavani, A., Mitchell, D.G., Ternovska, E.: New encoding for translating pseudo-boolean constraints into sat. In: SARA (2013)
2. Abiyev, R.H., Akkaya, N., Aytac, E.: Control of soccer robots using behaviour trees. In: 9th Asian Control Conference, ASCC 2013, Istanbul, Turkey, June 23-26, 2013. pp. 1–6. IEEE (2013). https://doi.org/10.1109/ASCC.2013.6606326, https://doi.org/10.1109/ASCC.2013.6606326
3. Annpureddy, Y., Liu, C., Fainekos, G., Sankaranarayanan, S.: S-taliro: A tool for temporal logic falsification for hybrid systems. In: Abdulla, P.A., Leino, K.R.M. (eds.) Tools and Algorithms for the Construction and Analysis of Systems - 17th International Conference, TACAS 2011, Held as Part of the Joint European Conferences on Theory and Practice of Software, ETAPS 2011, Saarbrücken, Germany, March 26-April 3, 2011. Proceedings. Lecture Notes in Computer Science, vol. 6605, pp. 254–257. Springer (2011). https://doi.org/10.1007/978-3-642-19835-9_21, https://doi.org/10.1007/978-3-642-19835-9_21
4. Baier, C., Coenen, N., Finkbeiner, B., Funke, F., Jantsch, S., Siber, J.: Causality-based game solving. In: Silva, A., Leino, K.R.M. (eds.) Computer Aided Verification - 33rd International Conference, CAV 2021, Virtual Event, July 20-23, 2021, Proceedings, Part I. Lecture Notes in Computer Science, vol. 12759, pp. 894–917. Springer (2021). https://doi.org/10.1007/978-3-030-81685-8_42, https://doi.org/10.1007/978-3-030-81685-8_42
5. Bemporad, A., Morari, M., Dua, V., Pistikopoulos, E.N.: The explicit linear quadratic regulator for constrained systems. Automatica **38**(1), 3–20 (2002). https://doi.org/https://doi.org/10.1016/S0005-1098(01)00174-1, https://www.sciencedirect.com/science/article/pii/S0005109801001741
6. Benedikt, M., Puppis, G., Riveros, C.: Regular repair of specifications. In: Proceedings of the 26th Annual IEEE Symposium on Logic in Computer Science, LICS 2011, June 21-24, 2011, Toronto, Ontario, Canada. pp. 335–344. IEEE Computer Society (2011). https://doi.org/10.1109/LICS.2011.43, https://doi.org/10.1109/LICS.2011.43
7. Ergurtuna, M., Yalcinkaya, B., Gol, E.A.: An automated system repair framework with signal temporal logic. Acta Informatica **59**(2-3), 183–209 (2022), https://doi.org/10.1007/s00236-021-00403-z
8. Ghosh, S., Sadigh, D., Nuzzo, P., Raman, V., Donzé, A., Sangiovanni-Vincentelli, A.L., Sastry, S.S., Seshia, S.A.: Diagnosis and repair for synthesis from signal temporal logic specifications. In: Proceedings of the 19th International Conference on Hybrid Systems: Computation and Control. p. 31–40. HSCC '16, Association for Computing Machinery, New York, NY, USA (2016). https://doi.org/10.1145/2883817.2883847, https://doi.org/10.1145/2883817.2883847
9. Ghzouli, R., Berger, T., Johnsen, E.B., Dragule, S., Wasowski, A.: Behavior trees in action: a study of robotics applications. In: Lämmel, R., Tratt, L., de Lara, J. (eds.) Proceedings of the 13th ACM SIGPLAN International Conference on Software Language Engineering, SLE 2020, Virtual Event, USA, November 16-17, 2020. pp. 196–209. ACM (2020). https://doi.org/10.1145/3426425.3426942, https://doi.org/10.1145/3426425.3426942
10. Gundana, D., Kress-Gazit, H.: Online modifications for event-based signal temporal logic specifications. IEEE Robotics and Automation Letters **9**(8), 6864–6871 (2024). https://doi.org/10.1109/LRA.2023.3343597

11. He, Z., Zhang, X., Jones, S., Hauert, S., Zhang, D., Lepora, N.F.: Tacmms: Tactile mobile manipulators for warehouse automation. IEEE Robotics and Automation Letters **8**(8), 4729–4736 (2023). https://doi.org/10.1109/LRA.2023.3287363
12. Hoffmann, J., Porteous, J., Sebastia, L.: Ordered landmarks in planning. CoRR **abs/1107.0052** (2011), http://arxiv.org/abs/1107.0052
13. Hu, H., Jia, X., Liu, K., Sun, B.: Self-adaptive traffic control model with behavior trees and reinforcement learning for agv in industry 4.0. IEEE Transactions on Industrial Informatics **17**(12), 7968–7979 (2021). https://doi.org/10.1109/TII.2021.3059676
14. Kapoor, P., Kang, E., Meira-Góes, R.: Safe planning through incremental decomposition of signal temporal logic specifications. In: NASA Formal Methods Symposium. pp. 377–396. Springer (2024)
15. Koo, T., Sastry, S.: Output tracking control design of a helicopter model based on approximate linearization. In: Proceedings of the 37th IEEE Conference on Decision and Control. vol. 4, pp. 3635–3640. IEEE (1998). https://doi.org/10.1109/CDC.1998.761745
16. Leucker, M., Sánchez, C.: Regular linear temporal logic. In: International colloquium on theoretical aspects of computing. pp. 291–305. Springer (2007)
17. Raman, V., Maasoumy, M., Donzé, A.: Model predictive control from signal temporal logic specifications: A case study. In: Proceedings of the 4th ACM SIGBED International Workshop on Design, Modeling, and Evaluation of Cyber-Physical Systems. pp. 52–55 (2014)
18. Sato, S., An, J., Zhang, Z., Hasuo, I.: Optimization-based model checking and trace synthesis for complex STL specifications. In: Gurfinkel, A., Ganesh, V. (eds.) Computer Aided Verification - 36th International Conference, CAV 2024, Montreal, QC, Canada, July 24-27, 2024, Proceedings, Part III. Lecture Notes in Computer Science, vol. 14683, pp. 282–306. Springer (2024). https://doi.org/10.1007/978-3-031-65633-0_13, https://doi.org/10.1007/978-3-031-65633-0_13
19. Scheper, K.Y.W., Tijmons, S., de Visser, C.C., de Croon, G.C.H.E.: Behavior Trees for Evolutionary Robotics†. Artificial Life **22**(1), 23–48 (02 2016). https://doi.org/10.1162/ARTL_a_00192, https://doi.org/10.1162/ARTL_a_00192
20. Schirmer, S., Singh, J., Jensen, E., Dauer, J., Finkbeiner, B., Sankaranarayanan, S.: Temporal behavior trees (Sep 2024). https://doi.org/10.5281/zenodo.13807484, https://doi.org/10.5281/zenodo.13807484
21. Schirmer, S., Singh, J., Jensen, E., Dauer, J., Finkbeiner, B., Sankaranarayanan, S.: Temporal behavior trees: Robustness and segmentation. In: Proceedings of the 27th ACM International Conference on Hybrid Systems: Computation and Control. HSCC '24, Association for Computing Machinery, New York, NY, USA (2024). https://doi.org/10.1145/3641513.3650180, https://doi.org/10.1145/3641513.3650180
22. Schmelz, T., Lantzsch, R.: Abschlussbericht: F&t studie - pilotenassistenz für schiffsdecklandungen (pilodeck)[final report: F&t study - pilot assitance for ship deck landing (pilodeck)],. Technical Note AHD-TN-ESPE-302-18 (2018)
23. Schuchardt, B.I., Dautermann, T., Donkels, A., Krause, S., Peinecke, N., Schwoch, G.: Maritime operation of an unmanned rotorcraft with tethered ship deck landing system. CEAS Aeronautical Journal **12**(1), 1–9 (9 2020), https://elib.dlr.de/140951/
24. Sidorenko, A., Hermann, J., Ruskowski, M.: Using behavior trees for coordination of skills in modular reconfigurable cppms. In: 2022 IEEE 27th International Conference on Emerging Technologies and Factory Automation (ETFA). pp. 1–8 (2022). https://doi.org/10.1109/ETFA52439.2022.9921558

25. Sun, Y., Poskitt, C.M., Zhang, X., Sun, J.: Redriver: Runtime enforcement for autonomous vehicles. In: Proceedings of the IEEE/ACM 46th International Conference on Software Engineering. ICSE '24, Association for Computing Machinery, New York, NY, USA (2024). https://doi.org/10.1145/3597503.3639151, https://doi.org/10.1145/3597503.3639151
26. Vanderbei, R.J.: Linear Programming: Foundations and Extensions. International Series in Operations Research & Management Science, Springer International Publishing, 5th edn. (2020)
27. Wagner, R.A.: Order-n correction for regular languages. Commun. ACM **17**(5), 265–268 (1974). https://doi.org/10.1145/360980.360995, https://doi.org/10.1145/360980.360995
28. Williams, H.P.: Model Building in Mathematical Programming. New York Academy of Sciences Series, John Wiley & Sons, Incorporated, 1st edn. (2013)

Author Index

© The Editor(s) (if applicable) and The Author(s) 2026
S. Junges and G. Katz (Eds.): TACAS 2026, LNCS 16505, pp. 681–682, 2026.
https://doi.org/10.1007/978-3-032-22752-2

GPSR Compliance
The European Union's (EU) General Product Safety Regulation (GPSR) is a set
of rules that requires consumer products to be safe and our obligations to
ensure this.

If you have any concerns about our products, you can contact us on

ProductSafety@springernature.com

In case Publisher is established outside the EU, the EU authorized
representative is:

Springer Nature Customer Service Center GmbH
Europaplatz 3
69115 Heidelberg, Germany